Ethical Lawyering

A Guide for the Well-Intentioned

ASPEN COURSEBOOK SERIES

Ethical Lawyering

A Guide for the Well-Intentioned

Bernard A. Burk
Former Assistant Professor of Law
University of North Carolina School of Law

Veronica J. Finkelstein
Adjunct Professor
Drexel University's Thomas R. Kline School of Law and Rutgers Law School

Nancy B. Rapoport
Garman Turner Gordon Professor of Law
William S. Boyd School of Law, University of Nevada, Las Vegas

ASPEN
PUBLISHING

Cover image: Lynn Del Vecchio

To contact Customer Service, e-mail customer.service@aspenpublishing.com, call 1-800-950-5259, or mail correspondence to:

    Aspen Publishing
    Attn: Order Department
    PO Box 990
    Frederick, MD 21705

Printed in the United States of America.

2 3 4 5 6 7 8 9 0

ISBN 978-1-4548-6155-3

Library of Congress Cataloging-in-Publication Data

Names: Burk, Bernard A., author. | Finkelstein, Veronica J., author. |
  Rapoport, Nancy B., author.
Title: Ethical lawyering : a guide for the well-intentioned / Bernard A.
  Burk, Veronica J. Finkelstein, Nancy B. Rapoport.
Description: Frederick, MD: Aspen Publishing, 2021. | Includes bibliographical
  references and index. | Summary: "Concise, accessible, and
  rules-and-problems-oriented coursebook for law school students taking
  Professional Responsibility courses"– Provided by publisher.
Identifiers: LCCN 2021019303 | ISBN 9781454861553 (hardcover) | ISBN
  9781543823271 (ebook)
Subjects: LCSH: Legal ethics–United States. | Practice of law–United
  States. | Attorney and client–United States.
Classification: LCC KF306 .B83 2021 | DDC 174/.30973–dc23
LC record available at https://lccn.loc.gov/202101930

About Aspen Publishing

Aspen Publishing is a leading provider of educational content and digital learning solutions to law schools in the U.S. and around the world. Aspen provides best-in-class solutions for legal education through authoritative textbooks, written by renowned authors, and breakthrough products such as Connected eBooks, Connected Quizzing, and PracticePerfect.

The Aspen Casebook Series (famously known among law faculty and students as the "red and black" casebooks) encompasses hundreds of highly regarded textbooks in more than eighty disciplines, from large enrollment courses, such as Torts and Contracts to emerging electives such as Sustainability and the Law of Policing. Study aids such as the *Examples & Explanations* and the *Emanuel Law Outlines* series, both highly popular collections, help law students master complex subject matter.

Major products, programs, and initiatives include:

- **Connected eBooks** are enhanced digital textbooks and study aids that come with a suite of online content and learning tools designed to maximize student success. Designed in collaboration with hundreds of faculty and students, the Connected eBook is a significant leap forward in the legal education learning tools available to students.

- **Connected Quizzing** is an easy-to-use formative assessment tool that tests law students' understanding and provides timely feedback to improve learning outcomes. Delivered through CasebookConnect.com, the learning platform already used by students to access their Aspen casebooks, Connected Quizzing is simple to implement and integrates seamlessly with law school course curricula.

- **PracticePerfect** is a visually engaging, interactive study aid to explain commonly encountered legal doctrines through easy-to-understand animated videos, illustrative examples, and numerous practice questions. Developed by a team of experts, PracticePerfect is the ideal study companion for today's law students.

- The **Aspen Learning Library** enables law schools to provide their students with access to the most popular study aids on the market across all of their courses. Available through an annual subscription, the online library consists of study aids in e-book, audio, and video formats with full text search, note-taking, and highlighting capabilities.

- Aspen's **Digital Bookshelf** is an institutional-level online education bookshelf, consolidating everything students and professors need to ensure success. This program ensures that every student has access to affordable course materials from day one.

- **Leading Edge** is a community centered on thinking differently about legal education and putting those thoughts into actionable strategies. At the core of the program is the Leading Edge Conference, an annual gathering of legal education thought leaders looking to pool ideas and identify promising directions of exploration.

To Amy Kaufman Burk, who makes all things possible;
to Anschel, Jared, and Ariela Burk, who cheered this project to the finish line;
and to Arnold Burk, who provided a lifetime of inspiration and example.
—BAB

To all the great teachers in my life, including: my fifth grade teacher, Mrs. Tuckman, who first inspired my love of learning; my high school art teacher, Mr. Kight, who taught me the value of hard work and patience; my college speech and debate coaches, Professor Bloomingdale and Professor Gehrke, who together played a formative role in setting me on my future path to the law; my college English Professor Selzer, who had a way of making students, including me, fall in love with anything he taught; and my law school Professor Witte, who set the standard of excellence I strive for every day.
—VJF

To my husband, Jeff Van Niel, and my father, Morris Rapoport,
who are both men of infinite patience with good senses of humor.
—NBR

Summary of Contents

Contents

UNIT III   Duties to Third Parties and the Public   *319*

UNIT IV   Some Realities of Practice

19   The Organizational Environment

UNIT V Challenges and Complications When Duties and Interests Collide 597

22 Conflicts of interest 599

UNIT VI   Judicial Ethics

Acknowledgments

We all want to acknowledge the exceptionally patient team at Aspen Publishing, which encouraged us throughout some long and unforeseeable delays, most especially Rick Mixter, who went to bat for our book over and over again despite those delays; Anton Yakovlev, who continued to keep us on track; Kathy Langone, whose eagle eyes and good judgment made our book better; and Sarah Hains, the person who made sure that our book read the way that it was supposed to, word by word. Thanks, too, to the original green-lighter of the book, Steve Errick, to John Devins, and to Alan Childress, who had the original vision for this book. Our individual acknowledgments are below.

—The Authors

My wife, Amy Kaufman Burk, made this project possible with her bottomless support. My adult children, Anschel, Jared, and Ariela Burk, were always ready with a kind word of encouragement. And my father, Arnold Burk, provided a lifetime of inspiration and example. My coauthors, Nancy Rapoport and Veronica Finkelstein, were such invaluable and creative collaborators and contributors that it is impossible to speak well enough of them. I'm also grateful to Alan Childress for his foundational contributions and to Mike Frisch and Julia Porter for their efforts and suggestions. I reiterate everyone's joint and several thanks to Aspen Publishing and its remarkable personnel, but in particular to Rick Mixter, who was not only a tireless advocate for continuing this project through endless setbacks but suggested innumerable improvements that proved instrumental. Rick is an extraordinary editor and human being. I'm grateful to Dean Katharine Traylor Schaffzin for making research assistance resources available. Appreciation also to Steven Liening for able research assistance.

—Bernie Burk

I cannot sufficiently thank everyone who made this book possible, but I will try my best. First, thank you to my coauthors Nancy Rapoport and Bernie Burk. Each one of you brought something different and valuable to this project, and the final book would not be the same without your contributions. Second, thank you to everyone at Aspen Publishing, especially Rick Mixter, who took a chance working with a mere adjunct professor after meeting her at a conference. He was a champion for me at every stage of this process. Third, thank you to my wonderful student research assistants, including Michael Lomtevas from University of Pennsylvania Carey Law School, Robert Lowmaster from Temple University Beasley School of Law, Kyle Lynch from Drexel University Thomas R. Kline School of Law, and Trevor Waldron from New England Law School. I am especially grateful to Abhinandan Pandhi from Drexel University Thomas R. Kline School of Law for his invaluable help with the Teacher's Manual. Fourth, thank you to my friend Lynn Del Vecchio for the beautiful artwork on the cover, which sets the tone for how special and different this book is from the average textbook. And, finally, thank you to my husband, Joseph S. Cohn, for being sympathetic when I was up late working on this project after work and for understanding every weekend I spent in front of the computer.

—Veronica Finkelstein

In addition to my husband, Jeff Van Niel, and my father, Morris Rapoport, I want to do a personal shout-out to my wonderful coauthors, who made this process fun and who made the book a joy to read; to Alan Childress for coming up with the idea for the book in the first place; to Rick Mixter, our book's champion; to Mike Frisch and Julia Porter for their involvement, even through some exceptionally tough times; to Steve Errick, who got me started on writing books with the misleading but useful phrase, "it's not going to be that hard or time-consuming"; to Nettie Mann, Jamilah Brewington, and Alicia Portillo, my amazing assistants over the years; to Daniel Brady, Brian Terrell, Blake Quackenbush, and Jarad Beckman, who took a look at earlier drafts; to my Spring 2019 Professional Responsibility students and to my COVID-hero Spring 2020 students, who—despite their displacement into little Zoom boxes—came up with great suggestions, especially Seth Wynn, Sam Bruketta, Andre Labonte, and Erika Smolya; to our de-snarkifier and intrepid cite-finder, Katrina Stark; to our research assistant who's helping us with our Teacher's Manual, Alexandra Mateo; to my law librarian partner in all things, Youngwoo Ban, and my former law librarian partner, Jennifer Gross; and to my buddy Walter Effross, who always has intriguing ideas and good suggestions.

—Nancy Rapoport

About the Authors

Bernard A. Burk graduated from Yale College in 1980, *summa cum laude* with distinction in English, and from Stanford Law School in 1983, Nathan Abbott Scholar and Order of the Coif. He was a Note Editor on the *Stanford Law Review*.

Burk clerked for Hon. William W. Schwarzer in the United States District Court for the Northern District of California and then spent 25 years at Howard Rice Nemerovski Canady Falk & Rabkin, A Professional Corporation, in San Francisco, 20 of them as a shareholder and director. That firm is now part of Arnold & Porter LLP. He chaired his firm's ethics function, represented other lawyers and law firms in ethics counseling and claims defense, and also represented a wide range of clients in commercial, intellectual property, and constitutional litigation and media and entertainment industry counseling and transactions. He was named a Best Lawyer in America in Commercial Litigation in 2009 and 2010.

Since leaving private practice in 2011, Burk has taught at a number of law schools. His research focuses on legal ethics and professional conduct as well as empirical study of the legal profession and the legal academy. He has served as a consultant and expert witness in multiple engagements involving legal ethics and professional conduct and continues to provide *pro bono* assistance to legal aid programs on regulatory and ethics questions. He blogs regularly on The Faculty Lounge, www.thefacultylounge.org. Unlike Prof. Rapoport, he cannot dance to save his life. He can, however, sing at least passably.

Veronica J. Finkelstein is a 2004 honors graduate of the Emory University School of Law and a 2001 graduate, with dual distinction and dual honors, of The Pennsylvania State University, where she majored in English and Speech Communication.

Finkelstein currently serves as an adjunct professor at Drexel Law, Emory Law, and Rutgers Law. She teaches a variety of classes including Professional Responsibility, Pretrial Advocacy, Trial Advocacy, Appellate Advocacy, Evidence, Litigation Practice Skills, Sales Law, Criminal Law, and Corrections Law.

Finkelstein currently works as an Assistant U.S. Attorney with the U.S. Department of Justice in Philadelphia, Pennsylvania. She served as the Civil Division's Training Officer and Paralegal Supervisor before being selected as Senior Litigation Counsel. At the Department of Justice, she has tried numerous cases to defense verdicts, including in tort, employment law, and medical malpractice cases. In addition to this defense work, Finkelstein investigates and prosecutes affirmative fraud claims, including *qui tam* actions. She also handles criminal child exploitation cases. In 2014, she was awarded the Executive Office of United States Attorneys Director's Award for Superior Performance as a Civil Assistant United States Attorney.

Prior to her government service, Finkelstein clerked for the Pennsylvania Supreme Court and was an associate at Duane Morris, LLP and Cohen Seglias Pallas Greenhall & Furman, PC. At both firms, she specialized in construction law.

She frequently serves as faculty in National Institute for Trial Advocacy programs across the country. She has taught at the National Advocacy Center on ethics, appellate advocacy, legal writing, and trial practice.

Finkelstein lives on a farm with an ever-evolving collection of cats, dogs, and horses. She is an avid cook and baker, well-known for her creative cupcakes.

Nancy B. Rapoport is the Garman Turner Gordon Professor of Law at the William S. Boyd School of Law, University of Nevada, Las Vegas, and an Affiliate Professor of Business Law and Ethics in the Lee Business School at UNLV. After receiving her B.A., *summa cum laude*, from Rice University in 1982 and her J.D. from Stanford Law School in 1985, she clerked for the Honorable Joseph T. Sneed III on the United States Court of Appeals for the Ninth Circuit and then practiced law (primarily bankruptcy law) with Morrison & Foerster in San Francisco from 1986-1991. She started her academic career at The Ohio State University College of Law in 1991, and she moved from Assistant Professor to Associate Professor with tenure in 1995 to Associate Dean for Student Affairs (1996) and Professor (1998) (just as she left Ohio State to become Dean and Professor of Law at the University of Nebraska College of Law). She served as Dean of the University of Nebraska College of Law from 1998-2000. She then served as Dean and Professor of Law at the University of Houston Law Center from July 2000-May 2006 and as Professor of Law from June 2006-June 2007, when she left to join the faculty at Boyd. She served as Interim Dean of Boyd from 2012-2013, as Senior Advisor to the President of UNLV from 2014-2015, as Acting Executive Vice President & Provost from 2015-2016, as Acting Senior Vice President for Finance and Business (for July and August 2017), and as Special Counsel to the President from May 2016-June 2018.

Her specialties are bankruptcy ethics, ethics in governance, law firm behavior, and the depiction of lawyers in popular culture. She is admitted to the bars of the states of California, Ohio, Nebraska, Texas, and Nevada and of the United States Supreme Court. In 2001, she was elected to membership in the American Law Institute, and in 2002, she received a Distinguished Alumna Award from Rice University. In 2017, she was inducted into Phi Kappa Phi (Chapter 100). She is the Secretary of the Board of Directors of the National Museum of Organized

Crime and Law Enforcement (the Mob Museum) and is a member of the Board of Trustees of Claremont Graduate University. She is also a Fellow of the American Bar Foundation and a Fellow of the American College of Bankruptcy. In 2009, the Association of Media and Entertainment Counsel presented her with the Public Service Counsel Award at the 4th Annual Counsel of the Year Awards. In 2017, she received the Commercial Law League of America's Lawrence P. King Award for Excellence in Bankruptcy, and in 2018, she was one of the recipients of the NAACP Legacy Builder Awards (Las Vegas Branch #1111). She has served as the fee examiner or as chair of the fee review committee in such large bankruptcy cases as *Zetta Jet, Toys R Us, Caesars, Station Casinos, Pilgrim's Pride,* and *Mirant.* She has also appeared in the Academy Award®-nominated movie, *Enron: The Smartest Guys in the Room* (Magnolia Pictures 2005) (as herself). Although the movie garnered her a listing in www.imdb.com, she still hasn't been able to join the Screen Actors Guild. In her spare time, she competes, pro-am, in American Rhythm and American Smooth ballroom dancing. The most interesting thing about her is that she is married to a former Marine Scout-Sniper.

Ethical Lawyering
A Guide for the Well-Intentioned

Introduction

No, OF COURSE you can't lie, cheat, or steal, whether or not you have a bar card. But if you didn't know that already, no book on legal ethics is likely to help.

Don't worry—that still leaves us plenty to talk about. In fact, we can guarantee that this will be the single most practically useful course that you'll take during your entire legal education. Why? Because in virtually any legal practice, some requirement of the Rules of Professional Conduct and the related law governing lawyers—in other words, what you'll learn in this course—will come up every single day of your career. Mastering this material is so important that, in 49 states and the District of Columbia, you must pass a standardized ethics test (the Multistate Professional Responsibility Examination, or "MPRE") in addition to the bar exam in order to get a license to practice law. In the remaining states (and Puerto Rico) you still must take and pass a professional responsibility course in law school.

And there's another reason that this course is essential: Even though everybody knows that you can't lie, cheat, or steal, and most of us take those prohibitions seriously, surprising numbers of lawyers run into trouble with their professional responsibilities. Thousands of lawyers every year face professional disciplinary proceedings brought by their state bar. And according to the American Bar Association, in the course of a career, *four out of five* practicing lawyers can expect to be sued (rightly or wrongly) on account of their professional activities.[1] Four out of five—meaning that one of them is likely to be you.

This is not because law school somehow Completes Your Journey to the Dark Side, or because lawyers as a species are more thoughtless or immoral than other Americans. Quite the contrary: One of the most important things we want you to know, right up front, is that most of the lawyers who run into trouble are every bit as honest, smart, and careful as you are. That's why we named this book "A Guide for the Well-Intentioned"—it's specifically meant for people like you, who really care about doing the right thing.

---

[1] Ways to avoid legal malpractice, as claims rise industry-wide, https://www.americanbar.org/publications/youraba/2016/december-2016/legal-malpractice-claims-are-on-the-rise--but-you-can-take-steps.html (December 2016).

The trick is using your good intentions well, and that's a lot harder than it sounds. The narratives we hear from lawyers in trouble are sad but strikingly similar, time after time:

- Facing professional discipline: "Why is the state bar wasting its time on a silly technicality like that?"
- Facing a malpractice claim: "All I was doing was trying to help my client, and this is the thanks I get."
- And in the most serious cases, when a lawyer is facing suspension, disbarment, or criminal penalties, we often hear the deeply felt heartbreak of hindsight: "As my family, friends, and community can tell you, I have always been a person who tries to do the right thing. I was proud to be a lawyer. I studied the law; I took my obligations seriously; I always did my best to meet them and to advise my clients to do the same. And yet, looking back, I now realize what I did here was terribly and inexcusably wrong. I'm not really sure how it happened. Little step by little step, I gradually but blindly advanced on the line between right and wrong. I seem to have crossed that line without noticing, and I suddenly awoke one morning to find it far behind me. I am anguished that I hurt people. I am ashamed. I am sorry."

At this clean, well-lighted point when your professional life is all before you, there aren't many of you who can easily imagine yourselves in a position that calls forth one of these sentiments. And yet four out of five of you will be. Like many others before you, someday you may look back on the road to the professional hell you are then enduring and, despite the fact that you were and remain a fundamentally good person, see that it has been paved with your good intentions. That's one reason that Professional Responsibility is a required law school course.

Does this mean that effort and good intentions don't matter? A thousand times no—of course they do. Effort and good intentions are the difference between the best and the worst of us who are called to the bar. Then why do so many well-intentioned lawyers face professional troubles? We would say that it's because they failed to use their efforts and good intentions *effectively*. The three most common paths to trouble are ignorance, negligence, and misperception. Our goal in this book is to help you learn to anticipate and avoid those troubled paths.

Banishing Ignorance. You've got to know the law to follow it. Much of the law governing what lawyers do is easy to anticipate and follow—once you understand it. But some of it can be intricate, subtle, or counterintuitive. Sometimes law that seems clear contains critical implications that may not be immediately obvious; sometimes, a clear rule may be difficult to apply. Sometimes there are good reasons for that, and sometimes there aren't.

We'll try throughout this book to point out when we think particular rules are grounded in good reasons and when they're not. But let us belabor the obvious for a moment and emphasize that, whether a rule is good or bad, it's still the law, and you have to follow it until it changes. (Imagine advising a client, "I agree with you—that's a dumb law that makes things harder for you. So go ahead and ignore it." Any takers?) And as we said before, you've got to know the law to follow it. To avoid trouble born from ignorance, knowledge is power. And if you'll work with us, we'll help you acquire that power by understanding how the law governing lawyers really works in the real-world circumstances in which you can expect to run into it.

Foreseeing Negligence and Avoidable Disputes. Lawyers also run into trouble because much of what we do is really important to our clients, and it's also really hard. We're regularly called upon to advise and protect people and organizations with respect to important matters that they often can't fully understand or navigate on their own. So when we make mistakes, the implications for those with whose affairs we've been entrusted can be terrible. Protection of the people for whose benefit we take on these awesome responsibilities—clients—is the main reason that the law has been a specially regulated learned profession for centuries, and why today you generally have to go to school for at least three years *and* pass a long and difficult exam in order to be allowed to practice.

And even when we don't make mistakes, clients often don't fully understand what we do, how we're required to do it, and how little control we often have over how their matters turn out. It doesn't help that we don't always explain things as well as we should. No law practice can exist without clients, of course. And often clients can make our work a joy with their support, appreciation, helpful collaboration, thoughtful use of our advice, and responsibility in paying their bills. But occasionally they can be unreasonable, ungrateful, mean-spirited, dishonest, or worse. Often you can see the bad ones coming. And even when you're working with a good one, bad results or bad communication can lead to bad feelings.

In short, because the job is so complex and difficult, it's easy to make mistakes. Even the very best lawyers sometimes do, and despite your best efforts, sooner or later you probably will, too. At the very least, sooner or later you're very likely to have a client accuse you of making a mistake even if you didn't—four out of five lawyers, remember?

Does this mean that you should just relax and let your clients' chips fall where they may? Once again, of course not: The price of your professional freedom as a lawyer is eternal vigilance. Often accusations arise out of circumstances that you might have foreseen and avoided. And if the mistakes you do make are ones that a reasonable lawyer wouldn't have made, the consequences will be serious no matter how hard you tried to avoid them. This course can teach you skills and methods that will help you avoid some disputes and mistakes and, at least as important, help you recognize and address any mistakes that you do make in ways that are best for all concerned (most especially your client).

Anticipating Misperception. Finally, sometimes we stumble into trouble simply because we're human. Like all human beings, lawyers can fall physically ill or develop illnesses such as anxiety, depression, or addiction. And, on top of those risks, we all grow older. Any of these can affect our focus, judgment, or the energy available to meet our responsibilities. No one is to blame for such things, but we are each still responsible for how we handle them if they overtake us.

These illnesses and impairments not only interfere with our ability to think clearly and work effectively, they can also affect our ability to recognize that our abilities and judgment have become impaired in the first place. And because our jobs can be so difficult and stressful, lawyers suffer from anxiety, depression, and substance abuse *two to three times more frequently* than the average nonlawyer, with younger and less experienced lawyers suffering most frequently of all.[2] Being able to see these problems coming and cope with them proactively when they do, as well as being able to guide others in seeing and coping with theirs, will help you avoid a great deal of pain and damage for yourself, your colleagues, and your clients.[3]

And even when we're fully healthy and functioning normally, limits on human perception and reason (often referred to as cognitive biases) can interfere with our ability to see a problem coming or to figure out how to handle it appropriately. *See* **Chapter 4.A at 70**. Such misperceptions can and often do distort our perception and reasoning in ways that may remain transparent to us until after an error or misconduct has occurred. But research tells us that the more we know about our normal human tendencies to misperceive in common and predictable ways, the more often we can catch ourselves in time. In other words, knowing about these normal but sometimes transparent human stumbling blocks—and keeping them in mind as you navigate your daily life—can help you see and avoid them.

So as you can see, we've got a lot of work to do. Let's get started.

---

[2] Patrick R. Krill, Ryan Johnson & Linda Albert, *The Prevalence of Substance Use and Other Mental Health Concerns Among American Attorneys*, 10 J. Addiction Medicine 46, https://journals.lww.com/journaladdictionmedicine/Fulltext/2016/02000/The_Prevalence_of_Substance_Use_and_Other_Mental.8.aspx (January/February 2016).

[3] You may know that you're susceptible to one of these illnesses, or even be suffering from one now. If that's true, there's no better time than now to address it. The sooner you do, the less likely it is to disrupt or outright ruin your life later. You don't need to be anywhere near trouble, let alone the proverbial rock bottom. There are things that you can do to prevent or manage these issues during law school and a legal career, and there are people and programs whose specific purpose is to help you, compassionately and confidentially. Right now. *See* **Chapter 4.C at 93**. Contact the professor teaching this course or reach out to anyone else you trust. But please, reach out.

1

How to Use This Book

WE WANT THIS BOOK TO BE DIFFERENT from the casebooks you're used to. One of the big differences that you'll notice right away is that there are no cases for you to read or analyze. That's not because caselaw is unimportant in the law governing lawyers. Caselaw often provides indispensable fact-specific interpretations of the generalized standards found in statutes, rules, or other caselaw. But we think that you've already had plenty of practice researching, reading, and analyzing caselaw in your first year; probably you'll get even more in your other courses this year. So we've decided to take a different approach.

A. Read the Rules

Legal ethics is predominantly rule-based: The law governing lawyers centers on the American Bar Association's Model Rules of Professional Conduct. As we'll explore with you in **Chapter 3.A at 32**, all 50 states and the District of Columbia have adopted the Model Rules, each with its own particular variations from the Model Rules version, as the principal body of law regulating attorney conduct. Most federal and territorial courts and administrative agencies have also adopted the Model Rules, or a particular state's version of them, to govern the conduct of the lawyers practicing before them. The MPRE is, accordingly, based in significant part on the ABA Model Rules as well. As a result, we'll spend a lot of time and attention on the text of the Model Rules and their Drafters' Comments.[1]

Our focus on the text of the Model Rules and Comments will also help you develop and refine your statutory construction skills, because we interpret the Model Rules (or a particular state's version of them) according to the same general principles that we apply to any rule or statute. And as we hope you recall, the place that you always, always, *always* start in interpreting a rule or statute is

---

[1] The Comments are, like the Drafters' Comments to other model statutes, nearly as powerful as the Rules themselves in setting the standards governing lawyer behavior. In fact, in some instances we'll see that the Comments not only offer interpretive guidance, they actually add enforceable legal requirements not stated in the Rule itself. (For those of you keeping score at home, yes, that is wonky drafting; and yes, it is unusual in the world of model rules and statutes. But as we'll see, sometimes that's just how it works.)

with its specific, actual words. So to make any sense of this book or to analyze most of its problems intelligently, you absolutely, positively *must* look at the text of the Rule or Comment under discussion. Every single time. No kidding.

One of the wonderful things about the twenty-first century is having the expertise of millions at your fingertips. Many of us are used to consulting the "hive mind" to get a quick take on a complex subject, and we encourage you to continue to make judicious and appropriate use of this powerful time-saving resource. But you're here in law school not just to find out what the law on some subject is right now—most folks can do that without three years of postgraduate education—but, much more important, to learn how to *read, interpret, and apply* the law. And you can't possibly learn to do that unless you actually read, interpret, and apply the law *yourself*. The alternative is like trying to learn to drive exclusively by watching someone else do it. That approach has predictable consequences the first time you get behind the wheel yourself.

Yes, learning how to make use of others' interpretations, especially authoritative ones, is another important skill. But there will often be lots of competing interpretations, all of them flawed in one way or another, and what you must be able to do is to filter your way through the noise to find the signals that matter most in the situation before you. So let's be absolutely clear: Being able to think for yourself and explain your thoughts to others are your superpowers as a lawyer. And the only way to learn to think for yourself is, well, to think for yourself.

One thing that your authors have learned during our collective years as practicing lawyers, consultants, and expert witnesses is that good lawyers routinely open a book or a window on their screen and consult the actual words of the rule or statute governing whatever they're doing, even though they may have done so dozens (or even hundreds) of times before. You'd be surprised how often you'll find that the specific words suggest or remind you of things you hadn't thought about, even when you thought you knew the law cold. And when you're learning a rule for the first time, of course, nothing can substitute for starting with the text. You should paraphrase the text to make sure you understand what it means (if you can't, then you don't), but that's the second step. Confronting the text in its pristine literal glory is always the first.

As discussed below, we try to make this easier in the digital version of this book by letting you click on a hyperlink — we call them law links — whenever a Rule is discussed. Clicking on that link will open a window containing the relevant text (*see* **Chapter 1.F at 14**). If you prefer hard copy, you can also find the text under discussion on the Internet or in a print Statutory Supplement. But one way or another, you really have to get out that text and read it.

Though the law governing lawyers *centers* on the ABA Model Rules, the Rules are only one of several bodies of law that affect your day-to-day work as a practicing attorney. As we'll see in **Chapter 3.A at 41**, the Rules of Professional

Conduct, by their literal terms, govern only professional discipline, that is, the standards under which a state's organized bar or other disciplinary authority may suspend or revoke a lawyer's license to practice law or impose some lesser disciplinary penalty, such as a formal reprimand.

Clients, former clients, and sometimes others may go to court to seek civil remedies such as money damages or **disqualification** (a court order directing a lawyer to get out of a particular engagement) against lawyers who have violated civil duties. The most common of these is a client's claim for damages in tort for what often is called legal malpractice—a term that we will see in **Chapter 3.B at 46** actually comprises a number of distinct kinds of claims, as well as several different formal causes of action in tort and contract.

In addition, procedural rules, such as the Federal Rules of Civil and Criminal Procedure and the similar rules applicable in state courts, impose various restrictions and obligations directly on the lawyers practicing in the courts in which those rules apply. A good example involves the signing and certification obligations of **Fed. R. Civ. P. 11(a) and (b)**, about which you learned in your first year and which are among a number of rules, statutes, and powers on the basis of whose violation state and federal courts and administrative tribunals may impose monetary or other sanctions. Other common examples in the federal system include **Fed. R. Civ. P. 11(c)**, **Fed. R. Civ. P. 37**, **Fed. R Crim. P. 42**, and the federal courts' "inherent" common-law powers to govern the conduct of the attorneys appearing before them. Many state courts have similar rules and powers. And as we will see, the standards for many of these other remedies are dictated—or at least influenced by—the terms of relevant Rules of Professional Conduct. *See* **Chapter 3.B at 49**.

Though we will focus principally on the Model Rules of Professional Conduct, we will also revisit several areas of the law that you studied during your first year. We'll also visit a few areas of the law that you'll be seeing this year or next for the first (or nearly first) time. Don't worry—we understand that your first year seems like a long time ago, and what you might run into this year or next seems a long way off. So we'll remind you of the relevant principles as we go. But expect to refamiliarize yourself with some civil procedure, contracts, torts, and even a little criminal law, and to learn (or perhaps revisit) some agency, business organizations, criminal procedure, and evidence. One of the great things about this course is that it will give you some insight into how areas of the law that you previously studied (or will study) in separate little jars of isolation actually interact with and complement one another in the real world of practice that you're about to enter.

B. The Ball Is in Plain Sight; Just Keep It There

We don't hide the ball. This book contains a lot more explanation than you're probably used to. That's because we want you to have a basic understanding of the principles at issue before we show you how they play out in the real world, as illustrated in the problems. So every topic contains a discussion of the law that you need to know to help you figure out what to do. That's why you'll be doing the assigned reading before class. That way, you'll have an idea of how to approach problems that your professor is likely to use your class time to discuss.

C. Work the Problems — No, Really: Work the Problems. Then Use the Big-Picture Takeaways and the Multiple-Choice Review Questions at the End of the Chapters and Chapter Sections for Review as You Prepare for Class

Instead of incomprehensible cases and imponderable questions, we've filled this book with impossible problems. (Just kidding—only some of them are impossible.) These problems are designed to address a pervasive challenge in law school that you experienced (maybe without fully realizing it) last year: It's often a lot easier to state a legal rule than it is to apply it, even in an everyday situation.

At this point, you've probably had a casebook or two that included hypotheticals and problems. We think that's a good way to approach this material. Professional responsibility issues arise in the real world of practicing lawyers. Some of the problems we've developed for you are based, closely or loosely, on actual fact patterns in decided cases or in the news; some are based on our experience as practitioners. But they're designed to resemble the kind of problems that you might realistically encounter once you leave the shelter of your classroom. So if you read the assigned text and work your way through the problems before class, you'll be preparing yourself to vanquish the ignorance, negligence, and misperception (*see* the **Introduction at 2**) that are lurking in the shadows of the practice world, crouching in quiet malevolence and awaiting the opportunity to leap out unseen and consume your mind and your livelihood.

Some of the problems will have clear solutions; some won't. But these problems are designed to look like ones you might realistically encounter in practice. So every time you address a problem, we and your professor want you to put yourself in the position of the lawyer in the problem. (You'll be meeting some of them later in this chapter, and they're a lot like you.) Then we want you to (1) identify the specific words in the Rules of Professional Conduct or formulate a precise statement of some other specific legal principle that applies to the problem; (2) say the words or statement out loud (and we really mean the "out loud" part; this tactic not only forces you to slow down and reason step by step, it also engages an additional part of your brain and makes what you're learning "stick" better); and then (3) explain (again, out loud in the simplest words you can) (a) what solutions to the problem the words of the Rule allow, and (b) which solutions are better or the best. This kind of analysis often works well in group study, and we encourage you to prepare the problems in small groups before class. Besides, we don't want you to be lonely.

One other important thing about the problems: Many of them explicitly involve a present and active client. The attorney-client relationship is the epicenter of a lawyer's professional life. Law practice is, after all, a service profession in which the client's needs and preferences largely define the services provided. We'll quickly see that this is not just a nice ideal; it's hard-wired into the legal obligations that structure the attorney-client relationship. *See* **Chapter 5 at 105**; **Chapter 6 at 131**. Given these facts, you may be surprised as you think back on the classes you've taken up to this point how few of them ever asked you to consider how your client might behave or what your client might need or want. This course is different: We'll offer you a toolkit of strategies for anticipating and managing clients' understandings, preferences, and needs (often under the signposts Tips & Tactics or Real World, *see* the discussion just following) and ask you to practice using those tools in common circumstances sketched out in the text or in the problems.

And, as an added bonus, we offer you two important review features, which we strongly suggest that you use as you prepare for class, and to which you should return at exam time. At the end of each chapter or section of a chapter that hangs together as a subunit, we've provided "Big-Picture Takeaways" that give you an aerial photograph of the material you just read. The Big-Picture Takeaways alone will *not* be enough for you to reason your way through most of the problems or to answer an MPRE or final exam question. But they will give you a sketch of the general principles that you've just been studying. They should remind you of the overall lay of the land, and if they seem surprising or unfamiliar, they should prompt you to review a portion of the preceding section of the book so that you can see how it fits into the big picture. Because we care about you, most of the Big-Picture Takeaways end with a cross-reference to specific pages so you can quickly and easily jump back and review the relevant portion of the chapter if the Takeaway or the principle it involves seems unclear. (You're welcome.)

After the Big-Picture Takeaways, we'll provide you with some multiple-choice questions. Some of these will just be reminders of useful points of information that were just covered; others will be MPRE-style, "reason your way to the best choice" questions. But they're designed to help cement into place what you just read. They'll also help get you ready for the MPRE, which we recommend that you register to take as soon after you finish this class as you can. (And yes, you're allowed to sit for the MPRE while you're still in law school.)

D. Follow the "Signposts"

Whether you're reading this book in physical book form or on a screen, you will see recurring "signposts" that are intended to alert you to categories of issues that commonly arise in legal ethics. In the print edition, signpost discussions will be marked at the beginning and the end with a colored text box shaped like an arrow: ⬛TʜɪS Oɴᴇ at the beginning of a signpost discussion, and Tʜɪꜱ Oɴᴇ⬛ at the end. In the digital edition (discussed in more detail in **Chapter 1.F at 13**), the introductory arrow boxes may be a different color or in black, and the ending arrow boxes will be black.

Here's a list of common signposts and why we're using them:

- ⬛Tᴀᴍɪɴɢ ᴛʜᴇ Tᴇxᴛ⬛: This book will usually start a new topic by discussing the text of a relevant Model Rule (or a portion of one) and work with you to interpret it according to ordinary principles of statutory construction. Sometimes that will be easy; sometimes, it won't be. (And every now and then, ordinary principles of statutory construction will yield an interpretation different from the one that has actually been adopted in one or many jurisdictions.) So any time you see the signpost ⬛Tᴀᴍɪɴɢ ᴛʜᴇ Tᴇxᴛ⬛, what follows will be a discussion of how the law governing lawyers ties into the specific words of the ABA Model Rules and its Drafters' Comments (or some other rule or statute relevant to the problem at hand). The actual language of the Model Rules and Comments is essential, because it's the starting point for analyzing most of the professional responsibility problems that you'll encounter in practice (as well as most of the problems in this book, not to mention much of the MPRE). ⬛Tᴀᴍɪɴɢ ᴛʜᴇ Tᴇxᴛ

- ⬛Rᴜʟᴇ Rᴏʟᴇꜱ⬛ The Rules of Professional Conduct by their terms set standards only for professional discipline. But as the law governing lawyers has developed, the Rules of Professional Conduct have come in many instances to define, and in other instances to influence, the legal standards for other **consequences** available under other bodies of law. In many states, for example, whether a lawyer's conduct violated an ethics rule can be relevant to (but not necessarily determinative of) whether the lawyer breached her duty in a civil case for professional liability or whether she is subject to some other civil remedy. Similarly, violations of the Rules of Professional Conduct have been held to set the legal standard for court-imposed sanctions under statutes and procedural rules that do not literally refer to those Rules. Whenever you see the signpost ⬛Rᴜʟᴇ Rᴏʟᴇꜱ⬛, what follows will be a discussion of how the terms of a particular Rule of Professional Conduct affect the standard for imposition of one or more **consequences** other than professional discipline. ⬛Rᴜʟᴇ Rᴏʟᴇꜱ

- ⬛Rᴇᴀꜱᴏɴ ꜰᴏʀ ᴛʜᴇ Rᴜʟᴇ⬛ One thing that we hope you learned in your first year of law school is that understanding *why* we have a legal rule helps us determine whether or how to apply it in unfamiliar situations. When you see the signpost ⬛Rᴇᴀꜱᴏɴ ꜰᴏʀ ᴛʜᴇ Rᴜʟᴇ⬛, we'll share justifications offered for an ethical rule's existence or scope. Sometimes ethical rules are over- or underinclusive of the situations that the reason might encompass, and sometimes the reasons offered for a rule may seem downright pretextual, or anachronistic, or wrong. We'll try to point out those instances too, but as we pointed out in the **Introduction at 2**, you still have to follow the law, no matter how worthy of criticism it may appear. REASON FOR THE RULE

■ CONSEQUENCES As discussed above and in **Chapter 3.F at 56**, professional trouble comes in many different forms and from many different sources. Different remedies can be imposed by different legal authorities under different bodies of law, each with its own legal standards. For example, only a state bar or other professional disciplinary authority can suspend or revoke a lawyer's license. Only a government prosecutor can charge a lawyer (or anyone else) with violations of the criminal law, with the criminal court imposing imprisonment, fines, or other criminal punishment upon conviction. Only a court or other tribunal can impose civil damages, **disqualification**, or sanctions.

All of these remedies, and the bodies of law that authorize them, are designed to regulate lawyer conduct (and sometimes the conduct of others as well); and all of them are pitfalls that you as a lawyer will naturally wish to avoid. One of the things you must always do in a risky situation is to ask yourself what different **consequences** could befall you if you mishandle things (or are accused of doing so), and where those **consequences** might come from. Many situations create risks of multiple different kinds of **consequences** from multiple different authorities: For example, a misjudgment on your part could result in both professional discipline administered by your state bar *and* a lawsuit against you for money damages brought by your client (who may also dispute your fees).

We will also use the term **consequences** to refer to *informal* phenomena that may result from your conduct. These informal **consequences** can be fantastically important as a practical matter, and they are often salient enough to guide or determine your conduct even before you start worrying about formal legal **consequences**. They can include your client's exercise of her right to terminate your services in the middle of the engagement (or not hire you in the future), and they can also include damage to your professional reputation.

When you see the signpost CONSEQUENCES , what follows will be a discussion of what could happen to you and who could make it happen. **Consequences** is also a defined term (*see* **Chapter 1.E at 12**, which immediately follows), so when used in text discussion, it will be displayed as one, in **bold**. Whenever you see the defined term **consequences**, stop and think about *all* the *different* kinds of retribution that could befall the lawyer in the situation under discussion. We discuss these more generally in **Chapter 3 at 41**. CONSEQUENCES

■ YOUR HOUSE; YOUR RULES : Remember that each state has adopted its own somewhat customized version of the Model Rules; no state has adopted all of the Model Rules verbatim. Similarly, though most states take similar approaches, each state has its own law regarding tort liability for professional negligence or breach of fiduciary duty, court-imposed sanctions, and other **consequences**.

When you see the signpost `Your House; Your Rules`, we'll try to point out areas where more jurisdictions tend to vary more widely in their approach, and we'll also try to describe common variations on the Model Rules and related law. `Your House; Your Rules`

In addition, your professor may supplement your course materials with pertinent Rule variations and other law specific to the state in which your law school is located or where many of its graduates practice. But this book is keyed to the Model Rules and what your first-year professors probably called the "general law" of torts, contracts, agency, and the like (that is, what most states do with a particular issue most of the time, sometimes summarized in a Restatement). So it's critical that you remember to check whether and how your state's version of a particular Rule or doctrine may differ before complying once you are in practice.

■ `Real World` What seems clear in theory may prove confusing in practice. One of the most important things that we try to show you in this book is how the law governing lawyers plays out in situations like those that practicing lawyers commonly confront. So when you see the signpost `Real World`, look for discussions of the practical implications of the issue under discussion. `Real World`

■ `Tips & Tactics`: There are many professional responsibility problems that can be addressed by commonly used good (or best) practices. These practices are not required by rule or common law, but they are widely recognized as effective or efficient ways to comply with the law. When you see the signpost `Tips & Tactics`, we'll offer examples of such good practices. `Tips & Tactics`

E. Remember Recurring Defined Terms

We will sometimes define recurring terms or principles and highlight them to remind you that they come up in a range of contexts. Some of these defined terms are fanciful nicknames that we've developed to help you remember them; others are in more common usage. Defined terms will appear in **bold**. Because we're getting to like you already, we've provided you with a **Glossary at 1031** containing definitions of defined terms as used in the book. (If you're using the printed version of the book, put one of those funny little tape flags on the first page of the Glossary (page 1031), so that you can find it easily when you need it.)

An example of a bolded defined term that will be used frequently is **consequences**, discussed above. Some other defined terms you'll see a lot are **must** or **must not**; **may**; and **should** or **should not**. The differences among these terms are critically important, and you need to pay attention to them every time you think about professional conduct. That's because professional responsibility is not only about understanding what you *have to* do or not do, but just as important, recognizing what *options* you may have and how to use your judgment to pick the better or best (or, in difficult times, the least bad) option. To emphasize the importance of these considerations, we emphasize those terms every time we use them:

- **Must** (or **must not**) refers to things that you have an *enforceable legal obligation* to do (or not do)—that is, an obligation whose violation can result in a formal **consequence** imposed by an authority legally empowered to do so—whether that obligation arises out of criminal law or procedure; civil statutory, rule, or common law; or an obligation stated in the applicable Rules of Professional Conduct.
- **May** refers to things that, under governing law, you have personal discretion to do or not do, as you choose.
- **Should** (or **should not**) refers to things that you **may** do (or not do), and that in the exercise of prudence and good judgment you (or we) deem it the better or best practice to do (or not do). A **should** judgment may be based on any or all of the available competing reasons to do or not do something, including (among many others) your personal moral or ethical values about whether something is or is not the right thing to do, or simple self-interest (such as making a profit, avoiding potential disputes or liability, or protecting your own reputation).

To use these terms in a practical example, if you see an apparently unaccompanied toddler on the sidewalk heading toward the street, you **must not** push him into traffic—you would quite probably be criminally prosecuted, and you would certainly be sued for damages in tort if the child or anyone else were hurt as a result. You **may** (but are not obligated to) stop him and try to find his parent or caretaker; and many people would say that you **should** do so, even though you don't have to (and you wouldn't be in trouble with the law if you didn't, though you might suffer other *informal* **consequences**, such as personal or public criticism).

An example of a common principle to which we give a nickname to help you remember it is what we call the **no-puppetry rule**. This principle is codified in **Model Rule 8.4(a)**, and it reminds us that, if you as a lawyer **must not** do something, you also **must not** ask or allow someone else to do it for you. The same idea is expressed in civil and criminal doctrines of secondary and vicarious liability, such as the principal's liability for her agent's actions in the course and scope of the agency (including *respondeat superior*), conspiracy, and aiding and abetting, so you already knew something about this concept. **Model Rule 8.4(a)** tells you that this same principle applies to professional conduct and discipline, too.

F. Enjoy the Advantages Offered by the Digital Edition

Thanks to our good friends at Wolters Kluwer, this book comes to you as a Connected Casebook. If you bought or rented the Connected Casebook (and we hope that you did—it's actually a better deal for you), what that means is that you get the use of a physical textbook and a statutory supplement and also a digital online edition (or perhaps you bought the digital-only package and saved some money). Thanks to the magic of computer technology (cue beeping sounds and an image of lights flashing on a control panel), the digital edition includes tools not available in print that are designed to make using the book to prepare for class and exams faster and easier. These include:

- *Highlighting and note-taking tools.* These allow you to highlight text in different colors (the colors may depend on the user platform that you're on), take notes, and export those notes into a document that you can save for class preparation or use in class.
- *An outlining tool.* This tool helps you prepare a course outline as you go, using notes that you may be taking as you read.
- *Law links.* Consistent with our exhortations to look at the text of the rule or statute under discussion (every single doggone time—did we mention that?), we've tried to make it easy to do. Every time that we refer to a rule or statute that you need to read, the citation will appear **linked** so that you can click to read the rule or statute. Clicking on the link will open a new tab in your browser containing the text of the authority, such as the language of a Model Rule or Comment. Similarly, clicking on a **bolded** defined term will open a new tab in your browser with the page containing the defined term's definition from the Glossary. We recommend placing and sizing that new tab on your screen so that you can look at the authority or definition and the page of the book discussing it side-by-side, but by all means do whatever works best for you. The only thing we insist on is that when we talk about a linked rule or statute, you must look at it so that you can understand the book's discussion of that rule or statute's specific wording.
- *Jump links.* You've probably heard that the law is a seamless web. That's because it is. Discussions at one point in this book inevitably relate to discussions in other parts. When they do, we'll tell you where with a cross-reference that will appear in **bold**. If you're using the digital edition, clicking on the bolded cross-reference will jump you to that place in the book. Just use the "back" button on your browser to get back to where you were before you jumped. If you make multiple jumps, you can use multiple clicks of the "back" button to retrace your steps. We've also provided cross-references by page for those using the book in hardcopy. Using these jump links is up to you; they're there if you want to remind yourself of something we've already covered or get a quick download on something that's coming up.

G. Meet Danielle, Frank, and Maya

We believe that the best way for you to get a feel for how the ethics rules fit together (or how they don't) is for you to think your way through (and, if necessary, around) hypothetical practice situations. Instead of having all sorts of characters crop up and giving you the misimpression that we'll let just about anybody in here, we want to introduce you to three recurring characters you'll see every day: in alphabetical order, Danielle, Frank, and Maya. Each of them has a backstory that lends context to the situations in which you'll find them. They have friends, colleagues, and adversaries you'll meet when they're relevant.

Danielle, Frank, and Maya will be making choices throughout the book, some of which build on earlier choices, and some of which don't. (Rather like real life.) They're in the beginning stages of their careers, and you can assume that they each had a good legal education—in fact, in a coincidence that can only be seen as magical, they attended *your* law school—and have had the benefit of some amazing professional responsibility professors included prominently in their list of "all-time greats." (Hey, we're writing the story, so we get to portray ourselves any way we like.[2]) Despite their strong preparation and good intentions, they will run into jams and even mess up now and then. In the immortal words of Merle Haggard, mama tried.

Maya Mendoza is a second-year associate at a big law firm with multiple offices in the United States and abroad. She's in the firm's main office, which is in a big city, but she herself is from a small town in west Texas. She was hired into her firm's Corporate Department, and her practice focuses on business transactions and finance.

Frank Freeland is in his third year as an associate at a small law firm in the Midwest that has four founding partners (one who litigates, named Harlan "Happy" Trials; one who does family law, named Sally Splitsville; one who does real estate, named Barney Blackacre; and one who does estate planning and some business and tax counseling, named Willie Willmaker), and a senior associate in addition to Frank (as well as various nonlawyer staff, of course). Like many smaller firms, Frank's firm does a wide range of legal work, including various kinds of litigation, transactional, and counseling work for individuals and smaller businesses in Frank's community.

Danielle Dutton recently graduated from law school and passed the bar exam, and has been working at the Medium County District Attorney's office for only three months.[3] Medium County has its share of street crime, but it's also a regional financial center, and thus Danielle's office prosecutes some white-collar crime as well. Danielle is originally from the East Coast, but Medium County is in the mid-South. Danielle works most of the time under the direction of a Supervising Deputy DA.

---

[2] Needless to say, for purposes of this book we are all charming, debonair, expensively but tastefully dressed, and really good dancers. Well, at least Rapoport is a good dancer.

[3] We've now confirmed reports that Medium County is in the State of Confusion. Would you really expect anything else from us? If you're looking for the State of Bliss, take a yoga class.

Though they were in different years, Maya, Frank, and Danielle knew each other in law school (and, yes, they became friends there). They keep in touch, mostly on social media.

With our *dramatis personae* thus dramatically personified (bet you see what we did there), let's get to work!

Big-Picture Takeaways from Chapter 1

1. We want you to treat this course as a statutory analysis class, and the best way to do that is to take the time to read the text of the Rule under discussion and the Comments related to the Rule. Don't just read our explanations; *always* read the actual language of the Rule and the Comments. *See* **Chapter 1.A at 5**.

2. The best process for you to show yourself that you understand the law governing lawyers is to work the problems before class, using our handy three-step approach:
   a. Identify the legal "phrase that pays"[4]—the specific words that matter when you apply the law to the facts in the problem.
   b. Say that phrase out loud (paraphrasing it, if you need to do so, to understand what it means).
   c. Then, in your answer to the problem, explain (again, out loud) what possible solutions there are, which solution is best, and why.
   d. While you're working a problem, pay special attention to any identified client's (or potential client's) preferences, needs, or understanding of the situation, and make sure that your solution takes them into account.

   This approach is also helpful if you prepare the problems in a small group, and we recommend that you use small-group study to prepare for class. Your professor may require it. *See* **Chapter 1.C at 8**.

3. Pay close attention to whether your conduct options in a given situation are **must** or **must nots**; **mays**; or **should** or **should nots**, and the differences among them. *See* **Chapter 1.E at 13**.

4. Keep the **Glossary at 1031** handy.

5. Have fun!

---

[4] We stole this phrase from one of our favorite articles on legal writing: Mary Beth Beazley, *The Self-Graded Draft: Teaching Students to Revise Using Guided Self-Critique,*3 J. L. WRITING INST. 175 (1997). You can find the discussion of the "phrase that pays" starting on page 182, and you can use the lessons gleaned from the article in diagnosing practice exam answers, too.

UNIT I

Working in a Regulated Profession

Okay, enough preliminaries. Before we get to the specifics at the heart of the course, however, we want to provide you with some concepts that underlie all of the details to come.

If you're the least bit typical, you came to law school with a limited view of the careers that lawyers pursue and the kinds of workplaces in which they pursue them. Most of your classmates are in the same position. The good news is that the menu of legal careers is much richer and more varied than you probably imagined. But this happy fact counsels thought and attention on your part. Choosing something that promises to consume most of your waking hours for most of your adult life deserves real care and forward thinking. So **Chapter 2 at 19** is a brief introduction to and overview of the many different kinds of things that lawyers do and where they do them. We want to get you thinking about what kinds of law-related work might prove most satisfying to you. We don't expect you (and you certainly shouldn't expect yourself) to make up your mind after you finish Chapter 2; we just want you to open your mind to the many possibilities before you and to help you start feeling your way toward the ones that draw you in (or repel you) so that you can start to forge a path out of law school toward something that seems worth pursuing. Just as important, professional responsibility issues always arise in a particular substantive and social context. Chapter 2 is a short and admittedly superficial survey of some of those contexts, so that you'll have some background as the issues and the problems we discuss get more specific.

Chapter 3 at 29 fleshes out the sources of legal governance (and thus the formal risk) with which you have to contend as a practicing lawyer. As we touched on in **Chapter 1.A at 7**, the Rules of Professional Conduct are just one of several different sources of legal regulation of your conduct as a lawyer. Each of those sources of regulation is controlled by different decision makers and carries different **consequences**, but all of these sources of regulation can have profoundly disruptive effects on your professional and personal life. Chapter 3 catalogues the many different places from which trouble may come.

Finally, you're probably wondering why, when what we do all day as lawyers is to help our clients understand and comply with the law, so many lawyers run into trouble with the law that governs their own conduct. (As we pointed out in the **Introduction at 1**, four out of five lawyers in the course of their careers run into legal trouble of their own.) Lawyers aren't, as a group, bad people, and lawyers as a group don't have uniquely bad judgment. In fact, quite the opposite is generally true. But professional responsibility issues always arise in a particular context, and that context often defines and may even create the issue. And context all too frequently makes risks or mistakes hard to discern or manage, even for people with excellent skills and judgment as well as the best intentions. **Chapter 4 at 69**, entitled "Why Smart People Do Stupid Things," gives you an overview of some of the powerful and universal human forces that can interfere with your good judgment and good intentions in many situations.

Let's explore!

2

What Lawyers Do, and Where They Do It

THIS BOOK IS ABOUT YOU—your training as a lawyer and how you can use what you'll learn about our profession and its values in whatever line of work you pursue. If you're a typical law student, then you came to law school without knowing a lot about the different kinds of careers that lawyers lead other than what you may have seen on television (which—spoiler alert—is narrowly limited to the kinds of things that make good television).[1]

Being a criminal trial lawyer like Jack McCoy (of *Law & Order* fame) or Perry Mason (a popular television series from the late 1950s and early 1960s that has recently been resurrected in a new and much darker remake on HBO) is a wonderful career choice for some people, but it leaves out hundreds of thousands of currently practicing lawyers who are happily earning a living with their law licenses in lines of work that have nothing to do with courtrooms. If you're a typical law student, then at this point in your legal education you're beginning to get a sense of the huge number of alternatives available with a bar card, and you're beginning to explore those possibilities. You'll probably try out some of these possibilities while you're in law school, and you'll probably make up your mind more than once before you graduate about what kind of career you want to pursue. For now, we urge two simple imperatives: Keep an open mind, and keep exploring the possibilities.

---

[1] One of us has written about how deceptive such fictional depictions can be. *See* Nancy B. Rapoport, *Dressed for Excess: How Hollywood Affects the Professional Behavior of Lawyers*, 14 NOTRE DAME J. OF LAW, ETHICS & PUBLIC POLICY 49 (2000), available at http://papers.ssrn.com/sol3/papers.cfm?abstract_id=936188; Nancy B. Rapoport, *Swimming with Shark*, in LAWYERS IN YOUR LIVING ROOM! LAW ON TELEVISION 163 (Michael Asimow, ed. 2009), chapter available at http://papers. ssrn.com/sol3/papers.cfm?abstract_id=1157053; Eric Van Horn & Nancy B. Rapoport, *Restructuring the Misperception of Lawyers: Another Task for Bankruptcy Professionals*, 28 AM. BANKR. INST. JOURNAL 44 (2009), available at http://papers.ssrn. com/sol3/papers.cfm?abstract_id=1472211; Nancy B. Rapoport, *Where Have All the (Legal) Stories Gone?*, M/E INSIGHTS 7 (Fall 2009) (publication of the Association of Media and Entertainment Counsel), available at http://papers.ssrn.com/ sol3/papers.cfm?abstract_id=1545443.

Even more important (and yes, we're cheating a little by sneaking an extra imperative in there after the two that we just promised), keep that open mind and spirit of exploration active *after* you graduate. Your first job will probably not be your last. It may or may not resemble the job you thought you wanted when you graduated, but if it doesn't, you've got to start somewhere; and even if it does, you may change your mind about your preferences as your life unfolds. The leading study on lawyer career paths found that the average person who graduated from law school at the turn of the century had changed jobs at least three times by around 12 years into his or her career. Each of your authors has already changed careers at least once. We've been in private practice, we've worked in government, we've done nonlegal work (not to be confused with "illegal" work), and we've taught in law schools and across our universities. Your career will probably take you in and out of a number of different jobs, too. You may be a lawyer all your life, or you may end up using your J.D. in other ways.

Law school is designed to teach you a way of approaching and analyzing complex issues.[2] This course in particular, though, is designed to help you understand our profession's ethics and values, and how those frequently interact with the kinds of problems that clients ask us to address. As we said in the **Introduction at 1,** we presume that you already know not to lie, cheat, or steal. A lot of the rules governing lawyer conduct reinforce and elaborate on those basic (and obvious) prohibitions, but still more of them speak in more detail to the special fiduciary relationship that lawyers have with our clients (*see* **Chapter 5 at 105** for an introduction to the lawyer's fiduciary duties). Others regulate how lawyers should behave in front of tribunals and with opposing parties, witnesses, or others. Some even address how lawyers should behave when we're not representing clients at all (*see, e.g.,* **Model Rules 8.4(b)-(c)**; **Chapter 18 at 473,** on advertising and solicitation). Our values represent the fact that the law is still a profession and not just a business (though yes, it is a business too, and the tension between being a professional and being a business person animates some of our ethical rules).[3]

So let's survey some of the more common career options that practicing lawyers choose.[4] We've broken them down into just a few categories, proving that

---

[2] We think that saying that law school "teaches you how to think" or that "thinking like a lawyer" is somehow radically different from or better than any other way is insulting to every other profession. Every profession has a way of critically approaching and analyzing the kinds of problems that it typically encounters, and many of those ways have a lot in common, though they're applied in very different contexts. (We're reminded of a remark overheard from the dean of a nationally prominent dental school, who gently and ironically chided the dean of the law school at his university about how long and arduously *his* faculty had to work to teach their students to "think like dentists.") That said, law school does teach you a particular method for analyzing practical problems. It's not the only way to approach a problem, but it's a pretty good one.

[3] Of course, businesses aren't supposed to encourage lying, cheating, or stealing, either. *But see* pretty much every corporate scandal that has occurred in your lifetime.

[4] We're going to focus on career options that directly involve practicing law, as these are the ones that new law graduates most commonly choose if they're available.

we can oversimplify with the best of 'em. Among other things, lawyers resolve conflicts, put together and document deals, provide advice to people trying to decide among various courses of action, help people and businesses follow the various statutes and regulations that govern their work, and draft and enforce those statutes and regulations. They can work in big firms, small firms, by themselves, inside companies, in government, and in nonprofit and public-interest organizations.[5]

As we skate through these categories, we encourage you to think about what's important to you in choosing a career. Everyone's relative preferences are different, but no matter who you are, no job is perfect; as the old saw goes, that's why they call it work. Most people find that they have to make career choices that trade off some of their preferences against others. But the fact that no one can find the *perfect* job doesn't mean that you shouldn't think long and hard about what kinds of work and work environments might be *better* for you. Thinking early and often about what you might especially like or dislike about a job can help you steer yourself toward something that you're more likely to enjoy overall.

So consider: What kinds of things are important enough to actively *pursue* at the possible expense of other goals? Work in a particular subject area? Work for a particular kind of client (e.g., needy people? wealthy people? big companies? startups or small businesses?)? High or above-average compensation? Accommodations for family or other commitments outside work? A collegial workplace? More or less independent responsibility early on?

And consider also: What kinds of things are important enough to actively *avoid* at the possible expense of other goals? Work in a particular subject area? Work for a particular kind of client? A competitive "everyone for themselves" workplace? Stressful work or work environment? Consuming and inflexible demands on your time? More or less independent responsibility early on?

A. Types of Work (a Gross Oversimplification)

1. Dispute Resolution

When nonlawyers think about lawyers, they probably think about the trials that they see on television or in the movies. Nonlawyers may not spend a lot of time thinking about the rest of what constitutes traditional litigation, such as investigation, discovery, data analysis, motions practice, settlement negotiations, appellate work, or, for that matter, resolving a dispute as a judge, arbitrator, or special master. They probably also don't think about alternative forms of dispute

---

[5] For a more in-depth discussion, *see* Andrew J. McClurg, Christine Coughlin & Nancy Levit, Law Jobs: The Complete Guide (2019); Catherine L. Fisk & Ann Southworth, What Lawyers Do: Understanding the Many American Legal Practices (2020).

resolution, such as mediation or something like collaborative divorce law. And they probably don't think about the countless times that lawyers wisely advise their clients "don't bother suing—it's not going to be worth it in terms of cost, distraction, and stress." Lawyers who are attracted to conflict resolution work are typically comfortable dealing with people who are angry or upset, and can disassociate themselves (most of the time, anyway) from the intense feelings of their clients or the people on the other side of the case.[6]

Litigators and trial lawyers serve an essential social purpose—they facilitate the resolution of disputes that the parties have not been able to resolve themselves in any other way, using our legal system in lieu of the kinds of violence and self-help that characterize less fortunate places in the world that lack the benefit of the rule of law.

Many traditional litigators seem to think that they've cornered the market on certain "constants" in law practice. Sure, they work hard, but most lawyers work hard, and many nonlitigators have experienced their share of short nights and weeks of little sleep and bad food. Good litigators write well and speak coherently, but so do good lawyers in every other type of practice. And most good lawyers are also good at thinking on their feet. There are other constants as well, none of which is limited to dispute resolution practice. Almost every lawyer has dealt with opposing counsel who are obstreperous or play games, and almost every lawyer has had his or her share of annoying clients who act irrationally, are too demanding, or may even lie to them.

2. Transactional ("Deal") Work

Not everything that lawyers do involves situations that have somehow devolved into the due process version of a street fight. Many lawyers help their clients make something new happen—start a business; merge, sell, or acquire a business or valuable assets; create new or renovate old buildings; protect or exploit technology; facilitate adoptions and prenuptial agreements or help warring spouses reorganize their families; and so on. If two or more people, or two or more organizations, want to make something that didn't exist before—and if what they want to do is more complicated than, say, selling a 1986 Dodge Colt on eBay—then they may want to use lawyers to help them. By the way, one of us is pretty insistent about letting you know that great bankruptcy lawyers are both great litigators and great deal lawyers. So that's something to consider if you're looking for a twofer.

---

[6] There are some interesting studies about law-student and lawyer personalities. For starters, *see, e.g.,* Lawrence S. Krieger & Kennon M. Sheldon, *What Makes Lawyers Happy?: A Data-Driven Prescription to Redefine Professional Success,* 83 Geo. Wash. L. Rev. 554 (2015); Susan Daicoff, *Making Law Therapeutic for Lawyers: Therapeutic Jurisprudence, Preventive Law, and the Psychology of Lawyers,* 5 Psychol. Pub. Pol'y & L. 811 (1999); Susan Daicoff, *Lawyer, Know Thyself: A Review of Empirical Research on Attorney Attributes Bearing on Professionalism,* 46 Am. U. L. Rev. 1337 (1997).

3. Counseling in General

Lawyers do one-on-one counseling, too, and they do it all the time: wills, trusts, tax advice, and plain, garden-variety "should I or shouldn't I" (or "what do I do now") advice about personal, family, or business matters, great and small. Not all of the advice that a lawyer gives a client may be, strictly speaking, legal advice—in fact, there's a lot of argument about where "legal advice" ends and other kinds of advice start. Some of the advice may be business or personal advice, either by itself or mixed up with more conventionally "legal" advice. But counseling is part of almost every area of practice, and a large part of some areas of practice. Many lawyers view the counseling part of their job as the most interesting and satisfying thing that they get to do.[7]

4. Compliance and Regulatory Work

Compliance generally describes helping clients with the vast array of federal, state, and local rules and regulations that govern their businesses and personal endeavors. Compliance lawyers like to catch problems before they happen by giving advice and developing systems that will help clients do the right thing now, so that they don't have to suffer the **consequences** of having already done the wrong thing later. Regulatory lawyers sometimes focus their work on particular regulatory agencies or regulated industries; there are dozens of them. Lawyers doing compliance work might help their clients set up ways of making sure that they follow the law (policies and protocols), or address whether a particular product or proposed course of action complies with existing rules. They may work closely with accountants and auditors, or directly with management.[8]

5. Legislative and Lobbying Work

Someone has to write the statutes and regulations that the rest of us have to deal with, and that someone is often a lawyer. The step-by-methodical-step and what-if process of thinking about the world that you're learning right now is a useful way of thinking about how to write a law. Other lawyers often act as lobbyists to encourage legislators and regulators to write laws and rules in ways more

---

[7] The role is so common that there's a whole section of the Model Rules (Section 2, "Counselor") generally addressing it (*see* **Model Rule 2.1**), and lots of Rules touching on what lawyers **must not** or **should not** advise their clients to do or not do (*see, e.g.,* **Model Rule 1.2(d)**, which states that you **must not** advise clients to violate the law, or advise them on how to do so).

[8] Just as many litigators mistakenly think that they've cornered the market on long hours, many compliance lawyers think that they've cornered the market on working with accountants and auditors. Nope: Many other types of lawyers do as well. If you think that you might be working with (or against) any kind of business (and almost all lawyers do), it would behoove you to understand how to read balance sheets and income statements yourself, so that you're not dependent on experts telling you how to understand them. Your law school probably offers "accounting for lawyers." If it doesn't, you can probably find an introductory financial accounting course at the university with which your law school is affiliated or elsewhere nearby. If you didn't study accounting in college, consider taking it.

favorable to their clients.[9] Some of the best lawyers around worked with federal and state legislatures and agencies early in their careers, so that, when they left to go into private practice, they understood every detail about "how the sausage is made."[10]

B. Types of Work Environments

Lawyers practice law in a variety of settings, from private practice (big firms, small firms, and solo practices) to organizations (for-profits, nonprofits, and public interest work). And it's possible to go from one type of work environment to another and back again. All three of us are proof of that.

1. Law Firms: Big Firms, Small Firms, and Solo Practitioners

Lawyers can group together in all sorts of organizations. The principals can join together as partners in a partnership, shareholders or directors of a professional corporation, or members of a limited liability company. There are a lot of different words for the owners of a law firm, depending on its organizational form. Depending on the state law governing professional organizations, law firms can organize as LLCs (limited liability companies), LLPs (limited liability partnerships), general partnerships, PCs (professional corporations), chartered organizations, and so on. Even solo practitioners need to consider the organizational form of their practice and the potential liability and tax consequences that might flow from the choice.

Nonowner lawyers may be called "associates" (employees on a track that, at least potentially, leads to an ownership role), contract attorneys (employees or independent contractors not on a path to ownership), or "of counsel" (which means different things in different places).[11] A firm can be local, regional, national, or international in scope.[12] It can offer a general practice or limit its practice to certain specialized areas of law.

---

[9] Lobbyists advocate for the interests of their clients with the government agencies and officials that make law and policy. They are often lawyers, though they are not required to be. (Legend has it that the term originated during the Ulysses S. Grant administration, when advocates would meet to seek the favor of the president or members of his cabinet or the Congress in the lobby of the Willard Hotel in Washington, D.C. The Willard still stands today, across the street from the Treasury Building and in view of, though a discreet mile and a half away from, the Capitol—and its lobby is still quite comfortable.) Lobbyists often have to register with the government as lobbyists (and if they are lobbying as an agent of a foreign government, they must register as a foreign government agent) to do official lobbying work.

[10] We've debated among ourselves to a stalemate over who originated this phrase, but we've found a site that narrows down the origin: http://quoteinvestigator.com/2010/07/08/laws-sausages/. It should not be confused with Ambrose Bierce's poignant definition of "litigation" as "[a] machine which you go into as a pig and come out of as a sausage." AMBROSE BIERCE, THE DEVIL'S DICTIONARY (1906).

[11] "Of Counsel" or "Counsel" can mean a lot of different things. In some places, "Of Counsel" lawyers are people who have stopped being "owners" as part of a multiyear path toward retirement. Often "Of Counsel," "Counsel," or the like means someone who is not an owner but not an associate either, but whose expected stay at the firm as a nonowner is indefinite.

[12] Different countries, of course, have different ethics rules. For example, some countries allow nonlawyers to be owners of the firm; others don't.

There are as many different kinds of law firms as there are different kinds of cats. (And law-firm managers often liken their jobs to "herding cats"; go figure.) Tigers and tabbies. Big, small, dainty, predatory, independent, lap-seeking, and so on, *ad infinitum*. We don't have the time or space to provide you with meaningful characterizations beyond a few gross, but not altogether inaccurate, generalizations: Larger law firms (50 to 100 lawyers or more) tend to serve medium-sized and larger companies and wealthy individuals in more complex legal matters. Their larger size generally supports a good deal more individual specialization, hierarchy, infrastructure, and nonlawyer staff. Smaller firms and solo practitioners tend to serve individuals and small businesses.[13] Maya works at a large firm; Frank at a small one. (Danielle works for state government as a prosecutor.)

About a third of all practicing lawyers practice on their own. Very few new law graduates (fewer than 2 percent) start practice as solos, and for good reason—for most new graduates, starting as a solo would be like completing a few driving lessons and then trying to start a career as a NASCAR driver. But after gaining supervised experience for several years in other practice environments, lots of lawyers strike out on their own and enjoy being their own bosses and clearing their own path to success. And for new law graduates, one great way to start a career is to get hired by an experienced solo who is willing to show you the ropes and supply clients for you to serve.

Like all organizations (and cats), law firms have personalities, often referred to in the profession as "firm culture." At large firms with many offices, the environment may be more locally determined by the particular office or practice group leaders, but generally each law firm has its own ethos. In choosing a firm, you need to be vigilantly attentive to the environment in which you are going to spend most of your waking hours. Some people thrive in a more competitive, "everyone for themselves" environment; others prefer something more familial. If, despite your efforts to find a good fit, you find yourself in an environment that you dislike, think about how to find another one more consistent with your temperament and needs. You don't get to choose your family, and you don't always get to choose your boss or colleagues, but you have a lot more control over the latter than the former. Make the most of it.

2. In-House Counsel

Many businesses have lawyer-employees who represent only the organization that employs them. They are referred to as "in-house" or "inside" counsel. The person managing the in-house lawyers and the company's internal legal functions

---

[13] Yes, of course there are exceptions. "Boutiques" are smaller firms that typically do complex or highly specialized work more commonly done by larger firms. Some big firms have substantial "emerging company" practices in which they represent small "startup" companies, each often centered around a novel technological development, that are just getting off the ground. Some small firms do this work, too. "Insurance defense" firms, which work with insurance companies and also defend the companies' insureds on covered claims, run the gamut from fairly large to quite small.

(often referred to as the "Law Department") is commonly called the company's "General Counsel" or "Chief Legal Officer"; often, that person is part of the highest level of company management. In-house counsel handle all sorts of legal tasks themselves, and many also supervise independent law firms engaged by the company ("outside counsel") on larger or more complex or specialized matters.[14]

It's currently rare to start your career inside a business, because most businesses hire only well-trained lawyers with plenty of experience (though this practice is gradually starting to change). Where do you get that experience? In other types of work environments. But many lawyers do make the switch from a private law firm or a governmental legal position to a company's legal department.

It can be both enjoyable and intellectually challenging to help a client run a business. The beauty of working "inside" is that you generally have a single client—your employer (or a family of companies affiliated with your employer). You develop a deep familiarity with your client's business and the people who make it happen. Many in-house lawyers find this close affiliation profoundly satisfying. And the hours in many legal departments can be more humane than at private firms, particularly larger ones.

But being an inside lawyer isn't a picnic. The hours at some companies can be as long and as unpredictable as law-firm hours are. And office politics are office politics, whether in a law firm, a company, a governmental unit or, well, anywhere. In addition, though having one client to care for can be a big upside to in-house work, it can also be a downside. You live or die (not literally, we hope, but professionally) on the success and longevity of your client. If a client of a law firm ceases to exist, the law firm will have to worry about how the loss of that client's work will affect the law firm's bottom line, but if the law firm's client base is reasonably diversified (and most are), losing a single client isn't a death knell for the law firm. If you're working in a business that fails or gets acquired, though, you may become unemployed.

Similarly, sometimes a client insists on doing something as a result of which you **may** or **must** withdraw from the engagement. *See* **Model Rule 1.16(a)-(b)**; **Chapter 9.D at 294**. Outside counsel who withdraw from an engagement usually have other clients, but withdrawing when you're working inside a company is generally called "quitting your job."

3. Government Service

Some governmental agencies do little other than legal work. Prosecutors' and public defenders' offices are good examples. For the rest, working as a government lawyer amounts to being in-house counsel for a governmental agency or officer, but with more restrictions on what you can and can't do. Those restrictions range from "ethics in government" (that is, anti-corruption) rules as detailed as how

---

[14] Depending on how the company chooses to organize its legal affairs, some in-house lawyers handle large deals or disputes themselves as well.

much someone can spend taking you to lunch to what you can do if you switch jobs ("revolving door" and other specialized conflict-of-interest rules).

Government lawyers do countless different kinds of work, as different as all the functions of federal, state, and local government. They enforce the criminal law as prosecutors and fulfill the Sixth Amendment right to counsel as public defenders. They pursue and defend civil claims by and against government. They help formulate, draft, promulgate, and enforce governmental rules and regulations. They negotiate and document all kinds of deals when the government buys and sells things. The possibilities are endless.

What's the advantage to being in government service? First, and we're not kidding around here, it can be deeply satisfying to work for "the people," which is the heart of government service. You also may get more hands-on experience more quickly, at least in some kinds of governmental units. And the work can often be quite interesting.

What's the downside? You may make less money, though the pay depends on what governmental agency you work for, how senior you are, and what your realistic alternatives to government service are. Unlike working at some companies, there are no stock options. Unlike working at many law firms, there are no (or at most small) bonuses. Some people have said that you make up in free time what you lose in salary by going from a law firm to a government position, but many government lawyers work long hours, too.

4. Nonprofits and Public-Interest Organizations

Don't think that all lawyers work in for-profit businesses.[15] Some don't. You can work in legal aid (representing the poor in pursuing their basic rights and needs) or at domestic or international human rights organizations, environmental organizations, or other organizations that pursue social or political issues. Nonprofits also serve the arts, community well-being, and lots of other causes. You can work in think tanks and other public policy organizations. And, of course, you can be law professors—even law professors who write textbooks about professional responsibility (but do us a favor and hold off for a few years until we sell this edition out).

Did we give you the impression that lawyers can do a lot of things and find satisfying careers in a lot of different environments? Good. The rest of this book is devoted to talking about how to use your good intentions to stay on the right side of the ethics rules in all of the different lines of work in which lawyers find themselves, and how to avoid some pitfalls that challenge even the best-intentioned among us.

---

[15] And don't think that you'll go broke if you work at a nonprofit. You might make less than you would at an available private-sector job, but you might not.

Big-Picture Takeaways from Chapter 2

1. There are countless uses for a law degree. When you're thinking about your future, don't limit yourself just to the types of lawyering that you see on TV or in the movies.

2. As you start to think about the type of practice and work environment in which you might want to build a career, spend a little time thinking about such things as:
    a. What level of compensation will be sufficient to satisfy your needs;
    b. How comfortable you are dealing with people who are angry or upset;
    c. Whether there are particular areas of the law that you especially like or dislike;
    d. Whether you are (or are willing to get) comfortable with business and financial concepts, and at what general level of depth and complexity;
    e. What kind of clients you would prefer to represent, and whether you want to work with a variety of clients or just one (such as a single organization or governmental entity);
    f. Whether you're comfortable getting "thrown in the deep end" with a lot of responsibility right away or whether you'd like more supervision while you're getting used to the practice of law;
    g. Whether you prefer a work schedule that more easily accommodates commitments outside of work, and whether you prefer a more flexible schedule (as in, "you can work any 80 hours a week that you want") or a more regimented one ("our hours are 8 a.m. to 5 p.m., Monday through Friday"); and
    h. What kinds of jobs are realistically available to you given your law school, class standing, extracurricular activities, background, and connections.

3

Regulating Lawyer Conduct:
Where Guidance and Consequences
Come From

As we'll explore in detail in **Chapter 5 at 105**, lawyers are fiduciaries. In broad outline, that means that we are entrusted with, and accept responsibility over, matters of great importance to our clients—matters that they often could not handle for themselves because they lack the necessary knowledge, skills, and experience. As a result, our conduct is subject to all kinds of scrutiny and constraints, both formal and informal. Any of them can bring unwelcome **consequences** if we wander from what the law allows. With great powers come great responsibilities.[1]

In this chapter, we'll introduce you to the many independent sources of scrutiny and constraints on lawyer conduct and to the **consequences** that they can bear. The fact that these sources are numerous and independent means that you have to keep *all* of them in mind as you decide what you **must**, **may**, or **should** do in your professional (and personal) life. To make the point a little more vividly (and figuratively), at every moment of every day that you are a lawyer, you will have multiple separate legal guns pointed at you. Any one of them could hurt or even kill you professionally, reputationally, or financially. You therefore would be wise to learn what those guns are, whose fingers are on their respective triggers, and what kinds of bullets they fire.

Let's survey the armory arrayed against you.

A. Government Regulation of Law Practice and Admission to the Bar

Since the founding of the Republic, the licensing and regulation of lawyers has been left exclusively to the States and the District of Columbia within their respective jurisdictions.

---

[1] The origin of this saying is disputed, though one of its best-loved users was Peter Parker's Uncle Ben. Voltaire also may have been responsible. *See, e.g.,* https://quoteinvestigator.com/2015/07/23/great-power/.

> The States prescribe the qualifications for admission to practice and the standards of professional conduct. They also are responsible for the discipline of lawyers.[2]

We'll see later in this chapter that this summary is a little overbroad—there are a few areas of lawyer licensing and regulation that fall outside the purview of the several states. *See* **Chapter 3.A at 42**. But there are only a few, and as a practical reference point, it's fair to say that both the authorization to practice law and the regulation of those who practice fall substantially to each individual American state and territory with respect to the practice of law within its boundaries. This creates a classic federalistic patchwork of law governing legal services. But even though every state regulates lawyering in its own way, we'll also see that all of them do a great deal of this oversight in similar fashion, so it's not hard to generalize about many important topics.

1. The Development of Lawyer Ethics Rules: From Professional Aspiration to Disciplinary Regulation

The practice of law in this country dates back to colonial times. The local trial courts in most American colonies, commonly called county courts, were usually presided over by local dignitaries rather than by law-trained judges. Most colonies discouraged the paid practice of law, with some colonies actually prohibiting it. As a result, there was little practical need for a formal code of lawyer ethics, because most people represented themselves.

But the legal profession put down strong roots in a constitutional republic that styled itself, in John Adams's memorable phrase, as "a nation of laws, not men," and soon began to grow. As early as the 1800s, states began to form bar associations and promulgate ethical codes. Lawyer-assisted profiteering during the Civil War and Reconstruction prompted state legislators to increase efforts to regulate the practice of law. In 1887, the Alabama Bar Association adopted the first comprehensive code of ethics. Other states followed, adopting their own ethics rules.

One of the first broad-membership lawyer organizations, the American Bar Association, began in New York in 1878. The ABA still exists today and is one of the world's largest voluntary professional organizations, with over 400,000 members. In addition to regulating and accrediting law schools, one of the ABA's other central missions is the promulgation of model ethics rules for lawyers.

After its creation, the ABA debated various ethical codes before adopting 32 Canons of Professional Ethics in 1908. The Canons were an array of mostly general and aspirational precepts, such as "[t]he obligation to represent the client with undivided loyalty and not to divulge his secrets or confidences forbids also the subsequent acceptance of retainers or employment from others in matters adversely affecting any interest of the client with respect to which confidence has been

---

[2] *Leis v. Flynt*, 439 U.S. 438, 442 (1979).

reposed" (Canon 6); and "[a] lawyer should endeavor to obtain full knowledge of his client's cause before advising thereon, and he is bound to give a candid opinion of the merits and probable result of pending or contemplated litigation" (Canon 8). Although the application of these general standards to specific situations was left to state disciplinary authorities, a great many of the concerns reflected in the current Model Rules of Professional Conduct can be found in the Canons.

The ABA replaced the Canons in 1969 with the Model Code of Professional Responsibility. The Model Code was structured as an array of general canons like the original 1908 Canons, each of which was associated with a set of more specific precatory ("**should**"-oriented) guidelines called Ethical Considerations ("ECs"), and specific disciplinary rules ("DRs") implementing the ECs. Only the DRs could form the basis for a disciplinary sanction. With its multiple levels of principles, the Code was difficult to interpret, and although it was adopted in many states, the Code was never very well-liked, either as a resource or as a source of positive law.

The Watergate scandal and related abuses by lawyers serving in government brought fresh attention to the importance of legal ethics in the 1970s.[3] In the wake of Watergate, the ABA's accreditation arm[4] first required American law schools to include mandatory instruction in professional responsibility in their curricula. And in 1983, the ABA replaced the Model Code with the Model Rules of Professional Conduct. The Model Rules consist of a series of rules with appended interpretive Comments. The Rules are organized into chapters that address a more general topic, such as the client-lawyer relationship (Chapter 1); the lawyer as counselor (Chapter 2); the lawyer as advocate (Chapter 3); and so on. With a few exceptions, each Model Rule is designed to state specific principles enforceable by professional discipline, completing the evolution of ethical regulation from aspirational guidelines to a detailed set of enforceable rules authorizing professional sanctions.

The Model Rules are like other influential uniform laws, such as the Uniform Commercial Code or the Uniform Probate Code, in that they are recommended prototypes for individual states and other jurisdictions to adopt in whatever form and with whatever modifications they see fit. The Model Rules themselves thus are not binding on anyone. As of today, however, all 50 states and the District of Columbia have adopted some version of the Model Rules. Because of that fact,

---

[3] If you're reading this book as a law student, chances are that you view Watergate as a somewhat distant historical episode with whose details you may not be entirely familiar. It's worth getting acquainted with the story. A sitting American President, Richard Nixon, orchestrated a cover-up of a government-sponsored attempted burglary and bugging of the headquarters of Nixon's rival political party. Nixon resigned shortly before he would have been impeached in 1974. His Vice-President, Spiro Agnew, had resigned the year before and pleaded no contest to tax evasion in connection with bribes and kickbacks that he had been collecting in his White House office and, before that, as Governor of Maryland. Nixon's Attorney General, Commerce Secretary, Chief of Staff, White House Counsel, and numerous other aides and advisors all went to prison for corruption, financial misdeeds, or perjury. Many of these people, from President Nixon on down, were lawyers.

[4] That's the ABA's Section of Legal Education and Admission to the Bar.

and because the MPRE tests the Model Rules rather than any particular state's enacted variation (just as the Multistate Bar Examination and the Uniform Bar Examination, discussed below, test the "general law" of the subjects that they address, rather than any particular state's actual law), this book will focus on the text of the Model Rules. YOUR HOUSE; YOUR RULES ▶ It's important to bear in mind, however, that no state has adopted the Model Rules verbatim, so you must always check whether any provision with which you may be concerned is noncon- forming in the jurisdiction in which you practice. Your professor may supplement your reading in this course with nonconforming versions of the Rules in effect in the state in which your law school is located or in which many of its graduates practice. ◀ YOUR HOUSE; YOUR RULES Even though no state has adopted the Model Rules unchanged, the problems and multiple-choice questions in this book will always refer to one or more of the Model Rules. Those references are each meant to be treated, for purposes of the problem or question, as the governing ethical rule adopted by the relevant jurisdiction.

The ABA's Standing Committee on Ethics and Professional Responsibility issues reasoned Ethics Opinions construing the Model Rules. Many state bar associations have similar standing committees that issue occasional guidance on the interpretation or application of their state's version of a Model Rule or Rules (which is often similar or identical to the Model Rules in relevant respects). Some larger urban areas with many practicing lawyers, such as New York City and Los Angeles, have county or municipal bar associations with similar commit- tees offering similar interpretive guidance. All such bar opinions are persua- sive authority for disciplinary adjudicators, as well as for courts and arbitrators relying on ethical rules to inform or determine standards of conduct governing civil issues such as civil damages liability, fee disputes, **disqualification**, or sanc- tions. These tribunals frequently rely on bar opinions from outside their own jurisdiction as persuasive authority if the other opinions construe identical or similar Rule language.

In addition, at the beginning of the twenty-first century, the American Law Institute (the "ALI") issued a Restatement of the Law Governing Lawyers. The ALI was established in 1923 to promote the clarification and simplification of the common law in the United States and its adaptation to changing social needs. One of the ALI's projects is the Restatement of the Law on various important topics, each of which might be generally described as a compendium of what most states do most of the time with the legal principles addressed. You probably saw excerpts from Restatements in some of your first-year courses, such as Contracts and Torts.

Like other restatements, the Restatement of the Law Governing Lawyers is not designed to be adopted as binding law in the way that the Model Rules are. Instead, it is intended to complement formal ethical rules and provide guidance for how such rules should be applied. It also addresses a good many civil rights and remedies arising out of lawyer conduct that the Model Rules don't address, or at least don't address directly. Where there is a gap in a state's law governing lawyers or that law is unclear, the Restatement can help fill the gap or suggest a refined interpretation.

2. State Regulation of Admission to Practice

Just as each state, U.S. territory, and the District of Columbia has adopted its own law governing lawyer conduct and the **consequences** for violating that law, each jurisdiction also has its own requirements for, and restrictions on admission to, the practice of law there. These admission requirements are typically promulgated by a jurisdiction's legislature, by its supreme court, or by powers delegated from one or the other to its state bar; and they are typically administered by an agency of the state supreme court or state bar referred to as a committee of bar examiners (or by a similar name).

There is no such thing as a license to practice law nationwide. Generally speaking, if you want to practice law in a particular jurisdiction, you must be licensed to practice *in* that jurisdiction *by* that jurisdiction. Being licensed to practice is also referred to as being "admitted to practice" (or "admitted to the bar"), or being "barred" in the relevant jurisdiction (which ironically means that you've been allowed into, not shut out of, the ranks of those licensed to practice). Practicing law in a jurisdiction in which you're not licensed to practice is called the unauthorized practice of law (often abbreviated "UPL"), and UPL is a misdemeanor in most states. And if you are licensed to practice in one state while engaging in unauthorized practice in another, that unauthorized practice may result in professional discipline in the state in which you engaged in the UPL as well as in the state that licensed you. *See* **Model Rule 8.5(a).**[5]

> **Problem 3A-1:** After graduating from law school, Maya's best friend takes a job with a large firm in its office in Philadelphia, Pennsylvania. She takes the Pennsylvania Bar Exam, passes, and is admitted to practice in Pennsylvania. Her office is right near the bridge across the Delaware River to New Jersey—so near, in fact, that she can walk to Camden, New Jersey, in five minutes. Her firm even has an office there. Barring (so to speak) an exception to the general rules of state regulation, can she practice in Camden?

---

[5] Defining just what constitutes "practicing law" turns out to be surprisingly difficult, because lawyers regularly do quite a few things that other people who lack a law license have always been allowed to do as well. The overlap includes such common tasks as negotiating and documenting contracts, giving business and tax advice, and preparing and filing many kinds of documents with various governmental authorities. To complicate things further, it turns out to be even harder to define what constitutes practicing law "in" a particular jurisdiction—does it matter where the lawyer is located, for example, or where the client is located, or where any forum that might be involved is located, or what kind of law is being interpreted or applied? Both of these concepts are incredibly important, because "practicing law" "in" a particular jurisdiction is what that jurisdiction's license to practice specifically authorizes and what the jurisdiction's laws specifically forbid without such a license. For now, however, we think it will suffice to say that, a fair amount of the time, these issues don't present any serious interpretive questions, and for purposes of the instant discussion, your intuitive sense of what it means to practice law in a particular state or territory will serve you just fine.

So what does it take to get a license to practice in the typical American jurisdiction? Although the requirements vary from state to state, in one way or another, all American jurisdictions require an applicant to demonstrate (1) minimum competence in the knowledge and application of important areas of the law, usually by passing tests on both substantive law and legal ethics; and (2) adequate honesty and trustworthiness to show no undue risk to the public by granting the applicant the power to represent others, usually referred to as a "moral character" or "character and fitness" evaluation. We'll provide a brief overview of each. But first:

a. An Introductory Observation: The Powers and Perils of Regulating Law Practice

The point of the remainder of this subchapter is not (unless your professor tells you otherwise) for you to learn the details of admission to practice in the United States, though we do provide some information to satisfy the curiosity that you probably have about the process that you'll soon have to navigate. We'll get to those details in a moment. Before we do, though, we need to introduce you to an important "big picture" concern about lawyer regulation in general, which we'll illustrate by discussing the regulatory function of controlling the admission to practice.

Like those in other learned professions, lawyers do important things for people who typically can't do those things for themselves. This puts lawyers in a position of power (and our clients in a corresponding position of vulnerability and dependence) that causes each jurisdiction to take care in selecting who will be allowed to exercise that power (by controlling admission to the bar) and vigilance over those who do to prevent and remedy its abuse (by the lawyer disciplinary system and related civil remedies).

As discussed at the beginning of the chapter, these powers of selection and oversight are exercised independently by each individual American state and territory. The requirements for licensure vary state to state, but every state jealously guards entry into the legal profession. The articulated purpose of these restrictions is to protect the public by limiting licensure to the competent and the trustworthy. Those are admirable goals, but these motives have often been mixed—consciously or unconsciously—with ones that are far less admirable. A number of observers have made convincing cases that some constraints on admission and practice are in significant part "guild restrictions" quietly (and perhaps even unconsciously) designed to limit competition and keep prices for legal services higher than might otherwise be the case.[6] Others have demon-

---

[6] *See* Robert C. Fellmeth, Bridget Fogarty Gramme, & C. Christopher Hayes, *Cartel Control of Attorney Licensure and the Public Interest*, 8 Brit. J. Am. Legal Stud. 193 (2019); Joel Henning, *Bar Associations, Law Firms, and Other Medieval Guilds*, 32:1 Litigation 17 (2005); Richard Posner, Overcoming Law 47-50 (1995); Deborah L. Rhode, *Moral Character as*

strated that, well into the twentieth century, moral character restrictions were systematically misused to exclude women and disfavored racial, ethnic, and religious minorities from the profession, on the view of those in power that women and minorities were not "the right kind of people" to share the privileges of bar membership with them.[7]

Our point as you go forward in this course is modest but fiendishly difficult to apply: There are many good reasons why not everyone should be allowed to do a lot of the things that lawyers do, but *which* people and activities should be restricted, *why* they should be restricted, and *how carefully tailored* the means of winnowing the worthy from the unworthy should be assessed with excruciating care.

Here's a good example of the problem: You're about to learn (or, more likely, you already knew) that almost every state requires almost everybody to pass a bar examination as a condition to licensure. The articulated purpose of the bar exam is to guarantee some minimum degree of substantive competence in those admitted to practice law, a goal that is difficult to fault. A majority of states now administer the Uniform Bar Examination, but with significant differences in the score necessary to pass and be granted admission to practice. There is currently no coherent explanation offered for these state-to-state differences in "cut scores," or more fundamentally, for exactly what ought to comprise minimum substantive competence, or how the Uniform Bar Examination or any state's variant might actually measure it.

We're not suggesting that ensuring the competence of new lawyers is a bad idea, of course. And unless you plan to work in a jurisdiction with a "diploma privilege" (and chose your law school accordingly), you will have to take the bar exam in your jurisdiction of choice, no matter what its purpose or efficacy. But we are suggesting that honest and serious scrutiny of what the bar exam—or any other restriction on the right to practice law—is for, and whether it achieves its goals, is more complicated than may first appear.

b. Substantive Competence

Most states require a four-year college degree and a post-graduate Juris Doctor (or as it is still occasionally called, a Bachelor of Laws ("LL.B.")) degree before you

---

a Professional Credential, 94 YALE. L.J. 494, 502 (1985). *See generally* RICHARD ABEL, AMERICAN LAWYERS (1985). For examples of contemporary restrictions on lawyer advertising that seem to serve no other purpose, *see* **Chapter 18.B at 478.** And to put this issue into a contemporary perspective, a few states are now experimenting with imposing more modest educational and testing requirements for "limited licenses" that allow people without the traditional qualifications required of lawyers to provide less complex legal services often needed by clients with limited resources, such as landlord-tenant advice and certain family law services. *See, e.g.,* Elizabeth Chambliss, *Law School Training for Licensed "Legal Technicians"? Implications for the Consumer Market*, 65 S. CAR. L. REV. 579 (2014). In June 2020, the first state to implement such a program ended it, asserting that the costs of continuing the program were not justified by the limited interest that it elicited. Bob Ambrogi, *Washington, State that Pioneered Licensed Legal Technicians, Cancels the Program*, https://www.lawsitesblog.com/2020/06/washington-state-that-pioneered-licensed-legal-technicians-cancels-the-program.html (June 9, 2020).

[7] *See, e.g.,* Rhode, *supra* note 6, 94 YALE. L.J. at 498-501.

can apply for admission to practice. A law degree from a law school that is accredited by the American Bar Association's Section of Legal Education and Admission to the Bar (there are currently just under 200 of these nationwide) will allow you to take any state's bar exam. A few states have certified additional law schools not accredited by the ABA to allow their graduates to sit for that state's bar exam. Even fewer will allow you to sit for the state's bar exam if you have "read the law" under the formal supervision of a practicing attorney licensed in that state for a period of years (a now-rare practice that, through much of the nineteenth century, was the most common way to prepare to become a lawyer).

And then you have to pass a bar examination.[8] In most states, the bar exam is actually two exams. (And yes, they're both hard, and the pass rate differs quite a bit from state to state, and within states from law school to law school, but generally speaking, about three-quarters of those nationwide with a J.D. from an accredited law school who take a bar exam pass on their first try.) The bigger and more demanding test—the one that people generally refer to when they talk about the bar exam—is a written test on numerous areas of substantive law and their application in certain lawyering skills. In most jurisdictions, that examination is at least two days long and consists of both essay and multiple-choice questions.

Almost every state's bar exam includes a day-long, nationally standardized multiple-choice test prepared by the National Conference of Bar Examiners (the "NCBE," an independent nonprofit organization that prepares standardized lawyer-licensing exams) called the Multistate Bar Examination ("MBE"). The MBE has 200 questions testing seven common-law subjects[9] and Article 2 of the Uniform Commercial Code.

Though some states supplement the MBE with specially prepared essay questions on local law, the NCBE has also developed a completely Uniform Bar Examination (the "UBE"). As of the time that this book went to press, 36 jurisdictions had adopted the UBE. Rather than test state-specific law, the UBE tests the "general law" in the United States, meaning the substantive rules that a majority of states apply regarding the tested subjects. The UBE has three parts: the MBE; the Multistate Essay Examination (the "MEE"), and the Multistate Performance Test (the "MPT").[10]

---

[8] Wisconsin offers a "diploma privilege"—that is, an automatic license to practice in the state without taking or passing a bar examination—if you graduate from either of the two accredited law schools located there. New Hampshire offers an alternative licensing program, called the Daniel Webster Honors Program, through the University of New Hampshire. As this book is going to press, the COVID-19 pandemic is causing several states to consider limited or modified diploma privileges for a period of time until it is considered safe to administer in-person bar examinations again.

[9] Civil Procedure, Constitutional Law, Contracts, Criminal Law and Procedure, Evidence, Property, and Torts.

[10] The MPT requires applicants to apply substantive law to some common lawyering tasks, such as writing an analytical office memorandum or a persuasive brief. In addition to the subjects tested on the MBE, the UBE and most non-UBE states often test additional subjects in the non-MBE portions of their examinations. These include Business Associations, Conflicts of Laws, Family Law, Trusts and Estates, and Secured Transactions (UCC Article 9).

The UBE is uniformly administered and scored, and an applicant's UBE score is "portable," meaning that an applicant's score on the UBE taken in any state that offers it can be used to apply for licensure in any other jurisdiction that has adopted the UBE. Although different states require different minimum scores on the UBE for admission, the UBE's portability is a very big deal, because it makes applying for licensure in other UBE jurisdictions much easier. Until recently, few states allowed licensing "reciprocity" with other states, so that moving or expanding your practice to another state typically required you to study for and take the new state's bar exam. The UBE can simplify this process considerably, and thus if you aren't sure where you might end up practicing by the time that you finish law school, you should seriously consider taking the bar examination in a state in which you *may* settle that offers the UBE. (MPRE scores are also portable in many jurisdictions.)

Most jurisdictions also require that applicants pass an ethics examination. Most use the Multistate Professional Responsibility Examination (the "MPRE"), which the NCBE administers three times a year. The MPRE is a two-hour, 60-question multiple-choice examination designed to test the applicant's knowledge of the ABA Model Rules of Professional Conduct, the ABA Model Code of Judicial Conduct, and some closely related subjects, such as civil remedies for the breach of a lawyer's duties. (A quick skim of this book's table of contents will show you that its scope is similar. This is not a coincidence.)

Passing the MPRE is required for admission to the bar in all but four U.S. jurisdictions. Each jurisdiction sets its own requirements for the minimum score necessary for admission, which varies between 75 and 86 on a scale that runs from approximately 50 to approximately 150.[11]

c. "Character" Evaluation

Aside from minimum educational requirements and competence assessment, every U.S. jurisdiction requires bar applicants to submit to and pass what is typically called a "moral character" or "character and fitness" evaluation. The stated purpose of this requirement is to protect the public by excluding persons determined not to be honest or trustworthy enough to assume the fiduciary responsibilities of law practice.[12] The burden is generally on the applicant to show that he or she possesses "good moral character."

Bar applicants are typically required to complete an extremely detailed personal background questionnaire and provide a list of references. Admission to practice may be denied if the facts disclosed raise sufficient doubt about the

---

[11] Wisconsin and Puerto Rico test their local rules of professional conduct on their bar examinations rather than with the MPRE. New Jersey and Connecticut waive the MPRE for applicants who earned a passing grade in a law school course in professional responsibility. For minimum passing scores state by state, *see* https://thebarexaminer.org/2019-statistics/the-multistate-professional-responsibility-examination-mpre/.

[12] *See* Rhode, *supra* note 6, 94 YALE. L.J. at 507-12.

applicant's integrity, but also if the applicant knowingly makes a false statement of **material** fact on the questionnaire, fails to disclose a fact necessary to correct a misapprehension that the applicant knows has arisen, or fails to respond to a demand for information from an admissions or disciplinary authority in connection with the application.[13]

Though you may not have realized it, your character and fitness evaluation began with your application to law school. Most law schools include a section in their applications eliciting personal information about the applicant that might trigger concern when the applicant, having graduated, later seeks admission to practice. What you disclose on your law school application is extremely important, because all state bars we know of contact any law school that a bar applicant attended and, in addition to asking the school to certify that the student graduated in good standing, will typically ask the school to share any information that the student may have disclosed on his or her law school application or any information on events that occurred during law school that the bar considers "character"-related. Because they want to see their graduates licensed to practice, schools virtually always cooperate.

Of course, by the time it contacts the law school, the state bar already has the graduate's detailed character and fitness questionnaire, and most state bars independently research applicants' personal backgrounds as well. Thus, any discrepancies between what you did or didn't disclose in your law school application and what you did or didn't disclose in your character and fitness questionnaire will trigger an inquiry. The point then becomes not only whether the omitted information is **material** to the state bar's character and fitness inquiry, but also whether you were dishonest with either your law school or the state bar in failing to disclose the information requested. Either could be grounds for the state bar to refuse you admission to practice. And anything significant that you failed to disclose to both your law school and the state bar, but that the state bar uncovers on its own, makes admission to practice even more difficult.[14]

This issue is sufficiently important (and comes up frequently enough) that your law school has probably brought it up not only on your original application, but at least once since you got there. Even though we're sure that you treated this inquiry with the gravity that it genuinely deserves, in the interest of ensuring that

---

[13] Similarly, if a lawyer makes a false statement of material fact, fails to correct a misapprehension, or fails to respond to a demand for information, that misconduct is typically grounds for professional discipline for that lawyer, unless there are any applicable **confidentiality** obligations that justify the lawyer's conduct (*see* **Chapter 8.A at 206**). *See* **Model Rule 8.1**; *Konigsberg v. State Bar*, 366 U.S. 36 (1961). The information requested must bear some rational relationship to fitness to practice law, but that still leaves the licensing authority with a great deal of latitude in deciding what information is pertinent to the character inquiry. *See Schware v. Board of Bar Examiners*, 353 U.S. 232 (1957).

[14] *See, e.g., In re Application of Phares*, Slip Op. No. 2020-Ohio-3346 (Ohio 2020) (bar applicant who failed to disclose being terminated from a job for a positive marijuana test denied admission to practice); *In re Grimsley*, 141 Ohio St. 3d 94 (2014) (failure to disclose underage drinking convictions on law school admissions and transfer applications, even though the convictions were later disclosed on the candidate's bar application, delayed permission to sit for bar exam).

all the effort and expense that you're currently enduring results in a license to practice, for heaven's sake, *please* pause for a moment and think back to whether there is anything in your past that, even arguably, should have been disclosed on your law school application. If you are in doubt about any detail, ask your dean of students or associate dean for academic affairs (or whoever at your law school oversees the school's interaction with state bars): Those people want you to become a lawyer, too, and will be happy to answer questions about these issues. The longer you wait, the more explaining you'll have to do later about why you waited, and the more likely it is that the detail (or your failure to disclose it) will be considered **material** to your application. Remember, if the state bar really cares about something, its character and fitness investigators will dig for it in your background, and they will find it. (On some law school applications and in some jurisdictions, this even includes juvenile and other convictions that have been legally expunged from your record. If you are in any doubt about what to disclose, check with your law school.) And if they find it before you disclose it, that will reflect badly on your candor, and it will likely hurt your chances for admission. The facts aren't going to change, and sooner is always better (*always!*) for disclosures of this kind.

Although protection of the public and the integrity of the legal system are undoubtedly admirable goals, there are serious questions about whether the currently prevalent "character" evaluation system works evenhandedly. Those questions arise not only because of the system's well-documented history of confusing the prediction of future ethical behavior with race, gender, ethnic, religious, class, sexual orientation, ideological, and other kinds of prejudice (*see* **Chapter 3.A at 35**), but also because predicting future misconduct in a system like the states' character and fitness assessments may be all but impossible in other-than-obvious cases.

In work that was in part the basis for a Nobel Prize in economics, psychologists Daniel Kahneman and Amos Tversky showed that predicting complex future behaviors based on a limited sample of current or past behavior was something that even well-resourced organizations that cared deeply about getting it right failed to achieve much more often than they would have by random chance.[15] So much here is imponderable: Assuming that you could reliably derive a probability of future professional misconduct (which, of course, you can't), what probability

---

[15] Two examples were the Israeli Army's efforts to identify future military leaders and an investment advisory's efforts to identify future success in securities trading. *See* Daniel Kahneman, *Don't Blink! The Hazards of Confidence*, https://www.nytimes.com/2011/10/23/magazine/dont-blink-the-hazards-of-confidence.html (Oct. 19, 2011). *See generally* Daniel Kahneman & Amos Tversky, *On the Psychology of Prediction*, 80 Psychological Rev. 237 (1973); Rhode, *supra* note 6, 94 Yale. L.J. at 555-62. Combine this human reality with the observation that when admitted lawyers are caught committing actual professional misconduct, they are only relatively rarely disbarred, while applicants presenting what bar examiners perceive to be a theoretical risk of such misconduct are excluded and effectively disbarred before they start (*see* Rhode, *supra* note 6, 94 Yale. L.J. at 546-51), and it's easy to wonder what state bars might be accomplishing.

would cause you to exclude an applicant from ever practicing law? Five percent? Ten percent? Fifty? You might think that it would be easy to conclude that someone with felony convictions ought to be denied admission, but the fact is that people can change (though they only sometimes do), and even bank robbers and carjackers have occasionally been found to have shown sufficient evidence of rehabilitation to be admitted to practice.[16] By contrast, a journalist who falsified sources in numerous magazine stories (and then lied repeatedly to cover it up), but later attended and excelled in law school, and spent years in psychotherapy and trying to make amends both to those he had harmed and by working (with a flawless and exemplary record) as a paralegal with a public interest law firm that served the homeless, was found to be inadequately trustworthy to merit bar admission.[17]

Problem 3A-2: Which of the following applicants for admission to practice should be denied admission? Be sure to explain carefully why you think so:

a. The applicant is in default on her six-figure student loans.[18]

b. The applicant has bounced 14 checks in the past year (but no criminal or civil proceedings resulted).

c. The applicant is a recovering alcoholic. Does it change your answer if the applicant has also pleaded guilty to driving while intoxicated before beginning recovery? What if someone was hurt while the applicant was driving drunk?

d. The applicant saw a psychotherapist during college and law school for anxiety and depression and is currently taking antidepressant medication. Does it change your answer if you know that 15 to 20 percent of the American population over age 12 is taking prescription antidepressants? What if the applicant has schizophrenia (a psychotic thought disorder that is generally viewed as incurable) that is currently controlled with antipsychotic medication?

---

[16] *See* Reginald Dwayne Betts, *Could an Ex-Convict Become an Attorney? I Intended to Find Out,* https://www.nytimes.com/2018/10/16/magazine/felon-attorney-crime-yale-law.html (Oct. 16, 2018); Katherine Long, *Former bank robber helped by Gates fund now professor at Georgetown Law School,* https://www.seattletimes.com/seattle-news/former-bank-robber-helped-by-gates-fund-now-professor-at-georgetown-law-school/ (April 7, 2017); *see also* Stephanie Francis Ward, *Recovering former convict defies odds, ends 'long and hard journey' after being sworn in as a lawyer,* http://www.abajournal.com/news/article/recovering_former_convict_defies_odds_ends_long_and_hard_journey_after_bein (June 18, 2018) (felony convictions for theft, drug possession, and gun possession; "in an April 2018 opinion explaining its decision reversing the character and fitness board finding [excluding the applicant], the [Washington] state supreme court wrote that 'one's past does not dictate one's future'").

[17] *In re Glass on Admission,* 58 Cal. 4th 500 (2014). Illustrating the difficulty of the case, the State Bar Court had found Mr. Glass had been rehabilitated adequately to merit admission. The California Supreme Court reversed. *See also* Hanna Rosin, *Hello, My Name Is Stephen Glass, and I'm Sorry,* http://www.newrepublic.com/article/120145/stephen-glass-new-republic-scandal-still-haunts-his-law-career (Nov. 10, 2014); David Plotz, *Stephen Glass Should Be a Lawyer,* http://www.slate.com/articles/news_and_politics/jurisprudence/2014/01/stephen_glass_of_shattered_glass_the_california_supreme_court_rejects_the.html (Jan. 27, 2014).

[18] *See* Adam S. Minsky, *Court Cites Student Loans as Reason to Deny Bar Admission to New Lawyer,* https://www.forbes.com/sites/adamminsky/2020/01/23/court-denies-bar-admission-to-new-lawyer-due-to-student-loans/#7f6ae572548f (Jan. 23, 2020).

e. The applicant has received eight speeding tickets in the past year.

f. The applicant was caught plagiarizing in high school. Does your answer change if the cheating occurred in middle school? College? Law school?

g. The applicant is an undocumented immigrant. Does it matter if the applicant illegally entered the country as a child?[19]

h. The applicant pleaded guilty to possession of small amounts of marijuana while a resident in a state in which, and at a time when, such possession was a felony. Does your answer change if the applicant is seeking admission in Colorado, where possession and use of marijuana are currently not crimes at all? What if the applicant is seeking admission in a state in which possession or use of marijuana is a crime and, as required by that state's law, has truthfully admitted on his moral character questionnaire to possession and use of marijuana in Colorado, where possession and use is now legal?

i. The applicant has been convicted of robbery.

j. The applicant has been convicted of domestic violence.

k. The applicant is currently a member of a white supremacist organization. Does it matter if members of the organization have attended rallies and assaulted demonstrators advocating civil rights? What if the organization itself advocates violent means to achieve its ends? Does it matter whether the applicant himself has ever endorsed or participated in such violence?

3. State Government's Regulation of Law Practice Through Professional Discipline

RULE ROLES As we noted at the outset, there are several independent sources of law governing what lawyers do after they are admitted to practice. At the center of this arrangement is each state's Rules of Professional Conduct, which are enforced by that state's system of professional discipline. The Rules aren't "central" because they're the most commonly brought to bear; in fact, civil claims for breaches of lawyers' duties are far more common than are disciplinary proceedings. But the Rules have come to serve as the central repository of rules and standards concerning lawyer conduct. As we will see, they are at the heart of each state's system of professional discipline, and are also influential in determining standards for civil remedies sought by private litigants, such as **disqualification** and damages for legal malpractice, as well as defenses to claims for fees and court sanctions. RULE ROLES

---

[19] Compare *Florida Board of Bar Examiners Re: Question as to Whether Undocumented Immigrants Are Eligible for Admission to The Florida Bar*, https://www.floridasupremecourt.org/content/download/242731/2141215/sc11-2568.pdf (No. SC11-2568, March 6, 2014) (undocumented immigrants may not be admitted to practice under Florida law) with *In re Sergio C. Garcia on Admission*, https://caselaw.findlaw.com/summary/opinion/ca-supreme-court/2014/01/02/268898.html (No. S202512, Jan. 2, 2014) (undocumented immigrants may be admitted to practice under California law). *See also* Kevin R. Johnson, *Bias in the Legal System? An Essay on the Eligibility of Undocumented Immigrants to Practice Law*, http://ssrn.com/abstract=2257026 (2013).

As noted above, each state, through its Supreme Court or its legislature, adopts rules and standards for the admission to and practice of law. In all 50 states and the District of Columbia, these rules comprise some version of the ABA Model Rules of Professional Conduct. The rules are enforced by the state's Supreme Court or some agency of the state, such as a state bar, and the **consequences** by which those rules are enforced involve professional discipline, such as suspension or exclusion from the practice of law, or a less severe sanction, such as a public or private reprimand.

4. Federal Regulation of Law Practice

Admission to practice in a particular state typically authorizes the licensee to practice before all of that state's courts (to appear as counsel of record, argue or question witnesses on behalf of a client, sign court pleadings and other papers as counsel, and question witnesses or object on the record in court-related proceedings such as depositions), as well as to do anything in that state outside of court that the state regulates as the "practice of law."[20]

But the Supremacy Clause of the U.S. Constitution (**Art. VI ¶ 2**) prevents states from imposing control over proceedings in or access to *federal* courts and administrative agencies. Thus, every federal district and appellate court is free to adopt its own rules about who may practice before it, the standards to which their conduct must conform while doing so, and the **consequences** for violating those standards.[21]

As a practical matter, this is usually less complicated than you might fear. You must apply and be admitted to practice in any federal district or appellate court before you can appear for a client or sign pleadings to be filed there. Most federal courts will admit anyone who is admitted to practice in the state in which

---

[20] We also briefly mention admission *pro hac vice*, a Latin phrase generally pronounced "pro hock [or hack] *vee*-chay" that means "for this occasion only." A lawyer who is not licensed to practice before a particular tribunal—for example, a lawyer licensed in Kansas who wishes to litigate a case in a Missouri state court—may ask that tribunal for permission to practice before the tribunal *pro hac vice* in that one particular case. Every state, territorial, and federal court has its own rules for admission *pro hac vice*. Those rules vary, but they often include requirements that the applicant-lawyer does not reside in the jurisdiction, that the applicant-lawyer has a clean disciplinary record, that the applicant-lawyer has associated local counsel who is licensed to practice before the tribunal and who has an office in the jurisdiction and will accept service of papers and pleadings in the case, and that the applicant-lawyer will learn and follow the procedural and ethical rules in force in the tribunal and submit to the jurisdiction of local disciplinary authorities. Admission *pro hac vice* is helpful for the litigator who wishes to handle the occasional out-of-state case before a tribunal in which she is not admitted, but it has no effect in any other lawyering context.

[21] The same is true of federal administrative agencies, many of which conduct legal proceedings of various kinds. Typically, federal agencies adopt simple standards of admission allowing any lawyer admitted in any U.S. jurisdiction to practice before the agency (and, in some cases, allowing anyone to appear before the agency regardless of training or licensure in the law) and adopt standards of conduct, such as the Model Rules, by reference. There is typically no separate procedure for admission to practice before a federal agency, but a few specialized agencies, such as the United States Patent and Trademark Office, require that a lawyer pass a special examination before the lawyer (or in the case of the PTO, a nonlawyer with the proper background) may appear before the agency. Most federal administrative agencies have adopted lawyer-disciplinary procedures by rule.

a district court sits, and some federal district courts and all of the federal appellate courts will admit any lawyer who is admitted to practice in *any* state (and is otherwise qualified).[22] Similarly, many federal courts have adopted the Rules of Professional Conduct in effect in the state in which they sit, or the Model Rules themselves, to govern the conduct of the lawyers in the proceedings before them.[23] As a result, the rules governing lawyer conduct may differ between a federal court and the state court next door, but they typically don't differ much. Each federal court has its own disciplinary function, separate from that of the state in which it sits and that of other federal courts, to adjudicate and mete out **consequences** to lawyers accused of violating standards of professional conduct in that particular court.

> **Problem 3A-3:** Frank and one of his supervising partners file a personal injury case based on a car accident for a client in their local state court of general jurisdiction. It turns out that the other driver (the defendant) lives in the adjacent state, and the defendant removes the case to the local federal district court on the basis of diversity of citizenship. Frank and his boss continue their prosecution of their client's case after removal, propounding interrogatories and document requests. Do their actions create any problems, and if so why, and what can they do about them?

What about lawyers who work exclusively for the federal government or one of its agencies? Like any other lawyers, those who practice before courts, agencies, and other tribunals must follow the rules that those tribunals have adopted. In addition, by statute and regulation, federal government lawyers are required to follow the state ethics rules and laws governing lawyer conduct in the state(s) in which the lawyer practices.[24] Federal government lawyers may also be subject to additional rules, including those set forth in presidential executive orders or the rules of the government agency or department by which they are employed. And even without a specific rule or executive order, federal courts have expressed heightened expectations of candor and civility from federal government lawyers because those lawyers speak for the government.[25] You'll learn more about the role and obligations of the government lawyer in **Chapter 25 at 907**.

5. Disciplinary Procedures (a Quick and Dirty Overview)

A lawyer who commits "professional misconduct" is subject to professional discipline. Take a look at **Model Rule 8.4**, which defines some of the most common

---

[22] *See, e.g.,* Fed. R. App. P 46(a); E.D. Pa. Local R. Civ. P. 83.5(a) (allowing admission of persons admitted to the Pennsylvania Bar); D.D.C. Civ. Local R. 83.8(a) (allowing admission of persons admitted to any state bar).

[23] *See, e.g.,* N.D. Cal. Civ. Local R. 11-4(a)(1) (adopting California's Rules of Professional Conduct).

[24] 28 U.S.C. § 530B(a) (known as the "McDade Amendment"); 28 C.F.R. §§ 77.2, .3.

[25] *See Berger v. United States,* 295 U.S. 78, 88 (1935); *Freeport-McMoRan Oil & Gas Co. v. FERC,* 962 F.2d 45 (D.C. Cir. 1992); *Reid v. INS,* 949 F.2d 287, 288 (9th Cir. 1991).

types of professional misconduct. Now let's walk through the Rule: Professional misconduct includes violation or attempted violation of any Rule of Professional Conduct, or being involved in someone else's violation (**Model Rule 8.4(a)**); commission of a crime "that reflects adversely on the lawyer's honesty, trustworthiness, or fitness as a lawyer in other respects" (**Model Rule 8.4(b)**); "conduct involving dishonesty, fraud, deceit or misrepresentation" (**Model Rule 8.4(c)**); "conduct prejudicial to the administration of justice" (**Model Rule 8.4(d)**); "stat[ing] or imply[ing] an ability to influence improperly a government official" or knowingly assisting a judicial officer in conduct contrary to the rules of judicial ethics (**Model Rules 8.4(e)-(f)**); engaging in invidious discrimination (**Model Rule 8.4(g)** (*see* **Chapter 15 at 427**); or doing anything else that the relevant jurisdiction defines as "professional misconduct." One thing that this list should make apparent is that you can be (and lawyers regularly are) disciplined for bad acts that are not necessarily tied to your activities as a lawyer or undertaken on behalf of a client.[26] Accepting the benefits of a professional license brings elevated expectations regarding almost anything you do, both formally and informally.

Although the specific procedures vary from state to state, the disciplinary process typically follows a similar trajectory:

- The process is initiated when the disciplinary authority receives notice that a lawyer may have committed misconduct. That notice can be informal, and may come from a client or other member of the public, another member of the bar, a referral from a court or other governmental body, or from facts that come to the attention of disciplinary prosecutors by other means. As a matter of public policy, to encourage the filing of complaints, the filing of a complaint is generally considered a privileged communication. (We don't mean "privileged" in the sense of the **attorney-client privilege**, which makes certain information immune from compelled disclosure, but "privileged" in the more general sense of being immune from use as a basis for civil liability.) As a result, in most jurisdictions, the complainant is shielded from any subsequent civil claim for defamation or malicious prosecution by the lawyer who has been accused of misconduct.

- Next, bar personnel or a similar reviewer (or panel of reviewers) appointed by the disciplinary authority screens initial complaints. Complaints that are facially invalid (that is, do not state a claim for professional misconduct) are dismissed at this point.

---

[26] Commission of a crime is a common reason for such discipline. State bars routinely suspend or disbar lawyers on the basis of guilty pleas and criminal convictions, whether or not practice-related. Tax evasion or drug dealing are just as suitable for discipline as stealing a client's funds or property or committing perjury. (A conviction itself is not required for discipline; all that is needed is the commission of a crime. But a conviction establishes the crime for purposes of issue preclusion, which makes the disciplinary proceeding very simple.) Commission of noncriminal acts of dishonesty, such as academic cheating, are also regularly the basis for professional discipline under **Model Rule 8.4(c)**.

- If the complaint is facially valid and plausible, the disciplinary authority may investigate. The nature and extent of the investigation is within the disciplinary prosecutors' discretion and may range from an interview with the accused lawyer or other witnesses to requesting documents and other information. In most jurisdictions, the lawyer is obligated to cooperate in the investigation, and (subject to the lawyer's Fifth Amendment rights against self-incrimination) the refusal to cooperate is in and of itself an act of professional misconduct.

- If the investigation shows no probable cause to believe that the lawyer has committed professional misconduct, the proceeding ends. If the investigation does show probable cause, then a formal disciplinary proceeding is convened. Usually this process is non-public. The Due Process Clauses of the Fourteenth Amendment and relevant state constitutions apply, and thus disciplinary proceedings typically include notice and an opportunity to be heard, usually in a hearing before a disciplinary judge or panel. Although the specific procedures vary by jurisdiction, a lawyer subject to a disciplinary hearing generally has the right to counsel, to present evidence and argument, and to cross-examine witnesses at the hearing.[27] The lawyer also has the right to invoke the Fifth Amendment protection against self-incrimination.[28]

- Following the hearing, the disciplinary adjudicator will make findings. Those findings usually include factual determinations about what the accused lawyer did (or did not do), and legal conclusions about how the lawyer's acts or omissions did or did not comprise professional misconduct. As part of these findings, the disciplinary authority may issue a sanction. The sanction must be designed not to punish the violator, but to protect the public from future harm. The most common penalties for unethical or unprofessional conduct are disbarment, which is the permanent revocation of the lawyer's law license; suspension, which is a temporary revocation of the lawyer's right to practice law; and public or private censure or reprimand (or reproval; the terminology varies) appended to the lawyer's professional record.[29]

As you previously learned, each state and federal court system separately admits lawyers to practice. They also separately impose discipline within their respective jurisdictions. Therefore, discipline imposed by one state would not, without more, have any effect on a lawyer's license in another jurisdiction, such as the right to practice before federal courts sitting in the same state, or a lawyer's

---

[27] *In re Ruffalo*, 390 U.S. 544 (1968).

[28] *Spevack v. Klein*, 385 U.S. 511 (1967).

[29] Although a reprimand is obviously less serious than a suspension or disbarment, you should not underestimate its significance. This sanction can be a basis for denial of admission to practice in other jurisdictions or *pro hac vice* (see **Chapter 3.A at 42 n**. 20); and if disciplinary issues arise in the future, the lawyer's history of professional discipline is taken into account in determining the severity of the **consequences**. Many legal employers and some potential clients will also view a public record of prior discipline as a "red flag" when they are selecting employees or counsel.

license to practice in another state. Nevertheless, most jurisdictions authorize (and regularly impose) "reciprocal discipline"—that is, imposing discipline of their own on the basis of another jurisdiction's disciplinary findings. As a result, a lawyer may be disciplined in multiple jurisdictions for the same conduct. *See* **Model Rule 8.5**.

B. Civil Consequences for Violating Duties Specific to Lawyers

All of the breaches of a lawyer's duties just discussed are ones whose **consequences** are sought by some representative of a governmental entity, and the **consequences** are exclusion or suspension from the practice of law or an official warning or condemnation of some kind on a lawyer's professional record—a record that is usually available to the public. In this section, we survey the **consequences** that may be brought to bear by private parties who claim to have been harmed by a lawyer's misconduct. These **consequences** are typically raised as claims or defenses in civil litigation.

1. Professional Liability Claims for Damages

Professional liability claims for damages are often referred to generically as "legal malpractice," but that term conceals a multitude of sins, and we discourage you from using it other than as a collective or generic term for *any* civil claim for damages against a lawyer. What is generally referred to as "legal malpractice" is a civil claim for damages for the breach of *any* duty arising out of or relating to the attorney-client relationship that causes monetary harm. As we will discuss in detail in **Chapter 5.D at 112**, there are at least four different basic duties arising out of the attorney-client relationship—**loyalty**, **confidentiality**, **care**, and **candor**—and multiple additional ones incidental to the particular activities in which the lawyer may be engaging. In this course, when you discuss a potential civil claim against a lawyer, you must identify it by the *specific* duty or duties that may have been breached. This identification is essential: Only by identifying the relevant duty will you be able to identify whether there is actionable harm, what the harm is, and what **consequences** may be available to remedy it.

a. Common Civil Causes of Action for Damages Asserted Against Lawyers

If a lawyer breaches any of his or her professional duties in a way that results in pecuniary (economic) harm, the person to whom the duty is owed may be able to assert a civil claim for damages. We survey here the causes of action commonly asserted, so that you can be alert to their possibilities as you learn more about the specific duties that lawyers owe.

Before we do, however, we remind you of a principle to which you were introduced in your first year. When considering a possible claim, don't fall into the trap of asking, "but he can't sue me for *that*, can he?" The short answer, as one of your first-year professors likely assured you, is: "This is America. Anybody can sue anybody for anything here. The question really is what's going to happen after that. Will the claim be dismissed, and if so, by what procedural mechanism, how quickly, and at what cost? Will the plaintiff recover, and if so, how much?"

We bring this up because even a frivolous civil claim is expensive, stressful, and distracting to the person against whom it is asserted. If that person is you, you'll have to notify your insurance carrier (if you have insurance), who may raise your rates in later years. You will have to defend the case, and in all but the simplest situations, you likely will have to (or at least **should**) hire counsel. Your professional liability insurance will probably have a "self-insured retention" or deductible, and that deductible often includes the costs of defense. You will have to spend time and effort defending yourself, or you'll have to work with your lawyer in the same way that you expect your clients to work with you. You'll be spending time and effort that you could be devoting to your clients (and the revenue and satisfaction that such work generates) in responding to the allegations against you. Not every civil claim can be avoided, but a fair number of the ones that get litigated could have been avoided with some relatively simple forward thinking and advance planning. Strive to be that one lawyer in five (*see* the **Introduction at 1**) who manages to get through a career *without* having been sued (rightly or wrongly) for alleged misconduct.

One way to pursue that goal is to be continually aware of how unhappy clients and **prospective clients** might express their grievances in a lawsuit. Common civil claims for damages include:

■ **Professional negligence.** The claimant must prove that she was owed a duty of care (*see* **Chapter 7.B at 180**); that the lawyer breached that duty; and that the breach actually and proximately caused monetary damages. The damages must be economic in nature; emotional distress damages are almost never recoverable in professional negligence cases.

■ **Breach of fiduciary duty.** Attorneys are fiduciaries to their clients, and so this cause of action can include claims for breach of the **duty of loyalty** (*see* **Chapter 5.D at 113**); breach of the **duty of confidentiality** (*see* **Chapter 5.D at 116; Chapter 8.A at 204**); and breach of the **duty of candor** (*see* **Chapter 5.D at 117**). The legal standard for each of these duties depends on the claim and the situation, and the elements don't always include alleging and then proving a lack of **care**, so don't fall into the trap of assuming that every civil claim against a lawyer requires some showing of negligence. The claim still requires an identified duty owed to the client; a breach of that duty; and actual and proximate cause of monetary harm, or the improper acquisition of monetary benefits that may be disgorged to the client under restitutionary measures of recovery.[30] Although emotional

---

[30] Though the differences between compensatory and restitutionary measures of recovery are properly the subject of a Remedies course (and we heartily recommend that you take one), a basic understanding is important in appreciating

distress is still only rarely recoverable, some jurisdictions will allow it if the lawyer's breach of duty was intentional. Intentional breaches of fiduciary duties can also bear punitive damages.

- **Breach of contract.** Most attorney-client relationships (the voluntary ones, as opposed to those imposed by court order or appointment by law) are contractual. Most jurisdictions hold that the attorney-client contract includes an implied obligation on the attorney's part to fulfill all the duties that a lawyer owes a client, including the canonical **duties of loyalty**, **confidentiality**, **care**, and **candor**. Thus a breach of a lawyer's duty to a client can be both a tort and a breach of contract. As with any claim for breach of contract, the plaintiff must plead and prove the formation of a contract, the lawyer's breach of the contract, and the actual and proximate causation of damages. The proof of causation and measure of damages for a breach of contract is different from that necessary for a tort, and although tort standards are usually more favorable to the plaintiff, in a few situations, contract measures may yield the plaintiff better results. In some states, the statutes of limitations for the two types of claim may also differ.

- **Abuse of process and malicious prosecution.** These two torts, generally viewed as "disfavored" because of their tendency to be wielded (often unwisely) for revenge, are available to those harmed by extreme and deliberate misuses of the legal system. They are specifically available against lawyers even when the acts at issue are ones that lawyers undertook on behalf of their clients. The issues of pleading and proof that these torts often present can be complex and difficult, and we won't devote much specific attention to them in this book other than to alert you to their existence. Here's the abbreviated version:

  - Abuse of process typically requires the plaintiff to plead and prove (1) the existence of an ulterior purpose or motive underlying the use of some legal process; and (2) some act in the use of the legal process that is not proper in the regular prosecution of the proceedings. A classic example is the filing of a *lis pendens*, or notice of pending action, on the title to real estate, which adversely affects the marketability and value of land

---

the risks that you face. Compensatory remedies are the ones most commonly sought in civil cases. They are designed to compensate the plaintiff for the losses that she suffered as a result of the defendant's wrong, and they try to put the plaintiff in the position that she would have been in had the wrong not occurred. For example, if the defendant negligently broke the plaintiff's leg, the plaintiff would be entitled to recover money to compensate for everything that the injury took from the plaintiff—for example, medical expenses and lost wages—as well as pain and suffering and emotional distress. Restitutionary remedies, by contrast, are available when the defendant has been unjustly enriched by benefits that should have belonged to the plaintiff. The recovery is measured not by what the *plaintiff lost*, but by what the *defendant* wrongfully *gained*. For example, suppose the defendant "borrows" the plaintiff's idle tractor without permission in order to grade the defendant's land. The plaintiff has lost nothing, because she wasn't using her tractor anyway. But the defendant would have had to buy or rent a tractor to do the grading. The value of the use of the plaintiff's tractor (or the increase in the value of the defendant's land as a result of having been graded) is unjust enrichment, and the plaintiff may recover that value as a restitutionary remedy.

and thus often creates a good deal of leverage for the filing party, under circumstances in which a *lis pendens* is not legally authorized.

- Malicious prosecution typically requires pleading and proof of (1) the institution (and in some states, the continuation) of a civil or criminal legal proceeding against the plaintiff (2) by, or abetted by, the defendant (the prosecutor or alleged crime victim or plaintiff in the underlying malicious action) (3) without probable cause and (4) with primarily malicious purpose (5) with termination of the proceeding on the merits in favor of the plaintiff (the defendant in the underlying maliciously prosecuted action) (6) causing damages.

Both are intentional torts, and thus they can bear punitive and well as compensatory damages in the rare cases in which their famously demanding elements are actually met.

b. A Note About the Relationship Between the Rules of Professional Conduct and the Elements of Duty and Breach in Civil Professional Liability Cases

You will have noticed that a specific duty and its breach are essential to any lawyer liability claim. That should come as no surprise; all tort and contract claims involve a duty and its breach. Tort law imposes duties on everyone in particular circumstances; contract law imposes duties on the parties to the contract. But how do we define the duties whose breach gives rise to these civil claims? Specifically, what is the relationship between all those handy Rules of Professional Conduct that establish so many **musts** and **must nots,** and the **duties of loyalty, confidentiality, care,** and **candor** whose breach can ground a civil claim for damages?

RULE ROLES That question turns out to be surprisingly difficult to answer. The answer starts with the principle that the Rules of Professional Conduct, by their terms, define only *disciplinary* offenses—that is, wrongs that can be pursued and remedied only by a disciplinary authority, and that result only in the **consequence** of professional discipline. The **Model Rules Preamble ¶ 20** is quite explicit in this regard:

> Violation of a Rule should not itself give rise to a cause of action against a lawyer nor should it create any presumption in such a case that a legal duty has been breached. In addition, violation of a Rule does not necessarily warrant any other nondisciplinary remedy, such as **disqualification** of a lawyer in pending litigation. The Rules are designed to provide guidance to lawyers and to provide a structure for regulating conduct through disciplinary agencies. They are not designed to be a basis for civil liability.

In other words, that stuff that you learned in Torts about how violation of a statute that harms a person the statute is intended to protect is negligence *per se*, and no further proof of duty or breach is needed—all of that doesn't apply here. (Sorry. We're not crazy about it either, but nobody asked us.)

So what role *do* the Rules play in lawyer litigation? The precise formulation of that role varies from state to state, but it's fair to generalize that most states view the Rules as setting forth standards of lawyer conduct that are *relevant to* but *not determinative of* standards of lawyer conduct that are enforceable by civil liability. We appreciate that this is not particularly precise, but it's the best we can do. As a practical matter, the Rules are quite influential in determining civil liability standards, but variations small and large abound, as do interjurisdictional differences about whether or how the Rules may be used to formulate or prove a standard of conduct or its violation. RULE ROLES

We will be vigilant throughout this book to point out instances where disciplinary, civil, and other standards of conduct diverge—that is, when different **consequences** for related acts require different proof (or may not be available at all). For your part, you should try always to keep in mind *all* of the different **consequences** that might follow from a particular type of conduct, and then ask yourself whether the standard for each potential **consequence** for that conduct is (or is not) the same. (Remember the "many different guns are trained on you" metaphor from the **chapter Introduction at 29**.)

c. A Note About Causation in Civil Professional Liability Cases

You will also have noticed that all the causes of action commonly asserted against lawyers require causation of damages. This too is hardly surprising; causation plays an essential role in most legal claims. And the standards for actual and proximate cause are generally no different in claims based on violations of a lawyer's duties than those used in any other tort or contract case. But in some lawyer liability cases, those standards play out in an unusual way. Specifically, suppose that you've agreed to represent a plaintiff in a personal injury case. And suppose further something that we assume would never actually happen to you (though it does happen to lawyers who don't maintain strong and reliable office systems (*see* **Chapter 7.A at 178**)): The client's file gets buried on your desk, and you neglect to file her action before the statute of limitations runs.

Classic professional negligence, right? You have a professional duty to meet deadlines; no reasonable lawyer would fail to file an action before the statute of limitations ran, so you breached that duty. But what damages did the breach of duty *cause*? Well, we generally measure tort damages by what the plaintiff lost as a result of the tort. Here, the plaintiff lost the right to prosecute her case: The breach of duty (the failure to file timely) prevented the plaintiff from recovering whatever she would have recovered in her case if it had been filed on time. But what if the case was a loser? Well, if the case was one that the plaintiff would have lost on the merits, then the damages are zero: The plaintiff would have recovered nothing even if the case had been timely filed. So in the professional negligence case that the plaintiff's new lawyer will pursue against you for blowing the statute on her case (sorry—it's just a hypothetical), she will have the burden of proving how her personal injury case would have come out. In the trial of the malpractice claim, the plaintiff's proof of causation and damages for professional negligence must include the trial of the underlying personal injury case that your negligence prevented from being tried. All the evidence; all the experts; the whole shebang.[31]

Similarly, if you fail in a business context to negotiate the inclusion (or exclusion) of a particular contract term that your client instructed you to pursue, that is not necessarily professional negligence. The client has the burden of showing that, but for some lack of reasonable care on your part, the desired agreement would have been reached, as well as the value of what the client would have had if the result had been achieved.[32]

This causation issue is referred to as the "case within a case" requirement, and it follows directly from the universal principle of tort and contract law that the plaintiff has the burden of proving what would have happened had the defendant's wrong not occurred. We bring it up here because while you're thinking through the potential **consequences** of your conduct, it's easy to glide over the rather complex causation and damage issues that commonly attend professional liability claims. These are an important part of the risks that you're managing, and they must be taken into account.

2. Disqualification

Disqualification, which is usually viewed as a remedy rather than a cause of action, is a court order directing a lawyer to get out or stay out of an engagement. It is available principally when a lawyer's breach of the **duty of loyalty** or **confidentiality** creates the opportunity for the lawyer to act contrary to the **interests** of a **current client** (loyalty, *see* **Chapter 22.B at 646**), or to the **interests** of a **former client** or **prospective client** (confidentiality, *see* **Chapter 22.C at 679**). These opportunities are typically created by **conflicts of interest**, situations in which lawyers have conflicting duties to two different clients or certain kinds of conflicts between their own interests and those of a client. *See* **Chapter 22 at 599. Disqualification** also may be available in situations in which a lawyer has broken rules limiting information-gathering and

---

[31] *See, e.g.*, Restatement (Third) of the Law Governing Lawyers § 53 (2000); *Myers v. Robert Lewis Seigle, P.C.*, 751 A.2d 1182 (Pa. Super. 2000).

[32] *See, e.g.*, *Viner v. Sweet*, 30 Cal. 4th 1232 (2003). Your House; Your Rules Although most states impose the requirement of "but for" cause on alleged professional wrongs, a few states use a "substantial factor" test. That is, these states hold that, if the professional breach of duty was a "substantial factor" in causing the plaintiff's loss, that loss is compensable even if the breach of duty was not a "but for" cause. In cases in which the chain of causation is complicated, this formulation can make a big difference. So be sure you find out what the rule is in the state in which you practice. Your House; Your Rules

has come to possess information that should not have been acquired. *See, e.g.,* **Chapter 11.G at 363**; **Chapter 12.B at 385**.

Disqualification is a prophylactic remedy—it's available when a lawyer merely has the *opportunity* and temptation to act adversely to a client's or former client's (or improperly treated third party's) **interests** but may not yet have done so. If the lawyer yields to the temptation and harms the client, damages for any actual harm that the client suffers may also be recoverable in addition to a **disqualification** order.

3. Fee Disputes

Many fee disputes center on whether lawyers working by the hour were inefficient, or they overstaffed the engagement, or they performed tasks that were not reasonably necessary or were tasks that the client directed the lawyer not to do. But an alleged breach of a lawyer's other duties can also form the basis for a challenge to a lawyer's fees.

Fee disputes can occur, for example, when a client claims that a breach of the lawyer's duties caused monetary harm, as in an ordinary professional liability case. If proved, the damages can be set off against (that is, deducted from) any unpaid fees that would otherwise still be due. These rights can be asserted as a counterclaim or by the affirmative defense of setoff to the lawyer's contractual claim for fees (and, commonly, both). A related but different defense available in these circumstances is the assertion that the lawyer's breach of duty comprised a breach of contract, in that the lawyer had contracted implicitly to provide services without breaching any lawyer duties. On the general contract principle that one measure of damages for breach is the difference in value between what was promised and what the nonbreaching party received, the lawyer's fee recovery may be limited by the actual value of the services provided rather than by the agreed-upon rates. In appropriate cases, the client may argue that the actual value of the lawyer's services was zero.

In addition, many jurisdictions hold as a matter of general fiduciary law that fees for services incurred while a fiduciary was acting under a significant **conflict of interest** or committing another significant breach of fiduciary duty were not properly earned at all.[33] Such a breach acts as a complete defense to a claim for fees, and may make any fees actually paid unjust enrichment subject to restitutionary disgorgement. That is, not only may you not get paid for the work you did under these circumstances, but you may also have to repay to the client anything that you received. Most lawyers view these potential **consequences** as a powerful motivation to avoid the kinds of conduct that could invoke them.

---

[33] *See* Restatement (Third) of the Law Governing Lawyers (2000) § 37 & Comment b.

C. Monetary Sanctions and Other Liability Imposed During Litigation

Besides conventional civil liability for breach of a lawyer's duties, lawyers can have monetary and other remedies imposed on them by courts under specific rules and statutory provisions. We will focus here on federal law, but most states have comparable rules or statutes. These remedies deal exclusively with abuse of the court system or the litigation process, and thus are available only in pending litigation—typically by motion of a party, but occasionally on the court's own motion:

- As you may recall from your Civil Procedure course, **Fed. R. Civ. P. 11(b)** provides that "[b]y presenting to the court a pleading, written motion, or other paper—whether by signing, filing, submitting, or later advocating its contents—" the presenter "certifies" to the court that, after a "reasonable inquiry," the position is not being presented for an improper purpose, is warranted under existing law (or a nonfrivolous argument for the extension or modification of existing law), and is justified by facts of which the presenter is aware or that the presenter reasonably believes will be revealed by discovery. Sanctions for violation can be sought by a party on motion or by the court on its own motion, and may include orders to pay money to compensate the party harmed by the wrongful conduct, a penalty paid into court, or "nonmonetary directives." **Fed. R. Civ. P. 11(c)**. An example of a nonmonetary sanction is a so-called "scarlet letter" sanction, in which misbehaving lawyers are required to notify the public, or clients, or other courts in which they practice, of their misconduct.[34] Significantly, "[a]bsent exceptional circumstances, a law firm must be held jointly responsible for a violation committed by its partner, associate, or employee." **Fed. R. Civ. P. 11(c)(1)**.
- **Fed. R. Civ. P. 26(g)** and **Fed. R. Civ. P. 37** are both focused on civil discovery misconduct, and they authorize the court to award sanctions against a party or its counsel (or both) if discovery is used for an improper purpose or is unnecessarily burdensome, or if discovery responses are not complete or accurate. As you probably discussed in Civil Procedure, these sanctions can run all the way from compensatory monetary sanctions up to evidentiary and terminating sanctions in appropriate cases.
- **Fed. R. Crim P. 42(b)** authorizes federal courts to sanction counsel in criminal cases for misconduct commited in the court's presence by means of "summary contempt" procedures.

---

[34] *See, e.g., In re Omnitron International, Inc. Securities* Litigation, No. C 92-4133, 1994 WL 476694, at *1 (N.D. Cal. Aug. 19, 1994) ("scarlet letter" order requiring a law firm to inform other courts before which it is seeking to serve as class counsel in class actions of its misconduct in the instant case; *see also Dignity Health v. Seare (In re Seare)*, 493 B.R. 158, 226 (Bankr. D. Nev. 2013) (requiring the attorney "to provide a copy of this opinion to every client in the next two years . . . who is sued in an adversary proceeding, but only if [the attorney] declines to represent them in that adversary proceeding for any reason").

- Federal courts are also vested with the inherent authority (deriving from the "judicial power of the United States" recognized in **Art. III § 1** of the Constitution) to regulate the parties and counsel in the litigation before them. This inherent authority authorizes courts to award sanctions against misbehaving counsel in both civil and criminal cases. The sanctions "may go no further than to redress the wronged party 'for the losses sustained' as a result of the litigation misconduct" and "may not impose an additional amount as punishment . . . ."[35] Most state courts are endowed with similar powers.

- **28 U.S.C. § 1927** authorizes federal courts to require an attorney who "multiplies the proceedings in any case unreasonably and vexatiously" to pay "the excess costs, expenses, and attorneys' fees reasonably incurred because of such conduct . . . ."

- Finally, some states require the lawyers they license to report to the state's disciplinary authority any sanctions awarded against them by any court or any other disciplinary authority. The report usually becomes part of the lawyer's publicly available disciplinary record and can also trigger professional discipline for the conduct that was sanctioned. Failure to report the sanction as required constitutes professional misconduct in and of itself.[36]

D. Civil or Criminal Liability for Violation of Duties Applicable to Everyone

Almost all of this book will be about your obligations specifically as a lawyer, with occasional references to generally applicable law that may be interpreted in particular ways when applied to your conduct because you are a lawyer, and some generally applicable law that you're more likely to run into (or afoul of) because of the kinds of things that lawyers do. *See, e.g.,* **Chapter 10 at 327**. Of course, you still have to follow the rules that everyone else does and do things such as pay your taxes and avoid illegal activity (everything from speeding to murder).

Though a law license can open many fascinating and rewarding career opportunities for you, in some meaningful ways it actually *reduces* your range of freedom (*see, e.g.,* **Chapter 11 at 341** and **Chapter 12 at 374**, discussing things that, as a lawyer, you **must not** do, even though regular folks **may**), and informally being a lawyer will cause many people to judge you by a higher—and, in cases of perceived wrongdoing, harsher—standard. Just remember that even though ignorance of the law is no excuse, knowledge of it is even less so.

---

[35] *Goodyear Tire & Rubber Co. v. Haeger,* 197 L.Ed.2d 585, 593 (U.S. 2017).
[36] *See, e.g.,* E.D. Mich. Local R. 83.22(e)(8); S.D.N.Y. Local Civ. R. 1.5(h); Cal. Bus. & Prof. Code § 6068(o).

E. Informal Consequences

Obviously, the formal **consequences** of misconduct—professional discipline, civil liability, sanctions—can be very costly. But the *informal* **consequences** of misconduct and of conduct that, though not forbidden, is unwise can be just as severe in their own ways.

Your reputation is your stock in trade; damage to your good name by association with conduct that others rightly condemn can take years to repair. A client who is unhappy with your performance—whether or not the source of the dissatisfaction amounts to a breach of your duties—can terminate your engagement (and in case you were wondering, clients are free to fire you at any time, and for any reason, *see* **Chapter 9.D at 294**), and may be tempted to dispute your fees or disseminate negative word-of-mouth that can hinder your ability to obtain new work. Many lawyers find that a lot of their referrals come not only from satisfied former clients, but from former opposing counsel who were better able to appreciate the lawyer's skill and diligence because she acted honorably and treated them with simple respect. And everybody remembers when opposing counsel was rude, gratuitously nasty, or unnecessarily unaccommodating. In short, you can make plenty of friends and influence a lot of people without ever acceding to an unreasonable demand simply by being polite. A little professional courtesy goes a long way.

The inverse is also true. Take, for example, a recent incident involving an experienced and generally well-regarded Texas lawyer whose opposing counsel accused him in a sanctions motion of shaking his rear end at the accusing lawyer and making obscene comments during a settlement conference, apparently as a means of taunting opposing counsel (who characterized the behavior as gay-baiting). The accused lawyer and his firm disputed the incident—exactly how is unclear because his firm took the position that the proceedings occurred during a settlement conference and thus were privileged, and accordingly, the law firm filed its response under seal. The court ultimately condemned the accused lawyer's conduct as "clearly outside professional bounds," and concluded that it had the power to sanction the lawyer, but decided that "[n]o further or formal sanction is necessary at this point."

You might be inclined to consider this substantially a victory for the accused lawyer—a verbal "slap on the wrist" with no formal sanctions. You would be terribly wrong. In the course of declining to award formal sanctions, the judge observed that the accused lawyer had "received national press coverage when the sanctions motion 'went viral.' [His] professional reputation, and the closely related ability to attract new business, will no doubt suffer, and they should." In addition, the accused lawyer's client, a Fortune 100 company, fired the lawyer and his firm and hired new counsel for the case. The accused lawyer left his firm on terms and for reasons that were not made public.[37] After a long and successful career, this lawyer may well be remembered not for his many accomplishments, but rather for one dumb gesture. There is no victory to be found here.

F. Summary: A Taxonomy of Professional Woes

What follows is a chart summarizing the **consequences** that we've surveyed in this chapter. Keep it handy as a reference when considering "what do you do now" sorts of questions, as every potential **consequence** is part of the strategic picture that you need to keep in mind.

In the next chapter, we consider the puzzling fact of human nature that good, sensible people sometimes make bad, senseless mistakes, and we try to help you understand how that can happen.

A Taxonomy of Professional Woes

RISK	ADVERSARY	REQUIREMENTS	REMEDY
Criminal liability	Prosecutor (state prosecutor or U.S. Attorney); often urged or supported by a victim	Violation of state or federal criminal law	Criminal sanction (fines; imprisonment) imposed by the government after conviction
Professional discipline	State bar prosecutor; investigation often (but not always) begins with a complaint to the state bar from a client or other victim of the alleged misconduct, or a "referral" from a tribunal concerned about conduct in a matter before it	Violation of a Rule of Professional Conduct	Professional discipline (warning; reproval; suspension from practice; disbarment; sometimes accompanied by restitution) imposed by the state disciplinary authority or the federal or administrative forum in which the alleged violation occurred
Civil remedies: a. Tort (or contract) liability	Usually a client or potential client, but claims may be asserted by nonclients owed duties (*see* **Chapter 9.B at 267**)	(1) A duty arising out of the attorney-client relationship or otherwise imposed on lawyers (2) Breached by the lawyer (3) Actually and proximately causing (4) Pecuniary harm (sometimes also styled as a breach of the contract creating a particular attorney-client relationship) Or tort claims for abuse of process or malicious prosecution	Money damages awarded by a court; additional punitive damages where authorized by governing law (almost always requires intentional, or in a few jurisdictions some level of reckless, wrongdoing)

[37] Angela Morris, *'Butt-Shaking' Houston Lawyer Escapes Sanctions, But No Longer Baker & Hostetler Partner*, https://www.law.com/texaslawyer/2020/05/05/butt-shaking-houston-lawyer-escapes-sanctions-but-is-no-longer-a-bakerhostetler-partner/ (May 5, 2020).

RISK	ADVERSARY	REQUIREMENTS	REMEDY
b. **Disqualifica-tion**	Usually a client or former client claiming a breach of a duty owed to that client (though standing can be broader), but nonclients can be owed relevant duties under limited circumstances	Breach of certain attorney duties in certain ways: usually a breach of either the **duty of loyalty** or the **duty of confidentiality** in a way that creates a **conflict of interest**; typically, no actual injury is required	**Disqualification** (an injunctive order forbidding a lawyer to accept or continue a particular representation) imposed by a court
c. Fee disputes or disgorge-ment	A client (or occasionally someone other than a client who has agreed to pay for the client's representation)	Damages for a breach of professional duty as an offset to fees owed, or a breach of professional duty asserted as devaluing or preventing the recovery of accrued fees	Reduction in the amount of, or a complete defense to, recovery of fees and/or an order to disgorge (in other words, to return) fees already paid, imposed by a court
d. Sanctions; contempt (can be civil or criminal)	Often an adversary in a proceeding; sometimes the court itself *sua sponte*	Violation of a statute or rule governing conduct of the proceeding (e.g., Fed. R. Civ. P. 11, 26(g), 37; 28 U.S.C. § 1927) or a court order, or conduct offensive to the "inherent power" that most courts have to govern the parties and proceedings before them	Sanction authorized by relevant rule or statute (typically an order to pay money to the adversary or to the court; fines and imprisonment are also possible sanctions for criminal contempt) imposed by the court in which the proceeding is pending (except for a criminal contempt not committed in the presence of the court, which is conducted as a stand-alone criminal prosecution)
e. Informal **consequences**	Clients; potential clients; courts; the public	Whatever the relevant observer finds offensive	Client termination of pending engagements; fee disputes; loss of future business; loss of credibility with courts and judges; reputational harm

Big-Picture Takeaways from Chapter 3

1. Every jurisdiction regulates the practice of law within its borders. All 50 states and the District of Columbia now use a version of the Model Rules of Professional Conduct as the basis for the ethics rules they apply, but the Model Rules themselves do not have the status of legally enforceable rules. *See* **Chapter 3.A at 32**.

2. If you want to practice law, you'll have to be admitted to the jurisdiction in which you want to practice. Admission usually requires a bar examination, an ethics exam (usually the MPRE), and a character-and-fitness review. *See* **Chapter 3.A at 33** .

3. The character-and-fitness process actually starts when you apply to law school, so if there are any discrepancies between your law school application and your bar application, or significant omissions from both, you need to correct them long before a bar examiner asks you about them. *See* **Chapter 3.A at 38**.

4. There is a process for professional discipline, and it follows roughly the due process format that you'd expect. The most common penalties for unethical or unprofessional conduct are disbarment, which is the permanent revocation of the lawyer's law license; suspension, which is a temporary revocation of the lawyer's right to practice law; and public or private censure or reprimand (or reproval; the terminology varies) appended to the lawyer's professional record. *See* **Chapter 3.A at 43**.

5. Discipline imposed by one state would not, without more, have any effect on a lawyer's license in another jurisdiction, but most jurisdictions authorize (and regularly impose) "reciprocal discipline"—that is, imposing discipline of their own on the basis of another jurisdiction's disciplinary findings. As a result, a lawyer may be disciplined in multiple jurisdictions for the same conduct. *See* **Chapter 3.A at 45**.

6. The Rules of Professional Conduct, by their terms, define only *disciplinary* offenses—that is, wrongs that can be pursued and remedied only by a disciplinary authority, and that result only in the **consequence** of professional discipline. But not only can you be disciplined for violating ethics rules, you can also be sued in civil court for alleged misconduct by a client or third party affected by the wrong. Common civil claims for damages include professional negligence; breach of fiduciary duty; breach of contract; and abuse of process and malicious prosecution. *See* **Chapter 3.B at 46**.

7. Other **consequences** for professional misconduct can include:

    - **Disqualification**
    - Fee disputes
    - Monetary sanctions
    - Rule 11 sanctions
    - Discovery sanctions
    - Contempt sanctions
    - Sanctions for "vexatious litigation"
    - Sanctions involving the inherent authority of the courts to regulate the behavior of the lawyers appearing before them.

    See **Chapter 3.B at 51**; **Chapter 3.C at 53**.

8. On top of all of the informal sanctions that a misbehaving lawyer might experience, one of the harshest **consequences** of all is informal but still powerful: the loss of a good reputation. *See* **Chapter 3.E at 55**.

Multiple-Choice Review Questions for Chapter 3

1. Recently barred lawyer Atkinson has just violated **Model Rule of Professional Conduct 1.1**, which deals with competence, because he failed to provide competent representation to a client. Although Atkinson knows nothing about patent law, he agreed to litigate a patent dispute. He never properly educated himself in this new area of the law and, due to his incompetence, he caused the client to lose the case entirely.

   The state in which Atkinson lives, New Columbia, has its own codified rules of professional conduct that closely mirror the Model Rules of Professional Conduct. These rules include a rule that closely tracks the language of **Model Rule 1.1**.

   Can Atkinson be disciplined for violating **Model Rule of Professional Conduct 1.1**?
   a. Yes. Violation of the Model Rules can be the basis for professional discipline.
   b. Yes. The Model Rules apply in all states and supersede states' rules of professional conduct.
   c. No. Atkinson might be subject to discipline pursuant to the New Columbia Rules of Professional Conduct, but not pursuant to the Model Rules.
   d. No. Violation of a state's professional rules cannot be the basis for discipline, but these rules can guide the court in assessing a malpractice claim.

2. Summer intern Sally was recently tasked with drafting a memo summarizing the major binding precedential authority in the State of New Jersey addressing client **confidentiality**. In her research, Sally comes across citations to:
   (1) the ABA Standing Committee on Ethics and Professional Responsibility's recently promulgated Formal Ethics Opinion No. 492, "Obligations to Prospective Clients: Confidentiality, Conflicts and 'Significantly Harmful' Information";
   (2) a recent on-point opinion from a New Jersey appellate court; and
   (3) § 15: A Lawyer's Duties to a Prospective Client as contained in the *Restatement (Third) of The Law Governing Lawyers*.

   Assuming Sally is providing only binding authority in her summary, which should she include?
   a. 1.
   b. 2 and 3.

c. 2.

d. 1 and 3.

3. Borris and his partner Norris graduated from law school in Hawaii. They have practiced law in the fictional U.S. territory of Great Pacific Island, where they have been duly admitted to the bar. Great Pacific Island does not have any reciprocity rules or similar rules or agreements with other jurisdictions. Borris and Norris move back to Hawaii, but only Norris gains admission to the Hawaii bar. They name their law practice "Borris and Norris, Attorneys at Law." Borris advises Norris on Great Pacific Island legal questions faced by Great Pacific Islanders in Hawaii, while Norris handles all other legal questions. Borris sometimes files documents in Hawaii courts, but he lets Norris handle all the oral arguments and trials. Is this arrangement proper?

    a. Yes, because admission to the bar in one U.S. territory authorizes lawyers for the practice of law in every other territory.

    b. Yes, because Borris avoids working on legal questions involving Hawaiian law.

    c. No, because it is unclear how long Borris has practiced Great Pacific Island law, and he needs to have practiced it for at least ten years before being allowed to practice in another jurisdiction.

    d. No, because Borris is engaged in the unauthorized practice of law.

4. Several years prior to enrolling in law school, Lexa was the director of a well-known think tank that was recently involved in a scandal over its questionable scientific research. Believing the think tank's mission to be especially important to American values, Lexa lied to the press to save the think tank's image. She has never mentioned this indiscretion to anyone outside of the think tank after these events occurred, and she did not disclose it on her law school application. Fortunately for her, this strategy worked, and the nonprofit continues to extol the virtues of clean coal.

    Lexa graduated from law school at the top of her class, and she even won the award for the most pro bono hours worked among the graduating class.

    On the character and fitness questionnaire, Lexa is asked, "Have you ever made a public false statement?" Lexa answers "No." She assumes that, because she was never caught in the lie and because her law school knows nothing about it, her lie will never be discovered. Unfortunately for Lexa, she is incorrect. A member of the committee is familiar with the the nonprofit's scientific research. Lexa's application piques his interest. He does a little digging and discovers what Lexa has done. If the committee rejects Lexa's application for admission to practice, what would be the most likely ground for that rejection?

a. Knowingly making a false statement of material fact on the background questionnaire.

b. Failing to correct a misapprehension about her application.

c. Failing to respond to a demand for information from an admissions or disciplinary authority in connection with the application.

d. All of the above.

5. Attorney Adam has successfully operated a mid-sized law firm specializing in a range of issues, including white-collar crime and patent litigation. Adam's hard work has helped the firm expand to 13 other states, in addition to the Great Pacific Island territory. Adam has been admitted to practice in each of these other jurisdictions. Unfortunately, due to his crippling fear of federal courts, Adam himself has never gained admission to any federal district or appellate courts.

One day, Adam's partner Eva, who is duly admitted to the local federal district court and who is unaware of Adam's crippling fear, asks Adam to make an initial appearance before the district court to represent a client in a potentially lucrative white-collar case. Adam is admitted in the state where the federal district court is located. He does not seek admission before the district court, but Eva assures him that it's fine because she will take over after the initial appearance.

Can Adam appear in court for this routine matter?

a. Adam may appear before the district court; he has significant legal experience, and other lawyers in his law firm have litigated several high-profile white-collar cases before this particular district court.

b. Adam may not appear before the district court; that would be the unauthorized practice of law.

c. Adam may appear before the district court; Adam is working only in the capacity of a coverage lawyer, and Eva will take over the case after the initial appearance.

d. Adam may not appear before the district court; he has not studied the local district court's rules of professional conduct.

6. One morning, client Chrissy retained attorney Allen to defend an action brought by Chrissy's neighbor, Nicole. Chrissy brought Nicole's complaint to Allen, who kept it on his desk.

Unfortunately, that was pretty much the extent of Allen's preparation for Chrissy's case. Allen failed to file an answer, neglected to appear in court multiple times, never filed the local jurisdiction's mandatory filings, and, on the single time that Allen did appear in court, he arrived unprepared. He reported to Chrissy, "The file was eaten by my dog, again!"

A default judgment is entered against Chrissy, who fires Allen and then sues him for malpractice. Assuming that Chrissy can prove all the elements of a professional negligence claim, what **consequences** might Allen face?

   a. **Disqualification**.
   b. Civil liability.
   c. Informal **consequences**.
   d. b and c.

7. Several years ago, the local district attorney's office successfully prosecuted Ivan Innocent for the murder of an ATM technician in a botched robbery, locking Ivan away for life. This prosecution was notable because it drew to a close the spate of crimes committed by the infamous and previously unidentified "ATM Bandit" and was conducted amid a storm of public pressure to hold the culprit accountable and bring justice to the victims' family. Unfortunately, another ATM robbery has just occurred that was eerily similar to the one for which Ivan was prosecuted, and DNA evidence recently came to light that strongly indicated Ivan's innocence.

   Deputy DA Anna only recently joined the DA's office and did not participate in Ivan's case but was assigned to investigate it in light of the new evidence. After looking into Ivan's case, Anna brought to her supervisors' attention her belief that Ivan was innocent. She was nonetheless ordered to defend the conviction.

   Anna then engaged in a deliberate effort to throw the case. She secretly communicated to defense counsel her research supporting Ivan's innocence and identified several witnesses that they could use. "What the office wants me to do is unethical!" she would frequently exclaim to opposing counsel. Ivan's conviction was overturned a few weeks later.

   Did Anna commit a tort?[38]

   a. No. The office wanted her to keep a person incarcerated for a crime that he did not commit, and she did her best to make sure that wouldn't happen. A lawyer who acts ethically cannot commit malpractice.
   b. Yes. She breached her fiduciary duty to the district attorney's office for which she works—specifically, her duty of loyalty. Anna should have withdrawn from the case or quit if she could not ethically pursue her client's objectives. Her failure to do so was tortious (though the damages may be difficult to quantify).

---

[38] For a different and deeply thoughtful perspective on this problem (which closely parallels an actual case), *see* David Luban, *The Conscience of a Prosecutor*, 45 Val. U. L. Rev. 1, https://ssrn.com/abstract=1614963 (2010).

    c. No. The only relevant duty that ADA Anna had was to the citizens of her jurisdiction. She fulfilled this duty by ensuring that justice was served. As long as the citizens approved of her actions, she did not commit malpractice.

    d. No. A prosecutor cannot commit malpractice.

8. Mr. Kent seeks the services of patent lawyer Lex Luthor. They are both located in a jurisdiction that observes the implied contractual obligation on the lawyer's part to fulfill all the duties that a lawyer owes a client. Mr. Kent wants to patent his invention; it is a device that he believes can locate a mysterious green crystal that he claims can be found all over their small town. Mr. Kent makes clear to Lex that he would not like others to know of his cutting-edge device before the world is ready for it. They execute a retainer agreement.

    Later that night, Lex Luthor decides to clue a few executives at LexCorp, a nearby company specializing in scientific research, in to the lucrative possibilities of finding this green crystal. He discloses Mr. Kent's design.

    A week later, Mr. Kent sees his exact device being used in fields near his farm and learns that Lex has violated his **duty of confidentiality**. "What should I do?" he asks his son, who advises him to bring a malpractice lawsuit against Lex. What claim could he bring?

    a. Breach of contract.

    b. Malicious prosecution.

    c. Abuse of process.

    d. None of the above.

9. Chip went for a walk to the nearby park one sunny afternoon in Philadelphia. While on his walk, he noticed that Max was not paying attention, because Max was about to walk right into Chip. Chip moved to the side so that the two of them would not collide. Realizing what had happened, Max took out his ear buds, and the following exchange took place:

Max exclaimed, "You were right to move aside, because if you didn't, I would have sued you!"

Chip responded, "Surely you couldn't sue me for something so trivial as being bumped into on the sidewalk. And what would you even sue me for? What probable cause do you have?"

Max retorted, "I don't need probable cause. This is America! Watch this."

The exchange having ended, Max and Chip went their separate ways.

    Max's lawyer, a family member who does pro bono legal work for Max, proceeded to initiate civil proceedings against Chip. The lawsuit was summarily dismissed as frivolous, leaving Chip saddled with legal bills for his defense.

Chip believes that he has recourse against Max and/or his lawyer for bringing this lawsuit. Assuming that Chip can prove that Max's lawyer acted with the requisite purpose, which of the following claims can he bring?

    a. Breach of fiduciary duty.

    b. Breach of contract.

    c. Unauthorized practice of law.

    d. Malicious prosecution.

10. Attorney Senior was recently retained by the plaintiff in a slip-and-fall lawsuit that is based on an injury that the plaintiff suffered earlier this year. Senior is especially proud of her daughter, attorney Junior, who works in Senior's firm, and whose life's calling is representing defendants whom Junior believes are being unfairly targeted by overly litigious plaintiffs. To the surprise of both attorneys, they realize that they are representing opposing sides in the same lawsuit. One day, they meet over a bowl of Senior's husband's beloved onion apple soup to discuss the lawsuit. They both decide to continue as counsel for the case, even though both admit that there is a **conflict of interest**.

The judge soon finds out about the **conflict of interest**. What remedy is the judge most likely to impose?

    a. None. There is no **conflict of interest**.

    b. The judge is likely to recuse herself.

    c. Professional discipline against Senior as the more experienced lawyer.

    d. **Disqualification** of Senior, Junior, or both lawyers.

11. Huey and Fred were next-door neighbors for quite a few years. Theirs was a tumultuous relationship. In the days of the COVID-19 lockdown, Fred especially appreciated his backyard space, because on sunny days, it was ideally suited for his newfound passion for pottery. After ensuring that it was legal for him to create pottery in his own backyard, Fred had a wheel (and even an outdoor kiln) set up. He loved pottery; it was his escape from social distancing and quarantine.

Huey could not stand Fred's constant state of self-righteous contentment and tranquility. One day, Huey warned him: "Fred, I don't like that you spend so much time in your backyard making bowls and mugs. I don't like Etsy! Stop!" Fred ignored him.

A few weeks later, with no end to the COVID lockdown in sight, Huey brought a lawsuit in the District of Keystone against Fred. Although Huey was not a lawyer, he managed to file a complaint that alleged that Fred had violated Huey's constitutional rights. Of course, there was no legal basis for Huey's lawsuit; Huey wanted only to waste Fred's time and bankrupt him with legal fees.

Despite the many chances that the district court gave to Huey to amend his pleadings or withdraw his complaint, Huey persisted to shower Fred with burdensome litigation. Ultimately, the case was thrown out on a motion to dismiss, but only after Huey spent several thousand dollars on attorney's fees.

What **consequences** could Huey face?

a. No consequences, because Huey is not a lawyer.

b. Per **Federal Rules of Civil Procedure 26(g)** and **37**, Huey faces sanctions due to discovery misconduct.

c. Per **Federal Rule of Civil Procedure 11(b)**, Huey faces sanctions for filing a frivolous lawsuit.

d. Huey has engaged in the unauthorized practice of law and has committed a criminal misdemeanor.

12. Lawyer Lee represents BigCorp. in a contract dispute. Lee's client gives him a box of documents that Lee reviews before disclosing them in discovery to opposing counsel. In the box is a memo that a BigCorp employee named Nelly, who helped negotiate the contract, wrote about the contract negotiations. Some parts of the memo help Lee's client, but the memo overall is harmful to his client's case. If the memo is disclosed, Lee realizes that his client may lose the case. Lee decides not to disclose the memo, even though it is responsive to opposing counsel's discovery requests and is not privileged.

During her deposition, Nelly is asked whether she ever wrote anything down about the contract negotiations. Nelly admits that she did and mentions the memo. When she is asked where the memo is located, she explains that she gave it to Lee. Ultimately, opposing counsel files a motion to compel production, seeking sanctions against Lee and his client for discovery misconduct.

If the motion is granted, what might the **consequences** be?

a. An award that Lee pay damages to his client for malpractice.

b. An award that Lee pay damages to opposing counsel for malpractice.

c. An order requiring Lee to pay discovery sanctions.

d. An order preventing the opposing party from relying on the memo at trial.

13. Early one morning, as you read the paper, you come across the following incident: During a recent deposition in an otherwise forgettable dispute in your jurisdiction between heirs to an estate, one of the lawyers was caught

attempting furtively to thumb his nose at the deponent. You remember reading that this deponent was blind, which meant that everyone else in the room treated the nose-thumbing as even more egregious.

Because you recently have read up on the rules of professional responsibility, you know that this is conduct unbecoming an officer of the court. "Harrumph," you think to yourself, "if a lawyer thumbed his nose at *me*, I'd do the one thing I know would be quickest, easiest, and cheapest way to get back at him. I would . . ."

    a. Let other lawyers know about the unprofessional behavior. Reputational damage is just one example of informal **consequences** that lawyers can face.

    b. Sue the lawyer for damages due to emotional distress.

    c. Refuse to cooperate in discovery and obstruct that lawyer's efforts in other cases.

    d. All of the above.

14. Jimmy, a local lawyer, prides himself on his dedication to his criminal defense practice and clients, all of whom he believes have gotten a hard bargain in life. One day, after getting one client a plea deal, Jimmy decided to get himself a celebratory drink at the nearby brewhouse. A few drinks later, Jimmy decided to drive home because he only lived a few minutes away. (Editorial aside from your friendly authors: Never do this.)

When he was stopped after running a red light, he pleaded with the officer to let him go, saying that he was very sorry and that he is a criminal defense lawyer. Smelling alcohol, the officer suspected that Jimmy was driving under the influence and placed Jimmy under arrest.

Jimmy does not think that he will be prosecuted because he is a hard-working lawyer and believes that he is well-respected.

Is he correct?

    a. Yes, lawyer privilege can be asserted to stave off prosecutions of lawyers, within the court's discretion.

    b. Yes, such infractions as this are commonly excused if they occur in connection with a lawyer's work.

    c. No, lawyers who violate the criminal law can be subject to criminal liability.

    d. No, because, contrary to his belief, he is actually not well-respected by other lawyers or judges in his area.

15. Lawyer James lives in a jurisdiction in which the rules of professional conduct are modeled exactly after the Model Rules. James sought to avoid jail time for his business partner and client, Hank. James thought that it would be a good idea to send a barrage of letters and postcards

from Hank's hometown in a neighboring state to the judge; according to James's plan, these letters and postcards would contain forged statements of support for Hank and other evidence of Hank's good character and strong community ties. Of course, none of these letters was actually written by anyone in Hank's hometown. In fact, very few people in Hank's hometown seemed to know who Hank was.

Fortunately for James, the plan worked. The judge, overwhelmed by the showing of support, gave Hank a reduced sentence accompanied by community service—virtually unheard of for Hank's offense. Unfortunately for James, his state bar association discovered the trickery after the prosecutor assigned to the case filed a complaint.

What **consequences** are in store for James?

a. Nothing. James zealously represented his client.

b. Professional discipline: by engaging in mail fraud to sway a judge, James violated **Model Rule 8.4(b), (c), and (d)**.

c. Informal **consequences**; the local bar association wrote about James's trickery in the latest issue of its magazine in order to alert prosecutors' offices to such strategies. James's reputation could suffer irreparable harm as a result.

d. b and c.

4

Why Smart People Do Stupid Things: Cognitive Biases and the Stresses of Practice

Every now and then, you'll find yourself wondering, "Why in the world did that person do that?" You'll probably have thoughts like that every time you read the back pages of your state bar journal—the part that lists why the bar imposed professional discipline on particular attorneys. Sometimes, of course, people do bad things for immoral reasons, or as a result of inexcusably habitual carelessness or incompetence. Some of the people in that back part of the state bar magazine probably had it coming for years. They were probably "bad apples."

But sooner or later, you may find yourself asking the same question about yourself: *"What was I thinking?"* We hope that the transgression you're remembering will be small and easily repaired. Sometimes the answer will be that you didn't have complete information, or that you were tired or distracted. Nobody's perfect; to err is human. After all, *you're* a good person, so you couldn't possibly have *intended* to do something really bad, right? Well, hold on; many of the lawyers who have been on the receiving end of a malpractice claim or bar discipline—or, worse, who are in prison for crimes that they committed as lawyers—thought of themselves as good people, too. And most of the time, in most quarters of their lives, they were. And yet, with disturbing frequency, good people do bad things without realizing until too late that they made bad decisions. *What were they thinking?*[1]

This chapter is designed to give you a feel for why smart, well-educated, well-intentioned people—people like you—can find themselves having done bad things. Those things often feel right to the person doing them at the time, but

---

[1] We can't help it. Whenever this phrase comes up, in our minds we hear Dr. Phil, in his Foghorn Leghorn drawl, honking *"Whut the hail were yewwwwwww thinkin'?"* If this earworm helps inspire you to avoid the need for the question in the first place, so much the better.

from a more objective point of view, they clearly weren't, and from that same objective point of view, they pretty clearly weren't *at the time*. You need to understand some of the glitches in perception and reasoning to which we humans are prone simply because of the way most human minds and personalities are put together. We aren't trying to urge you to become *inhuman*; not only would that be impossible, it would be counterproductive, because the same human characteristics that occasionally lead to these errors in perception and reasoning more often serve to make us stronger, better, and wiser people. That's why we have those characteristics in the first place. But you need to understand them, because the more that you're aware of their potential to lead you into occasional error, the more likely you'll be able to manage risks that could reduce your career to a paragraph at the back of a bar journal.

This chapter will be different from the ones that follow. We're not going to interpret or apply particular Rules of Professional Conduct to practical situations that lawyers encounter. Instead, this chapter will help you understand some general issues of professionalism and ethics. Think of it as a global primer on the cognitive biases and stresses of practice that might lead you to violate the specific rules that we discuss elsewhere.

A. Cognitive Biases

What do we mean by "cognitive biases"? Simply put, they are normal human tendencies to see or interpret things under certain circumstances in ways that are, objectively speaking, distorted or incomplete. It's important to keep in mind that these are not characteristics reserved to bad people; they are normal predispositions to which almost everyone is subject. We're going to discuss only a few here: those that can have more direct influence on your ethical decision-making as a lawyer. But these psychological forces are often at play in many tasks that lawyers regularly perform, so they deserve your broader attention.[2]

1. Bad Apples or Bad Barrels? The Role of Situational Pressures and Organizational Structures

When an individual misbehaves, we often dismiss the wrongdoer as a "bad apple" who just isn't like us honest, well-intentioned folks. When an organization goes off the rails—think of the company-wide fraud at Enron, for example, or the other corporate scandals of the early 2000s—we likewise tend to think that "a few bad apples" spoiled the whole corporate barrel. But what we know about human decision-making and behavior tells us a very different story—often, "bad apples" begin in bad barrels; that is, they emerge in environments that foster or

---

[2] For a more thorough discussion of cognitive biases, *see* Jean R. Sternlight & Jennifer K. Robbennolt, Psychology for Lawyers: Understanding the Human Factors in Negotiation, Litigation, and Decision Making (2013).

multiply individual misconduct. Here's what we mean, with particular reference to the environment in which you're likely to find yourself in your first law job.

a. The Challenges of Being a New Lawyer in an Unfamiliar Environment

We humans are social animals, and the communities in which we congregate develop common ways of interacting—summed up in what you could call "customs" or "culture"—that organize and simplify interactions and allow us to recognize who's part of our community. The rules can be explicit and formal: for example, the liturgy in your church, synagogue, or mosque, which may be different from the liturgy a couple of blocks over, even though both houses of worship may be part of the same or similar denominations. Culture also comprises innumerable informal conventions: for example, members of different groups in your community might greet one another by saying "howdy," or "hey," or "'sup." In Massachusetts, "howdy" sounds weird. In Texas, it doesn't.

Lawyers have conventional or customary ways of doing what they do, too. We don't spend a lot of time talking about these conventions in law school, because they are subtle, situational, and in some regards can vary from region to region and practice to practice. But when you go into practice, you will be a stranger in a land not yet your own, and some of the most important things that you'll be learning from the lawyers with whom you work is how "we" handle all kinds of common situations. This is one big reason why being a new lawyer is so difficult and stressful: You've just walked into an elaborate formal banquet in an exotic location where everyone else in the room knows what to do with the food, the utensils, and the dinner conversation—and expects you to know, too. And the penalties for disregarding or mistaking local custom could be severe.

Sometimes you'll ask, or be told, what to do, but often you'll just watch what's going on around you to see what people in your practice community do when they're interacting with (for example) clients, adversaries, or tribunals. You typically won't know whether what a partner or other supervisor is doing, or is telling you to do, is what "all lawyers do," what "most lawyers do," what "some lawyers do," or just "what I do," let alone whether it's what *good* lawyers do. Similarly, quite often you'll see someone in authority do something, or someone in authority will ask you to do something, that is not what you would have done if left to your own devices. You'll be left guessing whether the difference is because you don't know what you're doing, or whether it's based on personal style, accepted community norms, or formal obligations—or inversely, on the ignorance or bad intentions on the part of the person telling you what to do or how to do it. And you'll be working with someone who generally knows way more than you do, and who probably can have you penalized for messing up or disobeying.

Your overwhelming inclination will be to follow your boss's lead, and resolve doubts in favor of the assumption that the person for whom you're working is probably right (or at least not terribly wrong). That's one reason that it's important to pick a practice environment early in your career that is populated with the kind of lawyer you'd like to become.[3] But you need to stay vigilant to the possibility that the person in charge is wrong, whether innocently, negligently, or knowingly. If you've chosen your employer well, this issue will come up only rarely or not at all. But what if you haven't? How will you know?

One thing that we want to make dead sure you understand right up front is that, no matter how junior or inexperienced you are, you are *personally, independently* responsible for learning and complying with your legal and ethical obligations. You may *not* simply assume that what your supervisors tell you to do is okay. If you don't know what your obligations are, you have the personal, nondelegable duty to figure it out. "I was only following orders" is almost never an appropriate excuse for unethical conduct (or pretty much anything else). *See* **Model Rule 5.2(a)**; **Chapter 19.B at 507**.[4]

TIPS & TACTICS ▸ How will you know when to question authority? Nobel Prize–winning economist Daniel Kahneman, who has been a pioneer in showing the influence of cognitive biases both in important decisions and in daily life, has observed that

> [w]e would all like to have a warning bell that rings loudly whenever we are about to make a serious error, but no such bell is available, and cognitive illusions are generally more difficult to recognize than perceptual illusions. The voice of reason may be much fainter than the loud and clear voice of an erroneous intuition, and questioning your intuitions is unpleasant when you face the stress of a big decision.[5]

But even though the voice of reason may be faint, it's still there if you listen. If we keep our wits about us, each of us can sometimes hear a certain still, small voice asking us whether something makes sense, and urging us to take steps to satisfy ourselves that what we're being asked to do is really okay. Think back to a difficult circumstance that you've had to face, one in which there were pressures to do something that didn't seem entirely okay (or a decision not to step in and intervene when someone else was doing something that didn't seem entirely okay). Now remember that feeling. This quiet reminder isn't perfect, and it's easy

---

[3] In other words, when you're at an interview and your gut tells you that the place is filled with people who skate the edges of appropriate behavior, or who have adopted a style uncomfortably at odds with your own, listen to your gut.

[4] The only, very narrow, exception (in legal ethics, at least) is if you "act[] in accordance with a supervisory lawyer's *reasonable* resolution of an *arguable* question of professional duty." **Model Rule 5.2(b)** (emphasis added). In other words, it has to be a true judgment call, and your boss's judgment has to be objectively reasonable. How do you know if it's a judgment call, and that your boss's judgment is reasonable? You have a personal duty to figure that out. Yes, we know that you're new; we know that this means that the most available guidance may not be reliable, and we know that you may not know where to turn. You *still* may not simply rely blindly on your boss's presumed superior knowledge or judgment. That rule may seem overly harsh, but look at the bigger picture: You're only subject to professional discipline for following orders to do something that is *inarguably* unethical. How could a rational system shield you from responsibility for doing something that is inarguably wrong? *See* **Chapter 19.B at 509**.

[5] DANIEL KAHNEMAN, THINKING, FAST AND SLOW 417 (2011).

to miss in the hubbub of your busy day or the din of fraught events. But you know what it feels like when your conscience is tugging at your sleeve, however gently. Don't forget.

So you're feeling uncomfortable—now what? When you feel that tug of conscience, it means only that it's time to *inquire*. That tug tells you only that something *seems* off, that something *might* be amiss. There's usually no need for a nose-to-nose confrontation when you inquire; a simple, informational "why are we doing [this]?" or "why aren't we doing [that]?" or "what about our obligation to do X?" will probably get you a more thoughtful and less defensive answer. If your supervisor is not the sort of person who tolerates being asked for explanations (whether for lack of time, or lack of patience, or both), then do some research, or ask another lawyer in your office or another practitioner whose judgment you trust.[6] (Be careful, though—remember the rule about keeping client **confidences**, and be smart about whom you ask and how you do it. *See* **Chapter 4.B at 88; Chapter 8.B at 243.**)

And don't stop until you get an answer that satisfies you. Often you will find that a better understanding of the situation leaves you satisfied that things are being handled in an acceptable fashion, even if it's not one that you personally might have chosen. Every now and then, however, you won't be satisfied that there are reasons adequate to justify the course of action. At that point, duty calls, and you've got to do something. *See* **Chapter 4.B at 87**, "What Should You Do If You Wake Up on the Wrong Side of the Line?" Tips & Tactics

Real World Unfortunately, inquiring will rarely be easy. Here's an example from a famous ethical disaster from the 1970s, the *Kodak-Berkey* antitrust case.[7] Noted legal ethicist David Luban describes the mess succinctly. For now, let's focus on the agonies that the situation created for the law-firm associate involved:

> In the heat of adversarial combat, Mahlon Perkins, an admired senior litigator for the large New York firm representing Kodak, snapped. [Your authors would say he made a mistake and then couldn't bring himself to correct it, but on with the story. We'll talk about Mr. Perkins later.] For no apparent reason, he lied to his opponent to conceal documents from discovery, then perjured himself before a federal judge to cover up the lie. Eventually [much too late], he owned up, resigned from his firm, and served a month in prison. [Needless to say, he lost his law license as well.] Perhaps this sounds like an instance of chickens coming home to roost for a Rambo litigator. But by all accounts, Perkins was an upright and courtly man, the diametrical opposite of a Rambo litigator.
>
> Joseph Fortenberry, the associate working for him, knew that Perkins was perjuring himself and whispered a warning to him, but when Perkins ignored the warning,

---

[6] But be aware that a supervisor's consistent refusal to explain him- or herself and demand blind loyalty or obedience is itself a significant danger signal.

[7] You can read more about the case in Corporate Scandals and Their Implications Ch. 18 (N. Rapoport & J. Van Niel, eds., 3d ed. 2018).

Fortenberry did nothing further to correct his misstatements. "What happened," recalled another associate, "was that he saw Perkins lie and really couldn't believe it. And he had just no idea what to do. I mean, he . . . kept thinking there must be a reason. Besides, what do you do? The guy was his boss and a great guy!"

Notice the range of explanations here. *First*, the appeal to hierarchy: the guy was his boss. *Second*, to personal loyalty: the guy was a great guy. *Third*, to helplessness: Fortenberry had no idea what to do. *Fourth*, Fortenberry couldn't believe it. He kept thinking there must be a reason [—one that, as a less experienced lawyer, he just wasn't seeing].[8]

These explanations come not from Fortenberry himself, but from one of his fellow associates, who could imagine himself in Fortenberry's position and feel the confusion and helplessness that Fortenberry himself undoubtedly experienced. On a moment's reflection, you can probably imagine those feelings, too. And in this case, those feelings effectively paralyzed the associate, allowing a clear wrong to persist. The dilemma here is excruciating: Fortenberry's conduct (or lack of it) is completely understandable. But it's also unacceptable.

> **Problem 4A-1:** Put yourself in Joe Fortenberry's shoes. You've got your dream job at a big New York firm: big salary plus bonuses, and complex, interesting, high-profile work. You're working for a widely respected and well-liked senior litigation partner who has treated you really well. And now he appears, inexplicably, to have withheld responsive documents and submitted a perjured affidavit to cover it up. You've tried gently reminding him about the documents in his office closet by leaving a discreet note on his chair (less difficult than trying to discuss it face-to-face), and he hasn't responded. What do you do now?

Fortenberry's situation was relatively easy compared with the ways that this problem often arises. Fortenberry was surrounded by his firm's practice infrastructure and with high-quality lawyers who cared deeply about the firm's reputation. He had potential resources to address his problem. (Yes, that's a hint about one way to think about the last problem.) It's often much tougher to find any way at all out of the thicket. We'll get back to Frank, Maya, and Danielle later, but we want you to put yourself directly in the middle of this one:

> **Problem 4A-2:** Soon after you start working for a solo practitioner who does personal injury work, he gets you involved in a new medical malpractice case. The case is not an easy one, and it presents some arguable issues about duty (standard of care), causation, and damages. You ask your boss repeatedly when you should hire some expert witnesses to help address these issues and when you should start discovery. Your boss, who's often hard to reach because of his own busy schedule, keeps telling you to hold off because he thinks the case will settle. Early in the case, the defendants make a very modest lowball offer ($20,000) to

---

[8] David J. Luban, *The Ethics of Wrongful Obedience*, in ETHICS IN PRACTICE: LAWYERS' ROLES, RESPONSIBILITIES AND REGULATION 94, 95 (D. Rhode ed. 2000). The bracketed parts are our added comments.

settle the case. The client angrily instructs you and your boss to reject that offer, saying that the amount is "something I would never even consider."

Now the trial date has been postponed twice, and you still have retained no experts and taken no discovery. The trial court suggested at the last scheduling conference that requests for further continuances of the trial date would not be well received. The trial date is two weeks away, and your boss is in trial on another case. That trial may last until after the medical malpractice client's trial is supposed to start. Defense counsel (who is aware of your bind) sends an email reiterating the $20,000 settlement offer.

You reach your boss by phone at a break in his trial and tell him about the offer. "Take it," your boss directs. "But the client rejected that offer eight months ago," you helpfully remind him. "She said she'd never even consider an offer like that." "I'll get her to take it this time," your boss replies. "Call up defense counsel, say yes, draw up a stipulation with the other side that we'll exchange releases in the customary form, and dismiss the case with prejudice." "But shouldn't I at least call the client and ask her?" you ask. "No," says the partner. "Just do what I said. I'll take care of the client. I gotta go." And he hangs up.

What **must** or **should** you do now? Is there anything you **must** or **should** have done earlier?

REAL WORLD

b. The Invisibly Powerful Effect of Situational Pressures

Being a new and inexperienced lawyer in an unfamiliar practice environment is hard enough. But situational pressures can influence our perception and decision-making in ways that, though profound, we often barely see while they are influencing us.

i. Diffusion of Responsibility

There are important ways that people around us influence our behavior, even when they do nothing. Consider the situation in which a lot of people know that something bad is going on, but no one speaks up. No one wants to be the one to stick up out of the texture of inaction; no one's sure who's supposed to do something about the problem. This organizational stalemate is sometimes referred to as "diffusion of responsibility." If everyone hopes that someone else will speak up, often the result is that no one speaks up.

Let's assume that you're in an organization that includes a professional who's abusive to subordinates: screams at them, humiliates them, and maybe even throws things. Or maybe the offender is sexually inappropriate or makes offensive remarks about race or gender. Several people in the organization have seen this behavior firsthand. People giggle about it nervously in the halls; they pat the latest victim on the back and sympathize that they've been there, too. Yet no one brings it up with management.

Maybe management has no independent knowledge of the egregious behavior. Maybe management is aware that the professional isn't a nice person, and maybe management is even aware that there are behavioral issues, but assumes that if no one's complaining, the behavior probably isn't that bad. Or worse, maybe the professional is valuable to the business, so management is disinclined to interfere with the goose that lays the golden eggs, even though this particular goose spits and bites. If no one who has witnessed the behavior speaks up, management might not even know that there's a serious problem or might be inclined to ignore it—right up until the time that the organization is sued for tolerating the behavior.

Why wouldn't people who were witnesses speak up? They might be afraid of retaliation. After all, that professional with the hair-trigger temper and the mediocre throwing arm might go after the whistleblower next. But possibly they just assume that someone else has already spoken up. And that's even worse for the organization than the failure to speak up out of a fear of retaliation. If people can assume that someone *has* told the Powers That Be about the bad behavior and nothing happened, they're likely to assume also that the Powers That Be don't care. That assumption, in turn, may encourage others to believe that there will be no **consequences** if they act in a similar fashion. And the workplace gradually becomes a nightmare.

ii. Social Conformity

The invisible power of those around us is strong enough when people are silent, but even stronger when they speak. Solomon Asch did a series of experiments that demonstrated how just a few people can change a situation's dynamic. He held up a series of cards—two at a time—in front of a group of people. In each set, one card (let's call it Card A) had one line on it. The other card (Card B) had three lines, one of which was the same length as the line on Card A. Participants in the experiment were shown the series of cards and, each time, each participant was supposed to name the line on Card B that was the same length as the line on Card A. Simple, right? But, as psychology experiments sometimes are, this one was actually full of hired actors, with only one experimental subject. At first, each of the actors answered correctly. Then, over time, the actors started to pick the incorrect line in a card pair—first, one actor would pick the wrong line, then two actors would pick the same wrong line, and so on. A surprising amount of the time, the experimental subjects would go along with the wrong choice, and they did so more often when more of the actors were picking the same wrong line.

After the experiment, the experimental subjects were debriefed. Those who went along with the wrong answers typically explained that they did so because they thought their eyes were deceiving them ("I must have been at a bad angle") or because they wanted to fit in with the rest of the group ("I didn't want them to laugh at me"). Think of the Asch experiments as showing what happens when people around you seem to agree about something. The behavior of those around them made the test subjects doubt the plain evidence of their own eyes. Even when direct peer pressure to adopt a party line is absent, it's not hard to fall into lockstep with a larger group that's already marching together, although the effect of falling into lockstep can be reversed fairly easily by even one person who stops and speaks up. This is just the theme of "The Emperor's New Clothes" in a more chillingly realistic context.[9]

What does conformity mean for lawyers? If a few people in your law firm joke around about fudging their billable hours in order to "make their time quota" for the month, maybe you won't fudge your time, especially if those few people are vastly outnumbered by non-fudgers. But if your firm is relatively small or if a few people in your immediate practice group fudge their time (or your boss fudges his or hers), you may start fudging yours, too, either because you've convinced yourself that you must not understand how billing time works (at least not in the way that your colleagues understand it), or because you convince yourself that fudging isn't unethical because all the presumably good people around you are doing it.

iii. The Power of Authority

Now add to the practice context the existence of authority figures whose job it is to know how things are done and who have actual power over the circumstances of your employment, such as your supervisor. The effects of authority, even informal authority, can be stunning.

In the early 1960s, social psychologist Stanley Milgram developed a series of experiments to test how people's judgment might be influenced by authority figures.[10] Professor Luban describes the experiment vividly:

> Imagine, then, that you answer Milgram's newspaper advertisement, offering twenty dollars if you volunteer for a one-hour psychology experiment. When you enter the room, you meet the experimenter, dressed in a gray lab coat, and a second volunteer, a pleasant, bespectacled middle-aged man. What you don't know is that the second volunteer is in reality a confederate of the experimenter.
>
> The experimenter explains that the two volunteers will be participating in a study of the effect of punishment on memory and learning. One of you, the learner, will memorize word-pairs; the other, the teacher, will punish the learner with steadily increasing

---

[9] If you want a striking visual illustration of the social conformity effect, watch this famous *Candid Camera* clip illustrating what's known as the elevator experiment: https://www.youtube.com/watch?v=P00i7_C8tl8. Take two minutes and take a look. It's mind-blowing. Another television program showed the phenomenon's continuing power 50 years later: https://www.youtube.com/watch?v=dDAbdMv14Is.

[10] Milgram was inspired (if that's the right word) by the trial of Adolf Eichmann in 1960. Eichmann developed and administered the German concentration camps during World War II, and his trial was a reminder of the complicity of millions of ordinary German citizens in the horrific humanitarian catastrophes carried out under the Nazi regime. How, Milgram wondered (as had many before him), did large parts of an entire nation become party to such astoundingly obvious and inhuman brutality? What, or how, were they thinking?

electrical shocks each time he makes a mistake. A volunteer, rather than the experimenter, must administer the shocks because one aim of the experiment is to investigate punishments administered by very different kinds of people. The experimenter leads you to the shock-generator, a formidable-looking machine with thirty switches, marked from 15 volts to 450. Above the voltages, labels are printed. They range from "Slight Shock" (15-60 volts) through "Danger: Severe Shock" (375-420 volts); they culminate in an ominous-looking red label reading "XXX" above 435 and 450 volts. Both volunteers experience a 45-volt shock. Then they draw lots to determine their role. The drawing is rigged so that you become the teacher. [Remember, though you haven't been told, the "learner" is actually not a volunteer at all, but an actor who is in on how things work.] The learner mentions that he has a mild heart problem, and the experimenter replies rather nonresponsively that the shocks will cause no permanent tissue damage. The learner is strapped into the hot seat [which is out of sight; communication is by audio only], and the experiment gets under way.

The learner begins making mistakes, and as the shocks escalate he grunts in pain. Eventually he complains about the pain, and at 150 volts announces in some agitation that he wishes to stop the experiment. You look inquiringly at the man in the gray coat, but he says only, "The experiment requires that you continue." As you turn up the juice, the learner begins screaming. Finally, he shouts that he will answer no more questions. Unflapped, the experimenter instructs you to treat silences as wrong answers. You ask him who will take responsibility if the learner is injured, and he states that he will. You continue.

As the experiment proceeds, the agitated learner announces that his heart is starting to bother him. Again, you protest, and again the man in the lab coat replies, "The experiment requires that you continue." At 330 volts, the screams stop. The learner falls ominously silent, and remains silent until the bitter end.[11]

Disturbing, right? Stop and guess how many of Milgram's test subjects (the "teachers") followed the experimental protocol, through what were portrayed as thirty increasingly severe shocks, all the way to the end, to the switch ominously labeled "XXX" in red. Ready? *Nearly two-thirds* (63 percent). You need to pause and take that in. The "experimenter" had no formal authority over the test subjects; he couldn't punish *them* with electric shocks or with anything else. All he had was a lab coat, a clipboard, and the role of being the person who apparently knew how things were supposed to work: "The experiment requires that you continue." And yet two-thirds of the ordinary, regular people—people like you—who volunteered for the study found themselves pulling switches that, as they understood it, inflicted excruciating pain and serious, even fatal injuries on an innocent stranger.

---

[11] Luban, *supra* note 8, at 96-97. You can see a video clip from an actual session of the experiment at https://www.youtube.com/watch?v=Kzd6Ew3TraA.

For current purposes, we offer three lessons that we think the Milgram experiments teach that are profoundly important to you. *First*, an unfamiliar environment in which there are authority figures who appear to know what they're doing (like the "laboratory" presided over by the "experimenter" in the lab coat, and like the practice environments that you're likely to enter early in your career) tends to blunt any inclination to resist what you are being asked to do, even when it is blatantly and obviously wrong. If ordinary people could be induced to administer apparently fatal electrical shocks to an innocent stranger just by someone in charge telling them that "that's how things work around here," how easy do you think it will be to acquiesce when your supervisor suggests that you fudge the facts in a sworn statement or bill a client for time that you didn't spend, explaining (if any explanation is offered) that that's just how it's done?

Second, Milgram's test subjects knew something was wrong. They giggled nervously, they questioned the "experimenter" when the "learner" started showing distress (but generally returned to the shock generator when told that "the experiment" required them to do so); they sweated; they squirmed; they grew agitated.[12] The point for our purposes is that the sense of conscience tugging at your sleeve we just described is not some animated Jiminy Cricket that appears only in the movies[13]—it's real and physical, though not always as strong as what some of the Milgram subjects experienced in the extreme circumstances to which they were subjected. Your job is to be alert for it, and to pause, reflect, and act as appropriate when you feel it.

Third, we suspect that many of you are skeptical of this experiment's relevance to you. You're probably thinking that whatever those fools in Milgram's lab may have done, you'd never torture someone as part of a psych experiment. Most of you are wrong. Another feature of Milgram's work was to describe the experiment in all of its details to other test subjects, and then ask each how far they would have gone had they been the "teacher" in the experiment (not knowing all the details about the "learner" being in on the game). Everyone asked was positive that he or she would never have gotten anywhere near the end. Everyone. When asked what percentage of *other* people would go all the way to 450 volts, almost everyone guessed that almost no one would (other than the occasional deranged sadist). And yet two-thirds of the subjects drawn from the same population defied these expectations when put to the test.[14] The point for our purposes is not only

---

[12] An example of that agitation is apparent in the video clip cited in the previous footnote. Many subjects had lasting emotional effects from the experience. As an aside, the cruelty of Milgram's experiments to the test subjects (despite the experiments' unquestionable brilliance and significance) inspired reforms to the process by which social science experiments with human subjects are allowed to proceed. Imagine waking up the next day having learned that you were capable of administering a fatal electrical shock to an innocent stranger just because someone told you that it was a necessary part of a learning experiment *and* having thought that you might actually have killed someone.

[13] *See* https://www.youtube.com/watch?v=DOZzNOkcEgM.

[14] And if you're thinking that it must have had something to do with the selection of test subjects, forget it. The experiment was replicated with similar results whether the test subjects were men or women, and by using populations in Holland, Spain, Italy, Australia, South Africa, Germany, and Jordan. Luban, *supra* **Chapter 4.A at 74 n.8, at 97**.

that an environment with authority figures who seem to know how things are done is an incredibly powerful damper on independent moral judgment but that, unless we are knowledgeable and vigilant, *we are not aware of its power, either in anticipating its effects or while it is acting on us.*

2. Cognitive Biases Affecting Individual Perception and Reasoning

Leaving aside group and organizational effects, there are other normal human tendencies that can distort our perception and our reasoning and lead us into bad decisions. These are hard-wired into almost everybody, so (like responses to social and organizational pressures) there's nothing "wrong" with you if you experience them, yet we must all be alert to times when these normal tendencies may lead us into dangerous or destructive behaviors. We'll talk about a few of the most salient.

a. Cognitive Dissonance

Cognitive dissonance flows from the difficulty of holding two competing moral views of yourself simultaneously. If you think of yourself as a good, moral person (and who doesn't?) and you find yourself having done something bad or foolish, you may try to reconcile those competing moral views of yourself by unthinkingly adopting a good justification for your bad act. Cognitive dissonance played some role in the Milgram experiments. Remember, the "teacher" found himself in a position where, as a good person, he had just flipped the switch to "punish" the "learner." By refusing to flip the next switch, involving only a little more voltage, he would have had to conclude that there had been a similar (if slightly less serious) moral problem with his having flipped the last one. His cognitive dissonance would have subconsciously reassured him that good people don't flip switches to punish others for bad reasons, so if the last switch was one that would have been flipped by a good person, the next one would be okay, too.[15]

Cognitive dissonance can play two different roles in your practice environment: one for the supervising lawyer, who tells herself that what she's doing is ethical because she is, after all, a good person and an ethical professional, and one for the supervised lawyer, who tells himself that what the supervising lawyer wants him to do *must* be ethical because a good person wouldn't ask him to do bad things. Remember the observation of Joseph Fortenberry's fellow associate relating to the *Kodak-Berkey* case (*see* **Chapter 4.A at 73**): "And he had just no idea what to do. I mean, he . . . kept thinking there must be a reason."

---

[15] Notice, too, how much easier the gradual progression of the shocks' intensity made it for the "teachers" to adopt that silent rationalization. It's easy to imagine that the experiment would have ended a whole lot quicker if there had been one switch labeled "Danger—High Voltage" that the "teacher" was supposed to pull the first time the "learner" made a mistake. Most often, we are led (or lead ourselves) into evil one small step at a time.

Let's go back to *Kodak-Berkey* and focus on the partner, Mahlon Perkins. Remember, Perkins was a widely respected senior litigator at a large New York firm who had earned a reputation as a straight shooter over a long and successful career. Then he claimed that a cache of responsive documents did not exist (perhaps mistakenly; perhaps in a moment of bad judgment; but, in all events, he later learned the truth) and submitted a perjured affidavit to a federal court to cover up his blunder. Now, making a misstatement to a court is not, as a practical matter, a horrible, career-destroying problem *if* you correct the misstatement right away. We all make mistakes. That's part of what's baffling about the *Kodak-Berkey* case and what has inspired so much commentary about it: Whatever the reason for the original misstatement, Perkins could easily have fixed the problem in plenty of time to avoid any **consequences**. But instead, he realized his mistake, kept quiet, and began to compound his errors. *What was he thinking?*

Was it the heat of battle, the fog of war? One fascinating feature of this case is that the documents that Perkins withheld, while clearly responsive and producible, were not all that important to the merits of the case. So it's not like he was hiding the proverbial smoking gun to protect his client. (Not that that would have been remotely okay either, of course, but it might be more understandable as an excess of adversarial zeal.) So what was he thinking? At his criminal sentencing, he justified the time lag during which he concealed and then lied about the documents in part by saying:

> But I think on my own behalf I will say that it was not my intention to withhold documents from the plaintiff to which I thought they were entitled.
>
> The question is: Why didn't I verify from the suitcase [containing the documents, which he kept in his office closet the entire time] that I had indeed produced everything? I think I didn't know of everything. I had no reason to believe that there was anything of any substance or materiality that had not been produced to the plaintiff. I still believe that is true, your Honor. But I think I can say that in making that affidavit with the false statements in it I was horrified—I did it, but I was horrified at the time when I did it.[16]

Take a look at Perkins's sincere efforts to understand his own misconduct at his sentencing hearing: (1) "[I]t was not my intention" to withhold responsive documents (yet clearly he did, and by the time that he filed the perjured affidavit, he knew it); (2) "I had no reason to believe" that there was anything in those documents that would have mattered (yet they were unquestionably responsive to proper document requests, and he knew he had a legal obligation to produce them); and (3) I'm appalled by what I did—"I did it, but I was horrified at the time when I did it." Even in remarks presumably considered and prepared in

---

[16] The sentencing transcript, which was filed on February 2, 1979, is captioned *United States v. Perkins*, and this excerpt is from pages 3-5.

advance of his criminal sentencing, his mind recoiled at the idea of "hey, I did a really bad thing." That hesitation to recognize that you, a genuinely good person, can do really bad things is classic cognitive dissonance. Cognitive dissonance probably played an important role in Perkins's path from having withheld the documents to his written lie under oath that they didn't exist.

Another Wall Street lawyer, John Gellene, spent over a year in federal prison for failing to disclose **conflict-of-interest**-related information required to be disclosed by bankruptcy law.[17] His firm forfeited over $2 million in fees that it had earned on the case. The situation is similar to *Kodak-Berkey* in that the original omission may have been inadvertent, but Gellene then discovered the error and tried to cover it up by making knowingly false statements to the court. Also, just as with *Kodak-Berkey,* if the disclosures had been made in the ordinary course, or promptly corrected when the omission was first discovered, they might have proven insignificant. At his sentencing, Gellene did a somewhat better job than Mahlon Perkins at expressing an understanding of why he did what he did:

> I have not just for my adult life but before that I've been recognized as a person with gifts in terms of my intellect and my ability to deal with problems, and I've been very good and very competent at the kinds of problems presented [by] my clients in the practice of law and in academics and so on.
>
> And that is I think such a part of me and who I hold myself out to be and who I am that when I am confronted with a mistake, an act of inadvertence that is stupid that I'm—it is very difficult for me to stand up and say I did a stupid thing. . . . [T]hrough my adult life I have not been able to deal in a responsible and mature and forthright way with the imperfections that I like anyone else have and the shortcomings that I think any man or woman has in a world that's not perfect.[18]

REAL WORLD   Cognitive dissonance is the same cognitive bias that will cause someone to misrepresent material facts in a negotiation because "we're just negotiating, and I'm just posturing." (More later in this book about how much you can bluff in a negotiation before running into trouble. *See* **Chapter 10.B at 327**.) It's the same cognitive bias that many lawyers who "borrow" money from a client trust account to pay their personal bills have used. ("The client's not going to miss the money, because I'm going to pay it back with interest, and if I don't use the money, then I won't make this month's payroll, and I'll have to lay off some workers. *That* won't help the client, either.") It's the same cognitive bias that will lead someone to fib on time entries. ("It would have taken an average lawyer more time to research this issue, so I'm just going to put down how much time an

---

[17] Our choice of examples is in no way intended to imply that large New York law firms regularly engage in criminal behavior. To the contrary, such firms generally take great pride in handling the most complex and difficult matters in exemplary fashion, and they invest in personnel and infrastructure designed to ensure high-quality and highly ethical work. Our point is rather that, if it can happen there, it can happen anywhere.

[18] Milton C. Regan, Jr., Eat What You Kill: The Fall of a Wall Street Lawyer 262-63 (2004).

average person would have taken. It's not fair to punish me for being efficient.") All of these justifications just don't stand up to honest scrutiny, any more than Mr. Perkins's did, and yet when we offer them to ourselves in the quiet of our own internal dialogue, they *seem* to make sense and to justify our actions.

Because one of the first things that you may have to do once you start your career is to record your time, we want to emphasize how easily cognitive dissonance can creep into your timesheets:

> One day, not too long after you start practicing law, you will sit down at the end of a long, tiring day, and you just won't have much to show for your efforts in terms of billable hours. It will be near the end of the month. You will know that all of the partners will be looking at your monthly time report in a few days, so what you'll do is pad your time sheet just a bit. Maybe you will bill a client for ninety minutes for a task that really took you only sixty minutes to perform. However, you will promise yourself that you will repay the client at the first opportunity by doing thirty minutes of the work for the client for "free." In this way, you will be "borrowing," not "stealing."
>
> And then what will happen is that it will become easier and easier to take these little loans against future work. And then, after a while, you will stop paying back these little loans. You will convince yourself that, although you billed for ninety minutes and spent only sixty minutes on the project, you did such good work that your client should pay a bit more for it. After all, your billing rate is awfully low, and your client is awfully rich.
>
> And then you will pad more and more—every two minute telephone conversation will go down on the sheet as ten minutes, every three hour research project will go down with an extra quarter hour or so. You will continue to rationalize your dishonesty to yourself in various ways until one day you stop doing even that. And, before long—it won't take you much more than three or four years—you will be stealing from your clients almost every day, and you won't even notice it.[19]

And what's worse? You won't even think of it as stealing. But it is. `REAL WORLD`

`TIPS & TACTICS` **Getting a sense of when cognitive dissonance may be distorting your thinking.** One way to test yourself if you feel the tug of conscience at your sleeve (or really any time that you're in a situation that you recognize as difficult) is to drag your justifications out of your head and into the light and to try and look at them objectively, as if they were not your own rationalizations about yourself. We recommend a thought experiment that we didn't invent but that we like to call the **front-page test**: Imagine the conduct that you're trying to justify described in a simple, factual manner on the front page (or the home page) of the most widely

---

[19] Patrick J. Schiltz, *On Being a Happy, Healthy, and Ethical Member of an Unhappy, Unhealthy, and Unethical Profession*, 52 VAND. L. REV. 871, 917 (1999) (footnote omitted); quoted in Douglas R. Richmond, *For a Few Dollars More: The Perplexing Problem of Unethical Billing Practices by Lawyers*, 60 S.C. L. REV. 63, 107-08 (2008) (also quoted in Nancy B. Rapoport, *The Case for Value Billing in Chapter 11*, 7 J. BUS. & TECH. L.J. 117, 134-35 n. 99 (2012)).

read newspaper in your community. How would you feel if you saw it there? How would your nonlawyer friends and relatives react? If the conduct looks bad from that perspective, it probably is. If you start thinking about whether the newspaper would ever find out, you've got something to hide. And if you start trying to artfully edit the imaginary coverage rather than living with the plainly stated facts, then you know that something's not right. TIPS & TACTICS

b. Ethical Fading and Framing

Now that you have a handle on cognitive dissonance, let's talk about other tricks we let our minds play on us. Two of those are "ethical fading" (a reconceptualization that removes ethical considerations from decision-making) and the "framing" of ethics issues.[20] In both of these techniques, people shave the ethical issues off of difficult situations, often with tricks of language. If cognitive dissonance and diffusion of responsibility are types of biases in which people develop comforting excuses for not acting ethically, fading and framing try to wash ethical considerations out of a situation entirely. If Wells Fargo employees get bonuses for opening up as many customer accounts as humanly possible (even without telling the customers that they have been given new and unnecessary accounts), the employees may well be focusing on the business decision, rather than on the ethics of forcing new accounts on their customers. ("I get a bonus if I get X number of new accounts signed up this month.") If VW engineers decide to develop a way to skirt emissions testing because the testing is "unreasonable," they're probably doing so because they're looking through the frame of "impossible bureaucratic tests," rather than compliance with the law.

A telling example of ethical framing can be seen in a recent disciplinary case. A Nevada lawyer with 20 years of practice experience was defending himself in a defamation lawsuit (he was the named defendant, and was representing himself in the case). In his deposition of the plaintiff, he:

> used vulgarities, called the deponent derogatory names, aggressively interrupted the deponent and opposing counsel, answered questions for the deponent, and repeatedly made inappropriate statements on the record. [The lawyer] went on to ask the deponent if he was "ready for it" while positioning his hand near his hip. The deponent briefly left the room, but when he returned [the lawyer] displayed a firearm he had holstered on his hip to the deponent and opposing counsel.[21]

---

[20] Jennifer K. Robbennolt & Jean R. Sternlight, *Behavioral Legal Ethics*, 45 ARIZ. ST. L.J. 1107, 1120-22 (2013) ("Along these same lines, the language that we use to describe a particular act or decision can mask its ethical contours. Euphemisms—such as friendly fire, collateral damage, downsizing, strategic misrepresentation, creative time-keeping, bluffing, decedent, a case with bad facts, or Ford Pintos lighting up—can strip the decision of much of its ethical content. These effects of language can even be seen in the ways that lawyers prefer to talk about ethical issues. Lawyers tend to shy away from labeling behavior as 'misconduct,' and are seemingly more comfortable discussing issues involving 'gray areas' or 'incivility'") (footnote omitted).

[21] *In re Pengilly*, Case No. 74316, Supreme Court of Nevada, Sept. 8, 2018, at 1.

Pretty extreme, right? How many lawyers brandish a gun in a deposition? The lawyer who was disciplined had no history of similar behavior *as a lawyer*, but he did have a history with the defamation plaintiff, who he testified had threatened him personally several times. That prompted this not-unreasonable question at his disciplinary hearing: "If you were under the impression that [the plaintiff-deponent] was this violent individual and that you had had those threats made against you on at least four occasions in the past, why did you call him a dipsh[*]t at the deposition?" The answer in part: "I allowed myself to be a defendant, and I forgot that I was acting as an attorney."[22]

Notice the lawyer's use of framing: As a litigator, he was apparently able to keep his baser impulses in check. (That is, in broader perspective, an important part of the job.) But in this particular matter, he saw himself as a litigant, and apparently in his thought process, this entitled him to act like the litigant-plaintiff and be just as abusive and threatening as he perceived the plaintiff was to him. The lawyer's answer, though likely sincere and accurate, may have been a good explanation, but it was a bad excuse. He was suspended from practice for six months.

REAL WORLD ▶ **The non-excuse of "zealous advocacy."** Fading and framing can make extreme behavior seem acceptable, at least in the moment. One frame (that is, a frame of reference invoked to rationalize bad behavior) on which a certain kind of lawyer likes to rely is the frame of the zealous advocate. Verbal abuse, misrepresentation, even threats of violence are regularly attributed to the need—indeed, the claimed obligation—for zealous advocacy.

Let's be clear—this is usually the last refuge of the scoundrel. Nowhere is it written that a zealous advocate needs to be a liar, a blowhard, or a bully. To the contrary, the Model Rules explicitly tell us that "[t]he lawyer's duty to act with ['dedication to the interests of the client and with zeal in advocacy'] does not require the use of offensive tactics or preclude the treating of all persons involved in the legal process with courtesy and respect." **Model Rule 1.3 Comment [1]**.[23] In

---

[22] *State Bar of Nevada v. Pengilly*, Case Nos. OBC16-1169 & OBC16-1170, July 21, 2017, at 140-46.

[23] Think about it—the fact that the drafters of the Model Rules felt the need to insert this observation gives us a hint about how widespread the misimpression to the contrary is and how many lawyers claim to rely on that misimpression to justify inexcusable behavior. As Chief Justice Warren Burger remarked 50 years ago:

> [O]verzealous advocates seem to think the zeal and effectiveness of a lawyer depends on how thoroughly he can disrupt the proceedings or how loud he can shout or how close he can come to insulting all those he encounters. . . . [L]awyers who know how to think but have not learned how to behave are a menace and a liability . . . to the administration of justice. . . . [T]he necessity for civility is relevant to lawyers because they are the living exemplars—and thus teachers—every day in every case and in every court and their worst conduct will be emulated perhaps more readily than their best.

Address to the American Law Institute, 52 F.R.D. 211, 213-15 (1971) (paragraph breaks omitted). And yet so little seems have changed since Chief Justice Burger made those remarks. *See, e.g.,* Hon. Marvin E. Aspen, *A Response to the Civility Naysayers*, 28 STETSON L. REV. 253, 254-55 (1998) (a survey of lawyers in the Seventh Circuit revealed that over 40 percent "perceived a civility problem," with over 60 percent in the Chicago area agreeing). As an exasperated appellate court in California recently observed, "what we review in this case is not so much a failure of court and counsel as an insidious decline in the standards of the profession that must be addressed." *Lasalle v. Vogel*, 36 Al. App. 5th 127, 134 (Ct. App. 2019).

fact, these tactics are, at best, ineffective and are usually counterproductive. The most effective advocates we know are the most civil and courtly, which is in no way inconsistent with pursuing your client's cause tirelessly and forcefully.[24]

REAL WORLD

TIPS & TACTICS **Getting a sense when fading and framing may be distorting your thinking.** Remember that fading and framing are often carried out by using "**weasel-words**"—euphemisms, technical jargon, funny nicknames. Word choices like "bluffing" to describe lying during negotiations; "pre-billing my time" to describe billing fraud; "borrowing" to describe temporary misappropriations from a client's trust account. The verbal rationalizations that you or coworkers may offer to try to justify conduct that is just not okay are nearly unlimited, but one word that recurs during fading and framing is "technically." It's not bad to be technically proficient. Lawyers live and work in the realm of the technical, and learning to interpret and apply the law strictly and technically according to its terms is part of what law school is training you to do. But often the word "technically" can lead you astray:

> There are always line-drawing problems when it comes to giving legal advice. [A] client may want to "test" the line or urge that the line be moved in some way. [T]he line may not be well-defined at all when the client wants to take a particular action. And, of course, some clients (and some lawyers) couldn't . . . locate the line between right and wrong . . . if it were directly in front of them and labeled "LINE IS HERE". . . . [But one way to tell is that] if the advice uses the word "technically" in order to be accurate, then that advice is far too close to the line for comfort. So, for example, if an opinion letter suggests that a transaction will comply with the relevant regulations only if the words are read out of context and counter to the purpose of the regulations, that opinion letter likely will have some variant of the word "technically" in it. . . .[25]

So be alert for any discomfort or other sign of that "tug of conscience at your sleeve" that we've described. If you feel that tug, test the words that you're tempted to use to describe the conduct in question by using the **front-page test**: Imagine that front-page story about what's happened or is happening. Say out loud in plain terms, without euphemisms or jargon, what someone has done or proposes to do, and then say "They called it . . ." and use the words that are

---

[24] Many books addressing this subject provide pages and pages of examples of Horrible Lawyer Behavior, mostly from depositions. Rather than trotting out the usual Parade of Horribles, we'll ask you to trust us that far too many lawyers are capable of being colossal jerks, oddly enough even when a court reporter is present and transcribing their every word. We'll have more to say about incivility in the next section, but think about it—it may make *you* feel Great and Powerful, but what does it get your *client* when you gratuitously insult or threaten your opposing counsel or opposing parties? And if your client is the kind of person who gets off on hiring people to threaten or intimidate enemies, think carefully about (a) what that makes you; and (b) how that client is going to treat *you* in due course.

[25] Colin P. Marks & Nancy B. Rapoport, *The Corporate Lawyer's Role in a Contemporary Democracy*, 77 FORDHAM L. REV. 1269, 1290-91 (2009) (footnote omitted).

being applied. If they sound like **weasel-words** in this context, then they probably are. TIPS & TACTICS

B. What Should You Do If You Wake Up on the Wrong Side of the Line?

We've all done stupid or thoughtless things in our personal and professional lives. Sometimes we've realized, aghast, that we may have gotten ourselves into real trouble of one kind or another. You will, one day, look back on a serious misjudgment and realize, only in retrospect, that cognitive biases or the effects of stress may have led you there. In the unlikely event that you think you haven't made any significant personal or professional mistakes yet, interrogate yourself a little more closely before volunteering for sainthood. And if, miraculously, you still believe you haven't, rest assured that you will.

And when it happens, what then? The urge to sit paralyzed at your desk and hope that it will somehow go away can be overwhelming. At his criminal sentencing, John Gellene, the Wall Street lawyer who went to prison for failing to make legally required disclosures to a bankruptcy court (and then covering it up with perjury), described his reaction when he received an order to show cause indicating that the court had questions about what he'd done (or failed to do):

> I could not deal with it. I just fell apart . . . I didn't work. I didn't do anything. I would sit at my desk. And only when I absolutely had to did I zip up all of that and for whatever time it took put a face before the world that didn't reveal what was going on with me.[26]

He shoved the order into a drawer and told no one about it.

This is a common and very human reaction to discovering a potential mistake. It's also among the most self-destructive things that you can do. The most important thing that we can tell you is that error, like infection, festers and multiplies in darkness. A minor cut or scrape that could have been washed, dressed, and healed in short order will, if left unattended, rapidly go septic. So in the succinct phrasing of our friend, the noted lawyer and law professor David McGowan,

"When you mess up, 'fess up."[27]

But *how* and *to whom* you 'fess up is critically important. Start by reaching out to someone you trust to get perspective and advice. As hard as practicing law is, recognizing and responding to mistakes is even harder. There may be complex decisions about how to deal with your employer, your client, and your professional liability insurer (and most insurers require you to talk to them before

---

[26] Regan, *supra* **Chapter 4.A at 82 n. 18, at 263**.

[27] DAVID MCGOWAN, DEVELOPING JUDGMENT ABOUT PRACTICING LAW 15 (2d ed. 2013). For discussion of more of the **consequences** you can suffer by failing to come forward, *see* **Chapter 5.D at 120**.

confessing error to the client, on pain of losing your coverage for the error), as well as any tribunal involved and any affected third parties. No matter how clever and self-possessed you are, you need a calm and objective eye outside the morass to help you think these things through. And at least as important, no one—especially not you—deserves to face troubles like these alone.

If you have a supervisor in the matter in which you've erred, start there if you possibly can. If you can't, most **practice organizations** (law firms, corporate law departments, government agencies, etc.) have an "ethics czar," an ethics committee, or other persons designated to help with such matters. Or you can reach out to an experienced lawyer in your workplace whose personal and professional judgment you trust. And bear in mind that some professional liability insurers have a "help line" for their insureds where lawyers experienced in ethics and professional liability matters are available to give you free advice about the problem (it's part of what your employer's premiums pay for, and it's much better for you *and* the insurer if the insurer can give you good advice up front about handling the problem). If you can't get the advice you need in or through your workplace, contact a lawyer outside your work environment whom you trust—taking care to explicitly approach that person for legal advice from a lawyer (whether you get the advice for free (*pro bono*) or you have to pay for it), so that your communications can remain protected as **attorney-client privileged**. *See* **Chapter 8.B at 243**.

You may discover that you didn't make an actionable mistake after all. Often, newer lawyers confuse not living up to their own highest aspirations with disciplinary violations or breaches of their duties, or they simply misunderstand what the law requires in particular circumstances. Or you may find that you've made a mistake that, because you are attending to it early and thoughtfully, can be easily repaired. But even if you've made a serious and irreparable error, attending to it promptly and mindfully is *always* better than ignoring it and hoping that it will disappear. It won't. It will just get worse and worse for you and everyone else involved. Just ask Messrs. Perkins and Gellene.

C. Coping with the Stresses of Practice

1. Like Law School, Lawyering Is Stressful

You already know that law school is stressful. Unfortunately, and we're genuinely sorry to be the bearers of rough tidings, it doesn't end there. Law practice is stressful, too.

Any job has stresses, and the legal profession is no exception, except in the sense that it can be exceptionally stressful, considerably moreso than many other jobs. BigLaw is, of course, the most common source of stories in the popular press about soul-crushing hours at work, mind-numbing tasks thrown at inexperienced lawyers, thoughtless and narcissistic supervisors, and the ugliness of the competitive tournament that leads to partnership. (As discussed below, these stories, while real, can be exaggerated: There are plenty of happy lawyers in BigLaw, but they're the ones who have learned to cope with the very real stresses of the job.)

But BigLaw is not the only place in which lawyers—new and experienced—get stressed. Any workplace can be understaffed, a competitive battleground, or the home of indifferent, clueless, or abusive managers. If you're a solo practitioner, imagine your stress level skyrocketing when you or a loved one encounters illness, bereavement, or other pressing needs, or when you want to take a vacation but have no one to attend to your clients or their matters while you're away. And if you're in a small firm, the ebbs and flows of your colleagues' personal and professional lives can create some sharp-elbowed moments. Or imagine life as a government attorney when the person at the top of the food chain changes with each election, replacing old priorities and policies with new ones.

And then there's time, or more to the point, there usually isn't. Most lawyers work really, really hard, but constantly feel as though they're behind. (You're probably already familiar with that feeling in law school. Sorry, but for most of us that feeling doesn't let up after graduation.) Regardless of where you work, good lawyers (like you) generally want to produce good work, but rarely will the press of business or the client's budget accommodate all the time that you'd like to spend. You will always be asked to do more with less. The fear of error will chase you through sleepless nights. And the more success you achieve, the more you'll be asked to do.[28] In this environment, even family and friends can become stressors. Busy work lives impinge on home and personal lives. That elusive "work-life balance" often amounts to work-life juggling. Have you ever seen a relaxed juggler? (No? Now ask her to add in another chainsaw and keep going.)

And besides the unrelenting time pressure and fear of error, there's the incivility of other lawyers (and sometimes that of your own clients). You work in an adversary system, and for most lawyers—whether they are negotiators or litigators—conflict is part of the job. There's a certain kind of lawyer for whom the adversary system is just a playground for deep-seated personality defects. There are others, more calculating, who know that angry lawyers make mistakes, and who will work hard to make you angry for exactly that reason.

Just wait until you see what opposing counsel seem to enjoy doing to you. We're not just talking about sarcasm, shouting over you, hanging up on you, falsely accusing you of lying or malfeasance with exaggerated or made-up facts, or worse. We're talking about imposing deadlines that deliberately coincide with a holiday or a vacation that you've told them that you've already booked. We're talking about someone sending an email setting a 5:00 p.m. deadline at 4:55 p.m.

---

[28] Jokes often tell us important things about their subjects. If you haven't heard this one yet, let us be the first to share it with you: Law practice is a pie-eating contest in which the prize is another pie.

and then using your failure to respond in the five-minute gap as evidence that you've consented to something that the person knows that you oppose. We're talking about eye-rolling, sighing, and lengthy "speaking objections" in which opposing counsel coaches the witness in depositions. We're talking about failing to mark the changes on a draft document. You can comfort yourself by wondering which of these treasures of humanity were raised by wolves, how many divorces they've enjoyed, and how lonely they must be when they leave the office. But none of it will really help. Incivility has a corrosive way with decent people.[29]

2. How Do You Know When Practice Stresses Are More Than You Should Handle Alone?

You may think that we're trying to persuade you to reconsider your choice of career, but we're not. We think that lawyering is a great way to earn a living. We're each happy that we're lawyers, and we'd do it all again in a heartbeat. We know countless lawyers who feel very much the same. Practice is intellectually challenging, client service can be a joy, and the profession offers a wide range of career choices that also allow you help others and serve society. Lots of lawyers—including many of the lawyers in very stressful practices—are happy and healthy.

But we know our limitations, so we know that we can't tell *you* how to build *your* happy life. There's plenty of literature about finding joy among life's challenges, some of it focusing on the issues typical to lawyers. It can't be meaningfully summarized in the space that we have here, but research shows that autonomy, a sense of connectedness, and feelings of competence all contribute far more to many lawyers' sense of well-being than do being rich, having made good grades (or law review) in law school, or being in a job that's considered "high status."[30]

---

[29] Every decent lawyer develops techniques to try and keep indecent conduct at bay. A few of our favorites: Start by assuming (or pretending to assume) that the incivility was an aberration: "Oh, I thought that you remembered that I'll be on vacation when that discovery is due, so why don't we agree to an extension of time?" Another is to name the behavior calmly but directly: "I don't respond well to tantrums, so I'm going to end this call now, and we can resume when you've calmed down." (Our experience leads us to believe that jerks who need to calm down hate being told to calm down, thereby making a response of this type at least somewhat emotionally satisfying.) A third is to write the other lawyer, describing simply and plainly what happened (adjectives and adverbs in your description only antagonize, so avoid them) and explaining that, as a result, you will no longer deal with that person except in writing. (Some people like to copy writings describing bad behavior to the bad actor's boss or someone else in authority that might take a dim view of the behavior. We've found that such a plan rarely helps; people in an organization who behave a certain way usually have an understanding that they can get away with it. And whatever you do, don't copy the person's client. You can't communicate directly with a represented person without her lawyer's permission, no matter how terribly the lawyer is misbehaving. *See* **Chapter 11 at 341**.) What *doesn't* work? Seething about the behavior and doing nothing. Seething equals more stress, not less.

Even worse is trying to retaliate in kind. We share with you a lesson that each of us learned the hard way: There are at least three reasons you should never mud wrestle with a pig:

(1) The pig likes it.
(2) The pig is probably better at it than you are.
(3) It doesn't take long before it's hard to tell you from the pig.

[30] *See, e.g.,* Lawrence S. Krieger & Kennon M. Sheldon, *What Makes Lawyers Happy? Transcending the Anecdotes with Data from 6,200 Lawyers*, 83 Geo. Washington L. Rev. 554 (2015).

But wait, those of you who have been reading along alertly are now thinking, you just told us we won't *have* much autonomy, sense of connectedness, or feelings of competence when we're just starting out. To which we respond (in addition to thanking you for paying attention), that's true. The early years of practice can be among the hardest. Nevertheless, we offer you a glimpse of a happy and satisfying future worth waiting for as you settle in, and experience shows that if you're prepared for the challenges you face, they're much easier to master. The happy lawyers we know are all happy in their own way. So we'll just urge *you* to find *your* joy in your own way, too. Start by pursuing practice opportunities that you find interesting and personally rewarding. You will find them, and many lawyers find them early on. Add family and friends, civic or charitable engagement, pets, hobbies, or exercise—whatever floats your emotional boat. And try to be a little patient while you get there.[31]

One thing that is certain, though, is that you will face stresses, challenges, and setbacks throughout your career. Everyone does, and lawyers do, too. And (to turn Tolstoy on his head) while happy lawyers are each happy in their own way, unhappy lawyers have a lot in common.[32] The challenges in practice that we just surveyed share many characteristics, regardless of the type of work environment. Those stressors take a toll, particularly on highly motivated and ambitious people like you.

Some people cope with these stresses better than others. The reasons are disputed—some of it is probably innate; some probably learned—but none of it has anything to do with people's merits as human beings. Everyone is occasionally sad, anxious, or overwhelmed; that's normal. But for some of us, the sense of dread or misery can become commonplace or pervasive. Some suffer in silence; others "self-medicate" with alcohol or drugs, either to dull the discomfort or to force themselves to stay focused and alert when their minds and bodies are telling them that they'd rather be doing almost anything else.[33]

As we mentioned in the **Introduction at 4**, lawyers—and law students—suffer from anxiety, depression, and addiction at rates *two to three times higher* than the general population. In a recent large-scale study, 21 percent of lawyers—more than one in five—showed signs of abusive or problem alcohol use; up to 28

---

[31] We will also repeat the adage that no one ever said on his deathbed that he wished that he'd spent more time at the office, though one of us did have a couple of law partners for whom he wondered if it would be true. And if we had to give it to you in two words that were necessary if not sufficient, we'd venture: Take vacations. Overwork leads to burnout, which leads to greater suffering and many other evils.

[32] *Cf.* Leo Tolstoy, Anna Karenina 1 (1877) ("Happy families are all alike; every unhappy family is unhappy in its own way"). With all respect to a literary genius, we think Tolstoy got this famous observation, and its application to lawyers, exactly backwards.

[33] We're sad to report that some of the most commonly abused drugs in law school are attention deficit disorder medications such as Adderall or Ritalin. If you are taking these drugs without a prescription and the supervision of a doctor, get help now. They can be addictive, and misuse can have terrible consequences. Your authors have had students hospitalized with breakdowns triggered by misuse of these substances.

percent—more than one in four—exhibited symptoms of depression, anxiety, or severe stress.[34] The bad news is that these are serious and debilitating diseases that can rob you of your energy, attention, and competence, and can cause you to make mistakes or neglect your clients (or, in your current circumstances, your schoolwork), not to mention making you completely miserable. And that can lead to academic or workplace **consequences**, disciplinary charges, malpractice claims, and court sanctions.[35]

The good news is that anxiety, depression, and addiction are *diseases*, not failures of morality, willpower, or work ethic, though some people may try to tell you otherwise (and you may experience lingering questions of your own along those lines). And because they are diseases, they are treatable and beatable, and help is available so long as you will accept it.

How do you know if you or someone you care about is headed for this kind of trouble? Again, you must watch and listen, and be frank with yourself about what you see or feel. Some common warning signs of depression and anxiety include:

1. you've been sleeping too much or too little, or you're waking up early or having trouble falling asleep;
2. you've been eating too much or too little or are gaining or losing weight;
3. you're listless or having trouble concentrating or doing things that you used to find easy to do;
4. you're having difficulty making decisions;
5. you're having a hard time controlling your negative thoughts, or having trouble focusing on or thinking clearly about anything other than something you're worried about;

---

[34] Mark S. Goldstein, *"Scared. Ashamed. Crippled.": How One Lawyer Overcame Living With Depression in Big Law*, https://www.law.com/2019/02/12/scared-ashamed-crippled-how-one-lawyer-overcame-living-with-depression-in-big-law/?utm_source=email&utm_medium=enl&utm_campaign=morningminute&utm_content=20190213&utm_term=law (Feb. 12, 2019); Patrick R. Krill, Ryan Johnson & Linda Albert, *The Prevalence of Substance Use and Other Mental Health Concerns Among American Attorneys*, 10 Journal of Addiction Medicine 46, https://journals.lww.com/journaladdictionmedicine/Fulltext/2016/02000/The_Prevalence_of_Substance_Use_and_Other_Mental.8.aspx (January/February 2016). A growing literature documents the challenges that lawyers face in this regard. Alec Rothrock, *Lawyers Who Live in Pain: Mental Health Issues and Lawyer Misconduct*, 45-Aug Colo. Law 73 (2016); Debra S. Austin, *Drink Like a Lawyer: The Neuroscience of Substance Use and its Impact on Cognitive Wellness*, 15 Nev. L.J. 826 (2015); Dan T. Lukasik, *One Lawyer's Journey Through Depression*, 38-Feb Wyo. Law 26 (2015); also published in 62 La. B.J. 286 (December 2014/January 2015); Andrea Ciobanu & Stephen M. Terrell, *Out of the Darkness: Overcoming Depression Among Lawyers*, 32 No. 2 GPSolo 36 (March/April 2015); Brian S. Clarke, *Coming Out in the Classroom: Law Professors, Law Students and Depression*, 64 J. Legal Educ. 403 (2015); Robert B. Thornhill, *Attorney Suicide: A Discussion of Untreated Depression and Suicide*, 75 Ala. Law 388 (2014).

[35] Without attempting an exhaustive list: **Model Rule 1.1** requires you to remain competent in representing your clients, including thoroughness and preparation. **Model Rule 1.3** requires you to remain prompt and diligent. *See* **Chapter 7.A at 172**. **Model Rule 1.2(a)** and **Model Rule 1.4** require you to communicate and consult with your clients regularly and thoroughly. *See* **Chapter 5.D at 117**. These are among the duties enforced by the professional discipline of lawyers who succumb to depression, anxiety, and addiction. In addition, you have a civil duty, enforceable in tort (that is, by a civil lawsuit for legal malpractice), to exercise reasonable professional care. *See* **Chapter 7.B at 180**. Not surprisingly, addiction and depression also sometimes lead to financial mismanagement (or worse) of professional or client funds. *See* **Model Rule 1.15; Chapter 21 at 574**.

6. you frequently feel sad, helpless, irritable, or angry;
7. you frequently feel anxious (that is, feelings of tension, worry, fear, or dread);
8. you have thoughts about hurting yourself or others; or
9. you're engaging in unusually risky or reckless behavior.

If you think that two or more of these describe you, then there very likely is help that you can get that will significantly improve your life and outlook.

There are also common warning signs of problems with alcohol (and for concerns about prescription or recreational drugs, just substitute those for alcohol in these questions). One respected self-evaluation contains just four questions:

1. Have you ever felt that you should cut down on your drinking?
2. Have people annoyed you by criticizing your drinking?
3. Have you ever felt bad or guilty about your drinking?
4. Have you ever had a drink first thing in the morning to steady your nerves or to get over a hangover?

If your answer to two or more of these is "yes," it's worth consulting a medical or mental health professional. More generally, you should be alert for any of the following:

- Experiencing temporary blackouts or short-term memory loss;
- Exhibiting signs of frequent irritability or extreme mood swings;
- Making excuses for drinking, such as to relax, deal with stress, or feel normal;
- Feeling an urge or craving to drink;
- Choosing drinking over other responsibilities, obligations, or interests;
- Becoming isolated and distant from friends and family members;
- Drinking alone or in secrecy;
- Feeling hung over when not drinking;
- Hanging out with people now who are different in identity or appearance from the ones you used to hang out with; or
- Getting into situations while drinking that increase your chances of harming yourself or others (*e.g.,* drinking and driving), or getting in trouble with the law for conduct involving alcohol.

3. Getting Support

Being strong means being strong enough to accept help.

We don't want anyone to think that this advice is patronizing—and it's not merely theoretical for us. Your authors are experienced practitioners, expert witnesses, and law teachers. A majority of us have confronted anxiety and depression in law school and law practice. All of us are still lawyers, and we are still very happy that we are. The secret of our survival is simple—once you realize that you're miserable, don't hide or ignore it; don't assume that's just how it is; *do something*. We also don't want to sound glib. Doing something about one of these illnesses may very well be among the hardest things that you ever do, whether it concerns you or someone else. But though it may not be easy, it *is* possible. And necessary. Sooner or later—and usually sooner than you think—the option of doing nothing implodes in personal and professional disaster.

So what can you do? Help is available from many sources:

- While you are in law school, the Student Services department of your school's administration will have resources on site or be able to refer you to resources, all on a confidential basis. Rest assured that many, many students have asked for help before you did, and the staff know how to help, compassionately and quietly, including helping you manage any associated disruption to your schoolwork.

- Family and friends can help you find assistance, as can a trusted professional such as a personal or family doctor.

- Once you are employed, most employers of any size include among their benefits an Employee Assistance Program ("EAP") that typically makes all kinds of resources available at modest cost and that works with your employer to preserve your employment, if possible. A human resources officer or a trusted supervisor or coworker can get you to the available resources.

- Every state bar in the United States (including the District of Columbia) has a Lawyer Assistance Program ("LAP"). These are programs that help lawyers (and law students) address substance abuse and mental health issues; the American Bar Association keeps a directory of each one.[36] LAPs are typically staffed by professionals who can help a struggling lawyer find care *and* assist in the management of any ethical or practice issues that the problem may be causing. The assistance is confidential to the extent possible and typically will not be disclosed to the state's professional disciplinary authority so long as the lawyer sticks to the remedial plan. *See* **Model Rule 8.3(c)**.

YOUR HOUSE; YOUR RULES We'd be remiss if we didn't point out that there are variations among the many American jurisdictions in dealing with mental health and substance abuse issues, both in the workplace and among professionals (such as lawyers). But many states' policies are long on features emphasizing compassion and confidentiality, as well as protection of the ill person and others who could be affected. Most employers and state bars also make it easy to find out what assistance they have to offer. YOUR HOUSE; YOUR RULES

---

[36] https://www.americanbar.org/groups/lawyer_assistance/resources/lap_programs_by_state/.

D. It's Not All About You: Like It or Not, You Are Your Brothers' and Sisters' Keeper

In the immortal words of Albus Dumbledore, "It takes a great deal of bravery to stand up to our enemies, but just as much to stand up to our friends."[37] We would say that Professor Dumbledore understated this truth considerably: Intervening when your friends and colleagues need help in exiting the wrong path is likely one of the hardest things that you'll ever do, even when the need is obvious. And often it isn't, which makes the decision about what to do even harder. Let's face it: People rarely welcome the suggestion—no matter how right it may be—that they may be acting wrongfully or may need to address a mental illness or addiction.

CONSEQUENCES Yet often, you **must** bring it up. As a subordinate, you won't be protected from disciplinary liability for conduct in violation of the Rules of Professional Conduct just because your boss told you to do it (unless the situation truly called for a fairly arguable judgment call, and the boss's order was objectively reasonable, *see* **Chapter 4.A at 72 n. 4; Model Rule 5.2**). As a supervisor (whether of other lawyers, *see* **Model Rule 5.1**, or of nonlawyer staff, *see* **Model Rule 5.3**), you will be subject to discipline for any disciplinary violation your subordinate commits that you directed or knew of and could have prevented. *See* **Chapter 19.C at 516**. And in states that have adopted **Model Rule 8.3** (about half), if you know that another lawyer—*any* other lawyer—has committed a disciplinary offense "that raises a substantial question as to that lawyer's honesty, trustworthiness or fitness as a lawyer in other respects," you **must** inform your state's disciplinary authority so long as you can do so without disclosing information subject to your **duty of confidentiality** (*see* **Chapter 8.A at 206**); if you don't "rat" on that lawyer, you're subject to discipline yourself. *See* **Chapter 16.D at 446**.

As for civil liability, if you commit a tort in the course of your work, you will typically be personally liable for the damages, even if you did so at the direction of a supervisor. And if someone else within your firm commits a tort in the course of employment, in most states, you will personally be liable for that other person's tort if you directed or encouraged or, as a manager or supervisor, reasonably could have prevented it. This liability arises directly under torts such as negligence, negligent supervision, or breach of fiduciary duty; or under doctrines of

---

[37] J.K. ROWLING, HARRY POTTER AND THE SORCERER'S STONE 306 (1997). And after that heading, you probably thought we were going to go all biblical on you. Now that you mention it, though, the biblical story that gives rise to the heading is, regardless of your views regarding biblical teachings, deeply woven into the moral fabric of our culture: Cain murdered his brother, Abel, out of envy. "And the Lord said to Cain, 'Where is Abel your brother?' And he said, 'I do not know: am I my brother's keeper?'" Genesis 4:9. Cain's sullen response (to an omniscient God, no less, from whom the question "Where is Abel?" must be viewed as rhetorical—since God knows everything, he or she certainly knows what happened to Abel) suggests an answer from Cain's bad example—yes, we are all our brothers' (and sisters') keepers. Whether you accept that view as a matter of *morals*, and what it may call on you to do as a result, is up to you. But as we are about to see, the moral judgment implied in this story underpins some enforceable *legal* obligations as well. And those you can't ignore (not, at least, without **consequences**).

secondary or vicarious liability such as *respondeat superior,* aiding and abetting, or civil conspiracy. And of course in all these cases, your firm will be vicariously liable as a matter of *respondeat superior* as well. *See* **Chapter 19.C at 517**.[38] CONSEQUENCES

And even in circumstances in which you **may** refrain from addressing someone else's distress, think carefully about whether you **should**. Depending on the circumstances, stepping up can be personally difficult and professionally risky, and those are considerations that you'll inevitably take into account in deciding what to do. (Imagine yourself in a work situation in which your boss shows signs of a drinking problem.) But remember also that we are discussing debilitating illnesses that are not only personally devastating for the individual afflicted and those close to him or her, but potentially risky for your **practice organization** and its clients. Here too, consulting with someone you trust to determine how to react may be helpful.

> Problem 4D-1: One of the partners in Maya's firm, Ted Toughtimes, is going through a rough divorce. He is frequently down in the dumps, irritable, and distracted. He doesn't seem to be getting much work done, either. Lately, he's been regularly returning from lunch unsteady on his feet and smelling of liquor. One of the other partners, Sarah Steady, has just brought in a new matter in Ted's area of expertise. Hoping to help Ted get his hours up, Sarah asks Ted to handle the new matter, and he agrees. She also asks Maya to assist him. Under what circumstances might Sarah be subject to **consequences**? What **consequences** and why? Under what circumstances might Maya be subject to **consequences**? What **consequences** and why? Aside from anything that Sarah or Maya **must** or **must not** do, is there anything that they **should** or **should not** do?

So you see, though it *is* about you and your well-being, it's not *only* about you. Law practice regularly laces us into a web of relationships binding us to others through all kinds of moral and legal responsibilities. Sometimes it's tempting to view these obligations as dangers to be avoided, but they connect others to us as well. These ties are not just burdens, but affirmative benefits of practice in a service profession, and they can just as likely support us in moments of need as they may call upon us to support others.

* * *

From here, we go on to consider the particular rules and doctrines that govern your life as a lawyer. But we put this chapter near the beginning for a reason, and it's a reason that we hope you'll keep in mind for the rest of the term and, frankly, for the rest of your life: A working understanding of rules governing lawyer conduct is good, but a working understanding of all the things that can

---

[38] It's easy to shrug and assume that somebody's insurance will take care of this risk, but not every law firm carries professional liability insurance, and such insurance doesn't necessarily cover every kind of claim. *See* **Chapter 19.B at 508**. And never forget the importance of informal **consequences**. Most lawyers and law firms care deeply about their reputations, and for good reason: Neither lawsuits for professional negligence nor word of mouth from the unhappy people who filed those lawsuits is good for business.

keep you from making good *use* of your understanding of the rules—cognitive biases and stress-induced deficits in particular—is better.

Onward.

Big-Picture Takeaways from Chapter 4

1. Be aware that (a) you're human, and thus (b) you're subject to the same cognitive errors and stresses as everyone else. *See* **Chapter 4.A at 70**.

2. If you discover—or merely suspect or fear—that you've made a mistake or have otherwise done something wrong, there are a range of steps that you **should** and often **must** take very promptly. Although these steps will often be difficult for you, doing nothing (or worse, concealing the problem) will virtually always turn out much, much worse. *See* **Chapter 4.B at 87**.

3. Be mindful of your work and life stress and actively work to manage your reaction to it. *See* **Chapter 4.C at 88**.

4. Be vigilant for symptoms of anxiety, depression, and substance abuse in yourself and those around you. *See* **Chapter 4.C at 90**.

5. Understand that you have ethical duties (for example, the duty to supervise those who report to you) that will require you to think through how others might be responding to stress. *See* **Chapter 4.D at 95**.

Multiple-Choice Review Questions for Chapter 4

1. You are a new lawyer who has just started working at a large law firm. You have been assigned a mentor who is a third-year associate. Your mentor will not only be reviewing your work product but also assisting you as you acclimate to law-firm policies and procedures.

   During your first week, you spend ten hours drafting a motion to dismiss. You enter those ten hours into the firm's billing program. At the end of the week, your mentor sits down with you to review your timesheets for the week. She asks you why you billed only ten hours on the motion package. You respond that you billed exactly the time you spent: ten hours.

   Your mentor suggests that you add a few more hours to the bill. When you ask why, she explains that firm practice is to "round up" and that the client will be billed for 15 hours for the motion package.

   Can you take this advice at face value and add the five extra hours to the timesheets?

   a. Yes. Your mentor is far more experienced than you are with firm practice, and she was assigned to give you advice.

    b. Yes. Your mentor reviewed the motion package and believes that it should have taken 15 hours.

    c. No. You are personally responsible for complying with your ethical obligations and cannot misrepresent your time spent working on a matter, even if your mentor suggests that you do so.

    d. No. Your mentor is only an associate, not a partner, so she can't direct your work.

2. After a series of associates in your firm practice group quit, the firm's human resources department interviews all remaining associates to find out why. Your interview is scheduled for the last day. You suspect that many associates who quit did so because the head of the practice group makes insensitive comments about race. Although you have never been on the receiving end of such a comment, you have heard him make comments to and about other firm associates.

    During your interview with human resources, you are asked to disclose any problems in the workplace. You consider alerting human resources to the behavior of the practice group head, but ultimately you don't bother, because you assume that other associates would have raised the issue in their interviews. You never check with other associates to see whether they did indeed raise this issue.

    What situational pressure best explains your failure to raise the issue?

    a. Cognitive dissonance.

    b. The power of authority.

    c. Social conformity.

    d. Diffusion of responsibility.

3. Your state's rules of professional responsibility prohibit a lawyer from having a sexual relationship with a client. One reason for this prohibition (there are several, *see* **Chapter 5.C at 108**) is that the sexual relationship may cloud the lawyer's judgment and impede the lawyer's ability to give the client objective advice.

    Lawyer Louise begins sleeping with her client. Louise knows that the relationship is unethical, but she nonetheless justifies it because she's an excellent lawyer who is doing high-level work for her client.

    What might explain Louise's need to justify behavior that she knows is unethical?

    a. Cognitive dissonance.

    b. The power of authority.

    c. Social conformity.

    d. Diffusion of responsibility.

4. You are litigating your first major criminal defense trial with a partner from your firm. The case is almost over, and it looks likely that the prosecution will prevail. While strategizing with you over dinner, the partner suggests counseling a key witness to "bend the truth" on the stand during the next day of trial. When you object, the partner points out, "If we don't, we're going to lose the case. Don't you want to win?"

    The partner is engaging in what strategy?
    a. Groupthink.
    b. Ethical fading.
    c. Cognitive dissonance.
    d. Hedonism.

5. What is one benefit to owning up to a mistake?
    a. You may discover that the mistake bears no **consequences**.
    b. You may discover that you didn't actually make a mistake.
    c. You may discover that the mistake can be fixed.
    d. All of the above.

6. Which of the following is *not* a common warning sign of depression or anxiety?
    a. Changes in sleep patterns.
    b. Changes in eating patterns.
    c. Flashbacks during which you relive traumatic events.
    d. Having difficulty making decisions.

7. Lawyer Linda practices in the Commonwealth of Keystone. She realizes that she has a substance abuse problem that is affecting her work. She calls the Keystone Lawyer Assistance Program ("LAP") and asks for a referral to a counselor. Linda begins seeing the counselor and enters a treatment program. She is compliant with the program.

    Should Linda be concerned that the LAP will tell the Keystone professional disciplinary authority that she has a substance abuse problem?
    a. Yes. A LAP is usually obligated to disclose to the state's disciplinary authority the name of all lawyers who contact the LAP.
    b. Yes. Linda has been noncompliant in her treatment, which justifies the LAP's disclosing her identity so that the state disciplinary authority can take appropriate action.
    c. No. Linda never disclosed her name to the LAP, so there is no risk that her identity will be discovered.
    d. No. Assistance from a LAP is generally confidential and typically will not be disclosed to a state's professional disciplinary authority when a lawyer is compliant with a treatment program.

UNIT II

The Attorney-Client Relationship

As we saw in Unit I, there are multiple sources of law governing attorneys' conduct, each bearing its own standards and **consequences**.

Now we're going to get to the heart of things. As we mentioned in **Chapter 1.C at 9**, the attorney-client relationship is the epicenter of a lawyer's professional life. It is also the epicenter of the law governing lawyers. Most of the Rules of Professional Conduct are about what you **must** (or **must not**), **may**, or **should** do for, to, or with clients. Even the rules about interacting with *nonclients*, which we'll discuss in **Unit III at 319**, govern a range of conduct in which your client may want you to engage, or in which you might be tempted to engage for the benefit of your client, but which you **must** moderate or abstain from for various policy reasons. So pretty much any way you look at it, this course is all about our clients. Just about everything we do is judged from their point of view, not our own.

So let's get to it. In this unit, we're going to examine the attorney-client relationship, the duties that arise out of that relationship, and the **consequences** by which they are enforced. We'll begin with a general introduction to the lawyer's status as a fiduciary (and we'll explain what that means) and the fiduciary duties that lawyers owe their clients—principally **loyalty**, **care**, **confidentiality**, and **candor**. *See* **Chapter 5 at 105**. Then we'll turn to the agency character of the attorney-client relationship, and see what duties and powers it does—and does not—confer on lawyers. We'll show you a little agency law, which will come in handy not only in this course, but also in your Business Organizations course and likely one or two others that you have yet to enjoy. *See* **Chapter 6 at 131**. We'll also look into the **duties of competence**, **diligence**, and **care**, and how they affect the way that you **should** and **must** organize and conduct your practice. *See* **Chapter 7 at 171**. We'll do the same for the **duty of confidentiality**. *See* **Chapter 8 at 203**. Finally, we'll explore how a lawyer's duties to a client arise and terminate—that is, when you definitively become some-body's lawyer, when you stop, and how you may end up owing duties to someone who's never even been your client. *See* **Chapter 9 at 255**. This point is tremendously important, because if you have become (or remain) someone's lawyer (or owe that person duties for other reasons) and don't realize it, you won't do things that you're expected (and legally obligated) to do, almost inevitably leading to claims that you violated your duties.

Beginning with this unit, you'll see the standard model of exposition for the rest of the book: An explanation of governing law interspersed with problems illustrating how that law comes up in real-world situations. In preparation for that material, we offer a way of organizing your thinking when you confront a problem (in the book or in the real world). We're bringing it up now because, beginning with this unit, the rest of the course will be focused on what duties you have and what risks you face as a lawyer, and on how you **must** or **should** go about addressing them. Many common situations that practicing lawyers confront involve several different professional duties at once, and you need to have a method for unraveling these knots. Here's a good one.

A Suggested Approach for Analyzing Professional Responsibility Problems

Some professional responsibility issues are easy to spot and analyze. Some aren't. So it may not be long before you find yourself facing a situation in which you sense something is wrong, but you find yourself stuck at "I don't even know how to begin thinking about this." (We've had this experience countless times; we still do every now and then. So even experienced lawyers can find themselves at a loss for how to analyze an issue in the face of something new or unantici-pated. The question is what to do next.) With that in mind, we'd like to suggest an analytical framework that, more often than not, will provide you with a starting point for thinking your way through ethics problems. This approach won't solve every problem, but it will often give you a way in and a method for breaking complicated situations down into pieces that are easier to handle one at a time.

Just ask yourself four questions:

1. What duty (or duties; quite often, there are several) is or arguably might be at play in this situation, and to whom is each such duty owed?
2. How has (or arguably might have) each duty at issue been breached, or how *could* it be breached going forward?
3. What harm (if any) has been or might, in the future, be caused by each breach that you have identified, and to whom?
4. What **consequences** are or could become available for each breach that you have identified, and who could seek those **consequences**?

Once you have working answers to this series of questions (remembering that there may be, and often is, more than one duty and more than one potential breach at issue in any situation), you can start to figure out what you can do to avoid a problem that's coming right at you, or to address a problem that you have (or the person whom you're advising has) already stepped in.

Try using this approach on the problems in next few chapters as you prepare for class—it's also a great approach for analyzing MPRE or final exam questions.[1] You'll have to remind yourself at first to follow each of these steps, in order, but keep reminding yourself to follow the steps until they become a mental habit. That will serve you in good stead for the rest of your career.

Now we turn to an overview of the lawyer's basic fiduciary duties: **loyalty**, **care**, **confidentiality**, and **candor**.

---

[1] Caveat: As explained in **Chapter 6.A at 135**, when you're confronted with questions about what kind of authority you have to act on a client's behalf in your role as the client's agent, the analytical approach that you need to take is somewhat different. We'll tackle that when it comes up. But for now, keep the above four-step approach on your hip as your tool of choice to pry apart seemingly unbreakable problems (and seemingly simple ones, too, because this approach can expose otherwise unappreciated complications).

5

The Lawyer as Fiduciary

THIS UNIT OF THE BOOK explores the attorney-client relationship, mostly from the standpoint of the duties that typically arise between attorney and client, and how those duties dictate how we, as lawyers, **must** or **should** act in situations that practicing lawyers confront. We're going to consider some of those duties in greater detail—particularly the **duty of care** and the related **duties of competence** and **diligence** in **Chapter 7 at 171**, and the **duty of confidentiality** in **Chapter 8 at 203**. But we start the unit with an overview of what it means to be a fiduciary and how you know when you'll be held to a fiduciary standard. We'll then illustrate why lawyers are (and should be) regulated as fiduciaries, using the example of sex with clients, thus cleverly providing many of you with an incentive to keep reading. We'll round out the chapter with a survey of the basic fiduciary duties in the specific context of the attorney-client relationship.

A. What Does It Mean to Be a Fiduciary?

Lawyers are fiduciaries to their clients. "Fiduciary" is a fancy Latinate word, but what does it actually mean, and how do we know when and to whom we are fiduciaries? "Fiduciary" is a legal term of art (one that's not limited to legal practice) that comes packed with a complex bundle of obligations. Those obligations vary to some degree from situation to situation and from state to state, but generally they have a great deal in common.

The term "fiduciary" derives from the Latin *fidere*—to trust. And true to the word's roots, a fiduciary is a person who takes a position of trust and responsibility with respect to someone else's property or affairs. Often the fiduciary has the legal power to act or speak on behalf of, and bind, the beneficiary.[2] Often the fiduciary has superior knowledge or skill on which the beneficiary expects to rely in important decisions. (You will notice that both of these characterize much of

---

[2] "Beneficiary" and "principal" are general terms that refer to the person to whom the fiduciary's duties are owed. Other terms are used in more specific contexts. For example, the doctor's principal is the patient; the lawyer's principal is the client.

the work that lawyers do.) Beneficiaries' needs or desires for this assistance and advice cause them to *entrust* fiduciaries with something of theirs that is important to them—their legal matters; their healthcare decisions; their personal care; their money or property—and the fiduciary then has both personal influence and legal power over what is to be done with it.

To recall the wisdom of Peter Parker's Uncle Ben, with great powers come great responsibilities.[3] Fiduciaries are invested with a range of special and often highly demanding legal and ethical obligations, the violation of any of which bears **consequences**, often serious ones. We'll explore those duties (and the **consequences** that back them up) generally in **Chapter 5.D at 112**, but first let's discuss how you know when you're a fiduciary.

B. How Do You Know When You're a Fiduciary?

Because fiduciaries have great powers and great responsibilities, you need to know when you are one, so that you know what you have to do (or refrain from doing) and when. Broadly speaking, fiduciary duties arise in two general contexts: fiduciary duties created by *status*, and fiduciary duties created by *circumstances*.

1. Fiduciaries by Status

Generally speaking, certain kinds of status—positions, titles, professions— come with a bundle of fiduciary duties.[4] Here's an incomplete list of common examples:

- Lawyers are fiduciaries to their clients within the scope of the legal engagement (and in a number of broader respects as well).
- Agents are fiduciaries to their principals within the scope of the agency. *See Restatement (Third) of Agency* §§ 8.01, 8.08 (2006); **Chapter 6.A at 151.**
- Conservators and guardians are fiduciaries to their wards within the scope of the conservatorship or guardianship.
- Doctors are fiduciaries to their patients within the scope of the treatment relationship.
- Clergy are fiduciaries to their congregants within the scope of their pastoral responsibilities.

---

[3] *See* **Chapter 3 at 29 n.1.**

[4] By law, the degree to which any of these duties can be waived or disclaimed by agreement is limited—and for good reason. The kind of knowledge, skill, and persuasiveness that invites the beneficiary's trust in the fiduciary can easily be abused, and the law constrains the extent to which the fiduciary can simply induce the beneficiary to sign away the responsibilities that ensure the proper exercise of the fiduciary's duties. Imagine a lawyer saying to a client at their initial meeting: "Now, before you become my client so that I can provide you the expert services you so desperately need, please sign this form right here—all my clients do—saying that I won't be responsible no matter what I do wrong." You'd be right if you guessed that won't work. We hope you found that answer in the "duh" department.

- Trustees are fiduciaries to the beneficiaries of the trust within the scope of the trust's corpus and purposes.
- General partners in a partnership owe fiduciary duties to one another and the partnership itself within the scope of the partnership's affairs.
- Corporate directors are fiduciaries to the corporation and its shareholders with respect to the affairs of the corporation (and other high-level managers of various kinds of business organizations are often, as a matter of the law of business organizations, fiduciaries to the organization and its owners).

YOUR HOUSE; YOUR RULES Who is deemed a fiduciary by status as a matter of law varies a bit from state to state, as do the duties that attach to each status. In some states, for example, spouses are considered fiduciaries to one another for various purposes. Some states consider stockbrokers fiduciaries to their customers; many do not. The list that we just gave you provides just a few examples, applicable in most places in the United States, of the innumerable different situations in which a legal status carries with it special and demanding fiduciary duties. The two key points to take away here are (1) whether a particular legal status carries fiduciary duties, and how far those duties may extend, has some general consistency across the United States but also some state-to-state variation; and (2) most important for our purposes, *all lawyers in every state are virtually always considered fiduciaries to their clients* in almost any engagement, with some minor variations among the states in the extent of the duties, but no real variation in the application of fiduciary status. YOUR HOUSE; YOUR RULES

2. Fiduciaries by Circumstance

In many situations, a person's *legal status* by itself does not create any special duties, but the *particular circumstances of that person's relationship with someone* will. The circumstances typically involve the beneficiary's bestowing, and the (situational) fiduciary's accepting, the beneficiary's special trust or reliance. The beneficiary might repose that trust because of the nature of the relationship between the beneficiary and the fiduciary, or because the beneficiary believes that the fiduciary has superior knowledge, skills, or abilities in a particular area, or because the beneficiary has entrusted secret or confidential personal or business information to the fiduciary. Different jurisdictions may call this type of relationship a fiduciary relationship, even though it is not status-based, or they might refer to it instead as a "confidential relationship." A "confidential relationship" in this context can mean one that invokes the full panoply of fiduciary duties, but sometimes means that the trusted person has undertaken only a duty of confidentiality (that is, a duty to keep information entrusted in confidence to him- or herself). Let's give you a chance to think through some basics about the creation of a fiduciary relationship:

Problem 5B-1: Nora Neighbor has been good friends with her elderly next-door neighbor, Dale Doddering, for a number of years. Nora is a lawyer, but she has never represented Dale. After Dale's spouse passes away, his health and clarity of thinking deteriorate. Dale remains competent, but he needs help with some day-to-day activities. As a good neighbor and friend, Nora gradually begins to help Dale more and more, taking him to church with her on Sunday and assisting with his grocery shopping and other household chores. Eventually, Dale asks her to help with his banking and gives her signature authority over his bank accounts. Nora later invests a portion of Dale's savings in a small start-up technology company in which Nora's spouse is involved. Nora genuinely believes that there's a good chance that her spouse's start-up will hit it big, and that this is a good investment. Does Nora face any potential **consequences**? Why or why not, and if so, what are they?

C. Why Lawyers Are Fiduciaries: The Example of Sex with Clients

Why (other than a shameless appeal to your prurient interests, which we can't entirely deny) would we mix a discussion about lawyers' fiduciary duties with a discussion about sex? Well, as it turns out, there's an ethical rule about it. And thinking a little about why we have that rule ends up telling us a lot about the reason that lawyers have fiduciary duties.

So what's the rule? **Model Rule 1.8(j)** says, "A lawyer shall not have sexual relations with a client unless a consensual sexual relationship existed between them when the client-lawyer relationship commenced." Most states have adopted **Model Rule 1.8(j)** in one form or another.[5] But why do we have such a rule specifically for lawyers, and why might we need it?

REASON FOR THE RULE ▶ To think about these questions, let's start with a silly analogy: We can probably agree that you shouldn't put beans in your ears.[6] It's messy; it feels bad; it interferes with your hearing; it could actually result in serious and potentially permanent injuries. But despite its obvious dangers, there is no legislation forbidding it.[7] The alert reader might suggest that the lack of any formal

---

[5] North Carolina has a rule similar to **Model Rule 1.8(j)**, but it adds a prohibition on "requir[ing] or demand[ing] sexual relations incident to or as a condition of any professional representation." N.C. R. PROF. COND. 1.19. Texas considered a rule with a prohibition similar to North Carolina's, as well as one forbidding lawyers from soliciting sex in lieu of fees. The Texas bar rejected the proposed rule altogether, with some members expressing concerns about "frivolous malpractice claims." Rudolph Bush, *Texas Lawyers Divided over "Sex with Clients" rule*, https://www.dallasnews.com/news/texas/2010/10/04/20101003-Texas-lawyers-divided-over-sex-4374 (Oct. 2010). It's not unreasonable to assume that these extra prohibitions were considered or adopted to address existing issues. What do you imagine lawyers proposing those kinds of arrangements were thinking? Why did North Carolina adopt a disciplinary rule forbidding "requir[ing] or demand[ing] sexual relations incident to or as a condition of any professional representation"? What do you think of the reason articulated by many Texas lawyers to reject an outright ban on sex with clients—"frivolous malpractice claims"?

[6] Oddly enough, this is not an original thought. *See* https://www.youtube.com/watch?v=kO8iZIVZmsU.

[7] When the recording linked in the preceding footnote became popular in 1964, some children responded with early signs of oppositional defiant disorder (DSM V 313.81 (F91.3)), or perhaps sympathy with the contrarian sentiment then rising among American youth, and defied the recording's wholesome admonition. The great folk musician, activist, and civil disobedient Pete Seeger recorded his own version in 1966 on an album entitled *Dangerous Songs!? See* https://www.youtube.com/watch?v=LcvoC3u__xs. Parents and pediatricians raised the alarm, and a number of large cities,

prohibition is because the misconduct here (putting beans in your ears) is one that rational people can protect themselves (and their children) against without the intervention of the law, and to the extent that they can't, legally forbidding it wouldn't have any discernible deterrent effect on the limited number of oppositional children and perpetual adolescents inclined to do it, whether in some glorious gesture of personal autonomy or just because someone told them not to. Moreover, that alert reader might add, other than during an aberrational couple of years in the 1960s, pretty much nobody does it, so why bother with a law?[8]

So how is lawyers having sex with their clients different? Remember, we're talking about sex that is at least superficially consensual; anything nonconsensual is already forbidden as a crime and a tort. Why shouldn't lawyers be free to seek love where they can find it like everyone else, including some other fiduciaries?[9]

That alert reader, flush from her success two paragraphs ago, might press her luck and venture whether it could be something about the attorney-client relationship. Well done, reader! Now, what might that "something about the attorney-client relationship" be? Let's work from what probably seems like another silly comparison: How are auto mechanics like lawyers? (This is not a joke, but if you come up with a good punchline, send us and your professor an email.) The answer is that they are more alike than you might think at first. Auto mechanics, like lawyers, acquire and use a substantial body of technical skills and knowledge that most of the rest of us don't possess. As a result, we depend on them, as lay clients depend on lawyers, to figure out and provide what we need with respect to something that is important to us (our cars, which are substantial investments for most of us, and are important to conducting our daily lives). And as clients often do with lawyers, we entrust valuable property to our mechanics, and we expect to (and often do) end up better off as a result.

But people don't end up in bed with their mechanics very often, though they do with their lawyers often enough that the organized bar found it necessary to intervene.[10] So what's the difference? Well, car owners entrust important things

---

apparently including Pittsburgh and Boston (Beantown, no less!) passed ordinances banning the song. (Regrettably, perhaps, censorship is beyond the scope of this lesson, and perhaps even more regrettably for your authors, beyond their pathetically feeble powers as well.) For what it's worth, your authors' (very) limited research has disclosed no law forbidding the practice itself, and no incident in which any child was sent to juvie for this kind of civil disobedience. *See* https://en.wikipedia.org/wiki/Beans_in_My_Ears.

[8] *But see* What to Do When Something Gets Stuck in the Nose, https://www.whattoexpect.com/toddler/grooming/stuck-in-nose.aspx (Jan. 24, 2019).

[9] Well, not *everyone* else. Professionals (and fiduciaries) such as physicians and psychotherapists are also subject to restrictions on consensual sex with their patients in many states. Keep this in mind as the discussion continues, as the reasons are similar to those animating the constraint on lawyers.

[10] It is notoriously difficult to gather data on the prevalence of (assertedly) consensual sexual contact between lawyers and their clients; it's not the kind of thing that either is eager to confess, even in a survey answer. And relatively few such incidents turn into disciplinary cases or civil suits—as a practical matter, the issue comes to light more often when the client suffers ill effects or other bad behavior accompanies the lawyer's undue influence. One of the more extreme "you gotta be kiddin' me" examples we've seen is the Minnesota family lawyer who had an affair with his client (a woman undergoing a divorce that the lawyer was handling; the lawyer himself was also married) and actually billed the client

to mechanics just as clients entrust important things to lawyers, but let's focus on the *kinds* of important things. Think about how it feels to discuss the effects of a serious injury, yours or a loved one's; the awful details of a failing marriage; the life aspirations shattered in a personal bankruptcy or a criminal charge. (Compare that with how it feels to discuss that funny noise that your transmission is making.) Often, the subject matter that a client confides to a lawyer is intensely personal, even intimate. Opening up to someone about these sensitive personal issues requires a deeply personal kind of trust, one that, for most people, generates a certain vulnerability and connection. And because the client depends on the lawyer to advise on and handle these intensely personal issues, a more general dependence and susceptibility to influence can result. On the lawyer's side, receiving this kind of trust and reliance is deeply satisfying, and sometimes exhilarating. Serving in the role of comforting sage or protector and champion can engender strong feelings of attachment and affection. And quicker than you can say Bob's-your-uncle, Bob may not, um, be just your uncle anymore.

So how is this different from putting beans in your ears (other than the obvious physiological differences—keep your mind on the subject!)? Adults' decisions about whether to put beans in their ears are reached, in most cases, under circumstances in which their independent judgment is not threatened by *undue influence*; and their children's decisions can be made under the watchful protection of parents who (other than in pathological situations) have no independent interest in this issue that might diverge from their children's welfare.

By contrast, the client's emotional vulnerability, engendered by the intimate communications, trust, and reliance that the legal engagement often requires—as well as the client's important practical needs that the engagement often serves and the stressful personal circumstances that often create the need for legal representation in the first place—all can give the lawyer outsize influence and the opportunity, whether consciously or unconsciously, to exploit the client's practical and emotional dependence for the lawyer's own personal gratification. As in all situations presenting the risk of undue influence, the client's independent judgment can be compromised, and it becomes difficult to tell how freely the client decided to become physically intimate with the lawyer. In these

---

by the hour for the time they spent "meeting" in motel rooms. Sadly, the farce quickly devolved into tragedy. The client attempted suicide when the lawyer broke off the affair. The lawyer was suspended from practice "indefinitely." *See* Elie Mystal, *When I Get That Feeling, I Want Sexual Billing,* https://abovethelaw.com/2013/01/when-i-get-that-feeling-i-want-sexual-billing/ (Jan. 15, 2013).

When the organized bar began to consider a specific rule on the subject in the early 1990s (rather than using more general existing prohibitions to discipline more egregious cases, as had been the practice before then), some efforts were made to size up the problem. These efforts are mostly collections of anecdotes from reported disciplinary cases, followed by public policy arguments for regulation. One that does a nice job of collecting examples and exploring the human and gender dynamics of the problem is Caroline Forell, *Lawyers, Clients and Sex: Breaking the Silence on the Ethical and Liability Issues,* 22 GOLDEN GATE U. L. REV. 611, http://digitalcommons.law.ggu.edu/ggulrev/vol22/iss3/3 (1992); *see also* Nancy E. Goldberg, *Sex and the Attorney-Client Relationship: An Argument for a Prophylactic Rule,* 26 AKRON L. REV. 45 (1992).

circumstances (unlike the ones involving the temptation to put beans in one's ears), an enforceable legal rule constraining the party legally charged with maintaining clear and independent judgment—the lawyer—can and should change behavior in a way that is protective of clients. ⟨ REASON FOR THE RULE ⟩

> **Problem 5C-1:** Assuming that the foregoing analysis accurately describes some of the human dynamics that can arise in a lawyer-client relationship, which legal specialty do you guess might most commonly involve lawyers engaging in inappropriate sexual contact with their clients? Explain your reasoning.

⟨ REAL WORLD ⟩ Notice something very striking about the rule banning sex with clients—it has nothing to do with lawyering. After all, sex is *never* part of the professional services that clients hire lawyers to perform, and yet it's regulated as part of the rules governing the attorney-client relationship. How come? Well, what we hope you've gathered from the preceding discussion is that, although sex has nothing to do with lawyering, sex is a temptation that arises surprisingly commonly *in the attorney-client fiduciary relationship*, most likely because of the practical and emotional closeness that the relationship often fosters.

This is a good example of a broader truth about the regulation of the attorney-client relationship: That regulation extends not only to all the details of the professional services lawyers perform for their clients, but more broadly to many of the ways in which lawyers and clients can interact *outside the scope of ordinary professional services.* For example, business transactions between lawyers and their clients, even ones unrelated to the professional services that the lawyer has been engaged to perform, are subject to special scrutiny and constraints. *See* **Model Rule 1.8(a); Chapter 22.A at 617**. Similarly, there are special rules limiting when and how clients may give their lawyers a gift or bequest, however purely donative the clients' motives may actually be. *See* **Model Rule 1.8(c); Chapter 22.A at 612**.

What this means as a practical matter is that your conduct toward your client will likely be subjected to more exacting scrutiny even when you might be inclined to say that you weren't acting "as a lawyer." It also means that, as a practical matter, when questions of responsibility or blame arise, it will be the educated and trained professional owing fiduciary duties—you, the lawyer—who likely will be held to a higher standard of conduct in almost every context by judges and juries as well as by clients: to "the punctilio of an honor the most sensitive," in Judge Cardozo's memorable formulation, one of "unbending" and "[u]ncompromising rigidity" that is "stricter than the morals of the market place" (or the pick-up bar).[11]

Sometimes those standards will be imposed explicitly by the law, but even when they're not, you should generally expect others to expect more of you

---

[11] *Meinhard v. Salmon,* 249 NY 458, 464, 164 N.E. 545 (N.Y. 1928); *see* **Chapter 5.D at 112.**

in *every* context simply because you're a lawyer in *some* contexts. In fact, in a number of states, the existence of a fiduciary or confidential relationship reverses the burden of persuasion and requires holders of fiduciary duties to prove that they did *not* breach them. Regardless of the burden of proof, however, you will be expected to do the right thing the right way for the right reason no matter what's going on around you—or suffer the sharp disapproval of those in a position to judge you, whether formally or informally. And in many jurisdictions, you risk enhanced **consequences** (such as professional discipline, a more generous measure of damages, and even punitive damages) as well. If your own sense of integrity ever starts to flag, recalling the **consequences** that may follow from such judgments may help to reinforce your backbone. ⟨Real World⟩

D. The Lawyer's Fiduciary Duties: An Overview

Because lawyers are (by status) fiduciaries to their clients, they owe their clients the same general duties that all fiduciaries owe to their beneficiaries. But the general fiduciary duties that lawyers owe clients are, in many respects, tailored to common features of the attorney-client relationship. When you do research on the law in your state regarding your fiduciary duties as a lawyer, you will find that statutes and caselaw on fiduciaries generally will often be relevant, but you must also be alert to extensions, limitations, or refinements of those duties that are specific to lawyers. Among other sources of law defining lawyers' fiduciary duties, it is fair to say that many of the Model Rules of Professional Conduct are refinements on general fiduciary principles specifically applicable to lawyers and bearing the **consequence** of professional discipline for violations. And in the many states in which the Rules of Professional Conduct determine or influence standards for civil remedies, violation of the Rules may also contribute to a finding of tort liability for breach of fiduciary duty or similar claims. This is part of what we meant in **Chapter 1.C at 9** when we told you that the obligations to understand and attend to the client's preferences and needs are legal duties hard-wired into the law structuring the attorney-client relationship—specifically by considering virtually all lawyers to be fiduciaries to their clients, with the full panoply of duties that entails.

Fiduciary duties are among the most rigorous and demanding imposed by law. The especially exacting nature of fiduciary duties tends to be reflected in sweeping but imprecise rhetoric in caselaw, emphasizing how elevated the standards are that the fiduciary is expected to meet. A good example comes from an often-quoted decision of that old friend from several of your first-year courses, Judge Benjamin Cardozo:

> Many forms of conduct permissible in a workaday world for those acting at arm's length, are forbidden to those bound by fiduciary ties. A trustee is held to something stricter than the morals of the market place. Not honesty alone, but the punctilio of an honor the most sensitive, is then the standard of behavior. As to this there has developed a

tradition that is unbending and inveterate. Uncompromising rigidity has been the attitude of courts of equity when petitioned to undermine the rule of undivided loyalty by the "disintegrating erosion" of particular exceptions. Only thus has the level of conduct for fiduciaries been kept at a level higher than that trodden by the crowd.[12]

This kind of language is typical of many court decisions discussing fiduciary duty—long on rhetoric stressing the importance of the demanding standards imposed on fiduciary conduct, but short on practical guidance about how to decide what to do in real-world situations.

Fear not, your intrepid authors are here to help. What follows is a brief overview of the four canonical fiduciary duties that lawyers owe clients—**loyalty**, **care**, **confidentiality**, and **candor**. These four duties are related, and they often have overlapping application in many situations common to lawyering. But you should always analyze these duties separately—and in the order that we suggest—to define precisely the client's rights, the lawyer's duties, and the **consequences** that should follow.

1. The Duty of Loyalty

The **duty of loyalty** is the most general and fundamental duty of a fiduciary, and in some ways, the other fiduciary duties can be seen as logical and practical implications of the duty of loyalty. The basic idea of the duty of loyalty is a corollary of the Golden Rule[13]—fiduciaries **must** treat their beneficiaries at least as well as they would treat themselves (or perhaps more accurately and to rule out those drawn to self-abnegation, at least as well as reasonable people would treat themselves). Thus, lawyers **must not** act in a manner adverse to the interests of their clients and **must not** act for their own benefit in relation to the engagement, except to receive reasonable compensation for their services, if that is the parties' understanding.

> **Problem 5D-1:** Ending one of the most shocking series of crimes in the state in recent memory, local law enforcement captures a man they believe kidnapped and murdered several children. The defendant denies responsibility. Danielle's office takes the case to trial. The trial is front-page news, and the lawyer appointed to represent the defendant—who has his eye on the DA's job in the next election—holds daily press conferences. After the jury convicts the defendant on all counts on the basis of strong forensic evidence of his guilt, the defense lawyer stands before the gathered microphones and cameras on the courthouse

---

[12] *Meinhard v. Salmon*, 249 NY 458, 464, 164 N.E. 545 (N.Y. 1928) (citation omitted).

[13] You know, do unto others as you would have others do unto you. Or as Immanuel Kant put it in his famous *Prolegomena to Any Future Metaphysics That Will Be Able to Present Itself as a Science* (1783), it is a categorical imperative (basically, an unbending moral rule) that each of us should act toward others as we would want all other people to act toward all other people. We have now satisfied those who wear their Fancy Pants to work and believe that no legal textbook is complete without a meaningful reference to Kant. And now you know some Kant, too. Feel free to let the Order of the Fancy Pants know.

steps, and announces, "The defendant received a full and fair trial, and I thank the Lord Almighty that the jury in this case was able to carefully consider all the evidence and dispassionately reach a verdict that will remove this monster from our community forever." Has defense counsel done anything that he **must not** or **should not** do? Why or why not? If so, what **consequences** might he face?

Significantly, your **duty of loyalty** extends beyond the scope of whatever you've been asked to do as a fiduciary. A fiduciary may not act disloyally—that is, contrary to the interests of—the beneficiary in *any* respect, including one unrelated to the subject matter that has created the fiduciary relationship. In legal ethics, this is the source of the principle that you may not represent one client against another, even when you represent the other client in something completely unrelated to the matter in which you want to be adverse (unless both clients give **informed consent**). *See* **Chapter 22.B at 646.**

But a breach of the **duty of loyalty** does not always require an actual *act of disloyalty*. If lawyers put themselves in a position where the *opportunity* and *temptation* for disloyalty is too great, they have created a **conflict of interest** (a term you will hear a lot in this course), which is a wrong for which **consequences** (principally, **disqualification**) are available even if the lawyer never succumbs to the temptation, never acts disloyally, and thus never actually harms the client's interests. *See* **Chapter 22 at 603.**

CONSEQUENCES ▶ We'll be discussing these issues at length and in detail in **Chapter 22 at 599,** but let's take a high-level glance at the **consequences** that may result from a breach of the **duty of loyalty**. Unsurprisingly, they depend on the harm or risk that the breach creates.

First, let's talk about the **consequence** of professional discipline. One of the striking omissions from the Model Rules of Professional Conduct is any single Rule that imposes a general **duty of loyalty**. There are multiple Model Rules that forbid violating particular *aspects* of the **duty of loyalty**, or particular *instances of disloyal conduct*.[14] But basic principles of due process require that, before professional discipline may be imposed, a specific disciplinary rule that the attorney violated must be identified. There is no general power to discipline lawyers for disloyalty that's not specifically prohibited in a Rule of Professional Conduct or related statute carrying a disciplinary remedy.

Now let's switch focus to civil remedies. There are a variety of civil **consequences** for violation of the **duty of loyalty**. If a lawyer yields to temptation and acts in a manner that damages the client's interests, then a claim for damages for breach of fiduciary duty or "legal malpractice" (a general term that comprises any claim resulting from a breach of any duty arising out of the

---

[14] For example, **Model Rule 1.7(a)** forbids **conflicts of interest** based on the **duty of loyalty**; several subsections of **Model Rule 1.8** provide protections for clients against disloyalty or overreaching of various particular kinds; and **Model Rules 1.13(a), (b), and (c)** elaborate on how the **duty of loyalty** must be observed when the client is an organization.

attorney-client relationship, *see* **Chapter 3.B at 46**) will follow. But even lawyers who never succumb to the temptation created by a **conflict of interest** are subject to the **consequence** of **disqualification**—a quasi-injunctive court order directing a lawyer to get out or stay out of an engagement (*see* **Chapter 3.B at 51**). **Disqualification** is a prophylactic remedy that forces **conflicted** lawyers out of the range of temptation before they can do anything harmful. Professional discipline can also result from a **conflict of interest**, also in the absence of any actual harm to the client (but, as a practical matter, becoming more likely and more severe if actual harm results). *See* **Model Rule 1.7(a); Model Rules 1.9(a)-(b).** Not every temptation to disloyalty rises to the level of a **conflict of interest** from which **consequences** flow, and we'll spend a lot of time and effort in **Chapter 22 at 599** analyzing which ones do. For now, be aware that such **consequences** are available (and regularly imposed), and that one duty from which they commonly arise is the **duty of loyalty.** `CONSEQUENCES`

> **Problem 5D-2:** Maya's firm represents BigCo in intellectual property licensing work. That work is done in the office of the firm where Maya works. A partner in another office of Maya's firm, who has no connection to BigCo, is approached by VendorCorp, a trading partner of BigCo, to litigate a commercial contract dispute with BigCo over a large shipment of raw materials. No intellectual property issues are involved. The litigation partner wants to go ahead. **May** he? Why or why not?

2. The Duty of Care

As you may remember from your first-year Torts class, generally a lawyer must exercise a level of skill, diligence, and care—and possess (or acquire) a level of knowledge—that a reasonably careful and prudent lawyer would under the same or similar circumstances. The wording of this standard of reasonable professional care varies a bit from state to state, but it is generally well established in civil cases for professional negligence.[15]

`CONSEQUENCES` We will speak in detail in **Chapter 7.A at 172** about the related **duties of competence** and **diligence**, which are codified in **Model Rule 1.1** and **Model Rule 1.3** and are enforced by the **consequence** of professional discipline. The **duty of care** applicable to fiduciaries in general and to lawyer-fiduciaries in particular

---

[15] `YOUR HOUSE; YOUR RULES` Occasionally, you may see caselaw suggesting a higher standard of care for fiduciaries, referring to common formulations requiring a fiduciary to exercise "all of the skill, care and diligence at his [or her] disposal," or requiring the fiduciary's "best efforts," which might exceed "reasonable efforts" in one way or another. *See, e.g., FDIC v. Stahl*, 854 F. Supp. 1565 (S.D. Fla. 1994). You may also see caselaw suggesting that the **duty of care** is not a fiduciary duty at all—not that it doesn't exist, but that the **duty of care** exists independent of the fiduciary character of the relationship. *See, e.g., Tante v. Herring*, 264 Ga. 694, 453 S.E.2d 686 (1994). Obviously, you need to find and use the standard established in your jurisdiction. One place to start your research is your state's form jury instructions, which usually state the standard and provide citations for its origins. But you will generally find that, notwithstanding any caselaw whose dicta might suggest more highfalutin' aspirations, reasonable skill, diligence, care, and prudence is generally the applicable standard of care for lawyers. `YOUR HOUSE; YOUR RULES`

is generally enforced by the **consequence** of civil liability for professional negligence. Consequences

For now, your fond if bittersweet memories of all the medical malpractice and other professional negligence cases that you read in Torts (wait, they really cut off the *wrong leg?*) give you enough background to move on to the **duty of confidentiality**. We'll speak in more detail about the **duty of care** in **Chapter 7.B at 180.**

3. The Duty of Confidentiality

The **duty of confidentiality** is one of the most powerful and pervasive obligations to which lawyers must adhere. For centuries, protecting the integrity of the deeply personal and tactically sensitive information that clients entrust to us has been one of the most fundamental features of a lawyer's job. It comes up literally every day in practice, pretty much no matter what you do. We will explore the **duty of confidentiality** at length in **Chapter 8 at 203**, but here's a quick download to hold us until we get there:

- **Confidential information** protected by the **duty of confidentiality** includes *all* information of *any* kind that you learn in the course of representing a client, irrespective of its source, even information that the client may have disclosed to others, and even information that may be publicly available (unless it is so widely disseminated that it can be considered "generally known"). *See* **Chapter 8.A at 210.**[16]

- The **duty of confidentiality** forbids you from *voluntarily using* or *disclosing* a client's **confidential information** unless the client authorizes it or some other specific exception to the duty applies. Different **consequences** may flow from different violations. *See* **Chapter 8.A at 217.**[17]

- You must take all reasonable steps to protect your client's **confidential information**.

- Unlike the other fiduciary duties, which generally end when the engagement ends, the **duty of confidentiality** survives the end of the attorney-client relationship, in some jurisdictions lasting until the client's death, and in others lasting forever. *See* **Chapter 8.A at 224.**

---

[16] The range of **confidential information** protected by the **duty of confidentiality** is drastically different from the scope of the **attorney-client privilege**, which much more narrowly protects only communications between attorney and client made for the purpose of giving or receiving legal advice, and which is waived by even one voluntary disclosure outside the scope of the privilege. *See* **Chapter 8.A. at 225.**

[17] Again, notice how different this concept of **confidentiality** is from the **attorney-client privilege**: The **duty of confidentiality** must yield to legal compulsion, such as disclosure obligations in discovery or a subpoena. The **attorney-client privilege** is a privilege against compelled disclosure, and thus allows nondisclosure even in the face of most legal compulsion.

Problem 5D-3: Danielle attends an informal get-together of recent graduates of her law school living in her area. Everyone is glad to see old friends; most are excited about their new jobs, and all are curious about what everyone else is doing. Dramatic stories of big personalities and big confrontations start to flow. "You're not going to believe this one," says one of Danielle's classmates, who landed at a respected family law firm in town. She relates that her firm is handling the divorce of Sally Socialite, a doyenne of the local country club set whose husband walked out after she (allegedly) gave him a sexually-transmitted disease. Uproarious humor ensues. Is anything out of line in this gathering of friends? Is there anything that Danielle **must** or **should** do?

Problem 5D-4: Frank is working on a personal injury case, and propounds a set of interrogatories to the defendant, including several regarding the defendant's physical and emotional state at the time of the accident at issue. The defendant's responses to those particular interrogatories read, in their entirety: "Defendant objects to this interrogatory on the ground that it seeks information protected by the **duty of confidentiality**." Assuming that the information sought is in fact subject to opposing counsel's **duty of confidentiality**, are these interrogatory responses proper? If Frank and his client want the information, what **should** they do?

Problem 5D-5: Maya is working on her first initial public offering (a first sale of stock in a privately held company to the investing public), a big and exciting transaction. She comes in one morning to find an email from the supervising partner on the offering: "Maya, I stopped by your office early this morning to discuss the lockup agreement that you're drafting and saw that you had left materials regarding the offering on your desk. Please don't ever do that again." Is the partner being a bit of a neat freak here, or is she making a different point? If so, what might that point be? Are her concerns exaggerated?

4. The Duty of Candor

a. What You Must Disclose to Your Clients

In a relationship in which the beneficiary (client) is trusting the fiduciary (lawyer) to do important things for the beneficiary while often acting far from the beneficiary's immediate oversight, and with respect to subject matter that the beneficiary may not fully understand, it hardly seems surprising that a lawyer **must** fully, honestly, and promptly provide the client with all the information concerning the engagement that the client requests or reasonably needs to make informed decisions about the engagement. That's the **duty of candor** in a nutshell. Accordingly, **Model Rule 1.4** provides that lawyers **must**:

- Generally "explain a matter to the extent reasonably necessary to permit the client to make informed decisions regarding the representation" (**Model Rule 1.4(b)**);

- [K]eep the client reasonably informed about the status of the matter" and "promptly inform" the client of anything requiring the client's **informed consent**" (**Model Rule 1.4(a)(1), (3)**);[18]
- "[P]romptly comply with reasonable requests for information" (**Model Rule 1.4(a)(4)**); and
- Consult with the client about what the lawyer legally **may** or **must not** do when the lawyer knows the client expects assistance not permitted by law or that the lawyer is legally permitted to refuse (**Model Rule 1.4(a)(5)**).

Caselaw (and in some states statutory law as well) also expounds the civil fiduciary **duty of candor,** both for fiduciaries in general and for lawyers in particular.

As a practical matter, these requirements amount to saying that, if you have reason to believe that this client, or a reasonable client, would find an item of information significant in relation to the lawyer's engagement, then that information is **material** (a term of art used in many areas of the law to denote information that matters), and you **must** promptly disclose it to the client.

REAL WORLD Now, it's always easy to share good news, but bad news is a different matter. Your natural inclinations may not serve you well when something doesn't go as hoped or planned. And it is the rare engagement that goes flawlessly. Much more commonly, Murphy's Law is just another law with which you have to cope as things large or small go wrong. Motions or whole cases are lost; critical deal terms don't work out as desired; work takes longer to complete than anticipated.[19]

Even worse, *what if you think you made a mistake?* Not all bad news is somebody's fault, but as we discussed in **Chapter 4.B at 87**, mistakes happen, and even the best lawyers sometimes make them. Sometimes those mistakes are serious; sometimes, they're not. Sometimes they're mistakes that will matter down the road only

---

[18] TAMING THE TEXT **Informed consent** is an essential concept in legal ethics. We'll run into it many times in many different contexts. It's sufficiently vital and ubiquitous that it's defined in **Model Rule 1.0(e)**. Stop and read the definition. The "informed" part of **informed consent** is the tricky part. Sure, you need your client to approve (to *consent* to) important things—after all, it's the *client's* legal matter. *See* **Chapter 6.C at 161**. And sometimes the client's consent has to be given in a particular form or manner to be effective or it doesn't count (similar to the operation of the Statute of Frauds that you learned about in Contracts). We'll discuss those requirements later. But the client's consent also doesn't count unless it is "informed" consent. And *informed* consent must be based on (in the words of the Rule) "adequate information and explanation about the material risks of and reasonably available alternatives to the proposed course of conduct." That requirement means that this information and explanation must not only be provided in full, but in a form and manner that the client can understand and use to make an informed decision, taking into account the client's education, sophistication, and language and other skills. So the right way to provide a client the information necessary for the client to supply "informed consent" (and the right way to provide the "expla[nations]" required under **Model Rule 1.4(b)**) strongly depends on the client and the situation. For example, you probably need to explain things to an injured stevedore differently from the way that you would to the CEO of the big shipping company that employs her in order for each client to be adequately "informed." TAMING THE TEXT

[19] One of us had a colleague whose bicycle messenger was stopped and arrested for drug possession halfway to the courthouse while carrying an important filing that was due (in hard copy) in minutes. To euphemize, stuff happens.

if other events make them matter. Sometimes they're not mistakes in the literal sense of conduct falling below the applicable standard of care, but rather failures to meet the more elevated expectations that many of us impose on ourselves as a point of professional pride. But an important part of your job is to keep your client informed about what matters (or reasonably should matter) to the client, even when it may not be what the client wants (or what you want the client) to hear. Most clients are resilient and understanding about most setbacks, especially if their expectations have been sensibly managed from the outset. But regardless of temperament, and even on that rare occasion when you've made an error that you fear could result in your termination or in a malpractice claim, clients have a right to the whole truth and nothing but the truth when setbacks happen. REAL WORLD

TAMING THE TEXT There are times when, as a matter of your **duty of candor**, you or your firm **must** inform the client of bad news, including your own error or omission. How do we know when? Well, in the words of **Model Rule 1.4**, you **must** explain any situation to the client to the extent necessary to keep the client reasonably informed about the engagement or if the client reasonably needs the information to make informed decisions regarding the representation. In addition, you **must** "promptly comply with reasonable requests for information and "keep the client reasonably informed about the status of the matter." These are, of course, very general standards. For bad news generally, you have the **materiality** standard discussed above—loosely, whether a reasonable client, or this particular client, would consider the information to matter in relation to the engagement.[20]

An ABA Formal Ethics Opinion addresses when you **must** disclose your own mistake to the client, and it plausibly construes **Model Rule 1.4** to provide that you **must** promptly disclose if the error or omission is "**material**" (that word again!). In this context, the opinion defines "**material**" as "reasonably likely to harm or prejudice a client" or "of such a nature that it would reasonably cause a client to consider terminating the representation even in the absence of harm or prejudice."[21] ABA Formal Ethics Op. No. 18-481 (2018). TAMING THE TEXT

TIPS & TACTICS One way to assess when you **must** disclose unwelcome news is a thought experiment that we call the **don't-wanna test**. It's vexingly simple: The more you *don't wanna* disclose something to a client, the more likely it is to be

---

[20] Note the potential difference between what a reasonable client would want to know, and what you have reason to understand that *this particular client* wants to know. Sometimes, clients have unique practical needs, or just idiosyncratic interests, that lead them to want to know things about their engagements that the ordinary reasonable person might not care about. Because **Model Rule 1.4(a)(4)** says that you **must** "promptly comply with reasonable requests for information," what this particular client reasonably asks to be informed about is subject to the **duty of candor** even if an ordinary reasonable person might not have asked for it.

[21] Remember, **materiality** is a concept that comes up in many different situations. It generally refers to information that matters for a particular purpose in a particular context. So the definition that the ABA Formal Ethics Opinion offers for "**materiality**" is not intended to be general or universal, but is offered to help you understand specifically what kind of error or omission is "**material**" for the purpose of determining whether you **must** disclose it to the client under **Model Rule 1.4**. Other considerations will determine whether other information is **material** for other purposes.

something **material** that you **must** disclose. The **don't-wanna test** is a good practical way to alert yourself to the need to stop and examine carefully the reasons why you feel disinclined to bring something up. Sometimes there is a good and proper reason for your reticence—maybe you're forbidden to disclose the information by law or court order, for example; or maybe it's personally embarrassing to you but has nothing to do with, and has no effect on, the client's engagement. But more often you'll find that you're disinclined to tell clients about something because they're likely to care, and you fear that they'll react badly. And that's exactly why it's likely to be **material**.

A quick caution: We offer you the **don't-wanna test** because we think it will prove a useful guide when questions of **candor** arise. But the name is our invention, and the test is not a legal standard. Instead, it's a *practical* touchstone to help you get your bearings when you're facing a difficult decision about what to do with some awkward news that you may feel disinclined to share. In any context other than a class using this textbook, you'll need to explain the principle and its function to anyone with whom you're discussing the situation. TIPS & TACTICS

CONSEQUENCES What happens if you fail to disclose something to the client that **must** be disclosed? Well, the penalty for violation of **Model Rule 1.4** is professional discipline. The severity of the penalty will depend, as a practical matter, on any number of factors, likely including how serious the problem was, and whether the client suffered avoidable harm as a result of not knowing. But even a less severe penalty, such as a public reprimand, will require you to defend a disciplinary proceeding and could result in a public sanction that will follow you for the rest of your career (and can interfere with important professional needs, such as the availability or cost of professional liability insurance, or admission to practice in federal courts or sister states, or *pro hac vice* outside your jurisdiction).

And sometimes the failure to disclose can cause the client to suffer avoidable monetary harm. This happens most frequently when there is an issue that the client could have fixed or ameliorated had she known, and thus could have avoided losses that resulted from the lawyer's nondisclosure until after it was too late to fix the problem. In such situations, the client may seek to recover those avoidable losses from you or your firm in a legal malpractice action. The cause of action might be called breach of the **duty of candor**, or professional negligence (for failing to do what a reasonable attorney would have taken care to do), or breach of fiduciary duty, or fraud, but the costs of the nondisclosure will be visited on you or your firm, along with the effort and any costs of defense not covered by your insurance.[22]

And even if the nondisclosure causes zero compensable harm (because you fixed the problem, or because it ultimately didn't matter as a result of the way

---

[22] Most insurance policies have "self-insured retentions," or deductibles, and many of those require you to pay the initial costs of defense up to a defined limit before the insurance company's obligation to defend kicks in.

that events naturally played out), you may suffer what you might call procedural or evidentiary **consequences**. In a situation in which a client, angered by what is perceived as dishonesty, chooses to dispute your fees or seek damages, the client may argue that your nondisclosure is a "concealment" or "cover-up." Concealment can be argued to be evidence of guilty knowledge and deliberate wrongdoing, even in situations in which your mistake was at worst inadvertent, and your decision not to disclose it was an oversight or was based on a reasoned conclusion that you didn't need to disclose. The failure to disclose thus could be a basis on which a disgruntled client raises the stakes by seeking *punitive* damages for a knowing and willful violation of your duty to disclose which was actually, based on your knowledge of the facts and your intentions, just a mistaken failure to bring up a minor and inadvertent error—one that caused little or no harm. ⟨ CONSEQUENCES ⟩

> **Problem 5D-6:** One of Maya's friends at her firm is another associate in her practice group named Pete. Pete does corporate governance and transactional work for a regional chain of hunting, fishing, and camping equipment stores called Outdoors. Pete frequently interacts directly with various Outdoors officers and directors. The company's management has extremely strong religiously based views disapproving of homosexuality, and the company and its owners have contributed large amounts of money to political and other causes opposing LGBTQ rights and same-sex marriage. Pete is gay, but up until now, he has chosen to keep his sexual orientation largely to himself and a small circle of friends and family. Now Pete has fallen in love with someone with whom he wants to spend the rest of his life, and they've set a wedding date. Pete has every reason to believe that, if Outdoors knew that he was marrying another man, the company's owners and management would refuse to work with him and might even fire his firm. (The firm itself is aware of Pete's sexual orientation and marriage plans and has no issue with them.) **Must** Pete or the firm tell Outdoors about Pete's sexual orientation or impending marriage? **Should** they? Why or why not?

> **Problem 5D-7: Mess in the Press:** Michael Cohen was Donald Trump's personal lawyer for about ten years before Trump was elected president (and for a period of time after the election). After the FBI executed search warrants on Cohen's home and office, Cohen and Trump had a very public falling out. (Please bear in mind that this problem is about Mr. Cohen's conduct, not Mr. Trump's, and refrain from getting distracted by your feelings—whether positive or negative—about Mr. Trump. The same ethical rules apply no matter how famous or important the client—or the lawyer—may be.) Cohen eventually released to the public audiotapes of a telephone call that he'd had with Trump shortly before the 2016 election. In the conversation, they apparently discussed financial arrangements with a third party to pay a former *Playboy* model with whom Trump had earlier had an extramarital affair to buy her silence in exchange for a six-figure cash payment. Cohen later pleaded guilty to felony campaign-finance-law violations based on those arrangements. (After the FBI seized the materials, Trump waived his **attorney-client privilege** and **confidentiality** rights with respect to that and a number of other taped telephone conversations.) Assume that Cohen taped the phone conversation with

Trump without Trump's knowledge or consent, and that such secret taping was legal under applicable law. Did Cohen violate any of his fiduciary duties to his client? Which ones and why? Would your answer differ if the secretly taped telephone conversation had been with a nonclient witness to the transaction? Why or why not?[23]

Problem 5D-8: Maya's firm represents Saucy, a big company that makes and markets canned and bottled sauces and gravies. Saucy instructed a partner in Maya's practice group to negotiate an agreement with one of its principal suppliers of organic produce, Top Tomato Growers, for Saucy to purchase one million pounds of certified organic Roma tomatoes for delivery over 90 days. That delivery would help Saucy make one of its popular pasta sauces. Saucy told the partner up front that obtaining the full one million pounds of tomatoes within 90 days of contracting was critical, as Saucy had heard rumors of early infestations of cutworm in the tomato crop, and also because the prime growing season would be over in three months. Cutworm is a pest that destroys tomato plants and would be especially dangerous to organic tomato farms, which do not use chemical pesticides. From the first exchange of emails, Top Tomato told the partner that, because of cutworm problems, it could commit to deliver only 600,000 pounds of tomatoes over 90 days. The partner kept working on renegotiating the quantity to be delivered, but despite his best efforts and considerable creativity, Top Tomato never budged on quantity. By the time that the agreement was ready to sign, the cutworm infestation on organic produce farms had become serious, and the wholesale price of organic Roma tomatoes for delivery in the next 90 days had gone up from $1.10 per pound (the contract price on which the parties agreed at the beginning of the negotiation, and to which they adhered in the ultimate agreement) to $1.70 per pound. Saucy is surprised to be presented with a proposed contract that is 400,000 pounds short of its needs—the first that it had heard of the shortfall. To what formal or informal **consequences** might the partner and Maya's firm be subject, and why?

Problem 5D-9: Frank's firm represents Bob deBilder Co., a medium-sized excavation and construction company. The president and CEO, the company's namesake Bob deBilder, has decided to upgrade his company's heavy equipment and to sell a lot of its older equipment to another construction company to help defray the cost. Supervised by the partner with the primary client relationship, Frank negotiates and documents the deal with the buyer of the used equipment. The price for all the used equipment is $2.4 million, payable over two years at $100,000 per month plus interest at an agreed rate on the outstanding balance and secured by a lien on the used equipment. After the deal is done and signed, Frank is assembling a set of the executed documents for the client's records and discovers to his horror that, because of a couple of errant keystrokes while he was drafting the promissory note, he

---

[23] For some discussion of these issues that you may find helpful, *see* Bernie Burk, *Was Michael Cohen's Secret Taping of His Then-Client Donald Trump Improper?*, http://www.thefacultylounge.org/2018/07/was-michael-cohens-secret-taping-of-his-then-client-donald-trump-improper.html (July 26, 2018). On the doubtful wisdom of lawyers' taping their telephone conversations, *see id.*

inadvertently deleted the acceleration clause from the form of commercial promissory note that his boss gave him to use as a model. For those not familiar, an acceleration clause is a contractual term that is usually included in any agreement to pay money in installments over time. It provides that, if the obligor (the party owing the money) misses a payment, the entire amount of all remaining payments becomes immediately due and payable ("accelerating" the due date to the time of default; hence the name). In the absence of an acceleration clause, by the literal terms of the contract, the only payments owed would be the ones that had already come due and remained unpaid, meaning that the creditor might be forced to sue separately for each payment as it came due over months or years, even though the obligor was many payments behind. Like many small businesspeople in the construction business, Bob deBilder is a tough and crusty person with no patience for disorganization or delay. **Must** or **should** the firm tell Mr. deBilder about the inadvertent deletion of the acceleration clause, and if so, when? Please explain your answer.

Problem 5D-10: Same facts as **Problem 5D-9 at 122** (Frank has inadvertently left out an important acceleration clause in a loan agreement that is now signed and delivered). Put yourself in the shoes of Frank's firm. You've decided to talk to Bob deBilder about Frank's drafting error. Explain to Bob deBilder the absence of the acceleration clause and its implications. Don't wing it; take some time to specify in advance (1) who will speak to Mr. deBilder; (2) the subjects that will be addressed; and (3) the specific wording that will be used on each topic. (Note: This problem and **Problem 5D-9 at 122** are quite difficult. If you don't think that they're difficult, or you can't succinctly explain *why* they're difficult, you have missed a lot in this section on the **duty of candor**. Retrace your steps before it's too late: Go back to the beginning of **Chapter 5.D.4 at 117** and start over.)

b. TIPS & TACTICS What You Should Disclose to Your Clients

The previous discussion was all about what you **must** disclose to your clients (in the sense that, if you don't, you will likely suffer **consequences**). Because we're law professors and we know that you're going to have to take the MPRE, we're obligated to discuss these enforceable obligations, and you're obligated to understand them. But really, if you're thinking about the **duty of candor** in terms of "the minimum that I **must** disclose to clients," then as a *practical* matter, you're thinking about it all wrong.

REAL WORLD Why? Let's face it: "We do the minimum for you that the law requires" is not the motto that you want emblazoned below your smiling photograph on your website's home page. Open and complete communication with clients, regardless of their level of sophistication, is virtually always the best policy as a matter of good client relations and professional reputation—not just on things that meet some uncertain test for **materiality**, but on anything that you imagine the client might appreciate knowing, even if it's not good news. (Remember the **duty of loyalty's** golden rule: If you'd want to know the information if you were the client, then the client deserves at least as much. Or as we will urge you in **Chapter 7 at 172**, *be the lawyer you'd want to hire.*) Obviously you can set ground rules and develop an understanding with your clients about what kinds of things they do and don't want to hear about (and some definitely want to hear a lot more—and a lot more frequently—than others). But always remember that, as a rule in human relations,

Conversations that begin "why didn't you tell me . . ." rarely end well.

So conduct your client communications accordingly. REAL WORLD

If you're the person (or one of the people) responsible for communicating directly with the client, set up systems that remind you when to reach out and update the client. Part of planning these communications effectively involves reaching an understanding right off the bat on the kinds of things that this client wants or needs to know. Some, for example, will want to see copies of every pleading or other filing and every letter or email, and they'll want a report about every phone call. Others will be much more selective. Any significant development will be a natural moment to communicate with the client (and the development itself should naturally remind you to consider whether or how to report to the client), but most clients will want and appreciate periodic updates even if little is happening. Planning regular client updates is especially important in a practice with many small matters, any one of which can easily get lost in the hubbub of daily work. And nothing says to clients more effectively that you care about and are attending to their matters (and are earning the fees that they're paying you) than regular communications regarding status and developments. TIPS & TACTICS

C. TIPS & TACTICS What About Your Colleagues?

This subchapter is about when you **must** or **should** disclose information *to your client*. But when you're considering those issues, you also need to pay attention to anyone else to whom you answer in addition to the client, such as an employer or supervisor. In your early years of practice, you will almost certainly have people to whom you answer, and unless you eventually become a solo practitioner (and thus your own boss), you will have employers or supervisors or partners for your entire career.

If you're worried about whether or how to communicate something to a client, it's probably because you're worried about how that client may react, which in turn means that something potentially significant has happened. And when something potentially significant has happened, you virtually always **must** or at least **should** involve the person to whom you report in addition to the client, almost always *before* communicating with the client.

To begin with, your bosses expect to be kept abreast of what you're doing. It's part of their **duty to supervise** to know (*see* **Chapter 19.C at 513**), and part of your obligation to perform your duties ethically to keep them apprised (*see* **Chapter 19.D at 520**). However upset you imagine your employer may be, concealing problems from your employer (or neglecting to disclose them promptly) is generally viewed by employers and supervisors as a *much* more serious failing than creating those problems in the first place.

Just as important, as discussed in **Chapter 4.B at 87**, for both emotional and practical reasons, no one should ever try to address a practice dilemma alone. Most practice organizations have probably seen problems like whatever you're encountering, and others there may have some experience and perspective for dealing with it that you lack. Those around you will have a more objective outlook on whether there's a problem, what it is, and how to address and potentially ameliorate or remedy it. They're also likely to have valuable knowledge about how to interact constructively with any professional liability insurer, if appropriate, and to have suggestions for how to address the issue with the client (which, depending on your seniority in the organization, may very well fall to someone other than you).[24]

So when questions about disclosure to a client arise, always consider whom else you need to talk to, and talk with those people first. You can review **Chapter 4.B at 87** for a more detailed discussion about deciding whom to talk to and how to have that conversation. ⟨Tips & Tactics⟩

* * *

In the next chapter, we turn to a related perspective on the attorney-client relationship—the lawyer's power to speak and act on behalf of the client (and to bind the client) as the client's agent. Because agents are generally fiduciaries to their principals within the scope of the agency (*see* **Chapter 5.B at 106**), some concerns similar to those discussed in this chapter will arise when we talk about lawyers' duties as their client's agents. We will also see that, just as experience has tailored general fiduciary duties to the particular circumstances common to the attorney-client relationship, lawyers' duties as agents have also evolved to manage issues that lawyers naturally confront. Read on!

Big-Picture Takeaways from Chapter 5

1. You can become a fiduciary by status or by circumstances. Attorneys are, by status (that is, simply because they are attorneys), virtually always fiduciaries to their clients. But you can also develop fiduciary duties to nonclients because of things they and you say and do. *See* **Chapter 5.B at 106**.

2. Lawyers may not have sex with their clients unless the sexual relationship preexisted the attorney-client relationship. This issue arose

---

[24] That said, you need to examine your employer's steps critically; occasionally, bosses get it wrong, too.

frequently enough that almost every state has seen fit to adopt this rule. The fact that it was a commonly recurring issue probably results from the nature of common interactions between lawyers and their clients. *See* **Chapter 5.C at 108**.

3. Fiduciaries have four basic duties to their beneficiaries—**loyalty, confidentiality, care**, and **candor**. Each of those duties needs to be analyzed separately, not just in terms of the duties themselves but also in terms of the different **consequences** that can flow from the breach of each duty. *See* **Chapter 5.D at 113**.

4. The **duty of loyalty** requires you not to act adversely to your client's interests in any respect, even in respects unrelated to your engagement, and to treat your client at least as well as you would treat yourself. *See* **Chapter 5.D at 113**.

5. The **duty of confidentiality** requires you not to voluntarily use or disclose any information that you learn in connection with representing your client, unless that information is or becomes generally known, the client authorizes you to use or disclose it, or some other exception to the duty exists under the circumstances. *See* **Chapter 5.D at 116**.

6. The **duty of care** requires you to exercise a level of skill, diligence, and care—and possess (or acquire) a level of knowledge—that a reasonably careful and prudent lawyer would under the same or similar circumstances. *See* **Chapter 5.D at 115**.

7. The **duty of candor** requires you to:
   a. Generally explain a matter to the client to the extent reasonably necessary to permit the client to make informed decisions regarding the representation;
   b. Keep the client reasonably informed about the status of the matter and promptly inform the client of anything requiring the client's **informed consent**;
   c. Promptly comply with the client's reasonable requests for information about the engagement; and
   d. Consult with the client about what the lawyer legally **may** or **must not** do when the lawyer knows that the client expects assistance not permitted by law or that the lawyer is legally permitted to refuse.
   See **Model Rule 1.4; Chapter 5.D at 117**.

8. Both as a practical matter and because you have legal duties to your employer, if you think that you may have messed up, your first call should always be to the person to whom you report. *See* **Chapter 5.D at 124**.

Multiple-Choice Review Questions for Chapter 5

1. Which of the following best describes the fiduciary duty that a lawyer owes a client?
   a. The duty to secure the client's objectives at all costs.
   b. The duty to treat the client with the utmost loyalty.
   c. The duty to balance the lawyer's needs and desires equally with the client's needs and desires.
   d. The duty to treat the lawyer's needs and desires as paramount.

2. Lawyer Laura is defending her client, Clint, in a criminal embezzlement case. Clint must decide whether he will testify in his own defense. He has a constitutional right not to testify. If he does take the stand, he may be cross-examined and thoroughly discredited by the prosecution. Clint maintains his innocence and would testify that he had no involvement in the embezzlement scheme. The documents suggest otherwise: There are emails from Clint demonstrating his involvement in the scheme.

   Ultimately it is Clint, not Laura, who must decide whether he will testify. As a matter of strategy, Laura knows that Clint should not testify. She also knows that, if he does testify, it will attract media attention to the case. That media attention could boost Laura's career.

   May Laura suggest that Clint testify?
   a. Yes. Whether to testify is ultimately Clint's decision, and Laura's fiduciary duty does not require her to deny Clint his right to decide.
   b. Yes. Laura's fiduciary duty simply requires that she present the options to Clint; it does not require that she advise him as to which option is best.
   c. No. Laura has a fiduciary duty to make the best decision for Clint. If he wants to testify, she must prevent him from doing so.
   d. No. Laura has a fiduciary duty to advise Clint not to testify. She **must not** prefer her own career's interests over what is in his best interest.

3. Lawyer Leon is hired by Bullseye Corp. to represent the company in a breach of contract case asserted against the company by one of its suppliers. As Leon litigates the case, he realizes that Bullseye did indeed breach the contract. He urges Bullseye to settle, but Bullseye refuses. Desperate to ensure a just outcome in the case, Leon secretly leaks **attorney-client privileged** documents not otherwise called for in discovery to the supplier defendant. Relying on these documents, the defendant files a successful motion for summary judgment and wins the case.

   Did Leon act appropriately?

    a. Yes. Leon's **duty of candor to the tribunal** trumped his **duty of loyalty** to his client.

    b. Yes. Leon owed a fiduciary duty not only to his client but also to the opposing party.

    c. No. Leon breached his **duty of confidentiality** by secretly leaking the information. Leon should have done so overtly.

    d. No. Leon breached his **duty of confidentiality** to his client by assisting in securing a win for the opposing party. Leon had other options, including withdrawal, if his client refused to settle the case.

4. Which of the following is not an example of a fiduciary duty described in this chapter?

    a. The duty that a physician owes to the patient within the scope of the treatment relationship that prevents the physician from intentionally harming the patient.

    b. The duty that a lawyer owes to the client within the scope of the legal engagement that requires the lawyer to disclose **conflicts of interest**.

    c. The duty that an agent owes to the principal within the scope of the agency relationship that prohibits any self-dealing by the agent.

    d. The duty between a brother and a sister within the scope of the familial relationship that obligates them to care for one another in the case of illness.

5. Lawyer Louis is retained by Client Christine to defend Christine in a bribery case being prosecuted in the Commonwealth of Keystone. Both Louis and Christine are licensed in Keystone. Although Christine is an experienced criminal defense lawyer herself, she prefers not to handle her own defense. Under these facts, is Louis a fiduciary for Christine?

    a. Yes. Lawyers are almost always considered fiduciaries to their clients.

    b. Maybe. It depends whether Louis agreed to such a fiduciary duty in his retainer agreement.

    c. Maybe. It depends whether such a duty is implied in the Commonwealth of Keystone.

    d. No. Fiduciary duties arise because of superior knowledge, skills, or abilities, and here both the client and lawyer are on equal footing.

6. What are the four canonical fiduciary duties that lawyers owe clients?

    a. Professionalism, care, confidentiality, and candor.

    b. Loyalty, care, confidentiality, and candor.

    c. Professionalism, loyalty, care, and civility.

    d. Loyalty, care, confidentiality, and civility.

7. Lawyer Liam is representing FarmCorp, a large agricultural business seeking to acquire acreage in the Commonwealth of Keystone.

FarmCorp has tasked Liam with researching seven different land parcels that FarmCorp is considering purchasing. FarmCorp tells Liam that it would like to spend the minimum amount possible to purchase a suitable property.

As he researches the parcels, Liam discovers that one of the parcels is owned by landowner Lillian. Liam calls Lillian to inquire about the price. He is careful not to tell Lillian who is inquiring about the property. Lillian confides in Liam that she has a pressing family emergency and therefore would sell the property well below market value. Based on Liam's research, this parcel is the cheapest of all of the seven identified by FarmCorp.

Liam does not disclose anything about his conversation with Lillian to FarmCorp. He advises FarmCorp. to purchase an entirely different property. Liam then purchases Lillian's parcel for himself.

Has Liam violated any of his fiduciary duties?

a. Yes. Liam has breached his **duties of loyalty**, **confidentiality**, and **candor**. He furthered his own financial gain over that of FarmCorp using information obtained on the client's behalf. FarmCorp would have wanted to know that Lillian's parcel was available at a below-market price.

b. Yes. Liam has breached his **duty of care**. Liam did not exercise reasonable care in advising FarmCorp to buy a parcel other than Lillian's. His advice was negligent.

c. No. Liam did not breach his **duties of loyalty, confidentiality**, and **candor**. It is unclear whether FarmCorp would have purchased Lillian's parcel even with the information that Liam withheld. The parcel may not have been suitable for FarmCorp. Because it is uncertain whether FarmCorp was damaged, there has been no breach.

d. No. Liam did not breach his **duty of care**. He handled FarmCorp's purchase of the parcel that it bought carefully and competently.

8. Lawyer Lucy practices matrimonial law. She represents Hank, a man planning to divorce his wife, Wendy. Wendy does not yet know that Hank is planning to divorce her. The two still live together.

During a meeting, Hank asks Lucy if it will hurt his interests in the divorce proceedings if the court learns that he has a girlfriend. Lucy advises that it could. She asks whether Wendy is aware. Hank says Wendy is not and, although he is still intimate with Wendy, he has no plans to tell her about the girlfriend.

That night, Lucy tosses and turns. The next morning, she leaves an anonymous voicemail for Wendy, stating that a "concerned friend" wants her to know that Hank is being unfaithful and intends to divorce her.

Has Lucy violated her **duty of confidentiality**?

    a. Yes. She should not have disclosed any information that she learned from Hank about his infidelity or his plans to divorce Wendy.

    b. Yes. Lucy should not have disclosed to Wendy that Hank plans to divorce her. She was free to disclose that Hank has been unfaithful, however.

    c. No. Hank was concealing **material** information that Wendy had a right to know.

    d. No. The voicemail was anonymous.

6

The Lawyer as Agent

HORACE AND HELENA Homeowner sit down in a conference room with Frank and his boss, litigation partner Harlan "Happy" Trials. The Homeowners look distressed. "What brings you in today?" Happy asks. "The bank took our home," says Horace. "I'm very sorry," Happy says. "Can you tell me what happened?"

"I'm not sure," says Horace. "See, we paid our mortgage every month, but somehow the bank didn't think so. Our local Savings & Loan got bought out by a big out-of-state bank, and the bookkeeping must have gotten messed up. Maybe the bank lost our checks; maybe it credited the payments to someone else. But one day, this thing that says 'Notice of Default' appears in the mail. So we called the bank right away, and after hours on hold, we just got the runaround. Then this guy shows up at our front door and hands us an envelope that has something called a 'Complaint for Judicial Foreclosure.' It came along with a scary-looking paper that said, in big letters, '**Summons. Attention—you have been sued.**'

"So we hired a lawyer—'Honest Abe' Andon. He said that he was a foreclosure specialist. After that, things were quiet for a few months. We thought that he was doing a good job. We called a couple of times, and Abe said that our case was going well. Then suddenly a sheriff's deputy showed up, nailed a 'Notice of Sale' to our door, and a month or so later, we're told that the house was foreclosed and we had to leave. We frantically called and emailed the lawyer, but he stopped responding."

Frank uses his laptop to pull up the local court docket and finds the Homeowners' case. From the docket, it appears that after filing a Notice of Appearance, Abe Andon did . . . nothing. He didn't answer the complaint, didn't seek relief after default was entered, didn't show up at (or file anything before) a special hearing that the court had called before it entered a default judgment of foreclosure. He didn't even show up at a later "prove-up" hearing to determine the amount of any deficiency. Court records show that the home was sold at what looks to Frank like an amount well below its fair market value (not surprising for a sheriff's sale), and that a deficiency judgment (a money judgment for the amount of the mortgage loan left unpaid after applying the proceeds of sale to the loan) for about $45,000 has been entered against the Homeowners. Frank's heart sinks as he delivers the news.

"What can we do?" Helena asks. "Well," says Happy, "first of all, let me say again how sorry I am about what's happened to you. You were treated horribly, and what happened is completely unfair. But I'm afraid the question is what we can do now. We can help you lodge a complaint against the lawyer with the state bar. He'll likely get suspended from practice for a time or maybe even disbarred, which should stop him from doing this to anyone else. But I realize that won't help *you* much. You can also sue the lawyer for malpractice. Given how completely he ignored your matter and the strength of your defenses to foreclosure, that's a case that you're almost certain to win. The hitch is that, in my experience, lawyers who behave the way your lawyer did have often done the same thing to numerous other clients, too. So they often have no money to pay a malpractice judgment, and they usually don't have any malpractice insurance, either. What it comes down to is this: If Abe Andon can pay for what he did, we'd be happy to handle the case against him on a contingency fee—that is, we don't get paid unless you do. But we'd want to look into his ability to pay a judgment before we committed to filing your lawsuit against him in order to make sure that it's worth it."

"Malpractice suit!" sputters Horace. "Forget that. We paid our mortgage just like we were supposed to every month—the bank screwed up, and then that idiot lawyer screwed up. We did everything right. We want to get this fixed and get our home back!" Helena, tearful, nods emphatically.

Can this mess be fixed the way that Horace wants? Can the Homeowners get a "do-over" with a lawyer who actually shows up and does something this time? The answer to these questions lies in the law of agency, and it may surprise you.

* * *

Fair warning: This chapter is long and at times must work its way through some intricate technical details about how agency law works in the context of the attorney-client relationship. But as you'll see, these details form the framework for lawyers' powers to do most of the things that lawyers do, including negotiating, advocating, and generally speaking and acting on behalf of our clients. You need to understand this framework in order to understand what you **must** or **may** properly do and when you **must** or **may** do it and, conversely, when you've done more than the law allows or less than it requires, either of which can open you to a world of hurt. Because lawyers are virtually always their clients' agents (with all the duties and powers that this status carries with it), this is another important part of what we meant when we told you in **Chapter 1.C at 9** that obligations to understand and attend to the client's preferences and needs are legal duties hardwired into the law structuring the attorney-client relationship.

So work with us. You won't regret it.

A. The Lawyer as Agent

1. An Introduction to Agency[1]

Agency law governs a range of contractual, quasi-contractual, and non-contractual fiduciary relationships in which one person (the *principal*) authorizes another (the *agent*) to act on behalf of the principal within the scope of the *authority* that the principal confers on the agent.[2] This describes a lot of what lawyers do: Our clients authorize us to prosecute or defend a lawsuit, or negotiate a deal, or close a real estate transaction, and we act on behalf of our clients (not for ourselves) when we do so. So you won't be surprised to learn that the attorney-client relationship is (among other things) an agency relationship in which the client is the principal and the lawyer is the agent.

How do you know when you're someone's agent? An agency relationship is created when the principal objectively manifests the intention that the agent act on the principal's behalf, and the agent objectively manifests the intent to do so. *Restatement (Third) of Agency* § 1.01. This concept should remind you of the "objective theory" of contract formation that you learned in Contracts. Though only some agency relationships are contractual, the circumstances under which each relationship is formed are similar. When the parties by their words or actions each manifest to the other something that a reasonable person would understand to be an intent that the agent act on the principal's behalf (very much like that objective manifestation of mutual intent to be bound that you obsessed about in Contracts during your first year), the agency relationship is formed. As we will see in **Chapter 9.A at 259**, this test is also very similar to the test for when an attorney-client relationship is formed. As a practical matter, once you've determined whether you have an attorney-client relationship with someone, you will know whether you are that person's agent, because agency is virtually always a part of the attorney-client relationship.

---

[1] Your House; Your Rules Our overview of agency law draws extensively on the RESTATEMENT (THIRD) OF AGENCY (2006). As you learned in your first year, Restatements are expert summaries of what most states do, most of the time, in a particular area of the law. Your state may have its own little quirks that might be inconsistent with the Restatement approach. And remember that, although the agency law applicable to lawyers is generally consistent with that applicable to other types of agents, there are some specialized rules unique to lawyer-agents, many of which are found in the Rules of Professional Conduct. So when you're confronted with an agency question in the jurisdiction that you've come to call home, do your homework and check your state's consistency with the Restatement generally, and the consistency of its version of the Rules of Professional Conduct with the Model Rules with respect to the agency-oriented rules discussed in this chapter. Your House; Your Rules

[2] Please don't mix up "principal" and "principle." Although they sound the same, they're completely different words with completely different meanings. Generally speaking, *principal*, when used as a noun, refers to the person in charge (as in "the *principal* is in charge of the school," or as in "the *principal* determines which goals the agent is to pursue on the *principal's* behalf"). In other contexts, *principal* can also refer to a sum of money lent or invested on which interest is paid (as in "the loan *principal* is $1,000, with interest to be paid thereon at 2 percent per year"). As an adjective, *principal* means the main or most important (as in "my *principal* concern is that you not subject yourself to malpractice liability"). *Principle* is never an adjective. It is a noun that refers to a fundamental idea or general rule (as in "it is a *principle* of Anglo-American criminal law that the accused is innocent until proven guilty").

We know from **Chapter 5.B at 106** that lawyers are fiduciaries to their clients. And we just learned that lawyers are also agents for their clients. So the fact (which we also learned in **Chapter 5.B at 106**) that agents are fiduciaries to their principals (*see Restatement (Third) of Agency* §§ 8.01, 8.08) might not seem to add much to what we already knew.[3]

The alert readers are likely now feeling a little impatient: If agency law adds nothing new to the attorney-client relationship, then why are we bothering to discuss it? The answer is that agency *does* add something new. Fiduciary duties are almost entirely about the legal relations between the fiduciary and the beneficiary (here, the lawyer and the client)—but just between the two of them. Agency adds something that is not only new but breathtakingly important: *the agent's power to alter the principal's legal relations with third parties.* How? The essence of agency is that it gives the agent the power, within the scope of the agent's authority, to make representations, to enter into agreements, and to engage in conduct *as if those things were being done by the principal herself.*[4]

This is huge. Stop and think about how radical and world-altering this concept is. If an agent makes a contract within the scope of his authority, the principal is bound by that contract—even if the principal wasn't there, and even if the principal didn't know what the agent was doing![5]

The rest of this chapter will focus on how a lawyer's power to obligate a client-principal to third parties works, and what happens if lawyer-agents exceed their authority. As you'll see, these concepts are incredibly important in achieving the outcomes that you and your client want to achieve and in avoiding the outcomes that you don't. In thinking about this issue, the key point to keep in

---

[3] Other than a neat little syllogism of the kind at which you became adept when you were preparing for the LSAT, which at the least should remind you that you're having more fun now than you did then. (You're welcome.)

[4] This point highlights a daily reality worth noting—one that you will be discussing at much greater length in your Business Organizations and Employment Law courses (and which we'll revisit from time to time in this course): Business organizations (such as corporations, LLCs, and partnerships) are only abstract legal constructs that—having no arms, legs, minds, or mouths—cannot act, decide, or speak *except* through human agents whose principal is the disembodied entity. Employees are agents of their entity employers within the course and scope of their employment. And lawyers can, and frequently do, represent and act as agents for their clients that are business organizations. They *don't* necessarily also act for the organizations' other agents, such as its officers and employees, nor for the organizations' owners. *See* **Chapter 23 at 769**.

[5] An agent's contracts and an agent's torts are treated differently. If an agent is acting within the scope of his authority (say, someone who has been hired to drive the principal's truck for business and is doing so) and commits a tort (say, negligently runs down a neurosurgeon in a crosswalk), then legally *it's generally as if the principal had also committed the tort herself.* And that, ladies and gentlemen, is the origin of *respondeat superior*, which we hope you remember from Torts, and which can be fairly translated from the law Latin as "let the principal answer" (that is, answer for the agent's wrong). *See* Restatement (Third) of Agency § 2.04. But the principal's vicarious liability for the agent's torts committed within the scope of the agency does not exonerate the agent from the **consequences** of his tort; it just makes the principal equally responsible—that is, jointly and severally liable with the agent—for the agent's wrong. When an agent makes a *contract* within the scope of his authority, by contrast, *only* the principal is responsible for performing the contract. That's why, when a real estate agent makes a deal on your behalf for a new home, you (not the real estate agent) get to move in, but you (not the real estate agent) must pay the house's purchase price. (On the other hand, if your real estate agent is checking out an open house for you and accidentally smashes a priceless vase in the house, you're both on the hook.)

mind is that statements, agreements, and conduct *within the scope of the lawyer-agent's authority* are binding on the client-principal, but those *outside the scope of the lawyer-agent's authority* are not. As a result, the practical questions we're going to be addressing are:

- How do you know whether you have the authority to engage in a particular act or make a particular agreement on the client's behalf?
- How can you get the authority that you need if you don't yet have it?
- What are the **consequences** if you exceed the scope of your authority?

We're going to discuss those questions first as a matter of the general law of agency (in the next section of the chapter), then briefly review the duties that the lawyer-agent owes the client-principal so that the agency can be properly carried out (**Chapter 6.B at 151**). Then we'll apply those principles to questions of authority that come up frequently in law practice (**Chapter 6.A at 148; Chapter 6.C at 151**).

The analytical approach that we suggested in the **Introduction to this unit at 130** needs to be adjusted a little when dealing with questions of authority. Here, rather than focus on the *duties owed*, you should focus on the *existence and scope of the lawyer's authority*. Three questions will guide your analysis:

1. What kind or kinds of authority (out of the four kinds available) does the lawyer-agent have, what facts confer that authority, and why?
2. For each kind of authority available to the lawyer-agent, what is the scope of that authority (that is, what does it allow the lawyer-agent to do on the client-principal's behalf), what facts define that scope, and why?
3. If the lawyer-agent has acted without authority in any respect, what are the **consequences** and on whom will they fall?

Ask and answer these questions in addressing the problems in this chapter, and you are well on your way to understanding the lawyer's role as the client's agent.

2. Sources of the Lawyer-Agent's Authority to Bind the Client-Principal[6]

Model Rule 1.2(a) says that a lawyer "shall abide by a client's decisions concerning the objectives of representation." Because the Rule says "shall," this is something

---

[6] The aspiring business and transactional lawyers among you will notice, perhaps with some nagging sense of exclusion, that almost all of the examples and problems in this chapter arise in litigation. That's not because we've forgotten you, or don't care about your careers. It's because the most common difficult authority questions that lawyers confront have to do with litigation. Any time that you see a litigation settlement being discussed, imagine that you're negotiating a business deal, and ask yourself to which terms in that deal you can agree without your client's authority. Being sensible business lawyers, you'd instantly see that *of course* you can't agree to a price or any other **material** term in the transaction without your client's authority. But for reasons that you'll soon understand, in litigation these issues get more confusing, and the temptations to stray more alluring. So be patient with your warrior cousins, and pity their appetites for the battle scars that they'll soon be accumulating. Your work has other ethical challenges that will captivate us later in the book. And if you can think of any difficult authority questions that commonly arise in business work, send us an email. We'll consider them for the next edition.

that you **must** do or suffer the **consequences**. As we'll see in **Chapter 6.C at 151**, the "objectives of [the] representation" are those things over which the client has complete and ultimate control, and therefore the lawyer **must** have the client's authority to accomplish them on the client's behalf. One of those objectives is whether, when, and on what terms to settle a dispute (it says so in black and white right there in **Model Rule 1.2(a)**—quick, find the relevant phrase!), which is why we'll use the example of settlement in all of the problems in this section. (There are, of course, other "objectives of representation" besides settlement terms, and we'll discuss them in **Chapter 6.C at 151**, but using a settlement hypothetical in many of the problems and altering the facts step by step will allow us to show you in detail how the different kinds of client authority get conferred.)

There are four ways in which the lawyer-agent may acquire the authority to bind the client-principal to those things over which the client has the ultimate power: actual authority; implied authority; apparent authority; and ratification. We'll discuss each in turn.

a. Actual Authority

We start with the simplest and most intuitive form of authority: *actual authority*. A lawyer-agent has actual authority to act on behalf of and bind the client-principal to third parties when the client communicates to the lawyer that the lawyer is directed or permitted to do so. *Restatement (Third) of Agency* §§ 2.01, 3.01. Of course, clients grant lawyers actual authority all the time.

> Problem 6A-1: Frank is representing the plaintiff, Payne N. Suffern, in a fender-bender case (an intersection collision) with minor injuries. He calls her up. "I'm meeting with opposing counsel tomorrow to talk about discovery," he tells her. "If settlement comes up, what's the smallest amount that you'd accept?" After Frank and Payne discuss the settlement value of the case, she says, "OK, don't take less than $25,000." During the meeting the next day, while the lawyers are discussing the outstanding discovery, Frank's opposing counsel brings up settlement. After some sparring about the strengths and weaknesses of the case, the two start trading numbers, each justifying his or her counteroffers with comments about the claims, defenses, and damage figures. Opposing counsel finally offers $25,000, warning "but that's as far as I can go. And of course, we'll need written documentation, including a dismissal with prejudice, mutual releases, and the other typical terms." "You have a deal," Frank says. The next day, opposing counsel calls Frank, very embarrassed. "My client authorized me to offer you up to $25,000 yesterday, but today he's having buyer's remorse and has changed his mind. I'm afraid the deal's off." "The heck it is," says Frank. "You offered, I accepted, and a deal's a deal." Who's right, and why? Does your analysis change if opposing counsel offered, and Frank accepted, $30,000? If so, how and why; and if not, why not?

> Problem 6A-2: Same as **Problem 6A-1** (a fender-bender with minor injuries), but now the client, Payne, has developed very unreasonable expectations. "After what I went through,"

she says, "I won't take less than $250,000 to settle the case. I deserve it." Frank patiently explains that the evidence available would never allow a jury to award more than about $25,000, and that's only if all the disputed facts go her way. But Payne won't budge. The next day at the meeting, opposing counsel brings up settlement, and after some sparring on the merits of the case, opposing counsel offers $15,000. "My client won't take less than $250,000," Frank says, concealing his discomfort with his client's position. "She'd rather go to trial than accept less." Opposing counsel is quite surprised and, with admirable restraint, explains how absurd that demand is in light of the known facts (in terms quite similar to those Frank laid out to his client the day before). "Well," opposing counsel concludes, "let's cut to the chase here: $25,000 is the best I can possibly do, and really, the case isn't worth anything near that—but it'll cost us that much to try it." Frank knows that opposing counsel is right and that the offer is actually generous. What's more, Frank's firm is working on a contingency fee—that is, a fee calculated as a percentage of the client's settlement or verdict (after recouping costs advanced on the client's behalf). Because $25,000 is the best that Frank could reasonably do at trial, he's now in a position in which his firm gets a significantly better fee if the client settles right now than if the firm goes to all the effort of preparing and trying the case (advancing experts' and jury fees in the process)—effort that the firm could expend earning fees from other clients. Can Frank do the sensible thing and accept the $25,000 offer on Payne's behalf? Why or why not?

Problem 6A-3: Same as **Problem 6A-2 at 136** (fender-bender with minor injuries; client with unreasonable expectations), but in response to Frank's explanations the day before the meeting, Payne reluctantly agrees that Frank may settle the case at the meeting the next day for $25,000, but that he first must demand $250,000 and try to get as close to that amount as he can.

a. Opposing counsel eventually makes a $25,000 last, best, and final offer, and Frank accepts it on Payne's behalf on the spot. He returns to his office and calls Payne with the news. "But I changed my mind last night," she says. "I talked with my spouse and my minister— you can ask them—and they persuaded me that I should ask for what I thought was fair. So I told them that's what I was doing." Can Payne walk away from the $25,000 settlement? Why or why not?

b. Same as (a) (fender-bender with minor injuries; client with unreasonable expectations; client granted authority to settle for $25,000 the day before counsel meet), except Payne calls Frank the night before the meeting after talking with her spouse and her minister and informs Frank that she's changed her mind and must have at least $250,000 in order to settle the case. What is the extent of Frank's authority at the meeting of counsel the next day? (*Hint:* Take another look at *Restatement (Third) of Agency* § 2.01. There are 13 words, set off from the rest of the sentence by commas, that give you the principle needed to solve Problems 6A-3(a) and (b). What are those words, and how do they help you solve these problems?)

Now let's focus on how lawyers acquire actual authority. We already know that lawyers acquire actual authority when that authority is communicated ("manifested") by the client. But how do we know when the client is doing so? The answer (again, very much like the objective determination of intent to be bound in contract law) is when "the agent reasonably believes, in accordance with the principal's manifestations to the agent, that the principal wishes the agent so to act." *Restatement (Third) of Agency* § 2.01. That tells us that it doesn't matter what's in the client's head but unexpressed. (Why? How do the words in § 2.01 tell us that?)

So in determining whether the lawyer-agent has actual authority to do something on the client-principal's behalf, we just learned that what matters is *what a reasonable person would understand from the client's "manifestations"*—that is, the client's words and actions of which the lawyer is aware—in light of all of the known facts and circumstances. The client's intent can be manifested in any number of ways. If you have a client with a certain unusual way of expressing himself, and you know that he sometimes says "Thunderbuggies!" when he means "Heck, yes," then "Thunderbuggies" in answer to your request for settlement power is enough to give you actual authority. (Whether you should accept a client who invented and apparently regularly uses the word "Thunderbuggies" is a question that we leave you to debate with your classmates.) Similarly, a thumbs-up or nod of the head is enough to confer actual authority if that's what would reasonably be understood in context. Anything sufficient to make the client's assent understood by a reasonable person will do.

> **Problem 6A-4:** Same as **Problem 6A-2 at 136** (fender-bender with minor injuries; client has unreasonable settlement expectations). After Frank patiently explains that $250,000 is completely out of the realm of the possible, Payne gets sullen and angry. "So *you* say," she says, going on to suggest, rather uncharitably, that Frank's advice is motivated by his self-serving urge to avoid the work of preparing for trial, "settle quick, and leave me hanging." Frank, retaining his composure, explains why $25,000 would be about the best that Payne could expect after trial and asks if he can settle the case for that much if the opportunity presents itself at the meeting the next day. "I don't know. I guess. Maybe," Payne says dejectedly, slowly shaking her head and staring at the table. What is Frank's actual settlement authority at the meeting with opposing counsel tomorrow, and why?

Tips & Tactics As we will discuss in more detail in **Chapter 6.A at 145**, the **consequences** for you (and everyone else) can be very serious if it turns out that you acted on your client's behalf without the authority to do so. And if the client disputes your authority (rightly or wrongly), what follows is litigation over whether you reasonably understood from the client's manifestations of intent (words and actions) that you in fact had the authority that you exercised. In other words, in the event of a dispute over your authority, you and the parties won't know if there was (and still is) a deal until after evidentiary proceedings to determine whether you had the authority to make one. The moral here is simple:

When in doubt, speak out.

You can put that moral into practice in three simple steps:

- **Inquire:** If you have *any* doubt about the extent of your authority, *always ask.* Don't get tangled up in "what-ifs" about what happens if you ask and the client says no. If you ask and the client says no, then you don't have authority, and you need to know and conduct yourself accordingly. If the client says no beforehand, she likely would have asserted afterwards that she never authorized whatever it was that you did. Remember, if you think that you have actual authority and the client later asserts that you didn't, you now have a three-way fight on your hands among the client, the opposing party, and you. Such disputes can be protracted, expensive, and result in **consequences** to your client or to you and your firm. *See* **Chapter 6.A at 145**.

- **Explain:** If you have *any* doubt about the client's understanding of the implications of a grant of authority, *explain* those implications. Plaintiffs who are not well acquainted with the legal system may have no idea that their grant of authority to you may lead to a deal that can't be reconsidered, will end the lawsuit without the client's having had the opportunity to tell her story at trial, and will usually result in a settlement payment not of the full settlement amount, but that amount *minus* your fees and costs. Less sophisticated defendants may not have considered all the costs (monetary and practical) of settling the case, or what portion of those costs might or might not be borne by any insurer that may be involved. As discussed in **Chapter 5.D at 117** and **Chapter 6.B at 151**, you have a duty to make sure that your client understands *all* of the **material** implications of the decision that you're asking her to make.

- **Confirm:** If you have *any* doubt about the client's inclination to stick with the authority that she's granting or her general trustworthiness or reliability, then *confirm* your authority and any appropriate explanation of its consequences in a way that makes any question about it something more than a he-said/she-said later (sometimes referred to as a "swearing contest," because each of you swears under oath to a different version of who said what, and there's no corroborating evidence confirming either side). There's no one "right" way to make this confirmation: You can tailor your confirmation methods depending on the nature and degree of your concerns and the importance of the steps that you're being authorized to take. When you have confidence in the understanding and reliability of your client, no confirmatory steps may be needed at all (though some simple ones are often wise, no matter how much you trust your client). Or you can simply confirm the client's grant of authority in a short email to the client. If you are concerned that the client may later assert that she didn't manifest the intent you say she did, or didn't understand its implications, you can mitigate that risk by having the client sign a writing acknowledging the grant of authority and its implications. Confirmation in a brief writing to the client is common, and it is widely viewed as careful lawyering; having the client sign something is somewhat less common, but it's good practice with an unsophisticated client who is about to take an important step, and some lawyers make it a standard practice. You can also confirm the grant of authority orally in the presence of a witness (but beware having a witness who is clearly associated with you or the client, as that association can affect the witness's credibility in any later dispute—take a moment to think through why).

There are usually no formalities (such as a signed writing or specific "magic words") that are required for the client to confer actual authority. All that is typically required is that the client manifest the intent to authorize you to do or say something in any way reasonably understood as such. Confirming your authority as just described is usually for the purpose of having *evidence* of the client's manifestations of intent in case they are disputed later.[7] TIPS & TACTICS

b. Implied Authority

"Implied authority"

is often used to mean actual authority either (1) to do what is necessary, usual, and proper to accomplish or perform an agent's express responsibilities or (2) to act in a manner in which an agent believes the principal wishes the agent to act based on the agent's reasonable interpretation of the principal's manifestation in light of the principal's objectives and other facts known to the agent.

Restatement (Third) of Agency § 2.01 Comment b. So implied authority is really just a form of actual authority that depends on what the lawyer-agent reasonably understands to be implied by or contained in the broader grant of actual authority that the principal-client has explicitly conferred.

Often a lawyer's authority to speak or act on the client's behalf is implied simply from the client's retention of the lawyer for a particular purpose. **Model Rule 1.2(a)** confirms this view by pointing out that "[a] lawyer may take such action on behalf of the client as is impliedly authorized to carry out the representation." So when Horace and Helena Homeowner in **this chapter's Introduction at 131** retained Abe Andon to defend the foreclosure proceedings filed against them, they authorized him to do the things reasonably necessary to pursue that

---

[7] One important exception applicable in many jurisdictions is called the "Equal Dignities Rule." It holds that an agency to perform an act on the principal's behalf that legally requires a writing to be enforceable (such as a transfer of certain interests in land, or the making of contracts subject to the state's Statute of Frauds) must itself be documented **in a writing signed by the client**. *See* RESTATEMENT (THIRD) OF AGENCY § 3.02. Because some engagement terms **must** be documented **in a writing signed by the client**, and all engagements **should** be (*see* **Chapter 20. B at 539**), one convenient place to document an agency required by the Equal Dignities Rule to be in writing is in your engagement agreement with your client.

goal—for example, to prepare and file an answer and other pleadings; to appear at hearings and speak on their behalf; and so on. The fact that Abe didn't do those things was not because he lacked the authority to do them, but rather because of his lack of **competence** and **care**.

How do we determine the scope of our implied authority? The same way that we determine the scope of our actual authority: by determining what a reasonable person would understand from the client's manifestations of intent under all the known facts and circumstances. *Restatement (Third) of Agency* § 2.01 Comment b.

TIPS & TACTICS Often these determinations are easy, as when we conclude that the instruction to pursue a lawsuit authorizes us to prepare, file, and serve a summons and complaint even if the client doesn't specifically say so. Sometimes they are more difficult, and it's less clear that the client's more general directions encompass a particular act. The practical approach to these situations is the same as the approach that we just discussed for actual authority—**inquire**; **explain**; **confirm** (*see* **Chapter 6.A at 139**). We'll have more to say on the scope and significance of implied authority in **Chapter 6.C at 162**. TIPS & TACTICS

c. Apparent Authority

"Apparent authority," also referred to as "ostensible authority," is different from actual and implied authority and is widely misunderstood. Watch closely while we conjure up an agreement that is legally binding on the principal even though the principal may not have directly authorized the agent to make it.

Apparent authority is "the power held by an agent or other actor to affect a principal's legal relations with third parties when a third party reasonably believes the actor has authority to act on behalf of the principal and that belief is traceable to the principal's manifestations." *Restatement (Third) of Agency* § 2.03.

TAMING THE TEXT Let's take that apart. Unlike actual and implied authority, in which the agent's power to bind the principal is based on the principal's direct grant of authority to the agent (by manifesting that intent *to the agent*, expressly or by implication), apparent authority exists *independent of any actual or implied authority granted to the agent*. It allows an agent to make a deal with a third party that is binding on the principal ("to affect a principal's legal relations with third parties") *regardless of the agent's actual or implied authority to do so* "when [i] *the third party* reasonably believes" (emphasis added) that the agent "has authority to act on behalf of the principal" *and* [ii] the principal has said or done things to create the third party's reasonable belief ("that belief is traceable to the principal's manifestations"). These deals are binding on the principal *even if the agent does not have actual or implied authority* (or can't easily prove it). TAMING THE TEXT

One thing that confuses many people when they consider a lawyer's apparent authority is how much authority is apparently vested in the lawyer simply by the principal's having hired the lawyer to represent her. Just being hired as somebody's lawyer does *not* allow you to bind your client to objectives of the engagement with third parties unless the *client herself* indicated *to those third parties* that the lawyer had that power by something more specific than merely hiring the lawyer. Why? Because the Rules (and related civil law) tell us that the client has absolute and final say on the objectives of the engagement, and that client control over objectives would be frustrated if a lawyer could exercise power over objectives in every circumstance simply because the lawyer represented the client. So we require the principal-client to manifest to the third party *specifically* that the lawyer has the necessary authority to bind the client on an objective.

Now let's work our way through some problems that illustrate why many lawyers find apparent authority so counterintuitive and occasionally downright odd:

> **Problem 6A-5:** Same as **Problem 6A-2 at 136** (fender-bender with minor injuries and a best plausible outcome of $25,000; the client has unreasonable expectations and informs Frank the day before he meets with opposing counsel that she will not accept less than $250,000; opposing counsel makes a last, best, and final offer of $25,000, which is—as Frank advised his client—the plausible best outcome after trial), except here, Frank accepts the $25,000 offer on Payne's behalf. "Do you have your client's authority to make this deal?" opposing counsel asks, in a routine exercise of professional caution. "Well, I'm her lawyer, aren't I?" Frank replies, figuring that he can talk Payne into it if he can put a concrete sum of money in front of her.
>
> Frank takes the good news back to Payne, and he again tries to persuade her that the settlement is the sensible thing to do. Payne explodes in rage. "How dare you! I told you plain and simple just yesterday that I would never accept less than $250,000! No deal!"
>
> Is there an enforceable settlement or not? Why or why not? Does your answer change if, in answer to opposing counsel's question about whether Frank has authority, he falsely states, "Yes, I do"?

> **Problem 6A-6:** Same as **Problem 6A-5** (fender-bender with minor injuries and a best plausible outcome of $25,000; the client has unreasonable expectations and informs Frank the day before he meets with opposing counsel that she will not accept less than $250,000), except that, early in the case, Payne accompanies Frank to a status conference. When the case is called, the judge does some routine scheduling and then directs the parties to discuss the possibilities for settlement before leaving the courthouse. In the hallway, Frank introduces Payne to opposing counsel, with whom Frank has dealt before. "I don't have anything to offer today," says opposing counsel, "but I will talk with my client and the insurance company and get back to you." "Fine with me," says Payne, trying to be helpful and also appear in charge. "You just get in touch with Frank here. What's OK with him is OK with me."
>
> As in **Problem 6A-5**, Frank accepts opposing counsel's $25,000 offer on Payne's behalf at their meeting, and Payne refuses to ratify the deal. Is there an enforceable settlement or not? Why or why not?

Problem 6A-7: Same as **Problem 6A-6 at 142** (fender-bender with minor injuries and a best plausible outcome of $25,000; hallway discussion with opposing counsel after the early status conference in which the client tells opposing counsel "[w]hat's OK with [Frank] is OK with me"; client develops unreasonable expectations about the value of the case), except here, Frank manages to persuade Payne to accept $25,000 if that amount is offered at the meeting of counsel the next day. Frank accepts $25,000 on Payne's behalf at the meeting. When Frank tells her, Payne protests that she had changed her mind the night before, after discussions with her spouse and her minister. "I'm sorry, Payne," Frank explains. "It's too late to change your mind. You told me yesterday that you would take $25,000, and you didn't tell me that you'd changed your mind until after I had made the deal on your behalf." "What? I *never* told you I'd take $25,000," Payne hisses, falsely. "I'll swear to that on a stack of Bibles. There is no deal." Assume that the defendant in the fender-bender case seeks to enforce the settlement, and Payne testifies as she said she would. What effect, if any, will her testimony have on the outcome, and why?

d. Ratification

Ratification is "the affirmance of a prior act done by another, whereby the act is given effect as if done by an agent acting with actual authority." *Restatement (Third) of Agency* § 4.01(1). Ratification can occur by "(a) manifesting assent that the act shall affect the person's legal relations, or (b) conduct that justifies a reasonable assumption that the person so consents." *Restatement (Third) of Agency* § 4.01(2).

In other words, ratification provides a way for the client-principal to authorize an act done or an agreement made by the lawyer-agent without authority, and thus make it binding on herself, after the fact, retroactively. The principal must ratify the agent's entire unauthorized act or agreement to make the ratification effective, not just a part (*Restatement (Third) of Agency* § 4.07), and the ratification must occur before the third party shows any intention of walking away from the deal (or before other circumstances occur that would make the principal's ratification unfair) (*Restatement (Third) of Agency* § 4.05).

Problem 6A-8: Same as **Problem 6A-2 at 136** (fender-bender with minor injuries and a best plausible outcome of $25,000; the client has unreasonable expectations and informs Frank the day before he meets with opposing counsel that she will not accept less than $250,000; at the meeting, opposing counsel makes a last, best, and final offer of $25,000, which is—as Frank advised his client—the best plausible outcome after trial), except here, Frank accepts the $25,000 offer on Payne's behalf without Payne's authority. Frank reports back to Payne the next day, and she is quite taken aback. "I didn't say you could do that," she says. "No, you didn't," says Frank, "but here's why it's the best you could possibly do and why you should take it." Frank then explains again the extra risks, delays, and costs of trial, and the reasons why, given the facts in dispute, the settlement is about as good as a verdict for Payne that she will ever get. "OK, have it your way, then," Payne grumbles. She eventually signs the settlement agreement that the lawyers hammer out in the next few days. The following Monday, Payne calls Frank and says, "Forget it. I want to go to trial. You're fired. I'll find a lawyer who believes in my case." Will Payne be able to extricate herself from the settlement? Why or why not?

Problem 6A-9: Same as **Problem 6A-8 at 143** (fender-bender with minor injuries and a best plausible outcome of $25,000; the client has unreasonable expectations and informs Frank the day before he meets with opposing counsel that she will not accept less than $250,000; at the meeting, opposing counsel makes a last, best, and final offer of $25,000, which is—as Frank advised his client—the best plausible outcome after trial; Frank accepts the offer on Payne's behalf, despite his lack of authority), except here, Payne refuses to ratify the deal. Frank, very abashed, calls opposing counsel to say that his client won't go along with the settlement. After consulting with her client, opposing counsel calls back and says, "Fine with us. We're tired of this, and we think that we're gonna skunk you at trial. The deal's off."

When Frank reports the news to Payne, she is suddenly concerned: "Wait, are they right? Could we lose?" "Remember the day before I met with opposing counsel, when we talked about how a trial might go?" Frank begins, concealing his impatience. "The other driver tells a different story about who caused the collision. He says you had the red light. Now, I believe you, but if a jury believes *him*, you could lose." "Um, I think I wanna take the deal," says Payne. "You did settle the case, right? What do I have to sign?" If the defendant refuses to go ahead with the settlement at this point, can Payne enforce the settlement to which Frank and opposing counsel had previously agreed? Why or why not?

Problem 6A-10: Same as **Problem 6A-8 at 143** (fender-bender with minor injuries and a best plausible outcome of $25,000; the client has unreasonable expectations and informs Frank the day before he meets with opposing counsel that she will not accept less than $250,000; at the meeting, opposing counsel makes a last, best, and final offer of $25,000, which is—as Frank advised his client—the best plausible outcome after trial; Frank accepts the offer on Payne's behalf, despite his lack of authority), except here, when Frank urges Payne to ratify the deal, she says she'll think about it. Two weeks later, Frank sends Payne the settlement agreement that he's worked out with opposing counsel, along with the insurance company's check made payable to Payne for the $25,000 settlement amount, less Frank's fees and costs (which the insurance company has agreed to pay directly to Frank's firm by separate check as part of the settlement agreement). Payne sends back the settlement agreement with a big red "X" on each page and a note scrawled across the front that says, "When is the trial?" But Payne keeps and deposits the check, which she communicates in a cover note she returns with the unsigned settlement agreement that she considers "a down payment" on the damages she's owed. Is there an enforceable settlement? Why or why not?

TIPS & TACTICS ▶ Ratification is an important and valuable tool, but you shouldn't ever deliberately plan to use it as your means of acquiring authority. Remember, ratification is a way to bind the client *after the fact* to an act that you did or an agreement that you made *without the client's authority at the time*. As we're about to see, if you acted without authority, you've already violated the Rules of Professional Conduct, specifically **Model Rule 1.2(a)**. And you are left at the mercy of the client's choice as to whether to ratify whatever you did. If the client declines (as she has every right to do), then the **consequences** described in the next section of this chapter start raining down, both on you personally and on your firm. "I'll make the deal now while it's available and bring the client along later" is an unethical, risky, and very bad strategy. In short, ratification may be useful to try to clean up a mess that you've made inadvertently, but it's foolish to *plan in advance* to make a mess that you *might* be able to clean up later with ratification. ◀ TIPS & TACTICS

3. CONSEQUENCES ▶ What Happens If You Exceed the Scope of Your Authority?

a. CONSEQUENCES ▶ Professional Discipline

TAMING THE TEXT ▶ **Model Rule 1.2(a)** says that a lawyer "shall abide by a client's decisions concerning the objectives of representation." If you do something to decide the "objectives of [the] representation" without the client's authority, you have failed to "abide by [the] client's decisions" concerning that objective, and you have violated the Rule. (We'll tease out in more detail the "objectives" over which the client has ultimate control in **Chapter 6.C at 151**.) TAMING THE TEXT ◀ As you know, the **consequence** for violating a Rule of Professional Conduct is professional discipline.

b. CONSEQUENCES ▶ Undoing the Unauthorized Act or Agreement

As we've been discussing, a principal purpose of agency law is to define which acts by the agent are binding on the principal—acts that the agent does with authority of some kind are binding on the principal, but acts without authority are not. So let's suppose that a lawyer makes a contract, claiming to be acting on the client's behalf. And let's suppose that the client claims that the contract was unauthorized and refuses to ratify it, thus asserting that, legally, there's no enforceable contract. What happens next depends on what the lawyer and the opposing party have done, and what they choose to do next.

If the opposing party chooses to abide by the client's assertion that there's no deal, then both parties agree there is no deal, and there is nothing to fight about. Things go on pretty much as if nothing ever happened. (Take another look at **Problem 6A-9 at 144**.)

But what if the opposing party disagrees, and claims that the lawyer did in fact make a deal that's enforceable against his client? Then the opposing party may need to take formal steps to try to enforce the contract. Those steps could include a lawsuit by the opposing party against the client for breach of contract. That action could seek damages, declaratory relief (that is, a court order specifying that the parties do have an enforceable contract and stating its principal terms), or specific performance (that is, a court order directing the client to perform the contract according to its terms). That lawsuit could become part of existing litigation between the parties (if there is any), or it might be a separate lawsuit in a state or federal court that has jurisdiction over the parties and the subject matter. The outcome of that litigation will depend principally on whether the lawyer did or did not act with some kind of authority in making the disputed agreement.[8]

If the opposing party loses because the court finds that the lawyer acted outside the scope of his authority, then the contract is unenforceable. In that case, the client would have the right to undo anything that her lawyer and the opposing party might have done pursuant to the unenforceable agreement—again, with litigation as a likely next step to undo official actions. For example, if the lawyer recorded a change in title to land pursuant to what turned out to be an unenforceable deal, the client might need to get a court order correcting or quieting title. Or if the lawyer dismissed a pending action pursuant to a settlement that turned out to be unenforceable, the client could reinstate the lawsuit with a timely motion under **Fed. R. Civ. P. 60** ("Relief from a Judgment or Order") or its state-law equivalent.

C. CONSEQUENCES Lawyer Liability

A lawyer who undertakes a significant act or agreement on the client's behalf without authority faces potential liability from multiple directions. The **consequences** can be very serious.

i. CONSEQUENCES Consequences from the Client

A significant act that the lawyer claims to have undertaken on the client's behalf, but which the client repudiates, will likely have unpleasant informal **consequences**. A client who believes that her lawyer exceeded the scope of his authority to produce an undesired result is likely to terminate that lawyer's representation and will probably dispute his fees as well. And that's just the beginning.

Once the client asserts that the lawyer exceeded his authority, the lawyer has a potential **conflict of interest** with his client, creating a situation in which the lawyer **should** or **must** make detailed written disclosures and obtain the client's **informed consent**, or resign the engagement (if he hasn't already been fired). *See* **Chapter 22.A at 629**. The failure to do so could lead to formal **consequences** of its own.

---

[8] In many states and the federal system, many kinds of disputes over whether or not there has been an enforceable settlement of pending litigation can be determined as part of the pending case, sometimes by motion. *See, e.g., Kokkonen v. Guardian Life Ins. Co.*, 511 U.S. 375 (1994).

The possible formal **consequences** of exceeding your authority are even worse. A lawyer has a duty to act on the principal's behalf only with the client's authority to do so. As a result, acting without authority is a breach of the lawyer's duty to the client. Similarly, your actual and implied authority is based on what you reasonably believe it to be under all the known facts and circumstances, particularly the client-principal's manifestations of intent. *See* **Chapter 6.A at 136, 140**. So if you thought that you were acting with authority and you turn out to be wrong, your understanding that you had that authority was, by law and logic, unreasonable. Acting on the basis of an unreasonable belief is a breach of your **duty of care**.

If that breach causes monetary harm, the client may recover damages from the lawyer to compensate for that harm. Often, the monetary harm to the client comes in the form of the client's expenses to clean up the mess created by the lawyer's unauthorized acts. These expenses could include the cost of successfully defending the opposing party's lawsuit to bind the client to the unauthorized act, or to undo formal actions (such as the change in title or the dismissal referred to above) taken by the lawyer pursuant to an unauthorized deal.

ii. CONSEQUENCES Consequences from the Opposing Party

And that's not all. If you do or say something on your client's behalf without clarifying that you lack authority or that the act is otherwise subject to your client's approval, or if you claim authority based on what turns out to be an unreasonable or nonexistent belief that you have that authority, you have misrepresented or falsely warranted your authority to the opposing party. That representation or warranty of authority can be, and often is, implied in your actions, such as if you sign a stipulation or written agreement on your client's behalf. (In other words, in most states, executing a document as agent on behalf of a principal *implies* a representation or warranty that you have the authority to do so.) If you claim authority knowing that you don't have it, you have intentionally misrepresented your authority, and that (if reasonably relied upon in a way that causes harm) is the intentional tort of fraud.

The victim of these breaches of warranty and torts is the opposing party, who accordingly has an action against you *personally* and often against your law firm as well (as a matter of *respondeat superior*), should these wrongs cause the opposing party any monetary harm. That harm could be the cost of fighting over whether there was a deal, or conceivably the difference between the outcome that you promised in your unauthorized agreement and the outcome that the opposing party eventually got instead.[9] CONSEQUENCES

---

[9] Misrepresentation, negligent or intentional, is a tort. Breach of warranty is a claim in contract (that is, you promised something—specifically, that you had authority to bind your client—that you did not deliver, so you breached your promise). In most states, the measure of damages for misrepresentation and breach of warranty differs. Misrepresentation

> Problem 6A-11: Same as **Problem 6A-4 at 138** (Frank accepts a $25,000 settlement offer on the basis of the client's ambiguous behavior), except when Frank reports the settlement to the client, she repudiates it, insisting that she never authorized such a deal. If the opposing party insists that there is a deal and seeks to enforce it, what steps follow?

The overall point here is that taking action on your client's behalf without authority, or without a clear understanding that you definitely do have that authority, can create a complex chain of events running in many directions at once, almost all of which are really, really bad for your client, for your opposing party, and for you personally, as well as your law firm. We trust no more need be said. And yet . . .

4. REAL WORLD How Lawyers Negotiate Without Exceeding the Scope of Their Authority

Given what you now know about how lawyers get authority to bind their clients to things that require such authority, and what you just learned about how dangerous and ill-advised it is to exceed the scope of your authority, you may be wondering how you can safely negotiate on your client's behalf.

Sometimes negotiations are conducted in a highly formal fashion, with each step specifically approved by the client (in complex negotiations with many moving parts, approved in every detail), and exchanged in detailed writings. But often negotiations proceed informally, with hints and suggestions between lawyers designed to open doors to further the discussion without the complication of potentially legally binding moves such as offers or rejections and counteroffers. The good news is that there are some widely accepted conventions by which lawyers make the scope of their authority known to negotiating adversaries as a means of avoiding the kinds of disputes described in the preceding section.

There are two practical issues in play:

■   One practical issue is that adversaries in business negotiations or litigation naturally wish to extract the best deal they can from the other side, and they also often distrust one another. No one wants to be the first to extend an offer or express interest in a middle ground for fear of appearing "weak" or of "tipping your hand." Tipping your hand can include disclosing that your client is interested in a compromise, what concessions your client might be willing to make, or what terms might be more valuable to your client, giving the other side an informational negotiating advantage.

---

entitles the aggrieved party to compensation adequate to put her in the same position as if the wrong had never happened; breach of warranty entitles the aggrieved party to compensation adequate to put her in a position as if the warranty had been true. (Remember the "hairy hand" case, *Hawkins v. McGee*, which illustrates the difference and is discussed in **Chapter 7.B at 182**.) The differences between tort damages and contract damages are often misunderstood and can make any later dispute even more complex and contentious.

■ The other is that clients, particularly clients less familiar with the legal system, may be afraid of making a bad decision on something important enough that they hired a lawyer to handle it. Such clients may not have fully decided what they really need or want out of the matter in which they are represented. Only when presented with a concrete outcome do they feel able to decide whether or not that outcome is sufficient.

Given these realities, there are sometimes both informational and practical advantages to being able to "get out ahead of your client" in a way that is explicitly tentative and not tied to your client's position, and as a result not legally binding or a violation of anybody's rights.

How do lawyers do this? By overtly differentiating their own views from their clients' views, and by making it clear they're expressing their own opinion, not making a binding offer that the client has authorized. This technique is perfectly legal and proper if done correctly, and in the right circumstances, it can be a very effective negotiating tool. How does such an approach work? Like this:

■ To opposing counsel: "Given [X], [Y], and [Z], my own view is that we could easily hit the jackpot on the big-ticket claim in this case [say, a "reach" claim for punitive damages], but you and I both understand that's up to the jury. So I personally could see settling the case for [a lower amount that more closely approximates a more middling outcome]. Now, you need to know that my client is still furious about what happened and wants to ask the jury for his punitives. But if you think that your client might consider the figure that I just mentioned, and you're willing to recommend it to your folks, I would feel comfortable trying to talk my client off the ledge and recommend that he take it."

■ From opposing counsel in response: "Look, I appreciate your trying to find a middle ground here, but that number that you mentioned just isn't close to what I think my client might accept. They don't take the punitives claim seriously and won't let it influence settlement valuation. They're very focused on [A], [B], and [C] which, you have to admit, should play well for us at trial. We think there's an excellent chance that we win outright or end up with only small damages. So I'm constrained by some pretty strong client expectations myself. But I appreciate your effort, and I know there's always jury risk. I don't know how far I could drag them, but I think I might be able to get them to [a lower number closer to the middle]. Would you be willing to recommend that?"

Tentative, nonbinding discussions like this can go on for multiple rounds, sometimes for months.

■ To the client: "I had an interesting discussion with opposing counsel when she called the other day. She made the usual noises about how strongly her client felt about the case, but she said that her own opinion was that [$D] was an amount she was willing to try and persuade her side to take. This is not a formal offer, and of course I didn't commit you to anything, because this is your decision. But here's what I think about the settlement value of the case." [You give the client your honest assessment of the plausible range of outcomes and explain why you think that the other side's "non-offer offer" is—or is not—something to seriously consider. Then you recommend whether to pursue the other side's "non-offer offer," counter it with another "non-offer offer" by you or with a true, binding offer by the client, or terminate negotiations for the time being. And of course, the client makes the call after considering your advice.][10]

Similar kinds of negotiations take place all the time in business negotiations as well.

The main thing to appreciate about this example is that both lawyers are making it absolutely clear (in an informal, understated way, but absolutely clear nevertheless) that they do *not* have the authority to bind their clients to any particular agreement. If a negotiator makes it clear that she is speaking without her principal's authority, there can be no reasonable understanding by the other side that the lawyer can make a binding deal on the client's behalf, and nobody gets caught in a situation in which he or she has purported to commit the client to something to which the client never agreed.[11] Having always made it clear that you were hypothesizing without client authority, you're always free to come back to the table and say that you've overestimated your client's interest in whatever had been under discussion, and then either redirect the discussions or abandon them.[12] Real World

---

[10] Notice that the lawyer in this hypothetical is telling his client about an unauthorized, nonbinding invitation to negotiate that comes from the other side. When lawyers do this kind of thing, there is almost always a reason—either they believe that they can deliver a settlement that their client will accept, or they may even have received actual authority from the client to make this nonbinding invitation to negotiate. Either way, this is a material event that tells us something important about the prospects for settlement, and therefore is the kind of information that you **must** disclose to your client, after which you **must** discuss with the client whether or how to respond. *See* **Model Rule 1.4(a)-(b); Chapter 5.D at 117**.

[11] We're leaving aside the situation in which one of the negotiators just flat-out lies about what was said between them or if the client lies about what she authorized. Those things do happen, and you need to be constantly vigilant in your work as to how much you feel that you can trust everyone with whom you're dealing. If you find yourself with a client or an adversary whom you fear is untrustworthy enough to lie about your interactions, you need to work in ways that create an independent evidentiary record of what has been said—emails or draft agreements rather than oral negotiations or phone calls with opposing counsel; and if the client is unreliable, you'll want to confirm your authority and advice in writing, as discussed in **Chapter 6.A at 139** (or you might want to get out of the representation altogether).

[12] That is, you're free to do so without *legal* consequence. Making bad predictions about your client's inclinations to opposing counsel may affect opposing counsel's sense of your reliability the next time that you say that you'll be able to deliver something to move the process along. Negotiation is a subtle art in which trust and your reputation as an honest broker is a valuable currency.

B. The Lawyer-Agent's Duties to the Client-Principal

This part of the chapter won't take long. We know that lawyers are their clients' agents (*see* **Chapter 6.A at 133**), and we know that agents are fiduciaries to their principals (*see* **Chapter 5.B at 106**). So as a lawyer and as your client's agent, you owe your client the full panoply of fiduciary duties introduced in **Chapter 5.D at 112**—**loyalty**, **confidentiality**, **care**, and **candor**.

We won't repeat ourselves (this time, anyway), but we suggest that you consider taking a quick run back over **Chapter 5.D at 112** to remind yourself of what those important duties require from you, and the **consequences** of breaching them.

C. The Division of Authority Between the Client-Principal and the Lawyer-Agent

Now we get to some new and really important topics, specifically the application of the agency-law principles just discussed to the context of the attorney-client relationship. The text on which all these issues depend is **Model Rule 1.2(a)**, which sets up a fundamental distinction critical to understanding the lawyer-agent's authority: The "*objectives* of [the] representation" (emphasis added; sometimes also referred to as the "*ends*" of the engagement) are within the client's ultimate control; "the *means* by which they are to be pursued" (emphasis added) are lawyer decisions. The same distinction is reflected in the civil law governing a lawyer-agent's powers. Go read the Rule now and see how it expresses this dichotomy.

1. Client Control Over the Objectives of the Representation

Model Rule 1.2(a) says that a lawyer "shall abide by a client's decisions concerning the objectives of representation." As we explained in **Chapter 6.A at 145**, if you do something to decide the "objectives of [the] representation" without the client's authority, you have failed to "abide by [the] client's decisions" concerning that objective, and you have violated the Rule. So in order to comply with the Rule, you need to know (a) how to determine what the "objectives of [the] representation" are, and (b) what kinds of conduct would amount to a failure to "abide by a client's decisions" concerning them. In one of those strange convergences of fate, that's exactly what the next two sections happen to be about.

a. What Are the "Objectives of Representation" as Defined by Model Rule 1.2(a)?

TAMING THE TEXT Read **Model Rule 1.2(a)** again. As we just pointed out, the Rule says that a lawyer "shall abide by a client's decisions concerning the objectives of representation." But it also gives you several examples of "objectives" over which the client has ultimate control. What are they? (*Hint*: There are four.

You can find them because the Rule says that "a lawyer shall abide by a client's decisions concerning the objectives of representation," and then includes four specific things that it also says the lawyer "shall abide by the client's decisions" concerning. Yes, the drafters could have crafted this language more clearly, but we have to work with what they gave us.) If you found (1) the client's settlement of any case, civil or criminal; (2) the client's plea in a criminal case; (3) whether the client will waive a jury in a criminal case; and (4) whether the client will waive the right not to testify in a criminal case, then you are learning to read the Rules, and we applaud you. If you missed any of these or found any others, go back, reread the Rule, and puzzle out how these four are the examples of "objectives" that the Rule supplies.

Are the four enumerated objectives in **Model Rule 1.2(a)** the *only* objectives over which the client has ultimate control? No: "Objectives" is a general category of things of which the four objectives enumerated in the Rule are only some examples. How do we know? Well, when in doubt about the Rule, go to the Comments. Read **Model Rule 1.2(a) Comment [1]**. The Comment says the client has "ultimate authority" over "the purposes to be served by the legal representation," which is of course another word for the representation's objectives. Then the Comment says, "the decisions specified in paragraph (a) . . . must *also* be made by the client" (emphasis added). That "also" implies that the four enumerated objectives are *only a part of* the general category of "objectives" or "purposes." Yes, again, the drafters could have been a lot more explicit, but this is what they gave us. Courts and ethics bodies interpreting the Rule have consistently agreed with this interpretation, so you're in good company if you read the Rule that way.

And how do we know what kinds of things are "objectives" or "purposes" of the engagement over which the client has "ultimate control"? Well, applying general principles of statutory interpretation, we have the commonly understood meaning of "objective," and we have the four examples.[13] "Objective" is commonly understood to mean "something that one's efforts or actions are intended to attain or accomplish; purpose; goal; target";[14] and the examples that the Rule provides are either *basic procedural or substantive rights* (such as the right to a criminal jury trial as guaranteed by the Sixth Amendment, or the right not to testify in your own criminal case as guaranteed by the Fifth Amendment, or the right to choose your plea in a criminal case) or the *ultimate goals of a legal*

---

[13] The Law Latin League (resplendent in their Fancy Pants) is bursting out with two timeless canons of statutory construction: *ejusdem generis* (literally "of the same kind," a principle that dictates that an ambiguous word in a rule or statute that also provides examples should be construed to include things of similar nature); and *noscitur a sociis* (literally, "it is known by its associates," or more loosely "know it by the company it keeps," a similar canon of construction that suggests that ambiguous words in a rule or statute should be interpreted according to the words associated with them in the rule or statute).

[14] https://www.dictionary.com/browse/objective.

representation (that is, the results that the client hired the lawyer to accomplish, such as resolving a dispute by settlement). The client's plea in a criminal case is a critical step toward achieving the desired result in a criminal case, so it really fits in both categories.

In the real world, of course, some rights are more fundamental than others, and some goals are more ultimate, so we occasionally have categorization issues. Whether something rises to the level of an "objective" is critically important, because if it is an "objective," then the client has "ultimate control" over it, which means that *you, the lawyer-agent, can't take steps that bind the client regarding it without the client's authority*. If you try, your acts won't be binding on the client, the client can undo anything you did related to the unauthorized objective, and you may be fired, stiffed on your fees, and face malpractice claims for violating your **duties of loyalty** and **care**, not to mention the claims for misrepresentation and breach of warranty that may be asserted against you by the opposing party. *See* **Chapter 6.A at 145**.

There is no hard-and-fast rule about how to distinguish the "objectives of representation" from "the means by which they are to be pursued" beyond the word describing the category ("objectives"), and the four examples that Rule 1.2(a) supplies. Generally speaking, the more that something looks like a basic procedural or substantive right or a result that the client hired the lawyer to achieve, the more likely that it is an "objective." Advocates in the position of contesting or defending acts undertaken without client authority must argue how strong or weak the resemblance is in that particular case. Taming the Text

Problem 6C-1: Which of these qualifies as an "objective of representation" that the lawyer must have the client's authority to make binding on the client, and why?

a. Consenting to engage in mediation in a civil case.

b. Consenting to resolve a civil dispute by binding arbitration rather than by trial. *See Blanton v. Womancare Inc.*, 38 Cal. 3d 396 (1985).

c. Agreeing to a "high-low" (sometimes also called a "collar") arrangement in a civil case, in which the plaintiff will receive the amount of the jury's verdict after trial, but not less than $X nor more than $Y if the verdict falls outside those limits.

d. In a civil sexual harassment case in which the lawyer represents the plaintiff, accepting a confidentiality clause (sometimes referred to as a "gag clause") as part of a settlement that requires the plaintiff to speak to no one about what she asserts the harasser and their mutual employer did to her or what they paid her for her silence, on pain of liquidated damages (a payment back to the employer) in the amount of the settlement payment, in the event that she violates the confidentiality clause.

Tips & Tactics Questions about what qualifies as an "objective" requiring client authority are sometimes difficult. In questionable situations, you will have to research whether a relevant court or ethics body has addressed the question, and if authority is sparse, you may not know whether you've committed a disciplinary violation and a breach of your duties to your client until after a court tells you so, if you choose to proceed without clarifying matters with your client. As in all other questions of client authority, the practical approach is simple: When in doubt, speak out: **inquire; explain; confirm** (*see* **Chapter 6.A at 139**): *Ask* your client for permission; *explain* all the material implications of granting the permission that you seek; *document* that permission as the circumstances suggest. Don't jump into the void and hope that, somehow, you'll land on your feet. Tips & Tactics

b. What Kinds of Conduct Amount to a Failure to "Abide by a Client's Decisions" About an "Objective of Representation"?

At this point, we know that whether, when, and on what **material** terms to settle a dispute is an "objective of representation" over which the client has ultimate control. Often clients seek, and after consultation follow, our advice about the objectives of representation. But they don't have to, and sometimes they don't. As illustrated in some of the problems in **Chapter 6.A at 136**, sometimes their judgment or values differ from ours, and sometimes their choices can seem downright unreasonable or irrational to us. Worse, sometimes these client decisions on objectives of representation can impose inconvenience or unnecessary expense not just on the client herself, but directly on us. That's a hazard of our legal status as the client's agent.

Recall **Problem 6A-2 at 136**, in which Frank's client has put a settlement value on her case ten times greater than Frank (in his honest and objective professional opinion) believes is the best outcome that can reasonably be expected after trial. When an offer equal to that best plausible outcome after trial comes in, Frank faces a dilemma: He and his firm are working on a contingency fee (that is, a fee equal to a predefined percentage of any recovery or verdict, after his firm is reimbursed for the costs of suit they have advanced). So Frank's firm will recover roughly the same fee if the client accepts the offer right now, or if Frank and others in his firm work hard preparing and trying the case, advancing experts' fees and other expenses that, in a case of this value, might easily consume most of the verdict and leave a fee near zero. This is not a trivial or theoretical concern—many lawyers do plaintiff's-side contingency-fee work more or less exclusively, and disagreements with clients over when or for how much to settle, though not an everyday occurrence, are hardly unheard of.

By now, one thing should be perfectly clear: If Frank asks for authority to settle the case for the offered amount and the client refuses (or the client never provides any settlement authority in the first place), any deal that Frank makes without authority will be unenforceable, and Frank will be in civil and disciplinary trouble. Lawyers, being the too-clever creatures that we sometimes are, have tried a variety of ways to work around this problem and avoid Frank's dilemma. One is to put in their engagement agreements, presented to the client right at the beginning of the matter, that the client has the power to determine settlement but is irrevocably assigning all settlement authority to the lawyer. If the client consents by signing the agreement, the argument goes, then the lawyer has the authority, granted by the client, to decide whether, when, and on what material terms to settle the case. Lawyers using this tactic have argued that the Rule requires that they "abide by the client's decisions" on "objectives of representation" such as settlement, and that they have done exactly that because the client, presented with a choice whether or not to do so, has voluntarily decided to assign the power to make those decisions irrevocably to the lawyer. The choice, these lawyers argue, was freely and fairly agreed by client and lawyer alike—unless the client signs the agreement, the lawyer doesn't want the engagement—and this is a free country for both of us. Checkmate, right?

Nice try. The critical thing that you must understand is that the law governing lawyer conduct aggressively protects the *client* in this regard, and jealously guards the client's prerogatives regarding the "objectives of representation." Remember, the Rules of Professional Conduct are predominantly designed to protect the public from lawyers tempted to act badly or to overreach. So in most states, anything that the lawyer may try to do that "unduly" interferes with the client's power to make a specific decision about a concrete objective of representation is considered either void as against public policy or unconscionable. As a result, advance blanket assignments of settlement power to the lawyer are widely viewed not only as unenforceable, but also as a violation of **Model Rule 1.2(a)**—a "failure to abide by the client's decisions concerning the objectives of representation."[15] In short: Don't try this at home.

There are, of course, many ways in which the terms of an engagement can be used to create incentives for the client to reach a result that the lawyer prefers but that the client (for good reasons or bad) may not. Not all of them are improper, but some are. The standard to be applied is whether the incentives "unduly" interfere with the client's right to make decisions on the "objectives of representation." There is a smooth continuum from a little interference to a lot in which line-drawing is often difficult, and "unduly" (which amounts to "too much") doesn't provide a lot of guidance.

Problem 6C-2: Which of these is unenforceable as undue interference with the client's right to decide the objectives of representation, and why or why not? Make the best arguments on both sides of the question.

---

[15] *See, e.g., In re Grievance Proceeding,* 171 F. Supp. 2d 81 (D. Conn. 2001).

a. A term in an agreement for a contingent fee providing that, if the client refuses to follow the lawyer's advice as to settlement, then the lawyer will receive, in addition to the contingent fee stated in the agreement, additional compensation by the hour at his normal hourly rate after the time of the disagreement until the engagement is over.

b. A term in an agreement for a contingent fee providing that, if the client refuses to follow the lawyer's advice as to settlement, then the lawyer's fee for the engagement will automatically convert, retroactively to the beginning of the representation, to an hourly fee at his normal hourly rate.

c. A term in an hourly fee agreement providing that the lawyer may require the client to deposit in the lawyer's trust account, and leave there until earned, the reasonable estimated costs of the reasonably anticipated next steps in the engagement, with the lawyer returning any unearned amounts at the end of the engagement.

d. Same as (c), but the client has just rejected a settlement offer that the lawyer has strongly recommended, and now the lawyer is demanding that the client deposit a substantial sum of money in the lawyer's trust account that represents a reasonable estimate of the fees and costs for representation through the impending trial.

e. A term in the engagement agreement of a public-interest law firm that exclusively represents survivors of sexual assault and sexual harassment, and which is committed to "name and shame" the perpetrators of violence and harassment against women, in which the firm agrees to represent the client *pro bono* in return for which the survivor agrees, in advance, never to agree to any confidentiality provision ("gag clause") as part of a settlement.

f. Same as (e), except the term in the engagement agreement provides that the client may settle the matter on any terms, but if the client agrees to any confidentiality provision of any kind as part of a settlement, instead of being represented *pro bono*, the client must pay the law firm its hourly fees at its normal rates for all work done on the engagement. *See* Los Angeles County Bar Assn. Op. No. 505 (2000).

Problem 6C-3: Same as **Problem 6A-2 at 136** (fender-bender with minor injuries; client has unreasonable settlement expectations; opposing party makes a $25,000 offer equal to the plausible best outcome after trial; client resists Frank's recommendation to accept it; now Frank may have to do a lot more work for a much lower eventual contingent fee to try the case). Frank again reviews the logical and practical reasons why the $25,000 offer makes the most sense for the client. "And for you," Payne says, shrewdly. "Tell you what. If you give up your fee to me, I'll take the $25,000 settlement offer. I'll even reimburse your out-of-pocket costs" (which at this point in the case are just a few hundred dollars' worth of copying costs and filing fees). "And tell your boss that, if you refuse, I'll sue you for interfering with my right to settle my case on the terms that I choose. Deal or no deal?" **Must** Frank's firm accept Payne's proposal? **May** Frank's firm accept Payne's proposal? If the firm tries to collect its originally agreed fee after accepting Payne's proposal, can Payne enforce her revision of the fee deal?

2. Lawyer Control (of a Sort, and Subject to "Consultation" with the Client on Material Matters) Over the "Means" by Which the Client's Objectives Are Pursued

Although clients have ultimate control over the "objectives of representation," their lawyers have control over "the means by which they are to be pursued." **Model Rule 1.2(a)**. Right now, the alert readers are protesting that we just spent several pages talking about how the *client-principal* is in charge. More generally, everything you've been told in law school is probably about how it's the *client's* case or deal, and our work as lawyers is all about pursuing what the *client* needs and wants so long as it falls within the limits of the law. So where the heck do these "lawyer calls" even come from? (We appreciate you, alert readers.)

a. The Source of Lawyer Control Over Means Decisions

TAMING THE TEXT **Model Rule 1.2(a)** provides a hint about where in the law governing lawyers we find lawyer control over means decisions. The Rule reminds us that "[a] lawyer may take such action on behalf of the client as is impliedly authorized to carry out the representation." Think back to the four kinds of authority that lawyer-agents can acquire that we discussed earlier in the chapter. (Pop quiz: Name them. If you've forgotten, go back and look them up in **Chapter 6.A at 135**.)

As it turns out, *implied authority* (**Chapter 6.A at 140**) may be a lot more pervasive and important than you thought. Remember, implied authority is the authority that a reasonable person would infer from a broader grant of actual authority, even though the principal did not explicitly specify each and every little thing that would reasonably fall within the broader task. For example, when you hire a lawyer to handle your home purchase and you tell the lawyer that it's time to close the deal, you don't have to explicitly tell her, step by step, to transfer your down payment from her escrow or trust account to the seller, transfer the prorated portions of property tax back to the seller from your funds in that same escrow account, record the deed, and do the rest of the many important steps necessary to secure and document your ownership of your new home. You don't even have to know what all those steps might be, and in fact most people don't. That's part of the lawyer's job. The lawyer has the *implied authority* to do all those things on your behalf—authority implied from the simple instruction "close the deal."

More generally, once the client specifies an objective of the representation (which typically happens not only at the beginning of the engagement, when the client tells you why she's in your office, but during the engagement, as the client develops or revises her objectives as events unfold), "[a] lawyer may take such action on behalf of the client as is impliedly authorized to carry out the representation." **Model Rule 1.2(a)**. These are important words. They announce that you, the lawyer-agent, have the implied authority to select and implement, on the client's behalf, the "means" necessary or proper to achieve the client's objectives. *See* **Model Rule 1.2(a) Comment [3]**. TAMING THE TEXT The civil law determining your agency powers applies a similar principle.

Pause and marvel at what a broad range of discretion this simple grant of implied authority gives you. Within the grant of authority implied by being retained to handle the client's acquisition of a company, the business lawyer has the implied power to plan and carry out the nature and extent of due diligence (the investigation of the target company's business, personnel, and assets), the order and style in which issues are negotiated, the optimal wording of many needed contractual provisions, and so on. Within the grant of authority implied by being retained to handle a piece of litigation, the litigator has the implied power to select the causes of action or defenses pled (or not pled); what investigation or discovery will or will not be pursued; what legal or factual arguments, and what witnesses, documents, or other evidence will or will not be presented in motions or at trial; and so on. How powerful is this implied authority? Read on.

b. The Nature and Effects of "Consultation" with the Client on Means Decisions "As Required by Rule 1.4"

TAMING THE TEXT In making means decisions, the lawyer has a duty of client consultation. We find that duty in **Model Rule 1.2(a)** as well, in the requirement that "a lawyer. . . , as required by Rule 1.4, shall consult with the client as to the means by which [the client's objectives] are to be pursued." We discussed **Model Rule 1.4(a) and (b)'s** consultation requirements as a feature of the **duty of candor** in **Chapter 5.D at 117.** You'll recall that **Model Rule 1.4** generally requires lawyers to keep their clients informed about **material** events, to explain what they reasonably need or want to know, and to consult with them about **material** decisions in the engagement.

But let's be clear about the "consult[ation]" that **Model Rule 1.2(a)** and **Model Rule 1.4** require. In the dichotomy between "objectives" and "means" that **Model Rule 1.2(a)** creates, the lawyer must "abide by the client's decisions" on objectives, and "as required by Rule 1.4 . . . consult" with the client on means. The reference to the consultation "required by Rule 1.4" means that you have to consult about *material* means; that is, ones that a reasonable client would, or that this client does, want to know about or discuss. It doesn't mean that you have to consult about every little step that you take or choice that you make. And "consult" is a term the Rule expressly opposes to "abiding by the client's decisions"; that language shows that "consult" means to explain things to and discuss them with the client, but *without* any legal or ethical obligation to "abide by the client's decisions."

Adding all that up, these Rules (and related civil law) mean that *you* make the "means" decisions and carry them out on the client's behalf. If they're not **material** "means" decisions, you don't even have a duty to consult with the client about them;

and even when they're **material**, you're free to make and implement those decisions so long as you "consult" with the client beforehand. Under the literal meaning of the **Model Rule 1.2(a)** and **Model Rule 1.4,** then, you are free to make and carry out decisions on the client's behalf, even **material** ones, *and even if they are contrary to the client's express instructions,* so long as they are "means" decisions. TAMING THE TEXT

REAL WORLD That seems a little weird, doesn't it? The answer is yes, it *is* a little weird, but as a practical matter, lawyers don't disregard their clients' preferences on means decisions very often (even though they can) because of the practical realities of the attorney-client relationship. Put slightly differently, you may have the raw power to make means decisions contrary to the client's preferences, but it's usually a bad idea as a practical matter.

Why? Consider what happens when a lawyer consults with her client about a means decision and the client disagrees with the lawyer's call. For example, suppose the lawyer calls the client (or client representative when the client is a business organization) and tells him, "We're going to take witness X's deposition." What discovery to take (or not take) is a classic means decision, and thus within the lawyer's scope of authority. The client representative says, "Forget it; I don't want you to take witness X's deposition; it's not worth the cost," or maybe "Witness X is the CEO of a critical customer of my company, and I don't want to involve her in this."

Now at this point, the lawyer *could* say, "I, sir, am an attorney who knows things. And one of the things I know is that I have broad implied authority to select and implement the means by which your objectives are to be pursued. And I also know that this includes choices about what discovery to pursue and how. So this is my call. And despite your clearly expressed instructions, I intend to stand on my implied powers and proceed with this deposition."

Yes, the lawyer *could* say this, and proceed accordingly; the analysis is impeccable. But the choice to do so would be a really bad one from the standpoint of client relations. What do you suppose would happen once the lawyer announced her intentions to ignore the client's preferences on a means decision? The client would likely reply, "Fine, but I'm not paying for it"; or more likely, "Fine—you're fired; I'll find lawyers who can conduct this matter more consistently with my preferences." Is the client within his (or, in the case of an organization, its) rights to do either of these? Of course—clients are generally free to fire their lawyers at any time, and clients are not required to pay for services that they told their lawyer not to perform. Neither of those ideas should be much of a revelation.

So as a practical matter, even though lawyers have broad implied powers over means decisions, the consultation process usually results in clients having substantial input into such decisions, if they choose to do so.[16] And also as a practical matter,

---

[16] Of course, the degree of client input on means decisions depends on the client. As you can imagine, an unsophisticated client with no familiarity with the legal system will likely defer to the lawyer on what needs to be done and how; an in-house lawyer at a big company who supervises outside counsel every day will likely have lots of views on those issues.

this back-and-forth only rarely creates problems. Most of the time, the lawyer and the client develop a constructive working relationship, and most lawyers and most clients are reasonably good at understanding where the client's preferences or the lawyer's expertise ought to more strongly influence decisions about what things ought to be done and how to do them. For example, clients may offer a valuable sense of when business concerns might influence the manner in which an engagement is conducted or what kinds of additional effort are cost-justified given the size and purposes of the deal or dispute. And lawyers can offer guidance about the potential legal or tactical upsides or downsides of a particular choice. The circumstances under which lawyers find it necessary to exercise the raw power that they have to disregard the client's insistence on means decisions turn out to be rare. On the whole, then, consultation is not just the law; it's a good idea. It typically leads to better-considered legal services that are more consistent with the client's needs and with which the client is more satisfied. *See* **Model Rule 1.2 Comment [2]**.

That said, accommodating client preferences on means decisions is not *always* easy or advisable. A classic example is the party to a hotly contested dispute or a pitched and highly adversarial business negotiation who wants you to deny routine courtesies (say, a short extension of time to respond to a pleading or discovery request) or just to be personally nasty when interacting with opposing counsel. To be sure, some lawyers *enjoy* being discourteous and nasty (thus conveniently leveraging a personality disorder into a career), and clients who want such lawyers usually find them. We think that's a less effective way to practice (what goes around comes around, after all), and a worse way to live. But the point for now is that whether to extend professional courtesies or treat others with professional respect is a means decision that you get to make.[17] Someday you may find yourself representing a client who rejects your explanations of how professional courtesy makes things run more smoothly and efficiently and allows for dialogue on difficult issues, and specifically demands a "mad dog," while you are disinclined to be either rabid or a dog. Such lawyer-client mismatches can lead to hard choices on your part and may end in your withdrawal or termination. *See* **Model Rule 1.2 Comment [2]**. We'll talk in more detail about when you **may, should,** or **must** withdraw in **Chapter 9.D at 288.**

---

[17] Within limits. You **must not** needlessly embarrass, delay, or burden another person. *See* **Model Rule 4.4(a)**; **Chapter 14 at 413**. And you **should not** be a jerk just because you can, or even because your client wants you to be. If you need any incentives, courts have grown increasingly impatient with sharp practice:

> Our profession is rife with cynicism, awash in incivility. Lawyers and judges of our generation spend a great deal of time lamenting the loss of a golden age when lawyers treated each other with respect and courtesy. It's time to stop talking about the problem and act on it. For decades, our profession has given lip service to civility. All we have gotten from it is tired lips. We have reluctantly concluded lips cannot do the job; teeth are required. In this case, those teeth will take the form of sanctions.

Counsel in that case was sanctioned $10,000. *Lasalle v. Vogel,* 248 Cal. Rptr. 3d 263, 267 (2019) (*quoting Kim v. Westmoore Partners, Inc.,* 201 Cal. App.4th 267, 293 (2011)).

c. Unusual Cases in Which the Client's Right to Discharge Counsel Is Limited

One context in which we see the lawyer's implied authority to make means decisions collide head-on with conflicting client demands is when criminal defendants disagree with their public defenders about how their defense is to be conducted. Criminal defendants may terminate their court-appointed defenders under much more limited circumstances than can a client with a private attorney. Like other lawyers, court-appointed criminal defenders must comply with the defendant's "objectives" decisions regardless of their views on their wisdom; not doing so amounts to **ineffective assistance of counsel** in violation of the Sixth Amendment (*see* **Chapter 7.C at 184**). But the defender does have the power to, and sometimes does, make means decisions over the client's objections, and those choices are binding on the client.

Problem 6C-4: Barry Brute is on trial for domestic violence. Brute has certain strongly and sincerely held religious views that he believes justify the injuries that he inflicted on his spouse. He wants his lawyer to advance a "religious freedom" defense at trial. Brute's experienced public defender understands that Brute's argument that his spousal abuse was sanctioned by the Bible (and thus is not sanctionable by the State) would be not only legally defective (*see Employment Division v. Smith*, 494 U.S. 872 (1990)), but also seriously counterproductive with the jury. The defender explains all of this to her client, but he continues to insist that she present his "religious freedom" defense at trial. **Must** the defender present the defense the client demands? Why or why not?

Problem 6C-5: **Mess in the Press**: Robert McCoy was charged by the State of Louisiana with the murder of his wife's son, mother, and stepfather. The prosecution sought the death penalty. McCoy pleaded not guilty, and he wished to pursue a factual defense that he did not commit the murders, but rather was framed in an elaborate conspiracy by law enforcement. McCoy's lawyer believed (with considerable basis in the record) that the evidence against McCoy was overwhelming, and that the jury would be more likely to impose the death penalty if the defendant denied the obvious. McCoy insisted on pleading not guilty. Counsel accordingly elected to try the case by conceding in opening statement that McCoy had committed the murders, and then trying to portray the defendant and the circumstances in a more sympathetic light that might persuade the jury to forgo the death penalty. McCoy strenuously objected to this approach, insisting that his lawyer argue that McCoy was factually innocent. (McCoy's lawyer was private counsel paid for by his parents, but the judge denied McCoy's motion to discharge the lawyer because McCoy did not move to fire his lawyer until two days before trial. That decision was well within the trial judge's discretion.) **Must** defense counsel abandon his plans to concede guilt factually and plead for mercy in sentencing, and instead pursue the theories his client demands? Why or why not? *See McCoy v. Louisiana*, 138 S. Ct. 1500 (2018).

> **Problem 6C-6: Another Mess in the Press:** James "Whitey" Bulger was the boss of the orga-
> nized-crime Winter Hill Gang in the Boston area in the 1970s and 1980s. He was finally
> brought to trial at the age of 83, charged with numerous serious and violent crimes,
> including over a dozen murders, some of which (the FBI asserted, and Bulger denied) Bulger
> committed or ordered while he was an FBI informant. Bulger claimed to subscribe to a "code
> of conduct" in which murder for the good of the (criminal) organization was honorable,
> except for the murder of women (and two of the murders for which he was indicted were of
> women). Under Bulger's "code," being a government informant was supremely dishonorable.
> His instructions to his lawyer were clear and simple: He would not plead guilty because he
> insisted on contesting the government's evidence that he murdered women and that he was
> an FBI informant. At trial, his lawyer was to admit the murders of the male victims (which
> were "honorable" in Bulger's world), contest the murders of the female victims, and contest
> the government's assertions that Bulger informed for the FBI for part of his career as a way to
> avoid prosecution. What **must** his lawyer do under these circumstances? What, in your view,
> **should** he do?[18]

d. What Happens If the Lawyer-Agent Makes Incompetent or Careless Means Decisions?

This brings us full circle to the question posed in the **chapter's Introduction at
131**. (You thought that we forgot, didn't you?) Horace and Helena Homeowner
hired a lawyer, Abe Andon, to defend the foreclosure action on their home. He
did nothing, and the clients lost their home despite the apparent existence of
winning defenses that he simply never presented. Worse still, the lawyer is likely
judgment-proof, so that a malpractice case, however meritorious, would probably
be a waste of time. Do the Homeowners get a "do-over" with a competent lawyer?

Alas, no, at least as a matter of agency law. But let's play out why: The client's
retention of Abe Andon with the objective of defending the foreclosure action
endowed Andon with implied authority to select and implement the means by
which the defense would be conducted. The choices that he made (or failed to
make) were careless and incompetent, but he was authorized to act (or refrain
from acting) on the Homeowners' behalf, and because he acted with their
authority, they are bound by his choices. Their remedies are limited to those
available against the lawyer-agent, Andon, for exercising his implied authority
incompetently.[19]

---

[18] *See* Katherine Q. Seelye, *In Bulger's Underworld, 'a Judas Was the Worst,'* https://www.nytimes.com/2013/06/19/us/in-bulgers-underworld-a-judas-was-the-worst.html?nl=todaysheadlines&emc=edit_th_20130619#commentsContainer, (June 18, 2013).

[19] But never say never. Agency law may not be the only game in town. One thing that we didn't discuss in the **chapter's Introduction at 131** was the possibility that Horace and Helena Homeowner might get relief from the default judgment that Abe allowed to be entered (and thus a do-over) under **Fed. R. Civ. P. 60** (or its state-law equivalent) on the ground of "excusable neglect." The problem is that Abe Andon's neglect in this case looks pretty *inexcusable,* and courts generally require that the moving party show why the neglect is, in fact, excusable. *See Pioneer Electronics Serv. v. Brunswick Assocs.*

REASON FOR THE RULE ▶ If we step back, it's possible to see this horrendously unfair result in a broader context—one that justifies the more general rule that means decisions within an agent's implied authority are binding on the client. What if we allowed a principal to say "I authorize you to pursue my objective so long as you do so with due care" or "I authorize you to pursue my objective, but only in ways that I decide later that I like"? If the agent made a mistake, or in the case of the latter instruction, if the principal just disliked the outcome, the principal could claim that the agent had acted without authority (because the work or the result was bad and therefore "exceeded" the scope of the principal's instructions), and demand a "do-over" after the fact. The result would be that third parties dealing with agents would have to doubt whether *anything* that the agent *ever* did on the principal's behalf would "stick," which would erode or defeat the whole purpose of having the law of agency in the first place—to facilitate more efficient transactions by allowing third parties to rely on agents to transact business enforceably on the principal's behalf, without the principal's needing to possess all the necessary skills or expertise herself (or to be everywhere at once). And if that were the law, in a more typical foreclosure case, in which the debtor-homeowners just can't pay the mortgage and have no or only weak technical defenses, the debtors would have an incentive to play the system by hiring a lawyer to mess up just so they could demand a do-over, over and over again, and delay the inevitable loss of their home while they continued to occupy it.[20] That wouldn't be fair, either. ◀ REASON FOR THE RULE

The moral of the story? Even good general rules occasionally lead to unfair results, which is just another way of saying that hard cases make bad law. And to belabor the obvious, don't be like "Honest Abe" Andon.

Big-Picture Takeaways from Chapter 6

1. The *fiduciary* relationship between lawyer and client focuses on the duties that the lawyer owes the client. The *agency* relationship involves the ways

---

Ltd., 507 U.S. 380 (1993). Nevertheless, the facts that we gave you are so egregiously unfair to the Homeowners that there is some chance a court might grant the relief anyway. And never forget about the possibility of a business solution. During the wave of residential foreclosures in the Great Recession after 2007, banks become more willing to put debtors who were willing and able to resume their mortgage payments back in their homes rather than getting stuck with the responsibility for maintaining the homes and selling them at foreclosure sales. Creative and aggressive lawyering can get clients results that might initially seem beyond their reach. Did Happy Trials perhaps give up too easily?

[20] The law-and-economics mavens also like to argue that a rule allowing do-overs for principals with careless agents lessens principals' incentives to choose careful agents and supervise them adequately. *See, e.g., United States v. 7108 West Grand Avenue*, 15 F.3d 682 (7th Cir.), *cert. denied sub nom. Flores v. United States*, 512 U.S. 1212 (1994). We think that this argument presumes too much, given that many clients hire lawyers precisely because they don't know how to achieve their objectives, and as a result, those clients often lack the knowledge necessary to pick a better lawyer rather than a worse one, or to supervise the lawyer's work in any meaningful sense. This is true not only regarding lawyer-agents, but in any situation in which the principal needs and is depending on the agent's skill or expertise—which, realistically, is much of the time.

in which the lawyer-agent can bind the client-principal to obligations with *third parties. See* **Chapter 6.A at 134**.

2. There are four sources of authority that allow a lawyer to bind a client to obligations to third parties:
   a. **Actual or express authority**. The test for actual authority is what a reasonable person would understand that she is allowed or directed to do from the client's outward "manifestations" of intent. When in doubt, speak out, and **inquire; explain; confirm** (*see* **Chapter 6.A at 139**). *See* **Chapter 6.A at 136**.
   b. **Implied authority.** Implied authority flows from actual authority in one of two ways:
      i. The principal's express authority to do something empowers the agent to do what is necessary, usual, and proper in order to accomplish or perform those express responsibilities; or
      ii. The principal's actual authority to do something empowers the agent to act in a manner in which the agent reasonably believes the principal wishes the agent to act based on the agent's reasonable interpretation of the principal's manifestations in light of the principal's objectives and other facts known to the agent.
      See **Chapter 6.A at 140**.
   c. **Apparent or ostensible authority.** A lawyer has apparent authority to bind the client to obligations with a third party when the third party reasonably believes that that the lawyer had that authority *and* that belief is traceable to the *principal's* manifestations *to the third party*. Just being somebody's lawyer does *not* allow you to bind your client to objectives of the engagement with third parties unless the *client herself* indicated *to those third parties* that the lawyer had that power by something more specific than merely hiring the lawyer. *See* **Chapter 6.A at 141**.
   d. **Ratification (after-the-fact authority).** Ratification occurs when the principal affirms, approves, or adopts, by words or conduct after the fact, an act done by the agent that was outside the scope of the agent's authority when the agent did it. *See* **Chapter 6.A at 143**.

3. The **consequences** for exceeding your authority can include:
   a. Professional discipline. *See* **Chapter 6.A at 145**.
   b. An undoing of the unauthorized act, such as the rescission of a contract, the undoing of a change in title to property, or the reinstatement of an action that was dismissed. *See* **Chapter 6.A at 145**.
   c. A lawsuit to determine whether or not the act was authorized, in which the lawyer personally (and the lawyer's firm) are often parties. *See* **Chapter 6.A at 146**.

d. Personal liability on the part of the lawyer and the lawyer's firm:
  i. To the client for the costs of undoing the unauthorized act and any other monetary damages the client may have suffered from the unauthorized act itself; and
  ii. To the opposing party for damages for having misrepresented or miswarranted your authority.
  See **Chapter 6.A at 146**.
e. And once the client asserts that you've exceeded your authority, you've got a potential **conflict of interest** with your client, creating a situation in which you **should** or **must** make detailed written disclosures and obtain client consent or withdraw from the engagement (if you haven't already been fired). *See* **Chapter 6.A at 146**.

4. It's possible to negotiate without exceeding the scope of your authority. Lawyers have developed a number of conventions to clarify the negotiator's authority. They generally involve making clear what views are your client's and what views are your own (*e.g.*, "My own view is X, and I might be able to persuade my client to agree with me"). *See* **Chapter 6.A at 148**.

5. As an agent, you still owe your client the same fiduciary duties we discussed in the last chapter: **loyalty**, **confidentiality**, **care**, and **candor**. *See* **Chapter 6.B**.

6. The client controls the *objectives* (ends) of the representation, but the lawyer controls the *means* (how to achieve those objectives). Four objectives are specified in **Model Rule 1.2(a)**: whether, when, and on what terms to resolve a dispute; the defendant's plea in a criminal case; whether the defendant will exercise the Fifth Amendment right not to testify in a criminal case; and whether the defendant will waive the Sixth Amendment right to a jury in a criminal case. There are, however, other decisions that qualify as client "objectives," and it's not always easy to recognize them. Generally, objectives comprise basic procedural or substantive rights and purposes or goals for which the lawyer has been retained. *See* **Chapter 6.C at 151**.

7. Although the lawyer has the ultimate authority over means decisions, the lawyer **must** *consult* with the client about **material** means decisions (meaning ones that would matter to a reasonable client or that actually do matter to a particular client). After consultation, the lawyer is free to disregard the client's preferences or directions on means decisions, but the client (other than a client of court-appointed counsel) may dispute fees with or discharge a lawyer who insists on means decisions with which the client disagrees. Client consultation on means decisions

usually leads to decisions more consistent with the client's legitimate needs and preferences, so it's not only the law; it's actually a really good idea. *See* **Chapter 6.C at 157.**

Multiple-Choice Review Questions for Chapter 6

1. If a client tells a lawyer, "I want you to represent me," and the lawyer agrees, is this language sufficient to create an agency relationship?
   a. Yes. Viewed objectively, the client is consenting to entering into a lawyer-client relationship. This type of relationship is almost always an agency relationship.
   b. Yes. Viewed subjectively, the client is admitting to the formation of the lawyer-client relationship. This type of relationship is almost always an agency relationship.
   c. No. Viewed objectively, the client did not create a relationship because the client did not use the formal language necessary to create an agency relationship. The client asked only for legal representation and did not ask the lawyer to serve as an agent.
   d. No. Viewed subjectively, the lawyer may not have understood the client to be seeking an agency relationship because the client did not use the term "agent" in the request. When the lawyer agreed, the lawyer may not have understood the relationship to be one of agency.

2. After Christine slips and falls, she retains Lawyer Linda to represent her. Linda files a complaint, and the parties begin discovery. Linda expects that Christine (whose injuries are serious) may be able to recover $100,000 if she prevails in the litigation.

   Out of the blue, defense counsel calls with a settlement offer that seems overly generous to Linda: The defendant offers to pay $300,000 to settle the case. Defense counsel says that it is a "take it or leave it" offer that Linda must accept on the spot. Linda knows that $300,000 is far more than Christine expects and is probably more than she deserves.

   May Linda accept the offer without consulting with Christine?
   a. Yes, but only because it is self-evident that Christine will accept the offer.
   b. Yes, but only because it is a limited time offer that Christine will otherwise lose.
   c. No, because only Christine has the authority to decide whether she will settle and on what terms.
   d. No, because Linda has clearly undervalued the case and further negotiation may result in an even larger settlement offer.

3. As in question 2, after Christine slips and falls, she retains Lawyer Linda to represent her. Linda files a complaint, and the parties begin discovery. Linda expects that Christine may be able to recover $100,000 if she prevails in the litigation.

   Out of the blue, defense counsel calls with a settlement offer that seems overly generous to Linda: The defendant offers to pay $300,000 to settle the case. Defense counsel says that it is a "take it or leave it" offer that Linda must accept on the spot. Linda knows that $300,000 is far more than Christine expects and is probably more than she deserves. Linda accepts the offer.

   When she hangs up with defense counsel, Linda calls Christine. Christine agrees that the offer is generous and agrees to settle the case for $300,000.

   Linda calls defense counsel to make arrangements for the payment. Defense counsel now claims his client has had a change of heart and will not settle. Defense counsel claims that his client can back out of the settlement because Linda did not have authority when she agreed to the $300,000 settlement. Is defense counsel correct?

   a. Yes, the agreement was not binding because Linda lacked authority.
   b. Maybe; it depends whether defense counsel knew at the time that Linda lacked authority.
   c. Maybe; it depends whether the offer was reasonable under the circumstances.
   d. No; Christine has ratified Linda's actions.

4. Physician Phyllis retains Lawyer Leroy to defend her in a medical malpractice case. They sit down together during their first meeting, and Leroy explains the process of defending this type of case. He walks Phyllis through all the steps, describing discovery (which can include taking and defending depositions).

   Phyllis signs a retainer agreement that states that Leroy may take all steps necessary to defend the case. The agreement says nothing specific about the scope of discovery.

   One day, Phyllis opens a bill from Leroy and is shocked to discover that she is being charged for his time spent taking five depositions. She complains to Leroy that she never agreed that he could take any depositions. Leroy reminds her of their initial conversation and the retainer agreement.

   What type of authority best explains why Leroy believed that Phyllis authorized him to take the depositions?

   a. Actual authority.
   b. Implied authority.

   c. Apparent authority.
   d. Ratification.

5. Pursuant to **Model Rule 1.2(a)**, the client always has the final authority to decide which of the following?
   a. Whether to plead guilty in a criminal case.
   b. Whether to authorize extensions of time.
   c. Whether to file in state or federal court.
   d. Whether to raise a defense in an answer or as a motion to dismiss.

6. Lawyer Lydia is handling a breach of contract case for one of her longtime clients. Opposing counsel calls to ask whether Lydia would agree to have the case tried before a magistrate judge rather than before the assigned district court judge.

   Is Lydia obligated to discuss this strategy with her client before she agrees?
   a. Yes. This is an objective of litigation, so the client must not only be consulted but must independently decide whether to agree.
   b. Maybe. If it is clear that the magistrate judge will be better for the client, Lydia need not discuss this with the client but can use her own judgment.
   c. Maybe. If this is a **material** matter, the client is entitled to be consulted before Lydia agrees.
   d. No. Reassignment of the case is an administrative matter that Lydia can decide.

7. What is the main difference between the fiduciary relationship between the lawyer and client and the agency relationship that flows from the lawyer-client relationship?
   a. The fiduciary relationship creates obligations that the lawyer owes only to the client. The agency relationship allows the lawyer to create obligations that bind the client to third parties.
   b. The fiduciary relationship may create obligations that bind the client to third parties. The agency relationship creates obligations that the lawyer owes only to the client.
   c. The fiduciary relationship creates obligations that the client owes only to the lawyer. The agency relationship may create obligations that bind the lawyer to third parties.
   d. The fiduciary relationship may create obligations that bind the lawyer to third parties. The agency relationship creates obligations that the client owes only to the lawyer.

8. Marty and Rick get into a minor fender-bender. Rick immediately apologizes, hands Marty a business card for Joe Croft, Esq., and says, "I am so

sorry. I caused that accident. Joe is my lawyer. Please send him your bill for repairing the damage, and he will make sure that you get taken care of. I will pay for whatever it reasonably costs to repair your car."

Marty has his car repaired and sends his $750 bill to Joe Croft. Joe calls Marty a few days later and asks whether Marty would accept $650 to resolve the matter with Rick. Joe points out a few line items on the bill that appear to be inflated. Marty agrees. He says, "Tell Rick we have a deal. I will accept $650."

Marty waits for his check, but it never arrives. He ultimately sues Rick for breach of contract. Rick responds that he never authorized Joe to pay $650, and that the repairs should have cost no more than $500.

Is Marty out of luck?
- a. Yes. His agreement was with Joe, not Rick, so Marty has named the wrong party in his breach of contract suit.
- b. Yes. Marty cannot prove that Rick authorized Joe to offer $650, and he must prove that fact in order to prevail.
- c. No. Rick expressly promised to pay Marty in full for the damage to his car.
- d. No. Under the circumstances, it was reasonable for Marty to believe that Joe had authority to act on Rick's behalf.

9. Morris represents Gertrude, who has sued Patricia in a breach of contract action. Gertrude authorizes Morris to settle her case for $40,000. Morris thinks that Gertrude is being unreasonable, so he agrees to settle her case for $20,000. He negotiates with Patricia, who agrees to pay $20,000. What consequences might Morris face?
- a. Gertrude may sue him for breach of the **duty of care**.
- b. Patricia may sue him for misrepresentation.
- c. Both a and b.
- d. Neither a nor b.

10. Lawyer Lori represents Client Chris, who was injured in a car accident. Chris insists on suing the driver who hit him, Dave, as well as another driver, Susan, who claims that she was uninvolved in the accident. Although Susan's car was not involved in the accident, Chris insists that Susan stopped suddenly, causing the chain of events that led to the accident.

Lori believes that Chris's claim against Susan is weak, though not frivolous.

Susan's attorney calls Lori, urging Lori to dismiss the claim against Susan. Lori relays the contents of this conversation to Chris. She urges Chris to consider dismissing the claim. Chris refuses.

Which of the following would be an appropriate response to opposing counsel within Lori's authority?

a. I will dismiss Susan from the case.
b. My client insists on proceeding against Susan.
c. Either a or b.
d. Neither a nor b.

7

The Duties of Competence, Diligence, and Care

As a favor to a family friend, Maya has helped the friend's adult daughter organize a small corner grocery in a neighborhood of the city in which she lives. (Yes, Maya has cleared this with her firm, checked for conflicts of interest, and prepared an engagement letter describing the scope of the engagement and addressing the fact that she is jointly representing the founder and the resulting limited liability company operating the store, and doing so *pro bono*. She already took this class.) The clients picked a great location, and business is good. Now they would like Maya to help them figure out which items in the store are subject to state and local sales taxes, and advise them how to collect, account for, and remit those taxes. Maya likes tax law (like beets and soap carving, some otherwise normal people actually do like unusual things), and she recognizes that learning more about this area will come in handy throughout her career. The problem is, she doesn't know a thing about it. Can she expand her engagement as requested? How should she go about it?

* * *

Take a moment to think about what you want when you ask for help from someone with specialized knowledge. Maybe you're asking your doctor about some odd symptoms. Maybe you're asking your auto mechanic or your electrician about sparks that are coming from a place where there shouldn't be any sparks. What do you want? You want someone who knows what he or she is talking about, who will explain it to you in terms that you can understand, and who can do what's necessary to address the problem in a timely manner. If you or someone you care about has ever hired a lawyer, you know that's what you or your loved one wanted, too. And of course, that's what your clients are going to want from you, though they generally won't know how to tell whether you know what you're talking about, or what you're going to need to do to address the problem effectively.

TIPS & TACTICS We're not big fans of homilies. But this discussion nevertheless prompts us to offer a general guiding principle that, although it will rarely provide a specific answer to a question about lawyer conduct, is a useful touchstone for professionalism generally, especially in situations in which clients may not know what kind of lawyer they need or what they need that lawyer to do:

Be the lawyer you'd want to hire.[1]

What does this mean as a practical matter? Your clients are going to want you to know what you're talking about (legal knowledge), to be able to explain things to them in terms they can understand (communication skills), to be able to apply your knowledge to seek the desired outcome (legal skills), and to apply yourself to achieve their objectives (thoroughness, diligence, and preparation, also known as work ethic).[2] And they'll want you to get it done diligently and promptly. **TIPS & TACTICS**

Miraculously enough, there are rules about that. In fact, commensurate with their overall importance, they're among the first substantive rules in the Rules of Professional Conduct.

A. The Duties of Competence and Diligence

1. Getting Up to Speed

Model Rule 1.1 is simple: "A lawyer shall provide competent representation to a client." It goes on to provide a working definition of "competent representation": It "requires the legal knowledge, skill, thoroughness and preparation reasonably necessary for the representation." It's a "shall" rule, so we all **must** provide clients with competent representation. No surprise there. But the terms of the Rule provide guidance at the level of abstraction of the Scout Law ("Trustworthy, Loyal, Helpful, Friendly, Courteous, Kind, Obedient, Cheerful, Thrifty, Brave, Clean, and Reverent")—certainly words to live by, but ones that often need interpretation when applied in everyday situations.

The bind that Maya faces in the **chapter Introduction at 171** is one that new lawyers face all the time: Despite three long years in law school and intensive study for the bar exam, you won't know very much law yet, and (despite the best efforts of your clinical and skills professors) you'll still know very little about how lawyers go about doing what they do. (That's no knock on law school; it's just that

---

[1] The alert reader will recognize this exhortation as a corollary of the **duty of loyalty** (*see* **Chapter 5.D. at 113**). The **duty of loyalty** generally requires a fiduciary to treat her beneficiary as well as she would treat herself in similar circumstances. So if you're being the kind of lawyer that you'd want to hire for yourself, you're probably on the right track.

[2] They'd probably like you to like them as people, too. Maybe you will, but maybe you won't. We've liked many of our clients, though certainly not all of them. But we've always tried to do the best job possible for them, even when we didn't like them at all. And whether you like your clients personally or not, you must always—*always*—treat them with the dignity and respect that every human being deserves, especially those who have accorded *you* the incredible esteem of asking you to be their advocate or advisor.

lawyering requires a huge amount of information of many different kinds. It takes time to take it in and learn to use it.) And yet you'll be licensed to practice. When you're not competent at anything yet, and the only way to *get* competent is to practice (they don't call it "practice" for nothing, y'know),[3] you may wonder how you can practice "competently."

Nor does this dilemma end in your early years of practice. As you gain experience and skills, more principles and tasks become familiar, but lawyers with years of experience still regularly encounter things they haven't seen or done before. (That's one of the reasons that law practice remains exciting and engaging over a whole career.) And even in areas with which you're familiar, the law and its practice will change as courts, legislatures, and administrative agencies mess with things that you thought you finally understood, and as custom and technology evolve. (This is one of those sources of stress that we discussed in **Chapter 4.C at 88**—**competence** is a treadmill that never stops, and always seems to be speeding up. No wonder you're out of breath all the time.)

You'll be relieved to learn that the rules governing lawyer conduct accommodate both your need to learn your trade and the reality that all lawyers, regardless of experience, answer new questions and do new things all the time. In fact, your years in law school are preparing you for exactly that. If you think about it, what we're teaching you here in law school is not predominantly *what the law is* in any particular area right now (though of course we do talk about that, and it's not unimportant), but rather how to *find, interpret, and apply* the law, not only in areas with which you are familiar as they evolve, but also for questions that you've never seen before. After all, many lawyers end up practicing in subject areas that they barely touched in law school. Regardless of your intended practice area, much of the substantive and procedural law that you're learning today will be different in 10 or 20 years. So the most important thing that we're teaching you is to learn and interpret the law as it inevitably grows and changes, and new challenges arise.

TAMING THE TEXT ▶ **Model Rule 1.1 Comment [2]** explains that "competence" often just means applying the knowledge and skills that you already have *relating to how to acquire more knowledge and skills*:

> A lawyer need not necessarily have special training or prior experience to handle legal problems of a type with which the lawyer is unfamiliar. A newly admitted lawyer can be as competent as a practitioner with long experience. Some important legal skills, such as the analysis of precedent, the evaluation of evidence and legal drafting, are required in all legal problems. Perhaps the most fundamental legal skill consists of determining

---

[3] Actually, that's a joke. "Practice" derives from the Old French for "to do"; "to act"; or "to carry on a profession," and today it means actually doing the job, rather than rehearsing how to do it. That said, it's a convenient linguistic and (so to speak) practical fact that the way you get practice is to practice. We'll be here all term, folks.

what kind of legal problems a situation may involve, a skill that necessarily transcends any particular specialized knowledge.

That does *not*, of course, mean that you can just fake it, and make it up as you go along. If you're doing something new, you have to take the time and make the effort "reasonably necessary" to figure it out and do it right. Depending on how unfamiliar and how complicated the engagement is, that can be quite a lot. *See* **Model Rule 1.1 Comment [4]** ("A lawyer may accept representation where the requisite level of competence can be achieved by reasonable preparation."); **Model Rule 1.1 Comment [5]** (describing the kinds of preparation often required).[4] And in some intricate or highly specialized areas of practice, your own hard work may not be enough: "Expertise in a particular field of law may be required in some circumstances," and you may need to "consult with . . . a lawyer of established competence in the field in question" to get it. **Model Rule 1.1 Comment [1]**.

Model Rule 1.1 Comment [1] provides us with a nonexclusive list of factors to help "determine[e] whether a lawyer employs the requisite knowledge and skill in a particular matter," including "[i] the relative complexity and specialized nature of the matter, [ii] the lawyer's general experience, [iii] the lawyer's training and experience in the field in question, [iv] the preparation and study the lawyer is able to give the matter and [iv] whether it is feasible to refer the matter to, or associate or consult with, a lawyer of established competence in the field in question." If you find yourself in a position requiring you to determine whether to associate outside help, or refer the matter to someone more expert, these factors will help you decide, and each should be analyzed separately, with all then weighed together. But as with most multifactor tests, there is a lot of room for weighing and balancing, and you'll need to exercise reasonable judgment about when you need backup, and what kind of backup you need.[5] TAMING THE TEXT

---

[4] REAL WORLD The fact that you may become "competent" in something unfamiliar by hitting the books (or the keyboard) does not necessarily mean that you can charge your client for the effort. Developing knowledge and expertise is, to some degree, an investment that you may have to make in your own career. If you work for a firm, your supervising partners will adjust your rates and consider "writing off" (that is, not charging the client for) some of your learning and training time so that your charges are not excessive under the circumstances. (After all, one reason that less experienced lawyers have lower hourly rates is that they usually need to do more basic research and are less efficient than more experienced practitioners.) But if (for example) experienced practitioners in your community defend a DWI (driving while impaired) charge for a flat $5,000 and, even at a reasonable hourly rate, you end up doing $50,000 in hourly work to do the same job while teaching yourself DWI defense, it should be no surprise that there's going to be a problem with charging ten times as much as a more experienced lawyer does to accomplish the same task. *See* **Model Rule 1.5[a]** (no "unreasonable" fees); **Chapter 20.C at 546**; *In re Fordham*, 423 Mass. 481, 668 N.E.2d 816 (1996) (imposing discipline for charging a fee as just described). REAL WORLD

[5] TIPS & TACTICS But what if it's a true client emergency and so far as you know, no one else is available in time? Well, often that may mean that you simply might have to forgo this engagement. In a pinch, **Model Rule 1.1 Comment [3]** suggests you might be able to provide some limited help (and "limited" means the minimum "reasonably necessary under the circumstances") beyond your current experience and knowledge in a true emergency situation. But we want you to think hard before doing so, especially if you're providing that help without supervision. Remember the plight of the well-intentioned volunteer from Torts? You provide help as a volunteer (thereby earning the truly impressive common-law epithet of "officious intermeddler"); it's the wrong sort of help or not done quite right; the person receiving the help

So summing up where we are at this point, you can be "**competent**" doing things that you've never done before, so long as you apply a reasonable combination of your own research and more experienced backstopping. **Model Rule 1.1 Comments [1]-[2]**. And fortunately for most new lawyers, backup is often not far away. That's because almost all new lawyers start their law careers by working for other lawyers. The more experienced lawyers with whom you work can provide you with research leads, form pleadings and documents, archival memoranda, pointers on how it's done, and other pro tips. These are invaluable time-savers and **competence**-enhancers. If you're not getting that type of support, you need to ask for it, and if your requests are going unheard, you may have to insist, or take responsibility for finding help elsewhere. *See* **Chapter 19.D at 520** (on the **duty to be supervised**—which is not an actual duty but is a good way of thinking about your own responsibilities to get help when you need it).

Remember, you have a personal, nondelegable duty to comply with your ethical and legal obligations, including your **duties of competence** and **care**, and if your supervisor won't provide you the oversight that you need to fulfill that duty, it will be no excuse in a disciplinary proceeding or malpractice case that you asked and asked, but no one took the time to help. *See* **Model Rule 5.2**; **Chapter 19.D at 520**.[6] That's why it's so important to pick a workplace with other lawyers who are conscientious and helpful. There are many such workplaces; seek and ye shall find. But there are some where supervision is haphazard or absent, so you have to look and be sure.

> Problem 7A-1: Answer the questions in the first paragraph of the **Introduction to this chapter at 171**.

2. Tips & Tactics ▶ Using Forms

One way that lawyers help each other or research how to prepare a pleading or instrument is with an example previously used in similar circumstances. These are often called "forms" (or in some parts of the country, "go-bys," as in "do you have something I could go by?"). It is completely appropriate—in fact, highly advisable—to use a form as a basis for your drafting. After all, why spend the extra time and effort to reinvent the wheel if someone can give you something that is roughly the right size and shape to start with? But you **must** use that form correctly.

---

becomes worse off because of your help, or less well-off than reasonably competent assistance would have left him or her; and you become liable for the result in a situation in which you had no obligation to put yourself at risk in the first place and were just trying to be a good Samaritan. In other words, just because you have a newly minted bar card doesn't mean that you have to show off your skills every second of the day. The urge to provide aid to those in need is admirable, but do it in a manner and with resources calculated to leave everybody better off. Tips & Tactics

[6] To be sure, a supervisor who fails or refuses to supervise will probably be in trouble too if something goes badly wrong. But it won't get you off the hook, and it won't be much comfort, either. *See* **Model Rule 5.1(b)**; **Chapter 19.C at 515**. If you go outside your own **practice organization** to obtain the expertise or backstopping you need, there are additional steps you must take to protect client **confidentiality** and other concerns. *See* **Model Rule 1.1 Comments [6]-[7]**; **Chapter 8.B at 244**.

Let's say that again to make absolutely sure that you've heard us, because this is a mistake that inexperienced lawyers make with alarming frequency: *You **must** use forms properly.* The form may be *roughly* the right size and shape for your purposes, but it's up to you to determine how that size and shape must be adjusted to fit the vehicle that you're building in this particular instance. If you don't, and you just blindly jam it onto your axle without adjusting the fit, terrible accidents are just around the corner. (See how we used that colorful metaphor to illustrate the point? That's because this is really important.) The results from thoughtless adherence to a form range from embarrassing to disastrous.

You can often get forms from lawyers with whom you work just by asking. Some **practice organizations** actively maintain "knowledge banks" or "form files" that contain indexed stores of good examples of pleadings, briefs, and transactional documents for the kinds of things that the **practice organization** handles regularly. There are also commercially available "form books," found in most law libraries, focused on all kinds of practice situations, both litigation and transactional. And in some states, your state bar or another government agency has prepared printed forms for particular purposes (a form of summons, perhaps, or a form of subpoena, or a simple form promissory note or will; California even has form interrogatories asking for information often requested in many types of litigation and drafted to avoid most common objections). Sometimes these official forms are actually statutorily *required* for the purposes for which they were prepared; sometimes, they're optional. Even when optional, however, when properly used they are usually going to be viewed by local courts as legally sufficient, so they may be useful in avoiding unnecessary fighting over the adequacy of important instruments.

Forms can be tremendously helpful for a number of important purposes. A good form complaint or answer may provide you with language that has survived motions to dismiss for failure to state a claim or to strike an affirmative defense. A good form brief on a common issue may give you a big head start on the statutes and caselaw pertinent to making or opposing a particular kind of motion in particular circumstances. A good form contract for a particular kind of transaction will give you the benefit of a more experienced lawyer's thinking about what points ought to be addressed and how to address them clearly and consistently.

But it's up to you to determine whether what you have in front of you is in fact a *good* form, and even if it is, *how well it fits* the particular circumstances that you're addressing. Circumstances vary too much for us to give you a checklist of every way that you may need to determine fit, but three general imperatives will help:

First, always be sure what you have is a *good* example, at least for the purpose for which it was originally prepared. Do you know and respect the author? Do you know for what particular purposes the example was prepared? Remember the coder's creed: Garbage in, garbage out.

Second, even when you're sure that you're working with a good example, you must *never* allow any language or authority to remain in a form that you don't fully understand and for which you don't have an articulable good reason for using without changes. If you blindly assume that a smart lawyer had decided that certain language ought to be in there so you'll just follow along, you're committing your client to terms or assertions whose meaning you don't even know. ("Just sign here, Ms. Client." "Um, what does this mean?" "Heck if I know, but somebody else signed something just like it last year." "Right. You are so totally fired.") If, on the other hand, you just delete language that you don't understand, you may be eliminating something that your client actually needs. By the same token, consider whether your circumstances call for *adding* something that your example doesn't have. Failing to think about what's *not* in your example is just as dangerous as failing to think about what's there. Both are textbook examples of a lack of **competence** under **Model Rule 1.1**, and of a lack of due care for purposes of professional negligence liability.

Third and similarly, you **must** *always* assure yourself that you have *customized* the form to reflect your client's specific circumstances and needs. If the form relies on a statute or caselaw, *read the authority*; don't just assume that it's relevant. Check to see if the law has changed since the example was prepared. Make sure the document fits the facts and your client's needs. If it's a formal notice or agreement of some kind, make sure that it's got the right names, addresses, and dates in it (duh, you're thinking, but you would be astounded how often this mistake gets made). If it's a contract, make sure that its structure is right, that it complies with any regulations regarding the subject matter, and that it includes all the terms that your client wants. You get the idea.

In short, forms are great resources and time-savers, but they're only the beginning of your drafting. You will make us cry if you ever forget this. We'll be crying over the painful **consequences** and professional humiliation that you'll be experiencing because of this inexplicable lapse in judgment. We care about you. Don't make us cry.

And by the way, good lawyers build their own form files to help themselves get more efficient over time. After you've spent the time and effort to prepare something that you consider really well-thought-out and complete, put it aside in some kind of indexed source that you can consult when you need it again. Your index should include the type of document the form is (*e.g.*, Complaint—Breach of Contract, Money Had & Received; or Nondisclosure Agreement). You may be able to group similar kinds of documents together or otherwise organize your index for easy reference. Each entry should also describe the type of client for which you drafted the form as well as any pertinent circumstances in which the document was prepared (*e.g.*, Commercial Lease—Landlord; or Nondisclosure Agreement—New Product Submission). Think of all the time you'll save ransacking files you worked on five years ago to find that thing you did for that client whose name might have started with "G." A quick glance at your well-indexed form file, and you're ready to roll. And because you know a lot about the circumstances surrounding the creation of that document, you'll find it a lot easier to customize it for new facts and circumstances. TIPS & TACTICS

3. Exercising Reasonable Diligence and Promptness

Model Rule 1.3 elaborates on **Model Rule 1.1's** ideas of "thoroughness and preparation" by adding the complementary obligations of "reasonable diligence and promptness." The Comments elaborate, but not with anything that should surprise you. You must not only get up to speed substantively to the extent necessary to handle the matter, you must do so "reasonably" promptly. Then you must move the client's matter along with reasonable alacrity, find the time and energy necessary to do so, and finish what you undertook to do in a reasonable time. *See* **Model Rule 1.3 Comments [1]-[2], [4].**

REAL WORLD Duh, you may be thinking, what could be more basic than that? But one of the most common causes of disciplinary charges and malpractice claims is what is often called client neglect or abandonment.[7] It is especially prevalent in high-volume practices, such as intellectual property prosecution, smaller personal-injury or debt-collection claims, workers' compensation, consumer bankruptcy, and immigration, where the sheer number of "balls in the air" all the time can become overwhelming. But *all* law practice is inherently unruly. One big case or deal can have as many disparate moving parts and elusive details as many small ones. Whatever you do, you will constantly be interrupted and forced to switch your focus to something that claims to be more urgent than whatever it was you were doing at that moment—and from that to something else. It's hard to overstate how completely the daily array of fires on your desk can distract you from following up on important details. The results are never pretty:

> Perhaps no professional shortcoming is more widely resented than procrastination. A client's interests often can be adversely affected by the passage of time or the change of conditions; in extreme instances, as when a lawyer overlooks a statute of limitations, the client's legal position may be destroyed. Even when the client's interests are not affected in substance, however, unreasonable delay can cause a client needless anxiety and undermine confidence in the lawyer's trustworthiness.

Model Rule 1.3 Comment [3]. REAL WORLD

TIPS & TACTICS The cats will not herd themselves. You must find ways to catalogue and maintain order among the myriad details that are always trying to scurry off your desk and hide under the furniture. It's hard, but lawyers do it every day. If you

---

[7] For reasons that are apparent, lack of **competence** or **diligence** on a client's work is frequently accompanied by failure to communicate with the client as required or requested, a topic that we discussed in **Chapter 5.D at 117.**

work in a **practice organization** (law firm; government agency; nonprofit; company law department), your employer likely will provide you with computerized tools to help you. Maintain "tickler" and calendar systems that remind you of everything that's in play. If your employer provides you with secretarial or paralegal support early in your career, learn to collaborate with those essential colleagues to keep track of what's coming due and what needs to be done. Experienced legal secretaries and legal assistants are invaluable resources. They've seen it all and have made sure that everything has been completely finished and put away when it was done more times than you can count. Organization is a learnable skill, and one that almost everyone can improve. Watch practitioners whom you admire and see how they do it. Some people use specialized commercial personal-organizer software; others develop to-do lists in their own special format, which they update constantly. But in the immortal words of Larry the Cable Guy, Git-R-Done.[8] ⟨ TIPS & TACTICS ⟩

4. Keeping Up

As we've mentioned before, **competence** is the treadmill that never stops and always seems to be accelerating. The law and law practice change constantly. And the **duty of competence** not only requires you to acquire the skill and knowledge reasonably necessary to handle what's on your desk, but encourages you "[t]o *maintain* the requisite knowledge and skill" by "keep[ing] abreast of changes in the law and its practice, including the benefits and risks associated with relevant technology, [and] engaging in continuing study and education. . . ." **Model Rule 1.1 Comment [7]** (emphasis added).[9]

As an illustration of the constant and constantly accelerating change inherent in law practice, the language in **Model rule 1.1 Comment [7]** regarding the need to "keep abreast of . . . benefits and risks associated with relevant technology" was added in 2013 in light of growing concerns about the vulnerabilities to error, intrusion, and theft that dependence on changing technology creates. If you're a typical law student, you know about and are comfortable with a lot of information technology widely in use today, mainly because you've been using it. As you enter law practice, you will discover all kinds of specialized software to help you find, organize, and store information for clients. The only things that we know for sure about these tools are that they're changing all the time, and the rate of change has increased over time. The changes are usually for the better, making the software tools available more versatile and powerful. But with those changes come opportunities for

---

[8] *See* https://www.youtube.com/watch?v=xfbQ81SJn8s. We do not recommend Larry as a role model in any other respect.

[9] **Model Rule 1.1 Comment [7]** also reminds you to "comply with all continuing legal education requirements to which the lawyer is subject." In most states, continuing professional education is a *mandatory* condition of keeping your license, so it's more than just a good idea. Make sure you understand what your state requires, because the obligation starts on the day that you get your bar card.

you to make errors in using the software, as well as vulnerabilities to third-party misappropriation and misuse.

And where cybertools are pervasive, cybercrime is inevitable. As more and more client information is stored electronically, the risks of data breaches and similar cyber-invasions grows. Some of the largest and most prestigious law firms in America—firms with very substantial resources and infrastructure—have already suffered data breaches.[10] You and those with whom you work have personal duties to safeguard your clients' **confidential information**—which, as we will discuss in **Chapter 8.A at 210,** can be pretty much anything that you've gathered and stored in connection with representing them. So staying educated on the software tools currently in use and their potential risks becomes part of your duty of competence.[11]

Today, your **duty of** technological **competence** involves things that seem as simple as understanding how to protect information stored "in the cloud," how to scrub metadata from documents so that the other side can't see your side's thought process (that is, your **attorney work product**) as you developed the document, and how to keep your information secure. Information security could include things as simple as adopting passwords more secure than "password" or "12345678," or as complex as the evolving standards of practice in institutional cybersecurity. Right now, we imagine that this sounds insignificant, because you're likely comfortable with prevailing technology. But 10 or 20 years from now, with a busy law practice, a family, and countless other obligations and distractions, keeping up with The New Best Thing may seem more of a chore.

What you will need to know and do will depend on the tools you use and any changing industry standards. You don't have to add a degree in software engineering to your law degree; you can meet your technological **competence** obligations by working with reasonably reliable consultants and making appropriate use of their advice. But what you can't do is retreat into the twentieth century and hope that it will all leave you alone.

B. The Duty of Care

The **duty of care** shares many characteristics with the **duties of competence** and **diligence**, but it is by no means the same.

---

[10] *See, e.g.,* Nicole Hong & Robin Sidel, *Hackers Breach Law Firms, Including Cravath and Weil Gotshal,* https://www.wsj.com/articles/hackers-breach-cravath-swaine-other-big-law-firms-1459293504 (Mar. 29, 2016). The American Bar Association has issued a Formal Ethics Opinion regarding a lawyer or law firm's ethical duties to its clients in managing the risks and results of a data breach, including the obligation to maintain reasonable cybersecurity measures; monitor for breaches; and notify affected clients, stop any breach, and restore its systems if a breach occurs. ABA Formal Ethics Op. 18-483 (2018).

[11] A damaging misuse of software or a negligent failure to prevent a data breach could also entail very substantial civil liability. But just failing to keep up with technological developments can, in appropriate circumstances, result in professional discipline. *See State of Oklahoma ex rel. Oklahoma Bar Assn. v. Oliver,* 2016 OK 37, 369 P.3d 1074 (2016) (bankruptcy lawyer suspended from practice in bankruptcy court for repeatedly failing to learn how to comply with the court's electronic filing protocols, resulting in additional reciprocal state discipline).

CONSEQUENCES One way of distinguishing the **duty of care** from the **duties of competence** and **diligence** is by the **consequences** for violating them. The **duties of competence** and **diligence** are defined by Rules of Professional Conduct; by their terms, then, the **consequence** of violating those duties is professional discipline. The **duty of care**, by contrast, is enforced by civil claims, usually for money damages. In other words, the **duty of care** is one of the duties arising out of the attorney-client relationship whose breach may be remedied by a civil lawsuit when the breach causes pecuniary harm.[12]

A violation of the **duty of competence** or **diligence** does not require causation of harm to invoke professional discipline, although as a practical matter harm to one or more clients is typically what triggers attention from disciplinary authorities. The severity of the harm can affect the severity of the discipline, but the main purpose of professional discipline is not to punish the offender or to compensate the victim, but to protect the public from future harm. *See* **Chapter 3.A at 39**. So discernible breaches of the **duty of competence** or **diligence** may trigger professional discipline before anyone is hurt (though, as a practical matter, they usually don't, because bar prosecutors tend to pick and choose which cases to prosecute and lean toward using their scarce resources to press cases that protect the public from future harm *and* show the practical dangers of Rule violations). CONSEQUENCES

The **duty of care** is defined similarly, but not identically, to the duties of competence and diligence. Recall that the **duty of competence** requires "the legal knowledge, skill, thoroughness and preparation reasonably necessary for the representation" (**Model Rule 1.1**), and the **duty of diligence** requires "reasonable diligence and promptness" (**Model Rule 1.3**). The **duty of care** is one that we imagine you remember from your first-year Torts class: Lawyers must exercise reasonable care in their professional endeavors, and because they are trained professionals who hold themselves out as having specialized knowledge, they must exercise *a level of skill, diligence, and care, and possess (or acquire) a level of knowledge, that a reasonably careful and prudent lawyer would exercise or possess under the same or similar circumstances.*

The standard of care does not guarantee any particular *result* in any particular engagement. That makes sense if you think about it—after all, even the best lawyers lose cases with bad facts, or fail to negotiate deals between their clients and recalcitrant counterparties. Failing to achieve a result does not, by itself, show that you were negligent. Of course, if you fail to achieve a result that you otherwise would have achieved specifically because you did (or didn't do) something that any reasonable lawyer wouldn't (or would) have done, that's professional negligence, and **consequences** may follow.

---

[12] As discussed in **Chapter 3.B at 50**, causation and damages are also essential elements of a professional liability case, and they are often more difficult to establish than might appear at first glance. But here we're focused on the duty and breach elements of such claims.

TIPS & TACTICS You may also remember from your first-year Contracts class the celebrated "hairy hand" case, *Hawkins v. McGee*, 84 N.H. 114, 146 A. 641 (N.H. 1929). If you do, you'll recall that Dr. McGee "guarantee[d]" George Hawkins a "100% perfect hand" after treatment, and poor George ended up with anything but that "perfect" hand. In that case, Hawkins's claims against Dr. McGee for professional negligence (medical malpractice) were dismissed—Dr. McGee did no worse for George than any reasonable doctor would have done. But Hawkins recovered on a *contract* (warranty) theory based on the specific result that Dr. McGee had *promised* him.

The lesson of the hairy hand is simple: Don't ever promise results or do something that might leave your client believing that you're doing so. That means more than just avoiding boastful assurances that you'll have the adversary's head on a pike by Tuesday: If your client expresses unrealistic expectations, whether in the nature or the extent of the outcome that the client seems to expect, your silence may be taken as a guarantee. You **should**, and likely **must**, promptly find a gentle but direct way to make it clear that what your client wants is a kind or measure of justice that the legal system just won't provide.

Managing client expectations often feels painfully difficult and awkward—who wants to tell new clients (or worse, ones still deciding whether to hire you) that you can't bring them what they want? But if you don't, you've set yourself up as a failure in the client's eyes no matter how great a job you do, or how objectively excellent the result was that you achieved. And clients who view their lawyer as a failure have a nasty way of trying to impose **consequences** for their disappointment, formal or otherwise, and whether they're justified or not. For just this reason, many lawyers do (and all lawyers should) have a clause in their standard form of engagement letter, stating in essence that "we will use our professional knowledge and skill to try and achieve a favorable outcome in any matter that we agree to handle on your behalf, but we cannot promise or guarantee any particular result." **TIPS & TACTICS**

> **Problem 7B-1:** A new client, Dan Distraught, comes to see the litigation partner in Frank's firm, Harlan "Happy" Trials. Frank sits in. Dan's teenage daughter was sexually assaulted at a party by a boy who attends her high school. There was alcohol and a pointed he-said, she-said about whether Dan's daughter consented to the sexual contact, and on that basis, the local DA's office has declined to prosecute the boy. Dan wants to know what a "real lawyer" can do for his family. He wants to see the boy "get the prison term that he deserves" and force him to register as a sex offender. He also mentions that he and some friends from work are planning to "make it right." What **must** or **should** Happy say to Dan, and at least as important, how should he say it? (We acknowledge that there is a rich discussion to be had about the underlying situation and the prosecutors' reaction to it, but please focus only on the questions posed. Many of the clients who come through your doors will have suffered real and wrenching injustices, and even some who haven't will think they have. In each case,

you must find out what justice they'd like you to produce for them now, and then you need to be able to explain in a way that the client can understand what you and the legal system can realistically do for them.)

Problem 7B-2: **A** new client, Wanda Whiplash, comes to Frank's office. She has soft-tissue injuries from a rear-end automobile collision (that is, she didn't break anything, but her neck and back still hurt a lot, even months after the accident). She had hired local attorney Stanley Sloppy to handle the case, but nothing seems to have happened since she hired him, and lately, he hasn't even responded to her calls or emails. She's frustrated and wants to change lawyers. Frank asks her the date of the accident and realizes to his horror that the statute of limitations has run without Sloppy's having filed a complaint on Wanda's behalf. Has Sloppy violated his **duty of care** to Wanda? What **consequences** may Sloppy face, and what will Wanda need to prove to impose them?

REAL WORLD ❭ Knowing the standard of professional care for the lawyer-work that you do is important, but really it's just a beginning. Why? Think about it—the standard of care is the *absolute minimum* that you have to meet in order to avoid potential liability for professional negligence. Most lawyers aim to *exceed* the standard of care in everything they do. Aiming for best practices is most likely to lead to better outcomes for your clients and greater professional success for you; after all, being known as adequately competent in routine situations isn't likely to bring you many referrals. And being able to take pride in the quality of your work is one of the pleasures of law practice. Remember, *be the lawyer you'd want to hire.* REAL WORLD

Problem 7B-3: The partner in Frank's firm who handles trusts and estates matters, Willie Willmaker, is retained to help a prosperous married couple, John and Jane Jarndyce, prepare a joint estate plan. In order to avoid the delays, expenses, and complexities involved in probating a will, the estate plan's centerpiece is a "living trust" that is supposed to hold the couple's principal assets and that provides for the surviving spouse on a simple and tax-advantaged basis after one spouse dies. Willie meets with the Jarndyces, prepares the necessary documents reflecting their intentions, and has them come into the office to execute everything. Willie has a very busy practice, and trusts and estates work is very detail-oriented, with many small and urgent tasks arising every day, so he never quite gets around to the numerous and intricate (but relatively simple) tasks of putting title to all the significant assets that the Jarndyces own in the name of the couple's living trust. These assets include their home, a summer house on the lake, their cars, substantial retirement savings, and the shares in the corporation that operates their wholly owned family business. Eight months after the living trust and associated documents were duly witnessed, signed, and notarized, John has a sudden and unexpected heart attack and dies. Because the living trust does not yet hold title to anything, all of John's property will have to be probated, resulting in long delays, substantial legal fees, and some very significant adverse tax consequences for Jane and their children. What duties (if any) has Willie breached, and how? What **consequences** (if any) could Frank's firm and the responsible partner face as a result, and on what basis?

C. The Constitutional Right to Effective Assistance of Counsel in Criminal Cases

A criminal defendant's constitutional right to **effective assistance of counsel** creates a special set of competency, diligence, and care obligations for criminal defense lawyers. The accused's right to counsel applies at the latest when a formal criminal proceeding against the accused has begun, typically by a formal charge, preliminary hearing, indictment, information, or arraignment. These rights apply not only in court (for example, during trial), but even outside of court (for example, during a government interrogation). Once the right to counsel attaches, it continues throughout the criminal proceeding.[13]

1. The Source of the Right to Effective Assistance of Counsel

TAMING THE TEXT In addition to other procedural protections for those accused of crimes, the Sixth Amendment guarantees that "[i]n all criminal prosecutions, the accused shall enjoy the right . . . to have the Assistance of Counsel for his defence." The Supreme Court has held that this right is incorporated in the Fourteenth Amendment's Due Process Clause and thus is applicable to the States as well.[14] The literalists among you will have observed that the constitutional text refers only to "Assistance of Counsel," so it might seem that a law license and a pulse is all that the Bill of Rights requires. Confronted with cases in which appointed defense counsel with little more than these minimum attributes failed to raise substantial defenses that any reasonable lawyer would have interposed on the accused's behalf, however, the Supreme Court eventually decided that the "Assistance of Counsel" that the Sixth Amendment ensures had to be *effective* in order to satisfy the constitutional guarantee. And to be effective (at least for purposes of satisfying the Bill of Rights), the lawyer assisting in the accused's defense must act at least *competently*. Two United States Supreme Court cases, decided on the same day in 1984, set forth two alternative tests for determining

---

[13] There are lots of nuances to when a right to counsel may attach under the Bill of Rights or governing state law, but we have no desire to intrude on your Criminal Procedure course. For present purposes, we'll just note that the Sixth Amendment guarantees competent counsel to those accused of a crime at any "critical stage" of their criminal proceedings. *See Montejo v. Louisiana*, 556 U.S. 778 (2009), https://www.law.cornell.edu/constitution-conan/amendment-6/assistance-of-counsel. The Fifth Amendment separately guarantees a right to have counsel present during a custodial interrogation, which loosely corresponds with the period beginning with arrest (at least for relatively serious crimes), even if no formal proceeding against the accused has yet begun. *See generally Miranda v. Arizona*, 384 U.S. 436 (1966). This is no doubt something that you already knew from every cop show that you ever saw on television, even if you haven't taken Criminal Procedure yet. For an overview of constitutional rights to counsel that is more thorough, if less colorful, than television, *see generally* Akhil Reed Amar, The Constitution and Criminal Procedure: First Principles (1997); Martin R. Gardner, *The Sixth Amendment Right to Counsel and its Underlying Values: Defining the Scope of Privacy Protection*, 90 J. Crim. L. & Criminology 397 (2000); Note, *Rethinking the Boundaries of the Sixth Amendment Right to Choice of Counsel*, 124 Harv L. Rev. 1550 (2011).

[14] *See Gideon v. Wainwright*, 372 U.S. 335 (1963).

whether criminal defense counsel's assistance satisfies the Sixth Amendment.

Taming the Text

2. When Is Defense Counsel's Assistance "Ineffective"?

a. The *Strickland* "Presumption of Reasonableness" or "Deficiency and Prejudice" Test

In *Strickland v. Washington*, 466 U.S. 668 (1984), the United States Supreme Court imposed a minimum competence standard on criminal defense counsel by holding that such counsel will presumptively meet the Sixth Amendment standard for **effective assistance** *unless* (1) they did (or failed to do) something in defending the accused that no reasonable defense lawyer would have done (or failed to do); *and* (2) there is a reasonable probability that the case would have come out differently had counsel done what any reasonable defense lawyer would have done. We're going to discuss each of these elements in detail below. But let's start with the observation that, as the facts in *Strickland* show, this standard leaves a great deal of latitude for defense counsel to make tactical choices, even ones that end badly for their clients, so long as the choice is one that *some* reasonable criminal defense lawyer might have made under the circumstances.[15]

The defendant in *Strickland*, David Washington, pled guilty to three counts of capital murder.[16] As part of his plea, Washington was brought into court and asked questions by the presiding trial court judge to ensure that his guilty plea was knowing and voluntary. This process is known as a "plea colloquy" or "allocution." During the plea colloquy, Washington admitted that he had committed the murders but explained that he had been driven by extreme financial stress at the time. The trial judge commented favorably on Washington's admission of guilt, praising Washington's willingness to accept responsibility for his conduct.

Washington's case then proceeded to its sentencing phase. Because he had just pled guilty to multiple counts of capital murder, sentencing was literally a matter of life or death. During the sentencing phase in a death-penalty case, the defense has an opportunity to offer evidence of mitigating factors intended to explain the defendant's conduct or invite mercy, in order to persuade the sentencing authority (judge or jury) to refrain from imposing the death sentence.

---

[15] As you've probably noticed by this point, this book doesn't engage in much discussion or interpretation of any decided cases. That's mainly because most ethics cases simply apply a particular state's version of a particular Model Rule or Rules, have only persuasive effect outside their territorial jurisdiction, and are at best examples of issues that we illustrate as well or (we hope) better in the problems we have typed our fingers to the bone to provide you. (To the bone. Bony fingers, OK? For you.) But *Strickland* and its companion case, *Cronic*, are United States Supreme Court decisions interpreting the Constitution; they are not just authoritative, they are, in a very meaningful sense, *the law* on these issues. So this discussion will probably be a good deal more like your other law school classes. Consider it a temporary aberration.

[16] The Washington in *Strickland v. Washington* was a person, not a state. This is a strong hint that his Sixth Amendment rights were being adjudicated not on direct appeal from his conviction, but through the post-conviction remedy of *habeas corpus*, which challenges the propriety of the defendant's incarceration. Strickland was Mr. Washington's prison warden, the customary respondent in a *habeas corpus* proceeding.

The prosecution, for its part, may offer evidence of aggravating factors favoring a death sentence. Commonly, the prosecution will also rebut or challenge any mitigating evidence proffered by the defense.

At this stage of the litigation, then, Washington's lawyer had to decide whether to offer mitigating evidence. For example, the lawyer could have requested that Washington undergo a psychiatric examination, because a diagnosed mental illness could be a basis to argue for leniency. Similarly, defense counsel could have identified, interviewed, and prepared character witnesses to testify on Washington's behalf at the sentencing in support of an argument that, despite the bad things Washington had done, he was not such a bad person that he deserved to die. If these witnesses credibly testified to Washington's good character, the judge (the sentencing authority in this case) might have been moved to spare Washington's life.

You may be wondering how Washington's lawyer could even *consider* not offering mitigating evidence in an effort to save his client's life. It's a fair question. But in a vivid illustration of the challenges of criminal defense work, offering mitigating evidence created real and significant risks for Washington, and presenting no mitigating evidence created different risks of its own. For example, if Washington's lawyer ordered a psychiatric examination, he would be required to disclose the results to the prosecution. Anything negative, such as evidence that Washington had shown a lack of remorse during his psychiatric interview, would be admissible by the prosecution as evidence supporting a harsher sentence. And a psychiatric report fully supporting leniency might prompt the prosecution to order its own rebuttal psychiatric examination, presumably conducted by a mental health professional more sympathetic to the prosecution's view that Washington should be put to death.

Similarly, if Washington's lawyer called character witnesses, the prosecution would have the right to cross-examine those witnesses, which could undermine the witnesses' credibility or, worse, expose new aggravating evidence against Washington. And Washington had an extensive criminal record prior to the murders—a history that would be well known to any character witnesses—and would be ready impeachment material for any character witness who claimed not to know about (or just failed to mention) Washington's many previous crimes.

Faced with this dilemma, Washington's lawyer made a strategic decision *not* to order a psychiatric examination or call character witnesses to testify during the sentencing hearing. Instead, he introduced Washington's testimony from the plea colloquy and relied on this testimony to argue for mitigation.

The strategy was unsuccessful: The trial judge found no mitigating circumstances and sentenced Washington to death. After his direct appeals failed, Washington asserted a claim for **ineffective assistance of counsel** on *habeas corpus*. The

United States Supreme Court ultimately took the case in order to resolve conflicts in the legal standard for **effective assistance of counsel** under the Sixth Amendment that had developed among the lower federal and state courts.[17]

The *Strickland* Court reconfirmed that the Sixth Amendment right to "Assistance of Counsel" requires *competent* counsel providing reasonable professional assistance. It introduced a two-part test to determine when this competency standard was met: For a defendant to prevail on a claim that defense counsel had *not* met the Sixth Amendment's guarantee, the defendant had to show (1) deficient performance by counsel; and (2) prejudice to the outcome.

i. When Is Defense Counsel's Performance Constitutionally "Deficient"?

The Court held that defense counsel's performance was constitutionally "deficient" if it fell below an "objective standard of reasonableness" comprising the "skill, judgment, and diligence of a reasonably competent defense attorney."[18] As just discussed, litigation often involves strategic decisions between two or more highly imperfect alternatives, and Washington's sentencing was no exception. Washington's lawyer had made a tactical choice—ordering a psychiatric examination or calling character witnesses could have helped his client's chances of a more lenient sentence, but it also could have hurt those chances. Washington's counsel had concluded that the risks outweighed the benefits, and the Court could not say that *no* reasonable lawyer would have done the same.[19]

Because most cases involve tactical choices whose results are difficult to predict and thus could reasonably be made either way, the *Strickland* Court was reluctant to require defendants to be retried on grounds of **ineffective assistance** every time their lawyers' tactics failed to avert a conviction based on speculative arguments that a different choice in the heat of trial might have delivered a better result. As the Court put it, criminal defense counsel's performance is *presumed* to have been reasonable, and on review counsel is accorded "wide latitude" to have made "reasonable tactical decisions."[20]

---

[17] As we will discuss below in **Chapter 7.C at 194**, a finding that criminal defense counsel provided **ineffective assistance** in violation of the Sixth Amendment does not determine the defendant's innocence or guilt; it simply determines that the defendant did not receive a fair trial. Thus, the principal remedy for **ineffective assistance of criminal defense counsel** is a retrial with competent defense counsel, though the **ineffective** defense counsel may personally be subject to other **consequences** as well.

[18] 466 U.S. at 650.

[19] You'll recall that, because these decisions involve what evidence to present and what arguments to make, they are "means" decisions within counsel's legal and ethical powers to decide, even if the client demands otherwise. *See* **Chapter 6.C at 157**. To be clear, there is nothing in the record of the *Strickland* case suggesting that the client expressly disagreed with his lawyer's approach to the sentencing hearing. Rather, Washington argued post-conviction that he (like most clients) had depended on his lawyer to make good tactical decisions regarding his sentencing hearing, but that the decisions that his lawyer had made amounted to **ineffective assistance**.

[20] 466 U.S. at 689. Although there is a broad logic grounded in the necessities of a functioning criminal justice system to applying this rather modest standard to the performance of criminal defense counsel, it comes with a price. Criminal defendants, who face the highest stakes of anyone haled into our justice system—their freedom, and at times their very

ii. When Is Defense Counsel's "Deficient" Performance Unconstitutionally "Prejudicial"?

Even when the defendant can show that his attorney did something that no reasonable lawyer would have done, however, that showing alone is not sufficient to establish that counsel's assistance was **ineffective**. Not all errors on defense counsel's part justify setting aside the conviction and conducting a new trial.

Strickland articulated a standard for when defense counsel's unreasonably poor performance is unconstitutionally "prejudicial": when the identified "deficiencies" in counsel's performance give rise to a "reasonable probability" that the *result in the case* would have been different had counsel performed adequately.[21] Having concluded that Washington had not shown his counsel's performance to be "deficient," the *Strickland* Court did not determine the "prejudice" element of **ineffective assistance** in the case. It simply articulated the "reasonable probability of a different result" standard for the lower courts' future guidance.

But if the Supreme Court had considered prejudice, it likely would have found none in *Strickland*. The "result" at issue was the outcome of Washington's sentencing proceeding.[22] Washington had already pled guilty to three grisly murders. It's hard to see any mitigating evidence available to Washington's counsel that presented any reasonable likelihood of sparing him from the death penalty, especially given his substantial prior criminal record and its inevitable effect on any character determination. Quite probably, the Supreme Court would have found that, under these circumstances, there was no "reasonable probability" of a different outcome, and thus any deficiencies in counsel's performance were not unconstitutionally "prejudicial."

Although *Strickland*'s "prejudice" standard can be simply stated, applying it in actual cases can be difficult. So many things go into the ultimate result of a verdict or a sentence that it can be speculative to argue how likely it is that the result would have differed had counsel not made particular bad choices. Each case must be analyzed and argued closely on its own facts.[23]

---

lives—quite frequently do not have the resources to choose their own counsel. These unfortunates are not guaranteed the best defense, or even a particularly good one. Those privileges are reserved to those wealthy or lucky enough to retain the very best lawyers, lawyers who consistently make the very best choices under pressured conditions of uncertainty, investigate the underlying facts aggressively, and maintain a workload that allows them to devote the time and the resources needed to mount the strongest and best-supported defense that they can devise. As skilled, resourceful, and devoted as most public defenders are, in many jurisdictions they are systematically overworked and underfunded, and thus are simply unable as a practical matter to provide this kind of defense to every client. Donald J. Farole, Jr. & Lynn Langton, *A National Assessment of Public Defender Office Caseloads*, 94 Judicature 87 (2010). Under *Strickland*, all the Constitution requires is a *minimally competent* defense, one that will survive scrutiny unless *no* reasonable lawyer would ever have provided it.

[21] 466 U.S. at 694.

[22] This illustrates an important point about applying the "prejudice" element: You must always first identify *what* result might have been different but for counsel's deficient performance. Often, that result is a conviction. But as *Strickland* itself illustrates, sometimes it's something else, such as sentencing. *See Lafler v. Cooper*, 566 U.S. 156 (2012).

[23] Besides comprising some strong and serious legal and exam practice advice, this observation shows us another important shortcoming of the *Strickland* standard. Often, the most valuable and important thing that criminal defense counsel can

That said, we can offer some generalizations: The more serious the error, the more likely it may be deemed "prejudicial."[24] If, for example, the defendant had a viable defense, supported by credible evidence that could have resulted in acquittal, failure to pursue that defense might be "prejudicial."[25] If the error is repeated, it is more likely to be considered "prejudicial."[26] If improper character or other improper adverse evidence is admitted multiple times due to defense counsel's failure to object, that is more likely to be held "prejudicial."[27] The weaker the prosecution's case is, the easier it will be for the defendant to show that any **ineffective assistance** by counsel was "prejudicial."[28] Inversely, if the evidence of guilt was overwhelming, even a serious error may not have affected the outcome (that is, *no* reasonable defense lawyer could have won this case).[29]

Although the application of both the "deficiency" and "prejudice" elements of the *Strickland* standard are highly fact-specific and often doubtful, the results are usually profound. The *Strickland* Court held that David Washington received constitutionally adequate assistance of counsel in his sentencing proceeding. He was executed two months later.

iii. ⟨Rule Roles⟩ How Does the *Strickland* Ineffective Assistance Standard Interact with the Rules of Professional Conduct and Civil Liability Standards?

As we know from *Strickland*, the Sixth Amendment requires competent counsel. This requirement dovetails neatly with what the Model Rules and state tort law require. We discussed the **duties of competence**, **diligence**, and **care** in the first two sections of this chapter. **Model Rule 1.1** and **Model Rule 1.3** require that a

---

do is to investigate the underlying facts aggressively to find exculpatory witnesses and other evidence. Such investigation takes time and money (for investigators, personnel to review documents, experts, etc.). Time and money for investigation are just what defense counsel, especially public defenders, often lack. But the *Strickland* standard requires a defendant who is challenging the constitutional **effectiveness** of his counsel to show not only a failure to investigate something **material** ("deficiency") but *what that investigation would have found and why that would have changed the outcome* ("prejudice"). This means that appellate or post-conviction counsel actually has to conduct that investigation in order to develop and ground any viable **ineffective assistance** argument based on a failure to investigate. But indigent defendants whose appointed lawyers do little or no independent investigation because they lack the time or money are often succeeded by appointed appellate counsel who (through no fault of their own) also typically lack the same resources. Prejudicial deficiencies in defense counsel's performance thus may simply never come to light.

[24] 466 U.S. at 680-81.

[25] *See, e.g., Gennetten v. State,* 96 S.W.3d 143 (Mo. Ct. App. 2003) (finding that the *Strickland* standard was met where defense counsel failed to proffer expert testimony that would have created a viable defense to charges of child abuse by showing that the child's burns were accidental rather than intentional).

[26] *See, e.g., Rodriguez v. Hoke,* 928 F.2d 534, 535 (2d Cir. 1991) (finding that the *Strickland* standard was met based on cumulative errors, including repeated failures to discover exculpatory evidence).

[27] *See, e.g., Alvarado v. State,* 775 S.W.2d 851 (Tex. App. 1989) (finding that the *Strickland* standard was met where defense counsel failed to object to testimony by three different witnesses who each offered inadmissible testimony).

[28] *See Strickland,* 466 U.S. at 681, 695-96; *see also Luna v. Cambra,* 306 F.3d 954, *amended,* 311 F.3d 928 (9th Cir. 2002) (finding clear prejudice in an attempted murder and robbery case based in part upon the fact that the prosecution's evidence was relatively weak).

[29] *See Strickland,* 466 U.S. at 667; *see also United States v. Hatcher,* 541 F. App'x 951, 953 (11th Cir. 2013) (holding that an **ineffective assistance** claim failed due to the overwhelming evidence of guilt, including audio recordings where the defendant was heard discussing his participation in the crime).

lawyer have the "legal knowledge, skill, thoroughness and preparation reasonably necessary for the representation" and act with "reasonable diligence and promptness" (*see* **Chapter 7.A at 172; Chapter 7.A at 178**); and state tort law typically requires a lawyer to exercise a level of skill, diligence, and care, and possess (or acquire) a level of knowledge, that a reasonably careful and prudent lawyer would possess or exercise under the same or similar circumstances (*see* **Chapter 7.B at 180**).

Because of the myriad kinds of work that lawyers do, these standards are quite intentionally stated broadly. They apply to both civil and criminal cases, and in both litigation and nonlitigation contexts. But in the specific context of criminal defense, how much knowledge, skill, thoroughness, and preparation must defense counsel have, and how do the requirements of the Model Rules and state tort law fit with the constitutional standard for **ineffective assistance of counsel**? The Supreme Court recognized the difficulty of answering this question in *Strickland*, noting that "[n]o particular set of detailed rules for counsel's conduct can satisfactorily take account of the variety of circumstances faced by defense counsel or the range of legitimate decisions regarding how best to represent a criminal defendant."[30]

To harmonize ethics rules and professional liability standards with the Sixth Amendment, let's start by recalling that, under *Strickland*, "deficient" performance by criminal defense counsel is essentially defined as something that no reasonable criminal defense lawyer would do (or fail to do) under the circumstances. *See* **Chapter 7.C at 187**. In other words, prevailing professional norms and standards (that is, what a reasonable lawyer would do under the circumstances) will help guide an analysis of whether defense counsel's performance was "deficient." And once we understand *that*, it's easy to say that no reasonable lawyer would violate an applicable rule or standard of professional ethics or professional liability, so a Rule violation (or a violation of the standard of care adequate to support civil liability for professional negligence) will ordinarily satisfy the first element of the *Strickland* test.

But—and this is very important—not every violation of every legal or ethical rule can be shown to meet the second *Strickland* element: A reasonable likelihood that the result in the case would have differed had counsel acted properly. Criminal convictions have been affirmed on appeal and on post-conviction review even when the **ineffective assistance** claims involved such egregious conduct as defense counsel's falling asleep while his client was being cross-examined;[31] being drunk during the trial;[32] and discussing his own mental illness and paranoid delusions while giving an opening statement for the defense.[33]

---

[30] 466 U.S. at 688-89.

[31] *See Muniz v. Smith*, 647 F.3d 619 (6th Cir. 2011).

[32] *See People v. Garrison*, 47 Cal. 3d 746 (1989).

[33] *See Smith v. Ylst*, 826 F.2d 872 (9th Cir. 1987). On the irony of calling representation like this "effective assistance of counsel," *see* **Chapter 7.C at 187 n.20; Chapter 7.C at 188 n.23**, *supra*.

Although each of these examples undoubtedly violates one or more Rules of Professional Conduct (and the civil **duty of care** as well), the key additional requirement of "prejudice" was missing. In each of these cases, there was independent and substantial evidence of the defendant's guilt. The reviewing courts in each case concluded that the defendants in these cases still would have been convicted even if defense counsel had been awake, sober, and lucid throughout the trial.

In short, compliance with disciplinary and civil standards of lawyer conduct is highly relevant to the "deficiency" element of the *Strickland* test, but much less important to the "prejudice" element. Because of its powerful role in determining deficient performance, you should always consider defense counsel's compliance with ethical rules and practice standards when analyzing a Sixth Amendment claim of **ineffective assistance of counsel**. But never forget to reason out how the rule or standard violation may have affected the outcome of the case. 〈RULE ROLES〉

> **Problem 7C-1:** Danielle sometimes litigates against a private criminal defense attorney named Steve. From time to time, Steve and Danielle go out for drinks after work.
>
> a. One evening, Steve shows up at the bar, sighing heavily. Danielle asks Steve what's wrong. Steve explains that a client he defended on an armed robbery charge decided to testify in her own defense, got impeached very effectively on cross-examination for her three prior armed robbery convictions, and got convicted. Now her family has hired post-conviction (*habeas corpus*) counsel who has argued that Steve provided **ineffective assistance of counsel**. Danielle asks Steve whether he advised her about whether to testify. Steve replies that, though he cannot disclose **confidential** client communications, Danielle may assume that the defendant was fully informed about all of her Fifth Amendment rights and the probable effects of her criminal record if she testified, as well as the fact that the choice whether or not to testify was ultimately her call. Was Steve's advice "deficient"? Was it "prejudicial"?
>
> b. Same as (a), but assume that Steve had advised his client to testify based on the rather inexplicable guess that the jury would find her credible, though he made it clear that, ultimately, the choice whether to testify was hers and hers alone. Was Steve's advice "deficient"? Was it "prejudicial"?

b. The *Cronic* "Automatic Reversal" or "*Per Se*" Test

Although ordinarily a defendant must show "deficiency" and "prejudice," some situations are so offensive to the fair administration of criminal justice that such a showing is not required. If a defendant can show that counsel created or suffered one of these situations, counsel's performance is **ineffective** *per se*, and reversal for retrial is ordered automatically, without detailed inquiry into the deficiencies of counsel's performance or its effect on the outcome. On the same day that the Supreme Court decided *Strickland*, it also decided a second case involving **ineffective assistance of counsel**. In *United States v. Cronic*,[34] the Court held that where circumstances indicate that *no* competent lawyer could have provided constitutionally **effective assistance**, a reviewing court may reverse for retrial on Sixth Amendment grounds *without* an inquiry into exactly what defense counsel might have done wrong, and what effect it had on the outcome, but that such cases are rare. Again, the facts are instructive, so let's take a look.

Defendant Cronic had been indicted with two other co-defendants on mail-fraud charges involving a multimillion-dollar "check-kiting" scheme. Less than three weeks before trial, Cronic's lawyer withdrew, and the court appointed a new lawyer to defend him. This new lawyer practiced real estate law, had never tried a case to a jury, and was given only 25 days to review and prepare a case that the government had investigated and prepared over four and a half *years*, including thousands of documents. Cronic's two co-defendants cooperated with the government and testified against him. Unsurprisingly, Cronic was found guilty and was sentenced to 25 years in prison.

On appeal, Cronic (with new counsel) raised an **ineffective assistance** argument. The Tenth Circuit reversed and remanded for a new trial on the ground that the circumstances of the trial made counsel's **ineffective assistance** so likely that it could reverse *without any inquiry into counsel's actual performance or its effect on the outcome*. The appellate court was particularly concerned about (1) the time afforded for investigation and preparation, (2) the experience of counsel, (3) the gravity of the charge, (4) the complexity of possible defenses, and (5) the accessibility of witnesses to counsel.

The United States Supreme Court granted *certiorari* and considered the case along with *Strickland*. Reasoning that a complete denial of counsel would violate the Sixth Amendment, the *Cronic* Court observed that there could be circumstances in which "the likelihood that any lawyer, even a fully competent one, could provide effective assistance is so small that a presumption of prejudice is appropriate without inquiry into the actual conduct of the trial."[35]

Somewhat surprisingly, the Supreme Court then concluded that this was *not* such a case. The Court held that it was sufficiently possible, despite every obstacle to which he had been subjected, for Cronic's lawyer to have met *Strickland*'s minimum standards of competence.[36] Because the Tenth Circuit had never considered the actual performance of Cronic's lawyer at trial, the Supreme Court reversed the determination of *per se* **ineffective assistance** and remanded for an analysis under the *Strickland* standards whether defense

---

[34] 466 U.S. 648 (1984).

[35] 466 U.S. at 659-60.

[36] Or perhaps that there was no *Strickland* "prejudice" because any mistakes that Cronic's lawyer did make wouldn't have changed the outcome; or perhaps because, no matter how poorly Cronic's lawyer had performed, *no* reasonable lawyer could have won Cronic's case.

counsel performed deficiently in any respect, and if so, whether those deficiencies created the reasonable likelihood that the outcome would have differed had they not occurred.[37]

The facts of *Cronic* illustrate how hard this *per se* standard is to meet. The circumstances to which Cronic's new lawyer was subjected seem systematically engineered to force him to fail, yet they were not enough to justify reversal and retrial for **ineffective assistance** without a *Strickland* inquiry into his actual performance.[38] It bears remembering that the *Cronic* Court's reasoning that automatic retrial for **ineffective assistance** should be available only when "the likelihood that any lawyer, even a fully competent one, could provide effective assistance is so small that a presumption of prejudice is appropriate without inquiry into the actual conduct of the trial." Consistent with this reasoning, lower courts have generally limited automatic reversal under *Cronic* to cases in which the circumstances create the equivalent of having no counsel at all.[39]

---

[37] *Cronic*, 466 U.S. at 666 & n.41.

[38] You may be wondering what the pitiable inexperienced lawyer who received the last-minute appointment to represent Cronic in a serious, complex felony trial well beyond his experience could or should have done. Certainly he should have sought a continuance of the trial to allow him to prepare better. The record shows that he did so. He was appointed about two weeks before trial, but he asked the trial court for a total of only 30 days to prepare; the court's grant of 25 days looks rather less unreasonable in that light.

Nevertheless, one might conclude that counsel was in way over his head, and the request of only 30 days' preparation time (for a case that took the government four and a half years to investigate and develop) is some indication that he may not have fully appreciated how much work he needed to do. A real estate lawyer with no jury experience ought to question whether *any* amount of preparation would allow him to competently try to a jury a complex, multi-count federal financial fraud case based on thousands of documents. As the Model Rules point out, sometimes the law is so specialized or the facts so intricate that an inexperienced lawyer needs to involve, or refer the matter outright to, a more knowledgeable and experienced attorney. See **Model Rule 1.1 Comment [1]**; **Chapter 7.A at 174**. This may well have been such a case.

Whether or not it should have, however, that didn't happen. What then? **Model Rule 1.16(a)(1)** says a lawyer **must not** take on an engagement that "will result in violation of the rules of professional conduct or other law," and in this case that might arguably include the new counsel's **duty of competence** and the civil **duty of care**. But the Supreme Court held that Cronic's lawyer had enough of a chance to be competent that Cronic had to affirmatively show that he actually *wasn't* competent *in this case* (which is what *Strickland* requires). That holding implies that the engagement would not necessarily violate **Model Rule 1.16(a)**, a conclusion we're not so sure about (though, needless to say, the Supreme Court didn't consult us). Aside from mandatory withdrawal under Rule 1.16(a), **Model Rule 1.16(b)(6)** provides that a lawyer **may** withdraw from or refuse an engagement that "has been rendered unreasonably difficult by the client." But here it was the court, not the client, making the engagement unreasonably difficult. **Model Rule 1.16(b)(7)** says that a lawyer **may** withdraw when "other good cause for withdrawal exists." Such "good cause" likely did exist here (for the reasons that the Tenth Circuit identified—the conditions that made counsel's position all but impossible), but **Model Rule 1.16(c)** provides that, even when a lawyer **may** withdraw, he **must not** do so if a presiding court will not allow it. Under the circumstances, Cronic's new lawyer **should** at least have *asked* to be relieved as counsel. (*See* **Chapter 9.D at 294** on mandatory and permissive withdrawal.) It does not appear that he did; the only thing he asked for was a short continuance. To be sure, the trial court had appointed him, and it wouldn't even give the poor man 30 days to prepare. It thus seems unlikely that the court would have let him out even if he had asked. In short, there was no obvious solution available here. Sometimes all you can do is buckle your seatbelt, keep the airsickness bag at hand, and make your record for appeal.

[39] *See, e.g., Donald v. Rapelje*, 580 F. App'x 277 (6th Cir. 2014) (defendant's counsel absent from the courtroom during examination of an important witness); *Mitchell v. Mason*, 325 F.3d 732, 744 (6th Cir. 2003) (defendant saw his lawyer for only six minutes during a seven-month pretrial period); *United States v. Russell*, 205 F.3d 768 (5th Cir. 2000); (defense attorney absent for two days during a critical stage of defendant's trial); *United States ex rel. Thomas v. O'Leary*, 856 F.2d 1011 (7th Cir. 1988) (absence of counsel at resentencing hearing prejudicial *per se*).

3. CONSEQUENCES What Happens If a Criminal Defendant Receives Ineffective Assistance of Counsel?

Unlike a challenge on the merits, which tests the adequacy of the evidence and the proper application of substantive and procedural law, and thus the correctness of the verdict or other result, a Sixth Amendment **ineffective assistance** challenge tests only the adequacy of defense counsel's performance. If counsel's performance fell below constitutional standards, then the defendant did not receive the fair trial guaranteed by the Bill of Rights. The remedy is reversal or vacatur, and a new trial or hearing on whatever results were caused by counsel's **ineffective assistance.**[40]

But what are the **consequences** for the lawyer whose work failed to meet those constitutional standards? Well, if the failure violated a Rule of Professional Conduct, then the lawyer is subject to professional discipline, if disciplinary authorities choose to pursue it. In fact, disciplinary **consequences** may be available for a wide range of professional misconduct or incompetence that might *not* comprise **ineffective assistance of counsel** under the Sixth Amendment, because acts or omissions by counsel that violated a Rule of Professional Conduct may not have caused *Strickland* "prejudice" in a particular case, and thus would leave the results in the trial court unaffected. *See* **Chapter 7.C at 189**.

What about civil malpractice liability to the defendant-client for the **ineffective** counsel? Here, things get interesting: In most states, tort damages for professional negligence or breaches of other professional duties to a criminal defendant are available only if the client was *actually innocent* and the lawyer's error or omission more likely than not caused the client not to be acquitted.[41] Thus, as a practical matter, there are plenty of situations in which counsel may have provided assistance less **effective** than the Sixth Amendment demands, but nevertheless for which counsel will face no civil liability for legal malpractice.

REAL WORLD Ordinary professional pride, coupled with the fact that disciplinary **consequences** (and, at least now and then, civil liability) may be available against counsel accused of **ineffective assistance**, can create a peculiar reversal of loyalties. During the engagement, of course, defense counsel owes the defendant zealous representation and undivided loyalty. *See* **Chapter 5.D at 113**. Once the defendant accuses counsel of **ineffective assistance**, counsel may naturally feel inclined to defend her performance—and may have ample grounds to do so. (Statutory and constitutional criminal procedure protections for the accused exist because sometimes defendants really do get an unfair trial, but criminal defendants found guilty as charged may sometimes wish to blame their lawyer, the judge, or the

---

[40] "Vacatur" is the noun for what happens when a court vacates (that is, revokes or undoes) an order or judgment. "Vacation" is what you take with your friends or family when you take a break from asking for things like vacatur.

[41] *See, e.g., Coscia v. McKenna & Cuneo*, 25 Cal. 4th 1194 (2001); *Fink v. Banks*, 374 Ill. Dec. 722, 996 N.E.2d 169 (2013); *Dombrowski v. Bulson*, 19 N.Y.3d 347, 350-351 (2012); *Skindzelewski v. Smith*, 2020 WI 57 (2020).

jury rather than face the mirror and take responsibility for their actions.) Often, the defendant's accusation makes defense counsel into a reluctant (or even an enthusiastic) ally of the prosecutor, who will contest the **ineffective assistance** claim in order to preserve a conviction or other result that is favorable from the government's point of view.[42] This dynamic is similar to the reversal of allegiance that often occurs when clients accuse their lawyers of professional negligence or other misconduct in any context. Perhaps it proves little more than that litigation can make strange bedfellows. REAL WORLD CONSEQUENCES

Problem 7C-2: Danielle and Steve continue the conversation described in **Problem 7C-1(a) at 191**.

a. Steve goes on to relate that the reason that the robbery defendant's family hired new post-conviction counsel is that, although Steve had agreed to pursue an appeal on the defendant's behalf, he missed the deadline for filing a notice of appeal, which resulted in the loss of his client's rights of appeal. Is Steve's failure to meet the appellate filing deadline **ineffective assistance of counsel**? Why or why not?

b. Same facts as (a). Setting aside the **ineffective assistance** claim, what are the defendant's prospects for success if she sues Steve for damages for professional negligence? Why?

Problem 7C-3: Danielle and her supervisor are prosecuting Joe Jealous for attempted murder after he allegedly shot at his ex-girlfriend's new paramour. Jealous has retained private defense counsel. During opening statement, Danielle glances over to counsel table and realizes that defense counsel is asleep. Several jurors appear to have noticed that as well. Defense counsel quietly snores during the remainder of the prosecution's opening statement and elects not to cross-examine any prosecution witnesses. Danielle is surprised because her primary witness, Jealous's ex, could easily be impeached. She and Jealous ended their relationship on less-than-amicable terms, and it would not be difficult to argue that her testimony is shaded by animus.

To Danielle's surprise, Jealous takes the stand and testifies in his own defense. Midway through Danielle's withering cross-examination, defense counsel's phone rings. Defense counsel gets up and leaves the courtroom to answer the call. At the judge's direction, Danielle continues. She cross-examines Jealous for ten more minutes while defense counsel is outside of the courtroom. When defense counsel returns, the judge admonishes him in front of the jury. Defense counsel just shrugs.

When the time comes for closing arguments, the judge calls on defense counsel. Counsel stands, says "I can't give a closing. I agree with the prosecution—my client is guilty," and then sits down. Then defense counsel refuses to review the jury instructions, telling Danielle, "whatever you want to include is fine with me." He is absent when the jury renders its verdict: guilty.

---

[42] The accusation of **ineffective assistance** thus creates a **conflict of interest** between defense counsel and the defendant. *See* **Chapter 22.A at 629.** If the defense engagement is not completed by its terms at this point, the accusation and the conflict it creates will probably require counsel to withdraw, if the client has not already discharged her.

Under these circumstances, if Jealous asserts an **ineffective assistance of counsel** claim, is it likely that he will need to prove *Strickland* prejudice? What must he demonstrate to avoid having to prove prejudice, and why might he be able to do so here?

Big-Picture Takeaways from Chapter 7

1. Be the lawyer you'd want to hire. That's good advice no matter who the client is or what the engagement is. *See* **Chapter 7 at 172**.

2. **Model Rule 1.1** codifies the **duty of competence** and requires competent representation. Sometimes, "competence" just means the ability to analyze and research solutions to a problem; other times, it'll require highly specialized skills and knowledge. Your job is to identify whether you have the skills and knowledge to serve your client, whether you can acquire them with the amount of time and effort you're willing and able to expend to do so, whether you need to work with someone else who has the skills and knowledge that you don't (yet) have, or whether prudence dictates that you turn down the engagement. You can be "**competent**" doing things that you've never done before, so long as you apply a reasonable combination of your own research and more experienced backstopping. *See* **Chapter 7.A at 172**.

3. You **must** *stay* **competent** by keeping abreast of changes in the law and in practice technology. *See* **Chapter 7.A at 179**.

4. **Competence** also involves proper use of forms and examples. Before you use a form, think about which parts of the form might apply to whatever drafting you're doing, think about which ones won't apply, and make sure that you understand every term so that you can tailor the form to your client's needs. *See* **Chapter 7.A at 175**.

5. **Model Rule 1.3** codifies the **duty of diligence** and requires you to be reasonably diligent and prompt. Develop your own "to-do" checklist and your own calendaring system, in addition to or in combination with any such systems that your employer uses, to make sure that you remember and leave yourself enough time to complete whatever tasks are on your to-do list. *See* **Chapter 7.A at 178**.

6. The **duty of care** requires you to exercise reasonable care in your professional endeavors. When you're a lawyer, you'll be holding yourself out as having specialized knowledge, so you must exercise *a level of skill, diligence, and care, and possess (or acquire) a level of knowledge, that a*

reasonably careful and prudent lawyer would exercise or possess under the same or similar circumstances. See **Chapter 7.B at 181**.

7. If you were to violate the **duty of competence** or **diligence**, you'd be subject to professional discipline, and the disciplining authority doesn't need to prove actual harm. If you were to violate the **duty of care**, though, you'd be subject to a lawsuit for professional negligence, which can involve some hefty monetary damages against you personally or against your law firm, if such damages can be proved. Just because you didn't achieve the result that the client wanted doesn't mean that you violated your **duty of care**. But do yourself a favor: Don't promise what you can't deliver. Promising what you can't (and don't) deliver can set you up for a nasty lawsuit for breach of contract. *See* **Chapter 7.B at 181**.

8. Criminal defense lawyers have a special set of competence, diligence, and care obligations, referred to as the duty of **effective assistance of criminal defense counsel**, imposed by the Sixth Amendment (and similar provisions in many state constitutions). **Effective assistance of counsel** is governed by two alternative tests:
   a. The *Strickland* "deficiency and prejudice" test requires the criminal defense client claiming **ineffective assistance of counsel** to prove that (1) defense counsel did (or failed to do) something in defending the accused that no reasonable defense lawyer would have done (or failed to do); *and* (2) there was a reasonable probability that the case would have come out differently had counsel done what any reasonable defense lawyer would have done. *See* **Chapter 7.C at 185**.
   b. The *Cronic* test looks at whether the defendant was in (or defense counsel created) a situation in which *no* competent lawyer could have provided constitutionally **effective assistance**—but such cases are rare. *See* **Chapter 7.C at 191**.

9. A criminal defense lawyer who has provided **ineffective assistance** can, of course, be subject to professional discipline, but criminal defense clients will only be able to support a tort action against their (former) defense counsel if they can show that they were actually innocent and the lawyer's error or omission more likely than not caused the client not to be acquitted. *See* **Chapter 7.C at 194**.

Multiple-Choice Review Questions for Chapter 7

1. Lawyer Liam is an experienced trust and estates attorney. Business has been a bit slow, so he decides to branch out and accept a slip-and-fall case on behalf of a client who fell outside a United States

Postal Service station. Liam accepts the case one year and nine months from the date of the fall. He explains to the client that this is his first tort case.

Liam does not realize that the Federal Tort Claims Act applies and that there is a jurisdictional requirement to exhaust administrative remedies prior to filing in court. He files his complaint in court on the eve of the two-year statute of limitations, but he tenders no administrative claim. The court dismisses the complaint with prejudice for failure to exhaust administrative remedies. Liam's client is now out of time to exhaust her administrative remedies.

Has Liam violated **Model Rule 1.1**?

a. Yes. Liam was an experienced trust and estates lawyer but inexperienced in tort cases. He could only handle a slip-and-fall case if he worked with more experienced co-counsel.

b. Yes. Liam had a responsibility to educate himself enough to handle the representation, which would have included researching and understanding the application of the Federal Tort Claims Act.

c. No. Liam is charged with knowing only what an average lawyer would know. Because the Federal Tort Claims Act is not usually addressed in a first-year Torts class, a lawyer is not charged with knowing the nuances of this law.

d. No. Liam notified the client of his experience level. The client selected Liam as her lawyer notwithstanding his inexperience and therefore could only expect performance in line with his experience.

2. Mary is barred in Pennsylvania. She has never handled a medical malpractice case. A client approaches her about filing a case in Ohio. The last time that Mary had any legal education relating to this topic was her 1L Torts class.

Mary is admitted to the Ohio court where the case is filed *pro hac vice* on the motion of her local counsel, an Ohio attorney who then has no further involvement in the case. Mary is bright, motivated, and hardworking. She devotes sufficient time to bring herself up to speed and litigates the case through to summary judgment. Her performance is generally excellent.

Unfortunately, Mary's client ultimately loses because Mary was unaware of a particularity to the statute of limitations that is unique to Ohio law. Because of this detail, summary judgment is granted for the defendant. Unbeknownst to Mary, the statute of limitations had already passed before she even accepted the case.

Has Mary violated **Model Rule 1.1**?

a. Yes. Mary did not properly educate herself before undertaking the representation. The fact that her performance was generally good is irrelevant; she should have discovered the statute of limitations issue before expending the client's resources in litigating the case.

b. Yes. Mary should have required the Ohio-barred attorney to remain more involved in the case. Mary's failure to do so is the direct cause of the client's claim being lost.

c. No. The lawyer who got Mary admitted *pro hac vice* is at fault, but Mary is not. That lawyer should have educated Mary about any particularities of Ohio law.

d. No. There was no prejudice to Mary's client because the claim was not viable at the time that Mary undertook the representation.

3. Lawyer Leanne works for a law firm. Pursuant to the firm's procedures, Leanne's legal assistant enters key deadlines into Leanne's calendar for her.

Leanne has filed a motion in a securities case. Once the other side responds with an opposition, she will have an opportunity to file a reply. Leanne attends a status conference, and the judge orally changes some deadlines. Leanne forgets to alert her legal assistant, so the dates are never changed in Leanne's calendar. Due to the omission, Leanne fails to timely file her reply.

She realizes the error a few days later and requests permission to file a late reply. The court permits her to do so. Ultimately, Leanne's motion is granted.

Has Leanne violated **Model Rule 1.3**?

a. Yes. Leanne had an obligation to timely file the reply regardless of how her firm handled the internal scheduling of response dates.

b. Yes. Leanne had an obligation to calendar the reply date if she wasn't going to communicate the new date to her legal assistant.

c. No. Leanne filed the reply a few days later, and that passage of time was insignificant.

d. No. The court allowed Leanne to file the reply, and her client ultimately won that motion.

4. Alan is a solo practitioner assisted by a paralegal. Typically, his paralegal sends out his correspondence. The paralegal is off one day, and Alan sends out a draft contract to opposing counsel. Alan forgets to scrub the metadata from the draft, and as a result, opposing counsel can see the communications between Alan and his client as they exchanged comments on the draft contract. Those comments included details about the client's business that the client was adamant be kept **confidential**.

Has Alan violated **Model Rule 1.1**?

a. Yes. A lawyer **must** keep abreast of technology, including the fact that metadata may disclose lawyer-client communications.

b. Yes. **Model Rule 1.1** requires that a lawyer supervise subordinates, including the paralegal here.

c. No. **Model Rule 1.1** applies to the substance of legal action, not to procedural matters.

d. No. The disclosure of the client's **confidential information** caused no monetary harm.

5. What is one major difference between the **duties of competence** and **diligence**, on one hand, and the **duty of care**, on the other?

a. The **duties of competence** and **diligence** can be violated only where there is pecuniary harm to the client.

b. The **duties of competence** and **diligence** can be violated only where there is pecuniary harm to the lawyer.

c. The **consequence** for violation of the **duties of competence** and **diligence** is professional discipline, but the **consequence** for violation of the **duty of care** can be a civil claim for malpractice.

d. The **consequence** for violation of the **duties of competence** and **diligence** can be a civil claim for malpractice, but the **consequence** for violation of the **duty of care** is professional discipline.

6. Lawyer Louise has been litigating a breach of contract case. Despite her best efforts, she loses at trial.

After the verdict is read, Louise's client is upset. He turns to her and complains that she should have been more aggressive at trial. He tells her that she should have impeached a key witness for the other side. Louise did not impeach the witness. As a strategic matter, she thought it would be unhelpful to the client's case. She discussed this thoroughly with the client in advance, and the client had begrudgingly agreed to Louise's strategy.

Will the client prevail in a civil suit for legal malpractice?

a. Yes. The client lost the case, and Louise failed to impeach a witness. These actions constitute a violation of the **duty of care**.

b. Maybe. The client will need to demonstrate both a violation of the **duty of care** and that the violation caused the loss of the case. The mere fact that the case was lost or that Louise failed to impeach a witness is insufficient.

c. Maybe. The client will need to demonstrate that the decision as to whether to impeach the witness was a decision for the client and not the lawyer.

d. No. The client has not been prejudiced.

7. When does a defendant's constitutional right to **effective assistance of counsel** apply in criminal cases?
   a. After formal proceedings have been filed against the defendant.
   b. At trial.
   c. During an appeal.
   d. All of the above.

8. Lawyer Larry is appointed to defend Client Christopher, who is accused of criminal sexual assault. Larry meets with Christopher. Christopher claims that it is a case of mistaken identity, and that his sister, Suzanne, will provide him with a complete alibi.

   Larry does not believe Christopher. Larry feels strongly that Christopher is a danger to the community and should be imprisoned. Larry never meets with Suzanne and refuses to call her to testify at trial.

   Larry sits through the entirety of Christopher's trial. Larry is on time every day. Larry says nothing as the prosecution admits improper evidence. He simply sits in silence. He fails to raise numerous legal arguments that might result in a defense verdict. He puts on no defense case. He does not even call Christopher to testify. In closing, Larry simply argues that the prosecution failed to meet its burden of proof. The jury finds Christopher guilty.

   When Christopher tries to appeal the verdict, he learns that Larry's failure to object and raise legal arguments has waived those issues on appeal.

   Did Larry violate his duty to provide **effective assistance of counsel**? If so, in what way?
   a. Yes. He failed to call Suzanne to testify and failed to present a defense case. Suzanne would have provided testimony that could have exonerated Christopher.
   b. Yes. He failed to object to inadmissible evidence. This could have altered the outcome of the case and he was obligated to preserve the objection.
   c. No. He was present for all phases of trial.
   d. No. He was entitled to make the strategic decision whether to offer Suzanne's testimony or not.

9. For purposes of proving the element of prejudice for an **ineffective assistance of counsel** claim, what must be proven?
   a. The defendant must prove that defense counsel did something that no reasonable lawyer would have done.
   b. The defendant must prove that, but for defense counsel's error, it is reasonably likely that the result of the proceeding would have differed.

    c. The prosecution must prove that defense counsel's conduct was what a reasonable lawyer would have done.

    d. The prosecution must prove that, notwithstanding the error, the result of the proceeding would have been the same.

10. Danny serves as defense counsel in a felony criminal case. He oversleeps and misses his client's sentencing. His client, who is a first-time offender with significant mitigation evidence to present at sentencing, is sentenced well above the guidelines' maximum.

    If his client later asserts an **ineffective assistance of counsel** claim flowing from the harsh sentence imposed, will the client have to prove prejudice?

    a. Yes. The client must show both prejudice and an error by counsel.

    b. Yes. The client could have presented his own mitigation evidence.

    c. No. Danny could have committed no error because he was not present.

    d. No. Failure to attend a critical phase of trial is *per se* **ineffective**.

8

The Duty of Confidentiality

MAYA FINDS ONE of her supervising partners, Ron Rainmaker, in good spirits. "Today's a good day," he greets her. "What's going on?" Maya asks. "Well, I just got a call from Petrified Petroleum," Ron explains. "It's a petroleum-products supplier that has a broad relationship with Mojo Manufacturing to supply raw materials. The two of them have a big-dollar commercial dispute over the quality and timing of a series of deliveries. Petrified Petroleum is looking for litigation counsel."

Maya is a little confused. "Wait," she says. "I've heard of Mojo Manufacturing. Isn't it a client of the firm in several pending matters? We can't represent someone suing a current client of ours like Mojo, can we? And besides, you're not even a litigator; you do transactional work. Why is any of this good news for you?"

"Right on all three counts," Ron confirms, "but it's still a good day for me. Mojo's one of our best clients, which means they're really going to appreciate it when I call the Chief Operating Officer and let him know that Petrified is gunning for them. What's more, the general counsel of Petrified told me some of his concerns about the dispute—details about some of their vulnerabilities on the merits, and some of his management's business concerns about how Petrified would prefer to litigate or settle the thing. Imagine how Mojo's going to appreciate getting the inside scoop—it'll hire us to handle the case for sure, and maybe give us some other work besides!

"And as for the fact that I'm not a litigator and wouldn't be handling the case," Ron continues, "it's time you learned a little more about how law firms like ours work. See, our continuing existence depends on our ability to keep bringing new client work in the door, so everyone here keeps billing hours, and we keep earning income through fees as we finish up the work we already have. That's how we have the money to keep paying your exorbitant salary." They both grin. "To create incentives to bring in new work, we have a partner compensation system that is like many other law firms' systems—a significant part of what every partner gets paid depends on how much business he or she brought to the firm in the prior year. It's called 'origination credit'—credit for originating the work at the firm.

I don't have to *do* the work to get origination credit, and I don't have to be the only partner involved in bringing it in. In fact, this kind of origination is *better* for me—I pass the work on to a litigation partner who has the time to do it, and I still have time to do the transactional work that other clients ask me to handle myself while getting part of the credit for the revenue that the litigation matter brings to the firm. So y'see, this really is a good day for me."

Maya now understands why Ron Rainmaker is excited, but she remains somewhat unsettled. Is Ron headed for trouble?

A. The Scope and Nature of the Duty of Confidentiality

1. Introduction

The lawyer's **duty of confidentiality** is ancient. It was recognized in England under Elizabeth I, back in the sixteenth century, and it has been a fixed star in legal ethics and the law of lawyering here in the United States for centuries as well.[1]

The **duty of confidentiality** is venerated in terms reserved for few other lawyer obligations. It and the distinct but related **attorney-client privilege** have been called a "necessity"[2] that "promote[s] broad[] public interests in the observance of law and administration of justice."[3] The two are "rooted in the imperative need for confidence and trust . . . [and] rest[] on the need for the advocate and counselor to know all that relates to the client's reasons for seeking representation."[4]

REASON FOR THE RULE So what's the big deal? In a regulatory state like twenty-first-century America, detailed and technical requirements for business and industry abound, many of which carry serious **consequences** for their violation. And as you've certainly learned by now, even basic principles of tort, contract, property, and criminal law are often challenging to apply to real-world situations. Sometimes clients come to us needing to know how to conduct their affairs in compliance with the law (or whether what they've done or are planning to do is illegal) and what the **consequences** might be. Just as often, clients come to us accused of wrongdoing—sometimes serious wrongdoing. Sometimes they have been accused unfairly or out of proportion with whatever they actually did, and sometimes the accusations are entirely justified. Still other times, clients come to us believing that they have been wronged, but unsure about what they can prove and whether the justice system can provide them any redress. But in all events, they need our skill and knowledge to help them respond to the situation, to counsel

---

[1] *See, e.g.,* Geoffrey C. Hazard, Jr., *An Historical Perspective on the Lawyer-Client Privilege*, 66 CALIF. L. Rev. 1061, 1069-80 (1978).

[2] *Hunt v. Blackburn*, 128 U.S. 464, 470 (1888).

[3] *Upjohn Co. v. United States*, 449 U.S. 383, 389 (1981).

[4] *Trammel v. United States*, 445 U.S. 40, 51 (1980).

them on their duties and the best way to protect their rights, and to help them cope with the potential **consequences** when they get it wrong.

We can only rarely give our clients complete and informed advice unless they are prepared to tell us everything that might matter, no matter how embarrassing, incriminating, or otherwise inimical to their interests that information might be. And they'll never tell us everything that we need to know without being assured that we won't let that information fall into the hands of their adversaries. It's no accident that "confidence" means both "secret" ("I will keep your confidences") and "trust" ("you can have confidence that I will keep your confidences"). From this point of view, a strong **duty of confidentiality** not only "contributes to the trust that is the hallmark of the client-lawyer relationship" (**Model Rule 1.6 Comment [2]**), this shield for lawyer-client candor often makes it possible to provide complete and reliable advice about law-abiding conduct and the **consequences** of not following that advice. And without clients' ability to seek, and our ability to offer, that advice freely, voluntary lawfulness and the rule of law itself would likely suffer. *Id.*

Although there is a good deal of merit to these justifications of lawyer **confidentiality**, however, they are usually overstated. As we will see, the **duty of confidentiality** has always been a lot *less* impermeable than our self-congratulatory speeches typically suggest. There are multiple exceptions to the duty—occasions when we either **may** or **must** violate our clients' confidences in the service of some other interest—most of them arising when our clients would most want us *not* to do so. Half of this chapter (**Chapter 8.B at 235**) will be devoted to figuring out when and why some of those exceptions apply.

And secrets have a dark side. The ability and obligation to keep clients' secrets is also the ability, and the obligation, to withhold or conceal the truth. And those from whom the truth must be withheld often are people, such as regulators, law-enforcement officers, factfinders, and the victims of our clients' alleged wrongs, who have a serious and legitimate need to know. So though lawyer confidentiality is powerful and pervasive, and its justifications are substantial and serious, its consequences are not always pretty, and the **duty of confidentiality** is not absolute. REASON FOR THE RULE

Now prepare yourself: The **duty of confidentiality** is very broad and very powerful, affects a great deal of the information that you accumulate and learn in your practice, and is enforceable through a wide range of very serious **consequences**. It is an issue that comes up in almost every area of legal practice almost every day, and the stakes for compliance are high. So you really need to understand it. Unfortunately, this subject has many twists and turns. The boundaries of the duty as to both time and substantive coverage are sometimes difficult to determine and can vary from state to state. The scope of the duty differs depending on to whom it's owed, who is enforcing it, and what **consequence** is sought for its violation. The duty is easily confused with its sister doctrines, the **attorney-client privilege** and the **attorney work product doctrine**, but it is quite different in its scope and effect from either (just as they're quite different from one another). And it has multiple exceptions, each of them uncertain in its scope and complex in its application.

We have a lot of work to do here. Stick with us; we've got your back.

2. The Scope of the Duty of Confidentiality

Let's start by figuring out to whom the **duty of confidentiality** is owed, when it starts and ends, what information it covers, and what it requires us to do (or not do). We'll address each of those scope limits in order.

a. To Whom Is the Duty of Confidentiality Owed, and When Does It Start?

Read **Model Rule 1.6(a)** and **Model Rule 1.6 Comment [1]**; **Model Rule 1.8(b)** and **Comment [5]**; **Model Rule 1.9(c)** and **Model Rule 1.9 Comment [1]**; and **Model Rule 1.18(a) and (b)** and **Model Rule 1.18 Comments [1] and [2]**. Although all of the ethics rules are extremely important, Rules 1.6, 1.9, and 1.18 are among the most central to your day-to-day life as a lawyer. What those rules show us is that the **duty of confidentiality** is owed to three distinct categories of actors: **current clients**, **former clients**, and **prospective clients**.[5]

i. Current Clients

Current clients, obviously, are the people and organizations we currently represent. **Model Rule 1.6(a)** tells us so by requiring that a lawyer "shall not [that is, **must not**] reveal information relating to the representation of a client," which **Model Rule 1.6 Comment [1]** helpfully explains governs "disclosure . . . during the lawyer's representation of the client." **Model Rule 1.8(b)** adds a prohibition against *use* of a **current client's** information to the client's disadvantage. We'll discuss the details of how and when an attorney-client relationship is formed and ended in **Chapters 9.A at 257** and **9.D at 286**. But it will suffice for now to say that, though it isn't always as clear as we'd like it to be, we usually know who our clients are. And if they are our **current clients**, then we owe them a **duty of confidentiality**.

ii. Former Clients

Former clients, as the name suggests, are people and organizations whom we *used to* represent, but no longer do. *See* **Model Rule 1.9(c)** and **Model Rule 1.9 Comment [1]**. Again, we'll discuss in **Chapter 9.D at 286** how we know when an attorney-client relationship has ended, but it will suffice for now to say that, though it's not always

---

[5] We also owe the **duty of confidentiality** to a fourth category of persons and organizations—*non*-clients to whom we voluntarily create such duties. How and when that happens is discussed in **Chapter 9.B at 268**. That topic will make a lot more sense after we've talked about the much more common situations that we're about to address.

beyond argument, we often have a pretty good idea when our engagements are over and our **current clients** have become **former** ones.

iii. Prospective Clients

Prospective clients, in contrast, are *not* our clients. They are defined in **Model Rule 1.18(a)** as "person[s] who consult[] with a lawyer about the possibility of forming a client-lawyer relationship with respect to a matter. . . ." **Prospective clients** may eventually become **current clients**—if you think about it, most **current** and **former clients** were **prospective clients** first, at least briefly—but they may never become clients at all. Either the lawyer or the **prospective client** may decide, after "consult[ing] . . . about the possibility of forming a client-lawyer relationship," that the relationship should not be formed, and for any number of reasons. These reasons could include the **prospective client's** preference for someone else (yes, many clients shop around, and they have every right to do so), the lawyer's lack of time or relevant expertise to handle the matter, or a failure to reach consensus on mutually acceptable goals or fees for the engagement. But **prospective clients' confidentiality** is protected "*[e]ven when no client-lawyer relationship ensues. . . .*" **Model Rule 1.18(b)** (emphasis added). The key to **prospective client** status is "consultation with [the] lawyer about the possibility of forming a client-lawyer relationship with respect to a matter," whether or not the preliminary consultation actually ripens into an engagement.

It's worth noting that someone can be your **current client** with respect to some engagements and your **former client** with respect to others. (And, for that matter, your **prospective client** with respect to yet others.) That's because we define our attorney-client relationships by subject matter, so a lawyer can have several distinct and different relationships with the same client. When we agree to represent a client, usually it is not an undertaking to handle everything that may ever arise for that person or organization, but rather an agreement to handle or advise about a particular situation or set of related situations: a dispute; a transaction; a business's labor and employment issues (but not, say, its securities or tax issues). The Model Rules often refer to this defined scope of an engagement as a "matter," and we will use that terminology sometimes, too (as well as the common synonyms "engagement" and "representation"). We will further discuss how the scope of an engagement is defined, and how important it is to define it, in **Chapter 9.A at 262**.

> Problem 8A-1: Which of the following persons are Frank's **current clients**, **former clients**, and/or **prospective clients**? Pick all that apply, and explain why:
>
> a. Frank is counsel of record for the plaintiff in a pending personal injury action. (By the way, what does it mean to be "counsel of record" in an engagement? How do you know when you are?)

b. The personal injury action in (a) settles, the settlement documentation is signed, the settlement money is paid, and the action is dismissed. What is the plaintiff's client status now?

c. A few months after the completion of the settlement described in (b), the injured person calls Frank and says, "I'm thinking of revising my will to deal with the settlement money that you got me. Does anyone in your office do estate planning?" What is the former plaintiff's client status at that moment?

Problem 8A-2: Review the hypothetical in **this chapter's Introduction at 203**. Is Mojo Manufacturing a **current client**, **a former client**, or a **prospective client** (select any and all that apply)? What about Petrified Petroleum? What does your answer tell you about what Ron Rainmaker **must** or **must not** do, and why?

Problem 8A-3: One of the partners in Frank's firm, Sally Splitsville, specializes in family law. The mayor of the town in which Frank works comes in to see her. The mayor confides that she is thinking about divorce and is looking for a lawyer to represent her. After the mayor discusses her marital situation and her legal and practical concerns with Sally in some detail, the mayor decides that she's not ready to hire a divorce lawyer. With whom **may** Sally discuss what she's learned that day? What are the likely **consequences**, formal and informal, if she lets some juicy details slip out at happy hour? Explain your answer.

TAMING THE TEXT Sometimes it's easy to know when someone is consulting with you in contemplation of possible representation and thus is a **prospective client** to whom you owe a **duty of confidentiality**. Problem 8A-2 and Problem 8A-3 are classic examples of easy calls. But sometimes the situation is more ambiguous. So how do we know when someone is a **prospective client** and thus is owed a **duty of confidentiality**? **Model Rule 1.18 Comment [2]** tells us that whether communications with a lawyer amount to a consultation in contemplation of possible representation depends on the involved persons' mutual manifestations of intent in light of all of the surrounding facts and circumstances.

One useful way of summarizing a test that many jurisdictions use is whether the person communicating with the lawyer (the putative **prospective client**, we might say) *actually and reasonably believes it is a consultation in contemplation of possible representation.* This test has both a subjective element (the putative **prospective client** must actually subjectively think that she is talking to the lawyer because she is really considering hiring the lawyer), and an objective element (the putative **prospective client's** belief must be objectively reasonable, viewed from outside the putative **prospective client's** head). **Model Rule 1.18 Comment [2]** provides a couple of examples: People are likely to be considered **prospective clients** if they respond after a lawyer "specifically requests or invites the submission of information about a potential representation without clear and reasonably understandable warnings and cautionary statements that limit the lawyer's obligations." In contrast, people are unlikely to be considered **prospective clients** if they "commu-nicate[] information unilaterally to a lawyer, without any reasonable expectation that the lawyer is willing to discuss the possibility of forming a client-lawyer relationship . . . ," such as "in response to advertising that merely describes the lawyer's education, experience, areas of practice, and contact information, or provides legal information of general interest." TAMING THE TEXT

TIPS & TACTICS Because this test (which you should remember from here on, as it's similar to the test for whether someone has actually become your client, *see* **Chapter 9.A at 259**) focuses in part on what the person claiming a **duty of confidentiality** should reasonably understand from the circumstances, **Model Rule 1.18 Comment [2]** reminds us of the significance of "clear and reasonably understandable warnings and cautionary statements that limit the lawyer's obligations." *You* are the person who understands what a lawyer's duties are and when they are owed, so it should not surprise you that the law expects *you* to make it clear to nonlawyers what they should expect from you. And you need to think about whether you're dealing with people whom you may not be able to trust to relate their state of mind honestly later or to reasonably interpret situations that seem commonplace to you, so that you can take appropriate precautions. TIPS & TACTICS

> Problem 8A-4: Same as **Problem 8A-3 at 208** (the mayor speaks to Sally Splitsville about her potential divorce), except that Sally discovers that the mayor has "interviewed" every respected family lawyer in the county, disclosing only that she is considering divorce and asking each lawyer what his or her "philosophy of practice" is. **May** the partner tell her friends at happy hour that the mayor is having marital problems? (*Hint: See* ABA Formal Ethics Op. No. 492 at 3.) **Should** she? Please explain your answers.

> Problem 8A-5: Maya is attending a cocktail gathering at a neighbor's place. (a) She strikes up a conversation with someone she vaguely recognizes as living in the same apartment building as hers. (b) He quickly turns the conversation to the "mother of all divorces from hell" that he is going through. (c) He tells Maya that he thinks his lawyer is doing a lousy job. (d) He describes several pieces of advice that his lawyer has given him and asks Maya what she thinks. (e) Maya asks follow-up questions and (f) comments on each piece of advice about which her conversation partner is complaining. After each lettered piece of the conversation, what risk does Maya have of finding herself owing duties to the person to whom she's talking, and why? What duties might she owe the aspiring divorcé?

As these problems illustrate, ordinary social conversation concerning a person's law-related difficulties will not always turn that person into a **current client** or a **prospective client**, both because the nonlawyer isn't thinking about the conver-sation in that way (though he may say something different later), and because a reasonable person in the client's position wouldn't see a conversation in this context as involving an interview of potential counsel. Similarly, a person who tries to "lick all the cookies on the plate" and pretends to interview every good lawyer in town so that her adversary can't hire any of them (*see* **Model Rule 1.18(c)**) fails the subjective test—she wasn't really seeking a lawyer so much as seeking to deprive her adversary of one. **Model Rule 1.18 Comment [2]**.

REAL WORLD   TIPS & TACTICS The test for whether strangers have become **prospective clients** (or for that matter **current clients**, *see* **Chapter 9.A at 260**) is inherently fuzzy. It depends on what others may be thinking or might reasonably understand under all of the surrounding facts and circumstances—or what they might say that they were thinking or understood later. It thus is subject to uncertainty about what other people over whom you have no control were thinking, and subject to argument about what the surrounding facts and circumstances do or don't reasonably indicate. Uncertainty brings risk—the risk that others understand the situation differently from the way that you do or will portray the facts or their intentions opportunistically at a later date, or that a factfinder will understand the facts differently from the way that you did.

There's a simple, practical approach that helps you avoid, or at least manage, these risks—one that we've recommended to you in similar circumstances:

When in doubt, speak out.

Then **inquire**; **explain**; **confirm** (*see* **Chapter 6.A at 139**).

There are lots of polite ways to make it clear that you're not looking for a client during a conversation. For example, you can say that the law-related subject that someone is raising with you is not an area in which you practice: "I'm not a family lawyer, and I never handle divorces, but that does sound like a tough situation." Or if you might consider taking your conversational companion on as a client, and invite a real consultation at some other time, when you can check for **conflicts of interest** first (*see* **Chapter 22.F at 756**; what if someone in your firm already represents the party guest's wife?) and after that, if appropriate, give the potential matter your undivided professional attention: "We need to be careful talking about this kind of thing in public and before I know whether I might have a **conflict of interest**, but if you'd like me to take a look, here's my card. Come by my office next week, and we'll talk."

Be aware of your entrepreneurial instincts' natural drive to win clients, make friends, and influence people. It's a very good thing to have such instincts, and you should cultivate them. But you also have to manage them. If you leave anything to chance, the risk—and the potential **consequences**—are yours. REAL WORLD   TIPS & TACTICS

b. What Must Be Treated as Confidential Information Protected by the Duty of Confidentiality?

Now that we know to whom the **duty of confidentiality** is owed, let's explore what kinds of information it protects. Lawyers often refer to information subject to the

duty of confidentiality as "**confidential information**," "**client confidences**," or "**client confidential information**," and we'll use those phrases in that sense in this book, too. Although these phrases are accurately descriptive and frequently used, they appear nowhere in the Model Rules of Professional Conduct. The Rules instead use several other phrases to describe information protected by the **duty of confidentiality**, and you should remember them so that you can recognize them when they come up in the Rules. We'll give you those phrases in the next section. Remember: The scope of the information protected by the **duty of confidentiality** may differ depending on to whom the duty is owed and the **consequence** being sought.

i. The General Scope of the Duty of Confidentiality: *Any* "Information Relating to the Representation of a Client" Received from *Any* Source

Confidential information is described in **Model Rule 1.6(a)** and elsewhere as "information relating to the representation of a client."[6] Other Model Rules denote **confidential information** with the phrase "information protected by Rule 1.6" or "Rule 1.9" (which specifically addresses the **duty of confidentiality** to **former clients**); "information whose disclosure is prohibited by Rule 1.6," or "Rule 1.9"; or words to similar effect.[7]

TAMING THE TEXT ▶ Let's pause and take a hard look at the defining phrase "information relating to the representation of a client." First, we need to talk about how incredibly broad it is; then we'll explore the limits of its reach.

Let's start with its breadth: The **duty of confidentiality** is *not* limited to what the client confides to you; it includes almost *anything* pertaining to your engagement that you learn from *any* source, including from witnesses, documents, or your own investigation or research. It even includes the identity of a client or **prospective client** and the fact that you represent, represented, or considered representing that client. (Do you see why?) *See* **Model Rule 1.6 Comment [3]**. And, amazingly enough, even though we commonly refer to information subject to the **duty of confidentiality** as "**confidential information**," it does *not* have to be "confidential" in the conventional sense of being secret in order to be subject to the **duty of confidentiality**. If it "relat[es] to the representation of a client," then (within limits that we're about to discuss) you are duty-bound to treat it as **confidential information**, even if somebody else doesn't. ◀ TAMING THE TEXT

---

[6] *See* **Model Rules 1.6(a), (b), (c)**; **Model Rule 1.8(b)** (delineating the **duty of confidentiality** owed to current clients); **Model Rule 1.8(f) (3)** (requiring the lawyer to protect the client's **confidential information** when someone other than the client is paying the lawyer).
[7] *See, e.g.,* **Model Rules 1.9(b)(2), (c)** (delineating the **duty of confidentiality** owed to **former clients**); **Model Rule 1.10(b)(2)** (defining one circumstance in which a lawyer's **duty of confidentiality** is **imputed** to that lawyer's entire **practice organization**); **Model Rule 1.13(c)** (allowing disclosure of **confidential information** to protect an organization client against wrongs committed by its constituents); **Model Rule 2.3(c)** (confirming that information pertaining to the preparation of an "evaluation of a matter for the use of someone other than the client"—such as an opinion of counsel in a transaction—remains **confidential information** despite disclosure of the "evaluation"); **Model Rule 3.3(c)** (requiring disclosure of **confidential information** if necessary to correct a misrepresentation to a tribunal); **Model Rule 4.1(b)** (requiring correction of a misrepresentation to a third party to avoid "assisting" a client in a crime or fraud, unless the correction requires unauthorized disclosure of **confidential information**); **Model Rule 8.3(c)** (requiring reporting of serious ethical violations by other lawyers or judges unless the reporting requires unauthorized disclosure of **confidential information**).

Problem 8A-6: **Mess in the Press:** On the night of February 26, 2012, a Florida man named George Zimmerman shot and killed a 17-year-old African American named Trayvon Martin in a predominantly white neighborhood in Sanford, Florida. Martin was unarmed. The incident received broad attention from the press nationwide and was intensely controversial: Zimmerman (and many commentators) claimed that he had shot in self-defense; Martin's family (and many commentators) asserted that Zimmerman had racially profiled Martin and then engaged in a gratuitously violent, racist act, which they linked to increasingly widespread attention to shootings in many locales of unarmed young Black men.

Zimmerman was eventually charged with Martin's murder. Zimmerman's investigation and later prosecution was a very high-profile and challenging case, and there was widespread interest among Florida's criminal defense bar in representing Zimmerman. While the state of Florida's investigation was still pending and before any charges were handed up, Zimmerman reportedly agreed to be represented by two Florida criminal defense lawyers. Before the Special Prosecutor appointed by the Florida governor had made any charging decisions, those lawyers called a widely covered press conference in which they announced that they were withdrawing from representing Zimmerman. According to contemporaneous press reports, in the course of that press conference, they asserted:

a. The lawyers had previously spoken daily with Mr. Zimmerman but recently had "lost contact" with him and were worried about his emotional state. "He's gone on his own," said one of the lawyers. "I'm not sure what he's doing or who he's talking to."

b. The other lawyer said, "George Zimmerman, in our opinion, and from information made available to us, is not doing well emotionally, probably suffering from post-traumatic stress syndrome." He added that the pressure might have "pushed him a little over the edge and [Zimmerman] thought, 'I'm going to take care of it myself [referring to recent steps that Zimmerman had taken without consulting with his lawyers].'"

c. The lawyers argued at length that Zimmerman had acted in self-defense and without racial motivation. Said one, "There's no evidence since the day the Earth cooled whatsoever that George Zimmerman ever has been racially motivated."

d. The first lawyer asserted that Zimmerman had gone into hiding, and that no one knew where he was. The other lawyer said that those looking for Zimmerman "can stop looking in Florida," but the first lawyer stated he was "reasonably sure" that Zimmerman was still in the United States.

e. Zimmerman had contacted Fox News commentator Sean Hannity to discuss the incident, despite having been advised by his lawyers not to speak with anyone.

f. "The last straw," said one of the lawyers, was when they learned that Zimmerman had contacted the Special Prosecutor handling his matter and offered to come in on his own and answer questions.[8]

g. "Our thought process is, we're professionals," one of the lawyers told the gathered reporters. "We do this for a living. We try to do a good job of it, but we are not going to

---

[8] The prosecutor reportedly declined to speak with Zimmerman. Can you guess why? *See* **Chapter 11 at 341.**

put ourselves out to the public . . . unless he makes it clear to us that he wants us as his lawyers." The lawyers stated they would resume representing Zimmerman if he asked.[9]

So were these attorneys Knuckleheads or Big Freaking Knuckleheads? Now that we've gotten that out of our systems, let's talk a little more dispassionately (and compassionately) about how and why.

Let's start by emphasizing that, although this is a controversial event and many of you likely have extremely strong feelings about it, this discussion is not about those feelings or any of the very real issues that gave rise to them. It's about how these lawyers seriously violated their clear ethical obligations and what might have caused them to do so. We are not, of course, suggesting that the issues that Trayvon Martin's killing raised—or your views about those issues—are not important. They're incredibly important. But it's also important to be able to analyze dispassionately issues about which you have strong feelings, and to appreciate how your strong feelings or a hot public spotlight may cloud your vision about your legal and ethical obligations, which appears to be just what happened to these lawyers in this case.

Now, examine each of the lettered sets of statements in context. What professional duty or duties does each statement violate, and why? What are the implications for their **former client** of each statement that the lawyers made (and why are we referring to him as a **former client**)? What are the potential **consequences** for the lawyers? What might have motivated these lawyers to call this press conference and make these statements? Try and tie a specific motivation to specific statements. How could those motivations have affected their abilities to appreciate the nature and consequences of their actions?

Having discussed the exceptionally broad scope of **confidential client information**, now let's discuss its limits: The **duty of confidentiality** does not extend to *everything* "relating to the representation of a client." There are three important restrictions on the scope of **confidential information**.[10]

ii. Limit on the Scope of the Duty of Confidentiality: For a Prospective Client, Only Information "Learned . . . from [the] Prospective Client" Is Protected, Rather Than *Any* Information Relating to the Potential Representation

TAMING THE TEXT The very broad definition of **confidential information** as "information relating to the *representation of a client*" (emphasis added) applies, consistent with **Model Rule 1.6(a)'s** and **Model Rule 1.9(c)'s** explicit terms, only to information

---

[9] *See* http://www.foxnews.com/us/2012/04/10/zimmermans-lawyers-withdraw-from-shooting-case/; https://news.blogs.cnn.com/2012/04/10/zimmerman-attorneys-to-speak/.

[10] Don't confuse these *limitations* on the scope of the **duty of confidentiality** with the *exceptions* to the duty that are catalogued in **Model Rule 1.6(b)**, and which will be discussed the second half of this chapter. The *exceptions* allow the use or disclosure of information for various purposes *despite* the fact that the information is **confidential information** and is protected by the **duty of confidentiality**. In contrast, the *restrictions* that we are discussing here are limits on what is considered **confidential information** in the first place.

relating to actual "representation of a client"—that is, **current clients** and **former clients**. Where the source of the information is from a **prospective client, Model Rule 1.18(b)** more narrowly protects only information "learned . . . *from a prospective client*" (emphasis added). That would exclude information that the lawyer might learn from sources *other* than the **prospective client** (such as third-party witnesses or documents received from someone other than the **prospective client**, or the lawyer's own investigation or research) when the lawyer or the **prospective client** is still considering whether to enter into the engagement. `TAMING THE TEXT`

`REASON FOR THE RULE` **Model Rule 1.18 Comment [1]** explains the reason for this difference:

> A lawyer's consultations with a **prospective client** usually are limited in time and depth and leave both the **prospective client** and the lawyer free (and sometimes required) to proceed no further. Hence, **prospective clients** should receive some but not all of the protection afforded clients.[11] `REASON FOR THE RULE`

iii. Limit on the Scope of the Duty of Confidentiality: Information That Is "Generally Known"

`TAMING THE TEXT` Another limit on what qualifies as **confidential information** is that the **duty of confidentiality** does not extend to information that is (or becomes) "generally known." How do we know about this limit? **Model Rule 1.9(c)** and **Model Rule 1.9 Comment [8]** state that it is permissible for a lawyer to use a **former client's confidential information** that has become generally known. Other than that, the Rules are silent about any limit on **confidential information** that would be grounded in the information's public disclosure or availability. Despite the "general knowledge" limit's absence from some of the relevant Model Rules, however, in many jurisdictions, "general knowledge" is a recognized and accepted restriction on the **duty of confidentiality's** application to all the information otherwise "relating to the representation of a client" or "learned . . . from a **prospective client**" that you are obligated to keep confidential, especially where civil **consequences** are at stake. `TAMING THE TEXT`

What is required for information to be "generally known"? Let's start with what is *not* sufficient by comparing the scope of the **duty of confidentiality** with the scope of the **attorney-client privilege** and the **attorney work product doctrine**: When we are determining the scope or waiver of the **attorney-client privilege** or the **work product doctrine** (which we will discuss in more detail below), even a very minor or limited disclosure of privileged information to a third party usually serves to end the privileged status of the disclosed information in all contexts and for

---

[11] If the consultation with the **prospective client** in contemplation of possible representation ripens into an actual engagement, then any information gathered during the consultation becomes "information relating to the representation of a client," and all of it is subject to the lawyer's **duty of confidentiality. Model Rule 1.18** is more focused on what is protected "even when no lawyer-client relationship ensues. . . ."

all purposes (so long as it is voluntarily made or authorized by the client). The scope of the **duty of confidentiality** is very, very different. Information that has been disclosed or is known to others, even through voluntary acts of your client or other proper means, may still remain subject to your **duty of confidentiality**. *Even information that is a matter of public record may fall within your* **duty of confidentiality**, a point that vividly illustrates the difference between information's having been used or disclosed and its being "generally known."

What's the difference? Although jurisdictions differ, one useful test is that information is *not* "generally known" for this purpose even if it is *known* to persons other than you and the client, and *knowable* by others, but would require something more than minimal effort to discover. An ABA Formal Ethics Opinion defines "generally known" as "(a) . . . widely recognized by members of the public in the relevant geographic area; or (b) . . . widely recognized in the . . . client's industry, profession, or trade."[12] One thing that this test suggests is that there's a lot of information out there that no one could fairly describe as a "secret" that is nevertheless subject to your **duty of confidentiality** *if* you learn it in relation to the representation of a client.

YOUR HOUSE; YOUR RULES ▶ The scope of the **duty of confidentiality**, including what's "generally known" and thus not **confidential**, can vary from state to state. As we noted above, an explicit limit on the **duty of confidentiality** for information that is "generally known" appears only in **Model Rule 1.9(c)(1)** and not in any other Model Rule. The ABA Formal Ethics Opinion that we just cited interprets this drafting literally to conclude that, if otherwise **confidential information** is "generally known," a lawyer can *use* it but can't *disclose* it. And the lawyer can *use* this **confidential information** only if the **confidential information** pertains to a **former client**. This is the specific and limited scope of **Model Rule 1.9(c)(1)**.[13] Under this reading, the fact that a **current client's confidential information** is "generally known" doesn't affect its **confidentiality** at all. However, a number of states consider information's being "generally known" to limit its **confidentiality** in *all* circumstances.[14] Make sure you have a fix on where the line is drawn in the jurisdiction in which you practice before you use or disclose *anything* that you learn in the course of a client engagement, even things that you are confident that other people already know. ◀ YOUR HOUSE; YOUR RULES

> **Problem 8A-7:** Frank's firm is hired by a local real estate developer to obtain the land-use permissions necessary to build a big shopping center on some agricultural land that the developer has acquired on the outskirts of town near the highway. Many residents of the town like its small-town feel, and the developer is concerned that its project will be controversial.

---

[12] ABA Formal Op. No. 479 at 5 (2017).

[13] ABA Formal Op. No. 479 at 1-2 (2017). As we will discuss in more detail in **Chapter 8.A at 217**, the **duty of confidentiality** approaches different activities involving **confidential information** differently, explicitly differentiating between the *use* and the *disclosure* of such information under some circumstances.

[14] *See, e.g.,* N.Y. R. PROF. COND. 1.6(a) (express definition of "**confidential information**" excluding information that is "generally known").

Frank takes the completed permit applications down to the Planning Commission office and files them. Applications to local Planning Commissions are open to public inspection under state law.

a. Leaving the Planning Commission office, Frank runs into Frannie Farmer, a well-known local environmental activist who is concerned about preserving agricultural lands in the area. Frannie asks Frank what brings him down to the Planning Commission. What **must** or **must not** Frank say in reply? What **should** Frank say? Please explain your answers.

b. Frannie regularly checks the recent Planning Commission filings and discovers the new ones by Frank's firm on behalf of its developer client regarding the shopping center. Frannie alerts a reporter she knows who writes for the local newspaper, giving him copies of the permit applications and mentioning Frank's name. The reporter begins investigating a news story on the developer's plans and calls Frank for information and comment. What **must** or **must not** Frank say to the reporter? Is there anything Frank **must**, **must not**, or **should** do? Please explain your answers.

iv. Limit on the Scope of the Duty of Confidentiality: Information Not Obtained in Connection with the Representation

`TAMING THE TEXT` The third limit on the scope of the **duty of confidentiality** is that (despite the literal language of the Rules) it does not include "information *relating* to the representation of a client" (emphasis added) just because the information "relat[es]" (*i.e.*, is relevant) to the engagement. You learn new and different information every day in the course of your work. Most lawyers, except some government lawyers and in-house counsel, typically have more than one client. You may acquire information in the course of representing (or considering representing) one client that "relates" to the representation of another. You have a duty to the client in the course of whose representation or prospective representation you acquired the information not to disclose it to anyone else, *including* another client of yours. *See* **Model Rule 1.18 Comment [3]**. So although the Rules literally define **confidential information** as information "*relating to* the representation of a client" (emphasis added), this phrase is typically construed to mean information "*obtained in connection with* the representation of a client." The difference does not come up often, but when it does, it usually matters. `TAMING THE TEXT`

Problem 8A-8: Consider the problem in **this chapter's Introduction at 203**. What if Ron Rainmaker argues to his partners that their firm is allowed to disclose what he was told by Petrified Petroleum's general counsel to Mojo Manufacturing because it "relat[es] to the representation of a client"—specifically, to the representation of Mojo, which is a **current client** of the firm? What's more, Ron may argue, because Mojo is a **current client**, the firm has **duties of loyalty** and **candor** to Mojo, and it would be disloyal to Mojo, and a breach of the firm's **duty of candor**, *not* to tell Mojo what he knows about Petrified Petroleum. Thus, Ron would argue, not only is he *permitted* to (**may**) disclose the information to Mojo, he has an *obligation* to (**must**) do so.

Is Ron right? Should his partners allow Ron to go ahead and speak with Mojo on this basis? Why or why not?

c. What Does the Duty of Confidentiality Prohibit or Require?

Summarizing what we've done up to this point, you now know *to whom* you owe **duties of confidentiality**, *when* those duties start, and *what kinds of information* are protected by the **duty of confidentiality** as **confidential information**. (If you're having trouble stating any of those three things clearly, you should pause and review the chapter up to this point one more time.) It's finally time to talk about what the **duty of confidentiality** requires you to do and not do.

Simply and generally put (and although the **consequences** may differ depending on what you do and to whom the breached duty is owed), the **duty of confidentiality** forbids you from *voluntarily disclosing* or *using* **confidential information**, and requires you to *exercise reasonable efforts to protect* the confidentiality of the **confidential information** in your care.[15] Let's talk those three requirements through.

i. The Prohibition on *Voluntarily Disclosing* Confidential Information

TAMING THE TEXT The most basic and commonly applicable obligation of the **duty of confidentiality** is not to *voluntarily disclose* **confidential information** to anyone other than your client (or someone acting on your client's behalf), or to someone within your **practice organization** who needs to know it in order to help serve the client. **Model Rule 1.6(a) (current clients); Model Rule 1.9(c) (former clients); Model Rule 1.18(b) (prospective clients)**. The Model Rules use the word "disclose" as well as the word "reveal" to describe this prohibited act, but what's forbidden is clear—no divulging **confidential information** in any way or in any form, for any purpose, to anyone but the client or someone acting on her behalf, or to someone within your own **practice organization**.[16] TAMING THE TEXT

This prohibition is limited to *voluntary* disclosure. That means that you **must** still disclose **confidential information** to comply with a valid legal duty, such as a duty created by a subpoena or a discovery obligation. The **attorney-client privilege** and the **work product doctrine** provide immunity from *compelled* disclosure and thus allow you to withhold privileged matter despite an otherwise valid legal obligation to disclose it, but they cover a *much* narrower range of documents and information. *See* **Chapter 8.A at 225** (exploring the differences among the three). And because

---

[15] The **duty of confidentiality** also forbids you from putting yourself in situations in which you would have the *opportunity* and *temptation* wrongfully to disclose or use **confidential information**, even if you don't actually do so. That describes one important category of **conflicts of interest**, which we will discuss fully in **Chapter 22.C at 678**. But first let's get the basic **confidentiality** obligations under our belts.

[16] Unless an exception applies, of course. We'll discuss some of the major exceptions to the **duty of confidentiality** in **Chapter 8.B at 235**.

you **may** withhold privileged material, the **duty of confidentiality** says that you **must** do so until and unless a legal authority or your client directs otherwise.[17]

> **Problem 8A-9:** Frank is helping partner Sally Splitsville with a divorce case. The firm represents Husband. Husband was devoted to Wife, but when she filed for divorce, he became concerned that she had been cheating on him. Frank is reviewing some third-party discovery in the case and finds information establishing that Wife was, in fact, cheating with Husband's best friend. Wife's infidelity would not be relevant to any issue in the divorce under the matrimonial law in Frank's state. May Frank talk about the situation with or show the documents produced in discovery to:
>
> a. His supervising partner, Sally?
> b. The other associate at his firm, who isn't working on the case?
> c. His opposing counsel in the case, as part of a "suggestion" that Wife get "realistic" about negotiations over settling the couple's marital property division?
> d. His opposing counsel in the case, in response to Wife's document request calling for the documents?
> e. The client Husband, if Frank is concerned that telling him would be so devastating to him that it could threaten his physical or emotional health?
> f. A small group of Frank's law school classmates who meet weekly at a local bar to talk about their work in order to help one another improve their skills? Is there anything that Frank might do in such a discussion to comply with his **duty of confidentiality**? *Hint: See* **Model Rule 1.6 Comment [4].**

> **Problem 8A-10:** Same family law case as Problem 8A-9, but one of the couple's children showed up for Husband's period of shared custody recently with bruises on his torso. The nature and placement of the bruises has made Husband concerned that Wife has physically abused the children, and he has directed Frank to prepare a motion to revoke Wife's shared custody. In the meantime, he's consulting a forensic physician to see if the cause of the child's

---

[17] As we will see, the **duty of confidentiality**, the **attorney-client privilege**, and the **attorney work product doctrine** can overlap and apply to the same information or documents. And because anything that is subject to the **attorney-client privilege** or the **attorney work product doctrine** *must* be confidential (it's an element of both privileges), almost anything subject to either privilege is also subject to the **duty of confidentiality**. One important implication of these facts is that, because the **duty of confidentiality** requires you not to disclose anything that you don't have a legal obligation to disclose, you **must** always assert any privilege on your client's behalf that can be argued in good faith to be applicable unless your client has waived that privilege or has directed you to do so. But how far **must** you keep fighting to defend the client's claims of privilege? Everyone agrees that (in the absence of permission from your client) you **must** make reasonable efforts to quash or narrow the disclosure obligation (by asserting objections when reasonably available, then by negotiation, and then by litigation). But what if the tribunal to which your privilege objection is presented rules against you? **Must** you seek appellate remedies before disclosing? If the highest available authority directs you to disclose, does your **duty of confidentiality** force you to go to prison or suffer ruinous fines for contempt rather than comply? Although the law varies among the states, most jurisdictions do expect you to pursue available appellate remedies to protect a privilege claimed in good faith (unless your client directs you to give up), but they do *not* require you to violate a final court order or other final and binding determination requiring disclosure—to the contrary, you're required to comply with a final, legally binding determination. *See* **Model Rule 1.6(b)(6)** (providing an exception to the **duty of confidentiality** "to comply with other law or a court order"); **Chapter 8.B at 248.**

injury can be narrowed down. He is very concerned that, if Wife is advised that the motion might be coming, she might threaten or harm their children, and he has told Frank to "keep it quiet" until he has the doctor's report and decides how to proceed.

In the meantime, opposing counsel (with whom Frank has a decent working relationship) calls Frank up and says, "I hope Husband didn't freak out about the boy's bruises. It was just an ordinary fall on the playground. You're not going to do anything crazy with that, are you?" How **must** or must Frank **not** respond? How **should** he respond? *See In re Pressly*, 160 Vt. 319 (1993).

ii. The Prohibition on *Using* Confidential Information

TAMING THE TEXT The Model Rules forbid using **confidential information** "to the disadvantage of" a **current, former**, or **prospective client. Model Rule 1.8(b)** (**current client**); **Model Rule 1.9(c)(1)** (**former client**); **Model Rule 1.18(b)** (**prospective client**). The Model Rules' prohibitions on *disclosing* **confidential information** contain no similar qualification, forbidding disclosure for any purpose and whether or not it disadvantages the client. Why is the lawyer's *use* of **confidential information** not as broadly restricted? **TAMING THE TEXT**

REASON FOR THE RULE There are two reasons, corresponding to two different ways in which a lawyer might use a client's **confidential information** *without* harming the client. In some cases, a lawyer might be tempted to use **confidential information** in a way that doesn't harm the client but that allows the lawyer to profit wrongfully. One good example is insider trading—that is, buying or selling a client's publicly traded securities on the basis of **confidential information** not yet known in the securities markets. If you know something about an issuer to which others trading in the securities markets don't yet have access, you can predict movements in the stock price that will happen when the **confidential information** becomes public. That gives you an unfair (and profoundly illegal) advantage in trading. Such activities rarely harm the client in any direct or measurable way—the harm is usually to other participants in the securities markets and to the integrity of the markets as a whole, not to the client issuer of the securities.

Because the lawyer's use of the **confidential information** is not disadvantageous to the client, there is no disciplinary offense. But insider trading is a felony and a civil wrong under federal and state law, with powerful remedies available in addition to potential imprisonment and fines: The fiduciary **duties of loyalty** and **confidentiality** forbid a fiduciary (such as a lawyer) from profiting from his fiduciary position in any way other than reasonable compensation for services. There are civil restitutionary remedies (that is, monetary and in-kind remedies measured by the amount that the fiduciary wrongfully gained, rather than the amount that the beneficiary was harmed) designed to ensure that the fiduciary does not retain any wrongful profits, even when the client may not have been harmed. The Model Rules and Comments are silent on why wrongfully profitable use of

confidential information not disadvantageous to the client is not also a disciplinary offense, though it may well be that the drafters assumed that these civil and criminal protections would be both remedy and deterrent enough, as well as the fact that many such uses of **confidential information** will still violate other disciplinary rules. ◄ REASON FOR THE RULE

TAMING THE TEXT ► Another category of uses of **confidential information** not disadvantageous to the client is entirely proper and thus does not bear any **consequences**. These uses include the use of legal or factual research, instructive experience, or creative ideas developed in the course of representing one client in representing other clients without harming the original client. For example, a lawyer who studies a government agency's interpretation and application of its regulations in order to advise a client regarding compliance has acquired "information relating to [that] representation" within the meaning of **Model Rule 1.6(a)**. But it is well accepted that it is permissible—in fact, desirable—for the lawyer to use that same knowledge to advise other clients on similar questions, so long as she doesn't use any knowledge specifically about the first client to harm the original client or benefit the later ones. Similarly, if a lawyer develops a new and creative structure for a certain kind of transaction that provides economic or practical benefits for one client, or develops a particularly well-drafted form of agreement or new legal argument for another, the lawyer may reuse the form and ideas to benefit another client without **consequences**. That's how lawyers develop expertise and experience, characteristics that are beneficial to all clients seeking and employing lawyers.[18] *See* **Model Rule 1.8 Comment [5]**. ◄ TAMING THE TEXT

> Problem 8A-11: A real estate client of Frank's firm wants to sell a piece of commercial property that it owns. That property has an ideal location for many different kinds of consumer businesses. The client will handle the marketing but retains Frank's firm to advise on and prepare formal responses to any offers that the client receives. Which of the following **may** Frank do while representing this client, and of the ones that he **must not** do, what are the possible **consequences**?
>
> a. Tell a college friend who is looking for a location for a sporting goods store that the property is on the market.
>
> b. Use a form of Rejection and Counteroffer for Purchase and Sale of Commercial Property that his supervising partner developed in representing other clients as the basis for the

---

[18] In addition to being advantageous to all clients in the aggregate to allow the professional knowledge and expertise developed for one client to be used for the benefit of another, as a practical matter it would be impossible for a lawyer who had learned from arguing a particular kind of motion, trying a particular kind of case, appearing before a particular judge, or negotiating with a particular commercial trading partner to prevent herself from using that experience to benefit a different client under similar circumstances, at least in the absence of "brain-wipe" technology not currently (and hopefully never) extant. See the films *Payday* and *Eternal Sunshine of the Spotless Mind* for thought experiments concerning this proposition, and a well-deserved study break. (But not until after you finish the chapter.)

current client's response to an offer it has received for the property, customizing it for the current client's property and preferences, of course.

c. Prepare an offer on his own behalf to purchase the property on terms that Frank knows that the client prefers, and at a price a little higher than the best offer that the client has received, before the client has acted on any offer.

iii. CONSEQUENCES The Different Consequences that Can Result from Improper Disclosure or Use of Confidential Information

Let's sum up the preceding discussion about which kinds of breaches of the **duty of confidentiality** can lead to which kinds of **consequences**. A chart might be handy:

Consequences for Improper Use or Disclosure of Confidential Information

Act[19]	Professional Discipline	Civil Liability
Voluntary disclosure	**Model Rule 1.6(a) (current client); Model Rule 1.9(c) (former client); Model Rule 1.18(b) (prospective client)**	For damages (for harm caused) or restitutionary remedies (to recover wrongful profits) for breach of confidence or breach of fiduciary duty
Use to the client's disadvantage	**Model Rule 1.8(b) (current client); Model Rule 1.9(c) (former client); Model Rule 1.18(b) (prospective client)**	For damages (for harm caused) or restitutionary remedies (to recover wrongful profits) for breach of confidence or breach of fiduciary duty
Use *not* to the client's disadvantage but to profit wrongfully from the client's **confidential information**	No Rule regarding **duty of confidentiality**; may violate other disciplinary rules, depending on the circumstances	For restitutionary remedies (to recover wrongful profits) for breach of confidence or breach of fiduciary duty
Use *not* to the client's disadvantage but used as general knowledge or expertise developed while representing the original client to benefit another client without harming the original client	No breach of duty; no **consequence**	No breach of duty; no **consequence**

CONSEQUENCES

[19] Remember that we have deferred until later any discussion of the breach of the **duty of confidentiality** that is committed when a lawyer represents a new client who could use the original client's **confidential information** against the original client, even if the lawyer hasn't (yet) disclosed or used the original client's **confidential information** to the original client's disadvantage. This is one broad category of **conflicts of interest**, which we will discuss in detail in **Chapter 22.C at 678**. The **consequences** for such a **conflict of interest** are both professional discipline (**Model Rules 1.9(a)-(b); Model Rule 1.18(c)**) and **disqualification**—a court order directing the lawyer to get out and keep out of the new engagement. (And if the lawyer has actually disclosed or used the original client's **confidential information** to the original client's disadvantage, then discipline and civil liability, as described in the above chart, will likely follow.)

iv. Your Obligation to Exercise Reasonable Efforts to Preserve the Confidentiality of Confidential Information

In addition to what the **duty of confidentiality** *prohibits* you from doing with **confidential information**, the duty also carries an *affirmative obligation* to exercise reasonable care to keep **confidential information** in your possession from being improperly used or disclosed. This obligation is stated explicitly in **Model Rule 1.6(c)** and **Model Rule 1.6 Comments [18]-[19]** and is part of the lawyer's civil **duties of confidentiality** and **care**, so the **consequences** for a lack of due care in this regard can involve both discipline and civil liability. This duty has many important implications for the way that you conduct your day-to-day life.

To begin with, before talking about **confidential information** in any way, you must be fully aware of your surroundings: Is there—or might there be—anyone else within earshot who should not have access to the **confidential information** that you're about to mention? If you're anywhere where someone who shouldn't reasonably might overhear, then you should wait until you're in a suitably private place.

What this means as a practical matter is that *all* public places, including streets and sidewalks, airports, transit (planes, trains, buses, taxi cabs, and rideshares), restaurants, elevators, and even the publicly accessible portions of your workplace, such as its lobbies, hallways, and restrooms, are all very unwise places to discuss **confidential information**. And obviously that includes speaking on a cell phone in any of those places or using your phone to text or email where anyone might be able to see your screen.[20] For similar reasons, if you have **confidential information** in your car or suitcase, you can't let that information out of your control. That means no valet parking and no checking luggage with the bell stand. And if you're at any risk that someone could read over your shoulder while you're typing away at your laptop, invest in a screen guard that makes it much harder for that other person to snoop.

Next, you must take reasonable care to protect from exposure or loss the documents and electronic media entrusted to you that contain **confidential information**. The amount of care that is reasonable depends in part on the sensitivity of the information. Market-moving information, such as an impending merger or acquisition, or an impending major lawsuit attacking an important feature of

---

[20] Even experienced lawyers lose track of their surroundings sometimes, typically to their grave embarrassment, or worse. For example, a BigLaw partner was overheard talking on his cell phone on a train from Washington, D.C., to New York discussing his firm's plans to lay off a substantial number of associates. https://abovethelaw.com/2009/02/a-funny-thing-happened-on-the-way-to-new-yorkor-pillsbury-associates-brace-yourselves/. And two of President Trump's lawyers in Special Counsel Robert Mueller's investigation were overheard by a *New York Times* reporter discussing confidential details of their work over lunch at a popular Washington restaurant. http://www.americanlawyer.com/id=1202798245139/Trump-Lawyers-Loose-Lips-Find-Audience-in-DC-Power-Lunch-Scene?kw=Trump%20Lawyers%27%20Loose%20Lips%20Find%20Audience%20in%20DC%20Power%20Lunch%20Scene&et=editorial&bu=The%20American%20Lawyer&cn=20170919&src=EMC-Email&pt=Am%20Law%20Daily. Our advice to you is simple: Be mindful of your surroundings, and use your common sense.

the business of a publicly traded company, may need to be stored under lock and key (or the electronic equivalent) at all times when it's not actively in use, in files with dummy client and matter names so that even attorneys or staff within your firm who aren't working on the matter can't guess what's going on. Less exactingly sensitive but still **confidential information** might appropriately be left on your desk in your office overnight, but not carried with you in your briefcase or on the tablet or laptop that you bring with you to a gathering on your way home from the office (unless you're prepared to carry the briefcase or laptop on your person the whole time you're there).[21]

Finally, you must take steps reasonably proportional to the sensitivity of the information at issue to prevent interception or eavesdropping when you store or transmit information electronically. For example, the email application that you use when transmitting or writing about **confidential information** must be reasonably secure, and your workplace must take reasonable steps to protect its servers (electronic storage and transmission devices) from outside intrusion (that is, hacking). *See* ABA Formal Ethics Op. 477R (2017); **Chapter 7.A at 179** (discussing the **duty of competence** obligation to keep abreast of developments regarding the digital tools used in your practice).

Although this aspect of the **duty of confidentiality** does require reasonable and mindful effort, it does not require perfection. The history of spycraft teaches us that those with sufficient resources and resolve can eventually get their hands on even the best-protected secrets. Nor do you need to conduct every aspect of your affairs as if the National Security Agency or the CIA were trying to crack your office files. What the Rules of Professional Conduct and corresponding civil duties require is that you take *reasonable* steps that are proportional to the sensitivity of the information and the potential harm of its wrongful use or disclosure to protect **confidential information**. *See* **Model Rule 1.6 Comment [18]** ("The unauthorized access to, or the inadvertent or unauthorized disclosure of, information relating to the representation of a client does not constitute a violation of paragraph (c) if the lawyer has made reasonable efforts to prevent the access or disclosure. Factors to be considered in determining the reasonableness of the lawyer's efforts include, but are not limited to, the sensitivity of the information, the likelihood of disclosure if additional safeguards are not employed, the cost of employing additional safeguards, the difficulty of implementing the safeguards, and the extent to which the safeguards adversely affect the lawyer's ability to represent clients (e.g., by making a device or important piece of software excessively difficult to use).").

Problem 8A-12: Which of the following violates the lawyer's **duty of confidentiality**, and what are the potential **consequences** for those instances that do?

---

[21] *See* https://abovethelaw.com/2019/10/orlando-attorney-is-having-a-hell-of-a-hangover/ ("if your name is Christy and you're fighting a custody battle in Orlando[,] fire your lawyer bc I found your whole case file at the bar last night").

a. Maya is going to continue to work on a large commercial lending agreement at home this evening. She has a hard-copy folder of confidential background information that she needs to prepare the agreement. She locks the file in her trunk when she stops briefly to pick up her takeout dinner at a local eatery. Does your answer change if she leaves the file on the passenger seat of her locked car?

b. Maya is mugged while walking home from work one evening. Fortunately, she is not hurt, but her laptop, which has some client documents saved on its hard drive, is stolen.

c. Maya is working on a client company's initial public offering of stock to the public, and she leaves a draft of an agreement that will be used in the offering on her desk overnight. (*See* **Problem 5D-5 at 117.**)

d. Danielle leaves an outline of a cross-examination of a witness who's on the defense's witness list on her desk in the DA's office overnight.

e. You represent Mars, Inc. in patent prosecution matters. Mars has asked you to patent the formula for its popular Starburst® candies, which involves application of the Juicedratic Equation. You store the equation and related materials regarding the candy formula in a safe inside a vault inside a volcano.[22]

d. When Does the Duty of Confidentiality End?

We already know that the **duty of confidentiality** continues for a **prospective client** "[e]ven when no client-lawyer relationship ensues . . ." (**Model Rule 1.18(b)**) and continues for a **former client** even after any client-lawyer relationship has ended (**Rule 1.6 Comment [20]; Rule 1.9 Comment [1]**). But where does it all end? Are your lips sealed until you're moldering in the grave? Are the coworkers within your firm, law department, or government agency, and their successors after them, sworn to silence until the stars are but smoldering embers?

The answer may very well be yes. There are three ways that the **duty of confidentiality** may end:

First, the **current client, former client**, or **prospective client** who is owed the **duty** can waive it—narrowly and piecemeal for particular disclosures, uses, or applications; or broadly for all time or any purpose. We'll talk about such authorization more below (*see* **Chapter 8.B at 238**), but as a practical matter, something that fuels your desire to disclose or use the **confidential information** is likely to present a good reason for the person owed the duty *not* to want to waive. ("Would you mind if I regaled my golf foursome with the story about how you contracted that disease while cheating on your taxes? Just sign here.") And to be effective, the client's authorization has to meet the requirements for **informed consent**. *See* **Model Rule 1.0(e); Model Rule 1.0 Comments [6]-[7]**.

Second, **confidential information** can cease to be protected by becoming generally known. But remember that becoming "generally known" requires a lot more than just one-time or limited disclosure, and that some states allow you only to *use* but

---

[22] *See* https://www.ispot.tv/ad/IGgd/starburst-volcano.

not to *disclose* **confidential information** that has become "generally known," and then only if it is **confidential information** of a **former client.** *See* **Chapter 8.A at 214.**

Third, about half of the states provide that the **duty of confidentiality** (and the **attorney-client privilege**) terminate, at least in part, when the client dies. Most of the jurisdictions holding that the client's death affects the **duty of confidentiality** and the **attorney-client privilege** provide that they terminate upon the client's death only for limited purposes, principally to resolve disputes among the dead client's heirs. But most jurisdictions hold that the **duty of confidentiality** and the **attorney-client privilege** survive the client's death except for use in a testamentary dispute, and some hold that the two survive under any circumstances.[23]

Though it's usually clear when our human **current, former,** and **prospective clients** are deceased, this potential end to the **duty of confidentiality** and the **attorney-client privilege** does raise additional questions when the **current, former,** or **prospective client** was an organization. Most organizational forms can theoretically exist forever, but of course organizations can also terminate themselves or be terminated by the jurisdiction under whose laws they were organized. The law of the various states is both sparse and inconsistent in determining whether **the duty of confidentiality** and the **attorney-client privilege** continue in effect when an organizational **current, former,** or **prospective client** "dies," as well as when an organization will be considered "dead" for these purposes.[24]

YOUR HOUSE; YOUR RULES Because of the wide interstate variation on these issues, be aware that if you encounter any of them, that you will need to figure out which approach your jurisdiction has adopted. YOUR HOUSE; YOUR RULES

3. The Differences Among the Duty of Confidentiality, the Attorney-Client Privilege, and the Attorney Work Product Doctrine

The **duty of confidentiality,** the **attorney-client privilege,** and the **attorney work product doctrine** are different sides of the same coin.[25] We're going to leave it principally

---

[23] *See* Simon J. Frankel, *The Attorney-Client Privilege After the Death of the Client*, 6 GEO. J. LEGAL ETHICS 45 (1992). There is no federal **duty of attorney confidentiality**; that is a subject governed by state law alone. There is, of course, a federal **attorney-client privilege**, and the United States Supreme Court has held that it survives the death of the client. *Swidler & Berlin v. United States*, 524 U.S. 399 (1998). *Swidler* is a fascinating case adjudicating the privilege objection asserted against a grand jury subpoena issued at the behest of an Independent Counsel investigating President Bill Clinton. The subpoena sought the notes of an attorney who had provided Deputy White House Counsel Vince Foster personal legal advice nine days before Mr. Foster committed suicide, an event whose cause remained the subject of fascination among conspiracy theorists for years. Because the federal law of privilege is developed by common-law process "in light of reason and experience" (**Fed. R. Evid. 501**), the Court surveyed the law of the several states in reaching its conclusion. As we discuss in more detail below, the **attorney-client privilege** has a scope and effect that is very different from that of the **duty of confidentiality**.

[24] *See* Michael Riordan, *The Attorney-Client Privilege and the "Posthumous" Corporation—Should the Privilege Apply?*, 34 TEX. TECH L. REV. 237 (2003).

[25] If you didn't stop after that sentence to object that there's no such thing as a three-sided coin, then you're not reading as critically as you should be. Of course, now some smart-aleck with a STEM degree will point out that every modern coin actually does have three sides—heads, tails, and the surface on the edge. Others of you, of course, will note that, in 100 coin-flips, you probably won't get one that comes to rest on the coin's edge. At this point, you may be wondering what

to your Evidence and Skills classes to explore the details of the **attorney-client privilege** and the **attorney work product doctrine**, but it is extremely important for you to understand that there are very significant differences among them.

The differences may sometimes seem small or technical, but they can be world-changing: Information subject only to the **duty of confidentiality** and not also subject to a privilege **must not** be *voluntarily* disclosed, but it **must** be disclosed pursuant to any legal obligation to do so. The much narrower range of information and documents subject to a valid privilege is immune from compelled disclosure. So figuring out with care and precision which duties and protections apply to which information is frequently critically important.

It's our experience that many practicing lawyers don't fully appreciate the differences among the **duty of confidentiality**, the **attorney-client privilege**, and the **attorney work product doctrine**. So that you will have a leg up on those lawyers, here's a helpful chart:

The Duty of Confidentiality, Attorney-Client Privilege, and Attorney Work Product Doctrine Compared

	What It Covers	When It Applies	What It Does	Who Holds It
Duty of Confidentiality	All documents and information obtained in connection with the engagement except what is or becomes "generally known"; anything that is subject to the **attorney-client privilege** or the **attorney work product doctrine** is *also* subject to the **duty of confidentiality**	All the time	Prohibits voluntary disclosure or use of **confidential information** (except use in the lawyer's practice of general information, knowledge, or experience); requires reasonable care to prevent inadvertent or wrongful disclosure or use	**Client**
Attorney-Client Privilege	• Communications • In confidence • Between attorney and client (or someone acting on behalf of either) • For the purpose of giving, receiving, or transmitting legal advice • Unless the client waives the privilege (one authorized disclosure generally waives the privilege for the disclosed material for all time and all purposes)	In situations governed by the rules of evidence	Immunity from compelled disclosure (that is, a merited and timely assertion of the **attorney-client privilege** excuses compliance with an otherwise valid and binding legal obligation to disclose, such as a subpoena or a discovery obligation)	**Client**

the point of this footnote is. Our use of the failed "three-sided coin" metaphor had two purposes: First, to remind you to read carefully as you prepare for class, and not blindly to accept (or worse, slide your eyes over without reflecting on) everything that we tell you. And second, to point out that, although the **duty of confidentiality**, the **attorney-client privilege**, and the **attorney work product doctrine** have similar and related purposes and applications, they are also quite distinct in their scope and effects. We could have done at least the latter with a homier analogy, such as a three-legged stool. But what would have been the fun in that?

	What It Covers	When It Applies	What It Does	Who Holds It
Attorney Work Product Doctrine	• Documents and tangible things • Prepared in anticipation of litigation or for trial • By or for a party or its representative **(Fed. R. Civ. P. 26(b)(3)(A))**	In situations governed by the rules of evidence	Immunity from compelled disclosure (that is, a merited and timely assertion of the **work product doctrine** excuses compliance with an otherwise valid and binding legal obligation to disclose, such as a subpoena or a discovery obligation) • The immunity from compelled disclosure is conditional (that is, it can yield in proper circumstances to a showing of "substantial need" by the party seeking its disclosure and the absence of other sources to obtain the information sought without "undue hardship") **(Fed. R. Civ. P. 26(b)(3)(A)(ii))** • The signed or transcribed statement of any person **may** always be discovered by that person **(Fed. R. Civ. P 26(b)(3)(C))** • But the "mental impressions, conclusions, opinions, or legal theories of a party's attorney or other representative concerning the litigation" are virtually never discoverable **(Fed. R. Civ. P. 26(b)(3)(B))**	**Attorney** (but the client can require the attorney to waive)

Problem 8A-13: Which of the following is subject to the **duty of confidentiality**, the **attorney-client privilege**, or the **attorney work product doctrine** (choose any or all that apply)?

a. Clippings that Frank collects from local newspapers, news sites, and discussion boards regarding public reaction to the shopping center that his firm's client has proposed to build.

b. Notes that Danielle takes of her interview of a witness to a crime.

c. Notes that a nonattorney investigator employed by the District Attorney's office takes of an interview of a witness to a crime.

d. A written statement that the investigator in (c) prepares for the witness reflecting what she said and that the witness signs after reviewing it for accuracy.

e. What the lawyer representing the defendant in an assault case that Danielle is prosecuting knows about whether the defendant came to the lawyer's office on the evening of the alleged crime, and if the defendant did, whether he had blood on his shirt.

f. An email sent by one employee of the client company to another employee of the client company regarding a business dispute that the company is having with a customer.

g. Same as (f), but now the business dispute is on the verge of litigation, and the client company sends the already existing email to Frank to give him information that he needs to advise the company about whether to file a lawsuit.

h. A memorandum that Maya prepares for her supervising partner discussing her legal research on the enforceability of a particular contract clause that they're negotiating in a pending deal.

i. Same as (h), but now the partner has sent the memo to the client representative responsible for the negotiation to inform their discussions about how to proceed in the negotiation.

Big-Picture Takeaways from Chapter 8.A

1. You have a **duty of confidentiality** to **current clients**, **former clients**, and **prospective clients**. And remember: the status of **current**, **former**, or **prospective client** depends on which "matter" you're addressing; one person or organization can be a different kind of client in multiple different "matters" at once. *See* **Chapter 8.A at 206**.

2. **Prospective clients** are defined in **Model Rule 1.18(a)** as "person[s] who consult[] with a lawyer about the possibility of forming a client-lawyer relationship with respect to a matter . . . ." One useful way of summarizing a test that many jurisdictions use to determine if someone is a **prospective client** is whether the person communicating with the lawyer *actually and reasonably believes it is a consultation in contemplation of possible representation. See* **Chapter 8.A at 207**.

3. If you don't know whether you're dealing with a **current client**, a **former client**, a **prospective client**, or none of the above, then **inquire; explain; confirm** (*see* **Chapter 6.A at 139**). *See* **Chapter 8.A at 208**.

4. **Confidential information** is described in **Model Rule 1.6(a)** as "information relating to the representation of a client," and its scope is very broad. Other Model Rules denote **confidential information** with the phrase "information protected by Rule 1.6" or "Rule 1.9"; "information whose disclosure is prohibited by Rule 1.6" or "Rule 1.9"; or words to similar effect. The **duty of confidentiality** is not limited just to what your client tells you. It includes almost anything pertaining to the engagement that you learn from any source. It doesn't even have to be "confidential" in the dictionary sense of being "secret." *See* **Chapter 8.A at 210**.

5. There are three important restrictions on the scope of **confidential information:**

a. For a **prospective client**, only information "learned . . . from [the] **prospective client**" is protected, rather than *any* information relating to the potential representation. For **current** and **former clients**, though, the scope is broader and covers all information the lawyer gathers or receives from any source in connection with the representation. *See* **Chapter 8.A at 213**.

b. The **duty of confidentiality** does not extend to information that is or becomes "generally known." However, "generally known" means "(a) . . . widely recognized by members of the public in the relevant geographic area; or (b) . . . widely recognized in the . . . client's industry, profession, or trade." Even material that is a matter of public record is often considered *not* "generally known." *See* **Chapter 8.A at 214**.

c. If you didn't obtain the information *in connection with* the representation of a client, then it's not **confidential information** as to that client. *See* **Chapter 8.A at 216**.

6. The **duty of confidentiality** forbids you from *voluntarily disclosing* or *using* **confidential information**.

a. The most basic and commonly applicable obligation of the **duty of confidentiality** is not to *voluntarily disclose* **confidential information** to anyone other than the client (or someone acting on the client's behalf) or to someone within your **practice organization** who needs to know it in order to help serve the client. *See* **Chapter 8.A at 217**.

b. This prohibition is limited to *voluntary* disclosure. That means that you must still disclose **confidential information** to comply with a valid legal duty, such as a duty created by a subpoena or a discovery obligation. (*But see* the distinctions among the **duty of confidentiality**, the **attorney-client privilege**, and the **attorney work product doctrine**. And remember: even though you **may** withhold privileged material, the **duty of confidentiality** says that you **must** do so until and unless a legal authority or your client directs otherwise.) *See* **Chapter 8.A at 217**.

c. The **duty of confidentiality** not only prohibits you from *voluntarily disclosing* **confidential information**, but it also prohibits you from *using* **confidential information** in certain ways. Specifically, you **must not** use **confidential information** for your own benefit, even if your client isn't directly harmed by that use, *except* that you **may** use **confidential information** such as legal or factual research, instructive experience, or creative ideas developed in the course of representing one client when you're representing other clients without harming the original client—so long as you don't use any knowledge specifically about the first client to harm the original client or benefit the later ones. You **must not** use **confidential information** to benefit one client at another client's expense. *See* **Chapter 8.A at 219**.

7. In addition to what the **duty of confidentiality** *prohibits* you from doing with **confidential information**, the **duty of confidentiality** also carries an *affirmative obligation* to exercise reasonable care to keep **confidential information** in your possession from being improperly used or disclosed, whether by you or others. *See* **Chapter 8.A at 222.**

   a. Be fully aware of your surroundings at all times, and don't discuss **confidential information** where you could be overheard. *See* **Chapter 8.A at 222.**

   b. Take reasonable care to protect from exposure or loss the documents and electronic media entrusted to you that contain **confidential information.** *See* **Chapter 8.A at 222.**

   c. Take steps reasonably proportional to the sensitivity of the information at issue to prevent interception or eavesdropping when you store or transmit information, whether physically or electronically. *See* **Chapter 8.A at 223.**

8. There are three ways that the **duty of confidentiality** may end:

   a. *First*, the **current client, former client,** or **prospective client** who is owed the duty can waive it voluntarily after receiving sufficient information to determine whether waiver is advisable (that is, with **informed consent**). The waiver can be narrow and piecemeal for particular disclosures, uses, or applications, or it can be broad (for all time or any purpose). *See* **Chapter 8.A at 224.**

   b. *Second*, **confidential information** can cease to be protected by becoming "generally known." But remember that becoming "generally known" requires a lot more than just one-time or limited disclosure, and that some states allow you only to *use* but not to *disclose* **confidential information** that has become "generally known," and then only if it is **confidential information** of a **former client.** *See* **Chapter 8.A at 224.**

   c. *Third*, about half of the states provide that the **duty of confidentiality** (and the **attorney-client privilege**) terminate, at least in part, when the client dies. Most of the jurisdictions holding that the client's death affects the **duty of confidentiality** and the **attorney-client privilege** provide that they terminate upon the client's death only for limited purposes, principally to resolve disputes among the dead client's heirs. But most jurisdictions hold that the **duty of confidentiality** and the **attorney-client privilege** survive the client's death except for use in a testamentary dispute, and some hold that the two survive forever under any circumstances. *See* **Chapter 8.A at 225.**

9. Information subject only to the **duty of confidentiality** and not also subject to a privilege **must not** be *voluntarily* disclosed, but it **must** be disclosed pursuant to any legal obligation to do so. The much narrower range of

information and documents subject to a valid privilege is immune from compelled disclosure. *See* **Chapter 8.A at 226**.

Multiple-Choice Review Questions for Chapter 8.A

1. Lawyer Lisa does criminal defense. A new potential client, David, has been accused of fraudulently billing Medicare for mental health services that the government claims were never provided.

   Lisa interviews David. Lisa's paralegal sits in to take notes. Lisa explains that, before she will agree to undertake the representation, she needs to understand what happened. David tells her that he is anxious to retain a lawyer and hopes that she will represent him.

   During the interview, David admits that, although he billed the government as though he had provided half-hour sessions to his clients, in actuality he met with each client for approximately ten minutes. He insists, however, that he provided quality therapy during those sessions and that the government was not defrauded.

   Lisa agrees to represent David. Are the contents of their interview subject to the **duty of confidentiality**?
   a. Yes. David was a **prospective client** when he spoke with Lisa.
   b. Yes, but only if David again repeats this information to Lisa after she has agreed to retain him.
   c. No. David was not a client when the conversation occurred.
   d. No. The paralegal was present, so any **confidentiality** was waived.

2. Lawyer Luis represents BigCorp in a breach of contract case. In preparation for trial, Luis meets with Charlie, the CEO of BigCorp. Charlie negotiated the contact that is in dispute in the lawsuit. Luis and Charlie discuss the negotiations at length, and during the conversation, Luis learns how BigCorp sets the prices of its products. Trial is set to commence in a few weeks, and Luis feels ready.

   A few days after the trial preparation session, Luis is having drinks with his friend Maurice. Maurice operates a chain of local stores that competes with BigCorp. Maurice laments that BigCorp always under-prices his stores. Luis realizes that the information that he has learned from Charlie could provide Maurice with a competitive advantage.

   Can Luis disclose BigCorp's pricing policy in order to help a friend?
   a. Yes. Luis's client is BigCorp, not Charlie, so disclosure would not be a breach of the **duty of confidentiality**.
   b. Yes. This information may come out at trial anyway, so providing it to Maurice a few weeks in advance will have limited impact on BigCorp.

    c. No. Luis's client is BigCorp and under the circumstances, the information that Charlie communicated was on behalf of BigCorp.

    d. No. Luis only suspects that the information would help Maurice.

3. Divorce lawyer Lucretia represents Henrietta in a divorce proceeding. Over the months as the case proceeds, Henrietta tells Lucretia several lurid details about her extramarital affairs. Henrietta's spouse never asks about any affairs, and Lucretia never discloses anything about them. Lucretia urges Henrietta to "come clean" with her spouse, but Henrietta refuses.

    Once the divorce is final and Henrietta pays the final bill, Lucretia sends a letter to Henrietta's ex-spouse disclosing the affairs.

    Has Lucretia breached her **duty of confidentiality**?

    a. Yes. Lucretia owed a **duty of confidentiality** to Henrietta because Henrietta was a **former client**.

    b. Yes. Lucretia owed a **duty of confidentiality** to Henrietta because Henrietta was a **current client**.

    c. No. Lucretia owed Henrietta no **duty of confidentiality** once the representation ended.

    d. No. Lucretia gave Henrietta a chance to disclose the affairs herself and was entitled to disclose those affairs once Henrietta failed to self-disclose.

4. After a huge snowstorm, Alice (who is a lawyer) and her neighbor, Bernard, are shoveling their respective driveways. They take a break to catch their breath. During this five-minute conversation, Bernard asks how Alice's law practice is going. She tells him, "really well." Bernard then changes the subject and mentions his plans to install a pool on his property that spring. Alice says that she can't wait for the spring because she's had it with the snow. The two then go back to shoveling.

    A few weeks later, Alice bumps into another neighbor, Carly, in the supermarket, and they start chatting. Alice mentions Bernard's plans for a pool. Carly immediately files for an injunction to block Bernard from building the pool.

    Bernard calls Alice and demands why she shared this information when he expected it to be **confidential**.

    What is Alice's best response if she hopes to illustrate successfully why she has done nothing legally or ethically wrong? You may disregard any informal or moral judgments that might be made.

    a. Bernard never said that he wanted to retain Alice, so the conversation could not have been protected by the **duty of confidentiality**.

    b. Alice never said she would represent Bernard, so the conversation could not have been protected by the **duty of confidentiality**.

   c. Under the circumstances, Alice did not view the discussion as an interview of prospective counsel, so the **duty of confidentiality** is inapplicable.

   d. Under the circumstances, a reasonable person in Bernard's shoes would not have viewed the discussion as an interview of prospective counsel, so the **duty of confidentiality** is inapplicable.

5. Lawyer Lyle meets with a potential client, Cillian. Cillian claims that he was injured in a slip-and-fall outside the local library. Lyle interviews Cillian, who describes his recollection of the accident.

    Lyle then does some research on his own. He discovers that Cillian has filed at least ten other slip-and-fall lawsuits. Each was dismissed as frivolous. Lyle declines to take Cillian's case.

    A few weeks later, Lyle meets up with his friend from law school, Emily. Emily tells Lyle that she is excited because she just retained a new client who slipped and fell outside the local library. Lyle says "I hope his name isn't Cillian. That guy has filed ten other slip-and-fall cases that were dismissed as frivolous." Emily's face goes pale—indeed, her new client is Cillian.

    Has Lyle breached his **duty of confidentiality**?

   a. Yes. Lyle learned this information from Cillian.

   b. Yes. Lyle learned this information while researching whether he should agree to represent Cillian.

   c. No. The information that Lyle learned did not come from Cillian directly.

   d. No. Lyle did not represent Cillian, so he owed him no duty.

6. George learns information while defending his client Jacob. After the case is complete, Jacob gives an interview to his college newspaper, which is circulated only on the college campus. In the interview, Jacob discusses information that he told George in confidence.

    Is George now free to disclose that same information?

   a. Yes. Disclosure to a third party by Jacob waived any **confidentiality**.

   b. Maybe. It depends in part on the jurisdiction's rules and how easy it is for others to find this information, given the limited circulation of the newspaper.

   c. Maybe. It depends on whether Jacob intends to retain George to represent him in any future cases.

   d. No. All information communicated by a **former client** during the engagement always remains **confidential**.

7. While representing current client Zaphod, a lawyer learns information that might benefit another current client, Trillian. Can the lawyer disclose the information to Trillian?

   a. Yes. It is not **confidential** if it relates to both Zaphod and Trillian.
   b. Maybe. It depends on whether the information was communicated by Zaphod directly.
   c. Maybe. It depends on whether the information will substantially benefit Trillian and how detrimental disclosure would be to Zaphod.
   d. No. It is still **confidential** if it was discovered in the course of representing Zaphod.

8. Lawyer Lloyd receives a subpoena compelling him to produce **confidential information** provided to him by his **current client**. The information is not protected by either the **attorney-client privilege** or the **attorney work product doctrine**.

   Does **Model Rule 1.6(a)** apply to Lloyd's situation?
   a. Yes. The situation involves **confidential information** for a **current client**.
   b. Yes. The situation involves divulging information.
   c. No. The situation does not involve voluntary disclosure.
   d. No. The situation does not involve attorney-client communications.

9. While representing client Lisa, lawyer Nanette discovers a novel argument through legal research. Nanette makes this argument at trial and wins the case for Lisa. Lisa is thrilled.

   Nanette later takes on a new client, Steve. Steve says that he read about the trial, and he wants Nanette to make the same argument in his case.

   Assuming that the argument applies to Steve's case, is Nanette prohibited from making the argument on Steve's behalf?
   a. Yes. She learned this information while representing Lisa.
   b. Yes. Steve would be benefitting from work for which Lisa has paid.
   c. No. Lisa cannot limit Nanette's use of the argument that Nanette developed in ways that are not harmful to Lisa.
   d. No. Once the argument was made at trial, it was no longer **confidential**.

10. If a lawyer uses the **confidential information** of a **former client** to that **former client's** disadvantage, what are the likely **consequences**?
    a. Civil liability for breach of confidence.
    b. Civil liability for breach of confidence under **Model Rule 1.9(c)**.
    c. Restitutionary remedies for breach of confidence.
    d. Restitutionary remedies for breach of confidence under **Model Rule 1.9(c)**.

11. Lawyer Lonnie is discussing his client's case with the assigned paralegal at his firm over lunch at a restaurant. Lonnie's tone of voice is loud enough for anyone passing by to overhear. When his paralegal shushes him,

reminding him that the information is **confidential**, Lonnie says, "Everyone else should butt out; I'm allowed to talk about this in public because everyone else has to stop themselves from eavesdropping."

Is Lonnie correct?

a. Yes. As long as his intent is to speak only to the paralegal, he is meeting his duty to keep the information **confidential**.

b. Yes. It is not foreseeable that someone in the restaurant would know enough about the case to make use of any overheard information.

c. No. A restaurant is not a suitably private place for the conversation, especially in light of Lonnie's loud tone of voice.

d. No. Mere disclosure to the paralegal waives **confidentiality** without even considering whether anyone else in the restaurant hears the information.

12. Which is *not* a way that a **duty of confidentiality** can end?

a. Waiver of the **duty** by the client.

b. General knowledge of that information.

c. By death of the client.

d. By termination of the attorney-client relationship.

13. Two law students are arguing. Sally claims that anything that is **attorney-client privileged** is automatically covered by the **duty of confidentiality**. Barry disagrees.

Who is correct?

a. Sally. The **duty of confidentiality** applies to virtually all information obtained in connection with the engagement. A subset of this information would include attorney-client communications.

b. Sally. The **attorney-client privilege** applies to virtually all information obtained in connection with the engagement. A subset of these communications would include **confidential information**.

c. Barry. Information can be either **attorney-client privileged** or **confidential**, but not both.

d. Barry. The Federal Rules of Evidence define what is **attorney-client privileged**, and professional conduct rules define what is **confidential**. Because different sets of rules apply, no information can be both **attorney-client privileged** and **confidential**.

B. Exceptions to the Duty of Confidentiality Found in Model Rule 1.6

Now that we've explored the scope and limits of the **duty of confidentiality**, let's discuss some of its exceptions. Before we start, though, several introductory cautions are in order. We'll number them for easy reference.

1. When you are confronting **confidentiality** issues, don't analyze a whole conversation, an entire document or set of documents, or every aspect of an event all together. Instead, you should break the information down into the smallest salient units and consider them one at a time. You will frequently find that different pieces are subject to different analysis and, often, different treatment. If an exception to the **duty of confidentiality** applies only to a part of a document or communication, that's the only part that you **may** or **must** disclose.

2. As we've seen, the **duty of confidentiality** is very broad, but it doesn't cover *everything* that you've ever learned, seen, heard, or read. Before you start exploring whether a particular item of information is subject to an exception, start by figuring out whether it is subject to the **duty of confidentiality** (and other protections, such as the **attorney-client privilege** or the **attorney work product doctrine**) in the first place. If it isn't, then you don't need to worry about whether there's an exception that authorizes your use or disclosure; you already know that the information is unprotected. (Of course, if **confidentiality** protection even arguably exists, you'll want to explore potential exceptions, just to be safe.)

3. The fact that something is *not* subject to the **duty of confidentiality** means only that you **may** use or disclose it without concern that you're breaching your **duty of confidentiality**. There may be other reasons why you **must not** disclose or use it—for example, doing so might harm your client and thus violate your **duty of loyalty,** even though the **information** is not **confidential**. And even if you **may** use or disclose information, there are often very good reasons why you **should not**, such as preserving client relations or your reputation in your community for discretion and good judgment. Don't do something just because you can; think it through.

4. In the remainder of this chapter, we're going to discuss the exceptions to the **duty of confidentiality** set out in **Model Rule 1.6**. These are all important exceptions, but they're not the only ones in the Model Rules. Some important confidentiality exceptions appear in **Model Rule 1.13(c)** (regarding "reporting out" an organization's harmful activities that its highest management has failed or refused to address, *see* **Chapter 23.B at 791**), and **Model Rule 3.3** (regarding the **duty of candor to the tribunal** and the **duty to correct,** *see* **Chapter 24.C at 878**).

5. TAMING THE TEXT **Model Rule 1.6(b)** begins: "A lawyer may reveal information relating to the representation of a client to the extent the lawyer reasonably believes necessary . . ." and then lists multiple enumerated exceptions. This is critical language in several respects:

    a. All of the exceptions in **Model Rule 1.6(b)** are *permissive* ("may") and *not mandatory* ("shall" or "must"). As a practical matter, that means that, once you have determined that an exception applies to a particular piece of information, you still need to reason out whether you **should** or **should not** disclose it under the circumstances in which you find yourself. (A number of states take a different approach to some exceptions, so make sure you know what rules you need to follow.) Sometimes these practical "**should** or **should not**" decisions are easy; often, they're not.

b. The **Model Rule 1.6(b)** exceptions are limited to *disclosure* ("a lawyer may reveal") and do not authorize *use*.

c. Each **Model Rule 1.6(b)** exception has an explicitly defined scope and purpose. The introductory language's qualification that a lawyer may disclose **confidential information** "*to the extent* the lawyer reasonably believes necessary*" (emphasis added) to achieve an exception's purposes means that *you must always take great care to disclose only* (i) *the minimum amount of* **confidential information** *subject to the exception* (ii) *to the minimum number of people strictly necessary* (iii) *to serve the specific purpose of the exception at issue. See* **Model Rule 1.6 Comment [16]**. If you exceed the scope of the exception in *any* of these three respects, then you will have violated your **duty of confidentiality** and subjected yourself to all of the **consequences** that come with such a violation.

> TAMING THE TEXT

d. All of the **Model Rule 1.6(b)** exceptions are available on the condition that "the lawyer reasonably believes" that the disclosure is "necessary" to achieve the purpose of the exception. By its terms, this means that you must subjectively believe that the disclosure you make is "necessary" to achieve the exception's purpose, and your belief must be *objectively reasonable* ("reasonably believes necessary") based on the surrounding facts and circumstances that you know or reasonably should know.

6. YOUR HOUSE; YOUR RULES The exceptions enumerated in **Model Rule 1.6(b)** (which is all of the **Model Rule 1.6** exceptions except client consent, which is stated in **Model Rule 1.6(a)**) are subject to the widest and most prevalent interstate variation of any provisions in the Model Rules. It is likely that your state has departed from the standard text of **Model Rule 1.6(b)** in one way or another. Make sure that you know what your particular jurisdiction allows you and, in some cases, requires you, to disclose and when.

> YOUR HOUSE; YOUR RULES

7. RULE ROLES The following discussion will focus on the exceptions as provided in the Model Rules, which, as you know, govern the imposition of professional discipline. But for purposes of determining civil liability, most jurisdictions rely extensively on their Rules of Professional Conduct to define the scope, limits, and exceptions of the **duty of confidentiality** as well. Some states rely on the literal terms of their ethical rules; others hold that the rules are influential in defining the standards for civil liability but don't necessarily literally define them. Thus, although you will need to explore

the relationship between disciplinary and civil liability for **confidentiality** issues in your particular state, if you have a detailed understanding of what your state's Rules of Professional Conduct require, permit, or forbid, you will be most of the way to understanding what facts will and will not be sufficient to impose civil **consequences** as well. ⟨Rule Roles⟩

With these general concerns in mind, let's look at the **Model Rule 1.6** exceptions to the **duty of confidentiality**.

1. The Client's Informed Consent, Express or Implied

It should come as no surprise that you **may** use or disclose anything protected by the **duty of confidentiality** (or the **attorney-client privilege**) if your client says that you can.[26] **Model Rule 1.6(a)** provides that lawyers **must not** disclose **confidential information** "unless the client gives **informed consent**, the disclosure is impliedly authorized in order to carry out the representation or the disclosure is permitted by paragraph (b)."

The exceptions enumerated in **Model Rule 1.6(b)** will be covered in the remaining sections of this chapter, but we start with the client's "**informed consent**" or "**implied[] authoriz[ation]**" to disclose.

a. Express Informed Consent

As we've discussed before (*see* **Chapter 5.D at 118 n.18**), **informed consent** is a term of art in professional ethics. It requires not just the client's express *consent* (that's the easy part); in addition, in the words of the term's definition in **Model Rule 1.0(e)**, that consent must be based upon "adequate information and explanation about the material risks of and reasonably available alternatives to the proposed course of conduct." This information and explanation must not only be provided in full, but in a form and manner that the client can understand and use to make an informed decision, taking into account the client's education, sophistication, and language and other skills. Client consent that is not "informed" under this very demanding standard is no consent at all.[27]

Informed consent requires differing degrees of formality for different purposes provided in the Rules. **Informed consent** for disclosure of **confidential information** requires no special formalities; oral disclosures and oral authorization are sufficient. Of course, that doesn't mean that it's always *prudent* to use informal and undocumented disclosures and consent regarding **confidential information**. Informal oral consent may be fine for something small or insignificant, but any significant disclosure of

---

[26] The same is true of the **attorney work product doctrine**, but a little more indirectly. As you'll recall from our handy chart (**Chapter 8.A at 226**), the **work product doctrine** is in most jurisdictions held by the attorney, but in most jurisdictions, the client **may** direct the attorney to waive it, and the attorney **must** comply (even when the waiver would be inimical to the **interests** of the attorney).

[27] *See, e.g., McClure v. Thompson*, 323 F.3d 1233, 1244-45 (9th Cir. 2003).

confidential information—and by that we mean one that is reasonably likely to have significance to the client or to the legal matter you're handling—deserves your effort to **inquire; explain; confirm** (*see* **Chapter 6.A at 139**). Make sure the client understands all of the implications of disclosing the information in question. Explain and confirm these implications in writing. If you're concerned about the client's changing her mind or not remembering the discussion accurately, have her sign a copy of the disclosures after giving her time to review and consider them. And *when in doubt, speak out*—if you have any doubt about whether the client might have concerns about the disclosure (whether or not those concerns might be reasonable in your eyes) or may not fully appreciate the implications, then ask.

b. "Implied[] Authori[ty]" to Disclose Confidential Information "in Order to Carry Out the Representation"

Model Rule 1.6(a) states that a lawyer **may** disclose **confidential information** if "the disclosure is impliedly authorized in order to carry out the representation." Even in the absence of the client's **informed consent** for you to disclose **confidential information**, then, you may have *implied authority* to do so. Implied authority is a concept with which you became familiar in **Chapter 6.A at 140**. Recall that **Model Rule 1.2(a)** says that "[a] lawyer may take such action on behalf of the client as is impliedly authorized to carry out the representation." The reference to implied authority in **Model Rule 1.6(a)** is just a narrower instance of that broader principle.

For example, suppose that you're retained to file an action to recover damages for a claimant injured in an accident. Being a careful and thorough lawyer, you interview the claimant, inspect the accident site, obtain the client's medical records, and gather other information about the claim. All the information that you learned in the course of representing the client is, of course, **confidential information**. Then you put some of that information into the complaint that you prepare and file on the client's behalf. Where did you get the authority to disclose that **confidential information** by including it in a publicly filed pleading? You got it by *implication* when the client retained you to file an action to recover for her injuries, because you needed to disclose some of the information that you learned "in order to carry out the representation."

You should approach whether you have implied authority to disclose **confidential information** in the same way that you approach any question of your implied authority. Look at the surrounding facts and circumstances, and if you have any doubt about the client's understanding or intentions, **inquire; explain; confirm** (*see* **Chapter 6.A at 139**).

Problem 8B-1: Which of the following disclosures is made with the client's **informed consent** or implied authorization (pick any that apply)?

a. Another lawyer in your firm is helping you review the client's documents to select those that must be produced in response to a pending document request. You explain the claims and defenses in the case to the other lawyer, as well as some factual issues that the client has confided to you will be reflected in some of the documents that you are reviewing. (*Hint: See* **Model Rule 1.6 Comment [5]**.)

b. Your client is under suspicion of the murder of two missing teenage girls. He tells you that their bodies can be found off a little-used hiking trail in thick underbrush some miles from the trailhead. You tell him that disclosing the location of the bodies will allow the girls' families some relief from the uncertainty and allow them to give their loved ones a decent burial. This, you suggest, may buy some goodwill with the prosecutor, though (you also inform him) it will also be strong evidence that your client was involved in the murders. Your client agrees, and you tell the prosecutor where to find the girls' bodies.[28]

c. In your opening statement at trial, you lay out what the evidence you intend to introduce will show regarding the merits of the case, including previously undisclosed facts to which your client will testify (and about which opposing counsel failed to inquire in deposition). Your client has not heard you rehearse your opening statement.

2. Preventing Imminent and Serious Physical Harm

Model Rule 1.6(b)(1) provides that you **may** disclose **confidential information** "to the extent [that you] reasonably believe[] necessary . . . to prevent reasonably certain death or serious bodily harm. . . ." TAMING THE TEXT Let's start by exploring the implications of the Rule's specific language:

- The Rule says you **may** disclose **confidential information**, not that you **must**. That means that you don't have any *obligation* to do so, or put slightly differently, that you have *no legal duty to warn* someone who is in danger. As noted above, whether you **should** warn in these circumstances is often a very difficult moral and practical judgment. YOUR HOUSE; YOUR RULES But beware: A number of states have changed this "may" to a "shall" or "must," which *does* imply a duty to warn endangered third parties.[29] YOUR HOUSE; YOUR RULES

- The exception allows you to disclose **confidential information** to prevent "reasonably certain *death or serious bodily harm*" (emphasis added). If the threatened harm is something less serious than "death or serious bodily harm," then the exception is not available. YOUR HOUSE; YOUR RULES A number of states,

---

[28] These facts are loosely adapted from what is widely known as the "Buried Bodies Case," which unfolded in Lake Pleasant, New York in the 1970s. One major difference between the Buried Bodies Case and the hypothetical problem in the text was that the defense lawyers in New York did *not* disclose whether the missing girls were dead or where the bodies were located, even though the families begged the lawyers to tell them if indeed they knew. When the truth eventually emerged, the lawyers were ostracized in their communities, but lionized in the criminal defense bar. What might the different treatment the lawyers received in these two communities tell you about legal ethics in general, and the **duty of confidentiality** in particular? For a more detailed discussion of the facts, *see* Lisa G. Lerman, Frank H. Armani, Thomas D. Morgan, and Monroe H. Freedman, *The Buried Bodies Case: Alive and Well after 30 Years*, 2007 PROF. LAWYER 17.

[29] And if you genuinely believe that your client or someone else is reasonably certain to cause death or serious bodily harm, as part of your obligation to make the least disclosure reasonably necessary, your first duty (if it is in your reasonable judgment safe to do so) is to remonstrate with the client to refrain (or to urge the client to warn the potential victim, if the client knows that a third party intends to act). Only after you take those steps **may** you yourself act, and only if you still feel that it is reasonably necessary to do so.

however, have broadened the exception to allow disclosure to prevent the imminent commission of *any* crime, not just one involving "reasonably certain death or serious bodily harm." Know your state's rules. <small>YOUR HOUSE; YOUR RULES</small>

■ The exception allows disclosure only to the extent reasonably necessary "to *prevent* reasonably certain death or serious bodily harm" (emphasis added). If the harm has already occurred, it's too late to avail yourself of the exception, because you can no longer "prevent" it.

■ The exception allows disclosure only to the extent reasonably necessary "to prevent *reasonably certain* death or serious bodily harm" (emphasis added). "[H]arm is reasonably certain to occur if it will be suffered imminently or if there is a present and substantial threat that a person will suffer such harm at a later date if the lawyer fails to take action necessary to eliminate the threat." **Model Rule 1.6 Comment [6]**.

■ All **Model Rule 1.6(b)** exceptions must be strictly limited "to the extent the lawyer reasonably believes necessary" to achieve the purpose of the exception. You **must not** tell anyone about the impending risk to whom disclosure is not reasonably necessary to prevent the death or bodily harm.

■ The emphasized language in the four preceding bullet points is important because, if you disclose **confidential information** by warning a third person regarding your client's dangerous intentions, and the potential harm was not likely or imminent enough, or was not reasonably likely to be serious enough, or was not reasonably likely to be preventable, you will have **exceeded** the scope of the exception, violated your **duty of confidentiality**, and bought yourself a heap of trouble. <small>TAMING THE TEXT</small>

Problem 8B-2: Which of the following is a proper disclosure, and why or why not?

a. You are in-house counsel at a municipal water company. Recently, the company changed its treatment protocols to reduce the cost of purifying the city's drinking water. Now an engineer has come to you with the news that there could be levels of lead contamination in the water sufficient to cause neurological damage to children who drink the water over a period of months. You tell the consumer affairs reporter at the local newspaper.

b. You are a family lawyer. Your client, the husband in a bitter divorce, is beside himself at the extended impasse that he feels that his wife is causing. "Sometimes," he says to you, "I just want to wring her neck." You call the wife to warn her.

c. Same facts as in (b), but the husband-client is waiting at your office early one morning, looking panicked and bedraggled. "I lost it last night," he blurts out. "I choked her." As calmly as you can after getting him into your office, you ask, "Is she all right?" "I don't know," he answers, sobbing. "She wasn't moving when I ran out the door." You call 911 to summon aid for the wife.

d. A client meets with you in your office. He is walking unsteadily and smells of liquor. He cuts your meeting short because he has to drive to the next town over, about three-quarters of an hour away. You try to dissuade him from driving but are unable to do so; he insists that he's fine. You call the state troopers after he leaves in order to alert them to a drunk driver on the highway.

3. Preventing or Addressing Serious Economic Wrongs in Which the Client Used the Lawyer's Services

These exceptions are narrower than you might at first think. You have to puzzle it out from the language of **Model Rules 1.6(b)(2)-(3)**, which allow you to disclose **confidential information**

to the extent [you] reasonably believe[] necessary . . .

> (2) to prevent the client from committing a crime or fraud that is reasonably certain to result in substantial injury to the financial interests or property of another and in furtherance of which the client has used or is using the lawyer's services; [or]

> (3) to prevent, mitigate, or rectify substantial injury to the financial interests or property of another that is reasonably certain to result or has resulted from the client's commission of a crime or fraud in furtherance of which the client has used the lawyer's services. . . .

TAMING THE TEXT This is not beautiful drafting, but it's what the drafters gave us, so let's do the best we can to parse it out:

- Both exceptions focus on a client's actual or intended "crime or fraud" that is "reasonably certain" to cause or has actually caused "substantial injury to the financial interests or property of another." So the Model Rules limit these exceptions not to just any crime or fraud, but only to serious ones threatening or causing "substantial" financial harm.
- Both exceptions are limited to serious crimes or frauds "in furtherance of which the client has used or is using the lawyer's services." This is a significant restriction. If the client committed the crime or fraud *before* retaining you, or if the client effected the crime or fraud while you were representing him but without using your legal services, the exception does not apply.
- The **Model Rule 1.6(b)(1)** exception is limited to disclosure necessary to *prevent* serious bodily harm. **Model Rule 1.6(b)(2)** allows disclosure to "*prevent*" (emphasis added) qualifying crimes or frauds, but **Model Rule 1.6(b)(3)** broadens the exception to allow disclosure to "*mitigate or rectify*" (emphasis added) qualifying financial wrongs. Thus, in appropriate circumstances, the lawyer **may** take steps to alert the victims of financial wrongs that can no longer be prevented if it would help to mitigate or rectify the already-completed wrong. (Can you think of any circumstances in which this would be the case?)

■ Once again, the disclosure must be limited only to what is necessary to prevent, mitigate, or rectify the qualifying wrongs, and the steps that the lawyer takes **must** be limited to those that the lawyer reasonably believes are necessary to do so. TAMING THE TEXT

Problem 8B-3:

a. You represent a client who is seeking to raise money to fund a business through a private placement of securities. You discover, after preparing disclosure documentation based on information that the client supplies, that the financial information in the documentation is incomplete and is thus **materially** misleading. The client has already raised some money, and though you tell him to stop because of the serious **consequences** of continuing, he continues to use the documents that you prepared to solicit more investments. Whom **must**, **may**, or **should** you tell about this, if anyone?

b. A new client comes to see you. She is the business manager for a successful local small business. She tells you that, over the past three years, she has embezzled $600,000 from the business by submitting falsified invoices from nonexistent vendors and pocketing the payments. As she tells her story, you learn that she stopped embezzling several months ago, but needs advice about what to do now. Whom **must**, **may**, or **should** you tell about this, if anyone?

4. Obtaining Legal Advice About Compliance with the Lawyer's Own Legal or Ethical Obligations

When questions of professional ethics or liability arise, whether in mid-engagement or after the fact, it's often wise to consult someone knowledgeable about these issues (and who isn't involved in the events in question) for more informed and objective guidance (or, if disciplinary proceedings or civil claims are threatened or pending, for assistance with defense).

The preceding sentence was a polite way of making the point, but it really needs to be said more directly: Ethics compliance and risk management can involve really hard questions of legal interpretation and even harder questions of practical judgment. For novice and experienced lawyers alike, these are questions that those stuck in the mosh pit of the circumstances often lack perspective to resolve reliably on their own. When you're confronted with a difficult client or adversary, or feel threatened or vulnerable, you should never hesitate to consult a cooler head. The only dumb questions are the ones that you don't ask. But when you ask, you have to go about it in the right way so that you protect your client's **confidential information** *and* the **confidentiality** of your own consultation. We'll tell you how.

On its face, the **duty of confidentiality** would present impediments to lawyers' seeking advice about their own client engagements because, in order to inquire about the situation, you ordinarily would have to disclose it to the advisor.[30] **Model Rule 1.6(b)(4)** addresses this concern by allowing disclosure of **confidential information** "to the extent the lawyer reasonably believes necessary . . . to secure legal advice about the lawyer's compliance with these Rules . . . ."

There is a world of complications tucked into the phrase "to secure legal advice." To put it simply, "legal advice" has to come from a lawyer, and it has to come from not just any lawyer, but from a lawyer duly engaged to give you legal advice about the particular questions at issue. This is important not only to stay within the contours of the exception, but also to preserve the **confidential** and **attorney-client privileged** status of your own consultation.

Why should you care about preserving the **confidential** and **attorney-client privileged** status of your own consultation? Think it through: If disciplinary proceedings, a civil claim, or (heaven forbid) criminal charges result from the situation about which you are seeking advice, unless your communications with your own ethics counsel are privileged, an enterprising bar or public prosecutor or plaintiff's lawyer will be free to cross-examine you (or the person whom you consulted) about everything that you discussed, or subpoena your written communications. Because you were seeking advice about a problem engagement, this almost certainly includes your fears about all the worst facts and their potential implications. Surely you should treat your own consultations with counsel with the same care that you urge on your clients, and for the same reasons.

Okay, now that we're clear about why you should care, let's talk about how to protect your consultations. Lawyers frequently make the mistake of wandering down the hall (or down the block) to chat informally with a friend within their **practice organization** or a fellow practitioner in their line of practice about their concerns. Why is this a mistake? Well, just because you're speaking with a lawyer doesn't make your consultation **attorney-client privileged**. You have to consult someone duly engaged to advise you on these issues *for the purpose of getting legal advice.* And in order to prevent lawyers from swathing any conversation they have with another lawyer in secrecy, courts are typically very demanding that a lawyer who is claiming **attorney-client privilege** over a consultation regarding a client engagement or claim show that there was a demonstrable attorney-client relationship with the other lawyer concerning that specific subject matter before holding its contents **attorney-client privileged** from the client about whom the lawyer was seeking advice.[31]

---

[30] In some circumstances, it may be possible to get compliance advice with use of a "no-names" hypothetical that does not identify the client being described (and whose identity can't be inferred from the facts disclosed). This "I know a guy" approach would be permissible, and is sometimes used, without resort to the **Model Rule 1.6 (b)(4)** exception, because no **confidential information** is being divulged. (Do you see why?) But if the situation is complex or detailed, or if a disciplinary inquiry or civil litigation is pending, no-names hypotheticals will usually be insufficient to address the lawyer's needs.

[31] To put this issue in perspective, imagine one nonlawyer businessperson wandering down the hall to talk with another nonlawyer businessperson about a dispute developing with a problem customer. Their communications would not be **attorney-client privileged** and would be fully discoverable in later litigation. Courts are concerned that the answer be the

How do you do that? If the lawyer is outside your **practice organization**, you need to show that you expressly consulted the other lawyer as your counsel for legal advice on this situation. That doesn't mean that you necessarily have to pay that other lawyer; she can agree to advise you *pro bono* if she wishes. But a brief writing that confirms that you have retained her to discuss your concerns regarding your representation of a particular client (or some other subject matter) will go a long way toward persuading a judge in some later dispute that you were engaged in **attorney-client privileged** communications.

Within your own **practice organization**, authority is mixed. The **organization's** management should appoint one or more lawyers in the organization as in-house counsel whose specific job it is to field and address concerns about pending matters on a **confidential** and **attorney-client privileged** basis. Some **practice organizations** have designated "Firm Counsel," an "Ethics Partner," or an "Ethics Committee" for this purpose; government agencies often appoint "Professional Responsibility Counsel" within the agency for the same purpose. Regardless of the name, the fact and purpose of the appointment need to be formally stated and documented so that the **practice organization** can show that the consultations were intended to be, and properly were, **confidential** and **attorney-client privileged**. And you should be aware that some jurisdictions draw peculiar distinctions between in-firm and outside ethics counsel and forbid consultations between any two lawyers in the same firm to be privileged as against the firm's client.[32]

> **Problem 8B-4:** Which of the following is a proper disclosure? Which disclosures are likely to be treated as **confidential** and **attorney-client privileged** as against the lawyer's client and others?
>
> All of the problems below are based on the following: Your client, Perry Plexing, insists that you introduce evidence at the impending trial of his civil claims against his former employer—evidence that it's clear to you is relevant only to claims that the judge has already dismissed, but that the client wants you to argue to the jury. Plexing says that he'll refuse to pay your fees and sue you for malpractice unless you "try my case my way." To help assess your risk and manage the situation in the most prudent way, you consult an experienced trial lawyer, Gina Grayhair, and run the situation by her, including descriptions of the claims and defenses, the evidence available, and your conversations with your client. Her advice is very practical and very helpful.
>
> a. You are a solo practitioner. Gina Grayhair is your favorite aunt, who has retired from the practice of law and whose bar status is inactive.

---

same if the business in question happens to be a law firm, or if one or both of the businesspeople happens to have a law license but the search for legal advice isn't why one is consulting the other.

[32] *See, e.g., Bank Brussels Lambert v. Credit Lyonnais (Suisse) S.A.,* 220 F.Supp.2d 283 (S.D.N.Y. 2002). Later decisions by some state supreme courts protect such intra-firm consultations with designated firm counsel. *See, e.g., RFF Family Partnership v. Burns & Levinson, LLP,* 465 Mass. 702 (2013); *St. Simon's Waterfront LLC v. Hunter, Maclean, Exley & Dunn, P.C.,* 293 Ga. 419 (2013).

　　b. Same as (a), except Gina Grayhair has her own solo practice and rents space in your suite of offices.

　　c. Same as (b), except that before you begin the consultation, you confirm with Ms. Grayhair in a brief email that she has agreed to act as your attorney for the limited purpose of advising you regarding some tactical, legal, and client-dispute issues connected with your representation of Perry Plexing. How does it affect your analysis if you agree to pay Ms. Grayhair her ordinary hourly rate for the brief consultation?

　　d. You work in a medium-sized law firm. Gina Grayhair is an experienced trial lawyer, and she is the senior lawyer in your firm assigned to the Perry Plexing case, but she has been letting you handle the case and the contact with the client with minimal supervision.

　　e. You work in a medium-sized law firm. Gina Grayhair is the chair of the litigation group in your firm and has not been involved in the Plexing case.

5. Lawyer Self-Defense

Model Rule 1.6(b)(5) allows lawyers to use **confidential information** to protect their own interests in three limited circumstances:

> [i] to establish a claim or defense on behalf of the lawyer in a controversy between the lawyer and the client,
>
> [ii] to establish a defense to a criminal charge or civil claim against the lawyer based upon conduct in which the client was involved, or
>
> [iii] to respond to allegations in any proceeding concerning the lawyer's representation of the client. . . .

(Paragraph breaks and bracketed numerals added for convenience.)

▶ REASON FOR THE RULE ◀ It's not hard to see the need for these exceptions. It would hardly be fair for a client to complain about what his lawyer had done (or not done) during the engagement, or what the lawyer had charged for it, and then prevent the lawyer from refuting the complaint or explaining her conduct, which would almost always necessarily require the use of **confidential information**. Likewise, if a third party (say, an opposing party in a preceding deal or dispute) or a criminal or bar prosecutor accuses a lawyer of wrongdoing while representing a client, it would only be fair for the lawyer to be able to defend herself. *See* **Model Rule 1.6 Comments [10]-[11]**. In all of these circumstances, the lawyer is allowed to disclose the minimum **confidential information** reasonably necessary to pursue or defend her rights. ◀ REASON FOR THE RULE ▶

But it's important to understand the limits on this right. Not all **confidential information** available to the lawyer may be reasonably necessary to pursue or defend her rights, and not every accusation or insult justifies resort to these exceptions to the **duty of confidentiality**. Lawyers who feel unfairly accused (and most lawyers who are accused feel unfairly accused) transgress these limits with some frequency and at great cost to themselves.

One common mistake that accused lawyers make is to disclose **confidential information** that is embarrassing to the accuser (typically a current or former client) as a means of "defending themselves" against the accusations. Courts and bar prosecutors generally treat this tactic very harshly unless the embarrassing disclosure is directly relevant to a specific claim or defense in the controversy.[33]

Another common error that accused lawyers make is to forget the exception's limited scope—the lawyer self-defense exception has commonly been limited to accusations leveled in actual or threatened litigation. This is reflected in the exception's repeated use of words such as "claim or defense . . . in a controversy," "defense to a criminal charge or civil claim," and "allegations in any proceeding." Most states that have considered the issue have declined to allow lawyers to rely on **confidential information** to respond to bad-mouthing *outside* the litigation context, most commonly condemning the use of **confidential information** in responses to bad reviews on social media.[34]

> **Problem 8B-5:** Which of the following is a proper disclosure?
>
> a. Former client Bonnie Badmouth has refused to pay your hourly fees, asserting that your bills reflect work that she did not ask you to perform. In the fee arbitration convened to resolve the dispute, you introduce emails from Bonnie in which you inform her of your intent to perform those tasks and her responses in which she consents.
>
> b. Bonnie Badmouth claims that you failed to return unearned portions of a retainer at the end of your engagement. In response to the state bar's disciplinary inquiry, you provide the state bar records of your client trust account relevant to Bonnie's retainer, as well as email correspondence between the two of you on the subject.
>
> c. Dan Disappointed, the opposing party in the negotiation that you just completed on Bonnie Badmouth's behalf, has accused you of fraud, claiming that you misrepresented material facts during the negotiation. You supply Dan's lawyer with correspondence and documents that you had received from Bonnie that formed the basis for your representations during the negotiation, as well as a ten-year-old judgment against Bonnie for civil fraud in a different matter that you discovered while representing her.
>
> d. After church last Sunday, Carla Congregant mentioned that she had been thinking of asking you to prepare her will, but Bonnie Badmouth told Carla that you had messed

---

[33] *See, e.g.,* Debra Cassens Weiss, *Lawyer Is Suspended for Giving Client's Business a Bad Review in 'Good for the Gander' Retaliation,* https://www.abajournal.com/news/article/lawyer-suspended-for-giving-clients-business-a-bad-review-in-good-for-the-gander-retaliation (May 13, 2020) (lawyer suspended for disclosing client's criminal record in response to negative social media review); Stephanie Francis Ward, *Attorney Sued for Malpractice Is Suspended after Releasing Client's Psychiatric records,* http://www.abajournal.com/news/article/attorney_sued_for_malpractice_suspended_after_releasing_clients_psychiatric/?utm_source=maestro&utm_medium=email&utm_campaign=weekly_email (Sept. 18, 2018); *Dixon v. State Bar,* 32 Cal. 3d 728, 735 (1982) (lawyer disciplined for, among other things, gratuitously disclosing client's spouse's irrelevant extramarital affair).

[34] *See, e.g.,* ABA Formal Ethics Op. No. 496 (2021); Joan C. Rogers, *Lawyers Must Not Divulge Client Confidences When Responding to Negative Reviews Online,* http://lawyersmanual.bna.com/mopw2/3300/doc_display.adp?fedfid=41578824&vname=mopcnotallissues&jd=a0e5u7b9t5&split=0 (Jan. 29, 2014).

Bonnie's will up. Carla wonders what happened. You explain that Bonnie is developing early-onset dementia and gets confused sometimes, which you learned while preparing her estate plan.

e. Same as (d), except that you reply to Carla, "I can't discuss Bonnie's personal affairs, but I can assure you that what she said is not true."

6. To Comply with Other Law

One of the most basic aspects of the **duty of confidentiality** is that it prohibits only *voluntary* disclosure of **confidential information**. Unlike the **attorney-client privilege** and the **attorney work product doctrine,** the **duty of confidentiality** yields to any proper legal compulsion to disclose. *See* **Chapter 8.A at 226. Model Rule 1.6(b)(6)** reflects this feature of the **duty of confidentiality** by acknowledging that a lawyer **may** disclose **confidential information** to the extent reasonably necessary "to comply with other law or a court order."

"Other law" sufficient to compel disclosure of **confidential** (but not **attorney-client privileged**) **information** includes (by way of examples) discovery requests, such as those found in Fed. R. Civ. P. 28-37, disclosure obligations such as those found in **Fed. R. Civ. P. 26(a)**, and subpoenas authorized by any law, such as **Fed. R. Civ. P. 45**, as well as any court order compelling disclosure.

Problem 8B-6: Which of the following are proper disclosures?

a. You are a family lawyer. The matrimonial law in your state requires the parties to a divorce proceeding to fill out a court-mandated disclosure form listing all assets and liabilities in which each spouse has any interest and to serve it on the other spouse. Your client, the husband in a divorce, has given you a substantial retainer as a deposit against his future fees and expenses in the proceedings, which you are holding in your client trust account. That retainer was the contents of a secret offshore bank account that your client held in his own name, and of which his wife was unaware. When you tell the client that the amount of the retainer should be disclosed, he refuses, saying "that's between you and me." You accordingly add a notation to the form before serving it that disclosure of other assets is precluded by the attorney-client privilege and the attorney work product doctrine. The wife's lawyer moves to compel disclosure, contesting your claims of privilege. The court rules in the wife's favor, and orders the assets referred to in the objection disclosed. You supplement the disclosure to state the amounts held for the husband in your attorney trust account. What **must** or **should** you do if the client instructs you not to supplement the disclosure?

b. You represent the plaintiff in a trade-secret case. The court issues an order requiring your client to describe, in writing and under seal, the trade secrets that it claims the defendant misappropriated. You and your client believe that this order fails to protect the trade secret adequately from being viewed by certain personnel working for the defendant, and for that reason, the court order is legally erroneous. You seek interlocutory review of the order, but the appellate court does not stay the order before the date that the order requires compliance. You file the description of the trade secret as the trial court's order directs.

7. To Allow the Lawyer to Check for Conflicts of Interest

Model Rule 1.6(b)(7) "recognizes that lawyers in different firms may need to disclose limited information to each other to detect and resolve **conflicts of interest**, such as when a lawyer is considering an association with another firm, two or more firms are considering a merger, or a lawyer is considering the purchase of a law practice." **Model Rule 1.6 Comment [13]**. We will deal with the complex and difficult **conflict of interest** issues created when lawyers change firms or when firms merge when we get to **Chapter 22 at 597**, but for now, it is sufficient to say that lawyers **may** disclose **confidential information** in order to address these issues as long as the information is limited in amount and purpose and would not "compromise the **attorney-client privilege** or prejudice the client." **Model Rule 1.6 Comment [13]**.

Problem 8B-7: Which of the following is a proper disclosure?

a. Associate Gulliver Green is moving from Firm 1 to Firm 2. To ensure that Gulliver does not have **confidential information** that could create a **conflict of interest** for his new firm (*see* **Chapter 22.D at 709**), Firm 2 requests that Gulliver provide a list of each matter on which he worked at Firm 1, the names of the parties, and a very brief description of the subject matter. Gulliver does so.

b. One of the matters in (a) that Gulliver discloses to Firm 2 that he worked on at Firm 1 is a confidential investigation for Firm 1 client PubliCo concerning whether two senior officers engaged in insider trading of the firm's publicly traded securities. This investigation was conducted in strict secrecy and resulted in the forced retirement of the two officers.

c. Another of the matters in (a) that Gulliver discloses to Firm 2 involved the client in **Problem 8.B-3(b) at 243** (the business manager who embezzled funds from her employer). One of Firm 1's white-collar criminal defense lawyers tried to work out a deal with the district attorney on a "no-names" basis but was unable to reach an acceptable resolution, so the identities of Firm 1's client and her employer were never disclosed.

C. The Limits of the Duty of Confidentiality – How Hard Cases Can Test Your Ethical Tolerance

The **duty of confidentiality** is very broad and powerful in its reach, and as we've just seen, the exceptions to that reach are limited. Sometimes that breadth and power can create profoundly uncomfortable dilemmas for responsible counsel. Here are two particularly agonizing examples:

Problem 8C-1: The Miscarriage of Justice: The fact pattern recurs every few years, but the heartache remains the same.[35] A criminal defense lawyer learns in confidence from a client that the client previously committed a serious crime for which someone else who had no part in the crime has been wrongfully accused, tried, and convicted, and now is serving a lengthy prison sentence (or in the case of a murder, may even be sentenced to death). The only way to correct the miscarriage of justice is for the actual perpetrator (the lawyer's current client) to come forward, but of course he has no interest in confessing to another crime, and will never authorize his lawyer to alert the authorities to the problem. The lawyer is understandably horrified at the injustice and wants to do something to get the innocent person released. What, if anything, can the lawyer do? Are there changes in circumstances over time that could affect the lawyer's options and, if so, what are they and why? Does it change the analysis if the wrongfully convicted man is on death row and his execution date is approaching?

Problem 8C-2: The Kidnapped Children:[36] A single mother of two school-age children is violently murdered in her home. Her children are missing. Fingerprints in the mother's blood are found on the walls of her home; they belong to Defendant. Defendant, who has a history of mental illness and substance abuse, is promptly arrested. Defendant's counsel meets with Defendant in prison. Defendant is largely incoherent during the interview, but makes a few garbled remarks suggesting the vague possibility that the children may be alive and confined in a remote location.

Counsel pursues this idea with Defendant as the interview continues, and Defendant draws a map that may (or may not) indicate the location of the children (or their murdered bodies). If the map has anything to do with the location of the children or their bodies, it almost certainly implicates Defendant in two more gruesome crimes (either kidnapping or murder of the children). If the children are alive, they will likely die unless they are found and rescued. What, if anything, **must**, **may**, or **should** counsel do consistent with his professional obligations?

Big-Picture Takeaways from Chapter 8.B-.C

1. When you are analyzing **confidentiality** issues, break the information down into the smallest salient pieces and consider them one at a time. If only some of the information is not **confidential** or is subject to an exception to the **duty of confidentiality**, only that portion of the information **may** or **must** be disclosed. *See* **Chapter 8.B at 236**.

2. The fact that something is not subject to the **duty of confidentiality** (or is subject to an exception to the **duty of confidentiality**) means only that you

---

[35] *See, e.g.,* Associated Press, *A Killer's 26-Year-Old Secret May Set Inmate Free,* https://www.nbcnews.com/id/wbna24083675 (April 12, 2008).

[36] These facts are loosely adapted from *McClure v. Thompson*, 323 F.3d 1233, 1244-45 (9th Cir. 2003), a staple of many professional responsibility casebooks.

may use or disclose it without concern for its **confidentiality**. There may be other reasons why you **must not** disclose or use it even though the information is not **confidential**. And even if you **may** use or disclose the information, there are often very good reasons that you **should not**, such as preserving client relations or your reputation in your community for discretion and good judgment. *See* **Chapter 8.B at 236.**

3. All of the **confidentiality** exceptions in **Model Rule 1.6(b)** are *permissive* ("may") and not *mandatory* ("shall" or "must"). As a practical matter, that means that once you have determined that an exception applies to a particular piece of information, you still need to reason out whether you **should** or **should not** disclose it under the circumstances in which you find yourself. *See* **Chapter 8.B at 236.**

4. The **Model Rule 1.6(b)** exceptions to **confidentiality** are limited to *disclosure* ("a lawyer may reveal"), and do not authorize *use*. *See* **Chapter 8.B at 237.**

5. Each **Model Rule 1.6(b)** exception to **confidentiality** has an explicitly defined scope and purpose. The introductory language's qualification that a lawyer may disclose **confidential information** "*to the extent* the lawyer reasonably believes necessary" (emphasis added) to achieve an exception's purposes means that you **must** always take great care to disclose only (i) the minimum amount of **confidential information** subject to the exception (ii) to the minimum number of people strictly necessary (iii) to serve the specific purpose of the exception at issue. *See* **Chapter 8.B at 237.**

6. All of the **Model Rule 1.6(b)** exceptions to **confidentiality** are available on the condition that "the lawyer reasonably believes" the disclosure is "necessary" to achieve the purpose of the exception. *See* **Chapter 8.B at 237.**

7. Here is a list of all of the **Model Rule 1.6** exceptions to the **duty of confidentiality**. There are other Rules that cover additional exceptions (which we'll cover elsewhere in this book):
   a. When and to the extent the client has provided express **informed consent** to the disclosure or use. *See* **Chapter 8.B at 238.**
   b. When and to the extent "the disclosure is impliedly authorized in order to carry out the representation." *See* **Chapter 8.B at 239.**
   c. When and to the extent you reasonably believe that disclosure is necessary to prevent imminent and serious physical harm. *See* **Chapter 8.B at 240.**
   d. When and to the extent you reasonably believe that disclosure is necessary:
      i.   to prevent the client from committing a crime or fraud that is reasonably certain to result in substantial injury to the financial

interests or property of another and in furtherance of which the client has used or is using your legal services; or

ii. to prevent, mitigate, or rectify substantial injury to the financial interests or property of another that is reasonably certain to result or has resulted from the client's commission of a crime or fraud in furtherance of which the client has used your legal services.

See **Chapter 8.B at 242**.

e. When and to the extent reasonably necessary for you yourself to seek legal advice to help you determine how to comply with your own legal or ethical obligations (but be sure to seek that advice in a way that protects its **confidentiality** and **attorney-client privilege**). See **Chapter 8.B at 243**.

f. When and to the extent reasonably necessary, in your own self-defense, you use **confidential information** to establish a claim or defense on your behalf in a controversy between you and your client, to establish a defense to a criminal charge or civil claim against you based upon conduct in which your client was involved, or to respond to allegations in any proceeding concerning your representation of your client. See **Chapter 8.B at 246**.

g. When and to the extent reasonably necessary to comply with any legal compulsion ("other law or a court order") to disclose **confidential information**. See **Chapter 8.B at 248**.

h. When and to the extent reasonably necessary to determine whether you may have a **conflict of interest**. See **Chapter 8.B at 249**.

Multiple-Choice Review Questions for Chapter 8.B-.C

1. Lawyer Juanita is representing client Martin in a medical malpractice case arising from a botched surgery. During a routine visit to his physician, Martin learns that he has a rare genetic disorder known as Marfan syndrome. He experiences no symptoms now, but he could have heart problems in the future. In addition, any of his biological children would have a 50 percent chance of inheriting the condition. Martin communicates that information to Juanita. The information is not relevant to the medical malpractice case, so neither Juanita nor Martin tells anyone.

A few months after the malpractice case settles, Juanita receives a wedding invitation in the mail. It is from Martin and his fiancée Kristen. She calls Martin to offer her congratulations. During the conversation, she asks how Kristen feels about Martin's diagnosis. Martin says that he hasn't told her and that he's not planning to, because he wants to spare her any worry.

Juanita continues thinking about the conversation long after the call ends. She can't help but think that, if she were in Kristen's position, she would want to know.

Can Juanita disclose the information without violating her professional obligations?

a. Yes. Juanita **must** disclose the information.

b. Yes. Juanita **may** disclose the information if Kristen asks.

c. No. Juanita **must not** disclose the information.

d. No. Juanita **must not** disclose the information unless Kristen asks.

2. Allison is counsel to a school district embroiled in a breach of contract case with a general contractor. She receives document requests from the contractor. She reviews those requests with a representative of the school district and, together, they identify responsive documents to be produced in discovery. Allison copies those documents and provides a copy to the contractor.

Has Allison violated her **duty of confidentiality** by disclosing the documents?

a. Yes. There are no exceptions to the **duty of confidentiality** that would permit Allison to disclose the documents.

b. Yes. She did not have express **informed consent**, in writing, from the school district.

c. No. Documents cannot be **confidential**. Only communications can be **confidential**.

d. No. She had implied consent from the school district to disclose the documents because the understanding was that the documents would be produced.

3. Gertrude practices law in the State of Raptor, where the state has adopted verbatim the language of **Model Rule 1.6(b)(1)**. Gertrude represents Hank, a local businessman who sometimes enters into joint ventures for construction projects around the state.

One day, Hank storms into Gertrude's office. She asks him what's wrong. He says, "You know that power line project I was working on with Bob? The one you were drafting the contract for? Bob just decided to work on the project with someone else." Gertrude expresses her sympathy.

"Don't worry," Hank says, as he shows Gertrude the revolver tucked in the waistband of his jeans. "Double-crossing me is the last thing that Bob will ever do." Hank then leaves, slamming the front door on his way out. He peels out of the parking lot in the direction of Bob's house.

Assuming that Gertrude believes that Hank's threat is sincere, what can she do?

a. Gertrude **must** call Bob and warn him.

   b. Gertrude **may** call Bob and warn him.
   c. Gertrude **must not** call the police and alert them.
   d. Gertrude **must** call the police and alert them.

4. Jen, who practices in the Commonwealth of Keystone, is concerned that her client is using her services to commit fraud. She would like to solicit ethics advice from the Keystone ethics hotline. Keystone has adopted **Model Rule 1.6(b)** verbatim.

   What **confidential information may** Jen disclose to the ethics hotline under Keystone Rule 1.6(b)(4)?
   a. She **must not** disclose any **confidential information**.
   b. The minimum amount of **confidential information** necessary to get the advice Jen needs.
   c. All the **confidential information** she has regarding the client in question.
   d. Only the **confidential information** that her client agrees that she may disclose.

5. Under the Model Rules of Professional Conduct, if a client sues a lawyer alleging legal malpractice, might the lawyer be entitled to disclose relevant **confidential information** as part of the lawyer's defense, even without the client's consent?
   a. Yes, under **Model Rule 1.6(b)(5)**.
   b. Yes, under **Model Rule 1.6(a)**.
   c. No. **Model Rule 1.6(b)(5)** does not permit such a disclosure.
   d. No. **Model Rule 1.6(a)** requires consent for any disclosure, including under these circumstances.

9

Creation, Assumption, Disclaimer, and Termination of a Lawyer's Duties

FRANK AND HIS FIRM'S LITIGATION PARTNER, Harlan "Happy" Trials, are meeting with a potential new client, Bobby Boilermaker. Bobby is a welder. About a year and a half ago, he was injured on the job when he was hit by a piece of falling debris that someone knocked off a scaffolding at a construction site. The debris hit Bobby on the head just as he had taken off his hard hat for a few seconds to remove his welding mask. Bobby suffered a nasty scalp laceration that required over a dozen stitches. He also suffered a moderate concussion. He was out of work for several weeks.

Given his medical expenses and lost wages, not to mention his pain and suffering, Bobby went to see a lawyer about his accident. One of Bobby's coworkers recommended Charlie Comp, a workers' compensation lawyer in town. Charlie was happy to take the case. He explained in their initial meeting that workers' compensation is all that he does, and that he would handle Bobby's workers' compensation claim for this on-the-job injury. Bobby has brought Charlie's engagement letter with him to the meeting with Happy and Frank. Paragraph 3 of Charlie's engagement letter provides:

> 3. **Scope of Engagement**. The Law Offices of Charlie Comp handles workers' compensation claims. We're specialists, and that's all we do. We will handle your workers' compensation claim that arose out of your on-the-job injury on or about April 28, 2019, at the Ubetcha Industries job site in Ourtown. We will not handle any other claim or legal issue for you.

"So what happened with your comp claim?" Happy asks. "No problem," Bobby replies. "He filed the claim the week after we met, and he got me my money pretty quick." "But something's wrong," Happy prompts, gently. "Well," Bobby explains, "the other day, I was over at the union hall, and I ran into one of the folks who was working that Ubetcha job with me. She's an officer of our union local. She asked me how my head was doing, and I told her that it's healed up okay. She asked if I got paid for the injury, and I told her that I had gotten my workers' comp. Then she asked if I had sued anyone in court, and I said no, I didn't think so, unless that's what workers' comp is. She told me that Ubetcha was a multi-contractor job, and that there probably was a lawsuit that I could file in court that would pay me a bunch more money on top of the workers' comp. I don't know why Charlie didn't do that. Anyhow, she recommended you guys, so I'm here to see if I can get anything more coming my way because of that accident."

"Well," says Happy, "your friend was absolutely right to send you here. Workers' comp does provide prompt help for on-the-job injuries, but it doesn't pay as much as a lawsuit can for the same accident. Often, workers' comp is all that you can get, but for some kinds of on-the-job accidents, you can get money from both workers' comp and a separate lawsuit, and it does look like this could be one of those accidents. But . . ." (and here Happy's face turns serious), "I'm afraid that I have some bad news. There's this law called a statute of limitations. What it means is that you have to file your lawsuit within a limited time after you get hurt, or you lose your rights forever. And I'm sorry to have to tell you that the statute of limitations has run on the lawsuit that you could have filed, which means it's too late."

"What?" Bobby is startled and upset. "You mean I had a right to more money, but Charlie Comp didn't get it for me, and now it's too late?" "I'm afraid so," Happy answers. "Any way around it?" Bobby asks. "I'm afraid not," Happy replies.[1] "But there may be another way that we can help you. How would you feel about suing Charlie Comp for that extra money?" "Sue the lawyer? How would that work?" Bobby asks, dubiously. "Well, the claim would be for professional negligence; you've probably heard it called malpractice. The idea would be that Charlie didn't get you what he should have gotten you, and that's his fault, so he should pay you what he failed to get you from the company whose employee knocked that debris off the scaffolding and onto you." Bobby nods. "You're telling me that Charlie could have gotten me more money, but he didn't, and that's not fair, so he should pay." "Exactly," says Happy. Bobby thinks for a moment. "OK," he says. "Let's do it."

After Bobby leaves, Frank turns to his boss with a puzzled look. "I don't get it," Frank says. "The lawyer told Bobby that he was a workers' comp specialist, and that's all he did. The engagement letter specifically says that the lawyer is not going to handle anything other than Bobby's comp claim. The lawyer did exactly what he promised to do—handle the comp claim and nothing else—and he did it right. Where's the malpractice?"

Is Frank right? Should his firm take Bobby's case?[2]

---

[1] Admit it: You were waiting for us to say, "Happy replies, *sadly*." Forget it. Even we have standards.

[2] This hypothetical is based on *Nichols v. Keller*, 15 Cal. App. 4th 1672, 19 Cal. Rptr. 2d 601 (1993), a case that appears in many professional responsibility casebooks because it so beautifully illustrates the principles that it addresses.

A. Creation of the Attorney-Client Relationship

In this chapter, we're going to explore the contours of the attorney-client relationship. We'll discuss how you, as a practicing lawyer, develop obligations to others, what those obligations generally are, and how they begin and end. To start with, we'll explore where attorney-client relationships come from and what they mean by addressing three simple questions:

1. Why should you care whether you have (or want to have) an attorney-client relationship with someone?
2. How do you know whether you have an attorney-client relationship with someone?[3]
3. What is the scope of your attorney-client relationship in any given engagement?

Let's get started.

1. Why Should You Care Whether You Have an Attorney-Client Relationship with Someone?

This may seem like a silly question at first glance, but stick with us—its practical implications are deadly serious. From your reading in this course up to this point, you know that we lawyers are fiduciaries and agents to our clients (*see* **Chapter 5.B at 106**; **Chapter 6.A at 133**), and that as fiduciaries and agents, we owe each client a complex bundle of obligations, including **duties** of **loyalty**, **care**, **confidentiality**, and **candor**. When an attorney-client relationship is created, all of these duties instantly snap into being and become enforceable obligations that you owe from that moment onward. If you have these obligations but don't know it (or actively think that you don't have them), then you won't do any of the things that a lawyer would reasonably be expected to do for a client, and eventually the client will be harmed by this failure. For example, if someone reasonably believes that you've undertaken to get her compensation for an injury, but you don't think that you have, then you won't send a demand letter or file a complaint. The statute of limitations will run, the claim will be time-barred, and the "client" will assert that any reasonable lawyer would have filed a timely claim and that you breached your

---

[3] A quick reminder: The "someone" with whom you might initiate an attorney-client relationship could be a business organization, such as a corporation or a partnership, rather than an individual natural person. Of course, business organizations are just legal constructs; they can't speak or act other than through living, breathing human beings who act as their agents (in much the same way that you act as an agent for your client; *see* **Chapter 6.B at 134 & n.4**). But because business organizations are legally distinct from their owners, managers, and employees, representing a business organization is completely different from representing any of the organization's owners, managers, or employees. *See* **Model Rule 1.13(a)**; **Chapter 23.A at 770**. The point to remember for purposes of this discussion is that when you're agreeing to represent someone, you need to be very clear, both in your own mind and in your communications with everyone else, precisely *who* (or what) your client is: The business organization? One of its constituents (owners, managers, employees)? Some combination? (In the latter case, you must address possible **conflicts of interest** among your joint clients; *see* **Chapter 22.B at 645**; **Chapter 23.A at 772**.)

professional **duty of care** by failing to do so. And then the complaints to the state bar and the claims for civil liability will begin.

What's more, once someone is your client, you owe the full panoply of lawyer's duties to that client at least until the attorney-client relationship is over (and in the case of the **duty of confidentiality**, for a long time after that; *see* **Chapter 8.A at 224**), meaning that those substantial and serious obligations continue. If you know what they are, you can comply with them or, in appropriate cases, take steps to terminate the attorney-client relationship and limit those obligations.

In short, being someone's lawyer means you owe that someone a broad range of very serious and substantial duties—duties enforceable by very serious **consequences**. You'd best know who your clients are.

REAL WORLD Because the duties that you owe a client are so serious and substantial, you would be wise to consider at the outset whether the person in your office is someone you want to represent and whether the needs that the person wants you to address are ones that you feel comfortable addressing. Most professional liability insurers and professional liability defense counsel will tell you that one of the most common mistakes that lawyers make are "intake" mistakes—that is, taking on the wrong client or the wrong matter. Every intake decision requires judgment and a certain leap of faith, and in many kinds of practices, clients often arrive burdened with a range of difficult challenges and needs. But many lawyers looking back on problem clients, fee disputes, and client malpractice claims will concede that they had a bad feeling in that first meeting or soon after, should have seen the train wreck coming, and should have simply stayed off the train. No one sign will tell you to stay away, but there are some classic "red flags" that should prompt you to inquire and think about whether the engagement is well-advised:

- A potential new matter in an area in which you lack experience or expertise. Do you know what's going to be involved in getting up to speed? Can you do it in the time available? Can you afford the time investment? *See* **Chapter 7.A at 172**.

- A **prospective client** who wants to "make a point," obtain revenge, harass an enemy, or use the justice system for anything other than the remedies that the law conventionally supplies.

- A **prospective client** whose expectations regarding the process or outcome are unrealistic in terms of timing, type, or amount, and who resists your efforts to manage those expectations. (Always ask in that first meeting what the potential client would like to see happen as a result of the engagement; it's one of the most revealing questions that you can ask.)

- A **prospective client** who is looking to change lawyers, especially for the second (or third, or fourth) time.

- A **prospective client** who says, "I don't care what it costs." He will.

- Conversely, a **prospective client** who is single-mindedly focused on what it will cost, and how to reduce that cost. A corollary concern is the **prospective client** who aggressively seeks discounts on the current matter in return for vague promises of valuable future work or referrals.

- A **prospective client** who, without apparent relevant education, background, or experience (and there are plenty of clients who do have lots of one or more of these), tries to impress you with his knowledge of the governing law or procedure, especially if the source of that knowledge is television or the Internet.

- A **prospective client** who has trouble clearly and consistently answering your basic factual questions about what happened.

- A **prospective client** who gets angry or defensive if you probe the details of his story for consistency or plausibility.

- A **prospective client** with financial, lifestyle, or personal issues, past or present, such as substance abuse, mental illness, financial problems, or a bumpy employment history. To be clear, **prospective clients** with such issues may genuinely need and deserve your help, and in some practices, this kind of client background is common (and may be the specific problem for which the client is appropriately seeking legal help). But you need to know your client, so you know what you're taking on, whether you're able to help, and what your help may require.[4] REAL WORLD

2. How Do You Know Whether You Have an Attorney-Client Relationship with Someone?

Often, the existence of an attorney-client relationship is easy to determine. Sometimes it's created by court order or other law; public defenders acquire their attorney-client relationships with their clients this way. More often, the relationship arises by agreement: The client says something like, "I'd like you to represent me"; the lawyer replies something like, "I would be pleased to represent you"; and off they go. Terms like the fee arrangement and other details are resolved, and work begins (though not always in that order). But if you think back to your Contracts course, you'll recall that sometimes it was maddeningly uncertain whether or when legally binding commitments had been made, and that sometimes binding commitments are made before all the details of the commitments have been worked out (or even discussed).

---

[4] Reflecting the frequency with which intake problems ripen into other problems, there are a lot of "potential client red flag" lists out there. This one is indebted to Peter Geraghty & Susan Michmerhuizen, *Red Flags and White Whales: Beware of Problem Clients*, https://www.americanbar.org/news/abanews/publications/youraba/2017/november-2017/red-flags-and-white-whales--beware-of-problem-clients.html (Nov. 2017). *See also* Douglas R. Richmond, *Dishonest or Unworthy Clients: "Pink Flags,"* https://www.americanbar.org/groups/professional_responsibility/dishonest-or-unworthy-clients--pink-flags/.

Because of the high stakes that often attach to whether or when an attorney-client relationship has formed, we need a rule to guide the analysis of uncertain cases. Because of the myriad ways that humans interact as they are considering forming legally significant relationships, it's not possible to state a rule that answers this question with geometric precision, just as you discovered that the rules governing formation of a contract had some irreducible degree of uncertainty built in. Nevertheless, the *Restatement (Third) of the Law Governing Lawyers* § 14 provides a workable standard that approximates the law in most American jurisdictions. Here's what it says:

A relationship of lawyer and client arises when:

1. A person manifests to a lawyer the person's intent that the lawyer provide legal services to the person; and either

   a. The lawyer manifests to the person consent to do so; or

   b. The lawyer fails to manifest lack of consent to do so, and the lawyer knows or reasonably should know that the person reasonably relies on the lawyer to provide the services; or

2. A tribunal with power to do so appoints the lawyer to provide the services.

TAMING THE TEXT Take a moment and study Section 14(1). It's not literally the law on forming an attorney-client relationship, but it's a good description of what the law is in most U.S. jurisdictions. Note that formation depends on the manifestation of an intention on the *client's* part to have the lawyer provide legal services. And the attorney-client relationship is formed if the lawyer, in response, either manifests consent to provide services, or *fails to manifest lack of intent* to provide services under circumstances in which the lawyer reasonably should know that the client is relying on the lawyer to provide those services. Pay special attention to what this standard does *not* involve:

- Formation of an attorney-client relationship depends on the client's and the lawyer's "manifestation of intent" to one another (a phrase that should be familiar from Contracts), which means that what either of them may have been silently *thinking* doesn't matter. What does matter is what each person *says* and *does*—that's how we humans manifest intent.

- In terms of *what* intent must be manifested to form the relationship, look carefully at the Restatement section. It's quite clear that once a client manifests an intent to retain you, then you can form the attorney-client relationship *either* by manifesting "yes" ("[t]he lawyer manifests . . . consent") *or by failing to manifest "no"* ("[t]he lawyer fails to manifest lack of consent . . ."). In other words, your silence will often be construed as consent, and it's up to you to make the existence or nonexistence of the relationship clear to the **prospective client**.

- The standard is objective ("knows or reasonably should know that the [client] reasonably relies on the lawyer . . ."), which means the lawyer's protest that "I never thought that person was depending on me" is irrelevant unless it's reasonable and grounded in *objective* facts outside the lawyer's head.

- Formation of an attorney-client relationship doesn't depend on whether the parties have mutually manifested an intention as to precisely *what* services the lawyer will provide; a general expression of intent that "legal services" be provided (such as "handle my divorce" or, in some contexts, even something as general as "be my lawyer") is sufficient.

- Formation of an attorney-client relationship also doesn't necessarily depend on whether the parties have resolved any other details of the engagement, such as fees and expenses.

- Nor does formation depend on whether the lawyer has completed other preparatory steps in which the lawyer may customarily engage, such as checking for **conflicts of interest** or preparing an engagement agreement, unless the lawyer explicitly says so. In other words, "I can't represent you until I check for **conflicts** and we complete an engagement letter" is a way of "manifest[ing] lack of consent" to the client's request for services, at least right now, but it doesn't count unless you actually say it in a way that the **prospective client** reasonably ought to understand.

Add all this up, and what you get is the conclusion that it is breathtakingly simple to initiate an attorney-client relationship and to assume all of the duties that accompany it, even when you subjectively may not have meant to do so. This is another instance of a principle that we've already mentioned: That as the educated, knowledgeable, articulate, trained lawyer, it's up to you to clarify the situation, in this case to clarify whether or not an attorney-client relationship has been formed.

Put slightly differently, *you* bear the risk of any uncertainty that you allow to persist in this context. One good way to sum up this allocation of risk is that *an attorney-client relationship exists any time that the* **client** *actually and reasonably believes that such a relationship exists.* And consistent with the idea of putting the obligation to clarify on the party best situated to do it (the "cheapest cost avoider," as the law-and-econ folks would say), what the client reasonably believes is based not on what someone with a lawyer's knowledge and sophistication would bring to the judgment, but on what a person in the *client's* position, with the *client's* knowledge and background, would reasonably believe under the circumstances. Remember, what you do is usually judged from the *client's* (or **prospective client's**) point of view. Your role as the lawyer is to influence what the client actually and reasonably believes by making the situation clear, and you must do that by manifesting your consent or lack of it in terms the client understands. As your preschool teacher used to say, use your words. Or as we have advised you in much the same spirit,

When in doubt, speak out

and **inquire; explain; confirm** (*see* **Chapter 6.A at 139**). ⟨ TAMING THE TEXT ⟩

> **Problem 9A-1: The Accidental Client:** Maya attends a cocktail party hosted by another resident of her apartment building. Friends of the host and other residents of the building whom Maya knows only by sight attend as well. Maya strikes up a conversation with another guest at the party. Upon discovering that Maya is a lawyer, the guest reveals that he is suffering through a difficult divorce and is quite unhappy with his lawyer. He describes a number of recent events in the proceedings and asks Maya her opinion about whether his lawyer has handled them appropriately. Trying to be helpful, Maya reaches back to her Family Law course in law school and does her best to answer his questions. Her conversation partner is grateful for the advice, says that he really wants to change lawyers, and asks if they could speak again sometime. Maya offers him her business card with her contact information. What is the legal nature of their relationship at this point? Please explain your answer.

> **Problem 9A-2:** In a conference room in her offices, Maya hosts a meeting of three entrepreneurs who want to form a small technology company. The three founders include an inventor with the bright idea that the company will develop and exploit, a sales and marketing whiz, and a venture capitalist who will fund the venture. The venture capitalist is a longtime client of Maya's firm in connection with his various start-up investments, and he has made it clear to Maya and her supervising partner, in a phone call before the meeting, that he expects her and her firm to represent him and his interests in the formation of this new company. In the meeting, the three founders develop an understanding of what their respective contributions and responsibilities to the new company will be, as well as their respective management powers and ownership interests. Maya draws up papers consistent with this understanding, forms the company as a corporation, and issues the founders their shares. Who—or what—is (or are) Maya's client(s)? How do you know? (*Hint: See* **Chapter 23.A at 777**.)

3. What Is the Scope of Your Attorney-Client Relationship in Any Given Engagement?

It's time to introduce a very important concept: the *scope* of a lawyer's engagement. If you think about it for a second, every engagement has a scope. A client retains a lawyer for a particular purpose. Put simply, the purpose and scope of the engagement define what you're hired to do. That purpose could be (for example) to seek remedies for a particular injury or accident, to negotiate and document a particular transaction (or series of transactions), or to provide periodic consultation as requested in a specialized area of the law, such as antitrust, employment law, securities law, or tax. The purpose of the engagement defines the scope.

Defining the scope of an engagement is so important because the scope of the engagement defines the scope of your duties, specifically your **duties of care** and **candor**. Let's explore for a moment how your basic lawyer's duties interact with the scope of your engagement: Your **duty of loyalty** extends *beyond* the scope of your engagement: While you are representing a client, you **must not** be disloyal to that client (that is, act adversely to that client's interests) in *any* respect, even one unrelated to the engagement. *See* **Chapter 5.D at 114.** Similarly, your **duty of confidentiality** to a client covers *any* information that you learn in connection with representing that client, even information that may not be relevant to your engagement, as long as you happen to learn it in connection with representing that client. *See* **Chapter 8.A at 211.**

In contrast, your **duty of candor** is defined by the scope of your engagement: Your job is to keep your client informed regarding the engagement for which you were retained. *See* **Chapter 5.D at 117.** You have no legally enforceable *duty* to inform your client of matters that have no reasonable bearing on your engagement, even if they might be important to your client for other reasons. (Of course, you **may** inform your client of such things because you think that your client would appreciate it, unless you have a duty to someone else not to do so, for example, because it's another client's **confidential information**.) Similarly, your **duty of care** requires you to exercise the skill and diligence that a reasonable lawyer would exercise, including providing all the services that a reasonable lawyer would provide, *within the scope of your engagement.*

To illustrate the principle, imagine that you've been retained to represent a client in a personal injury case. April 15 comes around, and the client calls, exasperated, asking "Where are my tax returns?" "Your tax returns?" you say, genuinely perplexed. "Why would you be asking me about your tax returns?" "You were supposed to prepare them," the client says, slowly and emphatically, as if explaining something obvious to a four-year-old. "What gave you that idea?" you ask, confused. "You're my lawyer, aren't you?" the client demands. "So where are they?"

If you think that this client is way off base, you're right. But why? Because agreeing to represent a client in a personal injury case does not, under normal circumstances, imply any undertaking to provide other, unrelated legal services, such as preparing the client's tax returns.[5] And why is that? Because they are outside *the scope of the engagement*—it's not what you were hired to do. By the same token, however, services *within* the scope of your engagement are ones that you have a legal duty to perform whether the client asks for them specifically or not. After all, clients often need a lawyer precisely because they don't know exactly what needs to be done to address a particular problem or need. So the same client who hired you to handle that personal injury case would be well within his rights to blame you if you had failed to figure out when the statute of

---

[5] But beware—advising the client about the specific tax implications of the settlement or other result of the personal injury claim you're handling might well be within the scope of your engagement. *See* **Chapter 9.A at 266.** Do you see the difference? Explain it out loud.

limitations ran on his claim and then had failed to file a complaint in time. Determining and meeting filing deadlines is what any reasonable lawyer retained to handle a personal injury claim would do. And the client wouldn't have to ask you specifically to do those things, or even know that a statute of limitations existed; those tasks are still obviously within the scope of the engagement for which you were retained.

So how do we know what the scope of a particular engagement is, and what services it comprises? The test for the scope of an attorney-client relationship is very closely related to the test we discussed in the preceding section for whether there is an attorney-client relationship at all: The scope of the engagement includes anything that the *client* actually and reasonably believes is encompassed within what she hired the lawyer to do, judged from the *client's* point of view and the *client's* knowledge and experience.

Which brings us back to the tale of Bobby Boilermaker in **this chapter's Introduction at 255**. (Go take another look at it. We'll be here when you get back.) Charlie Comp's mistake was thinking about and explaining the situation in terms that were perfectly clear to Charlie, but that the ordinary working person would not reasonably understand. Charlie, being an experienced lawyer and, what's more, a workers' compensation specialist, understood that, though workers' comp is often the exclusive remedy available to a worker injured on the job, occasionally a conventional tort claim is also available and can combine with comp payments to increase the worker's recovery. Charlie had chosen, as some comp specialists do, to limit his practice to comp, because he doesn't want to litigate in court. (In the real world, some lawyers and firms do both comp work and court litigation, and others, like our hypothetical Charlie, limit their practice to comp only.) Charlie had every right to limit his practice in this fashion. *See* **Model Rule 1.2(c)**; **Chapter 9.C at 284**.

So what's the problem? Charlie's mistake was in not explaining this limitation on his practice in terms that his *client* could understand, and because Bobby Boilermaker couldn't (and couldn't reasonably be expected to) appreciate the distinctions that Charlie was making, Charlie's distinctions didn't affect Bobby's reasonable expectations. Think about this situation from Bobby's point of view. From his perspective, he got hit on the head by a piece of flying debris. He went to see a lawyer, as any layperson might sensibly do, to get legal remedies for his injury. He had no idea that there is an administrative system for workers' comp *and* a court system with separate remedies in tort, and he had no idea when one, the other, or both should be available to him. Nor should Bobby be expected to know these things. The whole point of his going to see a lawyer was to consult an expert who could tell him what could be done for him in a complex remedial system about which he knows nothing. (Think about it—chances are that *you* had no idea about the differences between workers' comp and tort litigation before you went to law school. We didn't. Most folks don't.)

So Bobby left Charlie Comp's office after their first meeting reasonably understanding that he had hired a lawyer to do whatever was reasonably possible to compensate him for his injury. The lawyer had said to him, "workers' compensation is all we do." From Bobby's point of view, that statement confirmed his understanding—he was a worker who was trying to get compensated. Bobby didn't realize that "workers' compensation" is the lawyer's equivalent of magic words with a particular, narrow meaning. Because the *client's* actual and reasonable understanding is what defines the scope of the engagement, if Charlie Comp wants to limit the scope of this engagement to workers' compensation only, *he has to do it in terms that Bobby Boilermaker can understand.* How could Charlie have done that? In the meeting and in his engagement letter, he should have explained:

> The most common way for workers to get compensated for an on-the-job injury is through the workers' compensation system. That's what we do here, and we will handle your workers' compensation claim for you. Sometimes it's possible for an injured worker to get compensation through a lawsuit in court in addition to what workers' compensation pays. It's possible that you might have such a litigation claim, and that claim might be valuable. This office does not handle court litigation, and we can't advise you on whether you might have a separate lawsuit that you could file. *We strongly suggest that you consult a lawyer who handles court litigation for injuries to see whether you have a separate lawsuit you could bring.* Any court lawsuit that you might have must be brought within a limited time after your injury or you will lose your rights, so we suggest that you locate and consult such a lawyer *immediately.* We can provide you with a list of lawyers who have gotten good results for our clients in the past (though we can't promise you any particular result in this case), or you can seek your own lawyer for these purposes. But please don't delay; any court litigation claims you may have must be pursued within legally defined time limits that can be quite short, and failure to seek them in time may cause you to lose those rights forever. In other words, by waiting, you may lose out on additional payment to which you may be entitled.

Why is this explanation effective? Because it affects Bobby's actual and reasonable understanding about what services Charlie will and will not provide. Once Charlie provides this explanation, it would not be reasonable for Bobby to continue to think that Charlie will get him all the compensation to which he might be legally entitled for his injury from any source. Bobby would know that there are two potential sources of compensation, that Charlie is pursuing only one of them, and that, if he wants to find out if the other is even available, he needs to add another lawyer to his team. Charlie has also offered to help him find one (though the referral is not something that Charlie has any obligation to do).[6]

---

[6] REAL WORLD TIPS & TACTICS It is not unusual for lawyers who do workers' comp exclusively to have a list of tort litigators with whom they have successfully worked in the past. The referral is an additional service that, though not required (or

Tips & Tactics Misunderstandings about the scope of the lawyer's engagement are a sufficiently common cause of client civil claims that many professional liability insurers require the lawyers that they insure to have a written agreement for each matter that includes a description of the scope of the engagement. Even if your insurance carrier doesn't require it, it is the much better practice to do so.

Although any engagement's scope may be subject to misunderstanding, there are three more common issues that come up often enough (usually in the form of claims for professional negligence) that we want to highlight them so that your future engagement letters and other disclosures will allow you to avoid them:

- **Post-trial proceedings in a litigation engagement**: When you undertake to handle a piece of litigation (civil or criminal), you need to define where your obligations stop. Some lawyers are happy to build post-trial motions, appeals, or enforcement of judgments into their engagements; others view those as separate matters that they either do not handle or would charge extra to take on. This point is especially important where the basic fee arrangement is a flat fee (common in criminal cases) or a contingent fee (common in civil cases on the plaintiff's side). *See* **Chapter 20.B at 538, 540, 541**. Make sure that you have a clear writing specifying whether there are limits on the stages or phases of litigation that you are prepared to handle for the agreed fee.

- **Tax issues**: Any time that money changes hands, the taxman is watching. The way in which a transaction or litigation settlement is structured and documented can make dramatic differences in its tax treatment, which in turn can affect the fundamental economics of the deal. Tax is a complex and technical area of the law, and many lawyers (especially litigators) don't have (and don't wish to spend the time and effort acquiring) the expertise necessary to consider the tax implications of the work that they're doing. If you don't intend to take responsibility for spotting and addressing any potential tax issues in the work that you've agreed to do, you need to say so and encourage the client to get the necessary advice somewhere else.

- **Insurance issues**: Whenever there's a loss or a dispute involved in your engagement, it becomes possible that your client or the opposing party may have insurance that covers the loss or dispute as well as the costs of litigation.

---

charged for), is often helpful to the client and appreciated by the recipient of the referral. Referring to other lawyers is not without risk, however; it has to be done with reasonable care. If the referred lawyer is hired and messes up the case, *and* if the referring lawyer should have known that the referred lawyer had competence issues (a disciplinary history; a drinking problem; etc.), the malpractice case against the referred lawyer may also include a claim against the original lawyer who made the referral for "negligent referral" (and yes, that's a thing). Most lawyers develop a short list of other lawyers whose skill and expertise they respect in specialties that they themselves don't handle (as well as lawyers who do what they do who can be referred those cases that the referring lawyer can't take because of a **conflict of interest** or for other reasons). The moral of this story is that, if you do refer, pick your referrals carefully, offer several alternatives where possible, and make sure that your clients understand that they need to exercise their own independent judgment about the choice.

REAL WORLD   Tips & Tactics

(Obviously, insurance that helps pay your fees is a benefit to your client and sometimes to you, but there are also complicated procedural and tactical issues that can arise in determining whether an opposing party has relevant insurance and whether to "plead into coverage" or otherwise invoke the insurance.) Insurance coverage issues can also be complex and technical. If you're not willing or able to help clients determine whether they might have relevant insurance and how best to achieve its benefits, or whether opposing parties might have relevant coverage and what to do about it, you again need to state this carve-out from your services clearly in your engagement letter and again encourage the client to get the necessary advice somewhere else. ⟨Tips & Tactics⟩

Problem 9A-3: With respect to each of the three common sources of misunderstandings regarding the scope of a lawyer's engagement just discussed above, explain how and why a misunderstanding could arise in the absence of a clear statement by the lawyer of the scope of the engagement and what a clear scope statement avoiding each potential misunderstanding might generally look like. (*Hint*: Look at the discussion of Bobby Boilermaker's problem immediately preceding the above Tips & Tactics section for an example of both.)

B. Assuming Duties to Non-Clients

In the preceding section, we saw that attorney-client relationships can be formed more easily and more inadvertently than you might think. As a result, whether or not you're forming an attorney-client relationship is something that you can and must consciously manage by being clear, both in your own mind and in your communications with others, precisely who your client is. In this section, we'll discuss the most common ways in which lawyers can assume duties to non-clients. "Duties to *non*-clients?" we hear you ask, your voices rising with anxiety. "Even after I've done everything that I reasonably can to make it clear that I *don't* represent them?" 'Fraid so. The good news is that these duties, like the attorney-client relationship, are created only by manifesting your intent, and once you understand how those choices are manifested, you can manage these obligations, too.

Here's one major difference between the duties that we discussed in the preceding section and the ones that we'll discuss in this one: When you initiate an attorney-client relationship, all the duties that a lawyer owes a client pop into being at once, and you owe your client all of them from that point on until each duty is terminated (and we'll discuss how *that* happens in **Chapter 9.D at 286**). This section discusses various ways in which you can assume *just one* type of duty to someone (or some organization) who is *not* your client and thus who is *not* owed all those other obligations. As we'll see, however, one duty is often more than enough to drag you into a heap of trouble, so you'll need to take vigilant and thoughtful care. The goal is not necessarily to avoid these duties altogether, but simply to assume them only when you affirmatively mean to do so (and when you know that you're doing it).[7]

The two duties lawyers most commonly assume to non-clients without becoming their lawyers are the **duties of confidentiality** and **care**. We'll discuss each in turn.

1. Assuming Duties of Confidentiality to Non-Clients

a. Assuming a Duty of Confidentiality by Consulting with a Prospective Client in Contemplation of Possible Representation

The first way that you can assume a **duty of confidentiality** to a non-client is one with which you're already familiar: by consulting with a **prospective client** in contemplation of possible representation. As you'll recall, as soon as such a consultation begins, and "even when no client-lawyer relationship ensues," the consultation creates a **duty of confidentiality** to the **prospective client**. **Model Rules 1.18(a)-(b); Chapter 8.A at 207**. As just discussed, the point here is not always to avoid this **duty of confidentiality**—consultations in contemplation of possible representation are where new engagements are often conceived, and new engagements are a good thing—but (1) to realize that what you learn is **confidential information** and must be treated as such; and (2) to assume this **duty of confidentiality** only when you actually mean to do so.[8]

b. Assuming a Duty of Confidentiality by Promise

You can also assume a **duty of confidentiality** by making a promise, express or implied. Two common contexts in which these promises of confidentiality are made are when witnesses ask for assurances of confidentiality, and when third parties who have some relationship with the client cooperate with the client on the understanding that some information that they supply will be kept confidential. The thing to keep in mind here is that such promises often create a **duty of confidentiality** for you, and thus should be made only when those promises would

---

[7] A research note: Court decisions in various jurisdictions, including the federal system (mostly older decisions), sometimes refer to a lawyer's assumption of a limited duty to a non-client as creating some kind of "implied attorney-client relationship" or other variations on that theme. A widely cited example is *Westinghouse Elec. Corp. v. Kerr-McGee Corp.*, 580 F.2d 1311, 1312, 1319 (1978). We (along with pretty much everybody else) think that the result in *Westinghouse*—that the lawyers involved owed the non-clients who were complaining a **duty of confidentiality**—is quite right. (**Problem 9B-2 at 269** in this section is based loosely on the facts of *Westinghouse*.) But we think that the analytical path by which the opinion reaches that result is a little wonky. Often (as in *Westinghouse*) only one kind of duty is at stake, and the resort to some kind of "implied" representation amounts to a search for a doctrinal vehicle capacious enough to carry the result that a duty is owed, though none of the other attorney-client duties are at issue and no mutual manifestation of the intent described by the *Restatement (Third)* and consistent state law (*see* **Chapter 9.A at 260**) is involved. You should use the legal lexicon of whatever jurisdiction you're in when arguing the law in that jurisdiction, of course, but for clarity of analysis, you also should strive to be aware of what kind of duties these authorities are implying and why.

[8] Recall also that the **duty of confidentiality** owed a **prospective client** is slightly narrower in scope than the one owed to an actual client. But it is a real and substantial duty nevertheless, backed up by significant **consequences,** both disciplinary and civil. *See* RESTATEMENT (THIRD) OF THE LAW GOVERNING LAWYERS § 15; **Chapter 8.A at 207; Chapter 8.A at 221.**

be consistent with your obligations to your actual clients, and with a view to the **consequences** that the promise may create if you don't honor it or if your client doesn't. CONSEQUENCES Under the right circumstances, those **consequences** could include civil liability in contract or tort, or disciplinary liability for misrepresentation under **Model Rule 4.1** (*see* **Chapter 10 at 323**). In addition, a promise that you're asked to make to keep something confidential from your client can create a **conflict of interest** between your obligation to keep your promise and your **duty of candor** to your client, which can result in **disqualification** as well as professional discipline and civil claims for damages.[9] CONSEQUENCES

Problem 9B-1: Frank is investigating revenue that seems to be missing from a small-business client of his firm, a local restaurant. A visibly uncomfortable Wendy Waitress reluctantly tells Frank that she knows something, but that she fears for her safety and can't tell unless Frank can promise her that the culprit will never know that she was the one who "ratted him out." Frank consults with the owner of the restaurant and, with the owner's permission, makes that promise. Wendy then reports she's seen one of the busboys, Buff Burly, skimming from the till after the restaurant has closed. Was Frank right to check with his client before making the promise? Why? How are Frank and the client constrained if they wish to report Burly to the local District Attorney for theft?

Problem 9B-2: Maya's firm is retained by a national trade association for cosmetic and fragrance manufacturers to prepare a report on the toxicity of their products—or more precisely, to prepare a report confirming that the members' products are *not* toxic, in order to allay public concerns that have arisen about that issue. The engagement letter makes clear that the sole client in the engagement is the trade association (an unincorporated association), and not any of its members. But the engagement letter also makes clear that the association members will be providing information about their products and manufacturing processes to the law firm—information that is necessary to prepare the report—and that the law firm will keep that information confidential, including keeping each association member's information confidential from other association members.

One of the association's members is D'Odore, a perfume manufacturer. Not long after work on the report begins, a litigator in another office of Maya's firm is approached to represent one of D'Odore's suppliers in a commercial dispute with D'Odore regarding contracts for deliveries of the roses that D'Odore uses in some of its perfumes. Can Maya's firm take this case? Why or why not?

Does your analysis change if we add the fact that D'Odore has rejected deliveries of the supplier's roses because it claims that those roses have been contaminated with a pesticide

---

[9] This problem can also arise when you're representing a business organization and one of the organization's **constituents** (an owner, manager, or employee, for example) wants to tell you something in confidence. You can't keep such third-party confidences from your client (unless your client consents to this unusual arrangement, which is almost never a good idea), and you must make the non-client **constituent** with whom you're communicating understand that. *See* **Model Rule 1.13(f)**; **Chapter 23.A at 781**.

that is dangerous to people and animals, while the supplier denies any such contamination and says that any problems are attributable to D'Odore's formulation and manufacturing practices and not to the supplier's roses? If so, how and why; and if not, why not?[10]

c. Assuming a Duty of Confidentiality by Representing a Client with Confidentiality Obligations to Third Parties

Occasionally, lawyers take on an engagement in which their client has **confidentiality** obligations to third parties who are involved in the engagement (but who are not also represented by the lawyers). The client's **confidentiality** obligations may arise by contract or as a matter of law. Engagements involving insurers are a common example. Some jurisdictions have found that lawyers are bound by the **confidentiality** obligations that their clients owe third parties in connection with the engagement, whether or not the lawyers make any direct promise of **confidentiality** to the third party. ⟨CONSEQUENCES⟩ In the event that the lawyers breach these **confidentiality** obligations, those obligations have been enforced by **disqualification** and civil liability for damages. ⟨CONSEQUENCES⟩

> **Problem 9B-3:** Frank's firm agrees to represent InsureCo, a local liability insurance company. The firm's job is to oversee the lawyers (not in Frank's firm) that the insurance company is paying to defend its insureds, and to make sure that they're doing a competent job and giving the insurance company its money's worth. In order to do that, Frank's firm must see what the defense lawyers are doing in the cases and discuss their tactics and strategy with them. Obviously, those discussions involve the insureds' **confidential information**. In Frank's state, insurance companies are entitled to know the **confidential** details of the defense of the claims that they cover, but they are obligated to keep those details **confidential** themselves.
>
> One of the cases that Frank's firm oversees for InsureCo involves a claim that a civil engineering company (a company that InsureCo covers) negligently designed a freeway overpass so that the roadway cracked, requiring expensive repairs. Now a local resident has approached Frank's firm, asking the firm to represent him in claims that the cracks in that overpass were so bad that they bent the frame of his car and injured his back when he drove on the overpass. Can Frank's firm take the personal injury and property damage case of the motorist? Why or why not?[11]

2. Assuming Duties of Care to Non-Clients

a. Assuming a Duty of Care by Offering Advice to a Non-Client

One of the instances in which lawyers may assume a **duty of care** to a non-client is the situation in which a lawyer quite explicitly rejects an engagement, but

---

[10] This problem is loosely based on the facts of *Westinghouse Elec. Corp. v. Kerr-McGee Corp.*, 580 F.2d 1311 (1978). *See* **Chapter 9.B at 268 n.7,** *supra.*

[11] *See Morrison Knudsen Corp. v. Hancock Rothert & Bunshoft*, 69 Cal. App. 4th 223, 81 Cal. Rptr. 2 (1999).

assumes duties to the non-client in the process anyway. These duties are usually enforced by civil liability for damages. In a well-known case reproduced in many professional responsibility casebooks,[12] a wife was concerned that her husband had been the victim of medical malpractice resulting in his partial paralysis. She consulted a law firm at the recommendation of a family friend. A lawyer from the firm met with the wife and, after listening to her concerns, said that he didn't want to take the case. The wife left with the clear understanding that she and her husband had *not* retained the lawyer. But the wife didn't consult any other lawyers until after the statute of limitations on the medical malpractice case had run, after which she discovered that the medical malpractice claim had merit after all. The Minnesota Supreme Court found these facts to state a claim for professional negligence against the lawyer and his firm and affirmed a jury verdict of over $600,000 (in 1980 dollars). The case is widely viewed as correctly decided.

Startled? Many law students are. After all, the lawyer explicitly said that he *didn't* want to take the case, and the **prospective client** understood that he hadn't taken it. How could this be legal malpractice? Where's the duty?

What made the substantial judgment against the lawyer possible was not that he had declined the case, but *the way in which he had done so.* The lawyer had passed on the case, he later testified, because he didn't do medical malpractice work. But the **prospective client** understood the lawyer to be saying that he was refusing the case because she didn't have a good case to pursue. (There was conflicting testimony about just what the lawyer said, and the jury apparently credited the wife's version.) In other words, the **prospective client** reasonably understood the lawyer *to have offered advice* on the strength of her case while turning it down. And as we've already discussed, it's all about what the **prospective client** reasonably understands (not what the lawyer silently thinks)—whether that's about if an attorney-client relationship has been formed, what the scope of that relationship will be or, as in this case, whether the lawyer was offering any advice.

Now, the lawyer had no *obligation* to offer advice on the merits of the case when he turned it down. But under generally applicable principles of tort law, whenever you do pretty much *anything*, even things that you aren't obligated to do, you **must** exercise reasonable care toward those foreseeably affected.[13] And it appears that the lawyer here didn't mean to offer any opinion on the merits of the case: He had no expertise in the subject matter; he didn't look at any medical records; he didn't consult any medical experts. He didn't conduct any investigation or analysis that would precede and inform any reasonably careful lawyer's opinion on a case's prospects (by turning it down, it would seem that

---

[12] *Togstad v. Vesely, Otto, Miller & Keefe*, 291 N.W.2d 686 (Minn. 1980). The facts in the text are simplified slightly in ways that we don't consider **material**.
[13] *See, e.g.*, Restatement (Second) of Torts § 324A (1965).

he was trying to avoid any obligations at all). But the jury concluded that what the lawyer said and how he had said it gave the **prospective client** the reasonable understanding that the lawyer thought that the case was not viable. And he never suggested that she consult someone who *did* do medical malpractice work, nor did he warn her about the statute of limitations. And *that* induced the **prospective client** not to pursue the case further until it was too late.

TIPS & TACTICS ▸ How do you avoid this bind? It's easier than you may think, but it takes some effort and presence of mind. When we are actively representing clients, we give them advice all the time, and we expect them to rely on it. But when dealing with a **prospective client**, or someone who might reasonably *think* that he or she is consulting you in contemplation of possible representation, express yourself clearly (and if you are concerned about being fully and accurately understood, do so in writing, to avoid a disagreement later about what you did or didn't say). We've already talked about avoiding "accidental clients" in informal situations (*see* **Chapter 9.A at 257** and **Problem 9A-1 at 262**), and this issue is closely related (can you see why?). In situations in which someone is explicitly offering or considering offering you work that you don't want to or can't do, be very clear:

1. You're not going to provide any services. You can say this as gently or as formally as the circumstances dictate. You don't have to say why you are passing on the engagement, but if you do, don't make something up. "I'm afraid I don't have the time to give your matter the attention it deserves" is one way to offer a reason if you feel compelled to do so. "I don't handle this kind of matter" is another (if it's true).

2. You're not offering any advice or opinion on the matter under discussion. Again, you can do this as gently or as formally as the circumstances dictate. If the lawyer in the case just under discussion had done this clearly enough, he would have had 600,000 reasons to be happier.

3. Encourage the **prospective client** to consult other counsel who may be able to handle the matter or provide a second opinion that may be different from yours. You can even suggest some, but be sure they're ones whom you trust and respect, and realize that someone may consider you responsible (rightly or wrongly) if things go badly with the referred counsel. *See* **Chapter 9.A at 265 n.6**.

4. If there's an applicable statute of limitations or other time or practical constraint (which is true for virtually any litigation claim), mention it specifically: "Your claims may be subject to time or other constraints that may require you to take action within a limited time, and if you fail to do so, you may lose your rights forever. Please act promptly, and don't wait."

5. Do it in writing. (Yes, we've already said that, but we want to make sure that you understand just how important a writing is in this type of situation.) The case that we were just discussing came down to a he-said/she-said situation

before a jury on what the **prospective client** was told and what could be reasonably understood from it. You can avoid that mistake (or at least manage the risk) with an email or letter. Many practitioners refer to such a writing as a "non-engagement letter"—a written communication clarifying what you said and what the person with whom you spoke can expect.   Tips & Tactics

Problem 9B-4: Frank and Happy Trials meet with a prospective new client who believes that she is the victim of medical malpractice. The case presents some difficult issues regarding standard of care, causation, damages, and the statute of limitations. Before looking into those, however, Frank discovers that one of the doctors involved is currently a client of the firm in a real estate transaction. This creates a **conflict of interest**, which prevents the firm from taking the new case unless the doctor-client gives **informed consent**. The firm's real estate partner, Barney Blackacre, does not wish to seek the doctor-client's consent (which, if given, would allow the firm to represent the patient against the doctor) because the doctor is a repeat client of the firm in real estate matters and, in his experience, doctors are very touchy about being accused of malpractice. What should Frank's firm do now?

b. Assuming a Duty of Care by Agreeing to Provide Services to a Client for the Benefit of a Non-Client

Occasionally, we are asked to provide services for the benefit of someone other than the client. Let's start by drawing an important distinction: Someone who agrees simply to pay our fees or costs for representing someone else is typically *not* our client. We have a legal relationship with the paying party—but it is an arm's-length contractual and financial relationship, not a fiduciary attorney-client relationship. Among other things, this difference means that

- there is no **attorney-client privilege** over our communications with the payor (and, in fact, disclosure to the non-client payor of **attorney-client privileged** communications with our actual client may waive the privilege);
- we **must not** disclose any **confidential information** to the payor without the client's **informed consent** (which **must** include the client's understanding of the risks that disclosure to the payor may waive **attorney-client privilege**); and
- we **must not** take instruction regarding the engagement from the payor, or allow the payor to interfere in the attorney-client relationship with our client or otherwise interfere with our independent professional judgment. *See* **Model Rule 5.4(c)**.

In fact, **Model Rule 1.8(f)** expressly requires us to obtain the client's **informed consent** to all of these constraints before we can allow someone other than the client to pay us. Simple prudence, if not the Model Rules, dictates that similar disclosures be made, and consent received, from non-client payors, so that they're not surprised later, either.

In contrast with an engagement involving a third-party payor, sometimes someone whom we actually represent asks us for services expressly for the benefit of a third-party non-client. Because estate planning is a discipline that frequently focuses on conveying benefits to someone other than the person whose estate is being planned, it is the most common source of such arrangements, though many other areas of practice can produce similar obligations. Case law in most jurisdictions finds (by different analytical approaches) that a client's provable intent to benefit a third party through the lawyer's services creates a **duty of care** owed *directly to the third-party non-client*.[14] Consequences That **duty of care** is usually enforced by a civil claim for damages for professional negligence. Consequences

> **Problem 9B-5:** The estate-planning partner in Frank's firm, Willie Willmaker, represented Theodore ("Ted") Testator during his lifetime. Ted had a carefully considered plan about the distribution of his wealth over the next few generations in his family, which he instructed Willie to effectuate in appropriate instruments. The plan was a good deal more complicated than the estate plans to which Willie was accustomed, and his documentation violated his state's Rule Against Perpetuities, making some of Ted's gifts to some of his descendants invalid. One of those descendants is now suing Willie and Frank's firm, claiming that Willie's professional negligence deprived the descendant of the bequest to which he was entitled. Willie denies that he owed the intended beneficiary any duty: "He wasn't even born when those documents were drafted and signed! Ted was my only client, and our engagement letter says so!" What result, and why?

> **Problem 9B-6:** During Ted Testator's lifetime (*see* **Problem 9B-5**), one of Ted's favorite nephews ran into a small jam: He was grilling dinner on the roof of his apartment building using a small charcoal grill, and he left the grill on the roof so that the coals could go out and cool.

---

[14] *See* Restatement (Third) of the Law Governing Lawyers § 51(3). The Restatement suggests that such liability to a non-client is available when "(a) the lawyer knows that a client intends as one of the primary objectives of the representation that the lawyer's services benefit the nonclient; (b) such a duty would not significantly impair the lawyer's performance of obligations to the client; and (c) the absence of such a duty would make enforcement of those obligations to the client unlikely. . . ." As an example, *see Lucas v. Hamm*, 56 Cal. 2d 583 (1961), whose facts are similar to **Problem 9B-5**. *Lucas* is distinguished by a separate holding that California's Rule Against Perpetuities is so difficult that it is not a breach of a lawyer's **duty of care** to violate it. *Id.* at 591-93. That is a unique feature of that case that no other jurisdiction that we know of has ever adopted, though many states have agreed with the portion of the decision finding duties to non-clients in this context in the years since *Lucas* was decided.

  Your House; Your Rules A number of states have applied this general idea in the trusts and estates context to find that lawyers for a fiduciary (such as a trustee or executor) owe a **duty of care** to beneficiaries of the trust or estate to advise a misbehaving fiduciary to act within his or her legal obligations to the beneficiaries. The Restatement (Third) of the Law Governing Lawyers § 51(4) describes that duty as arising when: "(a) the lawyer's client is a trustee, guardian, executor, or fiduciary acting primarily to perform similar functions for the nonclient; (b) the lawyer knows that appropriate action by the lawyer is necessary with respect to a matter within the scope of the representation to prevent or rectify the breach of a fiduciary duty owed by the client to the nonclient, where (i) the breach is a crime or fraud or (ii) the lawyer has assisted or is assisting the breach; (c) the non-client is not reasonably able to protect its rights; and (d) such a duty would not significantly impair the performance of the lawyer's obligations to the client." Application of these principles is not universal or particularly consistent. For current purposes, it's fair to say that to whom the fiduciary's lawyer owes duties beyond the fiduciary himself or herself is highly unsettled and varies from state to state. If you end up practicing in the trusts and estates area, beware. Your House; Your Rules

The wind blew the grill over, and the live coals started a small fire that caused several thousand dollars' worth of damage to the building's roof. The nephew was just out of college and had no significant resources, but the landlord sued him for negligently damaging the property. Ted asked Willie to get someone in his firm to defend the case, promising to pay the fees and costs. Willie got Frank to do so.

a. Who was or were the firm's client(s) in defending the Landlord v. Nephew case? Why?

b. The case settled after a few months. In investigating the circumstances, Frank discovered that the nephew was having a difficult patch in his life and was taking opioids. It appears that the influence of opioids caused the nephew to carelessly leave the grill in a position on the roof where it was easily blown over, causing the fire. Frank tells Willie what he has learned. Willie knows that Ted, who has more money than he knows what to do with, would be happy to provide resources to help his nephew address his drug issues before they become more serious. What should Willie do?

c. Assuming a Duty of Care to Third Parties by Providing Work Product on Which You Know the Client Intends Third Parties to Rely

Usually, the work product that we provide—the advice that we give; the pleadings and documents that we draft—is intended for the client's use and reliance. Occasionally, particularly in some transactional practices, we are asked to produce documents or other statements on which everyone understands that third parties will rely. *See* **Model Rule 2.3**. Though there are many different kinds of such statements, the classic example is the "opinion of counsel"—a document prepared by counsel to one party in a transaction providing counsel's opinion on a particular conclusion for the express purpose of its being relied upon *by another party to the transaction*. Its purpose is to provide the transactional counterparty with the additional assurance of a reputable bystander that certain basic and important legal conclusions are valid, for example that opining counsel's organizational client is duly organized and currently existing in good standing under the laws of the state in which it says it was formed.

There is an elaborate set of conventions and understandings about opinions of counsel, mostly focused on the specific conclusions to which counsel should, and should not, opine, and on what factual basis. This is a highly specialized area of business law, with some interstate variation regarding when third parties may rely on such opinions and what **consequences** may exist for opinions that prove incorrect.[15] We don't intend to delve into these details in this survey course. But legal opinions are just one very highly refined area of practice in which lawyers

---

[15] The American Bar Association publishes a three-volume treatise on opinion practice: ARTHUR NORMAN FIELD & JEFFREY M. SMITH, LEGAL OPINIONS IN BUSINESS TRANSACTIONS (4th ed. 2019). There are plenty of other resources on the subject as well. But we can't resist this opportunity to mention that two of your authors became acquainted on a case involving this very issue, and we've been fast friends ever since!

may make representations to third parties (oral or written) on which the third parties may reasonably understand that they are intended to rely. [CONSEQUENCES] Any time that this occurs, the third party may try to treat your statement as a representation or a warranty and hold you to it with claims in contract for breach of warranty or in tort for negligent misrepresentation or fraud if it proves to be incorrect. *See* **Model Rule 2.3 Comment [3]**.[16] [CONSEQUENCES]

Big-Picture Takeaways from Chapter 9.A-.B

1. Creation of the attorney-client relationship:
   a. Be clear about if and when an attorney-client relationship has begun. One good way to summarize the legal standard is that an attorney-client relationship exists any time that the *client* actually and reasonably believes that such a relationship exists. By being outspoken and clear about whether a representation has begun, you can adjust the **prospective client's** actual and reasonable expectations. Your silence will often be taken as consent. *See* **Chapter 9.A at 257**.
   b. Make sure that you want to take on the representation. Sometimes, the potential engagement or the **prospective client** shows warning signs ("red flags") that tell you to stay away. *See* **Chapter 9.A at 258**.

2. You need to worry not only about whether an attorney-client relationship has formed, but also about whether you've been clear about the *scope* of that relationship.
   a. A client retains a lawyer for a particular purpose. Put simply, the purpose, and the scope of the engagement, define what you've been hired to do. *See* **Chapter 9.A at 262**.
   b. The scope of the engagement generally defines the scope of your duties, specifically your **duties of care** and **candor**.

---

[16] *See* Restatement (Third) of the Law Governing Lawyers § 51(2). The Restatement suggests that such liability should be available to third parties when: "(a) the lawyer or (with the lawyer's acquiescence) the lawyer's client invites the nonclient to rely on the lawyer's opinion or provision of other legal services, and the nonclient so relies; and (b) the nonclient is not, under applicable tort law, too remote from the lawyer to be entitled to protection. . . ." As an example, *see Roberts v. Ball, Hunt, Brown & Baerwitz*, 57 Cal. App. 3d 105 (1976). Often this liability is limited rather strictly to those specifically to or for whom the professional's statements were made. *See e.g.*, Restatement (Second) of Torts § 522; *Bily v. Arthur Young & Co.*, 3 Cal. 4th 370 (1992). And of course the plaintiff's reliance on any statements must be reasonable, including a reasonable understanding that the statements were meant for the plaintiff to rely on. *See, e.g., Goodman v. Kennedy*, 18 Cal. 3d 335 (1976). [YOUR HOUSE; YOUR RULES] If you're noticing a lot of cases from California, it's not your imagination. California is the most populous state in the nation, and it has a very large practicing bar. As a result, it is the source of many court decisions on lawyer liability that have been influential in many other jurisdictions. The contours of lawyer liability vary a fair bit from state to state, so you must always check on the law in effect in your jurisdiction if issues like these arise. [YOUR HOUSE; YOUR RULES]

      i. Your **duty of candor** is defined by the scope of your engagement: Your job is to keep your client informed regarding the engagement for which you were retained. *See* **Chapter 9.A at 263**.

      ii. Similarly, your **duty of care** requires you to exercise the skill and diligence that a reasonable lawyer would exercise, including providing all the services that a reasonable lawyer would provide, *within the scope of your engagement. See* **Chapter 9.A at 263**.

      iii. In contrast, your **duty of loyalty** extends *beyond* the scope of your engagement: While you are representing a client, you **must not** be disloyal to that client (that is, act adversely to that client's interests) in *any* respect, even one unrelated to the engagement. *See* **Chapter 9.A at 263**.

      iv. And your **duty of confidentiality** to a client covers *any* information that you learn in connection with representing that client, even information that may not be relevant to your engagement as long as you happen to learn it in connection with representing that client. Your **duty of confidentiality** also continues in effect after the engagement is over. *See* **Chapter 9.A at 263**.

  c. The standard for determining the scope of an attorney-client relationship is very closely related to the test for whether there is an attorney-client relationship at all—the scope of the engagement includes anything that the *client* actually and reasonably believes is encompassed within what she hired the lawyer to do, judged from the *client's* point of view and the *client's* knowledge and experience. *See* **Chapter 9.A at 264**.

3. What about duties to non-clients? The two duties that lawyers most commonly assume to non-clients without becoming their lawyers are the **duties of confidentiality** and **care**.

  a. Assuming a **duty of confidentiality** to a non-client:

      i. You can assume a **duty of confidentiality** to a non-client by consulting with a **prospective client** in contemplation of possible representation. Remember **Model Rule 1.18**? *See* **Chapter 9.B at 268**.

      ii. You can also assume a **duty of confidentiality** by making a promise. Two common contexts in which these promises are made are when witnesses ask for assurances of confidentiality and when third parties who have some relationship with the client cooperate with the client and her (or, in the case of an organization, its) lawyer on the understanding that some information will be kept confidential. *See* **Chapter 9.B at 268**.

iii. In some jurisdictions, you can assume a **duty of confidentiality** to a non-client by taking on an engagement in which your client has **confidentiality** obligations to third parties who are involved in the engagement (but whom you don't also represent). Your client's **confidentiality** obligations to the third party may arise by contract or as a matter of law. Engagements involving insurers are a common example. *See* **Chapter 9.B at 270.**

b. Assuming a **duty of care** to a non-client:

i. You can assume a **duty of care** to a non-client by offering the non-client advice. One common way in which this occurs is when a lawyer turns down a case in a way that gives the impression the lawyer has doubts about the strength of the case, and doesn't warn the non-client that an important deadline, such as a statute of limitations, is coming up and that the non-client should seek another lawyer posthaste. *See* **Chapter 9.B at 270**.

ii. You can also assume a **duty of care** to a non-client if you are hired for the express purpose of conferring benefits on that non-client. A good example is estate-planning services in the common situation in which a testator or trustor wishes a gift or bequest to benefit a third party. *See* **Chapter 9.B at 274**.

iii. It's important not to confuse an engagement in which the client wants you to provide benefits to a third party with one in which a non-client is simply paying for your services to your client. You do have a legal relationship with the paying party, but it is an arm's-length contractual and financial relationship, not a fiduciary attorney-client relationship. Among other things, this difference means that:

A. There is no **attorney-client privilege** over your communications with the payor (and, in fact, disclosure to the non-client payor of **privileged** communications with your actual client may waive the **privilege**);

B. You **must not** disclose any **confidential information** to the payor without the client's consent; and

C. You **must not** take instruction regarding the engagement from the payor or allow the payor to interfere in the attorney-client relationship with your client or otherwise interfere with your independent professional judgment.

Model Rule 1.8(f) requires you to disclose these limitations to your client and obtain the client's **informed consent** to all of them. *See* **Chapter 9.B at 273.**

iv. Finally, you can also assume a **duty of care** (and obligations as a warrantor) to third parties when you produce documents or other statements on which you understand that those third parties will rely (such as opinion letters). *See* **Chapter 9.B at 275**.

Multiple-Choice Review Questions for Chapter 9.A-.B

1. Lawyer Abed is a general civil practitioner. Looking to expand his skill set, he agrees to have his name placed on a random-assignment list to represent indigent criminal defendants. Abed's name comes up in the rotation. The court appoints him to represent Troy, who has been accused of petty theft.

   In his civil cases, Abed has all of his clients execute a retainer agreement at the outset of the representation. Abed asks Troy to sign such an agreement, and Troy says that he will think about it.

   The date for Troy's arraignment arrives. Abed doesn't attend because Troy has yet to sign and return the agreement.

   Can Abed claim that he was not Troy's lawyer, and therefore that he didn't have to appear, because Troy never signed the agreement?

   a. Yes. The attorney-client relationship arises out of contract law. Although Abed made an offer to represent Troy, Troy had not yet accepted by the time of the arraignment. As a result, no contract was formed at that time.

   b. Yes. There was no meeting of the minds. At the time of the arraignment, it was still possible that Troy would decide not to retain Abed.

   c. No. Although attorney-client relationships often arise out of contract law, they can also arise by other means. Here, Abed was appointed, and that appointment created an attorney-client relationship.

   d. No. A lawyer who is court-appointed must serve through the entirety of a case. Abed had no means to withdraw once he was appointed.

2. Lawyer Logan meets with Connor, a man who slipped and fell outside the local United States Department of Veterans Affairs Hospital. Logan asks when Connor fell, and Connor discloses that it was approximately a year and nine months prior. The two do not discuss fees or costs. Logan does not tell Connor that he will send a retainer agreement.

   After Connor leaves the office, Logan writes "send Connor retainer agreement" on a Post-It® note. Logan sticks the note to his day-planner. While Logan is out at lunch, his legal assistant takes Logan's day-planner to enter some filing deadlines. In the process, the note falls to the floor and lands under a filing cabinet.

   Logan never sends Connor the retainer agreement, and he forgets to follow up. He doesn't complete a **conflicts** check. Connor, however, believes that he has retained Logan and does nothing further.

Four months later, Connor calls Logan to ask how the case is going. Logan realizes that the deadline to file an administrative claim has passed, and that Connor's claim is forever barred.

Did Logan and Connor create an attorney-client relationship that might expose Logan to a claim for malpractice?

- a. Yes, if an objective observer would believe that Connor was relying on Logan.
- b. Yes, because Connor subjectively believed that he could rely on Logan.
- c. No, because Connor and Logan never discussed specific details of the arrangement.
- d. No, because Logan never ran a **conflicts** check.

3. What is the main difference between the scope of a lawyer's various duties?

- a. The **duties of loyalty** and **confidentiality** are broader than the scope of the engagement, but the **duties of candor** and **care** are limited to the scope of the engagement.
- b. The **duties of loyalty** and **candor** are broader than the scope of the engagement, but the **duties of confidentiality** and **care** are limited to the scope of the engagement.
- c. The **duties of loyalty** and **care** are broader than the scope of the engagement, but the duties of **candor** and **confidentiality** are limited to the scope of the engagement.
- d. The **duties of candor** and **care** are broader than the scope of the engagement, but the **duties of loyalty** and **confidentiality** are limited to the scope of the engagement.

4. Which of the following is a benefit to having a written engagement agreement with a client?

- a. Such an agreement bars the client from suing for malpractice.
- b. Such an agreement prevents the lawyer from being disciplined for a breach of duty.
- c. Such an agreement constitutes a writing that meets the Statute of Frauds and therefore creates an enforceable contract.
- d. Such an agreement can clarify the scope of an attorney-client relationship.

5. Lawyer Lani agrees to represent client Caitlin, who has been injured in a slip and fall. The engagement agreement says that Caitlin will play a flat fee of $15,000 "to represent you in a slip and fall case."

Despite Lani's best efforts, Caitlin loses at trial. After the jury returns its verdict, Lani turns to Caitlin and says, "You really deserved to win, and I think there are legal grounds for appeal."

Lani assumes that her work is complete, and she sends Caitlin a final invoice. Caitlin calls Lani after receiving the invoice. To Lani's surprise, Caitlin is upset. "I thought that you'd file an appeal," Caitlin says. Lani responds, "I would be happy to, but that will take time, and I will have to charge you an additional $5,000 for handling the appeal."

Who is at fault for this misunderstanding about the scope of the engagement?

    a. Lani is. Lani's comment after the jury verdict implied that she would handle the appeal for no additional compensation.

    b. Lani is. Lani did not clearly define the term "a slip and fall case" in the retainer agreement to exclude handling appeals.

    c. Caitlin is. Caitlin should have known that the term "represent" in the retainer agreement did not include any appeals.

    d. No one is. Lani was willing to handle the appeal, and she simply requested additional compensation for additional work.

6. Shola feels that she has been the victim of employment discrimination. She meets with lawyer Marisa. During the meeting, Shola tells Marisa what happened at work. Shola also shares some personal details about her relationship with her direct supervisor. Shola makes it clear that she is embarrassed by the details and does not want them made public.

At the conclusion of the meeting, Shola decides that she would rather not retain Marisa. She tells Marisa so.

Marisa responds, "Then you shouldn't have told me all of those details about your employment. If you don't retain me, I'll share those publicly." Shola is taken aback. She says, "I shared those in **confidence** because I was considering hiring you to represent me." Marisa says, "Too bad. If I'm not your lawyer, then I don't have to keep that information **confidential**."

If Marisa follows her legal and ethical obligations, **may** Marisa share this information?

    a. Yes. There is no attorney-client relationship because Shola did not manifest an intent to create a relationship. Without a relationship, Marisa owes Shola no **duty of confidentiality**.

    b. Yes. There is no attorney-client relationship because Shola did not manifest an intent to create a relationship. As a result, there can be no **attorney-client privilege**.

    c. No. Even after an attorney-client relationship terminates, the **attorney-client privilege** remains. Here, Shola only terminated the relationship after disclosing the information, so it remains **attorney-client privileged**.

d. No. Even without an attorney-client relationship, there is a **duty of confidentiality** under these circumstances. Marisa must treat Shola's information as **confidential**.

7. Lawyer Hareem handles mainly commercial litigation. One day, he meets with prospective client Rose. Rose would like to file a lawsuit against a Federal Bureau of Investigation agent who caused an automobile collision injuring Rose. Hareem does not generally handle these types of personal injury cases, but he is familiar with the Federal Tort Claims Act, which is the applicable law.

   Hareem listens as Rose describes the accident at length. He does not say much, but he does take detailed notes.

   Hareem decides not to take the case. He tells Rose that he's not interested. Hareem knows that Rose cannot file suit under the Federal Tort Claims Act unless she first tenders an administrative claim. As the accident occurred only a few weeks prior, Rose has adequate time to do so, because she has two years from the date of the accident. Hareem doesn't bother to explain to Rose the intricacies of the Federal Tort Claims Act. He instead explains, truthfully, that he does not handle personal injury cases. He suggests that Rose consult with another lawyer. He provides the name of a lawyer who handles these types of cases.

   Rose does not consult with another lawyer. Instead, she waits several years and then files a complaint in state court. Because she is unaware of the administrative claim requirement, she never tenders one. The case is removed to federal court, and a motion to dismiss is filed. At this point, Rose is out of time to exhaust her administrative remedies, so her case is dismissed with prejudice.

   Did Hareem violate his duty of care?
   a. Yes. If Hareem was going to decline the case, he had to provide Rose with sufficient information to proceed *pro se*. He failed to properly educate Rose about the administrative exhaustion requirement.
   b. Maybe. It depends on whether Hareem exercised reasonable **care**. Given that Rose had plenty of time to tender a claim, and that Hareem suggested that she consult another lawyer, he may have exercised sufficient **care**, but he may not have, if he didn't explain the timing requirement and that there were other steps that Rose would have to take.
   c. Maybe. It depends whether Hareem was competent to handle the case. If he was, he owed Rose a duty to represent her until she could retain other counsel.
   d. No. A lawyer only owes a **duty of care** to his client. Here, Hareem never represented Rose, so he owed her no duty.

8. Keyan is in the midst of dissolving his domestic partnership with Amayah. Keyan asks his lawyer, Inez, to draft a qualified domestic relations order (a "QDRO") to ensure that Amayah receives half of Keyan's retirement assets in the divorce.

    To whom does Inez owe a **duty of care**?

    a. Keyan.

    b. Amayah.

    c. Keyan and Amayah.

    d. Neither Keyan nor Amayah.

9. Robin is the Chief Executive Officer of a major hospital. The hospital is currently under federal investigation. Another company is interested in purchasing the hospital but is concerned about the potential exposure from the investigation.

    Robin hires a lawyer, Owen, to provide an assessment of the possible exposure. She asks him to evaluate the likelihood that the hospital will face criminal charges and the potential range of any fine or civil liability. Robin makes it clear that the assessment will be shared with the interested purchaser.

    To whom does Owen owe a **duty of care**?

    a. No one.

    b. The hospital.

    c. The purchaser.

    d. Both b and c.

10. Lawyer Alex is retained by his client, Arianna, to provide an opinion of counsel to a third party, Gina. Alex makes a negligent mistake in his opinion, and Gina relies on it to her detriment.

    If Gina sues Alex, what is her most viable legal cause of action?

    a. Breach of fiduciary duty.

    b. Breach of warranty.

    c. Fraud.

    d. Violation of the Rules of Professional Conduct.

C. Disclaiming Duties

The first half of this chapter was about how you acquire duties. Now we're going to discuss how you get rid of them.

Just as duties can be acquired either within or outside the attorney-client relationship, they can also (within limits) be disclaimed. The most basic way to do so is by disclaiming *all* lawyer duties, and you can do that by making it clear to people whom you don't intend to represent that you're not their lawyer (*see* **Chapter 9.A at 261**), and don't offer them any advice or make any promises while doing so (*see* **Chapter 9.B at 268**). For those contexts in which you might be deemed to have acquired a duty to a non-client, you can usually expressly disclaim that duty by making it clear that you're not doing anything that would impose such a duty on you (*see* **Chapter 9.B at 270**).

In addition, we briefly consider some other ways in which lawyers sometimes try to limit their duties to both clients and non-clients.

1. Limiting the Scope of the Engagement

As we saw in **Chapter 9.A at 262**, the scope of your engagement defines the scope of some of your most important duties. It follows that you can limit your duties to your client by limiting the scope of your engagement. **Model Rule 1.2(c)** sets some boundaries on this practice, but they are not very restrictive. The Rule provides that you "may limit the scope of the representation if the limitation is reasonable under the circumstances and the client gives informed consent." Remember, **informed consent** requires you to explain everything that the client reasonably needs to know or has asked about concerning the choice the client is making, and you must include all reasonably foreseeable possible adverse consequences of consent. As for what limitations on the scope of the representation should be considered "reasonable," **Model Rule 1.2 Comment [6]** provides at least a little guidance by pointing out that, if counsel is being supplied by an insurer, the representation **may** generally be limited to what the insurer covers; that the scope of the representation **may** be tailored to the client's limited objectives for the engagement; and that the limitation **may** exclude specified actions or tactics that the client considers too costly or that the lawyer considers "repugnant or imprudent."

> **Problem 9C-1:** Assuming that the client provides **informed consent**, which of the following limitations on the scope of a lawyer's engagement are permissible under **Model Rule 1.2(c)**, and why? In each case, what kinds of disclosures **must** or **should** the lawyer make in order to support properly **informed consent?**
>
> a. The lawyer will represent the client in a dispute through settlement or trial and post-trial motions in the trial court, but not with respect to any appeals or proceedings regarding the enforcement of any judgment.
>
> b. The lawyer will investigate and prepare a complaint and related initiating papers for the plaintiff in a form suitable for filing, but will not file the complaint or appear as counsel of record on the plaintiff's behalf, and will not represent or advise the client further after the complaint and related papers are prepared and provided to the client.
>
> c. The lawyer will prepare pleadings and papers for the client and will advise the client regarding the proceedings, but the client will file all such pleadings and papers and will appear in court *in propria persona* (in her own name). The lawyer will not appear as counsel in the case in any respect.

d. The law firm is a public-interest firm that focuses on the representation of survivors of sexual assault and sexual harassment. The firm strongly believes in a "name and shame" approach to this issue. As a result, the firm includes a provision in its standard form engagement letter saying that it will not represent the client in negotiating any settlement that contains any confidentiality provision limiting the disclosure of the identity of anyone whom the client considers responsible for his or her assault or harassment or that contains a confidentiality provision concealing what the client contends that the person or company did. (Such provisions are common in settlements of claims of this kind.)

2. Client Waivers of Future Liability

Within an existing attorney-client relationship (or in creating one at the outset), a lawyer may occasionally wish to adjust the duties owed the client by asking the client to agree to waive some future breach of a duty that the lawyer owes. (You can phrase this as a prospective waiver of the duty itself; it amounts to the same thing and is subject to the same constraints.) This practice is more strictly limited than are agreements limiting the scope of the engagement, both substantively and procedurally.

Substantively, every state puts limits on prospective waivers of future torts as a matter of public policy, and many do so quite narrowly (you probably talked about these types of purported waivers in your Torts class—you know, "Skiing is dangerous, so if we fail to properly maintain the equipment that you rent and you break your leg, don't come running to us"). For current purposes, we're going to limit our discussion to the observations that this type of future waiver of lawyer liability is generally difficult to achieve, and that most states are particularly resistant to enforcing agreements limiting the fiduciary duties of *any* fiduciary by status (such as, say, a lawyer). So if you're going to try to limit your duties or your liability prospectively, you will need to research carefully the governing law in your state.

Procedurally, **Model Rule 1.8(h)(1)** restricts this kind of agreement further by providing that you **must not** "make an agreement prospectively limiting the lawyer's liability to a client for malpractice unless the client is independently represented in making the agreement." So anything that state law allows (and that may not be much to start with) will have to be reviewed by a separate and independent lawyer advising the client, and in many circumstances, independent counsel is likely to advise the client that such a waiver (if it is even enforceable in the first place) is a bad idea. (That's because, from the client's perspective, it usually *is* a bad idea. Why would anyone want to sign an agreement saying, "You have no remedies against your lawyer if she messes up"?)

In short, there may be the occasional situation in which some kind of limited prospective waiver makes sense and ought to be enforceable, but such a situation will be rare.

Problem 9C-2: Facts similar to the first paragraph of **Problem 9B-2 at 269**, but instead of representing the cosmetics and fragrances trade association, Maya's firm is retained to represent jointly eight of the association's member companies to prepare a report on the safety of their products. Each of the joint clients will need to supply Maya's firm with information regarding its formulation and manufacturing practices. Ordinarily, a lawyer's **duty of candor** to joint clients requires that the lawyer not withhold any **confidential information** supplied by one joint client (or acquired anywhere else) from all the other joint clients. Here, each company wants to keep information regarding its formulation and manufacturing practices, much of which are trade secrets, confidential from the other joint clients and is happy to have the other companies do the same. **May** Maya's firm and the clients agree that each joint client will waive the firm's **duty of candor** to that extent? Describe the steps that would need to be taken for such an agreement to be prepared.

D. Ending the Attorney-Client Relationship

1. How Do You Know When It's Over (and Why Should You Care)?

In broad outline, there are two general ways in which an engagement can end: When it's completed according to its terms, or when one or both parties to the relationship properly terminates it before it's completed.

Completion is often straightforward: The engagement was for a specific purpose, such as to litigate a dispute or to negotiate, document, and close a transaction, and all work related to that purpose is complete—the case has been won, lost, or settled; the deal is done. There's nothing more for you to do. *See* **Model Rule 1.16 Comment [1]**.

Sometimes, however, an engagement is open-ended, or one or both parties wish to terminate it before it's complete. A common example of an open-ended engagement is when a lawyer has been retained to consult on a particular subject on an occasional basis when the client requests it; for example, when small-business clients call their lawyer occasionally when legal issues in the business arise; or when specialists are consulted occasionally by a client in the specialist's area of expertise. Such an engagement is never completed according to its terms, as it has no defined endpoint. Common examples of termination before completion include a lawyer who is not getting paid and wishes to withdraw, or a client who is unhappy with the lawyer's charges or services and wishes to fire the lawyer. There's clearly more to do in these engagements before they would be over according to their own terms, but one or both of the parties to the engagement wants that work not to be done by the lawyer currently engaged.

There are also lots of situations in which the endpoint of the engagement may not be clearly defined. Sometimes there can be some residual ambiguity to the scope of the engagement, even when the basic work is complete—for example, were particular follow-up tasks supposed to be included or not? Perhaps you think that you've done everything that you agreed to do, but the client may not agree. And in open-ended engagements, the endpoint of the engagement is inherently undefined.

Because the existence and scope of the attorney-client relationship depends on what the *client* actually and reasonably believes, ambiguity about the scope or endpoint of the engagement could put you in a situation in which the client is expecting you to complete follow-up tasks that you had not contemplated doing, or the client believes that you continue to be available to her though you did not understand that to be the arrangement. Misunderstandings of this kind can lead to civil claims for damages or for **disqualification**, and even to possible professional discipline. The solution, of course, is prospective:

When in doubt, speak out

and **inquire; explain; confirm** (*see* **Chapter 6.A at 139**).

    TIPS & TACTICS   For that reason, it's always a very good idea to send an explicit written communication—some lawyers call it a "disengagement letter" or a "termination letter"—making it clear that you've completed the engagement. If there are follow-up tasks that are needed but that you don't think that you contracted to do as part of the original engagement, list them explicitly. This tactic avoids future disputes along the lines of "but I thought the lawyer was supposed to. . . ." And if there are reasonably foreseeable future tasks that the client should do (or have done) and that you don't intend to handle, it's part of your **duties of care** and **candor** to advise the client what those tasks are.

A satisfied customer is your best source of future business, and a disengagement letter doesn't need to be formal or confrontational. For example, you can say something as kind and simple as, "All requested services have been completed. It's been a pleasure representing you, and I hope that you'll consider retaining me again should the need arise." This is also an opportunity to have clients determine what to do with their files (*see* **Chapter 9.D at 303**). Finally, in a number of jurisdictions, the statute of limitations on legal malpractice claims is tolled (that is, suspended) during any time that the engagement in which the lawyer allegedly breached duties is still pending. In those jurisdictions, providing a defined endpoint can start the limitations clock. TIPS & TACTICS

> **Problem 9D-1:** The real estate partner at Frank's firm, Barney Blackacre, is consulted by Leo Landlord about the effect of certain local land-use regulations on his apartment buildings. Barney does some research, suggests some changes to the landlord's management practices and standard form lease, and sends Leo a bill for the work. Six months later, Leo calls back with a follow-up question; Barney responds appropriately and sends another small bill. Three months after that, a different local landowner contacts Frank's firm because he has a property-line dispute with a neighboring building. It turns out that the neighboring building belongs to Leo Landlord. Can Frank's firm take the matter on? Why or why not?

2. Terminating Pending Engagements

Termination is governed by a range of rules that may not always allow a person who *wants* out to *get* out. We realize that this may be a little surprising, so let's let it sink in—sometimes you can't quit, and sometimes a client can't fire you, even when that may be what one or even both of you may want.

a. Getting the Permission of Any Involved Tribunal

i. When Do You Need a Tribunal's Permission to End an Attorney-Client Relationship?

Model Rule 1.16 is all about terminating engagements, and although like all the Rules of Professional Conduct, it governs disciplinary **consequences**, many of its provisions also define the civil standards governing termination and its effects in most jurisdictions. Let's start in the middle with **Model Rule 1.16(c)**. Because it's so important (and somewhat counterintuitive), we'll quote it in full right here:

> A lawyer must comply with applicable law requiring notice to or permission of a tribunal when terminating a representation. When ordered to do so by a tribunal, a lawyer shall continue representation notwithstanding good cause for terminating the representation.

Now let's be clear on the context: Lots of lawyer engagements involve a tribunal—some adjudicator such as a court, an administrative agency, or an arbitrator. Let's also be clear that lots of lawyer engagements—including most business and transactional engagements—do *not* involve a tribunal. **Model Rule 1.16(c)** applies only to those engagements that do. If there is no tribunal involved in your engagement, you don't have to go out and find one in order to be relieved of your responsibilities as counsel. Of course, you still have to comply with all the other rules about when and how you may withdraw. Those are described in the sections that follow.

When a tribunal is involved, most tribunals (including virtually all courts) have rules that require lawyers who have appeared on behalf of parties before that tribunal to continue to be responsible for the matter before the tribunal until and unless the court excuses them from further service and allows them to withdraw (or the proceeding ends).[17] **Model Rule 1.16(c)** says that you are subject to professional discipline if you walk away from an engagement in which a tribunal is involved without the tribunal's permission (and as we'll see, related law provides other **consequences,** too).

---

[17] "Appearance" in this context is a term of art that comprises the various ways that lawyers may notify a court and the other parties that they represent a particular party in a particular proceeding. By "appearing," you become "counsel of record," another term that typically conveys the same thing. The most common ways of entering an appearance are filing a Notice of Appearance (which is a very brief pleading stating counsel's name, contact information, and the identity of the party represented), being listed as counsel to a party in the caption or signature block of a paper or pleading filed with the court, or speaking on the record at a hearing.

But surely, you're thinking (even though none of us is named Shirley), no court would ever *force* unwilling lawyers to continue to serve ungrateful or nonpaying clients or *force* dissatisfied clients to accept the services of lawyers that they do not wish to have speaking on their behalf. Wherever she is, though, Shirley has let you down.[18] In fact, courts actually can, and occasionally do, prevent withdrawal.

REASON FOR THE RULE ▶ How can this be? Because once a tribunal is involved, it's no longer just about you and your client. There is an important public interest in the regular and orderly processes of our tribunals, especially our public courts and agencies. And a tribunal typically takes an active interest in making sure that its processes are not misused for unjust purposes or otherwise disrupted.

Imagine, for example, that an individual is charged with a crime. He hires a lawyer, promising to pay by the hour. As trial approaches, he stops paying the lawyer. The lawyer quits (or maybe the client just fires the lawyer on the eve of trial). The client shows up at trial and says, "I have no lawyer and I want one. I have a Sixth Amendment right to counsel, and the trial can't go forward until I have one." The court, having learned that the client can afford and wishes to retain private counsel, postpones the trial so that the client can hire a new lawyer. The client pulls the same stunt with the new lawyer. The court, annoyed, asks if the client expects another trial continuance, and if so until when. "How about never?" the client asks. "Is never good for you? I'll keep firing my counsel right before trial as long as I need to, and you'll have to honor my Sixth Amendment rights every time." In the meantime, determination of the client's guilt or innocence (and from the client's tactics, it looks like he anticipates being convicted), and the imposition of any appropriate **consequences**, have been put off—something that the client has indicated that he would be happy to do indefinitely. In addition, the court's trial calendar has been disrupted, and the time that the court set aside to try this case will not be efficiently used, delaying other litigants' access.

Although we may admire this client's candor (and yes, the hypothetical is unrealistic—parties who manipulate counsel for procedural advantage rarely admit it—but it made our hypothetical work better), we can't admire much else here. To avoid this kind of opportunism and to protect the efficient use of the court's resources, almost all courts have rules preventing counsel from being relieved of their responsibilities without leave of court. And the courts in every jurisdiction have broad discretion to exercise this power to protect court processes. Thus, any tribunal that allows withdrawal only with permission (which is almost all of them, in civil as well as criminal matters) has lots of latitude to prevent counsel from quitting or being fired. ◀ REASON FOR THE RULE

---

[18] *Cf. Airplane!* (Paramount Pictures 1980) ("And don't call me Shirley."), https://www.imdb.com/title/tt0080339/quotes/?tab=qt&ref_=tt_trv_qu. One of your authors did have a beloved mother whose name actually *was* Shirley, so she always gets a kick out of that scene in the movie.

What this means as a practical matter is that when a lawyer is fired or wishes to quit in a matter in which the permission of a tribunal is required but not obtained—even when the client is the one in the wrong, for example, by refusing to pay the lawyer or by firing the lawyer without cause—the lawyer **must** continue to represent the client anyway. If you think that this rule can create situations that are profoundly awkward, you're right. But courts still do it sometimes. Worse still, the lawyer continues to have enforceable legal obligations to the client and the court.

CONSEQUENCES If you have obligations to do things (such as meet filing or other deadlines) under court order or the court's procedural rules, the court may impose **consequences** on you such as sanctions or contempt if you fail to comply. And the court's refusal to allow the attorney-client relationship to be terminated means that you continue to owe all of the usual duties to your client, even if the client is in breach of her obligations to you. Thus, the client may seek civil damages for breach of any of the lawyer's duties (most often, the **duties of care** or **candor**) if the lawyer fails to do things that need to be done or provide information that the client reasonably needs. And the lawyer may be subject to professional discipline for violating **Model Rule 1.16** or the **duties of competence** under **Model Rule 1.1** or **diligence** under **Model Rule 1.3** (*see* **Chapter 7.A at 172**). And forgive us for saying it again, but we've found that sometimes angry lawyers forget: All of these **consequences** will be imposed on the lawyer *even when the client is completely in the wrong, and the lawyer has every justification to quit or even has been unjustly fired.* CONSEQUENCES

Needless to say, then, the permission of any involved tribunal is really important. This naturally leads to the question of when courts tend to refuse counsel permission to withdraw or, conversely, what makes a motion to withdraw more likely to be granted. The good news is that most courts try to be fair to the needs of both the parties and their counsel, and when there's a good reason to end the lawyer's service and it's not unduly disruptive to the court's calendar, courts usually grant counsel leave to withdraw. But not always. By far the two most common circumstances in which courts deny leave is when the request is made close in time to an important filing or hearing in the case (especially when the request is made shortly before trial), so that the court's schedule would be disturbed if counsel is relieved of the engagement; or when the court is concerned that counsel or the client is acting opportunistically for the purpose of disruption or delay.

Problem 9D-2: Frank and Barney Blackacre are representing Aloysius Angry in real estate litigation. The dispute between Al and his residential neighbor is about trees on the neighbor's property near the property line; those trees are dropping debris and blocking Al's view. Owing to the difficult personalities involved, efforts to work the matter out have gone nowhere. At their initial meeting, Barney warned Al that the litigation process is expensive to start with and can get out of hand, so Al needed to be sure that he wanted to commit to the cost to deal with his neighbor's trees in this manner. Al was extremely frustrated at the time and made it table-poundingly clear that he didn't care how much it cost.

The neighbor turned out to be a lawyer who decided to represent himself, and that lawyer has amply shown how he was capable of driving Al so crazy. Halfway through the very disputatious discovery, Al started falling behind on his bills from Frank's firm. Despite repeated reminders and repeated promises, Al has fallen even further behind. Now trial is in two weeks, significant amounts of fees and costs remain unpaid, and Al is making noises indicating that maybe he really does care how much it costs. Requests that Al clear up his arrearages and deposit a retainer against the estimated cost of trial have gone unanswered. What should Frank's firm do now, and why? Is there something that that the firm should have done before now?

Problem 9D-3: Same facts as **Problem 9D-2 at 290** (Frank's firm is representing Aloysius Angry in a litigated real estate dispute that is set for trial in two weeks; the client stopped paying his bills some time ago). Barney writes Mr. Angry an email reminding the client of the amounts due and his repeated promises to clear up the arrearages.

a. The email goes on to say that, if Mr. Angry does not pay the overdue amounts in full by the end of the week, the firm will be unable to appear for trial a week after that. Is there anything that Barney should do in addition or instead? If so, what and why?

b. Mr. Angry doesn't pay his past-due bills by the deadline that Barney's email set. Frank's firm does not appear in court on the date set for trial. What's likely to happen now, and why?

ii. How Do You Get an Involved Tribunal's Permission to End an Attorney-Client Relationship?

A court that has a rule requiring leave to withdraw will typically include in that rule instructions on how to seek that leave. The two most common means are a substitution of counsel or a formal motion.

A substitution of counsel is a brief form of stipulation and proposed order that typically includes a statement identifying the counsel who is withdrawing, the name and contact information of the new lawyer appearing in place of the withdrawing counsel, signatures from both counsel and from the client to show everyone's agreement to the change, and a place for the court to indicate its approval. REAL WORLD Substitutions are almost always approved, because a new lawyer is stepping in without any change in the court's schedule, so there's usually no reason that the court would object. If you find yourself "substituting in" for withdrawing counsel, however, be aware that you're assuming the obligations on the court's then-current calendar with no guarantee that the court will extend or continue anything (and a real likelihood that it may not). In addition, you should never agree to step in to replace withdrawing counsel without a full understanding of *why* the other lawyer is withdrawing. Though some withdrawals are the withdrawing lawyer's fault or just a result of bad chemistry, a withdrawing lawyer in the current or prior engagements, and especially more than one, is a classic "red flag" warning of a potential "problem client"—not always, but often enough that it bespeaks caution. *See* **Chapter 9.A at 258.** Realistic evaluations of a client's complaints about quality of service, expected results, cost, and ability to pay may raise concerns that you won't be able to provide what this client demands any more than your predecessor could. And remember that, once you step in, the court has broad discretion whether to let you out. So look before you leap.

REAL WORLD

A formal motion to withdraw, which is typically the procedural route taken when there is no successor counsel who is both acceptable to the client and prepared to substitute in unconditionally, raises other issues. The form of the motion is usually prescribed by rule, and it usually requires advance written notice to the court, the opposing party, and the client, as well as a written statement of reasons, including any necessary supporting evidence (usually by affidavit or declaration). Last-minute oral motions to withdraw (for example, on the morning of a scheduled hearing or trial) are usually frowned upon, and often forbidden outright.[19]

The fundamental difficulty in moving to withdraw is one that we hope will be clear from your recent study of **Chapter 8 at 210.** The motion here is one to withdraw from an existing attorney-client relationship. Because the relationship is still in force, you still owe your client all the usual duties, specifically including the **duty of confidentiality.** But the motion to withdraw requires a showing of a proper reason to withdraw (and we'll be discussing what those are in the sections that follow). In order to show a proper reason to withdraw, you have to volunteer facts about how the attorney-client relationship has gone wrong, and that's almost always **confidential information:** that the client has failed to pay your fees when due, for example, or has demanded that you violate the law or ethics rules, or has made the engagement impossible by failing to respond to you, or even has discharged you. All of those reasons involve information learned in the course of the representation—in other words, **confidential information**—and that information **must not** be disclosed without the client's permission or some other applicable exception. The mere citation of a subsection of **Model Rule 1.16(a) or (b),** which enumerate the proper grounds for withdrawal, will often effectively disclose **confidential information.** The result is a classic dilemma: How do you show that you have a right to withdraw without violating your **duty of confidentiality?**

---

[19] A recurring principle to keep in mind in this context is one we think of as the Legal Secretary's Creed, a rule of respect for legal staff in every environment that is also adopted by many courts presented with last-minute motions to withdraw: "Your lack of planning is not my emergency." *See* **Problem 9D-2 at 290.**

Model Rule 1.16 Comment [3] recognizes the problem and suggests a solution that many courts will ordinarily honor:

> The court may request an explanation for the withdrawal, while the lawyer may be bound to keep **confidential** the facts that would constitute such an explanation. The lawyer's statement that professional considerations require termination of the representation ordinarily should be accepted as sufficient. Lawyers should be mindful of their obligations to both clients and the court under Rule[] 1.6. . . .

Consistent with this Comment, common evidentiary bases for a motion to withdraw are often little more than representations or statements under oath by the lawyer to the effect that "professional considerations require termination of the representation"; or "the attorney-client relationship has broken down, the details of which are confidential"; or "proper grounds for withdrawal under Rule of Professional Conduct 1.16 exist, but their factual basis is subject to counsel's **duty of confidentiality**." A statement of this kind is commonly accompanied by non-**confidential information** showing why the withdrawal is not unduly prejudicial to the client at this point in the proceedings (an important concern to most courts, *see* **Chapter 9.D at 289**). Most courts, under most circumstances, will be satisfied with this rather rudimentary showing.

Okay, we hear you thinking (actually, we don't really hear you thinking; it's just an expression), but what if the court demands a more detailed explanation? This does occasionally occur, particularly if the court has concerns that opportunistic conduct may be afoot. The short answer is that, consistent with your **duty of confidentiality**, you **must** do what you can to limit what is disclosed, as to both the amount and the manner of disclosure (*e.g.,* limiting disclosure by filing under seal or speaking *in camera*). But ultimately the Rules provide a solution to this problem, too: Once the court *orders* you to disclose **confidential information, Model Rule 1.6(b)(6)** provides an exception to the **duty of confidentiality** "to comply with . . . a court order." So you're acting within your ethical and legal duties if you argue for no disclosure (and if disclosure is ordered, then limited disclosure under seal or *in camera*) and withhold any arguably **confidential information** until the court orders you to do otherwise.[20]

---

[20] ABA Formal Ethics Op. No. 476 (2016) suggests that a lawyer withdrawing for nonpayment of fees may disclose the fact of nonpayment under the **Model Rule 1.6(b)(5)** confidentiality exception allowing disclosure "to establish a claim or defense on behalf of the lawyer in a controversy between the lawyer and a client," but that opinion recognizes that case authority on the topic is mixed at best, and advises avoiding such disclosure at least until the court demands it. We don't think that a motion to withdraw is a "claim or defense" at all (it's a motion!), which leaves only the "court order" exception of **Model Rule 1.6(b)(6)**. Only one state of which we are aware, California, does not have an exception to the **duty of confidentiality** allowing disclosure of **confidential information** to comply with a court order. The California State Bar has issued an ethics opinion that walks through the same suggestions as **Model Rule 1.16 Comment [3]**, and then helpfully concludes that, if the court ultimately orders counsel to disclose confidential information, *in camera* or otherwise, counsel faces a "dilemma" whose resolution is not clear. Cal. Formal Ethics Op. No. 2015-192 (2015).

Problem 9D-4: Same facts as **Problem 9D-3 at 291** (Frank's firm represents Aloysius Angry in a litigated real estate dispute; Frank's firm did not appear in court on the scheduled trial date when Mr. Angry failed to pay his past-due bills). The court has now issued an "Order to Show Cause Why Counsel Should Not Be Sanctioned" to Frank's firm for not showing up on the trial date. Concerned, the partner prepares a response to the Order to Show Cause in which he explains that Mr. Angry has failed to pay past-due bills, the amounts of which are confidential, and that the firm duly warned Mr. Angry in writing that the firm would not appear at trial unless he cleared up his arrearages. Should the partner have done anything differently or in addition? If so, what and why?

b. On What Grounds May the *Client* Terminate the Relationship?

Now that we know *how* the parties can terminate their attorney-client relationship, let's explore the grounds on which such termination is allowed. On the client's side, this is easy: "A client has a right to discharge a lawyer at any time, with or without cause. . . ." **Model Rule 1.16 Comment [4]**.[21] (The Comment goes on to say that any discharge is "subject to liability for payment for the lawyer's services," but all that means is that the client still owes any fees due upon discharge, leaving it to the lawyer to collect them if he can. It does *not* mean that the lawyer cannot be discharged until his bills are paid.) The client's power to terminate the engagement freely is so fundamental that, in most jurisdictions, it cannot be waived or contracted away, and in most states, features of any fee arrangement that unduly burden a client's right to terminate are considered void as against public policy.

The client's power to discharge the lawyer is much more constrained if the lawyer was court-appointed, such as a public defender. Here, the court has a much greater degree of control over the grounds on which termination by the client will be allowed. *See* **Model Rule 1.16 Comment [5]**. And even when the attorney-client relationship is fully consensual, an involved tribunal has the oversight powers described in the preceding sections and **Model Rule 1.16(c)**.

c. On What Grounds Must or May the *Lawyer* Terminate the Relationship?

Unlike clients, who are free to terminate their lawyers at any time for any reason (subject to the permission of any involved tribunal), lawyers may terminate their engagements before completion on only a limited set of enumerated grounds. These grounds are set out in **Model Rules 1.16(a)** and **(b)**. `CONSEQUENCES` `RULE ROLES` Although a lawyer's termination of an attorney-client relationship on a ground not enumerated in the Rules is a basis for professional discipline, courts considering leave to withdraw typically rely on the same Rules to define proper bases for withdrawal. In addition, the lawyer's civil **duties of care**, **candor**, and **loyalty**

---

[21] *Accord*, Restatement (Third) of the Law Governing Lawyers § 32(1).

end in conjunction with a proper termination of the attorney-client relationship. (As we'll see, they may call for a little mop-up after the relationship ends, so they're not exactly coextensive; and remember that your **duty of confidentiality** persists long after the engagement is over.) Standards for civil liability based on an improper termination (sometimes called "client abandonment") are typically grounded in the terms of **Model Rule 1.16** as well. Rule Roles Consequences

i. When a Lawyer Must Withdraw (or Seek to Withdraw)

Model Rule 1.16(a) lists three circumstances under which a lawyer **must** withdraw.[22] All three are, by the terms of the Rule, subject to the permission of any involved tribunal, so even if a Rule makes your withdrawal mandatory, you still must obtain the tribunal's permission (if there is one), and you **must not** withdraw if the tribunal refuses leave. The three grounds for mandatory withdrawal are:

1. "[T]he representation will result in violation of the rules of professional conduct or other law" (**Model Rule 1.16(a)(1)**). No surprise here. If continuing the engagement will result in your doing something illegal or unethical, and you can't avoid it, you **must** get out. Note that this ground is based on a *future* illegality ("will result"). *Past* illegal or unethical conduct on the part of the lawyer or the client will likely require action of one kind or another and bear **consequences**, but it doesn't necessarily require you to withdraw. One example falling under this Rule that doesn't immediately occur to everyone is the situation in which you have a **conflict of interest** (*see* **Chapter 22 at 603**). Your being in the engagement while **conflicted** is, in and of itself, a violation of the Rules, and unless you can immediately remedy the **conflict**, you **must** withdraw.

2. "[T]he lawyer's physical or mental condition materially impairs the lawyer's ability to represent the client" (**Model Rule 1.16(a)(2)**). Again, no surprise. If you simply can't do the job (*see* **Chapter 4.C at 90**), it's no good for anyone if you stay in, and you **must** get out, hopefully before someone's interests are harmed.

3. "[T]he lawyer is discharged" (**Model Rule 1.16(a)(3)**). If you're fired, you have to quit. Or if there is an involved tribunal, at least *seek leave* to quit. And if the client discharges you, whether for good reasons or bad ones, it remains *your* responsibility (not the client's) to obtain the permission of any involved tribunal to allow you to withdraw.

---

[22] The alert student (whose praises we sing once again) will have noticed that the title of **Model Rule 1.16** is "*Declining or Terminating Representation*" (emphasis added), but that the only reference in the Rule to *declining* an engagement is in **Model Rule 1.16(a)**, which requires you to turn down ("shall not represent") any engagement on the same grounds on which you would be required to withdraw from the representation once you were already in it. Obviously, you **must** refuse an engagement that you would be obligated to quit the minute that you took it on. The more interesting feature of the Rule is the absence of any grounds on which you **may** (but are not required to) decline any representation. That's because you **may** turn down any engagement for any reason you like (so long as you don't do so for a reason forbidden by rules outside legal ethics, for example because of illegal race or gender discrimination).

> Problem 9D-5: Same facts as **Problem 9D-2 at 290** (Frank's firm is representing Aloysius Angry in a litigated real-estate dispute that is set for trial in two weeks; the client stopped paying his bills some time ago, and the firm has sent a letter refusing to appear for trial unless the arrearages are resolved). Mr. Angry shoots back an email immediately that says, in its entirety, "No problem. You're fired." Barney (the partner) tells Frank not to prepare for trial and instead to prepare a complaint for filing against Mr. Angry to collect the fees he owes. Should the partner do anything differently or in addition? If so, what and why?

ii. When a Lawyer May Withdraw (or Seek to Withdraw)

The list of grounds on which a lawyer **may** withdraw is somewhat longer and is set out in **Model Rule 1.16(b)**. There is a much broader range of circumstances in which a lawyer **may** seek to quit (again, subject to the approval of any involved tribunal, if there is one):

1. "Withdrawal can be accomplished without **material** adverse effect on the interests of the client" (**Model Rule 1.16(b)(1)**). This is a broadly available basis to withdraw that doesn't require fault on anyone's part: If you can get out "without **material** adverse effect on the **interests** of the client" and with the approval of any involved tribunal, you're free to do so. The pressure point here is "**material** adverse effect." Any time that you withdraw, it inevitably adversely affects your client's **interests** in *some* ways and to *some* degree—the client has to find a new lawyer, get that lawyer up to speed, transfer files and other materials, and so on. But *some* identifiable adverse effect is generally not thought of as sufficient to prevent withdrawal; it must be a "*material* adverse effect" (emphasis added), which in this context is taken to imply something more substantial. The adverse effect most commonly relied upon as "**material**" is a withdrawal that leaves the client without reasonable time to obtain new lawyers and get them up to speed in time to meet an existing obligation or deadline. This is another reason why, if you see problems developing in a client relationship, taking action promptly either to solve the problems or to get out is so important (*see* **Problem 9D-2 at 290**). An oddity here: If a lawyer seeks to withdraw because the client can no longer pay her bills, you might think that the withdrawal would impose "**material** adverse effect[s]" on the client because her lack of resources will prevent her from hiring a replacement. But in both motions to withdraw and civil claims based on wrongful withdrawal (also referred to as "abandonment"), the lack of ability to pay replacement counsel is rarely considered adequate to make withdrawal improper.

2. "[T]he client persists in a course of action involving the lawyer's services that the lawyer reasonably believes is criminal or fraudulent" (**Model Rule 1.16(b)(2)**).

This ground involves the client's *prospectively* "persist[ing]" bad conduct. Clients come to us all the time having *already done* bad things and seeking our help regarding the **consequences**, or continuing to do bad things that we persuade them to stop doing (often by simply pointing out that what they're doing is illegal and will result in **consequences** for them). There is, of course, nothing the least bit wrong with our accepting an engagement of either kind; it's what we do. But if the client starts (or keeps) misbehaving *after* we're hired, then we may want or need to withdraw.

3. "[T]he client has used the lawyer's services to perpetrate a crime or fraud" (**Model Rule 1.16(b)(3)**). Unlike the **Model Rule 1.16(b)(2)** ground, this one is retrospective—you've discovered that the client has *already* used your services to commit a crime or fraud. In other words, this ground focuses on a *past* act by the client while using your services, not something that the client is "persist[ing]" in doing or planning to do later.

4. "[T]he client insists upon taking action that the lawyer considers repugnant or with which the lawyer has a fundamental disagreement" (**Model Rule 1.16(b)(4)**). This is another prospective ground; the client "action" to which the Rule refers is one not taken yet. As discussed above, clients often come to us having already done something repugnant; our job in those circumstances is to help them make the best of the bad situation they've already created for themselves. Take a moment to admire this permissible ground for withdrawal. It arises when your client insists on doing things to which you strongly object *not* because they violate any positive rule of law or ethics, but because you consider them wrong as a matter of morals or principle. This is one of a number of moments in the Rules of Professional Conduct in which the professional separation between you and your client, and the importance of your independent professional judgment, is vindicated.[23]

5. "[T]he client fails substantially to fulfill an obligation to the lawyer regarding the lawyer's services and has been given reasonable warning that the lawyer will withdraw unless the obligation is fulfilled" (**Model Rule 1.16(b)(5)**). This

---

[23] An important note of caution to those of you soon to enter legal workplaces as employees (that is, virtually all of you): The fact that, as a lawyer, you **may** decline to represent or withdraw from representing a client who is doing something that is legal, but of which you strongly disapprove, does *not* mean that your employer can't expect you to assist such clients, so long as their current and future conduct doesn't violate the law. (If your employer expects you to do or help the client do things that are affirmatively illegal, that's a whole different kettle of fish, a kettle out of which you should leap as soon as possible, with additional steps to follow.) But you should not expect your supervisors to tolerate what they will likely characterize as your being a "picky eater." In other words, you ethically **may** refuse to serve clients whose conduct going forward is objectionable but not illegal, but your employer generally has the right to fire you for it. (Imagine going to work for an oil company, and then refusing to do your job because of your sincere and deeply held views about climate change.) This disconnect emphasizes the importance of choosing a legal employer with a clientele with which you're generally comfortable.

is the ground that authorizes you to withdraw if the client fails or refuses to fulfill any of her obligations as your client, from failing to pay bills when due to failing to provide information or other cooperation in the process, to anything else **material** the client is supposed to or has agreed to do but doesn't. Note the requirement that the client have "been given reasonable warning that the lawyer will withdraw unless the obligation is fulfilled." That means that, when you are anticipating having to deal with a client problem before a court deadline or other obligation is too close to make withdrawal proper, you need to build in time to give the client reasonable notice and an opportunity to cure.

6. "[T]he representation will result in an unreasonable financial burden on the lawyer or has been rendered unreasonably difficult by the client" (**Model Rule 1.16(b)(6)**). To some degree, this ground overlaps with **Model Rule 1.16(b)(5)**. What constitutes an "unreasonable financial burden" is subject to the 20-20 hindsight of a judge or jury, however. If you take on a matter that is likely to take substantial amounts of time and effort, and then try to walk away on the ground that it's taking substantial amounts of time and effort, you may not be viewed with sympathy. The result could be a refusal to allow you to withdraw, or a successful claim by the client for wrongful withdrawal or breach of contract.

7. "[O]ther good cause for withdrawal exists" (**Model Rule 1.16(b)(7)**). This is a residual catchall. It still requires "good cause," which is an affirmative showing of a good reason, even if that reason may not neatly fall into **Model Rules 1.16(b)(1)-(b)(6)**.

3. What If Your Client Is Continuing to Violate the Law or Otherwise Exposing Third Parties to Torts or Crimes and You to Liability? The Challenges of the "Noisy Withdrawal"

When your client is engaging (or proposing to engage) in illegal conduct, you may be faced with difficult crosscurrents among the law constraining withdrawal, your **duty of confidentiality**, and the law of lawyer liability. Of course, we regularly serve clients who have been or may be accused of having *previously* violated the law, either civilly or criminally (and those clients may in fact have done so). In those cases, it's unequivocally our job to defend the client from liability and limit any **consequences** to the best of our ability within the bounds of proper advocacy. But what should you do when clients *continue* preexisting illegal conduct after retaining you, propose an illegal course of action from which they cannot be dissuaded, or use your services to break the law? This problem doesn't come up very often, but when it does, the risks and conflicting duties to which you are subjected can be agonizing.

As just discussed, **Model Rule 1.16(b)(2)** and **(3)** provide that you **may** withdraw under these circumstances (subject to the approval of any involved tribunal). But this discretionary right raises two very important practical questions.

First, having determined that you **may** withdraw, **should** you? Often you **should**, principally to protect yourself. You **may** remain in the engagement in the belief that you will be able to persuade the client to stop any "persist[ing]" wrongs and that, as to anything bad the client has already done during your representation, you will be able to distance yourself and your work from the client's wrongful conduct.

Bear in mind, however, that this is a risky endeavor: If the client "persists in a course of action involving the lawyer's services that the lawyer reasonably believes is criminal or fraudulent" (**Model Rule 1.16(b)(2)**), at some point, the victims of that continuing crime or fraud may blame you and seek to have you bear their losses. (After all, you make a good living and probably have insurance. The fraudster probably doesn't.) More pointedly, if the client has *already* used your work to commit a crime or fraud (**Model Rule 1.16(b)(3)**), this is an obvious breach of faith (in the moral sense) on the client's part. It doesn't take much imagination to appreciate why you might want to cut off relations—you would be wise to wonder if you could ever trust that client again. Assuming that the client used your services to perpetrate a crime or fraud without your knowledge or consent (and if that's not the case, you probably have bigger problems than this book can solve), you're likely to want to get out immediately and draw bright lines between yourself and whatever your client did. If you let the client continue to misuse your services to commit crimes or frauds, you become complicit and likely personally responsible disciplinarily, civilly, and criminally. This is typically a catastrophically bad idea.

Second, if you withdraw under these circumstances, is there anything you **must**, **must not**, **may**, or **should** say to anyone outside the attorney-client relationship? Warning third parties in this situation is referred to as a "noisy withdrawal," and whether or how to accomplish one can be quite difficult to figure out. *See* **Model Rule 1.2 Comment [10]**.

We necessarily begin answering this question with the **duty of confidentiality**, which you now know forbids you from voluntarily disclosing anything that you learned in the course of representing your client (*see* **Chapter 8.A at 210; Chapter 8.A at 217**) unless it is subject to an exception (*see* **Chapter 8.B at 235**). **Model Rule 4.1(b)** (which we'll discuss in more detail in **Chapter 10.C at 329**) says that you **must not** "fail to disclose a material fact to a third person when disclosure is necessary to avoid assisting a criminal or fraudulent act by a client, *unless disclosure is prohibited by Rule 1.6*" (emphasis added). Certainly, whether your client is currently committing, proposing to commit, or has used your services to commit crimes or frauds is **confidential information** protected by **Model Rule 1.6** in the absence of some applicable exception.

But an exception may exist. Recall that **Model Rules 1.6(b)(2)-(3)** provide that you **may** disclose **confidential information** to prevent your client from committing a serious financial crime or fraud "in furtherance of which the client has used or is using the lawyer's services," or to "prevent, mitigate or rectify" serious financial harm to third parties "that is reasonably certain to result or has resulted from the client's commission of a crime or fraud in furtherance of which the client has used the lawyer's services." Some states' exceptions are worded more broadly, and some such exceptions affirmatively *require* disclosure rather than merely permit it. What's more, the effect of **Model Rule 4.1(b)** in this context is that, if some **confidentiality** exception provides that you **may** disclose **confidential information** to prevent a client crime or fraud, then in situations described by **Model Rule 4.1(b)**, you **must** do so. (Do you see why?)[24]

When disclosure is mandatory, of course you **must** make it, whether you withdraw or not. When disclosure is discretionary, you must decide whether you **should**. As in any "**should**" decision, you may rely on any reasons that are persuasive to you. Those could include a sense that it is morally right to warn the potential victims of a serious crime or fraud (or morally wrong not to), especially if your client used or was planning to use your services to perpetrate the wrong. You also may want to protect yourself from potential liability, claims, and reputational harm—to "get out ahead of" and distance yourself from the client's bad acts, and make it clear that you not only didn't have anything to do with them, but tried to stop them or minimize their effects.

> **Problem 9D-6:** For each situation below, describe the steps the lawyer **must**, **must not**, **may**, and **should** take, and why:
>
> a. A solo practitioner has filed an antitrust class action against six major manufacturers of a common consumer item, alleging price-fixing. The initial wave of discovery has resulted in the defendants' production of several million documents. The solo does not have the resources to review and deal with a production anywhere close to this size, and this is not his only case.
>
> b. You work for an insurance defense firm. The firm gets a set of product liability cases against a cigarette manufacturer that it agrees to defend. Both of your parents died from smoking-related diseases, and you consider tobacco companies' widespread advertising when your parents took up the habit to be one reason that your parents smoked. You don't want to have anything to do with defending Big Tobacco.
>
> c. A solo practitioner, age 60, has decided to retire. He has a personal injury practice, but none of his pending cases are close to trial or any major motions practice.
>
> d. In a litigation matter, your client has had his deposition scheduled and noticed three times, and each time, the client has failed to appear with no advance warning to you.

---

[24] In addition, **Model Rule 1.13(c)** allows you to disclose seriously illegal activity by an organization or one of its **constituents** if you are unable to persuade its management to address the issue. *See* **Chapter 23.B at 798**. And **Model Rule 3.3** requires you to disclose and correct any false representation that you made to, or false evidence you introduced in, a tribunal, even if you believed it to be true at the time that you originally acted. *See* **Chapter 24.C at 878**.

e. Same as **Problem 8B-3(a) at 243**: You represent a client who is seeking to raise money to fund a business through a "private placement" of securities. You discover after preparing disclosure documentation based on information that the client has supplied that the financial information in the documentation is incomplete and **materially** misleading. The client has already raised some money, and though you tell him to stop because of the serious **consequences** of continuing, he continues to use the documents to solicit more investments.

4. What Are a Lawyer's Duties Upon Termination?

In baseball, as Yogi Berra sagely reminded us, it ain't over till it's over. For lawyers, though, it's worse: For us, it ain't over even when it's over. The end of the attorney-client relationship brings some final aspects of a lawyer's duties into play, ones that may be tempting to overlook or withhold.[25] Why? Well, when an engagement is terminated before its completion, it's typically because something has gone pretty badly wrong in the attorney-client relationship. The grounds for mandatory and permissive withdrawal that we just discussed give you a sense of what some of those things can be. Regardless of the reasons, though, termination can be accompanied, rightly or wrongly, by disagreements as well as bad feelings running both ways.

In another maddening instance of the asymmetry of the attorney-client relationship, "[e]ven if the lawyer has been unfairly discharged by the client, a lawyer must take all reasonable steps to mitigate the consequences to the client." **Model Rule 1.16 Comment [9]**. That usually requires nontrivial amounts of time and effort, frequently uncompensated, to facilitate a smooth transition. These obligations can be infuriating in a situation in which you are withdrawing because you believe that the client has misbehaved or has mistreated you. But you have to perform those obligations anyway. You're a fiduciary to the end. Actually, you're a fiduciary beyond the end, because termination invokes your existing duties as a lawyer to require you to bring your involvement to a graceful close even after it may have ended for most legal and practical purposes.

In that regard, **Model Rule 1.16(d)** reminds us that:

Upon termination of representation, a lawyer shall take steps to the extent reasonably practicable to protect a client's interests, such as giving reasonable notice to the client, allowing time for employment of other counsel, surrendering papers and property to which the client is entitled and refunding any advance payment of fee or expense that has not been earned or incurred.

CONSEQUENCES   RULE ROLES These obligations arise out of the basic fiduciary duties that the lawyer owes the client, and **Rule 1.16(d)** recognizes duties that not only are

---

[25] And, of course, there's the **duty of confidentiality**, which continues long after the termination of the engagement, at least until the client dies and, in some jurisdictions forever. *See* **Chapter 8.A at 224**.

enforceable by professional discipline, but also have been adopted in most states as bases for civil liability as well. RULE ROLES CONSEQUENCES

a. "Giving Reasonable Notice to the Client [and] Allowing Time for Employment of Other Counsel"

One part of a proper withdrawal requires notice and remaining available (and potentially on the job) for enough time to save the client from potentially being unduly disadvantaged in the pending engagement. Failure to provide these services "to the extent reasonably practicable" is sometimes referred to as "client abandonment" and is a basis for professional discipline and potential civil liability for any monetary harm that the client suffers as a result. Abandonment includes not only walking away without providing reasonable time to obtain a replacement, but also threatening to withhold services that can't be provided within a reasonable time from another source as a means of obtaining leverage over the client, for example, to pressure for the payment of past-due fees.

Notice and time to obtain replacement counsel are required only "to the extent reasonably practicable." If the basis on which the lawyer has withdrawn or the circumstances surrounding it limit what kinds of timing are "reasonably practicable," a hasty exit is permitted. A client who is perpetrating a significant business fraud and refuses to desist, for example, is unlikely to elicit much sympathy in complaining that his counsel resigned on short notice. If you've waited until the eve of trial or a closing to seek leave to withdraw, on the other hand, you have not given the client the time "reasonably practicable" because your delay created avoidable urgency (*see* **Chapter 9.D at 288**).

> **Problem 9D-7:** Same facts as **Problem 9D-2 at 290** (Frank's firm is representing Aloysius Angry in a litigated real-estate dispute that is set for trial in two weeks; the client stopped paying his bills some time ago, and the firm has sent a letter refusing to appear for trial unless the arrearages are resolved), except that when Mr. Angry fails to pay by the deadline a week before trial, Frank's firm moves to withdraw. Mindful of the terms of **Model Rule 1.16(d)** and the **duty of confidentiality**, the firm argues that it has provided Mr. Angry notice and time for employment of other counsel "to the extent reasonably practicable" because the attorney-client relationship had just broken down at the time the motion was made. In response, Mr. Angry produces the partner's email and announces that he disputes all the amounts that the firm claims are overdue, but he wants the trial to go forward as scheduled. What should the court do, and why?

b. "Refunding Any Advance Payment of Fees or Expenses That Have Not Been Earned or Incurred"

It's not unusual for clients to put money on deposit with their lawyers to cover future fees or costs.[26] (This money must be held segregated from the lawyer's own

---

[26] It's also not unusual to be loved by anyone, but that's not important now. https://www.youtube.com/watch?v=k-HdGnzYdFQ.

funds in the lawyer's client trust account until the fees are earned or the costs are incurred. *See* **Chapter 21.C at 578**.) When an engagement is over, the lawyer **must** return to the client those funds that, because they do not represent earned fees or costs incurred on the client's behalf, are still the client's money.

Occasionally it won't be easy to determine which funds have remained the client's funds. If a client has prepaid a flat fee to complete a defined task, or has entrusted the flat fee to you to be paid when the task is completed, it may be difficult to determine how much of the flat fee has been earned if the lawyer withdraws or is discharged before the agreed work is complete.[27]

Similarly, sometimes the client disputes some or all of the lawyer's charges, creating a dispute as to which portions of the deposited funds the lawyer has, in fact, earned. The way to handle client funds in the context of a fee dispute is discussed in **Chapter 21.C at 585**; the short preview is that you **must** return any funds that you do not dispute are the client's, and you usually **may** hold any disputed funds in your client trust account and take steps to resolve the dispute with all deliberate speed. What you **must not** ever do is exercise "self-help" and take disputed funds as your own money without a formal settlement or adjudication, no matter how strongly you believe that the client's disputes have no merit.

c. "Surrendering Papers and Property to Which the Client Is Entitled"

When an engagement is completed according to its terms, the client may not have any immediate need for the files and papers in your possession. It's not uncommon for the lawyer to hold onto the file, something that has become easier and less expensive in the last 20 years as more and more of the client's file has become digital.

There may be advantages to retaining the file for the client after completion, in particular because you may be the person the client needs to call if there are follow-up tasks or questions that arise later (which makes it more likely that you will be asked to do the work). But there are costs as well. Storing client files and papers can become expensive as time goes on and the number of your completed engagements (and volume of "closed" files) rises. In addition, if you're storing the file, then you're responsible for its safety, integrity, and **confidentiality**. What's more, if a third party thinks that there's something relevant to a pending investigation or dispute in there and you're holding the file, you may get served with a

---

[27] When a matter is terminated before completion, the question often arises how much in fees the lawyer has earned. A well-documented flat fee will allow the parties to determine how much of the flat fee has been earned at the stopping point. An hourly arrangement will usually make it easy to determine how many hours at what rates have been expended. But contingent fees are difficult. Although there is a good deal of variation from state to state, we can generally say that, in a contingent-fee engagement, (1) if the lawyer quits without good cause, or is fired for good cause, then the lawyer gets nothing; (2) if the lawyer quits for good cause or is fired without good cause, then the lawyer gets the reasonable value of her services (*quantum meruit*), usually measured by a reasonable hourly rate times the number of hours the lawyer had expended, plus expenses advanced, at the time of termination, but collectible only if and when the agreed contingency (typically a recovery by settlement or judgment) actually occurs. *See* Lester Brickman, *Setting the Fee When a Client Discharges a Contingent Fee Attorney*, 41 Emory L.J. 367 (1992).

subpoena (you *are* the custodian of those documents, after all). Your client **should** pay for your time in responding to the subpoena of files and papers belonging to the client, but if the client fails or refuses to do so, you still have to respond to the subpoena.

All of which is to say that the completion of an engagement is a very good time to ask your clients what they would like you to do with their files. Clients may have document retention policies that require saving or destroying portions of your client file at different times; they may wish to take possession of the materials and do that themselves, or they may prefer that you do it for them. But, as we're about to discuss in more detail, fundamentally the files and papers that you've accumulated on your client's behalf are your *client's* property, and as a result you **must not** simply dispose of them as you might wish. And even when you have instructions from the client to discard the file or portions of it (for example, often everyone agrees that extra copies of documents that were produced by one party or another in litigation can be destroyed), remember your duty to take reasonable care to protect **confidential information** (*see* **Model Rule 1.6(c)**; **Chapter 8.A at 222**), and be sure that any client papers are securely transported and shredded (or digitally scrubbed), and not just sent to the county landfill or recycling facility where anyone might see them (or left in recoverable form on a storage medium).

In situations in which the engagement has been terminated before completion, the client typically needs the file (or large parts of it) right away to protect or pursue whatever rights the engagement involved. In these circumstances, surrendering the papers and property in the lawyer's possession to which the client is entitled is an extremely important obligation—one that angry lawyers regularly incur discipline and civil liability for disregarding. The part of the Rule about client property is straightforward—if you're holding any of the client's tangible property as part of your engagement at the time that you withdraw or are discharged, you **must** give it back, and do so immediately. (We discussed money in the preceding section.) It doesn't matter how wrong the client was in firing you or making you quit; it's not your stuff, and you're still a fiduciary.

Client files and other papers (including digital files) are a little more complicated. The starting point in the analysis is that most states view most or all client files and papers as the *client's* property, *whether the client has paid for them yet or not.* One critical implication of this principle is that, in all but a few states (Illinois is one of the exceptions, for those of you keeping score), a lawyer **must not** withhold delivery of client files or papers after termination as security for unpaid fees or for any other reason. CONSEQUENCES If you violate this principle, you will suffer professional discipline, and civil liability for losses that the client incurs as a result of not having had access to materials needed to advance the client's

interests. CONSEQUENCES Seriously, don't let your frustration with a difficult client draw you into this blunder. Unless you are practicing in that small minority of states that allow it, you just can't do this, no matter how much you think that the client deserves it.

Now some details: The alert student (there you are again!) points out that **Model Rule 1.16(d)** says that you must turn over papers "to which the client is entitled," but it doesn't specify *which* papers those are. True enough (and kudos on your sharp eye, alert student), but this omission is less significant than you might think. Authority is spotty and a bit inconsistent, but (outside of the few states that allow you to withhold client files as security for payment) the most lawyer-favorable reading of the rule is that the "papers . . . to which the client is entitled" means *anything reasonably necessary for the client to protect or pursue her rights, paid for or not.*

TIPS & TACTICS There are some things that you might consider withholding and, in many states, would be allowed to withhold, but **should not** anyway:

- Papers *not* reasonably necessary for the client to protect or pursue her rights for which the client has not paid. In many states, you have no ethical obligation to turn these over upon withdrawal. As a practical matter, they're a very small portion of the client's file, and by definition, they're insignificant: If withholding them creates any kind of leverage, they're almost certainly necessary for the client to protect or pursue her rights, and you can't withhold them in the first place. The only thing that withholding such papers does is to give the client something to complain about, forcing you to argue later about how unimportant these papers actually were ("And if they were so unimportant, ladies and gentlemen, then why did he go to so much trouble to sort them out and hold them back?").

- Papers that make you look bad, such as uncomplimentary internal communications about the client or her matter, or documents that might indicate (or might be argued to indicate) errors or omissions on your part. The temptation to withhold such papers can be overwhelming. Don't succumb. Why? Well, some states look at these as papers reasonably necessary for the client to protect or pursue her rights—specifically, her rights against *you*. Regardless, they are unquestionably subject to discovery in any later fee dispute or malpractice litigation. If you turn over the client file minus papers that could be embarrassing to you, then when you are forced to hand them over in discovery later, you will be accused of a "cover-up," and you will have created a situation in which the initial withholding is convincingly marshalled as proof of bad acts and guilty knowledge ("Why else would he have hidden these critical papers, ladies and gentlemen?"), possibly turning what might have been at worst a professional negligence claim into an intentional tort case, subject to punitive damages.[28] And don't even think about destroying those documents or planning to withhold them in discovery later. Then you're looking at major ethical violations that will likely cost you your license (*see* **Model Rule 3.4(a), (d)**; **Chapter 24.B at 821**), as well as possible criminal **consequences** for obstruction of justice or similar charges. Given the options, just handing the whole file over at the first obligation to hand over any of it is usually the least bad option in a difficult situation.

In contrast, one kind of document that you **may**, and usually **should**, withhold is any paper or communication relating to any legal advice that you may have sought regarding *your own* rights and duties vis-à-vis the client. It is, of course, completely proper, and often advisable, to get legal advice regarding a developing client situation that could turn (or has turned) difficult. So long as that advice is sought in the proper way from another lawyer acting as your counsel (whether duly designated internal counsel to your firm or outside counsel), that material is subject to *your* **attorney-client privilege** as a client and may properly be withheld from the client as such in most jurisdictions. *See* **Chapter 8.B at 243**. (This is not really a part of your *client's* file; it is *your own* file in which *you* are the client, and thus should be kept separate from the client's papers from the moment it's created.) TIPS & TACTICS

Summing up your obligations regarding client files and other papers, here is a diagram dividing those materials up by practical category:

---

[28] To give you a sense of how these things often play out, consider the real-world client that felt that it was being overbilled in an insolvency matter. The client terminated the large law firm representing it and refused to pay the bill. It was a big matter, and there were hundreds of thousands of dollars in fees at stake. In the later fee litigation, the client's discovery demands eventually forced the disclosure of internal emails among lawyers at the firm joking about how the partners in charge were perceived to be overworking the matter. For example: "[partner] has random people working full time on random research projects in [his] standard 'churn that bill, baby' mode. That bill shall know no limits"; and "with the number of bodies being thrown at this thing it's going to stay stupidly high. . . ." https://archive.nytimes.com/www.nytimes.com/interactive/2013/03/26/business/dealbook/20130326law-documents.html?_r=0, Ex. 5 at 84, Ex. 6 at 87 (March 25, 2013). Needless to say, the dispute settled soon afterward. This incident also conveniently illustrates another lesson about how to express yourself (or really how not to) regarding clients and their matters, especially in writing, in internal communications that you don't expect the client to see. Humor almost never translates well in a later dispute. Remember the **front-page test**: Always talk and act as if everybody's watching, because sooner or later someone might be.

Client Files and Other Papers Upon Termination

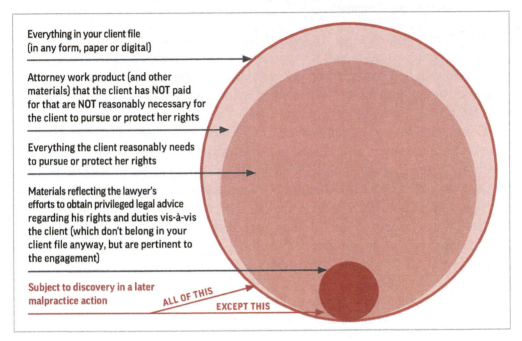

Everything in your client file
(in any form, paper or digital)

Attorney work product (and other
materials) that the client has NOT paid
for that are NOT reasonably necessary for
the client to pursue or protect her rights

Everything the client reasonably needs
to pursue or protect her rights

Materials reflecting the lawyer's
efforts to obtain privileged legal advice
regarding his rights and duties vis-à-vis
the client (which don't belong in your
client file anyway, but are pertinent to
the engagement)

Subject to discovery in a later
malpractice action   ALL OF THIS
                    EXCEPT THIS

Problem 9D-8: Which of the following **must**, **may**, or **should** be turned over to the client promptly after an engagement is terminated before completion, and why?

a. An expert report prepared in pending litigation with an approaching mandatory expert disclosure date for which the discharged lawyer has paid the expert, but the client has not yet reimbursed the lawyer.

b. The discharged lawyer's handwritten notes concerning his interview of a potential witness that the client, in consultation with the discharged lawyer, had already decided not to depose or call as a witness at trial.

c. The lead lawyer's notes on his conversation with his firm's managing partner over the likelihood that the client would dispute the firm's charges, and what should be done to prepare for that possibility. Does your analysis change if the notes reflect that the conversation included the partner at the firm designated as the firm's "Ethics Partner"?

d. A "to-do" list that the discharged lawyer prepared at some point in the litigation and left in his notes file, which includes a task that was never completed. Does your analysis change if the uncompleted task was underlined and had a big asterisk in red?

e. An email from the associate to the partner on the matter relating a conversation the associate had with the client, including: "He seems unhappy with the state of the deal, but I can't for the life of me figure out why. He's such a whiny pain in the a**."

d. Other Steps to Ensure a Reasonably Smooth Transition to Successor Counsel

Model Rule 1.16(d) says that "[u]pon termination of representation, a lawyer shall take steps to the extent reasonably practicable to protect a client's interests, *such as*" those discussed in the preceding sections (emphasis added). This language suggests that the described acts are only an incomplete list of examples. *See* **Chapter 6.C at 162 n.13**. So what else do we have to do? The Comments are silent.

Consistent with your **duties of care** and **candor**, you **must** notify the client as soon as possible after your discharge or withdrawal of all pending dates and deadlines in the matter (can you see why?), and doing so in writing is the only prudent course in order to avoid unnecessary confusion or disputes. Answering any reasonable number of reasonably focused questions about the matter from the client or successor counsel is also good practice and may even be required. And as time goes on, if you receive pleadings, papers, or other communications regarding the client's matter, you **must** make sure that the client or successor counsel receives them.[29]

Generally, you should consider doing anything not prohibitively difficult or expensive that makes the client's transition to successor counsel easier. This is true even when the client doesn't deserve it. If there's going to be a fee dispute or a malpractice claim, then withholding small favors just makes you look mean-spirited and gives the client something more to complain about. Take the opportunity to both be and appear to be gracious to anyone who might review the transition later.

> **Problem 9D-9:** Which of the following **must** or **should** a discharged lawyer do promptly after discharge?
>
> a. Remind the client of the trial date that the court has set and all the filing deadlines that arise out of that date according to the court's Local Rules, even though the lawyer included all those dates in an email sent to the client shortly after the trial date was set.
>
> b. Inform the client of a potential statute of limitations on a claim not yet included in the pending litigation.
>
> c. Take a phone call from successor counsel inquiring about the existence and location of several documents and pleadings.
>
> d. Prepare a detailed index of every document produced in pending litigation.
>
> e. Sit down with successor counsel for an afternoon for the discharged lawyer to answer questions and share her impressions of the strength and status of the case.

And that completes our overview of the attorney-client relationship. In the next unit, we'll broaden our perspective and consider the duties that you owe to people other than your clients. We can't wait!

---

[29] *See* Restatement (Third) of the Law Governing Lawyers § 33(2)(c).

Big-Picture Takeaways from Chapter 9.C-.D

1. Disclaiming duties:
    a. The best way to disclaim duties is to be specific. Tell someone whom you don't intend to represent that you don't intend to represent her (and do it in writing). Tell a non-client who may think that you owe him a duty that you don't (again, in writing). *See* **Chapter 9.C at 283**.
    b. Another way to disclaim duties to a client is to limit the scope of your engagement. **Model Rule 1.2(c)** provides that you "may limit the scope of the representation if the limitation is reasonable under the circumstances and the client gives informed consent." *See* **Chapter 9.C at 284**.
    c. Beware any attempt to waive future liability to a client. States frown upon fiduciaries (including lawyers) trying to limit their liability for future wrongs, so check your own state's law on this topic. And **Model Rule 1.8(h) (1)** provides that you **must not** "make an agreement prospectively limiting the lawyer's liability to a client for malpractice unless the client is independently represented in making the agreement." *See* **Chapter 9.C at 285**.

2. Ending the attorney-client relationship:
    a. There are two general ways in which an engagement can end: When it's completed according to its terms, or when one or both parties to the relationship properly terminates it before it's completed. A completed engagement is usually easy to spot, but you should write the client a lovely termination letter thanking the client for the opportunity to represent him or her. A friendly "disengagement letter" can generate goodwill at the same time as it clarifies the status of the relationship. *See* **Chapter 9.D at 286**.
    b. Sometimes, engagements are more open-ended. A common example of an open-ended engagement is when a lawyer has been retained to consult on a particular subject on an occasional basis when the client requests it. Such an engagement is never completed according to its terms, as it has no defined endpoint. *See* **Chapter 9.D at 286**.
    c. And sometimes either the lawyer or the client (or both) wants to terminate the engagement before it's completed. *See* **Chapter 9.D at 286**.
    d. Because the existence and scope of the attorney-client relationship depends on what the *client* actually and reasonably believes, when in doubt, speak out and **inquire; explain; confirm** (*see* **Chapter 6.A at 139**). *See* **Chapter 9.D at 287**.
    e. Termination is governed by a range of rules that may not always allow a person who *wants* out to *get* out. Sometimes you can't quit, and sometimes a client can't fire you, even when that may be what one or even both of you may want. *See* **Chapter 9.D at 288**.

    i. When you need a tribunal's permission to let you out of an engagement: When a tribunal is involved, most tribunals (including virtually all courts) have rules that require lawyers who have appeared on behalf of parties before that tribunal to continue to be responsible for the matter before the tribunal until and unless the court excuses them from further service and allows them to withdraw. **Model Rule 1.16(c)** says that you are subject to professional discipline if you walk away from an engagement in which a tribunal is involved without the tribunal's permission. You also have continuing civil duties to the client until the tribunal relieves you. *See* **Chapter 9.D at 288**.

    ii. How to get an involved tribunal's permission to withdraw: A court that has a rule requiring leave to withdraw will typically include in that rule instructions on how to seek that leave. The two most common means are a substitution of counsel or a formal motion. *See* **Chapter 9.D at 291**.

    iii. How to show that you have a right to withdraw without violating your **duty of confidentiality**: The lawyer's statement that professional considerations require termination of the representation ordinarily should be accepted as sufficient. In the event that the court demands details implicating **confidential information**, once the court *orders* you to disclose **confidential information**, **Model Rule 1.6(b)(6)** provides an exception to the **duty of confidentiality** "to comply with . . . a court order." So you're acting within your ethical and legal duties if you argue for no disclosure (and if disclosure is ordered, then limited disclosure under seal or *in camera*) and withhold any arguably **confidential information** until the court orders you to do otherwise. *See* **Chapter 9.D at 292**.

f. When a *client* may terminate the relationship: A client has a right to discharge a lawyer at any time, with or without cause, unless the lawyer was court-appointed, such as a public defender. And even when the attorney-client relationship is fully consensual, an involved tribunal has the oversight powers described in **Model Rule 1.16(c)**. *See* **Chapter 9.D at 294**.

g. When a *lawyer* **must** or **may** terminate the relationship: Lawyers **must** or **may** terminate their engagements before completion only on a limited set of enumerated grounds. These grounds are set out in **Model Rules 1.16(a)** and **(b)**.

    i. When **must** a lawyer withdraw? **Model Rule 1.16(a)** lists three circumstances under which a lawyer **must** withdraw. All three are, by the terms of the Rule, subject to the permission of any involved tribunal, so even if a Rule makes your withdrawal mandatory, you still must obtain the tribunal's permission (if there is one), and you **must not** withdraw if the tribunal refuses that permission.

A. "[T]he representation will result in violation of the rules of professional conduct or other law" (**Model Rule 1.16(a)(1)**).

B. "[T]he lawyer's physical or mental condition materially impairs the lawyer's ability to represent the client" (**Model Rule 1.16(a)(2)**).

C. "[T]he lawyer is discharged" (**Model Rule 1.16(a)(3)**). If you're fired, you have to quit. Or if there is an involved tribunal, at least *seek leave* to quit.

See **Chapter 9.D at 295**.

ii. When **may** a lawyer withdraw? The list of grounds on which a lawyer **may** withdraw is set out in **Model Rule 1.16(b)**.

A. "Withdrawal can be accomplished without material adverse effect on the interests of the client" (**Model Rule 1.16(b)(1)**).

B. "[T]he client persists in a course of action involving the lawyer's services that the lawyer reasonably believes is criminal or fraudulent" (**Model Rule 1.16(b)(2)**).

C. "[T]he client has used the lawyer's services to perpetrate a crime or fraud" (**Model Rule 1.16(b)(3)**). Unlike the **Model Rule 1.16(b)(2)** ground, this one is retrospective—you've discovered that the client has *already* used your services to commit a crime or fraud.

D. "[T]he client insists upon taking action that the lawyer considers repugnant or with which the lawyer has a fundamental disagreement" (**Model Rule 1.16(b)(4)**).

E. "[T]he client fails substantially to fulfill an obligation to the lawyer regarding the lawyer's services and has been given reasonable warning that the lawyer will withdraw unless the obligation is fulfilled" (**Model Rule 1.16(b)(5)**).

F. "[T]he representation will result in an unreasonable financial burden on the lawyer or has been rendered unreasonably difficult by the client" (**Model Rule 1.16(b)(6)**).

G. "[O]ther good cause for withdrawal exists" (**Model Rule 1.16(b)(7)**). This is a residual catchall. It still requires "good cause," which is an affirmative showing of a good reason, even if that reason may not neatly fall into **Model Rules 1.16(b)(1)-(b)(6)**.

See **Chapter 9.D at 296**.

h. "Noisy withdrawal": When your client is engaging (or proposing to engage) in illegal conduct, you may be faced with difficult crosscurrents among the law constraining withdrawal, your **duty of confidentiality,** and the law of lawyer liability. Whether your client is currently committing, proposing to commit, or has used your services to commit crimes or frauds is **confidential information** protected by **Model Rule 1.6** in the absence of some applicable exception. But **Model Rules 1.6(b)(2)-(3)** provide that you **may** disclose **confidential information** to prevent or address a serious financial crime or fraud in which your services are used. Some states' exceptions are worded more broadly, and some such exceptions *require* disclosure rather than merely permit it. What's more, the effect of **Model Rule 4.1(b)** in this context is that, if some **confidentiality** exception provides that you **may** disclose **confidential information** to prevent a client crime or fraud effected using your services, then under **Model Rule 4.1(b)** you **must** do so. *See* **Chapter 9.D at 298**.

3. The lawyer's duties upon completion or termination:
   a. "Even if the lawyer has been unfairly discharged by the client, a lawyer must take all reasonable steps to mitigate the consequences to the client." **Model Rule 1.16 Comment [9]**. Those steps include:
      i. When the engagement is terminating prematurely, to the extent reasonably practicable, you **must** give reasonable notice to the client and give the client time to hire replacement counsel. *See* **Chapter 9.D at 302**.
      ii. To the extent that the client has given you any advance payment of fees or expenses that you have not earned or incurred, you **must** refund that advance payment. *See* **Chapter 9.D at 302**.
      iii. You **should** ask your client what he or she (or it) would like you to do with the files related to the engagement. The files and papers that you've accumulated on your client's behalf are your *client's* property, *whether the client has paid for them yet or not*, and as a result, you **must not** simply dispose of them as you might wish. You **must** promptly give back any papers that might reasonably be necessary for the client to protect or pursue her rights. But one kind of document that you **may**, and usually **should**, withhold is any paper or communication relating to any legal advice that you may have sought regarding *your own* rights and duties vis-à-vis the client. This is not really a part of your *client's* file; it is *your own* file in which *you* are the client, and thus should be kept separate from the client's papers from the time it is created. *See* **Chapter 9.D at 303**.
      iv. Consistent with your **duties of care** and **candor**, you **must** notify the client as soon as possible after your discharge or withdrawal of all pending dates and deadlines in the matter, and doing so in writing is the only prudent course in order to avoid unnecessary confusion or disputes. Answering any reasonable number of reasonably focused questions about the matter from the client or successor

counsel is also good practice and may even be required. And as time goes on, if you receive pleadings, papers, or other communications regarding the client's matter, you **must** make sure that the client or successor counsel receives them. *See* **Chapter 9.D at 308**.

Multiple-Choice Review Questions for Chapter 9.C-.D

1. Merida, a contractor, has a dispute with one of her materials suppliers. When she can't work the problem out, she meets with Elias, a lawyer whose name she saw on a billboard. Merida tells Elias about the problem. She explains that her supplier misrepresented the quality of countertop materials supplied for a kitchen renovation. She shows Elias an email in which the supplier admitted that he knew the countertop was defective before it was delivered, and that he assumed that after he installed the countertop, Merida would simply accept the inferior product because removing it would be too much trouble. Although Merida tries to remain professional, it is clear that she is upset. "He duped me," she tells Elias, "it wasn't just an oversight. And it cost me a very important client."

   Elias explains that he would be happy to represent Merida and would be willing to file a breach of contract claim on Merida's behalf. "What would happen if I won?" Merida asks. Elias explains, "You would get back the difference in value between what you were promised and what you got, and maybe the cost of repair."

   Merida isn't completely satisfied, but she decides that getting her money back is better than nothing. Elias hands her a retainer agreement, which she signs immediately. The agreement specifies that Elias will file only a breach of contract claim.

   Elias files the claim, and after a few months, is able to settle the case. Merida is initially pleased.

   A few weeks later, Merida runs into a neighbor who also happens to be a lawyer. When she explains what happened, the neighbor asks, "Why didn't you file a fraud claim? You would have been entitled to three times the amount of the contract under a special statute." Merida says, "I didn't even know that was a possibility."

   Merida confronts Elias. He tells her, "You signed an agreement saying that we would only pursue breach of contract claims. That was the limited scope of our agreement."

   Did Elias properly limit the scope of his engagement?
   a. Yes. Although Elias presented Merida with the agreement during their initial meeting, she was not coerced into signing it immediately.
   b. Yes. Merida consented to a limited scope of engagement.

    c. No. Merida did not consent to the limited scope because she signed the agreement under duress.

    d. No. Merida may have consented to the limited scope, but her consent was not **informed consent**.

2. Timothy is a brand-new lawyer. In order to keep malpractice claims down, he inserts a clause in his standard retainer agreement that requires that the client waive any future claims for legal malpractice.

    Timothy plans simply to hand clients the agreement to sign when they first meet with him. If they will not sign the agreement at that initial meeting, he will tell them that he is unwilling to represent them.

    Timothy's jurisdiction has adopted **Model Rule 1.8(h)(1)** verbatim. There is no other state law addressing the issue.

    Can Timothy comply with his ethical obligations and limit liability in this way?

    a. Yes. A client may agree to limit the scope of representation.

    b. Maybe. The waiver may be valid, but only if the client gives **informed consent**.

    c. Maybe. The waiver may be valid, but only if the client is represented by independent counsel.

    d. No. A client may never waive future claims for legal malpractice.

3. Chandra is retained by BigBox Corp. to handle an employment discrimination case through all appeals. After her client wins at trial, the 30-day time period lapses for any appeal. The opposing party files no timely appeal.

    Six more months pass. Chandra hears nothing from her client or from opposing counsel. Chandra assumes the representation has concluded.

    Is she correct?

    a. Yes. Chandra agreed to represent her client through the appeals. At this point, there can be no timely appeals, so the representation has concluded.

    b. Yes. Chandra only agreed to represent her client if her client appealed. Here, her client won at trial, so the representation ended immediately upon that trial win.

    c. No. There were no appeals, so the condition precedent to concluding the representation never occurred. The representation continues.

    d. No. Chandra never unequivocally stated that she believed the representation to be concluded. Until she does so, the representation continues.

4. Gabrielle is a lawyer who occasionally provides advice to a real estate development firm. She never appears in court; rather, she provides research upon request to the client regarding real estate transactions.

Gabrielle decides to leave private practice to work for the United States Department of Housing and Urban Development, a federal administrative agency. She writes to her real estate client to let it know that she will no longer be able to provide legal advice. The owner of the firm calls Gabrielle to thank her and wish her luck in her new position. Does Gabrielle also need court permission to end this attorney-client relationship?

    a. Yes. Where a client contests withdrawal, a tribunal must be involved.

    b. Yes. A tribunal must always approve the termination of a representation.

    c. No. Because the client consented, the termination can end without involving a tribunal.

    d. No. Because the representation never involved a tribunal, Gabrielle need not involve one now.

5. Marta is a private criminal defense attorney. She represents Ashton, who has been accused of embezzlement. She appears on Ashton's behalf for a preliminary hearing and files several pretrial motions. When Ashton receives the bill for these services, he refuses to pay.

    Marta seeks court permission to withdraw from the representation. The court denies her request.

    She argues the motions and submits a bill to Ashton. He again refuses to pay. Because Marta has not been paid for months, she decides not to show up for trial.

    Can Marta be subject to discipline for failing to represent Ashton at trial?

    a. Yes. She lacked grounds to seek withdrawal, and her request to do so was frivolous.

    b. Yes. Until the court approved her withdrawal, she had a duty to represent Ashton.

    c. No. Ashton was in the wrong for refusing to pay, and Marta had grounds for withdrawal.

    d. No. The court erred in denying Marta's request in light of Ashton's conduct.

6. Max has agreed to take over as plaintiff's counsel in a medical malpractice case. Before agreeing to take over the case, Max meets with the plaintiff to learn the factual basis for the claims.

    Prior counsel files a stipulation to substitute signed by prior counsel, Max, and the client, which the court approves.

    Max is unaware that the deadline for serving expert reports is the following day. He does not timely serve a report. As a result, his client is barred from proceeding in the case.

Was Max responsible for serving the expert report?

a. Yes. Once Max took over as counsel, he was responsible for all filing deadlines.

b. Yes. Max should have asked his new client about any outstanding deadlines before agreeing to take over the case.

c. No. Prior counsel lacked diligence and should not have left the report for the last minute.

d. No. Max was unaware that the report was due, and prior counsel should have notified him.

7. Ruth is frustrated because she has had a hard time reaching her lawyer, Jeff. In all other respects, Jeff is complying with his obligations in the case. The case is scheduled for trial in a few weeks.

Can Ruth fire Jeff and replace him with another lawyer so long as the court allows it?

a. Yes. Jeff's lack of communication is sufficient cause for Ruth to fire him.

b. Yes. Ruth does not need cause to fire Jeff.

c. No. If Ruth fires Jeff, it may prejudice the ability of the trial to occur timely.

d. No. Jeff must consent before Ruth can fire him.

8. When **must** a lawyer withdraw?

a. Continued representation of the client will result in violation of the rules of professional conduct or other law.

b. The lawyer is physically or mentally impaired in a way that prejudices the client.

c. Both a and b.

d. None of the above.

9. When **may** a lawyer withdraw?

a. When it is possible to do so without material adverse effect on the client's interests.

b. When the client persists in a course of action involving the lawyer's services that the lawyer reasonably believes is criminal or fraudulent.

c. Both a and b.

d. None of the above.

10. Margaret is a solo practitioner in the State of Texas who agrees to represent Randy in a breach of contract case. After she files a complaint in state court initiating the case on Randy's behalf, Randy moves to Canada. Randy takes all the necessary documents with him. As a result of Randy's move, the litigation becomes more complex for Margaret. She must now

arrange to copy documents and have them shipped from another country. Randy refuses to coordinate with Margaret and insists that she come in person to review and copy the documents. Because Margaret is a solo practitioner, having to travel to copy the documents would affect her ability to take on other clients.

Does Margaret have grounds to seek withdrawal from the case?

a. Yes, if the representation will result in an unreasonable financial burden on Margaret or has been rendered unreasonably difficult by Randy.

b. Yes, if Randy misrepresented his intention to remain in Texas at the time that Margaret agreed to represent him.

c. No, because it was foreseeable to Margaret that Randy could relocate during the pendency of the case.

d. No, because Randy has committed no crime or fraud by moving to Canada.

11. If a lawyer has been terminated, what documents **must** the lawyer provide to the client?

a. All work product for which the client has paid.

b. All documents reasonably necessary for the client to protect or pursue his or her rights.

c. All documents containing information about the client's case.

d. All documents reflecting the lawyer's efforts to receive legal advice about his or her own rights or duties to the client.

UNIT III

Duties to Third Parties and the Public

LET'S RECONNOITER:

Unit I introduced you to the many different environments in which we lawyers practice (**Chapter 2 at 19**), the many different sources of regulation that govern our conduct as we do (**Chapter 3 at 29**), and the various, often-unseen forces that may drive us crosswise of that regulation before we know it (**Chapter 4 at 69**).

Unit II surveyed our principal obligations to our clients. We started with our duties as our clients' fiduciaries (**Chapter 5 at 105**), continued with our duties (and our powers) as our clients' agents (**Chapter 6 at 131**), and then focused on the details of our **duties of competence, diligence,** and **care** (**Chapter 7 at 171**) and our **duty of confidentiality** (**Chapter 8 at 203**). We wrapped up Unit II with a detailed exploration of how we can initiate the attorney-client relationship and acquire all the duties that come with it, how we can acquire duties to non-clients, how we may be able to disclaim some duties and, finally, how we can end the attorney-client relationship and what we're obligated to do when that happens (**Chapter 9 at 255**).

That's a lot, but there's even more that you need to know. As a lawyer, you have special duties to various third parties with whom you deal and to the public at large—duties that ordinary folks don't have, or don't have in quite the same way. These include the duty to refrain from misrepresentation (**Chapter 10 at 321**), special duties in communicating with people who have (or **must** be treated as if they have) lawyers of their own (**Chapter 11 at 339**), and with people who don't (**Chapter 12 at 373**). And, of course, you **must** avoid advising or assisting your clients to violate the law (**Chapter 13 at 391**). Further duties include refraining from unnecessarily embarrassing or burdening others (**Chapter 14 at 413**) and ethical duties (on top of the legal duties that you share with everyone) to avoid invidious discrimination

(**Chapter 15 at 427**). You even have duties to report other lawyers' ethical violations (**Chapter 16 at 439**), and duties to refrain from offering or agreeing to restrict the scope of your future practice (**Chapter 17 at 455**). Finally, you **must** comply with the regulations on lawyer advertising and solicitation (**Chapter 18 at 473**).

Some of these obligations will seem obvious; some won't; and some you won't have time to cover in this course, though you will have this book to consult if they ever come up. But as you can see, we still have a lot to do.

Let's get going.

10

Avoiding Misrepresentation

MAYA IS ASSISTING Ron Rainmaker, a partner in her firm, in a corporate acquisition. A large company that is a longtime client of the firm is acquiring a smaller company. It's a "cash-for-stock" deal—that is, Maya's client intends to purchase all the shares of the smaller target corporation for cash.

The basic framework and structure of the deal having been tentatively agreed upon, Maya sits in on the negotiating session in which the purchase price per share will be set. The two lead lawyers confirm that they have a common understanding of the number of shares outstanding and who owns them (the target is a closely held corporation with only a few shareholders, all of whom are represented by one law firm). Ron and the lawyer representing the shareholders then start discussing price per share. After some extensive sparring about the target company's assets and liabilities, and its past performance and future prospects, the shareholders' lawyer demands $320 per share. "You've got to be kidding," Ron sputters. "Not only is that ten times last year's earnings in an industry that averages sales at six times earnings, but it's beyond my authority. I can get you $280, and that's a stretch." The shareholders' lawyer argues that a higher multiple is appropriate because the target company's main product is positioned to become the industry leader in its niche—which, he points out, is undoubtedly why the larger company wants to acquire the target in the first place. Nevertheless, the shareholders are ready to sell, and he has authority to set the purchase price at $315 per share.

"Sorry, no can do," Ron says. "That is still beyond what I'm authorized to offer. My client has done its homework, there's a board resolution limiting what I can agree to, and my instructions are clear." After some concerted back-and-forth dressed up as debate about the company's value, the lawyers reach agreement (subject to documentation of all terms of the deal) at $305 per share. Everyone shakes hands, and the lawyers agree to meet back in few days to hammer out the documentation. Maya will prepare the first draft of the Acquisition Agreement.

Maya (to her credit) has remained carefully impassive during the negotiation, quietly taking notes. Once she and Ron have retired to his office, however, she allows her concern to show. "I'm confused," Maya says. "The board resolution that we prepared and that the board adopted authorized you to offer as much as $320 a share. But you told the shareholders' counsel that you didn't have the authority to pay that much. How does that work?" "Don't worry about it," Ron answers. "It's just negotiation." "But . . ." Maya interjects. "I said, don't worry about it," Ron repeats, with finality. "That's how it's done. I just saved our client over $8 million."

Are Maya's concerns well taken? If they are, what should the partner have done differently? To learn the answers, read on.

* * *

There are some rules that apply to everybody, lawyers included. To give an obvious example, no one is allowed to commit murder, whether or not you have a law license. But some rules governing lawyer conduct apply *only* to lawyers. For example, there are important limitations on what a lawyer may say in the course of representing a client to persons who have (or **must** be treated as if they had) their own lawyer (*see* **Model Rule 4.2**; **Chapter 11 at 339**), and to persons who don't have their own lawyer (*see* **Model Rule 4.3**; **Chapter 12 at 373**). Those particular constraints on what someone can say to represented and unrepresented persons don't apply to nonlawyers.

The rules forbidding misrepresentation by lawyers are somewhere in between these two categories. On the one hand, no one (lawyer or not) is allowed to make **material** factual misrepresentations. If someone reasonably relied upon those misrepresentations and is harmed as a result, those misrepresentations are a tort (negligent misrepresentation or fraud) and possibly a crime as well. On the other hand, we will see that there is a well-developed body of law that helps us *interpret* certain kinds of statements that lawyers make to determine whether or not they amount to factual misrepresentations. That body of law sometimes causes us to interpret some things that lawyers (and others undertaking similar tasks in similar contexts) say somewhat differently than we would if they were not lawyers.

Either way, make no mistake: Intentional misrepresentation is lying. Lying about facts that are **material** (that is, that matter in the context in which they are communicated) is wrong, and it can bear very serious **consequences**. But our first task is to figure out when something amounts to a misrepresentation.

We start, as we usually do, with the Rules. Please read **Model Rule 4.1**, including the Comments.

Having now done what's right and read the Rule, you will have noticed that **Model Rule 4.1(a)** forbids ("shall not") "a lawyer" from "knowingly" making a "false statement of material fact" to a "third person" while "in the course of representing a client." And you will also have noticed that **Model Rule 4.1(b)** forbids a lawyer from "knowingly" "fail[ing] to disclose a material fact" when "disclosure is necessary to avoid assisting a criminal or fraudulent act by a client," except when "disclosure is prohibited by Rule 1.6." Let's break those down.

A. The Scope of Rule 4.1: Communications and Failures to Disclose by "A Lawyer" "To a Third Person" Made "In the Course of Representing a Client"

TAMING THE TEXT The scope limitation of **Model Rule 4.1** (that is, which statements it covers) has three pieces. These scope restrictions apply to both false statements under **Model Rule 4.1(a)** and misleading **material** omissions under **Model Rule 4.1(b)**.

First, the statement or omission has to be made by a *lawyer*. Because of the **no-puppetry rule** (codified in **Model Rule 8.4(a)**, which forbids lawyers from using someone else to accomplish things that they are prohibited from doing themselves), this includes statements made *on behalf of* a lawyer, for example by the lawyer's office staff or by anyone else the lawyer induces to speak falsely.

Next, the only statements and omissions **Model Rule 4.1** covers are ones made "to a third person." This raises the question of who is *not* a "third person." The answer to that question is that your client is not a "third person" for these purposes. How do we know? We can infer it from the fact that the Chapter of the Model Rules containing Rule 4.1 (Chapter 4, Rules 4.1-4.4) is entitled "Transactions with Persons *Other Than Clients*" (emphasis added). And we already know that lawyers are fiduciaries to their clients (*see* **Chapter 5.B at 106**), with elevated **duties of candor** and disclosure that result from that special status. *See* **Chapter 5.D at 117**. As a result, there's a specific Rule that we've already talked about that governs communications with clients: **Model Rule 1.4**. It's different from, and *more* demanding than, **Model Rule 4.1**. So **Model Rule 4.1** forbids misrepresentations and misleading omissions made to anyone other than the lawyer's client in the matter at hand. That could include an opposing party or opposing counsel, or anyone else, such as a witness or other nonparty to the transaction or dispute at issue.

Finally, the statement or omission has to be by a lawyer "in the course of representing a client." If the lawyer is committing fraud or otherwise lying for his or her own benefit (or the benefit of someone other than a client, perhaps a family member whom the lawyer does not represent)—running her own Ponzi scheme, for example, or providing a false alibi for one of his adolescent children accused of a crime—**Model Rule 4.1** provides no **consequences**. TAMING THE TEXT

CONSEQUENCES Of course, tort and criminal law prohibiting fraud and other false statements provide other remedies for this kind of dishonesty.[1] In addition, misrepresentation (even innocent misrepresentation) material to the making

---

[1] As you probably learned in your first year, both criminal and tortious fraud generally require proof of (1) a false statement of material fact; (2) known by the speaker to be false; (3) reasonably relied upon by the victim; (4) causing (5) damages. Because it has five elements, this wrong is sometimes rather charmingly referred to as "five-finger fraud." Negligent misrepresentation is also actionable as a tort in many jurisdictions, but **Model Rule 4.1** refers only to "knowingly" false or misleading statements or omissions. A number of other torts and crimes involve false statements as well. The hypothetical in the text about a lawyer providing a false alibi for one of the lawyer's children, for example, amounts to obstruction of justice, hindering a police investigation, or similar crimes variously named and defined in different jurisdictions. And the *actus reus* for perjury is the making of a **material** false statement under oath.

of a contract is a defense to enforcement of that contract, making the contract voidable. *See, e.g., Restatement (Second) of Contracts* § 164. Please pause and note the difference between the two: Fraud as a tort or a crime brings civil liability or criminal penalties to those responsible for the lie. Misrepresentation in the formation of a contract is a *defense* to the formation or enforcement of the contract. This concept has tremendous practical importance because, in addition to any possible damages from a civil tort claim, a contract induced by misrepresentation may often be undone by rescission, and any exchanged consideration may be returned to restore the state of things to how they were before the deal was made (the *status quo ante*).

And if you are concerned that the Rules of Professional Conduct provide no *disciplinary* **consequences** for a lawyer lying for his or her own benefit rather than for a client's, fear not. **Model Rule 8.4(c)** quite explicitly designates as "professional misconduct" subject to professional discipline *any* "conduct involving dishonesty, fraud, deceit or misrepresentation."[2] Consequences

B. What Qualifies as a "False Statement of Material Fact" Under Model Rule 4.1(a)?

Once you find a statement covered by **Model Rule 4.1(a)**, you must determine whether it is a "false statement of material fact."

1. A "Statement"

Taming the Text Let's start with the easy part—what qualifies as a "statement." Lest there be any confusion, a "statement" covered by **Model Rule 4.1(a)** can be in any form: oral, written, head nod, hand gesture, whatever. Any communicative act will do. And, of course, that includes "incorporat[ing] or affirm[ing] a statement of another person that the lawyer knows is false." **Model Rule 4.1 Comment [1]**. Taming the Text

As for the rest of the phrase, there are three important concepts to unpack: To violate **Model Rule 4.1(a)**, a statement must be *material*, *factual*, and *false*.

---

[2] **Model Rule 8.4** is a catchall of sorts, and we urge you to keep it in mind whenever you find yourself wondering whether some bad act a lawyer commits is immune from professional discipline. Usually there is something in Rule 8.4 that provides disciplinary **consequences** when no more specific Rule of Professional Conduct quite gets there. *See* **Chapter 3.A at 43**.

It's worth asking yourself, hey, self, why would we have a rule like **Model Rule 8.4(c)**, which imposes *professional discipline* on a lawyer who engages in dishonesty or deceit even when the bad acts are done when *not* representing a client (and therefore when not acting "as a lawyer")? The answer is that this Rule represents a judgment that a lawyer who engages in dishonesty or deceit when *not* representing clients is, as a matter of human nature, a lot more likely to be dishonest when representing clients, too. (That's also the basic policy judgment underlying **Model Rule 8.4(b)**, which states that it is "professional misconduct" subject to discipline to "commit a criminal act that reflects adversely on the lawyer's honesty, trustworthiness or fitness as a lawyer in other respects." And because the purpose of professional discipline is to protect the public from a lawyer's future malfeasance (*see* **Chapter 3.A at 45**), these predictors of future malfeasance fit snugly into the disciplinary scheme.

2. "Material"

TAMING THE TEXT "**Materiality**" is a concept that we've explored before. (*See, e.g.,* **Chapter 6.C at 158**, in which we discussed how you know which "means" decisions in an engagement are important enough—sufficiently **material**—that you **must** consult with the client about them.) It comes up in many other legal contexts, too. Simply put, something is "**material**" if it meaningfully and reasonably matters or reasonably should matter to the person with whom you're dealing in the context at hand.

One thing that should be clear from this practical definition is that **materiality** is highly dependent on the situation in which the issue arises. For example, if you're representing a halal or kosher grocery store (which adheres strictly to dietary restrictions imposed by Islam or Judaism, respectively), it is material to your clients whether the products that you're helping them acquire for sale contain even miniscule amounts of pork or pork by-products, because observant Muslims and Jews may not eat even the tiniest bit of pork. If you're representing a general-purpose grocery store, this issue is probably not material to your client. So when you're determining whether a statement is material, the first questions you need to ask are "material *to whom*?" and "why does or should it matter to that particular person or company?" TAMING THE TEXT

3. "Factually False" (in General)

TAMING THE TEXT "False" and "factual" go hand-in-hand. Why? Only statements of fact can be false, that is, can be *objectively proven* not to be true. In this context, the opposite of "fact" is "opinion" (or, as we'll discuss in the next section, a "statement of position"). "Opinions" involve matters of evaluation or taste that cannot be objectively proven true or false. "Beets are delicious" is not a statement that can be proven true or false in any objective or universal sense. Some reasonable people like beets; some don't. By the same token, "the beets in the bowl on the table in front of us are red beets" is either true or false—there are also yellow beets, and red-and-white-striped Chioggia beets, and probably lots of other colorful beet hybrids, but the particular beets to which the statement refers are either all red or they're not—and thus, this statement is factual. TAMING THE TEXT

There are statements whose truth or falsity is hard to determine. These difficulties are often attributable to questions about the statement's precise meaning. For example, if there's a green blotch on one of the beets in the bowl, is the statement about the bowl of beets being red true or false? The important point here is that it's either one or the other—depending, perhaps, on whether the statement is understood to refer to a particular species of beets called "red beets," or whether it refers to the color of the beets in the bowl and, if the latter, how **material** that green blotch is when you say they're "red"—and, thus, "the beets in that bowl are red beets" is a statement of fact.

There are also statements that are close to the dividing line between facts and opinions, but the distinguishing feature that factual statements are *provably* true or false provides a useful and workable practical test much of the time. When a statement could be interpreted either as an assertion of fact or a statement of opinion, or if its meaning is otherwise ambiguous (like the reference to "red" beets in the previous paragraph), you interpret it as a reasonable person in the circumstances of the person receiving the communication, knowing what that person knows, would understand it. You must examine the totality of the circumstances, including the background or context in which the statement is made, the past relationship among the negotiating parties, their apparent sophistication, the statement's facial plausibility, the statement's phrasing, related communications, and other relevant circumstances.[3]

What about half-truths and other ambiguously misleading or incomplete statements? The interpretive test just provided gives you the answer: If a reasonable person in the position of the recipient of the communication would be misled into understanding the communication as a statement of fact that the speaker knows is false, it's a misrepresentation. *See* **Model Rule 4.1 Comment [1]**. In other words, a lawyer cannot exploit a misunderstanding that the lawyer helped to create. But we imagine (because we think the best of you) that your common sense told you that already.[4]

> **Problem 10B-1:** Frank is handling a trip-and-fall case. His client, Penelope Plaintiff, was walking in front of a local grocery store when she caught her toe in a crack in the sidewalk and fell. Frank is preparing to file a complaint on Penelope's behalf, and (to his credit) interviews her first. He asks where she was hurt after she fell. She replies that she experienced radiating pain in her lower back. When he asks how long the pain lasted, Penelope shrugs

---

[3] *See* **Model Rule 4.1 Comment [2]**. We caution care in using a turn of phrase now in vogue in which partisans express "opinions" or "feelings" about whether factual propositions are true or false. Scrutinize the speaker and context to figure out what is reasonably understood. Sometimes the speaker is making a prediction or inference about something that may turn out to be true or false after time or proof resolves uncertainty, or where uncertainty may never be resolved. Used in this sense, the speaker is not making a factual representation, but making an argument or stating a contestable belief based on incomplete or inconsistent evidence, something that humans in general and lawyers in particular do all the time.

Sometimes this turn of phrase is used to express the view that something is factually true simply because the speaker thinks that it is or wishes that it were, in the absence of any evidence or even in the presence of evidence to the contrary. This is a phenomenon that psychologists call "magical thinking." If such statements are made in a context that reasonably implies that the speaker has a factual or evidentiary basis for the statement, it is a representation of fact.

There are also all kinds of hyperfine distinctions about truth and falsity over which philosophers, logicians, linguists, and rhetoricians regularly tie themselves up into strangulating little knots. Many of them have to do with annoying self-referential paradoxes ("this statement is false") or contextual and interpretive problems (imagine a debate between a person who intensely dislikes the taste of beets and a person who is mortally allergic to them over whether the statement "beets are edible" is fact or opinion). Fortunately, you are not a philosopher, logician, linguist, or rhetorician. (Well, you might have studied those topics as an undergraduate.) You will soon be a lawyer. The practical and interpretive guidelines that we have provided in the text will be adequate to address almost any situation that you encounter as a lawyer. Though some situations may be harder to resolve than others, the guidance in the text will allow you to ask the right questions.

[4] There is a firm distinction, however, between speaking half a truth and then stopping or speaking ambiguously in a way that might suggest a fact that you know isn't true, on the one hand, and simply not disclosing facts that your adversary might really, really like to know, on the other hand. The latter is usually permissible, unless there is an affirmative duty to speak (which arises only relatively rarely). See **Chapter 10.C at 329**.

and says, "Not exactly sure; it was really bad for about two weeks, and then it started to get better as I did physical therapy. I was OK to go back to work after maybe three weeks." Before filing the complaint, Frank decides to send a demand letter to the grocery store. In his letter, he writes that Penelope suffered "severe back pain" that lasted "for weeks." Is this letter consistent with Frank's ethical obligations? Why or why not?

Problem 10B-2: Same as **Problem 10B-1 at 326**, but now Frank revises his letter to state that Penelope experienced "severe back pain" that lasted for "months." Is this letter consistent with Frank's ethical obligations? Why or why not?

Problem 10B-3: Same as **Problem 10B-1 at 326**. Penelope also missed about three weeks of work. She makes $17.92 per hour. Frank's demand letter includes a claim for lost wages, asserting that Penelope missed 120 hours of work at $18 per hour. Is this letter consistent with Frank's ethical obligations? Why or why not?

Problem 10B-4: Same as **Problem 10B-1 at 326**, but add that when Frank interviewed Penelope, he asked her if there was anything on the sidewalk to mark the crack on which she tripped. Penelope says she saw orange paint on the crack. Frank drafts a complaint that states what the client told him — that there was paint marking the crack. When he gives the draft to the partner to review, the partner crosses out this allegation and writes to Frank in the margin, "if we plead that there was paint marking the crack, we will lose the case." **Should** Frank follow the partner's direction, change the allegation regarding the paint, and file the complaint? If so, how **should** he change the allegation? If not, what **should** he do?

4. "Factually False" in the Context of Negotiation — Statements of Position vs. Statements of Fact

One place that things can get tricky is that, in some circumstances, a statement may seem more factual on its face, but under accepted interpretive understandings relating to how lawyers speak with one another, the statement should reasonably be understood as nonfactual. Specifically, in negotiation, certain types of statements are ordinarily understood to be statements of the negotiator's *position*, not as statements of *fact*:

> Under generally accepted conventions in negotiation, certain types of statements ordinarily are not taken as statements of **material** fact. Estimates of price or value placed on the subject of a transaction and a party's intentions as to an acceptable settlement of a claim are ordinarily in this category . . . .

Model Rule 4.1 Comment [2]. And a statement of position in negotiation (also referred to at times as "puffing" or "posturing") is conventionally understood as a statement of opinion regarding the value or outcome of a matter—a statement that is generally viewed as nonfactual. Why? Because a common and accepted feature of negotiation since the dawn of time is the legitimate and permissible effort on both sides to *conceal* their priorities and bottom-line needs in order to make the best deal that they can (not just the minimum deal that they need). And over time, accepted conventions arose about what kinds of "position concealment" were considered acceptable negotiating moves, and which needed to be understood as straight-up factual representations (or misrepresentations). As a result, as weird as it may sound, a "statement of position" does not have to, and quite often does not, represent the negotiator's actual position.

Problem 10B-5: In response to Frank's demand letter described in **Problem 10B-1 at 326**, defense counsel calls him. Defense counsel asks, "What's it going to take to settle this case?" Frank knows that Penelope would settle for $20,000. What if he answers "$80,000"? Is that a misrepresentation within the meaning of **Model Rule 4.1**?

Problem 10B-6: Same as **Problem 10B-5**, but instead of asking, "What is it going to take to settle this case?," defense counsel asks, "What is your client's bottom line?" Does Frank have to disclose that it's $20,000? Does he have to answer at all? If Frank responds by saying, "I could convince her to settle for $80,000," is that a misrepresentation within the meaning of **Model Rule 4.1**?

Problem 10B-7: Same as **Problem 10B-6**. What if, in answer to defense counsel's question, "What is your client's bottom line?" Frank simply answers "$80,000?" Is that a misrepresentation within the meaning of **Model Rule 4.1**?

Problem 10B-8: Same as **Problem 10B-5**, but in response to Frank's $80,000 demand, defense counsel (who has dealt with Frank and his firm on several occasions) says genially, "Frank, c'mon buddy, it's me. You and I both know that $80K is out of the ballpark. I can get her $20,000, but that's really as far as we're gonna go. Anything more than that exceeds the per-claim limit on the store's insurance policy." Although $20,000 is a fair settlement, the store actually has $100,000 per-claim policy limits.

Frank says, "Sorry, dude, she'll never take $20,000." "Well, then," says defense counsel, "what you're telling me is she really wants to roll the dice and try this case." In fact, Penelope has told Frank that she is risk-averse and really needs some money right away because she used up her modest savings when she was laid up from the accident. Frank is relieved at Penelope's urgency, because $20,000 is actually a good settlement, and the chances of getting a better result at trial are, in his view, low. "She's dying to try the case," says Frank. "So am I."

Is anything in this conversation a misrepresentation within the meaning of **Model Rule 4.1**?

Problem 10B-9: Go back and review the hypothetical in the **chapter Introduction at 319**. Has Maya's boss said anything that he shouldn't have? If so, what and why, and how could he have conveyed a similar sentiment more properly?

5. "Knowingly"

TAMING THE TEXT **Model Rule 4.1(a)** forbids only "false **material** statement[s] of fact" made "knowingly." In a strange and mysterious coincidence (well, not really), **Model Rule 1.0(f)** defines "knowingly" in pretty much the same way it is defined in many other legal contexts: with "actual knowledge of the fact in question," which "may be inferred from circumstances." **TAMING THE TEXT**

CONSEQUENCES What that definition means is that negligence regarding a statement's material falsity ("should have known") or a **material** but innocent mistake is not sufficient to violate **Model Rule 4.1(a)** and can't form the basis for professional discipline. On the other hand, justifiable reliance and causation of harm, which are necessary for civil remedies (except the avoidance of a contract, which does not require causation of harm but does require justified reliance inducing the contract), are *not* required in order to violate **Model Rule 4.1(a)**. It's really important to keep these differing requirements for different **consequences** straight. When you're confronting a real-world situation and trying to assess your or your client's risk, you need to assess the risk of each different **consequence** separately. **CONSEQUENCES**

C. Knowing "Fail[ure] to Disclose a Material Fact" When Necessary to Avoid Client Crime or Fraud Under Model Rule 4.1(b)

As you'll recall, although **Model Rule 4.1(a)** is about making *affirmative misstatements*, **Model Rule 4.1(b)** forbids "knowingly" "*fail[ing] to disclose* a material fact" (emphasis added) when "disclosure is necessary to avoid assisting a criminal or fraudulent act by a client," except when "disclosure is prohibited by Rule 1.6."

1. Knowing "Fail[ure] to Disclose a Material Fact"

TAMING THE TEXT From the preceding discussion, we already know what "knowingly," "**material**," and "fact" mean. The lawyer has to know the undisclosed fact, and know that it is **material** to whoever hasn't been told.[5] Does that mean that a lawyer has to spill the beans on everything of consequence that she knows or else suffer professional discipline? Absolutely not. "A lawyer is required to be truthful when dealing with others on a client's behalf, but generally has no affirmative duty to inform an opposing party of relevant facts." **Model Rule 4.1 Comment [1]**.
TAMING THE TEXT

Generally, a lawyer's duty to disclose **material** facts under **Model Rule 4.1** arises in only two circumstances: First, when the lawyer has said something that makes omitting the **material** fact misleading—that's the half-truths and strategic ambiguities covered by **Model Rule 4.1(a)** that we already discussed in **Chapter 10.B at 326**.

---

[5] As discussed above, the omission also has to be on the part of a lawyer, that lawyer has to fail to disclose to a "third party" (that is, someone other than the lawyer's own client), and the omission has to occur "in the course of representing a client" (that is, not when the lawyer is acting for his or her own benefit or for the benefit of someone other than a client). *See* **Chapter 10.A. at 323**.

And second, when "disclosure is necessary to avoid assisting a criminal or fraudulent act by a client."[6]

2. When Disclosure Is "Necessary to Avoid Assisting a Criminal or Fraudulent Act by a Client"

We can't anticipate every scenario in which you may find yourself (or your work product) involved in a client crime or fraud, but there are several more common ones: Sometimes you find that the client has provided you, whether innocently, negligently, or deliberately, with inaccurate information on which you have relied in making representations of your own to third parties; and when you discover the error or falsehood, the client refuses to allow you to correct the misstatement, which is **material** to the third party. Sometimes a statement was true when made, but circumstances change in a way that is **material**, and the client won't allow you to disclose that the statement has become inaccurate. Sometimes the client has taken your work product (reflecting an inaccurate understanding of something important that needed to be corrected before the work product was used), or altered it so that it is **materially** misleading or false, and presented it to third parties to induce their reliance.

These are, fortunately, nightmare scenarios that aren't very common. After all, though you can't spot every crook or grifter who walks into your office, anyone you believe you can't trust to keep you out of a mess like this should *never* be offered an engagement letter in the first place. Life is too short, and your license to practice too precious, to waste on human flotsam like that. Usually, if a mistake has been made or a situation has changed after you made statements about it, the client will be willing, sometimes grudgingly, to allow you to correct things. You can encourage the correction by pointing out that a failure to disclose would amount to a crime or fraud by the client him- or herself, which could carry terrible **consequences** for the client.

But what can you do if the client refuses anyway? A Comment to **Model Rule 4.1** offers guidance:

> Ordinarily, a lawyer can avoid assisting a client's crime or fraud by withdrawing from the representation. Sometimes it may be necessary for the lawyer to give notice of the fact of withdrawal and to disaffirm an opinion, document, affirmation or the like. In

---

[6] This discussion is limited to **material** omissions forbidden by **Model Rule 4.1**. Contract and tort law in many jurisdictions impose duties to disclose in various circumstances involving special relationships. In addition, the contractual defenses of unilateral mistake or misrepresentation become available if one party to a contract allows the other to enter into the contract knowing that the other is operating under a mistaken belief of various kinds, including one that will substantially decrease or deprive the opponent of the benefit of its bargain. *See* RESTATEMENT (SECOND) OF CONTRACTS § 161. Again, these defenses can be used to undo (rescind) deals that clients believe that they have made, and the risk that they may be asserted later by a party who finds him- or herself to have been mis- or uninformed can be a significant issue informing how the client should be advised to behave. Lawyers also have powerful duties to correct discovered falsities in representations made and evidence presented to a tribunal. These topics are discussed in detail in **Chapter 24.C at 878**. This discussion concerns "third parties" other than tribunals.

extreme cases, substantive law may require a lawyer to disclose information relating to the representation to avoid being deemed to have assisted the client's crime or fraud. If the lawyer can avoid assisting a client's crime or fraud only by disclosing this information, then under paragraph (b) the lawyer is required to do so, unless the disclosure is prohibited by Rule 1.6.

Model Rule 4.1 Comment [3]. The need and permissibility of giving interested third parties notice or information at the time you are constrained to quit—a so-called "noisy withdrawal"—thus depends on a detailed consideration of the rules governing **confidential client information**, which we addressed in **Chapter 9.D at 298**. For now, suffice it to say that, if the client refuses to allow you to disclose **material** facts that must be disclosed to avoid assisting the client's crime or fraud, you need to get out, and you need to make those disclosures despite the client's instructions not to disclose, *unless* they are "prohibited by Rule 1.6" (and not subject to an exception to your **duty of confidentiality**).

3. When Disclosures Are "Prohibited by Rule 1.6"

TAMING THE TEXT As you know, **Model Rule 1.6** states the basic principles governing **confidential client information**. In broad overview, any information obtained in the course of representing a client is **confidential**, and you **must not** voluntarily disclose it without the client's permission unless an exception to your **duty of confidentiality** exists. *See* **Chapter 8.A at 217**. The **material** facts that you have concluded that you need to disclose in order to avoid assisting a client's crime or fraud are usually considered to be **confidential information** protected by **Model Rule 1.6**. Thus, unless you can find an exception to your duty of confidentiality that permits (**may**) or requires (**must**) you to disclose this information, you are "prohibited by Rule 1.6" from disclosing, and you may be in a serious bind.

In addition, you know from **Chapter 8.B at 236** that all of the exceptions to the duty of confidentiality stated in **Model Rule 1.6(b)** are permissive in form (**may**), though other rules contain mandatory (**must**) overrides of **client confidentiality**—for example, the **duty to correct** false evidence presented or false representations made to a tribunal under **Model Rule 3.3** (*see* **Chapter 24.C at 878**).[7] Because **Model Rule 4.1** *requires* you to disclose **material** facts necessary to avoid assisting in a client's crime or fraud unless "*prohibited* by Rule 1.6" (emphasis added), you **must** exercise the permission granted in any permissive exception to confidentiality in these circumstances. *See* **Chapter 9.D at 300**. TAMING THE TEXT

---

[7] YOUR HOUSE; YOUR RULES And a number of jurisdictions have altered the model form of **Model Rule 1.6** to make some of the **Model Rule 1.6(b)** exceptions mandatory rather than permissive. So if you find yourself in the unfortunate situation of needing to disclose **material** facts to avoid assisting in a client's crime or fraud, check your state's version of the Rules carefully. YOUR HOUSE; YOUR RULES

Problem 10C-1: Maya has been working on a real estate investment fund headed up by Sherman Shady. The fund is raising money from investors that will be used to invest in commercial real estate. Maya uses her online investigation skills to find out more about Shady and discovers that, in addition to a number of successful ventures, he has been involved in two real estate companies that ended up in bankruptcy, had a personal bankruptcy himself around the same time, and pleaded *nolo contendere* to a state law securities fraud claim in connection with the failure of one of the companies. Shady failed to tell his lawyers about these events in his past, and they are currently not disclosed in the "Management" section of the fund's draft offering circular. Worse, Maya discovers that Shady has used the draft circular in his early efforts to start raising money for the fund. What **must**, **may**, and **should** Maya and her firm do now?

Big-Picture Takeaways from Chapter 10

1. **Model Rule 4.1** covers misrepresentations and misleading failures to disclose by a lawyer to a third person made in the course of representing a client. In other words, the statement has to be made by a lawyer (or on behalf of a lawyer); the statements have to be made to a third person (not a client; there are other Rules protecting clients); and the statements have to have been made to the third party in the course of representing a client. *See* **Chapter 10.A at 323**.

2. In addition to triggering professional discipline when a lawyer violates **Model Rule 4.1**, a misrepresentation can include such **consequences** as tort or criminal liability, or rescission of any agreement procured by that misrepresentation. *See* **Chapter 10.A at 323**.

3. A "statement" can be made by any means: oral, written, by context. And incorporating another's statement that the lawyer knows is false is also covered by **Model Rule 4.1**. But the statement in question must be (a) **material**, (b) factual (in other words, provably true or false, and not an opinion or a statement of position), and (c) false. *See* **Chapter 10.B at 324**. More specifically:
   a. If a reasonable person in the position of the recipient of the communication would be misled into understanding the communication as the statement of a fact that the speaker knows is false, it's a misrepresentation. *See* **Chapter 10.B at 326**.
   b. In negotiation, certain types of statements are ordinarily understood to be statements of the negotiator's *position*, not statements of *fact*. A statement of position in negotiation (also referred to at times as "puffing" or "posturing") is conventionally understood as a statement of opinion regarding the value or outcome of a matter—a statement that is not generally viewed as factual. *See* **Chapter 10.B at 327**.

    c. Because **Model Rule 4.1** requires a "knowing" misrepresentation regarding a statement's falsity, a **material** false statement that is negligent ("should have known") or innocent ("didn't know and shouldn't have known") is not sufficient to violate **Model Rule 4.1(a)**, and cannot form the basis for professional discipline. But under appropriate circumstances, a knowing or negligent misrepresentation can form a basis for tort liability, and a knowing, negligent, or even innocent misrepresentation can ground a defense to a contract claim or a claim for rescission of the contract. *See* **Chapter 10.B at 329**.

4. It's not just sins of *commission* (knowing, **material** misrepresentations) but also sins of *omission* that can cause a **Model Rule 4.1** violation. **Model Rule 4.1(b)** forbids "knowingly" "fail[ing] to disclose a material fact" when "disclosure is necessary to avoid assisting a criminal or fraudulent act by a client," except when "disclosure is prohibited by Rule 1.6." *See* **Chapter 10.C at 329**.

5. A lawyer's duty to disclose undisclosed **material** facts under **Model Rule 4.1** arises in only two circumstances:
    a. First, when the lawyer has said something that makes omitting the **material** fact misleading—that's the half-truths and strategic ambiguities covered by **Model Rule 4.1(a)**. *See* **Chapter 10.C at 329**.
    b. And second, when disclosure is necessary to avoid assisting a criminal or fraudulent act by a client. If the client refuses to allow you to disclose **material** facts that must be disclosed to avoid assisting a client's crime or fraud, you **should** withdraw from the engagement (or seek leave of court to withdraw where required), and you **must** make those disclosures despite the client's instructions not to disclose, *unless* they are "prohibited by Rule 1.6." Because **Model Rule 4.1(b)** *requires* you to disclose material facts necessary to avoid assisting in a client's crime or fraud unless "*prohibited* by Rule 1.6" (emphasis added), you **must** exercise the permission granted in any permissive ("**may**") exception to **confidentiality** in these circumstances. *See* **Chapter 10.C at 333**.

Multiple-Choice Review Questions for Chapter 10

1. Curly is an immigration lawyer. One day, he hears from a prospective client, Mo, who currently lives in Egypt. Mo wants to apply for asylum in the United States and eventually to seek lawful permanent resident status and naturalization. "Not a problem," Curly thinks, "I've done a hundred asylum applications before, and I run a respected immigration practice." Curly and Mo execute a retainer agreement, and Curly begins gathering more facts to file Mo's asylum application.

As his conversations with Mo progress, a few facts begin to worry Curly. Not only does Mo strangely refer to the United States as the "promised land" (a common name for the country among Egyptians seeking entry into the United States, he tells you), but he also confides to Curly that he recently killed an Egyptian security guard, Larry, and has yet to be prosecuted for it.

Mo assures Curly that Larry had it coming. Curly begins to suspect that the real reason for Mo's asylum application is to escape prosecution. Curly is also aware that the commission of aggravated felonies of the kind that Mo has admitted to Curly he committed can make him ineligible for admission to the United States.

The application form asks whether the asylum seeker has ever committed a violent act. Intent on assisting Mo, Curly omits the murder from Mo's application.

Has Curly committed professional misconduct?
  a. No. Mo may have a legal defense to murder.
  b. No. Curly owed Mo a fiduciary duty to do whatever he could to ensure Mo was granted asylum.
  c. Yes. Curly knowingly failed to disclose a **material** fact and allowed his services to be used to commit fraud.
  d. Yes. Curly should have waited until Mo was acquitted and then filed the same application, omitting the murder.

2. Lawyer Lawrence thinks that he is very clever. One day, it occurs to him that, because his legal assistant is not a lawyer, Lawrence can recruit his legal assistant to make false or misleading statements to his adversaries. The advantages that such a plan would create for his burgeoning law practice would be incalculable, he marvels.

    What, if anything, is wrong with Lawrence's plan?
    a. It runs afoul of **Model Rule 8.4(c)**, which prohibits any conduct involving dishonesty, fraud, deceit, or misrepresentation.
    b. It runs afoul of **Model Rule 8.4(a)**, which prohibits lawyers from having someone else do what they are prohibited from doing themselves.
    c. Both a and b.
    d. None of the above.

3. There has been a murder. In the criminal prosecution for that murder now pending against client Stacey, Stacey asked her lawyer, Lonnie, to promise that he'd never communicate with the prosecution.

    Lonnie does the best that he can for Stacey, including asking whether the prosecution might be willing to offer her a plea bargain. Unfortunately, the prosecution declines.

During one of their prep sessions, Stacey explains how relieved she is that Lonnie promised never to communicate with the prosecution. "They have no case, and I didn't do it," she said. Lonnie, cunning as he is, lies through his teeth when he says, "Of course, Stacey, I'd never lie to you." He does not tell her about his earlier discussions with the prosecution to seek a plea bargain.

Stacey later learns about those discussions.

What rule applies to Lonnie's conduct?

a. **Model Rule 8.4(a)**: The **no-puppetry rule** applies; in the course of their communication, someone undoubtedly made a false statement on behalf of lawyer Lonnie.

b. **Model Rule 4.1**: Lawyer Lonnie made a false statement to client Stacey.

c. **Model Rule 1.4**: Lawyer Lonnie's communication with his client is subject to ethical constraints.

d. None of the above. Lonnie acted in his client's best interest. He could be sued for malpractice for not seeking a plea bargain for his client.

4. Recently barred lawyer Percy has a significant number of outstanding student loans. To supplement his income as a practicing attorney, he joins a multi-level marketing (pyramid) scheme selling essential oils.

When meeting with potential recruits to the scheme, Percy lies to the recruits. He promises them that if they invest $100, they can earn back $1,000 in a matter of months. He shows them doctored financial statements that suggest that he has earned over $50,000 that year from selling essential oils. Actually, Percy has not made a single sale. Moreover, he knows that his representations are false and misleading—virtually no one at the bottom of the pyramid scheme makes any money at all.

Might Percy be subject to professional discipline?

a. Yes, under his state's enactment of **Model Rule 8.4**.

b. Yes, under his state's enactment of **Model Rule 1.4**.

c. No, because the recruits are not clients (as defined under the professional rules).

d. No, because Percy was not acting as a lawyer when promoting the pyramid scheme.

5. Which of the following qualifies as a "statement" within the meaning of **Model Rule 4.1**?

a. Using your and your client's trusty hand-signal technique when you want the client to know something during cross-examination.

b. A lawyer presenting a statement made by her client as true that she knows is false during a deposition.

c. Nodding one's head.

d. All of the above.

6. Counsel for Widgets 'R' Us is negotiating a contract between her client and Annie. According to the terms of the contract, if Annie can sell 100,000 widgets in the Commonwealth of Keystone by year's end, Annie will earn $1 million. If Annie fails to meet this goal, Widgets 'R' Us will pay her nothing.

   Assuming that the following facts are true, which statements by Counsel for Widgets 'R' Us constitute a misrepresentation within the meaning of **Model Rule 4.1**?

   I. Counsel for Widgets 'R' Us knows that the market for widgets in Keystone has plummeted. No one, not even the best salesperson, could hope to sell 100,000 widgets there. When Annie asks, "How many people are making the million-dollar threshold in Keystone?" counsel responds, "Not everyone, but I'd bet you can do it."

   II. Counsel for Widgets 'R' Us has no idea how much demand there is for widgets in Keystone. In an effort to close the deal, counsel tells Annie that, if she is an excellent salesperson and works hard, she might meet her sales target.

   III. Counsel for Widgets 'R' Us thinks it would be difficult to sell 100,000 widgets in Keystone in a year. She tells Annie that she thinks the sales goal will be difficult to meet. Annie assures counsel that she can meet the goal.

   a. I.
   b. II.
   c. III.
   d. All of the above.

7. Tom was driving home after a long day at work. He narrowly avoided colliding with Pam, who was walking on the sidewalk. She dodged out of the way of his car, avoiding being hit but spraining her ankle in the process. Pam incurred $20,000 in damages and lost wages due to her sprained ankle.

   Pam sued Tom. Counsel discuss settlement, and Tom's lawyer makes the following statements:

   I. Tom's lawyer knows that Tom's liability insurance limit is $100,000. Tom's lawyer instead tells Pam's lawyer that the limit is $15,000.

   II. Tom's lawyer claims to have found an eyewitness who will testify that Pam jumped in front of Tom's car on purpose, hoping to get hurt so that she could sue him. There is no such eyewitness.

   III. Tom's lawyer claims that Pam's case isn't worth more than $10,000 because some of her damages are inflated. He claims that Tom will pay no more than $10,000. Actually, Tom told his lawyer that he would be willing to pay up to $20,000.

IV. Tom's lawyer says that Tom earns only $25,000 per year and therefore cannot afford to pay a settlement of $20,000. Tom's lawyer knows that Tom earns in excess of $1 million per year.

Which statements count as permissible posturing?

a. I.

b. I and II.

c. III.

d. III and IV.

8. Spike represents Jerry, a defendant in a slip-and-fall case. Jerry is not a lawyer. Spike is attempting to negotiate a settlement of the case. He asks Jerry how much Jerry earns. Jerry tells Spike that he earns $30,000 per year. This is a lie. Jerry actually earns $250,000 per year.

There is no way that Spike could have known how much Jerry was actually earning; Spike took this matter *pro bono* as a favor to Jerry's family.

Spike negotiates the settlement. During the negotiations, he tells opposing counsel that Jerry earns only $30,000. Opposing counsel agrees to settle for less because he believes that Jerry cannot afford to pay more.

After the settlement is negotiated and signed, opposing counsel learns that Jerry earns much more than he had been told.

If opposing counsel refers Spike to the applicable disciplinary authority, what is likely to happen?

a. Jerry can be held civilly liable for lying to his attorney, but Spike did not commit a tort.

b. Spike misrepresented a **material** fact to opposing counsel, which is a violation of the rules of professional conduct; Spike is subject to professional discipline.

c. Spike did not misrepresent Jerry's salary knowingly, so he did not violate a professional obligation. Spike is not subject to professional discipline.

d. Spike and Jerry can both be held civilly liable for misrepresentations.

11

Duties to People Who Have (or Must Be Treated as If They Had) Their Own Lawyers

FRANK REPRESENTS A CLIENT who has been injured in an accident. His client knows little about the legal system. One day, Frank learns that the defendant's lawyer has spoken directly with Frank's client about the accident. The defense lawyer is (as many lawyers are, when they want to be) affable and friendly. She finds Frank's client at his favorite local watering hole one evening, truthfully introduces herself as the lawyer representing the defendant, and chats Frank's client up while buying him several drinks. In the course of their conversation, she learns a great deal about the accident, its cause, the client's injuries and similar prior injuries, his current financial needs, and even some of the advice that Frank has given his client about the settlement value of his case. The defense lawyer then persuades Frank's client how much easier it would be to get a check right now rather than to endure a long, contentious, and uncertain lawsuit. The client calls Frank to announce that he signed a release last night and has his settlement money in hand this morning. He's wondering why he bothered to hire Frank and his firm.[1]

Frank is horrified. He thinks that his client had a good chance of recovering a lot more at trial than defense counsel talked him into accepting, and he would have argued forcefully to his client that the defendant's offer was much too low. Has defense counsel done anything wrong, and if so, what can Frank do about it?

Defense counsel didn't mislead Frank's client about who she was or what she was trying to accomplish (*see* **Model Rule 4.1** (no misrepresentations while representing a client); **Model Rule 8.4(c)** (no dishonesty or deceit in any circumstances); **Chapter 10 at 323**). And even if Frank can find a Rule that she broke, he has the

---

[1] The client says that he shouldn't have to pay Frank's firm the contingent fee to which he agreed in their engagement agreement, given that he made the deal without them. Is he right? *See* **Chapter 20.B at 541 n.5**.

dual problem that the client has already handed his adversary a lot of important information about his case, and now has signed and accepted the benefits of a settlement deal as well. How do you get all that toothpaste back in the tube?

You may breathe a sigh of relief. **Model Rule 4.2**, which is sometimes referred to (with considerable oversimplification, if not downright inaccuracy) as the "**no-contact rule**," restricts when and how lawyers may communicate with people who are represented by other lawyers. Better yet, the legal system has also developed civil remedies that both deter and mend violations.

REASON FOR THE RULE▶ Why do we have this Rule? As **Model Rule 4.2 Comment [1]** explains, the **no-contact rule** supports two important features of the lawyer's role as client-protector. One is to defend one of your most basic functions as a lawyer—making sure that your clients have and understand the information and opportunities that your services provide so that they can make fully informed decisions about what to do, free from the influence of those who don't have their best interests at heart. Here, defense counsel talked Frank's client into a settlement deal before Frank had the opportunity to provide additional information that could have changed the client's mind about how much to accept. The hypothetical just above illustrates how someone with anything less than undivided loyalty to the well-being of your clients can exploit superior learning and communications skills to interfere with your clients' pursuit of their own best interests.

The other protective function the **no-contact rule** serves is to help you manage when, how, and to whom information about your engagement gets out. After all, knowledge is power: The more information you have, the more power you have to win your case or out-negotiate your adversary. There are essentially two ways that we gather information about our engagements—investigation and discovery. (Yes, we know this seems elementary, but bear with us.)

Discovery has the advantage of being coercive—that is, you can force the production of documents and information that someone won't provide voluntarily. But when investigation is possible, it's usually superior. Why? Because good old, uninhibited personal conversation is almost always easier, quicker, less expensive, and less encumbered by the efforts of opposing counsel to interfere. Think about it: Would you rather have a direct, informal one-on-one interview with an important witness, or take that witness's deposition after the witness has been extensively prepared by opposing counsel to testify, and during which counsel is present to object, whisper advice to the witness at breaks, and otherwise remind the witness to be more guarded and scripted? The **no-contact rule** puts represented persons (as defined by the Rule) off-limits for the kind of direct contact necessary for informal investigation, unless the represented person's lawyer consents.

Of course, speed, simplicity, and cost-effectiveness are also important values in our legal system. *See* **Fed. R. Civ. P. 1**. So is developing some good-faith basis to make factual allegations before formally asserting them (and thus before coercive discovery is generally available). In fact, **Fed. R. Civ. P. 11(b)** *requires* investigation where reasonably possible as a basis for the allegations in any pleading or paper submitted to the court. As a result, informal investigation with the voluntary cooperation of those having information or documents is broadly permitted *except* when another value outweighs it. Here, that value is preserving the information-protective function that counsel is hired to perform (and that unsophisticated clients don't always realize that they need). As we will see, the tension between the desire for broad access to cheap and effective informal investigation and the protection of counsel's information-protective function helps to shape the scope and contours of the **no-contact rule.** REASON FOR THE RULE

TIPS & TACTICS It goes without saying, but we'll say it anyway: Voluntary cooperation in informal investigation is exactly that—voluntary. Witnesses or others who possess evidence or other information and who are not protected by the **no-contact rule** are nevertheless free to refuse to cooperate with you for any reason, or for no reason at all. One thing that lawyers can lose sight of is that, when others' cooperation is voluntary, in addition to complying with all applicable legal and ethical rules prohibiting misleading or abusive conduct, if you want cooperation, you need to present yourself as the sort of person with whom others want to cooperate. TIPS & TACTICS

Now take a look at **Model Rule 4.2.** Please don't ignore the Comments; they're essential to understanding the Rule. We're feeling generous today, so we'll even give you a quick-and-dirty paraphrase: You **must not** communicate directly with non-clients represented by their own lawyer, if that lawyer is representing them on the subject of the intended communication, unless that other lawyer gives you permission.[2]

There are two basic things that you really need to know at the beginning of what's going to be a fairly long and complicated discussion:

First, Model Rule 4.2 comes up all the time. Model Rule 4.2 potentially affects your interactions with *anyone* you don't represent. That means you'll have the opportunity to violate it pretty much every single day, as it's hard to imagine a day in practice in which you don't communicate with *someone* who is not your client about the engagements on which you're working.[3]

---

[2] Remember, one way to understand statutory language is to paraphrase it yourself in a way that summarizes the basic gist. Assume that friends or relatives who are not lawyers and not in law school have asked you what that rule or statute means, and answer them in terms that they'd understand. You should do this every time that you encounter a new rule or statute. If you can't do it, you don't understand the rule yourself yet.

[3] And, as we'll see in **Chapter 12 at 373, Rule 4.2** regulates your communications with nonclients who *do* have their own lawyers, and **Model Rule 4.3** and **Model Rule 3.4(f)** regulate your communications with nonclients who *don't. See* **Model Rule 4.2 Comment [9]**. So it turns out that, as a lawyer, you have special responsibilities to pretty much everyone—clients, non-clients with lawyers, and non-clients without lawyers. Those responsibilities differ depending on which kind of person you're dealing with, so the moral of the story is to understand up front with whom you're dealing and act accordingly. If you think about the issue before communicating, you're much better off. If you don't, your prospects for regret are excellent.

Second, the scope and application of Model Rule 4.2 is a lot more complicated than it looks. The **no-contact rule**'s simple-looking language conceals a host of complications, most of which are not reflected in that paraphrase we just gave you, so stay tuned and be prepared to refine your understanding. In the coming pages we'll talk about at least seven critically important ones. In yet another jaw-dropping coincidence, the subject headings in this chapter will be the same seven questions, all grounded in the specific language of the Rule:[4]

A. Who has to follow **Model Rule 4.2**?

B. Who is protected by **Model Rule 4.2**—when is someone "represented by another lawyer" within the meaning of the Rule?

C. When do you "know" that someone is protected by other counsel within the meaning of the Rule?

D. When are you "communicat[ing]" with a protected person within the meaning of the Rule?

E. How do you know when the other lawyer has "consent[ed]" within the meaning of the Rule (the main way that the **no-contact rule** actually allows contact with represented persons)?

F. What communications with a protected person does the Rule permit *without* counsel's consent (the other ways that the **no-contact rule** allows contact with represented persons)?

G. CONSEQUENCES What happens if you violate the **no-contact rule**? CONSEQUENCES

CONSEQUENCES Though we'll talk about the various **consequences** of violating the **no-contact rule** in detail in **Chapter 11.G at 362**, here's a quick overview to give you a sense of the stakes.

Because **Model Rule 4.2** is a Rule of Professional Conduct, violating it can be a basis for professional discipline. In addition, a court may **disqualify** a lawyer and that lawyer's firm (that is, issue an order enjoining that lawyer and firm to get out and stay out of the client engagement in which she violated the Rule) if the lawyer obtained information in violation of the Rule that would not otherwise have been available.

Other civil remedies also allow the victim of the Rule violation (the client who was improperly contacted) to neutralize any advantage that the client surrendered, or undo any decisions the client was induced to make, in violation of the Rule. Thus, if the violation allowed the violator access to evidence that would otherwise have not been available, the court might impose an evidentiary sanction precluding that evidence's use in the proceeding by the party who wrongfully obtained it. If the violation caused the client to make an agreement that she otherwise would not have made (such as a settlement agreement like the one in **this chapter's Introduction at 339**), that contract may be rescinded and the parties

---

[4] Don't ask us how we do it; we wouldn't tell you, even if we knew.

returned to the *status quo ante*. And if the violation induced procedural steps that would not otherwise have been taken in litigation (up to and including dismissal of the case, as also occurred in **the chapter Introduction at 339**), those steps can be undone under **Fed. R. Civ. P. 60(b)** or similar state law.

The presiding court also can impose monetary sanctions on the lawyer who violated the rule. Those sanctions are designed to compensate for any monetary harm that the violation caused (such as, for example, the attorneys' fees that the victim of the violation has incurred in order to fix the mess that the violation caused). CONSEQUENCES

So to put it mildly, a violation can be very costly. Now let's see how the **no-contact rule** works.

A. Who Has to Follow the No-Contact Rule?

TAMING THE TEXT Take another look at **Model Rule 4.2**. It says that "a lawyer" may not engage in the communications that the Rule prohibits. Could the Rule really be that narrow?

Problem 11A-1: Same as **this chapter's Introduction at 339** (defense lawyer chats up Frank's client in a bar), except defense counsel sends a private investigator who is a retired police officer to chat up the client instead of going herself. When Frank finds out and protests that defense counsel has violated **Model Rule 4.2**, she points out that the Rule says only what "a lawyer" can't do, and the investigator isn't a lawyer—he's a retired police officer. What's more, the investigator isn't even defense counsel's employee; he's an independent contractor who has his own business. And opposing counsel says (you may assume truthfully) that the investigator didn't even know about the Rule in the first place. Opposing counsel suggests that Frank quit whining before she's forced to seek sanctions. Should Frank back off? *Hint:* In analyzing this problem, use your common sense and read the Rules as a whole. Could it really be that easy to dodge the Rule? Don't forget:

- The **no-puppetry rule** (**Model Rule 8.4(a)**) comes directly into play in this context (*see* **Model Rule 4.2 Comment [4]**), and says that anything that you aren't allowed to do yourself can't be accomplished "through the acts of another"; and
- The **duty to supervise** (**Model Rule 5.3(b)**); *see* **Chapter 19.C at 516**) makes a lawyer responsible for supervising the conduct of any nonlawyer whom the lawyer "employed or retained" or who the lawyer is "associated with," and over whom the lawyer has supervisory authority, including taking reasonable steps to ensure that those subordinates understand the legal and ethical constraints on their conduct, and do nothing that the supervising lawyer herself **must not** do. TAMING THE TEXT

B. Who Is Protected by the No-Contact Rule — When Is Someone "Represented by Another Lawyer" Within the Meaning of the Rule?

[TAMING THE TEXT] **Model Rule 4.2** limits your communications with someone "represented by another lawyer." Is this part really that simple? In some ways, it is. (In other ways it very much isn't, so keep reading.) To start with, **Model Rule 4.2** is much broader than it needs to be: Even though the reason for the Rule is to prevent lawyers from taking advantage of less-sophisticated laypersons, the language of the Rule broadly applies to *anyone* "represented by another lawyer," no matter how smart, knowledgeable, or experienced that represented person may be. In other words, the Rule is overbroad. [TAMING THE TEXT]

> **Problem 11B-1:** Maya represents a small technology company (SmallTech) that is being acquired by a much bigger one (BigTech). BigTech has assigned one of its vice-presidents for business development to run the acquisition. The VP is not a lawyer, but he has overseen dozens of acquisitions, and he is completely familiar with all of the ins and outs of a deal like this one. One day, he calls up Maya to discuss the latest draft of the Acquisition Agreement that Maya has just sent to opposing counsel. Maya promptly and politely informs the VP, "I'm really sorry, but I can't speak with you directly without your lawyer's permission." "Bullpucky!" the VP cheerfully responds. "I do these deals all the time. I really don't want to pay my lawyer to hammer out stuff I can handle myself. I speak for BigTech on this. I'm the client, and I get to call the shots." What **must**, **may**, and **should** Maya do?

Now we know that everyone who is "represented by another lawyer" is protected by **Model Rule 4.2**, whether they need (or want) that protection or not. But just when is someone "represented by another lawyer" within the meaning of the Rule? Should we take that phrase literally to mean that *only* those with their own personal counsel are protected? Alas, no. We regret to inform you that this is one of those rare occasions when the Rules of Professional Conduct mean something very different from what they seem to say. So pay close attention—this is an area where it's easy to mess up.

There are two ways that people can come within the protection of the **no-contact rule**: (1) by their direct retention of their own personal counsel; and (2) by having the right kind of relationship with an organization that has counsel. We'll discuss each in turn.

1. Direct Retention of Personal Counsel

One way to gain the protection of the **no-contact rule** is simple: Agree to be personally represented by an attorney in a conventional, direct attorney-client relationship. The lawyer can be paid by the client herself, by an insurance company, by a family member, or—not uncommonly in a work-related situation—by the person's employer, which is usually some kind of business organization. The terms of the engagement may vary: The lawyer may have other joint clients in the same engagement or may represent only the single individual. The **consequences** to which the joint clients may have agreed if their interests come into conflict can vary, too. (*See* **Chapter 22.B at 656**; **Chapter 22.E at 746**.) But the focus here is an actual, direct, consensual attorney-client relationship between the lawyer and the represented person.

By the same token, remember that just because an organization has a lawyer does *not* necessarily mean that any particular organizational **constituent**— individuals such as directors, officers, agents, or employees—is personally represented by that lawyer. Company counsel often interview employees for information or give them advice or direction regarding company business on the company's behalf. That doesn't necessarily mean that company counsel represents those individuals directly. *See* **Model Rule 1.13(a)**; **Chapter 23.A at 770**.[5]

REAL WORLD Responsible organization counsel represent **constituents** jointly with the organization client only when necessary, and only with everyone's detailed knowledge and **informed consent**. It's wonderful to have clients, but it's a lot less wonderful when their **interests** start to **conflict** with one another. *See* **Chapter 22.B at 657**; **Chapter 22.E at 745**. One thing that this means is that when the BigTech VP in **Problem 11B-1 at 344** says "I'm the client," he's literally incorrect. And he probably knows it, but he's indulging in a manner of speaking that's common in the business world. When you're dealing with business organizations, you *always* deal with the human agents of those organizations. Those human agents are the only way that a company thinks, speaks, or does things. And those agents often get confused about the nature of their personal relationship with company counsel, sometimes just in the way they speak about it, and sometimes more fundamentally in mistaking company counsel for their personal lawyer when company counsel's only client is (and all that counsel's duties are owed to) the organization itself. You don't have the luxury of these confusions—at least not if you want to stay out of trouble. You must always have an ironclad understanding of who (or what) is, and is not, your client, and it's your responsibility to make sure that no one else is confused, either. *See* **Model Rules 1.13(a), (f)**; **Chapter 23.A at 781** on representing business organizations and *Upjohn* warnings. REAL WORLD

2. Protection of an Organizational Constituent Through Organization Counsel Without Actual Personal Representation

Look back at **Problem 11B-1 at 344**. BigTech is acquiring SmallTech. BigTech (a business organization of some kind, distinct from its human **constituents**) is

---

[5] As we'll discuss again in **Chapter 23.A at 770**, counsel representing only the organization may have **attorney-client privileged** communications with some of the organization's employees or other **constituents** without representing them personally. The **attorney-client privilege** arises out of the attorney-client relationship between the lawyer and her or his organizational client, even when there is no personal attorney-client relationship between the lawyer and the individual.

doing the acquiring and paying the money, and will own SmallTech or its assets when the deal is done. In this context, company counsel would not represent the VP *personally*; they would represent BigTech (the company), and the VP would provide instructions *on behalf of the company* to the company's counsel. The VP of business development in the problem is just an *agent* of BigTech—someone who speaks and acts on the company's behalf. But Maya treated the VP as protected by the **no-contact rule**, even though he legally and literally was *not* "represented by another lawyer." Was she right?

TAMING THE TEXT Oddly enough, she was. Why is this odd? Because Maya correctly treated the VP as "represented by other counsel" within the meaning of the **no-contact rule** when he literally wasn't (despite his loose language about whom BigTech's lawyers represented). So where in the language of **Model Rule 4.2** do we find the authority for this result? Nowhere! Instead—and we think that this is as bizarre as you probably do—this elaboration on the scope of the Rule is found not in the text of the Rule, but in the Comments. And what's worse, back in 2002 when the ABA wanted to clarify this feature of the Rule, it amended the *Comments* rather than amending the *Rule itself.* We offer no excuses for this peculiar approach, but it does serve as a good reminder that you must always read the Comments as well as the Rule. You never know what might be in there.

So let's start by reading the relevant Comment: **Model Rule 4.2 Comment [7]**. (This is a really important Comment that, in effect, amends the Rule, so you need to go read it. Take your time and identify the three groups of organizational **constituents** the Comment specifies as being protected when their *employer* has counsel. We'll cool our heels—or more accurately our fingers—right here till you get back.) In general terms, the Comment says that when an organization is represented, **Model Rule 4.2** protects *some* but *not all* of its "**constituents**" (that is, human beings who have some role in the organization), *even though they are not literally, personally represented by company counsel.*

Lawyers sometimes talk about this as "deeming" these **constituents** to be represented by company counsel, but don't be fooled. They are *protected by the **no-contact rule**,* but they are *not represented by company counsel* in the absence of a direct, personal engagement. This point matters because, in the absence of a direct, personal engagement by the **constituent**, the only **attorney-client privilege** available for communications with an organization's **constituents** is the organization's, and company counsel owes the individual **constituent** no client **duties of loyalty, confidentiality, care**, or **candor**—company counsel owes those duties only to the company itself.

Because you seem like a nice person, and because this is a very technical set of issues, let's sum up where we are: People are protected by the **no-contact rule** if they have their own personal lawyers. In addition, *some* people who are affiliated with a company that has *company* counsel are protected by the **no-contact rule**, too. We sometimes say that those people are "deemed" to be represented by company counsel for purposes of the **no-contact rule**, *even though they are not personally represented by company counsel and enjoy no other benefits of an attorney-client relationship with company counsel.* Weird? Definitely. Important? Absolutely, because you'll want to have direct contact with many witnesses precisely because they have a relationship with a company involved in the dispute or the deal that you're handling. This aspect of the **no-contact rule** tells you whether or not you can interview them without their company counsel's knowledge or permission. ⟨Taming the Text⟩

Determining when an individual **constituent** is protected by company counsel always raises two issues: (a) When is a company "represented" so that some of its **constituents** are protected; and (b) once it's determined that a company is "represented" within the meaning of the Rule, *which* **constituents** are protected (remember, only *some* of them are)? We bet you can guess what we're going to talk about next.

a. When Is an Organization "Represented" So That Some of Its Constituents Are Protected by the No-Contact Rule?

⟨Taming the Text⟩ The first thing that we hope you noticed about **Model Rule 4.2 Comment [7]** is that it begins "[i]n the case of a represented organization . . . ." So the organization has to be represented in order for any of its **constituents** to be protected. Is it enough to have a lawyer for *any* purpose?

Problem 11B-2(a): Frank's supervising partner, Harlan "Happy" Trials, is retained by Wanda Worker, who is seeking remedies for having been sexually harassed at work. Her employer was BCraftyCo, a company that operates a regional chain of brick-and-mortar stores selling craft materials and equipment. Wanda reports that the harasser was her supervisor, Gary Grabby, the store manager at the BCrafty store where Wanda worked. Before initiating any legal or administrative proceedings, Happy sends Frank out to the store where Wanda worked, so that Frank can investigate. He interviews a number of witnesses, including the alleged harasser, Gary Grabby. All the witnesses voluntarily speak with Frank at length. Later, BCrafty complains that the company was "represented" within the meaning of **Model Rule 4.2** at the time because it had counsel working with that store on how state sales taxes apply to the products the store sells. Are Frank and Happy in trouble? *Hint*: There is a three-word phrase in the language of **Model Rule 4.2** itself that answers this question for you. Find it.

Problem 11B-2(b): Same as Problem 11B-2(a) (Frank conducts a pre-filing investigation by interviewing store employees), but BCrafty also complains that the company was "represented" within the meaning of **Model Rule 4.2** at the time of Frank's interviews because BCrafty has several full-time employment lawyers in its in-house Legal Department whose job it is to advise the company about its employment practices and liability exposure. These in-house lawyers also sometimes appear in court and administrative proceedings as counsel to defend employment claims. Are Frank and Happy in trouble now? *Hint*: What are the best arguments for and against the conclusion that BCrafty is represented "in the matter" that Frank is investigating? What public policy arguments might support or deter either conclusion? *See Jorgenson v. Taco Bell Corp.*, 50 Cal. App. 4th 1398 (1996).

Problem 11B-2(c): Same as (a), except that in Frank's investigation of Wanda Worker's sexual harassment claim, he looks into Wanda's reports that she complained to a lawyer in BCrafty-Co's legal department about her harassment before she left her job. Is BCrafty "represented by counsel" within the meaning of the **no-contact rule** now? TAMING THE TEXT

b. When the Organization Is "Represented," Which Constituents Are Protected?

When an organization is "represented," some, but nowhere close to all, of its **constituents** (that is, officers, employees, etc.) are protected by the **no-contact rule**, even though they have no personal counsel. There are three general categories of such protected **constituents**. The three categories are described in the Comment to the Rule that addresses this issue, **Model Rule 4.2 Comment [7]**. These categories make a lot of sense if you think about them in terms of the protective functions that the **no-contact rule** is supposed to support.

i. Current *Upjohn* Management

One category of organizational **constituents** protected by the **no-contact rule** when the organization has counsel is any manager who "supervises, directs or regularly consults with the organization's lawyer concerning the matter [that is the subject of organization lawyer's engagement]." **Model Rule 4.2 Comment [7]**. This is, and apparently is intended to be, a pretty good description of those communications with organization counsel by **constituents** whose communications with company counsel are protected by the *organization's* **attorney-client privilege** under the "subject-matter test" of *Upjohn v. United States*, 449 U.S. 383 (1981). *See* **Chapter 23.A at 784**. In other words, **constituents** who can have privileged communications with company counsel concerning counsel's legal work for the organization are protected from prying investigative eyes by the **no-contact rule**.

Before **Model Rule 4.2 Comment [7]** was amended in 2002, the Rule was generally understood to protect only "an officer, director or managing agent of the company." This language was apparently intended to focus on an organization's so-called "control group," a term of art generally understood to include only top managers, such as corporate directors and high-level officers and managers, and those employees whose advisory roles to top management indicate that a decision would not normally be made without those employees' advice or opinion. This was the same test used to define those organizational **constituents** whose communications with company counsel were considered protected by the organization's **attorney-client privilege** before *Upjohn*. The 2002 amendment was designed to substitute *Upjohn*'s more functional selection of communications between company counsel and those **constituents** who request and receive legal advice on the company's behalf and instruct company lawyers, regardless of the **constituent's** position on the company's organizational chart.

> YOUR HOUSE; YOUR RULES ▶ Needless to say, *Upjohn* defines the scope of an organization's **attorney-client privilege** only under *federal* evidence law, **Fed. R. Evid. 501.** Since *Upjohn* was decided, however, a great many states have adopted *Upjohn*'s subject-matter test to define the scope of an organization's **attorney-client privilege** under state law as well. The **attorney-client privilege** varies from state to state, so make sure you understand what your state does once you're admitted to practice somewhere, and (if they differ) when state or federal evidence law might apply to any situation in which you are involved.

In addition, beware: Not every state has adopted the 2002 Model Rules amendment, so some states still construe the **no-contact rule** to protect only "control group" management, regardless of their application of the organizational **attorney-client privilege**. And a number of states have adopted idiosyncratic interpretations of **Model Rule 4.2** in this regard that don't strictly follow either the original Comment [7] or the revised 2002 version. Once you know where you're practicing, make sure you know what version of **Model Rule 4.2** and its Comments your state has adopted and how it affects this issue.
◀ YOUR HOUSE; YOUR RULES

ii. Current Organization Constituents Whose Conduct Can Be Imputed to the Organization for Purposes of Liability

The second category of organization **constituents** protected by the **no-contact rule** when the organization has counsel is any **constituent** "whose act or omission in connection with the matter may be imputed to the organization for purposes of civil or criminal liability." **Model Rule 4.2 Comment [7].** These are the people whose conduct is part of the transactions or events at issue in the engagement, people whose behavior *is* the behavior of the organization under the doctrine of *respondeat superior* or other rules of imputed or vicarious civil or criminal liability, such as conspiracy or aiding and abetting.

This category's focus on the organizational **constituents** whose behavior is at issue in the engagement leaves out a great many witnesses who may have information about the transaction or event at issue. Unless they fall within some other category of protected persons, they remain fair game for direct informal contact.

Problem 11B-2(d): In Frank's investigation of Wanda Worker's sexual harassment claim, Frank visits the BCrafty store where Wanda used to work. Frank speaks with several employees who observed Wanda's interactions with her supervisor, along with some other female employees who also experienced unwanted sexual advances from the same store manager, Gary Grabby. Frank also speaks with Grabby himself. Any problems? If so, what and why?

iii. Current Organization Constituents Whose Words Can Bind the Organization

The third category of **constituents** protected by the **no-contact rule** are those who have "authority to obligate the organization with respect to the matter [that is the subject of organization lawyer's engagement]." **Model Rule 4.2 Comment [7]**. Note the difference between this category and the one that we just discussed: The second category includes **constituents** *whose speech or conduct is a part of the events* comprising the claims or defenses the organization has engaged counsel to handle. The third category is **constituents** *who have the authority to make an agreement or admission that is legally binding on the organization* about an issue that counsel has been engaged to handle. This category of employees is sometimes referred to as "managing-speaking agents."

Before the 2002 amendments to **Model Rule 4.2 Comment [7]**, this portion of the Comment referred much more broadly to **constituents** "whose statement[s] may constitute an admission on the part of the organization." This phrase was often understood (or misunderstood) to mean anyone whose out-of-court statements concerning the matter would be admissible in evidence against the organization for the truth of their contents, despite the hearsay rule, as a party-admission—that is, as a statement made on behalf of the organization itself. *See* **Fed. R. Evid. 801(d)(2)**. Such party-admissions comprise a much broader category of statements, including most statements by employees concerning something within the scope of their employment (*see* **Fed. R. Evid. 801(d)(2)(D)**). The 2002 amendments eliminated the quoted phrase in order to narrow the scope of this category to the very limited class of people ("managing-speaking agents") who can *legally bind* the organization with their statements, and not just any employee speaking about his or her work.

YOUR HOUSE; YOUR RULES ▶ Again, beware: Some states have not adopted the 2002 amendment, and some states interpret the scope of this category of protected persons differently, regardless of which version of Comment [7] is on their books. So be sure you know who it's safe to interview before you or your investigator heads out into enemy territory. ◀ YOUR HOUSE; YOUR RULES

Problem 11B-2(e): In Frank's investigation of Wanda Worker's sexual harassment claim, Frank contacts the Regional Director of Human Resources for BCraftyCo, who enforces the company's policies regarding workplace conduct in numerous BCrafty stores, including the one at which Wanda worked, and who has the power to hire, discipline, and fire employees as well as to resolve employment disputes within certain monetary limits. Has Frank violated **Model Rule 4.2**? If so, why; and if not, why not?

iv. Other Organization Constituents *Not* Protected by Organization Counsel

(A) What If a Protected Constituent Has Left the Represented Company?

"Consent of the organization's lawyer is not required for communication with a former **constituent**." **Model Rule 4.2 Comment [7]**. In other words, former employees and other former **constituents**, even ones who dealt with organization counsel while employed or who (allegedly) committed the wrong at issue, are fair game for direct informal contact unless they have agreed to be personally represented, either jointly by the organization's lawyers or separately by their own personal counsel. In your interviews, you still **must** respect the sanctity of any legally privileged information or communications such former employees may possess, such as trade secrets or **attorney-client privileged** communications to which former employees may have been exposed while employed. *See* **Model Rule 4.4(a)**; **Chapter 11.G at 365**.

> Problem 11B-2(f): In Frank's investigation of Wanda Worker's sexual harassment claim, Frank learns that Gary Grabby has been fired. Can Frank find and speak with him without opposing counsel's permission? What additional facts would you need to know in order to answer this question, and how could you find out?

> Problem 11B-2(g): Same facts as (f) (Gary Grabby has been fired), except that the counsel that BCrafty has retained to deal with Wanda's situation is interested in keeping Grabby from making things any worse for the company (and for Grabby himself) by running his mouth as the situation develops. What can BCrafty's counsel do?

The deemed protection of the **no-contact rule** can raise complications of its own.

(B) What If Someone Deemed Protected But Not Personally Represented by Organization Counsel Has Counsel of His Own?

> Problem 11B-2(h): Same facts as (f) (Frank is investigating Wanda's claim), except Gary Grabby is still employed by BCrafty. However, Grabby is afraid that he's going to get fired and has hired his own personal lawyer to advise him about the situation. Grabby's personal lawyer contacts Frank. He points out that Grabby is pretty much judgment-proof (that is, like many working people, Grabby lives paycheck to paycheck, and has no significant savings or assets to satisfy any judgment that might be entered against him), but in return for a small settlement, he will make himself available for an interview with Frank and share documents with him. **May** Frank properly meet with Grabby? **Should** he? *Hint:* Take a look at **Model Rule 4.2 Comment [7]**. A sentence in the Comment is very helpful here. Which one is it?

(C) What If a Constituent Deemed Protected But Not Personally Represented by Organization Counsel Is Him- or Herself an In-House Lawyer for the Organization?

Problem 11B-2(i): Same as **Problem 11B-2(e) at 350**: Frank contacts the Regional Director of Human Resources for BCraftyCo. Mindful of the **no-contact rule**, Frank immediately asks whether BCrafty has lawyers working on Wanda's claim, and the HR director informs him that it does. The HR director goes on to point out that she herself is also a licensed lawyer. May Frank continue the conversation? *Hint*: ABA Formal Ethics Op. 06-443 (2006) suggests that organization counsel's consent is still required if the **constituent** is in one of the protected categories, even if the protected **constituent** is a lawyer in his or her own right. Not everyone agrees. Why might that opinion make, or not make, practical sense?

(D) What If Someone Deemed Protected But Not Personally Represented by Organization Counsel Does Not Want to Be "Protected" by Organization Counsel and Welcomes Direct Contact with Opposing Counsel?

Problem 11B-2(j): Same as (i) (Frank is in contact with BCrafty's HR director), except this time the HR director is not a lawyer. In her conversation with Frank, the HR director goes on to complain that the company has now hired outside counsel to "whitewash this and a bunch of similar messes"; that her job is impossible because of senior management's "stone-age" attitudes; that she doesn't want anything to do with the counsel BCrafty has hired to deal with the situation; and that she would like to talk to Frank about all of this. **May** Frank speak with her? **Should** he?

Problem 11B-2(k): Same as (j), but here the investigating lawyer is Danielle (not Frank), who is investigating allegations that several employees have been embezzling money from BCrafty. No charges have been filed. **May** Danielle, or a police detective she sends to see the HR director, speak with her? **Should** they? *Hint*: Go back and look at **Problem 11B-1 at 344**. In that problem, a **constituent** deemed protected but not represented by organization counsel felt (with some justification) that he could safely engage directly with opposing counsel and didn't want to bother with getting organization counsel's consent to do so. How are these problems different? Should that lead to a different result? *See United States v. Talao*, 222 F.3d 1133 (9th Cir. 2000).

C. When Do You "Know" Someone Is Represented by Other Counsel?

TAMING THE TEXT **Model Rule 4.2** is quite explicit in protecting only "a person the [investigating] lawyer *knows* to be represented . . ." (emphasis added). As **Model Rule 1.0(f)** (defining "knows") and **Model Rule 4.2 Comment [8]** emphasize, "knows" means "actual knowledge" of the contacted person's representation. "Should have known" (negligence) is not enough. Taming the Text

> **Problem 11C-1:** Early in the investigation of Wanda Worker's harassment case, Frank contacts the assistant store manager at the store where Wanda worked. Frank carefully asks her right up front if she has consulted her own lawyer or if the company has a lawyer dealing with the situation. (Why might this witness be deemed protected under the **no-contact rule** by company counsel in this situation? Make the arguments for and against.) She says nope, no lawyers, and answers Frank's questions, mostly siding with her employer and professing no knowledge of any harassment that Wanda might have experienced. In fact, an in-house lawyer at BCrafty has been directly involved in complaints concerning Grabby's workplace behavior for some time now and spoke with Grabby several weeks ago. The assistant manager just didn't know about it. Is Frank in trouble? Does your analysis change if the assistant manager *did* know about it and lied to Frank? If so, how and why; and if not, why not?

> **Problem 11C-2:** Early in the investigation of Wanda Worker's harassment case, Happy Trials comes into Frank's office, beaming. "I just called Gary Grabby to see what I could learn," he says. "The guy's still living in the *Mad Men* era. He admitted that he made lots of suggestive remarks to Wanda and several other female employees, and touched them on a number of occasions. He called it 'locker-room talk' and 'roughhousing.'" Frank, slightly alarmed, asks, "Is it OK to talk with him directly when he or the company might have a lawyer?" "Well," Frank's boss replies, "I wasn't about to ask him if he or the company had a lawyer, and he didn't tell me. So *to my knowledge*"—he says the words slowly and deliberately—"there's no lawyer involved." In fact, an in-house lawyer at BCrafty has been directly involved in complaints concerning Grabby's workplace behavior for some time now and spoke with Grabby several weeks ago. Has Happy created a problem?

Most of us flunked out of mind-reading school, which is why we find ourselves relegated to studying the law. So in most circumstances in which we need to know someone's state of mind, we have to infer it from what they do and say, and from the surrounding circumstances. Lawyers trying to be too clever by "evad[ing]" actual knowledge by "closing their eyes to the obvious," and not asking under circumstances in which the contacted person is reasonably likely to have a lawyer (or be protected by organization counsel), may find a court *inferring* actual knowledge of the contacted person's representation from the circumstances and the contacting lawyer's willful blindness to that likelihood. **Model Rule 4.2 Comment [8]**.[6]

---

[6] This is a good example of the doctrine of "willful blindness" or "conscious avoidance," a rule of inference used in most jurisdictions to infer knowledge of a fact from behavior that avoids actually learning something that someone thinks is probably true. The Supreme Court of the United States and many state supreme courts have used the concept of willful blindness as a proper means of inferring actual knowledge in a wide range of civil and criminal contexts. *See, e.g., Global-Tech Appliances, Inc. v. SEB S.A.*, 563 U.S. 754 (2011). **Model Rule 4.2 Comment [8]** makes it clear that the drafters of **Model Rule 4.2** meant for that inference to be used with the **no-contact rule.**

If you start a conversation innocently ignorant of the contacted person's representation, you must still "terminate the conversation immediately" upon discovering that the person is protected by the **no-contact rule. Model Rule 4.2 Comment [3]**. And of course it doesn't matter if the protected person initiates or consents to the communication; to protect the lawyer's role, it is the protected person's *lawyer* who has to consent; the *client's* consent alone is not enough. *Id.*

TIPS & TACTICS You can always take your chances that someone with whom you want to speak is not protected by the **no-contact rule** and hope that in fact they're not or that, if they are, a court later believes that you didn't actually know or willfully blind yourself. *See* ABA Formal Ethics Op. No. 95-396 (1995) (no enforceable legal duty to ask if a contacted person is represented). But the risk is professional discipline, monetary or evidentiary sanctions, or **disqualification**, and given the willful blindness doctrine and **Model Rule 4.2 Comment [8]**, that risk is considerable. From that observation, you've probably figured out that "don't ask; hope they don't tell" is not a wise approach. There's a simple way to make sure you're on the right side of the law here—ask. TIPS & TACTICS

> **Problem 11C-3:** Frank takes a phone call in his office. The caller introduces himself as Gary Grabby. "Mr. Grabby, haven't you spoken with a lawyer?" Frank asks. "Well, yeah," Grabby replies, "but he's an idiot and thinks that I'll get in trouble for some plain old-fashioned locker-room talk and roughhousing. I'm gonna fire him. Wanda's got completely the wrong idea, and I'd like to straighten this out." What should Frank do? Should he continue the conversation? Either way, **must** he advise Grabby's (or BCrafty's) lawyer that Grabby called? **Should** he? Why or why not?

> **Problem 11C-4:** Frank is working on a small case in which the opposing party files all his pleadings *in propria persona* (literally, in his own person; that is, on his own behalf, representing himself). The opposing party has limited education and no discernible experience with the legal system, but his pleadings are all in proper form, citing relevant rules and statutes. The *pro se* litigant calls Frank to discuss resolving the case. What **must** or **should** Frank do? *See* ABA Formal Ethics Op. 15-472 (2015).

D. When Are You "Communicat[ing]" with a Protected Person?

TAMING THE TEXT **Model Rule 4.2** says that you must not "communicate" with a person protected by the Rule. What exactly does that mean? "Communicate" is another one of those words that seems painfully simple until, suddenly, it painfully isn't. Conventional two-way conversations are easy to categorize as "communicat[ion]," but there are a surprising number of difficult situations. TAMING THE TEXT

> **Problem 11D-1:** Same facts as **Problem 11C-2 at 353** (Gary Grabby calls Frank directly). Frank tells Grabby that, because Grabby has a lawyer—even if Grabby doesn't like him—Frank is ethically forbidden from speaking with Grabby without the permission of Grabby's lawyer.

"OK," says Grabby, "don't speak. Just listen. If you'll just hear me out, I think we can get this straight." What **must** or **should** Frank do, and why?[7]

Problem 11D-2: Instead of the phone call described in **Problem 11C-2 at 353**, Frank receives an unsolicited email directly from Gary Grabby, which contains the same content as the phone call described in the problem. The email goes on to describe a number of things that Grabby did and said to Wanda, what he "meant" by them, and why, in his view, none of this is any big deal. What **must** or **should** Frank do now?

Problem 11D-3: In investigating Wanda's claims, Frank sends a private investigator over to the BCrafty store where she used to work. The investigator does not speak with Grabby, but observes him in the public parts of the store touching female store employees unnecessarily, calling several "honey" and "sweetheart," and making jokes about their physical appearance. Has Frank created a problem for himself?

Problem 11D-4: Same facts as Problem 11D-3 (Frank sends a private investigator over to the store to observe), except that Frank encourages the investigator to approach Grabby, speak to him conspiratorially about the appearance of some of the female store employees, and try to get him talking about what it's like to have them as his subordinates. Has Frank created a problem?

Problem 11D-5: Same facts as Problems 11D-3 and 11D-4 (Frank sends a private investigator over to the store to observe), but the investigator records Grabby's words and actions with a concealed miniature video camera. Does Frank have a problem now?

Problem 11D-6: Early in his investigation, Frank explores Gary Grabby's social media presence:

a. Frank visits Grabby's Facebook page. Grabby's privacy is set very low (meaning anyone can access anything on his page), and Frank takes screenshots of various posts and photographs portraying Grabby's exceptionally retrograde attitudes about women.

b. Frank subscribes to Grabby's Twitter feed, on which he regularly posts his thoughts about the appearance of his female subordinates and what's going on at work.

c. Frank visits Grabby's Facebook page, and finds that Grabby's privacy settings show almost none of his page unless you're one of his 3,682 Facebook friends. Frank asks Wanda if anyone she knows has friended Grabby on Facebook. Wanda herself is Grabby's Facebook friend (he encourages all BCrafty employees to friend him), and she gives Frank permission to use her account to explore Grabby's Facebook page. Does your analysis change if Wanda does it herself? What if the Facebook friend is instead an acquaintance of an acquaintance of a friend of Wanda's? What if Grabby has only four Facebook friends, and Wanda is one of them? If any of these new facts change your analysis, how and why; and if not, why not?

---

[7] *See In re Howes,* https://caselaw.findlaw.com/nm-supreme-court/1100584.html (N.M. 1997).

d. To get at Grabby's Facebook page, Frank sends Grabby a friend request in his own name. Does it matter if Frank instead has a female friend of Wanda's send the friend request so that Frank can gain access? What if Frank sets up a dummy Facebook account in a different name and sends the friend request from that account? If any of the additional facts change your analysis, why and how; and if not, why not?[8]

Problem 11D-7: Maya is advising SmallTech on its acquisition by BigTech; Maya's client contact is the founder and President of SmallTech, Sally Small. BigTech's VP of business development, who is not a lawyer but does acquisitions like this all the time, contacts Sally and suggests that "we all save some money" by negotiating the business terms directly between the two of them without involving "the lawyers, who are always complicating everything to run up their bills." Sally, who is well aware that BigTech's VP knows a lot more about this kind of deal than she does, reluctantly agrees, but seeks out Maya's assistance behind the scenes. Maya is happy to help.

a. In preparation for a meeting to negotiate the business terms, Maya walks Sally through the typical structure and most common variations of the major business terms for an acquisition of this kind. Sally goes into the meeting feeling much more confident and prepared. Any problem?

b. Sally and the VP are negotiating the critical price and payment terms. They are still fairly far apart, and the discussions feel stuck. Maya comes up with a clever compromise, which adjusts several moving parts in the deal in a way that helps everyone get a lot more of what they need to make the deal work. Maya gives Sally a written "cheat sheet" summarizing the compromise for her to use in the continuing negotiations. Any problem now?

c. Same as (b), but in addition Maya gives Sally a script detailing, word for word, how to describe the compromise to the BigTech VP.

d. Same as (b), but Maya writes an email for Sally to send to the VP describing the compromise and why it is a good idea for both sides. Sally sends the email that Maya writes, under her own name, as Maya suggests.

E. How Do You Know When the Other Lawyer Has "Consent[ed]" to Your Communicating with That Lawyer's Client?

Direct contact with a person protected by the **no-contact rule** is allowed "with the consent of the other lawyer." **Model Rule 4.2**.

REAL WORLD Opposing counsel's consent is by far the easiest and most common solution to the **no-contact rule**'s interference with direct contact between non-lawyers and opposing lawyers, especially when that contact is genuinely desirable and useful for both sides. Counsel's consent is often used to allow direct contact between sophisticated business people and opposing counsel during business

---

[8] *See In re Robertelli*, https://images.law.com/contrib/content/uploads/documents/399/43490/Robertelli-Majority.pdf (No. DRB 19-266, N.J. Rev. Bd. April 30, 2020).

negotiations, particularly in smaller deals. *See* **Problem 11B-1 at 344**. Of course, in any situation in which information or client control is of any concern, opposing counsel will typically refuse (as they should, and you should, too). Real World

Taming the Text But how do we know when opposing counsel has consented? Are there required formalities to make the consent effective? Well, the Model Rules define "writing" (**Model Rule 1.0(n)**), "signed writing" (*id.*), and **confirmed in writing**" (**Model Rule 1.0(a)**), and the Rules generally call for such formalities explicitly when they are either required or recommended. *See, e.g.,* **Model Rule 1.5(c)** (requiring that a contingent fee "shall be **in a writing signed by the client**"); **Model Rule 1.5(b)** (requiring lawyers to communicate the scope of the engagement and the basis for the fees and costs to be charged, "preferably in writing"); **Model Rule 1.7(b) (4)** (requiring that a client waive a **conflict of interest** by "**informed consent, confirmed in writing**"). None of these formalities are required for opposing counsel's consent to waive the **no-contact rule**. So we may safely infer that no particular formality is required to consent; a simple, oral "go ahead" from opposing counsel over the phone is sufficient. Taming the Text

Tips & Tactics But why forgo a written consent just because you can? Counsel's oral consent is sufficient to satisfy the Rule, but when you can dash off an email in a minute or less, why leave a later dispute about whether consent was given to a situation of one lawyer's word against another? What can you do? Get opposing counsel to send you a one-line consent: "Dear Maya, Feel free to communicate directly with BigTech's VP business development regarding the SmallTech acquisition." (*See* **Problem 11B-1 at 344**.) Or get opposing counsel to reply to your email asking for consent with a simple "yes." Or if you can't get opposing counsel's attention (which is, unfortunately, an inconvenient practice reality sometimes), then at least send opposing counsel a written note (electronic or otherwise) confirming the oral consent that you received.

Sometimes whether opposing counsel consented is a matter of interpretation. Once again, the prudent approach is not to risk serious **consequences** to the outcome of a later interpretive dispute. If you're not sure, *get* sure before you do something that could cost you your engagement—or your law license. **Inquire**; **explain**; **confirm** (see **Chapter 6.A at 139**). Tips & Tactics

Problem 11E-1: Same facts as **Problem 11B-1 at 344** (the non-lawyer VP insists on negotiating a transaction directly with Maya), except that Maya has been unable to reach opposing counsel to get the consent necessary to deal directly with BigTech's VP. Her client, SmallTech, is upset at the delay. In frustration, she writes an email to opposing counsel: "I have called and emailed you three times in the past five days seeking your consent to negotiate directly with your VP BizDev as he has requested. I still have no response. We're not getting anywhere on this deal, and both our clients have become quite impatient. Unless I hear from you by next Tuesday, I will assume that you have consented and proceed accordingly." If opposing counsel continues to ignore her, has Maya complied with **Model Rule 4.2**?

Problem 11E-2: In connection with Wanda Worker's employment claim (*see* **Problem 11B-2(a) at 347**), Frank has now exhausted administrative remedies and filed suit on Wanda's behalf against BCraftyCo and Gary Grabby for gender discrimination and related torts. BCrafty's litigation counsel sends a settlement proposal to Frank by email, with a "cc" on the email to the business person at BCrafty with settlement authority and to Grabby. After appropriately conferring with Wanda, Frank prepares a response rejecting the offer and describing the strengths of Wanda's case and the litigation agonies that await his adversaries. He sends it by clicking "reply all." Has Frank violated the **no-contact rule**? What are the best arguments that he has and that he hasn't?

F. What Communications with a Protected Person Are Permitted *Without* Counsel's Consent?

Although many direct communications with a represented person that matter to you will require opposing counsel's consent, there are some that don't. Here's a quick inventory.

1. Communications Not Concerning "the Matter" with Respect to Which the Contacted Person Is Protected

TAMING THE TEXT **Model Rule 4.2** is explicit that the communications that it forbids without counsel's consent are ones "about the subject of the representation . . . ." So no consent is needed for a lawyer to walk right up to an opposing party and ask "Manchester United or Arsenal?"—unless someone's favorite European soccer (excuse us—*football*) club is at issue in the dispute that you're handling. TAMING THE TEXT

REAL WORLD As a practical matter, this exception doesn't come up all that often. In most situations, the only thing about which you'd *want* to speak directly with a represented person would be your deal or dispute. So if you find yourself tempted to make small talk directly with the opposing party without opposing counsel's knowledge or permission, ask yourself why. You may find that you're hoping that the small talk will shift over into improvident admissions in this unguarded context. Of course, that's exactly what you're not allowed to elicit, so you're flirting with trouble. REAL WORLD

Problem 11F-1: The family that lives two doors down the street from Frank in his small town has a dispute with the neighbor who lives between them. The dispute relates to the middle neighbor's trees. The trees are big, they drip copious amounts of sap, and they overhang the property line. The middle neighbor is inordinately fond of these trees despite the corrosive mess that they make most of the time, and he hasn't trimmed them in years. As a favor, Frank is representing the homeowner two doors down. The middle neighbor has made it clear that he's consulted what he calls a specialist in "tree law." Frank bumps into the middle neighbor at a PTA meeting. What **must** he **not** do? What **may** he do?

2. Communications as a Party

TAMING THE TEXT As discussed above, the parties themselves are always free to speak directly to one another if they wish. *See* **Rule 4.2 Comment [4]**. It's widely understood that this applies equally to parties who happen to have a law license, so when you're actually a party to a negotiation or dispute (rather than a lawyer representing a party), you're free to deal directly with your adversaries if you wish and if they're willing.

What's the textual basis for this exception in the Rule? The closest we get is that **Model Rule 4.2** is qualified at the beginning by limiting a lawyer's communications "[d]uring the representation of a client . . . ." This language indicates that you are not constrained by the Rule when you're not representing a client in connection with the communication. But quite frequently in small disputes (and occasionally in big ones), lawyers represent themselves, and it is widely understood that lawyers representing themselves as parties to a deal or dispute are still free to contact represented persons directly. In other words, this is another situation in which there is no coherent textual explanation; it's just the way the Rule is understood despite *not* literally saying "during the representation of a client other than himself or herself . . . ." TAMING THE TEXT

> Problem 11F-2: Same facts as **Problem 11F-1 at 358** (two of Frank's neighbors have a dispute about trees overhanging the property line), but the trees overhang Frank's driveway, too, and Frank is tired of the sap damaging his car's paint. Frank bumps into the middle neighbor at a PTA meeting. What **must** Frank **not** do? What **may** he do?

3. Communications with Someone You Also Represent or Are Asked to Represent

TAMING THE TEXT **Model Rule 4.2** also doesn't apply if you also represent the person contacted in the same matter as co-counsel. The words of the Rule don't seem to accommodate this exception—after all, you're "communicat[ing] about the subject of the representation with a person the lawyer knows to be represented by another lawyer in the matter." But it is universally understood that **Model Rule 4.2** does not constrain your communications with your own client just because you have co-counsel.

The same is true if you're approached by someone looking to replace current counsel or seeking a second opinion. Once again, the words of the Rule seem literally to forbid the substitution or consultation, but once again, it is universally understood that you don't need current counsel's permission to consult with the **prospective client** about current counsel or otherwise not on behalf of an adverse party. This exception is confirmed in **Rule 4.2 Comment [4]**. Can you identify the relevant sentence? (Of course you can.) TAMING THE TEXT

But if you already represent (or have previously represented) *another* player in the same engagement, then you may have a **conflict of interest**. We'll discuss these in excruciating detail in **Chapter 22 at 599**, but it should not surprise you that you can't advise two opposing parties in the same dispute, nor can you advise one party when you have **confidential information** from another that you could misuse. Because of the **conflict of interest**, you must terminate the conversation and refuse the engagement to avoid becoming **conflicted** out of the engagement that you already have.

> **Problem 11F-3:** Same facts as **Problem 11C-1 at 353** (Gary Grabby calls Frank and tells him that he dislikes his personal counsel), but now Grabby tells Frank that he's very concerned that he's not being portrayed fairly and asks Frank whether Frank thinks that his lawyer is doing a good job. What **must** or **should** Frank do?

> **Problem 11F-4:** A woman who works at the same BCrafty store as Wanda did contacts Frank. She has consulted another employment lawyer in town about her own harassment by Gary Grabby and BCrafty's failure to do anything about it, but she is having doubts about that lawyer's ability to handle her case. She'd like to talk with Frank about it. What **must** or **should** Frank do?

4. Communications Authorized by Law or Court Order

Rule 4.2 also says no consent from counsel is necessary when the communication is "is authorized . . . by law or a court order."

a. Statutory Authorization of Governmental Lawyers for Certain Prefiling Investigative Purposes

Probably the most common example of communications with represented persons that are "authorized . . . by law" is "investigative activities of lawyers representing governmental entities, directly or through investigative agents, prior to the commencement of criminal or civil enforcement proceedings." *See* **Rule 4.2 Comment [5]**. In other words, most states by law expressly allow governmental lawyers and law enforcement officers to make direct contact with someone represented by counsel—sometimes even the "target" of a criminal investigation—*before* that person is arrested or indicted. (After arrest or indictment, the Fifth and Sixth Amendments and other protections come into play.[9])

YOUR HOUSE; YOUR RULES ▸ This state law varies among jurisdictions, so if your practice involves the criminal law or certain civil enforcement proceedings (the range of which varies from state to state), you need to learn what the state in which

---

[9] We're oversimplifying a little, but federal prosecutors are generally required by a federal statute called the McDade Amendment to follow the law of the state in which they are conducting an investigation regarding contacting represented persons, as well as following other state-law ethical constraints. **28 U.S.C. § 530B(a)**.

you practice does or does not allow. If your practice includes federal law, there are provisions of federal law in specialized areas, such as tax or securities law, that may authorize federal lawyers or their agents to contact represented persons directly for particular purposes. ◁ Your House; Your Rules ▷

Problem 11F-5: Danielle's office is investigating alleged embezzlement at a local investment company. The investigation is just beginning, triggered by a whistleblower who has come to the DA's office with stories of misappropriated funds. No one has yet been arrested or charged. Danielle's supervisor suggests that they refer the matter "to the feds," by which he means the local U.S. Attorney's office. Danielle asks why—at this point, the case appears limited to a few people at this one company in this one state. Her supervisor says that he understands that, because of federal preemption of state law, federal prosecutors don't have to follow state rules of professional conduct during criminal investigations, just federal law and the Constitution. Because there have been no charges or arrests, he reasons, the Fifth and Sixth Amendment aren't going to constrain things much for them, making their investigative options a lot broader. Is he right?

Problem 11F-6: The DA's offices in Danielle's state are charged with enforcing certain civil obligations as well as the criminal law. One of these state civil laws forbids race discrimination in housing. Danielle has been assigned to investigate complaints that her office has received that a particular landlord who owns two large apartment buildings in the county seat has been discriminating on account of race. The landlord is already being sued by the Downforda County DA's office on the other side of the state for fair housing violations in that county. To investigate the issue in her county, Danielle sends "testers" to interview for vacant apartments in the landlord's local buildings. Sets of "testers" have indistinguishable employment, credit, and rental histories, but some are White, some are Hispanic, and some are Black. Has Danielle violated the **no-contact rule**?

b. Communication with Represented Governmental Agencies or Officers

Another example of "authorization . . . by law" is communications in furtherance of the right to petition government for redress, which is protected by the First Amendment. This right has been broadly held to authorize many direct communications between a citizen's lawyer and a local, state, or federal government official, even when the citizen is in a dispute with the government and the official or her governmental agency is represented by counsel. *See* **Rule 4.2 Comment [5]**.

Problem 11F-7: Frank represents Cindy Citizen, a resident of his town who tripped on an uneven section of sidewalk and injured herself. Cindy has filed a lawsuit against the town for maintaining the sidewalk negligently. The town has retained counsel to defend the lawsuit. Cindy directs Frank to go with her to visit a member of the Town Council whom she has actively supported in the last several elections and with whom she is personally friendly "to see if we can get him to work this thing out with the town." **May** Frank do so? Why or why not?

The courts are generally available to regulate contact between counsel and represented (or arguably represented) persons, and in a situation in which the stakes are high enough, you can always seek guidance or permission from a court with jurisdiction over the parties and the subject matter.

c. Collective Proceedings Such as Class Actions

Class actions are a good example of a proceeding in which the supervising court can and often does take an active role in regulating contact between opposing counsel and actual or potential class members. Generally speaking, most federal and state courts consider persons who are not named class representatives but are potential members of a class not yet certified not to be represented by counsel for purposes of **Model Rule 4.2**, and thus available to be contacted directly by defense counsel. But the court is free to change that by order if it is persuaded that there is good cause to do so. And once a class is certified, the class-action court typically takes an active role in regulating contact between counsel and the absent members of the class.

> **Problem 11F-8:** In investigating Wanda Worker's claims against BCrafty, Frank and Happy find that gender discrimination in hiring, promotion, and pay is pervasive at the company. Wanda agrees to be a class representative, and Frank's firm files a class action on behalf of all women working in BCrafty retail stores in several states. BCrafty hires experienced labor and employment counsel, who begin a campaign of rather pushy "interviews" trying to persuade female employees not to cooperate with Frank's firm in the guise of "investigating" the claims made in the class-action suit among their employees. Have BCrafty's lawyers violated **Model Rule 4.2**? If BCrafty's tactics turn out to be permissible, what **may** Frank try to do about it?

G. CONSEQUENCES What Happens If You Violate the No-Contact Rule?

1. CONSEQUENCES Professional Discipline

RULE ROLES **Model Rule 4.2** is a Rule of Professional Conduct, and as such, it is a basis for your state's disciplinary authority to censure, suspend, or disbar you. But suspending the lawyer who violated the Rule won't protect against the misuse of wrongfully extracted information that has already been disclosed, or undo unfairly induced conduct such as settlements or dismissals. (Take another look at the hypothetical at the beginning of **this chapter's Introduction at 339**.)

As is true of many other Rules of Professional Conduct, however, courts in many states have relied on **Model Rule 4.2** as a standard for civil remedies designed to undo the practical harm that a violation of the Rule may have caused. Note that there is nothing in the Rule that says that any court has to do that—in fact, there's nothing in the Rule that governs court-imposed remedies at all. *See* **Model Rules Preamble ¶ [20]**. This is yet another example of state and federal courts adopting ethical standards drafted to govern professional discipline in order to administer their own processes and remedies. RULE ROLES

As in most remedies inquiries, the questions that the court must address are what wrong the Rule is supposed to prevent, what actual harm the claimed violation of the Rule has caused (or will cause if it's not remedied), and how closely the remedy can be tailored to the problem that needs to be addressed without causing disproportionate harm in other respects.

TIPS & TACTICS As you're about to see, seeking remedies for a **no-contact rule** violation involves a lot of effort and uncertainty. Often, the best defense is client education. For many people, crossing paths with lawyers and the legal system is a new experience and a big deal, and they will be inclined to discuss these important events with relatives, friends, and others—all outside the ambit of applicable privileges. Take care at the outset and at reasonable intervals throughout the engagement (perhaps even, depending on the client, as often as every time you communicate) to caution your client and the client representatives with whom you interact about the importance of preserving the **confidentiality** of your communications, the implications of failing to do so (waiver of privileges; release of valuable cats from important bags), and the surprisingly short list of people with whom the matter can be safely discussed. An ounce of prevention is worth a pound of motions practice trying to get that cat back in the bag. TIPS & TACTICS

Given the purposes of the Rule discussed above, and entirely separate from any disciplinary **consequences** in which a **no-contact rule** violation could incur, courts have developed four basic categories of nondisciplinary **consequences** to remedy violations of the **no-contact rule**. We'll discuss each in turn.

2. CONSEQUENCES Nondisciplinary Consequences When the Information-Protective Purpose of the Rule Is Violated

In the **chapter Introduction at 339**, the defense lawyer who violated the **no-contact rule** was able to find out all kinds of things from Frank's client that ordinarily would have required formal discovery and that, in some instances (for example, Frank's views of the settlement value of the case), were **attorney-client privileged** and would never, in the absence of defense counsel's misconduct, have been disclosed at all. When lawyers or those working with them gain access to information that would not have been obtained had they obeyed the **no-contact rule**, the challenge is how to undo that wrong without doing too much collateral damage. Two common responses are **disqualification** and evidentiary sanctions.

a. CONSEQUENCES Disqualification

Disqualification, you'll recall, is a court order directing counsel to get out and stay out of an engagement. In the context of a **no-contact rule** violation, such an order is often coupled, explicitly or implicitly, with a direction that disqualified counsel—and the client, if the client knows—not convey any improperly obtained information to successor counsel or disclose or use it in any other respect.[10]

Disqualification solves the problem of preventing unfair use of improperly obtained information, but at a significant cost: The client (who often had nothing to do with her lawyer's violation) loses her chosen counsel and must find new lawyers who will have to incur effort and cost to become familiar with the matter. Courts thus usually impose this **consequence** only when no other step will prevent misuse of information that was improperly elicited. Often a violation **disqualifying** one lawyer in a firm results in an order disqualifying the entire firm (on the presumption that lawyers in a single firm tend to share information; *see* **Model Rule 1.10(a)**), but sometimes a court **disqualifies** only the individual lawyer who violated the Rule.

> **Problem 11G-1:** Frank successfully **disqualifies** the defense counsel in **this chapter's Introduction at 339**, as well as her firm, for violating **Model Rule 4.2**. As a result, the defendant must now find a new lawyer and pay the new lawyer's hourly rate as she gets up to speed on the proceedings, investigation, and discovery that the original defense lawyer conducted. How might the defendant, who is forced to incur these costs by counsel's violation of the **no-contact rule,** try to recover them? What legal grounds and remedies might exist?

> **Problem 11G-2:** Defense counsel in **this chapter's Introduction at 339** approaches Frank's client as described. But as defense counsel tries to chat the client up about his injury and understanding of his case ("Wow, that must have hurt; how come you didn't see the shovel on the sidewalk?"), the client remembers Frank's admonitions about **confidentiality.** "Look," the client says, "my lawyer says that I have a really good case, but I really think you ought to talk with him about this." The defense lawyer says she understands, pays for the drinks, and politely takes her leave. Has she violated **Model Rule 4.2**? Has she obtained any **confidential** or **attorney-client privileged information**? Should she and her firm be **disqualified**?

b. CONSEQUENCES Evidentiary or Other Informational Sanctions

Sometimes it's possible to identify information wrongfully obtained in violation of the **no-contact rule** for which the court can structure an evidentiary or similar sanction that neutralizes the harm. The sanction often takes the form of an exclusionary order forbidding a party from introducing or otherwise relying on the tainted evidence. Unfortunately, this approach is not always an effective solution to the problem that the violation created.

---

[10] **Disqualification** is most commonly invoked as a civil **consequence** to address lawyer **conflicts of interest**. *See* **Chapter 22 at 603**. Here, the same remedy may be used to address a different wrong.

The plaintiff and his counsel's view of the settlement value of the case the client disclosed in **the chapter Introduction at 339** is valuable for tactical rather than evidentiary reasons—that is, it unfairly helps opposing counsel negotiate a more favorable resolution to the case, but it would almost never be allowed into evidence at trial. (Do you see why?) An evidentiary sanction excluding it thus would be pointless. Material protected by the **attorney-client privilege** or the **attorney work product doctrine** is the kind of "bell that can't be unrung" information that is difficult to prevent the misbehaving lawyer from using. **Disqualification** of the errant lawyer may be the only feasible option to protect this kind of information, despite the collateral damage that **disqualification** also inflicts.

TIPS & TACTICS   The most common fruit of a **no-contact rule** violation that cause courts to **disqualify** the violating counsel is information protected by the **attorney-client privilege** or the **work product doctrine**. Inducing someone to disclose **privileged** information violates the represented party's **confidentiality** and privacy rights, and thus violates **Model Rule 4.4(a)** (which forbids the "use [of] methods of obtaining evidence that violate the legal rights of [a third] person"). It may also comprise a tort under state law. Thus, in any situation in which you are unsure about whether your direct contact with someone might implicate the **no-contact rule**, or whether someone might later accuse you of doing so, make sure to caution the person with whom you are trying to speak not to tell you anything that her (or her company's) lawyer might have told her or anyone else. TIPS & TACTICS

An evidentiary sanction can also be overinclusive: Some of the information defense counsel extracted from Frank's client, such as the facts about the client's injury and similar prior injuries, would have emerged routinely in discovery.[11] It would unfairly punish the other party to preclude him from ever using that information just because his current lawyer behaved badly and got it by cutting ethical corners, when any competent lawyer could and would have gotten the same information by proper means.

> **Problem 11G-3:** Same as **Problem 11G-2 at 364** (the client cuts off conversation with the defense's investigator), but before cutting off the conversation, the client mentions a nurse who lives three doors down from the client and who took a look at the injury the day after it happened (as a "friendly neighbor") before the client had surgery to repair the injury. The client doesn't mention it, but the nurse noticed some details destroyed by the surgery that could be relevant to how much of the client's time out of work might be attributable to a previous injury with which she was familiar as his neighbor but of which the emergency room doctor and orthopedic surgeon were unaware. Frank seeks remedies for defense counsel's violation of **Model Rule 4.2**. Should the court **disqualify** defense counsel? Order an evidentiary sanction? If the latter, how should the evidentiary sanction be formulated?

---

[11] The idea is similar to the "inevitable discovery" exception to the Fourth Amendment's Exclusionary Rule (*see Nix v. Williams*, 467 U.S. 431 (1984)), or the "inevitable disclosure" doctrine in trade secret law (*see* Ryan M. Wiesner, *A State-By-State Analysis of Inevitable Disclosure: A Need for Uniformity and a Universal Standard*, 16 MARQUETTE INTELLECTUAL PROPERTY L. REV. 211 (2012)).

Problem 11G-4: Same as **Problem 11G-2 at 364** (the client cuts off conversation with the defense's investigator), but the court has now decided that the information that Frank's client was fooled into divulging is not significant enough to justify **disqualifying** defense counsel. What alternative remedy **should** the court order instead?

c. CONSEQUENCES Monetary Sanctions

Under a court's so-called inherent power to govern the conduct before it, as well as statutory and rule provisions that vary among jurisdictions, courts may also impose monetary sanctions to help remedy violations of the **no-contact rule**. These sanctions are usually not allowed to be *punitive* (that is, no fines or penalties), but they may be imposed to *compensate* the party who was wronged for the cost of the discovery or motions practice necessary to prove and address the violation (or any other monetary harm the violation caused).

Problem 11G-5: Same as **Problem 11G-2 at 364** (the client cuts off conversation with the defense lawyer). The court has decided against **disqualifying** defense counsel but wishes to impose monetary sanctions for counsel's violation of **Model Rule 4.2**. On what expenses can the court rely as the basis for a compensatory sanction?

3. CONSEQUENCES Nondisciplinary Consequences When the Decision-Protective Purpose of the Rule Is Violated — Relief from Client Action Obtained in Violation of the Rule

The hypothetical in the **chapter Introduction at 339** also involved a violation of the **no-contact rule** that induced Frank's client to enter into an unfavorable settlement of his case. When improper contacts with a represented person result in unfairly induced procedural or substantive decisions, there are remedies. Contract law provides the remedy of rescission to undo a deal that's been induced by undue influence, fraud, or other wrongful conduct. The dismissal of a civil case or a similar procedural step can be undone by motion under such provisions as **Fed. R. Civ. P. 60(b)**, which allows a court to grant relief from a judgment or order on a variety of grounds including "misconduct by an opposing party." Similarly, a court may grant relief from an improperly induced guilty plea in a criminal case. *See, e.g.,* **Fed. R. Crim. P. 11(d)**.

Problem 11G-6: Assume all the facts as presented in the **chapter Introduction at 339** (defense lawyer chats up Frank's client in a bar and talks him into settling the case on unfavorable terms). Lay out the basic court powers and the arguments to invoke them that would allow Frank and his client to undo the settlement into which the client entered and to reinstate the client's court case against the defendant after the client dismissed it with prejudice pursuant to the settlement. How much time does Frank have to make these motions? (*Hint:* Take a look at **Fed. R. Civ. P. 60**.) CONSEQUENCES

At this point, it should be clear how complex and dangerous things can get when a party or a witness, or a company with which a party or a witness is associated, has a lawyer. But what if someone doesn't have a lawyer (and is not protected as if they did)? The next chapter addresses the special duties that lawyers have in dealing with persons who are *not* represented by counsel.

Big-Picture Takeaways from Chapter 11

1. You need to be clear about which world you're in: Are you communicating with someone who is represented (or **must** be treated as if he or she were represented) by counsel, or are you communicating with someone who's not represented? That will determine which Rule governs your communications. *See* **Chapter 11 at 341**.

2. Even though the **no-contact rule** says that "a lawyer" can't talk with a represented person about the subject of the representation without the consent of the represented person's counsel, the Rule includes those acting under a lawyer's direction or on a lawyer's behalf. *See* **Chapter 11.A at 343**.

3. In terms of which organization **constituents** are protected by the **no-contact rule** when the organization is represented, there are three categories:
   a. Any organization **constituent** who supervises, directs, or regularly consults with the organization's lawyer concerning the matter in question (sometimes referred to as *Upjohn* management because they are the **constituents** who can have communications with company counsel protected by the company's **attorney-client privilege**) (*see* **Chapter 11.B at 348**).
   b. Any organization **constituent** whose act or omission in connection with the matter may be imputed to the organization for purposes of the organization's civil or criminal liability (*see* **Chapter 11.B at 349**); and
   c. Any organization **constituent** whose words can legally bind the organization concerning the matter in question (*see* **Chapter 11.B at 350**).
   But beware, because older versions of **Model Rule 4.2** and its Comments still in effect in some states define these categories somewhat differently. And a number of other states have adopted idiosyncratic approaches to the question of which employees of a represented organization are protected by **Model Rule 4.2** that don't square with older or newer versions of **Model Rule 4.2 Comment [7]**. *See* **Chapter 11.B at 349**.

4. You must actually "know" that the person with whom you are communicating is represented by counsel, but willfully blinding yourself to this knowledge is treated the same as actually knowing. *See* **Chapter 11.C at 352**.

5. Investigation that does not involve "communication" with a protected person does not violate the **no-contact rule**. *See* **Chapter 11.D at 354**.

6. There are several categories of communications with represented persons that do not violate the **no-contact rule,** including:
    a. Communications made with opposing counsel's consent (*see* **Chapter 11.E at 356**);
    b. Communications not concerning "the matter" with respect to which the contacted person is protected (*see* **Chapter 11.F at 358**);
    c. Communications you make as a party to the matter (even though you may be a lawyer) (*see* **Chapter 11.F at 359**);
    d. Communications with someone you also represent or are asked to represent (*see* **Chapter 11.F at 359**); and
    e. Communications authorized by law or court order (*see* **Chapter 11.F at 360**).

7. In addition to disciplinary penalties for violating the **no-contact rule,** there are other remedies as well: **disqualification**, evidentiary sanctions, and monetary sanctions. In addition, there are contract remedies, such as rescission, as well as procedural remedies that a court can impose to undo decisions improperly induced in violation of the Rule. *See* **Chapter 11.G at 362**.

Multiple-Choice Review Questions for Chapter 11

1. Alec has been litigating a contingent-fee tort case for over a year. His client, Betty, slipped and fell outside the town's elementary school. Counsel for the school district, Carl, has generally been difficult to reach, so most of Alec's emails and calls to Carl go unanswered.

    Early on in the case, the parties engage in mediation. Although the school district's representative, Donna, seems reasonable, the case does not settle.

    A few weeks before trial, Betty authorizes Alec to settle the case for $25,000 if the school district will offer to pay that amount.

    Alec immediately reaches out to Carl and leaves several voicemails explaining that Betty would settle for $25,000. The calls go unanswered. Alec sends several emails but also receives no response.

    Alec now has a difficult decision. If he does not settle the case soon, he will have to prepare for trial. This will take significant time and effort, in essence taking a big chunk out of the value of his contingent fee if the school district ultimately decides to pay the $25,000. Alec would really like an answer from the school district now so that he knows whether to prepare for trial or to draft a settlement agreement instead.

The next day at the supermarket, Alec bumps into Donna at the checkout line. Is there anything he can say to her without violating his professional responsibility obligations?

    a. Yes. He can communicate the same information that he left in the messages for Carl, namely, that Betty would settle for $25,000.

    b. Yes. He can communicate that he has tried to reach Carl to convey a settlement demand but that Carl has not been responsive.

    c. No. He cannot communicate anything about the case to Donna without Carl's permission in advance.

    d. No. He cannot communicate anything to Donna in the supermarket, but he can ask Donna to call him at his office and can then discuss the case when they are in a more private setting.

2. Ellie represents Fred, a plaintiff in a defamation case against Gertie. Gertie is represented by counsel in the case.

    Ellie and Gertie both attend the same church. One day after services, Gertie approaches Ellie and begins chatting about the weather and politics.

    Can Ellie discuss these topics with Gertie without breaching her professional responsibility obligations?

    a. Yes. So long as the topics of discussion are unrelated to the litigation, Ellie can speak with Gertie without violating the **no-contact rule**.

    b. Yes. Because Gertie initiated the conversation, Ellie is free to discuss any subject with Gertie that Gertie feels comfortable discussing.

    c. No. Ellie may not speak with Gertie about any subject matter unless Gertie's counsel consents to the discussion.

    d. No. Ellie may only speak with Gertie when Gertie's counsel is present.

3. Hans represents a real estate developer, Isabelle, who is negotiating a contract with a landowner, John. John is represented by counsel, Kathryn.

    Kathryn recently left town to care for an ailing relative. Hans would like to get the contract finished in her absence. He realizes that he should have asked Kathryn for her consent to contact John in Kathryn's absence. Unfortunately, he didn't.

    Hans asks his legal assistant, Lauren, to contact John to iron out some contractual language. Lauren and John email several times until they reach agreement. Lauren then sends the language to Hans, who incorporates the language into the contract.

    When Kathryn returns, she is upset. She informs Hans that he has violated the **no-contact rule**. Has he?

    a. Yes. Through Lauren, his agent, he contacted John without Kathryn's consent.

    b. Yes. He should have first contacted Kathryn and only contacted John directly when a reasonable period of time had passed with no reply from Kathryn.

    c. No. Lauren is not a lawyer and the **no-contact rule** prohibits only lawyers from contacting a represented party.

    d. No. This is a business transaction, and the **no-contact rule** applies only in litigation.

4. Maria is a newly hired assistant United States attorney. She represents the postmaster general of the United States Postal Service in an employment discrimination case. Under Title VII of the Civil Rights Act of 1964, the only proper party in this type of lawsuit is the head of the agency (regardless of who is alleged to have committed the discrimination).

    The plaintiff alleges that she was subjected to discrimination based on her sex when she was disciplined by her manager, Norman. The complaint details Norman's alleged conduct and asserts that the agency is responsible for that conduct. The only named defendant in the case caption is the postmaster general. One day, out of the blue, Norman calls Maria to notify Maria that plaintiff's counsel tried to set up a meeting with him. Maria knew nothing about any such meeting and did not authorize it.

    Has opposing counsel contacted a represented party?

    a. Yes. Maria represents all United States Postal Service employees.

    b. Yes. Maria represents the United States Postal Service, which is being sued through the postmaster general. Norman is an employee of the Postal Service whose acts may be attributed to the Postal Service for purposes of liability, so he is protected by **Model Rule 4.2**.

    c. Maybe. It depends on the terms of Maria's representation agreement with the United States Postal Service.

    d. No. Maria only represents the postmaster.

5. Opal represents Percy, a defendant charged with criminal assault and battery in the State of Raptor. Opal wants to interview the alleged victim, Quinn. Quinn claims that Percy hit her during a bar fight. Percy claims that Quinn instigated the fight.

    On the day of the alleged assault, law enforcement interviewed Quinn. Quinn has since met with the prosecution.

    At trial, the prosecution plans to call Quinn to testify in its case in chief. Can Opal speak with Quinn without the prosecution's permission?

    a. Yes. Quinn is not represented by the prosecution, and Opal does not know that she has other counsel.

    b. Yes. The prosecution has already had a chance to meet with Quinn.

    c. No. Although not formally a party to the case, Quinn is closely aligned with the prosecution.

    d. No. Quinn is not a party to the case, but she is a prosecution witness.

6. Ralph is a plaintiff in a car-accident case. One day, on the way home from work, Ralph was rear-ended by another driver, Sally. Ralph retained lawyer Trudy to represent him in a lawsuit against Sally. Sally is represented by lawyer Usain.

   Trudy has just filed a complaint in the Commonwealth of Keystone. She has met with Ralph a few times and is in the process of preparing for discovery.

   Keystone has adopted the entirety of **Model Rule 4.2** in its Keystone Rule of Professional Conduct 4.2.

   Usain calls Ralph directly and urges him to dismiss the lawsuit voluntarily. Usain explains that the case is frivolous, and he threatens to move for sanctions under Keystone's version of Federal Rule of Civil Procedure 11 if Ralph does not comply. Ralph asks whether he should speak to Trudy. Usain advises Ralph against it, telling Ralph that "time is of the essence" if Ralph wants to avoid having to pay a hefty fine.

   Ralph goes to the courthouse and files a *pro se* form to dismiss the lawsuit.

   When Trudy discovers what has happened, she reports Usain to the appropriate disciplinary authority, and she moves to reinstate the case and for attorney's fees.

   What might the court do procedurally to correct the consequences of Usain's improper contact with Ralph?
   a. Discipline Usain for violation of Model Rule of Professional Conduct 4.2.
   b. Discipline Usain for violation of Keystone Rule of Professional Conduct 4.2.
   c. Grant attorney's fees in favor of Usain under Federal Rule of Civil Procedure 60(b).
   d. Grant a motion under Federal Rule of Civil Procedure 60(b) to reinstate the case.

7. Vivian was recently retained to represent a sole proprietorship that had filed a *pro se* breach of contract complaint. She asks whether the opposing party is represented. Her client says, "I don't think so."

   No lawyer has yet entered an appearance in the case. Vivian calls the opposing party and asks "Have you retained counsel in this case?" The party says "I have, but I'd still be happy to talk to you without my lawyer being involved."

   What is Vivian's wisest course of action?
   a. Discuss the case.
   b. Conference her client into the conversation as a witness.
   c. End the conversation.
   d. Withdraw from the case.

8. If opposing counsel is a lawyer who is representing herself in litigation, does the **no-contact rule** mean that she is protected from any contact?
   a. Yes. No one may ever contact that lawyer, because she's representing herself.
   b. Maybe. It depends on the type of case.
   c. Maybe. The contact is permitted but only with court approval.
   d. No. It is widely understood that the rule does not apply in this scenario.

9. Zed is preparing to file a lawsuit on behalf of his client, Allie, against Bob. According to Allie, Bob trespassed on her lawn and damaged her rare roses. At the time, Allie told Bob, "You'll be hearing from my lawyer, I'll see you in court!" Bob said, "Super! I have a lawyer on retainer, I'll tell him about this, and I'd be happy to give you his number."

   Zed and Allie meet, and she tells Zed everything about what happened—including the discussion with Bob about having "a lawyer on retainer." Zed asks whether Bob ever provided his lawyer's name. Allie says, "We never spoke again."

   Zed has not filed the complaint yet. He suspects, given the low-dollar value of the case, that an early informal resolution would be best for both Allie and Bob.

   Can Zed contact Bob now, before the complaint is filed, without violating the **no-contact rule**?
   a. Yes. The **no-contact rule** is inapplicable because Zed is acting in both Allie and Bob's best interests.
   b. Yes. The **no-contact rule** is inapplicable because there can be no represented party until a case is filed.
   c. No. The **no-contact rule** applies because there may be a matter even before a case is filed, if Zed knows that Bob is represented by counsel.
   d. No. The **no-contact rule** applies because Allie is represented by Zed.

10. BigCorp is the defendant in trade-secret litigation. During the case, one of its district managers leaves the company.

    In this jurisdiction, **Model Rule 4.2** and its comments are applied verbatim.

    Is permission from BigCorp's counsel required before the district manager is contacted about the case by plaintiff's counsel?
    a. Yes. Consent of the organization's lawyer is required for communication with a district manager.
    b. Maybe. It depends on the circumstances under which the **constituent** left.
    c. Maybe. It depends on whether the district manager retained his own counsel.
    d. No. Consent of the organization's lawyer is not required for communication with a former **constituent**.

12

Duties to Unrepresented Persons

While Frank's boss is out of the office, his secretary sends Frank a call from a potential new client. Madison (Maddy) Malle broke her arm a while back in a fall at home, and a doctor (who seemed rather out of it) in the emergency department of the local community hospital appears to have mis-set the broken bone. Now Maddy will need orthopedic surgery and a lengthy recovery to correct the doctor's mistake. When Maddy recently visited the hospital to get her medical records, a lawyer for the hospital brought her the records. He explained that the staff physician who had treated her, Dr. Al K. Holic, was now in rehab ("Such a shame about his illness!"), and that multiple malpractice claims had left him flat broke and without a medical license. The lawyer suggested that Maddy accept a nominal payment from the hospital for her injury. Maddy asked him if the payment was fair. "It's a good deal," he assured her; "the best you can do under these unfortunate circumstances." Maddy doesn't remember the lawyer mentioning whether the hospital could be responsible for her injury, or whether the hospital or Dr. Holic had liability insurance. She signed the release and has cashed the check. What can Frank do to help her?

At the outset, we want to emphasize two things. They will sound similar to the two things that we emphasized at the beginning of **Chapter 11 at 341** regarding your duties to represented persons under **Model Rule 4.2**:

First, issues like the one that started this chapter arise frequently, hand in hand with questions about your duties to represented persons. That's because people either have a lawyer representing them on a particular subject or they don't. More specifically, those who are not your clients (and not clients of your firm) either have lawyers of their own with respect to the subject that they're discussing with you (or are deemed to be protected by the **no-contact rule** as if they did; *see* **Chapter 11.B at 345**), or else they don't. If they do (or are deemed protected by the **no-contact rule** as if they did), then your duties to them are defined by **Model Rule 4.2**, discussed in **Chapter 11 at 339**. If they don't have a lawyer, then your duties are defined by **Model Rule 4.3** and **Model Rule 3.4(f)**, and we're going to discuss your duties under those rules now. These two sets of duties are very different, but the **consequences**

of violating whichever set applies can be serious, so you need to figure out right away whether the person in front of you is represented or unrepresented, and then act accordingly.

Second, like the no-contact rule, the rules for dealing with unrepresented persons seem simple, but they can be difficult to apply in real-world situations. Subtle differences in phrasing and circumstance can distinguish compliance from violation. Who knew that dealing with ordinary folks could be this tricky?

Fear not. You have us, your faithful guides, to lead you through it. We'll start by looking at the governing Model Rules. They tell you that there are four things that you either **must** or **must not** do when you're acting as someone's lawyer and dealing with unrepresented persons. We'll give you a paraphrase of the four basic tenets of dealing with unrepresented persons. Then we'll talk about why these Rules exist and the **consequences** if you violate them. And then we'll walk through the requirements and show you how they can be hard to apply. Ready?

TAMING THE TEXT ▶ You know the drill by now: Read **Model Rule 4.3** (including the Comments) and **Model Rule 3.4(f)** (including **Model Rule 3.4 Comment [4]**). Now match up our paraphrase with the corresponding language in the Rules. When acting as a lawyer and dealing with an unrepresented person:

1. You **must not** "state or imply that [you are] disinterested." You're acting on behalf of a client, and you're there to advance your client's interests, so no suggesting or implying otherwise.

2. If you know or reasonably should know that an unrepresented person doesn't fully understand who you are or what you're doing there, you **must** make "reasonable efforts to correct the misunderstanding." So even if you never misled the unrepresented person, you **must** affirmatively correct any apparent misimpression about your role and loyalties.

3. If the unrepresented person's **interests** are or could be in **conflict** with your client's (that is, they're not fully aligned in all relevant respects), you **must not** give *any legal advice at all* to the unrepresented person except the advice to get a lawyer of his or her own. Aside from *advice*, you remain free to (**may**) answer questions, to offer information, and even to advocate for your client (so long as you tell the truth and don't dress any of it up as advice to the unrepresented person).

4. You **must not** "request a person other than a client" (or a relative, employee, or agent of a client) "to refrain from voluntarily giving relevant information to another party" unless you actually and reasonably believe that the person won't suffer any problems as a result. TAMING THE TEXT

REASON FOR THE RULE ▶ So why do we have such restrictive rules sucking all the fun out of everything?[1] Remember, in the **Introduction to Chapter 11 at 339**, we talked

---

[1] For those still trying to figure us out, yes, we're being ironic here. You're spending three long years in school and then a whole career training to be an intellectual black-belt in high-stakes battles of wits. As Peter Parker's Uncle Ben reminded him (and as

about how the **no-contact rule** is intended to stop clever, resourceful lawyers like you from getting around the protections that prompted others to get a lawyer of their own? Those protections are preserved in **Model Rule 4.2** by preventing you (the lawyer) from dealing directly with the represented person unless the represented person's lawyer feels confident that her client can handle the interaction with you and consents.

But an unrepresented person doesn't have a lawyer in his corner, ready to jump into the ring and fight for him. Most people don't have regular contact with lawyers or the legal system, and many of them don't know, or can be easily confused about, what a lawyer in a particular situation is supposed to be doing there and where his or her loyalties may lie. The ethical rules want to make sure that, at the least, the unrepresented person is aware who's in the other corner before the bell rings.[2] So although you generally **must not** deal directly with a represented person at all, you **may** deal with an unrepresented person directly, *but* you have special duties of care and candor designed to keep the unrepresented person at least somewhat better informed about who you are and what your role is in the matters at hand, in order to limit your opportunities to take unfair advantage. REASON FOR THE RULE

CONSEQUENCES We'll discuss the potential **consequences** for treating unrepresented persons improperly in more detail in **Chapter 12.B at 385**, but they're similar to those available for violation of the **no-contact rule**. This isn't surprising, because **Model Rule 4.3** and **Model Rule 3.4(f)** serve information- and decision-protective purposes for unrepresented persons similar to those of **Model Rule 4.2** for represented persons (*see* **Chapter 11 at 340**. Possible **consequences** for violation of **Model Rule 4.3** or **Model Rule 3.4(f)** include professional discipline, possible **disqualification**, possible court-imposed evidentiary or monetary sanctions, and possible civil liability if the violation causes the unrepresented person monetary harm (as well as civil remedies designed to undo any decisions or actions induced unfairly). As with violations of **Model Rule 4.2**, then, the stakes are high. CONSEQUENCES

Now that we've got the gist of the Rules and the **consequences** by which they're enforced, let's talk about how you might violate or, better yet, avoid violating them.

---

we reminded you in **Chapter 5.A at 106**), with great powers come great responsibilities. The system frowns on your using your superpowers to take advantage of those who lack your training and skills. **Consequences** will ensue if you try.

[2] That doesn't mean the fight will always be fairly matched. Sadly, it sometimes isn't. The world is full of low-income workers, tenants, and persons in need of governmental benefits who simply lack the resources to obtain the legal representation that might make their pursuit of their rights a fairer fight. But sometimes sophisticated nonlawyers can deal with lawyers well enough to accomplish their goals without spending money on legal fees, and they may prefer to do so (*see* **Problem 11B-1 at 344** to remind you of a common example); and sometimes—Abraham Lincoln's admonitions about those who represent themselves notwithstanding—nonlawyers who actually have a choice choose to represent themselves, whether it's wise or not.

A. How Do You Violate the Protections for Unrepresented Persons (or Better Yet, How Do You *Avoid* Violating Them)?

1. Creating or Failing to Dispel Misimpressions Regarding your Role

Remember, there are four basic prohibitions concerning unrepresented persons laid out by **Model Rule 4.3** and **Model Rule 3.4(f)**. Go back to the **Introduction to this chapter at 374** and review them.

The first two are (1) you **must not** give unrepresented persons the misimpression that you're "disinterested"; and (2) if there is any reasonable possibility that an unrepresented person doesn't understand your role, you **must** take reasonable care to explain it. Together, these principles require you *affirmatively* to make it clear that you are a lawyer representing a client and that your only job is to do what's best for that client. The first sentence of **Model Rule 4.3** says that you **must not** "state" or "imply" that you're "disinterested"—that is, you can't imply that you "don't have a dog in the hunt," as Texans say.[3] The second sentence goes a lot further: It says that if there is any reasonable chance that an unrepresented person might misunderstand your "role in the matter" *in any way*, regardless of the origin of or reason for the possible misunderstanding, you—the lawyer—**must** "correct" it.[4]

REASON FOR THE RULE Why is it up to you to correct any misimpressions that a third party, or even an adversary who lacks a lawyer, might have, even if you had no role in creating them? Why not just leave it as "everyone for themselves"? Simply put, it's because many people don't have your knowledge, training, and experience, so in the typical situation, it's more likely that unrepresented persons may have or develop misimpressions about your role that could allow you to take advantage of them. You, as the lawyer in the room, are more likely to spot this problem, and you have the knowledge of law and legal ethics, and the communication skills, to prevent it. From the perspective of fairness, the Rules don't allow you to take advantage of a less knowledgeable and less educated layperson. From the standpoint of efficiency, you are the "cheapest cost avoider"—that is, if the rule were "fend for yourself," people would need to spend a lot more time and money

---

[3] People other than Texans may also use this phrase, but we know that the Texan author among us most certainly uses it. She also uses "not my circus, not my clowns," but less often (and particularly not now, because it has no application here).

[4] There is one specific situation in which you **must** provide additional admonitions to an unrepresented person—when you are settling a malpractice claim asserted against you by *your own client*. (Just to be clear, in this situation, even if you continue to represent the client in the matter you are accused of having botched or in other matters, you are *not* representing the client with respect to his or her claims against *you*. You have a direct and unwaivable **conflict of interest** that would make that impossible, even if any client were foolish enough to consider it in the first place. *See* **Model Rule 1.7(b)(3); Chapter 22.E at 739**.) In that situation, **Model Rule 1.8(h)(2)** *adds* to the requirements that you make sure the claimant does not misunderstand your role (representing yourself, and not representing the claimant), and that you not give the client any legal advice on the subject, the additional requirement that the claimant **must** be "advised in writing of the desirability of seeking and is given a reasonable opportunity to seek the advice of independent legal counsel in connection therewith."

getting legal and other advice and knowledge just to make sure they knew with whom they were dealing, when you're already there on the scene with all the knowledge that you need to avoid this problem. `Reason for the Rule`

> **Problem 12A-1:** Same facts as in **this chapter's Introduction at 373**. State every way in which the hospital's lawyer violated the first two sentences of **Model Rule 4.3**. (If you think that he didn't, go back to the beginning of the chapter and start over.) Specifically, identify each thing that the hospital's lawyer said that violated his legal and ethical obligations, and explain why it did. Then identify anything that he was obligated to say that he didn't, and why.

> **Problem 12A-2:** Frank represents a client in a dispute in which the client "t-boned" (ran broadside into) an uninsured driver's car. Fortunately, no one was hurt, but the other driver's car has several thousand dollars' worth of body damage. The client doesn't want to involve his insurance company because he can afford to repair the damage caused and doesn't want his insurance rates to go up or to get "points" on his driving record. Having ascertained that the other driver has no lawyer, and having easily concluded that the driver's **interests** and his client's are in **conflict** (quick—explain why), Frank is trying to negotiate a resolution with the unrepresented driver. The unrepresented driver is not knowledgeable about the legal system. He begins the conversation by saying, "OK, so you're the lawyer; tell me what I get for the accident." What **must** or **should** Frank say now, and why?

> **Problem 12A-3:** In a conference room in her offices, Maya hosts a meeting of three entrepreneurs who want to form a small technology company. The three founders include an inventor with the bright idea that the company will develop and exploit, a sales and marketing whiz, and a venture capitalist who will fund the venture. The venture capitalist is a longtime client of Maya's firm in connection with his various start-up investments, and he has made it clear to Maya that he expects her and her firm to represent him and his **interests** in the formation of this new company, and no one else's. What **must** or **should** Maya say and do to comply with the first two sentences of **Model Rule 4.3**? Which participants in the meeting might develop misimpressions about Maya's role if she said nothing about it, and why? What might Maya be implying if she conducted the meeting without clarifying her role? Why would Maya and her firm be stuck with those implications if Maya remained silent on the subject?

`Tips & Tactics` Bear in mind that when **Model Rule 4.3** says that you can't "state or imply" that you're disinterested, it assumes that you can "imply" something under the right circumstances simply by saying and doing nothing. Similarly, when the Rule says that you **must** correct any misunderstanding about your role that you "know[]" or "reasonably should know" that an unrepresented person has, it leaves the determination about what you know or reasonably should know until later, when someone claims that you failed to correct a misunderstanding that you were required to rectify. It's human nature for honest people to remember a conversation consistently with whatever general understanding they have developed about the other person's role and purposes. (And, sadly, when the chips are down, some people may "remember" things self-interestedly.) Why would you want to leave the possibility of professional discipline and the undoing of things that you thought you'd accomplished for your client to guesses about what an unrepresented person you don't know might be thinking—or worse yet, to an opportunistic effort to revise history when someone later regrets a decision? It's easy to make your role clear, and you **should** make it a habit whenever you are representing a client in the presence of someone who is not represented.

- Make a point of clarifying your identity and your role. There are lots of ways to do this, and no one way is inherently more effective than another, but at in-person meetings, one way is to give unrepresented people your business card and write "representing" and the name of your client on the card. With or without the business card, be very explicit about who you are, whom you represent, what your job is and isn't, and what kinds of information you can and can't offer to unrepresented persons. You can (and **should**) do this very gently and politely; it's easier than you might think.

- If an unrepresented person with **interests** different from your client's asks you a question, make it clear in your answer that you can't give that person any legal advice because you represent someone else. And if you're providing a statement of fact or of your client's negotiating position (things we talked about in **Chapter 10.B at 327**), make it very explicit that that's what you're doing. Don't leave anything to doubt, guesswork, or misunderstanding (whether accidental or opportunistic). The sometimes subtle differences between things that you **may** properly say and things that you **must not** say are not always obvious to a lay person who has no reason to be sensitive to the fine distinctions that you're learning in this course.

- Advising unrepresented persons that they may need to consult a lawyer of their own is often a good idea. If you find yourself hesitating to do this—or to clarify your role in any other way—ask yourself why. If it's because you don't want the person to think as independently as he or she otherwise might, then you've confronted the exact reason why you **should**, and probably **must**, advise him or her to get a lawyer. Why? Because your temptation to remain silent about your role probably stems from the possibility that the unrepresented person's **interests** differ from your client's, and that the unrepresented person would listen to you more skeptically if your true loyalties and purpose were fully understood. As a collateral benefit, you may be surprised at how often it enhances your credibility to make it clear to unrepresented people that they should get independent advice—in doing so, you portray yourself as someone who is honest and has integrity. Decent folks respect that.

- Though clarifying your role orally at meetings or on the phone is essential, don't stop there. Avoid the possibility of he said/she said (or to de-gender it, I said/you said) disputes later. Make a contemporaneous durable record. Communicate in writing if you can. If you can't, confirm what you said and didn't say in a letter or email immediately afterwards. **Inquire; explain; confirm** (*see* **Chapter 6.A at 139**).

Recording phone calls or meetings is, in our view, usually not a very good idea, and sometimes (depending on the law of the state where the conversation is taking place) it's illegal. Even with notice and consent, recording may make for a stilted and uncomfortable conversation, and it often doesn't produce all that clear a record, anyway. Do not record a meeting or phone conversation without the other person's consent unless you have determined that your jurisdiction (and, if different, the other person's jurisdiction) allows it. (Some don't.) Even then, be sensitive to how it looks to record things secretly. ⟨ TIPS & TACTICS ⟩

> **Problem 12A-4:** Write an email for Maya to the participants in the meeting described in **Problem 12A-3 at 377**, to be sent after the meeting, confirming her role and her obligations. You can do it in about three sentences.

2. Giving Advice to Unrepresented Persons

The third sentence of **Model Rule 4.3** says that, if you "know or reasonably should know" that an unrepresented person's **interests** "are or have a reasonable possibility of being" in **conflict** with your client's, then you **must not** give the unrepresented person any "legal advice" "other than the advice to secure counsel." This is an area in which it's easy to make mistakes with significant **consequences**.

⟨ TAMING THE TEXT ⟩ Let's break this down. This part of the Rule is limited in scope in two important ways: First, if the unrepresented person's **interests** are and will stay completely aligned with your client's, you can advise the unrepresented person in any way that's acceptable to your client and consistent with basic honesty. The two following subsections elaborate on how to know when those **interests** are aligned. But even if unrepresented people's **interests** are hostile to your client's, you **may** communicate and negotiate directly with them. You often have no other choice, because they have no lawyer or other representative with whom you can deal. But what you **must not** do is give such people (that is, unrepresented persons with **interests** not aligned with your client's) "legal advice," other than to get their own lawyer. That's discussed in the third subsection below. ⟨ TAMING THE TEXT ⟩

a. When the Unrepresented Person's Interests "Are or Have a Reasonable Possibility of Being in Conflict" with Your Client's Interests[5]

This is the key trigger of your obligation not to "give legal advice to" the unrepresented person. The "**conflict**" refers to the possibility that some of the things that the unrepresented person may want out of the issues at hand could be

---

[5] **Conflict of interest** is a defined term that you can find in the Glossary, and to which we devote an entire lengthy chapter of this book, **Chapter 22 at 599**. A person's "**interests**" in this context amount to what that person wants or needs, or may reasonably be assumed to want or need, in the situation presented. One person's **interests** are in **conflict** with another's when the two want or need, or may reasonably be presumed to want or need, any **materially** inconsistent things.

materially different from things that your client may want. The actual or potential "**conflict**" doesn't have to be diametrically opposed to your client's **interests** in order to invoke the no-legal-advice rule (though it often is). It's enough that what your client may want and what the unrepresented person may want may end up not being the same in some **material** respect.

Nor does the **conflict** have to be on every issue. **Conflict** on one **material** issue is enough to trigger the obligation not to offer *any* "legal advice" to the unrepresented person.

Similarly, the Rule says that you **must not** give "legal advice" to the unrepresented person if that person's **interests** "are or have a reasonable possibility of being in **conflict**" with your client's. If you know (or should know) that **interests** "are" in **conflict** right now, that's easy: Don't give any legal advice to the unrepresented person. But what if **conflict** is just a "maybe" right now? The "reasonable possibility of being in **conflict**" covers two possibilities—one right now, and one in the future. Right now, if it's reasonably possible that the unrepresented person might have wants or needs about which you don't know and that could be different from your client's wants or needs, the no-advice rule is in effect. And even if the unrepresented person and your client's **interests** seem fully aligned right now, if it's reasonably possible that this alignment could later change in ways that could create a **conflict** in the future, that's enough to preclude your giving any legal advice to the unrepresented person now, even when there's no current **conflict**.

b. When You "Know or Reasonably Should Know" About the "Reasonable Possibility" of a Conflict Between Your Client's Interests and the Interests of the Unrepresented Person

Ignorance is no excuse if you should know better. And because you're a smart, educated, experienced lawyer, most courts and disciplinary authorities are likely to assume that you "reasonably should know" a great deal.

REAL WORLD **The organizational constituent:** One situation that comes up so frequently that it has specific ethical rules attached to it in addition to the general principles of **Model Rule 4.3** is when counsel for an organization communicates with a "**constituent**" of the organization. A **constituent** is an individual associated with the organization who works or speaks for the organization, or has an ownership interest or management powers in it, such as an officer, director, shareholder, manager, employee, or agent. As we'll discuss in more detail in **Chapter 23.A at 770**, company counsel represents the company, not any of the **constituents** with whom they deal, unless affirmative steps are taken to represent a particular **constituent** in addition to the company, and address any **conflicts of interest** that this **concurrent representation** may create. *See* **Model Rule 1.13(a), (g)**. Because the potential for confusion in these common circumstances is so great, a special rule requires company counsel to remind the company **constituents** with whom they are dealing that they represent only the company, not the individual **constituent**, any time that company counsel knows that the company's **interests** are "adverse" to the **constituent's**. **Model Rule 1.13(f)**; *see* **Chapter 23.A at 781**. (Can you see how this specific rule amounts to a special application of the general rule provided by **Model Rule 4.3**?) REAL WORLD

> **Problem 12A-5:** Maya provides advice on a range of subjects to one of her firm's clients, Infinity Investing, Inc., an investment advisory firm (that is, a company that gives individuals and businesses advice about how they should invest their money). Maya has dealt with a number of different people who work there. Artie Advisor is an investment advisor at Infinity. Maya has spoken with him before about securities and investment-advisor regulation issues pertinent to his customers. "What can I do for you today?" Maya asks. "Send a sympathy bouquet," Artie responds, glumly. "Gee, Artie, I'm sorry—what's going on?" Maya inquires. "Word is that we're going to have a round of layoffs here," Artie says. "I haven't been here that long, so my head is likely headed for the chopping block." "Dang, I'm sorry," says Maya. "Have you talked to a lawyer?" "Nah," replies Artie, "I'd rather not spend the money. You seem to know the company pretty well. What should I ask for in my severance package?" What **must** or **should** Maya do now, and why?

Lawyers also deal with unrepresented persons who may not understand the lawyer's role in a wide range of other circumstances. Here are some examples:

> **Problem 12A-6:** Frank's client has a small business dispute with Clarence Clever, which the client has asked Frank to handle. Clarence calls Frank to negotiate a resolution to the dispute, and starts asking Frank about the law on various questions pertinent to the dispute. "I'm sorry, Mr. Clever, but I'm not your lawyer, and I can't give you legal advice," Frank cautions him. "Well, your client wants to work this out, right?" says Mr. Clever. "Um, sure, on appropriate terms," says Frank. "Well, that's what I want, too," replies Mr. Clever. "We want the same thing. So how about helping me out here?" **May** Frank now give Mr. Clever the legal advice that he's requested? Why or why not?

> **Problem 12A-7:** Danielle is prosecuting a robbery case in which the state alleges that the defendant mugged Valerie Victim. Valerie will be the state's principal witness at trial. Danielle meets with Valerie to prepare her to testify, and in the process gives her a good deal of advice about how to present herself, how to explain what happened to her, how to indicate who did it (consistent, of course, with the truth), and what to expect when defense counsel cross-examines her. Has Danielle violated **Model Rule 4.3**? Why or why not? Is there anything else that Danielle **must** or **should** say to Valerie?

c. When You Are Giving "Legal Advice" to an Unrepresented Person as Opposed to Making Statements of Fact or Negotiating Position

Once there's a reasonable possibility that the unrepresented person's **interests** may not be aligned with your client's, the third sentence of **Model Rule 4.3** says that you **must not** give the unrepresented person any "legal advice . . . other than the advice to secure counsel." This part of the Rule does *not* mean that you can't speak to the unrepresented person under any circumstances. Remember, many people end up representing themselves in negotiations and disputes, and you may have no alternative but to deal with the unrepresented person. Direct, adversarial discussions between an unrepresented lay person and the other party's lawyer happen all the time.

So what *can* you say? The distinction that is typically drawn is between "giv[ing] legal advice" and making a *statement of fact* or *negotiating position*. The complication is that the difference between these two often comes down to subtle differences in context or word choice. And remember that the import of what you say will be judged from what the unrepresented person reasonably understood (we know this because the first sentence of the Rule says that you have to "correct" *any* misunderstanding that you reasonably ought to know the unrepresented person has, whether that misunderstanding is *itself* unreasonable or not). *See* **Model Rule 4.3 Comments [1]-[2]**.

> Problem 12A-8: Frank is involved in a hard-fought case between two former business partners who are dissolving their partnership. Frank's firm represents one of the partners. Each partner accuses the other of bad conduct. As in many such disputes, neither partner is entirely blameless. The partnership had several employees, one of whom—Wally Witness—is close friends with Frank's client but witnessed the client do a number of things in anger that the client is not proud of today (and that are harmful to his case). Wally isn't accused of anything, has no lawyer, and doesn't really appreciate the significance of what he knows. Trial is approaching, and the other side subpoenas Wally for a deposition. Wally is now retired and is shortly going to leave for a lengthy trip abroad that will not bring him back into the United States until after the scheduled trial. Wally calls up Frank. "I'm about to leave on this big trip," Wally explains, "and I really don't have time for this. Do I have to show up?" What **must** or **must** Frank **not** do or say, and why? What **may** he do or say to help his client's case, within the limits of his ethical obligations?

> Problem 12A-9: Same as **Problem 12A-2 at 377** (Frank represents a client who damaged another driver's car; the other driver, a nonlawyer, is representing himself in negotiating a resolution), but the other driver begins the conversation instead with the question, "So, what do you think my case is worth?" Which of the following **must** Frank **not** say, and why? Which **may** he say, and why? Are there other things that Frank **must** or **should** say in the course of the conversation? (You may assume all the statements are accurate.)
>
> a. "I've handled fender-benders before, and if I took this one to trial, you'd get about $4,000."
> b. "No way your claim is worth more than $4,000."
> c. "Based on the photographs you sent, I priced out the damage to your car with Shoddy Roddy's Auto Body, and it comes to about $4,000."
> d. "My client won't pay more than $4,000."

Does your answer to any of the questions change if the opposing party works as a claims adjuster for an auto insurance company but is not a lawyer, and has decided that he doesn't want to use one to resolve this claim?

Problem 12A-10: Mess in the Press:[6] For a brief time during 2017, Marc Kasowitz was one of President Donald Trump's personal lawyers. (That means that Mr. Kasowitz and his New York law firm represented Mr. Trump regarding personal legal issues arising from his public behavior, rather than having specific duties to the United States, the executive branch of the federal government, or the Office of the Presidency. The precise loyalties and identity of the clients of lawyers representing governmental agencies or officers can be subtle and confusing. *See* **Chapter 25.C at 911.**) Kasowitz promptly started meeting with White House staff, individually and in groups. Many of those people might have witnessed or participated in events that were, at that time, under investigation by federal prosecutors, including Special Counsel Robert Mueller, and thus faced the possibility of law-enforcement interviews, grand-jury subpoenas, and even possibly indictments, depending on their involvement in the particular events under investigation. When asked at a group meeting with White House staff whether they should get their own attorneys, Kasowitz answered that it was not yet necessary. Under the **no-contact rule**, of course, Kasowitz could meet one-on-one with individuals who did not have their own counsel without the consent or presence of another lawyer, which Kasowitz immediately began doing.

(A quick caution: Some of you reading this problem likely have strong feelings about President Trump, the Mueller investigation, and related issues, no matter which side of the political divide you're on. Don't let those feelings (whatever they are) cloud your views about whether this particular lawyer did or did not act consistently with his legal and ethical obligations on this particular occasion. The law and the rules of lawyer ethics apply equally and must be applied evenhandedly to all lawyers, no matter who their clients are.)

a. Kasowitz was criticized for his view of his ethical obligations to White House staff. Were his critics right? Why or why not? What constraints (if any) would have existed on what Kasowitz could say or do during his one-on-one meetings with White House staff?[7]

b. Kasowitz reportedly liked to boast that he was "the toughest lawyer on Wall Street." "Toughness" can mean a number of different things. What does it mean to be a "tough" lawyer, and why would someone want to be thought of as one? This is a serious question. Forget about armchair psychologizing and think of some practical reasons why some lawyers might rationally want to cultivate such an image. What kind of reputation for "toughness" might be a benefit in practice, and why? What kind of "toughness" is reflected

---

[6] Rebecca R. Ruiz & Sharon Lafraniere, *Role of Trump's Personal Lawyer Blurs Public and Private Lines,* https://www.nytimes.com/2017/06/11/us/politics/trump-lawyer-marc-kasowitz.html?_r=0 (June 11, 2017).

[7] After media coverage of his efforts on Mr. Trump's behalf, Kasowitz received a critical email from a private citizen calling on him to resign his engagement. The president's personal lawyer responded with several profanity-laden emails in response. The recipient released them to the media. Justin Elliott, *Trump Lawyer Marc Kasowitz Threatens Stranger in Emails: 'Watch Your Back, Bitch',* https://www.propublica.org/article/marc-kasowitz-trump-lawyer-threat-emails-maddow (July 13, 2017). Kasowitz publicly apologized later the next day, but he withdrew from the representation a few days later.

in emails saying things like "I already know where you live, I'm on you. You might as well call me. You will see me. I promise. Bro."? What kind of practical results might the "toughness" reflected in these emails cause?

3. Requesting That Someone Withhold Relevant Information

Model Rule 3.4(f) forbids you from "request[ing]" anyone other than a client (or a relative, employee, or agent of a client) "to refrain from voluntarily giving information to another party." This prohibition is not limited to unrepresented persons. But because you generally can't speak with a represented (or deemed protected) person under the **no-contact rule**, as a practical matter the issue usually comes up when lawyers are dealing with unrepresented persons.

Even when you're allowed to request that someone refrain from voluntary cooperation with another party because that someone is your client or your client's relative, employee, or agent, **Model Rule 3.4(f)(2)** says you **must not** do so unless you "reasonably believe[] that the person's **interests** will not be adversely affected" by complying with the request.

Once again, the rules may seem clear enough, but the difference between compliance and violation often amounts to subtle differences in context or wording.

Problem 12A-11: Same as **Problem 12A-8 at 382** (dispute between two business partners; third party Wally Witness has relevant knowledge but is reluctant to get involved), except that it's much earlier in the case, before any discovery has been taken. Wally has voluntarily come to speak with Frank because of his friendship with Frank's client. In interviewing Wally, Frank quickly realizes that Wally is a witness to facts that are quite bad for Frank's client, though Wally himself doesn't really appreciate this point. Wally is understandably uncomfortable being stuck in the middle of this fight between the two former partners. He asks Frank what he should do if the other partner or his lawyer calls him. The last thing that Frank and his client want is for Wally to tell the other side what he knows. What **must** Frank or **must** Frank **not** say or do? What **may** he say or do? What **should** he say or do?

Problem 12A-12: Maya's firm does a range of work for One Mississippi ("OM"), a large online retailer. To give its litigation associates some front-line experience, the firm has taken on, at reduced rates, the defense of personal injury and worker's compensation claims arising out of OM's warehouse operations. Recently, there was a serious accident at one of OM's warehouses in which a forklift ran amok. There was property damage and several serious injuries; one worker died. Maya's friend, litigation associate Leo Litigator, is representing OM. He has interviewed numerous people who were on the warehouse floor that day, including Sally Sawitall. Sally was not involved in the accident, but she witnessed some of the events at issue. She told Leo that the forklift involved in the accident was "going way faster than any of the others and weaving all the heck over the floor." She also says that, on the day of the accident, she saw the driver of the forklift passing a hip flask back and forth with his boss, the warehouse manager, before their shift started. Leo explains to Sally that the company really appreciates her cooperation, and if any law enforcement officers or lawyers or investigators for injured workers or the forklift manufacturer contact her, she should decline to speak to them and let Leo know. Is Sally protected from such inquiries by the **no-contact rule**? Why or why not? Has Leo complied with his ethical obligations? Why or why not?

B. CONSEQUENCES What Happens If You Violate the Rules Protecting Unrepresented Persons?

1. CONSEQUENCES Professional Discipline

RULE ROLES Like all the Rules of Professional Conduct, **Model Rule 4.3** and **Model Rule 3.4(f)** are by their terms disciplinary rules, so their violation can lead to professional discipline by your state bar or other disciplinary authority. But like the **no-contact rule** codified in **Model Rule 4.2**, courts have relied on **Model Rule 4.3** and **Model Rule 3.4(f)** to set standards for civil **consequences** that they may impose for violation of these Rules in matters before them. The choice of remedy is, as it usually is, driven by the harm that the lawyer's wrongful conduct caused. RULE ROLES

2. CONSEQUENCES Nondisciplinary Consequences When the Information-Protective Purpose of the Rules Is Violated

As a practical matter, parties and witnesses who have gotten (or been given) lawyers are more likely to have information with adversarial value, and more likely to have **confidential** or **attorney-client privileged** information. If an unrepresented witness were fooled into divulging something **confidential** or **attorney-client privileged**, the remedies would likely be similar to those invoked for similar violations of the **no-contact rule: Disqualification** if no other consequence could remedy the wrong; otherwise, evidentiary or monetary sanctions. *See* **Chapter 11.G at 363**. But sanctions are relatively uncommon as a practical matter. Unrepresented persons are less likely to be party to **confidential** or **attorney-client privileged** information because (by definition) they don't have lawyers with whom to have **attorney-client privileged** communications—and by the terms of the **no-contact rule**, they're less likely to be among those deemed protected by company counsel, again because that rule tends to protect people more likely to have had **attorney-client privileged** communications with company counsel (*see* **Chapter 11.B at 348**). Still, it can happen:

Problem 12B-1: Same as **Problem 11B-2(f) at 351**—Frank represents Wanda Worker, who has been sexually harassed on the job by her manager, Gary Grabby. Their employer, BCraftyCo, has decided to blame it all on Gary (colloquially referred to as "throwing him under the bus"), portraying Gary as a serial harasser about whom BCraftyCo was uninformed until the incidents with Wanda came to light. BCrafty fires Gary and provides him no company lawyer or independent counsel, so the **no-contact rule** does not apply. Happy Trials interviews Gary, and questions him extensively about his conversations with BCrafty's counsel while he was still employed. Has Frank's boss violated any ethical rules? What **consequences** might BCrafty seek?

3. CONSEQUENCES **Nondisciplinary Consequences When the Decision-Protective Purpose of the Rules Is Violated — Relief from Action Obtained in Violation of the Rules**

The much more commonly claimed **consequence** of a violation of **Model Rule 4.3** and **Model Rule 3.4(f)** is that an unrepresented person will claim that the lawyer for the other side unfairly induced her to make a decision that she now regrets. When there is fraud or undue influence—whether under common-law principles or as described by the governing Rules—the contract law remedy of rescission is usually available to undo an agreement (such as a settlement) induced by those improper means. And **Fed. R. Civ. P. 60(b)** authorizes the court to grant relief from an order or judgment resulting from "misconduct by an opposing party," such as a dismissal of a pending case as part of a settlement obtained in violation of the rule.

Problem 12B-2: Review the hypothetical in **this chapter's Introduction at 373**. Describe each step that Frank **should** take so that Maddy can pursue her rights in full, as well as the general authority allowing him to take each step on her behalf. CONSEQUENCES

Big-Picture Takeaways from Chapter 12

1. There are four things you either **must** or **must not** do when you are acting as someone's lawyer and dealing with unrepresented persons:
    a. You **must not** "state or imply that [you are] disinterested."
    b. If you know or reasonably should know that an unrepresented person doesn't fully understand who you are or what you're doing there, regardless of the reason for the potential misunderstanding you **must** make "reasonable efforts to correct [it]."
    c. If the unrepresented person's **interests** are or could be in **conflict** with your client's (that is, they're not fully aligned in all relevant respects), you **must not** give *any legal advice at all* to the unrepresented person except the advice to get a lawyer of her own. Aside from *advice*, you remain free to (**may**) answer factual questions, offer information, and even advocate for your client (so long as you tell the truth, and don't dress any of it up as advice to the unrepresented person).
    d. You **must not** "request a person other than a client" (or a relative, employee, or agent of a client) "to refrain from voluntarily giving relevant

information to another party" unless you actually and reasonably believe that the person won't suffer any problems as a result. *See* **this chapter's Introduction at 374**.

2. One situation that comes up so frequently that it has specific ethical rules attached to it in addition to the general principles of **Model Rule 4.3** is when counsel for an organization communicates with a **constituent** of the organization. Company counsel **must** remind the company **constituents** with whom they are dealing that they represent only the company, not the individual **constituent**, any time that company counsel knows that the company's **interests** are "adverse" to the **constituent's**. *See* **Model Rule 1.13(a), (f)**; **Chapter 12.A at 380**.

3. There's a distinction that is typically drawn between "giv[ing] legal advice" to an unrepresented person (which **Model Rule 4.3** forbids) and making a *statement of fact* or stating a *negotiating position* to an unrepresented person (which the Rules do not forbid). The complication is that the difference between these two often comes down to subtle differences in context or word choice. *See* **Chapter 12.A at 381**.

4. You are generally not allowed to request that someone refrain from voluntary cooperation in providing information to another party. Even when you are allowed to do so because that someone is your client or your client's relative, employee, or agent, **Model Rule 3.4(f)(2)** says you **must not** do so unless you "reasonably believe[] that the person's **interests** will not be adversely affected" by complying with the request. *See* **Chapter 12.A at 384**.

5. The **consequence** for violating **Model Rule 4.3** (or **Model Rule 3.4(f)**) is professional discipline. But these Rules also state the standards for various civil remedies, which can include **disqualification**, evidentiary sanctions, and monetary sanctions. Also available is the common-law remedy of rescission of any agreement into which the unrepresented person was unfairly induced to enter. And **Fed. R. Civ. P. 60(b)** and similar state laws are available to provide relief for judgments or orders obtained by a lawyer's unfair influence over an unrepresented person. *See* **Chapter 12.B at 385**.

Multiple-Choice Review Questions for Chapter 12

1. Andrew represents Balthazar, a pedestrian who was injured when a piano fell out of a third-story window. Balthazar wants to sue the moving company that was transporting the piano at the time that it fell.

    Before filing a complaint, Andrew interviews Balthazar to learn what happened. Balthazar says that he was walking down the sidewalk, minding his own business, when a piano fell on him, crushing his leg.

Andrew learns that there is an eyewitness to the accident named Cammie. Cammie was another pedestrian walking on the sidewalk that day. After the piano fell, Cammie rushed to help Balthazar. She gave Balthazar her name and contact information, which he retained.

Andrew calls Cammie to learn her version of events prior to filing the complaint. When she asks whether Andrew represents Balthazar or the moving company, he says "I just want to know what happened." Andrew asks "Do you have a lawyer?," and Cammie says "No." Andrew then interviews her about what she saw on the day of the accident.

Has Andrew violated his obligations when dealing with an unrepresented person?

a. Yes. He stated that he was disinterested.

b. Yes. He implied that he was disinterested.

c. No. He is disinterested because no complaint has yet been filed.

d. No. A lawyer may discuss any subject with an unrepresented person.

2. Darla is a criminal defense attorney handling an assault case. Darla's client Fay is accused of assaulting George during a bar fight. Fay and her friend Evie admit that they were in the bar when the fight broke out. Many people were involved in the scuffle. Fay claims that it was Evie who hit George and that she is innocent of the charges.

Darla interviews Evie, who is not represented by counsel. Darla begins the interview by explaining that she represents Fay.

During the interview, Evie expresses discomfort at having to testify at trial. She explains that she saw Fay hit George. Evie says, "I hate to testify against my friend. I just want to stay out of the case entirely." Darla explains that the defense does not intend to call Evie to testify but that the prosecution might do so.

Evie asks, "Can the prosecution force me to testify?" Darla explains that the prosecution can subpoena her to testify unless Evie is unavailable. Darla then explains that Evie would be deemed unavailable if she is out of town when the trial occurs. Darla also explains to Evie, "If you do decide to testify and the prosecution believes that you're lying, you could go to prison for perjury." Although it is true that such a penalty can flow from perjury, Darla knows that it is extremely unlikely that Evie would be prosecuted under these circumstances. Darla simply hopes to scare Evie away from testifying.

Has Darla violated her obligations when dealing with an unrepresented person?

a. Yes, but only because she gave Evie legal advice that was misleading.

b. Yes, because she should not have given Evie any legal advice.

    c. No, because her advice was technically correct even if it discouraged Evie from testifying.

    d. No, because she did not claim to be disinterested.

3. Horatio is suing his employer BigBox Co., claiming that he was fired because of his religion. Horatio's brother, Ignacio, also works for BigBox Co. Ignacio is not represented by counsel.

    Horatio's lawyer instructs Ignacio not to speak with counsel for BigBox Co. unless Ignacio receives a subpoena.

    Is this instruction proper?

    a. Yes. Ignacio is Horatio's brother, and a lawyer may instruct any family member of his client not to speak with opposing counsel.

    b. Maybe. It depends on whether Horatio is likely to suffer any adverse consequences from Ignacio's refusal to speak with BigBox Co.'s counsel.

    c. Maybe. It depends on whether Ignacio is likely to suffer any adverse consequences from refusing to speak with BigBox Co.'s counsel.

    d. No. It does not matter whether Ignacio is Horatio's brother. A lawyer may never instruct an unrepresented person to refrain from speaking with opposing counsel.

4. Assistant United States Attorney Marvin represents a government-owned hospital that has been sued by a patient. The patient asserted a medical malpractice claim against the hospital after the patient learned that a sponge was left in his abdominal cavity after an emergency appendectomy.

    As part of this representation, Marvin meets with Norris, one of the surgeons who works for the hospital. Norris seems relieved to meet with Marvin. Norris explains, "I know that hospital policy required me to double-check for any sponges before closing an incision, but I was in a hurry to get to my tee time, so I decided not to bother." Martin realizes that Norris could be fired for this conduct and, moreover, that the hospital may assert a cross-claim against him in the malpractice case.

    What should Marvin do, if he has not already done so?

    a. Explain that he represents only the hospital.

    b. Explain that he represents only Norris.

    c. Explain that he represents both the hospital and Norris.

    d. Explain that he currently represents the hospital but will also represent Norris if a cross-claim is filed.

5. Lawyer Lincoln represents the plaintiff in a slip-and-fall case asserted against a property owner. Lincoln is still determining whether the adjacent property owner should be joined as a co-defendant.

Lincoln is speaking with the adjacent property owner, Olivia, who is unrepresented. He has made it clear that he represents the plaintiff in the case. Olivia asks, "Has a complaint been filed?" and "What possible defenses could I raise?"

What may Lincoln say in response?

a. Nothing.

b. He may state that a complaint has been filed.

c. He may advise Olivia to seek the advice of counsel.

d. Both b and c.

6. Lawyer Shruti represents WorstBuy, a company that sells consumer electronics. WorstBuy is being sued by an employee, Ralph, who claims he was sexually harassed at work.

Shruti meets with Tom, Ralph's supervisor. She does not explain that she represents WorstBuy. During the meeting, Tom several times refers to Shruti as "my attorney." She does not correct him.

Tom admits to all of the conduct that Ralph has alleged.

After the meeting, Shruti turns her interview notes over to WorstBuy's Chief Executive Officer. Tom is fired.

The case proceeds to trial, and Tom is expected to testify for the plaintiff.

What consequences might Shruti face?

a. Professional discipline.

b. **Disqualification**.

c. Both a and b.

d. Neither a nor b.

13

Involvement in a Client's Wrongdoing: Advising, Assisting, Condoning, Aiding and Abetting, Conspiring

FRANK HAS JOINED his firm's family law partner, Sally Splitsville, for a meeting with an existing client, Narley Natrimony. Narley is in the midst of a divorce that is exceptionally bitter, even by the nuclear-winter standards of matrimonial practice, and recently things have gotten even worse. The court initially ordered an interim shared-custody arrangement in which Narley's ex-wife had custody of the couple's two primary-school-age children during the school week. Narley saw the children on the weekends, and he was given extra time with them during school holidays. Now, as the second week of winter vacation comes to a close, Narley has become convinced that his ex-wife has been physically abusing their children. He has made a doctor's appointment for them on Monday morning (the first day of school in January) to see if he can get a medical opinion confirming his fears regarding some bruises that he's noticed during the past week while the children have been with him.

Narley shared his concerns with Sally soon after his kids began their visit on Christmas Day, and at Narley's request, Sally made an emergency application to the court to change the interim custody arrangement. The court, mindful of the hyperbolic accusations that these spouses have exchanged in the course of the case, denied the application but set an evidentiary hearing for the first week in January, at which time the issue will be considered more fully. In the meantime, the court ordered the children returned to their mother on the coming Sunday evening.

Narley is distraught. "She's hurting them," he whispers, struggling to maintain control. "If I return them on Sunday, I can't take them to the doctor on Monday. And I'd be shoving them back into the hornets' nest. I can't do that. What do I do?" "Well," Sally tries, gently, "the full hearing is set for Thursday. Can't you leave them with her for a few days until then?" "Not safe, not safe," Narley says, shaking his head. "I can't." "But . . . ," Sally begins again. "No," says Narley, decisively. "I can't."

"Okay," says Sally, slowly. "If you can't, you can't. Why don't you just hold onto the kids until the hearing Thursday, and we'll see what the judge does then. Let your ex know where the kids are so that she doesn't get too worried. And we'll see what kind of evidence your doctor can provide."

Narley, deeply relieved, volubly thanks Sally and Frank and goes home. But Frank is not entirely comfortable. "Um," he says to Sally, with whom he works only occasionally, "I'm really sorry if this is a dumb question, but didn't the judge order Narley to return the kids to their mom just a few days ago in denying our emergency application?" "Yes, he did," Sally replies, "and we're definitely going to have some explaining to do on Thursday. But desperate times require desperate measures, as the saying goes."

"Look, I'm sorry if I'm not getting it, but *are* these desperate times?" Frank asks. "We don't know how well-justified Narley's suspicions are. I read the file last night, and he has accused his ex of some other stuff that I'm sure he believed at the time, but that didn't prove out. And it looks like she's done the same thing to him." Sally shrugs. "You're right; we can't be sure. But he does have a real basis to be worried, and we can all agree that he *could* be right." Frank nods. "And besides, you saw him," Sally continues. "He was never going to return those kids on Sunday. When in doubt, support the client, right?"

Frank remains disquieted. Is Sally right? Have the lawyers handled this situation appropriately?

A. The Ethical Prohibition on Advising or Assisting a Client to Engage in Illegal Conduct

Not infrequently, clients come to us having already violated (or having been accused of having violated) the law. Under those circumstances, it's our job to keep their **confidences** and defend them as best we can within the limits of the law and fidelity to the facts regarding their past acts. But that's not what this chapter is about. This chapter is about what we **must**, **must not**, and **should** do about what our clients *intend* to do—or what we suspect that they *may* intend to do—in the *future*. We can break these concerns out into four related scenarios:

1. **May** we ever counsel or assist a client to break the law?
2. A client proposes something unlawful. How **must** or **should** we respond?
3. A client insists on or persists in doing something unlawful without telling us, or despite our advice not to, and we find out about it. What now?
4. We develop concerns that a client *may* be doing or planning something unlawful. How **must** or **should** we respond?

In yet another of those mind-blowing coincidences that you've come to expect from us, this chapter discusses these very challenges, and then turns its attention to some nondisciplinary **consequences** of lawyers' involvement in client wrongdoing.

1. May We Ever Counsel or Assist a Client to Break the Law?

The answer to this first question is easy: virtually never. Let's tie that answer to the Rules of Professional Conduct. Any discussion of the constraints on lawyers' involvement in their clients' wrongdoing necessarily begins with the first clause of **Model Rule 1.2(d)**. We'll provide it for you right here. It's mercifully short:

> A lawyer shall not counsel a client to engage, or assist a client, in conduct that the lawyer knows is criminal or fraudulent. . . .

We hope that this Rule was a "duh" moment for you—*of course* we can't counsel or assist our clients to commit crimes or frauds. What kind of a system would this be if we were allowed to coach our clients on how to break the law?

TAMING THE TEXT So that much is easy. But let's focus on the precise terms of **Model Rule 1.2(d)**'s prohibition for a moment so that we understand its scope. The Rule says that you **must not** "counsel" or "assist" a client to engage in unlawful conduct. In other words, counseling and assisting are the forbidden acts, and they must involve a client to violate this Rule. The Rule also says that what you **must not** counsel or assist in is "conduct that [you] know[] is criminal or fraudulent." So apparently torts other than fraud that are also not crimes aren't included within the scope of this Rule. But we're just exploring the limits of this particular Rule. If you counsel or assist a *non*-client in illegal conduct, or break the law yourself, you won't violate **Model Rule 1.2(d)**, but you'll almost certainly violate other Rules of Professional Conduct, and likely you'll also commit crimes or torts for which you will be personally responsible. *See, e.g.,* **Model Rule 8.4(a)-(d)**; **Model Rule 4.1**; **Chapter 3.D at 64**; **Chapter 13.B at 401**. Similarly, you probably won't violate **Model Rule 1.2(d)** if you counsel or assist someone to commit a noncriminal tort other than fraud, but you will likely be vicariously liable for the tort. *See* **Chapter 13.B at 403**.

Model Rule 1.2(d) is also limited to client conduct that the lawyer "knows" is criminal or fraudulent. **Model Rule 1.0(f)** confirms that "knowledge" means "actual knowledge," but also reminds us that such knowledge "may be inferred from circumstances." This qualification, common in many areas of the law, is important because it frees factfinders to infer what you knew from the surrounding circumstances of which you were aware. One common corollary is the "willful blindness" or "conscious avoidance" doctrine, which allows a factfinder to infer actual knowledge of something from the fact that the person whose knowledge is in question (here that's you, the lawyer) failed to take steps to learn things that the person consciously suspected were true and that would have been discovered with reasonable effort. *See* **Chapter 11.C at 353 n.6.** ⟨ TAMING THE TEXT ⟩

There's also one small exception: **Model Rule 1.2 Comment [12]** observes that a lawyer's advice about how and when to test the validity or interpretation of a statute or regulation by disobeying it may be the proper subject of legal advice. That's true as far as it goes, but it doesn't go very far, and it also cautions great care in determining and advising *when* such tactics are in the client's best interests. The validity of some legal directives—for example, court orders—may almost never be tested by disobeying them. Disobeying a court order is contempt of court, pure and simple, and it is not a defense to the contempt that the order (or the statute or regulation on which it was based) is invalid, unless (and this situation almost never happens) there's *no* colorable legal basis of any kind for the order. In other words, if you violate a court order, the court *can't* consider a defense that the order or the law on which it was based is unconstitutional or otherwise invalid, even if it is.[1]

> **Problem 13A-1:** Maya provides *pro bono* assistance to PeaceOut, an organization that promotes civil rights in her community. She formed PeaceOut as a tax-exempt nonprofit corporation and attends its board meetings to supply the board with organizational and other advice. Recently, the local police shot and killed a young Black man. There are pointedly differing reports of the events leading to the shooting, and tempers are running high. At a regularly scheduled board meeting held soon after the shooting, the PeaceOut board and many of its members decide to conduct a protest of the shooting in which members will splash themselves in blood-colored paint and lie down in several of the busiest intersections downtown at the time of day when the young man was killed (5:30 p.m., during rush hour). They're calling the demonstration a "die-in." Maya (who is, you remember, a business lawyer with no criminal law experience) explains rather nervously that the interference with car and pedestrian traffic will likely be a violation of state and local law and will almost certainly get them arrested for trespass and similar crimes. The chair of the board responds, "If that's trouble, then it's good trouble!" to vocal assent and thunderous applause.[2] What **must** or **should** Maya do now?

2. A Client Proposes Something Unlawful. How Must or Should We Respond?

Having just confirmed that we can't "counsel" or "assist" a client to break the law, a practical question presents itself: What do you do if the client proposes

---

[1] *See Walker v. City of Birmingham,* 308 U.S. 307 (1967). We don't attempt to explore here the complex and difficult topic of when violating a law is necessary or advisable as a basis for a good-faith challenge to its validity or interpretation. Instead, we offer the more modest suggestion that whether and when a lawyer's advice suggesting such disobedience is legally and ethically proper requires not only careful investigation of the governing law and relevant facts, but an equally careful exploration with the client of the violation's potential **consequences** for the client.

[2] *See* Rashawn Ray, *Five Things John Lewis Taught Us About Getting in "Good Trouble,"* https://www.brookings.edu/blog/how-we-rise/2020/07/23/five-things-john-lewis-taught-us-about-getting-in-good-trouble/ (July 23, 2020).

doing something unlawful? We already know from the first clause in **Model Rule 1.2(d)** that we **must not** respond with the equivalent of "sure, go ahead" (or worse, "sure, but if you do x, y, and z, you're a lot less likely to get caught"). But what **may** and what **should** we do? The part of **Model Rule 1.2(d)** that we haven't talked about yet provides some helpful guidance:

> [A] lawyer **may** discuss the legal consequences of any proposed course of conduct with a client and **may** counsel or assist a client to make a good faith effort to determine the validity, scope, meaning or application of the law.

See also **Model Rule 2.1** (from the chapter of the Rules on the lawyer as advisor: "In rendering advice, a lawyer **may** refer not only to law but to other considerations such as moral, economic, social and political factors, that may be relevant to the client's situation").

REAL WORLD The Model Rules just quoted, both of which are, importantly, "**may**" rules elaborating your options, reflect an essential reality about lawyering: Most clients—even highly legally sophisticated ones, but especially ones with less familiarity with the legal system—often lack clarity on just what is proper or permissible. They often don't know the law, and even if they do, they may wonder whether people "really" comply with it. That's one reason that they've consulted a lawyer in the first place. So it's neither unusual nor surprising to have clients ask about, or express a preference for, a course of action that is, whether subtly or blatantly, unlawful. It's an important show of trust on most clients' parts to raise possibilities with you that they may have an uncomfortable sense may not be okay. The way in which you respond will affect the openness of the client's communications with you in the future. Often, all you have to do is to explain respectfully that the course of action under discussion is unlawful (or is just a bad idea as a practical matter), playing out the possible **consequences** of pursuing it. Based on your discussion, nine times out of ten your client will agree that it's not the way to go.

Realistically, though, it can be hard to say no, whether gently or forcefully, to someone whose continuing allegiance contributes to our livelihood. Nevertheless, sometimes that's our job. Take a moment and think about what it might be like to experience a common dilemma of professional practice: We depend on our clients to make a living; our clients can discharge us at any time for any reason, so keeping them satisfied is essential to our livelihoods; and a basic and non-negotiable part of our job sometimes is to tell clients that they can't do something that they would like to do (or that we can't do something that they'd like us to do for them). As the Comments counsel, "[i]n presenting advice, a lawyer endeavors to sustain the client's morale and may put advice in as acceptable a form as honesty permits. However, a lawyer should not be deterred from giving candid advice by the prospect that the advice will be unpalatable to the client." **Model Rule 2.1**

Comment [1]. Yes, keeping clients happy and making them feel supported, especially in difficult circumstances, is an important part of good client service, but you must never do that at the expense of making yourself complicit in a client's wrongful conduct. It never ends well. The client will pay for it in hard **consequences**, and so will you. Personally. REAL WORLD

> Problem 13A-2: Go back and review the problem that begins the **Introduction to this chapter at 391**.
>
> a. Did the partner handle the situation properly? Why or why not? If not, can you identify the specific point in the conversation at which the partner departed from the right way to do things? If so, identify what she **must not** or **should not** have said, and why.
>
> b. Suppose the hypothetical in the **chapter Introduction at 391** had facts that indicated that Narley's concerns about his ex-wife's abuse of their children were more than suspicions and instead would make a reasonable person confident that the abuse was actually occurring. Does your answer to (a) change? If so, why and how; and if not, why not?
>
> c. If you've identified things that the partner **must not** or **should not** have said, describe what you would have said instead. Please be very specific about the words and the tone that you would have used.

3. A Client Insists on or Persists in Doing Something Unlawful Without Telling Us, or Despite Our Advice Not To. What Now?

Although clients often take our advice, especially when that advice is to avoid a course of action that is illegal, they don't always do so. And sometimes they refrain from asking because they don't want to be discouraged from unlawful conduct that they've already decided to pursue. What **must** or **should** we do if we discover that clients are acting unlawfully without having consulted us in advance, or are doing so despite having told us that they wouldn't, or that they would stop?

These are difficult circumstances, but they do happen from time to time. **Model Rule 1.2(d)** says that you **must not** "counsel" or "assist" illegal conduct. **May** you remain silent in the face of knowledge that the client is breaking the law? After all, you could argue, saying nothing isn't really "counsel[ing]" or "assist[ing]." This is another one of those arguments that's too clever by half: If mom watches you jumping on the bed and says nothing, you're likely to assume that it's OK—right up to the point when you smash your face on the headboard. Thus, the Comments suggest that you may have a duty to say something to your client when you see your client doing something that your client **must not** be doing. Remember that **Model Rule 1.4(b)**, codifying your **duty of candor**, requires you to explain things relevant to your engagement to the extent reasonably necessary to allow your client to make informed decisions. It's not hard to infer that one of those required communications would be: "You know, you could go to prison or incur ruinous money damages for that." *See* **Model Rule 2.1 Comment [5]** ("when a lawyer knows that a client proposes a course of action that is likely to result in substantial adverse legal consequences to the client, the lawyer's duty to the client under Rule 1.4 may require that the lawyer offer advice if the client's course of action is related to the representation").

Now, what happens if your client refuses to take your advice to refrain from unlawful conduct? As you might imagine, this situation is even more awkward and complicated. Let's start with the easier scenario, the one in which your services are not being and will not be used in whatever unlawful conduct your client is planning or continuing. In that situation, you **may** (but are not required to) withdraw from the engagement (subject, as always, to the permission of any involved tribunal). Your choice will probably depend on whether you consider the client's intended conduct to be something with which you want no association. This is not always true: Lawyers sometimes choose to continue to represent clients planning civil disobedience or other, perhaps less admirable, behavior that's likely to get the clients into trouble. *See* **Model Rule 1.16(b)(4)**; **Model Rule 1.16 Comment [7]** (you **may** withdraw if "the client insists upon taking action that the lawyer considers repugnant or with which the lawyer has a fundamental disagreement"); **Problem 13A-1 at 394; Chapter 9.D at 297.**[3]

Things get even more awkward and complicated when clients have used or intend to use your services in the course of their unlawful conduct. Here again, you **may** (but are not required to) withdraw, subject to the permission of any involved tribunal. **Model Rule 1.16(b)(2)-(3)**; **Chapter 9.D at 298**. And if the client's use of your work in unlawful conduct involves you in the illegal acts, then you **must** withdraw. **Model Rule 1.16(a)(1)**; **Model Rule 1.2 Comment [10]**. But even if your withdrawal is discretionary, you are much more likely to *want* to withdraw under these circumstances than when your client is acting unlawfully without involving you or your services in the wrongdoing. That's because of the risk to you of having a client who wants to involve you and your work in unlawful conduct, and because of the inherent untrustworthiness of a client who behaves in this fashion. If you decide to withdraw (which you likely **should**), then you also must decide whether the withdrawal **should** be "noisy"; that is, with notice to those who may have relied on your work as part of the client's malfeasance, giving due regard to your **confidentiality** obligations to your client and any exceptions to them that may apply. These issues are discussed in detail in **Chapter 9.D at 298**.

---

[3] Let's be clear that the situations we are discussing are ones in which the person engaging in or planning unlawful conduct is the *client*. In those cases, you have the options sketched out by the **"may"** rules discussed in the text. In any situation in which continuing "the representation will result in violation of the rules of professional conduct or other law" by *you* (the lawyer), you **must** withdraw immediately (subject to the permission of any involved tribunal), something you're almost certain to want to do anyway. **Model Rule 1.16(a)(1)**; **Model Rule 1.16 Comment [2]**; **Chapter 9.D at 295**.

Problem 13A-3: Maya works with a firm client, Living Loans, whose business model is to raise funds, mostly through small investments by working people in the Latinx community in the area. Living Loans uses the invested funds to make home and small-business loans to people in the same community, many of whom have been unable to get credit from conventional banks. The interest on the loans provides a return to the investors. For the last several years, the model has worked well to support a financially underserved population in Maya's area. Living Loans and its principal, Lorenzo Lones, have been lionized in the local press as outstanding examples of community-based financing.

Lately, however, the economy has been weakening, unemployment is rising, and Lorenzo just called Maya to report that the company is not going to be able to make its scheduled quarterly distribution to investors next month because so many of Living Loans's borrowers are not making their loan payments. He tells Maya that his plan is to go out and raise additional funds from existing and new investors so that he can make the quarterly payment to investors and give the economy a chance to improve. "You can't do that," Maya responds, with some concern. "The documents that you use to solicit investments are based on the financial performance of Living Loans before this recession, and they're no longer accurate. Using that information to raise new money would be a violation of federal and state securities laws and other laws, too. Those are felonies; you could go to prison. This is really serious."

"Look," says Lorenzo, "if I raise the money, we stay in business, we can carry the nonpaying borrowers for a while without putting them out on the street or out of business, the investors get paid, and we stay alive to wait out the recession. If I don't, then the whole thing falls apart: The borrowers get foreclosed on and lose their homes and businesses, and the investors lose their savings, all during a recession when a lot of folks in our community are already out of work. I'm just looking for a bridge to carry us over until next year, when things will be better and we can resume normal operations. I have to do this, or else everyone loses—everyone. I already did it once to pay the investors last quarter. How much is one more time gonna hurt?" What **must** or **should** Maya say or do now? (And if you're struggling with Lorenzo's reasoning, go back and look at the discussion in **Chapter 4.A at 80** of the cognitive errors to which most human beings are subject. This is a good example.)

4. We Develop Concerns That a Client *May* Be Doing or Planning Something Unlawful. How Must or Should We Respond?

In the preceding sections, we've been talking about situations in which you *know* that your client is doing or planning something unlawful—the client, or someone or something else, has brought the relevant facts to your attention, and you're in no real doubt. Sometimes, however, things just aren't that clear: We don't *know* what the client is actually planning or doing, but we have concerns. And concerns come in every degree of intensity, from whispers of suspicion to clanging alarm bells. Maybe the circumstances surrounding the engagement strike you as sketchy. Maybe you notice potential patterns in an individual client's spending habits, or a client company's finances or claims history, that raise questions in your mind. Maybe a routine inquiry in the course of the engagement goes repeatedly unanswered or is answered implausibly. Maybe a self-styled whistleblower (perhaps someone with an axe to grind, such as someone who was recently fired) offers you allegations of improprieties. You don't *know* that something improper is going on, but you're starting to wonder, and maybe you're outright worried. What **must** or **should** you do?

These are challenging circumstances, and it's difficult to generalize about how to handle them. These difficulties are complicated by the fact that the limited authority available is impossible to reconcile. Let's start with the Rules and Comments themselves: **Model Rule 2.1 Comment [5]** advises that "[a] lawyer ordinarily has no duty to initiate investigation of a client's affairs or to give advice that the client has indicated is unwanted, but a lawyer **may** initiate advice to a client when doing so appears to be in the client's interest." So if you "ordinarily" have no duty to initiate investigation but "**may**" initiate unrequested advice, does that mean that you equally **may** remain silent, regardless of the potential **consequences** to the client or those with whom the client is dealing? Perhaps not: **Model Rule 1.2 Comment [13]** advises, apparently inconsistently, that because of the **duty of candor** codified in **Model Rule 1.4(a)(5)**, "If a lawyer comes to know or reasonably should know that a client expects assistance not permitted by the Rules of Professional Conduct or other law or if the lawyer intends to act contrary to the client's instructions, the lawyer **must** consult with the client regarding the limitations on the lawyer's conduct"—those "limitations" being your inability to be party to any illegal activity the client might be planning (*see* **Model Rule 1.16(a)(1)**). But where does the Comment derive a negligence standard ("reasonably should know") when **Model Rule 1.2(d)** requires actual knowledge ("conduct the lawyer knows is criminal or fraudulent")?

YOUR HOUSE; YOUR RULES ▸ To make things worse, if you laid the various state disciplinary decisions and bar ethics opinions on this question end to end, they'd all point in different directions. (That's a joke people sometimes make about economists, but it seemed apt here. We take our material wherever we can find it; don't judge.) Some of these authorities take **Model Rule 1.2(d)** literally and hold that there is no disciplinary liability unless the lawyer *actually knows* that the client intends to act unlawfully.[4] Others take **Model Rule 1.2 Comment [13]** literally and hold that lawyers **must** inquire further if they *reasonably should know* of a client's unlawful intentions, even if they lack all conscious suspicion.[5] And yet others take a middle path and, relying on the "willful blindness" or "conscious avoidance" doctrine

---

[4] *See, e.g., In re Tocco*, 984 P.2d 539, 543 (Ariz. 1999). This appears to be the *Restatement* view as well. RESTATEMENT (THIRD) OF THE LAW GOVERNING LAWYERS § 94(2) & cmt. g.

[5] *See, e.g., In re Dobson*, 427 S.E. 2d 166 (S.C. 1993) (but also stating that the lawyer "deliberately evaded knowledge" of the client's fraudulent scheme).

(*see* **Chapter 11.C at 353 n.6**) as a means of inferring (or simply as a substitute for) actual knowledge, hold that if you are consciously aware of a substantial probability that your client is up to no good, you **must** inquire, and you are subject to discipline if a reasonable inquiry would have yielded knowledge of the client's intentions.[6] Your House; Your Rules

Although your licensing jurisdiction is going to supply the disciplinary standard for your activities, an ABA Formal Ethics Opinion provides useful guidance on the kinds of facts that can raise an inference of the lawyer's complicity in the client's wrong.[7] Limiting itself to non-litigation contexts, the opinion examines **Model Rule 1.2(d)** and a range of other Rules to reason that

> [t]he kinds of facts and circumstances that would trigger a duty to inquire under these rules include, for example, (i) the identity of the client, (ii) the lawyer's familiarity with the client, (iii) the nature of the matter (particularly whether such matters are frequently associated with criminal or fraudulent activity), (iv) the relevant jurisdictions (especially whether any jurisdiction is classified as high risk by credible sources), (v) the likelihood and gravity of harm associated with the proposed activity, (vi) the nature and depth of the lawyer's expertise in the relevant field of practice, (vii) other facts going to the reasonableness of reposing trust in the client, and (viii) any other factors traditionally associated with providing competent representation in the field.[8]

Real World Given the uncertainty about the disciplinary standard and its application, how **should** you proceed when you feel some concern about whether your client is operating on the level? The practical answer is that you **should** virtually always ask about it. After all, you don't want to be associated with your client's crime or fraud, if that's where the client is headed. The more blindly you stay involved, the more likely it is that you will be blindsided by any crimes or torts that may be brewing, the less opportunity you'll have to intervene, and the more

---

[6] *See, e.g.*, N.Y. City Bar Assn. Formal Op. No. 2018-4 (2018) (a lawyer **must** inquire "where a *reasonable* lawyer prompted by *serious doubts* would have refrained from providing assistance or would have investigated to allay suspicions before rendering or continuing to render legal assistance" (emphasis added)).

[7] ABA Formal Ethics Op. No. 491 (2020). The opinion chooses the middle standard described above, arguing that a lawyer with knowledge of facts that create a "high probability" that a client is seeking the lawyer's services to further criminal or fraudulent activity **must** inquire further, with failure to do so amounting to conscious avoidance of what the inquiry would have revealed (*id.* at 2), but acknowledges wide interjurisdictional variation (*id.* at 3-6). For a thoughtful critique of the 2020 opinion's analysis (though not necessarily questioning the wisdom of its policy), *see* Peter A. Joy & Kevin C. McMunigal, *A Lawyer's Obligation to Avoid Assisting in a Crime or Fraud*, 35 ABA Criminal Justice 74 (2020).

[8] ABA Formal Ethics Op. No. 491 (2020) at 7 (footnote omitted). The ABA may have been motivated to address this issue by the federal government's increasing attention to money-laundering and other misuses of the domestic and international banking system to facilitate terrorism and other criminal enterprises. These issues, which are beyond the scope of this course, are a growing preoccupation in financial-services-related legal practice. *See* ABA Task Force on Gatekeeper Regulation and the Profession, Voluntary Good Practices Guidance for Lawyers to Detect and Combat Money Laundering and Terrorist Financing (2010). Although the opinion does not explain why, we'd guess its focus on transactional work is meant to compensate for the relative lack of attention to that context before now. As we'll see in **Chapter 24 at 813**, there already exists an array of disciplinary and civil standards for different kinds of lawyer misconduct in litigation.

likely that the client's eventual victims will argue, after the fact, that you were complicit (or willfully blind) and thus personally responsible. And where enough information is in front of you to raise real questions about what might be going on, what might seem like the expedient approach in the short term (why insult the client by questioning his motives; why not let sleeping dogs lie; why come to know something that you don't know now; you know—the usual refuges of the timid) may leave you with no better explanation to state bar prosecutors than that you did nothing because you were too dumb or distracted to wonder what was really going on. That's rarely a good look for a sophisticated, educated professional like you.

Frequently, this inquiry will require no more than a simple conversation with your client (or with your customary client contact at an organizational client), who will usually be able to dispel your concerns. In other words, we're not necessarily talking about full-blown investigations with witness interviews and document examination under these circumstances. In a situation in which your client has generally proved trustworthy and a proffered explanation is plausible, a reasonable lawyer likely would no longer have doubts that would require further inquiry. But if your client refuses to answer a simple question, acts insulted or angry that you asked, or provides an answer that doesn't make sense to you, your concerns may be unfurling into a real red flag. At that point, digging deeper, and if necessary refusing to proceed (or withdrawing) unless your concerns are addressed, may well be the right thing to do. *See* ABA Formal Ethics Op. No. 491 (2020) at 9-11. REAL WORLD

> **Problem 13A-4:** Maya is working with a closely held corporation that owns and operates several hardware stores. The corporation is owned by members of an extended family. Some of the relatives work in the company; others don't. By agreement, all shareholders get detailed financial reports quarterly so that everyone can see how the business is doing. Maya works with the president of the company (one of the family shareholders) each quarter to prepare the financial reports. As Maya looks over the third-quarter financials, she notices a five-figure payment to College Preparatory Academy. It's one of a number of expenses that the president intends to fold into one item on the financial report designated "Miscellaneous Expenses." Maya can't imagine what a prep school would be supplying to this hardware company, but she's aware that the president has two high-school-age children. What **must** or **should** Maya do about this puzzling fact, and why?

B. CONSEQUENCES Nondisciplinary Consequences of Involvement in a Client's Wrongdoing

The duties that we've been discussing up to this point in the chapter are duties based on the Rules of Professional Conduct, and thus are enforceable by professional discipline. In appropriate circumstances, however, duties provided by other law can give rise to other **consequences.**

1. CONSEQUENCES Vicarious Criminal Liability

Needless to say, you're personally responsible for any crimes that you yourself commit, whether or not you're acting as a lawyer. But what about when your client commits a crime while using your work or advice in the process? Generally applicable principles of vicarious criminal liability apply to lawyers as well as to nonprofessional participants involved in criminal activity:

- Aiding and abetting: Aiding and abetting is an independent basis for criminal liability and generally requires (1) specific intent to facilitate someone else's commission of a crime; (2) assisting or participating in the underlying crime; and (3) the commission of the underlying crime by the person aided or abetted.[9]
- Conspiracy: Conspiracy is also an independent basis for criminal liability and generally requires (1) agreement with one or more other people that one or more of them will commit a crime, or agreement to assist in the planning or commission of a crime; and (2) commission of an overt act in furtherance of the conspiracy by any conspirator.[10]

In other words, under long-standing and generally applicable principles of the criminal law, you don't have to commit the crime yourself in order to go to prison for it. All you have to do is to know what your client is doing (or willfully blind yourself to it) and do things that help the client carry it out, or agree with the client's course of action followed by anyone taking a step to put the plan into action.

Problem 13B-1: Danielle has been assigned a welfare fraud case. About a dozen local residents consulted lawyer "Swifty" Smith about their eligibility for government benefits. Swifty advised each of them that they were eligible for the benefits, and he filled out the application form for each of them to sign and submit. The facts stated on the applications are all the same, and they don't describe the actual circumstances of any of the applicants, each of whom, for various reasons, is not benefits-eligible. As is the case with some kinds of government benefits, Swifty's fee was set by statute and paid out of the benefits that the clients were awarded. It is a crime in Danielle's state to submit a government benefits application with a knowingly false factual representation. May Swifty be prosecuted for welfare fraud? Does it matter whether or not the applicant-clients understood what was on the benefits applications that they submitted?

Problem 13B-2: Danielle is assisting in the investigation of an alleged financial fraud. A small, state-chartered bank was offering above-competitive rates on certificates of deposit (bank savings accounts that the customers agree to leave on deposit for fixed periods of time),

---

[9] See, e.g., **18 U.S.C. § 2**; *United States v. Griffin*, 84 F.3d 912, 928 (7th Cir.), *cert. denied sub nom. Scurlock v. United States*, 519 U.S. 1020 (1996).

[10] See, e.g., MODEL PENAL CODE § 5.03 (2007).

and attracting large amounts of deposits because of the superior rate. In fact, the CDs were a Ponzi scheme in which the bank's president used new depositors' money to pay the interest on older deposits and bought fancy cars, houses, and vacations for himself with much of the rest. A local lawyer and personal friend of the president, Coster "Co" Opted, represented the bank during this period. Co was aware of the bank president's personal expenditures, and he even accompanied the president on a high-flying trip to Monte Carlo and the Cannes Film Festival at the president's expense, yet he prepared financial statements for the bank to present to its regulator and shareholders that reflected only a modest salary for the bank president. The lawyer was paid his ordinary hourly rate for the work that he did for the bank. Danielle is confident that she has the evidence to indict and convict the bank president on a variety of state-law financial crimes. Can she also prosecute the lawyer? Why or why not?

2. CONSEQUENCES Vicarious Civil Liability

Now we know that the principles of vicarious *criminal* liability are applied to lawyers the same way that they are to everyone else. What about *civil* liability? Specifically, when are lawyers vicariously liable to third parties for torts committed by their clients? Here, things get messy.

We start with the basic rules of vicarious liability in tort, as summarized in Section 863 of the *Restatement (Second) of Torts*:

> For harm resulting to a third person from the tortious conduct of another, one is subject to liability if he
>
> (a) does a tortious act in concert with the other or pursuant to a common design with him, or
>
> (b) knows that the other's conduct constitutes a breach of duty and gives substantial assistance or encouragement to the other so to conduct himself, or
>
> (c) gives substantial assistance to the other in accomplishing a tortious result and his own conduct, separately considered, constitutes a breach of duty to the third person.

This Restatement section may seem straightforward enough: If you advise your client to commit a tort against a third party knowing that the conduct that you're advising is in fact a tort, then you are jointly and severally liable with your client for any resulting damage to the tortfeasor's victim. If you've remonstrated with your client and advised her *not* to commit the tort and she does so anyway, you haven't given "substantial assistance or encouragement" to the client (just the opposite, in fact), so you're not personally vicariously liable. And in a situation in which the law is uncertain, you wouldn't "*know*" that the conduct under discussion constituted a breach of duty (emphasis added), and thus should not meet the standard for vicarious liability even if it turned out that the client's conduct was tortious.[11]

---

[11] Let's be clear that this discussion is about the rather unusual situation in which a *third party*—usually someone with whom your client is dealing—is claiming that you (the lawyer) are liable in tort *to the third party* because of what you helped or

Nevertheless, it's fundamental to a lawyer's role in our system to advise clients on potential courses of action whose legal treatment is uncertain. And if the legal status of the conduct is unclear, then you may find yourself forced to argue later about how much you "knew" about how risky the course of action was and how much you encouraged or assisted your client in carrying it out. Under these circumstances, all that a third party has to do in order to drag you (the lawyer) into the dispute between the third party and your client is to allege, under our procedural system's permissive pleading rules, that you knew that the course of conduct was tortious and advised the client to engage in it. Now you've become a defendant alongside your client, likely creating a **conflict of interest** between your-self and the client (basically because what you might want to argue about the law and the facts in order to exonerate yourself may not be the same as what your client would want you to argue; *see* **Model Rule 1.7(a)**; **Chapter 22.A at 603**), requiring you to withdraw, notify your insurance carrier, and probably hire a lawyer of your own, and requiring the client to get counsel other than you to handle the dispute. The **confidentiality** and **attorney-client privilege** of the lawyer-client communications forming the basis of the lawyer's alleged vicarious liability might be subject to inva-sion under exceptions applicable under the circumstances. And everyone has to scramble and incur significant extra expense. All of which creates a lot of leverage for the third party on the strength of some simple allegations in an initial pleading.

For this reason, a number of states have adopted a rule that imposes a common-law privilege (that is, an immunity from vicarious liability), or cuts off vicarious liability otherwise available under rules like *Restatement (Second)* Section 863, for advice and other services that a lawyer commonly provides within the scope of an attorney-client relationship, and that the accused lawyer in fact did provide in the course of such a relationship in that particular case.[12] Your House; Your Rules This is an area in which authority is sparse and what little authority there is varies widely in its terms and application. The existing authorities tend to articulate rules that are difficult to apply to actual cases. If a problem like this comes up, you will need to do some careful and thoughtful digging to figure out how the state in which you practice addresses this issue, and how any available law in your jurisdiction applies to the facts of your case.

Your House; Your Rules   Consequences

---

advised your client to do. Your duties *to your client* are different: In any situation in which a proposed course of action might be tortious (for example, because there is uncertainty about the interpretation or application of the law), your **duties of candor** and **care** to your *client* (*see* **Model Rule 1.4(b)**; **Chapter 5.D at 117**) will require you to explain the contours of the risk and uncertainty to the client so that your client can make an informed decision about how to proceed. If you fail to do so and the client chooses a course of conduct that is eventually determined to be unlawful *without* having been counseled that it might turn out that way, you may find yourself facing claims *by your client* for professional negligence or breach of fiduciary duty.

[12] *See, e.g., Reynolds v. Schrock*, 341 Or. 338 (2006), and cases cited; *Joel v. Weber*, 602 N.Y.S.2d 383 (1993); *see also Pacific Gas & Elec. Co. v. Bear Stearns & Co.*, 50 Cal. 3d 1118 (1990) (no liability for inducing breach of contract or similar torts for advice — by nonlawyers, but the principle is also applicable to lawyers — to a party to the contract to initiate potentially meritorious litigation about the terminability of a contract, but it "may be actionable to induce a party to a contract to terminate the contract according to its terms").

Problem 13B-3: Maya is assisting her firm's internal counsel in analyzing a claim that has been asserted against the firm. A partner in the corporate group represented the majority shareholder in a closely held corporation. In Maya's state, the majority shareholder of a corporation owes fiduciary duties to the minority shareholders, but the contours of that duty are not well-defined. The partner developed a strategy that made it easier for the majority shareholder to acquire a larger stake in the company relative to the minority. This strategy was arguably consistent with the majority shareholder's fiduciary duties under applicable law, but it also arguably violated those duties. The partner advised the majority-shareholder client fully about the doubts and risks, and the client decided that it was worth it to him to implement the strategy. Maya has concluded that the partner's analysis and advice to the client was complete and accurate. The minority shareholders have sued the majority share-holder for breach of fiduciary duty, and now the minority shareholders have amended their complaint to add the partner and Maya's firm, alleging that they are vicariously liable for the majority shareholder's wrongdoing. What are the lawyer-defendants' chances of success on a motion to dismiss for failure to state a claim under Maya's state's version of **Fed. R. Civ. P. 12(b)(6)**?

Problem 13B-4: Frank is working with the real estate partner in his office, Barney Blackacre. A client, Teri Tenant, hired Barney for some advice about Teri's office lease. Teri wanted to know under what circumstances she might be able to terminate her lease, and what the economics of that termination would be. Barney analyzed the termination clause in the lease and concluded that Teri had the right to terminate almost immediately under the terms of her lease. He also advised her to do so, because office rents in town have fallen since Teri entered into the lease, and she can get a much better deal on an office lease right now. Frank has reviewed this advice, and he has concluded that it's clearly correct. Nevertheless, Teri's landlord has now sued Barney and Frank's firm for intentional interference with contract and interference with potential economic advantage in a complaint alleging the facts set out in this problem. What are the chances of success on a motion to dismiss for failure to state a claim under Frank's state's version of **Fed. R. Civ. P. 12(b)(6)**?

Big-Picture Takeaways from Chapter 13

1. **Model Rule 1.2(d)** says that you **must not** "counsel" or "assist" a client to engage in "conduct that [you] know[] is criminal or fraudulent." **Model Rule 1.0(f)** confirms that "knowledge" means "actual knowledge," but it also reminds us that such knowledge "may be inferred from circumstances." These inferences include the "willful blindness" or "conscious avoidance" doctrine, which allows a factfinder to infer actual knowledge of something from the fact that the person whose knowledge is in question (here, that's you—the lawyer) failed to take steps to learn things that the person consciously suspected were true and would have been discovered with reasonable effort. *See* **Chapter 13.A at 392.**

2. There are very few circumstances under which you may properly counsel your client to break the law despite **Model Rule 1.2(d)**. **Model Rule 1.2 Comment [12]** observes that a lawyer's advice about how and when to test the validity or interpretation of a statute or regulation by disobeying it may be a proper subject of legal advice. But counseling a client to disobey a court order, even if you think the order is legally erroneous? Don't do it. *See* **Chapter 13.A at 394.**

3. If a client proposes something unlawful, you **must not** counsel or assist the client in the proposed unlawful conduct, but you **may** and **should** (and likely **must**) counsel the client as to the likely **consequences** of doing the unlawful thing (**Model Rule 1.2(d)** again), and you **may** and usually **should** give your client extra-legal advice about the advisability of, and the **consequences** for, what the client wants to do (**Model Rule 2.1**). A lawyer should not be deterred from giving candid advice by the prospect that the advice will be unpalatable to the client. Never keep a client "happy" by counseling the client that it's okay to do something unlawful at the expense of making yourself complicit in a client's wrongful conduct. It never ends well for the client or for you. *See* **Chapter 13.A at 394.**

4. If a client insists on or persists in doing something unlawful without telling you, or despite your advice not to do it, **may** you remain silent? Remaining silent doesn't absolve you of the application of **Model Rule 1.2(d)**. In fact, the Comments to the Rule suggest that you have a duty to (**must**) say something to your client when you see your client doing something that your client **must not** be doing. *See* **Chapter 13.A at 396.**
   a. When clients refuse to take your advice to refrain from unlawful conduct and are not using your services to do the unlawful thing, you **may** (but are not required to) withdraw from the engagement (subject, as always, to the permission of any involved tribunal) (**Model Rule 1.16(b)(4)**; **Model Rule 1.16 Comment [7]**). *See* **Chapter 13.A at 397.**
   b. When clients have used or intend to use your services in the course of their unlawful conduct, you **may** (but are not required to) withdraw, and probably **should**, subject to the permission of any involved tribunal (**Model Rule 1.16(b)(2)-(3)**)—but if the client's use of your work in unlawful conduct implicates you in the illegal acts, then you **must** withdraw (**Model Rule 1.16(a)(1)**; **Model Rule 1.2 Comment [10]**). Think, too, about whether you **must** or **should** withdraw "noisily" if you are in a situation in which you **must** or **may** withdraw. (Can't remember "noisy withdrawals"? **Chapter 9.D at 298** can help you here.) *See* **Chapter 13.A at 397.**

5. If you develop concerns that a client *may* be doing or planning something unlawful, but you don't *know* that the client is doing or planning to

do something unlawful, then you have to consider whether you **must** or **should** do something to explore the issue further. Disciplinary standards on whether or when to inquire about any concerns you have or reasonably should have vary widely from state to state. Whether or not there is an affirmative *duty* to investigate, you **should** investigate to confirm or allay your suspicions, and manage your own risks. *See* **Chapter 13.A at 398**.

6. In addition to professional discipline, there are some scary nondisciplinary **consequences** to burying your head in the sand, also known as "willful blindness" or "conscious avoidance," or worse, agreeing or assisting with a client's criminal or tortious activity. Those **consequences** can include vicarious criminal liability and vicarious civil liability as well. The standard for vicarious civil liability is uncertain and varies state to state. *See* **Chapter 13.B at 401**.

Multiple-Choice Review Questions for Chapter 13

1. Abbie was an Assistant United States Attorney but is now working at a law firm. One day, she receives a telephone call from Bethany, a long time client. Bethany is the chief financial officer for a large area hospital. Bethany asks if she can run an idea past Abbie. Abbie says, "Sure." Bethany describes installing a computer program at the hospital that will automatically review all billing records and inflate the bills by a modest amount—no more than 1 percent.

   Abbie knows that this conduct could be considered healthcare fraud, but she also knows that it is unlikely to raise any alarm bells so long as the increases are small. In fact, from her time at the Department of Justice, Abbie knows precisely the dollar threshold at which there is a risk of prosecution.

   Should Abbie advise Bethany of the specific threshold at which the hospital risks prosecution?

   a. Yes. A lawyer can discuss the legal consequences of any proposed course of conduct with a client. It would not be possible for Abbie to give Bethany complete legal advice without explaining to Bethany the benefits and the risks associated with the proposed conduct. If the hospital inflates the bills by only a small amount, the benefits may outweigh the risks.

   b. Yes. A lawyer may counsel or assist a client in making a good-faith effort to determine the validity, scope, meaning, or application of the law. Bethany may want to test the threshold at which the U.S. Attorney's Office prosecutes, and Abbie can assist her in doing so.

   c. No. Doing so may be recommending to Bethany a means by which the hospital may engage in healthcare fraud with impunity. Abbie should instead explain why this conduct constitutes fraud and counsel Bethany against the plan.

d. No. A lawyer may never present any analysis of questionable conduct. Doing so would only encourage Bethany to follow this course of conduct. Abbie must decline to give any advice, including advising Bethany that this conduct constitutes healthcare fraud.

2. Nicholas is an experienced methamphetamine manufacturer and dealer who employs numerous underlings who sell the meth on street corners throughout the city. Nicholas asks his lawyer, Oliver, to educate him about the potential sentences that he or his underlings might face if caught and convicted. Oliver is well aware of Nicholas's activities, though he has no involvement in them. Without endorsing or encouraging Nicholas, Oliver conducts the research and provides Nicholas with a detailed memorandum. Among other things, Oliver explains that, if someone is arrested with drugs in his possession, and that person is within five miles of a school, there are enhanced penalties. After receiving the memorandum, Nicholas instructs his underlings to move their "offices" so that they are slightly more than five miles away from all area schools. Through his underlings, Nicholas continues to deal drugs from these new locations.

   Was Oliver's legal advice proper?

   a. Yes. Oliver did not advise or assist Nicholas to do anything illegal. Oliver simply explained to Nicholas how Nicholas might minimize the negative consequences from his illegal action.

   b. Yes. Oliver's advice helped Nicholas avoid committing a worse crime, because Nicholas relocated his drug operations away from schools.

   c. No. Oliver knew that his advice would be used by Nicholas to escape liability for his criminal activity.

   d. No. Oliver knew Nicholas was less likely to be caught if he was farther from schools, so Oliver helped Nicholas evade detection for his crimes.

3. Chun represents a contracting company, Bolts Inc. Bolts Inc. typically does private work but recently landed a sizeable contract to work on a federal office building.

   Midway through the project, the owner of Bolts Inc., Dory, calls Chun in a panic. According to Dory, she did not read the terms of her contract closely, and she failed to realize that she was required to pay all employees a federal prevailing wage. She was supposed to pay them $50 per hour. Instead, she paid them $30 per hour.

   Chun reviews the payroll and realizes that Dory is correct—Bolts Inc. has violated the contract and underpaid the workers. The payroll clearly shows that all employees were paid only $30 per hour. By failing to pay $50 per hour, Bolts Inc. violated a federal statute: the Davis Bacon Wage Act.

May Chun counsel Dory to disclose this conduct to the federal government?

a. Yes. Chun **may** advise Dory first to pay the back wages owed. After Dory does this, she can tell the government that the $30 per hour shown on the payroll was a typo because the employees were actually paid $50 per hour and were never underpaid.

b. Yes. If self-disclosure could minimize legal exposure to Bolts Inc. (which is the case in many regulated industries), then Chun **may** and **should** counsel Dory to disclose to the government that she had underpaid the employees by $20 per hour for the work done so far.

c. No. He **should** instead advise Dory to pay correct wages going forward and hope that the prior underpayment goes undetected.

d. No. He **must not** give Dory any advice because doing so would be assisting Bolts Inc. in illegal behavior.

4. For several weeks, Eli's client Ferdinand has been calling to ask for advice. Eli knows that Ferdinand's marriage is on the rocks and that Ferdinand's wife has been threatening to divorce him and seek full custody of their children. At first, Ferdinand was asking fairly straightforward questions about alimony and marital property issues. Lately Ferdinand's questions have been more unusual: He has been asking about whether criminal kidnapping statutes apply to noncustodial parents, and whether different countries have extradition treaties with the United States.

Eli never asks Ferdinand what he is planning to do or why he is asking these questions. Ferdinand never tells him.

Eli patiently explains that it is a crime for a parent to take a child out of the country without the consent of the child's other parent but that many countries, including Morocco and Qatar, would not extradite a father for violation of those criminal statutes. Two days later, Ferdinand takes his children to Morocco and refuses to return with them.

Has Eli violated his obligations under **Model Rule 1.2(d)**?

a. Yes. Under the circumstances, Eli was aware of facts that would have prompted a reasonable lawyer to have serious doubts that Ferdinand intended to conform his conduct to the law and would have inquired or investigated before giving Ferdinand information that would assist him in committing a crime.

b. Yes. Under the circumstances, Eli should have known Ferdinand's plan.

    c. No. Eli did not actually know Ferdinand's plan, and the rule requires knowledge, not constructive knowledge.

    d. No. Ferdinand did not tell Eli his intentions, so Eli could not have known with certainty what Ferdinand would do.

5. George dies intestate. His stepson, Hadrian, contacts a lawyer, Irene. Irene explains that, because there was no will, George's estate will pass to his wife, Jackie, and not to Hadrian. Hadrian asks Irene to draft a back-dated will and sign George's name. Irene refuses.

    A few days later, Hadrian calls Irene again. He offers to draft the backdated will and sign George's name himself. He simply asks that Irene present the will to Jackie and tell Jackie that it is indeed George's will. He suggests that Irene simply say that George gave Irene the will for safe-keeping.

    Should Irene agree?

    a. Yes. As long as she does not draft the will, her legal services are not being used to perpetuate a fraud.

    b. Yes. She does not know with certainty that the will is fraudulent.

    c. No. She should instead draft the will herself.

    d. No. If she does, her legal services will be used in furtherance of a fraud.

6. Kabir represents Lionel, who claims that he was fired because he is a vegan. Lionel feels strongly about his vegan principles; to him, they are akin to a religion. Kabir explains to Lionel that, although federal employ-ment laws protect employees who are fired because of their religion, to date, no court has accepted veganism as a religion. Lionel tells Kabir that he understands Kabir's point, but that he wants to file suit anyway and argue that his veganism is a protected religion. Kabir files a complaint on behalf of Lionel.

    During discovery, Lionel's former employer serves discovery requests. Kabir advises Lionel that they can ignore the requests because they exceed what is permitted under the applicable rules. Notwithstanding Kabir's belief that the requests are excessive, the court orders Lionel to produce the requested information or face sanctions. Kabir advises Lionel that he can ignore that order.

    Which, if any, of Kabir's actions violated Rule 1.2(d)?

    a. Filing the complaint.

    b. Advising Lionel to ignore the discovery order.

    c. Both a and b.

    d. Neither a nor b.

7. Maureen represents a major pharmaceutical company, PharmCo. For years, PharmCo.'s most profitable drug was an injectable treatment for

rheumatoid arthritis. As competing products in the form of oral pills hit the market, sales of PharmCo.'s injectable drug fell.

PharmCo.'s chief executive officer asks Maureen's advice on the company's plan to invigorate sales. PharmCo. plans to give free samples of its drug to doctors and to counsel the doctors that they can sell this free product to their patients. The CEO explains that the sales representatives will give the samples with an insert that explains how the samples can be sold.

Maureen does some research. She discovers that, although there are anti-kickback statutes that prohibit a pharmaceutical company from giving bribes to doctors in exchange for referrals, there is no caselaw exactly on point. Maureen meets with PharmCo.'s CEO and presents him with her research. She carefully defines a kickback and points out why the company's plan would likely be considered to be a kickback even though there is no caselaw exactly on point. She notes that it is the combination of the free samples and the advice as to how those samples may be used that could create the appearance of a kickback. She urges PharmCo. not to engage in its plan because of the serious **consequences** that could result.

PharmCo.'s CEO uses Maureen's advice. He retools the plan to make it more subtle and harder to detect. He does not include an insert with the samples. Rather, he invites the doctors to an educational seminar during which it is explained that PharmCo. does not track the use of its samples. The samples are provided several weeks later by sales representatives who had no involvement in the seminar. The plan is extremely successful. Thanks to the tweaks made after Maureen gave her advice, PharmCo. evades detection and successfully uses kickbacks to promote its product.

Is Maureen a party to PharmCo.'s conduct?

a. Yes. There is no distinction between presenting an analysis of legal aspects of questionable conduct and recommending the means by which a crime or fraud might be committed with impunity.

b. Yes. A lawyer may not discuss the legal consequences of any proposed criminal course of conduct with a client or counsel a client to determine the validity, scope, meaning, or application of the law.

c. No. For a lawyer to be a party to fraudulent conduct, the lawyer must have drafted a fraudulent document. The mere giving of advice cannot be the basis for a lawyer's participation in fraudulent conduct.

d. No. The mere fact that a client uses advice in a course of action that is criminal or fraudulent does not, in itself, make a lawyer a party to the course of action.

8. If you advise your client not to engage in illegal conduct and your client nonetheless persists, which of the following is true?

    a. You **may** withdraw if your client has not involved you in the illegal conduct, but you **must** withdraw if your client has involved you in the illegal conduct.

    b. You **may** withdraw whether or not your client has involved you in the illegal conduct.

    c. You **may** withdraw if your client has involved you in the illegal conduct, but you **must** withdraw if your client has not involved you in the illegal conduct.

    d. You **must** withdraw whether or not your client has involved you in the illegal conduct.

9. If a lawyer allows a client to use his or her services in furtherance of a crime, who may be held criminally liable?

    a. The client.

    b. The lawyer.

    c. Both a and b.

    d. Neither a nor b.

14

Unnecessarily Embarrassing, Delaying, or Burdening Others

DANIELLE IS PROSECUTING a misdemeanor assault case. The defendant has hired a private lawyer known around town for his bad manners and surly demeanor. After the arraignment, counsel confer in the hall to discuss initial procedural matters, as is routine in the courthouse in which Danielle works. "Hah," says defense counsel, looking at Danielle and adding an oblique reference to her race. "I beg your pardon?" says Danielle (who, we may not have mentioned, is Black), startled and struggling to retain her composure. "You heard me, young lady," the defense lawyer sneers. "Tell your boss to send me a real lawyer." He stalks off down the hall.

Danielle is understandably shaken and furious. Defense counsel's behavior obviously transgresses the limits of acceptable civil (let alone professional) discourse; this guy has indelibly labeled himself an unreconstructed jerk (and a racist and sexist one to boot). But are there **consequences** for this kind of abuse? Let's talk about it.

* * *

Some lawyers live for the kill. Much lawyering is adversarial—litigation quite explicitly is, of course—but business or transactional negotiations of any kind are usually about each party seeking the outcome that is most favorable to that party, and there are always trade-offs to be made. The "killers" will do whatever they think it takes, often (to put it politely) testing the limits of the law, to get a "win," whatever that may comprise at any given moment.

Some lawyers, understanding that angry adversaries make mistakes, do everything they can to make their adversaries angry. The "provokers" will keep searching for your buttons relentlessly until they find one that they can push. They're well-practiced at it. Some are rather less calculating, but they allow their anger-management problems or sadistic impulses to distort their professional conduct, leveraging personality defects into a practice style.

You'll meet one of these lawyers before long; you'll meet a fair number of them in your career, no matter what career you choose. More often, though, you'll confront bad behavior from well-intentioned lawyers who have, however briefly, lost their way. The adversary process, whatever its many virtues (and there are plenty of them), can also overexcite impulses that, in proper measure, are appropriate and necessary. The heat of battle and the fog of war may compound a toxic brew that can asphyxiate, or at least temporarily anesthetize, our perspective and better judgment. It can happen to anyone, which doesn't make it okay when it happens to you or anyone with whom you're dealing.

But what should you do when you're confronted with personal or procedural abuse? As a practical matter, your first line of defense is simply to be prepared for whatever provocations get thrown your way so that you can keep a perspective on your reaction. You can't stop yourself from getting mad, but surprise is a gateway out of which you can lose your temper, and forewarned is forearmed.[1] You will probably fume and fantasize about revenge later (it's unavoidably human), but at least you will have prevented your adversary from knocking you off your stride.

The old saying goes, "Don't get mad; get even." We're skeptical on both counts. As just discussed, most normal human beings can't stop themselves from getting mad, so you're doomed to failure if you try. What you *can* do is prepare yourself for and learn to *manage* your anger in ways that are healthier for you and less harmful for your client. As for getting even, we're sad to report that it happens a lot less than you'll probably wish. Achieving your client's objectives is always the best (and often a very satisfying) result, and it's not always consistent with a snappy comeback, a retaliation in kind, or creating what may develop into a dilatory and expensive sideshow—in fact, such a sideshow may be exactly what a provocative adversary wants. But there are legal and ethical limits on abusive professional conduct, and more courts and state bars are becoming more sensitive to, and willing to impose **consequences** for, the kind of verbal assaults to which Danielle was subjected in the above illustration.

To be clear, this chapter is mostly not about how you **should** behave professionally; it's about the limits on the extreme behavior in which you **must not** engage on pain of formal **consequences**. We strongly believe that you **should** always behave with civility and professional courtesy, no matter how profoundly your patience is tested, and no matter how little your civility is reciprocated. This advice is based not only on the sandbox principle that two wrongs don't make a right, but also on the reality that important observers, such as other professionals and any involved court official, invariably admire the restraint required for a firm but civil and controlled

---

[1] There is a huge difference between getting angry and losing your temper. Losing your temper involves losing perspective, judgment, and control over your behavior. That's when angry lawyers make mistakes, and mistakes hurt your client (and often you as well). As a fiduciary, you don't have the luxury of indulging your impulses at your client's expense.

rebuke to provocative conduct, and invariably show distaste for the opposite approach. Remember, your reputation is your stock in trade.

Nor should the preceding discussion be taken as any condemnation of what is generally referred to as "aggressive" advocacy. But it all depends on how you advocate. All good lawyers are "aggressive" in the sense of taking calculated risks in litigation and negotiation by selectively staking out justifiable positions that may be greater than they expect the other side to give or the court to award. There is a broad range of plausible outcomes in any situation, and your job is to press, credibly and effectively, for the best one that you can achieve on your client's behalf. And the best lawyers we've known do so, but always in a manner that is civil and courtly—in a word, professional. The iron hand in the velvet glove, so to speak. You generally don't have to say "no" loudly or with insults appended to convey that you really mean "no."

All that said, there are lines (generally not very well-defined lines, but lines nevertheless) beyond which nasty conduct bears formal **consequences**. That's what we're going to discuss now.

A. Tactics with No Substantial Purpose Other Than to Embarrass, Delay, or Burden a Third Person

Model Rule 4.4(a) says that "[i]n representing a client, a lawyer shall not use means that have no substantial purpose other than to embarrass, delay, or burden a third person . . . ."[2] There are multiple pieces to unpack here.

1. TAMING THE TEXT ▶ "In Representing a Client"

First, this prohibition applies only when you are "representing a client"; in other words, when you're acting on a client's behalf. If you're being a jerk on your own time, the Rule does not apply, though your conduct may violate other Rules, depending on its nature. For example, discriminatory epithets demeaning someone because of their perceived membership in a protected class, whether or not in the course of representing a client, are also disciplined as violations of **Model Rule 8.4(g)**, which prohibits "harassment or discrimination" on the basis of a protected category. **Model Rule 8.4(g)** is discussed more fully in **Chapter 15 at 427**.

2. TAMING THE TEXT ▶ "Third Persons"

Next, let's take note of whom this Rule protects. It refers to "third persons." Here, as in **Model Rule 4.1** (*see* **Chapter 10.A at 323**), that phrase refers to anyone other than a client, whether an adversary or a true third party—for example, other attorneys and parties, witnesses, jurors, judges, court staff, and bystanders.

---

[2] The remainder of **Model Rule 4.4(a)** provides that you **must not** "use methods of obtaining evidence that violate the legal rights of [a third] person." We'll discuss that prohibition in **Chapter 24.B at 816**.

REASON FOR THE RULE Why exclude clients? Because your fiduciary duties to your client generally require *better* behavior than merely avoiding the abuse that this Rule forbids. So conduct toward your client is governed by other law. *See* **Chapter 5.D at 112.** REASON FOR THE RULE

3. TAMING THE TEXT "No Substantial Purpose Other Than to Embarrass, Delay, or Burden"

In addition, there is a very important qualification to the kinds of tactics that the Rule prohibits: It proscribes not *any* means that "embarrass[es], delay[s], or burden[s] a third person," but only those "that have *no substantial purpose other than* to embarrass, delay, or burden a third person" (emphasis added). REASON FOR THE RULE How come? Well, legal affairs in general, and litigation in particular, is by its very nature sometimes unavoidably embarrassing, often slow, and almost always burdensome. Genuinely relevant allegations of crime, dishonesty, or sexual harassment, for example, are likely to be embarrassing to their subject when made and again when proved. Legal matters often take longer than your client wants, with the delay not infrequently creating frustration, inconvenience, or worse. And even when the price is fair and the services efficient, lawyers are expensive. On top of that purely monetary burden, providing lawyers with the information, documentation, and cooperation that they frequently need in order to do their work often demands time, attention, and effort that the parties (who have their own lives to live and jobs to work or businesses to run) feel that they can ill afford. REASON FOR THE RULE

So some degree, and not infrequently a large degree, of embarrassment, delay, or burden may be an inevitable feature of any legal engagement. What **Model Rule 4.4(a)** prohibits is tactics that "have no substantial purpose *other than*" inflicting this kind of harm (emphasis added). This suggests that the forbidden tactic must be intended to add harm that is *not reasonably necessary* beyond any embarrassment, delay, or burden that the engagement might legitimately require. And because the Rule prohibits such tactics with "no . . . *purpose* other than" such unnecessary harm (emphasis added), we must look at the lawyer's subjective "purpose." It's worth observing that the Rule's language requires *only* an assessment of the lawyer's subjective "purpose" and does not mention its actual *effect*. So it's fair to say that you have violated the Rule as soon as you undertake "means" (that is, actual speech or conduct) with the requisite bad intent. REASON FOR THE RULE Recall, for example, why we punish criminal attempts, because the analogy is a good one here: The wrongdoer has done something worthy of discipline as soon as he takes steps to carry out his abusive "purpose," and we won't forgive him just because he may have failed to achieve it. REASON FOR THE RULE

And because the Rule prohibits such tactics with "no *substantial* purpose other than" unnecessary harm (emphasis added), the lawyer must have a legitimate "purpose" for the tactic that is "substantial"—that is, more than merely incidental or *de minimis* (but, on the other hand, not necessarily primary or exclusive, either). All in all, the Rule's bar is set fairly high in order to tolerate the many difficulties that participation in ordinary adversary engagements may entail.

A "substantial" purpose must also be a legitimate one. To eliminate one common confusion, it's not enough to justify your purpose by saying that your abusive tactic will help your client achieve a better outcome in your engagement or that the client asked or directed you to employ it. Yes, achieving the best outcome and honoring your client's requests are both proper (and often mandatory) ambitions for you to pursue, but blackmail or lying would meet that test as well, and everyone knows that those tactics aren't okay. What the "substantial purpose" requirement of **Model Rule 4.4(a)** requires is to serve your client's interests and preferences by pursuing the client's legitimate objectives by "means" that are intended to accomplish some "substantial purpose" *other than by* imposing embarrassment, delay, or burden.

4. ▌Taming the Text▐ "Embarrass, Delay, or Burden"

That brings us to the heart of the Rule: "to embarrass, delay, or burden." These terms are meant literally, and they are largely self-explanatory. Disclosing an adversary's irrelevant personal indiscretions, for example, is embarrassing. (Disclosing an adversary's personal indiscretions that are genuinely relevant to and probative on a real issue in your engagement endows the disclosure with a "substantial purpose" that takes it outside the Rule's prohibitions, even though the disclosure is also embarrassing to your adversary.) Repeatedly refusing to produce witnesses for deposition or drawing out negotiations with repeated changes of position for extended periods of time with no substantial purpose other than to delay things similarly falls within the Rule. Propounding a document request or subpoena demanding review or production of large volumes of documents for irrelevant, barely relevant, or redundant information is delay-inducing and burdensome.

▌Real World▐ Because many legal engagements inevitably involve embarrassment, burden, or delay, and because we don't want to overheat the professional disciplinary system with the ordinary frictions of legal practice, even when those frictions could be avoided, **Model Rule 4.4(a)** has generally been construed to require what might be described as a disgust-level response from the sophisticated legal observer. Although we now know you well enough to know that you wouldn't dream of indulging in petty cruelties or abuse just because you probably won't be punished for it, others may not be so civilized. As a practical matter, save your motions for sanctions or disciplinary reports for the kind of behavior likely to elicit a sharply drawn breath from a neutral observer. Lesser insults are, unfortunately, usually better viewed as a cost of doing business in our world. ▌Real World▐

▌Taming the Text▐

Problem 14A-1: Which of the following violate **Model Rule 4.4(a)**? Explain why or why not.

a. Frank represents a tenant in a landlord-tenant dispute. His tenant client is suing the landlord because the tenant's apartment had no heat for a month during a midwestern winter. After Frank files suit, the landlord knocks on the tenant's door at all hours of the day and night. When the tenant opens her door, the landlord suggests that she drop the case if she ever wants to get some sleep.

b. Same landlord-tenant case as in (a). Frank is defending his client's deposition. Defense counsel asks the tenant whether her husband divorced her because she cheated on him, and how often she has "male friends sleep over." When Frank objects to defense counsel's questions, counsel speaks over Frank, making it difficult for the court reporter to note Frank's objections for the record. Defense counsel does this several times in a row. What if defense counsel does it every time that Frank tries to object?

c. Same case and deposition as in (b). During the lunch break, Frank leaves his notebook, containing his preparation and deposition notes as well as potential exhibits, in the conference room. While he is gone, defense counsel reads and photocopies Frank's notes. Frank never realizes that his notes have been copied.

d. Same case as in (a)-(c). In deposition, defense counsel asks about plaintiff's religion, and over Frank's objection, discovers that she is Muslim. Religion is not relevant to any of the issues in the case. Defense counsel asked the question because he plans to assert in closing argument at trial that the jury should not believe the plaintiff's testimony because the testimonial oath does not affect Muslims the way that it does "Christians like us." Does your analysis change if defense counsel changes his mind and does not make this argument in closing? If so, how and why; and if not, why not?

e. Same case as in (a)-(d). A few weeks after the deposition is concluded, defense counsel sends Frank an email lambasting him for doing a "half-hearted" job at the deposition. The email suggests that Frank is too inexperienced to handle the case. Defense counsel copies all the partners at Frank's firm on the letter, all but one of whom are uninvolved in the case.

f. Same case as in (a)-(e). When Frank appears for a settlement conference, defense counsel shoves him in the hallway.

g. Same case as in (a)-(f). When Frank gets up to question the defendant at trial, defense counsel starts screaming objections. When the judge suggests that defense counsel calm down, defense counsel throws his files on the floor in disgust.

h. Same case as in (a)-(g). Once the trial has concluded, the judge tells counsel that they may contact jurors, but only those who consent. Defense counsel calls juror No. 4, but the juror does not return the call. The lawyer calls this juror every day for a week.

i. Maya is having lunch with Leo Litigator, a friend who is an associate in her firm's litigation group. They're having sandwiches in Leo's office so that they can talk freely about what they've been up to. (*See* **Chapter 8.A at 222**) Leo's been working on a big antitrust case in which the firm's client, a medium-sized company, is accusing its biggest and most powerful competitor of various anticompetitive trade practices. The defendant is despised in its industry as a ruthless, take-no-prisoners competitor, and the firm's client feels that way about the defendant as much as anyone else. The parties are in the midst of discovery, and a fever-pitched dispute is coming to a head over whether the defendant will have to produce millions of emails with its customers concerning the pricing and related marketing issues that are the basis for the plaintiff's claims. Leo says the litigation team thinks that the defendant will settle the case if it loses the discovery dispute, not only because the search for and production of responsive documents will cost many millions of dollars, but because the information contained is confidential, difficult to protect by the means conventionally used to protect confidential information in discovery, and likely shows the defendant in an unflattering light (though they won't know that until they see how well it substantiates the plaintiff's antitrust claims). "Wait," says Maya, "so they'd settle rather than comply with document requests that are burdensome, expensive, and embarrassing?" "Yup, I sure hope so," Leo replies and grins. "Couldn't happen to a nicer bunch of folks."

j. Maya is negotiating a commercial transaction. Her opposing counsel sends back a revised draft of the agreement under discussion with a cover email that begins, "attached is a blackline of the Agreement," and goes on to discuss a number of the more important substantive changes that the other side is requesting. (For those unfamiliar with the process, a "blackline" (also called a "redline," from a time when documents were marked up by hand with a red pen) is a revised draft in which changes from the prior draft are highlighted by graphic conventions such as underlining new text, displaying deleted text in strikeout, etc. This is one common way in which complex written agreements are negotiated.) Maya happens to notice that, in one fairly important provision, opposing counsel has inserted a "not" that significantly changes the meaning of the term and is not underlined as new text.

k. Review the conduct of Danielle's opposing counsel in the **Introduction to this chapter at 413**. If you conclude any of that conduct violates **Model Rule 4.4**, specify exactly which conduct and why.

Problem 14A-2: **Mess in the Press**: Matt Gaetz is a lawyer licensed to practice in Florida and at the time relevant to this problem was a member of the U.S. House of Representatives. Michael Cohen was Donald Trump's lawyer prior to his election as president and for a time afterwards. Cohen came under the scrutiny of federal prosecutors for various activities in which he engaged as Trump's lawyer. He eventually pleaded guilty to several felonies. In February 2019, it was announced that Cohen would testify before a House committee regarding some of his activities representing Mr. Trump. On the eve of that testimony, Representative Gaetz, a vocal supporter of the president, tweeted to Cohen: "Do your wife & father-in-law know about your girlfriends? Maybe tonight would be a good time for that chat. I wonder if she'll remain faithful to you in prison. She's about to learn a lot." Concerned about the tweet's potential for witness intimidation, the House Ethics Committee opened an investigation. Gaetz later deleted the tweet and apologized, acknowledging that he had acted improperly.

> The Ethics Committee formally admonished Gaetz in August 2020. The Florida State Bar also opened a disciplinary inquiry and found the tweet "unprofessional, reckless, insensitive, and demonstrated poor judgment." Did the tweet violate Florida's enactment of **Model Rule 4.4(a)** or any other Rule of Professional Conduct? Why or why not? If you think it did, what discipline do you think the state bar should have imposed, and why?[3]

B. Court Sanctions and Civil Liability for Conduct of the Kind Prohibited by Model Rule 4.4(a)

CONSEQUENCES Because **Model Rule 4.4(a)** is a Rule of Professional Conduct, the **consequence** for its violation is professional discipline. In addition, a great deal of the conduct that violates **Model Rule 4.4(a)** overlaps with various other prohibitions of abusive conduct. In appropriate circumstances, a violation of **Model Rule 4.4(a)** could violate **Fed. R Civ. P. 11**, **Fed. R. Civ. P. 26(g)**, or **Fed. R Civ. P. 37**; **Fed. R. Crim. P. 42(b)**; **28 U.S.C. § 1927**; the federal courts' inherent power to control the proceedings before them; or similar state laws. *See* **Chapter 3.C at 53**. When such misconduct occurs in litigation, court sanctions are probably the most commonly imposed **consequence** (and imposed much more commonly than professional discipline). But violations of **Model Rule 4.4(a)** could also, on appropriate facts, comprise abuse of process, misrepresentation, or other torts and, in the case of threats, the tort (and potentially the crime) of extortion. *See* **Chapter 3.B at 48**; **Chapter 16.A at 440**.

Suffice for now to say there are many ways that you can get burned for such excesses of zeal, not the least of which is the informal **consequence** of harm to your professional reputation. Everyone in your practice community knows who the jerks in town are. If you're on that list, expect to be treated accordingly by opposing counsel, referral sources, potential clients, and even judges (yes, they do talk to each other about the conduct of the lawyers who appear before them and about who deserves to be considered reliable and credible). CONSEQUENCES

C. The Constitution's Uncertain Role in Limiting Regulation of Abusive Lawyer Conduct

Generally speaking, the Constitution leaves plenty of room to regulate lawyer conduct that most people would consider abusive. But the prohibitions have to be articulated clearly enough to satisfy due process (under the vagueness and overbreadth principles requiring you to have a clear enough idea of what not to do before you can be penalized for doing it, especially where protected speech may be at stake). And when the behavior in question is speech (such as name-calling, racist or sexist epithets, or threats), the First Amendment can come into play.

---

[3] *See* Melanie Zanona, *House Ethics Panel Admonishes Gaetz over Michael Cohen Tweet*, https://www.msn.com/en-us/news/politics/house-ethics-panel-admonishes-gaetz-over-michael-cohen-tweet/ar-BB18eIYx (Aug. 21, 2020).

The application of these principles in this particular context is regrettably unclear. The Supreme Court has held that the First Amendment forbids the imposition on lawyers of professional discipline or other sanctions based on protected speech.[4] But lower appellate courts have also found lawyers' First Amendment rights to be more limited than other folks' when lawyers are speaking under the auspices of their professional licenses, and many courts and disciplinary authorities appear to consider any constitutional constraints on their powers to punish offensive speech in this context to be narrow.[5] We leave a more detailed understanding of what kinds of communicative activity might be protected from **consequences** to your Constitutional Law classes. But to give you a general sense of the contours of the uncertainty, consider a few examples.

California law provided for nearly 150 years that "it is the duty of any attorney . . . to abstain from all offensive personality."[6] Leaving aside the well-rehearsed japes wondering how California nevertheless managed to accumulate the largest state bar in the nation (and yes, that was a lawyer joke), the Ninth Circuit found this provision an unconstitutionally vague and overbroad basis for a federal court's sanction of an attorney who, outside the courtroom and after he was no longer involved in the proceedings, sent his female former opposing counsel a letter containing the following statement (in all capital letters):

MALE LAWYERS PLAY BY THE RULES, DISCOVER TRUTH AND RESTORE ORDER. FEMALE LAWYERS ARE OUTSIDE THE LAW, CLOUD TRUTH AND DESTROY ORDER.

The Ninth Circuit suggested that a similar "deplorable lack of sensitivity" might properly be subject to sanction if it had "interfered with the administration of justice," but that that had not occurred here because the lawyer had sent his offensive communication to opposing counsel after he was no longer involved in the case. The court reasoned that an interference with the administration of justice would offer a ground for **consequences** that was narrow enough to satisfy the First and Fifth Amendments.[7]

The California Legislature repealed the statute at issue in in 2001. Other states still have, and enforce, similar provisions. Wisconsin, for example, includes in the oath that all lawyers must take to be licensed to practice in the state a promise

---

[4] *Gentile v. State Bar of Nevada*, 501 U.S. 1030 (1991).

[5] *United States District Court v. Sandlin*, 12 F.3d 861, 866 (9th Cir. 1993) ("once a lawyer is admitted to the bar, although he does not surrender his freedom of expression, he must temper his criticisms in accordance with professional standards of conduct").

[6] Cal. Bus. & Prof. Code § 6068(f) (repealed 2001).

[7] *United States v. Wunsch*, 54 F.3d 579, 584-86 (9th Cir. 1995), 84 F.3d 1110 (9th Cir. 1996) (on rehearing), and cases cited.

to refrain from "offensive personality," and the Wisconsin Supreme Court apparently still considers its violation a proper basis for professional discipline.[8]

Similarly, in a recent Indiana case, a lawyer was suspended from practice for 30 days for writing a letter to his opposing counsel in a family law matter (and copying the presiding judge) saying, "[y]our client doesn't understand what laws and court orders are. Probably because she's an illegal alien to begin with." The Indiana Supreme Court rejected the suggestion that the comment was "legitimate advocacy" and concluded that it had no purpose other than to embarrass or burden the opposing party. The First Amendment wasn't even considered.[9]

Finally, in California (again!), a lawyer who sent over 100 emails to his opposing counsel laced with flagrantly obscene and discriminatory epithets and threats was sanctioned nearly $18,000 by the federal district court presiding over the underlying dispute under its inherent powers to compensate an "innocent party" for "bad faith" conduct by the opposing party or his counsel (*see* **Chapter 3.C at 54**). The lawyer opposed the sanctions request on (among others) First Amendment grounds, which the court summarily rejected.[10]

To sum up the state of play, there are all kinds of nonlegal reasons to avoid (and informal **consequences** for using) expletives, insults, discriminatory epithets, threats, or disruptive conduct in your professional endeavors, whether for emphasis, to make a point, because of a lack of self-control, or just because you think you can. Courts and disciplinary authorities also regularly impose formal

---

[8] *See In re Beaver*, 181 Wis. 2d 12, 510 N.W. 2d 129, 133 (1994) (upholding Wisconsin's "offensive personality" statute against a vagueness challenge similar to the one that succeeded in *Wunsch*, **Chapter 14.C at 421 n.7**, in part because of the context in which the phrase is used and the knowledge of ethical standards that is imputed to lawyers).

Does it matter *whom you* insult? For example, is there a difference between calling your opposing counsel dishonest and calling a sitting judge the same thing? Insults to judicial officers (at least ones made in open court) are regularly punished as contempts, as well as by professional discipline as conduct "prejudicial to the administration of justice" in violation of **Model Rule 8.4(d)**. Punishing disrespect to judicial officers is ordinarily justified as vindicating the dignity and authority of the court, a value apparently considered sufficient to overcome First Amendment concerns. *See, e.g., Sacher v. United States*, 343 U.S. 1, 5–7 (1952) (affirming summary contempt for insulting the judge); *In re Cordova-Gonzalez*, 996 F.2d 1334, 1335 (1st Cir. 1993) (affirming disbarment for violation of (among others) **Model Rule 8.4(d)** by filing "pleadings containing vitriolic slurs on judges and lawyers").

[9] *In re Barker*, 993 N.E.2d 1138, https://www.in.gov/judiciary/files/order-discipline-2013-55S00-1008-DI-429.pdf (Ind. 2013). Discriminatory epithets of the kind implied in *Barker*, demeaning someone because of the person's asserted or perceived membership in a protected class, can also be disciplined as violations of **Model Rule 8.4(g)**, which prohibits "harassment or discrimination" on the basis of a protected category. **Model Rule 8.4(g)** is discussed more fully in **Chapter 15 at 427**. Similar (and similarly difficult) free expression concerns may be raised by discipline on these grounds.

[10] *Baker v. Allstate Ins. Co.*, No. 2:19-cv-08024-ODW (JCx), 2020 U.S. Dist. LEXIS 34774, https://www.bloomberglaw.com/public/desktop/document/BakervAllstateInsCoNo219cv08024ODWJCx2020BL75073CDCalFeb282020Cou?1596481255 (C.D. Cal. Feb. 28, 2020); *see also* Porter Wells, *Profanity-Laden Emails Earn Sanctions for California Lawyer*, https://news.bloomberglaw.com/legal-ethics/profanity-laden-emails-earn-sanctions-for-california-attorney (March 2, 2020) (giving examples of some of the lawyer's saltier turns of phrase). When the offending lawyer raised his First Amendment rights at the hearing on sanctions, the judge reportedly responded: "You honestly believe the First Amendment extends to anything? . . . You did go to law school, right?" *Id.* As this book went to press, the district court's ruling imposing the monetary sanctions was on appeal. Whether or not the offending lawyer earned the style points he seemed to believe that his scatological flair justified, he clearly didn't stick the landing. By the time of the hearing, his client had discharged him, professing ignorance of and disgust with his conduct. *Id.*

consequences for such tactics, usually with no or minimal regard for any free expression or vagueness concerns that they may raise. Where does that leave you? As a practical matter, you proceed in communications or conduct of this kind at your peril: Leaving aside the informal **consequences** likely to result, the law remains highly unsettled as to when you may be subject to formal sanction by courts or disciplinary authorities and when your speech or conduct is or should be constitutionally protected by what Justice Holmes memorably referred to as "freedom for the thought that we hate."[11] You should not expect to have an easy time defining or vindicating these rights.

Big-Picture Takeaways from Chapter 14

1. **Model Rule 4.4(a)** says that, while you're representing a client (as opposed, say, to going grocery shopping or doing laundry), you **must not** "use means that have no substantial purpose other than to embarrass, delay, or burden a third person . . . ."

   a. "Third person" means someone other than your client. Your fiduciary duties to your client generally require *better* behavior than merely avoiding the abuse that this Rule forbids. *See* **Chapter 14.A at 415**.

   b. Contrast **Model Rule 4.4(a)** with **Model Rule 8.4(g)**, which prohibits "harassment or discrimination" on the basis of a protected category, whether or not you're doing so while representing a client. *See* **Chapter 14.A at 415**.

   c. **Model Rule 4.4(a)** doesn't say that you have to avoid *all* embarrassment, delay, or burden; that would often be impossible. But you **must not** employ tactics that impose embarrassment, delay, or burden that is *not reasonably necessary* and that has "no substantial purpose other than" to make someone else miserable. You have violated the Rule as soon as you undertake "means" (that is, actual speech or conduct) with the requisite bad intent. *See* **Chapter 14.A at 416**.

2. Much conduct that violates **Model Rule 4.4(a)** also violates another Rule of Professional Conduct. Much of that conduct also violates rules and statutes authorizing courts to impose civil sanctions on the misbehaving counsel. Some such conduct may also form a basis for civil tort liability on the lawyer's part. *See* **Chapter 14.B at 420**.

---

[11] *United States v. Schwimmer*, 279 U.S. 649, 654-55 (1929) (Holmes, J., dissenting) ("if there is any principle of the Constitution that more imperatively calls for attachment than any other, it is the principle of free thought—not free thought for those who agree with us, but freedom for the thought that we hate"). For a brief but thoughtful debate on the policy issue, see Roberta M. Ikemi and Carol A. Sobel, *Should Sexist Comments Be a Disciplinary Offense?*, 81 A.B.A. J. 40 (August 1995).

3. The First Amendment prohibits imposing any formal **consequences** on lawyers based on protected speech. However, the case law deciding what speech is protected in this context is very confused, and courts tend to take a narrow view of what lawyer speech the First Amendment protects. *See* **Chapter 14.C at 420**.

Multiple-Choice Review Questions for Chapter 14

1. Lawyer Hannibal represents June, a plaintiff in an employment discrimination case. Hannibal is preparing to depose June's supervisor, Kate. June claims that she was passed over for a promotion because of her religion. Kate disputes this allegation and claims that June was not eligible for a promotion because June had not met certain performance goals.

   A few days before the scheduled deposition, June calls Hannibal's office. June explains to Hannibal that she had created a fake name so that she could follow Kate's husband on his private social media pages. As a result, June has learned that Kate's husband has been cheating on her. June suggests that Hannibal question Kate about her husband's marital infidelity at the outset of the deposition. "It will throw her off," explains June, "and then she'll be flustered when you question her about the promotion."

   Should Hannibal question Kate as June suggests?
   a. Yes. Based on June's information, Hannibal has a good-faith basis for this questioning.
   b. Yes. Hannibal is entitled to find out whether Kate may have been distracted by her husband's affair and thus overlooked June for promotion as a result.
   c. No. Even if there is some tangential evidentiary value to the questioning, its primary purpose is to embarrass Kate.
   d. No. Hannibal must first do his own investigation to determine if Kate's husband is having an affair and may only question her about this topic if he has a good-faith basis to believe that the affair is occurring.

2. Laurie dreads litigating against Matthew, but both are construction litigators in a small town, so they often find themselves representing parties who are suing each other. Laurie currently represents a general contractor suing a material supplier who is Matthew's client.

   Matthew serves narrow discovery requests on Laurie, seeking production of the contract and any addenda thereto. The requests do not indicate what file format Matthew would like for any responses. The requests seek a response within 30 days, which is the timeframe provided in the applicable rules of procedure.

Laurie could easily produce those documents in hard copy, as scanned images, or in their native format. To spite Matthew, Laurie has the files converted to WordImperfect, a long-obsolete file format that she knows that Matthew does not use. This conversion takes a few weeks, because virtually no copy services are capable of handling the conversion. Laurie produces the responses 29 days after she receives the document requests.

Has Laurie met her professional obligations?

a. Yes. Her responses were timely.

b. Yes. Matthew could have requested a specific format if he had wanted to.

c. No. She should have produced the responses as quickly as possible.

d. No. She has rendered discovery unnecessarily more burdensome for Matthew.

3. Nabilla is a patent lawyer who represents biologist-inventors. She is representing a client involved in a patent dispute over a new drug. Opposing counsel asks in discovery for all research supporting the patent. Opposing counsel also asks that all responsive documents be produced as they are maintained "in the ordinary course of business." Nabilla produces the documents to her in a proprietary database, which is how the client accesses and keeps the documents. Nabilla suspects that opposing counsel will have to buy a license for the database in order to view the document production.

Has Nabilla unduly burdened opposing counsel as defined by **Model Rule 4.4(a)**?

a. Yes. She was aware that the documents would be difficult to access and should have converted them to a more accessible format.

b. Yes. She should have provided a license to the database if she was going to produce the documents in that format.

c. No. She took no extra steps to make the documents more difficult for opposing counsel to access.

d. No. Opposing counsel asked for documents to be produced this way, and therefore, Nabilla would have been justified in making the documents even less accessible had she wished.

4. Oscar's client is being deposed. Despite copious preparation in advance, his client is giving terrible answers that jeopardize the case. Opposing counsel's questions are all proper; the client is just responding poorly.

Can Oscar threaten to walk out of the deposition with his client even though he knows that there is no justification to do so?

a. Yes. Oscar must zealously advocate for his client.

b. Yes. Oscar may do so to signal to his client that his answers are terrible.

    c. No. Oscar would be improperly bluffing, because he has no basis to end the deposition.

    d. No. Oscar must first object, then call the judge, then he may threaten to walk out.

15

Avoiding Invidious Discrimination

MAYA HAS BEEN directed to see a partner in the corporate group (one she hasn't met before) regarding a new assignment. As she enters his open office door, Roy Roughshod looks her up and down. "You are . . . ?" he asks. "Maya Mendoza," she replies. "Right. Mendoza. Where you from?" Maya freezes. "Um, I was born in a small town outside Midland, Texas." "Well, I love all things Mexican," says Roughshod. Maya doesn't know what to say. "C'mon, no reason to get anything in a twist," the partner grins. "Sit down." Maya forces herself to smile and sits down, legal pad and pen at the ready.

You probably felt squeamish reading that hypothetical. We certainly felt squeamish writing it. But even a cursory glance at the headlines, and quite possibly your own lived experience as well, reveal that bias, harassment, and discrimination are still a part of our world. It's also a part of the world of legal practice, and no sector is immune. A lawyer may make suggestive or embarrassing comments about dress or appearance, or even proposition a subordinate lawyer or staff person for sexual favors. A female associate at a law firm may be overlooked for promotion in favor of a male colleague because she is perceived as "less dedicated" to her career, or "not aggressive enough," or "strident" when a male peer would be considered "assertive."[1] A Black prosecutor may be criticized as "angry" when he's forceful, or as a less effective advocate based on an unfair assessment of his litigation skills, viewed through the veil of cultural insensitivity. The objects of these affronts usually have little recourse, as a practical matter, without resort to processes that can put substantial organizational machinery into motion. That machinery can operate without doing much to fix the problem, and invoking it may even characterize those seeking redress as "not a team player," "oversensitive," or a malcontent. If we can't assure fair treatment for those within our own ranks, how can we hope to achieve fair outcomes for our clients? The practice of law, the legal system, and the rule of law suffer when wrongful bias, harassment, and discrimination go unchecked.

---

[1] This is not merely theoretical. One of these things happened to one of your authors, and she's not alone.

Although some people still stubbornly resist the "self-evident" "truth[]" on which our nation was founded that "all [people] are created equal," the vast majority of Americans agree that discriminatory or harassing conduct is wrong. And yet it persists. There are a great many reasons why it's hard to eradicate bias, harassment, and discrimination, and many of them don't have to do with bad motives. There may be generational differences that are resistant to change. There may be cultural miscommunication. There may be an overarching problem of people not seeing themselves as others see them. Most of us come to work genuinely believing in our own good intentions, and we struggle to see how those good intentions don't always stop us from behaving in ways that discomfit, insult, or unfairly disadvantage others. Understanding ourselves and others who may seem different involves a process of self-examination and empathy that can be hard to undertake, let alone change behavior.

Nor can we simply legislate inequity away. Although many types of harassment and discrimination are prohibited by law (and have been for decades), people still suffer this kind of treatment every day in forms both great and small. You've seen some of this anti-harassment and antidiscrimination law if you've taken a course in employment discrimination or civil rights. But as it turns out, the Model Rules of Professional Conduct address this issue, too. No professional disciplinary rule alone could possibly hope to end bias, harassment, or discrimination in legal practice, of course. But an ethics rule can help as a statement of commitment and purpose, as a reminder to confront our own stereotypes and biases and make them less transparent to ourselves, and as a corrective to wrongful conduct within the bar. These are the goals of **Model Rule 8.4(g)**, which was added to the Model Rules in 2016 to address harassment and discrimination on the basis of protected status.[2]

A. Understanding Model Rule 8.4(g)

Please pause and read **Model Rule 8.4(g)** and **Model Rule 8.4 Comments [3]-[5]**. The critical language, of course, is the Rule's declaration that it constitutes "professional misconduct" subject to discipline for a lawyer to "engage in conduct that the lawyer knows or reasonably should know is harassment or discrimination on

---

[2] As this book was going to press, attention to these issues had considerably intensified by the currency of the "#metoo" and "#blacklivesmatter" initiatives. This more intensive focus seems to have made the issues at once both more fraught and difficult to discuss and more urgently in need of discussion than ever. If you have something to say to your classmates on these topics (and we hope that you do), we urge you to think carefully about not only *what* you say but *how* you say it. We also urge you to please listen open-mindedly to them in turn, giving their intentions the benefit of the doubt as you would have them give the same to yours. Remember that we gather to educate and be educated by one another. For just one example of how easy it is for intelligent and well-intentioned people to fail to engage constructively on these issues, *see, e.g.,* Conor Friedersdorf, *Anti-racist Arguments Are Tearing People Apart: What a Viral Story Reveals about Contemporary Leftist Discourse,* https://www.theatlantic.com/ideas/archive/2020/08/meta-arguments-about-anti-racism/615424/?utm_source=newsletter&utm_medium=email&utm_campaign=masthead-newsletter&utm_content=20200822&silverid=MzEwMTU3MjA3MzI0S0 (Aug. 20, 2020).

the basis of race, sex, religion, national origin, ethnicity, disability, age, sexual orientation, gender identity, marital status or socioeconomic status in conduct related to the practice of law." Let's break that down.[3]

1. TAMING THE TEXT "Harassment or Discrimination on the Basis of" Protected Status

Because you're becoming adept at interpreting the language of the Rules, you immediately noticed that what **Model Rule 8.4(g)** prohibits is "harassment or discrimination." You also noticed that it doesn't prohibit just *any* harassment or discrimination; the Rule's prohibition is limited to harassment or discrimination "*on the basis of*" numerous protected categories (emphasis added), in particular "race, sex, religion, national origin, ethnicity, disability, age, sexual orientation, gender identity, marital status or socioeconomic status." Now, harassment as such for pretty much any reason is almost certain to be a very bad idea; on its face, conduct that meets the definition of "harassment" is likely to have no substantial purpose other than to embarrass, burden, or delay a third party, and thus will violate **Model Rule 4.4(a)**—and possibly other Rules of Professional Conduct, as well as nondisciplinary law bearing other **consequences**. *See* **Chapter 14 at 415.**

Discrimination, by contrast, must be scrutinized a little more carefully. Discrimination literally means only to make a distinction between things or people (and to treat them differently based on that distinction). Some distinctions are just fine. For example, if you want to hire a lawyer (whether you are a client or a law firm seeking to employ an additional attorney), no one would ever fault you if you required candidates to have a license to practice in the state in which the desired services would be provided. In this situation, you would literally be discriminating against persons who lacked a law license. And that would be completely proper; in fact, it would be legally *required* in all 50 states and the District of Columbia. But discriminating among people based on characteristics not relevant to the purpose for which you are making your choices is usually unwise, is frequently offensive to others and, depending on the characteristic relied upon, can be outright unlawful. Title VII of the Civil Rights Act of 1964, for example, forbids (and provides a range of **consequences** to remedy) discrimination in employment and harassment in the workplace on account of race, color, religion, sex, or national origin.[4] Other state and federal laws prohibit and

---

[3] YOUR HOUSE; YOUR RULES As discussed in **Chapter 15.B at 433** below, **Model Rule 8.4(g)** is relatively new and quite controversial, and it has been adopted verbatim in only three states. However, about half the states have, in their Rules of Professional Conduct, some form of prohibition on harassment or discrimination by lawyers based on protected status, and virtually every state has generally applicable anti-harassment and antidiscrimination laws that supplement the federal law in this area. That federal law applies in a broad range of contexts, most particularly in employment and the workplace. So regardless of exactly what your state's ethics rules have to say about invidious discrimination, these issues will inevitably affect your day-to-day life and that of your clients. YOUR HOUSE; YOUR RULES

[4] 42 U.S.C. §§ 2000e *et seq.*

remedy discrimination based on membership or perceived membership in other protected classes, and in other situations. **Model Rule 8.4(g)** adds to this patchwork by forbidding harassment or discrimination by lawyers licensed or practicing in the state in which the Rule is in force based on the specific protected classes enumerated above.[5]

There is a rich and complex jurisprudence arising under the many existing state and federal antidiscrimination laws—jurisprudence that defines the boundaries of protected classes and the kinds of conduct that do or do not constitute "harassment" or "discrimination." These concerns are important, and they apply to nearly all commercial activities and to many private ones as well. We urge you to become familiar with your obligations (and those of your future clients) in these regards; they are pervasive and the **consequences** for their violation can be very serious. Unfortunately, we won't have time in this course to explore those issues in the detail that they deserve (unless your professor wishes to make time to focus on them now, in which case you can expect some supplemental materials accompanying this chapter).

What does **Model Rule 8.4(g)** mean by "harassment" and "discrimination"? **Model Rule 8.4 Comment [3]** provides some guidance by explaining that

> discrimination [within the meaning of **Model Rule 8.4(g)**] includes harmful verbal or physical conduct that manifests bias or prejudice towards others. Harassment includes sexual harassment and derogatory or demeaning verbal or physical conduct. Sexual harassment includes unwelcome sexual advances, requests for sexual favors, and other unwelcome verbal or physical conduct of a sexual nature.

That is, of course, only a bare beginning to understanding the lines between actionable and nonactionable conduct drawn under other antidiscrimination laws. It may, however, be possible to provide a convenient, if imprecise, formulation of the relationship between those issues and the application of **Model Rule 8.4(g)**: **Model Rule 8.4 Comment [3]** suggests that "[t]he substantive law of antidiscrimination and anti-harassment statutes and caselaw may guide application of [**Model Rule 8.4(g)**]." Remember that **Model Rule 8.4(g)** is (where it or something like it is in force) an addition to an already robust array of regulation governing the same kinds of behavior in many of the same situations. In other words (and admittedly oversimplifying a little), if you are violating **Model Rule 8.4(g)**, you are most probably also violating other state or federal anti-harassment or antidiscrimination laws, and you can expect **consequences** from multiple directions. Although the overlap between the conduct forbidden by **Model Rule 8.4(g)** and conduct forbidden by other state and federal law may not be absolute, it is quite substantial.

---

[5] We realize that this explanation will seem elementary and unnecessary for anyone who has had any exposure to these issues in other courses. Please bear with us; we just want to make sure that those who haven't yet confronted these matters get some context.

2. TAMING THE TEXT ▸ "Knows or Reasonably Should Know"

Model Rule 8.4(g) forbids conduct that a lawyer "knows or reasonably should know" is harassment or discrimination on the basis of a protected class. Other antidiscrimination laws have differing intent requirements and complex judge-made law on how that intent may be inferred. This disciplinary rule appears to be somewhat simpler and more direct in that respect.

3. TAMING THE TEXT ▸ "In Conduct Related to the Practice of Law"

You'll recall that a number of Rules of Professional Conduct govern only conduct in which a lawyer engages "in representing a client." *See, e.g.*, **Model Rule 4.1**; **Chapter 10.A at 323**; **Model Rule 4.4(a)**; **Chapter 14.A at 415**. **Model Rule 8.4(g)** more broadly reaches any "conduct *related to the practice of law*" (emphasis added). **Model Rule 8.4 Comment [4]** explains that "conduct related to the practice of law" "includes representing clients; interacting with witnesses, coworkers, court personnel, lawyers and others while engaged in the practice of law; operating or managing a law firm or law practice; and participating in bar association, business or social activities in connection with the practice of law." This list makes it clear that **Model Rule 8.4(g)** covers a range of activities a good deal wider than simply doing legal work for a client.

4. TAMING THE TEXT ▸ Other Scope Limitations

Model Rule 8.4(g) and some of the Comments explaining it also provide some suggestions about conduct that the Rule is *not* intended to reach. These qualifications were prompted by concerns, expressed while the Rule was being drafted, about its potential to interfere with legitimate speech or advocacy. They are not precise in their limits, but they do give a helpful sense of what its drafters were *not* intending:

- The Rule itself disclaims any intent to interfere with a lawyer's power "to accept, decline or withdraw from a representation in accordance with Rule 1.16." So if **Model Rule 1.16** allows it (*see* **Chapter 9.D at 294**), **Model Rule 8.4(g)** probably doesn't prohibit it. (*But see* **Problem 15A-3 at 433** below.)
- The Rule also disclaims any power to "preclude legitimate advice or advocacy consistent with these Rules." Our legal system and the First Amendment grant extremely broad latitude to advocate (whether in formal proceedings or in public discourse) ideas, policies, or results that others may find hateful, discriminatory, or upsetting. The Rule is not intended to limit these activities.
- From the other side of the political spectrum, some people believe that taking race, ethnicity, or similar characteristics into account in hiring or promotion as a means of increasing inclusiveness or diversity is discriminatory. **Model Rule 8.4 Comment [4]** makes clear that conduct

undertaken by lawyers or law firms to promote inclusiveness or diversity in the workplace or the bar permitted under other applicable law doesn't violate **Model Rule 8.4(g)**.

- Addressing a concern of criminal law practitioners (principally prosecutors), **Model Rule 8.4 Comment [5]** makes clear that a judge's finding that peremptory challenges to potential jurors were exercised discriminatorily in violation of *Batson v. Kentucky*[6] "does not alone establish a violation" of **Model Rule 8.4(g)**. What additional findings or conduct would make discriminatory exercise of peremptories a violation is not explained. This sentence predates **Model Rule 8.4(g)**'s adoption in 2016, and it was previously part of a Comment addressing "conduct prejudicial to the administration of justice" under **Model Rule 8.4(d)**.

- **Model Rule 8.4 Comment [5]** also makes clear that lawyers do not violate Rule 8.4(g) by "limiting the scope or subject matter of the lawyer's practice or by limiting the lawyer's practice to members of underserved populations in accordance with these Rules and other law." The Comment does not say why this might be a concern, but presumably such common and widely accepted practices could have the effect of limiting the access of some protected groups to the lawyer's services (or causing a lawyer to prefer members of some protected classes as clients). Likely for the same reasons, the same Comment confirms that a lawyer may charge any fee authorized by **Model Rule 1.5** (*see* **Chapter 20.B at 537**; **Chapter 20.C at 546**). Taming the Text

These glosses are helpful, but the Rule remains challenging to apply. Consider the following problems:

Problem 15A-1: Go back and review Maya's experience in meeting partner Roy Roughshod in the first paragraph of **this chapter's Introduction at 427**. Did Roughshod violate **Model Rule 8.4(g)**? Why or why not? Put yourself in Maya's shoes. What (if anything) would you have done in her situation, and why?

Problem 15A-2: Frank meets with a potential new client, Polly Penurious. Polly owns a small residential lot that she inherited from her mother, and she has a boundary dispute with her neighbor. Frank reviews the firm's regular rate schedule with Polly. She says, quite directly, that she's been out of work for some time and can't afford the firm's regular rates. "I'm very sorry," says Frank, "but in that case, I don't think we can help you." "Wait a second," Polly interjects. "You're telling me that you won't represent me because I'm too poor to afford your hourly rates?" "Yes," says Frank, "I'm afraid so. I hope you can appreciate that it's nothing personal, and we'd be happy to help if you were able to pay us." "That," says Polly, "is

---

[6] 476 U.S. 79 (1986). *Batson* and its progeny hold that exercise of peremptory challenges in a manner intended to exclude jurors solely because they are members of the same protected class as a criminal defendant, or based on the assumption that all jurors in a protected class are unfit for jury service, is a violation of a criminal defendant's constitutional rights.

discrimination based on socioeconomic status. I'm reporting you to the state bar." What is the bar's response to the complaint likely to be, and why? *Hint*: Review **Model Rule 8.4 Comment [5]**. Does anything in the Comment help you predict the bar's response? What, and why?

Problem 15A-3: Frank joins the family law partner at his firm, Sally Splitsville, for a meeting with a potential new client, Peter Paterfamilias. Peter and his soon-to-be-ex-wife have been married for 12 years and have two children; Peter's wife worked as an investment banker throughout their marriage, while Peter took on the role of stay-at-home dad. Now the wife is divorcing Peter, and Peter believes that he should remain the children's principal caregiver, receiving custody of the children, child support, and alimony. Peter tells Sally and Frank that he went to see another family lawyer in town known for representing stay-at-home parents in divorces, but that lawyer said that she represented only women in divorce cases, using what she called a feminist orientation toward valuing the services of stay-at-home moms, and that she could not help Peter. Frank can't help wondering if that other family lawyer is complying with **Model Rule 8.4(g)**. Is she? Why or why not?[7]

Problem 15A-4: Ned Narrow is running for president of the County Bar Association in Danielle's county. His opponent is Nabilla Narahany, another lawyer in town who is a practicing Muslim and wears a head covering (a *hijab*). Ned has been stumping for votes by suggesting, without evidence other than Nabilla's religious affiliation, that Nabilla might try to impose "Sharia Law" on the Bar Association, and he has made pointed references to her *hijab*. Is Ned violating **Model Rule 8.4(g)**? Why or why not? Does your answer change if Ned and Nabilla are, instead, running for the City Council in Danielle's city? What if Ned's campaign posters for City Council feature his smiling photograph superimposed with the caption: "Trusted advocate and counselor for citizens and families in our community since 1994"? What if Ned has persuaded his law partners that running for City Council justifies his time and effort away from their practice because it's a "guaranteed magnet for new clients"?

B. Understanding Why Model Rule 8.4(g) Is Controversial

The Model Rules have always addressed concerns about bias and discrimination in legal practice. The original version of the Model Rules, promulgated in 1983, contained a Comment explicating the meaning of the phrase "conduct prejudicial to the administration of justice" in **Model Rule 8.4(d)** (which forbids such conduct). The Comment said: "A lawyer who, in the course of representing a client, knowingly manifests, by words or conduct, bias or prejudice based on race, sex, religion, national origin, disability, age, sexual orientation, or socioeconomic status violates [**Model Rule 8.4(d)**] when such actions are prejudicial to the administration of justice."

---

[7] This problem is based loosely on the facts of *Stropnicky v. Nathanson*, 19 M.D.L.R. (Landlaw, Inc.) 39 (MCAD Feb. 25, 1997), another favorite of many casebook authors.

The ABA added **Model Rule 8.4(g)** and **Model Rule 8.4 Comments [3]-[5]** in 2016. As you can see by comparing the two, **Model Rule 8.4(g)** is broader than the original Comment to Rule 8.4(d). It adds a reference to "harassment," increases the number of protected classes, relaxes the intent standard from actual knowledge to negligence ("knows or reasonably should know"), and broadens the scope of regulated activities from actual law practice ("in the course of representing a client") to "conduct related to the practice of law," and by eliminating the limitation that only discrimination "prejudicial to the administration of justice" is prohibited. By the time that the ABA incorporated **Model Rule 8.4(g)** into the Model Rules in 2016, between 20 and 30 states had adopted Rules or Comments addressing the issue, mostly in terms along the lines of the original Comment to Rule 8.4(d). Since that time, only three states (Pennsylvania, Vermont, and Maine) and three U.S. territories have adopted Model Rule 8.4(g) verbatim.[8]

Why the tepid response? The opponents of **Model Rule 8.4(g)** don't generally favor harassment or invidious discrimination. Instead, they argue principally that the Rule is so broadly and generally worded that it could cover constitutionally protected speech and advocacy. A number of state supreme courts, state attorneys general, and prominent academics have expressed that concern as well. Proponents of the Rule describe it as the culmination of a decades-long effort by the ABA to stop harassment and discrimination in law practice, arguing that the new rule has important educational and symbolic value for the organized bar. Proponents also argue that the scope-limiting qualifications contained in the Rule and the Comments (*see* **Chapter 15.A at 431**) adequately address any overbreadth concerns.[9]

As of the time that this book went to print, adoption of the model form of the Rule appears to have stalled. This emphatically does *not* leave law practice free from **consequences** for bias, discrimination, or harassment: As both the headlines and the case reporters reflect, lawyers are subject to all existing state and federal law of this kind, and many all too regularly experience its application.[10] The organized bar's contribution to eradication of harassment and discrimination in law practice through professional discipline remains, for the time being, a patchwork.

---

[8] *See* Kristine A. Kubes, Cara D. Davis, and Mary E. Schwind, *The Evolution of Model Rule 8.4(g): Working to Eliminate Bias, Discrimination, and Harassment in the Practice of Law*, https://www.americanbar.org/groups/construction_industry/publications/under_construction/2019/spring/model-rule-8-4/ (March 12, 2019). For an opposition point of view, see Bradley Abramson, *The ABA Was Dead Wrong About Model Rule 8.4(g)*, https://www.law360.com/articles/1091613#:~:text=Law360%20%28October%2012%2C%202018%2C%202%3A53%20PM%20EDT%29%20--.,8.4%20%28g%29%2C%20its%20controversial%20anti-discrimination%20and%20harassment%20 (Oct. 12, 2018).

[9] *See* authorities cited in note 8, *supra*; *see also* **Chapter 14.C at 420**. Nonetheless, a federal district judge in Pennsylvania enjoined enforcement of Rule 8.4(g) shortly after the state's adoption of Rule in 2020 on the ground it was unconstitutionally vague and overbroad. *Greenberg v. Haggerty*, No. 2:20-cv-03822-CFK (Docket No. 29, Dec. 8, 2020).

[10] *See, e.g., Price Waterhouse v. Hopkins*, 490 U.S. 228 (1989) (U.S. Supreme Court confirms that Title VII, forbidding discrimination in employment, applies to professional partnerships); *Weeks v. Baker & McKenzie*, 63 Cal. App. 4th 1128, 74 Cal. Rptr. 2d 510 (1998) (affirming compensatory and punitive damages awards against both a law firm partner who engaged in serial harassment of subordinate women and the law firm that failed to curb his conduct).

Big-Picture Takeaways from Chapter 15

1. The legal profession is filled with humans, and humans have a way of believing that their good intentions are all that they need to ensure that they treat everyone else fairly and with respect, and that they themselves are free of bias. In reality, good intentions get us only part of the way there. That's why the American Bar Association proposed **Model Rule 8.4(g)**—to educate the bar about and take action against the invidious discrimination still faced by some of our colleagues. *See* **Chapter 15 at 428**.

2. **Model Rule 8.4(g)** states that, when a lawyer "engage[s] in conduct that the lawyer knows or reasonably should know is harassment or discrimination on the basis of race, sex, religion, national origin, ethnicity, disability, age, sexual orientation, gender identity, marital status or socioeconomic status in conduct related to the practice of law," that lawyer is subject to professional discipline. *See* **Chapter 15.A at 428**.

3. **Model Rule 8.4(g)** prohibits "harassment or discrimination," but not *all* harassment or discrimination. For the Rule to apply, the harassment or discrimination must be *"on the basis of"* one or more protected categories enumerated in the Rule. *See* **Chapter 15.A at 429**.

4. "[H]arassment" and "discrimination" are defined in generally applicable state and federal statutes and caselaw, and those definitions inform their use in **Model Rule 8.4(g)**. A Comment to the Rule also explains that "discrimination includes harmful verbal or physical conduct that manifests bias or prejudice towards others," that "harassment includes sexual harassment and derogatory or demeaning verbal or physical conduct," and that "[s]exual harassment includes unwelcome sexual advances, requests for sexual favors, and other unwelcome verbal or physical conduct of a sexual nature." **Model Rule 8.4 Comment [3]**. *See* **Chapter 15.A at 429**.

5. **Model Rule 8.4(g)** limits its scope to conduct that a lawyer "knows or reasonably should know" is harassment or discrimination on the basis of a protected class. *See* **Chapter 15.A at 431**.

6. **Model Rule 8.4(g)** covers any "conduct *related to the practice of law*" (emphasis added), and **Model Rule 8.4 Comment [4]** explains that "conduct related to the practice of law" covers a range of activities a good deal wider than simply doing legal work for a client. *See* **Chapter 15.A at 431**.

7. **Model Rule 8.4(g)** and Comments to the Rule also provide some limits on the Rule's scope:

a. The text of the Rule itself disclaims any intent to interfere with a lawyer's power "to accept, decline or withdraw from a representation in accordance with Rule 1.16." So if **Model Rule 1.16** allows it (*see* **Chapter 9.D at 294**), **Model Rule 8.4(g)** probably doesn't prohibit it.

b. The Rule also disclaims any power to "preclude legitimate advice or advocacy consistent with these Rules" and consistent with First Amendment rights of free expression and petition, even if others might find the ideas advocated discriminatory or hateful.

c. In addition, conduct undertaken by lawyers or law firms to promote inclusiveness or diversity in the workplace or the bar that are permitted under other applicable law do not violate the rule. Nor do peremptory challenges to potential criminal jurors that violate *Batson v. Kentucky* (though that bears other **consequences**), limiting practice by subject matter or to underserved populations, or insisting on charging otherwise lawful fees. **Model Rule 8.4 Comments [4]-[5]**.

See **Chapter 15.A at 431**.

8. **Model Rule 8.4(g)** is new and controversial. Only three states have adopted it verbatim, though about half the states have in their Rules of Professional Conduct or Comments some kind of prohibition against discriminatory conduct, and virtually every state and the United States have generally applicable laws against discrimination and harassment. *See* **Chapter 15.B at 433**.

Multiple-Choice Review Questions for Chapter 15

1. A law firm is hiring five second-year law students for its summer associate class. The hiring committee, which comprises firm lawyers from various practice groups, meets to discuss eight potential candidates. Of those candidates, only one is an ethnic minority. Each of the eight candidates has different strengths and weaknesses.

    The committee discusses the candidates and determines that any of them would be appropriate members of the summer class. The committee ultimately selects the minority candidate and four other candidates. The minority candidate is selected, in part, because his inclusion will increase the overall diversity of the summer class.

    Does the committee's decision violate **Model Rule 8.4(g)**?

    a. No. **Model Rule 8.4(g)** applies only to lawyers. The second-year law students are not yet lawyers, so they are not bound by rules of professional conduct.

    b. No. **Model Rule 8.4(g)** prohibits only invidious discrimination. The rule permits efforts to promote diversity in hiring.

    c. Yes. **Model Rule 8.4(g)** prohibits discrimination. Selecting the minority candidate on the basis of his status prejudiced some of the nonminority candidates.

    d. Yes. **Model Rule 8.4(g)** requires that hiring processes be entirely neutral. The minority status of any candidate should not have been considered.

2. A young female associate arrives at a bar association networking event. The organizers, who are lawyers, inform her that she is seated at a table with other female associates. When she asks to move her seat so that she can network with more senior partners seated at other tables, she is told that she can't change her seat and that she should "lean in" with the other female associates.

    Does **Model Rule 8.4(g)** apply to this situation?

    a. Yes, even though the conduct does not relate to litigation of a specific case.

    b. Yes, because the conduct constitutes an unwelcome sexual advance.

    c. No, because assigning female lawyers to sit together is not prejudicial to the administration of justice.

    d. No, because this conduct is unrelated to the representation of a client.

3. A private defense lawyer is a practicing Seventh Day Adventist whose religion forbids working on the Sabbath. Although he generally accepts all sorts of criminal defense work, he refuses to accept domestic violence cases. He has a reason: Domestic violence cases often require that the lawyer seek a temporary restraining order on the client's behalf, and the emergent nature of these cases can require the lawyer to work on the weekend. Many, but not all, domestic violence cases are initiated by wives against their husbands.

    Does the lawyer's refusal to accept these types of cases violate **Model Rule 8.4(g)**?

    a. Yes. The effect of his refusal to accept domestic violence cases is tantamount to a refusal to represent women.

    b. Yes. His refusal to accept domestic violence cases is discrimination on the basis of a protected status, namely the status of being a crime victim.

    c. No. A lawyer has the autonomy to limit his practice, and this lawyer is not refusing to represent female clients.

    d. No. A lawyer may discriminate against women so long as the lawyer is guided by a sincerely held religious belief.

16

Threatening to Report and Reporting Wrongdoing

RATHER THAN DEPEND on our usual cast of characters, we'll start this chapter with a real, live, ripped-from-the-headlines "Mess in the Press": Michael Flatley is a successful dance producer known for developing the hit show *Riverdance* and other productions involving Irish folk dancing. Dean Mauro is a lawyer who threatened that unless he and his client (a young woman) immediately received a million-dollar "settlement" from Flatley, his client would sue Flatley for sexual assault. This is how a court reviewing the facts described Mauro's "settlement" demand:

> The key passage in Mauro's letter is at page 3 where Flatley is warned that, unless he settles, "an in-depth investigation" will be conducted into his personal assets to determine punitive damages and this information will then "BECOME A MATTER OF PUBLIC RECORD, AS IT MUST BE FILED WITH THE COURT. . . . Any and all information, including Immigration, Social Security Issuances and Use, and IRS and various State Tax Levies and information will be exposed. We are positive the media worldwide will enjoy what they find." This warning is repeated in the fifth paragraph: "[A]ll pertinent information and documentation, if in violation of any U.S. Federal, Immigration, I.R.S., S.S. Admin., U.S. State, Local, Commonwealth U.K., or International Laws, shall immediately [be] turned over to any and all appropriate authorities." Finally, Flatley is warned that once the lawsuit is filed additional causes of action "shall arise" including "Defamatory comments, Civil Conspiracy, Reckless Supervision" which are "just the beginning" and that "ample evidence" exists "to prove each and every element for all these additional causes of action. Again, these actions allow for Punitive Damages." At the top of the final page of the letter is the caption: "FIRST & FINAL TIME-LIMIT SETTLEMENT DEMAND." Beneath it a paragraph warns that there shall be "no continuances nor any delays." At the bottom of the page, beneath Mauro's signature, a final

paragraph warns Flatley that, along with the filing of suit, press releases will be disseminated to numerous media sources and placed on the Internet.[1]

Before we start, let's focus on the particular kinds of threats and reporting that we'll be discussing in this chapter. We're *not* going to talk here about lawyers' rights and duties in remonstrating with clients about the disclosure of, or actually disclosing, bad or embarrassing facts about, or conduct by, the clients themselves. These issues implicate the **duty of confidentiality** and related concerns about when you **may** or **must** disclose **confidential information**. *See* **Chapter 8.B at 235**; **Chapter 9.D at 298**; **Chapter 24.C at 878**. Instead, we'll focus on lawyers' threats to third parties, including opposing parties, opposing counsel, and true third parties—specifically, threats to disclose those third parties' alleged bad acts or to engage in other conduct adverse to their interests. We'll also focus on the related issue of simply making the disclosures or engaging in the adverse conduct without threatening first.

A. Threats

Some lawyers treat their bar cards as licenses to intimidate. Threats (broadly construed) do have a proper role in good advocacy, but that role, and the types of threats that the law actually permits, are far more limited than many lawyers seem to understand. Let's make sure that you won't suffer the **consequences** for that kind of mistake. To explain what's okay and what's not requires a little historical background, along with the context of other applicable law.[2]

Everyone has always agreed that "threatening" to pursue a civil process or remedy that the law actually provides as a means to resolve a civil dispute is perfectly proper. For example, ever since there have been civil actions, lawyers have been "threatening" that they will pursue a civil action on a client's behalf to collect a legitimate debt unless the debtor pays it promptly. But the propriety of threats that don't fit into this rather narrow category is more complicated.

The set of model ethical rules that the ABA promulgated before the Model Rules of Professional Conduct was called the Model Code of Professional Responsibility. The Model Code was first proposed in 1969, and for a time it was widely (though not universally) adopted by many state bars and other disciplinary

---

[1] *Flatley v. Mauro*, 39 Cal. 4th 299, 329-330 (2006) (paragraph breaks omitted). Rather than pay Mauro and his client, Flatley sued them for (among other things) civil extortion and defamation. The California Supreme Court concluded that Mauro's demand was "criminal extortion as a matter of law." *Id.* at 325. The Supreme Court of Illinois, where Mauro was licensed to practice, suspended Mauro for one year. *In re Mauro*, No. M.R. 21548, https://courts.illinois.gov/SupremeCourt/Announce/2007/051807.pdf (May 18, 2007). Mauro eventually paid Flatley $400,000 to resolve Flatley's claims against him; https://www.lawyersandsettlements.com/settlements/09208/creator-defamation.html (Aug. 31, 2007).

[2] For detailed and thoughtful expositions of these issues, *see* David McGowan, *Lawyer Threats*, https://papers.ssrn.com/sol3/papers.cfm?abstract_id=3756363 (2020); Douglas A. Richmond, *Saber-Rattling and the Sound of Professional Responsibility*, 34 Am. J. Trial Advoc. 27 (2010).

authorities. *See* **Chapter 3.A at 31**. One of the Model Code's disciplinary rules was **Model Code DR 7-105(A)**, which stated:

> A lawyer shall not present, participate in presenting or threaten to present criminal charges solely to obtain an advantage in a civil matter.

The "criminal charges" referred to in the Model Code were generally understood to include not only reports of alleged criminal conduct to prosecutors or law enforcement, but also complaints of professional misconduct to a professional licensing or disciplinary authority (which were and are considered "quasi-criminal" for due process purposes; that is, they involve what is viewed as a fundamental right to earn a livelihood by practicing law or some other licensed profession). The professional discipline available for such improper threats was independent of any court sanctions or tort or criminal liability that, depending on the circumstances and applicable law, might also result from the same conduct.[3]

The drafters of the Model Rules took a different approach to this issue. There is no corresponding provision to the predecessor **Model Code DR 7-105(A)** in the Model Rules. An ABA Ethics Opinion explains that the provision was "deliberately omitted as redundant or overbroad or both,"[4] and that the omission "rested on the drafters' position that 'extortionate, fraudulent, or otherwise abusive threats were covered by other, more general prohibitions in the Model Rules and thus that there was no need to outlaw such threats specifically.'"[5]

The Model Rules thus take a somewhat broader view of when threats of criminal or quasi-criminal charges **may** be made in order to achieve an advantage in the resolution of civil disputes. According to the ABA Opinion, a lawyer may threaten to lodge (or may negotiate an agreement not to lodge) criminal or quasi-criminal charges in order to obtain an advantage in a civil dispute if three criteria are met:

1. The criminal charge is "related to the civil claim";
2. The lawyer has a "well-founded belief that both the civil claim and the possible criminal charges are warranted by the law and the facts"; and
3. The lawyer does not "attempt to exert or suggest improper influence over the criminal process."[6]

Your House; Your Rules▸ A number of states have retained more restrictive disciplinary rules on threats of criminal or quasi-criminal charges similar to **Model**

---

[3] For this reason, you'll run into older lawyers who will insist, as they learned when they were in law school before the Model Rules were widely adopted, that *any* threat of a criminal or quasi-criminal charge is strictly forbidden. And as we'll discuss below, this is still the rule in some states. But as we'll now see, the Model Rules have relaxed this restriction, and a majority of states now follow the more permissive approach of the Model Rules.

[4] ABA Formal Ethics Op. No. 92-363 (1992) at 3 (quoting 2 G.C. HAZARD, JR. & W.W. HODES, THE LAW OF LAWYERING (2nd ed. 1990) § 4.4:103).

[5] *Id.* (quoting C.W. WOLFRAM, MODERN LEGAL ETHICS § 13.5.5, at 718 (1986)).

[6] *Id.* at 2.

Code DR 7-105(A).[7] Obviously, you must follow the rules of your licensing jurisdiction. YOUR HOUSE; YOUR RULES

Even in states that have adopted the less-restrictive Model Rules approach, it's worth reviewing what kinds of threats are still *never* allowed. Anything that amounts to the tort or crime of extortion (blackmail) is forbidden. The precise definition of extortion varies from state to state, but unsurprisingly, it's unlawful everywhere. Among others, the following threats are considered extortionate and, if made by a lawyer, can comprise a disciplinary violation in most jurisdictions that follow the Model Rules:

- Threats to make criminal or quasi-criminal charges unrelated to, or to disclose embarrassing or otherwise prejudicial facts not genuinely relevant to, a civil dispute under discussion;
- Threats to make criminal or quasi-criminal charges that have no substantial basis in fact or law (*see also* **Model Rule 3.1**, prohibiting "frivolous" claims; **Model Rule 8.4(d)**, prohibiting conduct "prejudicial to the administration of justice");
- Threats to engage in otherwise lawful conduct without any actual intention to do so (*see* **Model Rule 4.1(a)** and **Chapter 10.A at 323**; ABA Formal Ethics Op. No. 92-363 (1992) at 4);
- Threats based on an effort to improperly influence, or suggesting an ability to improperly influence, government officials (*see* **Model Rule 8.4(e)**, prohibiting such conduct); and
- Threats to inflict violence or to engage in any other illegal conduct in order to secure any advantage of any kind.

These threats are generally tortious and potentially criminal even when the threatened charges or disclosures are completely true (and threats like this are even worse if they're unfounded). That's why blackmailers still go to prison for threatening to disclose authentic compromising photographs unless they are paid sums of money by the person in the photographs. In addition to the specific disciplinary rules just cited, all of these threats are subject to professional discipline under **Model Rule 4.4(a)** and many also are subject to discipline under **Model Rule 8.4(b)** (prohibiting conduct that comprises "a criminal act that reflects adversely on the lawyer's honesty, trustworthiness or fitness as a lawyer in other respects"). *See* **Chapter 14.A at 415; Chapter 14.B at 420**. In sum, extortion (and attempted extortion) are disciplinary offenses, torts, and also potentially crimes. That adds up to a really bad idea any way you look at it.

Another common mistake that lawyers make is to believe, as the lawyer in the **chapter Introduction at 439** apparently did, that the rules of evidence or other

---

[7] *See id.* at 5-6 (Connecticut, Illinois, Maine, New Jersey, Texas, Wisconsin); California, New York, and Tennessee also take a similar approach. As with everything else in this book, please check your own jurisdiction's Rules before acting.

law somehow negate these restrictions on threatening speech or conduct if the threats are clothed in demands to "settle" a civil dispute. **Federal Rule of Evidence 408(a)** (and similar state evidentiary rules) makes any offer in compromise or other conduct during negotiation inadmissible "to prove or disprove the validity or amount of a disputed claim." Lawyers sometimes misinterpret these laws to provide that they can threaten anything during settlement negotiations and never have it used against them. That's simply wrong: If you demand that your opposing party settle a civil claim or else you will report her for an unrelated crime, or will publish compromising photographs of her with a paramour, Rule 408 will not protect you. (Why? Because the evidence of your extortionate threats will not be used "to prove or disprove the validity or amount of a disputed claim"; it will be used to prove that you actually committed a crime, tort, or disciplinary violation. *See* **Fed. R. Evid 408(b)**.)

[TIPS & TACTICS] The above discussion is about the threats that you **must not** make, and it does not address whether you **should** or **should not** use threats that your jurisdiction actually permits, even when you have the opportunity. We can group potential threats into three categories, each with different practical implications that you should consider when a threat is not forbidden and you're tempted to make it:

1. If you see the need to threaten to pursue civil causes of action or remedies to which your client has a substantial claim as part of a negotiated resolution of that claim, feel free. This kind of "threat" is universally accepted as proper, and it is the essence of any standard demand letter.

2. If you're thinking about threatening to report a significant ethics violation by your opposing counsel to the relevant disciplinary authority in order to achieve some advantage in a civil dispute, don't. In jurisdictions that follow **Model Code DR 7-105(A)**, this threat is flatly forbidden. Even in jurisdictions that follow the more relaxed restrictions of the Model Rules, your *opposing counsel's* ethical violation is going to have to be related to your client's civil claim against your *opposing party*, which is not always true and not always easy to determine. Most important, a threat to disclose the violation implies an invitation to bargain for something in exchange for *not* disclosing it. But in the states (about 35 of them) that have adopted **Model Rule 8.3**, a Rule we will discuss in detail in **Chapter 16.D at 446** below, you **must** promptly disclose to your bar disciplinary authority any ethical violation by another lawyer "that raises a substantial question as to that lawyer's honesty, trustworthiness or fitness as a lawyer in other respects" unless the violation is **confidential information**. That effectively prevents you from using it to bargain in the matter you're handling.

3. Any time that you think that you might have the power under governing law to threaten something other than to pursue civil causes of action or remedies to which your client has a substantial claim, think twice. The

line in many jurisdictions between a proper and an illegal threat can be razor-thin. Unless you're sure that you and your client are well within your rights, you may find yourself embroiled in a protracted, embarrassing, and expensive sideshow over whether or not you just attempted extortion. If that dispute is at all arguable, you and your client will end it worse off than when you started, even if you eventually prevail. The judge will likely be at best annoyed that she has to determine whether you did something arguably unethical and perhaps illegal; the results if you lose will be exceedingly painful for both you and your client; your client will be unhappy about the delay and expense, regardless of the outcome; and the accusation may stick in public memory even if the allegation that you attempted extortion is eventually rejected: Your reputation may linger among those who read about the dustup in the local or legal press but who don't remember the result—you'll be "that" lawyer who might have tried to leverage a law license into a protection racket. So consider the risks and potential rewards carefully before proceeding. **Tips & Tactics**

B. Presenting Criminal Charges to Gain Advantage in a Civil Matter

OK, the alert reader is now thinking, if threats can be so risky, then what if I forget about *threatening* and just *do* things *without* any advance threat, such as seeking an advantage in a civil case by reporting an adverse party's alleged criminal behavior, or disclosing embarrassing facts not genuinely relevant to the dispute, without threatening to do it first? (Great question, alert reader; we'd throw you a parade if we had the trombones!) Once again, however, nuance and interjurisdictional variations abound.

Model Code DR 7-105(A) expressly prohibits "present[ing]" or "participat[ing] in presenting" criminal charges "solely to obtain an advantage in a civil dispute" as well as "threatening" to present such charges for that purpose. In jurisdictions that still follow the old rule literally, then, just *reporting* criminal charges without threatening to do so beforehand, even if those charges are valid and well-grounded in fact, may not be used to leverage the resolution of a civil matter. **Your House; Your Rules** And by now, you should be expecting this sentence from us: Not all jurisdictions have adopted the prohibitions on "present[ing]" criminal charges in DR 7-105(A), and some have interpreted those prohibitions partially or entirely out of the Rule, so figuring out what's actually allowed in your specific state is (as it always is) a really good idea.[8] **Your House; Your Rules**

---

[8] *See* ABA Informal Ethics Op. No. 1484 (1981) (reporting criminal charges without a prior threat in order to gain advantage in a civil matter does not violate Model Code DR 7-105(A), at least where the criminal charges are based on the same conduct as the civil dispute). The alert reader (that's you!) will have noticed that, though perhaps justified by practical concerns, this conclusion is difficult to reconcile with the literal language of the Disciplinary Rule.

Jurisdictions that have adopted the Model Rules approach generally apply the same restrictions to simply *presenting* criminal charges that they apply to *threatening to present* them: You may present or participate in presenting criminal charges to gain an advantage in a civil matter if (1) the criminal charges are related to the civil dispute; (2) you have a well-founded belief that both the civil claim and the possible criminal charges are warranted by the law and the facts; and (3) you do not attempt to exert or suggest improper influence over the criminal process. ABA Formal Ethics Op. No. 92-363 (1992) at 2 n.3. In other words, in these jurisdictions, if you **may** threaten it, you **may** also just go ahead and do it without threatening; and if you **must not** threaten it, you apparently **must not** just do it, either (though this is not entirely clear in some states).

C. CONSEQUENCES Consequences for Improper Threats

As just discussed, some states still have an express disciplinary rule forbidding a lawyer from threatening to present or presenting criminal charges to gain advantage in a civil matter. In addition (and more generally), improper threats are frequently found to violate **Model Rule 4.4(a)**, because the effort to secure an unfair or improper advantage in a civil matter usually "has no substantial purpose other than to embarrass, delay, or burden"—the "burden" here being the one imposed by obtaining that improper advantage. *See* **Chapter 14.A at 415**. Depending on the nature of the threat or related conduct, improper threats can also violate other disciplinary rules. *See* **Chapter 14.B at 420**.

As is the case with other violations of **Model Rule 4.4(a)**, improper threats can result not only in professional discipline but also in court-imposed sanctions and tort liability. *See* **Chapter 14.B at 420**. As noted in the **chapter Introduction at 439**, in response to lawyer Dean Mauro's threats, Michael Flatley sued Mauro for (among other things) civil extortion and defamation; in addition to being suspended from practice, Mauro paid Flatley $400,000 to resolve those claims. CONSEQUENCES

> **Problem 16C-1:** Go back to **this chapter's Introduction at 439** and review Mauro's "settlement" demand to Michael Flatley. Do you agree with the California Supreme Court that the demand was extortionate on its face? If not, why not? If so, what specifically about the demand transformed it from what might have been a proper effort to resolve a civil claim into an improper attempt at blackmail?

> **Problem 16C-2:** Which of the following actions violate **Model Code DR-7-105(A)**? Which violate **Model Rule 4.4(a)** or another Model Rule? For each scenario, identify the Rule(s) and explain your conclusion(s).
>
> a. Frank is litigating the landlord-tenant case described in **Problem 14A-1(a) at 418**. The defendant's response to Frank's initial document request contains a number of what Frank

considers facially defective objections. Frank sends a meet-and-confer letter to opposing counsel, identifying the offending objections and demanding their withdrawal and the production of responsive documents within two weeks, "or we will be forced to seek all available remedies, including Rule 37 sanctions." (Rule 37 in Frank's state is the same as **Fed. R. Civ. P. 37**.)

b. Same case as in (a). Frank receives an email from defense counsel threatening to report Frank to the state bar's disciplinary committee for pursuing his client's "frivolous" claim unless Frank settles the case immediately.

c. Same landlord-tenant case as in (a)-(b). Frank receives an email from opposing counsel that says, in part, "My client's recent inspection of your client's unit revealed what appears to be a marijuana plant growing in the living room. Perhaps you should consider settling this case before the police find out."

d. Same as in (c), except opposing counsel simply informs the police about the marijuana plant without telling Frank or his client.

D. Reporting Another Lawyer's Wrongful Conduct

The preceding discussion has surveyed the kinds of threats and reporting in which a lawyer **must not** or **may** (but is not required to) engage. Many students are surprised to learn that there is one category of wrongful behavior by third parties that lawyers **must** report: serious ethical violations by another lawyer. Specifically, **Model Rule 8.3(a)** states:

> A lawyer who knows that another lawyer has committed a violation of the Rules of Professional Conduct that raises a substantial question as to that lawyer's honesty, trustworthiness or fitness as a lawyer in other respects, shall inform the appropriate professional authority.[9]

This mandatory reporting provision, which is sometimes demeaningly referred to as the "tattletale" or "rat-on" rule, is controversial. Critics believe that the Rule unnecessarily creates moral or personal dilemmas for lawyers who may find themselves required to report colleagues, friends, or relations. Proponents argue that the duty to report other lawyers' misconduct is part of the Rules' general project of protecting the public and has strong precedents in university and military service academy honor codes with similar terms.[10] *See* **Model Rule 8.3 Comment [1]**. Your House; Your Rules Regardless of your views on its wisdom, this Rule is the law in roughly 35 states, and you need to know whether it applies in yours. Your House; Your Rules

---

[9] **Model Rule 8.3(b)** requires lawyers to report serious ethical lapses by judges in similar terms.

[10] Take a look at your own law school's Honor Code and see if it includes a similar rule. (**Hint**: It probably does.) For precedent from our military service academies, *see* https://en.wikipedia.org/wiki/Cadet_Honor_Code#:~:text=The%20 code%20adopted%20was%20based%20largely%20on%20West,which%20was%20to%20be%20taken%20by%20 all%20cadets.

Now, in order to make sure that we understand the details of this obligation, let's break down the reporting requirement using that phrase-by-phrase method that we're hoping is now second nature to you.

1. [Taming the Text] "Knows"

Before any reporting obligation arises under **Model Rule 8.3**, a lawyer has to "know[]" about another lawyer's ethical violation. As you'll recall, "know" means "actual knowledge" (**Model Rule 1.0(e)**); thus "should have known" is not sufficient to invoke the reporting requirement, but "willful blindness" or "conscious avoidance" probably is. (*See* **Chapter 13.A at 393**.) Similarly, the Rule's knowledge requirement does not carry with it a requirement to investigate, but a conscious refusal to confirm something that you think (or fear) might be true may be seen as "willful blindness," and thus may be considered equivalent to actual knowledge.

2. [Taming the Text] "Another Lawyer"

The required reporting is of serious ethical violations by "another lawyer." Thus, the Rule doesn't apply to misconduct by unlicensed lay people. But it does apply to *any* other lawyer, whether that lawyer is your opposing counsel, law partner, friend, relative, or a total stranger about whom you have acquired knowledge of wrongdoing.

3. [Taming the Text] "A Violation of the Rules of Professional Conduct That Raises a Substantial Question as to That Lawyer's Honesty, Trustworthiness or Fitness as a Lawyer in Other Respects"

The Rule does not require reporting of just *any* wrong by another lawyer. It is limited in two important respects: First, reporting is limited to "a violation of the Rules of Professional Conduct." As we've learned, the Rules don't forbid every conceivable crime, tort, or other wrong, but because of the broad "catchall" provisions of **Model Rules 8.4(b), (c), and (d)**, they do cover a lot of them.

Second, the violation of a Rule of Professional Conduct has to be one "that raises a substantial question as to [the misbehaving] lawyer's honesty, trustworthiness or fitness as a lawyer in other respects." In other words, minor or technical Rules violations generally don't fall within **Model Rule 8.3(a)**. Only ones that carry an element of serious blameworthiness or dishonesty, sometimes referred to as "moral turpitude," **must** be reported. *See* **Model Rule 8.3 Comment [3]** (the requirement that the violation raise a "substantial" question about the lawyer's fitness "limits the reporting obligation to those offenses that a self-regulating profession must vigorously endeavor to prevent").

4. [Taming the Text] "Shall Inform the Appropriate Professional Authority"

The use of "shall" makes clear that this is a **"must"** Rule. As for the identity of the "appropriate professional authority" that must be informed, that will usually be the bar disciplinary authority of the jurisdiction in which the misbehaving lawyer is licensed (and, if different, also the jurisdiction in which the violation was committed). If the violation occurred in a tribunal with its own disciplinary mechanism (for example, a federal court or administrative agency), that disciplinary authority must also be informed, as well as the one for any other licensing jurisdiction (such as the state that granted the misbehaving lawyer a license to practice).

5. TAMING THE TEXT Exceptions to the Mandatory Reporting Requirement

The broad reporting mandate in **Model Rule 8.3(a)** is limited by two exceptions stated in **Model Rule 8.3(c)**. Both are important from a policy standpoint, but one comes up a lot more frequently than the other.

a. TAMING THE TEXT "Information Otherwise Protected by Rule 1.6"

First, **Model Rule 8.3(c)** says that you are not required to report "information otherwise protected by Rule 1.6." As you'll recall (*see* **Chapter 8.A at 211**), this is one of the phrases that the Rules use to describe **confidential information**. So if you can't report a serious ethical violation by another lawyer without disclosing information that you **must not** disclose under your **duty of confidentiality**, you are not required to report it. In other words, your **duty of confidentiality** trumps your reporting duty under **Model Rule 8.3**.

b. TAMING THE TEXT "Information Gained . . . While Participating in an Approved Lawyers Assistance Program"

The other exception to the mandatory reporting requirement of **Model Rule 8.3(a)** is information learned "while participating in an approved lawyers assistance program." Every state and the District of Columbia has a program created by rule, statute, or court order designed to assist lawyers and law students who are struggling with substance abuse, anxiety, depression, or other illness. Illnesses like these are often accompanied by practice, personal, or academic mishaps, and lawyer assistance programs are generally endowed with resources and authority to assist the struggling lawyer in managing them. In order to encourage participation, most of these programs also incorporate broad **confidentiality** guarantees that protect participants from being reported to disciplinary authorities by program officers while the lawyer is cooperating with the assistance program in managing the situation. *See* **Chapter 4.C at 94. Model Rule 8.3(c)** formalizes the programs' **confidentiality** guarantees and avoids creating conflicting disclosure obligations. TAMING THE TEXT

6. CONSEQUENCES Consequences for Violation of Model Rule 8.3

Model Rule 8.3 is a Rule of Professional Conduct. As a result, the **consequence** for its violation is professional discipline. Whether this ethical reporting duty influences civil duties enforceable in damages or sanctions remains largely unexplored. CONSEQUENCES

Problem 16D-1: Danielle has become friendly with her principal supervisor, who is becoming a mentor. While they're at lunch one day, the supervisor looks shaken and upset. Danielle asks what's bothering him. He tells her that he recently went to see an old friend with whom he had worked in the DA's office for many years, but who recently retired for health reasons. His friend had just learned that the cancer that caused him to retire had not responded to treatment, and that he had just a few weeks to live. In the course of their reminiscing about their years together in the DA's office, the friend expressed remorse about a murder case that he had prosecuted some years before. He confided that he had concealed forensic evidence that would have exonerated the defendant, who was convicted and is now sitting on death row. "He had a couple of felonies on his record," the friend said, "and I figured, what the hell, he's a bad guy we need to get off the street. I wonder about that now."

"What did you say? Danielle asks. "I told him there was an innocent guy on death row, and he needed to fix it," the supervisor replies. "He said that the guy wasn't innocent; he just probably didn't commit the murder he was convicted of. I pointed out that just wasn't right, and he said he'd think about it."

"What happened?" Danielle asks. "He died this past Monday," the supervisor says, sadly. "I don't think he got around to dealing with it." "What are you going to do?" Danielle asks. "I haven't decided yet," her supervisor replies. "The guy was a legend in the office, and he was one of my closest friends." What **must, may,** or **should** the supervisor do, and why? What about Danielle?[11]

Problem 16D-2: Frank has just settled a small personal injury case. In completing the settlement, defense counsel has just sent over what he describes in his cover letter as "a duplicate original settlement agreement countersigned by my client, and a check in the settlement amount drawn on our office's account on behalf of our client." The settlement documentation is in order, and the check is in the right amount. Frank is relieved, because this opposing counsel had been unreliable and quite difficult to deal with, and Frank really dislikes him.

Frank recently worked with his firm's bookkeeper on a routine state bar audit of his firm's trust accounts, and he learned that, under the Rules of Professional Conduct in force in his state, checks drawn on an attorney trust account **must** have, in the drawer information in the upper left corner of the check, the name of the lawyer or law firm maintaining the account and the words "ATTORNEY TRUST ACCOUNT" in at least 12-point font. The settlement check opposing counsel just delivered has only the attorney's name and address

---

[11] This problem is loosely based on the facts of *In re Riehlmann*, 891 So.2d 1239 (La. 2005).

in the upper left corner. **Must** Frank report this violation to the state bar? If reporting the violation is not required, **may** Frank report it? **Should** he? Does your answer to any of those questions change if Frank calls the bank on which the check is drawn and is told that the account on which the check is drawn is not an attorney trust account? Please explain your answers.

Problem 16D-3: Same as **Problem 16D-2 at 449**, except that opposing counsel sends over only the fully executed settlement agreement, without the check for the settlement amount. When Frank calls opposing counsel to ask about the money, opposing counsel is evasive. "Have you got the money in your trust account?" Frank asks. "No," replies opposing counsel, "I don't keep a trust account. That's an extra expense I don't need. But I do have the money." "Could I ask you please to send it over?" Frank says, working hard to conceal his surprise. "My client needs the money." "When I get around to it," says opposing counsel.

Frank receives the settlement funds the next week and decides to leave the whole experience behind him. A couple of months later, however, Frank reads in the local paper that his former opposing counsel filed bankruptcy after his ex-wife cleaned out his bank account to collect unpaid child support, leaving numerous other parties that had settled with the broke lawyer's clients (represented by lawyers other than Frank's firm) without the settlement money that the opposing counsel's insurance company clients had entrusted to him, because he had kept the settlement funds in his personal bank account. "Couldn't have happened to a nicer guy," Frank thinks to himself. But then he starts to wonder: Should he have reported opposing counsel's failure to maintain a trust account to the state bar? If he had, the bar might have stepped in, and those other plaintiffs might have gotten their money by now. Frank starts to worry whether he might face any **consequences** from those other plaintiffs. Does he? Why or why not? Please explain your answers.

Problem 16D-4: Frank is helping the litigation partner at his firm, "Happy" Trials, oppose a motion for summary judgment in a pending case. Key evidence creating disputed issues of material fact will come from a declaration (a form of witness statement signed under penalty of perjury that is permitted in Frank's state in lieu of an affidavit) provided by a third-party witness. Frank and Happy have been in contact with the witness, and they have worked out a statement with her that she has indicated is accurate. After they submit the filing, Frank and Happy sit down over a beer to catch their breath. "Whew!" Happy says. "That was a close one." "What do you mean?" Frank asks. "Well, I found out yesterday that, before signing her declaration, our key witness left on a trip to rural Sub-Saharan Africa with a relief organization, and was essentially unreachable." Frank suddenly feels a little sick. "What did you do?" he asks. "Well," says Happy, "she had said the statement was accurate when we discussed it, so I just signed it for her." **Must** Frank report this to the state bar? If reporting the violation is not required, **may** Frank report it? **Should** he? What else, if anything, **must, may,** or **should** Frank do? Please explain your answers.

Big-Picture Takeaways from Chapter 16

1. In terms of when you can "threaten" someone with **consequences** of some sort:

    a. The now-superseded Model Code of Professional Responsibility prohibited all threats of criminal or quasi-criminal **consequences** and allowed only threats to pursue a civil action or remedy to which the lawyer's client had a well-grounded right. A significant minority of jurisdictions that have generally adopted the Model Rules have nevertheless retained this provision from the Model Code, or something like it. *See* **Chapter 16.A at 440**.

    b. The Model Rules take a somewhat broader view of what kinds of threats of criminal or quasi-criminal charges may be threatened in order to achieve an advantage in the negotiation of civil disputes. According to an ABA Formal Ethics Opinion, in addition to what was permitted under the Model Code, a lawyer may threaten to lodge (or may negotiate an agreement not to lodge) criminal or quasi-criminal charges in order to obtain an advantage in a civil dispute if three criteria are met: (1) the criminal charge is "related to the civil claim"; (2) the lawyer has a "well-founded belief that both the civil claim and the possible criminal charges are warranted by the law and the facts"; and (3) the lawyer does not "attempt to exert or suggest improper influence over the criminal process." *See* **Chapter 16.A at 441**.

    c. Even though some threats are permitted, many kinds are still not okay in any jurisdiction. *See* **Chapter 16.A at 442** for an inventory of those you must always avoid.

    d. And even if you wish to go straight to reporting without threatening to report first, remember that the minority rule under the Model Code forbids you from "presenting" any charge that you **must not** threaten. The majority view under the Model Rules appears to be that if you **may** threaten to make a criminal or quasi-criminal charge, then you **may** present it without threatening it first, but if you **may not** threaten it, then you **may not** just present it without threatening, either. *See* **Chapter 16.B at 444**.

2. There is one category of wrongful behavior by third parties that lawyers **must** report: serious ethical violations by another lawyer. **Model Rule 8.3(a).** A lawyer **must** report to the appropriate disciplinary authority any violation of the Rules of Professional Conduct that the lawyer "knows" about (which includes actual knowledge and willful blindness) by "another lawyer" (*any* other lawyer) "that raises a substantial question as to [the

misbehaving] lawyer's honesty, trustworthiness or fitness as a lawyer in other respects." The Rule has two express exceptions: (a) your **duty of confidentiality** trumps your reporting duty under **Model Rule 8.3**, so you **must not** report any violation if the report requires disclosure of **confidential information** not subject to an exception to the **duty of confidentiality**; and (b) any information that you've learned "while participating in an approved lawyers' assistance program" is also protected. (That second exception means that if you're volunteering as a program officer in a LAP ("lawyers' assistance program"), you **must** keep confidential anything that you learn from a lawyer who's participating in that program to the extent required by the LAP's rules. *See* **Chapter 16.D at 446**.

Multiple-Choice Review Questions for Chapter 16

1. Cliff, a stuntman, has been sued in a civil case alleging breach of contract after he got in a fight on a movie set and broke another stuntman's nose. His employment contract with the production company required him to refrain from any contact with the other stuntman, but several witnesses have indicated that Cliff started the fight. The fight was also caught on video, and it shows Cliff slamming the other stuntman face-first into a car. The video was produced to Cliff's counsel in discovery.

   Cliff is being a jerk during his deposition. He put his boots up on the table, ignores questions asked of him, and lights a cigarette. His lawyer is doing nothing to control his client.

   Counsel for the production company has been trying to get Cliff under control for over an hour. In frustration, counsel says "Cliff, if you don't answer my questions, I'll send the video to the local prosecutor's office—they might charge you with assault."

   Does this statement violate **Model Rule 4.4(a)**?

   a. Yes, because the threat was made in an effort to gain an advantage for the production company. Specifically, counsel was using a threat of criminal prosecution as leverage to get Cliff to cooperate and testify during the deposition.

   b. Yes, because had counsel truly believed that the video showed an assault, she would have sent it to the prosecutor's office long before the deposition.

   c. No, because the Rules do not prohibit a lawyer from using the possibility of presenting criminal charges against the opposing party in a civil matter to gain relief for her client, provided that the criminal matter is related to the civil claim, the lawyer has a well-founded belief that both the civil claim and the possible criminal charges are warranted by the law and the facts, and the lawyer does not attempt to exert or suggest improper influence over the criminal process.

d. No, because the language of the Rule prohibits a lawyer only from making a threat of a criminal referral where the "sole purpose" of the threat is to gain an advantage in a civil case. Here, counsel has articulated two purposes, both to gain an advantage in the civil case but also to ensure Cliff is brought to justice for the assault.

2. Can a lawyer threaten to report another lawyer to a disciplinary authority?
   a. Yes. The lawyer can threaten to report misconduct as long as the threat does not amount to a violation of any Model Rule.
   b. Yes. A lawyer must first threaten and allow an opportunity to cure before reporting misconduct.
   c. No. The lawyer must simply report the misconduct. Threats are never permitted.
   d. No. Any threat to report a lawyer constitutes harassment and is prohibited.

3. Your client, Gambino, owner of a local diner, is being sued by Genovese, the owner of a neighboring café, for allegedly dishonest advertisements that have resulted in a loss of business for Genovese and his cafe's decline. During discovery, you receive a call from Genovese's lawyer, who is threatening to take evidence of Gambino's possible tax fraud to the authorities. This act would ruin your client's reputation in the community and would surely invite criminal charges from the relevant taxing authorities. Genovese's lawyer promises that all of this could be avoided if Gambino agrees to what is effectively a punitive settlement. "I'm doing this because false advertisements are bad for everybody," Genovese's lawyer explains. Do you have recourse against Genovese's lawyer?
   a. No. The Model Code of Professional Responsibility has prohibited lawyers from threatening to present criminal charges *solely* to obtain an advantage in a civil matter. Genovese's lawyer said that he had another reason for the threat.
   b. No. Genovese's lawyer has a point: Crime doesn't pay.
   c. Yes. The Model Rules prohibit engaging in conduct that is prejudicial to the administration of justice or has no substantial purpose other than to embarrass, delay, or burden someone else. Assuming that you can show that opposing counsel's conduct meets either of these standards, you may have recourse.
   d. Yes. Model Rule 3.1 bars frivolous claims.

4. Assume the same facts as in the previous question. After reviewing the options with your client, Gambino, he agrees to settle the case on the terms demanded. You do nothing with respect to the threats made by Genovese's lawyer, though Gambino has indicated to you that he has no objection to your doing so. Assuming that you know that Genovese's lawyer committed a violation of the Rules that raises a question as to his honesty, trustworthiness, or fitness as a lawyer, have you violated the Model Rules?

   a. No. The Model Rules do not require the reporting of your opposing counsel's violations of the Model Rules.

   b. No. You have not violated the Model Rules, and thus this entire episode falls outside the authority of the Model Rules.

   c. Yes. You have committed an ethics violation for failing to represent your client zealously.

   d. Yes. Genovese's lawyer's conduct has raised serious questions about his honesty, trustworthiness, or fitness as a lawyer.

17

Offering or Agreeing to Restrict Your Future Practice

FRANK AND HIS firm's litigation partner, Harlan "Happy" Trials, have been pursuing a products-liability case. The firm's client, Holly Hydrate, got seriously ill after drinking a bottle of "intelligent water"—advertised as purified water with some healthy additives, such as vitamins and electrolytes—prepared and distributed by a company called H2Whoa. By investing in some first-rate medical and chemical experts early in the case, then fighting tooth-and-nail through an extensive series of motions to force H2Whoa to cough up some critical discovery, and *then* laboriously sorting through the hundreds of thousands of pages of documents that H2Whoa eventually produced, Frank's firm has gathered evidence showing that a manufacturing lot of H2Whoa's smart water was accidentally contaminated with small amounts of a solvent called Toxate. Toxate is used to clean industrial equipment, and H2Whoa used it to clean its bottling equipment. Toxate ordinarily breaks down soon after exposure to the air and rinses off with water, but in this case, H2Whoa didn't rinse the equipment thoroughly enough and then used it too soon after cleaning. As a result, small amounts of Toxate were sealed into bottles of H2Whoa. Unfortunately, even small amounts of Toxate in this form can cause liver damage, and the plaintiff's experts have concluded that this is what happened to Holly Hydrate. H2Whoa has insisted throughout the litigation that its product had nothing to do with Holly's injuries. Frank's firm hasn't yet let on to the other side what it has discovered.

Soon after producing documents, H2Whoa's lawyers reach out to Frank's firm and suggest a meeting to discuss settlement. This has been an exceptionally hard-fought case at every step, but now the lead lawyer at the big firm representing H2Whoa—Lamont Libben of Libben Large—is all smiles and hospitality. As coffee and soft drinks are handed around, he gets to the matter at hand. "Well, gentlemen, you certainly put us through our paces," Lamont begins, "and my team remains confident that you won't be able to prove that H2Whoa is what caused Ms. Hydrate's health issues. But H2Whoa is getting tired of our bills, and they've asked us to see if we can get this matter resolved."

"We're always open to discussion," says Happy, pleasantly. "Glad to hear it," replies Lamont. "Then let's talk some numbers. As I understand it, Ms. Hydrate's medical expenses were $100,000 . . . ." "Actually, $150,000," Happy interjects, gently. "You have the medical records. She spent nearly a month in the hospital, and though she did manage to avoid a liver transplant, she may have permanent liver damage." Happy then goes on to summarize future medical expenses, loss of consortium, and past and future pain and suffering. Lamont, assisted by members of his team attending the meeting, responds on the damage issues and provides a detailed argument on causation. After considerable back-and-forth, Lamont offers $1.2 million "in full settlement of everything."

Frank tries hard to control his expression. This is an amount recognizably in excess of the reasonable settlement value of Holly's case alone. They must be really worried that we'll find out about the Toxate, Frank thinks. There must be other victims out there.

"Just so we're clear," Happy says, "that settlement includes a release and dismissal from our client in the usual form?" "Sure, but that's not all," says Lamont. "H2Whoa sells a mass-marketed product. We can't let this tarnish its good name. So we'd have to have a very strict confidentiality provision preventing your client from mentioning the suit or the settlement to anyone." "We can discuss that with her," Happy responds. "Anything else?" "I need you and Ms. Hydrate to understand that the confidentiality provision is indispensable," Lamont replies. "We can't make a deal without it. And, of course, it would include terms preventing you and your firm from bringing any claims against H2Whoa or anyone associated with it on behalf of anybody else."

"Wait, what?" Happy looks surprised. "I get that you want to end the dispute with Holly once and for all, and that's fine. But you're asking *me and my firm* to make an agreement with H2Whoa that *we* won't ever represent *another, different client* with claims of his own against the company?" "Exactly, or disclose anything about Ms. Hydrate's case to anyone else," says Lamont, cheerfully. He adds, with a conspiratorial grin, "If that's an issue for you, we can make it worth your while."

Happy seems intrigued. "How would that work?" he asks. "Easy," says Lamont, "I'd need to confirm authority for this with our client, but in consideration for your firm's agreement, H2Whoa would directly pay your firm, say, an additional $100,000 upon completion of the settlement with Ms. Hydrate. "Y'know," says Happy, warming to the subject, "if the settlement that you've proposed works out, our fee for this case alone will be four times that." "I take your point," says Lamont. "Let me see what I can do."

The lawyers shake hands and part ways. Driving back to the office, Frank is curious about the last part of the conversation. "Great deal for Holly—congratulations," he enthuses to his boss, "but I've never heard of a defendant paying opposing counsel not to bring new cases. Can you do that?"

"Seems to me," Happy reasons, "it's a free country, and we ought to be free to make any deal we like, so long was we don't take anything that belongs to Holly. You heard Libben—Holly is getting a generous settlement, and the offer to the firm was separate and apart from Holly's case; it was about future cases with different clients. What's wrong with that?"

Is Happy right, or is there more mischief afoot than he currently realizes?

* * *

This chapter is about some of the agreements that lawyers are not allowed to make specifically because they're lawyers. In fact, there are some agreements that are so problematic for lawyers that we aren't even allowed to *offer* them, whether for our own benefit or for anybody else's, including a client's. The relevant ethical rule is **Model Rule 5.6**, and it addresses two different kinds of prohibited agreements. We'll talk first about the kind of agreements addressed in **Model Rule 5.6(b)**—agreements that restrict a lawyer's future practice as part of a client's settlement—in some detail, because you're more likely to encounter that kind in the early years of your career than the kind addressed in **Model Rule 5.6(a)**. We'll touch briefly after that on the kind of agreements addressed in **Model Rule 5.6(a)**.

A. The Prohibition on Lawyers' Offering or Agreeing to Restrict Their Future Practice as Part of the Settlement of a Client Controversy

Take a good hard look at **Model Rule 5.6(b)**. Let's focus on the precise wording, which we know has become a habit for you by now.

1. TAMING THE TEXT "Shall Not"

The introductory words say that a lawyer "shall not" be involved in the agreements described in subsections (a) and (b), so we know that this is a "**must not**" rule. But the exact words delineating what we **must not** do are very important.

2. TAMING THE TEXT "Participate in Offering or Making"

The Rule says we **must not** "participate in offering or making" certain kinds of agreements. Clearly, this means we can't make such agreements for ourselves—that is, enter into such agreements on our own behalf as direct parties to a contract. But it means more than that: By prohibiting lawyers from "*participating in* offering or making" the specified kinds of agreements (emphasis added), the drafters are telling us that we **must not** even be *involved in negotiating* such agreements, whether on our own behalf or for the benefit of anybody else, such as a client.

3. TAMING THE TEXT "An Agreement . . . That Is Part of the Settlement of a Client Controversy"

This language limits the forbidden agreement by context: In order to fall within the Rule's prohibition, the agreement has to be "part of the settlement of a client controversy." The words "settlement" and "controversy" make it clear that the prohibited agreement has to be one that is part of the resolution of a client's dispute. This phrase doesn't necessarily mean as part of a settlement of pending litigation; sometimes we help clients resolve "controvers[ies]" before they land in court. But to fall within the Rule's scope, there has to be a real and identifiable dispute of which the agreement in question is "a part" of the resolution.

4. TAMING THE TEXT▸ "An Agreement in Which a Restriction on the Lawyer's Right to Practice Is Part of the Settlement"

Up to this point, understanding this Rule has been pretty easy. Now things get more complicated. What does the Rule mean by an agreement including "a restriction on the lawyer's right to practice"? Well, let's start with the literal meaning: Lawyers are generally free to represent whomever they wish in whatever matters they wish. To be sure, there are limitations on what engagements a lawyer can take on: You can't agree to represent a client who creates a **disqualifying conflict of interest**, for example (*see* **Model Rule 1.7**; **Model Rule 1.9(a)-(b)**; **Chapter 22.B at 646**; **Chapter 22.C at 679**), or accept an engagement to assert a frivolous claim or defense on a client's behalf (*see, e.g.,* **Model Rule 1.16(a)**; **Model Rule 3.1**; **Chapter 3.C at 53**; **Chapter 24.C at 845**, but these are limitations imposed by rule or statute. **Model Rule 5.6(b)** has to do with *agreements* (contracts) not to take on engagements that otherwise would be legally allowed—in other words, agreements that "restrict[]" a lawyer's "right to practice."

If you look back at the **Introduction to the chapter at 455**, you'll see a classic example of such an agreement: The arrangement proposed by Lamont Libben on behalf of his client, H2Whoa, for Frank's firm to restrict its practice by agreeing not to represent any other client in future claims against H2Whoa. These are engagements that it would otherwise be fully proper for Frank's firm to take on. In fact, any such future clients who were also poisoned by the bad lot of H2Whoa that the firm discovered would enjoy a big advantage in retaining Frank's firm because of all the extremely valuable and pertinent information that the firm developed while representing Holly Hydrate. TAMING THE TEXT

5. REASON FOR THE RULE▸ Why Does Model Rule 5.6(b) Forbid the Agreements That It Does?

Why isn't Frank's boss right when he reasons that "it's a free country, and we ought to be free to make any deal we like, so long was we don't take anything that belongs to Holly"? There are at least four different policies underlying the ban on the agreements identified by **Model Rule 5.6(b)**.[1] *First,* we generally believe in giving clients as many choices among counsel as reasonably possible, especially

---

[1] *See* ABA Formal Op. No. 93-371 (1993).

counsel who may have specialized knowledge or expertise that may make them particularly effective or efficient for a client with specific needs. So when the law governing lawyers prevents a lawyer from taking or continuing a particular engagement (and thus depriving a client of his or her counsel of choice), we want to be sure that there is a good reason justifying it.

Second (and related), as a practical matter, most of the agreements that someone would want to make with a lawyer that restricted the lawyer's future practice as part of the settlement of a client controversy are motivated by intentions of which the law disapproves, and disapproves quite sensibly. Consider the hypothetical in the **chapter Introduction at 455**. Why is H2Whoa so interested in benching Frank's firm from any future cases against it? Because through substantial investment of time and effort, Frank's firm now knows of evidence that likely proves that H2Whoa distributed a contaminated and dangerous product to a lot of people. Holly Hydrate might have considered her injuries an isolated incident or just bad luck, but Frank's firm laboriously compiled the information necessary for a roadmap through unknown territory to a settlement based on her likely recovery of substantial damages. For this very reason, they're the *last* lawyers H2Whoa wants involved in the next case against it. New lawyers starting from scratch may not be nearly so industrious or effective. Given the potential number of plaintiffs like Holly out there, and the possible extent of the harm that they've suffered, it's worth a lot of money to H2Whoa to make Frank's firm, and everything that it has uncovered about the facts, disappear from view. Although H2Whoa's intentions may be economically rational from its own narrow point of view, they are hardly admirable, and in a broader context, they are unfair and immoral (hiding, rather than accepting, responsibility for a dangerous mistake that has harmed innocent third parties), and also economically wasteful (frustrating our tort system's goal of forcing those responsible for injuring others to bear the cost of those injuries).[2]

Third, the Rule prevents the opposing party from creating a **conflict of interest** between lawyer and client. To see why, let's reimagine the hypothetical in the **chapter Introduction at 455** as involving a very generous settlement offer to the client, but nothing additional for the lawyers, who are nevertheless required to agree as part of H2Whoa's settlement with Holly Hydrate to refuse any future engagements against H2Whoa. The lawyers may not want to make such an

---

[2] Some of the same kinds of concerns have been raised about secrecy provisions in settlements like the one offered to Holly—that they tend to obscure patterns of harm or wrongdoing that society as a whole would be better off knowing about and addressing. (Such secrecy provisions usually don't implicate **Model Rule 5.6** because they are agreed to by, and govern the behavior of, the *client*, not the lawyer, *but see* **Problems 17A-1(d) and (e) at 461**.) Although confidentiality provisions in settlement agreements remain generally lawful almost everywhere, they are becoming increasingly controversial and are coming under greater scrutiny. *See, e.g.,* Vasundhara Prasad, *If Anyone Is Listening, #MeToo: Breaking the Culture of Silence Around Sexual Abuse Through Regulating Non-Disclosure Agreements and Secret Settlements*, 59 B.C. L. Rev. 2507 (2018); Jillian Smith, *Secret Settlements: What You Don't Know Can Kill You!*, 2004 Mich. St. L. Rev. 237 (2004). *See also The Public's Right To Know—Ending Secret Settlements to Protect Public Safety*, Seattle Times (Feb. 5, 1992), https://archive.seattletimes.com/archive/?date=19920205&slug=1474080 (discussing proposed "right to know" bills that didn't make it into law).

agreement, keeping themselves available to represent future clients with strong and valuable claims like Holly's, and also possibly feeling a moral imperative to help the innocent victims of the water company's tort. Holly naturally wants her settlement, and she wants her lawyers to do whatever is required of them to get it for her. An independent lawyer representing Holly's interests would point out that Holly's lawyers (Frank's firm), as Holly's fiduciaries, have a duty to put Holly's interests before their own. As a result of the demand that the settlement include restrictions on the party's lawyers, the client's interests and those of the lawyers are now in conflict. As we'll see in **Chapter 22.A at 626**, this is where things get messy. Frank's firm will, at a minimum, have to make elaborate disclosures and get Holly's informed consent to the **conflict of interest**; the firm may need to disqualify itself and withdraw; or Holly may need to get independent counsel—all because the defendant made a settlement offer that (ahem) might have been calculated to create exactly this kind of disruption.

The way that **Model Rule 5.6(b)** addresses this problem is to make an unbending rule that lawyers simply aren't allowed to make this kind of agreement. If they can't make the agreement, no **conflict** of this kind is created between their **interests** and their client's, even if the other side asks for one. (Do you see why? Explain it out loud.) So the Rule also helps avoid potentially disruptive **conflicts of interest**.

Fourth and finally, the lawyers' fiduciary status has another implication: Fiduciaries may not profit from the fiduciary relationship other than by receiving ordinary compensation for their services. *See* **Chapter 5.D at 113**. Any additional compensation that the lawyers might receive for agreeing not to sue H2Whoa, such as the additional money that Lamont Libben has offered Frank's firm in the **chapter Introduction at 455**, is exactly the kind of "ill-gotten gains" that fiduciary law forbids, even if those gains take nothing away from the client. ◀ REASON FOR THE RULE

6. CONSEQUENCES ▶ Consequences of Violating Model Rule 5.6(b)

Model Rule 5.6(b) is a Rule of Professional Conduct whose violation is addressed by professional discipline. But as we've just discussed, the Rule is grounded in fiduciary principles that separately give rise to civil remedies. If a lawyer agrees to a restriction on practice as part of the settlement of a client controversy in return for which the lawyer receives value that otherwise would have gone to the client, the lawyer has breached fiduciary duties by misappropriating property or opportunities belonging to the beneficiary, and and will be liable to pay that value over to the client.

But what if the lawyer accepts consideration for the restriction on practice that the client would not otherwise have received, as Lamont Libben offered Frank's firm in the hypothetical in our **chapter Introduction at 455**? Well, remember that a fiduciary may not profit from the fiduciary relationship other than by ordinary compensation for services. The **consequence** when a fiduciary receives such improper profits is being required to "disgorge" them (that is, pay them over) to the beneficiary—here, the client. The remedial doctrine in play here is not damages, but restitution, which focuses not on what the plaintiff *lost*, but on what the defendant (here, the lawyers) improperly *gained*. Tying this concern to the hypothetical in the **chapter Introduction at 455**, Frank's boss was missing an important point when he argued that "we ought to be free to make any deal we like, so long was we don't take anything that belongs to Holly." Fiduciary duties prevent fiduciaries not only from misappropriating the beneficiary's property or opportunities, but also from profiting from the fiduciary relationship.[3]

Finally, because **Model Rule 5.6(b)** is animated by the broader public-policy concerns discussed above, many jurisdictions will find that a contract that violates the Rule is voidable as against public policy and will refuse to enforce it or, if it has been performed, will rescind it.[4] All told, then, there is little upside and a great deal of downside in attempting to make any agreement inconsistent with **Model Rule 5.6(b)**. Consequences

> **Problem 17A-1:** Which of the following proposals would violate **Model Rule 5.6(b)**, and why or why not?
>
> a. H2Whoa makes the settlement offer described in the **chapter Introduction at 455**, except that all the money that Lamont Libben was discussing will be paid to Holly Hydrate.
>
> b. H2Whoa offers $1.2 million to Holly Hydrate to resolve all her claims. In addition, instead of asking the lawyers to agree not to sue H2Whoa on behalf of anyone else, H2Whoa makes it a condition of the settlement with Holly that Frank's firm agree that, as soon as Holly is paid and her action dismissed, the firm will agree to represent H2Whoa on an ongoing basis: The firm will be paid a flat fee of $100,000 to advise H2Whoa on any claims regarding the health effects of its water, including suggestions for improving product safety and avoiding future claims, as well as strategies and tactics for defending any such claims. The engagement will last until the statute of limitations runs on any claims based on H2Whoa tainted by Toxate.
>
> c. H2Whoa offers $1.2 million to Holly Hydrate to resolve all her claims, with no additional terms with respect to her lawyers. Soon after Holly is paid and her action dismissed, H2Whoa reaches out to Frank's firm and offers to engage the firm as counsel to H2Whoa, for which the firm will be paid a flat fee of $100,000 to advise H2Whoa on any claims regarding the health effects of its water, including suggestions for improving product safety and avoiding future claims, as well as strategies and tactics for defending any such claims. The engagement will last until the statute of limitations runs on any claims based on H2Whoa tainted by Toxate.
>
> d. H2Whoa offers $1.2 million to Holly Hydrate to resolve all her claims. The confidentiality provision in the draft settlement agreement that Lamont tenders provides that Holly agrees

---

[3] This is another opportunity for us to urge you to take that Remedies course before you graduate.
[4] *See* RESTATEMENT (SECOND) OF CONTRACTS § 178 (1981).

to instruct her lawyers irrevocably not to use or reveal any information that they learned in the course of representing her. The lawyers themselves are not asked to agree to anything. Does your analysis change if the relevant provision in the settlement agreement requires Holly to instruct her lawyers not to *reveal* information they learned in the course of representing her, but does not require Holly to forbid them from *using* any of that information? If so, how and why; and if not, why not? (*Hint: See* ABA Formal Ethics Op. 00-417 (2000).)

e. Maya's friend and fellow associate Leo Litigator has been working on a patent-infringement case brought against one of the firm's clients by a nonpracticing entity ("NPE"), commonly referred to as a "patent troll." (NPEs acquire patents from others with the purpose not of using the patented technology, but of suing others who they can claim make, use, or sell what the patent covers, and thus infringe.) The NPE plaintiff's counsel has been outrageously difficult—making unreasonable demands and fighting about everything, refusing routine courtesies, breaking promises, and generally making the litigation much more complicated and expensive than it needed to be. Leo's client operates in an industry in which the NPE acquires patents, and thus the client expects to see the NPE in court again someday. The client has suggested a settlement offer of $100,000 to resolve the patent-infringement claims (which is not a bad estimate of the settlement value of the plaintiff's claims), or $150,000 if the NPE will agree never to hire the lawyer who represented it in this case again.

f. Maya's firm is being considered by a new potential client, National Communications Corporation ("NCC"), for a modest-sized acquisition. NCC is a very big company, with several hundred subsidiaries and affiliates. As a condition of hiring Maya's firm, NCC is requiring Maya's firm (as it requires all its outside counsel) to agree that the firm will not represent any client in any matter adverse to *any* NCC subsidiary or affiliate, whether or not the firm is representing that affiliate, and even if the affiliate and the subject matter of the adverse matter are so remote from the firm's work that no **conflict of interest** is created.

B. Organizational or Employment Agreements That Restrict a Lawyer's Practice Upon Changing Jobs

Now let's take a look at **Model Rule 5.6(a)**. It addresses a context separate and quite different from **Model Rule 5.6(b)**. **Model Rule 5.6(b)** focuses on agreements to restrict a lawyer's future practice as "part of the settlement of a client controversy." **Model Rule 5.6(a)** focuses on agreements to restrict future practice as part of getting employed by, or affiliated with, a **practice organization**, specifically by "a partnership, shareholders, operating, employment, or other similar type of agreement that restricts the right of a lawyer to practice after termination of the relationship . . . ." What is this about? Well, the typical kind of agreement that the Rule forbids is one that provides that, as a condition of becoming a partner in a law partnership or a lawyer-employee of a law firm, you will not compete for clients with the **practice organization** after leaving your job there, at least for a period of time (and often within a particular geographic area).

REASON FOR THE RULE Why should we worry about this kind of agreement? This type of restriction on future practice finds itself at the center of a tug-of-war between opposed but legitimate policies, and seeks to strike a balance between them. As we discussed in the previous section, there is a strong policy in Anglo-American jurisprudence favoring clients' having as wide a choice of potential counsel as is reasonably possible, and also a strong policy favoring giving clients broad discretion to hire or fire their counsel as they wish (the principal impediment to the latter being the permission of any involved tribunal, for policy reasons discussed in **Chapter 9.D at 289**). In addition, there is a policy in our economic system favoring employee mobility—that is, the right of an employee to get a better job (however the employee defines a "better job," whether it's kinder management, better pay, more interesting work, etc.) by changing employers. An agreement that prevents, or makes it unreasonably difficult, for lawyers to change jobs, or for clients to choose to continue being represented by a lawyer who is leaving a **practice organization**, disserves these important policies. *See* **Model Rule 5.6 Comment [1]**.

The countervailing concern becomes apparent when you think about things from the point of view of a **practice organization** taking on a new lawyer, whether that lawyer will be a new partner or a new associate. A successful **practice organization**—one that is better than the sum of its parts—is one in which members collaborate with one another and invest in one another. If one partner is too busy or lacks the expertise to serve a new client, she can arrange for another partner who has the time and skills to handle the engagement; they share the revenue, and both of them are better off, as is the client. Similarly, a good employer not only provides clients for a junior lawyer to serve, but invests time and other resources in training and mentoring its younger lawyers, so that they learn to be better lawyers, and they learn more quickly and with fewer mistakes than if they had to pick up all of this knowledge on their own. In short, there are real advantages to teaching, training, collaborating, and sharing clients, both to the members of the **practice organization** and to their clients.

Given the choice, **practice organizations** would prefer to reap the benefits of their investments in their colleagues rather than have those benefits accompany a departing lawyer out the door. But if any member of the **practice organization** is free to leave at any time, perhaps taking with her the clients to whom her colleagues may have introduced her (and using the knowledge and skills that her former colleagues invested their time and abilities imparting to her to compete with her former colleagues), the **practice organization** loses the benefit of its investment in the departing individual, and in many cases sees that investment actively leveraged against it. You can hardly blame the **practice organization** for resenting this outcome and wishing to prevent it.

For that reason, some **practice organizations** may attempt to impose on new partners or new hires "a partnership, shareholders, operating, employment, or other similar type of agreement that restricts the right of a lawyer to practice after termination of the relationship." Lawyers, being more subtle than most beasts of the field,[5] have creatively tried many different ways to accomplish this goal, from outright prohibitions on a departing lawyer's competing with the former firm or representing any of its clients to imposing various financial incentives to discourage or offset the losses that the departing lawyer's competition with her former firm may create.   REASON FOR THE RULE

The balance that **Model Rule 5.6(a)** strikes between these competing priorities varies from state to state, but generally drops a thumb on the scale in favor of client choice and lawyer mobility. Most states find that outright prohibitions, such as a covenant not to compete or an agreement not to "poach" firm clients when departing (sometimes called a non-solicitation agreement), violate the Rule, but other states import a "reasonableness" standard that a restriction must transgress before the agreement falls into forbidden territory. The nuances under a reasonableness standard often focus on whether the restriction is a financial or cost-sharing provision rather than a direct prohibition, and whether the restriction is imposed on a partner in a partnership or the organizational equivalent (rather than an associate).[6] The Rule incorporates two express exceptions that are generally deemed acceptable: Restrictions in an "an agreement concerning benefits upon retirement" (**Model Rule 5.6(a)**); and restrictions that are part of the terms of lawyers' sales of their law practices (**Model Rule 5.6 Comment [3]**; *see* **Model Rule 1.17**). It's easy to reconcile these exceptions with the policy balance that informs the Rule: A lawyer who is retiring or selling her practice would reasonably be expected not to serve clients after leaving her current position, so the concerns about client choice and lawyer mobility in this context are minimal.

YOUR HOUSE; YOUR RULES It's very difficult to generalize how these issues are resolved in different states, so we'll leave this at a reminder to be aware of the need to determine what your state does, and the suggestion that such restrictions on more junior lawyers are relatively uncommon and are more likely to be found to violate the Rule.   YOUR HOUSE; YOUR RULES

CONSEQUENCES   **Model Rule 5.6(a)** is, again, a Rule of Professional Conduct, so the **consequence** for its violation is professional discipline. It's worth noting that the Rule forbids lawyers from "participating in offering or making" any agreement improperly restricting future practice, meaning that you are subject to discipline for agreeing to any such restriction, even though the restriction is one that your new employer is probably demanding for its own benefit. There also may be civil **consequences**: As is the case with **Model Rule 5.6(b)**, any restriction appropriating something that would have gone to a client or causing a lawyer to benefit beyond

---

[5] *See* Genesis 3:1, and yes, we're joking about the comparison.
[6] *See* RESTATEMENT (THIRD) OF THE LAW GOVERNING LAWYERS § 13 Reporter's Note, Restrictions on the Right to Practice (2000) (collecting cases).

ordinary compensation for services is likely to result in disgorgement of the benefit. Restrictions that violate the rule are also likely to be found voidable as against public policy and either not enforced or rescinded. CONSEQUENCES

Problem 17B-1: Which of the following proposals would violate **Model Rule 5.6(a)**, and why or why not?

a. Maya's friend Mark works at another large law firm with an office in her city. Mark has been suggesting that Maya might want to leave her firm and join his firm. Mostly to placate her friend, Maya meets with the firm's recruiting partner. The partner describes the practice opportunities, salary, and benefits that his firm can offer to Maya. He adds, "We can sweeten the deal if you decide to join us. We offer a $25,000 bonus for any associate who is still employed at our firm three years after starting." What if, instead of a three-year bonus, the firm has an employment agreement that requires new hires to remain for three years, points out the substantial expense involved in hiring, orienting, and training a new lawyer, and provides that the firm's liquidated damages for breach of the three-year requirement will be $10,000?[7] What if, instead of a liquidated damages clause, the firm agreed to lend new associates bar expenses and to forgive one-third of the loan for each full year that the associate remains employed at the firm?

b. Same as (a), but in addition, the partner explains that the firm is looking for an associate in its ERISA department. (ERISA is a big, complicated federal statute that governs employee pensions and benefits.) ERISA work is highly technical and specialized, and Maya will have to agree to practice exclusively in the ERISA area while she is with Mark's firm if she takes a job there.

c. Law firms (whatever their organizational structure) typically require partners to contribute money for capital—that is, to cover the cost of obtaining fixed assets like furniture, computers, and leasehold improvements, and invest in initiatives such as training and marketing. When partners leave a firm, they are generally entitled to the return of their capital contributions. In some firms, the amount of a partner's capital contribution can be quite substantial—hundreds of thousands of dollars or more. Maya's firm is considering changing its partnership agreement to provide that partners who leave the firm *and* take any firm client with them forfeit 50 percent of their capital.[8]

d. Same as (c), except that the proposed change to the partnership agreement is that partners who leave the firm *and* take any firm client with them must pay the firm 75 percent of the fees that they earn from that client during the two years following their departure. Does your answer change if the fee "rebate" is 50 percent? 25 percent? 10 percent? If

---

[7] Think we're kidding? *See* Debra Cassens Weiss, *Law Firm Sues Associate for Alleged Breach of Employment Contract*, https://www.abajournal.com/news/article/law-firm-sues-associate-for-leaving-too-soon (March 6, 2019). A note of comfort: This situation made the industry press because it's extremely rare (though seeking return of bar expenses or moving allowances from new hires who don't show up or stay a very short time is less uncommon).

[8] *Compare Howard v. Babcock*, 6 Cal. 4th 409, 863 P. 2d 150 (1993) *with Moskowitz v. Jacobson Holmon, PLLC*, No. 1:2015cv00336, 2015 WL 6830266 (E.D. Va. Nov. 6, 2015).

there is no time limit on the period during which the rebate is in effect? Should it matter whether the partner voluntarily quits or is involuntarily removed from the partnership?

e. A friend and coworker of Danielle's recently left the DA's office to become a solo practitioner in a small town in Danielle's county. He plans to do criminal defense and personal injury work. Recently, he applied to be put on the roster of court-appointed defense counsel to which the court resorts when the public defender's office has a **conflict of interest** and is unable to take on a case. The paperwork requires Danielle's friend to agree not to bring any civil claim on behalf of a client against the county or any local government agency within the county as a condition of inclusion on the court-appointment list. Does this proposed agreement violate **Model Rule 5.6(a)**? What about **Model Rule 5.6(b)**?

f. A large pharmaceutical company is seeking to hire someone to serve in a dual role, both as an in-house lawyer and also as the company's executive vice president. The employment agreement that the company is offering contains a provision in which the employee agrees not to serve as an executive vice president or any comparable or higher office for any other pharmaceutical company for one year after she leaves this job. The agreement does not restrict her from joining another pharmaceutical company as in-house counsel.

Big-Picture Takeaways from Chapter 17

1. **Model Rule 5.6(b)** prohibits lawyers from even "*participating in* offering or making" an agreement that, as part of the resolution of a client's dispute, includes "a restriction on the lawyer's right to practice."

    a. **Consequences** for violating the Rule include professional discipline.

    b. In addition, conduct violating this Rule may breach the lawyer's fiduciary duties by misappropriating property or opportunities belonging to her beneficiary (the client) or improperly profiting from the fiduciary relationship. Under the concept of restitution, the lawyer would be liable to pay her ill-gotten gains directly to the client. Moreover, courts have a good record of finding such agreements unenforceable as a matter of contract law.

2. **Model Rule 5.6(a)** focuses on agreements to restrict future practice as part of *getting employed by, or affiliated with, a **practice organization***, specifically by "a partnership, shareholders, operating, employment, or other similar type of agreement that restricts the right of a lawyer to practice after termination of the relationship . . . ."

    a. **Model Rule 5.6(a)** prohibits the kind of agreement that provides that, as a condition of becoming a partner in a law partnership or a lawyer-employee of a law firm, you will not compete for clients with the **organization** after leaving your job there for a period of time (and often within a particular geographic area).

b. The Rule incorporates two express exceptions that are generally viewed as acceptable:
   i. Restrictions in an "an agreement concerning benefits upon retirement" (**Model Rule 5.6(a)**); and
   ii. Restrictions that are part of the terms of lawyers' sales of their law practices (**Model Rule 5.6 Comment [3]**; *see* **Model Rule 1.17**).
c. As with **Model Rule 5.6(b)**, **Model Rule 5.6(a)** is a Rule of Professional Conduct, so the **consequence** for its violation is professional discipline.
d. There also may be civil **consequences**: As is the case with **Model Rule 5.6(b)**, any restriction appropriating something that would have gone to a client, or causing a lawyer to benefit beyond ordinary compensation for services, is likely to result in the lawyer's disgorgement of the benefit. Restrictions that violate the Rule are also likely to be found void as against public policy and thus subject to nonenforcement or rescission.

Multiple-Choice Review Questions for Chapter 17

1. Marlene has given her two-week notice to the firm at which she is a senior associate. During her exit interview, Neil, the hiring partner, gives her two options. She can leave and receive no severance. If she chooses this option, Neil explains, she is free to work for any other firm that she chooses. Or, if she accepts a $20,000 severance, Marlene can work for any firm other than the firm's biggest competitor. Knowing that she intends to join a small public interest organization anyway, Marlene accepts.

   Has anyone violated **Model Rule 5.6**?
   a. Neil, because he offered Marlene an agreement to restrict her future practice.
   b. Marlene, because she agreed to restrict her future practice.
   c. Both a and b.
   d. Neither a nor b.

2. Ori is an associate at a firm that handles personal injury cases. He works closely with Patricia, one of the named partners of the firm. Most of the firm's cases are taken on a contingency basis. Associates receive a salary regardless of the outcome of any of their cases, but when there is a favorable settlement or verdict in a case on which the associate worked, the associate receives a bonus from that amount. The firm characterizes the bonus payments as "deferred compensation" for work done earlier in the case.

   After several years of practice, Ori decides to hang out his own shingle and become a solo practitioner. At the time that Ori gives his notice, he and Patricia have a major case for which they have just agreed to a settlement. The settlement agreement is in the process of being drafted, so the defendant has not yet tendered the settlement payment. Under the practice described in the previous paragraph, Ori is entitled to $30,000 once the payment is made.

Patricia sits Ori down and tells him that it's a shame that he won't be getting the $30,000 for which he worked so hard. She says, "Let me do you a favor. If you agree not to poach any of the firm's clients, we'll remit half of your portion of the settlement payment."

Does this agreement comply with **Model Rule 5.6**?

    a. Yes. Ori is only owed the money once it is paid, and it was his choice to leave before that occurred. The firm is under no obligation to offer him anything.

    b. Yes. The firm is not forcing Ori to forgo representing existing firm clients in the future; it is merely providing a financial disincentive for doing so.

    c. No. The agreement would only be proper if the firm offered Ori the full amount due in exchange for his agreement not to compete.

    d. No. This arrangement imposes an unreasonable financial disincentive on Ori if he competes with the firm.

3. Querelle has been a solo practitioner for the past two decades. He has built a solid reputation and book of business over that time. He decides to join a large law firm with an office in his city as a partner. The firm offers great compensation and benefits, including participation in a 401(k) plan. Partners at the firm can contribute up to 2 percent of their salary to the plan, and the firm will match the amount.

    Before Querelle's first day at the firm, he is presented with a partnership agreement. According to the agreement, if Querelle ever leaves the firm, he is barred from representing any of the firm's clients in the future. If Querelle chooses to represent any firm client, he forfeits the employer match in his 401(k). Is this agreement proper?

    a. Yes. Querelle was never entitled to the employer matching contributions. The employer had no obligation to offer them and therefore can withhold them for any reason.

    b. Yes. Querelle was under no duress when presented with the agreement. He was able to negotiate and should be held to any terms to which he agreed.

    c. No. Querelle would be agreeing to restrict his future practice. This is impermissible.

    d. No. Querelle is entitled to his own contributions to the plan. The firm could withhold its matching contributions but must allow employees to take any amounts they contributed personally.

4. Rhoni is a partner at a law firm. According to her partnership agreement, if she leaves the firm and any firm clients follow her, she must remit to the firm 5 percent of any contingent fees that she is paid by those clients.

Does this agreement comply with **Model Rule 5.6**?

a. Yes. This is a retirement agreement and is therefore a recognized exception to the general rule in **Model Rule 5.6**.

b. Yes. This does not restrict future practice in violation of **Model Rule 5.6**; it simply requires fee sharing.

c. No. This constitutes an unreasonable restraint on the practice of law, which is prohibited by **Model Rule 5.6**.

d. No. The firm must do some work on the cases or assume joint liability for the representation in order to be entitled to share fees under **Model Rule 5.6**.

5. On the eve of trial in a products-liability suit, plaintiff's counsel Steven is contacted by in-house counsel for the defendant company, Tricia. Tricia offers Steven's client, Ushi, $500,000 to settle all of the claims in the case. Steven conveys this offer to Ushi, who happily accepts it.

   When Steven calls Tricia back to accept the settlement on Ushi's behalf, Tricia offers him a side agreement. "We won't call it a settlement agreement," she says "and it will only be signed by the two of us—not by our clients. For an additional $500,000 payable to you, you'll agree not to represent anyone else who wants to sue the company."

   Is it possible that the agreement could violate **Model Rule 5.6**?

   a. Yes, if the parties view the two agreements as related or if **Model Rule 5.6** is read broadly. The agreement restricts the access of the members of the public to the lawyer of their choice, and this is a primary policy motivation underpinning **Model Rule 5.6**.

   b. Yes, because the term "settlement" is defined in **Model Rule 1.2**, which states that a lawyer "shall abide by a client's decision whether to accept an offer of settlement of a matter." If Steven accepts the agreement without Ushi's consent, he violates **Model Rule 1.2**.

   c. No, because the agreement is not called a "settlement," and the parties' characterization of the nature of this document controls.

   d. No, because **Model Rule 5.6** applies exclusively to pending litigation, and this agreement relates to future litigation.

6. After five years of marriage, Vivian and Walter decided to agree to an amicable split. The couple were able to work out a shared custody agreement for their two children. Although there was a sleazy lawyer in town, Xavier, who handled divorce cases, neither Vivian nor Walter retained him because he was known for making cases acrimonious.

   Vivian's lawyer, Yolanda, cautioned her, "I know that you're on good terms with Walter now, but that might not be true in the future. As a condition to the divorce agreement, we should prohibit Walter from hiring Xavier for any future child support or custody cases." Vivian agreed. Yolanda suggested the term to Walter's attorney, Zaphod. Zaphod said, "What's good for the goose is good for the gander, so we can agree to that so long as Vivian also agrees not to hire him." Vivian and Walter, represented by their counsel, agreed to a divorce settlement containing the term.

A few months later, disgusted with Walter's failure to comply with the custody arrangement, Vivian filed a motion for child support. She hired Xavier to handle the motion. What is Vivian's best defense for her action?

- a. She has no defense, because she was represented by counsel when she agreed.
- b. The term was void as against public policy because it impermissibly restricts her freedom to choose an attorney.
- c. The agreement was outside the scope of the divorce settlement because it related to future litigation and not to the divorce itself.
- d. Walter violated the custody arrangement first and therefore voided the agreement.

7. For many years, Alvin was a partner at a large firm. All partners at the firm were charged a portion of the firm's operating costs for leasing office space. Because the lease was paid monthly, the partnership agreement provided that any partner who left the firm mid-month would have the full month's share of the lease payment deducted from his or her final partnership draw.

Betty, one of the firm's partners, was appointed to the federal bench as an Article III judge. She left the firm in the middle of January. The firm did not deduct the last two weeks' worth of her share of the rent from her final partnership draw.

Carole left the firm to retire. She left in the middle of February. The firm did not deduct the last two weeks' worth of her share of the rent from her final partnership draw.

Alvin left the firm to work for another large firm in the city. He left in the middle of March. The firm deducted the last two weeks' worth of rent from his final partnership draw.

Could the firm's selective enforcement of the partnership agreement violate **Model Rule 5.6**?

- a. Yes, if the selective enforcement is designed to discourage competition from departing partners.
- b. Yes, if the selective enforcement is based on sex (namely, that the firm prefers women over men).
- c. No, because the agreement is neutral on its face and does not mention future competition from departing partners.

d. No, because what matters is the plain text of the agreement, not its enforcement.

8. Dee is a solo practitioner who practices in the State of Raptor. Dee is diagnosed with breast cancer and begins treatment. She finds that she can't keep up with her practice while undergoing the cancer treatment, so she decides to sell her entire practice to Ellen. According to the terms of the sale agreement, Dee will never again practice law in Raptor—even if she goes into remission and is totally cured.

    Is the agreement proper under **Model Rule 5.6**?

    a. Yes. Restrictions on the right to practice do not apply to the sale of a law practice.
    b. Yes. The restriction is only in one jurisdiction and does not bar practice elsewhere.
    c. No. This is a restriction on the right to practice, which is never permissible.
    d. No. This is a sales agreement, not a retirement agreement, and restrictions on the right to practice are only permitted in retirement agreements.

9. Attorney Fred is 62 years old and owns his own firm. Fred decides to work only on a part-time basis. He hires Gary, a young partner, to help with the firm's cases. The partnership agreement provides that, after Fred retires at age 65, the firm will pay him retirement benefits in the amount of $3,500 per month as long as Fred does not practice law.

    Which of the following is a true statement about this partnership agreement?

    a. The agreement is proper under the Rules of Professional Conduct.
    b. The agreement is unenforceable under the Rules of Professional Conduct.
    c. Fred is subject to discipline for creating this partnership agreement, in which he agrees never to practice law again as a condition of receiving a retirement benefit.
    d. Gary is subject to discipline for entering into this type of partnership agreement, which restrains Fred from practicing law.

10. Helena is an associate at a law firm. After she gives her two-week notice, the firm offers to pay her a $15,000 severance payment if she will stay an extra two weeks and assist with onboarding her replacement.

    Does this agreement violate **Model Rule 5.6**?

    a. Yes, because it restricts Helena's future practice, even if only for two weeks.

b. Yes, because it conditions financial payment upon Helena's agreement to comply with the firm's limitations on her future employment.

c. No, because it only restricts Helena's future practice for two weeks and thus meets the "de minimis" exception in **Model Rule 5.6**.

d. No, because it does not restrict Helena's practice after the termination of her relationship with her current firm, but rather compensates her for something that she will do before she leaves.

18

Advertising and Solicitation

YES, THIS IS A REAL lawyer ad. What does it make you think of the law firm that put it on the front window of its storefront office? How do you think the typical client that this firm wishes to serve might react (the living ones, anyway)?

Although nobody particularly likes advertising, it has real value, and not just to those hawking their wares. Truthful advertising, broadly conceived, makes information about the availability, price, and quality of goods and services available to consumers so that they can make better-informed buying decisions. This information makes it easier for consumers to get the goods and services that they prefer at the most favorable available

price, and that's good not only for the public, but for the economy as a whole.[1]

One of the dirty secrets of the history of professional regulation is how much of it originated in practices that did much more to stifle competition among members of the profession than to protect members of the public. As we'll shortly see, regulation of lawyer advertising is a good example. These kinds of effects are

---

[1] Remember, competition is good for consumers precisely because it's tough on competitors: Consumers like competition because it allows them more choices at better prices; competitors dislike it because it forces scrutiny of their products' quality and price, which makes them work harder and price their goods and services lower to keep up with the competition. In the big picture, competition allows those who make products that are better or cheaper to succeed in the marketplace, and it generally broadens consumers' choices, saves them money, and increases the overall efficiency of the economy.

sometimes referred to as "guild-protective," a historical reference to the medieval and Renaissance associations of craftsmen and professionals that developed codes of conduct that were not infrequently self-serving.

Often, restraints on competition among lawyers have been dressed up in such high-flung values as dignity, decorum, respect for public institutions, and relief from the abrasions of petty commerce. The lawyers defending those restraints were probably both sincere in their concerns and focused on the restraints' perceived advantages over their anticompetitive effects. But whatever you may think of these justifications, it's worth bearing in mind that, overall, restricting advertising generally favors more established lawyers over newer ones, regardless of their relative skills or work ethic, and frustrates better-informed decision-making by potential clients. We ask you to keep these concerns in mind as you consider the past and present of lawyer advertising.

A quick use advisory: This chapter is a little different from the others in that we're going to be showing you examples of lawyer advertising using that miracle of digital technology (cue those flashing lights and beeping sounds!), the Internet. Hyperlinks to lawyer ads are interspersed throughout the text. Please use them—we've chosen examples that we think you'll find entertaining as well as enlightening, and they'll be worth your time. If you have the Connected Casebook digital edition of this book, then you have access to this chapter in a form that allows you to click on the links to see the linked content. If you have a hard copy of the book, please remind your professor to distribute a digital copy of this chapter to the class so that you can access the links. (We're reminding your professor to do this, too.)

A. A Brutally Short History of the Regulation of Lawyer Advertising, and an Equally Short Summary of the Constitutional and Other Safeguards Limiting State Bars' Regulatory Powers

These days, anyone who watches television or reads billboards sees lawyer advertising. That wasn't always true. In fact, until the late 1970s, most U.S. jurisdictions completely banned lawyer advertising of any kind, even ads in the yellow pages.[2] Public dissemination of a lawyer's rates was also forbidden, which made price competition all but impossible.[3] The concerns on which these bans were

---

[2] For you Millennials and members of Generation Z out there, the yellow pages were printed telephone directories of local businesses whose pages were—you guessed it—yellow. The telephone company created and distributed them free to telephone-service subscribers. In addition to a regular listing, including an address and phone number, merchants could buy ads in the yellow pages to highlight their goods or services. The yellow pages were a principal source of information for consumers for decades until the Internet changed everything. Now there are digital "yellow pages" on the Internet, though their pages are no longer yellow. And now you know why we use the term "yellow pages." And yes, there was television when your authors were young. Internal combustion engines, too. No, no email. Stop asking.

[3] *See* https://sociallyawkwardlaw.com/attorney-advertising-regulation/history-of-attorney-advertising/. For a more detailed history, *see, e.g.,* William E. Hornsby, Jr., *Ad Rules Infinitum: The Need for Alternatives to State-Based Ethics Governing Legal Services Marketing,* 36 U. Rich. L. Rev. 49, 51-63 (2002).

based focused on preserving the decorum of, and public respect for, the profession, as well as preventing advertising that could "mislead" consumers.

A great deal changed in 1977, when the United States Supreme Court decided *Bates v. State Bar of Arizona*.[4] *Bates* holds that lawyer advertising is what eventually came to be called "commercial speech" protected by the First Amendment. As the Supreme Court fleshed out commercial speech protections over the next few years, it became clear that government regulation of such speech must be subjected to "intermediate scrutiny," a standard that you may have encountered, or soon will, in a constitutional law or civil liberties course. As the test is still generally articulated, a government seeking to regulate commercial advertising is required to prove that a regulation (1) was adopted in the service of a "substantial" state interest; (2) "directly advances" that government interest; and (3) is "no more extensive than necessary" to serve that interest.[5] More recently, the Supreme Court has suggested that there may also be antitrust constraints when a state delegates governing power to a self-regulating profession (such as a state bar) and the profession adopts anti-competitive rules.[6] Lawyer advertising has proliferated since the late 1970s. We'll look at some examples later in **Chapter 18.E at 493**.

Problem solved, right? Of course not. Most state bars and other disciplinary authorities continue to claim broad authority to regulate the form and content of lawyer advertising, and some continue to do so aggressively. The caselaw defining limits on this power is very difficult (this is a nice way of saying "impossible") to reconcile. For example, wide gray areas remain within which it is uncertain how "substantial" a state interest is found in preserving decorum in and public respect for the legal profession—a concern that would command no respect as a ground for limiting advertising for, say, auto mechanics or information technology services. Equally unclear is how aggressively state bars may regulate lawyer advertising by declaring entire categories of promotion to be "inherently misleading" while keeping their rules "no more extensive than necessary" to protect the public. *See* **Chapter 18.B at 478**. And the developing antitrust constraints on regulation of lawyer advertising and other business practices are still in their infancy.

To give you a sense of just how resistant state bars can be to change in this area, nearly 20 years after the *Bates* decision, the State of Florida disciplined Sylvia Ibanez for having included on her business cards and letterhead (stationery), truthfully, that she was a Certified Public Accountant and a Certified Financial Planner as well as a lawyer—all undisputed facts that the Florida

---

[4] 433 U.S. 350 (1977).

[5] *Central Hudson Gas & Electric v. Public Service Commission of New York*, 447 U.S. 557, 564 (1980). *See generally* Michael R. Hoefges, *Regulating Professional Services Advertising: Current Constitutional Parameters and Issues under the First Amendment Commercial Speech Doctrine*, 24 CARDOZO ARTS & ENT. L.J. 953 (2006–2007).

[6] *North Carolina State Board of Dental Examiners v. Federal Trade Commission*, 574 U.S. 494 (2015). Before the *North Carolina Dental* decision, professional regulation of anything other than the charges allowed for particular services was widely believed to be exempt from the antitrust laws under the "state immunity" doctrine of *Parker v. Brown*, 317 U.S. 341 (1943).

Department of Business and Professional Regulation inexplicably characterized as "false, deceptive, and misleading." Ms. Ibanez had to litigate her way all the way to the Supreme Court of the United States to strike down this disciplinary sanction under the First Amendment.[7]

REAL WORLD ▸ All of which leads us to offer you some practical advice:

- YOUR HOUSE; YOUR RULES ▸ We'll discuss the most common and pervasive forms of advertising regulation in **Chapter 18.B at 477**, but be aware that many states have adopted supplementary bodies of rules limiting whole categories of lawyer advertising. Each state seems to have its own pet peeves. Before you put anything out there in any medium, including anything that you put on the Internet as part of a law firm website (which, we'll shortly see, qualifies as regulated "lawyer advertising" just about everywhere), you need to know exactly what your state bar considers objectionable. As a practical matter, if your state bar has taken the trouble to regulate it, then it's more likely to take the trouble to call it out in a disciplinary charge. ◂ YOUR HOUSE; YOUR RULES

- Although the limited advertising and solicitation restrictions incorporated in the Model Rules are for the most part beyond reproach, a certain amount of the supplementary state regulation just discussed may arguably, and sometimes even obviously, violate the First Amendment or the Sherman Antitrust Act. Nevertheless, before you disseminate any advertising that violates some arguably invalid state regulation, think twice. Unconstitutional or anticompetitive state regulation is unjust, but you'll be the test case for just how unjust it is. And the law in this area is, to put it politely, still developing. Although we hate to suggest that you consider not challenging *any* unjust law, realistically you need to ask yourself how much justice you can afford, and whether this particular justice is worth its cost to you. How important is this specific form of advertisement to your practice? Can you tailor your ads to live within your state's constraints without losing too much of what you consider to be valuable about the ads?

- Only about 1-2 percent of law school graduates immediately start a practice on their own. The overwhelming majority of new law grads go to work for someone else. As a result, advertising is not a significant concern for most new lawyers in their early years of practice, beyond being sure that whatever their employer is saying about them on a website, a business card, or any other communication with the public is generally consistent with their own state's regulations and with the truth. You are personally responsible for ensuring that statements about you comply with the law, meaning that you can't simply assume that whatever your firm is doing with your good name is okay. As a practical matter, though, you will probably have only a modest

---

[7] *Ibanez v. Florida Dept. of Bus. & Prof. Reg.*, 512 U.S. 136 (1994).

interaction with this area of professional regulation in your early years as a lawyer. (Nevertheless, lawyer advertising rules will be on the MPRE, so stick with us.) REAL WORLD

With that background, let's talk about the important topics that you really need to know, both for the MPRE and as a practitioner.

B. The Prohibition on False or Misleading Communications

We'll start this discussion with two basic concepts: What kinds of communications from lawyers are regulated, and what the principal standard is that governs such communications. The Rule at issue is **Model Rule 7.1**, which we'd like you to read carefully right now. Don't worry—it's quite short.

1. TAMING THE TEXT "Communications"

The scope of **Model Rule 7.1** is simple and sweeping: "communication[s] about the lawyer or the lawyer's services" that are "ma[d]e" by (or on behalf of) the lawyer. To whom? To *anyone*, from a specific targeted individual to the general public. "This Rule governs all communications about a lawyer's services, including advertising." **Model Rule 7.1 Comment [1]**. Note that the scope word in the Rule is "communication[s]"; "advertising" is not a term that is used in the Rule or that is even formally defined; all the Comments tell us is that "advertising" is one form of "communication."

> **Problem 18B-1:** Which of these falls within the scope of **Model Rule 7.1**?
>
> a. A television message describing recent discoveries that a widely prescribed drug is showing serious side effects and inviting calls to a law firm to get more information.
>
> b. A blog post, written by a lawyer, on a website that curates information from many different kinds of experts about drugs with adverse health effects and that describes recent discoveries that a widely prescribed drug is showing serious side effects.
>
> c. A listing in the Martindale-Hubbell lawyers' directory stating only a lawyer's name, **practice organization** (if any), address, and postsecondary education.
>
> d. A law firm's website.
>
> e. A lawyer's business card.
>
> f. A law firm's name. (*Hint: See* **Model Rule 7.1 Comments [5]-[8]**.)

2. TAMING THE TEXT "False or Misleading" Communications

a. In General

Now, what kind of "communication[s] about the lawyer or the lawyer's services" does **Model Rule 7.1** prohibit? It's right there in the Rule: "false or misleading" ones. This is a phrase that is by now familiar to you from **Model Rule 4.1** and **Chapter 10.A at 325**. Nevertheless, **Model Rule 7.1** explains that

[a] communication is false or misleading if it contains a material misrepresentation of fact or law, or omits a fact necessary to make the statement considered as a whole not materially misleading.

And **Model Rule 7.1 Comment [2]** elaborates on what is considered "misleading":

A truthful statement is misleading if it omits a fact necessary to make the lawyer's communication considered as a whole not materially misleading. A truthful statement is misleading if a substantial likelihood exists that it will lead a reasonable person to formulate a specific conclusion about the lawyer or the lawyer's services for which there is no reasonable factual foundation. A truthful statement is also misleading if presented in a way that creates a substantial likelihood that a reasonable person would believe the lawyer's communication requires that person to take further action when, in fact, no action is required.

All of which should remind you of your work on misrepresentation, and should be about what you expected.

Determining whether a statement is false or misleading in violation of **Model Rule 4.1**, in violation of the tort or criminal law forbidding misrepresentation, or in violation of **Model Rule 7.1** are all similar inquiries. For any of these purposes, whether a statement should reasonably be understood to contain or imply a false statement of **material** fact or to be something else (such as an opinion or a statement of position) is a judgment that must be made in light of all the relevant surrounding facts and circumstances. Sometimes that judgment is obvious, and sometimes you will have to reason your way carefully through all the facts and the context surrounding the making of the statement to answer the question. *See* **Chapter 10.B at 325.**   TAMING THE TEXT

Problem 18B-2: Which of these is false or misleading within the meaning of **Model Rule 7.1**?

a. An audiovisual lawyer ad in which the lawyer is shown standing in front of a top-ten law school in the city in which he practices, talking about what he learned about justice in law school, though the lawyer did not attend that (or any other) prestigious law school.

b. An audiovisual lawyer ad in which the lawyer portrays himself as a superhero in tights and a cape, with superpowers that allow him to fly to the rescue of innocent victims and vanquish their menacing adversaries.

c. A print lawyer ad in a city with a large Latinx population, placed in a Spanish-language newspaper that serves that community, depicting the lawyer and a message in Spanish, when the lawyer herself does not speak Spanish.

b. The Organized Bar's Continuing Aversion to Lawyer Advertising

No thinking person is going to want lawyer advertising to be false or misleading. But the widespread resistance in the organized bar to lawyer advertising of any kind has often hijacked this unexceptionable idea and pushed it well beyond its reasonable boundaries. Strikingly, when someone complains to a disciplinary authority about a lawyer's "false and misleading" advertising, it is usually another lawyer, and quite frequently another lawyer in the same line of practice. Coincidence? Perhaps, but the pattern should be prompting you to ask what interests may be driving those attitudes, consciously or not.[8]

Consider the reaction to what has become possibly the most famous lawyer television ad in history: a two-minute spot that aired locally in Georgia during the 2014 Super Bowl written and directed by (and, of course, starring) Savannah, Georgia, personal-injury lawyer Jamie Casino. In it, Mr. Casino, using vivid imagery and a throbbing heavy metal soundtrack, tells the story of how he abandoned a successful criminal-defense practice representing "cold-hearted villains" after his brother was murdered, possibly in a shootout with police (the dramatization is vague on what might have happened), and devoted his life instead to a personal-injury practice speaking for "innocent victims who cannot speak for themselves." In the climactic scene, Mr. Casino appears to wield a flaming sledgehammer emblazoned with a cross to smash his brother's headstone.[9]

Not long after the ad aired, the sitting president of the State Bar of Georgia published a Letter to the Editor in the Fulton County *Daily Report*:

> I AND OTHER GEORGIA lawyers have received calls and emails about the local advertisement that a Savannah-area lawyer ran during the Super Bowl.
>
> Although I cannot speak for all lawyers, I firmly believe most members of the State Bar of Georgia do not condone or approve of advertising that uses sensationalism and "over-the-top" graphics in an attempt to get business. Nonetheless, the right to free speech is guaranteed by the First Amendment of the U.S. Constitution. The U.S. Supreme Court has recognized that lawyer advertising is protected under the First Amendment. Therefore, the Bar's ability to control the content of ads is very limited.
>
> Notwithstanding, I assure you that Georgia lawyers engage in a level of professionalism beyond the bare minimum. Most of us follow The Lawyers' Creed, an aspirational statement endorsed by the Supreme Court of Georgia, which states in part: "As a lawyer, I will aspire . . . (b) To consider the effect of my conduct on the image of our systems of justice including the social effect of advertising methods. As a professional, I should ensure that any advertisement of my services: (1) Is consistent with the dignity of the justice system and a learned profession."

---

[8] *See* Ronald D. Rotunda, *Regulating Lawyer Advertising When It Is Not Misleading*, https://verdict.justia.com/2015/10/12/regulating-lawyer-advertising-when-it-is-not-misleading (Oct. 12, 2015).

[9] No, we don't get the symbolism, either. And as we'll explore further in **Chapter 18.E at 493**, what is it about lawyers and hammers, anyway?

The best lawyer advertising is designed to educate the public about the law or to help people in need find a lawyer. I encourage any member of the public to fully investigate the qualifications of a lawyer and not select a lawyer solely based upon the content of an advertisement.

Charles Ruffin
President
State Bar of Georgia[10]

The state bar president is appropriately careful *not* to argue that the ad is false or misleading, and thus forthrightly concedes that the bar cannot censor it. Just what, then, is he criticizing about it? Its flamboyant imagery? Its dramatic soundtrack? Its melodramatic story? Why does the state bar president disapprove of using "sensationalism and 'over-the-top' graphics in an attempt to get business"? Do you agree with him? If it doesn't work, then Mr. Casino just wasted a whole lot of money making a spectacle of himself. But what would the problem be if it did work? (That is a serious question, and the answer is not obvious. Think about it for a moment, and formulate an answer in your head.)

Oddly, the state bar president does *not* criticize a feature of the ad that a number of professional responsibility commentators have found troubling: Its flagrant disrespect for Mr. Casino's own former clients, whom he refers to as "cold-hearted villains." Would it have been acceptable for criminal-defense-lawyer Casino to hold a press conference after one of his clients was convicted to say: "I'm pleased to report that justice was done, and thank goodness the jury had the sense to keep that monster I represented off the streets"? Is that aspect of the ad merely unprofessional, or does it go far enough that it violates any professional duty that you can identify? (*Hint: See* **Chapter 5.D at 113** and **Problem 5D-1 at 113**.)

Whatever you may think of Mr. Casino's ad, consider his response to the state bar president in a Letter to the Editor of his own:

I RESPECT THE State Bar President's opinion on all points. I respect everyone's opinion. However, I have had significantly more lawyers and non-lawyers commend me than ridicule me for taking a much needed, bold stand in Savannah. I addressed in a powerful manner an epidemic in Savannah—police department corruption.

A few additional points must be made as to the content of the spot. My TV spot was not begging for people to call me. It had no phone number in the most important part of the message, so people could easily ". . . call me NOW." It had no website listed. It had no call to action, like "I can get you 1 million dollars!" It had no catchy slogans.

---

[10] 125 *Fulton County Daily Report*, Issue 27, at 2 (Feb. 10, 2014).

It had no elements of your typical personal injury commercial that you see airing on TV in Georgia and almost all other states, which most non-TV lawyers passionately despise.

Therefore, I want to make it clear that my intent was not to drum up car wrecks, slip and falls, dog bites; but more importantly, I am fairly certain its message ruffled some very dirty feathers in the leadership of our scandal-riddled police department. Continually condemning me will surely have those who are corrupt in our police department cheering my accusers on.

Jamie Casino
Savannah[11]

What do you think of Mr. Casino's response? Do you agree that his advertisement is not commercial and that its sole purpose was to take a "bold stand" against the "epidemic in Savannah" of "police department corruption"? Why does Mr. Casino seem to care whether the ad's intent was to attract clients, as the state bar president implied? Should he care? And why would a crusader convinced of the local police's "epidemic" corruption abandon a practice defending those arrested or abused by that police force in favor of the victims of car crashes?[12]

c. Categories of Communications That State Bars Condemn as "False or Misleading," Whether All of Them Are or Not

Public criticism by other lawyers is hardly the only response to lawyer advertising. Many states have regulations, some very detailed, specifying particular advertising tactics that the state considers "inherently misleading" and thus in violation of their adoption of **Model Rule 7.1**. This kind of category-based regulation has been the subject of a continuing game of constitutional whack-a-mole over the last several decades, with some state bars continuing to propose overbroad rule after overbroad rule after the prior rules succumb to First Amendment challenges.[13]

These regulations often have their roots in **Model Rule 7.1 Comment [3]**. Please pause and read that comment carefully right now. The guidelines set out in Comment [3] respond to lawyer marketing tactics that have shown up more commonly in genuinely overreaching ads.

---

[11] *Id.*

[12] Watch the opening seconds of the spot again and some of Mr. Casino's earlier television ads, *e.g.*, **here** and **here**. Though civil rights and civil tort claims are certainly available to remedy police misconduct, those are not the kind of claims about which Mr. Casino has generally advertised.

[13] *See, e.g., Zauderer v. Office of Disciplinary Counsel*, 471 U.S. 626, 633 (1985) (striking down attorney discipline based on a rule prohibiting print or broadcast advertising that was not "presented in a dignified manner without the use of drawings, illustrations, animations, portrayals, dramatizations, slogans, music, lyrics or the use of pictures, except for the use of pictures of the advertising lawyer or the use of a portrayal of the scales of justice"). *See generally* Rodney A. Smolla, *The Puffery of Lawyers*, 36 U. Rich. L. Rev. 1 (2002); American Bar Assn., *Lawyer Advertising and Solicitation Chapter from Lawyer Advertising at the Crossroads*, https://www.americanbar.org/groups/professional_responsibility/resources/professionalism/crossroads/ (reviewing developments into the mid-1990s).

i. Testimonials and Past Results

Take, for example, the Comment's concern that "[a] communication that truthfully reports a lawyer's achievements on behalf of clients or former clients may be misleading if presented so as to lead a reasonable person to form an unjustified expectation that the same results could be obtained for other clients in similar matters without reference to the specific factual and legal circumstances of each client's case." It's not hard to see the vice in a spot in which a former client, "making it rain" with coins and bills, exults that a particular lawyer "got me ONE MILLION DOLLARS, and he can do that for you, too!" After all, very few clients end up having million-dollar cases, and no one should be drawn to a particular lawyer on the premise that he can conjure one out of thin air. But the response of some state bars was to outlaw *any* ads with "endorsements," "testimonials," or "dramatizations," all of which are practices that some lawyers may see as cheesy or indecorous but are not necessarily misleading.[14]

> **Problem 18B-3:** Which of the following statements in a lawyer's advertisement is "false or misleading" within the meaning of **Model Rule 7.1 & Comment [3]**? Please explain your answer.
>
> a. A former client: "Lonnie Lawyer returned my phone calls and kept me informed at every step in my case."
>
> b. A former client: "Lonnie Lawyer got me a lot more than I thought I'd get." (*See* the first ad linked in **Chapter 18.B at 481 n.12**.)
>
> c. A former client: "Lonnie Lawyer got me a *fantastic* settlement!" Does your analysis change if the speaker is not a former client, but instead is an actor?

ii. Comparisons and Superlatives

Similarly, it's not hard to see the justice in **Model Rule 7.1 Comment [3]**'s warning that "an unsubstantiated comparison of the lawyer's or law firm's services or fees with those of other lawyers or law firms[] may be misleading if presented with such specificity as would lead a reasonable person to conclude that the comparison or claim can be substantiated." But, apparently based on these concerns, there have been state regulations forbidding *any* direct or indirect comparison with other lawyers in any ad.[15]

---

[14] *See, e.g., The Florida Bar: Petition to Amend the Rules Regulating the Florida Bar — Advertising Issues*, 571 So.2d 451, 452-53 (Fla. 1990) (no endorsements, testimonials, or dramatizations).

[15] *See Florida Bar Petition, supra* note 14, 571 So. 2d at 452 (no comparisons; no "self-laudatory" statements; no stating that "the lawyer or the lawyer's firm is 'the best,' 'one of the best,' or 'one of the most experienced' in a field of law"). Though the other restrictions have since been relaxed, the prohibition on superlatives remains part of Florida law. Fl. R. Prof. Cond. 4-7.13, Comments on "Comparisons" and "Characterization of Skills, Experience, Reputation or Record" (2020).

Problem 18B-4: Which of the following statements in a lawyer's advertisement is "false or misleading" within the meaning of **Model Rule 7.1 & Comment [3]**? Please explain your answer.

a. "Don't settle for less than the best!"
b. "The best DUI defense in Yoknapatawpha County."
c. "The lowest cost for a will in Yoknapatawpha County."

iii. Claims of Expertise or Specialization

Another preoccupation of sweeping state regulations has involved claims of specialization or expertise. Many states now have official certifications based on proof of knowledge and experience in common specialties, such as family law and criminal defense. There are also national organizations that focus on particular practice areas and offer achievement-based certifications in those areas. Although many states have detailed rules about when and how lawyers may claim specialization or expertise in particular subject areas, **Model Rule 7.2(c)** offers an approach that simply requires any lawyer who is claiming to be "certified as a specialist in a particular field of law" to have an actual certification from a state or national organization identified in the ad and recognized by the state bar in the jurisdiction in which the lawyer is advertising or by the ABA.

Problem 18B-5: Which of the following statements in a lawyer's advertisement violates **Model Rule 7.2(c)**? Please explain your answer.

a. "Twenty years' experience in family law."
b. "Specializing in immigration law." (*Hint: See* **Model Rule 7.2 Comment [9]**. It may help with (a) too.)
c. A lawyer's profile on a business networking social media site that lists, in pre-existing and standard fields on the profile, "skills" in the lawyer's areas of practice.
d. "A nationally recognized expert in taxation."

iv. Stuff That Just Makes You Wonder

Sometimes state bars consider regulations so sweeping, or so particularized, as to prompt curiosity about what might have motivated them.[16] In 2013, for example, Florida adopted regulations prohibiting any content in lawyer advertising that is not "objectively verifiable." This rule appears to prohibit any opinion at all, including common testimonials such as "Lonnie Lawyer did a great job in my case," or common personal-injury advertising themes such as "insurance companies don't want to pay you what you deserve." In fact, as a lawsuit challenging those regulations pointed out, they would have prohibited Abraham Lincoln's 1852

---

[16] In the same way that we sometimes wonder what prompted a warning label on an iron that said, "Do not use while asleep."

newspaper advertisement (allowed, surprisingly enough, under the Illinois law of the day) that his law firm handled its matters with "promptness and fidelity."[17]

To give you a sense of how far this proposed regulation may have strayed from the First Amendment roots from which lawyer advertising has sprung since the *Bates* decision, Florida banned any lawyer ad containing statements that are *not* "objectively verifiable." Yet long-standing Supreme Court precedent establishes that *only* statements that *are* objectively verifiable (and "provably false") may be subject to legal remedy; statements *not* "provably false"—what in First Amendment jurisprudence used to be called "opinions"—are broadly constitutionally protected. What do you imagine the Florida Bar was thinking?[18]

Bar regulation can aspire not only to the sweepingly overbroad, but the peculiarly detail-obsessed. In 2012, for example, Tennessee was considering adopting a suite of lawyer-advertising regulations. Some were characteristically overinclusive, such as the provision that limited the images used in any ad to scales of justice, the Statue of Liberty, flags, eagles, courthouses, columns, law books, or photos of attorneys "against a plain, single-colored background or unadorned set of law books." (We're still wondering what an "adorned" set of law books might look like, but that's probably beside the point now.) But the same set of regulations went to the trouble of specifically prohibiting talking dogs and space aliens in lawyer advertising. A Tennessee personal injury lawyer who favored the regulations wrote in a petition to the state Supreme Court that "some current and past lawyer advertisements rely on outrageous, misleading, and deceptive advertising techniques. These forms of advertising do not educate the public on the services performed by attorneys in this state, but rather distract, confuse, and mislead . . . ."[19]

Talking dogs and space aliens? How do you suppose the Tennessee personal injury lawyer who brought his concerns to his state Supreme Court thinks that these advertising techniques "distract, confuse, and mislead" the public? Is he afraid of a ***War of the Worlds***–style panic? Is he concerned that the gentle citizens of Tennessee will be misled into believing that a lawyer who has a talking dog is a better choice for trial counsel than he? Sadly, it appears to be the latter: Sample a few of the television advertisements of one of his competitors, a personal injury lawyer from Kentucky, the state immediately to Tennessee's north, who calls himself "**The Heavy Hitter**."[20]

---

[17] Max Kennerly, *The Florida Bar Sued for Prohibiting Lawyers from Having Opinions*, https://www.litigationandtrial.com/2013/12/articles/attorney/florida-bar-attorney-speech/ (Dec. 18, 2013) (contains link to the Complaint; *see* Introduction to Complaint at 2).

[18] *See, e.g., Milkovich v. Lorain Journal*, 497 U.S. 1 (1990). In *Searcy v. Florida State Bar*, 140 F. Supp. 3d 1290 (2015), a federal district court questioned the constitutionality of Florida's "objectively verifiable" rule, but found a challenge to the rule not yet ripe. In response, the Florida State Bar diluted the prohibition to allow a range of common opinions. Fl. R. Prof. Cond. 4-7.13, Comment on "Characterization of Skills, Experience, Reputation or Record" (2020).

[19] Jenna Greene, *FTC Urges Tennessee Court to Ease Off Lawyer Ad Restrictions*, https://legaltimes.typepad.com/blt/2013/01/ftc-urges-tennessee-court-to-ease-off-lawyer-ad-restrictions.html (Jan. 25, 2013).

[20] The Federal Trade Commission's Bureau of Regulation filed objections to the proposed regulations on the ground that they were anticompetitive. *Id.* Apparently, the Tennessee Supreme Court saw the merit in the FTC's concerns and did not

Does this advocacy in favor of the proposed regulations in Tennessee affect your perspective on the concerns for consumer welfare, decorum, and respect for a learned profession that have long been the centerpiece of arguments in favor of restricting professional advertising?

C. Prohibited Economics and Mechanics

In addition to the regulations on advertising *content* just discussed, the Model Rules contain a number of restrictions on the *economics* and *mechanics* of lawyer advertising.

1. *Quid Pro Quos;* "Capping" and "Running"

Take a hard look at **Model Rule 7.2(b)**. The structure of the Rule should be familiar to you—a general prohibition followed by a few enumerated exceptions to the prohibition. TAMING THE TEXT Let's start with the general rule: A lawyer "shall not" (that is, **must not**) "compensate, give or promise anything of value to a person for recommending the lawyer's services . . . ." What this Rule prohibits is often denoted with the Latin phrase *quid pro quo*, literally meaning "this for that," and referring to an intended exchange transaction. In the simplest terms, this means that you can't pay (with cash or anything else of value) for client referrals. TAMING THE TEXT

REASON FOR THE RULE The need for such a rule should be apparent. In order to encourage lawyers to provide the most efficient and effective service, we want consumers to choose a lawyer for *those* reasons, not because the lawyer can afford to pay someone to say that those things are true (whether they are or not). As for advertising, consumers generally understand that it comes from the advertiser, so they evaluate it accordingly. A recommendation from a purportedly neutral source likely would be viewed differently, which is why we have the rule forbidding *quid pro quos*.[21] REASON FOR THE RULE

One thing that **Model Rule 7.2(b)** forbids is conduct known as "capping" and "running." The origin of the terms is obscure, and they are used synonymously (and not infrequently together), but they refer to paying nonlawyers—such as emergency medical technicians, hospital staff, funeral directors, medical examiners, and others who commonly interact with people who have been injured or their families—to tout a particular lawyer's services. Such arrangements can

---

adopt the restrictions. For those of you who might have been considering attitudes of regional superiority, these issues are by no means limited to the South. *Zauderer* (**Chapter 18.B at 481 n.13**) addressed overreaching regulations in Ohio. Other Southwestern and Midwestern states still maintain what we would consider inappropriately restrictive rules, although most states are more readily recognizing the First Amendment and other limits on their powers today than they did in the 1990s.

[21] States have differing approaches to the use of paid spokespersons or celebrity endorsements for lawyers. Most have a requirement for an adequately visible disclaimer that the person making the recommendation is a paid spokesperson, which again allows consumers to evaluate the recommendation with complete information. *See* **Chapter 18.E at 494**.

include cash payments to hand out a lawyer's business cards to those who might be in a position to hire a lawyer, or a kickback arrangement based on the number or value of the clients that the third party actually steers to the lawyer. (Can you see how this falls within the language of **Model Rule 7.2(b)**? Pause and explain how the conduct fits the Rule's words.) CONSEQUENCES Capping and running have been outlawed for centuries, and they are still misdemeanors in most states, as well as triggering disciplinary violations for the involved lawyers in all of them. In addition, in many states, engagement agreements procured by capping or running are voidable as against public policy. CONSEQUENCES

The exceptions to the Rule are consistent with its purpose:

- You **may** pay the "reasonable costs" of creating and disseminating legitimate advertising. **Model Rule 7.2(b)(1).** This is not surprising: The people who help you create or distribute an ad aren't "recommending" your services to others within the meaning of the Rule; they're behind the scenes, helping you do that for yourself.

- You **may** "pay the usual charges of a legal service plan or a not-for-profit or qualified lawyer referral service." **Model Rule 7.2(b)(2).** The programs referred to are group-, insurance-, or bar-sponsored services that provide lists of lawyers to those whom they serve. You can also pay others to provide you with client leads (that is, the identity of people who may want or need a lawyer), so long as the lead provider does not *recommend* you. **Model Rule 7.2 Comment [5].**

- You **may** buy another law firm's practice, if that law firm is ceasing practice in a particular geographical or practice area and the other rules regarding this kind of transaction are followed. **Model Rule 7.2(c); Model Rule 1.17.**

- You **may** agree to refer matters to another lawyer or "nonlawyer professional" in return for that person's agreeing to refer matters to you, provided that the arrangement "is not exclusive" and that "the client is informed of the existence and nature of the agreement." (Can you see how this would fit the reason for the rule?) **Model Rule 7.2(b)(4).** And you **may** always accept a client referred or recommended by someone else (whether or not a lawyer) if you don't pay for the referral (with money or anything else). You **may**, however, give the referring person a "gift[] as an expression of appreciation." **Model Rule 7.2(b)(5).** "The gift may not be more than a token item as might be given for holidays, or other ordinary social hospitality" and may not be intended as compensation for the referral. **Model Rule 7.2 Comment [4].**

Problem 18C-1: Which of the following violates **Model Rule 7.2(b)**? Do any of them violate another Model Rule also or instead? Please explain your answers.

a. A bank offers to include local lawyers on a list of "approved counsel" provided to borrowers from the bank if the lawyers pay 10 percent of the fees earned on any engagement obtained this way back to the bank.

b. Same as (a), except instead of the bank asking for a portion of the fees, the bank requires lawyers added to its list of "approved counsel" to add the bank to their list of "recommended lenders" provided to their business and real estate clients.

c. SuperDuperLawyers, Inc. is a company started by a group of Chicagoland attorneys who will certify you as a "Chicago SuperDuperLawyer" and give you a framed certificate to that effect with your name on it for $500 and proof of an Illinois law license. You can hang that certificate in your office or reception area, reproduce it in your advertising, etc. Does this create any issues under **Model Rule 7.2(b)**? Does it raise concerns under any other subsection of **Model Rule 7.2**?

d. Happy Trials, the litigation partner in Frank's firm, went to law school and has remained close friends with Judge Trudy, a former state-court judge who now stars on a popular regional reality show in which she adjudicates small disputes colorfully. As a favor to her friend, Judge Trudy agrees to appear in a newspaper ad that the firm intends to place in the local paper and on the paper's website in which she, smiling and wearing her judicial robe (and sitting in her studio courtroom), points to Frank's boss at counsel table and says, "My judgment? This guy!" followed by the name of the firm and a short list of the kinds of cases that they do. Does this create any issues under **Model Rule 7.2(b)**? Does it raise concerns under **Model Rule 7.1**?

e. Frank recently helped a member of his church congregation, an elderly widow who lives on Social Security and has no liability insurance, *pro bono*. (*Of course* he got the partners' approval, did a **conflicts** check, and had her sign an appropriate engagement letter. How could you even ask?) Frank defended the widow in a claim by a delivery person from a package service who alleged that he tripped and fell on the widow's front walk because the path was not properly maintained. The engagement ended favorably. Frank's pastor learned of Frank's kindness and, in a recent sermon on charity, brought it to the congregation's attention. Quoting the famed nineteenth-century cleric Henry Ward Beecher, the pastor reminded the congregation that "[e]very charitable act is a stepping stone toward heaven," and urged the assembled to show some love back. Several phone calls from fellow congregants in need of a lawyer (and able to pay) followed in the next few weeks, all of which Frank happily arranges for his firm to accept.

f. Frank and Maya both maintain profiles on LinkedIn, a large business networking social media site. LinkedIn allows people to "endorse" others for a particular skill and write a brief "recommendation" to accompany it. The "endorsements" and "recommendations" are then reflected on their public profiles. Maya calls Frank (remember, they were at the same law school at the same time) and offers to endorse and recommend Frank for litigation on LinkedIn if he will endorse and recommend her for business and transactional law. Frank agrees.

g. Frank, newly attuned to the possibilities of marketing through social media (*see* (f)), proposes to his firms' partners that the firm offer a 10 percent discount on one monthly bill to any client who will endorse and recommend the firm or its lawyers on LinkedIn.

h. "Swifty" Smith, a personal injury lawyer in town, has discovered a new revenue stream. Swifty strongly recommends that all his injured clients get their prescriptions filled at

Phavorate Pharmacy. Phavorate Pharmacy sometimes charges more than the big chain drugstores in town, but its owners have agreed to pay Swifty one-third of their profits on the prescriptions of every customer that Swifty refers.

2. Advertising Mechanics

YOUR HOUSE; YOUR RULES Among the widely varying approaches of the several states, some have some rigid mechanical rules about lawyers' "communications" with the public. Many states have detailed record-keeping requirements concerning the content of a lawyer's advertising and the media in which it was placed. Many also have requirements that "communications" inviting client business be labeled "Lawyer Advertising" in some prominent form. Some states require that most kinds of lawyer advertisements be submitted to the state bar at or before the time they are published, to facilitate the bar's policing of lawyer advertising; some of those states will offer, on request, an "advisory opinion" on whether the ad will comply with the state's rules. At least one state (Texas) requires the state bar's advance approval before most ads can be published. As you're now used to hearing us say, you will need to figure out whether you and your **practice organization** are subject to any of these requirements. YOUR HOUSE; YOUR RULES

The Model Rules are less ambitious in this regard. **Model Rule 7.2(d)** requires only that "[a]ny communication . . . must include the name and contact information of at least one lawyer or law firm responsible for its content." Given that this information would naturally appear in almost any communication from lawyers about their services, it is not a very demanding obligation.

D. Solicitation

1. Solicitation Defined

Solicitation is a special category of lawyer communications subject to special rules. Though this is another area in which there is a good deal of interjurisdictional variation on the details, the Model Rule addressing this issue, **Model Rule 7.3(a)**, begins by defining which lawyer communications are "solicitations":

a communication initiated by or on behalf of a lawyer or law firm that is directed to a specific person the lawyer knows or reasonably should know needs legal services in a particular matter and that offers to provide, or reasonably can be understood as offering to provide, legal services for that matter.

TAMING THE TEXT Let's study the text of the Rule to determine what sets solicitation off from other lawyer communications. We'll get right to it, but first we'd like you to try and paraphrase the Rule's definition, because this is a good way to figure out what statutory language means and to make its meaning stick in your memory.

Done? Okay, now let's do it together: The wording tells us it has to be a communication "initiated" by (or on behalf of) a lawyer, meaning that solicitations don't include any conversation started by someone other than the lawyer. (Think of an example that does, and an example that does not, fit this portion of the definition.)

The heart of what makes solicitation different from other lawyer communications is found in the next phrase: It is a communication that *targets* a particular person—is "directed to a specific person." And what's more, that particular person must be someone who needs a lawyer *for a particular purpose* ("a specific person the lawyer knows or reasonably should know needs legal services *in a particular matter*" (emphasis added)), and it's about *that particular purpose* that the lawyer is communicating ("a communication . . . that offers to provide, or reasonably can be understood as offering to provide, legal services *for that matter*" (emphasis added)). ⟨Taming the Text⟩

> **Problem 18D-1:** Which of the following is a "solicitation" within the meaning of **Model Rule 7.3(a)**? Please explain your answer.
>
> a. Handing your business card to a pedestrian whom you just saw trip and fall on a crack in the sidewalk.
> b. Phoning the family of someone killed in a recent industrial accident and offering to help with the legal issues that the accident has created. Does your analysis change if the family member you're phoning is a **former client** of yours? How about if it's your brother-in-law? If so, how and why; and if not, why not?
> c. Returning a phone call from a family member of someone killed in a recent industrial accident who saw one of your ads and left a message asking what you could do to help.
> d. Placing an ad in the local paper including the words, "Everyone needs an estate plan. We can help you take care of your family at a very reasonable cost." (*Hint: See* **Model Rule 7.3 Comment [1]**.)
> e. Sending a mailing to everyone in your town's zip code with the same content as in (d).
> f. Subscribing to a service that checks public police records daily for reports of traffic tickets and accidents and sending a mailing to the people listed in those records including the words, "Traffic citation? Collision? Don't take on the cops or the insurance company alone!"

2. Types of Solicitation That Are Prohibited

Now that we know what solicitation is, let's figure out why we care about it. Not every kind of solicitation is prohibited, but there are several categories that are strictly forbidden. We'll look at them one by one, but first, our alert readers (blessings in abundance be upon them!) are quite sensibly asking why the Rules treat solicitation differently from other lawyer communications.

⟨Reason for the Rule⟩ Solicitation, we just learned, is different from other lawyer communications because it targets particular individuals whom the lawyer knows (or should know) to have particular legal needs and focuses the communication on those particular needs. A person who has particular legal needs (for example, someone who was just charged with a crime or someone who was just hurt or whose loved one was just injured or killed in an accident) is more likely to be emotionally distressed and vulnerable, less able to exercise detached and independent judgment, and thus more subject to influence, than someone in ordinary circumstances. And so we will see that the types of solicitation that the Rules prohibit are those generally presenting a greater risk of a lawyer's exercising undue influence to compromise a potential client's independent choice of counsel. Reason for the Rule

a. Live Person-to-Person Contact for Profit

The central category of forbidden solicitations is the solicitation of "professional employment by live person-to-person contact when a significant motive for the lawyer's doing so is the lawyer's or law firm's pecuniary gain . . . ." **Model Rule 7.3(b)**. Taming the Text From the Rule's wording, we know that the communication has to be a "solicitation" as defined by **Model Rule 7.3(a)**, and that the lawyer must be seeking "professional employment." We also know that the solicitation is not forbidden unless "a significant motive" is "pecuniary gain." The use of "significant" indicates that there can be (and often are) other motives for the solicitation in addition to profit, such as sympathy, a desire to help another in need, or a thirst for justice. The profit motivation thus need not be exclusive or even primary or predominant—just "significant." And to be forbidden, the solicitation must be made by "live person-to-person contact." Obviously, this includes face-to-face communication, but could also involve "other remote but instantaneous means of communication, such as the telephone and other real-time visual or auditory person-to-person communications in which the person is subject to a direct personal encounter without time for reflection." **Model Rule 7.3 Comment [2]**. The same Comment helpfully elaborates that "[s]uch person-to-person contact does *not* include chat rooms, text messages or other written communications that recipients may easily disregard" (emphasis added). Taming the Text

Reason for the Rule Consistent with the reasons just discussed about why we pay more attention to solicitation than to other forms of attorney communication, you could infer that the reason that this particular category of solicitation is banned is that live person-to-person contact (from which it is more difficult for the potential client to withdraw and "cool off" before deciding) by a lawyer pressing to make a profit (and thus more likely to be more insistent than if he were motivated exclusively by kinder and gentler human sentiments) would make it more likely that the lawyer might take advantage of a distressed potential client's emotional vulnerability and practical needs, possibly without even meaning to do so. *See* **Model Rule 7.3 Comment [2]**. In addition, "[t]he contents of live person-to-person contact can be disputed and may not be subject to third-party scrutiny. Consequently, they are much more likely to approach (and occasionally cross) the dividing line between accurate representations and those that are false and misleading." **Model Rule 7.3 Comment [4].** Reason for the Rule

For the same reasons, the exceptions to this prohibition are all situations in which this risk is mitigated by some other fact:

- When the contact is with another lawyer. **Model Rule 7.3(b)(1).** Another lawyer would more likely have the training and experience to resist a hard sell. *See* **Model Rule 7.3 Comment [5].**
- When the contact is with a "person who routinely uses for business purposes the type of legal services offered by the lawyer." **Model Rule 7.3(b)(3).** "Examples include persons who routinely hire outside counsel to represent the entity; entrepreneurs who regularly engage business, employment law or intellectual property lawyers; small business proprietors who routinely hire lawyers for lease or contract issues; and other people who routinely retain lawyers for business transactions or formations." **Model Rule 7.3 Comment [5].** Here again, a sophisticated and experienced buyer of legal services in business is more likely to have the experience and perspective to withstand any efforts at undue influence.
- When the contact is with someone who has a pre-existing close personal, family, business, or professional relationship with the lawyer. **Model Rule 7.3(b) (2). Model Rule 7.3 Comment [5]** explains the drafters' convictions that "[t]here is far less likelihood that a lawyer would engage in overreaching against a former client, or a person with whom the lawyer has a close personal, family, business or professional relationship." We wonder how true this is in general, though it does seem to us that, depending on how good or bad that pre-existing relationship is, people with whom the lawyer has these kinds of pre-existing relationships are either a lot more or a lot less likely to want to hire the lawyer for the work being sought than a stranger. So in either case, the risk of undue influence by the lawyer is mitigated to some degree.

Be aware that this category of forbidden solicitations and its exceptions are defined based on the *risk* or *probability* of undue influence. No *proof* of *actual* undue influence (or its absence for an exception) is required to show a violation or the availability of an exception. The Rule and its exceptions thus apply whether a particular individual or situation fits the generalization on which the Rule is based or not. Thus, as a practical matter, both the Rule and the exceptions are overbroad, and each will inevitably include (or in the case of the exceptions, exclude) situations in which the risk of undue influence is nothing like what the Rule assumes will generally be the case.

b. Contacting Someone Who Has Discouraged Solicitation

The remaining categories of prohibited solicitation are ones that you probably could have predicted without ever reading the Rule. **Model Rule 7.3(c)(1)** prohibits any solicitation when "the target of the solicitation has made known to the lawyer a desire not to be solicited by the lawyer." No big surprise there.

c. Any Solicitation Involving Coercion, Duress, or Harassment

Although **Model Rule 7.3(b)** prohibits the defined category of solicitation (and its exceptions) because of the *risk* of undue influence, **Model Rule 7.3(c)(2)** makes clear that, even if a solicitation is permitted under **Model Rule 7.3(b)**, it is forbidden if it *actually* involves "coercion, duress, or harassment." Again, no surprise, but this means that, even if your conduct fits into a **Model Rule 7.3(b)** exception, you can still violate **Model Rule 7.3** and suffer all the **consequences** by engaging in coercion, duress, or harassment.

d. Any Solicitation That Is Materially False or Misleading

Finally, don't forget that solicitation is a subset of the broader category of lawyer communications, and **Model Rule 7.1** forbids *any* lawyer communication that is false or misleading. *See* **Chapter 18.B at 477**. So a solicitation that is otherwise permissible, and even one lacking in any coercion, duress, or harassment, can still land you in hot water if it contains or implies **material** statements of fact that are false or misleading.

3. CONSEQUENCES Consequences of Engaging in Prohibited Solicitation

As you're now accustomed to our pointing out, **Model Rule 7.3** is a Rule of Professional Conduct, so the **consequence** for its violation is professional discipline. The same state bars that seek to regulate lawyer advertising aggressively are also, likely for the same reasons, especially vigilant about prohibited solicitation, so disciplining solicitation is a fairly typical preoccupation for bar prosecutors in many states.

In addition, recall that the policy motivation underlying regulation of solicitation is the avoidance of undue influence. **Model Rule 7.3** prohibits some of the categories of solicitation that it does because of the *risk* of undue influence, so a violation of the Rule does not necessarily establish that the lawyer *in fact* exercised undue influence. In those cases in which actual undue influence can be proven, however, there are civil remedies in addition to any disciplinary **consequences**. You may recall from your Contracts course that undue influence is a defense to the enforcement of a contract and is a ground for rescission.[22] These principles allow unduly influenced clients or potential clients to undo any agreement that they later regret, likely requiring the overreaching lawyer to pay over any excessive profits earned, or to compensate clients for any unfair losses that the clients may have incurred, as a result. It also is not unusual for a civil court to avoid (that is, undo) as against public policy an engagement agreement based on a prohibited solicitation as defined by the state's ethical rules. CONSEQUENCES

---

[22] *See* Restatement (Second) of Contracts § 177 (1981).

Problem 18D-2: Which of the following solicitations is a violation of **Model Rule 7.3**?

a. There has been a factory explosion in the town where lawyer "Swifty" Smith lives and works. A number of workers were killed or seriously injured. Swifty obtains a list of the casualties and sends letters to the victims or their survivors, describing his skill and experience in personal injury cases.

b. One victim of the factory explosion is Swifty's brother-in-law. Swifty goes to see his sister, with whom he has never gotten along, to console her in her time of need. While he is visiting, Swifty talks about the great job that he could do for her in her wrongful death case. Does your analysis change if he offers to represent his sister *pro bono*? If so, why and how; and if not, why not?

c. Same as (b), but Swifty's sister turns him down, saying "I really don't want to talk about this with you." Swifty calls her ten days later, asks her how she's doing, and then says, "I'd really like to see if I could discuss your case with you." Does your analysis change if Swifty communicates by email? If so, why and how; and if not, why not?

d. Swifty goes to the hospital to visit a worker injured in the explosion. Swifty and the worker attend the same church in town. After making some small talk, Swifty gives the worker his business card.

e. Swifty attends the wake of one of the workers with whose family he is acquainted. He takes the opportunity to draw the worker's widow into a corner and press her to sign an engagement agreement hiring him to represent her in her wrongful death case. "You'll be safe with me," Swifty assures her. "I've never lost a case." This is, of course, inaccurate—Swifty (like pretty much everybody) has lost cases before. Does your analysis change if Swifty doesn't say the words just quoted? If so, why and how; and if not, why not?

E. Lawyer Advertising in the Wild

We think that no examination of lawyer advertising or solicitation would be complete without a look at what some real lawyers actually do. You're going to be a lawyer soon, and at some point in your career, you may well consider advertising of one kind or another, even if it's only something as basic as a website or a printed brochure. You'll need to consider the image or message that you wish to convey and how you expect that image or message to affect the people you hope to reach. Those are questions that we'd like you to ask yourself about the lawyers whose communications we offer as examples to consider.

It is often said that private-sector client-service divides into two "hemispheres"—the lawyers, mostly in larger law firms and a few specialized high-end "boutiques," who generally serve larger companies and very wealthy individuals; and the lawyers, mostly solos and members of smaller firms, who serve individuals and small businesses. Lawyers in both hemispheres advertise, but the nature of the advertisements differs substantially between the two worlds. These differences likely correspond to the lawyers' perceptions of what might impress the clients that each seeks to reach.

Large-firm advertising is ubiquitous but is targeted mostly outside mass media. Every large law firm has a professionally designed website with carefully curated summaries and press releases regarding its highly sophisticated, high-stakes specialties, usually punctuated with tasteful photographs of client-industry facilities (factories; refineries; the stock exchange; banks of computers) and attractive people in business clothing meeting in elegantly appointed conference rooms or shaking hands. Pick any larger firm (if you can't think of one, consult the **Vault 100** or another large-law-firm prestige ranking to find one), and take a look.

Advertising in the other hemisphere, serving individuals and small businesses, is completely different and a lot more variable. We want you to think about why that might be so.

Let's start with a typical and relatively restrained ad for **a personal injury firm** focused specifically on an asbestos-related disease called mesothelioma. There are many examples of advertising like this one running on late-night (and occasionally prime-time) television all over the country.

Even with the most restrained and tasteful consumer advertising, however, all may not be as it seems. Here is a typical television ad for **The Law Offices of James Scott Farrin**, a successful personal injury firm in North Carolina. But the nice-looking, well-spoken gentleman with the lawyerly repp tie and suit vest is not James Scott Farrin or any other lawyer in his office. He is Robert Vaughn, an actor, whom some of you may have seen in the great western *The Magnificent Seven* (the original American version from 1960) and, less memorably, as Napoleon Solo in the 1960s television series *The Man from U.N.C.L.E.* Mr. Vaughn never practiced law. The ads reproduced on YouTube have a quick flash of small print stating "Robert Vaughn is a paid spokesperson for the Law Offices of James Scott Farrin." Can you find a requirement for such a disclosure in **Model Rule 7.2**? How likely is it that personal injury victims might imagine from these ads that the guy who was going to stand up for them to the insurance company and in court is that fellow on the screen? At what point (if ever) might this amount to a violation of **Model Rule 7.1** or **Model Rule 7.2**?

A great deal of the lawyer advertising that you see today is like the examples just discussed. We assume, without having the benefit of any actual data, that the lawyer advertising that you typically see is commercially effective—that is, it probably attracts more in client fees than it costs to make and disseminate. But features that are common to most lawyer ads are sometimes exaggerated in ways that, at the very least, tell us some interesting things about what some lawyers think may appeal to the kinds of clients they typically serve (or perhaps more generally, what appeals to the lawyers themselves about who they imagine themselves to be). The recurring elements of typical lawyer advertising are not hard to isolate. Here are some good examples of the "tough-talking lawyer" genre:

"Let's make 'em pay" (it's worth noting that this is the same firm that produced the mesothelioma ad linked above)

"I am the hammer; they are the nails" (and, yes, his phone number really is 459-CASH)

The **"Texas Hammer" – "I bite"** (perhaps carnivorous hammers are indigenous to Texas?)

Are these spots effective? To which kind of clients do you think they are directed, and how well do you think they work? And what the heck is it about lawyers and hammers? Is it that when you're a hammer, everything (or perhaps everybody) looks like a nail—or if you're the Texas Hammer and you bite, maybe you bite your nails?[23]

The "tough-talking lawyer" themes sometimes combine into deliberately exaggerated over-the-top spectacles involving shouting, explosions, and crashes. Consider this BBC News piece on a Fort Worth, Texas, criminal defense lawyer who calls himself the **Texas Law Hawk**.

A related take is the smirky suggestion that a lawyer may just be *too* good at what he or she does. Take a look at this humorously exaggerated puff piece for a criminal defense lawyer whose clients are portrayed in mid-felony, grinning at the camera and saying, **"Thanks, Dan!"** If you were in need of a criminal defense lawyer, would this ad persuade you to hire Dan? Why or why not? The real-life Pittsburgh criminal-defense lawyer featured in the ad, Daniel Muessig, was interviewed by a local news team about his ad's origins and motivations. **Listen to** his strikingly thoughtful reflections—and his reports of the ad's great success in generating new clients.

The "tough talking lawyer" genre also sometimes stumbles into the more disturbing (and here your authors paraphrase what we interpret to be the message of these ads): "Wouldn't it be cool to turn an abusive jerk like me loose on your enemies?" Check out this 2020 Super Bowl ad aired in the Mobile, Alabama area:

"The Godfather of Personal Injury"

And to the best of our knowledge this is a real ad for a real divorce attorney:

Divorce EZ

Here are some examples of *deliberately* humorous lawyer television advertising:

Poking fun at the struggle to extract compensation from an insurer
Ham Law

---

[23] Florida, perhaps unsurprisingly in these days of rising ocean levels, is still the high-water mark of advertising regulation and would apparently discipline the subject of such an ad: "The Supreme Court of Florida found that lawyer advertisements containing an illustration of a pit bull canine and the telephone number 1-800-pitbull were false, misleading, and manipulative, because use of that animal implied that the advertising lawyers would engage in "combative and vicious tactics" that would violate the Rules of Professional Conduct. *Fla. Bar v. Pape*, 918 So. 2d 240 (Fla. 2005)." Fl. R. Prof. Cond. 4-7.13, Comment on "Implying Lawyer Will Violate Rules of Conduct or Law" (2020).

"You really have to be injured":
>   **Example 1**
>   **Example 2**
>   **Example 3**
>   **Pete Reid — I'm the One**

Take a moment and note the different perspectives on lawyers and legal disputes on which each of these advertisements draws. Leaving aside your aesthetic preferences, which of these do you think would be most *effective* for its intended purpose—attracting the kinds of cases and clients that you imagine the advertisement was designed to attract? What does each of these styles of advertising say about what the lawyers who produced them think is important to potential clients? What do they say about the lawyers who produced them and how they see themselves and their competitors?

Along with the many other things that it protects, the First Amendment guarantees us the right to make fools of ourselves in ways limited only by the human imagination (and legitimate concerns for public safety and welfare). If in the course of making fools of themselves, the lawyers gain supporters or attract customers, we think that you shouldn't blame the messenger, or, for that matter, the message. What do you think?

Crazy Eddie, *requiescat in pace.*

Big-Picture Takeaways from Chapter 18

1. Lawyers have a First Amendment right to advertise, thanks to Supreme Court cases beginning with *Bates v. State Bar of Arizona* in 1977. Many states have nevertheless adopted supplementary bodies of rules limiting whole categories of lawyer advertising. Some of these categories are in whole or in part unconstitutional, but you will likely have to fight for your right to violate an overbroad rule. So before you put anything out there in any medium, including anything that you put on the Internet as part of a law firm website (which qualifies as regulated "lawyer advertising" just about everywhere), you need to know exactly what your state bar considers objectionable. If your ad violates bar rules, and you're sure that the rules are wrong, you still need to decide whether the fight is worth it. *See* **Chapter 18.A at 474.**

2. **Model Rule 7.1** encompasses all "communication[s] about the lawyer or the lawyer's services" that are "ma[d]e" by (or on behalf of) the lawyer. The Rule prohibits "false or misleading" communications. **Model Rule 7.1(a)** explains that a communication is false or misleading if it contains a material misrepresentation of fact or law or omits a fact necessary to

make the statement considered as a whole not materially misleading. *See* **Chapter 18.B at 477.**

3. **Model Rule 7.2(b)** provides that a lawyer "shall not" pay (with cash or anything else of value) for client referrals. One thing that **Model Rule 7.2(b)** forbids is conduct known as "capping" and "running": paying nonlawyers, such as emergency medical technicians, hospital staff, funeral directors, medical examiners, and others to tout a particular lawyer's services. Such arrangements can include cash payments to hand out a lawyer's business cards to those who might need one, or a kickback arrangement based on the number or value of the clients that the third party actually steers to the lawyer. The exceptions to the Rule are consistent with its purpose: You **may** pay the "reasonable costs" of creating and disseminating proper advertising; you **may** "pay the usual charges of a legal service plan or a not-for-profit or qualified lawyer referral service"; you **may** buy another law firm's practice, if that law firm is ceasing practice in a particular geographical or practice area and the other rules regarding this kind of transaction are followed; and you **may** agree to refer matters to another lawyer or "nonlawyer professional" in return for that person agreeing to refer matters to you, provided that the arrangement "is not exclusive" and that "the client is informed of the existence and nature of the agreement." *See* **Chapter 18.C at 485.**

4. As for what must be in every ad, **Model Rule 7.2(d)** requires only that "[a]ny "communication . . . must include the name and contact information of at least one lawyer or law firm responsible for its content." Many states have additional requirements regarding the form of advertisements or the records that you must keep. *See* **Chapter 18.C at 488.**

5. **Model Rule 7.3** governs solicitations, which the Rule defines as communications "initiated" by (or on behalf of) a lawyer that *target* a particular person who needs a lawyer *for a particular purpose* and that focus on *that particular purpose*. Not all solicitations are prohibited. But a person who has particular legal needs (for example, someone who was just charged with a crime, or someone whose loved one was just injured or killed in an accident) is more likely to be emotionally distressed and vulnerable, less able to exercise detached and independent judgment, and thus more subject to influence, than someone in ordinary circumstances. So the types of solicitation that the Rules prohibit are those generally presenting a greater risk of a lawyer's exercising undue influence to compromise a potential client's independent choice of counsel. The categories of solicitation that are prohibited (and the exceptions within those categories that are permitted) are defined in **Model Rule 7.3.** *See* **Chapter 18.D at 488.**

6. Don't forget that solicitation is a subset of the broader category of lawyer communications, and **Model Rule 7.1** forbids *any* lawyer communication that is false or misleading. So a solicitation that is otherwise permissible, and even one lacking in any coercion, duress, or harassment, can still land you in hot water if it contains or implies **material** statements of fact that are false or misleading. *See* **Chapter 18.D at 492**.

Multiple-Choice Review Questions for Chapter 18

1. Why were lawyers prohibited from advertising prior to the 1970s?
   a. To preserve the decorum of the profession.
   b. To prevent misleading potential clients.
   c. Both a and b.
   d. Neither a nor b.

2. The State of Raptor has rules restricting lawyer advertising. One such rule is that all advertising must be "dignified." The rule provides that a lawyer may not use any illustrations, cartoons, or animations as part of his or her advertising. Jeff is a lawyer barred in Raptor. His television commercial features an opening graphic showing him, in cartoon form, dressed to look like Superman. The cartoon Jeff swoops down and saves a woman from being hit by a car. The commercial then cuts to footage of Jeff sitting in his office, explaining that he handles motor vehicle cases. Jeff is disciplined for his commercial. What must be shown if Jeff challenges the constitutionality of the statute?
   a. The State must show a substantial state interest in dignified advertising, that its rule directly advances that interest, and that the rule is no more extensive than necessary to serve the interest.
   b. Jeff must show that his advertisement was broadcast for the purpose of free expression.
   c. The State must show the rule is narrowly tailored to achieve a compelling government interest.
   d. The State must show that the regulation has a rational relation to a legitimate state interest.

3. Kira is a lawyer practicing in the Commonwealth of Keystone. She takes out a full-page advertisement in a local newspaper. The ad says, "There's no fee unless we get money for you." Kira's contingent-fee arrangement with her clients provides that no attorney fees need to be paid unless the client recovers. Pursuant to the agreement, however, the client is responsible for paying all costs incurred during litigation, regardless of the outcome of the case. Kira reasons that there is a difference between a "fee" and a "cost," and although many lay people may not realize the

distinction, it is technically true that clients are not responsible for any "fees" unless they recover. Is Kira's advertisement likely to be protected by the First Amendment?

    a. Yes. All lawyer advertising is entitled to protection.

    b. Yes. It is not technically false and therefore it is entitled to protection.

    c. No. All lawyer advertising is unprotected.

    d. No. It may be deemed to be misleading and therefore unprotected.

4. A few months after passing the bar exam, Lottie hung out her shingle as a solo practitioner. She invested a few hundred dollars in some Facebook advertisements that include a flattering photo of her posing in a courtroom. Underneath the photo was her slogan: "I've never lost a single personal injury trial!" The ads also list the phone number for her firm. Her statement was technically true—she had never lost a trial. She had also never *litigated* one—in fact, she had only handled a few transactional real estate matters at the time that the advertising was placed. Is this advertisement likely to be deemed a violation of **Model Rule 7.1**?

    a. Yes. It contained no information about the types of cases that Lottie had handled and therefore deprived potential clients of the necessary context to understand why she had never lost a case.

    b. Yes. It might lead a potential client to conclude that Lottie had won trials for former clients and therefore could create an unjustified expectation that she could similarly win a trial for that potential client.

    c. No. The outcomes of trials are a matter of public record, and any potential client could check the court dockets and confirm that indeed Lottie had never lost a trial.

    d. No. It cannot be misleading because it is true. Lottie indeed had never lost a single trial, and therefore the advertisement was truthful.

5. Manny would like to run an advertisement that states he has the lowest rates in his county. Is such an advertisement prohibited by **Model Rule 7.1**?

    a. Yes. No advertisement may contain information about fees.

    b. Yes. This statement is only permitted if Manny also discloses the fees of all lawyers in the county as part of the advertisement.

    c. Maybe. This statement is permitted if indeed Manny is able to show that he has the lowest rates in the county.

    d. No. An advertisement may contain any information about fees.

6. Nora is a lawyer in the state of Peach. In addition to her law practice, Nora also sells essential oils as a "side hustle." She considers herself a

"board-certified aromatherapist." There is no such certification recognized by the state of Peach, nor is there any national organization for aromatherapy. The pyramid scheme for which she sells essential oils, however, deems all members to be so certified. May Nora include this title on the business cards that she uses for her law practice?

    a. Yes. This is a nonlegal specialization, so it falls outside **Model Rule 7.1**.

    b. Yes. She has this certification, so her communication meets the requirements of **Model Rule 7.2**.

    c. No. She must also indicate the authority issuing the certification to comply with **Model Rule 7.2**.

    d. No. Although this is a nonlegal specialization, it may nonetheless be misleading in violation of **Model Rule 7.1**.

7. Raquel went to Colombia Law School—not the prestigious Ivy League law school at Columbia University in New York City, but rather a lesser known law school in the country of Colombia at University of the Andes, Colombia in Bogotá. Can Raquel, who now practices in New York City, advertise that she is a graduate of "Colombia Law School"?

    a. Yes, because this is true. She did graduate from "Colombia Law School."

    b. Yes, so long as she does not use the term "Columbia University."

    c. No, because under the circumstances, a viewer may be misled into believing she graduated from "Columbia University," when in fact she graduated from "University of the Andes, Colombia."

    d. No, because this is untrue. She did not graduate from "Colombia Law School."

8. Olive is a personal injury lawyer. Her neighbor, Pilar, is a physician who both works in the emergency room of a local hospital and also has a private clinic. They have an exclusive arrangement. If a patient is admitted to the emergency room after a motor vehicle accident, Pilar hands the patient Olive's business card and recommends that the patient retain Olive. In exchange, any time that Olive has a client who needs medical care, she hands the client Pilar's business card and sends the client to Pilar's clinic. Could this arrangement violate **Model Rule 7.2**?

    a. Yes, because the reciprocal referral arrangement is exclusive.

    b. Yes, because a nonlawyer like Pilar is prohibited from recommending a lawyer. It does not matter whether Olive pays for the recommendation; the arrangement violates the Rule.

    c. No, because there is no direct *quid pro quo*. Olive generally funnels business to Pilar and Pilar generally funnels business to Olive. Their arrangement is built on mutual respect.

d. No, because Pilar's patients are not obligated to retain Olive. Pilar is simply suggesting Olive's services, and therefore this activity does not constitute a recommendation that could be governed by the Rule.

9. What is the difference between advertising and solicitation?
   a. Solicitation is more targeted than advertising.
   b. Advertising is more targeted than solicitation.
   c. Advertising is aimed at individuals, but solicitation is aimed at corporations.
   d. Solicitation is aimed at individuals, but advertising is aimed at corporations.

10. What **must** be in any advertisement pursuant to **Model Rule 7.2**?
    a. A list of where the lawyers in the firm are licensed to practice.
    b. The firm's areas of practice.
    c. The address of all firm offices.
    d. The contact information for a lawyer responsible for the advertisement.

11. Quincy handles personal injury litigation. One day, he reads an article in the paper about a serious construction accident in which debris fell on a pedestrian passing by. It includes the name of the pedestrian. He is able to find her address and Facebook account. Assuming that Quincy is interested in representing her in a lawsuit for which he will charge fees, which of the following is *not* a way he can contact her?
    a. Email.
    b. Postal mail.
    c. Social media.
    d. By knocking on her door and talking to her.

12. Solo practitioner Suzette advertises on the back of park benches in her hometown of Grittydelphia. The advertisements say nothing about whether she is the best lawyer in Grittydelphia. They do, however, contain her phone number: 1-800-BEST-ATTY. Is this advertisement proper?
    a. Yes. Suzette does not suggest that she is the best lawyer. If viewers draw that conclusion from the advertisement, that is their own inference.
    b. Yes. Had Suzette stated that she was the best lawyer in the text of the ad, this might be misleading, but it is not misleading to suggest so by using the phone number.
    c. No. It implies that Suzette is the best lawyer in the area and, without providing any basis for that comparison, it is misleading.
    d. No. The advertisement does not contain contact information for a lawyer responsible for its content.

13. Trudy won a $2 million judgment in a contingent-fee medical malpractice case for her client, Ulrich. Ulrich was thrilled with the result and offered to provide a testimonial for Trudy. Pursuant to their agreement, Trudy was entitled to 40 percent of the judgment as her fee. Because Ulrich was extremely handsome, Trudy asked Ulrich if she could instead use a testimonial and a picture of him in her future advertising. In exchange, she offered to take only 35 percent of the judgment as her fee. Ulrich agreed, and Trudy posted a billboard with a photo of the two of them and her contact information. Under Ulrich's photo was his testimonial: "Trudy fought for me every step of the way. I could not be happier with the outcome in my case." Was what Trudy did proper?
    a. Yes. Ulrich offered to recommend Trudy before she offered him the discounted fee.
    b. Yes. A discount of 5 percent is a *de minimis* amount, and the recommendation was sincere.
    c. No. Discounting the fee was a way of paying Ulrich for a recommendation.
    d. No. There was no guarantee that other clients would be awarded amounts as significant as Ulrich was awarded or that they would be as happy with Trudy as Ulrich was.

14. Vance is a lawyer who handles construction litigation. His sister, Wendy, is a construction project manager. At Thanksgiving dinner, Vance asks Wendy to please recommend his law firm to all the contractors and subcontractors with whom she deals. Although she finds the request annoying and has no intention of complying, she bites her tongue for the sake of family unity at the dinner table. Was Vance's request permitted under **Model Rule 7.3**?
    a. Yes, because Vance and Wendy are siblings.
    b. Yes, because Vance was not soliciting Wendy for legal services.
    c. No, because Wendy found the request annoying.
    d. No, because the solicitation was in person.

UNIT IV

Some Realities of Practice

THE LAST TWO UNITS were about the duties that lawyers owe, whether those duties are owed to their clients or to others. We still have more rights and duties to discuss, but in this unit, we consider them in the context of a lawyer's workplace. As we discussed way back in **Chapter 2 at 19**, there are lots of different kinds of workplaces, each with its own special mix of stresses and tensions and benefits and rewards. In this unit, we'll explore some of the legal features common to many of the kinds of workplaces in which you're likely to land during the early years of your work as a lawyer.

In **Chapter 19 at 505**, we'll consider the rights and duties inherent in working in a **practice organization**. In **Chapter 20 at 535**, we'll talk about fees. And in **Chapter 21 at 573**, we'll explore the sometimes complex and technical rules that govern how practicing lawyers must handle the money and property of clients and others with which they are frequently entrusted.

We'll continue to use the methods to which you've now become accustomed (or at least stoically resigned): We'll focus on the Model Rules, see how what the Rules require has influenced other potentially applicable areas of the law, and talk about the practical implications of the law's requirements on your day-to-day conduct.

Ready to get to work? *Of course* you are!

19

The Organizational Environment

DANIELLE IS HAVING LUNCH with a friend and law school classmate, Fiona Forsaken. Fiona works at a small firm in town that serves mainly small businesses. Both Danielle and Fiona are just a year out of law school, so nearly everything is still new to them. Fiona asks, a little hesitantly, what kind of training Danielle is getting. "Pretty good, really," Danielle answers. "The new deputies get brown-bag lectures now and then on basic stuff, like common evidence and procedural issues and voir dire. And my supervisor is great. He's a good teacher, and he often has the time to help. Even with all that, I still spend most days feeling like I got dropped in the deep end, wondering how long I can keep treading water. What about you?"

Fiona sighs. "At this point, the deep end sounds pretty good to me. I feel like I got dropped in the middle of the Bermuda Triangle. Most of the stuff we do I never heard a word about in law school. Property tax? Casualty insurance? Incentive stock option plans? Last month, I got handed a file for some company that wants to offer deals for equipment and business plans for fitness centers. Apparently, that might be a 'franchise.' Franchises? Do you even know what those are?" "Um, McDonald's?" Danielle guesses. "Don't feel bad; I didn't, either," Fiona shoots back with a smile. "McDonald's is an example of a company that offers franchises, but our state has this long, complicated statute and all these administrative regulations that define what a franchise is, when you have to register a franchise offering with the Secretary of State, and all the things you have to do or not do if you offer franchises. I've spent a solid week online, and I still don't really understand how it works."

"Can you get any help from your supervisor?" Danielle asks. "Supervisor?" Fiona snorts. "That's a good one. They sent me to the first client meeting with Andy Absent, a young partner who told the client's president that I knew all about franchising and was the perfect person to help his company. I nodded and played along. After the meeting, Andy told me to feel free to bring him any questions that I might have. Then he vanished. He hardly ever returns phone calls or answers emails, and he's out of the office most of the time. When I do get him, I get answers like, 'I think there's something about that in the statute.' The one thing I feel pretty confident I understand about this whole franchise thing is that if you do it wrong, the client is in big trouble: fines; rescission of the franchise agreements the client has made with franchisees; real 'wrath of God' stuff—maybe even criminal penalties. I'm scared out of my wits."

"I wish I could help," Danielle sympathizes, "but I've never come near franchise regulation in my job. What if you talk to one of the two senior partners at your firm about getting some help?" Fiona shakes her head. "And rat out Andy? Not good for job security." "Hmm," says Danielle, seeing her point. "Well then, I guess all you can do is do your best, and make sure that you keep copies of all your emails looking for backup on the law and asking for a review of your drafting. Then, if things go badly, at least it will be clear whose fault it is." "I guess you're right," sighs Fiona. "Thanks for the advice."

Is Danielle's strategy a good one for coping with this difficult situation within Fiona's small firm? What happens if things go wrong for the client?

* * *

This chapter is about the structure of obligations within a **practice organization**. Model Rules of Professional Conduct 5.1 through 5.3 govern the ethical obligations of lawyers working in organizational settings. Some Rules apply to subordinate lawyers, other Rules apply to managerial and supervisory lawyers, and still others apply to nonlawyer staff, such as legal assistants, investigators, and secretaries (more commonly called "administrative assistants" these days). There are corresponding legal rules governing the civil liability of a **practice organization's constituents**, both to one another and to third parties outside the **practice organization**.

As a new lawyer, you likely will be supervised by more senior lawyers, and you will also have some responsibility for supervising support staff. It is therefore essential that you understand how responsibility flows among the lawyers and nonlawyers in a **practice organization**. Let's get to it.

A. Defining a Practice Organization

When someone says "law firm," you probably think of a conventional private, for-profit, fee-for-service law practice. Most people do. But the drafters of the Model Rules had something much broader in mind. We know that they did because they defined "firm" and "law firm" in **Model Rule 1.0(c)**. Take a look at that Rule now.

TAMING THE TEXT What should emerge from the Rules' definition of "firm" or "law firm" is that *any* organization that offers legal services on *any* basis is treated as a "law firm" under the Model Rules. This definition extends not only to the common

forms in which private for-profit law firms are organized (including a solo practitioner's practice), but "a legal services organization or the legal department of a
corporation or other organization." The definition thus includes nonprofit legal
services organizations, government agencies that provide legal services (such as
district attorneys' offices, public defenders' offices, and city or county attorneys'
offices), and the legal departments of for-profit and nonprofit companies, as well
as the legal departments of government agencies whose principal purpose is to do
things other than provide legal services. We will sometimes use the term **practice
organization** to refer to this broad range of groups and organizations that provide
legal services in order to avoid any confusion that the conventional understanding
of "law firm" might cause. TAMING THE TEXT

Unlike most of the Model Rules, which focus exclusively on what an individual
"lawyer" **must**, **must not**, **may**, or **should** do, **Model Rule 5.1, Model Rule 5.2**, and **Model
Rule 5.3** focus on professional responsibility within **practice organizations**. The Model
Rules are the first rules of lawyer ethics that explicitly consider ethical responsibility
within **practice organizations**, an innovation long overdue given the fact that almost all
lawyers work in multiperson **practice organizations** — even if they are the sole lawyer
in the workplace. And as we discussed in **Chapter 4.A at 71**, the **practice organization**
within which you work has a powerful influence on your personal conduct and what
you learn (consciously or unconsciously) about how things are done.

B. The Duty of Each Individual Lawyer Within a Practice Organization to Comply with Applicable Rules of Professional Conduct and Other Law

1. The Broad Rule of Individual Responsibility

We begin the discussion of professional responsibility in a **practice organization** with an essential basic principle: Acting within an organizational structure
virtually never shields individual lawyers from responsibility for their own acts or
omissions. CONSEQUENCES For purposes of professional discipline, each lawyer within
a **practice organization** has a nondelegable, personal duty to comply with the Rules
of Professional Conduct as they apply to his or her individual circumstances. Civil
tort law applies a similar principle that agents (whether employees of an organization or lawyers acting for their clients) are *personally* liable for any tort that
they commit within the course and scope of the agency.[1] And, of course, if you
commit a crime on the job, you're responsible for it — no one is going to go to
prison for you. CONSEQUENCES

Some of you are probably thinking, "But what about all that *respondeat superior* stuff we talked about in Torts? Doesn't that affect this issue?" The answer

---

[1] RESTATEMENT (THIRD) OF AGENCY § 7.01 (2006).

is yes, but not in the way that you might wish. If you think back to your Torts course (we know, but take a deep breath and probe the wound), what you learned was that *respondeat superior expands* the number of persons liable for a tort by making the principal (employer) liable for torts committed by an agent (employee) in the course and scope of the agency (employment).[2] For example, if Frank commits professional negligence while representing a client, his firm will be jointly and severally liable to that client for Frank's negligence *vicariously*, that is, *in addition to* but not *instead of* Frank. Frank will be *personally* jointly and severally liable, too.[3]

REAL WORLD In the real world, a lot of these details become a lot less relevant if your **practice organization** has professional liability insurance. Virtually all professional liability policies cover both the **practice organization** and everyone working for it, at least for things done in the course of the **practice organization's** professional activities. Because the firm and everyone in it is covered, distinctions about who is liable for what portion of a tort liability often become irrelevant.

But don't assume that's the end of the discussion: Although many **practice organizations** have professional liability insurance, many don't.[4] Only two states (Oregon and Idaho) currently *require* lawyers to have insurance, and even in those states, if your **practice organization** violates the Rule and fails to insure itself, you're still "bare." And even if your **practice organization** has professional liability insurance, all insurance policies have a "policy limit"—that is, a maximum amount that the insurer will pay out no matter how much the actual liability turns out to be. In addition, many professional liability policies include the cost of defense within the policy limits (these are referred to as "wasting" policies), meaning that the fees and costs that the insurer pays to defend the insureds are part of what uses up the policy limits. (Common consumer insurance, such as automobile and homeowners' or renters' liability insurance, are typically *not* like this, so the "wasting" feature is a surprise to many new lawyers.) Most professional liability policies also have a "self-insured retention" or deductible; that is, an initial amount of any liability (and, often, any costs of defense) that you have to pay for yourself before the insurer becomes responsible for

---

[2] *See* RESTATEMENT (THIRD) OF AGENCY § 7.07 (2006). As you may recall from your Torts course, *respondeat superior* is not just the law; it's a good idea. Not only does it ensure compensation for the innocent victims of torts that are committed by employees of businesses, but it also creates financial incentives for employers to supervise and manage their employees in order to try to avoid accidents or to minimize their effects.

[3] The person harmed by the tort is entitled to recover no more than 100 percent of her damages no matter how many people are liable for the wrong, but she can recover it from anyone, or any combination of people, who is (or are) jointly and severally liable. People who end up paying the plaintiff more than their fair share of the liability may even the score with those who underpaid the plaintiff through the doctrines of contribution and indemnity, which are rife with interjurisdictional differences of their own. Here endeth the Torts lesson, and thanks for accompanying us on what might have been a somewhat rocky stroll down memory lane. Remember, we mean well.

[4] Although many private law firms and nonprofit legal services organizations have malpractice insurance, in-house law departments and government agencies often do not. How these **practice organizations** deal with lawyer-employee errors and omissions will differ.

anything. Depending on the policy, that amount can be quite substantial. What's more, most professional liability policies *don't* cover a number of important things: Most don't cover allegedly intentional torts; most don't cover the cost of defending professional disciplinary charges or any fines or expenses assessed as discipline; very few cover torts not committed in the course of the **practice organization**'s professional activities; and almost none cover fee disputes or court-imposed sanctions. It can be a big, cold world out there when something goes wrong. REAL WORLD

2. The Narrow Exception for Complying with a Supervisor's Reasonable Resolutions of Genuinely Arguable Questions of Professional Duty

Some of you, we would guess, are now thinking, "Okay, so *respondeat superior* doesn't help me, and professional liability insurance won't always help, either, but the whole point of going to work for an employer is to make sure that there are more experienced, wiser heads around to provide me with training and guidance. And what's more, I have to do what my boss tells me to, so I'm really off the hook, right?" Sorry, no. Yes, you should go to work for an employer that can provide you with training and guidance. And yes, you have to do what your boss tells you, in the limited sense that serious *employment* **consequences** are likely to follow if you don't. But you nevertheless remain *individually* responsible for your own compliance with the Rules of Professional Conduct. **Model Rule 5.2(a)** confirms exactly that. (Please read it now; it's short.) If you violate a Rule of Professional Conduct, you will be personally subject to the **consequence** of professional discipline, even if someone in authority told you to do it.

The same is, of course, true as to civil tort liability: Generally speaking, you are individually liable for the torts that you yourself commit. Someone who directed or encouraged you to commit a tort may *also* be *vicariously* liable, but that in no way relieves you of the **consequence** of personal liability if you're the tortfeasor.

There is one extremely narrow exception to the general rule of personal responsibility for Rules violations, and it's set out in **Model Rule 5.2(b)**:

> A subordinate lawyer does not violate the Rules of Professional Conduct if that lawyer acts in accordance with a supervisory lawyer's reasonable resolution of an arguable question of professional duty.

TAMING THE TEXT Let's take a hard look at this Rule to understand how very narrow this exception is. If you're working in a **practice organization** and a supervisor tells you to do something that turns out to be a violation of the Rules of Professional Conduct, you're protected from discipline if, but *only* if, what you're told to do raises "an *arguable* question of professional duty" (emphasis added), and the directions that you follow amount to a "*reasonable* resolution" (emphasis added) of that "arguable question." In other words, it has to be genuinely unclear how to comply with the Rules under the prevailing circumstances, and what you're told to do has to be a "reasonable" way of complying in the face of that uncertainty. Otherwise, "I was only following orders" is no defense.[5] TAMING THE TEXT

CONSEQUENCES Although **Model Rule 5.2(b)** may limit your exposure to professional discipline in a few situations, it remains unsettled whether the **Model Rule 5.2(b)** exception, narrow though it is, has any analogue in civil tort liability. CONSEQUENCES

REAL WORLD **Model Rule 5.2** highlights how broad every practicing lawyer's individual responsibility truly is. If you *should have known* that what you were being asked to do was wrong, then it is very difficult for you to argue later that you were faced with an "*arguable* question of professional duty" (emphasis added). "Should have known" usually means that a reasonable person *would* have known, and if a reasonable person would have known that the supervisor's direction was unlawful, then the question would not appear to be "arguable." (That said, ignorance of the law is still no excuse, and you can be liable for a violation whether or not you knew that it was wrong; the question under **Model Rule 5.2(b)** is whether the violation was, in actuality, objectively *arguable*, not whether you *thought* or *knew* that it was arguable.) To be sure, there are ethical questions for which a clear resolution by a reasonable lawyer is difficult, and those fall within the safe harbor of **Model Rule 5.2(b)**—but only if your supervisor resolves those ethical questions *reasonably*. In short, when your duty to follow your supervisor's directions conflicts with your duty to follow the Rules of Professional Conduct, the Rules win every time.

The day therefore may come when you are faced with the choice between refusing to follow an unlawful order and violating your ethical—and, quite probably, also your legal—duties to a client, a third party, or the state bar. The good news (such as it is) is that this horrible situation doesn't happen to most people, and it doesn't happen to anyone very often. If it does happen, however, it can be one of the most fraught and stressful moments of your career.

TIPS & TACTICS If that moment comes for you (and we hope that it never does), here's a little practical advice:

- Be sure that you've understood the supervisor's specific instruction that's in question. Especially early in your career, it's not hard to misunderstand a supervisor's instructions.
- If at all possible, discuss the issue with the supervisor who's giving the instructions. You may discover that you've misunderstood the supervisor;

---

[5] This phrase remains in the idiom decades after its repeated use by Nazi soldiers and government officials at the Nuremburg war-crimes trials that took place just after World War II. ("*Befehl ist Befehl*," many defendants pleaded; literally, "orders are orders.") One of the lasting effects of the Nuremburg proceedings was to discredit the "superior orders" defense for almost any purpose. **Model Rule 5.2** makes it clear that this is the rule in professional ethics as well. In a situation in which a subordinate legitimately did not know that the order was wrongful, the blameworthiness of the violation, and thus the attendant **consequence**, might be reduced, but lack of knowledge does not excuse the violation itself, unless the violation required the specific intent of *knowing* the order was unlawful. The same is true in professional ethics. *See* **Model Rule 5.2 Comment [1]**.

you may receive a satisfying and legally correct explanation as to why what you're being told to do is permissible (or, at worst, a reasonable resolution of an arguable question of professional duty); or you may be able to point out something that your supervisor hasn't considered, which could change the course of events.

■ Be sure that you're right that what you're being asked to do is unlawful (that is, that it's a violation of one or more Rules of Professional Conduct, a tort, or a crime). You may wish to, and probably should, seek advice from someone else within your **practice organization**. Many **practice organizations** have personnel specifically designated to handle such inquiries with whom, as counsel to the **practice organization**, your communications are privileged (not as to you personally, but as communications between the **practice organization** and its counsel; do you see why?). If such a person isn't available (or gives you advice that you believe to be wrong, which can occasionally happen), consider seeking advice from a lawyer outside the **practice organization**. See if you can retain that person as your personal counsel to protect your communications as privileged (with any luck, on a *pro bono* basis, but pay if you must to get independent, knowledgeable advice). *See* **Chapter 4.A at 71; Chapter 4.B at 87; Chapter 8.B at 243**. Some state bars maintain advice lines for such purposes that can point you to relevant research resources or, in some states, even provide opinions on which you can rely in determining your course of conduct.

■ All of this will be unimaginably difficult and stressful and will probably occur under significant time pressure. You have to do it anyway. If, after all your efforts, you remain convinced that you are being given unlawful instructions, you **must not** follow them. Be explicit that you are refusing to comply; don't hide it or lie about it. Document the reason that you're refusing to follow directions. Given that you are now disregarding a direct order from your supervisor, you may have to quit your job (or you may get fired). Although quitting or getting fired are serious **consequences** that will likely result in real hardship to you, remember that there are some jobs (not many, thankfully) that are worse than being unemployed. (After all, who really wants to work someplace where part of your job is to break the law?) Without getting overdramatic, at this extreme point in this inquiry—and we stress that, even when an issue of this kind arises, it hardly ever gets to this point—you are choosing between unemployment and committing disciplinary violations, torts, or crimes that could ruin your career. And no, it's not fair that someone may put you to that choice someday. But be mentally prepared for the possibility, however remote, that someday, someone might.

■ If you must quit or are fired, assess whether there is anyone else (a client; an organizational client contact; a third party; a tribunal) that you **must**, or **may** and **should**, inform about anything. *See* **Chapter 8.B at 235** (exceptions to the

duty of confidentiality); **Chapter 9.D at 298** ("noisy" withdrawals); **Chapter 9.D at 301** (duties upon withdrawal); **Chapter 23.B at 791** (**reporting up** within or **reporting out** of an organizational client); **Chapter 24.C at 878** (the duty to correct false evidence). If you personally are counsel of record in any proceedings before a tribunal, you may (and in most jurisdictions, do) need to seek the tribunal's permission in order to withdraw. *See* **Chapter 9.D at 288**. Tips & Tactics   Real World

Problem 19B-1: In each of the following situations, which lawyer(s) will be subject to one or more **consequences**, and what **consequences** are those likely to be? Please explain your answers.

a. As a new prosecutor, Danielle reports to the chief of her unit. Although the chief has no direct involvement in most of Danielle's cases, the chief must review all charges before they are filed. Danielle has a case that she thinks most likely should be charged as a simple assault. It would improve her statistics (which the office tracks as part of performance reviews) if she instead charges it as attempted murder. Danielle does not believe that a reasonable grand juror would find probable cause to believe that the defendant had an intent to kill (which is a necessary element of attempted murder in Danielle's state), but she reasons that the chief will review the charges and can direct her to pursue a lesser charge; and in all events, she can always bargain the charge down later, or drop it before trial. Danielle goes ahead and charges the more serious crime. (*Hint: See* **Model Rule 3.8(a)**.)

b. Under applicable law (in particular, *Brady v. Maryland*, 373 U.S. 83 (1963)), prosecutors have an obligation to disclose **material** exculpatory evidence to defense counsel. (*See* **Chapter 25.D at 945**.) Danielle has an interview report from a witness confessing that he actually committed the crime with which the defendant is charged. Although Danielle does not find the witness's confession credible, she fears that she will lose the case if she turns over the statement. Danielle reviews the witness report with her supervisor, who agrees that she will likely lose the case if she discloses it to the defense, and he directs her not to turn it over. Danielle follows her boss's instructions.

c. Same as (b), except that the statement that the witness gave gets all the details of the crime in question wrong, and Danielle has determined that the witness was in fact in jail himself at the time that he claims to have committed the crime. Danielle's supervisor concludes that the witness's statement is not **material** exculpatory evidence under prevailing law, and he directs Danielle not to turn it over. Danielle follows her boss's instructions.

d. Frank is representing the plaintiff in a personal injury case. Unfortunately, "Swifty" Smith is on the other side. Swifty's associate, a recent law graduate named Dan DeDupe, notices the deposition of the plaintiff's principal doctor treating the injury and two treating specialists. Because the doctors are not parties, they must be personally served with a deposition subpoena in order to be required to appear. Three Proofs of Service appear, stating that each doctor was personally served at his or her office on a particular date and time. Frank checks with the principal treating doctor, and he finds out that she is unaware of the impending deposition, was not served with a subpoena, and was out of the office playing golf at the time specified on the Proof of Service. The specialists tell similar stories: One was at a lunch engagement at the time that the Proof asserts she was served in her office; the other was attending rounds at a hospital. Frank calls Dan to find out what's going on. "Yeah, Swifty told me to just send those Proofs out because he said you guys would show up at the depos anyway," Dan explains, with refreshing, if unexpected, candor. "If you want different dates for the depos, we can do that."

C. The Duties to Manage and Supervise

Lawyers can have two different kinds of oversight obligations within a **practice organization**. Some lawyers have *management* responsibilities, and some have *supervisorial* responsibilities. (Some, of course, have neither, and some have both, but first let's get clear on the difference between the two.) When we're referring generally to managerial or supervisory authority, we'll sometimes use the term *oversight* responsibilities.

Some lawyers serve as firm managers. These managerial lawyers may not have day-to-day interaction with each lawyer in the firm, and they don't personally oversee or direct everyone's professional activities. Instead, managing lawyers have indirect, generalized authority over the professional work of the firm, either as a whole or as to some portion or aspect of the firm's work, such as a practice-group leader or the managing partner of one office of a multi-office firm. Because they generally oversee the professional work of the firm (as a whole or as to some portion of the firm or its practice), they *manage* both the lawyers and the nonlawyer staff who contribute to the firm's professional services within the scope of their oversight.

Supervisory authority involves responsibility on a day-to-day basis for overseeing the work of specific personnel. Unlike managerial lawyers, who often (but not always) have titles indicating their management powers and responsibilities, often a supervising lawyer has no formal title denoting this role. For example, a senior associate in a larger law firm may delegate work to a more junior associate. Although the senior associate cannot single-handedly fire or discipline the junior associate (both actions indicating managerial authority), the senior associate may nonetheless be responsible for ensuring that the junior associate's work product meets the client's needs and professional standards. Lawyers may directly supervise other lawyers, and they may supervise nonlawyer staff, such as legal assistants, investigators, and secretaries. It may be a while before you're supervising other lawyers, but you'll likely be supervising nonlawyers in your **practice organization** soon after you start work.

This distinction between managerial and supervisorial roles is reflected in the structure of the two Model Rules of Professional Conduct that address oversight responsibilities: **Model Rule 5.1** addresses management and supervision of other lawyers; **Model Rule 5.3** addresses management and supervision of nonlawyer staff. We'll consider each in turn.

1. The Duty to Manage Other Lawyers

Take a careful look at **Model Rules 5.1(a) and (b)**. They address the two different kinds of oversight authority that some lawyers may have over other lawyers within a **practice organization**, and the different kinds of responsibilities that each role carries.

TAMING THE TEXT **Model Rule 5.1(a)** defines the role and duties of managerial lawyers in a **practice organization**. How do we know? Because the Rule begins with a definition of the general managerial role discussed above. Management is not a role that can be defined with geometric precision, but the Rule gives us a sense of the kinds of positions and responsibilities that amount to managerial authority—"[a] partner in a law firm, or a lawyer who individually or together with other lawyers possesses comparable managerial authority in a law firm." *See also* **Model Rule 5.1 Comment [1]**.

The Rule also tells us that managerial lawyers have specific ethical duties attached to their managerial powers. What duties? They **must** ("shall") "make reasonable efforts to ensure that the firm has in effect measures giving reasonable assurance that all lawyers in the firm conform to the Rules of Professional Conduct."

Look carefully at what this Rule expects lawyer-managers to do. It does *not* expect them to directly oversee the work or work habits of every other lawyer in their firm and make sure that everyone is always in compliance with the Rules. In a **practice organization** of any significant size, that would be impossible. Instead, managers must make "reasonable efforts" to see that the **practice organization** (or that portion of it for which the manger is responsible) has "*internal policies and procedures* designed to provide *reasonable assurance*" that everyone will continue to comply with the Rules of Professional Conduct. **Model Rule 5.1 Comment [2]** (emphasis added). This includes adopting and using information systems (such as **conflicts**-checking and calendaring systems; *see* **Chapter 7.A at 178**) as well as policies and practices that are intended to keep everyone in compliance with all ethical obligations. Managerial lawyers must also make sure that everyone understands what the firm's policies and systems are and how to use and follow them through dissemination and training, and they must also promulgate and carry out appropriate staffing policies to ensure that less experienced lawyers (and nonlawyers) are properly supervised.

There is no one "right" way to do any of these things, and the Rule does not prescribe one. Instead, it recognizes that many different approaches to ethical compliance could be "reasonable" in different **practice organizations**, and that what's reasonable for any particular **practice organization** will depend on its characteristics—among other things, its size, structure, staffing, and the nature of its practice. *See* **Model Rule 5.1 Comment [3]**. What **Model Rule 5.1(a)** makes clear, though, is that managers **must** affirmatively *manage*—there **must** be "measures" adopted and publicized within the **practice organization** that are "reasonably designed" to ensure **practice-organization**-wide ethical compliance. ⟨ TAMING THE TEXT ⟩

2. The Duty to Manage Nonlawyers

⟨ TAMING THE TEXT ⟩ Now take a look at **Model Rule 5.3(a)**, which codifies managerial lawyers' **duty to manage** *non*lawyers who work for or with the lawyer's **practice organization**. If you compare it with **Model Rule 5.1(a)**, you'll see that the wording is similar, with two significant differences. One difference is that **Model Rule 5.3** is about managing and supervising a "nonlawyer employed or retained by or associated with a" **practice organization**. **Model Rule 5.3 Comment [3]** clarifies that this disjunctive ("or") wording is designed to cover the full range of nonlicensed "employees [and] independent contractors" who "act for the lawyer in rendition of the lawyer's professional services," such as "secretaries, investigators, law student interns, and paraprofessionals" as well as independent consultants and service providers outside the **practice organization** who are retained for specific cases or tasks.

The other difference is that, while a managing lawyer **must** take reasonable steps to ensure that other lawyers in the **practice organization** comply with the Rules of Professional Conduct, with respect to nonlawyers, those managers must ensure that that the nonlawyers' "conduct is compatible with the professional obligations of the lawyer." Why? Well, nonlawyers are not directly bound by the Rules of Professional Conduct: They aren't licensed and can't be professionally disciplined by a state bar. Does that mean that a lawyer can use unlicensed people to do things for him that he is banned from doing himself? Of course not—remember the **no-puppetry rule** codified in **Model Rule 8.4(a)**, which dictates just the opposite. **Model Rule 5.3(a)** thus is just an extension of the **no-puppetry rule**: The **no-puppetry rule** says if you can't do it yourself, you can't have someone do it for you. **Model Rule 5.3(a)** takes that idea a step further, and requires that you also **must** take reasonable steps, including instruction, training, and supervision, to ensure that the nonlawyers whom you employ or retain don't do what you're forbidden to do—even without your asking them to do something wrong, even without your knowing, and even without *their* knowing (for example, out of ignorance or mistake) that they're doing something wrong. *See* **Model Rule 5.3 Comment [2]**. ⟨ TAMING THE TEXT ⟩

3. The Duty to Supervise Other Lawyers

What about lawyers who *supervise* other lawyers? There's a Rule for that too—**Model Rule 5.1(b)**. It provides that a lawyer who has "direct supervisory authority over another lawyer shall make reasonable efforts to ensure that the other lawyer conforms to the Rules of Professional Conduct." How? In any ways that are reasonable under the circumstances. Again, the Rules don't try to tell every supervisor how to do his or her job. But again, we may infer that supervisors **must** affirmatively *supervise*—they **must** ("shall") "make reasonable efforts." This duty does *not* mean that supervisors must do *everything conceivable* to keep their subordinates' toes behind the line. But supervisors must make "reasonable efforts" to oversee subordinates' activities in a manner reasonably calculated to ensure their compliance with the ethics rules.

4. The Duty to Supervise Nonlawyers

Similarly, **Model Rule 5.3(b)** defines the **duty** of a lawyer with supervisorial powers **to supervise** nonlawyers who contribute to the **practice organization**'s professional services. And in a precise parallel to **Model Rule 5.1(b)**, lawyers who supervise nonlawyers **must** make "reasonable efforts to ensure that the [nonlawyer's] conduct is compatible with the professional obligations of the lawyer."

The Comments make clear that the "reasonable efforts" involved in managing and supervising nonlawyers **must** take into account the fact that these personnel have different backgrounds, training, and experience from lawyers. Accordingly, managing and supervising lawyers **must** give nonlawyers "appropriate instruction and supervision concerning the ethical aspects of their employment," especially regarding **confidential information**. **Model Rule 5.3 Comment [2]**.

5. The Vicarious Disciplinary Liability of Managerial and Supervisorial Lawyers for the Misconduct of Those Whom They Manage or Supervise

Let's pause for a moment and reconnoiter: We've learned that every lawyer in a **practice organization** is personally responsible for his or her own compliance with the Rules of Professional Conduct and other law, and that it's almost never an excuse to say, "But I did what I was told." **Chapter 19.B at 507**. We've also learned that lawyers with managerial or supervisory powers within a **practice organization** have an affirmative **duty to manage** or **supervise**—to make reasonable efforts to ensure that those within their oversight (both lawyers and nonlawyers) comply with governing law. **Chapter 19.C at 513**.

Does that mean that managerial or supervisory lawyers have breached their **duty to manage** or **supervise**, and thus are subject to professional discipline for violating **Model Rule 5.1** or **Model Rule 5.3**, any time one of the people they oversee violates the Rules? No, it doesn't. Why? Because what the **duty to manage** and the **duty to supervise** require is that managers and supervisors make *"reasonable efforts"* (emphasis added) to ensure that their subordinates follow the Rules. Reasonable efforts don't include stalking your subordinates all day, scrutinizing their every move. That would be crazy—no one would ever get anything done. So if, despite a manager's or supervisor's reasonable efforts, a subordinate violates the Rules, we don't hold the manager or supervisor personally ethically responsible for the wrong. Managers and supervisors are only subject to professional discipline when they fail to manage or supervise; that is, fail to exercise "reasonable efforts" to keep those they oversee in compliance.

So now we know that we don't *generally* hold a manager or supervisor personally responsible for a subordinate's wrong. But are there *ever* circumstances in which we will hold a manager or supervisor responsible for an ethical wrong committed by someone else—that is, *vicariously* liable for the violations of a subordinate? Yes, there are, and those circumstances are described in **Model Rule 5.1(c)** and **Model Rule 5.3(c)**. These Rules state that a lawyer "shall be responsible for another lawyer's violation of the Rules of Professional Conduct" or for a nonlawyer's "conduct . . . that would be a violation of the Rules of Professional Conduct if engaged in by a lawyer" under either of two conditions: (1) "the lawyer orders or, with knowledge of the specific conduct, ratifies the conduct involved";[6] or (2) a lawyer with managerial or supervisorial authority "knows of the conduct at a time when its consequences can be avoided or mitigated but fails to take reasonable remedial action." Take a look at **Model Rule 5.1(c)** and **Model Rule 5.3(c)** and trace how their words apply these vicarious liability rules equally to the misconduct of lawyer and nonlawyer subordinates. (And remember that "knows" means "actual knowledge," not "should have known." **Model Rule 1.0(f)**.)

How does the **duty to manage** or **supervise** codified in **Model Rule 5.1(a)-(b)** and **Model Rule 5.3(a)-(b)** interact with the rule of vicarious ethical responsibility in **Model Rule 5.1(c)** and **Model Rule 5.3(c)**? As **Model Rule 5.1 Comment [6]** points out, "[p]rofessional misconduct by a lawyer under supervision could reveal a violation of paragraph (b) on the part of the supervisory lawyer even though it does not entail a violation of paragraph (c) because there was no direction, ratification or knowledge of the violation." In other words, imagine a situation in which a subordinate lawyer violated a Rule of Professional Conduct. Imagine further that the misbehaving subordinate wasn't ordered to commit the wrong, nor did any manager or supervisor know that the wrong was going to happen and then fail to prevent it. Although the manager or supervisor would not be *vicariously* liable for the subordinate's wrong, the fact that the wrong occurred raises questions about whether the manager or supervisor made reasonable efforts to manage or supervise that would have prevented the subordinate's wrongful conduct, and the wrong is *potential evidence* of a failure to manage or supervise. It's often when internal policies, procedures, and practices break down that people on the front lines end up committing misconduct because of lack of training or oversight. That's why we have **duties to manage** and **supervise** in the first place.

6. CONSEQUENCES Consequences for Failing to Manage or Supervise (or Causing a Subordinate to Act Unlawfully)

Model Rule 5.1 and **Model Rule 5.3** are Rules of Professional Conduct, and they govern managerial and supervisory lawyers' direct and vicarious liability for professional discipline. What about civil liability? These are questions of tort law,

---

[6] To remind yourself about ratification, *see* **Chapter 6.A at 143**.

and they vary from state to state. We can safely generalize that, when managers or supervisors do the kinds of things described in **Model Rule 5.1(c)** and **Model Rule 5.3(c)** with respect to tortious activity—order or ratify another's tort, or fail to take steps within their authority to stop tortious conduct that they know is going to happen—they will likely be vicariously liable for the subordinate's wrong under general principles of vicarious tort liability, such as aiding and abetting and civil conspiracy.[7] The civil liability resulting from a manager's or supervisor's *negligent* failure to prevent a subordinate's wrong is more complicated and more variable across jurisdictions. ⟨ CONSEQUENCES ⟩

> **Problem 19C-1:** Which lawyers are exposed to **consequences** in the following situations? Please identify which **consequences** and explain why:
>
> a. **Mess in the Press:** Harry Connick, Jr. is a singer, jazz pianist, and actor (and a very good one). His father, Harry Connick, Sr., was the District Attorney of Orleans Parish (the parish—which is what Louisiana calls counties—in which New Orleans is located) from 1973 to 2003. After Mr. Connick, Sr. retired, numerous cases emerged reflecting a prejudicial failure by the DA's office to observe criminal defendants' constitutional rights during Sr.'s tenure as District Attorney. Most famous among these was *Connick v. Thompson*, a case in which John Thompson sat on death row for many years because the prosecutor who tried Thompson's case hid exculpatory blood evidence. There were other egregious examples as well.[8] "The district attorney, Harry Connick Sr., acknowledged the need for this training but said he had long since 'stopped reading law books' so he didn't understand the duty he was supposed to impart."[9]
>
> b. You are a solo practitioner sharing office space and a secretary with another solo. The two of you occasionally discuss your cases in terms that respect your clients' **confidentiality** rights. The other lawyer makes a serious mistake in a matter that the two of you had discussed.
>
> c. Same as (b), except that neither you nor the other lawyer has ever instructed your shared secretary on setting up a calendaring system for the deadlines in your respective practices. Although your shared secretary usually reminds each of you of your impending deadlines,

---

[7] Don't get confused and mix *respondeat superior* in here. Remember, *respondeat superior* holds the *employer* or *principal* vicariously responsible for the employee or agent's wrong. In the situations that we're considering, that would be the **practice organization** itself—the partnership, the professional corporation or other business organization or, in the case of a government agency, the agency itself—not any individual manager or supervisor.

[8] 563 U.S. 51 (2011). *See generally* John Simerman, *Former DA Harry Connick Defends His Leadership, Reputation*, https://www.nola.com/news/crime_police/article_c59c8c19-8f0a-5e85-9144-cfb789576a35.html (April 1, 2012). *See also* **Problem 16D-1 at 449**. The Supreme Court reversed a $14 million judgment in Mr. Thompson's favor for his wrongful imprisonment on the ground that he did not present adequate evidence of a municipal pattern or practice required for liability under special rules that apply in civil rights cases under 42 U.S.C. § 1983. The majority opinion was widely criticized for its failure to account for the evidence in the record of what Justice Ginsburg for the four-justice minority referred to as a "culture of inattention" to defendants' rights in the office. 563 U.S. at 100 (Ginsburg, J., dissenting).

[9] *Failure of Empathy and Justice*, https://www.nytimes.com/2011/04/01/opinion/01fri2.html?partner=rss&emc=rss (March 31, 2011).

this time she forgets to remind the other lawyer of an important deadline. As a result, the other lawyer blows the deadline.

d. Frank's firm employs an administrative assistant who answers the phones, manages the firm's reception area, and handles other administrative tasks, such as ordering office supplies. He has worked for the firm for several years, and he does a good job. One day, an advertising company calls and offers to create a website for the firm. The administrative assistant has a $500 purchase limit. The advertising company offers to prepare the website for $350, and the assistant agrees. The advertising company is not familiar with the rules governing lawyer advertising, and the website violates several Rules of Professional Conduct.

i. How (if at all) does your analysis change if the firm had a policy that a specific partner at the firm is in charge of marketing and has to approve any advertising—and the administrative assistant knows that? Does it matter if the assistant didn't make the connection that websites are "advertising" or if, instead, the assistant knew that websites fall within the firm's policy on advertising, but went ahead without approval so that the firm didn't miss out on the great promotional deal while the partner in charge of marketing was out of the office on a client matter?

ii. What if, in the marketing partner's absence, the assistant gets approval for the website from another partner who *is* in the office that day?

e. A corporate client has numerous matters pending with Maya's firm. Maya handles one of them. The relationship partner assigns another associate to handle quarterly filings regarding the client's securities that under state law must be made with the Secretary of State. That associate goes out on maternity leave. No one picks up the required quarterly filings, and the next filing deadline gets missed.

f. Frank and the firm's real estate partner, Barney Blackacre, are working on a landlord-tenant case in a building in which there appear to be widespread violations of the warranty of habitability. Tenants in two units have retained the firm, but Frank and Barney believe that there are numerous other units whose residents have good claims. Barney tasks Frank with going to the building, knocking on doors, and seeing if there are other tenants who have claims that they are willing to pursue. Frank, concerned that tenants won't answer the door to a stranger, comes to work on the day he is going out to the building wearing a City Gas & Electric uniform shirt with his first name on it—one that he was required to wear in a summer job for the local utility during college. He stops in to see Barney on his way out. "Happy hunting," Barney says.

g. Same as **Problem 19B-1(b) at 512** (a senior deputy in Danielle's office agrees with her that disclosing exculpatory evidence would harm Danielle's case and directs her not to do so), except that now the senior deputy is her assigned "mentor" in the DA's office. Under the office's mentorship program, each new deputy is assigned a more experienced prosecutor as a mentor. Mentors make themselves available to their mentees to answer questions and offer advice about substantive law and office practices and procedures.[10]

---

[10] *Mentos*, on the other hand, retain their customary responsibility to generate copious amounts of carbon dioxide foam upon exposure to diet soda. Just sayin'. https://www.youtube.com/watch?v=h_2osOb2SMU.

D. The Duty to Be Supervised Appropriately (in Other Words, the Duty to Get Help When You Need It)

Knowing what we now know, let's take a look back at the hypothetical in the **chapter Introduction at 505**. (Go back and remind yourself of the details. It's a story in which you can easily imagine yourself as Fiona Forsaken.) Who's responsible if Fiona moves ahead and, despite having tried her best to figure out the very complex and technical area of the law that she's been assigned to learn, she gets something important wrong? Certainly, Andy Absent has breached his **duty to supervise** Fiona by failing to oversee her work and failing to get her the resources and backstopping that she needs to fulfill her own **duty of competence** under **Model Rule 1.1** (*see* **Chapter 7.A at 172**) and her civil **duty of care** (*see* **Chapter 7.B at 180**). We'd need more detailed facts, but maybe the two senior partners have also breached their **duties** to **manage** and **supervise** by failing to instruct and train Andy on how to supervise a junior lawyer, or by failing to have policies or practices in place that ensure that a client with specialized legal needs gets them addressed with the requisite competence.

All of these could be grounds for professional discipline of the more senior lawyers. And if Fiona ends up committing professional negligence by making a mistake that a reasonably skilled and knowledgeable lawyer would not have made, and that mistake causes the client monetary harm, her firm will be liable to the client as a matter of *respondeat superior*. Andy would also most probably be personally liable to the client for negligent supervision and professional negligence in failing to ensure the adequacy of Fiona's work product.

But what about Fiona? She's really, really tried to do everything right here. She's worked hard to understand the law and related business needs, though she's not sure that she does. And she's chased Andy for backstopping and advice energetically and assiduously; his failure to respond is hardly her fault. Surely that's enough to insulate her from personal **consequences**, isn't it? Sadly, no; it isn't.

We suspect that you'll find that answer disturbing, so let's fill in the details. As one of the lawyers assigned to serve the client in its franchising matter, Fiona owes that client the full panoply of duties that every lawyer owes her clients. That includes, of course, the **duty of competence**, as well as the civil **duty of care**. Because we know that you've been paying careful attention all semester, you remember that "[a] lawyer need not necessarily have special training or prior experience to handle legal problems of a type with which the lawyer is unfamiliar" (**Model Rule 1.1 Comment [2]**), but "[e]xpertise in a particular field of law may be required in some circumstances" involving complex or specialized knowledge, and you may need to "consult with . . . a lawyer of established competence in the field in question" to get it (**Model Rule 1.1 Comment [1]**). *See* **Chapter 7.A at 173**.

At the point in the engagement when Fiona is talking with Danielle, Fiona has a strong sense that she can't master this complex and specialized area of the law on her own, and because Andy Absent is living up to his name, no one is available to backstop her or check her work. Proceeding on this basis is a violation of Fiona's **duty of competence** (because she hasn't developed or consulted the expertise needed to do the job), and if it results in an error or omission that a reasonably skilled and knowledgeable lawyer wouldn't have made, it's a breach of her civil **duty of care** as well. The fact that Andy may *also* be subject to discipline, and that Andy and the firm may *also* be jointly and severally liable for any professional negligence, does not relieve Fiona of her own personal responsibility, and with it, her own personal liability. And if Fiona's small firm is one that doesn't have professional liability insurance, a money judgment for malpractice could follow her around, even potentially garnishing her earnings, for the next 10 or 20 years. And even with insurance, she could have professional discipline on her permanent bar record for the rest of her career. Ouch.[11]

What this unpleasant reality amounts to as a practical matter is what we would call a **duty to be supervised** appropriately. There is no such duty literally stated in the Rules of Professional Conduct or in tort law. But such a duty is an important implication of the **duties of competence**, **diligence**, and **care**. You have a personal, nondelegable duty owed directly to your client to ensure that you get whatever supervision, backstopping, and support that you may need to handle your client's work with the knowledge and skill that a reasonable lawyer would bring to the task. It is one of the regrettable and inevitable paradoxes of early practice that you will not always have the perspective or assistance that you need in order to decide whether you're getting it.

[REAL WORLD] Please be assured that we take this issue seriously, and you should, too. But let's put the problem in context:

- Most practicing lawyers taking on an inexperienced associate understand that their own client relationships, reputations, and personal and firm liability are on the line if the associate messes up. Most of them react as the legal and ethical rules intend them to—by delegating and supervising judiciously. So although you will not always get the backstopping that you *want*, there's a decent chance that you'll get at least the backstopping that you *need*.

- Most self-respecting beginners who care about doing a good job (that's you!) are frequently worried not only by what they don't know, but by what they *don't know* that they don't know. It's the mistake that we don't see coming that

---

[11] Lest you think that this is one of those theoretical problems that never really happens, it was the result in *Beverly Hills Concepts, Inc. v. Schatz & Schatz, Ribicoff & Kotkin*, 247 Conn. 48 (1998). The junior associate in *Beverly Hills Concepts*, who got supervision (or the lack of it) very much like Fiona's, testified that she "assume[d] somebody was . . . watching, taking care of looking at my work." The court held that "this passivity departed from the applicable standard of care" and found her jointly and severally liable for the professional negligence that her firm had committed. *Id.* at 56. The lawyer-defendants ultimately escaped liability because the plaintiffs failed to prove their damages with sufficient certainty, but the standard of care, including a duty to "seek appropriate supervision" applicable to the junior lawyer (*id.*), was unanimously affirmed.

keeps most of us up at night. In fact, if you're not worried about doing a good job, then we're worried about you. (Pride goeth before a fall, and all that.) The first time (and, really, the first few times) that you do anything nontrivial, you will probably find yourself feeling somewhere between nervous and terrified. Nevertheless, if you've finished law school and have passed a bar exam, chances are pretty good that, for all you have yet to discover, you do have research and learning skills that allow you to do new things competently. (Remember **Model Rule 1.1 Comment [2]**: "A lawyer need not necessarily have special training or prior experience to handle legal problems of a type with which the lawyer is unfamiliar.") The fact that you're scared and you doubt yourself doesn't necessarily mean that you can't do or shouldn't be doing something, and often, your supervisor will have concluded that, despite your trepidations, you're ready for the job.[12]

- All that said, there may come a time when, like Fiona, you really don't have the backstopping and support necessary to do a competent job. Part of what's challenging about starting out is that, early on, it can be hard to tell when you're simply confronting new responsibilities that you can learn to handle by studying and then doing, and when you're actually in over your head. If, like Fiona, you're confident that it's the latter and you can't get any meaningful confirmation that you're simply more worried than actually incapable, you can't just stumble ahead, confident in the knowledge that your supervisor is at least as negligent as you are. (Danielle, though an excellent young lawyer, got that one wrong. Many new lawyers do, which is why we gave you the hypothetical.) You have personal **duties of competence** and **care** owed directly to the client, and you have to do something.

- Your solution will usually involve working within your **practice organization** (assuming that you're part of one; if you're not, then this is one of those situations in which you may need to associate knowledgeable co-counsel). That will usually be uncomfortable, because you'll need to raise the concern, whether subtly or directly, that someone with whom you work is not doing his or her job in supervising you. The supervisor whose judgment was bad enough to have tossed you in over your head is likely to be neither a willing nor

---

[12] We illustrate with a story from one of your authors' early days of practice. The first task he was assigned in his new law-firm job was to work on a real estate deal. After he had read up, studied forms, and formulated comments on a draft deal document, the assigning partner tasked him with calling up opposing counsel and negotiating changes to the document. "But," your author protested, with perhaps a bit too much candor, "I've never done anything like that before, and I don't know how." "Don't worry," the partner deadpanned. "That's why we have insurance."

At the time, it didn't seem the least bit funny (to your author, at least). But the partner was a deeply knowledgeable and meticulous business lawyer (with, we might add, a strikingly dry sense of humor). He knew that the associate had done his homework, and that the partner had spent time discussing the draft and suggested changes with him so that the associate knew more than he thought he did about how the deal terms fit together. Your author reluctantly advanced into battle and discovered what the assigning partner already knew—that your author wasn't going to do the best job in the history of dealmaking, but that he was ready to do a job that was good enough for this particular task. No notice to the firm's insurance carrier was required that day.

an able supervisor when you ask for help, and may be perversely irritated (or worse) when you demand what you have every right to expect. Others within the **practice organization** may be reluctant to intrude on an existing supervisory relationship. How to effectively get the help you need is always dependent on the personalities and organizational structure around you, but in general, you can imagine that it is better to do so by gently enlisting assistance with your duties than by pointing fingers at the person or persons at fault. Don't wait until the last minute; leave time for those who may be able to help to be able do so.

■ If you can't get the supervision you need, or if you find yourself constantly fighting for it, you may not have a job worth keeping. A boss who keeps dropping you on the brink of malpractice (or worse, recall **Problem 4A-2 at 74**) is not a boss you want. If you need to leave your job, bear in mind that you may have duties directly to the clients that you serve (and any involved tribunals) to withdraw with adequate notice and attention to the clients' needs. *See* **Chapter 9.D at 288**.

Problem 19D-1: Revisit Fiona Forsaken's situation as described in the **chapter Introduction at 505**. What **must, may,** and **should** Fiona do, and how should she go about it?

E. Lawyers' Obligations to Their Practice Organizations

1. The General Duty of Loyalty That Lawyers Owe Their Practice Organizations

When you work for a firm or other **practice organization**, you're not an army of one. Through a combination of general employment law and the special duties imposed on lawyers, you owe obligations to the **practice organization** and to the other lawyers in it. These obligations include a duty of loyalty. This duty is a form of the same fiduciary duty we learned about in **Chapter 5.D at 113** that lawyers and **practice organizations** owe their clients. Lawyers at a firm generally owe each other a fiduciary duty of loyalty to be forthright and honest in their dealings with each other and with their shared **practice organization**. This is true whether you are a partner or an associate (though, under partnership law, partners in a partnership may have special heightened duties to one another and the partnership). Nor can you put your self-interest above the interest of your **practice organization:** No lawyer at a firm may exploit his or her firm position for personal benefit (beyond the regular rewards, such as compensation and benefits, that the **practice organization** generally provides). Nor can a lawyer at a firm interfere with the law firm's business or personally appropriate any practice opportunities that belong to the firm.

CONSEQUENCES There are no specific Model Rules addressing these duties, but they are well recognized. State bars have disciplined self-dealing within law firms as acts of dishonesty or fraud under **Model Rule 8.4(c)**. And civil employment and fiduciary law impose liability on disloyal or self-dealing lawyers within a **practice organization** to disgorge any ill-gotten gains, and to make up the cost of any resulting losses. In addition, disloyalty or self-dealing is very likely to result in employment **consequences**. Unsurprisingly, general employment law and most partnership agreements or other governance documents recognize such conduct as grounds for the most serious employment **consequences**, up to and including termination. ⟨CONSEQUENCES⟩

Problem 19E-1: Which of the following lawyers are subject to **consequences**? Please explain which **consequences** and why:

a. Frank is saving up for a downpayment on a house. He secretly takes a second job as a contract attorney for another firm in town. Does your analysis change if Frank takes a second job as a bartender instead? What if either job occupies a few hours a couple of days a week during ordinary business hours?

b. The other associate in Frank's firm confides to him that the associate missed a filing deadline. The associate says that he's handling it, and he asks Frank to "keep it to yourself for now, okay?" Frank knows that the issue could prejudice the client's rights.

c. A cousin of Frank's has been seriously injured in a small-plane crash. When the cousin has recovered enough to attend to it, he calls Frank for advice about choosing a lawyer to handle any case that he may have arising out of the crash. Frank and the litigation partner with whom he often works, Harlan "Happy" Trials, have never handled an aviation case, though they are good personal-injury lawyers. One of Frank's law school classmates went to work at a firm that focuses on aviation work, and that firm is widely viewed as having several of the best aviation lawyers in the state. Frank recommends his classmate's firm to his cousin. Does your analysis change if Frank's state allows the payment of referral fees (many states restrict or forbid them; *see* **Chapter 20.F at 559**), and the aviation firm pays such fees to referring lawyers? What **must** or **should** Frank do with the referral fee (which, for a case like this in a state in which they are allowed, is likely to be substantial)?

d. A client whom Frank represented last year in a personal-injury case calls Frank to report that he now, unfortunately, needs help with a divorce. He tells Frank that he really liked him and his work and that he is wondering if they can work something out about the divorce. When Frank asks the **former client** what he has in mind, the **former client** suggests that Frank handle the divorce "on his own" for one-third less than the rate that Frank's firm charges for his work. The now-**prospective client** proposes to pay these fees directly to Frank. Frank agrees. Does your analysis change if Frank gets assistance from his secretary and legal assistant and uses his office computerized research account for research on the divorce matter?

e. The managing partner of the office of the firm in which Maya works has had some health issues and is out on temporary disability leave. The managing partner is expected to recover and return to work, but in the meantime, the management of the office has been assigned to another partner. In Maya's firm, office managing partners are generally paid an extra $50,000 per year for handling those administrative responsibilities. The lawyer who has been asked to step in for the ailing managing partner is assured that his extra responsibilities will be reflected in his year-end bonus, but when he receives the bonus, he doesn't consider it adequate. To make up the difference, he arranges to be paid an additional $30,000 out of a general administrative office account.

2. Conflicting Duties and Interests That May Arise When a Lawyer Changes Jobs

The preceding problems all assume as a basic premise a lawyer who intends to remain employed at his or her current **practice organization**. But the reality of practice is that you probably won't work for one **practice organization** for your entire career: Most lawyers end up having several different jobs in the course of a career.

Many issues relating to lawyers' duties of loyalty to their **practice organizations** and their clients arise in the context of lawyers who leave those **practice organizations** in order to take another job. When you leave a **practice organization**, you don't automatically and immediately sever all responsibilities. You continue to owe duties to all the clients you represented while you were at your former job. If you are leaving **current clients** behind, you have all the duties of a withdrawing lawyer, including notice to the client, reasonable steps to ensure a smooth transition to other counsel at the **practice organization**, and the permission of any tribunal, if required. *See* **Chapter 9.D at 288.** (The **practice organization** will usually help a departing junior lawyer comply with these duties.) Once you leave, all the clients you served at your former **practice organization** (in the past or at the time of your departure) are your **former clients** for the rest of your career, regardless of how many other lawyers at your **practice organization** may also have represented that client or may still be doing so. Your **duty of confidentiality** to **former clients** continues (*see* **Chapter 8.A at 224**), as does your duty to avoid **conflicts of interest** with **former clients** (*see* **Chapter 22.C at 679**).

You also owe duties to your **practice organization** even as you head out the door, a time when you can easily imagine that lots of lawyers are naturally disinclined to keep a soon-to-be-ex-employer's rights in mind, especially if the departure is not entirely amicable. Complications often arise from the fact that lawyers in **practice organizations** owe fiduciary duties to more than one beneficiary, and often have their own **interests** to attend to as part of the mix: Lawyers usually change jobs in the hope of improving their professional lives. They have the natural inclination to look out for their own **interests** in the process, and they have the right to do so except to the extent that their personal **interests conflict** with an equal or higher duty to someone else. But those other duties exist. As just discussed, lawyers have duties of loyalty to their **practice organizations**. And as we've been discussing all term, lawyers also owe duties directly to their **current** and **former clients**, one of which is to respect their clients' fundamental right to choose their own counsel. Sometimes, these **interests** and duties **conflict**.

One situation in which they often **conflict** is when departing lawyers would like to continue to represent clients they had represented as part of the **practice organization** they're leaving. (This usually comes up as a problem when the **practice organization** in question is a private law firm.) It may be difficult for you to imagine having clients of your own right now, but much sooner than you think, people will start looking to you as "their" lawyer—the person to whom they look for successful resolution of their legal matter. There is no greater professional compliment. And on the most basic level, in private practice, we make our living from the fees that clients pay us. So if you find yourself switching law firms (or deciding that you're ready to hang out your own shingle as a solo practitioner), you will naturally think about which clients you're serving at your current firm who might like to come along with you. Equally naturally, the firm that you're leaving will generally want nothing of the kind.

Because of the **duty of candor** (*see* **Model Rule 1.4; Chapter 5.D at 117**), the departing lawyer and the firm both have a duty to inform clients of any **material** change in the representation, including the departure of a lawyer who had substantial responsibility for a matter. The client must consent to how that case will be handled going forward, including the ultimate decision as to who her counsel will be: The client may decide to continue to work with the firm, to follow the departing lawyer, to choose to preserve continuity by working with both, or to choose none of these options and retain entirely new and different counsel.

Departing lawyers thus **may** inform clients about their impending departure, remind them that they have the right to choose their counsel, and offer their services. But departing lawyers still have residual duties of loyalty to the firm they're leaving and to the client. The precise contours of these duties vary by state, but they generally preclude misstating the facts or interfering with the freedom of the client's choice. They may preclude or limit a departing lawyer's ability to invite other lawyers or support staff to join him before departing, particularly if those personnel are uniquely valuable to the firm or to a client that the departing lawyer hopes will follow him. In cases in which the departure is amicable, the departing lawyer and the firm usually deal with one another openly and develop a joint plan for informing clients and transitioning files. But as you might imagine, such cooperation is not always forthcoming when the departure has been prompted by dissatisfaction on one or both sides, or when competition to handle valuable client work is in the offing.[13]

---

[13] Leaving a **practice organization** with any of the **organization**'s clients or personnel is a complicated and potentially risky endeavor. The brief discussion in the text is good enough for now, but if you find yourself in this situation, you should research your rights and duties in your state, and you should seriously consider consulting a lawyer who is an expert in these matters. *See generally* Robert W. Hillman & Alison Martin Rhodes, Hillman on Lawyer Mobility: The Law and Ethics of Partner Withdrawals and Law Firm Breakups (3d ed. 2020).

Problem 19E-2: A partner in Maya's practice group has decided to move to a different law firm to start an office for that firm. Which of the following could subject the partner (or someone else) to **consequences**? Please explain who, which **consequences,** and why:

a. The partner has been covertly downloading copies of all the deal documentation on which she's worked in her years at the firm to use as a "knowledge bank" at her new firm.

b. The partner hopes to take a number of substantial corporate clients with her to the new firm. She has made arrangements to have a team of outside movers and IT professionals pack up and remove those clients' physical files, and to copy and then delete those clients' digital files, the night before she announces that she is leaving to start at the new firm.

c. The partner plans to tell the clients whose files she is moving to her new firm that she has their complete files at her new office and will continue their work without interruption.

d. Instead of (b) and (c), the partner offers to have her new firm serve the clients she hopes to take with her, making clear that the clients are free to choose their counsel going forward. Some of those clients agree to retain the partner and her new firm. The partner assists those clients in requesting that her former firm transfer all physical and digital files to her new firm. The old firm refuses to do so.

e. The partner has spoken to Maya and two other associates with whom she regularly works, as well as to a young partner, about moving with her. The departing partner is involved in firm management and knows how much each is paid. She offers each a signing bonus and a raise. Does your analysis change if the partner has not spoken to any of these people yet but calls each of these lawyers after she has moved to the new firm and then invites them to join her?

f. The old firm reaches out to the clients that the departing partner has solicited and discourages them from leaving, offering those clients a 20 percent discount on the fees incurred in their pending matters going forward if they stay with the old firm. Does your analysis change if the old firm also tells the clients that the departing partner was fired for incompetence? What if the old firm's management committee hastily convenes a meeting, adopts a resolution that the partner is incompetent, and expels her from the partnership?

g. The old firm reaches out to all clients for whom the departing partner was working and informs them of new staffing arrangements on their matters. The old firm touts the skill and expertise of the new personnel assigned to the clients' matters, but it does not explain the reason for the change. Some clients are aware of the reason and ask for the departing partner's contact information. The old firm doesn't answer the question.

Big-Picture Takeaways from Chapter 19

1. *Any* organization that offers legal services on *any* basis is called a "law firm" under the Model Rules. We also use the term **"practice organization"** for this purpose. **Model Rule 5.1**, **Model Rule 5.2**, and **Model Rule 5.3** focus on professional responsibility within **practice organizations**. *See* **Chapter 19.A at 506**.

2. Acting within an organizational structure virtually never shields individual lawyers from responsibility for their own acts or omissions. Each

lawyer within a **practice organization** has a nondelegable, personal duty to comply with the Rules of Professional Conduct as they apply to his or her individual circumstances. There's also potential tort liability as well as potential criminal liability: Agents (whether employees of an organization or lawyers acting for their clients) are personally liable for any tort that they commit within the course and scope of their agency, and if you commit a crime on the job, you're responsible for it—no one is going to go to prison for you. *See* **Chapter 19.B at 507**.

3. **Model Rule 5.2(a)** makes it clear that you remain *individually* responsible for your own compliance with the Rules of Professional Conduct. If you violate a Rule of Professional Conduct, you will be personally subject to the **consequence** of professional discipline, even if someone in authority told you to do it. There is one extremely narrow exception to the general rule of personal responsibility for Rules violations, and it's set out in **Model Rule 5.2(b)**. This narrow exception provides that a subordinate lawyer will be excused from professional discipline for conduct in which a supervisor instructed her to engage that is determined to violate a Rule of Professional Conduct, but only if it was genuinely unclear how to comply with the Rules under the circumstances, and the instructions from the supervisory lawyer were a "reasonable" way of complying in the face of that uncertainty. *See* **Chapter 19.B at 509**.

4. Lawyers can have two different kinds of oversight obligations within a **practice organization**. Some lawyers have *management* responsibilities, and some have *supervisorial* responsibilities. (Some have neither or both.)
   a. Managing lawyers have indirect, generalized authority over the professional work of the firm, either as a whole or as to some portion or aspect of the firm's work, such as a practice-group leader or the managing partner of one office of a multi-office firm. Because they generally oversee the professional work of the firm (as a whole or as to some portion of the firm), they manage both lawyers and the nonlawyer staff who contribute to the firm's professional services. *See* **Chapter 19.C at 513**.
   b. Supervisory authority involves responsibility on a day-to-day basis for overseeing the work of specific personnel. *See* **Chapter 19.C at 513**.
   c. Lawyers may manage or supervise other lawyers, and they may manage or supervise nonlawyer staff, such as legal assistants, investigators, and secretaries. This distinction between managerial and supervisorial roles is reflected in the structure of the two Rules of Professional Conduct that address oversight responsibilities: **Model Rule 5.1** addresses management and supervision of other lawyers; **Model Rule 5.3** addresses management and supervision of nonlawyer staff. *See* **Chapter 19.C at 513**.

d. **Model Rule 5.1(a)** defines the role and duties of managerial lawyers in a **practice organization**. Managerial lawyers have specific ethical duties attached to their managerial powers. They **must** ("shall") "make reasonable efforts to ensure that the firm has in effect measures [that is, policies and procedures] giving reasonable assurance that all lawyers in the firm conform to the Rules of Professional Conduct." This imperative defines the **duty to manage** other lawyers. *See* **Chapter 19.C at 514.**

e. **Model Rule 5.3(a)** codifies managerial lawyers' **duty to manage** nonlawyers who work for or with the **practice organization**. Here, the **duty to manage** requires the managerial lawyer to "make reasonable efforts to ensure that the firm has in effect measures giving reasonable assurance that [each nonlawyer's] conduct is compatible with the professional obligations of the lawyer"—that is, policies and procedures designed to ensure that nonlawyers don't do anything that lawyers are forbidden from doing. *See* **Chapter 19.C at 515.**

f. **Model Rule 5.1(b)** states that a lawyer who has "direct supervisory authority over another lawyer shall make reasonable efforts to ensure that the other lawyer conforms to the Rules of Professional Conduct." This imperative defines the **duty to supervise** other lawyers. *See* **Chapter 19.C at 515.**

g. **Model Rule 5.3(b)** defines the **duty** of a lawyer with supervisorial powers **to supervise** nonlawyers who contribute to the **practice organization**'s professional services. And in a precise parallel to **Model Rule 5.1(b)**, lawyers who supervise nonlawyers **must** make "reasonable efforts to ensure that the [nonlawyer's] conduct is compatible with the professional obligations of the lawyer"—that is, reasonable efforts to ensure that the nonlawyer doesn't do anything that lawyers are forbidden from doing. *See* **Chapter 19.C at 516.**

h. **Model Rule 5.1(c)** and **Model Rule 5.3(c)** define when a lawyer will be *vicariously* responsible for someone else's disciplinary violation. These Rules state that a lawyer "shall be responsible for another lawyer's violation of the Rules of Professional Conduct" or for a nonlawyer's "conduct . . . that would be a violation of the Rules of Professional Conduct if engaged in by a lawyer" under either of two conditions: If (1) "the lawyer orders or, with knowledge of the specific conduct, ratifies the conduct involved"; or (2) a lawyer with managerial or supervisorial authority "knows of the conduct at a time when its consequences can be avoided or mitigated but fails to take reasonable remedial action." *See* **Chapter 19.C at 516.**

5. Subordinate lawyers have a **duty to be supervised**—that is, to get the supervision they need to do their jobs competently. This is not so much a separate and independent duty so much as it is a feature of the subordinate lawyer's **duties of competence** and **care**. *See* **Chapter 19.D at 520.**

6. Through a combination of general employment law and the special duties imposed on lawyers, lawyers who work for a **practice organization** owe obligations to the **practice organization** and to the other lawyers in it. These obligations include a duty of loyalty. This duty is a form of the same fiduciary duty that lawyers and **practice organizations** owe their clients. Lawyers at a firm owe each other a fiduciary duty of loyalty to be forthright and honest in their dealings with each other and with their shared **practice organization**. Nor can you put your self-interest above the interest of your **practice organization:** No lawyer at a firm may exploit his or her firm position for personal benefit (beyond the regular rewards, such as compensation and benefits, that the **practice organization** generally provides). Nor can a lawyer at a firm interfere with the law firm's business or personally appropriate any practice opportunities that belong to the firm. Violations of these duties can have disciplinary **consequences** as well as creating civil liability. In addition, disloyalty or self-dealing is very likely to result in employment **consequences**. *See* **Chapter 19.E at 523.**

7. When you leave a **practice organization**, you don't automatically and immediately sever all responsibilities.

   a. You continue to owe duties to all the clients you represented while you were at your former job. If you are leaving **current clients** behind, you have all the duties of a withdrawing lawyer, including giving notice to the client, taking reasonable steps to ensure a smooth transition to other counsel at the **practice organization**, and seeking the permission of any tribunal, if required. Once you leave, all the clients whom you served at your **practice organization** (in the past or at the time of your departure) are your **former clients** for the rest of your career, regardless of how many other lawyers at your **practice organization** may also have represented that client or may still be doing so. Your **duty of confidentiality** to **former clients** continues, as does your duty to avoid **conflicts of interest** with **former clients**. *See* **Chapter 19.E at 525.**

   b. One difficult circumstance that arises when lawyers leave **practice organizations** (usually private law firms) is when the departing lawyers would like clients of the **practice organization** to follow them to a new **practice organization**. Because of the **duty of candor**, the departing lawyer and the former firm both have a duty to inform clients of any **material** change in the representation, including the departure of a lawyer who had substantial responsibility for a matter. Clients have the right to consent to how their matters will be handled going forward, including the ultimate decision as to who their counsel will be. Despite the departing lawyer's duty of loyalty to the **practice organization**, the departing lawyer may generally inform clients of her impending departure and of the clients' right to choose counsel. The interplay of these duties is complex, varies among jurisdictions, and can affect the content and timing of any communications on these subjects. *See* **Chapter 19.E at 525**.

Multiple-Choice Review Questions for Chapter 19

1. Gertrude works for the U.S. Attorney's Office for the Eastern District of Keystone in its civil division, defending government agencies against employment discrimination lawsuits. Assuming that the Rules of Professional Conduct in the state of Keystone track the Model Rules, are she and her fellow civil assistant U.S. attorneys subject to **Model Rules 5.1 through 5.3**?
   a. Yes, because the term "firm" is defined to include a government agency.
   b. Yes, because they are civil litigators and not criminal prosecutors.
   c. No, because a government agency is not a "firm."
   d. No, because prosecutors are subject to **Model Rule 3.8**.

2. Helen is a new lawyer who just started working at a large law firm. She has been assigned a mentor, Irene, who is a third-year associate. During orientation, Helen is told that Irene will not only be reviewing Helen's work product but will also be assisting Helen as she acclimates to law firm policies and procedures.

   During Helen's first week, she spends ten hours drafting a motion to dismiss. Helen enters those ten hours into the firm's billing system. This client is billed on an hourly rate basis—so for each hour that Helen spent working for the client, the client will be billed $250.

   At the end of the week, Irene sits down with Helen to review Helen's timesheets for the week. Irene asks Helen why Helen only billed ten hours on the motion package. Helen responds that she billed the time she spent, which was ten hours. Irene suggests that Helen add a few more hours to the bill. When Helen asks why, Irene explains that firm practice is to "round up," and that the client should be billed for closer to 15 hours for the motion package. After all, Irene reasons, a less efficient associate could have actually spent that much time working on the motion package.

   Helen feels uncomfortable. This sort of padding of timesheets seems unethical to her. Yet she also realizes that Irene is much more familiar with the firm's practices.

   May Helen follow Irene's advice and add five hours to the timesheets?
   a. Yes. Irene is far more experienced than Helen, and she was assigned to give Helen advice. As long as Helen follows Irene's direction, Helen cannot violate her professional responsibility.

    b. Yes. Irene reviewed the motion package and believes that it should have taken Helen 15 hours. A client should be billed for the expected time spent, not the actual time. Regardless of whose idea it is to change the hours, it is not a violation of professional responsibility to bill the client for 15 hours of work.

    c. No. Irene is only an associate, not a partner, so she cannot direct Helen's work. Had Irene been a partner, she could have authorized Helen to add time to the bill and Helen would have been immunized if Irene's direction was incorrect.

    d. No. Helen is personally responsible for complying with all ethical obligations and cannot misrepresent the time spent working on a matter, even if Irene suggests that she do so.

3. Jack is a partner at a midsized law firm. Every summer, the firm hires a class of a dozen law students as summer associates. Jack supervises the students. Jack assigns one student, Kirk, to draft a motion to dismiss in a case pending in a federal district court in the Second Circuit. Jack tells Kirk that there are many cases decided by judges in the district court that support their argument, but that Kirk should double-check that those cases are still good law.

    During his research, Kirk discovers an older Second Circuit case that goes against the argument in the motion. Kirk doesn't tell Jack and does not cite the case in the motion.

    Jack reviews the motion and files it. After the motion is filed but before oral argument on the motion, Jack congratulates Kirk on his excellent work. Feeling guilty, Kirk tells Jack about the case. The two pull it up and read it together—it is adverse and controlling.

    Jack decides not to disclose the case to the court, reasoning that it was Kirk who drafted the motion and therefore Jack cannot be responsible for any violation of professional responsibility. Jack argues the motion, and it is granted in his client's favor—apparently, both the opposing counsel and the court failed to discover the adverse, controlling authority.

    Did Jack comply with the Rules of Professional Conduct?

    a. Yes, Jack was not the one who drafted the motion and did not know about the case when the motion was filed. He was entitled reasonably to rely on Kirk's research.

    b. Yes, Kirk was a nonlawyer and therefore not subject to the rules of professional conduct.

    c. No, Jack ratified Kirk's unethical conduct by failing to disclose the case once he realized that it existed.

    d. No, a lawyer like Jack cannot rely on the work of nonlawyers like Kirk.

4. Lloyd is a midlevel associate at a large law firm. He works in a practice group with three partners, two midlevel associates, two first-year associates, and one paralegal. Lloyd assigns work to the first-year associates and the paralegal. He reviews this work and gives feedback. He has no formal title and no input in hiring, firing, or promotions, either in the practice group or in the firm itself. What Model Rules might apply to Lloyd?

    a. He is a managerial lawyer subject to **Model Rule 5.1**.
    b. He is a supervisory lawyer subject to **Model Rule 5.1**.
    c. He is a managerial lawyer subject to **Model Rule 5.1** and **Model Rule 5.3**.
    d. He is a supervisory lawyer subject to **Model Rule 5.1** and **Model Rule 5.3**.

5. Molly is a solo practitioner. She puts out an ad for a paralegal and interviews several candidates. One is Nelson. During the interview, Nelson freely admits to having previously been convicted for embezzlement. Believing that everyone deserves a second chance, Molly hires him.

    About a month later, $5,000 goes missing from a client trust account. Only Molly and Nelson had access to the account. Molly asks Nelson whether he knows anything about the missing money. He denies knowing anything. Molly allows him to keep his job. The following month, another $10,000 is missing from the account. Nelson never comes back to work, and Molly is unable to find him. Could Molly be subject to professional discipline?

    a. Yes, because a lawyer is always responsible for the actions of subordinates.
    b. Yes, because she was negligent in both hiring and supervision.
    c. No, because Nelson is not a lawyer and therefore not subject to discipline.
    d. No, because she did not personally misappropriate client funds.

6. Orin is a young partner at a boutique employment law firm. At the firm's inception, the partnership voted only to represent employers. They agreed not to represent employees, because representing employees could create **conflicts of interest** with their employer clients, or prevent the firm from accepting new employer clients.

    As a young partner, Orin struggles to build his own book of business. All the large employers in town are already clients of the firm's more senior partners. Orin decides to represent some employees. None of these employees work for any clients of the firm, and Orin figures that, if **conflicts of interest** arise later, the firm can figure out how to deal with them. Has Orin violated any legal or ethical obligations?

    a. Yes, his fiduciary duty to his firm.
    b. Yes, his fiduciary duty to his new client.

    c. No, provided there is no client **conflict**, there is no breach of fiduciary duty.

    d. No, provided no other lawyer at the firm represents the employer being sued by Orin's new client.

7. For decades, Don Vito has used Tom as his lawyer. Tom has been employed as an associate at the law firm of Puzo and Coppola for five years. Recently, Tom decided to go out on his own as a solo practitioner. Don Vito has one pending matter at the time that Tom decides to leave the firm: Don Vito is trying to purchase a share in a thoroughbred race horse. Tom has been handling the negotiation.

    The day that he gives his notice, Tom asks the firm whether he can contact Don Vito to inform him that he is leaving the firm. The firm's managing partner says no and tells Tom to pack up his things and leave. Tom asks what will happen with the pending matter. The managing partner says that the firm will assign another firm lawyer to finish the deal.

    Assuming that no one contacts Don Vito, what Rules of Professional Conduct have been violated?

    a. **Model Rule 1.4**, by the partners of Puzo and Coppola only.

    b. **Model Rule 1.4**, by Tom and the partners of Puzo and Coppola.

    c. **Model Rule 5.1**, by Tom only.

    d. **Model Rule 5.1**, by Tom and the partners of Puzo and Coppola.

8. Fletcher is a successful lawyer who is often dishonest. He wakes up one day and discovers that he cannot lie. He has an important case going to trial before Judge Stevens, and Fletcher fears that he will lose if he must be truthful.

    He calls Judge Stevens to ask for a continuance, and the judge asks why. Fletcher hands the phone to his legal assistant, Greta, and asks her to tell the judge that he's sick. Greta says, "You're not sick, are you?" Fletcher (who, remember, is unable to tell a lie), says, "No, I feel healthy as a horse."

    It would be unethical and a violation of **Model Rule 3.3(a)(1)** to lie to Judge Stevens. Who could be professionally disciplined under the relevant state's enactment of **Model Rule 5.3** if Greta indeed lied about the reason for the continuance as Fletcher has asked her to do?

    a. Greta.

    b. Fletcher.

    c. Greta and Fletcher.

    d. Judge Stevens.

20

Fees and Fee-Sharing

FRANK WANDERS INTO the break room for a cup of coffee and finds the firm's estate-planning partner, Willie Willmaker, in a foul mood. "Ingrates!" he seethes, as Frank walks in. "Excuse me?" says Frank, hoping *he* hasn't done anything. "The Hands," says Willie, as if it were invective. "What hands?" Frank asks, confused now. "My clients—or, I guess, my *former* clients," Willie explains. "Harry and Helping Hand." "Ah," says Frank. "What happened?" "They're a well-off couple in their fifties. Harry runs a family business. They came in for me to redo their estate plan."

"That's good, right?" Frank interjects. "I thought so," Willie replies, continuing. "Their estate is more complicated than most, and I quoted them a flat fee of $10,000 to redo all the documents, make sure that all the assets were titled correctly—you know the drill." "Right," says Frank, thinking back to his Wills and Trusts class in law school. "It turned out to be a lot more complicated than I thought," Willie says. "There were several tricky gift and estate tax issues I had to figure out to make their plan work, along with a bunch of specialized drafting. I ended up spending over $15,000 worth of time structuring the estate plan and drafting the documents. Then Harry calls and says it's taking too long and they've decided to use someone else—*after* I spent the time and had the documents done, except for final proofreading. We deserve to be paid for all that work."

"OK," says Frank, who learned in law school that a lawyer should always start the analysis of a contract problem with the words in the contract. "So what does our engagement agreement say?" "It says, 'We will charge a flat fee of $10,000 to prepare and implement your new estate plan'—the language I usually use," says Willie, glumly. "Have they paid anything?" Frank asks, guessing that he already knows the answer. "No, I usually present the invoice when I show the clients the documents that they've come in to sign," Willie replies. "And what's even worse, I already sent the lawyer who represents the family business and who sent them over here a $1,000 referral fee. Argh."

Does Frank's firm have the right to collect any fees from the Hands? Are there any issues with the referral fee that Willie paid to the other lawyer? Read on.

* * *

Even with all of the fiduciary and other duties that we owe, lawyers are entitled (and deserve) to be paid for their work like anyone else. Most lawyers earn what the Model Rules delicately refer to as a "satisfactory living" (**Model Rules, Preamble ¶ [9]**), and some do much better than that. That's wonderful. But because of our fiduciary and other duties, there are some special constraints on how and how much we can be paid—constraints that don't apply to other service providers. Some of them will strike you as common sense, others as picky and hyper-technical, but all of them are the law, and the **consequences** of disregarding any of them can deprive you, in one way or another, of the fruits of your labors.

Model Rule 1.5 sets the general formal and substantive limits on fees and related expenses. That Rule and **Model Rule 5.4** provide limits on the persons with whom you can divide the fees that clients pay you and the circumstances under which you can divide fees when it's allowed. Once you know these constraints, they're generally not very difficult to follow. So work through this chapter with us, and you'll be ready to go.[1]

A. Fees and Expenses

We've talked in passing before about "fees" and about "expenses" or "costs." You're probably familiar with the difference, but let's pause for a moment and make sure that you're clear about where they fit into the amounts that lawyers charge clients.

When a lawyer or **practice organization** represents a client on a service-for-payment basis, the charges fall into one of two basic categories. "Fees" are direct charges for the professional services that the lawyer provides. "Expenses" or "costs" are interchangeable terms for out-of-pocket amounts for additional goods and services necessary to provide the professional services specific to this client. Expenses can include such items as travel, photocopying, data or document processing, filing and transcript charges, investigation, consultant and expert charges, and the like. Lawyers are allowed to, and frequently do, pay expenses to third parties directly at the time that those expenses are incurred (often referred to as "advancing" the expenses, because the economic reality is that the lawyer is lending the client the amount of the expenses), and then the lawyers recoup those already-advanced expenses from the client as part of the billing arrangement.

Lawyers are generally not allowed to bill to a client as expenses the lawyer's general personal expenses or the general "overhead" costs associated with staffing and maintaining an office. A client may be billed only for specific expenses incurred as a result of that client's own matter.

---

[1] Some related topics: Fee disputes are discussed in **Chapter 3.B at 52** (generally) and **Chapter 21.C at 585** (regarding the treatment of disputed funds in the lawyer's possession). Issues created by the use of liens (security interests) to secure the payment of fees and expenses are discussed in **Chapter 22.A at 603**.

B. Common Fee and Expense Arrangements, and the Formalities Necessary to Make Them Enforceable

Let's start with an overview of the most common arrangements by which we lawyers get paid and the formalities required to make them enforceable. All of these structures are, first and foremost, matters of contract: Usually as part of the initial engagement agreement, the lawyer (or law firm) and client agree what fee structure they will use, and also elaborate on the details of that particular structure in the matter at hand. **Model Rule 1.5(b) and (c)** provide various formal and mechanical requirements for agreements about fees, such as which terms **must** or **should** be stated in writing.[2]

Before we jump into descriptions of the most common fee and expense arrangements, let's provide a little context by being sure that we understand how we know what the fee arrangement in any particular matter is. Leaving aside the situations in which fees are set by statute or court order, a fee agreement between a lawyer or **practice organization** and a client is simply a contract. Its existence, interpretation, and enforceability are determined according to the principles of contract law that apply to all contracts. Though there are some special rules that apply uniquely to lawyer-client fee contracts, they fit neatly into the overall contract scheme: Formal requirements are analogous to the Statutes of Frauds that you learned about in Contracts, and can form defenses to formation or enforcement of the fee agreement. Forbidden fee arrangements are voidable as against public policy, a defense to enforcement.

Now let's look at some typical structures.

1. Regular Salary or Wages

Most individual lawyers get paid the way that most other people do—by receiving a periodic salary or a per-hour wage. Sometimes, this includes a

---

[2] Because the formalities of fee arrangements differ depending on the type of fee arrangement, this is a good time to review the three levels of formality specified in the Model Rules. Most agreements or consents require no particular level of formality; they **may** be made or given orally or in a writing of any form. Some terms of fee arrangements **must** be **confirmed in writing** in order to be effective. **Model Rule 1.0(n)** defines "writing" in part as "a tangible or electronic record of a communication or representation," and **Model Rule 1.0(a)** defines "confirmed in writing" as "consent that is given in writing . . . or a writing that a lawyer promptly transmits . . . confirming an oral . . . consent" transmitted at or within a reasonable time after the consent is given. Thus, an agreement or consent that is **confirmed in writing may** be, but is *not* required to be, signed by the person agreeing or consenting; it **may** simply confirm the terms agreed or consented to orally in a writing produced after the fact and sent to the client. Other fee terms **must** be contained **in a writing signed by the client** in order to be effective. **Model Rule 1.0(n)** defines a "signed" writing as a writing including "an electronic sound, symbol or process attached to or logically associated with a writing and executed or adopted by a person with the intent to sign the writing." Therefore, a term that **must** be **in a writing signed by the client** requires *both* a writing stating to what the client is agreeing or consenting *and* the client's signature on that writing (in some recognized form) indicating the client's agreement or consent. TIPS AND TACTICS As we will see, the formal requirements of the Model Rules are just the *minimum* steps required to make particular fee arrangements enforceable. The better practice for all terms, in virtually all circumstances, is to memorialize *every* **material** term of the engagement (including fees and expenses) **in a writing signed by the client**. This approach helps avoid disputes and ensures that the client has understood—and has knowingly agreed to—every detail of the arrangement. TIPS AND TACTICS

periodic bonus of some kind based on the individual's or the **practice organization**'s performance. Sometimes this compensation is, in effect, a fee paid to the lawyer by a client; sometimes it's payment from an employer **practice organization** to an employee lawyer.

If you work for a **practice organization** (other than being your own boss as a solo practitioner), then receiving an hourly or salaried wage is usually how your compensation is structured. Think about it: In government and in-house counsel work, almost all lawyers are paid this way, and given that they represent the government agency or company by which they are employed, they are being paid by their respective clients. In private law firms, the firm's clients pay their fees to the *law firm*, and then those fees are used to pay the law firm's expenses and compensate owners (partners and the like) and employees (associates, staff, and the like) according to the firm **constituents**' pre-existing understandings.

One thing that emerges from this perspective is that, when clients pay fees, they are often paying them to the **practice organization** that provided the legal services rather than to any individual lawyer who participated in providing the services. The constraints on fees and fee-sharing under the Model Rules and other law apply both to any involved **practice organization** and to any involved individual lawyers, though the professional discipline for any violation will be visited on those lawyers personally responsible for the violation.

2. Flat-Rate Fees

Flat-rate legal fees are exactly what they sound like—a sum certain, usually agreed in advance, for a specified task or set of tasks. The fee does not change, no matter how many hours the lawyer works (unless otherwise agreed). The fee is also unaffected by the outcome of the matter. Expenses **may**, by agreement, be included in the flat fee, or they **may** be itemized and charged in addition to the flat fee. Flat fees were very common before the 1970s, and they are becoming increasingly popular again, especially where the task is relatively straightforward and the amount of time and effort necessary to complete it is relatively easy to anticipate. Flat fees offer a degree of predictability that clients appreciate, and flat fees can also reward lawyers who can work more efficiently.[3]

---

[3] A historical note: Before the 1970s, many medium-sized and larger companies had long-term, comprehensive arrangements for all or nearly all of their legal needs, using just one law firm. (Significant numbers of in-house lawyers at any one company were rare at this time.) As part of such an arrangement, the law firm characteristically billed the company periodically, either for particular tasks (say, a securities offering) or for a set of tasks (say, general corporate and governance advice or, in some cases, for everything that the firm had done in the prior billing period) in unelaborated, one-page invoices that simply said, "For services rendered," followed by a single dollar amount. Where the parties had a long-term, comprehensive arrangement, this practice was satisfactory to both the client companies and to their outside law firms: The parties developed a consensus over time as to what the outside firm's services were worth. The bill varied from period to period, depending on the amount and type of work provided, but both parties had a general and predictable sense of roughly what the amount was going to be.

Because a flat-rate fee is (like almost all other fee structures) a creature of contract, it is essential to agree to the details, "preferably in writing" (**Model Rule 1.5(b)**), at the outset (in the terms of the Rule, "before or within a reasonable time after commencing the representation"). Those details **must** or **should** include the following terms:

- A definition of the task or tasks the lawyer is expected to complete in return for the flat fee (the scope of the engagement) **must** be agreed upon and **should** be **confirmed in writing. Model Rule 1.5(b).** *See* **Chapter 9.A at 262** on defining the scope of the engagement.
- The amount of the flat fee **must** be agreed upon and **should** be **confirmed in writing. Model Rule 1.5(b).**
- Whether the flat fee includes expenses and, if not, how expenses will be billed and paid, **must** be agreed upon, and **should** be **confirmed in writing. Model Rule 1.5(b).**
- When the client **must** *pay* the fee, which could be entirely up front, entirely on completion, or in installments as various defined milestones in the engagement are reached (some states have constraints, not included in the Model Rules, limiting these arrangements)—again, this issue **should** be agreed upon and **confirmed in writing.**
- At what point in the engagement the lawyer has *earned* the fee or portions of it, so that the parties understand what portion of a flat fee is unearned if the engagement terminates before it's completed—the issue of when a flat fee has been (or portions of it have been) earned **should** be agreed upon and **confirmed in writing.** *See* **Model Rule 1.5 Comment [4]; Chapter 9.D at 302.**

[TIPS AND TACTICS] Although **Model Rule 1.5(b)** provides that some of these terms **must** be agreed to at the outset and **should** be **confirmed in writing**, it also states that they need not be agreed to and confirmed in writing "when the lawyer will charge a regularly represented client on the same basis or rate." Regardless of what is required, however, the best practice is always to memorialize *all* terms **in a writing signed by the client** at or near the beginning of the engagement. This additional formality makes it more certain that the client has understood and agreed to the fee arrangement, avoiding misunderstandings, and a signed writing also provides

---

This arrangement does not fall neatly into any of the categories discussed in this chapter. It is a flat fee of sorts, but typically not one to which clients agreed in advance. It is an hourly fee of sorts, in that it varied to some degree based on how much work the outside firm did, but not in any way strictly proportional to "hours times hourly rates" agreed on in advance, which is the essence of an hourly fee. This billing method is a relic of a gentler time, when institutional law firms and institutional clients were much less adversarial and much more collaborative regarding the nature and pricing of the services that outside firms provided. The practice fell out of use as specialization became more important, outside counsel firms became more competitive, and companies started bringing more work in-house and distributing their outside work among different firms. *See* Bernard A. Burk & David McGowan, *Big But Brittle: Economic Perspectives on the Future of the Law Firm in the New Economy*, 2011 COLUM. BUS. L. REV. 1, 8, 23, 65-66 (2011).

evidence of the agreement in the event of a later fee dispute. *See* **Model Rule 1.5 Comment [2]**. Tips and Tactics

3. Hourly Fees

Hourly fee arrangements are common. As you would expect, under an hourly arrangement, the fee charged is equal to the number of hours worked times an hourly rate agreed to in advance. Different lawyers (and other timekeepers within a **practice organization** charging hourly fees, such as legal assistants) **may** and typically do have different hourly rates depending on their relative seniority, skill, and experience. Within a **practice organization** that charges hourly fees, the hourly rate for any one timekeeper may also differ depending on the nature of the matter or the work to be performed.

Rates also vary by geography and practice area. Typical hourly rates can be as low as $100 per hour or less in more rural areas for less complex work, all the way up to rates in excess of $1,500 per hour (catch your breath; check for nosebleeds) for senior lawyers specializing in complex or specialized matters at large firms (or smaller specialized boutiques) in larger cities.

Lawyers who bill by the hour usually bill in increments of one-tenth of an hour, meaning that the client is charged one-tenth of the hourly rate for every six minutes that the lawyer spends on the matter. Most firms employ timekeeping software that allows lawyers to capture all their time and to ensure that clients are billed properly. If you go to work with a **practice organization** that requires you to record your time, you may be surprised to learn how much time you spend doing just that: keeping a record of what you did, for whom, and for how long. Proper timekeeping is a key skill necessary for lawyers in private practice.[4]

In terms of how regularly the client receives a bill for hourly fees, the most common billing interval is monthly. Some lawyers will send bills more frequently, others less so. The Rules do not require any specific billing interval or any particular detail on hourly billing statements, though some states do have additional provisions not included in the Model Rules requiring specific details on written bills. Matters in which a court or some other authority must approve professional fees (such as lawyers representing debtors or other estate-paid representatives in bankruptcy court, and lawyers representing trusts or estates in many jurisdictions) are also often subject to special rules requiring specific details in timekeeping and billing.

As with other types of fee arrangements, it is essential to agree to the details of an hourly arrangement at or near the beginning of the engagement (again,

---

[4] Many lawyers who don't bill by the hour also keep track of their time. Timekeeping helps lawyers measure their efficiency as well as the time typically required for particular tasks for purposes of internal management, performance review, and future fee-setting. It's also valuable if a court awards a party attorneys' fees authorized by contract or statute, or as sanctions, and the lawyer thus needs to quantify the award.

unless you "will charge a regularly represented client on the same basis or rate"), and again, "preferably in writing." **Model Rule 1.5(b)**. Those details **must** or **should** include the following terms:

- A definition of the task or tasks that the lawyer is expected to complete in return for the hourly fees (the scope of the engagement) **must** be agreed upon and **should** be **confirmed in writing. Model Rule 1.5(b)**. Again, *see* **Chapter 9.A at 262** on defining the scope of the engagement.
- How expenses will be billed and paid **must** be agreed upon and **should** be **confirmed in writing. Model Rule 1.5(b)**.
- The hourly rate of each timekeeper who will work on the matter ("the basis or rate of the fee") **must** be agreed upon and **should** be **confirmed in writing. Model Rule 1.5(b)**.
- How and when the client will be billed, and how long, after receiving the bill, the client's payment is due, **should** be agreed upon, and **should** be **confirmed in writing**.
- In addition, if anything changes during the engagement (for example, if the firm adjusts its rates, or if a new timekeeper becomes involved), the client **must** be notified. Some firms notify the client by reflecting the new rates or timekeepers on a bill after the charges have been incurred, but advance notice is the better practice and in some states is required. **Model Rule 1.5(b)**.

TIPS AND TACTICS As is the case with flat fees, although **Model Rule 1.5(b)** provides that some of these terms **must** be agreed to at the outset and **should** be **confirmed in writing**, the best practice is to memorialize all of them **in a writing signed by the client** at or near the beginning of the engagement. TIPS AND TACTICS

4. Contingent Fees

A contingent fee is one in which the entitlement to or amount of the lawyer's fee, in whole or in part, is *contingent* (that is, conditioned) on something. A contingent fee can be conditioned on anything (or at least anything not prohibited by public policy), but by far the most common agreed fee contingency is the collection by or on behalf of the client of a settlement or judgment on the client's claim. The contingent portion of the fee **may** similarly be measured in any manner on which the lawyer and client agree, but the most common measure is a percentage of the amounts collected on the client's claim.[5]

---

[5] That arrangement in a plaintiff's-side engagement is usually stated more or less like this: "Our fee in this matter will be XX percent of anything of value recovered, whether by settlement, judgment, or otherwise, on account of the Incident [defined elsewhere to be the accident or other event that caused the plaintiff's harm]." Language like this has been construed to allow the lawyers to recover their contingent portion of a settlement obtained directly by the client or by someone else while the lawyers remain the client's counsel. If a contingent-fee engagement is terminated before the contingency occurs, the fee arrangement changes by operation of law, usually (depending on the jurisdiction) providing the lawyer the reasonable value of her services (*quantum meruit*, typically on an hourly basis) up to the time of termination,

In plaintiff's-side litigation engagements in which the claimant does not have the means to pay conventional hourly rates (which includes many personal-injury and employment cases with low- or middle-income claimants), contingent fees give claimants access to counsel that they otherwise could not afford. More generally, contingent fees allow lawyers to share some of the client's risk in the engagement in return for what may turn out to be a more substantial fee upon success. Contingent fees can incentivize lawyers to achieve better results by giving them a share of the "upside."

Although contingent fees often align the **interests** of lawyer and client to achieve optimal results, sometimes they can cause those **interests** to diverge. Recall **Problem 6A-2**, in which Frank finds himself in a bind because he and his client disagree about the settlement value of her case. In the problem, Frank is confident that a pending settlement offer is a generous resolution of the claim—as good as the client is likely to get at trial—and that the client should take it. The client is convinced that the offer is much too small and insists that Frank reject it and take the case to trial. If Frank takes the case to trial, his firm will spend a great deal more effort on the case (effort that the firm could be using to serve other paying clients) and will have to advance substantial amounts of experts' fees and other costs, all to achieve a result that Frank (in his honest professional opinion) believes will be no better than what's on the table already. Frank **must**, of course, follow his client's instructions on a settlement call, even when he believes that the client's decision is dead wrong and will likely cost his firm dearly. Frank's firm may even try to withdraw rather than take the case to trial, but the client may fight the necessary motion to be relieved as counsel. For our purposes right now, though, note how the economic incentives created by the contingent fee cause the **interests** of lawyer and client to diverge under these circumstances. For contrast, imagine how different everyone might feel if Frank's firm were getting paid in the same case by the hour.

Contingent-fee arrangements require heightened formalities. Under **Model Rule 1.5(c)**, a contingent fee **must** be memorialized **in a writing signed by the client**, and under **Model Rules 1.5(b)-(c)**, the writing **must** or **should** include the following terms:

- A definition of the task or tasks that the lawyer is expected to complete in return for the contingent fee (the scope of the engagement) **must** be agreed upon, **should** be in writing under **Model Rule 1.5(b)**, and, under best practices, **should** be **in a writing signed by the client**. Defining the scope of the engagement (*see* **Chapter 9.A at 262**) is especially important here, because if the need for additional services related to the engagement arises, the client will probably expect the lawyer to perform them without additional compensation unless their fee agreement specifically says otherwise.

---

but sometimes providing the lawyer nothing if the lawyer quits without justification or is terminated for good cause. *See* **Chapter 9.D at 303 n.27**.

- The contingency that triggers the client's obligation to pay the contingent portion of the fee **must** be included **in a writing signed by the client** under **Model Rule 1.5(c)**.
- "The method by which the fee is to be determined, including the percentage or percentages that shall accrue to the lawyer in the event of settlement, trial or appeal" **must** be included **in a writing signed by the client** under **Model Rule 1.5(c)**. Although the Rule is phrased in terms of the common contingent-fee arrangement used in representing a plaintiff in litigation, contingent fees are not limited to representing plaintiffs, or even to litigation. The contingent fee **may** be measured by a fixed sum or a defined percentage of some asset or fund other than a settlement or judgment.
- How "litigation and other expenses" will be billed and paid **must** be included **in a writing signed by the client,** per **Model Rule 1.5(c)**.
- More specifically, "whether [litigation and other] expenses are to be deducted before or after the contingent fee is calculated" **must** be included **in a writing signed by the client,** per **Model Rule 1.5(c)**.

  Either approach is permitted, but deducting expenses first is generally more favorable to the client, and is the more common approach. It may not be obvious at first, but whether expenses are deducted before or after the percentage fee is taken can have a significant effect on how much of the recovery (or other asset on which the fee is based) the client gets to keep. As an illustration, consider the difference in a personal injury case in which the lawyer and the client have agreed to a contingency fee of 30 percent of any settlement or judgment collected, the lawyer has advanced $100,000 in expenses during the litigation, and the case has settled for $1 million (all of which are plausible numbers for a case of this kind):

Deduction of expenses *before* assessing contingency fee (more common approach):	Deduction of expenses *after* assessing contingency fee (less common approach):
$1,000,000 recovery	$1,000,000 recovery
-100,000 subtract litigation expenses	-300,000 take 30% contingency fee
$900,000 basis for contingency fee	$700,000 recovery net of fees
-270,000 take 30% contingency fee	-100,000 subtract litigation expenses
$630,000 net amount client receives from settlement	**$600,000** net amount client receives from settlement

- "[A]ny expenses for which the client will be liable whether or not the client is the prevailing party." **Model Rule 1.5(c)**. TAMING THE TEXT There is an ambiguity buried in this portion of the Rule. As we will see in **Chapter 22.A at XX**, lawyers are allowed to advance litigation expenses on behalf of clients in contingent-fee matters on the understanding that they will not seek reimbursement of those costs from their clients if the contingency (usually a judgment or settlement in the client's favor) does not occur. **Model Rule 1.8(e)(1).** If the lawyer instead expects to recoup any litigation expenses from the client, those expenses subject to recoupment regardless of the outcome of the case **must** be specified **in a writing signed by the client**.

It is also possible that this clause in **Rule 1.5(c)** requires written disclosure of the client's potential obligation to pay *opposing parties'* litigation costs in a litigation matter if the client loses. In most jurisdictions, the prevailing party recovers its costs of litigation (specified by statute, but including items like filing and jury fees, transcript fees and, in some cases, experts' fees and even attorneys' fees if authorized by contract or statute) from the nonprevailing party. If the plaintiff-client loses in a contingent-fee matter, she may owe no fees and no costs to her own lawyer, but she may be taxed costs payable to the opposing party. Most clients have no idea that this possibility exists. This clause in **Model Rule 1.5(c)** may require written disclosure of that possibility, though the fact that it refers to "expenses for which the client will be liable *whether or not* the client is the prevailing party" makes that interpretation doubtful, as the opposing parties' litigation costs are generally assessed *only* if the client is *not* the prevailing party.

Even if this disclosure is not required by **Model Rule 1.5(c)**, however, it would appear to be required by the **duty of candor** in **Model Rule 1.4**, as part of the information that a reasonable client would want to know in order to grant **informed consent** to a fee arrangement. And common phrases by which some lawyers oversimplify contingent fees in advertising, such as "you pay nothing unless we get you something," could be considered **materially** misleading and thus in violation of **Model Rule 7.1**, **Model Rule 4.1**, and civil tort law's prohibitions on misrepresentation (*see* **Chapter 10.B at 324**). TAMING THE TEXT

- In addition, **Model Rule 1.5(c)** imposes a disclosure and accounting requirement at the conclusion of contingent-fee matters: "Upon conclusion of a contingent fee matter, the lawyer shall provide the client with a written statement stating the outcome of the matter and, if there is a recovery, showing the remittance to the client and the method of its determination." TIPS AND TACTICS There is no requirement that clients sign and return this accounting before receiving their portion of a judgment or settlement in their lawyers' hands, but as with other disclosures and agreements, it's the best practice. It allows you to confirm that your and your client's respective portions of the payout are consistent with your original agreement and helps to surface any dispute that may be brewing. TIPS AND TACTICS

5. "Alternative" Fee Arrangements

The fee and expense arrangements described above are by no means the only ways that clients can agree to pay their lawyers; they're just the most common.

Within a few substantive limits discussed in the next section, fee structures are limited only by the parties' imaginations and their ability to describe their arrangements precisely in contractual terms. Currently, lawyers, particularly at larger firms, are cultivating broader and longer-term arrangements with larger institutional clients, using creative arrangements that build various financial incentives for both parties into the firms' handling of larger blocks of work. They also are experimenting with risk-sharing arrangements in one-off engagements. These arrangements can, and often do, combine features of the more common arrangements just discussed, with other terms devised for the needs at hand.[6] Some of the problems below provide examples of these "mix and match" arrangements.

There are generally only two things to recall about such "alternative" fee arrangements. One is that they must remain within the substantive limits on fees discussed in the next section (and, more generally, any other public policy concerns; for example, a client could not agree to pay for a lawyer's services by donating one of her kidneys). The other is that the arrangement **must** conform to the formal requirements of **Model Rules 1.5(b)-(c)** and **should** conform to best practices. Thus *any* fee agreement **must** have a scope of engagement and the "basis or rate of the fee and expenses for which the client will be responsible" agreed at or near the outset of the engagement, "preferably" (that is, these terms **should** be) **confirmed in writing**; and the client **must** be notified of any changes (**Model Rule 1.5(b)**). Any fee arrangement in which *any* portion of the arrangement is "contingent" **must** have all aspects of the contingency fee that are set out in **Model Rule 1.5(c)** stated **in a writing signed by the client** (*see* **Chapter 20.B at 542**). TIPS AND TACTICS And the best practice is to clearly describe *all* aspects of *any* fee arrangement **in a writing signed by the client**, whether or not any Rule literally requires it. TIPS AND TACTICS

Problem 20B-1: Go back and take a look at the hypothetical described in **this chapter's Introduction** opening. How much do the Hands owe Frank's firm? Please explain your answer and the best arguments for and against your calculation. How could Willie Willmaker have made this an easier question to resolve?

Problem 20B-2: Maya's firm agrees to do employment counseling for a large company client. The engagement agreement addressing this engagement provides (in part): "We will provide the Company all requested employment counseling, including drafting agreements and drafting or amending company policies and procedures, for the next twelve (12) months for a flat fee of $120,000, payable at the rate of $10,000 per month in arrears. This agreement does not include services involving litigation or administrative proceedings." Is this agreement enforceable? Why or why not?

---

[6] And of course lawyers are free to discount or waive their fees as an accommodation to a client, to underprice a competitor, or as a matter of charity in *pro bono* engagements. The only time that a fee discount or other accommodation is not allowed is if it is payment for some kind of forbidden *quid pro quo*. *See, e.g.,* **Model Rule 7.2(b)**; **Chapter 18.C at 485**.

> **Problem 20B-3:** Frank's firm agrees to take a personal injury case on contingency. The firm's client is the plaintiff. The agreement states that costs will be advanced by the firm but are to be deducted from any judgment or settlement before the lawyer's fees are calculated. Regardless of outcome, the client is responsible for reimbursing the firm for any expenses. The agreement states that Frank's firm is entitled to 20 percent of any settlement reached pretrial and 30 percent of any award at (or settlement during) trial. The remainder, after any costs and fees are paid, will go to the client.
>
> a. The firm spends $5,000 in filing and deposition fees, and the case settles before trial for $200,000. How much does the client recover? How much goes to the firm?
>
> b. Same as (a), but the client rejects the settlement offer. After efforts to settle fail, the case goes to trial, and the firm incurs another $35,000 in transcript, jury, and expert witness fees. The jury awards the plaintiff $210,000. How much does the client receive? How much goes to the firm? If the client is unhappy, how might the firm explain the difference in its share of the judgment?
>
> c. Same as (b), except the client loses at trial (defense verdict). What does the client receive? What does the firm receive, and from whom? What does the opposing party likely receive, and from whom?

> **Problem 20B-4:** Frank's firm does not usually change its rates in a pending matter. Instead, it keeps the same rates in effect throughout any particular matter, and applies any new rates to new matters as they come in. One of the partners in Frank's firm points out that many law firms adjust their rates annually in pending matters. He proposes that the firm add a provision to its form engagement agreement stating, "We will adjust our hourly rates annually, effective January 1 of each calendar year, to reflect the increasing seniority and experience of our personnel, and also to reflect inflation generally." Is there any problem with this approach? If so, what is it, and why? If there is, what could the firm do to avoid it?

C. Substantive Limits on Fees and Expenses

So far, we've talked about the common ways that clients agree to pay their lawyers, and we've laid out the formal requirements for fee agreements: what terms **must** or **should** be part of an agreement regarding fees and expenses, and what terms **must** or **should** be **confirmed in writing** or set out **in a writing signed by the client**.

There are also a few substantive limits on fees and expenses—that is, some fees or expenses that you simply can't charge, no matter how willing the client is to pay them. As we'll see, these limits leave a lot of room for lawyers and clients to make mutually acceptable fee agreements responsive to their circumstances. But this freedom (much like "freedom of contract" generally), though broad, is not boundless.

1. The General Prohibition on Unreasonable Fees or Expenses

The one limit that applies to *all* voluntary fee arrangements is that "[a] lawyer shall not make an agreement for, charge, or collect an unreasonable fee or an unreasonable amount for expenses." **Model Rule 1.5(a)**. It's worth noting that, given the quoted language, a lawyer has violated this Rule, and is subject to discipline, the moment he *agrees to* or *charges* an unreasonable fee or expense, even if he never tries to collect it.

"Unreasonable" is one of those fuzzy standards of which it's difficult to get a clear picture, but the Rules offer some guidance. We are told that the reasonableness of a fee will be judged under all the relevant facts and circumstances, and **Model Rule 1.5(a)** offers a list of eight factors to be considered, not all of which will necessarily be relevant in any particular case, and no single one of which is necessarily dispositive (**Model Rule 1.5 Comment [1]**):

1. "[T]he time and labor required, the novelty and difficulty of the questions involved, and the skill requisite to perform the legal service properly" (**Model Rule 1.5(a)(1)**). A bigger commitment of the lawyer's or law firm's available time, or a more challenging engagement, **may** reasonably command a higher fee than a smaller or less difficult one. And though the parties are broadly free to negotiate a scope of engagement that limits the lawyer's work to only a portion of the case, it would be unreasonable for the lawyer to agree to a limited scope that would leave the client in immediate need of additional services when the agreed work was complete. *See* **Model Rule 1.5 Comment [5]**.

2. "[T]he likelihood, if apparent to the client, that the acceptance of the particular employment will preclude other employment by the lawyer" (**Model Rule 1.5(a)(2)**). Where the lawyer is forgoing other paying work to devote her time to the client's matter, an overall higher fee **may** be reasonable.

3. "[T]he fee customarily charged in the locality for similar legal services" (**Model Rule 1.5(a)(3)**). As discussed above, fees vary geographically and according to the nature and difficulty of the services. The benchmark of the going rate (or range of rates) for similar services in the community is an important measure of what's reasonable.

4. "[T]he amount involved and the results obtained" (**Model Rule 1.5(a)(4)**). This factor is less simple than it sounds. With respect to the amount involved, generally speaking, it **may** be reasonable to charge a higher fee for higher-stakes work. This may not always be true, however. For example, the bigger that the plausible outcome of a contingent-fee matter seems at the outset, the smaller the percentage of the recovery may be needed to provide the lawyer with a reasonable fee (though the larger the overall fee will probably turn out to be, relative to other, lower-stakes matters).

   "The results obtained" is also sometimes a difficult factor to apply. Generally, we judge the reasonableness of a fee at the time that the fee agreement is made, which is of course before the result is known. But some kinds of fees, particularly hourly ones, won't be known until the matter is over, and the total number of hours expended can be counted. And it would be reasonable to expect a lawyer to litigate a $10,000 case differently from a $1 million case, so that a very high hourly bill for a case that never had the prospect of a substantial result (or some important nonmonetary effect) **may** be considered unreasonable.

This factor can also pose challenges when applied to a contingent fee. When a lawyer agrees to a contingent fee, she takes some risks. The case may settle immediately, or it may have to be litigated through trial (and, perhaps, through multiple levels of appeals). Under the contingent-fee agreement, the law firm gets the same percentage of the recovery, whether it ultimately requires only a few hours or hundreds (or thousands!) of hours of work. (Some contingent fees increase the percentage as the case advances procedurally, *e.g.*, 25 percent of the recovery if the case settles before trial, or 33 percent if the case settles after trial has begun or is litigated to judgment. Such arrangements allocate back to the client some of the risk that the lawyer is taking.) Part of the contingent fee is compensation for the risk that the lawyer takes regarding how much of her own labor she'll have to expend to earn the fee. The risk that the lawyer took at the outset needs to be taken into account in judging the reasonableness of a contingent fee on commonly negotiated terms when the case happens to resolve quickly and easily.

5. "[T]he time limitations imposed by the client or by the circumstances" (**Model Rule 1.5(a)(5)**). Time-pressured matters are more stressful and can temporarily crowd out lawyers' other pre-existing obligations, forcing them to scramble to "keep all the plates spinning." Such matters thus **may** justify a higher fee than a comparable matter that is less time-pressured.

6. "[T]he nature and length of the professional relationship with the client" (**Model Rule 1.5(a)(6)**). The longer and deeper the relationship of mutual trust, the more likely it is that the lawyers have institutional knowledge about the client, and its preferred ways of conducting its business, that may create efficiencies and more effective service that are worth more to the client. In addition, the more sophisticated and capable the client is of judging what legal services may be worth to him, her, or it (in the case of an organization) under the prevailing circumstances, the more latitude the parties are likely to be given to negotiate a fee deal to which they will be held.

7. "[T]he experience, reputation, and ability of the lawyer or lawyers performing the services" (**Model Rule 1.5(a)(7)**). More experienced, better regarded, and more skilled lawyers **may** generally charge higher fees than others, within reason.

8. "[W]hether the fee is fixed or contingent (**Model Rule 1.5(a)(8)**). A fixed or contingent fee is set (or in the case of a contingent fee, the contingency and percentage are set) at the outset, when there can be significant uncertainty about how much work will be required and, in the case of a contingent fee, what the outcome will be. That risk may make a fee seem high in retrospect

when things break the lawyer's way and a quick result or a bigger-than-expected outcome materializes. Better-reasoned caselaw looks at whether the fee was reasonable at the time at which it was agreed and takes into account any risk that the lawyer had assumed at that time.

REAL WORLD The number and complexity of all these factors can seem overwhelming. One perspective that may help limit this difficulty is that, as a practical matter, clients who are reasonably well informed and exercise free choice have to show that a fee is *very* unfair in order to get much traction in attacking it. The most common kind of fee dispute is over hourly fees when (usually after the fact) the client claims that the law firm devoted significantly more time than was reasonable to the entire matter or to portions of it, allowed more senior timekeepers with higher hourly rates to perform simple tasks that a more junior lawyer or a nonlawyer could have performed less expensively, or simply "padded" the bill with time or tasks that were unnecessary, or not cost-justified, or never even performed. But whatever the nature of the dispute, tribunals asked to judge the reasonableness of fees tend to set the "unreasonableness" bar fairly high, though lawyers do nevertheless manage to clear it.[7]

Similarly, challenged expenses generally have to be seen as quite excessive or fabricated before they are branded as unreasonable. Lavish travel, meal, and lodging expenses that are well beyond "comfortable" have been condemned, as have expenses that were unnecessary or inflated, or that proved to be ordinary living or general office expenses. Again, tribunals generally need to see expenses well beyond reason to label them unreasonable, though some lawyers seem willing to show judgment (or the lack of it) bad enough to raise the question.[8]

REAL WORLD

---

[7] One of us has served as a fee examiner in several large bankruptcy cases, and she routinely looks at these factors. Lawyers often have legitimately earned the fees they charge but, occasionally, matters do get out of hand. The list of such matters is long, but *see, e.g.,* **Chapter 9.D at 306 n.28**; Roy Strom, *Former Kirkland, Chicago Boutique Lawyer Confesses to Years of Overbilling,* https://www.law.com/americanlawyer/2019/01/17/former-kirkland-chicago-boutique-lawyer-confesses-to-years-of-overbilling/ (Jan. 17, 2019). Webster Hubbell (the No. 3 person in President Clinton's Justice Department, former Chief Justice of the Arkansas Supreme Court, and before that a partner with Mrs. Clinton in a prominent Little Rock, Arkansas law firm) went to federal prison for billing clients (and his firm) hundreds of thousands of dollars in fees and expenses that he never incurred on behalf of clients while in private practice. Jeff Gerth, *Ex-Clinton Confidant Gets 21 Months,* https://www.nytimes.com/1995/06/29/us/ex-clinton-confidant-gets-21-months.html (June 29, 1995).

[8] *See, e.g.,* Willem Gravett, '*I am not overcompensated enough': The Moral Compass of the American Lawyer,* 25 ADVOCATE 43, 44, https://www.gcbsa.co.za/law-journals/2012/april/2012-april-vol025-no1-pp43-48.pdf (April 2012) ("massages during litigation; dry cleaning of a toupee; a Chicago lawyer who charged his client $25,000 for 'ground transportation' during an assignment in San Francisco; and a lawyer in Cleveland who charged his client for the suit, shirts, and underwear he purchased in the midst of a trial that took longer than expected"); Nancy B. Rapoport, *Rethinking Professional Fees in Chapter 11 Cases,* 5 J. BUS. & TECH. L. 263, 279-80 (2010) ($140 shirt billed to client); Sara Randazzo, *Ex-Sidley Partner Admits Faking Bills, But Not for Gain,* http://www.americanlawyer.com/PubArticleALD.jsp?id=1202610355577&kw=Ex-Sidley%20Partner%20Admits%20Faking%20Bills%2C%20But%20Not%20For%20Gain&et=editorial&bu=The%20American%20Lawyer&cn=20130711&src=EMC-Email&pt=Am%20Law%20Daily (July 10, 2013). In a scandal featured prominently in *The American Lawyer* at the time, a BigLaw firm was discovered to be marking up various expenses over their actual cost without telling its clients. S. Beck & M. Orey, *Skaddenomics,* THE AMERICAN LAWYER 3 (September 1991).

2. Prohibited Contingent Fees and Other Substantive Limits

In addition to the general requirement that no fee or expense be unreasonable, there are particular kinds of fees that it is unlawful to charge. For example, a lawyer may not charge a contingent fee "in a domestic relations matter, the payment or amount of which is contingent upon the securing of a divorce or upon the amount of alimony or support, or property settlement in lieu thereof" (**Model Rule 1.5(d)(1)**), or "a contingent fee for representing a defendant in a criminal case" (**Model Rule 1.5(d)(2)**).

REASON FOR THE RULE ▶ These constraints are difficult to justify. The traditional prohibition on a fee contingent on securing a divorce was adopted at a time when a divorce was difficult to obtain, and there were strong public policies in the Anglo-American legal system favoring marriage and disfavoring divorce.[9] The Rule makes no sense in an age in which no-fault divorce is freely and nearly universally available, but the fee constraint persists. As for the prohibition on a fee contingent on the amount of alimony or support awarded, it too was originally adopted as a means of limiting incentives to "break up families" or "paint a false picture" of the family's finances because it would not reflect the lawyer's contingent-fee interest.[10] Realistically, however, when the parties are determining alimony or child support, the family is *already* broken up, and the lawyers are simply helping the court and the parties figure out how to divide the formerly unified marital economic unit to meet the practical realities already established. The lawyers in this context get paid one way or another, and everyone knows it.

There is also gender politics hidden here: In adversary proceedings of this kind, it is typically the spouse *not* in need of alimony or child support (that is, the principal breadwinner, historically the husband in a heterosexual couple) who can afford more expensive advocates and pay for more of their time, so limiting the ways in which the non-breadwinner spouse can pay counsel just increases the disparity in power and resources. Given that the non-breadwinner spouse (again, historically the wife in a heterosexual couple) often receives significantly more custody time with any children and typically needs to seek child support, the children often suffer as well.

---

[9] *See, e.g., McCarthy v. Santangelo*, 137 Conn. 410, 412 (1951) ("The state does not favor divorces"); *In re Fisher*, 15 Ill. 2d 139, 152-55 (1958) (affirming discipline for an attorney for a contingent fee based on collecting back alimony: "[M]ost courts have based their holdings upon the premise that assignments of alimony tend to deter or prevent reconciliation between husband [and] wife"; citing cases). RESTATEMENT (FIRST) OF CONTRACTS § 542 (1933).

[10] *See, e.g., McCarthy, supra* note 9, 137 Conn. at 412 ("The vice of an agreement like that into which the plaintiff entered lies in the strong inducement which it offers to an attorney to ignore the possibility of reconciliation and to press, for personal gain, the dissolution of a marriage which patience and effort might salvage"); *In re Cooper*, 81 N.C. App. 27, 344 S.E.2d 27 (1986) (contingency arrangement in support case might paint a false financial picture to the court because the money intended for support might end up in the attorney's pocket).

The ban on contingent fees in criminal matters is equally difficult to justify. Apparently, it arose out of a concern that private criminal defense lawyers might bend the rules of advocacy to achieve acquittals in pursuit of a higher fee.[11] Yet we already freely allow contingent fees in civil matters, permitting lawyers to collect a greater fee when they achieve a better result, without (or at least suppressing) any concern that this fee structure might induce improper advocacy. Needless to say, however, though these Rules may seem irrational or anachronistic, they remain the law and continue to bear serious **consequences** if violated. ❰REASON FOR THE RULE❱

In addition, many states and the federal system have statutory limits on the fees that may be charged for certain kinds of work. Common examples include workers' compensation benefits, contingent-fee arrangements for certain kinds of claims (most commonly, medical malpractice claims), and many kinds of government benefits and court-supervised matters, such as Social Security claims, claims by military employees against the government, probate and guardianship matters, and representation of indigents in criminal proceedings. If you're new to an area of practice, you should check to see whether any such limits apply in the state in which you practice to be sure you don't charge an illegal fee.[12]

> **Problem 20C-1:** Maya's firm charges a flat fee of $750 to handle a simple residential real estate closing, which takes approximately two hours of lawyer time and another two hours of a legal assistant's time. This work could also be handled by a realtor or a title company, though some of the firm's clients prefer to have a lawyer at the closing. Her firm also has intellectual property litigators. Some of these lawyers charge $750 per hour to handle complex patent litigation disputes. **May** the firm charge some clients $750 per hour and others a rate tantamount to less than half of that? Why or why not?

> **Problem 20C-2:** Frank's firm does construction-dispute work and has represented mostly contractors and subcontractors. The firm charges those clients $250 per hour for partners' time and $150 per hour for associates' time. Recently, the firm was approached by an architect seeking representation in a number of construction disputes. If the firm represents the architect, the firm will likely have **conflicts of interest** preventing it from handling a significant number of future cases on behalf of contractors and subcontractors. In light of this reality, if the firm decides to take this engagement, **may** the firm charge the architect hourly rates higher than the rates that it charges contractors and subcontractors? Is this true even if the

---

[11] *See, e.g., Peyton v. Margiotti*, 398 Pa. 86, 90 (1959) ("In criminal cases the rule [limiting contingent fees] is stricter because of the danger of corrupting justice"); RESTATEMENT (FIRST) OF CONTRACTS § 542 (1933).

[12] Fees set or limited by self-regulating state bars exercising delegated government power have been struck down as anticompetitive. *Goldfarb v. Virginia State Bar*, 4 U.S. 773 (1975) (minimum fees for common tasks performed by private lawyers struck down under antitrust law). When fees are set or limited by duly-enacted state or federal statutes, they are protected from antitrust scrutiny by the "state action" doctrine and are generally considered enforceable. *See* **Chapter 18.A at 475 n.6.**

type of case is similar to the cases in which the firm represents contractors and subcontractors and would involve a similar amount of work? Please explain your answers.

Problem 20C-3: The family law partner in Frank's firm, Sally Splitsville, has a new client who is the wife in a wealthy divorcing couple. The case promises to be interesting and challenging, with lots of issues about how the parties' substantial amount of property is to be characterized and divided. Sally is proposing to offer the wife a fee of 10 percent of the wife's ultimate share of the property division, exclusive of any amounts awarded as alimony or child support. **May** she do so? Why or why not?

Problem 20C-4: In your area, lawyers handle simpler divorce cases for a flat rate between $1,000 and $5,000. A prospective client approaches you, asking you to handle his straightforward divorce. You have minimal experience in family law and would prefer not to take the case, as you will have to do a lot of studying up to get familiar with the governing law and procedure, but instead of declining the representation entirely, you offer to handle the case for $10,000. **May** you do this? Why or why not? (*Hint: See* **Chapter 7.A at 174 n.4.**)

Problem 20C-5: Maya's firm has a deal with the major computerized legal research platforms (Lexis and Westlaw) for unlimited use of their services in exchange for a monthly flat fee. Because Maya's firm has many lawyers in multiple offices, this monthly amount is quite substantial. (This is a deal that these services offer all private law firms, with the flat fee negotiated based on their size and their typical use profile.) To recoup what the firm pays Lexis and Westlaw, the firm charges clients $100 per hour of computerized legal research in addition to the timekeeper's hourly rate while conducting the research. The firm set this rate to approximate between 100 percent and 120 percent of the firm's flat-rate payment to the services in any given month, depending on overall client need for computerized research at the firm that month. Is that OK? Is there anything that the firm **must** or **should** do in addition to listing the amount charged to each client for "computerized legal research" on its monthly bills? Please explain your answers. (*Hint: See* **Model Rule 1.5 Comment [1].**)

Problem 20C-6: You are not licensed to practice law in New York. You are licensed to practice in New Jersey. Lawyers in New York charge in excess of $500 per hour to do the kind of work you do. **May** you offer your services in New York for a highly discounted rate of $300 per hour? Why or why not?

Problem 20C-7: The intellectual property litigators in Maya's firm are approached by a **prospective** start-up **client** whose entire business rests upon proving that its medical device patent is valid in litigation with an alleged infringer. If the client loses the case, the business will fold. The firm's intellectual-property litigators do some patent litigation on a contingent-fee basis and usually charge 30 percent of any recovery after recouping expenses. In this case, they propose to charge 40 percent of any recovery after recouping expenses, plus a $100,000 bonus if the patent is found valid. **May** they do so? Why or why not?

Problem 20C-8: A **prospective client** approaches Maya's practice group with an acquisition that, for legitimate business reasons, needs to be completed much more quickly than the typical transaction of this kind. Maya's team will have to work very long hours, including nights and weekends, for two weeks straight in order to get the job done, all while juggling their other pending matters. The partners are considering asking for a premium over the firm's usual hourly rate for this engagement. **May** they do so? Why or why not?

Problem 20C-9: Over the past decade, Maya's firm has handled 40 small acquisitions for Hugeola-Cola Company, a giant international corporation that makes the most popular soft drink in the world. On the most recent acquisition, the firm is charging $100 per hour more than other lawyers of comparable skill and experience in the same market would charge. Is this OK? Does the fact that the firm has a long-standing relationship with the client matter when assessing the rates' reasonableness? Should it? Does it matter whether the client has ever complained? Does it matter whether the client knows what other firms charge? Does it matter that the client has in-house counsel, and that those company lawyers are comfortable with the rate being charged? Please explain your answers.

Problem 20C-10: In a drug case on which Danielle is working, investigation is suggesting that the alleged drug dealer used some of his profits to buy several very fancy automobiles. Danielle and her boss initiate forfeiture proceedings on the cars. (Most jurisdictions by statute allow the state to "forfeit"—that is, take and sell or use for its own purposes—any property that the defendant acquired with the fruits of his crime.)

Yakety Yaxon, a criminal defense lawyer in town, is approached by the defendant with an offer for Yakety to defend the forfeiture proceedings in exchange for 25 percent of the appraised values of any cars that he saves from being forfeited. The defendant insists that he bought all the cars with money earned from the auto-body shop that he owns. Another lawyer will be defending the drug charges. **May** Yakety enter into this fee arrangement? Why or why not?

Problem 20C-11: Frank's firm has two billing structures that it offers clients for non-catastrophic slip-and-fall claims—either a $200 "blended" hourly rate (that is, the same hourly rate for any lawyer in the firm) or a 33 percent contingent fee. Frank's firm knows from experience that, though any particular case can vary, on average, such cases take approximately 50 hours of lawyer time and settle (or go to judgment) for about $40,000.

a. Is it permissible for the firm to charge the 33 percent contingency to some clients? Does it matter that cases taken on contingency are likely to net the firm significantly more in fees than if the same matter had been billed hourly? Please explain your answers.

b. Assume that a client elects the hourly structure. This particular case is aggressively defended by the property owner's insurance company, and Frank's firm must take the case to trial. The firm spends 100 hours on the case and charges the client $20,000. Unfortunately, the client loses and is awarded nothing at trial. **May** the client now challenge that $20,000 fee bill? Is the client entitled to a refund in whole or part? Why or why not?

c. Assume that the client in (b) instead elects the contingent-fee structure. Unexpectedly, the property owner's insurer offers $50,000 to settle the case before Frank's firm has even made its involvement known to the property owner or prepared a complaint. The client is thrilled and accepts the $50,000 offer. The client then balks at paying the firm 33 percent of the settlement, reasoning that the firm did nothing to earn its fee. How strong is the client's position? Why?

Problem 20C-12: Simon Sore, a potential client, approaches Frank's firm, seeking representation in a minor car accident. The accident was little more than a fender-bender, but Simon did suffer whiplash. (Whiplash is damage to the soft tissue in someone's neck or upper back, resulting from the sudden head movements that can be forced by automobile collisions. It is quite real, can be extremely painful, and can last a long time, or it can be modest and resolve itself quickly. Its existence and severity are notoriously difficult to diagnose.) Simon's medical bills (for imaging, diagnosis, tests, drugs, and physical therapy) are $5,000. His car suffered only minor damage. At the time of the accident, Simon was unemployed, so he has no claim for lost wages. His pain and suffering was modest, and he recovered quickly.

Simon has $10,000 worth of "personal injury protection" on his automobile insurance. All that Frank's firm has to do is present a claim that Simon was injured in his car to Simon's insurance company, and it will pay up to $10,000. Insurers usually will not dispute medical bills, and they typically agree to pay roughly an additional one-third of any medical bills to compensate for pain and suffering. The firm generally handles automobile accident cases pursuant to a 33 percent contingent-fee agreement with the client. Can the firm charge Simon 33 percent of what the firm knows will be a quick, easy, painless (so to speak), open-and-shut case? Please explain your answer.

D. CONSEQUENCES Consequences for Violating Formal or Substantive Requirements Regarding Fees or Expenses

Violation of any of the Model Rules regarding necessary terms, documentation, or the substantive terms of fees or expenses can result in professional discipline. Charging a client for services that were not provided or expenses that were not incurred also can be charged criminally, typically as fraud or theft (larceny by false pretenses). In the federal system, these offenses can be charged as mail or wire fraud if the offending bill was transmitted by mail or wire.

The civil **consequences** are a bit more variable. If you charge or collect a fee that is substantively prohibited, you have made a contract that is voidable as against public policy. The result is that the client has a defense against collection of the fee, and if the fee has already been collected, it's subject to disgorgement under principles of unjust enrichment. Similarly, the civil **consequence** of a failure to comply with formal requirements (for example, by failing to properly document terms that are required to be memorialized **in a writing signed by the client**) is usually that the agreed fee may not be enforced (or, if it's already paid, is subject to disgorgement). These are strong practical reasons to follow the Rules.

Your House; Your Rules ▸ Where state law varies is whether a lawyer who violates these requirements is allowed to recover anything at all. Some states may prevent a lawyer from collecting anything, most commonly for having charged or collected a substantively prohibited fee. Many states, especially in the case of a lawyer's failure to follow formal requirements, allow lawyers to recover the reasonable value of their work (*quantum meruit*) in lieu of the agreed contractual fee.

Determining the reasonable value of the services may strike you as an odd question—other than in cases in which a tribunal has found a fee unreasonable, the fee to which the lawyer and client agreed is likely what they thought was the reasonable value of the services. We can generalize by saying that, in these circumstances, the reasonable value of the services is typically found to be significantly less than the agreed-to amount. Usually, contingent fees are eliminated, and the court uses a "lodestar" method based on a "reasonable" rate (often lower than any contractually agreed rate) times a "reasonable" number of hours. Both tend to be less than the lawyer might otherwise have received. Either way, violators almost always find themselves worse off than if they had complied with the rules and had been allowed to collect their contractually agreed-upon fee.

◂ Your House; Your Rules Consequences

> **Problem 20D-1:** Maya's firm will be representing an individual who, though he has not had significant resources up until now, just inherited a significant minority block of stock in a publicly traded company. He wants to turn the inheritance into cash in an orderly way. This will require a lot of legal work, as the shares are currently unregistered, and there may be shareholder agreements that limit his range of action. Maya's firm offers to represent him for 10 percent of the value of his shares, to be paid upon the shares' sale or exchange.
>
> a. Maya and one of the firm's securities partners, Celia Deal, meet with the potential client, and they describe the kinds of work that the firm will likely need to do, as well as this proposed fee arrangement. The prospective client is glad to be able to defer payment for the work until he has the money to pay for it, and he agrees to the arrangement. Celia sends a detailed memo confirming the fee arrangement to the client later that week. Any problems? Why or why not?
>
> b. After a good deal of aggressive and creative lawyering, Maya's firm has registered the client's shares and resolved all other potential impediments to their sale. Maya and Celia meet with the client and explain that he has a green light to sell his shares. He responds, "That's great, and thanks for your hard work. But I've hired an investment advisor. She has advised me that the market for the company's stock is poor right now, and I shouldn't sell the shares yet." When Celia asks when he might be planning to sell any of the shares, he says he doesn't know and will have to see how things go. **Must** the client pay the firm now? Why or why not, and if so, how much? Does it matter whether the investment advice on

which the client claims to be relying may not exist, and that the overwhelming consensus among experts is that the company's stock is at a historic peak and likely to "plateau" there for a long time?

Problem 20D-2: Maya's firm is retained to defend a substantial securities class action. The securities litigators meet with the issuer-company's general counsel and make an impressive presentation regarding their relevant skill and experience. They also offer to defend the case for 20 percent off of the firm's regular hourly rates (plus expenses as incurred), billed monthly. When the class action is resolved, the firm will receive 5 percent of any amount that the company pays in settlement or judgment that is less than $100 million and more than $50 million, and 10 percent of any amount that the company pays in settlement or judgment that is less than $50 million. The general counsel is pleased with the arrangement and hires the firm. The lead securities partner confirms this arrangement in an email that she sends the general counsel the next week. Any problems? Why or why not?

E. Retainers and Deposits, and Their Role in Fee and Expense Arrangements

No discussion of fee and expense arrangements would be complete without a survey of what are loosely referred to as "retainers" and "deposits." These terms are not used with any precision in ordinary lawyer-speak, so we'll explain the different things that they can mean and encourage you to go out of your way to be extra clear when you are communicating with anyone on these subjects.

1. "True" Retainers

The "true" or "classic" retainer is a payment of money by a client for the specific purpose of *ensuring that a lawyer is available to perform described services when requested*. Sometimes the true retainer covers both the fee for the lawyers' holding themselves available and a flat fee for all services within the scope of the engagement requested during the term of the engagement; sometimes, the retainer covers only the fee for availability, and the client and lawyer agree that any actual services provided will be charged in addition to the true retainer, on some specified basis. For this reason, true retainers are typically paid at the outset of the engagement and are almost always considered fully earned by the lawyer when they are paid. Because all these are possible features of a true retainer arrangement, the details **should** be documented with precision.

True retainers were somewhat more common 50 or more years ago, but they are rare today. In fact, a number of states now forbid true retainers altogether or require that they be rigorously documented **in a writing signed by the client**, stating with particularity what the client is paying for and when the lawyer has earned the retainer, and requiring the lawyer to state expressly whether or not the retainer is nonrefundable.

2. Retainers as Security

Much more common today are retainers "as security" or "as deposits." These are sums of money that, by agreement, clients put on deposit with their lawyers to be used to pay *future* fees or expenses under agreed conditions. The parties can agree that the retainer will be used only like a security deposit under a lease: that is, only if the client fails or refuses to pay amounts billed when due. The parties can agree instead that the lawyers may draw on the retainer each time that fees or expenses are billed to the client in order to pay those bills. Part of such an agreement can be that the client has to replenish the retainer to its original amount as the lawyers draw down on it to pay billed fees and expenses; this arrangement is often referred to as an "evergreen" retainer. Or the parties can agree that the retainer is just a one-time deposit that does not need to be replenished and will eventually be exhausted; this arrangement is often referred to as a "wasting" retainer. Choosing whether to have a retainer as security and what its terms should be is generally a question of how confident you are that the client is willing and able to pay fees and expenses when due.[13]

The critical thing about a retainer as security is that, until the specified conditions have occurred that allow the lawyers to use those funds to pay themselves, *the retainer remains the client's money.* As we will explore in more detail in **Chapter 21.C**, you **must** keep any funds that belong to a client in your client trust account separate from your own money, and you **must** promptly take those funds out of the client trust account and transfer them to your firm when they have been earned. (Failure to do so is a common source of professional discipline, even for inadvertent errors of this kind, and you must pay excruciatingly close attention to the details that the rules in your state may impose.) Any unearned funds on deposit **must** be returned to the client promptly upon the engagement's termination or completion. *See* **Model Rule 1.16(d)**; **Chapter 9.D at 302**.

TIPS AND TACTICS ▶ Any time that you propose to have a client provide a retainer as security, you **should** be stringently precise in your fee agreement about how much the retainer as security will be, whether and when it **must** be replenished, and under what circumstances you can draw on the retainer to pay amounts that you are owed. Some states have rules that require this sort of documentation; the Model Rules do not. ◀ TIPS AND TACTICS

---

[13] TIPS AND TACTICS ▶ A retainer of some kind is often a good idea in hourly or flat-fee engagements with a new client, both to ensure that the client can afford you and so that the client can show some commitment to the engagement as you start work. Many lawyers use retainers for security in any engagement in which significant amounts of effort may be expended before a bill can be rendered. Make sure that the client understands whether a retainer for security represents your estimate as to the full extent of the fees and expenses to be incurred in the matter or is just an initial "down payment" on a larger expected expenditure, as is more often the case. Many fee disputes are grounded in clients' assertions, often sincerely, that they already paid you for all the work at the beginning through the retainer, when it was never your intention that the amount of the retainer would be anywhere near what the engagement would ultimately cost. Remember: **inquire; explain; confirm**. ◀ TIPS AND TACTICS

Problem 20E-1: A potential new client comes in to see Barney Blackacre, the real estate partner in Frank's firm. The client is a dentist who is having a dispute with her office land-lord. After an hour and a half of discussion, she has gotten the advice that she needs in order to take the next steps in addressing her issues with her landlord. She writes out a $1,000 check to the firm as she is leaving, commenting, "This should cover it if I have any follow-up questions." Barney charges $250 per hour. What should he do with the check?

Problem 20E-2: The dentist in **Problem 20E-1** can't resolve her dispute with her landlord, and litigation looks imminent. Frank's firm agrees to represent her. The engagement agreement provides that the firm will charge $150 per hour for Frank's time and $250 per hour for the litigation partner's and Barney's time. The agreement also states, "You will deposit with us a $5,000 retainer. We will draw on this retainer as fees and expenses in your matter are billed to you." The client promptly brings her deposit with the firm to $5,000. (You may assume that this takes into account any funds discussed in the previous problem.)

  a. A week into the matter, Frank has spent eight hours, and the litigation partner has spent two. How much money should the firm have on deposit in its client trust account for the dentist-client? Please explain your answer.

  b. The engagement agreement also has a provision that states, "If we anticipate that there will be an event requiring substantial amounts of fees or expenses occurring soon, we may ask you to deposit additional funds as security for those future fees or expenses in an amount equal to our reasonable estimate of the anticipated fees and expenses." A trial date has been set a month away. The litigation partner asks the dentist-client to deposit an additional $20,000 with the firm. She declines, explaining that she can't afford that. What **must**, **may**, or **should** Frank's firm do? Please explain your answer, identifying which steps are **musts**, **mays**, or **shoulds**.

  c. Same as (b), except that the firm and the client compromise on a $10,000 additional retainer, which the client has deposited. The case settles a week later. What **must**, **may**, or **should** the firm do with the $10,000 on deposit? Please explain your answer, identifying which steps are **musts**, **mays**, or **shoulds**.

F. Sharing Fees

Lawyers share the fees that they receive for their services with other people all the time. Some fee-sharing arrangements are perfectly permissible. Some are not. In this section, we'll give you a general overview of the difference.

Before we get to what kinds of fee-sharing are and are not OK, let's start by understanding what the Model Rules mean by "sharing" or "dividing" lawyers' fees. If you think about it, virtually all of the income from a fee-for-service law practice comes from client fees. Out of that income, the firm (whether it's a one-lawyer solo practice or a thousand-lawyer international behemoth) pays its bills, including compensating its lawyer and nonlawyer personnel for their work. On the face of things, then, you could say that any time a law practice pays any obligation it owes, it's "dividing" client fees that it has collected with the recipient of the payment—after all, that's where the money came from. Although there is an undeniable economic reality to that description, the Model Rules take a much narrower view of what it means to "share" or "divide" a fee. In essence, what the Model Rules call "fee-sharing" arrangements are ones in which the payment by the lawyer or law firm that earned the fee is measured by *direct reference* to fees that one or more clients paid (or the practice's profit on those fees). This is a definition with a certain amount of gray area at the margins, but it's often fairly easy to apply. The examples in **Problem 20F-1** below will help you appreciate where the line is.

Now that we have some idea what qualifies as "sharing" or "division" of fees, let's explore what kinds are permitted and what kinds are prohibited.

1. Sharing Fees with Other Lawyers

If you go into private practice, unless you become a solo practitioner, you will likely share clients' fees with other lawyers in your firm. The Rules allow this kind of sharing on any terms upon which the lawyers within the firm agree. As long as you are not **screened** from a case due to a **conflict of interest** (*see* **Chapter 22.E at XX**), you may freely share the fees earned and collected by another lawyer at your firm.

What about sharing fees with a lawyer *outside* your firm? Here there are stringent limitations. Suppose a business lawyer in town has a client who has been injured in an accident. The client asks the business lawyer for legal help. The business lawyer doesn't litigate and can't handle the injury case. He calls up "Swifty" Smith and wonders aloud what the case might be worth. Swifty offers to pay the business lawyer 10 percent of any contingent fee that he collects on the injury case if the lawyer will steer the client his way. The business lawyer agrees.

Is everybody happy? They shouldn't be. Swifty just agreed to give something of value to the business lawyer for recommending Swifty's services, a flat-out violation of **Model Rule 7.2(b)** (*see* **Chapter 18.C at 485**). The same, of course, would be true if Swifty had instead promised the business lawyer a sum certain untethered to the amount of any fees Swifty might earn on the case—it's still a classic forbidden *quid pro quo*. Hello, disciplinary committee. Plus Swifty may even be able to weasel out of his commitment to pay because he's made an illegal promise that many states would refuse to enforce.

So is it *ever* possible to share the benefits of a referral with the referral source? **Model Rule 1.5(e)** provides a very narrow exception to **Model Rule 7.2(b)**'s prohibition on *quid pro quos*. Although **Model Rule 1.5(e)** doesn't allow undifferentiated lump-sum payments for referrals, it does allow a lawyer receiving a referral from another lawyer to share the fees earned in the referred engagement under very narrow and demanding conditions, specifically:

1. The division is in proportion to the services performed by each lawyer, or each lawyer assumes joint responsibility for the representation;

2. The client agrees to the arrangement, including the share that each lawyer will receive, and the agreement is **confirmed in writing**; and

3. The total fee is reasonable.

What **Model Rule 1.5(e)** really authorizes is not *referral* fees, but rather *co-counseling* arrangements between lawyers not at the same firm, with one narrow exception. The Rule generally requires the fee-share to be proportional to the amount of work that each lawyer does on the matter. In other words, the lawyer with whom fees are shared has to *earn* those fees the old-fashioned way—by providing legal services and being compensated for those services by a portion of the fees that is proportional to the overall amount of work that the lawyer does on the matter. In addition, the fee-sharing arrangement has to be fully disclosed to the client in an agreement **confirmed in writing** *and* must not increase the overall fee that the client pays to an unreasonable level.

The only exception to the requirement that each lawyer receiving a share of the fees must provide an amount of work proportional to the fee-share is if "each lawyer assumes joint responsibility for the representation." What this phrase means is that a lawyer who is receiving a share of the fees that is greater than the proportion of the work that she agrees to do (and that she does do) on the matter must unconditionally undertake (promise) to the client to be jointly and severally liable, both financially and ethically, for anything that the *other* lawyer does wrong. **Model Rule 1.5 Comment [7]**. This undertaking obligates the lawyer to bear the **consequences** for the other lawyer's wrongdoing, irrespective of whether the promising lawyer had anything to do with the other lawyer's misconduct or even knew about it. And that undertaking has to be made directly to the client and **confirmed in writing**. That's taking a very big risk: You're basically guaranteeing that your co-counsel, over whom you will have no formal powers of oversight or control, won't do anything wrong, and you'll personally pay for it *and* accept professional discipline for it if he does. And a contractual undertaking of this kind is typically excluded from professional liability insurance coverage, so you're unlikely to get any backup there.

CONSEQUENCES▶ If you fail to meet these requirements (including the formal requirements of disclosure, client agreement, and **confirmation in writing**), what you've done is an unlawful *quid pro quo* in violation of **Model Rule 7.2**, an unlawful division of fees in violation of **Model Rule 1.5(e)**, or both. These violations both subject you to professional discipline and in many states, the fee-sharing agreement between the lawyers likely will also be unenforceable as an unlawful arrangement. ◀CONSEQUENCES

2. Sharing Fees with Nonlawyers

Sharing fees with nonlawyers is restricted even more stringently than sharing fees with other lawyers. The basic Rule is that you can't: Lawyers **must not** share fees with nonlawyers, whether they work inside or outside the lawyer's firm.

Model Rule 5.4(a). There are three very narrow exceptions (enumerated in four subparts of the Rule):

1. Payment of a share of fees to a lawyer's estate or family for a period of time as a death benefit for a deceased lawyer, or as part of the consideration for the purchase of the practice of a "deceased, disabled, or disappeared lawyer" under **Model Rule 1.17 (Model Rule 5.4(a)(1)-(2))**;
2. The inclusion of nonlawyers as beneficiaries of a **practice organization**'s "compensation or retirement plan" (**Model Rule 5.4(a)(3)**); or
3. Sharing "court-awarded legal fees with a nonprofit organization that employed, retained or recommended employment of the lawyer in the matter" (**Model Rule 5.4(a)(4)**).

In addition, the remaining parts of **Model Rule 5.4** cut off what might otherwise be alternative means of sharing legal fees with nonlawyers by forbidding any lawyer from having an ownership interest in or working for any for-profit law practice that also has nonlawyer owners, or has officers, directors, or other managers who have "the right to direct or control the professional judgment of a lawyer." Take a look at **Model Rule 5.4(b) and (d)**.

REASON FOR THE RULE The justification offered for these restrictions is that it is anathema to risk nonlawyers' influence over the independent professional judgment of practicing lawyers. **Model Rule 5.4 Comments [1]-[2].** (That's reflected and reinforced by **Model Rule 5.4(c) and (d)(3)**—can you see how?) Although this restriction is ancient, it doesn't really make much sense as anything other than guild-protection. We already trust lawyers to resist clients' requests that their lawyers act unlawfully, even though it may cost us the engagement. *See* **Model Rule 1.16(a) (1)**; **Model Rule 1.16(b)(4)**. And we already allow third parties to pay a client's fees and expenses, and we think that a rule requiring the lawyer to remain loyal to the client rather than the paying party is sufficient protection. *See* **Model Rule 1.8(f)**; **Model Rule 5.4(c)**. It's difficult to see how fee-sharing or firm co-ownership with a nonlawyer within the same firm presents greater risks. Nevertheless, it is the law almost everywhere (at least in the United States). REASON FOR THE RULE

A few jurisdictions have recently begun to relax the **practice organization** co-ownership rules to allow experimentation with alternative financing and management arrangements for legal-service providers, notably Washington, D.C., Arizona, and Utah (as well as Australia and England). Whether these experiments will prove successful in improving lawyers' lives or clients' access to justice remains to be seen.

Problem 20F-1: Which of these qualifies as a "sharing" or "division" of fees within the meaning of **Model Rule 1.5(e)** or **Model Rule 5.4(a)**? Please explain your answers.

a. Frank's firm uses the money that it just collected from a client in fees to make its monthly payment to the bank on the firm's loan to construct the improvements in its office space.

b. Frank's firm pays Frank a bonus at the end of the year that is bigger than the bonus he got last year because the firm had a better year this year than last year. Does it matter if the firm did 10 percent better and decided to pay Frank a 10 percent bigger bonus?

c. Frank's firm collects a substantial contingency fee in a successful client matter. The four partners in the firm cause the firm to pay each of them 25 percent of the fee.

d. Frank brings a new personal-injury case to the firm. As a reward for his entrepreneurial success, the firm promises him a special bonus of 10 percent of any contingency fee that the firm ultimately collects on the matter.

e. The legal assistant in Frank's firm brings to the firm a personal-injury case involving her next-door neighbor. As a reward for her entrepreneurial success, the firm promises her a special bonus of 10 percent of any contingency fee that the firm ultimately collects on the matter. Does your analysis change if the firm gives the legal assistant a special bonus of $5,000 instead? What if $5,000 is 10 percent of the fees the firm collects in the case?

f. Frank's firm establishes a tax-advantaged profit-sharing plan. The firm commits to pay a fixed percentage of its profits at the end of each year into the profit-sharing plan. Every employee at the firm who has been at the firm for at least one year will receive a share of those profits credited to an account in the plan that the employee is entitled to receive upon retirement or upon leaving the firm.

g. In the **Introduction to this chapter**, Willie Willmaker pays $1,000 to the lawyer who referred him the Hands' estate-planning engagement.

Problem 20F-2: Which of the arrangements described in **Problem 20F-1** is permissible? Why or why not?

Problem 20F-3: Frick and Frack were partners in a two-person law firm. They worked cases together and evenly split the fees they collected. Now they have each decided to go out on their own. They've split up their pending contingent-fee cases. They've also agreed that they will split the contingency fees from the contingent-fee cases by paying two-thirds to the ex-partner who finishes the case and one-third to the ex-partner who ceases work on it. (Reality check: Partnership breakups are rarely this easy or straightforward, but let's pretend that this one was.) **May** Frick and Frack make this agreement? Why or why not? Please explain your answer. (*Hint: See* **Model Rule 1.5 Comment [8]**.)

Problem 20F-4: Darnell's Delight is a company that owns three popular community grocery stores. Darnell's has run into some trouble with a watchdog group that has filed litigation challenging the stores' labeling of foods that they prepare, package, and sell from their deli counters. Darnell's has relied for its legal services since its founding on a solo practitioner who is a business and commercial lawyer. That solo practitioner contacts Frank's firm and offers to refer the defense of the labeling litigation to the firm. Normally, lawyers in this jurisdiction would charge $150 for less experienced lawyers and $250 per hour for more experienced lawyers to defend a case like this. Frank's firm charges these rates.

a. The solo practitioner says that he wants to work on the case, too, and that he'll charge the rate that he usually charges Darnell's ($350 per hour) to do so. The solo, who is a good business lawyer, has no expertise in litigation or food-labeling regulation, but he says that he will read all the pleadings and discovery and consult on strategy and tactics. He says he expects to be able to accomplish that in 20 to 30 hours per week. **May** Frank's firm agree to this arrangement? **Should** they? Why or why not?

b. Instead of (a), the solo practitioner says that he's too busy to work on the case and that it's not the type of work that he does, anyway. Instead, he just wants to refer the case to Frank's firm and then be kept apprised of developments without working on the case. In exchange for the referral, the solo practitioner wants a 10 percent finder's fee, taken off all fees billed and collected by Frank's firm. **May** Frank's firm agree to this arrangement? **Should** they? Why or why not?

c. Assume instead that the solo practitioner is an experienced trial lawyer, but as a solo, he doesn't have the personnel or facilities to handle the document-heavy discovery that this case will likely involve. He agrees with Frank's firm that the firm can handle all the pre-trial motions and discovery work, and bill Darnell's at the firm's regular rates. The solo practitioner will then take over the case for trial. The solo will try the case to verdict and bill Darnell's for his work during that phase of the case at his ordinary hourly rates. Frank's firm will handle any post-trial motions. **May** Frank's firm agree to this arrangement? **Should** they? Why or why not? Is there anything else that Frank's firm **must** or **should** do with respect to the fee arrangement?

Big-Picture Takeaways from Chapter 20

1. "Fees" are direct charges for the professional services that a lawyer provides. "Expenses" or "costs" are interchangeable terms for out-of-pocket amounts for additional goods and services necessary to provide the professional services specific to a particular client. *See* **Chapter 20.A**.

2. Usually as part of the initial engagement agreement, the lawyer (or law firm) and client agree what fee structure they will use and also elaborate on the details of that particular structure in the matter. **Model Rules 1.5(b) and (c)** provide various formal and mechanical requirements for agreements about fees, such as which terms **must** or **should** be stated in writing. *See* **Chapter 20.B**.

3. **Model Rule 1.5(b)** provides that the understanding between the client and the lawyer concerning the scope of the engagement and the lawyer's fees and expenses **must** be agreed to at or near the outset of the engagement and **should** be **confirmed in writing**, "except when the lawyer will charge a regularly represented client on the same basis or rate." But the best practice is to memorialize *all* of the **material** terms of the engagement **in a**

writing signed by the client at or near the beginning of the engagement. **Model Rule 1.5(b)** also requires that the client **must** be notified of any changes to the fee arrangement. The best practice is to do so in advance of implementing the change, in writing. *See* **Chapter 20.B at 539**.

4. Contingent-fee arrangements require heightened formalities. *See* **Model Rule 1.5(c)**. Any fee agreement **must** have a scope of engagement and "basis or rate of the fee and expenses for which the client will be responsible" agreed at or near the outset of the engagement, "preferably" (that is, these terms **should** be) **confirmed in writing** (**Model Rule 1.5(b)**). Any fee arrangement in which *any* portion of the arrangement is "contingent" **must** have all aspects of the contingency fee that are mentioned in **Model Rule 1.5(c)** stated **in a writing signed by the client**, and the best practice is to clearly describe *all* aspects of *any* fee arrangement **in a writing signed by the client**, whether or not any Rule of Professional Conduct literally requires it. *See* **Chapter 20.B at 541**.

5. The one limit that applies to *all* voluntary fee arrangements is that "[a] lawyer shall not make an agreement for, charge, or collect an unreasonable fee or an unreasonable amount for expenses." **Model Rule 1.5(a)**. Reasonableness is judged by a multifactor test. A lawyer has violated this Rule, and is subject to discipline, the moment that he *agrees to* or *charges* an unreasonable fee or expense, even if he never tries to collect it. *See* **Chapter 20.C at 546**.

6. Some fees are unlawful: A lawyer may not charge a contingent fee "in a domestic relations matter, the payment or amount of which is contingent upon the securing of a divorce or upon the amount of alimony or support, or property settlement in lieu thereof" (**Model Rule 1.5(d)(1)**), or "a contingent fee for representing a defendant in a criminal case" (**Model Rule 1.5(d) (2)**). In addition, many states and the federal system have statutory limits on the fees that may be charged for certain kinds of work. *See* **Chapter 20.C at 550**.

7. Violation of any of the Model Rules regarding necessary terms, documentation, or the substantive terms of fees or expenses is a basis for professional discipline. Charging a client for services that were not provided or expenses that were not incurred can also be charged criminally, typically as fraud or theft (larceny by false pretenses). In the federal system, these offenses can be charged as mail or wire fraud if the offending bill was transmitted by mail or wire. The civil **consequences** are a bit more variable. If you charge or collect a fee that is substantively prohibited, the client has a defense against collection of the fee, and if the fee has already been collected, it's subject to disgorgement (compelled repayment)

under principles of unjust enrichment. Similarly, the civil **consequence** of a failure to comply with formal requirements (for example, by failing to properly document terms that are required to be memorialized **in a writing signed by the client**), is usually that the agreed fee may not be enforced (or, if it's already paid, is subject to disgorgement). *See* **Chapter 20.D.**

8. "Retainers" or "deposits" are a part of many fee arrangements.
   a. "True" or "classic" retainers are payments by a client simply to ensure that a lawyer is available to perform services upon request. The payment may also be a flat-fee payment for the services to be performed, or services may be billed separately. "True" retainers are generally viewed as fully earned when paid. "True" retainers are heavily regulated in many states and are rare. *See* **Chapter 20.E at 556.**
   b. Retainers or deposits "as security" are funds transferred to a lawyer for use in paying *future* fees or expenses not yet incurred. The terms on which these funds may be drawn down by the lawyer are subject to agreement and **should** be documented carefully. Because they are intended to be used to pay future fees or expenses, these amounts remain the client's property until earned and **must** be treated accordingly. *See* **Chapter 20.E at 557.**

9. "Sharing" or "dividing" fees, as the Model Rules use those terms, involves paying someone an amount determined by *direct reference* to the fees that one or more clients paid (or the practice's profit on those fees). *See* **Chapter 20.F at 558.**
   a. **Sharing fees with other lawyers in the same firm:** If you go into private practice, unless you become a solo practitioner, you will likely share clients' fees with other lawyers in your firm. The Rules allow this kind of sharing on any terms upon which the lawyers within the firm agree. As long as you are not **screened** from a case due to a **conflict of interest** (*see* **Chapter 22.E at XX**), you may freely share the fees earned and collected by another lawyer at your firm. *See* **Chapter 20.F at 559.**
   b. **Sharing fees with other lawyers not in the same firm:** Model Rule 7.2(b) prohibits a lawyer from giving something of value to someone in exchange for recommending the lawyer's services. This kind of forbidden arrangement is often referred to as a *quid pro quo.* (*See* **Chapter 18.C at 485.**) Model **Rule 1.5(e)** provides a very narrow exception to **Model Rule 7.2(b)**'s prohibition on *quid pro quos.* Although **Model Rule 1.5(e)** doesn't allow undifferentiated lump-sum payments for referrals, it does allow a lawyer who is receiving a referral from another lawyer outside the referring lawyer's firm to share the fees earned in the referred engagement under very narrow and

demanding conditions, specifically: (1) the division is in proportion to the services performed by each lawyer, or each lawyer assumes joint responsibility for the representation; (2) the client agrees to the arrangement, including the share that each lawyer will receive (and the agreement is **confirmed in writing**); and (3) the total fee is reasonable. In other words, what **Model Rule 1.5(e)** really authorizes is not *referral* fees, but rather *co-counseling* arrangements between lawyers not at the same firm, with one narrow exception. The one narrow exception is that lawyers in different firms **may** share fees in the same engagement not in proportion to the relative amount of work they contribute if "each lawyer assumes joint responsibility for the representation," meaning that each agrees to be personally responsible to the client and the state bar for any misconduct committed by the other. *See* **Chapter 20.F at 559**.

c. **Sharing fees with nonlawyers:** Sharing fees with nonlawyers is restricted even more stringently than sharing fees with other lawyers. The basic rule is that you can't: Lawyers **must not** share fees with nonlawyers, whether they work inside or outside the lawyer's firm. **Model Rule 5.4(a)**. There are three very narrow exceptions (enumerated in four subparts of the Rule): (1) payment of a share of fees to a lawyer's estate or family for a period of time as a death benefit for a deceased lawyer, or as part of the consideration for the purchase of the practice of a "deceased, disabled, or disappeared lawyer" under **Model Rule 1.17** (**Model Rule 5.4(a)(1)-(2)**); (2) the inclusion of nonlawyers as beneficiaries of a **practice organization**'s "compensation or retirement plan" (**Model Rule 5.4(a)(3)**); or (3) sharing "court-awarded legal fees with a nonprofit organization that employed, retained or recommended employment of the lawyer in the matter" (**Model Rule 5.4(a)(4)**). In addition, the remaining parts of **Model Rule 5.4** cut off what might otherwise be alternative means of sharing legal fees with nonlawyers by forbidding any lawyer from having an ownership interest in or working for any for-profit law practice that also has nonlawyer owners, or has officers, directors, or other managers who have "the right to direct or control the professional judgment of a lawyer." **Model Rule 5.4(b) and (d)**. *See* **Chapter 20.F at 560**.

Multiple-Choice Review Questions for Chapter 20

1. Which of the following is *not* a litigation expense?
   a. Travel costs expended by an attorney to attend trial.
   b. Photocopying costs to duplicate exhibits to a motion for summary judgment.

    c. The payment made to a court reporter for transcribing a deposition.

    d. The hourly rate for a partner's time spent arguing a motion to dismiss.

2. Jan is the managing partner of a small personal injury firm. The firm pays $10,000 per month to rent its office space. The office space includes several attorneys' offices and one large conference room. The conference room takes up half of the total area rented by the firm.

    The firm is currently representing a new client, Kip. Kip's case presents some unique wrinkles that haven't previously arisen in other cases. As a result, the firm lawyers spend substantially more time meeting with Kip than with other firm clients. In fact, 50 percent of the time spent in the conference room is spent meeting with Kip and working on his case. How much of the monthly rent can the firm ask Kip to pay?

    a. $10,000.

    b. $5,000.

    c. $2,500.

    d. None.

3. Lupita does trust and estates work. She charges her clients $2,500 for a simple will, no matter how long it takes her to draft it. What type of fee is this?

    a. Hourly.

    b. Salary.

    c. Contingent.

    d. Flat-rate.

4. According to **Model Rule 1.5**, when **must** lawyer and client agree upon a fee?

    a. Within 48 hours after the initial client meeting.

    b. Before any work is done by the attorney.

    c. Within a reasonable period of time after commencing representation.

    d. Before the lawyer bills for work performed.

5. Under **Model Rule 1.5(b)**, if a lawyer and client agree to an hourly billing arrangement, which of these **must** be agreed upon at or near the beginning of the engagement?

    a. The scope of the engagement.

    b. How frequently the client will be billed.

    c. How long after billing payment is expected.

    d. That the lawyer's rates will not increase during the representation.

6. Which of the following is *not* an advantage of contingent fees?

    a. They provide access to the courts for those who might not otherwise have access.

    b. They often motivate the lawyer to work diligently to secure a good result for the client.

    c. They reduce the number of frivolous lawsuits.

    d. They often align the interests of lawyer and client regarding the optimal outcome of the engagement.

7. Under the plain text of **Model Rule 1.5**, a lawyer **must not** enter into a contingent-fee arrangement for what type of case?

    a. Litigation of a domestic relations case where the fee is contingent on the amount of alimony awarded.

    b. Prosecution of a criminal case where the fee is contingent on the amount of restitution that the defendant is ordered to pay.

    c. Both a and b.

    d. None of the above.

8. The Model Rules of Professional Conduct list several factors that should be used in assessing the reasonableness of a fee. Which of these is *not* one of those factors?

    a. Whether the defendant is guilty or innocent.

    b. The time and labor required.

    c. The skill necessary.

    d. How much is customarily charged for similar services in the same region.

9. The Federal Tort Claims Act limits attorneys' fees to 25 percent of any settlement or judgment in favor of the claimant. Attorney Alec uses a standard retainer agreement in personal injury cases that permits him to recover a 35 percent contingent fee. If Alec's client provides written consent, and assuming that 35 percent is generally considered a reasonable fee in personal injury cases, is Alec subject to discipline if he collects 35 percent of a judgment in his client's favor in an FCTA case?

    a. Yes, because a federal law can be the basis of professional discipline.

    b. Yes, because the Rules of Professional Conduct require that a fee be reasonable and 35 percent is an unreasonable contingency fee in this type of case.

    c. No, because laws like the FTCA can limit the amount that an attorney may charge as a fee.

    d. No, because a personal injury case may never be subject to a contingent-fee arrangement.

10. Lawyer Lorenzo has represented his client, Marnie, on four prior occasions. Marnie owns a small chain of grocery stores and is sued from time to time by customers who claim that they have slipped and fallen in one of

the stores. Each time that Lorenzo has defended Marnie in these slip-and-fall lawsuits, he has charged her $200 per hour for the representation.

One Friday at 4:55 p.m., Lorenzo receives a panicked call from Marnie. She was served with a new slip-and-fall complaint a while back but forgot about it, and the answer is due on the following Monday. She begs Lorenzo to represent her. He agrees but explains that his hourly rate will be $300 per hour to prepare a response to the complaint.

Is that rate unreasonable?

a. Yes, because Marnie and Lorenzo have an existing relationship, and Lorenzo is exploiting Marnie's desperation in order to extract a higher rate than he previously charged.

b. Maybe, depending on how much time has passed since the last time that Lorenzo represented Marnie.

c. Maybe, depending on the merits of Marnie's case and how much she stands to lose if she does not prevail.

d. No, because the reasonableness of a fee depends in part upon time limitations, and here Lorenzo will have to work over the weekend due to Marnie's delay.

11. Orville hires Polly to represent him as a plaintiff in an employment discrimination lawsuit. According to their agreement, Polly will advance all litigation costs. If Orville prevails, Polly is entitled to 30 percent of all front and back pay awarded. If Orville loses, Polly is entitled to no payment whatsoever.

Despite Polly's best efforts, Orville loses at trial. He refuses to reimburse Polly for the costs that she advanced. Can Polly force him to pay?

a. Yes, because even in a contingent-fee arrangement, the client is always responsible for costs.

b. Yes, because a lawyer is entitled to reimbursement of the advanced expenses under a theory of *quantum meruit*.

c. No, because the agreement did not say that Polly could recover the litigation costs that she advanced even if Orville lost.

d. No, because a lawyer may not advance litigation costs on behalf of a client.

12. Quinn is an experienced immigration attorney. She knows that a typical mandamus case requires about 40 hours of work. She is approached by a potential client, Rose, who asks to retain her. After interviewing Rose, Quinn anticipates that Rose's case will take the usual 40 hours. Quinn advises Rose that her hourly rate is $250 per hour, so she anticipates that the representation will cost Rose around $10,000. Rose tells Quinn that she can only afford to pay $3,000. Quinn tells Rose that she could file a

complaint for Rose for that amount. As Quinn truthfully explains, sometimes the government resolves the case immediately once a complaint is filed. If that happens, there will be no additional work necessary.

Rose agrees to retain Quinn. Quinn files a complaint. Unfortunately, the government aggressively litigates the case by filing a motion to dismiss the complaint. Rather than file an opposition to the government's motion, Quinn files a motion to withdraw and tells Rose that she must find a new attorney.

Could Quinn be subject to discipline?

a. Yes, because Quinn could not withdraw until after she filed an opposition.

b. Yes, because Quinn understood that Rose's matter would likely require additional work beyond a complaint and did not properly explain this to Rose.

c. No, because Rose understood that Quinn was agreeing to limit her representation.

d. No, because Quinn did $3,000 worth of work, and that is all the work for which Rose paid.

13. Sullivan contacts Tracey and asks her to represent him in a patent dispute. Although Tracey is a lawyer, she has no experience in that type of case. She refers Sullivan to another lawyer in town, Umar. Umar is an experienced intellectual property attorney who agrees to take the case. He litigates the case to a positive outcome for Sullivan.

The work is profitable for Umar. As a thank-you gift to Tracey, who had no involvement in the case, Umar sends her a $100 gift card. Sullivan does not object. In fact, he signs the greeting card enclosing the gift card.

Has Umar violated the Rules of Professional Conduct?

a. Yes, because this constitutes an improper *quid pro quo*.

b. Yes, because this is a fee division not permitted by **Model Rule 1.5(e)**.

c. No, because the client agreed in writing.

d. No, because this is a nominal thank-you gift permitted by **Model Rule 7.2**.

14. Victor works for a large law firm that employs Wendy, a nonlawyer, as its head of information technology. Victor has a contingent-fee case scheduled for trial that is worth millions of dollars. He relies heavily on Wendy to scan documents into trial presentation software so he can present them at trial. She works around the clock. Thanks in no small part to her efforts, the trial goes flawlessly, and Victor's client wins.

The firm collects a $500,000 contingent fee from Victor's client. From this amount, the firm pays Victor a $20,000 bonus. Victor asks that a portion of his bonus instead be paid to Wendy in appreciation for her help. Can the firm do so?

a. Yes, but only in proportion to the amount of work that Wendy performed.

b. Yes, because this is not a division of fees under the Model Rules.

c. No, because Wendy is a nonlawyer.

d. No, because the client did not consent.

21

Safeguarding, Segregating, and Accounting for Others' Funds and Property

Maya is back in Ron Rainmaker's office. The corporate acquisition on which they were working in the **Introduction to Chapter 10 at 321** has been documented and will be closing at the end of next week. The firm's client (a big company that is buying a smaller company's stock for cash) has provided the purchase amount to Ron's and Maya's law firm so that the firm will have the funds on hand when the deal is ready to close. The firm has deposited those funds in the firm's trust account (something about which you'll be fully informed by the time you finish this chapter) until the closing. The fee deal that the firm made with its client on this transaction included a bonus for the firm if the deal closed within a certain time and under a certain price per share, which happily will have happened when the deal closes as scheduled. The bonus is $50,000 in additional fees, and the client has sent that payment to the law firm in addition to the agreed purchase price.

"You know Lucy in accounting?" Ron asks. "Sure," Maya replies. Lucy is one of two or three accounting staff who handle disbursements from the firm's bank accounts. "Go see her. We need to get her to set up a wire transfer for the purchase price from the client's funds in our trust account on the closing date next week. No transfer until we close, of course. We'll tell her when to let it go on the closing day." "Got it," Maya replies. She's seen this before; it's a common way to transfer funds when a deal closes. She gets up to go.

"Oh, and one other thing," Ron adds. "When you talk to Lucy, have her take the $50,000 bonus in the trust account and pay it over to the firm." "At the closing?" Maya asks. She's familiar with the fee deal and proud of her role in bringing the performance bonus to the firm. "No, now," Ron replies.

"But we haven't closed yet," Maya points out. "Well," says Ron, "I don't see anything out there with any chance of interfering. I feel confident that we're going to close on schedule next week, don't you?" "Um, yeah," Maya responds, "but. . . ."

"Look," Ron interrupts, "the end of this week is the deadline for collections that determine this quarter's partner bonuses. I want that fee bonus in my column." Now Maya understands. "OK, but what happens if, y'know, lightning strikes, and something unexpected delays or prevents the closing?" she asks. "It won't, but even if it did, that's easy," says Ron. "The firm just puts the bonus amount back into the firm's trust account, credited to the client. Our revenues are over $600 million annually; we've obviously got the money. No harm; no foul." He grins.

Maya smiles back as she leaves Ron's office, but she remains uncomfortable. No one else at her firm has asked her to do something like this before. On the other hand, she's only been practicing for a year and a half, and there's a lot that she doesn't know. Still, this seems odd. How is Lucy in accounting going to react to this request? And even if Lucy just follows directions, is this really okay?

*　*　*

As we discussed in **Chapter 6.A at 133**, the essence of being an agent for your client is that you are entrusted to take care of your clients' affairs within the scope of your engagement. Quite frequently, that involves taking care of your clients' money or property as well as their legal rights and duties. Your clients may entrust important documents to you, such as an original will, trust, deed, or contract. Your clients may entrust you with physical evidence important to a dispute, or valuable property pertinent to your engagement. And frequently you will find yourself in possession of money that belongs not to you, but to your client or to a third party, or whose ownership is disputed.

There are very strict and uncompromising rules about what you as a lawyer **must**, **must not**, and **may** do with money or property that is not your own. The **consequences** for violation of these rules, even for what may seem like minor or technical violations regarding matters of form rather than substance, can be (and often are) quite severe. This is an area in which scrutiny is uncompromising, square corners are essential, and "substantial compliance" is hardly ever sufficient. So stick with us—this is a realm of practice management in which the details really, really matter.

A. Background: The Lawyer's Three Basic Duties with Other People's Money and Property, and the Tools That We Use to Comply with Them

1. The Lawyer's Three Basic Duties with Other People's Money and Property

Model Rule 1.15 sets forth many of the ethical duties you must fulfill when you are entrusted with someone else's money or other property. As we're about to see, **Model Rule 1.15,** and the corresponding civil fiduciary duties to which lawyers are held, articulate three primary duties: the **duty to safeguard**, the **duty to segregate**, and the **duty to account**.

Before we delve into the details, we pause to emphasize that the **duty to segregate** and the **duty to account** are *nondelegable*. This is a massively important principle. As a practical matter, what it means is that the ultimate responsibility for complying with both duties remains with the lawyer, no matter what. Although lawyers are permitted to (and regularly do) authorize nonlawyer employees or independent contractors to assist them in complying with these duties, the lawyers retain both disciplinary and financial responsibility if anything goes wrong for any reason, no matter how skilled or trustworthy the delegee may appear. Similarly, a lawyer cannot escape discipline or liability by blaming delegee employees or contractors when something goes wrong, even when it's obviously and fully the delegee's fault. Nor will the lawyer be excused by any showing that relying on the delegee employees or contractors was reasonable, or that the delegee's error or dishonesty was not foreseeable. In other words, when it comes to segregating and accounting for other people's money and property, the buck always stops with you. Always. No exceptions.

REAL WORLD This principle doesn't mean that you personally have to do everything relating to other people's money or property yourself; many lawyers and law firms employ the assistance of skilled and reliable nonlawyer staff in safeguarding others' property and managing funds held in trust. But the nondelegability of these duties does require you to use exceptional caution and diligent oversight when you rely on others to help you. So delegate; don't abdicate. And trust, but verify. REAL WORLD

Now that we know how powerful and inescapable these duties are, you may be wondering how they relate to the duties generally arising out of your status as a lawyer. The answer is that they are a component of your fiduciary duties. As a fiduciary, you have special responsibilities to take care of your clients' (and others') money or property within your oversight or care. This special responsibility means not only treating others' money or property at least as carefully as you would your own, but often it requires taking *additional* steps to safeguard and keep track of others' property—steps that you might not bother to take with your own money or property. **Model Rule 1.15** sets forth several essential requirements for how you handle others' property, and a great many states have additional detailed regulations regarding how you **must** keep track of the money or property that you handle. These requirements are all intended to reduce any risk that you (or someone else provided access) will take or misplace others' money or property in your care, whether deliberately or inadvertently.

2. Tools for Compliance: The Two Kinds of Bank Accounts That Lawyers Maintain

Tangible property is usually relatively easy to keep track of—you put it in a labeled container; you put the container somewhere very safe (such as a safe or a safe-deposit box—the repetition of "safe" in the names of those places is no accident); and absent pathological circumstances (such as the kind of ingenious and not reasonably preventable heists that happen mostly in the movies), it's still there in the condition in which you left it when you go back to retrieve it. Even things that look similar to one another—for example, suppose both you and your client collect antique English marbles—can be separated, labeled, and kept in a place that is secure from most predation and disaster, most of the time, without too much advanced engineering.

Money, however, is different. Other than when money is embodied in bills and coins, it is an intangible obligation rather than a physical thing. When you deposit different sums of money into a single bank account, you can't point to some pile of bills in a pigeonhole at the bank that represents those deposits. Hence the metaphor of money as "liquid"—it all gets indissolubly mixed up when different sums get deposited in the same place. And because we lawyers deal with other people's money more commonly than any other form of property, we have all kinds of tools, and all kinds of rules, for separating and keeping track of other people's money.

One of the main tools we use for these purposes—and it's a focus of the relevant ethical rules—is that we are required to use different kinds of bank accounts for different kinds of money. The two basic categories of bank accounts that lawyers and **practice organizations** maintain are "trust accounts" and "operating" or "office" accounts.

Both are bank deposit accounts, and each **may** be a checking or an ordinary deposit account (what might be colloquially referred to as a "savings" account). One **practice organization** can have as many of each as it feels that it needs, so long as it has at least one trust account.

The basic distinction between trust accounts and operating accounts is that (with only a few minor and short-term exceptions discussed below) trust accounts **must** hold *only* money belonging to people and organizations other than the **practice organization**; operating accounts **must** hold *only* money belonging to the **practice organization**.

As we'll also see, trust accounts are subject to a bevy of technical requirements that vary from state to state, but often include requirements that such accounts be maintained at only state-bar-approved financial institutions located within the state. *See* **Chapter 21.A at 578 & n.3**. In addition, many states require that financial institutions notify the state bar if a lawyer's trust account is ever overdrawn. This requirement helps the disciplinary authority in its oversight of lawyers' safekeeping of others' property, because there is *never* a proper reason for a trust account to be overdrawn. After all, it's supposed to hold only other people's money, and if a lawyer tries to draw on money that isn't there (which is what an overdraft is), then somebody else's money has either been taken, misplaced, or wrongly accounted for, and the disciplinary authority ought to (and always does) step in and investigate. Finally, many states require that interest earned on most or all lawyers' trust accounts be paid by the bank directly to the state bar to support legal services for the indigent and other public goals. *See* **Chapter 21.C at 581**. Rules also require that lawyers keep excruciatingly detailed records of whose money goes in and out of the trust account and for what purposes; some states have detailed rules dictating precisely how those accounting records must be set up and maintained. *See* **Chapter 21.D at 587**.

Operating accounts, by contrast, are subject to far fewer restrictions and are used by the **practice organization** maintaining them to hold the **practice organization's** own money and to pay the **practice organization's** own operating expenses, such as its personnel's wages, salaries, and partnership draws; its rent; its purchases of equipment and services for its own use; and so on.[1]

Now let's look at each primary duty in turn.

B. The Duty to Safeguard

Model Rule 1.15 is entitled "Safekeeping Property." It would be fair to say that the **duties to segregate** and **account** for others' money and property are aspects of the **duty to safeguard**. Simply put, the **duty to safeguard** means that you're responsible for keeping others' money and property safe and secure when it is in your care. **Model Rule 1.15 Comment [1]** explains that "[a] lawyer should hold property of others with the care required of a professional fiduciary." What that requires varies according to the kind of property and the surrounding circumstances, but it implies an obligation to be more than ordinarily careful. Many attorneys use bank safe-deposit boxes for others' important or valuable documents or tangible property; many maintain a fireproof safe in their offices.[2]

Clients' and third parties' funds must be kept in a trust account in a bank. **Model Rule 1.15 Comment [1]**. Many states specifically require the bank to be one that the state bar or state supreme court has approved for this purpose (though

---

[1] YOUR HOUSE; YOUR RULES Some states require lawyers to maintain a third category of deposit account, often referred to as a "fiduciary account," if the lawyer undertakes certain specialized duties. Specifically, these fiduciary accounts are for the purpose of holding money belonging to others as to whom the lawyer acts as a non-attorney fiduciary, such as a trustee or conservator. Other states allow attorneys serving in these special roles to use their trust accounts for these purposes, if they wish. The Model Rules suggest that you **should** maintain separate trust accounts for such purposes, but they do not require it. *See* **Model Rule 1.15 Comment [1]**. TIPS AND TACTICS If you're asked to undertake such duties (even when you do so without charge for friends or family), you should take care to understand what your state bar requires of you in terms of segregating and accounting for the money and property you handle in those nonlawyer capacities. And maintaining separate fiduciary accounts if you act as a nonlawyer fiduciary is the better practice, even if your state does not require it. TIPS AND TACTICS   YOUR HOUSE; YOUR RULES

[2] Unlike the **duty to segregate** and the **duty to account**, most jurisdictions don't view the **duty to safeguard** as nondelegable or absolute. The duty to safeguard is based on a standard of care: "the care required of a professional fiduciary." If you meet that standard, you won't be responsible if the unforeseeable occurs. For example, if you store securities in a bank safe-deposit box, and the bank is unforeseeably blown up or robbed, you won't be held personally responsible for the loss.

Model Rule 1.15(a) says only that the bank has to be in the state in which the lawyer practices, or outside that state if the client consents).[3]

> **Problem 21B-1:** Maya is working with a client to prepare to close a deal. The client provides her with a number of things that will be needed in the closing. Using her firm's filing system, Maya has her office staff prepare special files for each of the following, which will be stored in her firm's file room, along with the other files pertinent to the deal, and many files pertaining to other clients and other matters. Has she done everything that she needs to do?
>
> a. Multiple contracts with original ink signatures pertaining to lines of business at issue in the deal.
>
> b. Original grant deeds for several parcels of the client's real property being transferred in the deal.
>
> c. Stock certificates evidencing ownership of several of the client's subsidiaries involved in the deal.
>
> d. Bearer bonds (a debt instrument that is payable to the person who possesses it, and thus is like money in terms of liquidity) issued by the client.

> **Problem 21B-2:** Your client is a bit of a conspiracy theorist and keeps her money stuffed under her mattress. Can she ask you to do the same with her retainer?

C. The Duty to Segregate

1. Generally

The **duty to segregate** requires lawyers to keep clients' and third parties' property separate from the lawyer's own property. **Model Rule 1.15(a)** lays out the basic duty to segregate. Pause right here and give it a quick read. As **Model Rule 1.15(a)** explains, in the case of tangible property, you must segregate others' property from your own with some kind of physical separation between your stuff and everybody else's, with due regard for its safekeeping. In the case of money, you must deposit other people's money in a trust account that you maintain for that purpose. **Model Rule 1.15 Comment [1].**

REASON FOR THE RULE ▶ Why have a rule requiring that lawyers keep their own money separate from other people's money with which they are entrusted? There are at

---

[3] REASON FOR THE RULE ▶ Why do many jurisdictions insist that client trust accounts be maintained by a bank within that jurisdiction? Motivations likely vary (and may include simple parochialism or a desire to favor local businesses), but states that specifically approve the financial institutions eligible to maintain lawyer trust accounts usually employ financial strength and integrity standards that are designed to protect those whose funds are on deposit in trust. It is also a legitimate concern that out-of-state bank accounts may be outside the jurisdictional reach of state law and process. By mandating that the trust account be located within the state licensing the lawyer, these jurisdictions ensure that clients within the state will have the option to prevail upon the courts of that state to seize or freeze those funds. This option gives clients (and third parties) additional protection if there is a later dispute between the lawyer and the owner of the funds regarding the money held in trust. ◀ REASON FOR THE RULE

least three good reasons. *First*, many lawyers are not particularly adept at, nor interested in, accounting. Requiring that funds be segregated reduces the chance that a lawyer accidentally spends someone else's money. *Second*, some lawyers might be more tempted to take or "borrow" others' money if it were commingled with their own. Requiring separation reduces the temptation of theft or conversion, temporarily or otherwise. And *third*, the lawyer may owe money to creditors. Requiring lawyers to keep their own funds separate from others' protects other people's money from seizure by the lawyer's creditors in the mistaken belief that the money is the lawyer's own property (even though the seizure may only be temporary). ◂ REASON FOR THE RULE

With the **duty to segregate** in mind, let's look at some problems regarding the handling of money:

Problem 21C-1: Your mother sends you a $500 check for your birthday. Your client trust account pays a higher rate of interest than your personal checking account. Can you deposit the check in your client trust account to take advantage of the superior returns? Why or why not?

Problem 21C-2: A client hands you a $3,000 retainer check—that is, a deposit against future fees and costs. You have not yet done any work on the case. Where should you deposit the check, and why? *Hint: See* **Model Rule 1.15(c)**.

Problem 21C-3: You want to make sure that you don't bounce any checks drawn on your trust account, and particularly to make sure that you don't get overdrawn because of the regular fees that the bank charges you to maintain the account, which the bank deducts from the account balance monthly. What if you keep a few thousand extra dollars of your own money in your trust account, just to be safe? *Hint: See* **Model Rule 1.15(b)**.

Problem 21C-4: You have a balance of $3,000 in your client trust account. Your state bar dues this year are $350. Can you pay your state bar dues out of your client trust account? Why or why not?

Problem 21C-5: You are litigating a case on behalf of a client. An expert witness demands to be paid in advance, before the expert has done any work. Can you pay the expert's fees out of your client trust account? Why or why not?

Problem 21C-6: Take another look at the **chapter Introduction at 573.** Are Maya's concerns well taken? Explain them briefly in terms of the principles that we've just been discussing.

2. Avoiding Commingling

"Commingling" is the word that is usually used to describe a breach of the **duty to segregate**. Commingling *what* with *what?* Commingling other people's money or property with your own. It's worth emphasizing that commingling is, in and of itself, a wrongful act that, without further action and even if corrected before anything is misappropriated or misplaced, bears serious **consequences**. In other words, you can (and will) be disciplined for commingling even if the commingling occurs temporarily, is quickly rectified without confusion or harm to anyone, and every single dollar of other people's money is still present and accounted for. Civil liability would ordinarily not be available unless some monetary loss also resulted, but the disciplinary rules are strict, uncompromising, and in no way dependent on anyone's suffering any actual loss.

TIPS & TACTICS If you are a solo practitioner, establishing your trust account in compliance with applicable ethical rules and local law should be high on your list of initial priorities before you hang out a shingle. You might consider using a different bank from the one that you intend to use for your own office or personal accounts. Although the Model Rules don't require such separation, it reduces the risk of accidentally commingling funds. You might also consider ordering trust account checks that look visually different from any other checks you use so that you don't accidentally write a check from the wrong account. Anything that you can do when setting up your accounts to ensure that you don't accidentally confuse them will decrease the odds of an ethical violation in the future. We cannot stress strongly enough that even minor and innocent mistakes are Rules violations that are regularly prosecuted and disciplined. **TIPS & TACTICS**

The problems above illustrate a number of common situations in which you need to figure out to whom particular sums of money belong, and to make sure that other people's money goes into your trust account while your own money goes somewhere else. Although the obligation to avoid commingling is nearly absolute, there are some minor and mostly time-limited exceptions. We'll run through the most common ones now.

a. Combining Different Clients' and Third Parties' Funds in a Single Trust Account Is Permitted

The commingling that the Rules prohibit is specifically *and only* the mixing of other people's money with your own. Nothing in the Rules prohibits you from combining various different clients' and third parties' funds into a single trust account, and, in fact, most lawyers do so. Though you can have as many different trust accounts as you and your clients wish, you are only legally required to have one. And that one can hold money belonging to many different people and organizations, so long as none of them is you.

b. Keeping a Small Amount of Your Own Money in Your Trust Account to Cover Anticipated Routine Banking Charges Is Permitted

One small but clear exception to the duty to segregate is stated in **Model Rule 1.15(b)**—take a look at it now. **Model Rule 1.15(b)** allows you to keep a small amount of your own money in your trust account to cover ordinary "bank service charges" for maintaining the trust account, "but only in an amount necessary for that purpose." You can keep that small amount of your own funds in your trust account indefinitely and replenish it from time to time, so long as you limit it to just that minimal amount necessary to cover the account's routine banking fees.

c. Interest on Trust Accounts

We know that other people's money **must** be kept in trust accounts. And we know that trust accounts **must** be deposit accounts at a bank (in many states, a bank specifically approved by the state bar for that purpose). Most deposit accounts at most banks earn interest. This raises the question of to whom the interest belongs. The answer may surprise you.

Most state bars raise money by appropriating Interest on Lawyer Trust Accounts ("IOLTA"). In those jurisdictions, the financial institutions that maintain trust accounts are legally required to remit the interest on those accounts to the state bar. These IOLTA funds are generally used to support legal services for indigent persons or to create a publicly administered fund to help compensate clients who have lost money or property as a result of lawyer misconduct.

Most states allow lawyers to agree with their clients that a client's funds held in trust (at least when substantial or to be held for a longer period of time) may be held in an interest-bearing trust account separate from any others that the lawyer maintains and containing only that client's funds. The interest on such a separate interest-bearing trust accounts may accrue to the benefit of the client (and is reported by the bank to the Internal Revenue Service as the client's income), rather than being paid over to the state bar by the bank. But when smaller or shorter-term funds are pooled together in a single trust account, these states typically require the interest to be remitted to the state bar. Where remittance of interest on a pooled trust account to an IOLTA fund is not required, the interest accrues to each client or third party whose funds are pooled in the account (proportionally to the amount of each one's funds), and it is the lawyer's responsibility to account for and divide the interest accordingly.[4]

d. When Ownership of Money in a Trust Account Changes, the Money Must Be Promptly Handled in Accordance with the Change in Ownership

One complication that arises quite frequently in complying with your **duty to segregate** is that the ownership of money in your possession can suddenly change. For example, as part of their fee arrangements, lawyers frequently negotiate a

---

[4] Most jurisdictions require that lawyers participate in the state's IOLTA program on these terms. Only Alaska, Kansas, Nebraska, and Virginia allow attorneys to opt out. Even in jurisdictions that make participation voluntary, **Model Rule 1.15 Comment [6]** suggests that lawyers **should** opt in.

retainer as security, meaning a deposit of the client's funds against fees and costs not yet incurred. *See* **Chapter 20.E at 557**. Because the fees have not yet been earned nor the costs yet incurred, this money still belongs to the client (or to a third party who has agreed to pay the client's fees and expenses for the engagement). Thus, these funds must be held in the lawyer's trust account until the fees are earned or the costs are actually incurred. This situation is so common that **Model Rule 1.15(c)** expressly describes it (and yes, that means you should read that part of the Rule again now).

Now let's think through what happens when you're holding a deposit against future fees in your trust account. For simplicity, let's assume that you have an engagement with your client for which you bill by the hour. You work on the case for a month and then submit a monthly bill (and let's assume that months of work are still left to do before you're finished with the matter). At some point around the time of billing—maybe when you submit the bill; maybe when the client approves it—you've earned the fees reflected on that bill. Suddenly, part of the client's funds on deposit in your trust account belongs to you. Shazam! Without having done anything wrong (in fact, as a result of having done everything right), your money is suddenly commingled with the client's in your trust account. Fear not: This is a common and expected situation, so you're not in trouble so long as you react appropriately: This particular instance of commingling is unavoidable, and your duty is simply to address it in a timely manner so that the funds are only commingled briefly. You must promptly remove the earned fees from the trust account and move them to your operating account. This doesn't mean instantaneously, of course, but it does mean reasonably quickly. Lawyers properly do this every day.

TIPS & TACTICS So how do you know when your fees are earned, and thus subject to withdrawal from the retainer on deposit in your trust account? This is a very important question, because if you don't remove funds from your trust account promptly once they belong to you, you're commingling your money with the client's, and you're subject to discipline. On the other hand, if you withdraw funds from the trust account *before* you've earned them, you're misappropriating your client's money, and that's a serious violation, too.

The answer is that the precise moment when your fees are earned (that is, due and payable) is determined by your fee contract with your client. It is very much in your interest (and your client's) to define that moment in your engagement agreement precisely. It is not uncommon in an hourly or flat-fee engagement for the engagement agreement to provide for periodic billing and to specify that the lawyer may withdraw the billed fees from any funds on deposit with the firm upon rendering (that is, transmission of) the bill. Sometimes, the client insists on approving the bill for payment before the fees are considered "earned" and subject to the lawyer's withdrawal. But our point is that, if you haven't made clear when your fees are due and payable, you risk withdrawing them from your trust account too early or too late, and as a result, you risk incurring discipline and possibly civil liability as well. TIPS & TACTICS

e. Funds That Arrive in Your Hands Pre-Commingled in a Single Instrument May Be Deposited in Your Trust Account and Then Segregated When the Funds Are Available

It's not unusual in a contingent-fee arrangement for a settlement payment or payment in satisfaction of a judgment to be remitted to the claimant's lawyer. In fact, many lawyers who regularly represent claimants in contingent-fee engagements include a provision in their engagement agreements in which the client expressly authorizes recoveries to be paid directly to the lawyer precisely so that the lawyer will not have to chase her fee; this is perfectly permissible. For example, suppose that a lawyer has represented a client on a 30 percent contingent fee with costs taken "off the top," and has finally settled the case for $100,000 after incurring $10,000 in costs. The defendant's insurance company cuts a single check to the lawyer, "as trustee" for the client, in the amount of the full $100,000. Of the $100,000 represented by that check, $37,000 belongs to the lawyer (that's $10,000 in cost reimbursements off the top, plus a fee of 30% × $90,000 = $27,000).

If the lawyer deposits the check in her operating account and then pays over the client's share to the client, the lawyer will have had client funds in her operating account, and that is strictly forbidden. (*Never* do that. You will get into very bad trouble.) The accepted way to handle this check is for the lawyer to deposit it in her trust account, wait for the check to clear, and then promptly remit the client's portion to the client, and the lawyer's fee to the lawyer's operating account.[5] Yes, this process means that the lawyer's fee (which was earned when the insurance company paid up) was temporarily commingled with the client's share of the settlement in the lawyer's trust account. By promptly removing the earned fee as soon as it is available (but not before), the lawyer is doing what lawyers regularly and properly do when a single instrument combines funds belonging to the lawyer and funds belonging to the client.

REAL WORLD You'll also note that we mentioned that the right way to handle this situation involves waiting for the check to "clear." The underlying legal basis for this practice is very important. If you haven't taken a Payment Systems course, you may not know that there is an elaborate network of rules and practices that define the process and timing by which checks, electronic funds transfers, and similar financial instruments actually cause the transfer of money from the drawer's (that is, the check-writer's or wire transferor's) bank account to the

---

[5] At the same time as the payment comes in, of course, you **must** provide prompt notice of your receipt of the check as required by **Model Rule 1.15(d)**, as well as the written accounting for the lawyer's and the client's respective portions of the funds as required by the last sentence of **Model Rule 1.5(c)**. *See* **Chapter 20.B at 544**.

payee's bank account. Often, that money pinballs through multiple intermediary institutions during this process, and if at any point the check or other payment order is "dishonored" (bounced) because of a stop order, insufficient funds, or some other problem, the bank at which the payee deposited the check is told that the check or other payment is no good. In the meantime, the payee's bank may have given the payee "provisional credit" for the check, meaning that the bank will let the payee draw on the money even though the final steps of the funds transfer are not yet completed, but the bank will take that provisional credit back ("charge back" the credit and pull the funds out of the account) if the check is dishonored.

In other words, the fact that the bank will let you withdraw the money does *not* necessarily mean that the money is definitively and irreversibly available to you. The full process can take days or, in some cases, weeks. And if you've withdrawn the money from your trust account because the bank said that you could, and then the bank learns that the check has bounced, the bank will charge those amounts back against your trust account. You will have used someone else's money in your trust account to pay your client and your fee, and you will have violated the **duty to segregate**. You will be personally responsible for the shortfall—and be subject to discipline as well.

Fraudsters have taken advantage of the check-clearing process in recent years by "retaining" a lawyer, tendering a forged or nonsufficient-funds retainer check that the lawyer deposits in her trust account, then immediately announcing that the matter has suddenly resolved and demanding their "retainer" back immediately. Because it can take days or weeks for the forged or kited check to bounce (even a forged cashier's check!), lawyers who pay the "client" back its "retainer" out of their trust accounts before the forged "retainer" check is dishonored end up violating the integrity of their trust account and financially holding the bag after the fraudster disappears with the money.[6] And they often suffer a suspension of their license to practice as well. And *that* is one bad day at the office. ⟨ Real World ⟩

---

[6] Make sure that you're clear on why this is true. Suppose you have $1,000 in various clients' money in your trust account. The fraudster gives you a bad check for $1,000 as a "retainer," drawn on an overseas bank (those take an especially long time to clear). You deposit it in your trust account, and your bank gives you $1,000 in "provisional" credit on that foreign check, so now your nominal trust account balance is $2,000—except the money isn't really there yet. Your bank has just lent you that additional $1,000 while you wait for the check to clear. (This is a service that banks offer to good customers all the time, because it almost always works out just fine—the check eventually clears, and everybody's happy.) In the meantime, the fraudster-"client" announces that its dispute has resolved and it wants its money back immediately. You write a check on your trust account to the fraudster for the $1,000—the bank has told you that it will honor the check—and the fraudster cashes it and disappears. *Then* the foreign check that the fraudster gave you originally bounces. The $1,000 sitting in the trust account is taken by the bank as it "charges back" your account for the $1,000 credit based on the check that has now bounced. The $1,000 you sent "back" to the fraudster is gone. Your trust account now has a balance of $0, but you had put other clients' funds (totaling $1,000) in there at various times in the past. You just gave the other clients' $1,000 to the fraudster. And you have entered a world of hurt. Regrettably, these fraudsters succeed with some regularity. Don't fall prey to their wiles. *See, e.g.,* Martha Neil, *Law Firm Loses Bid to Hold Banks Accountable for its $287K Loss in Cashier's Check Fraud*, http://www.abajournal.com/news/article/law_firm_loses_bid_to_hold_banks_accountable_for_its_287k_loss_in_cashiers/?utm_source=maestro&utm_medium=email&utm_campaign=weekly_

f. Disputed Funds: You Must Not Pay Out Funds Subject to Any Colorable Claim or Dispute to Yourself or Any Third Party; You May Hold Disputed Funds in Your Trust Account Until the Dispute Is Resolved

Occasionally, you may find yourself in possession of money or property whose ownership is disputed. The dispute can arise from various causes. For example, you might have settlement money that just arrived in your trust account, and a creditor of your client levies on all or part of the funds. Or a creditor of your client (such as a healthcare provider who provided needed medical services to an accident victim whom you represent) may claim a lien on some or all of the settlement funds and take the steps necessary to perfect that lien on the money in your hands. Or your trust account may hold funds that the client has deposited against future fees, and you have done legal work and submitted a bill, but the client disputes the charges, claiming that they are excessive or that they included unauthorized services (so, in this case, the dispute over who owns those funds is between the client and you). How do you address the fact that the funds are in dispute?

Model Rule 1.15(e) answers this question. Please take a close look at it now—its terms are very important, because sooner or later most lawyers find themselves in possession of disputed funds, and there are a lot of ways to mishandle the situation that may seem intuitive but that can result in terrible trouble. **Rule 1.15(e)** tells us that "[w]hen in the course of representation a lawyer is in possession of property in which two or more persons (one of whom may be the lawyer) claim interests, the property shall be kept separate by the lawyer until the dispute is resolved."

The Rule is also clear that "[t]he lawyer shall promptly distribute all portions of the property as to which the interests are not in dispute," and hold onto only the disputed portions. But as to the disputed amounts, regardless of how the lawyer feels about the merits of the dispute, "[a] lawyer should not unilaterally assume to arbitrate [or otherwise resolve] a dispute between the client and the third party. . . ." **Model Rule 1.15 Comment [4]**. Similarly, when the dispute over the trust account funds is between the client and the lawyer, "[t]he lawyer is not required to remit to the client funds that the lawyer reasonably believes represent fees owed . . . [but also] may not hold funds to coerce a client into accepting the lawyer's contention." **Model Rule 1.15 Comment [3]**.

The right way to resolve the dispute is also clear: "The disputed portion of the funds must be kept in a trust account and the lawyer should suggest means for prompt resolution of the dispute [with the client], such as arbitration."[7] *Id.* When

---

email (May 23, 2016); David Donovan, *Law Firm That Fell for Scam Can't Collect on Insurance, Court Rules*, NC LAWYERS WEEKLY (April 2, 2014).

[7] Your House; Your Rules ▷ Many states have state bar-sponsored programs that encourage, or even require, arbitration of attorney-client fee disputes by specialized tribunals. Be sure that you know what your state encourages or requires if you're holding client funds that are subject to a fee dispute. Failure to comply with those rules is typically a disciplinary offense. Your House; Your Rules

the dispute is between the client and a third party, "the lawyer may file an action to have a court resolve the dispute." **Model Rule 1.15 Comment [4]**. That action usually takes the form of an interpleader in a court of competent jurisdiction, in which a stakeholder (such as the attorney here) pays the disputed funds or deposits the property into court and invites the disputing claimants to fight it out while the stakeholder retreats to a neutral corner. *See, e.g.,* **Fed. R. Civ. P. 22; 28 U.S.C. § 1335**.

The converse of these rules is equally clear: If you take it upon yourself to decide where disputed funds or property belong, you are not only subject to professional discipline (even if you eventually turn out to have been right), but you will be personally liable to the disappointed claimant if that claimant eventually makes out a good claim (because you gave away what turned out to be that claimant's money or property). That's another bad day at the office that you don't want to have.

> Problem 21C-7: Your client has deposited $10,000 in your trust account as a deposit against future fees and costs.
>
> a. You billed $1,000 worth of work this month, and your client has agreed to pay the bill. What should you do?
> b. You billed $1,000 worth of work this month, and your client has agreed to pay half the bill, but disputes the other half. What should you do?
> c. You billed $1,000 worth of work this month, and your client disputes the entire bill. What should you do? Does your analysis change if you have documents that show that the client's dispute is meritless? If so, why and how; and if not, why not?
> d. You billed $1,000 worth of work this month, and your client has disputed the entire bill. When you get a settlement check for that client, can you refuse to remit the settlement funds until the fee dispute is resolved?

D. The Duty to Account

1. Delivering Others' Property

Model Rule 1.15(d) provides that you **must** "promptly deliver to the client or third person any funds or other property that the client or third person is entitled to receive . . ." except as otherwise provided by the Rules, other law, or by agreement with the client. The most common exception is property subject to dispute (*see* **Chapter 21.C at 585**), but generally speaking, if you're holding somebody else's property, you **must** give it back when asked for it unless there is a well-defined reason why you **mustn't**. This requirement involves "accounting" for property in the ancient equitable sense, which includes an obligation to provide others what belongs to them that you possess.

2. Notifying Others When You Are in Possession of Their Property

Model Rule 1.15(d) also requires you to "promptly notify" anyone who has an interest in money or property "[u]pon receiving" that money or property. Again, no big surprise; we have to keep those with legitimate interests in property that's in our custody informed that we have that property. Note that the Rule refers to a client or third person who "has an interest" in the property; this language appears designed to broaden the scope of your notice obligations to anyone who might have a colorable claim on (and thus an "interest" in) the property, or any portion of it, rather than limiting it to anybody who definitively owns the property.

3. Maintaining Detailed Records in Proper Form, and Providing Them to Those Legitimately Interested on Request

Not only must others' money and property be safeguarded and segregated, but you must account for it in a manner consistent with both generally accepted accounting practices and any other specific recordkeeping rules established by law or court order. With respect to tangible property with which you have been entrusted, you have a duty to keep records about what you received, when you received it, where it's being kept, and when you have returned it to the client or other owner. Those records must be maintained not only throughout the representation but for five years (or whatever alternative period your state requires) after the representation ends. **Model Rule 1.15(a)**.

As for accounting for others' funds held in your trust accounts, at the most basic level, your trust accounting should track all deposits and disbursements with a method for associating each transaction with a specific client and purpose for that transaction. Typically, lawyers keep written or electronic ledgers detailing every monetary transaction for each particular client. In addition, lawyers should maintain account journals for each account. At the end of each month, the ledgers and journals should be reconciled.

YOUR HOUSE; YOUR RULES Every state has different trust accounting requirements. Most of them are extremely detailed, and many can fairly be described as persnickety. They often describe what the checks drawn on a trust account have to look like or say on them; how to organize and maintain the accounting records for each trust account; what methods and how frequently these accounting records must be reconciled; and so on. The American Bar Association has promulgated a Model Rule on Financial Recordkeeping,[8] but many states have adopted their own, much more elaborate, requirements. YOUR HOUSE; YOUR RULES

The important point here is that you have to do whatever your particular state requires, no matter how idiosyncratic, tedious or, in your view, repetitious or unnecessary. The failure to keep or reconcile trust account records as prescribed is a disciplinary violation in and of itself, so that *even if every dollar is present and accounted for*, and even if you maintained an accurate accounting in a manner different than your state's Rules require, you will still be subject to significant disciplinary penalties if your records are imperfect in any way. You may complain that this is a little

---

[8] https://www.americanbar.org/groups/professional_responsibility/resources/client_protection/fpreface/.

like prosecuting Al Capone for tax evasion, but don't forget that Al Capone spent a good long time in Alcatraz (when it was a federal prison, not a national park).[9]

What's more, you **must**, "upon request by [a] client or third person" whose property you are holding or have held, "promptly render a full accounting regarding such property." That "full accounting" presumably includes any records that you have been required by state rule or law to maintain regarding the property, taking care not to disclose any information that you've created or maintained about any other person's property that is subject to your **duty of confidentiality. Model Rule 1.15(d)**.[10]

> **Problem 21D-1:** You have settled a case, and the other party has agreed to pay the $50,000 settlement in two installments. In addition, $5,000 in your fees are outstanding, to be paid when settlement is complete and final. When the first $25,000 check comes, you deposit it in your trust account. When the second $25,000 check comes, you again deposit it in your trust account. Then you write two checks: one to yourself for $5,000 and one to the client for $45,000. Is this acceptable accounting?

> **Problem 21D-2:** Assume that you are a solo practitioner with two accounts: your operating account and a single trust account. Each account requires that $200 be deposited in that account to avoid a minimum balance service charge of $50. Both accounts pay 4 percent interest on the last day of the month. You have $8,000 in your operating account.
>
> a. Your new client, Cynthia Client, has retained you to represent her in the purchase of a piece of property for her business. On January 1, Cynthia gives you two checks: a $10,000 check that will ultimately be used as a down payment at closing, and a $1,000 check as a retainer against future fees and costs. Where do you deposit these checks?
>
> b. On January 15, you do one hour of work for Cynthia at an hourly rate of $200 per hour. You send her an invoice, and she does not dispute the fees. She communicates to you the following day that she agrees to pay these fees. What do you now do? How much should be in each account?
>
> c. On February 8, you do an additional two hours of work at the same rate. This time, when you send Cynthia the invoice, she questions whether both hours of work were necessary. That same day she agrees to pay only for one hour's worth of work. What do you do now? How much should be in each account?
>
> d. On February 10, you pay the appraiser (whom the bank required as a condition of Cynthia's loan to purchase the property) $250. Against which account do you write that check? How much should be in each account now?

---

[9] Kelly Phillips Erb, *Al Capone Sentenced to Prison for Tax Evasion on This Day in 1931,* https://www.forbes.com/sites/kellyphillipserb/2018/10/17/al-capone-sentenced-to-prison-for-tax-evasion-on-this-day-in-1931/#5d698e2a7c4c (Oct. 17, 2018).

[10] There are, of course, other accounting obligations in other parts of the Rules. **Model Rule 1.5(c)**, for example, requires you to prepare an accounting of the lawyer's and the client's respective shares of a settlement or other payment in a contingent-fee matter; **Model Rule 1.16(d)** requires you, upon termination of an engagement, to return any unearned fees that you are holding.

e. On February 12, you resolve the fee dispute. You agree to charge Cynthia only $100 for the second hour of work. What do you now do? How much should be in each account?

f. On March 1, you attend the closing and pay over the $10,000 to the seller. What do you now do? How much should be in each account?

g. Following the closing, you submit your final bill to Cynthia showing one more hour of work for the time attending the closing. On March 2, Cynthia agrees to pay the bill. There is no further work for you to do for this client. What do you now do? How much should be in each account?

Big-Picture Takeaways from Chapter 21

1. You have three basic duties in handling other people's money and property: The **duty to safeguard**; the **duty to segregate**; and the **duty to account**. *See* **Chapter 21.A at 574**.

2. The **duty to safeguard** requires you to keep safe and secure any money or property that is in your care but belongs to others (or whose ownership is disputed). In doing so, you must exercise the care with other people's money and property of a reasonable professional fiduciary. *See* **Chapter 21.B at 577**.

3. The **duty to segregate** requires you to keep other people's money and property separate from your own. *See* **Chapter 21.C at 578**.
   a. With tangible property, the duty to segregate requires you to keep other people's property physically separate from yours. *See* **Chapter 21.C at 578**.
   b. With money, the duty to segregate requires you to keep other people's funds in a trust account created and maintained specifically for that purpose. *See* **Chapter 21.A at 575; Chapter 21.C at 579**.
   c. Other people's funds and your funds must never be commingled in your trust account (or any other account), with the following exceptions:
      i. You **may** pool different clients' and third parties' funds (but not your own) in a single trust account. *See* **Chapter 21.C at 580**.
      ii. You **may** keep a small amount of your own money in your trust account to cover anticipated routine banking charges for the account, but only so much as is reasonably necessary for that purpose. *See* **Chapter 21.C at 580**.
      iii. Interest on your trust account accrues to the clients and others whose money is in the account in proportion to their share of the deposited funds, unless your state requires you or the bank to pay the interest directly to the state bar for public purposes (which most do). *See* **Chapter 21.C at 581**.

    iv. When ownership of any money in a trust account changes, the money **must** be promptly handled in accordance with the change in ownership. *See* **Chapter 21.C at 581**.

    v. Funds that arrive in your hands pre-commingled in a single instrument **may** be deposited in a trust account (but no other account) and segregated when the funds are available. *See* **Chapter 21.C at 583**.

    vi. You **must not** pay out funds subject to any colorable claim or dispute to yourself or any third party; you **may** hold disputed funds in your trust account until the dispute is resolved. *See* **Chapter 21.C at 585**.

  d. You **must not** draw on funds deposited in your trust account until the funds have completely "cleared" and are unconditionally available. *See* **Chapter 21.C at 583**.

4. The **duty to account** requires you to:
   a. Promptly deliver to a client or third person any funds or other property that the client or third person is entitled to receive except as otherwise provided by the Rules, other law, or by agreement with the client. *See* **Chapter 21.D at 586**.
   b. Notify those with a colorable claim on money or property when you receive it. *See* **Chapter 21.D at 586**.
   c. Maintain detailed records regarding the money and property in your custody that are strictly consistent with the requirements of your state's laws and rules, and provide copies of those records regarding particular money or property to those with a legitimate claim on it if they request them. *See* **Chapter 21.D at 587**.

Multiple-Choice Review Questions for Chapter 21

1. After a few years working for a more experienced lawyer, Salvador hangs out his shingle as a solo practitioner. He immediately attracts a client, Company Inc., which buys and sells small commercial properties. Company Inc. tasks Salvador with negotiating the sale of an empty parking lot it owns that can be developed into a small strip mall. Salvador is successful, and the buyer, Mall Inc., agrees to purchase the property for $50,000. At the closing, the representative for Mall Inc. pulls out a checkbook. Salvador is the only representative of Company Inc. present at the closing. Because Salvador has not had time to set up a client trust account, he asks Mall Inc. to make the check out to him personally. Salvador deposits the check into his personal bank account. Once the check clears, he writes a $50,000 check to Company Inc. Company Inc. is thrilled with Salvador's work and subsequently pays his fees in full.

Has Salvador violated his professional obligations?
a. Yes, because he could not hold the funds in any account for any period of time.
b. Yes, because he held the funds in his personal account rather than a client trust account.
c. No, because he promptly remitted the funds to his client, who was paid in full.
d. No, because his client did not object to his handling of the funds.

2. Theo represents plaintiffs in personal injury cases. His cases are always handled on a contingent-fee basis, with the firm charging the plaintiff 30 percent of any settlement or judgment collected. The firm maintains an interest-bearing client trust account for each client at a local bank. As long as these accounts have an average monthly balance of $500 or more, there is no fee charged by the bank. When a case settles or a judgment is paid, the firm deposits the funds in the account for that specific client and notifies the client. Although the firm pays its clients their portion of the funds immediately, the firm sometimes leaves a few hundred dollars' worth of its fee in the account to prevent fees from the bank. Does this violate **Model Rule 1.15**?
a. Yes, because as soon as the funds become firm property, they must be transferred out of the client trust account.
b. Yes, because the funds should have never been deposited in the client trust fund to begin with.
c. No, because the firm is simply trying to avoid bank fees that otherwise would have diminished the amount paid to the client.
d. No, because the amount left in each account is *de minimis*.

3. Ulysses is a solo practitioner whose office is located in the Commonwealth of Keystone. He maintains a client trust account and a separate operating account for his firm. When he receives a settlement or judgment for a client, he deposits the funds into the client trust account. He keeps careful records to indicate what funds in the client trust account belong to which client. Ulysses uses a bank located in the State of Raptor. Has he violated **Model Rule 1.15(a)**?
a. Yes. He used a bank that was not located in the state in which his office is located.
b. Maybe. It depends on whether his clients have consented to the use of this bank.
c. Maybe. It depends on whether the bank account is interest-bearing.
d. No. He is properly safeguarding the funds by depositing them in a bank.

4. The firm of Smith and Jones, LLC maintains complete records of any client trust accounts or property held by the firm on behalf of a client for a period of six years from the time that a case is initiated. The records are then destroyed. The firm handles basic personal injury cases, which typically are in litigation for a year or more. Does this practice comply with the requirements of **Model Rule 1.15**?

   a. Yes. The records are already being retained for longer than is required.

   b. Maybe. It depends on whether the bank also maintains the records.

   c. Maybe. It depends on whether the client consented to the destruction of the records.

   d. No. Complete records may need to be maintained for a longer period.

5. Valancy is a solo practitioner. She maintains two bank accounts: a client trust account and a firm account. When a client pays her a retainer, she deposits that into the client trust account. As she earns attorney fees, she transfers the amount earned from the client trust account to her firm account. At the beginning of each month, she also transfers money from the firm account to the client trust account to pay bank service charges. Does this system comply with **Model Rule 1.15**?

   a. Yes. She is permitted to transfer firm monies into the client trust account to pay bank fees.

   b. Maybe. She must only transfer from the firm account to the client trust account the amount necessary to pay the bank fees.

   c. Maybe. It depends on whether the client has consented to this arrangement.

   d. No. She can never mix firm monies and client monies in a single account.

6. What does the acronym "IOLTA" stand for?

   a. Internet Only Legal Transaction Accounts.

   b. Internal Oversight Lawyer Trust Accounts.

   c. Interest on Lawyer Trust Accounts.

   d. In-House, Of-counsel, and Law Firm Transaction Accounts.

7. How should a lawyer handle a settlement check in a contingent-fee arrangement when the client disputes the attorney's fee?

   a. Deposit the check in the firm's operating account. Then transfer the amount due to the client to a client trust account. Hold the remaining amount in the firm's operating account.

   b. Deposit the check in the client trust account. Once the check has cleared, transfer any amounts of the settlement that are not disputed to the client or to the firm's operating account, according to who owns them. Once any disputes are resolved, transfer the lawyer's fee to the firm's operating account and any remaining amounts to the client.

c. Deposit the check in the firm's operating account. Hold all funds there until all disputes over fees are resolved. Then issue a check to the client for the client's share from the firm's operating account.

d. Deposit the check in the client trust account. Hold all funds there until all disputes are resolved. Then issue a check to the client for the client's share from the trust account, and transfer the firm's fees to the firm's operating account.

8. Can a firm have a single client trust account?
    a. Yes, if the firm has only one client.
    b. Yes, if there is a separate accounting for each client.
    c. No, unless all clients consent.
    d. No, because each client must have a separate account.

9. Which of the following **must not** be held in a client trust account?
    a. Funds given to the lawyer by the client that are to be applied against future legal fees.
    b. Funds received by the lawyer for the benefit of the client.
    c. Funds given to the lawyer by the client for future use on the client's behalf.
    d. Funds paid by the client for legal fees that have already been earned.

10. Which of the following justifies a lawyer's commingling his funds with client funds?
    a. Maintaining a sufficient balance in the client trust account to avoid bank fees.
    b. Sheltering the lawyer's money from creditors.
    c. Managing firm cash flow efficiently.
    d. None of the above.

11. A massive alien head appears over the Earth, interfering with Earth's gravity and spawning several global disasters in the process. When the head exclaims, "Show me what you got," lawyer Rick immediately leaves for Washington to inform the President of the United States that the alien head is a Cromulon. Rick has previously dealt with the Cromulons and knows what to expect. They will continue to cause global disasters until the Earth gives in to their demands.

Rick is in such a hurry to leave that he forgets to lock his first-floor office door on his way out. He also forgets to close the window and to lock the door to the firm. On his desk is client Morty's secret recipe for dark matter, for which Morty wants Rick to apply for a patent.

Moments after Rick leaves, a great wind raised by the Cromulons blows in Rick's office window and causes everything on Rick's desk to fly out into the street. Included in the papers now strewn across the street is Morty's secret recipe. Nebulon Zigerion finds the recipe and publicizes it.

Has Rick violated any of the Model Rules of Professional Conduct?

a. Yes. He failed to take reasonable care to protect against the inadvertent disclosure of **confidential information** under **Model Rule 1.6.**

b. Yes. He failed to adequately safeguard client property under **Model Rule 1.15.**

c. Yes. Both a and b.

d. No. Neither a nor b.

12. Client Cathy provides lawyer Lucille with a stock certificate and asks that Lucille hold the certificate during the pendency of a divorce. The stock is a marital asset that Cathy anticipates will have to be liquidated as part of any division of assets. Assuming no special circumstances are present, what should Lucille do with the stock certificate?

a. Carry it in her briefcase.

b. Lock it in a drawer in her office.

c. Deposit it in a safe-deposit box.

d. Turn it over to counsel for Lucille's spouse.

13. Anthony has successfully litigated a slip-and-fall case on behalf of his client, Barbara. At the conclusion of trial, the jury awards Barbara $300,000. Barbara has agreed to pay Anthony a 30 percent contingent fee, and Barbara paid litigation expenses out of her own pocket as the case was ongoing. The defendant hands Anthony a check for the amount of the judgment, and he is preparing to deposit it in his client trust account when he learns that Barbara's medical insurance company claims that it has a lien on the judgment and its proceeds for $10,000 due to medical bills that it paid on Barbara's behalf following her accident. Anthony reviews the file, and it seems likely that the medical insurance paid that much but he cannot tell whether the lien is valid or not. What should Anthony do?

a. Deposit the check in his client trust account. Pay no one anything until Barbara and the insurance company resolve the lien.

b. Deposit the check in his client trust account. Transfer $90,000 to his firm's account for attorney's fees and then pay Barbara the remaining $210,000.

c. Deposit the check in his client trust account. Transfer $90,000 to his firm's account for attorney's fees, pay Barbara $200,000, and pay the insurance company $10,000.

d. Deposit the check in his client trust account. Transfer $90,000 to his firm's account for attorney's fees and pay Barbara $200,000. Hold the remaining $10,000 in the trust account until Barbara and the insurance company resolve the lien.

UNIT V

Challenges and Complications When Duties and Interests Collide

You now know a great deal about lawyers' duties to their clients, to their **practice organizations,** and to third parties. Thanks for sticking with us.

We still have a ways to go, though, and we've saved what are, in some ways, the most difficult issues for last, when we knew that you'd be ready for them. What makes these issues difficult? Well, sometimes lawyers confront situations in which they face two or more duties or **interests** at the same time, and those duties or **interests** are simply not compatible with one another. We've seen this problem before: When we learned about fiduciary duties, for example, we encountered the general rule that lawyers, as fiduciaries, must honor their clients' **interests** over their own. We also learned that this principle is not absolute—if a client demanded that you waive your substantively proper and duly agreed fee because it would be better for her not to have to pay you (and, after all, her **interests** come first), you would not have to comply with the demand. That raises the question of when, generally, lawyers **must** prioritize clients' **interests** over their own when the lawyers' and the clients' **interests conflict.** That's what the first section of the chapter on **conflicts of interest, Chapter 22.A at 603,** is about.

After that, much of Chapter 22 is about the **conflicts of interest** in which lawyers can entangle themselves when they take on duties to two or more different clients, and *those* duties **conflict**. Often each duty is, by itself, valid and honorable; the problem is that the lawyer has committed to two different duties that will be difficult or impossible to perform at the same time. **Chapter 22.B at 645** addresses **conflicts of interest** that are grounded in the lawyer's **duty of loyalty**; **Chapter 22.C at 678** addresses **conflicts of interest** that are grounded in the lawyer's **duty of confidentiality**. The remainder of Chapter 22 is about how we treat **conflicts of interest** in **practice organizations** (**Chapter 22.D at 701**, on **imputation** and **screening**); how some **conflicts** may be addressed with the affected clients' **informed consent** (**Chapter 22.E at 733**); and how **practice organizations** keep track of and use the information necessary to see **conflicts** coming so they can be properly avoided or addressed before they become problems (**Chapter 22.F at 753**).

Chapter 23 at 769 addresses the confusions and complications that can arise when your client is an organization and when different individuals within the organization (often referred to as "**constituents**"), or some of those **constituents** and the organization itself, may have differing **interests** with respect to the organization's conduct or affairs.

Chapter 24 at 813 is about ethics in advocacy and the problems that can arise when you have inconsistent duties to your client and duties to the tribunal as an "officer of the court."

Finally, **Chapter 25 at 907** is about the special obligations of government lawyers. Ready? Let's get to it.

22

Conflicts of Interest

CONFLICTS OF INTEREST is a big subject, and this is going to be a long chapter. In fact, it's really several chapters in one. We'll start with an overview.

The **Preamble to the Model Rules ¶ [9]** points out that "[v]irtually all difficult ethical problems arise from **conflict** between a lawyer's responsibilities to clients, to the legal system and to the lawyer's own **interest** in remaining an ethical person while earning a satisfactory living." Truer words were never spoken. Conflicts between our duties to our clients and our duties to the legal system will be discussed in **Chapter 24 at 813**. The remaining kinds of **conflicts of interest** break down into three categories:

1. There are **conflicts of interest** between your own personal **interests** and the **interests** of a client or third party. These amount to a hodgepodge of concerns that arise in lawyers' personal and financial dealings with their clients and others, and they're addressed in a hodgepodge of situation-specific Rules. We'll cover these **conflicts of interest** in **Chapter 22.A at 603**.

2. There are **conflicts of interest** based on *whom* you know and have ongoing relationships with, and your possible temptation to favor one client over another. These **conflicts** are grounded in your **duty of loyalty** and are governed by something often referred to as the "**concurrent client rule**." We'll cover these **conflicts of interest** in **Chapter 22.B at 645**.

3. And there are **conflicts of interest** based on *what* you know in **confidence**, and your possible temptation to share **confidential information** with (or use that **confidential information** on behalf of) another client to the original client's disadvantage. These **conflicts** are grounded in your **duty of confidentiality** and are governed by something often referred to as the "**successive client**" or "**former client rule**" (which is a little weird, because the rule applies to **prospective clients** and **current clients** too). We'll cover these **conflicts of interest** in **Chapter 22.C at 678**.

After we discuss the three main categories of **conflicts of interest**, we'll offer some broadly applicable principles about how **conflicts of interest** work within **practice organizations** (**Chapter 22.D at 701**, on **imputation** and **screening**). We'll then discuss how and when you can address **conflicts of interest** either through avoiding getting hooked on both horns of the dilemma (often referred to as "abstaining" from the **conflict**), or through the **informed consent** of those affected (**Chapter 22.E at 733**). Finally, we'll talk a little about how **practice organizations** keep track of and use the information necessary to recognize **conflicts of interest** and to avoid or address them before they become problems (**Chapter 22.F at 753**).

But let's begin by asking just what a **conflict of interest** is. By **interest**, we simply mean anything someone wants or needs. You have an **interest** in getting paid for your work, for example. You also have an **interest** in complying with the duties that the law governing lawyers imposes on you and in avoiding the **consequences** that could result from failing to do so. So a **conflict of interest** is a situation in which you (the lawyer) have more than one **interest** that you may have normal human incli-nations—or enforceable legal duties—to serve, but those **interests** (and duties) are in **conflict** with each other. In a situation like that, you can't serve one **interest** without harming the other—the **interests** *conflict*; hence the name. Consider the hypothetical in the **Introduction to Chapter 8 at 203** involving one of Maya's super-vising partners, Ron Rainmaker. (It's been a while, so take a moment to go back and take a look. We're going to use it as an example repeatedly throughout this chapter, so it's worth your time to refresh yourself. Besides, it's just a page. We'll wait right here.)

As you've now reminded yourself, Ron received a phone call from the general counsel of a potential new client, Petrified Petroleum, in which he learned that Petrified had a substantial commercial dispute with one of its customers—a dispute that was likely to lead to litigation. Ron also learned a number of important things from Petrified's general counsel about Petrified's perspective on the dispute, and the company's needs and preferences regarding how it wished the dispute to be litigated and resolved. And he learned that the customer with which Petri-fied was going to war was Mojo Manufacturing, a client of Ron's firm in other matters. Petrified is, of course, a **prospective client** of Ron and his firm (because Petrified consulted with Ron in contemplation of possible representation (*see* **Model Rule 1.18(a)**), and what Petrified's general counsel told him on that call was classic **confidential information**. Ron thus has a **duty of confidentiality** not to disclose that information. **Model Rule 1.18(b)**, remember? (*See* **Chapter 8.A at 207** if you need to brush up.) But Ron wants to expand his firm's relationship with Mojo by repre-senting *Mojo* in the dispute with Petrified because that will be both good for his firm and good for him personally (by likely increasing his personal compensation by bringing in new business).[1] And he even thinks that he might have a **duty of**

---

[1] And for reasons that will become clearer in **Chapter 22.B at 645**, Ron's firm *couldn't* take Petrified's side of this fight unless Mojo voluntarily gave the firm its **informed consent** to do so (**Model Rule 1.7(a)(1)**), which Mojo is unlikely to do for a dispute of this size. In fact, the firm's management might not even want to *ask* Mojo to consent to the firm's representing Petrified against Mojo, given the possibility that Mojo not only would refuse, but could be insulted by the disloyalty implied in the request ("Hey, would you mind if a team of our most skilled litigators tried to rip your lungs out? Just this once? We'll keep doing the same great work that you've come to expect from us on your pending matters . . .").

loyalty to Mojo as the firm's **current client** (*see* **Chapter 5.D at 113**) that may *obligate* him to tell Mojo what he's learned about Petrified's concerns and plans.

And there's the rub: If Ron complies with his **duty of confidentiality** to Petrified, then he can't tell Mojo anything, so he can't get the benefits that he would have liked to get for his firm and himself. If Ron discloses that information to Mojo, and thus wins some new business for his firm *and* a bump in compensation for himself, he will be violating his **duty of confidentiality** to Petrified. Moreover, if Ron and his firm now take Mojo's side in the dispute with Petrified, they're in a position to use the valuable tactical information that Petrified provided to Ron in **confidence**, in violation of the firm's **duty of confidentiality** to Petrified. Ron can't do right by one party without doing wrong by another. He has a **conflict of interest**.[2]

The most vexing thing about **conflicts of interest** is that the **interests** on either side of a **conflict** are often *both* legitimate. The problem is that they're also irreconcilable—that is, they *conflict*. That's what distinguishes **conflicts of interest** from most other ethical problems, in which some course of conduct may be tempting, but it's *wrong*—it's a disciplinary violation, or a tort, or a crime. In a **conflict of interest**, the lawyer's wrong lies in getting himself into a situation in which he has undertaken *two or more independently legitimate obligations that* ***conflict***, or at the least, in which he has an **interest** that he would like to pursue that also **conflicts** with a legitimate obligation. If the lawyer had just one of these obligations or **interests**, satisfying it would not be wrong; in fact, it would often be the necessary performance of a duty. But with two or more **conflicting** obligations, whenever you serve one, you disserve the other.

The observation that **conflicts of interest** always involve at least two **interests** that **conflict** with each other leads to a handy method for approaching potentially **conflicted** situations: Ask yourself (as we will do with you throughout this chapter), "What's the **conflict**?" Identify the **interests** of the people—lawyers and clients—involved in the situation. See how the clients' **interests** affect the lawyers' **interests**—they often will, because lawyers often have duties to do whatever they can within the limits of the law to serve their clients' **interests**. See whether and how the **interests** at play **conflict**. Once you've decided whether there is a **conflict of interest** and which **interests conflict**, you will have laid the groundwork for figuring out what you **must** or **may** do about it.

We'll talk later in the chapter about how to avoid **conflicts of interest** and what some of your options or obligations may be if you fail to avoid them. But first, let's explore a couple of important general observations: The *first* general observation about **conflicts of interest** that we want you to keep in mind

---

[2] To clarify something important, Ron's and his firm's **duty of loyalty** to their current client, Mojo, does *not* obligate Ron or anyone else at his firm to tell Mojo what they know about Petrified and its dispute with Mojo. The **duty of loyalty** never obligates you to violate another legally binding duty, just as the duty of zealous representation (a feature of the **duty of loyalty**) never obligates you to do anything for your client that the law does not allow. Ron has no duty to violate his **confidentiality** obligations to **prospective client** Petrified, just as he would have no duty to perjure himself if another client asked him to. So Ron is wrong about that.

throughout this chapter is this: *How much* the **interests** in play **conflict** with one another (that is, how bad the **conflict** is) can fall anywhere on a continuum from hardly any **conflict** at all to direct, zero-sum, mutual opposition. There are lots of **conflicting interests** in law practice that are sufficiently mild or manageable that you don't have to do anything special to avoid or address them (beyond applying your usual decency and common sense). For example, when your bill comes due, the client would generally prefer to pay later, or less, or not at all, but you're free to refuse the client's request to do so and insist that the client honor your fee agreement and pay what's owed when it's due—even though you owe the client fiduciary duties that are (in Judge Cardozo's memorable formulation) much "stricter than the morals of the market place."[3]

The client's financial **interests** and yours are in **conflict** in this situation, but you don't have to do anything special about it. There are no particular obligations to refrain from, to disclose, to explain, or to obtain the client's consent to these **conflicts**, most likely because everyone can be expected to understand this kind of inevitable divergence between your own financial interests and the client's, as well as the assumed ability of both parties to protect themselves in these circumstances. But as we will see, there are other divergences between the client's **interests** and your own that are more subtle and uncertain than the ones that we just described and that *do* require you to take special action.

When we talk about **conflicts of interest**, then, we are really talking about the ones in which the **conflict** between the relevant **interests** is sufficiently great in either importance or degree that something has to be done about it—or **consequences** for the lawyer will follow. There are, generally speaking, two kinds of rules defining the **conflicts of interest** that require some kind of action to prevent **consequences**. Some issues have crystallized into bright-line rules categorically forbidding certain defined situations or conduct or requiring formal steps to address them, such as explicit disclosure to and **informed consent** by the client. The Rule forbidding lawyers from giving most kinds of financial assistance to litigation clients (**Model Rule 1.8(e); Chapter 22.A at 606**) is an example of a bright-line prohibition; the Rule requiring special written disclosures and the client's **informed consent** for any transaction between lawyer and client other than an agreement to pay fees for legal services (**Model Rule 1.8(a); Chapter 22.A at 617**) is an example of a bright-line rule requiring special formal precautions. Some of these Rules, by contrast, are more general standards that call for avoidance or special precautions for **conflicts of interest** that meet a more general, fuzzily described threshold of concern. For example, **Model Rule 1.7(a)(2)** (**Chapter 22.A at 626; Chapter 22.B at 654**) requires action in the face of a "*significant risk* that the representation of one or more clients will be *materially* limited by the lawyer's responsibilities to another client, a former client or a third person or by a personal interest of the

---

[3] *Meinhard v. Salmon,* 249 NY 458, 464, 164 N.E. 545 (N.Y. 1928).

lawyer" (emphases added). Tests such as "significant risk" and "material[] limit[a-tion]" are general standards that must be evaluated on a relative, practical scale in each case, based on all of the surrounding facts and circumstances; they can't be weighed or measured with scientific precision.

CONSEQUENCES The *second* general observation we want you to remember throughout this chapter is that **conflicts of interest** that are sufficiently serious that they have to be avoided or addressed don't have to have caused *any* actual harm to the client in order for **consequences** to be imposed on the **conflicted** lawyer. The mere *existence* of the **conflicting interests** and the *potential* that they *might* cause the lawyer to harm a client is sufficient to comprise a breach of the lawyer's duty all by itself and to justify **consequences**. If harm to the client results from the **conflict**, of course, there will be *additional* **consequences** for that. But the most common **consequence** for a **conflict of interest** is **disqualification**—an order from a tribunal requiring a lawyer (and usually anyone associated with that lawyer in a **practice organization**) to get out and stay out of the **conflicted** engagement. The effect of the **disqualification** order is to get the lawyer out of the **conflicted** situation *before* any actual harm to any affected client (or any more of it) occurs.

And, of course, **conflicts of interest** in violation of the Rules of Professional Conduct can result in professional discipline. But in addition, because fiduciaries who act under a significant **conflict of interest** are not, under general fiduciary law, entitled to be compensated for their services, a serious enough **conflict** is not only a complete defense to a lawyer's claim for fees, it means that any compensation actually received while the lawyer had the **conflict** was not properly earned, and the lawyer may be sued in unjust enrichment for restitutionary disgorgement of those fees (that is, the lawyer may be required to *return* fees already paid if they were incurred while acting under a serious **conflict of interest**). In most states, the lawyer is entitled to *nothing* for her work under these circumstances—no claim in *quantum meruit* for the reasonable value of the services is available. And if the lawyer has succumbed to temptation and actually harmed a client because of **conflicting interests**—for example, by disclosing or using **confidential information** or by favoring one client at the expense of another—damages in tort (for breaching one or more of the duties arising out of the attorney-client relationship) are available to compensate the client for the harm. CONSEQUENCES

One thing that emerges from what we just discussed is that the stakes involved in recognizing and responding to **conflicts of interest** can be very high. So let's get to work understanding what matters and how to deal with it.

A. Conflicts of Interest Created by Conflicts Between the Lawyer's Personal Interests and a Client's Interests

The **conflicts of interest** that we're going to explore in this subchapter typically involve, on one side of the **conflict of interest**, the lawyer's legitimate **interest** in earning a living, or in maintaining a personal as well as a professional relationship with a client or someone else. (Remember, the thing about **conflicts of interest** is that the **interests** on either side of a **conflict** are often *both* legitimate, but they **conflict**, which is the problem.) It's important to recognize that lawyers are usually paid for their work, and that there is nothing inherently wrong with trying to maximize your income in order to reward yourself for your skills and industry, to support your family, to donate to causes that you favor, or to make any other use of your assets that our society allows. But our legal system imposes all kinds of limits on the ways in which you may seek to earn a living: No one is allowed to commit fraud or theft, for example. And because of lawyers' special role as fiduciaries to their clients and as participants in the operation of the legal system, in addition to the usual limits on profit-seeking that are imposed on everyone, lawyers are subject to additional, special limitations on their commercial conduct with their clients.

We'll warn you in advance—the kinds of commercial and personal conduct by lawyers that are regulated, and how they are regulated, are somewhat arbitrary and don't always make sense. But whether these rules are wise or foolish, they're the law, and until they're changed, they will carry serious **consequences** that can cost you your law license and your livelihood. So listen up.[4]

1. Forbidden Financial Assistance to Litigation Clients

A potential new client comes into the office to meet with Frank and the firm's litigation partner, Harlan "Happy" Trials. Peggy Plaintiff is a kind, grandmotherly woman who recently retired from her job as a fourth-grade teacher after 40 years in the local schools. She's very well-known and universally admired in her community for her years of devotion both to the area's children and to her many civic and church-related activities. Recently, she was rather unceremoniously run down in a crosswalk by the driver of a big, expensive sedan who has admitted that he was texting when he hit her, and who is overcome with remorse at his inattention. Peggy's injuries were serious, and her recovery will be long and difficult.

This is an easy liability case with big potential damages, and (with all due respect for the pain and expense that Peggy is suffering) Happy is delighted at the opportunity to get the engagement. All of the better personal injury lawyers in town (and quite a few from cities nearby) have heard about this accident and would also love to get the case. The driver's auto insurance company, aware of its substantial exposure, has hired one of its most effective and tenacious defense

---

[4] In addition to the personal-**interest conflicts** that will be addressed in this subchapter, there are several that we've already discussed. These include the restrictions on accepting compensation from someone other than the client (**Model Rule 1.8(f)**; *see* **Chapter 9.B at 273**); the restrictions on clients' prospective waivers of a lawyer's malpractice liability and on settling a malpractice claim with a **current** or **former client** who is not independently represented (**Model Rule 1.8(h)**; *see* **Chapter 9.C at 285**); and the prohibition on sex with clients (**Model Rule 1.8(j)**; *see* **Chapter 5.C at 108**). Make sure you're clear on how each of these presents a conflict between an interest of the lawyer (identify it) and of a client (identify that too).

counsel to handle the inevitable claim and do her best to hold down the eventual payout.

"The insurance company has hired Rhonda Resolute to defend the driver, which is some indication of how seriously it takes this case," Happy says to Peggy. "I have to tell you with all honesty that she's the best insurance defense lawyer around, and she never gives up. But we've taken her on a number of times, and we've always gotten our clients good results. We have the resources and the resolve to do what's necessary to get you what you deserve, all the way through trial and appeal." "How long might that take?" Peggy asks. "Well, given docket congestion in our local courts, I would guess 12-18 months, maybe longer," Happy responds.

"Then I've got a problem," Peggy explains. "My husband and I used most of our savings to remodel our house a few years ago, getting it ready for our retirement. In fact, we borrowed to get the work done, and then he died suddenly." "I'm very sorry," says Happy. "Well, thank you," says Peggy, "but the problem is that primary-school teachers don't get paid much, and my pension is pretty small. Social Security helps, but it's not much, either. Medicare covers only part of the expenses for my accident, which were a lot. And I have months, maybe years, of medical follow-up and physical therapy as well. I'm not getting any younger, you know. I was pretty shocked at how much that stuff costs these days. When I was planning my retirement, I didn't figure that something like this was going to be a part of it. I just don't know how I can pay my share of the medical bills, maybe get some Medicare supplemental insurance, and keep a roof over my head and food on the table at the same time."

"I'm very sorry to hear that," Happy responds, "but the good news is that the driver who hit you was clearly in the wrong and has a lot of insurance coverage. We can feel very confident that you will be recovering a big settlement or judgment, enough to pay your bills several times over."

"You're not the first lawyer to tell me that," says Peggy. "But the problem is timing. Those bills are due now, and they're going to keep coming due for as far as I can see. Some of the treatments that my doctors have recommended aren't covered by Medicare at all, and the providers won't see me without some guarantee of payment. I need money to live on now; I can't wait a year or more. I asked my bank if it could make me a loan, and the loan officer pointed out that the bank already holds the mortgage on my home. I have to say that I like you, and I'd like to see you take my case. Maybe you could lend me something to help tide me over? Of course you could take it out of whatever you get paid on my case when you get it. A couple of the other lawyers I've talked to hinted that they might be able to help in that way. What about you?"

Let's start with the subject of the Introduction to this subchapter—financial assistance to litigation clients.

a.　The General Rule: Financial Assistance to a Litigation Client Is Forbidden

TAMING THE TEXT ▶ **Model Rule 1.8(e)** categorically forbids a lawyer from "provid[ing] financial assistance to a client in connection with pending or contemplated litigation . . . ." (There are a few important exceptions, which we'll get to below, but the general rule is a **must not**.) This prohibition applies to almost any kind of financial assistance, including lending money to the client (whether or not secured by a lien on the client's litigation claims or by any other property), as Peggy Plaintiff had in mind in the **subchapter Introduction at 604**, or by guaranteeing a loan that the client gets from a third party. It also forbids any gift that you might give a litigation client beyond a *de minimis* token of personal appreciation—say, a hospitality basket or a coffee-table book at the holidays, or a bottle of wine on a birthday.

The prohibition of **Model Rule 1.8(e)** applies uniquely and specifically to lawyers' providing financial assistance to *their own* litigation clients. It does *not* prevent lawyers from providing assistance (whether in the form of loans, loan guarantees, or gifts) to litigants who are not their clients, or to clients in an engagement other than litigation. Nor does it prevent litigants from obtaining financial assistance from a bank, or a rich uncle, or anyone else who is not their litigation lawyer (though some jurisdictions have other laws restricting the use of a cause of action or its proceeds as security for a loan or as basis for a third party's investment). ◀ TAMING THE TEXT

REASON FOR THE RULE ▶ (or, in this case, the lack of any persuasive ones): **Model Rule 1.8(e)** may strike you as a bit odd. Why do we specifically forbid lawyers from lending (or giving) money or other things of value to their own litigation clients, when the lawyer is in a very good (perhaps the best) position to estimate the value of the claim and the client's needs, and should naturally have strong economic incentives to provide only the assistance that, in the lawyer's own financial judgment and at the lawyer's own financial risk, is worth it?

Whenever you think that you may be looking at a **conflict of interest** of any kind, it's always a good idea to identify the players on the board and how their rights, duties, and **interests** may **conflict**. (In other words, get into the habit of asking yourself, "What's the **conflict**?") This whole subchapter is about **conflicts** between the lawyer's personal **interests** and a client's. Here, the lawyer's **interest** is clear—lawyers would like to be able to persuade a client to retain them by supplying financial assistance that the client wants or needs (such as the loan that Peggy Plaintiff requests). Generally speaking, rational lawyers will not make an offer of this kind unless they expect to see it pay off in the fees that the matter will eventually generate. So the lawyer is, in effect, negotiating the overall terms of the fee to offer the client a better deal on the engagement as an inducement to hire that lawyer. Usually, we encourage that kind of thing, because competition among lawyers is generally good for clients.

And the client's **interest**? Well, a client who wants financial assistance or some other kind of "sweetener" added to the fee deal is simply trying to get the best fee arrangement available, and to address pressing financial needs that must be addressed before the claim will pay off. This puts pressure on lawyers to offer more competitive fee arrangements. That's generally good for clients, too.

So where's the **conflict**? The Drafters of the Model Rules suggest that here the **conflicting interest** is in the integrity of the civil justice system. The Comments to **Model Rule 1.8(e)** provide the traditional justifications: To allow lawyers to provide financial assistance to litigation clients "would encourage clients to pursue lawsuits that might not otherwise be brought and because such assistance gives lawyers too great a financial stake in the litigation." **Model Rule 1.8 Comment [10]**.[5] It's difficult to find firm grounding for either of these justifications in the real world.

Let's examine the first justification—"to do so would encourage clients to pursue lawsuits that might not otherwise be brought." You might ask what's wrong with that. If clients have legal rights that could be vindicated by suit, shouldn't they be advised or even encouraged to assert their claims? If the financial assistance is charity (perhaps Peggy Plaintiff's church congregation wants to give her a gift or make her a reduced-rate loan to see her through her lawsuit so that she can get the medical care, food, and shelter that she needs), why is charity bad? And if her lawyer engages in the same charity, how is that any worse? Alternatively, if lawyers want to invest in the litigation claim because they believe that it's strong enough to support a return on the investment, they do so at their own risk, and thus are very likely to do so only when the claim is meritorious (so that the investment or loan will be repaid).

In such cases, there is an obvious interest in seeing wrongfully harmed persons recover fair compensation for the violations of their legal rights, and the litigation "should" in that sense be brought. Restricting financial assistance to people like Peggy Plaintiff just leaves needy victims of torts and other violations of legal and civil rights in a position in which their financial needs will force them to settle their claims early and cheap so that they can pay their bills on time. That leaves those who wronged them bearing less than the full cost of their wrongs, and those who have been wronged not compensated by the full measure that the law provides. (Do you see why?) Where's the justice in that? We already

---

[5] This is our opportunity to introduce you to some quaint common-law terms that are still used in some jurisdictions when someone wants to call arrangements of this kind a nasty name. "Champerty" and "maintenance" were the terms at common law for providing financial assistance to litigation clients or investing in a litigation claim. (The adjectival form is "champertous," and at common law, an arrangement in which a lawyer or third party took a financial interest in a litigation claim or financed the litigation was often referred to as a "champertous connivance," in case you were wondering how the system felt about such things.) "Barratry" was the term used for conduct that incited litigation that might otherwise not have been brought or continued, often by means of champerty or offering a litigant other financial incentives. Under evolving definitions, both have been misdemeanors and violations of professional ethics for hundreds of years. As discussed in the text, the reasons for this condemnation may be more deeply rooted in guild protections limiting competition among lawyers to the general detriment of clients (*see* **Chapter 3.A at 34**) than in any sound public policy interests.

have strong rules, with strong **consequences**, forbidding lawyers from bringing or advising clients to bring *frivolous* claims or engaging in frivolous or abusive tactics (*see* **Chapter 3.B at 48**; **Chapter 3.C at 53**; **Chapter 24.C at 841**), so adding a prohibition on providing a client financial assistance to bring *meritorious* claims throws out a lot of babies with little or no bathwater.

The other traditional justification for forbidding financial assistance to clients—that allowing lawyers to invest in their clients' litigation claims "gives lawyers too great a financial stake in the litigation"—fares little better under scrutiny. Lawyers are, of course, always required "to exercise independent professional judgment and render candid advice" in advising their clients. **Model Rule 2.1**. And lawyers in every American jurisdiction are already allowed to invest in their clients' litigation claims by entering into contingent-fee agreements in which their compensation depends entirely or in part on the amount the client recovers (*see* **Chapter 20.B at 541**). Lawyers also invest in clients' claims by advancing out-of-pocket costs, which can be substantial and whose recovery from the client **may** be made contingent on the outcome of the case (*see* **Chapter 22.A at 609**). No one has ever really tried to explain how adding a loan for living expenses would throw the lawyer's independent judgment uncontrollably out of whack when the lawyer is already free to gamble that she'll receive no fee at all and lose tens or potentially hundreds of thousands of dollars in court, deposition, and travel costs, as well as experts' fees, unless the client recovers.[6] REASON FOR THE RULE

All told, then, the general prohibition on financial assistance to litigation clients seems very difficult to justify on any consistent policy rationale. Nevertheless, it is the law in virtually every state and is enthusiastically enforced by Bar prosecutors everywhere—with serious **consequences** up to and including suspension and disbarment. Don't try this at home.[7]

---

[6] **Model Rule 1.8 Comment [10]** goes on to say that the "dangers" of inciting frivolous litigation and losing professional judgment "do not warrant a prohibition on a lawyer lending a client court costs and litigation expenses, including the expenses of medical examinations and the costs of obtaining and presenting evidence, because these advances are virtually indistinguishable from contingent fees and help ensure access to the courts." True enough, but why are the "dangers" of a loan covering living expenses—so that the client can wait out the litigation process rather than being forced to the bargaining table by fundamental needs—any more serious? By way of comparison, the English legal system, where the ban on financial assistance to clients originated, also banned contingency fees in favor of a system in which the loser in litigation paid the winner's legal fees (or, more accurately, paid a portion of them according to a scale of presumed fees). But even England legalized contingency fees (which are often referred to there as "damages-based agreements" or "DBAs") in 2013. The justification offered was the same one relied on here in the United States, which indistinguishably supports other financial assistance to claimants—namely, furnishing the victims of legal wrongs easier access to the courts to vindicate their rights.

[7] The ban is nearly, but not entirely, universal. California—usually among the more restrictive jurisdictions in lawyer regulation—is one of the few states that allows a loan from litigation lawyer to litigation client of the kind about which Peggy Plaintiff inquires in the **subchapter Introduction at 604**, subject to complete and proper disclosures and consents. *See* CAL. R. PROF. COND. 1.8.5(b)(2).

b. Implicit Exceptions to the General Prohibition on Lawyers' Providing Financial Assistance to Clients

Though **Model Rule 1.8(e)** doesn't explicitly say so, in addition to the exceptions expressly written into the Rule that are discussed below, there are three implicit exceptions to the Rule that each allow financial assistance to clients in several forms:

First, you're always free to defer collection of your fee until some later date, such as the end of the case, to discount your fees from what you usually charge (before or after they are incurred), or to represent a client entirely free of charge (*pro bono*).[8]

Second, you are also free to negotiate and charge a contingent fee, in which the payment and the amount of any fee depends on (is "contingent" on) the outcome of the case. As you may recall from **Chapter 20.B at 541**, the most common use of contingent fees is in representing claimants in litigation, where the contingent fee is typically agreed to be a percentage of any eventual settlement or recovery. But contingent-fee agreements that vary the lawyer's fee depending on the success of the outcome are freely negotiated and perfectly permissible in representing other kinds of clients in most other kinds of engagement as well.[9]

Third and finally, given that the Rule limits its prohibition to assistance "in connection with pending or contemplated litigation," you **may** provide financial assistance to non-litigation clients. There is no widely understood policy basis for limiting financial assistance to litigation clients only, but the Rule is limited in this way virtually everywhere.

c. Express Exceptions to the General Prohibition on Lawyers' Providing Financial Assistance to Clients

In addition to the three implicit exceptions to the general prohibition on lawyers' providing financial assistance to clients just discussed, **Model Rule 1.8(e)** also articulates three exceptions expressly stated in the Rule itself:

i. Advancing Litigation Costs, Whether or Not Repayment Is Contingent on the Case's Outcome

Model Rule 1.8(e)(1) provides that, despite the general ban on furnishing financial assistance to litigation clients, "a lawyer **may** advance court costs and

---

[8] *Pro bono*, as you probably already know, is short for *pro bono publico*—literally, "for the good of the public." It means to represent a client without charging a fee (and usually, but not always, bearing the client's out-of-pocket costs as well, subject to the requirements of **Model Rule 1.8(e)**, discussed below). You don't actually have to show what benefit to the public you believe is served by representing the client without charge; it is simply an act of charity whose motivations and benefits are almost never questioned.

[9] But not every kind. As we discussed in **Chapter 20.C at 550**, most states prohibit contingent fees in most criminal and divorce cases. *See* **Model Rule 1.5(d)**.

expenses of litigation, the repayment of which **may** be contingent on the outcome of the matter." The court costs and expenses of litigation include expenses such as filing fees, deposition costs, reasonably necessary travel expenses, photocopying and other document processing, and (perhaps most significantly) experts' fees, which can be very substantial. Lawyers frequently pay such expenses directly out of their own pockets, with an understanding with their clients as to when and how the lawyers will be reimbursed. In effect, then, the lawyers are lending the amount of these advanced expenses to their clients, a loan that is just as real as if they had lent the client living expenses. *See* **Chapter 20.A at 536**. But advancing a client's litigation expenses, unlike other financial assistance to a litigation client, is allowed.

Model Rule 1.8(e)(1) further allows lawyers to agree that their clients' reimbursement of those expenses "**may** be contingent on the outcome of the matter"—in other words, lawyers **may** agree to bear the costs advanced *without reimbursement* (sometimes colloquially referred to as the lawyer "eating" the costs, one of the most unappetizing meals in law practice) if there is no (or insufficient) recovery from which they can be reimbursed. Such arrangements are quite common in cases in which the lawyer's fee is also contingent on the outcome and the client is unable to pay litigation costs as the matter unfolds.

ii. Paying Litigation Expenses Without Expectation of Repayment for an Indigent Client

The second express exception to the ban on financial assistance to litigation clients is **Model Rule 1.8(e)(2)**, which allows a lawyer to "pay court costs and expenses of litigation on behalf of" an "indigent" client. In other words, if the client is indigent (a term that the Rule doesn't define, but that generally means impoverished), a lawyer (or a legal aid program or other legal nonprofit that regularly serves indigent clients) may agree at the outset to pay the client's litigation costs and not to seek reimbursement. Ironically, a client in straitened circumstances but not obviously "indigent," such as Peggy Plaintiff, who has a home and a modest pension but can't afford big-case litigation expenses without real hardship and maybe not even then, apparently can't have her litigation expenses paid as part of a fee deal; clients like Peggy **must** agree to reimburse litigation costs that the lawyer advances on her behalf out of any recovery as allowed by **Model Rule 1.8(e)(1)**.

iii. *Pro Bono* Counsel's "Modest" Gifts to Indigent Clients for Living Expenses

Finally, **Model Rule 1.8(e)(3)** slightly expands the range of financial assistance that may be offered to indigent *pro bono* clients (but *only* to indigent *pro bono* clients). If a lawyer is representing an indigent client *pro bono* (whether through the lawyer's own **practice organization**, "through a nonprofit legal services or public interest organization," or "through a law school clinical or pro bono program"), then the lawyer **may** "provide modest gifts to the client for food, rent, transportation, medicine and other basic living expenses." As you can see, this exception somewhat broadens the exception in **Model Rule 1.8(e)(2)**, which already allows a lawyer to pay an indigent client's litigation expenses without expectation of reimbursement. This exception allows those lawyers assisting the indigent client *pro bono* to add "modest" living expenses to the arrangement. The Rule forbids such lawyers from promising such support as a means of getting or keeping the engagement (**Model Rule 1.8(e)(3)(i)**); seeking reimbursement from the client or anyone associated with the client (**Model Rule 1.8(e)(3)(ii)**); or "publiciz[ing] or advertis[ing] a willingness to provide such gifts to prospective clients" (**Model Rule 1.8(e)(3) (iii)**). Consistent with the guild-protective origins of the prohibition on financial assistance generally, it's hard to see these restrictions on the exception as doing anything other than limiting the ability to help clients in need to circumstances in which the lawyer making the gift is not competing for the engagement with anyone who's practicing for profit (do you see why?).

> **Problem 22A-1:** Which of the following arrangements violates **Model Rule 1.8(e)**, and why?
>
> a. Peggy Plaintiff (from the **Introduction to this subchapter at 604**) informs Frank and Happy that she is going to meet with the bank again later that afternoon to try and get a loan to cover her medical and living expenses while her case is pending. She was wearing her only business suit when she was run over in the accident and needs to dress appropriately for the meeting. Happy takes Peggy down the street to a local haberdasher and buys her a business suit for her meeting. He throws in a string of pearls to "dress it up." He arranges to meet her and her minister after the bank meeting at Exley's Exorbitantly Expensive Eating Establishment where, he announces, dinner will be on him.
>
> b. Peggy needs regular physical therapy to help her recover from the injuries she suffered in the accident as to which Frank's firm represents her. The physical therapist recommended by her orthopedist is in the next town over, about a half-hour's drive away. Peggy's car breaks down, and she can't afford the repairs. Happy lends Peggy an extra car that his college-age daughter drives when she's home from school so that Peggy can get to physical therapy. Does your analysis change if the partner also lets Peggy use the car to drive to the grocery store, to church, and to visit friends? If so, how and why; and if not, why not?
>
> c. When the physical therapist presses Peggy for payment for her treatments, Happy intervenes and persuades the physical therapist to wait for the outcome of Peggy's case to be paid. He negotiates and drafts an agreement for Peggy by which she promises to pay the charges out of any recovery in her case. Frank's firm does not charge Peggy for these extra services.
>
> d. Same as (c), except Frank's firm pays the physical therapist's charges and bills them to Peggy as a litigation expense to be reimbursed out of Peggy's eventual recovery in her personal injury case, with no reimbursement required if there's no recovery. Happy reasons

that these are medical expenses caused by her accident, and thus are recoverable items of damage in her case. Does your analysis change if Peggy must repay these charges at the conclusion of the case, even if there is no recovery? If so, how and why; and if not, why not?

e. Maya's firm is seeking to represent Danny Devisee, an heir of the founder of a successful publicly traded company, who has inherited a minority block of unregistered stock in the company. The engagement, if the firm can get it, is to find a buyer and negotiate and document the registration and sale of the shares. The shares are worth several million dollars and maybe a good deal more, but Danny has no liquid (currently spendable) assets at all. Maya's firm offers to lend Danny $100,000, secured by his shares or their proceeds, so that he can live "comfortably" during the six months or so while the firm registers the shares, helps find a buyer, and negotiates the transaction. The firm also asks that the shares secure the future payment of the firm's fees and costs, which will be paid upon sale of the stock.

2. Forbidden Conduct in Connection with Gifts and Bequests from Clients

Model Rule 1.8(e), which we just discussed, is about limits on lawyers' *giving* financial assistance *to* their clients. **Model Rule 1.8(c)** is about lawyers' *receiving* gifts and bequests *from* their clients. It prohibits two things: A lawyer **must not** "solicit any substantial gift from a client, including a testamentary gift"; and a lawyer **must not** "prepare on behalf of a client an instrument giving the lawyer or a person related to the lawyer any substantial gift unless the lawyer or other recipient of the gift is related to the client." Let's break that down.

TAMING THE TEXT The first phrase in the first sentence of **Model Rule 1.8(c)** says that you **must not** "solicit any substantial gift from a client, including a testamentary gift." The two key words there are "solicit" and "substantial." "Solicit" is an important word because it makes clear that the forbidden conduct is not *receiving* the client's gift, but rather *asking the client for it* ("soliciting" it).[10] Nothing in the Rule says that you can't keep and enjoy a gift, even a substantial gift, that a client gives you without your asking for it. "Substantial" is the other important word in the Rule because it makes clear that non-extravagant tokens of personal esteem, such as moderate gifts from a client in appreciation of a good result or as acts of holiday generosity, are fully permissible even if you solicit them (as graceless as that might be under the circumstances).

Similarly, the second phrase of **Model Rule 1.8(c)** says that you **must not** "prepare on behalf of a client an instrument giving the lawyer or a person related to the lawyer any substantial gift unless the lawyer or other recipient of the gift is related to the client." So even if you've been scrupulously careful about not soliciting anything, if the client asks you to amend her will to include a specific bequest to

---

[10] And, needless to say, you can "solicit" a gift in violation of the Rule indirectly or by implication, for example by inducing someone close to the client suggest it, or by dropping what might seem to you to be discreet hints. If you think that you're asking, or if a reasonable person in the client's position thinks that you are, then you're "soliciting" the gift, and you're on the wrong side of the Rule.

you (or someone related to you—say, your spouse), or asks you (out of the blue!) to prepare a Deed of Gift transferring that sweet little weekend house on the lake to you in appreciation for your years of loyal service, you **must not** do it (though an independent lawyer **may**). You **must not**, that is, unless you are (or the person related to you who is to receive the gift is) also related to the client. And the Rule helpfully defines "related" as a "spouse, child, grandchild, parent, grandparent or other relative or individual with whom the lawyer or the client maintains a close, familial relationship."

In other words, you may document a client's gifts or bequests to you or to members of your family if you (or another recipient related to you) and the client are family to one another, but not otherwise. Similarly to the other restriction in this Rule, this one also does not prevent you from *accepting* the client's gift or bequest; it simply forbids you from *documenting* it on the client's behalf.

Nothing in **Model Rule 1.8** forbids you from requesting more legal work from a client (or documenting a new engagement), either. Presumably this is implicit because a new or expanded engagement is not a "gift"—it is an exchange agreement for you to do more work in return for additional compensation. **Model Rule 1.8 Comment [8]** touches on this point by addressing a context that often arises for lawyers involved in helping clients plan gifts or bequests: Under the Model Rules, you are not precluded from seeking to have yourself or someone in your firm appointed "executor of the client's estate or to another potentially lucrative fiduciary position," an appointment that is often made, in advance, in a client's trust instrument or will. But, the Comment points out, seeking such an appointment can itself result in **conflicts of interest** "when there is a significant risk that the lawyer's interest in obtaining the appointment will materially limit the lawyer's independent professional judgment in advising the client concerning the choice of an executor or other fiduciary." *See* **Model Rule 1.7(a)(2)**; **Chapter 22.A. at 626**. That is, if you're preparing a will or trust for a client and the client needs to choose a trustee or executor, you are hardly disinterested in advising the client to consider you or one of your partners for that position (and the compensation that comes with it), rather than the client's family member, a trusted friend, or a professional fiduciary such as a bank or trust company. Similarly, when you are seeking compensation for yourself or your firm as the duly appointed trustee of a client's trust, and beneficiaries are objecting, you may have **conflicts of interest** that will need to be addressed.[11] `Taming the Text`

---

[11] `Your House; Your Rules` Some jurisdictions have special rules in their Rules of Professional Conduct, or as part of their law of trusts and estates, about when a lawyer for a trustor, trustee, beneficiary, or testator may serve as a trust or estate fiduciary. Be sure you know what your state allows. `Your House; Your Rules`

`Tips & Tactics` In addition, not all professional liability insurance policies cover claims that may be asserted against you because of your conduct as a trust or estate fiduciary (that is, serving in a position such as a trustee, executor, administrator, guardian, or conservator, rather than as a lawyer)—or at least not without a special "rider" that requires an extra premium. So before you agree to serve in a fiduciary capacity other than as an attorney (even for your own family members, and even without compensation), make sure that you know your local law and your professional liability insurance policy. `Tips & Tactics`

REASON FOR THE RULE Why all the restrictions on soliciting and documenting gifts when the gifts themselves are permitted if given in the proper way? Well, let's identify the **conflicting interests**: Lawyers would naturally like to receive gifts or bequests—who wouldn't? Clients, however, have a strong **interest** in exercising their own independent judgment about who should receive gifts or bequests of their property. And there is some real risk that the lawyer's self-**interest** in receiving a client gift could cause the lawyer, consciously or unconsciously, to press the client for gifts that the client otherwise might be less inclined to make. Think back to **Chapter 5.C at 108**—lawyers are held to fiduciary duties to their clients because the nature of the attorney-client relationship can cultivate a trust and dependence on the client's part that can make it easy for the lawyer to exercise undue influence over the client's judgment—even, at times, unconsciously. That can make it hard to determine how freely the client may really have chosen to favor the lawyer. To say that you can receive a gift but not ask for one is to shut down one avenue by which a lawyer might unfairly induce a client to indulge in a kind or degree of generosity that more detached and sober judgment might refuse. Similarly, disabling a lawyer from documenting a gift from the client to the lawyer or a member of the lawyer's family makes it less likely that the lawyer will slip something in front of the client in a moment of the client's pliability (or perhaps unbeknownst to the client altogether), and more likely that an independent advisor with no **interest** in the transaction will have to be brought in to consult and advise the client on the nature and significance of the proposed gift. *See* **Model Rule 1.8 Comments [6]-[7]**. **REASON FOR THE RULE**

In fact, **Model Rule 1.8 Comment [6]** reminds us that, in addition to the conduct expressly prohibited by the disciplinary rules, the civil law of fiduciary duty in most states also *presumes* that any gift from a client-beneficiary to a lawyer-fiduciary is the product of the lawyer's undue influence, rendering the gift voidable by the client or someone acting in the client's place (for example, an executor or heir after the client's death), unless the lawyer can meet her burden of proving that the gift was *not* the product of undue influence.

CONSEQUENCES Gifts improperly solicited or documented in violation of **Model Rule 1.8(c)** can result not only in professional discipline but in restitutionary remedies, including the return of the gift in kind if the donee still has it, or its appreciated value if the donee does not—in either case, plus any interest or profits made on the gift or its proceeds while they were in the donee's hands. Under more extreme circumstances involving an elderly or impaired donor, a lawyer may be accused of "elder abuse" (a tort-like protection variously defined in different states) or even fraud or theft. And remember that, even if the donor has no regrets, his or her successors or heirs may feel very differently about your receipt of property that they may perceive as their birthright. In short, the **consequences**

of violating the relevant Rules or violating your civil fiduciary duty without necessarily violating one of the specific prohibitions of **Model Rule 1.8** can be, and often are, very serious. CONSEQUENCES

> **Problem 22A-2:** Which of the following are violations of **Model Rule 1.8(c)**? Why or why not, and for those that are, what might the **consequences** be?
>
> a. Peggy Plaintiff (from the **Introduction to this subchapter at 604**) hires Frank's firm to handle her personal injury case. The firm achieves an excellent result: A substantial sum of money. Peggy tells Happy that she is deeply grateful and would like to give him a special token of her appreciation. She's been thinking of a very fancy wristwatch and asks him if he prefers Rolex or Breitling. Happy, genuinely moved, thanks Peggy for her generosity, sincerely reminds Peggy that she really doesn't need to do that, but if she really wants to know, he's always wanted a Rolex. Peggy delivers a gold Rolex watch costing over $5,000 to Happy, engraved "With gratitude" on the back of the case.
>
> b. The estate-planning partner in Frank's firm, Willie Willmaker, has a number of high-net-worth clients. He is meeting with one of them, an older gentleman named Richie Rich, at Richie's home and notices that, in addition to some impressive vintage cars, Richie has three Lincoln Continentals in the huge garage adjacent to his house. Richie explains that, before he retired, he used to have a staff of drivers to take guests and business associates around town, but he doesn't use them much anymore. Willie asks if his college-age son could borrow one of the Lincolns when he comes home for the summer to be able to commute to his summer job. Richie says, "Sure, for an old friend like you. Just write down something for us to sign that he's responsible for insurance, gas, and repairs, and has to return it by Labor Day." Willie does so.

3. Forbidden Negotiation for or Acquisition of Literary or Media Rights Related to an Engagement While the Engagement Is Pending

Model Rule 1.8(d) says you **must not** "make or negotiate an agreement" in which you obtain "literary or media rights to a portrayal or account based in substantial part on information relating to the representation until the engagement is over."

REASON FOR THE RULE The concern reflected here is that a lawyer who holds book, television, or motion picture rights to portray a sensational or celebrated legal matter might be tempted to handle the matter so as to be able to tell (and sell) a more compelling story later, while the client's best **interests** might lie in a different approach. Thus there would be potential **conflicts of interest** between the lawyer's personal **interests** and the client's regarding the conduct of the engagement, and we try to avoid them in this instance by prohibiting the lawyer from holding (or even asking for) any interest in media rights until after the matter itself is over. *See* **Model Rule 1.8 Comment [9]**. REASON FOR THE RULE

4. Forbidden Acquisition of Proprietary Interests in the Client's Cause of Action or in the Subject Matter of the Litigation

Model Rule 1.8(i) is a little more complicated. It says a lawyer **must not** "acquire a proprietary interest in the cause of action or subject matter of litigation the lawyer is conducting for a client . . . ." In simple terms, this means that, generally, you may not take a security or other ownership interest in the client's cause of action, or in the subject matter of the litigation that you're handling—for example, a disputed piece of property involved in a case in which you represent one of the parties to the dispute. There are two exceptions.

The *first* exception is that you **may** "acquire a lien authorized by law to secure the lawyer's fee or expenses." **Model Rule 1.8(i)(1); Model Rule 1.8 Comment [19]**. Such a security interest in the claims that you're litigating on the client's behalf is generally called an "attorney's lien" or a "charging lien," and it is among the most common means that lawyers use to ensure payment of their fees or costs in a litigation matter. Your House; Your Rules Charging liens differ state to state in how they may be obtained, perfected (that is, made enforceable against third parties), and documented, so be sure to learn what your state requires. In some states, they arise as a matter of law when the lawyer works on the case or appears as counsel of record; in other states, an express agreement with the client, or notice of some kind to the client, the court, or third parties is required. If you don't create, perfect, or document your charging lien properly under governing state law, you may lose this source of payment of your fees (or only get what's left after the client's other creditors have been paid). Your House; Your Rules Note that the Rule limits use of the lien on the claim that you're litigating to securing the payment of your fees or expenses, which implies that you **must not** use the cause of action or subject matter of the litigation that you're handling to secure any *other* debt that the client may owe you.

The *second* exception is that you **may** "contract with a client for a reasonable contingent fee in a civil case." **Model Rule 1.8(i)(2); Model Rule 1.8 Comment [19]**. As we've already discussed (*see* **Chapter 20.B at 541**), contingent fees in most civil cases are permissible in every American state. But because a contingent fee gives the lawyer an interest in the recovery on the claims being litigated, it must be called out here as an exception to the general prohibition on taking any interest in the client's cause of action.

> Problem 22A-3: Which of the following arrangements violate **Model Rule 1.8**, which subsection, and why?
>
> a. A colleague of Danielle's in the DA's office prosecutes sex crimes. She routinely asks the survivors of sexual assaults that she is investigating to agree to her use of the facts that she learns from the survivors and the things that the survivors say to her in a book on which she is working, tentatively entitled "Reports from the Front Lines in the #MeToo Wars."

Some survivors agree. When the DA asks the prosecutor whether this is a good idea, she points out that prosecutors represent the State, not crime victims. Does your analysis change if Danielle's colleague uses a form of agreement that promises not to publish anything regarding the survivor's case until after the prosecution involving the survivor is over? How about if the agreement promises not to use the survivor's name or any other identifying detail? If so, how and why; and if not, why not?

b. Same as **Problem 22A-1(e) at 612** (Maya's firm takes a lien on client Danny Devisee's inherited block of unregistered stock in a publicly traded company in order to secure a $100,000 loan that the firm makes to Danny to cover his living expenses while the firm helps to register the shares, find a buyer, and negotiate a sale). Then litigation breaks out among the shareholders of the company. The claims flying among the shareholders include a challenge to the will under which Danny inherited his shares which, if successful, will result in the shares going to other heirs. Can Maya's firm represent Danny in this litigation? Can it do so on a contingent fee basis, where the fee will be measured by a percentage of the amount for which the shares are eventually sold? Can Danny and the firm also agree that the firm will advance the costs of the litigation, and that Danny will repay those costs only out of the sales proceeds of his shares?

c. Frank's firm has decided to upgrade its computer systems. To help defray the cost, the firm is going to sell its old computers to Regina Recycler, who deals in used computer equipment, for $10,000. As it turns out, Regina is also in a commercial dispute with another of her customers and asks the firm if it can represent her in collecting amounts due to her. The litigation partner, Happy Trials, evaluates Regina's claim and offers to represent Regina in collecting the debt for a contingent fee equal to a percentage of her recovery in that case. Just in case, Happy asks that Regina grant the firm a lien on the recovery in the collection case that secures both the firm's fee in that case and the $10,000 that Regina owes the firm for its old equipment. Regina agrees. Does it matter if part of the agreement is that Regina need not pay the amounts that she owes the firm for the computer equipment until the collection case is over? If so, how and why; and if not, why not?

5. Substantive and Formal Requirements for Those Transactions with Clients That Are Not Forbidden

As just discussed, **Model Rules 1.8(c), (d), (e), and (i)** and the civil law of fiduciary duty make a range of gifts to or from, or transactions with, a client, as well as certain conduct in connection with such transfers, completely impermissible. But many transactions with clients (and conduct in connection with them) don't fall within any of those prohibitions. That's where **Model Rule 1.8(a)** comes in. The Rule covers any transaction with a client that other Rules do not forbid (with some important exceptions not obvious from the Rule's language that we'll discuss below). Let's pause and read the Rule together—we'll do it out here while you open your rule book or click on the link. Ready? Go.

a. The Scope of Model Rule 1.8(a): Any "Business Transaction with a Client," or Any Acquisition of Any Kind of Proprietary "Interest Adverse to a Client"

Having read the Rule, you now know that **Model Rule 1.8(a)** literally covers *any* "business transaction with a client" and *any* "knowing[] acqui[sition of] an ownership, possessory, security or other pecuniary **interest** adverse to a client."

TAMING THE TEXT ▶ "Business transaction" is broadly construed to mean any exchange of any kind, and there are even a few court decisions that seem to say that the client's investment in a business or property owned by someone else in which the lawyer also has an **interest** is a "business transaction" between the lawyer and the client for this purpose.[12] There is no requirement that the transaction have any relation to the services that the lawyer is providing to the client for the transaction to be covered by the Rule, providing another example of ways in which the Rules are careful to guard against any broader lawyer influence outside the particular legal services provided.

"[K]nowing[] acqui[sition of] an ownership, possessory, security or other pecuniary **interest** adverse to a client" is interpreted similarly broadly. The acquisition has to be "knowing[]" in the sense that you're not to blame if you don't know that the **interest** you're acquiring is "adverse to a client." Though it's not particularly common, that could happen if, for example, your client sells things on eBay using a screen name unknown to you, and you happen to buy something from that seller. If you knew that the seller was your client, however, **Model Rule 1.8(a)** would apply, regardless of whether the item you bought had anything to do with the work you were doing for the client.

And "adverse to a client" means that whatever interest you're acquiring is one with respect to which the client is, in one way or another, on the other side of the interest. If you take a lien in a client's property, for example, that's a classic "interest adverse to a client." It's not unusual for a lawyer to take a security interest in a client's property in order to secure the payment of the lawyer's fees and costs. That security interest can be in property involved in the lawyer's engagement, but it doesn't have to be. If you secured payment of your fees or costs with a lien on a client's business assets, or her home, or her block of shares in a publicly traded company that had nothing to do with your engagement, any of those would be the acquisition of an interest adverse to your client within the scope of **Model Rule 1.8(a)**.[13]

Beyond that, any interest you acquired that could be seen as "adverse" to your clients' **interests**—whether or not related to the legal work you're doing for that

---

[12] *See, e.g., Beery v. State Bar*, 43 Cal. 3d 802 (1987). Try to explain out loud why a client's investment in a company or property in which the lawyer is also an investor is not, at least on its face, a "business transaction" (or any other kind of transaction) between the lawyer and the client.

[13] And remember that **Model Rule 1.8(i)** provides that, although you **must not** take a security interest in the client's cause of action or the subject matter of the litigation to secure a debt that the client owes to you *other than* what you are owed for fees or expenses, you **may** take a security interest in such property to secure the payment of your fees and expenses. *See* **Chapter 22.A at 616**. What we're learning now is that, though such a transaction isn't forbidden, it **must** still comply with **Model Rule 1.8(a)**.

client—falls within the Rule. So if you rent office space in a building owned by your client (that is, the client is your landlord), or conversely if a client sublets a little of your extra office space from you, the creation of that landlord-tenant relationship counts as the acquisition of an interest adverse to your client within the meaning of **Model Rule 1.8(a)**, even if the work that you do for that client has nothing to do with the building. <small>TAMING THE TEXT</small>

b. Implicit Exceptions to the Scope of Model Rule 1.8(a)

There are no explicit exceptions to the scope of **Model Rule 1.8(a)** stated in the Rule itself. But there are three recognized categories of transactions to which **Model Rule 1.8(a)** does not apply despite the Rule's sweepingly broad language. Perversely, they are the most common kinds of transactions in which lawyers and clients engage.[14]

i. Exception: The Basic Fee Agreement Between Lawyer and Client

By far the most common "business transaction" between lawyer and client is their agreement regarding the services that the lawyer will provide and the fees and costs that the client will pay for those services. Most such transactions are *not* covered by **Model Rule 1.8(a)** despite their literal description in the Rule. **Model Rule 1.8 Comment [1]** makes it clear that the Rule "does not apply to ordinary fee arrangements between client and lawyer, which are governed by **[Model] Rule 1.5**, although [**Model Rule 1.8(a)'s**] requirements must be met when the lawyer accepts an interest in the client's business or other nonmonetary property as payment of all or part of a fee."

So an ordinary fee agreement (that is, one in which the client agrees to pay with consideration in the form of money, rather than a transfer of some other species of property in kind) **must** comply with the formal and substantive requirements of **Model Rule 1.5** (*see* **Chapter 20.B at 537**), but not the more intensive requirements of **Model Rule 1.8(a)**.

ii. Exception: An Agreement in Which the Lawyer Takes a Security Interest in the Client's Litigation Claims to Secure Payment of Fees and Costs, at Least as to a Contingent Fee

And here's where it gets even weirder: The most common arrangement in which a lawyer "accepts an interest in the client's . . . nonmonetary property" is an attorney's lien or the grant of a consensual security interest by the client in a litigation claim that the lawyer is handling on the client's behalf. Lawyers

---

[14] We've seen this rather strange drafting strategy before in the Model Rules—broad, inclusive language in the Rule itself, with significant modifications or exceptions suggested in the Comments. *See, e.g.,* **Chapter 11.B at 346**. All three implicit exceptions to **Model Rule 1.8(a)** meet this description as well. No, we don't think it's a very good way to write rules either, but nobody asked us.

commonly take such liens on the client's claims and their proceeds to secure payment of the lawyer's fees and costs in litigation matters, especially if the fee is a contingent fee based on the matter's outcome. (As discussed above, in some states, that attorney's lien arises automatically as a matter of law when the lawyer is retained to litigate the claim on the client's behalf; in other states, the lien must be obtained by agreement and possibly by other steps as well.)

TAMING THE TEXT Many states, however, do *not* require compliance with **Model Rule 1.8(a)** in connection with obtaining such a lien, despite its obvious and literal inclusion in the scope language of the Rule. The Model Rules don't address this exclusion directly, but **Model Rule 1.8 Comment [16]** states that "[w]hen a lawyer acquires by contract a security interest in property *other than that recovered through the lawyer's efforts in the litigation*, such an acquisition is a business or financial transaction with a client and is governed by the requirements of [**Model Rule 1.8(a)**]" (emphasis added). The strong implication of that statement is that security interests in the claims that the lawyer is handling, or their proceeds, are *not* governed by **Model Rule 1.8(a)**. (Do you see why?) And **Model Rule 1.8 Comment [16]** goes on to say that "[c]ontracts for contingent fees are governed by [**Model**] **Rule 1.5**." This language also suggests that they are *not* covered by **Model Rule 1.8**. And as previously discussed in **Chapter 20.B at 541**, **Model Rule 1.5(a)** requires contingent fees to be "reasonable," and **Model Rule 1.5(c)** provides a number of formal requirements that must be met for a contingent fee to be enforceable, including that it be **in a writing signed by the client** that discloses various important terms. Those requirements are significant, but as we'll see shortly, they are less demanding than those set out in **Model Rule 1.8(a)**. **TAMING THE TEXT**

YOUR HOUSE; YOUR RULES Unfortunately, it gets even more confusing than that. At least a few states say that you don't have to follow **Model Rule 1.8(a)** when you acquire a security interest in the client's litigation claim to secure a *contingent* fee in the litigation, but you *do* have to follow the Rule if you acquire a security interest in the client's litigation claim to secure payment of a *non-contingent* fee (for example, an hourly fee or a flat fee) for the litigation.[15] Finding out what your jurisdiction expects on this point is quite important, because compliance with the applicable requirements is necessary for your lien to be enforceable (and that lien is often important to getting your fees paid). **YOUR HOUSE; YOUR RULES**

TIPS & TACTICS One safe way to deal with this rather messy uncertainty is simply to comply with the most demanding standard once you determine that the transaction is permissible. As a practical matter, that means full compliance with **Model Rule 1.5** to document your fee arrangement (if the transaction in question is a fee arrangement), with additional disclosures and consent built into your engagement letter that are sufficient to comply fully with **Model Rule 1.8(a)**, which

---

[15] *See, e.g.,* Cal. R. Prof. Cond. 1.8.1 Comment [1]; *Fletcher v. Davis,* 33 Cal.4th 61, 68 (2004).

we will see shortly is more demanding than **Model Rule 1.5**. Then you're likely safe, no matter what your jurisdiction requires. (Tips & Tactics)

iii. Exception: Ordinary Commercial Transactions That the Client Offers to the Public on Similar Terms

Model Rule 1.8(a) also doesn't apply to "standard commercial transactions between the lawyer and the client for products or services that the client generally markets to others, for example, banking or brokerage services, medical services, products manufactured or distributed by the client, and utilities' services." **Model Rule 1.8 Comment [1]**. For example, if you represent a commercial bank in your town (say, in debt collection work) and also happen to do your personal (or, for that matter, your law office's professional) banking there, then even though those banking transactions literally meet the description of a "business transaction with a client," they are excluded from **Model Rule 1.8(a)'s** requirements and require no special attention or documentation.

Problem 22A-4: Which of the following arrangements fall within the scope of **Model Rule 1.8(a)**, and why?

a. Maya's firm represents Moosey's, a high-quality department-store chain. Maya shops there occasionally and applies for a store credit card.

b. Same as (a). Moosey's stock is publicly traded. After being sure that no one in her firm has any inside information (Maya's firm and those like it that represent public companies have policies that allow employees to find out when it is proper to trade in the securities of client companies without violating insider trading laws), Maya buys 100 shares of Moosey's for her 401k retirement account.

c. Same as **Problem 22.A-2(b) at 615** (Willie Willmaker is admiring the many automobiles that his wealthy client, Richie Rich, owns), except that Richie announces that he intends to dispose of his late-model Lincoln Continentals, which he no longer uses. Needing an extra car for his son returning from college for the summer, Willie asks what Richie wants for one of the Lincolns. They agree on the Kelley Blue Book wholesale price for the car.

d. Frank's firm takes on a real estate dispute on an hourly basis. In the written engagement agreement, the client agrees to a retainer of $10,000 as a deposit against future fees and costs.

e. Same as (d), but the engagement agreement also says, "we [the firm] will have a lien on your retainer, which will be deposited in our firm's client trust account."

f. Same as (d), but the engagement agreement also says, "we [the firm] will have a lien on your claims and rights asserted in the Action [defined elsewhere in the fee agreement as the dispute the firm is engaged to handle], and on any recovery, whether by settlement, judgment, or otherwise, you obtain in or in connection with the Action."

c. What Model Rule 1.8(a) Requires in the Transactions That It Covers

i. Substantive Requirement: The Terms of the Transaction Must Be "Fair and Reasonable to the Client"

Model Rule 1.8(a)(1) requires that any transaction or acquisition of an adverse interest covered by the Rule **must** be "fair and reasonable to the client." This is a striking departure from the law governing ordinary commercial transactions. As you probably recall from your Contracts class, usually we make no effort to scrutinize the adequacy of contractual consideration; once we've satisfied ourselves that there is *some* consideration exchanged (remember that peppercorn?), we consider that requirement for enforceability of the contract satisfied.[16] Here, because the contract is between a fiduciary (lawyer) and beneficiary (client), any transaction within the scope of **Model Rule 1.8(a)** will be scrutinized vigorously for substantive fairness. In fact, under the general fiduciary law applicable in most states, any transaction between fiduciary and beneficiary is *presumed to be **unfair***, and the fiduciary (lawyer) bears the burden of proving that it is fair and reasonable to the beneficiary (client). *See* **Model Rule 1.8 Comment [6]**.

TIPS & TACTICS Needless to say, the requirement of fairness in fact opens the door to second-guessing the transaction later with the benefit of 20-20 hindsight and the possibility of the client's or a successor's undoing a transaction that has proved unfavorable (with a possible helping of professional discipline for the lawyer on the side). All in all, that's a pretty wretched day at the office, and it strongly suggests that any transactions with clients, including transactions to secure the payment of fees and costs that fall within **Model Rule 1.8(a)**, **should** be undertaken with great care. TIPS & TACTICS

As we will now see, not only must the transaction be substantively fair and reasonable to the client, it must also be disclosed and documented elaborately and precisely, with any failure to do so leading to the same **consequences** as if the transaction were substantively unfair.

ii. Formal Requirement: The Terms of the Transaction Must Be Fully Disclosed to the Client in Writing

In addition to being substantively fair and reasonable, the terms of the transaction with or acquisition of an interest adverse to the client **must** be "fully disclosed and transmitted in writing in a manner that can be reasonably understood by the client . . . ." **Model Rule 1.8(a)(1)**. Let's break that down and examine how demanding this part of the Rule is. There are three distinct requirements in that short phrase: (1) The terms of the lawyer-client transaction must be fully disclosed; that is, everything **material** about the transaction has to be laid out.

---

[16] Yes, we have doctrines like duress and unconscionability to provide relief in extreme circumstances, but the standards to establish them are demanding.

(2) This disclosure has to be "transmitted in writing"; that is, you've got to do it in durable form so that a disciplinary prosecutor or a court can scrutinize its adequacy later. (3) The written disclosure of the terms of the transaction must be accomplished in terms that the client can reasonably understand. In other words, just presenting an agreement written in the kind of legalese that a lawyer could follow will rarely be sufficient. In disclosing the terms of the transaction, you must take into account the legal sophistication, literacy, education, English language skills, and cognitive abilities of the *actual client* with whom you're dealing, not some hypothetical reasonable person with whom your client may have little in common. Quite frequently, then, just making sure that the client has the opportunity to review the writing memorializing the deal between lawyer and client will *not* be sufficient to satisfy this requirement. For anyone other than a legally sophisticated client, you'll need to provide a separate, more accessible summary of the deal terms; a "Reader's Digest" version, if you will.

iii. Formal Requirement: The Client Must Be Advised in Writing of the Desirability of Consulting Independent Counsel and Given a Reasonable Opportunity to Do So

In addition to the written disclosure of all the terms of the transaction in a form the client can reasonably understand, the client **must** also be "advised in writing of the desirability of seeking . . . independent legal counsel on the transaction" and be "given a reasonable opportunity" to do so. **Model Rule 1.8(a)(2)**.
‹ REASON FOR THE RULE › The reason for this rule is rooted in the possibilities for subtle (or not-so-subtle) misuse of the lawyer's fiduciary role of trust and confidence. One way to guard against the lawyer's possible undue influence in inducing a client to enter into a transaction that might be ill-advised for the client is to introduce an independent advisor (or at least the opportunity to get one) to provide the client with perspective and disinterested advice. ‹ REASON FOR THE RULE ›

‹ TAMING THE TEXT › **Model Rule 1.8(a)(2)** does *not* go so far as to *require* independent counsel in a lawyer-client transaction covered by **Model Rule 1.8(a)**, but it does try to make certain that the client is made fully aware of this right and is advised that it would be a good idea to exercise it.[17] And not only **must** the client be advised of the right to independent advice on the transaction *and* the wisdom of getting it, she **must** also be given "a reasonable opportunity to seek" it. That means giving the client all the time that she reasonably needs to get any outside advice that she wishes and making it clear that she has all the time that she wants to do so. ‹ TAMING THE TEXT ›

---

[17] Compare **Model Rule 1.8(c)**, which affirmatively requires independent counsel to draft any instrument of gift or bequest in which the beneficiary is the lawyer herself or a member of her family. *See* **Chapter 22.A at 612**.

iv. Formal Requirement: The Client Must Give Informed Consent, in a Writing Signed by the Client, to the Principal Terms of the Transaction and the Lawyer's Role in It

Having received the written disclosure of all the terms of the transaction and the lawyer's role, as well as the admonition and opportunity to seek independent advice, there is yet another formal requirement: The client **must** "give[] **informed consent, in a writing signed by the client**, to the essential terms of the transaction and the lawyer's role in the transaction, including whether the lawyer is representing the client in the transaction." **Model Rule 1.8(a)(3)**. Remember, **informed consent** is consent "after the lawyer has communicated adequate information and explanation about the **material** risks of and reasonably available alternatives to the proposed course of conduct." **Model Rule 1.0(e)**. Consent without the disclosure of complete information regarding "**material** risks of and reasonably available alternatives to the proposed course of conduct" is the equivalent of no consent at all.

TIPS & TACTICS One good way to document that all the formal requirements for a transaction with a client governed by **Model Rule 1.8(a)** have been met is to create a single writing that states all the main terms of the transaction and transmit that to the client in a way that memorializes the date that the client receives it. That separate cover letter or memo accompanying the agreement memorializing the transaction **should** summarize (i) the principal terms of the transaction, (ii) the lawyer's role in the transaction (including whether you are representing the client in the transaction), (iii) the **material** risks of, and reasonably available alternatives to, the proposed transaction, and (iv) the admonition that the client has the right to seek independent legal and other advice, should get that advice, and should take all the time that she reasonably needs to do so.

Then, either right before or after (and if possible on the same page as) the client's signature agreeing to the transaction, or in a separate writing attached to the writing memorializing the agreement, you should create a separate statement in which the client acknowledges receiving full written disclosure of (i) all the terms of the transaction and a summary of its principal terms, (ii) the lawyer's role in the transaction, (iii) the **material** risks of, and reasonably available alternatives to, the proposed transaction, and (iv) the right to independent legal and other advice, the desirability of seeking it, and the right to take all the time that the client reasonably needs to do so, as well as the fact that the client has in fact sought any independent advice that she wished, and that the client is voluntarily agreeing to the terms of the transaction in light of all those disclosures.

When the client is ready to go ahead, she may use this document to confirm her agreement to the transaction by signing and dating this document, which contains all the necessary disclosures and consents, a reasonable period *after* the disclosures were transmitted (showing the client did in fact take some time to think about it and get any advice she wanted). The urgency of pending events may make it tempting to call the client into your office and rush any review and signature of a detailed disclosure and consent while you sit there impatiently, but this is a very bad idea if you want your agreement to remain enforceable if the client (or a successor-in-interest) develops buyer's remorse. Remember, if you fail to meet any formal (that is, process-oriented) requirement of **Model Rule 1.8(a)**, you are not only subject to professional discipline, the transaction is subject to rescission and restitution at the client's request, *even if the transaction was completely fair and reasonable.*

If this makes it sound rather difficult and effortful to undertake a transaction with your client other than the common ones excluded from the scope of **Model Rule 1.8(a)** (*see* **Chapter 22.A at 618**), that's because that's pretty much what the Rule intends. Transactions outside the range of ordinary fee agreements are unusual and easily subject to abuse, and thus subjected to unusually exacting scrutiny. If you're going to enter into one, then you'd best be sure that everything is meticulously documented and fully in order. **Tips & Tactics**

v. **Consequences** What Happens If You Fail to Meet the Formal and Substantive Requirements That Model Rule 1.8(a) Demands of All Lawyer-Client Transactions Within Its Scope?

If the lawyer fails to meet her burden of proving that the transaction was fair and reasonable to the client *or* fails to show that she met each of the formal requirements of **Model Rule 1.8(a)**, professional discipline can result. In addition, the client **may** rescind (undo) the transaction. In that event, the client **may** recover any consideration that the client gave in the transaction, plus any profits or appreciation that accrued to the lawyer under restitutionary principles of unjust enrichment. In addition or instead, the client **may** recover any monetary damage that the client may have suffered as a result of the violation. In short, substantive or technical failures to comply with **Model Rule 1.8(a)** put the client in the classic "heads, I win; tails, you lose" situation vis-à-vis a lawyer who didn't play by the rules. You can see where that leaves the lawyer. **Consequences**

> **Problem 22A-5:** Which of the following situations violate **Model Rule 1.8(a)**, and why?
>
> a. Same as **Problem 22.A-4(c) at 621** (Willie Willmaker is buying one of Richie Rich's Lincoln Continentals for his son to use), except Richie says, "heck, you'd be doing me a favor taking one off my hands," and offers to sell it to Willie for half of the Kelley Blue Book wholesale value. Willie accepts and writes Richie a check on the spot.
>
> b. Same as (a), but Willie provides all required disclosures and gets all required consents in writing. The Purchase and Sale Agreement for the Lincoln includes a clause stating, "The parties understand and agree that the sale price for the Vehicle to which they are agreeing is significantly less than the Vehicle's fair market value. Buyer is accepting this price as an accommodation to Seller, who wishes to dispose of the Vehicle promptly."

c. Same as (a), except that the purchase price is agreed to be the Kelley Blue Book wholesale price. Willie pulls a standard form Purchase and Sale Agreement for a car out of his form file from some work that he did once for an auto dealership, fills in the blanks, and offers it to Richie to sign.

d. Same as (c), except Willie types in on the bottom, near the signature lines, "Seller acknowledges that he has the right to consult independent counsel regarding this transaction." Willie runs back to Richie's house that afternoon, and they sign the agreement.

e. Same as (d), except Willie also types on the form at the bottom, "Seller also acknowledges that Buyer is his attorney in various matters, including Seller's estate planning."

6. Restrictions on Situations in Which There Is a "Significant Risk" That the Representation of a Client Will Be "Materially Limited" by a "Personal Interest of the Lawyer"

Way back in the **chapter Introduction at 602** (we know, it was a pretty long way back at this point, and we still have a long way to go; sorry), we pointed out that some **conflicts** issues have crystallized into bright-line rules categorically forbidding, or requiring explicit disclosure of and **informed consent** to, certain defined arrangements or conduct, while others are judged by fuzzier general standards to determine whether protective action need be taken. The situations discussed in the first five subsections of **Chapter 22.A at 604**—described in **Model Rules 1.8(a), (c), (d), (e), and (i)**—are governed by bright-line rules. For example, you **must not** document a client's gift or bequest to yourself or a member of your own family, and no amount of explaining how the circumstances in one particular case address all the potential risks will relax the rule.

But there is also a general and more flexible Rule that addresses any situation not covered by the specific protections in **Model Rule 1.8** in which the lawyer's personal **interests** and the client's **interests** may be in **conflict**. That Rule is **Model Rule 1.7(a)(2)**.

We'll come back to this Rule again in the next subchapter (because it also applies when a lawyer has **conflicting** duties to two or more clients), but now let's focus on the aspects of the Rule that address **conflicts** between a lawyer's personal **interests** and those of a client. In relevant part, **Model Rule 1.7(a)(2)** provides:

> [A] lawyer shall not represent a client if . . . there is a significant risk that the representation of one or more clients will be **materially** limited by . . . a personal **interest** of the lawyer [unless the affected client(s) give **informed consent, confirmed in writing**].[18]

TAMING THE TEXT The Rule is mandatory ("shall not"), and what a lawyer **must not** do is governed by two rather fuzzy standards: The engagement is forbidden (or requires the client's **informed** written **consent**) if there is a *"significant risk"* that the

---

[18] We'll talk about **informed consent** to a **conflict of interest** in **Chapter 22.E at 733**. Here, we'll discuss what you **must not** do in the absence of such **informed** written **consent**.

client's representation will be "*materially*" limited by a personal interest of the lawyer (emphases added; "materially" is also bolded because it's a defined term that you can look up in the **Glossary**). Why these standards? Well, they tell us that, in order to be something that the lawyer **must** refrain from (or seek the client's **informed consent** to before proceeding), this personal **interest** has to be quite strong: Not just the daily kinds of temptations that everyone feels—say, to be liked, or to do a favor so that you can be owed one, or the general temptation that might present itself to increase a bill or make more money on an engagement—but something so strong and personal that it genuinely creates a "significant risk" that it could adversely affect the way you treat or represent your client. And not just a little, but "**materially**"—that is, in a way that really matters. And you can see that the standard is a *predictive* one—that is, one that asks us to judge the *risk* that something bad *could* happen under these circumstances *before* anything bad *actually* happens, and even though nothing bad may ever actually happen.

Taming the Text

Perhaps the best way to help you get a feel for what rises to the level of a **Model Rule 1.7(a)(2) conflict of interest** (as opposed to the milder garden-variety temptations that you need not address, other than by being sensible) is to talk about the most common kinds of personal interests that require serious scrutiny to determine whether they've reached the threshold that the Rule sets. When a lawyer's personal interests are at stake, the situation often involves an important personal relationship or potential relationship with opposing counsel or an opposing party.

a. Close Personal Relationships

Imagine, for example, discovering that opposing counsel in a new dispute or deal is your spouse or sibling. Or discovering that a close friend or relation is employed by, or has an investment in, the business organization that your client is suing. You might be concerned about how the dynamics of that close personal relationship might alchemize in the crucible of the adversary process. (Pop quiz: What's the **conflict**? Describe the **conflicting interests** on either side of this situation, something that it's always important to do when you're faced with a potential **conflict of interest**.) Certainly a reasonable client would have such concerns. And, in fact, the Drafters of the Model Rules reflected exactly that concern in **Model Rule 1.7 Comment [11]**:

> When lawyers representing different clients in the same matter or in substantially related matters are closely related by blood or marriage, there may be a significant risk that client **confidences** will be revealed and that the lawyer's family relationship will interfere with both **loyalty** and independent professional judgment. As a result, each client is entitled to know of the existence and implications of the relationship between the lawyers before the lawyer agrees to undertake the representation. Thus, a lawyer related to another lawyer, e.g., as parent, child, sibling or spouse, ordinarily may not represent a client in a matter where that lawyer is representing another party, unless each client gives **informed consent**.

So marital or close blood relations with opposing counsel must either be avoided or be given **informed consent** by both clients after full disclosure of all the facts and potential risks. But what if a spouse or close relation is not literally on the other side of the table, but another member of his or her **practice organization** is? **Model Rule 1.7 Comment [11]** again provides guidance: "The disqualification arising from a close family relationship is personal and ordinarily is not **imputed** to members of firms with whom the lawyers are associated."[19] Notice that the Comment says that a close relationship with a member of a **practice organization** not personally involved in the matter at hand is "ordinarily" not disqualifying. The Comment is telling us that, in those circumstances, we still need to evaluate whether there is nevertheless a "significant risk" that the relationship could "materially" affect your conduct of the matter because of features unique to the situation that create such a risk.

Of course, beyond marital and close blood relations, which usually involve strong emotional connections, most of us have relationships of varying intensities with lots of people, from people with whom we're cohabiting, to lifelong best friends, to people we're dating, to fellow members of a club or organization, to people with whom we recently had a cordial conversation (or an argument) at a potluck. The fact that there's a smooth continuum of relational intimacy in human affairs from quite a lot to none at all means that there are line-drawing challenges in determining who is sufficiently close to you to create a "significant risk" the relationship could "**materially**" affect your representation if that person becomes your opposing counsel or otherwise involved in your engagement.

Just as importantly, some relationships might not rise to the level of creating a "significant risk" of "**material**" adverse effects on your client but could be of the kind that a reasonable client would, or your actual client might, reasonably want to know, in which case your **duty of candor** and **Model Rule 1.4** require you to disclose them (*see* **Chapter 5.D at 117**). Still other connections that we have with others require nothing more than good common sense.

ABA Formal Ethics Opinion No. 494 (2020) provides a framework for analyzing how to draw these lines in situations involving close personal relationships. It suggests a number of nonexclusive factors to consider in describing what steps might be necessary or appropriate, including the degree to which the nature or strength of the relationship might affect the matter; each lawyer's role in the matter; any risks to the integrity of **confidential information**; and whether the relationship changes in any **material** way over time.[20]

---

[19] "**Imputation**" is the attribution of one lawyer's **conflict of interest** to other lawyers in the same **practice organization**. Comment [11]'s guidance is based on **Model Rule 1.10(a)(1)**, which provides that a "prohibition" to participate in an engagement is not **imputed** to other lawyers in the same **practice organization** if "the prohibition is based on a personal **interest** of the disqualified lawyer and does not present a significant risk of **materially** limiting the representation of the client by the remaining lawyers in the firm." We'll discuss **imputation** in detail in **Chapter 22.D at 702**.

[20] *Id.* at 3-5.

The Opinion loosely divides personal relationships into three categories:

1. "Intimate relationships" such as cohabitation, engagement, or other "exclusive intimate relationships," which "should be treated similarly to married couples for **conflicts** purposes." Less exclusive intimate relationships require careful evaluation and judgment, but generally **should** be disclosed and given **informed consent** by both clients.[21]

2. "Friendships may be the most difficult category to navigate," the Opinion warns. "[O]pposing lawyers who are friends are not *for that reason* alone prohibited from representing adverse clients. The analysis turns on the closeness of the friendship" (emphasis in original). The depth, frequency, and nature of the friends' contacts will determine if the situation requires the clients' **informed consent**, whether it needs only to be disclosed under the lawyers' **duty of candor**, or whether no action is required.[22]

3. "Acquaintances are relationships that do not carry the familiarity, affinity or attachment of friendships." They generally do not create any ethical obligations of disclosure or consent.[23]

b. Other Personal Interests Creating Significant Risks of Material Effects on the Lawyer's Conduct

What about other personal interests of a lawyer besides those created by close personal relationships? Once again, the standard is whether, under all the relevant facts and circumstances, there is a "significant risk" that the lawyer's interest will "**materially**" affect the lawyer's conduct of the engagement. Sometimes there will be such risks. As **Model Rule 1.7 Comment [10]** elaborates:

> For example, if the probity of a lawyer's own conduct in a transaction is in serious question, it may be difficult or impossible for the lawyer to give a client detached advice. Similarly, when a lawyer has discussions concerning possible employment with an opponent of the lawyer's client, or with a law firm representing the opponent, such discussions could materially limit the lawyer's representation of the client. In addition, a lawyer may not allow related business interests to affect representation, for example, by referring clients to an enterprise in which the lawyer has an undisclosed financial interest.

Similarly, any situation in which you owe fiduciary duties of **loyalty** not grounded in an attorney-client relationship to someone other than your client that may **conflict** with your client's **interests**—for example, if you serve as a corporate director or as an estate fiduciary, such as a trustee, executor, conservator, or guardian—you are at risk that those duties could **conflict** with duties to your client, and **Model Rule 1.7(a)(2)** comes into play. *See* **Model Rule 1.7 Comment [9]**.

---

[21] *Id.* at 5-6.
[22] *Id.* at 6-7 (emphasis in original).
[23] *Id.* at 7-8.

TIPS & TACTICS The inherent uncertainty in determining when circumstances create a "significant risk" that a lawyer's personal interest could "**materially**" affect the engagement (requiring abstention from the engagement or disclosure to and consent by the clients), or when a reasonable client would (or your actual client reasonably does) want to know about the circumstances (requiring disclosure as a matter of **candor**) will usually leave lingering questions when you fail to disclose and obtain **informed consent** in any but the most obviously innocuous situations.

The best practice is simple: If there's any question about whether the client might care, either now or eventually, then disclose, obtain the clients' **informed consent in a writing signed by the client**, and if for some reason that isn't possible, bow out—either for another lawyer in your **practice organization**, or for a separate **practice organization** altogether. Don't hesitate to raise the issue because you're concerned that the client is going to be upset: If the client is going to be upset about the situation *now*, imagine how outraged he'll be if something goes wrong, or he is displeased with the conduct or outcome of the engagement, and *then* finds out. As we reminded you in **Chapter 5.D at 124**,

Conversations that begin "Why didn't you tell me . . ." rarely end well.

And don't forget the **don't-wanna test**: The more strongly you feel the urge *not* to disclose your personal relationship or **interest** and ask the client for consent, the more likely that it is, as a practical matter, something that the client would consider important to know. (No, not always, but often enough that this is a good practical measure of what you need to do, or at least when you need to inquire of yourself more searchingly why you're hesitating.) At a minimum, you're risking the loss of good client relations and trust, and often the result of 'fessing up too late leads to much worse. In fact, our collective experience is that clients generally appreciate this kind of information and trust a lawyer's considered advice about whether or not it's a problem. Quite often, transparency strengthens client relations.

And when in doubt, get a second opinion. If you're the junior lawyer on a team and this kind of issue arises for you, tell your supervisors and let them help you decide what to do. If you're the sole lawyer on the matter, consult a wise head in your **practice organization** (with appropriate steps to make the consultation **confidential** and **attorney-client privileged**, *see* **Chapter 8.B at 244**), or another source of **privileged** advice. When there are personal **interests** that arguably could interfere with your own judgment, backstop your judgment with someone you trust. TIPS & TACTICS

Problem 22A-6: What steps, if any, **must** or **should** each of these lawyers take to address the following circumstances? In each case, please explain each thing the lawyer **must** or **should** do, explain whether it's a **must** or a **should**, and explain why.

a. **Mess in the Press:** A lawyer served as in-house general counsel to the Indiana Utility Regulatory Commission. The Commission is a state government agency that regulates and sets rates for the public utilities (gas, electric, water, etc.) in Indiana. A large electric utility applied for a rate increase; whether to grant the increase, and if so in what amount, were both fairly arguable questions under state law on which interested constituencies disagreed. The Commission lawyer was under consideration for an in-house job at the electric utility during the pendency of the rate-increase application on which the lawyer was advising the Commission.[24]

b. Danielle is prosecuting a joy-riding case. The District Attorney who has been elected to run the county DA's office has an adolescent son, and defense counsel has just notified Danielle that the DA's son will be testifying at trial to provide the defendant with an alibi.

c. Maya is working on a contentious hostile takeover fight. Opposing counsel is another big firm with an office in town. In another, unrelated matter, Maya's firm is representing the opposing firm in defending a malpractice claim that a former client of the other firm has made against the other firm. Does your analysis change if the malpractice claim is based on a different hostile takeover? How about if one of the litigation partners in Maya's firm working on the current takeover (litigators and business lawyers typically collaborate on these kinds of disputes) is involved in opposing counsel's defense? Please explain why your analysis would or would not change, and if it would, how and why; or if not, why not.

d. Frank's firm is representing a products-liability plaintiff who was seriously injured by a malfunctioning power tool made by a small local manufacturer of tools and supplies for home hobbyists called Garage Gear. If the plaintiff prevails, the liability could put Garage Gear out of business. Real estate partner Barney Blackacre, visibly distressed, just saw the **conflicts** check memo that Frank's firm circulates to all lawyers in the firm for each new matter and walks into Happy Trials's office to ask about the case. "Garage Gear, Gary Geary's business?" Barney asks. "Well, I understand he's the majority shareholder and the company's president," Happy replies. "But we have no plans to name Geary personally as a defendant in the case." "Geez, Happy," Barney says, "Gary and I have been best friends since second grade. I'm closer to him than I am to my own brother. If we win this case, looks to me like he'll lose his entire investment in the company, which is most of what he has, and be out of a job besides." Does your analysis change if Gary Geary has the relationship described with Happy instead of with Barney? If so, how and why; and if not, why not?

e. Same as (d), except Gary Geary retired from his job running Garage Gear several years ago and has gifted most of his stock in the company to his adult children.

f. For several months, Frank has been dating a lawyer who works at another small firm in town. Her firm is opposing counsel on a case on which Frank has substantial responsibilities. Does your analysis change if Frank's girlfriend is assigned to write a set of document requests in the case? How about if she shows up to defend a deposition that he's taking?

---

[24] *See* Sue Reisinger, *General Counsel's Hiring at Duke Energy Sparks Ethics Firestorm*, https://www.law.com/corpcounsel/almID/1202473377204/ (Oct. 15, 2010). It is very much worth reading this short news item. It contains excerpts from emails between the lawyer and those at the utility considering hiring him that show how the prospect of the new job affected the lawyer's attitude, or at least the way he presented himself. The end result? Not pretty. Sue Reisinger, *Final Ethics Reprimand for Ex-GC in Indiana*, http://www.corpcounsel.com/id=1202642104576/Final-Ethics-Reprimand-for-Ex-GC-in-Indiana#ixzz2wizp0w1c (Feb. 7, 2014).

What happens if, six months into the case, Frank and his girlfriend decide that it's serious and they move in together? If any of these facts would change your analysis, please explain how and why, and if not, why not.

g. Maya is a baseball fan, and joins a group of her fellow associates and some of their friends in buying a set of four season tickets to the local Major League Baseball franchise. Everybody in the group gets to go to about eight home games a year, along with whoever else in the group selected tickets to that particular game (there's a lottery system to resolve conflicting claims to especially desirable games). A friend of one of Maya's colleagues, with whom she's sat at several ballgames, calls up Maya to negotiate the terms of a piece of a deal on which Maya is working. Does your analysis change if the other lawyer has asked Maya out several times, and she (being uninterested) has declined? If so, how and why; and if not, why not?

h. In a case on which Frank is working with his firm's litigation partner, Happy Trials, Happy confides to Frank that he is having an extramarital affair with their opposing counsel. Happy has no interest in breaking up his marriage and doesn't wish to disclose the affair to anyone. Happy is confident that opposing counsel feels the same way. Happy says he is trusting Frank's discretion to honor his preference to keep the affair quiet and told him only so that he would understand the dynamics between counsel if they get (as Happy put it) "weird."

i. In a case in which Frank is working with his firm's family law partner, Sally Splitsville, Frank handles some very hard-fought discovery motions. He does an excellent job and gets the firm's client most of what she was seeking. Opposing counsel, a highly respected family lawyer in town, congratulates Frank for his good work after the hearing. She says, "You're really a fine young lawyer, Frank. We're always looking for up-and-comers like you. We should talk about whether there might be a place for you at our firm. I'm sure that we could pay you a good deal better than Sally does." Does your analysis change if opposing counsel adds, "Let's wait until this case is over, and then let's have lunch"? If so, how and why; and if not, why not?

j. Reconsider **Problem 5D-9 at 122** (Frank has inadvertently left an important acceleration clause out of a loan agreement he drafted that is now signed and delivered). The client has not been informed of the error. The borrower has just defaulted on a loan payment, and the client (Bob deBilder Co.) contacts Frank's firm about initiating collection proceedings.

7. Summary: Situations Creating Conflicts of Interest Between a Lawyer's Personal Interests and a Client's Interests That Are Regulated by the Model Rules of Professional Conduct

We've just thrown a lot of very detailed information at you. Much of it comes up fairly frequently in many different kinds of law practices, so the details are ones that you need to know. We've become quite fond of you, and we want to help. (And there are still another five subchapters to go before you've mastered **conflicts of interest**, one of the most frequently and broadly tested subjects on the MPRE, so we feel sympathy for you, too.) All of which has inspired us to put together a meticulously organized chart to help you keep personal-**interest conflicts** straight.

Situations Creating Conflicts of Interest Between a Lawyer's Personal Interests and a Client's Interests That Are Regulated by the Model Rules of Professional Conduct

SITUATION	MODEL RULE	SUBSTANTIVE RESTRICTIONS	FORMAL OR CONSENT REQUIREMENTS
"[F]inancial assistance to a client in connection with pending or contemplated litigation" (*See* **Chapter 22.A at 606**)	1.8(e)	**Forbidden** *except for*: 1. Advancing litigation expenses, repayment of which may be contingent on the outcome of the litigation; 2. Paying litigation expenses on behalf of an indigent client with no expectation of repayment; or 3. "[M]odest gifts . . . for food, rent, transportation, medicine and other basic living expenses" to an indigent client represented *pro bono* (with restrictions elaborated in the Rule)	Not applicable, except Exception (1) must be agreed and documented as described in **Model Rules 1.5(b)-(c)** (*see* **Chapter 20.B at 539, 541, 543**)
Gift or bequest from client to lawyer (*See* **Chapter 22.A at 612**)	1.8(c)	Lawyer **must not** "solicit" any "substantial" gift or bequest from a client; lawyer **must not** prepare any document giving the lawyer or a member of the lawyer's family a gift or bequest *unless* the lawyer or the donee is a member of the client's family	Not applicable
Negotiation by the lawyer for, or acquisition by the lawyer of, "literary or media rights to a portrayal or account based in substantial part on information relating to the representation" before the representation is over (*See* **Chapter 22.A at 615**)	1.8(d)	**Forbidden**	Not applicable

SITUATION	MODEL RULE	SUBSTANTIVE RESTRICTIONS	FORMAL OR CONSENT REQUIREMENTS
Acquisition by the lawyer of "a proprietary interest [including a lien] in the cause of action or subject matter of litigation the lawyer is conducting for a client" (*See* **Chapter 22.A at 616**)	1.8(i)	**Forbidden** *except for*: 1. "[A] lien authorized by law to secure the lawyer's fee or expenses"; or 2. Agreement to "a reasonable contingent fee in a civil case"	1. The lien referred to in Exception (1) must be documented and perfected as required by governing state law and in some cases also as required by **Model Rule 1.8(a)**; 2. The contingent fee referred to in Exception (2) must be agreed and documented as provided in **Model Rules 1.5(b)-(c)** (*see* **Chapter 20.B at 542**)
A "business transaction with a client"; or The lawyer's "knowing[] acqui[sition] of an ownership, possessory, security or other pecuniary interest adverse to a client" that is not forbidden under another Rule (*See* **Chapter 22.A at 617**)	1.8(a)	The transaction's terms **must** be "fair and reasonable to the client"	1. The terms **must** be "fully disclosed and transmitted in writing in a manner that can be reasonably understood by the client; and 2. The client **must** be "advised in writing of the desirability of seeking and . . . given a reasonable opportunity to seek the advice of independent legal counsel on the transaction"; and 3. The client **must** "give[] **informed consent, in a writing signed by the client**, to the essential terms of the transaction and the lawyer's role in the transaction, including whether the lawyer is representing the client in the transaction."
Any other situation in which there is a "significant risk" that the representation of a client will be "**materially limited**" by a "**personal interest of the lawyer**" that is not forbidden under another Rule (*See* **Chapter 22.A at 626**)	1.7(a)(2)	The lawyer **must** "reasonably believe[] that the lawyer will be able to provide competent and diligent representation to each affected client" (**Model Rule 1.7(b)(1)**)	The affected client **must** "give[] **informed consent, confirmed in writing**" (**Model Rule 1.7(b)(4)**); even in situations in which the client's **informed consent** is not required, the lawyer's **duty of candor** and **Model Rule 1.4** may require disclosure without requiring consent if a reasonable client would, or this particular client reasonably would, want to know

Big-Picture Takeaways from Chapter 22.A

1. There are three basic types of **conflicts of interest**:
    a. There can be **conflicts of interest** between your own personal **interests** and the **interests** of a client.
    b. There can be **conflicts of interest** based on *whom* you know and have ongoing relationships with and the possible temptation to favor one client over another. These **conflicts** are grounded in the **duty of loyalty** and are governed by something often referred to as the "**concurrent client rule.**"
    c. There can be **conflicts of interest** based on *what* you know in **confidence** and the possible temptation to share that **confidential information** with

(or use that **information** on behalf of) another client, to the original client's disadvantage. These **conflicts** are grounded in the **duty of confidentiality** and are governed by something often referred to as the "**successive client**" or "**former client rule**" (which is a little weird, because the rule applies to **prospective clients** and **current clients**, too).
See **Chapter 22 at 599.**

2. The *first* general observation about **conflicts of interest** that we want you to keep in mind throughout this entire chapter is that *how much* the **interests** in play **conflict** with one another (that is, how bad the **conflict** is) can fall anywhere on a continuum from hardly any **conflict** at all to direct, zero-sum, mutual opposition. There are lots of **conflicting interests** in law practice that are sufficiently mild or manageable that you don't have to do anything special to avoid or address them (beyond your usual decency and common sense). *See* **Chapter 22 at 601.**

3. The *second* general observation that we want you to remember throughout this entire chapter is that **conflicts of interest** that are sufficiently serious that they have to be avoided or addressed don't have to have caused *any* actual harm to the client in order for **consequences** to be imposed. The mere existence of the **conflicting interests** and the *potential* that they *might* cause the **conflicted** lawyer to harm a client is sufficient to comprise a breach of the lawyer's duty all by itself, and to justify **consequences**. *See* **Chapter 22 at 603.**

4. The most common **consequence** for a **conflict of interest** is **disqualification**—an order from a tribunal requiring a lawyer (and usually anyone associated with that lawyer in a **practice organization**) to get out and stay out of the **conflicted** engagement. The effect of the **disqualification** order is to get the lawyer out of the **conflicted** situation *before* any actual harm to any affected client (or any more of it) occurs. In addition, **conflicts of interest** in violation of the Rules of Professional Conduct can result in professional discipline, again whether or not the client suffered actual harm. And a serious enough **conflict of interest** can result in the lawyer's forfeiting fees incurred while under the **conflict** and having to pay back any such fees that were already paid, yet again whether or not the client suffered actual harm. Any actual harm that the client suffered may be additionally compensated in damages. *See* **Chapter 22 at 603.**

5. There are (generally speaking) two kinds of rules defining the **conflicts of interest** that require some kind of action to prevent **consequences**. Some issues have crystallized into bright-line rules categorically forbidding (or requiring formal steps such as explicit disclosure of and **informed consent**

to) certain defined arrangements or conduct. Some of these Rules, by contrast, are more general standards that call for avoidance or special precautions for **conflicts of interest** that meet a more general, fuzzily described threshold of concern. *See* **Chapter 22 at 602**.

6. **Financial assistance to litigation clients. Model Rule 1.8(e)** categorically forbids a lawyer from "provid[ing] financial assistance to a client in connection with pending or contemplated litigation . . ." with only a few exceptions. This prohibition applies to almost any kind of financial assistance, whether a loan, guarantee, or gift. *See* **Chapter 22.A at 606**.

   a. There are three implicit exceptions to **Model Rule 1.8(e)**:

      i.   You **may** delay collection of or discount your fees, or represent a client *pro bono*;

      ii. You **may** negotiate and charge a contingent fee; and

      iii. Given that the Rule limits its prohibition to assistance to a client "in connection with pending or contemplated litigation," you **may** provide financial assistance to non-litigation clients, or to non-clients.

   See **Chapter 22.A at 609**.

   b. **Model Rule 1.8(e)** also articulates three exceptions expressly stated in the Rule itself:

      i.   You **may** "advance court costs and expenses of litigation, the repayment of which **may** be contingent on the outcome of the matter" (**Model Rule 1.8(e)(1)**);

      ii. You **may** "pay court costs and expenses of litigation on behalf of" an "indigent" client (**Model Rule 1.8(e)(2)**); and

      iii. You **may** "provide modest gifts to the client for food, rent, transportation, medicine and other basic living expenses" if you are representing an indigent client *pro bono* (whether through your own **practice organization**, "through a nonprofit legal services or public interest organization," or "through a law school clinical or *pro bono* program") (**Model Rule 1.8(e)(3)**), so long as you don't do so as a means of getting or keeping the engagement (**Model Rule 1.8(e)(3)(i)**), don't seek reimbursement from the client or anyone associated with the client (**Model Rule 1.8(e)(3)(ii)**); and don't "publicize or advertise a willingness to provide such gifts to prospective clients" (**Model Rule 1.8(e)(3)(iii)**).

   See **Chapter 22.A at 609**.

7. **Receiving gifts or bequests from clients. Model Rule 1.8(c)** is about lawyers' *receiving* gifts or bequests *from* their clients. It prohibits two things: A lawyer **must not** "solicit any substantial gift from a client, including a

testamentary gift"; and a lawyer **must not** "prepare on behalf of a client an instrument giving the lawyer or a person related to the lawyer any substantial gift unless the lawyer or other recipient of the gift is related to the client." *See* **Chapter 22.A at 612**.

8. **Literary or media rights**. **Model Rule 1.8(d)** says that you **must not** "make or negotiate an agreement" in which you obtain "literary or media rights to a portrayal or account based in substantial part on information relating to the representation" before the engagement is over. *See* **Chapter 22.A at 615**.

9. **Proprietary interests in the client's cause of action or in the subject matter of the litigation**. **Model Rule 1.8(i)** says that a lawyer **must not** "acquire a proprietary interest in the cause of action or subject matter of litigation the lawyer is conducting for a client . . . ." In simple terms, this means that, generally, you **must not** take a security or other ownership interest in the client's cause of action or in the subject matter of the litigation that you're handling—for example, a disputed piece of property involved in a case in which you represent one of the parties to the dispute. There are two exceptions: (1) you **may** "acquire a lien authorized by law to secure your fee or expenses" and (2) you **may** "contract with a client for a reasonable contingent fee in a civil case." *See* **Chapter 22.A at 616**.

10. **Requirements for non-forbidden transactions with clients**. **Model Rule 1.8(a)** governs any transaction with a client that other Rules do not forbid. The Rule literally covers *any* "business transaction with a client" and *any* "knowing[] acqui[sition of]" an ownership, possessory, security or other pecuniary interest adverse to a client." (A lien on a client's property is a classic example of an "interest adverse to a client.") *See* **Chapter 22.A at 618**.

    a. There are three recognized categories of transactions to which **Model Rule 1.8(a)** does *not* apply, despite the Rule's sweepingly broad language.

        i. An ordinary fee agreement (that is, one in which the client agrees to pay a lawyer for legal services with consideration in the form of money, rather than a transfer of some other species of property in kind) **must** comply with the formal and substantive requirements of **Model Rule 1.5** (*see* **Chapter 20.B at 537**), but not the more intensive requirements of **Model Rule 1.8(a)**. *See* **Chapter 22.A at 619**.

        ii. The most common arrangement in which the lawyer "accepts an interest in the client's . . . nonmonetary property" is an attorney's lien or the grant of a consensual security interest by the client in a litigation claim that the lawyer is handling on the client's behalf, or in the claim's proceeds. Many states, however, do *not* require compliance with **Model Rule 1.8(a)** in connection with obtaining such a lien, despite its literal inclusion in the scope language of the Rule.

Some states say that you don't have to follow **Model Rule 1.8(a)** when you acquire a security interest in the client's litigation claim to secure a *contingent* fee in the litigation, but you *do* have to follow **Model Rule 1.8(a)** if you acquire a security interest in the client's litigation claim to secure payment of a *noncontingent* fee (for example, an hourly fee or a flat fee) in the litigation. *See* **Chapter 22.A at 619.**

iii. **Model Rule 1.8(a)** also does not apply to "standard commercial transactions between the lawyer and the client for products or services that the client generally markets to others . . . ." *See* **Chapter 22.A at 621.**

b. For those transactions that it covers, **Model Rule 1.8(a)** requires:

i. Substantively, any transaction or acquisition of an adverse interest **must** be "fair and reasonable to the client" (**Model Rule 1.8(a)(1)**). *See* **Chapter 22.A at 622.**

ii. In addition to being *substantively* fair and reasonable, there are three *formal* requirements applicable to any transaction governed by **Model Rule 1.8(a):**

A. The terms of the transaction with or acquisition of an interest adverse to the client **must** be "fully disclosed and transmitted in writing in a manner that can be reasonably understood by the client . . ." (**Model Rule 1.8(a)(1)**). There are three distinct requirements in that short phrase: (1) The terms of the lawyer-client transaction must be fully disclosed; that is, everything **material** about the transaction has to be laid out; (2) this disclosure has to be "transmitted in writing"; and (3) the written disclosure of the terms of the transaction must be accomplished in terms that the client can reasonably understand. *See* **Chapter 22.A at 622.**

B. The client **must** be "advised in writing of the desirability of seeking . . . independent legal counsel on the transaction," and be "given a reasonable opportunity" to do so (**Model Rule 1.8(a)(2)**). *See* **Chapter 22.A at 623.**

C. The client **must** also "give[] **informed consent, in a writing signed by the client,** to the essential terms of the transaction and the lawyer's role in the transaction, including whether the lawyer is representing the client in the transaction" (**Model Rule 1.8(a) (3)**). *See* **Chapter 22.A at 624.**

If you fail to meet any of these formal (that is, process-oriented) requirements of **Model Rule 1.8(a)**, you are subject to professional discipline, and the transaction is subject to rescission and restitution, *even if the transaction was completely fair and reasonable*. *See* **Chapter 22.A at 625**.

11. **Personal interests creating a "significant risk" of "materially limiting" the lawyer's conduct of the engagement. Model Rule 1.7(a)(2)** provides that a lawyer **must not** take on or continue an engagement in which there is a *"significant risk"* that the client's representation will be *"**materially**"* limited by a personal interest of the lawyer (unless the client gives **informed** written **consent**).

    a. The standard is a *predictive* one—that is, one that asks us to judge the *risk* that something bad *could* happen under these circumstances *before* anything bad *actually* happens, and even though nothing bad might ever happen. *See* **Chapter 22.A at 627**.

    b. When a lawyer's personal interests are at stake, the situation often involves an important personal relationship or potential relationship with opposing counsel or an opposing party. The nature and strength of the connection between the lawyer and the opposing lawyer or party must be assessed in each case. An ABA Formal Ethics Opinion provides guidelines for assessing the significance of different kinds of personal relationships, with "intimate" and close familial relationships almost certain to create personal-interest **conflicts**; "friendships" potentially able to create personal-interest **conflicts** depending on the nature and strength of the friendship; and acquaintanceships unlikely to create a personal-interest **conflict**. *See* **Chapter 22.A at 627**.

    c. Even if the connection between the lawyer and the opposing lawyer or party is not one that creates a personal-interest **conflict** that requires the lawyer to abstain from involvement in the engagement or obtain the client's **informed consent**, it may be salient enough to require disclosure to the client under the lawyer's **duty of candor** and **Model Rule 1.4**. Good practice dictates erring on the side of disclosure and **informed consent** whenever there could be any reasonable doubt. *See* **Chapter 22.A at 628**.

    d. Personal-interest **conflicts** of this kind are generally not **imputed** to other lawyers in the **conflicted** lawyer's **practice organization** unless other lawyers in the **organization** are likely to be similarly affected. *See* **Chapter 22.A at 628; Chapter 22.D at 707**.

Multiple-Choice Review Questions for Chapter 22.A

1. Which of the following is *not* a major category of **conflicts of interest** discussed in this chapter?

    a. **Conflicts** based on **conflicting duties of loyalty** that a lawyer owes to more than one client.

b. **Conflicts** between personal **interests** of the lawyer and the **interests** of a client.

c. **Conflicts** between the client's duty to the lawyer and the lawyer's duty to the legal system.

d. **Conflicts** based on what a lawyer has learned **in confidence** and may be tempted to share with other clients to the original client's disadvantage.

2. Margaret works for the construction law department of a large law firm. She represents the owner of a new casino that is suing the general contractor who built the casino. She decides to take a break from firm life and to clerk for a judge for a year. Instead of returning to the law firm post-clerkship, she becomes a solo practitioner.

   The litigation is still ongoing. The general contractor, frustrated with the delay, fires its lawyer and retains Margaret. When her old law firm finds out, she receives an angry call from her former boss, threatening to take action. Assuming that there is a **conflict of interest** and she experiences the most common **consequence**, what is likely to happen?

   a. Margaret will be ordered to represent the owner rather than the general contractor.

   b. Margaret will be **disqualified** from representing the general contractor.

   c. Margaret will be disbarred.

   d. Margaret will be sued for malicious prosecution.

3. Lawyer Veronica is a loyal Diet Coke drinker. If she goes to a restaurant that offers Pepsi products, she orders water instead; she hates the taste of Diet Pepsi that much. One day, she is approached by Pepsi Co. and asked whether she would represent the company in a trademark dispute against the Coca-Cola Company. **Must** Veronica decline due to a **conflict of interest**?

   a. Yes. She would be representing a party **directly adverse** to her preferred brand.

   b. Yes. It would create a **positional conflict** because she would be required to argue that Pepsi's brand deserves protection when she actually believes that it does not.

   c. No. This is not a **conflict of interest** that requires a lawyer to decline representation. A lawyer may represent a company even if she prefers a competitor's product.

   d. No. She only need withdraw from representation if she is asked to represent Coca-Cola (the beverage). A **conflict** arises only from representing two adverse parties in the same litigation.

4. Lawyer Elaine is approached by a potential client, Freida. Freida works for a major pharmaceutical company. She has learned that the company

engaged in a cover-up to prevent the public from learning about the potential side effects of one of its drugs, which the company supplies to the military. Freida asks Elaine to file a *qui tam* complaint (a kind of whistleblower case created by statute) based on the allegations. Such a complaint would allow Freida to recover a share of any profits if the government intervenes and litigates the case.

Elaine thinks the case has merit. Not only that, but Elaine badly wants to handle the case because she knows that it will be high-profile and could attract future clients to Elaine's firm.

Unfortunately, Freida cannot afford to pay Elaine's usual $650 hourly rate. Although Freida is far from indigent, she simply does not have sufficient savings to pay fees on an ongoing basis.

Which of the following is Elaine prohibited from offering Freida?

a. That Freida pay a discounted rate of $350 per hour, rather than Elaine's usual hourly rate.

b. That Freida pay no hourly rate but instead pay Elaine a 40 percent contingent fee from any recovery in the case.

c. That Freida pay no attorneys' fees but, instead, Frieda will provide Elaine with all media and literary rights relating to the litigation.

d. That Freida take out a bank loan to pay Elaine's hourly rate.

5. Lawyer Sally represents a wealthy landowner named Marcus. Marcus tells Sally that he has $1 million to spend and would like to purchase a horse farm. Sally does some research and identifies a farm that meets all of Marcus's criteria. It is listed for $1.1 million.

Sally inquires whether the owners are willing to negotiate the price. They tell her that they would sell the property for $750,000 in a quick cash sale.

Sally creates a shell corporation for herself and has that corporation buy the farm for $750,000. Sally then has the corporation sell the farm to Marcus for $1 million. She does 20 hours of work drafting the sales contract. Her hourly rate is $350 per hour. Sally pockets the profit on the sale of the farm and sends Marcus a bill for $7,000, which he pays. Marcus is thrilled with his new farm and recommends Sally's services to all of his friends.

Was Sally entitled to the $7,000?

a. Yes. She did the work and was entitled to bill for her time.

b. Yes. Marcus is not dissatisfied and did not dispute the bill.

c. No. She was sufficiently compensated by the profit on the sale of the farm and should not have charged Marcus anything additional.

d. No. She breached her fiduciary duty and forfeited her fees by purchasing the farm for $750,000 rather than allowing Marcus to buy it for that price.

6. Which of the following is *not* the subject of an implicit exception to the rule against a lawyer providing financial assistance to a client?
   a. Offering to handle a case for a litigation client for a fee discounted below fair market value.
   b. Agreeing to handle a non-litigation matter on a contingent-fee basis even though most lawyers would insist on an up-front retainer.
   c. Lending money to a non-litigation client so that the client may invest in real estate.
   d. Lending a litigation client money for living expenses so that the client can litigate a claim, but taking a lien on the client's car as collateral.

7. Josie is a young associate at a large law firm. The firm allows associates to handle *pro bono* cases. Josie decides she would like to handle a discrimination case *pro bono*. After doing research, Josie finds a public university that changed its definition of a "female athlete" to exclude a transgender female student, Gabrielle, from its swim team.

   Josie realizes that this case could make history. She notifies the firm's managing partner, Devon. Devon is very supportive of Josie's representing Gabrielle in litigation against the university. Devon's support of the case stems in part from the fact that the case will likely reach the United States Supreme Court. Devon realizes that handling the case could elevate the firm's reputation nationwide. Devon also believes in *pro bono* work and thinks that Gabrielle deserves to have her rights vindicated.

   Josie and Devon call Gabrielle and arrange to meet with her. Although Gabrielle is upset about what happened, she seems reticent to sue the university. She is indigent and fears the university will retaliate by kicking her out of student housing.

   Before Josie can say anything, Devon tells Gabrielle, "Don't worry. If you let us handle the case as a *pro bono* matter, our firm will find you an apartment near campus and pay the rent for you." Has Devon violated **Model Rule 1.8**?
   a. Yes, because the firm has not promised not to publicize or advertise the gift.
   b. Yes, because the offer was promised to get the engagement.
   c. No, because the client is indigent, and the case will be handled *pro bono*.
   d. No, because the gift is from the lawyer to the client and not vice versa.

8. Lawyer Gertrude represents client Harriet in a trip-and-fall case. Harriet agrees to pay Gertrude a 33 percent contingent fee if she wins and recovers money. If she loses, Harriet agrees to pay Gertrude $10,000. As security in case Harriet loses, Gertrude takes out a mortgage on Harriet's home. Is this arrangement permissible?

a. Yes, because a lawyer may take a lien to pay a contingent fee.

b. Yes, if the arrangement is fair and reasonable and the client gives **informed consent** in writing after being advised to seek the advice of independent counsel.

c. No, because it creates an appearance of impropriety.

d. No, because it is a prohibited business transaction between a lawyer and a client.

9. Lawyer Lauren drafts a will on behalf of client Corrine. In the will, Corrine leaves three expensive oil paintings to Lauren. Does this violate **Model Rule 1.8(c)**?

a. Yes. A lawyer can never draft a will in which she is a beneficiary.

b. Maybe. It depends whether Lauren and Corrine are closely enough related to each other.

c. Maybe. It depends whether Lauren accepts the paintings after Corrine's death.

d. No. A client can agree to include a lawyer in her will.

10. Nancy is a lawyer who represents Bullseye Corp., a general merchandise retailer with stores across the country. Her local Bullseye store offers a "buy one, get one free" sale on canned goods. If Nancy accepts free canned goods as part of this promotion, would she violate **Model Rule 1.8(a)**?

a. Yes. She is receiving a "gift" from a client.

b. Yes. This creates an impermissible **conflict of interest** that Bullseye Corp. cannot waive.

c. No. The free canned goods do not constitute a "gift," as defined in the rule.

d. No. The Rule does not apply to commercial transactions generally offered to the public.

11. Lawyer Brent represents his client, Carl. Carl asks Brent to file a complaint against a local store, Stop-N-Spend, after Carl slipped and fell on the sidewalk outside the store. Which of the following scenarios might create a **conflict of interest** for Brent?

a. Brent is a transactional lawyer who primarily negotiates and drafts contracts. He feels ill-prepared to litigate a tort claim.

b. Brent has an overwhelming caseload and is unsure whether he has time to handle Carl's case.

c. Brent is not admitted to practice in the state where the fall occurred. Although he could be admitted *pro hac vice*, he has not yet moved for such admission.

d. Stop-N-Spend is owned by Brent's sister, Diane.

12. Rick drafts a contract on behalf of his architect client, who has been retained to design a home. A few years later, when the construction is complete, the homeowner sues the architect, claiming that the architect breached the contract. The lawsuit turns on a dispute over the interpretation of the contract regarding what the contract required Rick's client to do. The architect asks Rick to represent her in the breach of contract claim. Would this engagement create a **conflict of interest** under the state's enactment of **Model Rule 1.7**?

    a. Yes, because Rick will be tempted not to make certain arguments that might advantage his client, because the arguments will make him look bad.

    b. Yes, because litigating the breach of contract case may uncover malpractice by Rick in his initial drafting of the contract.

    c. No, because it is to the client's benefit. Rick will not need to spend time familiarizing himself with the contractual terms, as he is already familiar with them.

    d. No, because the architect was the client when the contract was drafted, and the architect is still the client in the breach of contract litigation. There does not appear to be a situation where there will be a **conflict** between two different **concurrent clients**.

13. Lawyer Ilana represents a large chain of high-end boutique grocery stores, Trader Joel's. Trader Joel's asks Ilana to negotiate with the owner of a retail parcel that Trader Joel's would like to purchase. Ilana realizes that the parcel is owned by Kim—someone who Ilana knows because she attends the same church that Ilana does. Ilana speaks to Kim in passing and considers her an acquaintance. Ilana does not think that this will cause a **conflict of interest**.

    What **should** Ilana do?

    a. Notify Trader Joel's and not proceed with the engagement unless Trader Joel's provides **informed consent, confirmed in writing**.

    b. Notify Trader Joel's and then proceed with the engagement unless Trader Joel's objects.

    c. Notify Kim and get her **informed consent, confirmed in writing**.

    d. Accept the representation and represent Trader Joel's without disclosing the issue.

14. Same facts as Question 13, but Kim is instead Ilana's ex-wife.

    a. Notify Trader Joel's and not proceed with the engagement unless Trader Joel's provides **informed consent, confirmed in writing**.

    b. Notify Trader Joel's and then proceed with the engagement unless Trader Joel's objects.

    c. Notify Kim and get her **informed consent, confirmed in writing**.

    d. Accept the representation and represent Trader Joel's without disclosing the issue.

B. Conflicts of Interest Created by Current Clients and Grounded in the Duty of Loyalty: The "Concurrent Client Rule"

Maya finds partner Ron Rainmaker looking a little down-in-the-mouth. "Everything okay?" she asks. "I guess," he says, glumly. "Seriously, what's up?" Maya presses. Ron sighs. "Well, remember that call that I got from the general counsel of Petrified Petroleum, and how it wants to sue Mojo Manufacturing? And how excited I was about getting the firm to represent Mojo against Petrified in that case?" "Sure," Maya responds. (*See* the **Introduction to Chapter 8 at 203** to remind yourself of the details.) "Well, the Intake Committee says we can't do that," says Ron.

"What's the Intake Committee?" Maya asks, appreciative that Ron is often willing to share information on how the firm operates. "Most large firms, including ours, have a committee of partners that has to approve the intake of any new matter," Ron replies. "At a firm with many lawyers in many offices, some people believe that you need centralized oversight and coordination. Our Intake Committee makes sure that the proposed new matter doesn't create any **conflicts of interest** (or that the affected clients have all consented to any **conflicts** that can be handled by client consent); that it won't create future **conflicts of interest** or client relations issues with the types of work or clients that we're interested in getting or keeping; and that it has appropriate initial staffing in terms of the seniority and expertise of the lawyers involved. They also make sure that the fee arrangement is good for the firm, properly documented, and involves a client that is capable of paying the likely charges." "Wow," says Maya, a little startled at all the issues to which she hadn't given much thought. "That's a lot of details." "Yeah, well," Ron replies, "I think of it as a private-sector Nanny State. Just gets in the way of entre-preneurial partners like me trying to keep this place afloat.

"So anyway," Ron continues, "after the Intake Committee spiked my idea about spilling the beans to Mojo and getting them to hire us against Petrified, I had another idea: If we can't represent Mojo because we have **confidential infor-mation** from Petrified, then, okay, let's represent Petrified against Mojo. After all, Petrified called us on this first; they oughta have first dibs." "Hmm," says Maya, wondering if that's a good idea. "What did the Intake Committee say?"

"Hard no." Ron sighs, shaking his head. "The partner with the main relation-ship with Mojo was opposed even to *asking* Mojo for consent to our being on the other side of such a big fight; she was afraid that Mojo would be offended and would withhold future business. The Intake Committee took her side. I really don't get it. Why do we have to *ask* Mojo if we can represent someone else who's suing them? It's not like we have **confidential information** about Mojo's side of this dispute like we do with Petrified. And there's loads of law firms out there who'd love to defend Mojo in this case, so they're gonna find good lawyers no matter what. Doesn't anybody around here want to make a living?"

Is Ron right? Is the firm getting in the way of its own success by turning away good, paying work? Let's think it through.

* * *

First, let's situate ourselves on the map of this area of the law governing lawyers by reminding ourselves of the three basic types of **conflicts of interest**:

- There can be **conflicts of interest** between your own personal **interests** and the **interests** of a client. We covered those in glorious detail in **Chapter 22.A at 603**.
- There can be **conflicts of interest** based on *whom* you know and have ongoing relationships with, and the possible temptation to favor one client over another. These **conflicts** are grounded in the **duty of loyalty** and are addressed by what is often referred to as the "**concurrent client rule**." That's what this subchapter is about.
- And there can be **conflicts of interest** based on *what* you know in **confidence**, and the possible temptation to share that **confidential information** with (or use that **information** on behalf of) another client, to the original client's disadvantage. These **conflicts** are grounded in the **duty of confidentiality** and are governed by something often referred to as the "**successive client**" or "**former client rule**" (even though, perversely, the rule really applies to **prospective clients** and **current clients**, too). We'll cover those next, in **Chapter 22.C at 678**.

Now that we know where we are and where we're headed, let's get going. A quick admonition before we start: Analyzing **conflicts of interest** can be intricate and difficult, and the interaction of the various governing rules can initially seem confusing. If you hang in there, we'll lay it out for you step by step, so that you'll be able to put the whole thing together and work your way through the different kinds of problems that come up in law practice (and on the MPRE). Try not to get too frustrated; if you're finding the analysis difficult, that's because it is. Try to slow down your thinking and take it one step at a time. We'll walk those steps with you.

1. The Concurrent Client Rule

What is generally referred to as the **concurrent client rule** is codified in **Model Rule 1.7(a)**. The basic rule is stated in **Model Rule 1.7(a)(1)**:

> [A] lawyer shall not represent a client if the representation involves a **concurrent conflict of interest**. A **concurrent conflict of interest** exists if . . . the representation of one client will be **directly adverse** to another client . . . .[25]

---

[25] **Concurrent conflicts of interest may** often be waived (or to use an equivalent term found in the Model Rules, consented to) by the affected clients, and then the **concurrent conflicting** engagements may proceed. Under what circumstances a **conflict of interest** is "**consentable**," and the formalities of how clients **must** consent in order for that consent to be effective, is the

TAMING THE TEXT We're going to talk about some of the other key terms in this Rule in the sections that follow, but let's start with the word "client." What creates a **concurrent conflict of interest**, the Rule tells us, is "if the lawyer's representation of one client will be **directly adverse** to another client." "Client" here means **current client**. There are other, different **conflicts** rules concerning **former** and **prospective clients**, and we'll talk about them in **Chapter 22.C at 678**.

Thus, the classic (but by no means exclusive) example of a **concurrent conflict of interest** is representing one **current client** in litigation or negotiation against another **current client** (who is represented by another lawyer in the matter). You just can't do that—the "shall not" means that the rule is mandatory, of course—at least without the affected clients' **informed consent, confirmed in writing,** as provided in **Model Rule 1.7(b)** (*see* **Chapter 22.E at 733**).[26]

Prospective clients (such as Petrified Petroleum in our hypothetical) enter the picture because, when we're presented with a potential new matter, we **must** always ask whether there *would be* a **concurrent conflict** between the **interests** of the new client and another **current client** if the **prospective client** *became* a **current client**—much as Ron Rainmaker wants to do in the **Introduction to this subchapter at 645** (where Ron's new plan is for the firm to represent a new client, Petrified Petroleum, against an existing firm client, Mojo Manufacturing, in commercial litigation). If taking on a **prospective client** would create a **concurrent conflict of interest** with another of your **current clients**, you **must** decline the engagement (or get a waiver, if it's permissible and the affected clients will agree, *see* **Chapter 22.E at 733**). *See* **Model Rule 1.7 Comment [3]**. Similarly, if the **concurrent conflict** arises after both engagements are underway (or if you don't discover it until then), you **must** withdraw as soon as possible, probably from *both* engagements that created the **conflict**. *See* **Model Rule 1.7 Comment [4]**.

Why? Because of good ol' **Model Rule 1.16(a)(1)** (*see* **Chapter 9.D at 295**), which says that you **must not** "represent a client or, where representation has commenced, shall withdraw from the representation of a client if . . . the representation will result in violation of the rules of professional conduct or other law . . . ." In this instance, the taking on or continuation of a **concurrent conflict of interest** is a "violation of the rules of professional conduct"—namely **Model Rule 1.7(a)**—so you **must** abstain or withdraw (subject to the approval of any involved tribunal). *See* **Model Rule 1.7 Comment [4]**. And if you don't, then a court will **disqualify** you, and additional unpleasant **consequences** will likely follow (*see* **Chapter 22.B at 663**). **TAMING THE TEXT**

To understand how **concurrent conflicts of interest** work, let's start by asking (as we always should whenever there might be a **conflict of interest**), what's the **conflict**?

---

subject of **Chapter 22.E at 733**. In this subchapter, our project is just to explore which situations fall within the scope of **Model Rule 1.7(a)** and the **concurrent client rule**.

[26] As we will discuss in detail in **Chapter 22.D at 678**, concurrent conflicts are **imputed** within a **practice organization**. That means that if one lawyer in a **practice organization** has a **concurrent conflict** (or one side of a **concurrent conflict**), then every other lawyer in that **practice organization** is deemed to have that **conflict**, too. *See* **Model Rule 1.10(a)(1)**; **Chapter 22.D at 707**.

Consider the classic **concurrent conflict** created by a lawyer representing one **current client** against another **current client** (which has its own counsel in that case or deal). The client getting sued (or being negotiated against) is confronted with his own counsel (his own counsel in a different matter, but his own counsel nevertheless) helping someone else do everything within the limits of the law to defeat the client who's getting sued (or being negotiated against). And the client doing the suing (or negotiating) has to stop and wonder: Is my lawyer doing everything for me that zealous advocacy allows, or is she pulling punches because she's worried about offending her other **current client** and losing *that* client's business? In short, the more that you help one client, the more you hurt the other, and vice versa.

Because of the nature of the **conflict**, the adversity between the **concurrent clients** need not be in the same or in substantively related matters in order to violate **Model Rule 1.7(a)** and create a **disqualifying conflict of interest**. **Concurrent conflicts** are grounded in the **duty of loyalty**, and that **duty** forbids you from acting adversely to a **current client** *in any material* respect, not just ones that are substantively related to the subject matter of the current engagement.

Consider Ron Rainmaker's new proposal in the **Introduction to this subchapter at 645**: Ron's firm currently represents Mojo Manufacturing in a variety of matters that have nothing to do with Petrified Petroleum or its commercial relationship with Mojo. Now Ron wants the firm to represent Petrified in suing Mojo in a commercial dispute. The firm has no **confidential information** of Mojo's that could be used against Mojo in the proposed new engagement for Petrified. (The firm *does* have **confidential information** of *Petrified's* that Ron acquired in speaking with Petrified as a **prospective client**. That **confidential information**, which could be used against Petrified by Mojo in the commercial dispute, is the reason why the firm can't represent Mojo against Petrified, as Ron first proposed, and why Ron can't disclose that **information** to Mojo to curry favor. *See* **Chapter 8.A at 217**; **Chapter 22.C at 683**.) The problem with Ron's new proposal is that Ron's firm has a **duty of loyalty** to Mojo as a **current client**. And the **duty of loyalty** forbids Ron and his firm from acting adversely to the **interests** of their **current client**, not just with respect to the subject matter of their pending engagements, but in *any* **material** respect. *See* **Chapter 5.D at 113**. So even when you're considering acting adversely to the interests of a **current client** in a way that has nothing to do with what you're doing for that client and implicates none of its **confidential information**, the answer is still no—your **duty of loyalty**, codified in **Model Rule 1.7(a)** for disciplinary purposes, says so. *See* **Model Rule 1.7 Comment [6]**.

2.   When Is a Client a Current Client?

a.   Generally

The **concurrent client rule** applies to **current clients** *only*. That's because it's based in the **duty of loyalty**, and the **duty of loyalty** ends (more or less) when the engagement ends. *See* **Chapter 5.D at 114**. And we already know what a **current client** is: A person or organization that we currently represent in an ongoing engagement. But what if the endpoint of the engagement is unclear? How do we know when a **current client** (who can create a **concurrent conflict of interest**) has become a **former client** (who can't)?

We discussed this problem in **Chapter 9.D at 286** when we were talking about how engagements end, and how you know when they're over. (Feel free to go back and take a look; it will be helpful in understanding the **conflicts** issue that we're discussing in this section, which comes up fairly often in practice.) In summary:

- Some engagements are completed according to their terms—you simply finish everything that you had agreed to do, and you're done.
- Some engagements are terminated before they're completed; these situations are typically punctuated by some version of "you're fired" or "I quit."
- And some engagements have an endpoint that is either ambiguous or deliberately undefined:
  - An example of an ambiguous endpoint is when it's not entirely clear from the parties' agreement whether or not there are additional tasks to accomplish before completion, so maybe you're done, and maybe you're not.
  - Another example of an ambiguous endpoint is when lawyer-client relations are bad, but it's not entirely clear whether the client has definitively said "you're fired," or the lawyer has plainly said "I quit" (and has also gotten the necessary approval from any involved tribunal).
  - A common example of an engagement with an undefined endpoint is one involving occasional consultation: The understanding in such an engagement is that the client will call upon the lawyer from time to time as needed to get advice or other services that the lawyer has agreed to provide upon request. It's very difficult to say when such an engagement is over unless one party or the other affirmatively communicates that the engagement has been terminated; otherwise, the fact that nothing has happened in a while might mean that the client no longer considers you her lawyer, or it might mean that she still does and expects to continue to consult you as needed, but that she doesn't happen to need you right now.

Again, why does this matter? Because under the **concurrent client rule**, you **must not** represent anyone else adversely to any **current client**, but you **may** represent clients who sue (or otherwise act adversely to) **former clients** in any matter in which you can't use the **former clients' confidential information** against them (*see* **Chapter 22.C at 678**). For that reason, the difference between a client's being a **current client** or a **former client** often amounts to the difference between your being able to take on a new engagement and your being **conflicted** out of it.

So that difference can be a meat-and-potatoes issue for practicing lawyers. And speaking of potatoes . . .

b. The "Hot-Potato Rule"

The **concurrent client rule** has an important corollary, born of hard experience, that bears the implausible but widely used nickname of the "**hot-potato rule**." A good way to illustrate what the **hot-potato rule** is and why clients need it is to return to Ron Rainmaker's efforts to bring his firm new work by representing Petrified Petroleum against Mojo Manufacturing. When we last left this hypothetical, Ron was hoping to see the firm represent Petrified (which would be a new client) against Mojo (which is a **current client**), but the firm's Intake Committee had, quite correctly, put the kibosh on that idea because it would create a **concurrent conflict of interest** to represent a **current client** (which Petrified would become) in suing another **current client** (Mojo).

Now let's change up the facts a little. Up until now, we've postulated that Mojo is an important and substantial client of Ron's firm, one that, for sensible business and client-relations reasons, the firm would strongly prefer not to offend. But suppose Mojo were not a significant client of the firm; suppose that the only business that the firm had been able to get from Mojo was about a dozen hours of employment counseling a year, and the firm's efforts to expand the relationship just hadn't borne fruit. Now the prospect of losing Mojo as a client doesn't sound so bad, especially if it were done for the purpose of taking on the big, new, lucrative engagement for Petrified instead (and remember, the whole point of the **concurrent client rule** is that the firm can't do both, because you can't be adverse to a **current client**).

Suppose Ron, in that, um, creative way he has (that's what *he* calls it, anyway) proposes that the firm simply terminate the employment counseling engagement with Mojo (which, under our facts now, is the only connection that the firm has to Mojo—one that's of trivial economic value to the firm). Under these circumstances, Ron would like to send Mojo a very polite termination letter ending the engagement with a courteous but definitive "We quit." Shazam—Mojo transforms instantly from a **current client** owed **duties of loyalty** to a **former client**, who isn't. Then the firm is free to sign up Petrified and get to work suing Mojo into the stone age, because the firm is suddenly free to be adverse to a **former client** (Mojo) about which it possesses no **confidential information** relating to the new adverse engagement.[27]

---

[27] REAL WORLD We make light of Ron, but he's not an unusual character in the real world, and he's not a bad guy. Look how supportively and respectfully he treats junior lawyers like Maya. **Practice organizations** are full of lawyers like Ron Rainmaker—excellent attorneys who are valued by their clients and their colleagues for their skill and expertise, but who get so focused on the success of their practice that they can lose perspective and judgment on other issues. As Upton Sinclair famously observed, "It is difficult to get a man to understand something, when his salary depends on his not understanding

"Can they do that?" the alert student gasps. "Sounds too clever by half." This is why the alert student is our Special Co-Star in these hypothetical flights of fancy. The alert student is absolutely right—it *is* too clever by half. "But what's wrong with it?" the alert student asks, struggling with the fact that it all sounds quite logical. Well, the **duty of loyalty** is a powerful binding force in the lawyer-client universe. It is the touchstone of the lawyer's fiduciary duties. It holds engagements together. And it would be a violation of the **duty of loyalty** itself for the lawyer-fiduciary to terminate the relationship with a client—to the client's detriment and against the client's will—for the purpose of making an extra buck or two (or 2 million) off some other engagement adverse to the original client. In short, it would be a violation of the lawyer's **duty of loyalty** to "drop the client [here, Mojo] like a hot potato" for the purpose of avoiding a **conflict of interest** with another client the lawyer suddenly prefers. Hence the rule's funny name.

`CONSEQUENCES` So what happens if you violate the **hot-potato rule**? An excellent question. (The alert student is killing it today.) If you go back and look at **Model Rule 1.7(a)**, you'll see that, although it explicitly forbids **concurrent conflicts of interest**, it says nothing about *dropping* one **current client** in order to *avoid* a **concurrent conflict** with the other. In the absence of an explicit prohibition in the Rules of Professional Conduct, violation of the **hot-potato rule** will not subject you to professional discipline (unless you go about the violation in a way that violates some other Rule—for example, by dumping the less-preferred client in a manner inconsistent with your obligations under **Model Rule 1.16(d)**, amounting to client abandonment, *see* **Chapter 9.D at 302**). What a violation of the **hot-potato rule** *will* get you is **disqualification** from the engagement for which you dropped the less-favored "hot-potato" client. The result is basically as if you had never disloyally dropped that client in the first place and had to face **consequences** for the **conflict of interest**, which removes any incentive to violate the **hot-potato rule** at all. `CONSEQUENCES`

3. Concurrent Conflicts of Interest Created by "Direct Adversity" Between Concurrent Clients: When Are Concurrent Clients' Interests "Directly Adverse"?

Go back and take a look at **Model Rule 1.7(a)(1)'s** definition of a **concurrent conflict of interest**. The Rule specifies that one way that a **concurrent conflict** is created is when "the representation of one client will be ***directly adverse*** to another client" (emphasis added). So what does it mean for the representation of one client to be **"directly adverse"** to another?

---

it." UPTON SINCLAIR, I, CANDIDATE FOR GOVERNOR: AND HOW I GOT LICKED 109 (1934). Many of the principles explored in this course require you to forgo real and substantial short-term advantages in the service of higher obligations. And although virtue is its own reward, by now you know that the law governing lawyers is also enforced by significant and serious **consequences**. Many **practice organizations** have formal or informal mechanisms, such as the Intake Committee at Maya's firm or an Ethics Committee or ethics "czar," to keep impulses like Ron's in check. Find out what those mechanisms are in your practice organization when you get there. They can help when questions or problems arise. `REAL WORLD`

The problem here is that the various things that we do as lawyers can have varying degrees of adverse effect on someone else, from very little to a whole lot, and the connection between what you do and the adverse effect ultimately visited on that someone else can be anywhere from completely "in your face" to highly attenuated. **"Direct" adversity** is most commonly thought of as head-on or "nose-to-nose" adversity—for example, when the affected person or organization is your or your client's opposing party (or otherwise the direct object of your adversarial efforts) or is your or your client's negotiating adversary in a business context.

Does the affected person or organization literally have to be a *party* on the other side of the "v." in the caption, or on the other side of the negotiating table to be **directly adverse**? No. For example, **Model Rule 1.7 Comment [6]** points out that "a **directly adverse** conflict may arise when a lawyer is required to cross-examine a client who appears as a witness in a lawsuit involving another client." Why? Because while representing one client in the litigation, you are face-to-face with another client (not your client in this matter, but in another, unrelated matter) who is testifying as a witness, and your job is to discredit that witness's testimony with your cross-examination. That effort to discredit your witness-client is **directly adverse** to that client's interests (after all, who wants to be made to look like a fool or a liar?). A similar non-party **direct adversity** could arise if you, representing a party in litigation, were to serve a third-party document subpoena on a person or organization who is your **practice organization's** client in some unrelated matter.

At the other extreme is a situation in which you represent two competitors in the same industry on matters not related to one another. In a very real sense, the better the job that you do for one client, the better (to some degree) that client will fare in competing with the other client in the marketplace, and vice versa. But so long as what you're doing is not going nose-to-nose at one competitor on behalf of the other, the effects of your good work may still be *somewhat* "adverse" to the other competitor without being "**directly adverse.**" *See* **Model Rule 1.7 Comment [6]**.[28]

---

[28] A vexing problem that occasionally arises in practices that represent larger companies is when **conflicts of interest** arise among organizational affiliates. Many large companies have large numbers of affiliates; that is, other companies with which they share some degree of common ownership or control. Sometimes, a family of organizational affiliates can be so sprawling that many affiliates have little or nothing to do with each other; other times, ownership and control are tightly centralized for all the affiliates. The question then arises whether one lawyer or **practice organization** may represent one affiliate while acting adversely to another. You might think that, because we have a law of business organizations that creates organizational distinctions among commonly owned or managed companies, the law of legal ethics would respect those distinctions except when the governing organizational law did not (that is, when there are grounds to disregard the corporate form, or as it is sometimes put, "pierce the corporate veil"). That is generally true, but not always. Rules in different jurisdictions take different approaches to this problem. An ABA Formal Ethics Opinion suggests that organizational distinctions should generally be respected in determining **conflicts of interest** between affiliates but lists several factors that should cause a lawyer to treat an affiliate of a client as another client of the same lawyer while still respecting its organizational separateness for other purposes. ABA Formal Ethics Op. No. 95-390 (1995). The opinion is not nearly as helpful as might be hoped, with multiple "dissents" among the authors and little clear guidance. For purposes of this introductory course, we will leave you with the caution that, if you or your **practice organization** represent one company and are asked to be adverse to another with which your client shares any common ownership or control (or vice versa), you have some careful analysis to do before proceeding.

Problem 22B-1: Which of the following describe "**directly adverse**" **concurrent conflicts of interest** within the meaning of **Model Rule 1.7(a)(1)?** Please explain your answers.

a. Maya's firm represents Mojo Manufacturing. Mojo has asked Maya's firm to represent it in negotiating a long-term supply contract with Slick Industries for its widely used industrial lubricant, Slick. Lawyers in another office of Maya's firm represent Slick Industries in negotiating long-term supply contracts for other items in Slick's product line (but not Slick).

b. Same as (a), except that the lawyers in another office of Maya's firm represent Slick Industries in labor and employment matters.

c. Same as (b), except that the employment lawyers in the other office have represented Slick only in negotiating executive employment agreements for Slick's top management last year as part of a major management change the company was going through at the time. It's been nine months since the employment group has heard from Slick. Does it matter if it's been only three months? A year and a half? What other facts would you want to know to help you answer this question?

d. Same as (a), except the sole matter in which Maya's firm is currently representing Slick is a modest collection action in state court. Maya's firm informs its client contact at Slick in a clear but polite email that the firm cannot continue representing Slick in the action.

e. Frank's firm represents a local bank, the Bank of Ourtown, in occasional loan and credit-card collection cases. Frank's firm also represents a local homebuilder, Better Builders Co., in land use matters. Times get hard, and Better Builders gets overextended. Better Builders has a credit line from the Bank of Ourtown to finance Better Builders' operations, and Better Builders misses several payments on that loan. The Bank hires Killer Karl's Kollection Kollective, a law firm specializing in loan-collection work, to represent the Bank in collecting on Better Builders' defaulted loan. Frank's firm continues to represent Better Builders in land use matters. Does Frank's firm have a **concurrent conflict of interest**?

f. Frank's firm has represented Diaper Dan, LLC, a local cloth-diaper pickup-and-delivery service, for a number of years in various business matters. The firm's tax and estate-planning partner, Willie Willmaker, has done the estate plan for the company's founder and general manager, Dan DeLivers, and fields Dan's occasional questions about his personal federal and state income tax. Now a national baby products company, Baby World, has acquired Diaper Dan, LLC as part of an effort to develop a region-wide cloth-diaper business by acquiring numerous local diaper services. Frank's firm represented the LLC in the acquisition. The general counsel of Baby World has reached out to Frank's firm and informed the firm that Baby World is willing to have the firm continue to advise Diaper Dan, LLC, at least for the time being. As the first order of business, Baby World would like Frank's firm to represent Diaper Dan, LLC in terminating the employment of Dan DeLivers so that Baby World can put its own general manager in charge.

g. Maya's firm represents Mojo Manufacturing in litigation against Qualter Quisling, a former engineering manager at Mojo who oversaw the processes by which Mojo makes soles for shoes, which Mojo sells to shoe manufacturers. Quisling left the company after downloading substantial amounts of information from Mojo's computer system and photocopying operating manuals regarding Mojo's manufacturing processes. Mojo regards significant amounts of those materials as trade secrets. Maya's firm filed the action against Quisling on Mojo's behalf last year, and the case is in discovery. Mojo just discovered that Quisling has taken a job with NordWay Shoes, a shoe designer and manufacturer that buys shoe soles from Mojo. Mojo wants its litigators at Maya's firm to amend Mojo's complaint in the trade-secrets case to add NordWay as a defendant. Maya's firm advises NordWay Shoes on import and export restrictions and tariffs. Does your analysis change if NordWay Shoes is one of several subsidiaries of Big Brother Holding Company, and Maya's firm represents only Big Brother in connection with securities regulation affecting Big Brother's publicly traded stock and bonds? If so, how and why, and if not, why not?

h. Maya's firm represents Quick & Nimble, a boutique law firm that does business and intellectual property litigation, in connection with Quick & Nimble's office lease and some ongoing leasehold issues. When Mojo, represented by Maya's firm, sues Qualter Quisling for trade-secret theft (*see* (g)), Quick & Nimble appears in the case as Quisling's counsel.

i. Same as (h), but now Quisling is failing to comply with his discovery obligations. On behalf of Mojo, Maya's firm moves to compel and for discovery sanctions against Quisling and/or his counsel under **Fed. R. Civ. P. 37(a)(5)(A)**.

4. Indirect Concurrent Conflicts of Interest Created by a "Significant Risk" That the Interests of Concurrent Clients May Conflict and "Materially" Limit the Lawyer's Ability to Represent All Concurrent Clients with Undivided Loyalty

So now you know that "**direct adversity**" between **concurrent clients** creates a **concurrent conflict of interest**. But is "**direct adversity**" the *only* kind or degree of adversity sufficient to create a **concurrent conflict**? Absolutely not. How do we know? Well, take another look at **Model Rule 1.7(a)**. The structure of the Rule is quite clear: The first sentence says that you **must not** have a **concurrent conflict of interest**. The second sentence defines a **concurrent conflict of interest** with two numbered alternatives; we know that they're alternatives because they're separated by an "or." Subsection (a)(1), which we discussed in the previous section, tells you that you have a **concurrent conflict of interest** if you have **concurrent clients** whose interests are "**directly adverse**." But subsection (a)(2) goes on to say that you *also* have a **concurrent conflict of interest** if

> there is a significant risk that the representation of one or more clients will be **materially** limited by the lawyer's responsibilities to another client, a former client or a third person or by a personal **interest** of the lawyer.

Because the **concurrent conflicts of interest** defined by **Model Rule 1.7(a)(1)** are often referred to as **direct concurrent conflicts**, the **concurrent conflicts of interest** defined by **Model Rule 1.7(a)(2)** are frequently referred to as "**indirect**" **concurrent conflicts**. The **indirect concurrent conflicts of interest** described by **Model Rule 1.7(a)(2)** fall into two rough categories. These categories are convenient for analysis and understanding, but they are both **concurrent conflicts** and must be addressed in similar ways. So if you're analyzing a possible **conflict** and you determine that there is no **direct adversity** between **current clients**, you're not done. You need to move on to the next category—**indirect concurrent conflicts**—and see if that applies.

As we just mentioned, there are two types of **indirect concurrent conflicts**. One category is *currently* **indirect**—that is, two **current clients** of the same lawyer or **practice organization** are not "nose-to-nose" in the same proceeding or transaction, but nevertheless the adversity of their **interests** is sufficiently strong or serious *at the moment that you evaluate it* that you have to do something about it. The other category of **indirect concurrent conflicts** presents an insignificant **conflict** or no **conflict** at all *right now* but exists in circumstances in which there is some reasonable possibility that, *in the future*, the adversity between the **current clients** may *become* either sufficiently serious or sufficiently **direct** that it would be a **conflict** *then*. We'll talk about each of these in turn.

a. Concurrent Conflicts of Interest Created by *Current* Duties or Connections to Clients or Others Not Directly Adverse to Your Client

Sometimes you or your **practice organization** will have clients who are not **directly** adverse to a **current client**, but that nevertheless seem likely to experience **material** bad effects from the engagement. This is very much the same kind of situation as the **conflict of interest** created by a "significant risk" of a "**material**" limitation on the engagement that we discussed in **Chapter 22.A at 626**. There, the **conflicting interest** was the lawyer's own personal **interest** (because of a financial **interest** or a personal connection to someone who is not a client). Here, the **conflicting interest** involves the lawyer's **duties of loyalty** to another **current client** who is **indirectly** but significantly ("**materially**") affected by the new engagement.

The factors that must be weighed in these situations to determine whether you have a **concurrent conflict of interest** that must be avoided or addressed are *how* the client **indirectly** affected by the engagement will be affected, and *how adverse* those effects are likely to be. These issues feed into the Rule's inquiry as to whether there is a "significant risk" that your representation in the new engagement will be "**materially** limited" by its **indirect** effects on someone else. Some examples are contained in the problems below.

One specific example of this kind of **indirect** conflict that arises occasionally is referred to as a "**positional conflict**." The name describes the problem: One lawyer or **practice organization** takes inconsistent positions on a specific issue of law or fact in two different proceedings on behalf of two different clients. This is the rare situation in which a Comment (**Model Rule 1.7 Comment [24]**) explains the general rule and its application so thoroughly we're simply going to quote it for you at length:

> Ordinarily a lawyer may take inconsistent legal positions in different tribunals at different times on behalf of different clients. The mere fact that advocating a legal

position on behalf of one client might create precedent adverse to the **interests** of a client represented by the lawyer in an unrelated matter does not create a **conflict of interest**. A **conflict of interest** exists, however, if there is a significant risk that a lawyer's action on behalf of one client will materially limit the lawyer's effectiveness in representing another client in a different case; for example, when a decision favoring one client will create a precedent likely to seriously weaken the position taken on behalf of the other client. Factors relevant in determining whether the clients need to be advised of the risk include: where the cases are pending, whether the issue is substantive or procedural, the temporal relationship between the matters, the significance of the issue to the immediate and long-term **interests** of the clients involved and the clients' reasonable expectations in retaining the lawyer. If there is significant risk of **material** limitation, then absent **informed consent** of the affected clients, the lawyer must refuse one of the representations or withdraw from one or both matters.

REAL WORLD Even in situations in which a **positional conflict** does not create a significant risk of **material** limitation on any affected client's representation, and thus requires neither abstention nor consent, it may create significant informal **consequences** in client relations. A client whose business or policy goals are adversely affected by legal precedents created in litigation to which the client is not a party may be quite displeased with the result you achieved for someone else and may make its displeasure felt by withdrawing or withholding ongoing or future work. Clients are of course free to retain or discharge counsel for any reason they see fit. If your practice is of a kind in which you can't please everyone you serve with the results in particular matters, you (or those in charge of the issue in your **practice organization**, such as the Intake Committee at Maya's firm) will have to make decisions about whom you wish to keep happy and whose displeasure (and its informal **consequences**) you're prepared to live with. These decisions are not always easy. REAL WORLD

b. Concurrent Conflicts of Interest Created by *Possibilities* of *Future Direct or Serious Indirect Concurrent Conflicts That Do Not Currently Exist, and May Never Develop, Including Joint Representations*

There are many situations in which there is no apparent **conflict** between the **interests** of your client in a new engagement and the **interests** of your other clients, but there is a realistic concern that such **conflicts** *could* develop later, depending on how the engagement unfolds. By far the most common of these is joint representation.

i. Joint Representation

(A) The Nature and Potential Advantages of Joint Representation

Joint representation occurs when one lawyer or **practice organization** represents more than one client jointly in the same engagement to help the joint clients achieve shared goals. Suppose, for example, that a company's truck driver has had an accident while driving a company truck, and that someone injured in the accident has sued both the driver, who (the plaintiff alleges) negligently caused the accident, and the driver's corporate employer, who (the plaintiff alleges) is vicariously liable for the driver's negligence by *respondeat superior*. In most such cases, one lawyer or **practice organization** represents *both* the driver *and* the employer in the lawsuit.

Why? Easy—it's usually cheaper, simpler, and more effective to have one lawyer representing the two co-parties in the case: It avoids duplicated effort and expense and makes it much more straightforward to ensure that the two co-defendants' defenses are coordinated and consistent. And it's easy to assume that both co-defendants *want* their defenses coordinated and consistent: Both wish to defeat liability and minimize any damages assessed. A good deal of the time, that stays true throughout the engagement: A single defense lawyer or firm represents the joint clients seamlessly because what's best for either is best for both.

(B) The Possibility That Conflicts May Later Develop Among the Joint Clients' Interests

But what happens if a rift develops between the joint clients—that is, their **interests** later come into **conflict**? For example, suppose that it turns out that the driver was abusing alcohol or drugs around the time of the accident. Suddenly, what may be best for each joint client may diverge: The driver, who may face the loss of his commercial driver's license (and thus his livelihood) and even criminal prosecution, may wish to argue—or might be advised to argue by independent counsel who had only his **interests** in mind—that he wasn't under the influence at the time of the accident, or that the accident had nothing to do with his driving (for example, that the truck's brakes failed because the employer neglected to maintain them). The employer, understandably concerned about the reaction of a jury to allegations that the employer had kept an impaired driver on its payroll and had regularly turned him loose on the motoring public (facts that make the employer look irresponsible and that might, in the employer's state, implicate other laws bringing more serious **consequences** into play for the employer), might want to distance itself from the driver. The employer might consider firing the driver, arguing that it had no idea that he was a secret addict, and blaming everything on him. Now what's best for one joint client is *not* good for the other.

At this point in the joint engagement, a **direct concurrent conflict of interest** within the meaning of **Model Rule 1.7(a)(1)** has developed, one that didn't exist when the lawyer undertook to represent both clients jointly but that very much exists right now. The lawyer can't help one client in important ways without hurting the other. As a result, the joint lawyer is going to have to withdraw from the engagement, probably with respect to *both* joint clients, or at the least get

informed consent, confirmed in writing, from both clients as to which one of the two the lawyer will continue to represent. (*See* **Chapter 22.B at 663**; **Chapter 22.E at 733**.)

But, the alert reader points out, you said that this part of this subchapter was about how to address *possible future* **concurrent conflicts** *before* they develop. (Bravo, alert reader!) We know from the previous section on **direct concurrent conflicts** that we have a problem that has to be addressed once the previously nonexistent **direct conflict** materializes. But is there anything that we need to talk about at that happy moment, *at the beginning* of the joint engagement, when the joint clients' interests genuinely seem aligned and reasonably likely to stay that way, and no **direct concurrent conflict** exists?

You bet there is. One thing that **Model Rule 1.7(a)(2)** cares about is assessing the likelihood that the *possibility* of *future* direct **concurrent conflicts** that don't exist now but might develop later *currently* presents a "significant risk" that could "**materially limit[]**" your representation of one or more of your clients *later* in the engagement. *See* **Model Rule 1.7 Comment [8]**. In this context, a "significant risk" doesn't mean "likely," or even "more likely than not." Think about it—if it were likely, or more likely than not, that your joint representation of two co-defendants in tort litigation were going to devolve into finger-pointing and blame-shifting, it would be very unwise even to *begin* the engagement as joint counsel for both. When you know that a train wreck is likely, you stay off the train; getting **informed consent** from all the passengers that they're unlikely to reach their destination because of impending disaster seems pointless at best (except to keep them off the train). So when we're talking about possible future serious or **direct conflicts**, what we're really worried about is the engagements in which such **conflicts** appear relatively *unlikely* to materialize, but where there is *some reasonable possibility* that they *might*. And if there's *any reasonable possibility* that a serious or **direct concurrent conflict** might materialize later in the engagement, then what **Model Rule 1.7(a)(2)** tells us is that you **must not** proceed with the engagement unless you inform all the affected clients about the possibility of the future **conflict**, and either obtain their **informed consent, confirmed in writing**, before going ahead, or refuse to represent more than one of the clients.

Let's explore further: What kinds of possible future **concurrent conflicts of interest** within the joint representation are we worried about here? Well, a **direct concurrent conflict** involves *any* situation in which you have two clients nose-to-nose and where what you do for one client hurts the other. Certainly that includes a situation in which codefendants decide to blame the other for whatever went wrong—that difference in their respective theories of the case will create **conflicts** in advocacy and proof that are sufficient to create a **direct concurrent conflict** even without the co-defendants' asserting formal cross-claims against one another. But it also includes more subtle differences, and you need to be alert to the possibility that those might arise, too. For example, if one joint litigation client might claim that the other is legally responsible for her defense costs, while the other might disclaim that responsibility, that's a possible future **direct concurrent conflict**. If there's any reasonable possibility that one joint client might give you instructions on any **material** feature of the engagement that differ from the instructions given by other joint clients, that's a possible future **direct concurrent conflict**. The possibilities are endless, and they depend on the nature of the engagement and the **interests** of the clients involved. Your job at the very beginning of the joint representation is to think through the plausible ways in which the engagement could play out and see if any of those possibilities end in a **concurrent conflict** that doesn't exist yet, but that might materialize later. *See* **Model Rule 1.7 Comment [23]**.

(C) Engagements as "Scrivener"

One kind of joint representation involves not only possible *future* **direct conflicts** among the jointly represented clients, but **conflicts** that pretty immediately are or will be current and **direct**. While some such situations are not workable as joint representations and should simply be avoided, others can be managed.

Consider the formation of a small business. Several individuals are each going to contribute different kinds and amounts of property and future effort to make that business work. Some (and maybe all) of them anticipate having ownership interests in the business they want to form; similarly, some (and maybe all) of them anticipate having different kinds of management authority in the business. One thing we know for sure is that this is a zero-sum game: There's only 100 percent of the ownership and management authority to divide up among the founders. What that means is that every bit of ownership or authority that one founder gets is a bit that another founder won't get. In creating and structuring this new business (whatever the form of its organization), the founders' **interests** will be in immediate, actual, and **direct conflict**. *See* **Model Rule 1.7 Comment [8]**.[29]

What if you're the lawyer asked to assist the founders in structuring and creating their new business? One way you can avoid any **conflict of interest** is to pick one client out of the several potential clients milling around your office. That way you can advocate for one client's **interests** in the structuring and formation of the business, and you don't have to worry about **conflicts** with the others' **interests** because, well, they're on their own. (Of course, you'd better be sure that everyone involved understands clearly whom you represent, in order to avoid disputes later in which people you never represented claim they believed you were there to protect them. *See* **Chapter 9.A at 257.**)

---

[29] The fact that the founders may ultimately agree on how the ownership and authority in their new shared enterprise will be divided doesn't matter for these purposes. While that agreement is being made, their **interests** are openly being traded off against one another. And that is a classic **concurrent conflict of interest**. This **conflict** is not necessarily an ethical crisis; it's simply a business reality that any lawyer consulted in the matter has to manage, part of which is to explain to anyone being jointly represented (and obtain those joint clients' **informed consent**) how the joint clients' **interests conflict**, and what the lawyer will and will not be able to do as joint counsel.

But that means all the founders will need their own lawyers, and will need to pay them, which will often strike the founders as duplicative and wasteful, particularly if this is a small business with limited resources. Is there anything that can be done? Yes, but it's a difficult balancing act that requires a lot of subtlety and presence of mind. *See* **Model Rule 1.7 Comment [28]** (which is uncomfortably vague on how the lawyer ought to approach the situation).

Most jurisdictions hold that a lawyer **may** (with proper disclosures and **informed consents**) jointly represent several clients and help them resolve their **conflicting interests** to achieve a common goal. That role is sometimes referred to as "scrivener," from the name originally given to an archaic trade common in times of limited literacy that was carried out by people who could read and write, and who wrote down or copied things for people who couldn't or didn't have time to do so.[30]

What lawyers acting as scriveners among joint clients **must not** do is advocate or negotiate for the **interests** of one joint client over another (regardless of how right or wrong they may think any particular joint client's position is). Why? Because that would violate the scrivener-lawyer's **duty of loyalty** to the joint client whose position or **interests** she advocated against. Instead, the scrivener stands in the middle of the trade-offs, and explains and documents without advocating. The scrivener explains to all the joint clients what each joint client's **interests** are, different ways the trade-offs among the joint clients could be resolved (without advocating for one or another), and the advantages and disadvantages of each possible solution for each joint client. The scrivener then clearly and accurately documents the resolutions the joint clients reach by negotiating among themselves (without the lawyer's advocacy for or against any of them). As we'll discuss further in **Chapter 22.E at 733**, these limitations on the lawyer-scrivener's role must not only be respected by the lawyer, they must be fully disclosed and explained to, and consented to by, all the joint clients at the outset of the engagement. *See* **Model Rule 1.7 Comment [32]**.[31]

(D) The Special Requirements for Aggregate Litigation Settlements Involving Two or More Joint Clients

Another kind of future **concurrent conflict** among jointly represented litigation clients is so common that it has its own special Rule. That's an aggregate

---

[30] If you took an American Literature course in college, you probably read Herman Melville's tale of Bartleby the Scrivener. Bartleby worked in a law office, and made his living making handwritten copies of legal documents in a time before photocopiers (or typewriters) existed. Scriveners (or "scribes") like Bartleby were common employees in law offices (well, nobody was quite like Bartleby, but many people did the same kind of work) for hundreds of years, until technology transformed office practices.

[31] Don't confuse the role of a lawyer as scrivener with the role of a mediator. Mediators are sometimes (but not always) lawyers, but when acting as mediators, they don't represent *any* of the parties who are participating in the mediation. In contrast, the lawyer as scrivener jointly represents some or all of the joint clients whose **interests** are in **conflict**, and thus has **duties of loyalty** to *all* of the clients jointly represented. The parties to a mediation are often separately represented, and they are always given reason to understand that the mediator is not their personal advocate or representative. Mediators **may**, and sometimes do, advocate for a particular solution to the dispute under mediation, advocating to one or more sides to moderate their respective positions and find a middle. A lawyer acting as scrivener **must not** assume this role.

settlement among joint litigation clients, which is addressed in **Model Rule 1.8(g)**. To appreciate why this situation deserves special attention, consider the cross-currents that can arise when one lawyer represents two or more co-parties in litigation (civil or criminal). At the beginning of the engagement, all of your joint clients look as if they have similar goals and no obvious differences in approach, so although there's some theoretical possibility that they'll come to disagree about something **material** later, it seems unlikely now.

Under those circumstances, you can make the required disclosures and get the required consents (*see* **Chapter 22.E at 741**), and off you go. Maybe the case goes to verdict without **material** differences among your co-clients; maybe one of your co-clients settles (or pleads) out while others remain in the case. No problems there. But look what happens if settlement (or plea) discussions start that involve two or more joint clients at the same time: The other side may make proposals that quite explicitly trade the joint clients' interests off against each other—for example, "We'll let your client Defendant Y plead guilty to a lesser-included misdemeanor, but only if your client Defendant X pleads guilty to the top-count felony"; or "we'll settle this case for $50,000 total, and your clients Plaintiff X and Plaintiff Y can divide it up any way they want." Even in a situation in which the trade-offs are not explicit, when joint clients are involved in the same settlement discussion, it may be hard to tell whether their interests are implicitly being traded off against each other. Suddenly, what's best for one of your joint clients may not be what's best for the other (or others).

Model Rule 1.8(g) provides that *any time* that there's an aggregate litigation settlement involving two or more jointly represented clients, without regard to whether anyone thinks that his or her **interests** have been traded off against the others' in reaching the settlement, the joint clients' lawyer **must** either (a) not participate in the settlement discussions on behalf of any client; or (b) before either client enters into any aggregate settlement, make complete disclosure about all the ways in which the clients' **interests** may have been or may be in **conflict** in the settlement process or terms, including "the existence and nature of all the claims or pleas involved and of the participation of each person in the settlement," and obtain each affected joint client's **informed consent, in a writing signed by the client**. (Note that this particular consent requires the highest level of formality, **in a writing signed by the client**, although most **conflicts** consents require only that the client's **informed consent** be **confirmed in writing**. Regardless, we'll urge you to follow best practices and obtain **informed consent** to any **conflict of interest in a writing signed by** each affected **client**, not just **confirm** the client's consent **in writing**. *See* **Chapter 22.E at 751**.)

Step back and marvel (or tremble) at everything that this situation requires from you. At the outset of the joint representation, there are possible future **concurrent conflicts** among your joint clients. As a result, you have a **Rule 1.7(a)(2) conflict** right then and there that requires all joint clients' **informed consent, confirmed in**

writing. Possible future "[d]ifferences in willingness to make or accept an offer of settlement are among the risks of common representation of multiple clients by a single lawyer"; therefore, "this is one of the risks that should be discussed before undertaking the representation, as part of the process of obtaining the clients' **informed consent**." **Model Rule 1.8 Comment [16]**. And what happens if an aggregate settlement involving two or more of your joint clients is on the table later? Under **Model Rule 1.8(g)**, you **must** obtain a *second* **informed consent** from each affected joint client at that later time, **in a writing signed by each client**, that discusses all of the terms of the aggregate settlement (including what all the other settling co-clients are getting), what the possible trade-offs and other risks of the aggregate settlement are, and what the alternatives to the offered settlement are, before any of the joint clients agree to the deal.

(E) Tips & Tactics Best Practices in Representing Joint Clients

What all this means, as a practical matter, is that virtually *any* joint representation presents a **Model Rule 1.7(a)(2)** future **concurrent conflict**, right at the outset. Why? Because there is *some reasonable possibility* in pretty much *any* joint representation that two or more of those clients' **interests** *could* come into direct **conflict** at some point before you're done. (It may be possible to imagine a joint representation in which there is *no* reasonable possibility that the joint clients' interests will diverge, but it would be difficult, and in the real world, it's rare. And remember, the question is not whether it's *likely*, but whether there's *any reasonable possibility* that it could happen.)

And because virtually any joint representation likely presents a **Model Rule 1.7(a)(2)** possible future **concurrent conflict** right at the outset, the only sensible way to approach any joint representation that you are asked to undertake is in two steps:

First, ask yourself how likely the proposed joint clients' **interests** are to diverge. If such a crash seems likely, joint representation is a bad idea, and you should either stay out altogether or choose one of the proposed joint clients to represent independently. And you need to make it clear to the others that you are *not* their lawyer in order to avoid obtaining any "accidental" clients to whom you owe duties you don't think you agreed to(*see* **Chapter 9.A at 257**).

Then, *second*, if you have identified joint clients whose **interests** seem unlikely to diverge (but a future **conflict** is still theoretically possible), then you must document the joint representation as if the *indirect* **concurrent conflict** actually exists (which it almost certainly does). That means evaluating whether the **conflict** is **consentable** (which many such **conflicts** are), and then properly obtaining and documenting **informed consent, confirmed in writing** (or better yet, consent **in a writing signed by the client**). *See* **Chapter 22.E at 733**.

Later, once your joint representation is underway, you **must** constantly be alert to the potential that the risks about which you warned the joint clients at the outset are becoming actual, **direct concurrent conflicts of interest**. You may have addressed what was going to happen in that event in your original consent, in which case you still have to notify everyone and take the steps on which everyone agreed. And if no plan was agreed on up front about what to do if the potential future **conflicts** became actual and **direct**, then further steps on your part will be immediately required. We'll discuss those steps in Section 5 below and in **Chapter 22.E at 745.** ╰ TIPS & TACTICS ╯

ii. Other Possible Future Concurrent Conflicts Not Involving Joint Representation

Are **indirect concurrent conflicts** created by possible future **conflicts** presented *only* in joint representations? No. Joint representations are the most common situation in which such **indirect** possible future **concurrent conflicts** are presented, but they're not the only one. Outside of joint representations, there are other situations in which there is some reasonable possibility that two or more of your clients' **interests** could later come into **direct** or serious **conflict** in the course of the engagement.[32] Explore the problems below for some examples.

5. ╰ CONSEQUENCES ╯ What Happens If You Have or Develop a Concurrent Conflict of Interest?

Although the **concurrent conflicts of interest** described in the preceding sections arise in somewhat different ways, they are all **concurrent conflicts of interest** as defined by one of the two subsections of **Model Rule 1.7(a)** and related civil law. And the Rule says that you **must not** get into a **concurrent conflict of interest**, whether it's a **direct** one under **Model Rule 1.7(a)(1)** or an **indirect** one under **Model Rule 1.7(a)(2)**. For that reason, if you find yourself in the middle of any **concurrent conflict**, you are subject to professional discipline "except as provided in [**Model Rule 1.7(b)**]."

We'll discuss in **Chapter 22.E at 733** how **Model Rule 1.7(b)** defines which **concurrent conflicts of interest may** be addressed by the affected clients' **informed consent, confirmed in writing**, and how you can properly obtain that consent. But the practical upshot is that, once you have a **concurrent conflict**, you **must** either (i) abstain or withdraw from the **conflicted** engagement or engagements; or (ii) obtain all affected clients' **informed consent, confirmed in writing** (and preferably **in a writing signed by** each **client**), if that is permitted and if the clients are willing. If you fail to do one or the other, professional discipline can follow.

If you take another look at **Model Rule 1.7(a)**, you'll also see that the existence of a **concurrent conflict of interest** exists *immediately* once two clients' **interests** are in **conflict**, or the circumstances present a "significant risk" of "**materially**" interfering

---

[32] For a discussion of these issues in the complicated multiparty environment of bankruptcy, *see, e.g.,* Nancy B. Rapoport, *Our House, Our Rules: The Need for a Uniform Code of Bankruptcy Ethics,* 6 AM. BANKR. INST. L. REV. 45 (1998); Nancy B. Rapoport, *Seeing the Forest and The Trees: The Proper Role of the Bankruptcy Attorney,* 70 IND. L.J. 783 (1995); Nancy B. Rapoport, *Turning and Turning in the Widening Gyre: The Problem of Potential Conflicts of Interest in Bankruptcy,* 26 CONN. L. REV. 913 (1994).

with the representation of one or both either now or later. *No actual harm to either affected client is required for the **concurrent conflict** to exist*, or for the **conflicted** lawyer to face professional discipline for violating **Model Rule 1.7(a)**.

RULE ROLES **Disqualification** is a civil remedy imposed by courts, usually authorized under the inherent power granted to courts under Article III of the Constitution or similar state law to control the conduct of lawyers and parties in the matters before them.[33] **Conflicts of interest** are the most common grounds on which courts **disqualify** a lawyer or **practice organization**. In most states and the federal system, the standard that a court applies to determine **disqualification** is very closely based on the standards for professional discipline set out in **Model Rule 1.7** (and, as we'll see in **Chapter 22.C at 690**, also based on **Model Rule 1.9** and **Model Rule 1.18** with respect to the types of **conflicts of interest** that those Rules define).

You'll find a lot of authority that purports to order (or refuse) **disqualification** "under" one of these Rules of Professional Conduct. That's an inaccurate analytical shorthand: No Rule of Professional Conduct authorizes a court to **disqualify** a lawyer (*see* **Model Rules Preamble ¶ [20]**), but most courts have adopted civil standards for **disqualification** that are very similar to the standards defining **conflicts of interest** stated in that jurisdiction's ethical rules. Accordingly, just as no actual harm to any client is necessary for a disciplinable violation of **Rule 1.7(a)**, no actual harm to any client is necessary to **disqualify** a lawyer with a **conflict of interest**. As we've discussed before, **disqualification** is a prophylactic remedy designed to get a lawyer out of a situation creating undue risks of harm before any (or any more) actual harm has occurred.

Ordinarily, **disqualification** follows immediately and unconditionally from the finding that counsel has a **concurrent conflict of interest**. However, there is one situation in which a court may refrain from **disqualifying** counsel caught in a **direct concurrent conflict of interest** (and disciplinary authorities might refrain from asserting a Rule violation): If the **conflict** was created by the client alone, without any contributing conduct by counsel. This relatively uncommon situation is often referred to as a "thrust-upon" **conflict**, because counsel has the **conflict** "thrust upon" them through no fault or action of their own.[34] For example, suppose that a law firm is representing Client A in Case A and representing Client B in Case B, suing Company X. Client A decides to acquire Company X and absorbs it into Client A. Suddenly, through no action or fault on counsel's part, counsel is representing Client B in Case B suing the acquiror, Client A, a classic "thrust-upon" **direct concurrent conflict**.

---

[33] **Disqualification** most commonly arises in the course of pending litigation and is usually raised by motion within the litigation in which the **conflict** has arisen. But **conflicts of interest** can just as easily arise in business or transactional matters in which no tribunal is involved. In such situations, the client aggrieved by a lawyer's failure or refusal to address a **conflict of interest** in a business or transactional environment may initiate litigation for the sole purpose of raising the **conflict of interest** and **disqualifying** the **conflicted** lawyer or **practice organization** from the business or transactional engagement.

[34] The literary mavens among you will recognize the origin of the term in Shakespeare's *Twelfth Night* (Act II, Sc. 5): "Be not afraid of greatness. Some are born great, some achieve greatness, and others have greatness thrust upon them." We have serious questions about whether **conflicts of interest** are synonymous with greatness, though we can't help but admire the recourse to such a venerable turn of phrase.

Under these very limited circumstances, some courts may refrain from the immediate **disqualification** in both **conflicted** engagements that would ordinarily follow the disclosure of a **direct concurrent conflict** like this and try to work with the parties to craft a solution, such as allowing counsel to withdraw from one engagement while continuing the other, or even to continue with both engagements subject to protections for any **confidential information** that might otherwise be at risk. *See* **Model Rule 1.7 Comment [5]**. But this situation, and the leniency it often prompts, is rare and narrowly construed.

As just noted, no actual harm from a **concurrent conflict** is necessary to invoke the **consequence** of **disqualification**. But if the **conflict of interest** has caused a client actual harm, then damages in tort are also available to compensate for the harm. The cause of action is typically denominated by one or more variations on what is generally referred to as "legal malpractice"—that is, a lawyer's breach of a duty arising out of the attorney-client relationship that has caused compensable harm. *See* **Chapter 3.B at 46**. The duty and breach may be described as a breach of the lawyer's **duty of loyalty** (for a **concurrent conflict**); a breach of the **duty of confidentiality** (for a **successive conflict**, *see* **Chapter 22.C at 678**); or a breach of the **duty of care** (because the **conflict of interest** has induced the lawyer to do something that no reasonable lawyer would ever do and that has harmed the client, *see* **Chapter 7.B at 180**).

Finally, as discussed in the **Introduction to this chapter at 645**, many jurisdictions apply to lawyers a general principle of fiduciary law that fees incurred while a lawyer is under a serious and unwaived **conflict of interest** are not considered to be properly earned. The result is that the **conflict of interest** is a complete defense to any claim for fees incurred while the **conflict** existed, and the lawyer may be compelled to disgorge any such fees already paid under principles of unjust enrichment. Once again, these **consequences** are not authorized or dictated by any Rule of Professional Conduct; they flow from the general civil law governing fiduciaries. <small>RULE ROLES</small> <small>CONSEQUENCES</small>

> Problem 22B-2: Which of the following situations describe **indirect concurrent conflicts of interest** within the meaning of **Model Rule 1.7(a)(2)** and related civil law? In each case, please explain why or why not, and specify whether the **indirect concurrent conflict** (if any) is one that is based on the state of the facts at the time the potential **conflict** is evaluated or is one that is based on the possibility of a future **concurrent conflict**. In addition, in any case that qualifies as a **concurrent conflict**, please identify the **consequences** that could be imposed as a result.
>
> a. Maya's firm represents Scooter's Computers, a large computer retailer. Scooter's is a publicly traded company, and the company and some of its managers have just been sued for securities fraud under Sections 10(b) and 20(a) of the Securities Exchange Act of 1934, and Rule 10b-5 promulgated by the SEC. The principal claim is that the company misled investors by overstating the sales in one of its biggest regional units. The defendants named in the action include the company, its Chief Financial Officer, and the Sales

Manager for the region accused of overstating sales. Scooter's asks a securities litigation team in Maya's firm to defend the company and the individuals named in the case.

b. Frank's firm is retained by a real estate developer who wants to purchase a parcel of land on the outskirts of town that is about to come on the market. A few weeks later, another **prospective client** contacts the real estate partner, Barney Blackacre, seeking advice about purchasing the same parcel.

c. Frank's firm is approached by three machinists. They have decided to pool their skill, customer lists, and equipment to form a bigger and more versatile machine shop than any of them has been able to establish alone. They are expert at their work and their business, but they don't know much about business law. They have come to Frank's firm for advice about what kind of business organization they should form, how it should work, and how to document it.

d. Maya's firm represents Guber, a company that uses technology to match people who need errands run for them with people to run those errands. The customers pay Guber. The helpers use their own cars and other equipment, but they receive their assignments from, and are paid through, Guber. Maya's firm is defending a class action brought on behalf of all Guber helpers in Maya's state seeking to determine that all Guber helpers are employees rather than independent contractors. Guber currently treats the helpers as independent contractors. Employee status would entitle the helpers to valuable wage and benefit protections under state law, which would be massively expensive for Guber.

    Over on the other side of Maya's state, two drivers for a ride-share app called Myffed sued Myffed, claiming that they should be treated as employees rather than as independent contractors under state law. The drivers lost and have appealed. An associate in the litigation department of Maya's firm is helping the Myffed drivers with their appeal *pro bono*. Does your analysis change if Maya's firm does not represent Guber in the class action described in the first paragraph of this problem, but only in a number of other matters unrelated to employment law? If so, why and how; and if not, why not?

e. One of the employment law partners at Maya's firm is contacted by Marla Manager, an experienced business executive who needs a lawyer to help her negotiate and document her new executive employment agreement with a large company. (Maya's firm does not represent the company.) Marla is going to head up an important division at the large company. The company has decided to put a whole new management team in place for the division, reporting to Marla. Marla has been introduced to the company's first choices for the three new managers who will report to her, and she approves of all of them. In order to save money and avoid "reinventing the wheel," Marla has suggested to the employment partner at Maya's firm and to each of the other three new managers that the employment partner represent each of the four of them in negotiating their respective employment agreements with the company.

f. Maya's firm represents Conglomerate Corporation in a variety of business and transactional matters. The firm also represents Murder, Inc. in a substantial piece of commercial litigation against Independent Co. Then Conglomerate acquires Independent and absorbs

Independent so that it is an unincorporated division of Conglomerate (that is, Independent no longer has any separate existence as a business organization in its own right).

Big-Picture Takeaways from Chapter 22.B

1. The **concurrent client rule** of **Model Rule 1.7(a)(1)** is triggered "if the lawyer's representation of one client will be **directly adverse** to another client." The classic (but by no means exclusive) example of a **concurrent conflict of interest** is representing one **current client** in litigation or negotiation against another **current client** (who is represented by another lawyer in that matter). Such an engagement is forbidden without the affected clients' **informed consent, confirmed in writing**. The **concurrent client rule** applies to **conflicts** between two **current clients** only. *See* **Chapter 22.B at 646**.

2. **Prospective clients** (such as Petrified Petroleum in our recurring hypothetical) enter the picture because, when we're presented with a potential new matter, we **must** always ask whether there *would be* a **concurrent conflict** between the **interests** of the new client and another **current client** if the **prospective client** *became* a **current client**. If taking on a **prospective client** would create a **concurrent conflict of interest** with another of your **current clients**, you **must** decline the engagement (or get a waiver from the affected clients, if it's permissible and the clients will agree). *See* **Chapter 22.B at 647**.

3. If a **concurrent conflict** arises after both engagements are underway (or if you don't discover it until then), you **must** withdraw as soon as possible, probably from *both* engagements that created the **conflict**. *See* **Chapter 22.B at 647**.

4. Because the **concurrent client rule** is grounded in the **duty of loyalty**, and because you **must not** be disloyal to a **current client** in *any* **material** respect, the adversity between the **concurrent clients** need not be in the same or substantively related matters to violate **Model Rule 1.7(a)** and create a **disqualifying conflict of interest**. So even when you're considering acting adversely to the interests of a **current client** in a way that has nothing to do with what you're doing for that client and implicates none of its **confidential information**, the answer is still no—your **duty of loyalty**, codified in **Model Rule 1.7(a)** for disciplinary purposes, says so. *See* **Chapter 22.B at 648**.

5. Because the **concurrent client rule** applies only to **current clients**, you must determine whether the involved clients are **current** or **former clients**. Sometimes the endpoint of an engagement is unclear (either because the endpoint is ambiguous or because the parties deliberately did not specify one). That matters because under the **concurrent client rule**, you **must not**

represent anyone else adversely to any **current client**, but you **may** represent clients who sue (or otherwise act adversely to) **former clients** in any matter in which you can't use the **former clients' confidential information** against them. For that reason, the difference between a client's being a **current client** or a **former client** often amounts to the difference between your being able to take on a new engagement and your being **conflicted** out of it. *See* **Chapter 22.B at 648**.

6. The **concurrent client rule** has an important corollary that bears the implausible but widely used nickname of the "**hot-potato rule**." It's called that because it involves dropping one **current client** "like a hot potato" in order to make it a **former client** so that you can represent another client that, for whatever reason, you like better *against* the "hot-potato" client. A violation of the **hot-potato rule** is *not* a violation of **Model Rule 1.7**, and thus will not result in professional discipline. What a violation of the **hot-potato rule** *will* get you is **disqualification** from the engagement for which you dropped the less-favored "hot-potato" client. *See* **Chapter 22.B at 650**.

7. **Model Rule 1.7(a)(1)** specifies that one way that a **concurrent conflict of interest** is created is when "the representation of one client will be *directly adverse* to another client" (emphasis added). So what does it mean for the representation of one client to be "**directly adverse**" to another? Generally, **direct adversity** is considered to be head-on or "nose-to-nose" adversity—that is, two **current clients** have opposed interests in the same litigation or transaction. *See* **Chapter 22.B at 651**.

8. Although **Model Rule 1.7(a)(1)** tells you that you have a **concurrent conflict of interest** if you have **concurrent clients** whose interests are "**directly adverse**," **Model Rule 1.7(a)(2)** goes on to say that you *also* have a **concurrent conflict of interest** if "there is a significant risk that the representation of one or more clients will be **materially** limited by the lawyer's responsibilities to another client, a former client or a third person or by a personal interest of the lawyer." *See* **Chapter 22.B at 654**. The **indirect concurrent conflicts of interest** described by **Model Rule 1.7(a)(2)** fall into two rough categories (which we describe only for clarity and convenience of analysis; they **must** be treated the same):

    a. One category of **indirect concurrent conflicts** is *currently* **indirect concurrent conflicts**—situations in which the adversity between the **concurrent clients** is not "nose-to-nose" in the same proceeding or transaction, but nevertheless is sufficiently strong or serious *at the moment that you evaluate it* that you have to do something about it. *See* **Chapter 22.B at 655**.

        i. For example, sometimes you or your **practice organization** will have clients who are not "directly" adverse to an existing client that you're representing, but who nevertheless seem likely to experience **material** bad effects from the engagement. The factors that must be weighed in these situations to determine whether you have a **concurrent conflict of interest** that must be avoided or addressed are *how* the client indirectly affected by the engagement will be affected and *how adverse* those effects are likely to be. *See* **Chapter 22.B at 655**. The standard for a **conflict of interest** that must be addressed, quoted above, is whether there is a significant risk that the potential **conflict** will **materially** limit the representation of one or both clients.

    ii. One specific example of this kind of **indirect concurrent conflict** that arises occasionally is referred to as a **"positional conflict."** The name describes the problem: One lawyer or **practice organization** takes inconsistent positions on a specific issue of law or fact in two different proceedings on behalf of two different clients. **Positional conflicts** generally do not amount to **conflicts of interest** requiring abstention or client consent *unless* "there is a significant risk that a lawyer's action on behalf of one client will materially limit the lawyer's effectiveness in representing another client in a different case; for example, when a decision favoring one client will create a precedent likely to seriously weaken the position taken on behalf of the other client." **Model Rule 1.7 Comment [24]**. *See* **Chapter 22.B at 655**. A **positional conflict** that is not sufficiently serious to require abstention or consent can still create significant informal **consequences** in client relations.

b. The other category of **indirect concurrent conflicts** is *possible future* **concurrent conflicts**—situations in which the adversity between the concurrent clients is insignificant or nonexistent *right now*, but there is some reasonable possibility that, *in the future*, it may *become* either sufficiently serious or sufficiently **direct** that something would have to be done **then**. *See* **Chapter 22.B at 656**.

    i. What we're worried about here is the situation in which such **conflicts** appear relatively unlikely to materialize, but where there is *some reasonable possibility* that they might. And if there's *any reasonable possibility* at the beginning that a serious or **direct concurrent conflict** might materialize later in the engagement, then what **Model Rule 1.7(a)(2)** tells us is that you **must not** proceed with the engagement unless you inform all the affected clients about the possibility of the future **conflict** and either obtain their **informed consent, confirmed in writing,** before going ahead—or refuse to represent more than one of the clients. *See* **Chapter 22.B at 656**.

    ii. The most common example of such possible future **concurrent conflicts** is joint representation. There is virtually always some possibility that joint clients' **interests** could diverge in the course of the engagement, and this possibility creates a possible future **concurrent conflict** right at the outset of the joint representation that requires disclosure and all joint clients' **informed consent, confirmed in writing**. If the possible future **concurrent conflict** becomes **direct** or actual later, additional steps may be necessary. *See* **Chapter 22.B at 657**.

    iii. Other issues of joint representation may arise when a lawyer represents multiple clients as "scrivener" (*see* **Chapter 22.B at 659**) or when joint clients are negotiating or entering into an aggregate settlement of a dispute (*see* **Chapter 22.B at 660**).

9. Once you have a **concurrent conflict**:
   a. You **must** either (i) abstain or withdraw from the engagement; or (ii) obtain all affected clients' **informed consent, confirmed in writing** (or better yet, confirmed **in a writing signed by** each affected **client**), if that is permitted and if the clients are willing.
   b. If you fail to do one or the other, professional discipline and **disqualification** can follow. The existence of a **concurrent conflict of interest** exists *immediately* once two clients' **interests** are in **conflict**, or the circumstances present a "significant risk" of **materially** interfering with the representation of one or both either now or later. *No actual harm to either affected client is required for the* **concurrent conflict** *to exist*, or for the **conflicted** lawyer to face professional discipline for violating **Model Rule 1.7(a)**, or to be **disqualified**.
   c. If the **conflict of interest** has caused a client actual harm, then damages in tort are also available to compensate for the harm.
   d. And many jurisdictions apply to lawyers a general principle of fiduciary law that fees incurred while a lawyer is under a serious and unwaived **conflict of interest** are not considered to be properly earned and thus are forfeited. *See* **Chapter 22.B at 663**.

Multiple-Choice Review Questions for Chapter 22.B

1. Lawyer Marie meets with a prospective client named Nona. Nona's case will be highly profitable for Marie, but if Marie takes it on, it will create a **conflict of interest** with her existing client, Opal. What **may** Marie do?
   a. Agree to represent Nona.
   b. Withdraw from representing Opal and then represent Nona.
   c. Ask Opal for a waiver and represent Nona if Opal gives **informed consent, confirmed in writing**.

    d. Decline the engagement unless both Opal and Nona properly waive the **conflict**.

2. A law firm represents client Gemma, who is suing Henrietta for breach of contract. If the same law firm enters an appearance on behalf of Henrietta in this same litigation, what type of **conflict of interest** would this create?

    a. A potential **conflict of interest**.

    b. A **concurrent conflict of interest**.

    c. A personal-**interest conflict**.

    d. A **successive conflict of interest**.

3. Dylan is a lawyer who represents Elaine, a nurse suing her former employer, a local hospital, for wrongful termination. The case is small; Dylan expects to collect no more than $10,000 in fees for litigating the case.

    One night, Dylan is out at a bar and he strikes up a conversation with Frannie. Frannie tells him that she is the general counsel for the hospital and that the hospital is under investigation by the federal government for health-care fraud. She also tells Dylan that the hospital is desperate to find competent counsel to handle the case.

    Dylan realizes that defending the hospital would be extremely lucrative and interesting. He promptly fires Elaine as a client so that he can represent the hospital. The hospital is indicted, and Dylan enters his appearance as defense counsel.

    Assuming that Dylan violated the **hot-potato rule** by firing Elaine but that he otherwise violated no Rules of Professional Conduct, what is the likely **consequence** that Dylan will experience?

    a. Being forced to withdraw from representing the hospital and being ordered to again represent Elaine.

    b. Being **disqualified** from representing the hospital.

    c. Being professionally disciplined for firing Elaine.

    d. Being professionally disciplined for representing the hospital.

4. Lawyer Gargamel represents Azrael, a plaintiff in a medical malpractice case. X-rays show that the hospital left a sponge in Azrael's abdomen during surgery.

    Gargamel also represents Hogatha, a plaintiff in an employment discrimination case. Hogatha claims that her supervisor made numerous derogatory comments about her race in front of other employees, creating a hostile work environment.

    It turns out that Azrael and Hogatha are coworkers and that Azrael was one of the employees who was present when the supervisor's comments were allegedly made. Azrael is listed as a witness for the employer because

Azrael claims that he never heard the supervisor make any derogatory comments. Many other employees claim that they did hear the comments. There is reason to suspect that Azrael is lying.

Might this present a **conflict of interest** for Gargamel?

    a. Yes, because he may be forced into a choice between cross-examining Azrael or pulling punches in his representation of Hogatha.

    b. Yes, because if Azrael is lying, Gargamel will have to withdraw from representing Azrael in the medical malpractice case.

    c. No, because Azrael and Hogatha are not opposing parties, and there is no substantive overlap between Azrael and Hogatha's cases.

    d. No, because Gargamel need not call Azrael to testify because there are other employees who will substantiate Hogatha's version of events.

5. Alan and Bertha are partners in the same law firm. On behalf of a firm client, Alan argues that a local ordinance is unconstitutional. On behalf of a different firm client, in a different case between different parties in the same court, Bertha argues that the same ordinance is constitutional. Do these circumstances create a **disqualifying conflict of interest**?

    a. Yes. The two partners' clients have **conflicting interests**, and both are **current clients**.

    b. Yes. A decision favoring one client will create a precedent likely to seriously weaken the position taken on behalf of the other client.

    c. No. This is merely a **positional conflict**, which is not **disqualifying**.

    d. No. Each partner has only a personal **interest** in representing his or her client.

6. Civil damages are likely to be awarded in a case of a **conflict of interest** only where the following is also present:

    a. Specific intent.

    b. Pecuniary harm.

    c. Malice.

    d. Fraud.

7. A law firm represents a commercial developer planning to build a drug treatment facility on an empty lot. The firm negotiated (on behalf of the developer) to purchase the lot and now has been assisting the developer in having the lot rezoned. There has been some press coverage of the planned construction, and several neighborhood groups have opposed the rezoning. A final zoning hearing has been scheduled, and public comment is invited. Following the hearing, the zoning board will issue its final approval or disapproval of the rezoning. The firm is prepared to represent the developer at this hearing. The developer had not previously

been a client of the firm, and the representation has been ongoing for only a few months.

A few days before the hearing, the firm receives a call from another long-standing firm client, a doctor. The firm is representing the doctor in a medical malpractice case. The firm has represented her in many medical malpractice cases over more than a decade. The doctor owns a home near the proposed development site and asks the firm to represent her at the zoning hearing, where she would like to challenge the construction of the drug treatment facility.

The firm declines the representation. The doctor declares that she will nonetheless speak against the rezoning at the hearing.

Must the firm now withdraw from representing the developer?
a. Yes, because the firm has a stronger relationship with the doctor, who has been a long-standing client with multiple cases over the years.
b. Yes, unless the doctor agrees to waive the **conflict of interest**.
c. No, because the firm did not realize there would be a **conflict** at the time that it agreed to represent the developer.
d. No, because the firm represents the doctor and the developer in separate matters.

8. Lawyer Priya represents a company, JC LLC, which is jointly owned by Joseph and Corey. The company owns and rents carnival equipment. Priya has negotiated for the purchase of that equipment on behalf of the company. Priya's main contact has always been Joseph, because Corey is less involved in the day-to-day operation of the business.

Priya is approached by Corey's spouse, Hailey. Hailey tells Priya that she intends to divorce Corey, and she would like to retain Priya as her counsel in the divorce.

If Priya agrees to represent Hailey in her divorce from Corey, does that create a **concurrent conflict of interest**?
a. Yes, because JC LLC is jointly owned, and Corey is one of the owners.
b. Yes, unless JC LLC consents to the representation.
c. No, because Priya's main contact is Joseph and not Corey.
d. No, because Priya represents JC LLC and not Corey.

9. For many years, you have represented a large retailer, Bullseye Corp., in employment discrimination cases brought by its employees in the State of Raptor. You are approached by the general counsel of Bullseye's biggest competitor, Wal-Mark Co. Wal-Mark's general counsel tells you that she is impressed with the work that you've done for Bullseye, and she would like you to represent Wal-Mark in its employment discrimination cases brought in the Commonwealth of Dragon, where you are also licensed to practice.

If you agree, does this create a **concurrent conflict of interest**?

a. Yes, because you may learn information while representing Bullseye that you can use to benefit Wal-Mark.

b. Yes, because the companies are economically adverse, given that Bullseye and Wal-Mark compete for the same customers.

c. No, because Bullseye and Wal-Mark will not be adverse; each will be sued by its own employees and not by each other.

d. No, because the litigation will be commenced in different jurisdictions.

10. You work at a law firm that represents a local bank. Another client of the firm, Bob, has filed a fraud case against Angelique. The bank is not a party to Bob's fraud case, but the bank may have information relevant to that case, because Angelique has an account at the bank that Bob thinks Angelique used in the course of the fraud. On behalf of Bob, can you subpoena the bank for information?

a. Yes, because the bank is a third party, not a litigant, and therefore you would not be representing two adverse parties in the fraud litigation. The fraud litigation involves only Bob and Angelique, so there can be no **concurrent conflict**.

b. Yes, so long as you are sure that the information provided by the bank will not implicate it in any wrongdoing. If you are confident that the bank did not assist Angelique in the fraud, you may subpoena the bank for Angelique's records.

c. No, because doing so could make you adverse to a **current client**. If the bank resists complying with Bob's subpoena, you will be forced to negotiate or litigate against the bank in order to gain compliance.

d. No, because if you uncover wrongdoing by the bank, you will be forced to withdraw from representing Bob. You must do everything in your power to avoid uncovering wrongdoing by the bank.

11. For years, lawyer Christine has represented client Donald in small commercial disputes. Donald has been a regular client and always pays his bills on time. Christine, however, dislikes these types of cases and would prefer to handle products liability cases instead.

Christine is currently handling a small commercial dispute on Donald's behalf. He is being sued by Evelyn.

During a settlement conference, Evelyn discloses that she is contemplating bringing a products liability case against K&K, a talcum powder manufacturer. Christine thinks that the case sounds interesting, so she asks Evelyn if Evelyn has retained counsel. Evelyn says that she hasn't, but she'd love to discuss the possibility of Christine representing her.

What is the likely consequence if Christine withdraws from representing Donald so that she can instead represent Evelyn?

    a. Nothing, because Christine may withdraw at any time and for any reason.

    b. Christine may be **disqualified** from representing Donald in the future.

    c. Christine may be **disqualified** in representing Evelyn in her case against K&K.

    d. Christine may be **disqualified** from representing K&K in all cases going forward.

12. Lawyer Steve is litigating a car accident case on behalf of two plaintiffs. He represents the driver, Theo, and Theo's passenger, Una. Theo and Una claim that they were injured when defendant Victoria negligently rear-ended Theo's car.

    During settlement negotiations, Victoria (and her insurer) offer to settle the case for $500,000, to be divided between the two plaintiffs. In Steve's honest professional judgment, this is a very good deal for his two clients. What should Steve do?

    a. Accept the offer.

    b. Continue the negotiations and see if he can get the defendant to divide the offer between the two plaintiffs in a way that is fair to each plaintiff.

    c. Not continue the negotiations unless both Theo and Una give **informed consent, confirmed in writing**, allowing him to do so.

    d. Withdraw from representing both clients.

13. Same facts as Question 12, but now Steve accepts the offer on behalf of Theo and Una to settle the case for $500,000, to be divided among the two plaintiffs. Theo claims his injures are more severe than Una's, so he should get more than half of the settlement. Una disagrees.

    Steve agrees with Theo, who was, in fact, the more seriously injured person. What should Steve do?

    a. Terminate his representation of Una, and then negotiate with Una on behalf of Steve regarding the plaintiff's respective shares of the settlement money so that he can advocate for the party he thinks is right.

    b. Terminate his representation of Theo, and then negotiate with Theo on behalf of Una, so that he can advise Una that she is asking for too great a share of the settlement money.

    c. Terminate his representation of both Theo and Una, unless both give **informed consent, confirmed in writing**, to his continuing to represent both of them in the negotiations between them regarding division of the settlement money, and then not advocate for either Theo or Una during the negotiations.

    d. Terminate his representation of both Theo and Una.

14. For many years, lawyer Franklin has represented his client, GeoCare Co., a skilled nursing facility, when GeoCare received subpoenas for records

from its residents in malpractice cases. Under applicable state law, hospitals must retain records for five years after a "patient" is discharged, but "non-hospital health care providers" need only retain records for three years. Franklin has argued that the term "hospital" in a state statute does not apply to skilled nursing facilities. Using this argument, Franklin has successfully defended GeoCare from allegations that it committed spoliation (that is, the improper destruction of potential evidence) by discarding records after only three years.

Franklin represents another client, HomeCare Inc. HomeCare Inc. also owns and operates skilled nursing facilities. HomeCare received a citation from the state for having too few handicapped parking spaces at one of its facilities. HomeCare has asked Franklin to argue that it is a "hospital" as defined by the state statute. If its facility is indeed classified as a hospital, HomeCare has the required number of spaces. If it is not so classified, it has too few spaces.

Both GeoCare and HomeCare are Franklin's current clients.

What must Franklin consider in determining whether making this argument on HomeCare's behalf creates a **conflict of interest** that must be avoided or addressed before Franklin can proceed?

  a. Whether there is a significant risk that Franklin will be materially limited in representing GeoCare or HomeCare in the future, based on the argument for HomeCare.
  b. Whether Franklin agrees, as a substantive matter, that the term "hospital" applies to HomeCare's facilities.
  c. Whether HomeCare is likely to pay more attorney's fees in the future, as compared to GeoCare.
  d. Whether GeoCare had good cause to discard records after only three years.

15. Marley is an Assistant United States Attorney defending the Federal Bureau of Prisons in a prisoner civil rights claim brought by an inmate who claims that correctional officer Bane Batterer used excessive force by using a twist lock to restrain her during a fight. Marley has been asked to defend the Bureau and Batterer, both of whom are named defendants.

When she initially meets with Batterer, he denies using a twist lock on the inmate. Marley presses him on this point, because she knows that this type of restraint is against Bureau policy and is grounds for discipline.

Marley files an answer to the complaint on behalf of both defendants, denying that Batterer applied a twist lock. She further pleads that Bureau policy prohibits the use of such a restraint and that the Bureau should not be held liable, because it promulgated appropriate policies and procedures.

Two months into discovery, Marley learns that there is surveillance video of the fight. It plainly shows that Batterer used a twist lock on the inmate.

Does Marley now have an obligation to withdraw from representing one or more defendants in this litigation?

a. Yes. She should withdraw from representing both defendants, because there may now be a **conflict of interest** between the Bureau and Batterer. The prison may want to argue that Batterer is solely responsible because it was his violation of Bureau policy that caused the inmate's rights to be violated.

b. Yes. She should withdraw from representing Batterer. He lied to her and caused her to file a pleading with false information, which violated Marley's **duty of candor to the tribunal**. As she can no longer trust Batterer, she should withdraw from representing him and defend only the Bureau going forward.

c. No. She cannot withdraw because both Batterer and the Bureau are current clients and she owes both a **duty of diligence** to see the litigation through to completion. Unless she is fired, she must continue to defend both Batterer and the Bureau.

d. No. She cannot withdraw from either client without harming the **interests** of the other. She should instead try to settle the case as quickly as possible before the inmate discovers that the video exists.

16. Niola is a lawyer who represents small businesses. Three people come to see her and ask her to represent the three of them in forming a business that will operate a corner bodega. Can Niola take on this engagement?

a. Yes, so long as Niola has a written engagement agreement with all three clients confirming the terms of her fee.

b. Yes, so long as Niola has each client's **informed consent, confirmed in writing**, regarding the **conflicts** among their **interests** in forming the business, and regarding Niola's inability to advocate for the interests of any one client during the formation negotiations.

c. No, Niola **must not** represent more than one of the three because their **interests conflict** regarding the formation of the business.

d. No, because Niola **must not** have more than one client in a business transaction, and she **must not** choose among the three **prospective clients**.

17. Wendy is a passenger in a car driven by Cheryl. Cheryl's car is rear-ended by Rick, who is speeding and runs a red light. How might there be a **conflict of interest** if Wendy and Cheryl retain the same lawyer to initiate a tort lawsuit against Rick?

a. There is no **conflict**. Their **interests** are all aligned because Rick caused the accident.

b. There is no **conflict**. A **conflict** would arise only if the lawyer also represented Rick.

c. There could be a **conflict** if Wendy decides that she wants to dismiss the case but Cheryl wants to litigate her claim.

d. There could be a **conflict** if the evidence leads Wendy to want to assert a cross-claim against Cheryl.

18. Jordan and Kenny live in the Commonwealth of Keystone, which does not recognize "no fault" or "collaborative" divorces. All divorce proceedings are considered adversarial. Jordan is divorcing his spouse, Kenny. The split is amicable; Jordan and Kenny wish to part ways but hold no animosity toward each other. To save on costs, they hire one lawyer— Alexis—to represent them both. She drafts the necessary paperwork to divide their assets. The court approves the divorce and the two men go on their way, both pleased with the representation. Could Alexis be disciplined for violating the rules prohibiting **conflicts of interest**?

a. Yes. It does not matter whether there was harm to either client; representing two divorcing spouses is a **direct concurrent conflict of interest** in a jurisdiction in which all divorce proceedings are considered fault-based and adversarial.

b. Yes. The clients may be happy now but may later dispute the division of assets. If they become unhappy with the representation, then the lawyer might be sued for malpractice.

c. No. There was no **conflict** here because both clients agreed on the division of assets.

d. No. A court approved the divorce. This approves the lawyer's conduct and shields her from discipline.

C. Conflicts of Interest Grounded in the Duty of Confidentiality: The "Successive Client" or "Former Client Rule" (Which, Ironically, Also Applies to Current Clients and Prospective Clients)

Let's go back to Ron Rainmaker's original plan to enrich his partners and himself. Take another look at the **Introduction to Chapter 8 at 203**. Ron has gotten a call from the general counsel of Petrified Petroleum. Petrified is not currently a client of the firm, though it becomes a **prospective client** in the course of the call by consulting with Ron concerning possible representation in a commercial dispute with Mojo Manufacturing. (*See* **Model Rule 1.18(a)**; **Chapter 8.A at 207.**) As you'll recall, originally Ron isn't interested in having the firm represent Petrified. What he really wants to do is curry favor with **current** firm **client** Mojo Manufacturing by telling Mojo that a fight with Petrified is brewing, and that Ron knows useful things about Petrified's goals and preferences for the litigation, so that Mojo will hire the firm to handle Mojo's side of the dispute *against* Petrified, expanding his firm's relationship with Mojo.

But the firm's Intake Committee has killed Ron's idea because it would create a **conflict of interest** for the firm. (*See* the **Introduction to Chapter 22.B at 645**.) So—as we always encourage you to ask when a **conflict of interest** may exist—what's the **conflict**? Well, we know that there are three basic kinds of **conflicts of interest**; let's check them one at a time.[35]

Is there a **conflict** between Ron's personal **interests** and the **interests** of a client (*see* **Chapter 22.A at 603**)? No—both Ron and his firm have a financial interest in expanding their relationship with Mojo, but the firm's only client right now is Mojo; Petrified Petroleum is *not* a client, and at least in his original plan, Ron doesn't intend to make it one.

Is there a **conflict** between two **current clients** grounded in the **duty of loyalty** (*see* **Chapter 22.B at 645**)? No, again, Petrified is not a client (and in Ron's original plan, won't become one).

Where the **conflict** lies is in the fact that, during the phone call that Ron had with Petrified's general counsel, the general counsel **confided** to Ron valuable information regarding Petrified's needs and preferences in the conduct and resolution of its impending litigation with Mojo—all of which are classic examples of a **prospective client's confidential information** (*see* **Model Rule 1.18(b)**; **Chapter 8.A at 207**). So now Ron and his firm have a **duty of confidentiality** to Petrified, as a **prospective client,** not to use or reveal the **confidential information** that Petrified imparted to Ron in that phone call. And as we'll now see, that **duty of confidentiality** also creates a duty not to get or stay involved in any engagement in which Ron or his firm could use or reveal Petrified's **confidential information** to Petrified's disadvantage.[36]

1. The "Successive Client" or "Former Client Rule"

a. The Basic Protection Afforded Former Clients

Let's take a hard look at **Model Rule 1.9(a)**, which articulates what is often referred to (interchangeably) as the **successive client rule** or the **former client rule**:

---

[35] TIPS & TACTICS We're walking you through this analysis because we think that it demonstrates a good way to assess a potentially complicated situation for possible **conflicts of interest**. But your analysis has got to be thorough and complete: Look at *every* person and organization who might have an **interest** in the situation (including yourself and your **practice organization**) and assess *each* such person's or organization's **interests** to see if they are meaningfully in **conflict** with anyone else's. Many situations can present multiple different **conflicts of interest** in more than one category; you'll have to assess and address every single one. TIPS & TACTICS

[36] You're probably starting to notice that, as we get into the material in this unit, you're seeing a lot more bolded defined terms gathered together in the same sentences and paragraphs. That's because this unit is about what happens when duties and connections about which we've already learned start to collide with each other. So the increasing number of defined terms per column inch reflects the fact that we're picking up a lot of concepts from previous chapters and seeing what happens when they run into each other. That's also why we saved this material for the last section of the book. You could only make sense of the conflicts and collisions between different ethical rights and duties after we had spent most of the course introducing you to those rights and duties one by one. The proliferation of defined terms in this last section of the book is a good measure of how much of the law governing lawyers you've already learned. At least *that's* good news!

A lawyer who has formerly represented a client in a matter shall not thereafter represent another person in the same or a **substantially related** matter in which that person's **interests** are **materially** adverse to the **interests** of the **former client** . . . ."

TAMING THE TEXT This is very dense stuff (frankly, it reminds us of trying to swim through a vat of strawberry jam), so let's paddle through it slowly. It starts with "[a] lawyer who has formerly represented a client." So we're talking in this particular Rule about the rights of **former clients**. What rights do **former clients** have? They have rights of **confidentiality** owed to them by their former lawyers with respect to the **confidential information** that their lawyers obtained during the now-ended engagement. And we know that the **duty of confidentiality** survives after the end of the engagement at least until the client dies, and maybe after that. *See* **Chapter 8.A at 224**. So we're talking about a protection for **former clients** owed a **duty of confidentiality**.

Now let's figure out what that protection is. We already know that the lawyer who owes that **duty of confidentiality** generally can't use or disclose any of that **confidential information**, with some limited exceptions not relevant here (*see* **Model Rule 1.6(a)**; **Model Rule 1.8(b)**; **Model Rule 1.9(c)**; **Chapter 8.A at 217**). But **Model Rule 1.9(a)** adds a new and different protection for **former clients** and their **confidential information**. That additional protection is that the lawyer who formerly represented the **former client** cannot now take on or continue certain kinds of *new* engagements for "another person"; that is, a person other than the **former client**.

What kind of new engagement for another person is forbidden? A new engagement in "the same or a **substantially related** matter in which that [new] person's interests are **materially** adverse to the interests of the **former client**." So the new engagement has to be "in the same or a **substantially related** matter" as the one in which the lawyer represented the **former client**. That is, the old engagement for the **former client** and any new engagement for any new client **must not** involve the same thing—the same dispute or deal—or something "**substantially related**"—that is, something substantively similar. And in that new engagement involving the same or **substantially related** subject matter, the new person's **interests** in the new engagement **must not** be "**materially** adverse to the **interests** of the **former client**."[37]

Now that we can describe the kind of new engagement that the lawyer is forbidden from taking on, let's think of a concrete example: One example would be a lawyer who is representing client A in *A v. B*, and who then withdraws from the case, leaves his firm (so A is now his **former client**), and goes to work at his new firm representing B in the very same case, *A v. B*.

---

[37] **Model Rule 1.9(a)** goes on to say that there is an escape hatch from this prohibition: "unless the **former client** gives **informed consent, confirmed in writing**." The requirements for consent to **conflicts of interest** by the affected client or clients are discussed in **Chapter 22.E at 733**. In this subchapter, we'll explore what is prohibited; we'll discuss whether and how you can properly get around the prohibition through client consent in **Chapter 22.E at 733**.

Model Rule 1.9(a) says that you can't do that, which should hardly be surprising. But *why* do we have this Rule against switching sides in the same case? Because in representing A, the lawyer acquired all kinds of **confidential information** from A. If the lawyer then jumps over to another firm to represent B in the same case, he is in a position to use A's **confidential information** *against his former client*, A, on behalf of his new client, B. But the **duty of confidentiality** says the lawyer **must not** use A's **confidential information** against A, or disclose it to B.

True enough, but the alert student points out that the lawyer hasn't necessarily done that yet, and might never do so (a very fair point of the kind that we've come to treasure from the alert student). In response, we remind you that **conflicts of interest** act *prophylactically* and exist the moment that a lawyer is *in a position* to violate a relevant duty, even if he hasn't yet done so yet (and might never do so). So the moment that the lawyer steps in to represent the new client (B) who is adverse to the old client (A) in a matter (*A v. B*) in which the lawyer *could* use A's **confidential information** against A, the rule is broken, and **consequences** follow. In short, *the **successive client rule** protects the lawyer's **former client** (A) and A's **confidential information*** by forbidding A's lawyer from putting himself in a situation where he could use A's **confidential information** against A.

Now that we understand what the Rule is for and how it works, the last piece of the Rule's language falls neatly into place. The new engagement adverse to the **former client must not** be in the same matter *or* a matter "**substantially related**" to the one in which the lawyer represented the original **former client**. Why? Because, similar to what happens when a lawyer switches sides in the *same* matter, a matter that is "***substantially related***" to the original one is also one in which the lawyer will have the opportunity to use the **former client's confidential information** from the original matter against the **former client**. The "**substantial relationship**" between the old engagement and the new one makes the **confidential information** from the old engagement likely to be useful to the adverse party in the new one. So the "**substantial relationship**" language broadens **Model Rule 1.9(a)'s** prohibition to better fit the purpose for which the Rule was created. We'll talk more about how to determine when a new engagement is **substantially related** to an old one within the meaning of **Model Rule 1.9** in just a moment in **Chapter 22.C at 683**.

b. Extension of the Successive Client Rule to Prospective Clients and Current Clients

So far, we've focused on **Model Rule 1.9(a)** alone. But **Model Rule 1.9(a)**, by its terms, concerns the protection of **former clients** only. If this new idea is about protecting **confidential information** by enforcing the **duty of confidentiality** prophylactically (do you see why?), what about the fact that lawyers owe **duties of confidentiality** to **prospective clients** (**Model Rule 1.18(b)**; **Chapter 8.A at 207**), and **current clients**, too (**Model Rule 1.6(a)**; **Model Rule 1.8(b)**; **Chapter 8.A at 206**)?

Fear not; there are Rules for that, too. Take a look at **Model Rule 1.18(c)**. What you'll see is language similar to **Model Rule 1.9(a)** that forbids a lawyer from putting himself in a position to misuse **confidential information** obtained from a **prospective client** against the **prospective client** (even when the **prospective client** never becomes an actual **current client**). One small difference when we're dealing with **prospective clients** is that the lawyer's new engagement adverse to the **prospective client** is forbidden only if the **confidential information** "could be significantly harmful" to the **prospective client** in the new matter. (Remember, **Model Rule 1.9(a)** says that you can't be involved in a new engagement **materially** adverse to the **former client** that is "**substantially related**" to the old one, so the **confidential information** could be harmful, but not necessarily "significantly harmful," to the **former client**.)

This limitation to "significantly harmful" **confidential information** makes the protection of **prospective clients** a little narrower than the protection for **former clients**; **Model Rule 1.18 Comment [1]** explains that "[a] lawyer's consultations with a **prospective client** usually are limited in time and depth and leave both the **prospective client** and the lawyer free (and sometimes required) to proceed no further. Hence, **prospective clients** should receive some but not all of the protection afforded clients."[38]

What about **current clients**? There is no specific Rule prohibiting **confidentiality-based conflicts of interest** between **current clients**. How come? Well, let's think back to the **concurrent client rule (Model Rule 1.7(a); Chapter 22.B at 646)**. It says you **must not** *ever* be **materially** adverse to a **current client**, whether you have relevant **confidential information** or not. In other words, the **concurrent client rule** is sufficiently broad that it encompasses any situation in which **confidential information** might matter. An additional rule focused on **conflicts of interest** created by the opportunity to use a **current client's confidential information** against the **current client** would just cover the same ground that the **concurrent client rule** already occupies (albeit based on a different duty—the **duty of loyalty**). So **current clients' confidential information** is protected, too.

c. A Practical Paraphrase of the Successive Client Rule

If all that statutory construction that we just did was exhausting, don't blame us. Our job is to immerse you in the actual language of the Model Rules, so that you can make sense of the Rules in the terms that they actually use. That said, we admire your fortitude and patience, and as a token of our admiration, we're going to offer you a practical paraphrase of the **successive client rule**. This paraphrase isn't perfect—as we'll discuss below, the relevant Rules of Professional Conduct are

---

[38] The second sentence of **Model Rule 1.18(c)**, like **Model Rule 1.9(b)**, addresses the details of how and when a **conflict of interest** based on the **duty of confidentiality** is **imputed** from an individual lawyer to all the other lawyers in that lawyer's **practice organization**, as well as the **practice organization** itself. We'll discuss **imputation** in **Chapter 22.D at 702**, and **imputation** of a **prospective client's confidential information** in **Chapter 22.D at 724**.

somewhat narrower than this paraphrase, though the paraphrase is a good approximation of the civil standard for **disqualification** in most states. *See* **Chapter 22.C at 690**.

And in any situation in which the application of the rule is in doubt, you really need to consult the actual words of the relevant Rules and Comments (and all the other authorities that you'd typically consult in order to figure out an arguable interpretation question, such as caselaw, bar opinions, and secondary materials). But our paraphrase gets at the gist and purpose of this particular **conflicts** rule in a way that is more explicitly grounded in the rule's purposes than the literal language of the Model Rules themselves. So if you're looking at a situation and wondering whether there might be a **confidentiality**-based **conflict of interest**, you can start here:

> When a lawyer has a **duty of confidentiality** to anyone (whether a **prospective client**, **current client**, **former client**, or someone else), the lawyer **must not** take on or continue an engagement in which the lawyer might reasonably be able to use any **confidential information** protected by that **duty of confidentiality** against the person to whom the lawyer owes that **duty of confidentiality**.

With that general paraphrase in mind, let's now address how we determine whether the lawyer might reasonably be able to use **confidential information** against the person to whom the **duty of confidentiality** is owed—the "**substantial relationship**" test.

2. How We Know When the Lawyer's New Engagement Is in "the Same or a Substantially Related Matter": The "Substantial Relationship" Test

Let's review what we know about the **successive client rule**: It prohibits lawyers and **practice organizations** from taking on or continuing an engagement in which they will be able to use or disclose **confidential information** belonging to someone else in a manner disadvantageous to the person to whom the lawyers owe that **duty of confidentiality**. But how do we know when we are in a situation in which a lawyer has *enough*, or *important enough*, relevant **confidential information** so that something has to be done about it? The Rules use the phrase "in the same or a **substantially related** matter" to describe when the old engagement (in which the **confidential information** was imparted to the lawyer) and the new engagement (for a new client adverse to the old one) are closely enough related that the risk of misuse of **confidential information** is great enough that something **must** be done.

a. Why Setting and Applying a Standard Is Difficult

Some situations are easy to judge, such as when a lawyer flat-out switches sides in the middle of the same deal or dispute, as in our *A v. B* hypothetical discussed above (*see* **Chapter 22.C at 680**). But such situations are so obviously inappropriate that they are rare. Much more common is the situation in which a lawyer finds herself asked to represent a new client adverse to someone to whom she owes a **duty of confidentiality**, and the new engagement has *some* degree of connection or similarity to the one in which the lawyer acquired the **confidential information**. Obviously, there's a smooth continuum of such situations, from ones in which the **confidential information** has no connection to or meaningful use in the new engagement at all, to ones in which the connection or potential use is only vague or general, to ones in which the **confidential information** has a great deal to do with what is happening or is likely to happen in the new engagement. So we have a line-drawing problem that is frequently difficult.

And that line-drawing is especially tricky to figure out in any situation in which the application of the **successive client rule** is in dispute, because in those situations someone *outside* the lawyer's **duty of confidentiality**, such as a court or a disciplinary prosecutor, has to make judgments about the utility of the **confidential information** in the new engagement, while keeping the aggrieved person's **confidential information** (as its name demands) confidential. Does the beneficiary of the **duty of confidentiality** have to disclose to the court or the disciplinary authorities the very **confidential information** she wants to protect in order to protect it? That could waive the **attorney-client privilege** or other applicable privileges or could make the **confidential information** known to the very person (the lawyer's new client who is the adversary in the new engagement) from whom she wants to keep it secret.

b. The "Substantial Relationship" Test

The solution that we've developed to these very real challenges is referred to as the **substantial relationship** test. The name of the test derives from the words of the governing Rules of Professional Conduct which, as you recall, forbid the lawyer from undertaking a new engagement in "the same or a **substantially related** matter" to the one in which the **duty of confidentiality** arose (and in which the new client's interests are "**materially** adverse" to those of the person to whom the lawyer owes the **duty of confidentiality**). **Model Rule 1.9(a)**; **Model Rule 1.18(b)**. And just to be clear about what we need to focus on, the **substantial relationship test** has nothing whatsoever to do with the *personal* or *professional* relationship between the potentially **conflicted** lawyer and her **former** or potential new **client**; the relationship we are assessing is the *substantive* relationship between the *subject matter of the old engagement* for the **former client**, and the *subject matter of the proposed new engagement* for the new client.[39]

The **substantial relationship** test is used almost exclusively in disciplinary and civil **disqualification** proceedings. Bar prosecutors enforcing the **successive client rule** and people or organizations seeking to protect their **confidential information** by seeking to **disqualify** their former lawyer typically invoke the test by two methods, which can be (and often are) mixed and matched to meet the demands of the situation at hand.

---

[39] The words are easy to confuse. One of us was involved in a hotly litigated **disqualification** motion in which a respected trial court judge wrote a decision assessing how "substantial" he considered the "relationship" between the allegedly **conflicted** counsel and his **former client**, an irrelevant question that neither side had argued. Yes, we wept.

i. Showing the Existence of a Substantial Relationship: Describing Generally or Disclosing Under Wraps the Confidential Information to Be Protected

The *first* method by which we test whether the **relationship** between the old engagement and the new one is **substantial** enough to require protective action or justify **consequences** is for the person seeking protection to describe the **confidential information** actually confided to the lawyer. This portrayal is typically accomplished through some combination of general description at a level of abstraction that doesn't let the cat out of the bag but does convey the nature and basic features of the cat that's in there (so to speak), sometimes with a more specific description of particular items whose misuse might be particularly prejudicial. When actual **confidential information** needs to be disclosed in some detail in order to be protected, that disclosure is typically accomplished under seal or *in camera* to retain its **confidentiality**. The person seeking protection then provides some practical explanation of how the **confidential information** that has been identified could be used against the person seeking protection in the new engagement. If it's reasonably likely that the **confidential information** identified could be used to the disadvantage of the party seeking protection, the two engagements will be considered "**substantially related**" and **consequences** will follow.

> **Problem 22C-1:** Let's return to the Petrified Petroleum/Mojo Manufacturing hypothetical in the **Introduction to Chapter 8 at 203**. Imagine that the firm's Intake Committee had allowed Ron Rainmaker's original plan to proceed, and the firm had agreed to defend Mojo in the commercial dispute against Petrified. Petrified now seeks to **disqualify** Ron's and Maya's firm from representing Mojo in the case by presenting a sworn statement from Petrified's general counsel in support of a motion to **disqualify** that Petrified makes shortly after Ron's firm appears as Mojo's counsel. In that statement, the general counsel says:
>
> > I contacted Ron Rainmaker by telephone on [date] to discuss with him the possibility of his firm's representing Petrified Petroleum in this dispute with Mojo Manufacturing. In that conversation, I discussed Petrified's views regarding the impending lawsuit in some detail. I reviewed the company's thoughts on some of the strengths and weaknesses of Petrified's claims on the merits, and I also discussed company management's concerns about ways in which Petrified would prefer to litigate or settle the matter. All of this was conveyed in confidence with a view to soliciting Mr. Rainmaker's advice about Petrified's concerns and the possibility of retaining litigation attorneys at his firm to represent Petrified in connection with the dispute. Needless to say, that information amounts to a roadmap on how to litigate this matter against us, and its disclosure to or use by Mojo or its litigation lawyers at Mr. Rainmaker's firm would be highly prejudicial to Petrified.
>
> Has Petrified Petroleum established a right to **disqualify** Ron's firm? Why or why not? Has Petrified disclosed any **attorney-client privileged** or **confidential information**? If so, which information and what will the effects of the disclosure be? If not, how did Petrified avoid doing so?

ii. Showing the Existence of a Substantial Relationship: Inferring the Confidential Information to Be Protected and How It Could Be Misused from an Objective Comparison of the Two Engagements Based Only on Nonconfidential Information

The *second* and other way that the party seeking protection may proceed can be pursued without directly disclosing or describing any of the **confidential information** that the party seeking protection imparted to the lawyer. In this approach (which, we should caution you, is the only one that some people call the **substantial relationship** test, even though some features of the approach described just above are usually mixed in), the party seeking protection describes the earlier engagement in which the lawyer received the **confidential information** at issue. This description is provided *from the outside* of the engagement—that is, by what anyone could see or know about the engagement from **non**confidential sources. From that outside view, the adjudicator (typically a disciplinary board or a judge entertaining a motion to **disqualify**) is invited to *infer* the kinds of **confidential information** that the party seeking protection *likely would have* imparted to the lawyer given the terms and nature of the dispute. Then the adjudicator takes a similar look from the outside at the new engagement and again *infers* what kind of legal and factual issues it involves or is likely to involve. Finally, the adjudicator takes the **confidential information** *inferred* to have been imparted, lays it against the legal and factual issues *inferred* to be presented or to be likely to be presented in the new engagement, and decides whether it is reasonably likely that the former could be used in a direct and specific way in handling the latter. *See* **Model Rule 1.9 Comment [3]**.

In applying the **substantial relationship** test, the adjudicator considers all of the features of the old and new engagements that could bear on whether **confidential information** gained in the old engagement could be misused in the new one. Commonly considered factors include:

- The legal issues presented in the old and new engagements;
- The factual issues presented in the old and new engagements;
- The witnesses and evidence presented in the old engagement, and likely to be presented in the new one;
- Whether the passage of time or intervening events since the old engagement have made any **confidential information nonconfidential** or less significant to the new engagement; and
- To what kind of **confidential information** the lawyers were likely exposed in the old engagement in light of their role and involvement in the old engagement; for example, if a **practice organization's** sole involvement in an earlier dispute was that it now employs an associate who researched and wrote a memo on a single legal issue at her prior firm, the **substantial relationship** test will not necessarily assume that that associate possesses all of the **confidential information** that her former firm might have about that prior case.

See **Model Rule 1.9 Comments [2-3]**.

Problem 22C-2: Last year, Frank's firm was retained by Seamy Sawmill, Inc. a local lumber company, to collect monies owed for a big delivery of lumber to a local builder. The builder contended that the delivery was not as warranted in quality or quantity. The parties engaged in discovery and motions practice; the case was tried; and Seamy got some but not all of what it sought.

A year later, Bob deBilder Co., a construction company that is a longtime client of Frank's firm, takes a big delivery of lumber from Seamy Sawmill and is unhappy with it. Bob claims that there are quality and quantity issues, and he asks Frank's firm to represent it in the brewing dispute. The firm agrees to do so.

A few days later, the general manager and part-owner of the sawmill, Seamus Seamy, calls the litigation partner at Frank's firm, "Happy" Trials, and tells Happy that he's got another collection case for him. Happy says that he's sorry, but he's going to be representing Bob deBilder in this one. "What?" says Seamus, "You can't do that. You're my lawyer." Happy patiently explains that the other case ended a year ago, and because the Sawmill is no longer the firm's client, the firm can represent other clients in suing the mill. (*See* **Chapter 22.B at 648**.) Happy says that he really is sorry and wishes he could help, but Bob deBilder Co. is a longtime client of the firm, and Bob asked first.

"But it's the same case!" Seamus insists. "You can't do that!" Happy gently points out that it's the same *kind* of case, not the *same* case, and the parties ring off.

Sure enough, shortly after the lawsuit is filed, Seamy Sawmill seeks to **disqualify** Frank's firm from representing Bob deBilder Co. in the pending case. The Sawmill's motion requests judicial notice of the court file of the collection case in which Frank's firm represented the Sawmill and of the complaint and answer in the pending case (which is all that there is in that case right now, as it's just getting started). The Sawmill argues, based on the court records from the two cases, that they are **substantially related**: Both involve sizable deliveries of lumber from Seamy Sawmill to local builders, and both builders claim breach of warranty with respect to both the quality and the quantity of the lumber delivered. Seamy argues that, from these court records, it can be inferred that Frank's firm learned a wealth of **confidential information** from the Sawmill in the first case about how the Sawmill does business, the quality and quantity of its deliveries, and the way that it litigates commercial disputes. These, the Sawmill argues, are the very issues presented in the second case, but now Frank's firm has switched sides. As a result, Seamy concludes in a dramatic peroration, Frank's firm must be **disqualified** so as to preserve the integrity of the local bar and of Sawmill's invaluable **confidential information**.

Has Seamy Sawmill established a right to **disqualify** Frank's firm in *Seamy Sawmill, Inc. v. Bob deBilder Co.*? Why or why not?

Let's pause and examine this second version of the **substantial relationship** test: Why is there all of this *inferring* about what *might have* happened or *will* happen, rather than just getting at the facts of what actually *did* happen? With respect to the question of how the **confidential information** could be misused in the new engagement, bear in mind that motions to **disqualify** are often made very early in the new engagement, so that all that we can do is make educated guesses about what legal and factual issues are likely to be presented as that new engagement unfolds. With respect to the question of what **confidential information** was imparted to the lawyers in the former engagement, remember that what's at stake is the protection of the **confidential information**. In many situations, discussion about the **confidential information** itself risks waiving the **attorney-client privilege** or other privileges, or compromising the secrecy that makes the information worth protecting as **confidential** in the first place. So we give the party seeking protection the option to choose how to put what it wishes to protect and why it needs to be protected before the adjudicator. As noted above, in many situations, the party seeking protections employs a mix of both methods, offering an objective description of the issues in the two engagements from the outside, with a little or a lot of general description or shielded disclosure of particularly salient **confidential information** (*see* **Chapter 22.C at 685**) for focus and emphasis.

c. The "Playbook Information" Problem

Problem 22C-2 at 687 is also an example of what is sometimes referred to as the "**playbook information**" problem. When you represent almost any client in almost any kind of engagement, you learn some general, practical information about that client. For example, you may learn about the personalities, temperaments, or business style of the client or the client's management; the structure of and identity of knowledgeable personnel in the system by which the client creates, organizes, and maintains its records; the client's approach to issues that recur in his or her life, or its business; and the client's general approach to the kind of issues you're handling. (For example, generally when does the client settle? When does it fight and what kinds of issues does it fight about?)

Because this information is learned in the course of representing the client, it's **confidential information** protected by the **duty of confidentiality**. (*See* **Chapter 8.A at 210**.) This kind of **confidential information**—information generally about the client, its personnel, or about a *type* of dispute or deal rather than information *specific* to a *particular* dispute or deal—is sometimes referred to as **playbook information**, because the person owed the **duty of confidentiality** sometimes complains that this kind of information allows an adversary to know (as in sports) generally what kinds of "plays" the client runs or how it runs those "plays."

You can see the difference between general **playbook information** and **confidential information** specific to a particular case by comparing **Problem 22C-1 at 685** (the Petrified Petroleum case) with **Problem 22C-2 at 687** (the Seamy Sawmill case). In **Problem 22C-1 at 685**, Petrified Petroleum has imparted to Ron Rainmaker and his firm **confidential information** concerning its assessment of the strengths and weaknesses in Petrified's claims in the case to be litigated, and its preferences regarding how that specific litigation should be conducted and might be settled—that is, detailed **confidences** on the *actual issues* presented in the *specific dispute* that the general counsel is discussing with Ron. In contrast, in **Problem 22C-2 at 687**, in representing Seamy Sawmill in the earlier case, Frank's firm learned something about Seamus Seamy's general personality and how he approaches customer disputes, and generally about how Seamy handled a customer dispute regarding the quality or quantity of product delivered. But the new dispute with Bob deBilder involves a different customer and a different delivery of lumber. Knowing what Frank's firm knows about Seamy from the single earlier case may have some limited utility in litigating against Seamy in the new one, but that utility is general and of minor significance.

And that's the problem with **playbook information**. It *is* **confidential information**, and it *does* have *some* utility in acting adversely to the former client in the new engagement, but usually not very much. How useful particular **playbook information** might be depends on the client, the information, and the deal or dispute, which means that we face another problem in which we need to draw a dividing line along a continuum of that information's usefulness that runs smoothly from a little to a lot.

The general rule regarding **playbook information** is that it is *not* sufficient to create a **substantial relationship** between the old engagements in which the **playbook information** was acquired and the new one that might create a **conflict of interest** unless it is so voluminous, detailed, or specifically applicable in the new engagement that it creates a substantial unfair advantage. *See* **Model Rule 1.9 Comment [2]** ("a lawyer who recurrently handled a type of problem for a former client is not precluded from later representing another client in a factually distinct problem of that type even though the subsequent representation involves a position adverse to the prior client"); **Model Rule 1.9 Comment [3]** ("In the case of an organizational client, general knowledge of the client's policies and practices ordinarily will not preclude a subsequent representation; on the other hand, knowledge of specific facts gained in a prior representation that are relevant to the matter in question ordinarily will preclude such a representation").

REASON FOR THE RULE This approach balances two important competing policy concerns: On the one hand, we don't want lawyers ever to take unfair advantage of the **confidences** that their clients impart to them. That would discourage clients from speaking with us freely. But the range of what is protected as **confidential information** is exceptionally broad, and if lawyers were forbidden to proceed when *any* **confidential information** had *any* relevance in a new engagement for a new client, then the old client could effectively prevent the lawyer from representing anyone adverse to the old client on almost anything, almost forever. ("You know about the general manager's general temperament and business style from your one engagement for the company years ago, and that could be helpful in this new engagement against the company that is otherwise substantively unrelated. Get out.") A rule like that generally would make it a lot harder for clients to find an **unconflicted** lawyer, and it would force lawyers to decline engagements in which the possibilities for mischief were small. So when we're looking at **playbook information**, or any other arguably relevant but peripheral **confidential information** that the lawyer may have acquired, we require the relationship between that **confidential information** and the new engagement to be, as the Rules expressly state, **substantial**. ◄ REASON FOR THE RULE

3. CONSEQUENCES ► What Happens If You Violate the Successive Client Rule?

If you violate **Model Rule 1.9(a)** (as to **former clients**) or **Model Rule 1.18(b)** (as to **prospective clients**), you are subject to professional discipline. By their express terms, these Rules are limited to **conflicts of interest** created by **confidential information** received from a **former client** (**Model Rule 1.9(a)**) or a **prospective client** (**Model Rule 1.18(b)**).

The civil remedy of **disqualification** extends somewhat more broadly than the Model Rules do in most states. **Disqualification** is available (and regularly ordered) if a lawyer holds **substantially related confidential information** from a **former client** or **prospective client**, but it is also available in many jurisdictions if a lawyer holds **substantially related confidential information** from *any* persons or organizations to whom the lawyer assumed a **duty of confidentiality** outside of an actual or **prospective** attorney-client relationship. *See* **Chapter 9.B at 268**.[40] Hence our broader practical paraphrase of the **successive client rule** (*see* **Chapter 22.C at 682**).

A **confidentiality**-based **conflict of interest** that is sufficiently substantial and serious will also in many jurisdictions invoke the equitable rule that attorneys' fees incurred under a significant **conflict of interest** are not properly earned, resulting in a complete defense to the lawyer's claim for fees and possible restitutionary disgorgement by the lawyer of fees already paid. *See* **Chapter 22.B at 665**.

As for civil damages or restitution, those are available if the **confidentiality**-based **conflict of interest** causes the person owed the **duty of confidentiality** on which the **conflict** is based any compensable pecuniary harm, or confers some ill-gotten gain on the lawyer. For the kinds of **conflicts** discussed in this subchapter, that harm would necessarily result from the lawyers' improper use or disclosure of the original client's **confidential information** (do you see why?). Remember that no such improper use or disclosure, and no resulting harm, is required for **disqualification**, which is a prophylactic remedy designed to remove the lawyer from the **conflicted** situation before causing any (or any more) actual harm. Damages and restitution, by contrast, do require actual compensable harm (or an ill-gotten gain), which can be substantial when lawyers actually betray their **duties of confidentiality**.

---

[40] *See, e.g., Westinghouse Elec. Corp. v. Kerr-McGee Corp.*, 580 F.2d 1311 (7th Cir. 1978) (**disqualified** lawyers acquired a **duty of confidentiality** to third parties because the engagement involved promising such **confidentiality** to the third parties); *Morrison Knudsen Corp. v. Hancock Rothert & Bunshoft*, 69 Cal. App. 4th 223, 81 Cal. Rptr. 2 (Cal. Ct. App. 1999) (**disqualified** lawyers acquired a **duty of confidentiality** to a third party because their client in the old engagement had assumed such a **duty** to that third party).

Problem 22C-3: Which of these situations describes a violation of the **successive client rule**, and why or why not? In any that do, describe the **consequences** that may result, and why.

a. The tax and estate-planning partner in Frank's firm, Willie Willmaker, represented Salim Siddiqui in personal tax and financial advice for a number of years. Salim moved this work to a different tax adviser last year. Now Salim's wife, Shahed, has approached Frank's firm seeking representation in divorcing Salim. The firm's family law partner, Sally Splitsville, accepts the engagement.

b. Tax lawyers in Maya's firm represented Charlie Chiseler several years ago. Charlie had been cheating on his taxes for a number of years, and the firm's tax lawyers negotiated Charlie's way out of the problem with an agreement that he pay certain back taxes, interest, and penalties. Now, a few years later, an employment lawyer at Maya's firm is contacted by one of the firm's employer clients. The company needs advice about how to fire a manager who has been inflating his division's reported revenues in order to increase his quarterly bonuses. The employee is Charlie Chiseler.

c. The real estate partner in Frank's firm, Barney Blackacre, represented a local real estate developer in acquiring a parcel of land, obtaining the necessary land-use permissions to build a shopping center, and preparing standard forms of leases for the different kinds of tenants likely to occupy space there. All requested legal work was completed, and the shopping center was built and leased out, three years ago. Two years ago, the developer sold the shopping center to an established shopping center operator. Now a retail tenant in that shopping center has a dispute with the shopping center owner concerning the interpretation of the "percentage rent" clause in her lease, and asks Frank's firm to represent her. (For those who are not familiar with this term, commercial leases of retail premises sometimes include a clause providing that the rent includes some small percentage of the sales in the store; these are often referred to as "percentage rent" clauses.) The firm's litigation partner, "Happy" Trials, agrees to handle the matter. Does your analysis change if the landlord-tenant dispute is based on the fact that local government authorities have issued a cease-and-desist order against the tenant, asserting that the tenant is selling goods and services not authorized by applicable zoning ordinances? Why or why not, and if so, how?

d. Same as **Problem 22C-2 at 687** (Frank's firm represented Seamy Sawmill in one customer dispute and now wishes to represent a different customer against Seamy in a similar kind of dispute), except that Frank's firm has represented Seamy Sawmill in five previous customer disputes over the last three years, all now completed. Does your analysis change if Frank's firm has been representing the Sawmill on all of its litigated customer disputes, amounting to two dozen of them over the last six years? What if the former general counsel of Seamy Sawmill just became a partner in Frank's firm? If any of these facts would change your analysis, please explain how and why, or if not, why not.

e. Rocky Rhoades was general counsel working in-house for Frannie's Frozen Frolics, an ice-cream manufacturing and packing company, for ten years. Now he is practicing business law on his own. Mary's Dairies, a dairy-farming operation, approaches Rocky to represent Mary's in negotiating a long-term contract to supply milk and cream to Frannie's.

692 Chapter 22 Conflicts of Interest

f. Danielle's office prosecuted Paul Poverty for petty theft (he stole three packs of cigarettes from a convenience store). Paul was convicted and served ten days in the county jail. The prosecutor who handled *State v. Poverty* has since left the DA's office and has gone into private practice. He has just filed a lawsuit claiming civil-rights violations and related torts on behalf of Paul Poverty against the city government, the police department, and two police officers. The complaint alleges that the police officers used excessive force on Paul and badly beat him up while falsely claiming that he was resisting arrest. Are there other facts that you would want to know in analyzing this problem? If so, what are they, and why do they matter?

g. Same facts as **Problem 22B-2(c) at 666** (Frank's firm represents three machinists jointly in the formation of a partnership among them), except that now the partnership has been formed among the three machinists and has been operating for some time. Unfortunately, one of the partners has developed an opioid addiction, and the other two partners would like to expel him from the partnership. They request help from Frank's firm.

Big-Picture Takeaways from Chapter 22.C

1. **Model Rule 1.9(a)**, which focuses on the **duties of confidentiality** owed to **former clients**, makes clear that a lawyer who formerly represented a **former client** cannot now take on or continue certain kinds of new engagements for "another person" (without the **former client's informed consent, confirmed in writing**). The prohibited kind of new engagement is one that's in "the same or a **substantially related** matter," and "in which that [new] person's **interests** are **materially** adverse to the **interests** of the **former client**." In other words, **Model Rule 1.9(a)** says that the old engagement for the **former client** and any new engagement for any new client **must not** involve the same thing—the same dispute or deal—or something "**substantially related**"—that is, something substantively similar. And in that new engagement involving the same or **substantially related** subject matter, the new person's **interests** in the new engagement **must not** be "**materially** adverse to the **interests** of the **former client**." *See* **Chapter 22.C at 679.**

   a. What about the fact that lawyers also owe **duties of confidentiality** to **prospective clients (Model Rule 1.18(b); Chapter 8.A at 207)**, and **current clients (Model Rule 1.8(b); Chapter 8.A at 206)**?

      i. With respect to **prospective clients, Model Rule 1.18(c)** uses language similar to **Model Rule 1.9(a)** and forbids a lawyer from putting himself in a position to misuse **confidential information** obtained from a **prospective client** against the **prospective client** (without the **prospective client's informed consent, confirmed in writing**). One small difference when you're dealing with **prospective clients** is that the lawyer's new engagement adverse to the **prospective client** is forbidden only if the **confidential information** "could be significantly harmful" to the **prospective client** in the new matter. This limitation to "significantly harmful" **confidential information** makes the protection of **prospective clients** a little narrower than the protection for **former clients**. *See* **Chapter 22.C at 681**.

ii. As for **current clients**, the **concurrent client rule** (**Model Rule 1.7(a)**; **Chapter 22.B at 646**) forbids acting adversely to a **current client** in *any* respect, whether or not **confidential information** might be involved (again, unless all affected clients give **informed consent, confirmed in writing**). So **current clients' confidential information** is protected by this broader rule. *See* **Chapter 22.C at 681**.

b. Here's a useful paraphrase of the **successive client rule**: *When a lawyer has a* **duty of confidentiality** *to anyone (whether a* **prospective client**, **current client**, **former client**, *or someone else), the lawyer* **must not** *take on or continue an engagement in which the lawyer might reasonably be able to use any* **confidential information** *protected by that* **duty of confidentiality** *against the person to whom the lawyer owes that* **duty of confidentiality**. *See* **Chapter 22.C at 682**.

2. The **successive client rule** prohibits lawyers and **practice organizations** from taking on or continuing an engagement in which they will be able to use or disclose **confidential information** belonging to someone else in a manner disadvantageous to the person to whom the lawyers owe that **duty of confidentiality**. But how do we know when we are in a situation in which a lawyer has *enough*, or *important enough*, relevant **confidential information** so that something has to be done about it? The rules use the phrase "in the same or a substantially related matter" to describe when the old engagement (in which the **confidential information** was imparted to the lawyer) and the new engagement (for a new client adverse to the old one) are closely enough related that the risk of misuse of **confidential information** is great enough that something **must** be done. The solution that we've developed to these very real challenges is referred to as the **substantial relationship** test. *See* **Chapter 22.C at 683**.

a. The **substantial relationship** test is most commonly used in disciplinary and civil **disqualification** proceedings. *See* **Chapter 22.C at 684**.

b. Bar prosecutors enforcing the **successive client rule** and people or organizations seeking to protect their **confidential information** by **disqualifying** counsel in a position to misuse it typically invoke the test by two methods, which can be (and often are) mixed and matched to meet the demands of the situation at hand. *See* **Chapter 22.C at 684**.

i. The *first* method by which we test whether the **relationship** between the old engagement and the new one is **substantial** enough to justify **consequences** is for the person seeking protection to describe in general terms the **confidential information** actually confided to the lawyer, or to disclose specific **confidences** from the old engagement that could be misused in the new one under seal or *in camera*. *See* **Chapter 22.C at 685**.

ii. The *second* and other way that the party seeking protection may proceed can be pursued without directly disclosing or describing any of the **confidential information** that the party seeking protection imparted to the lawyer. The party seeking protection describes the earlier engagement in which the lawyer received the **confidential information** at issue. This description is provided *from the outside* of the engagement—that is, by what anyone could see or know about the engagement from **non**confidential sources. Then the adjudicator looks at the proposed new engagement adverse to the **former client**—again from the outside—and infers what kinds of **confidential information** are reasonably likely to matter in that new engagement. By comparing the **confidential information** that the court infers was imparted in the former engagement with the **confidential information** the court infers is reasonably likely to matter in the new one, the court assesses whether the two engagements are **substantially related**. *See* **Chapter 22.C at 686**.

c. One area in which it can be difficult to apply the **substantial relationship** test involves "**playbook information**." When you represent almost any client in almost any kind of engagement, you gain some general, practical information about the client. Because this "**playbook information**" is learned in the course of representing the client, it's **confidential information** protected by the **duty of confidentiality**. This kind of **confidential information**—information generally about the client or about a *type* of dispute or deal rather than information *specific* to a *particular* dispute or deal—is sometimes referred to as **playbook information**, because the person owed the **duty of confidentiality** sometimes complains that this kind of information allows an adversary to know (as in sports) generally what kinds of "plays" the client runs or how it runs those "plays." The general rule regarding **playbook information** is that it is *not* sufficient to create a **substantial relationship** between the old engagements in which the **playbook information** was acquired and the new one that might create a **conflict of interest** unless it is so voluminous, detailed, or specifically applicable in the new engagement that it creates a substantial unfair advantage. *See* **Chapter 22.C at 688**.

3. If you violate **Model Rule 1.9(a)** (as to **former clients**) or **Model Rule 1.18(b)** (as to **prospective clients**):

a. You are subject to professional discipline. By their express terms, these Rules are limited to **conflicts of interest** created by **confidential**

information received from a **former client** (**Model Rule 1.9(a)**) or a **prospective client** (**Model Rule 1.18(b)**). *See* **Chapter 22.C at 690.**

b. The civil remedy of **disqualification** extends somewhat more broadly than the Model Rules do in most states. **Disqualification** is available (and regularly ordered) if a lawyer holds **substantially related confidential information** from a **former client** or **prospective client**, **but disqualification** is also available in many jurisdictions if a lawyer holds **substantially related confidential information** from *any* persons or organizations to whom the lawyer assumed a **duty of confidentiality** outside of an actual or **prospective** attorney-client relationship. *See* **Chapter 22.C at 690.**

c. A **confidentiality**-based **conflict of interest** that is sufficiently substantial and serious will also invoke the equitable rule that attorneys' fees incurred under a significant **conflict of interest** are not properly earned, resulting in a complete defense to the lawyer's claim for fees, and possible restitutionary disgorgement by the lawyer of fees already paid. *See* **Chapter 22.C at 690.**

d. As for civil damages or restitution, those are available if the **confidentiality**-based **conflict of interest** causes the person owed the **duty of confidentiality** on which the **conflict** is based any compensable pecuniary harm, or confers an ill-gotten gain on the lawyer. That will typically occur only if the **conflicted** counsel actually used or disclosed the **confidential information** in a way that harms the person owed the **duty of confidentiality** (or confers an ill-gotten gain). Remember that no such improper use or disclosure, and no resulting harm, is required for **disqualification**, which is a prophylactic remedy designed to remove the lawyer from the **conflicted** situation before causing any (or any more) actual harm. Damages and restitution, by contrast, do require actual compensable harm, which can be substantial when lawyers actually betray their **duties of confidentiality**. *See* **Chapter 22.C at 690.**

Multiple-Choice Review Questions for Chapter 22.C

1. David works at a large firm that represents owners, architects, and engineers in construction law disputes. He is assigned to represent the owner of a casino suing the general contractor for construction delays. Dissatisfied with firm life, David leaves the firm while the case is pending to clerk for a judge for a year.

   When his clerkship ends, instead of returning to his former firm, David goes to work at a small boutique construction law firm that generally represents contractors and subcontractors. On his first day at the firm, a partner leaves a Redweld folder (an accordion-pleated folder with an open top, often used for organizing large amounts of paperwork) on David's desk. To his surprise, it relates to the litigation over the casino, which is still ongoing. David's new firm represents the general contractor in the case.

David asks the partner why he was given the file. The partner explains, "I need you to go to a deposition tomorrow to defend our client, the general contractor." When David protests, the partner assures him, "it's fine; our client, the general contractor, has waived any **conflicts of interest**." Is such a waiver sufficient?

a. Yes, so long as David zealously represents the **interests** of the general contractor going forward and does not feel any loyalty to the owner.

b. Yes, so long as the general contractor gave **informed consent**, **confirmed in writing**.

c. No, because the general contractor's waiver is not sufficient to address the **conflict of interest**.

d. No, unless David actually uses **confidential information** obtained from the general contractor against the former client's interest.

2. For several years, Erin defended a local hospital and its employees when they were sued for medical malpractice. Over the years, Erin learned a lot about how the hospital operated. In particular, she learned a lot about each of the hospital's surgeons. Erin represented one surgeon, Henry Hacker, on several occasions. During the defense of one case, Erin learned that Henry went through a bitter divorce in April 2017 and that, as a result, he made several errors at work that spring. Luckily for the hospital and Henry, Erin settled the cases involving Henry's errors so that they did not become public knowledge.

Over the years, Erin also developed a good working relationship with the hospital's in-house counsel, Felicity. Felicity retired a few years ago, and the work dried up for Erin. Despite her efforts to make inroads with Felicity's replacement, the hospital retained different counsel for its medical malpractice defense work. Erin was upset.

Erin was recently approached by Greta, who claims that her April 2017 surgery was botched at the hospital. A quick glance at Greta's medical records reveals that Henry Hacker was the surgeon.

With her knowledge of the hospital's policies and procedures and its tolerances for litigation, Erin figures she can help Greta settle, likely for a hefty sum. She also assumes she can use the information about Henry's divorce to impeach Henry at trial if the case does not settle.

Can Erin now represent Greta in litigation against the hospital?

a. Yes, because the hospital fired Erin. Had it wanted to keep her from litigating against it, the hospital could have kept her on retainer.

b. Yes, because Erin never defended the hospital against claims by Greta in the past. Erin is not switching sides.

c. No, because Erin previously defended the hospital on **substantially related** matters. She could use the information that she had gained from representing the hospital to Greta's benefit now.

    d. No, because Erin has a personal-interest **conflict** caused by her bitterness over losing the hospital's business. This **conflict** could cloud her judgment.

3. The Internal Revenue Service opens an administrative investigation of Igor's personal income tax filings. The IRS believes that Igor hid certain offshore investments in order to avoid paying income tax on those investments. Igor hires a lawyer, Jane, to represent him in the administrative proceedings. They meet dozens of times, and Jane pores over all of Igor's financial records. She represents him before the IRS and resolves the dispute. Ultimately, the IRS agrees that Igor's actions were legal.

    Several years later, Jane is contacted by Igor's spouse, Kerry. Kerry asks Jane to represent her in her divorce proceedings against Igor. Kerry discovered that Igor had an affair, and she seeks to gain half of all Igor's assets in the divorce. Jane agrees to handle the case for Kerry.

    When Igor learns about this, he hires his own lawyer, who moves to disqualify Jane. In response, Jane argues that the IRS administrative investigation and divorce are not **substantially related**. Is this a valid argument?

    a. Yes, because the legal issues are wholly distinct. Jane was previously defending Igor against accusations that he improperly hid income to avoid taxes. That legal issue is not relevant in the divorce.

    b. Yes, because Jane has no **confidential information** that can be used against Igor. He was found to have acted properly by the IRS and, therefore, Jane knows nothing that could be used against him.

    c. No, because there is no reason to believe that the IRS investigation caused marital strife. In actuality, it was the affair, and not the investigation, that led to the divorce.

    d. No, because in the tax engagement for Igor, Jane may have learned **confidential information** about Igor's assets that she could now use to Kerry's benefit in seeking to have those assets awarded to Kerry in the divorce.

4. Why do **prospective clients** receive fewer **confidentiality** protections than actual clients?

    a. Consultations with **prospective clients** are usually more limited in time and depth.

    b. Many lawyers do not charge a fee for an initial consultation, and therefore should not have future representation limited by these free consultations.

    c. Prospective clients do not share **confidential information** with lawyers, because the **duty of confidentiality** attaches only once a retainer agreement is signed.

    d. A lawyer owes no duty of zealous advocacy to **prospective clients**.

5. One day at a party, lawyer Annalise strikes up a conversation with Bart. Bart is general counsel for a large insurance company. Annalise invites Bart to her firm's offices for a formal pitch meeting. During the meeting, Bart shares **confidential information** about how the insurance company litigates its cases. In particular, Bart discusses a potential claim by one of its insureds, although it does not mention her by name. Although the meeting goes well, Bart never follows up, and the insurance company does not retain Annalise or any of her colleagues.

    Months later, Annalise is approached by one of her regular clients, Carrie, who is considering bringing a claim against her insurance company. Carrie asks Annalise if she has any information about how the insurance company might handle the claim. Annalise realizes that Carrie is the insured Bart mentioned during the pitch meeting.

    How should Annalise respond?
    a. She should disclose the information shared by Bart during the pitch meeting. The insurance company is not a client and neither Annalise nor her firm owe it any **duty of confidentiality**, because Bart did not identify Carrie specifically.
    b. She should disclose the information shared by Bart during the pitch meeting. The insurance company was only a **prospective client**, but Carrie is a **current client**. **Current clients** are owed more duties than **prospective clients**.
    c. She should not disclose the information shared by Bart during the pitch meeting. Carrie and the insurance company are adverse to one another, and disclosing the information will cause Annalise to have to **disqualify** herself from representing Carrie.
    d. She should not disclose the information shared by Bart during the pitch meeting. As a **prospective client**, the insurance company was owed a **duty of confidentiality** by Annalise and her firm.

6. Lawyer Don defended Dr. Jones in a medical malpractice case brought by plaintiff Edgar, alleging that Dr. Jones left a sponge in Edgar's abdomen after a 2018 bladder surgery at Grittydelphia General Hospital. The legal issues in this case were specific to the standard of care for a surgeon. The case ultimately settled, and Dr. Jones paid Edgar $750,000.

    Which client **must** Don **not** represent under **Model Rule 1.9(a)**? (Assume no **informed consent** from anyone who would be required to give one.)
    a. Edgar, asserting a medical malpractice case against Dr. Franks arising from a 2019 failure to diagnose skin cancer. The legal issues in this case are specific to the standard of care for a dermatologist.
    b. The hospital, which terminated Dr. Jones due to the poor outcome in Edgar's surgery and is now being sued by Dr. Jones for wrongful termination.

    c. Dr. Jones, in a contribution and indemnity claim against one of the residents who participated in Don's 2018 bladder surgery, based upon the resident's failure to count the sponges before Dr. Jones closed the incision.

    d. Dr. Jones, in a claim against his insurance company after the company denied his client's request to pay a portion of the $750,000 settlement that Dr. Jones paid to Edgar.

7. **Model Rule 1.9(a)** adds what duty to the existing **duty of confidentiality** to **former clients** that generally applies under **Model Rule 1.9(c)** (unless an exception applies)?

    a. The duty not to use **confidential information.**

    b. The duty not to disclose **confidential information.**

    c. The duty not to take on certain future engagements.

    d. No additional duties are added.

8. Lawyer Allison represents Bernard, a plaintiff in a car accident case filed against defendant Chris. Bernard agrees to pay Allison on a monthly basis. Although she repeatedly sends him invoices, he fails to pay for her work on the case.

    With the court's permission, Allison withdraws from representing Bernard. She then enters her appearance in the case on Chris's behalf.

    Bernard hires new counsel, Dolores, who files a motion to **disqualify** Allison. Allison responds that she has not used any of Bernard's **confidential information** to Chris's advantage.

    Is this a viable defense to the motion to **disqualify**?

    a. Yes. Allison does not violate the **successive client rule** if she does not use or disclose Bernard's **confidential information.**

    b. Yes. Allison's withdrawal was approved by the court, so she is in compliance with the **successive client rule.**

    c. No. Allison needed the court's approval to enter her appearance. Only if the court approves may she represent Chris without violating the **successive client rule.**

    d. No. Merely by switching sides in the case, Allison violated the **successive client rule**; no proof of actual use or disclosure of Bernard's **confidential information** is needed.

9. When is a new matter "**substantially related**" to an older one, as defined by **Model Rule 1.9(a)**?

    a. If there is a reasonable likelihood that the **confidential information** that would normally have been obtained in the prior representation would **materially** assist the new client in the subsequent matter.

    b. If the lawyer has been directly involved in a specific transaction and now is representing a client **materially** adverse to the lawyer's former client.

    c. If the lawyer's past legal training, experience, and expertise could be used to benefit a new client.

    d. When the lawyer may be called upon to serve as both counsel and a witness in a particular case.

10. Polly is a prosecutor for the State of Raptor. She successfully tries and convicts defendant Rochelle for criminal fraud. Six months later, Polly leaves the government and joins a law firm that handles civil rights cases. She is asked to handle a case on behalf of Rochelle, who is asserting a civil rights claim against the State of Raptor. Rochelle claims that the state violated her constitutional right to be free from unreasonable searches and seizures in obtaining and executing an overbroad search warrant against her while investigating the fraud case, even though the evidence wrongfully seized was later suppressed.

    Can Polly handle this case?

    a. Yes. Because one case is civil and one is criminal, they are not **substantially related** under **Model Rule 1.9**.

    b. Yes. Because she was a government lawyer, she is exempt from **Model Rule 1.9**.

    c. No. Polly would be handling a **substantially related** matter.

    d. No. A government lawyer can never handle a case asserted against her former employer.

11. Which of the following information that a lawyer gains as part of a prior representation of a **former client** is generally **disqualifying** under the **successive client rule** when that lawyer seeks to undertake a new representation adverse to the **former client**?

    a. Knowledge of specific facts gained in a prior representation that are relevant in the new representation.

    b. Knowledge of an organizational client's general policies and practices.

    c. Information disclosed to the public.

    d. Information rendered obsolete by the passage of time.

12. What is the primary difference between **Model Rule 1.9(a)** and **Model Rule 1.18(c)**?

    a. A lawyer is not forbidden from taking a new engagement involving **confidential information** that would be "significantly harmful" to a **former client** but is forbidden from taking a new engagement that is "**substantially related**" to an engagement for a **prospective client**.

    b. A lawyer is forbidden from taking a new engagement involving **confidential information** that would be "significantly harmful" to a **prospective client** and is also forbidden from taking a new engagement that is "**substantially related**" to an engagement for a **former client**.

c. A lawyer is forbidden from being **directly adverse** to a **former client** on behalf of a **current client** in the same matter in which the lawyer represented the **former client**.

d. A lawyer is forbidden from being **directly adverse** to a **current client** on behalf of a **former client** in the same matter in which the lawyer represented the **former client**.

13. Which factor is generally *not* considered under the **substantial relationship** test?

a. The legal issues presented in the old and new engagements.

b. The factual issues presented in the old and new engagements.

c. The witnesses in the old and new engagements.

d. The judge in the old and new engagements.

14. Wade represents a bank foreclosing on a house. The bank had lent the homeowner, Xander, $250,000 to renovate the property. Xander then defaulted and failed to repay the bank.

Before he agreed to represent the bank, Wade conducted a **conflicts** check. The check revealed that, ten years prior, Wade's firm had represented Xander in drafting a purchase agreement. No one at the firm could remember the details of the representation, and neither Wade nor the firm had represented Xander in any other matters.

After Wade filed a notice of foreclosure on behalf of the bank, Xander filed an ethics complaint against Wade. As detailed in the ethics complaint, Wade's firm had drafted the purchase agreement pursuant to which Xander purchased the home from Zeke. Xander alleges that it is a **conflict of interest** for Wade or his firm to foreclose on a home that they helped Xander buy.

Is Xander correct?

a. Yes. The two matters are likely to be deemed **substantially related** because they involve the same property.

b. Yes. The two matters are likely to be deemed **substantially related** because Xander was a party to both.

c. No. The two matters are not likely to be deemed **substantially related** because the foreclosure involves Xander's debt to the bank, but his purchase of the property was a transaction between Xander and Zeke.

d. No. The two matters are not likely to be deemed **substantially related** because Wade would not be forced to take a position in the foreclosure matter that is antithetical to a position his firm took when drafting the purchase agreement.

D. Imputation and Screening

"I had a new idea about that Petrified thing," Ron Rainmaker announces when Maya stops by his office to check in with him on another project. "Okay,"

Maya says slowly, with the drawn-out vowels and rising tone that she uses when she's not sure where a conversation is going. "How does it work?"

"Let's review the bidding," Ron begins. "Petrified's general counsel calls me, looking for a sounding board on their problems with Mojo and some litigation counsel. I say that we should pitch Mojo on representing Mojo in that case, so we can broaden our existing relationship with Mojo. The Intake Committee says no, because I've gotten **confidential information** from Petrified about the dispute with Mojo, which means there's a **successive conflict of interest**." (*See* **Chapter 22.C at 682.**)

"So then I say, fine—then let's just represent Petrified against Mojo. The Intake Committee says no, this time because Mojo is our **current client** and representing Petrified against Mojo would create a **concurrent conflict of interest** (*see* **Chapter 22.B at 646**), and the firm doesn't want to even *ask* Mojo to consent to that. But I am not deterred!" Here, Ron grins at the self-consciously dramatic tone that he's adopted; Maya grins back.

"I start thinking about my original idea again—pitching Mojo to represent Mojo against Petrified. And about how the Intake Committee said that the problem was that Petrified's general counsel had given me **confidential information**. I gotta admit, that's probably right. But then I realize: Hey, I'm the *only one* at the whole firm who knows Petrified's **confidential information**! And that's when I figured out how we thread this labyrinth. The litigators who would actually work on the case don't know anything about my conversation with Petrified's GC. And I won't tell 'em—cross my heart and hope to die. I'll take an oath; I'll lock my notes in the firm's fire safe; I'll promise to have no contact with those litigators until the case is over; whatever it takes. Petrified's secrets are safe with me! Then the litigators can get us Mojo's side of the case, and Petrified can't stop us! Pretty clever, huh?"

It *is* pretty clever, Maya thinks. She wonders what the Intake Committee will say to Ron this time.

1. What Imputation Is

Simply put, **imputation** dictates how **conflicts of interest** are treated within a **practice organization**. After all, most lawyers work in **practice organizations** of two or more lawyers, but in many circumstances, the representation of a **current client** creating a **concurrent conflict of interest**, or the knowledge of **confidential information** creating a **successive conflict of interest**, involves only one, or only a few, of the lawyers in the **practice organization**. The others don't personally have the connection that it takes to create the **conflict**, so—as Ron Rainmaker reasons above—why should they be **conflicted** out of the new engagement?

Not so fast. The general rule, which is codified in **Model Rule 1.10(a)** and incorporated in the civil **disqualification** law of every jurisdiction, is that if *any* lawyer in a **practice organization** has a **conflict of interest**, then *every* lawyer in the same **practice organization** is *deemed* to have the same **conflict of interest**. In other words, each lawyer's **conflicts of interest** (and each lawyer's relationships or knowledge that could create a **conflict of interest**) are **imputed** to every other lawyer in the same **practice organization**. (Take a look at **Model Rule 1.10(a)** and explain out loud how the words of the Rule amount to the paraphrase that we just supplied. Seriously, pause and do it; you need to see how the words in the Rule create the result we just described.) As we'll see, there are a few exceptions to this general rule, but only a few, and the general rule of **imputation** is where you should always start your analysis once you've determined that any individual lawyer in a **practice organization** has a **conflict** of any kind, or a relationship or knowledge that could create one.

    REASON FOR THE RULE Why not just keep things simple and limit the effects of any **conflict of interest** to the lawyer or lawyers within a **practice organization** who actually *have* the **conflict of interest** personally? Why do we have a Rule that instead multiplies the **conflicts of interest** within any **practice organization**? The reasons trace back to the reasons that we pay attention to **conflicts of interest** in the first place, and to the general nature of **practice organizations**.

    The individual lawyers who appear on a client's behalf are not the only ones who owe a **duty of loyalty** to the client they represent: so does the **practice organization** of which those lawyers are a part. Like wolves, lawyers hunt in packs. Lawyers go into battle wearing the colors of their **practice organization**, and when clients retain lawyers, they also retain the lawyers' **practice organizations**. This organizational duty is reflected in the fact that, when lawyers appear in litigation, they appear under the name of their firm or other **practice organization**; similarly, when lawyers communicate in writing, they usually sign their correspondence as a representative of their **practice organization**. So when a **conflict of interest** is grounded in the **duty of loyalty**, that **duty**—including the duty to avoid putting yourself in a position in which you could help one **current client** by hurting another—applies to the **organization** as a whole and, by extension, to any lawyer within the **practice organization**. *See* **Model Rule 1.10 Comment [2]**.

    The same is true of the **duty of confidentiality**, with an added practical component: Experience has taught us that lawyers within the same **practice organization** talk to each other about their work. This is not only natural human behavior; it helps the **practice organization** provide better and more thoughtful services through collaboration, training, and oversight. Thus in addition to ordinary social interaction ("What are you up to lately?"), lawyers within **practice organizations** often consult each other informally for advice ("Can I run something by you?"), training and morale-building exercises often focus on pending matters ("We'll have a brown-bag Thursday, where Jane and JaRon will tell us about lessons learned in the Schmerdley deal"), and lawyers with management or supervisory responsibilities are often broadly exposed to many details of matters staffed by others but within their purview.

    Obviously, not every lawyer in every **practice organization** knows everything about what's going on with every other lawyer in the **organization**, and the development of the multi-office megafirm over the last 30 years has made universal sharing much less common in that sector of the bar. But the general proposition that client **confidences** are often held more by **practice organizations** than by individual lawyers remains true enough to be meaningful, and that proposition is reflected in the law governing lawyers. So the presumption of **imputation** of **confidential information** within a **practice organization** reflects both a legal reality (that the **practice organization** as a whole, as well as its individual lawyers, will owe clients **duties of confidentiality**) and a commonplace practical reality (that lawyers within a **practice organization** share information, including clients' **confidential information**, in a variety of contexts and for a variety of reasons).　REASON FOR THE RULE

2. When Imputation Is *Conclusively* Presumed

In most situations, the **imputation** of **conflicts of interest** within a **practice organization** is not only presumed, it is presumed *conclusively*. Other than the exceptions to the general rule of **imputation** discussed below, if a single lawyer in a **practice organization** has a **conflict of interest** (or a relationship or knowledge that could create one), every other lawyer in the **organization** is deemed to have it, too. Thus, courts (which is where **conflicts** issues are often disputed) will not even *consider* any factual argument that other lawyers within the **organization** are not actually subject to the **conflict** for any reason. This conclusive presumption applies equally whether the **conflict of interest** is **loyalty**- or **confidentiality**-based, and whether the **consequence** under consideration is professional discipline or **disqualification**.

REASON FOR THE RULE　Why presume **imputation** *conclusively* most of the time? Why not give lawyers a chance to show that, in a particular case, there is no factual basis to **impute**? Besides the conventional understanding that a **practice organization** generally owes all of the same duties that its individual lawyers owe (*see* **Model Rule 1.10 Comment [2]**), disputes about **conflicts of interest** often develop into expensive and contentious sideshows to the client matters in which they arise, inviting parties to fight about who's going to fight for them rather than about whatever the parties are actually trying to accomplish. A rule of conclusive presumption in most cases has the advantage of being simple and easy to apply.　REASON FOR THE RULE

> **Problem 22D-1:** Think back to the version of the Petrified/Mojo hypothetical in the **Introduction to this subchapter at 701** (Ron Rainmaker will keep Petrified's **confidential information** to himself, in the hope that his decision will allow other lawyers at his firm to represent Mojo against Petrified).
>
> a. Based only on what you know now, how **must** or **should** the firm's Intake Committee respond to Ron's suggestion? Please explain which parts of the response are **musts** and which are **shoulds**, and why.
>
> b. What if Ron takes a different tack and tries a new idea to represent Petrified against Mojo instead: He will find a team of litigators at the firm with no connections to Mojo—that is, they don't represent Mojo in any of the firm's currently pending matters. That group will represent Petrified against Mojo; no firm lawyer with any connection to Mojo or its

pending matters will come anywhere near the litigation in which the firm will represent Petrified. Does this approach address the Intake Committee's concerns? Why or why not? Does your analysis change if all the lawyers in the Petrified group live and work in an office of the firm that's located in a different state? If so, how and why; if not, why not?

c. Same as (b), except now Ron takes the idea a step further, and proposes that for the *Petrified v. Mojo* matter, and for that matter only, the group of lawyers representing Petrified will be acting on their own, as their own little firm for this matter alone, and not on behalf of the firm they generally work for. Their own names, and not the firm's name, will appear on any pleadings and correspondence. These lawyers will continue working on their other matters as part of the firm, just not in the Petrified case. Does this approach address the Intake Committee's concerns? Why or why not?

3. When Imputation Is Only *Rebuttably* Presumed, How It May Be Rebutted, and Why You Should Care

There are several situations in which the presumption that **conflicts of interest** are **imputed** throughout the **conflicted** lawyer's **practice organization** is *rebuttable*— that is, other lawyers in the **practice organization**, and the **practice organization** itself, may show facts that will cut off **imputation** from the **conflicted** lawyer to others within the **practice organization**, allowing other lawyers in the **practice organization** to proceed with an engagement that would otherwise be prohibited, even without the consent of any affected client. CONSEQUENCES These exceptions are codified in portions of **Model Rule 1.9** and **Model Rule 1.10**, and thus block the imposition of professional discipline that would otherwise be based on an **imputed conflict of interest**. Most jurisdictions have also adopted the same exceptions on the same terms as a defense to **disqualification**. CONSEQUENCES

a. Why Imputation of a Conflict of Interest Should Not Always Be Conclusively Presumed, and Why You Should Care

But wait, the alert student urges. You just finished telling us all the good reasons for a general rule that **conflicts of interest** are not only **imputed** within **practice organizations**, but that this **imputation** is usually presumed *conclusively*. Now you're saying that there are multiple situations in which that's not the law after all. What gives?

REASON FOR THE RULE The alert student has (as usual) asked an excellent question. For the reasons discussed above (**Chapter 22.D at 703**), a general rule of **imputation** both reflects practice realities and discourages lawyers and parties from gaming the **conflicts** rules by not allowing a **practice organization** to try and engineer some too-clever solution that puts clients' **interests** at risk (*see* **Problem 22D-1 at 704**) or waste resources on litigating a procedural distraction. The presumption of **imputation** also allows the client to stay in the driver's seat, because (as we'll see in **Chapter 22.E at 739**), many **conflicts of interest** are "**consentable**"—that is, the affected clients **may** choose to allow the **conflicting** engagements to go forward despite the **conflict of interest** in situations in which the risks to the client's interests are manageable and acceptable to the client. (The choice about when that's true remains, as it usually should, with the client. But we'll get to that.)

Still, a conclusive presumption of **imputation** has its own problems. It **disqualifies practice organizations** from proceeding with engagements under circumstances in which another client is being deprived of its counsel of choice, even when any risks to the first client's **interests** are genuinely minimal. That kind of rule is bad for clients in general because its overbroad nature limits clients' choices for counsel unnecessarily, and of course it's bad for lawyers too by precluding from doing work that they'd like to do, without supplying any real counterbalancing advantage. And putting control of consent into the client's hands can sometimes endow the client with the power to withhold consent in order to deprive an adversary of counsel of choice for tactically opportunistic reasons rather than legitimately self-protective ones. So limiting the rule of client control over consent can make sense in situations in which we feel we can adequately protect the client in other ways. ◂ Reason for the Rule

As a result, the Rules of Professional Conduct have identified several specific situations (seven, if we're counting, which, apparently, we are) in which the conclusive presumption of **imputation** is relaxed. In these situations, the presumption of **imputation** remains, but it is rebuttable, and the party seeking to rebut it bears the burden of proving facts defining a situation identified in the Rules in which we can feel reasonably sure that the affected clients' legitimate **interests** remain protected.

Before we explore these situations, let's be clear about why they matter. In the first step of any analysis of a **conflict of interest**, the **conflict** involves only the lawyer (or few lawyers) who are actually and personally involved in whatever is creating the **conflict**—for example, the individual lawyer who has a personal **interest** that conflicts with a client's **interests** (a personal-**interest conflict**); or the individual lawyer who is representing one **current client** against another **current client** (whom the **practice organization** typically represents in some other matter—a **loyalty**-based **concurrent conflict**); or a lawyer who has been exposed to **confidential information** of a **former** or **prospective client,** and now the **practice organization** proposes to represent a different client against that **former** or **prospective client** in a matter in which the **practice organization** can use the **former** or **prospective client's confidential information** against it (a **confidentiality**-based **successive conflict**). The Rules and Comments sometimes refer to this lawyer as "personally **disqualified**" or as "the **disqualified** lawyer," focusing on the fact that this lawyer is *personally* subject to the **conflict of interest** because of some personal **interest** that she herself holds, some client relationship that she herself has, or some **confidential information** that she herself knows. If the personally **disqualified** lawyer is part of a **practice organization** (as the majority of practicing lawyers are), every other lawyer in the **practice organization** doesn't have that personal **conflict of interest** and is therefore not personally **disqualified**.

But the rule of **imputation** says that, when one lawyer in a **practice organization** is personally **disqualified** (or has relationships or knowledge that, combined with the relationships or knowledge of another lawyer in the **practice organization, disqualify** both of them), then every other lawyer in the **practice organization** is also **disqualified**—that is, the **conflict of interest** (or individual lawyer's relationship or knowledge) is **imputed** to every other lawyer in the **organization** (and the **organization** itself). Thus, when a **conflict** is **imputed**, the only way that the **practice organization** can be involved in the **conflicted** engagement is if the affected clients all give **informed consent, confirmed in writing**, which any affected client may withhold for any reason or no reason at all. In situations in which one lawyer's personal **conflict of interest** is *not* **imputed**, however, any *other* lawyer in the same **practice organization may** go ahead with the **conflicted** engagement, as long as the personally **disqualified** lawyer is not involved. And no client consent of any kind is required. In short, the ability to rebut the presumption of **imputation** in some limited circumstances can make the difference between a **practice organization's** taking on a new case or deal and its being prevented from doing so.

In the rest of this subchapter, we'll explain the situations in which **imputation** of a **conflict of interest** is only rebuttably presumed, and how it is rebutted in each case. But as you're walking through them with us, bear in mind that each of these is a narrow exception to the general rule that **imputation** is not only presumed but is usually presumed conclusively for purposes of both professional discipline and **disqualification**. As for the exceptions, generally speaking, they break down into two groups: Those in which the presumption of **imputation may** be rebutted by specific situational facts, and those in which the presumption of **imputation may** be rebutted by proof of a timely implemented and properly maintained **ethical screen** (and yes, we promise to explain what that is). As you've probably already guessed, we'll talk about each in turn.

b. Situations in Which the Presumption of Imputation May Be Rebutted by Specific Situational Facts

i. No Imputation When "the Conflict Is Based on a Personal Interest of the Disqualified Lawyer and Does Not Present a Significant Risk of Materially Limiting the Representation of the Client by the Remaining Lawyers in the Firm"

TAMING THE TEXT The heading quotes the applicable portion of **Model Rule 1.10(a)(1)**. The Rule provides a two-part test, and both parts have to be met before **imputation** is rebutted. (We know it's a conjunctive test because the word "and" appears between the two halves.)

First, "the prohibition" (that is, the prohibition against taking on or continuing the engagement because of the **conflict of interest**) **must** be "based on a personal **interest** of the **disqualified** lawyer." Here the "**disqualified** lawyer" refers to the individual lawyer within the **practice group** prohibited from taking on or continuing the engagement because of the personal-**interest conflict of interest**. And you'll recall from **Chapter 22.A at 626** that a personal-**interest conflict** is one in which something that the lawyer wants *personally* conflicts with the **interests** of a client (rather than the more common situation in which the lawyer is subjected to **conflicting** duties to two different clients).

The *second* half of the test requires the lawyer or **practice organization** seeking to rebut the presumption of **imputation** to show that there is no "significant risk" that the personal-**interest conflict** of the individual **disqualified** lawyer will **materially** affect the conduct of the other lawyers in the firm. That's a lot narrower than it sounds. Why? Because most of the "personal-**interest**" **conflicts** that we discussed in **Chapter 22.A** and elsewhere in this book are already *conclusively* presumed to be **imputed** within the **practice organization** under **Model Rule 1.8(k)**. *See* **Model Rule 1.10 Comment [12]**. Pause and take a look at **Model Rule 1.8(k)** so that you can appreciate its breadth and importance.[41]

In fact, there are only two kinds of personal-**interest conflicts** *not* conclusively **imputed** from the individual lawyer with the **conflicting** personal interest to every other lawyer in the **practice organization**. One is the restrictions on sex with a client. **Model Rule 1.8(j)**; *see* **Chapter 5.C at 108**. A close personal relationship of this kind thus **must** be analyzed under standard of the second half of **Model Rule 1.10(a)(1)**, namely whether there is a "significant risk" that the personal-interest conflict of the individual **disqualified** lawyer will **materially** affect the conduct of the other lawyers in the firm.

The other type of personal-**interest conflict** not conclusively **imputed** to every other lawyer in the **conflicted** lawyer's **practice organization** is the kind created when an individual lawyer's personal **interests** or connections create a "significant risk of **materially** limiting" a client's representation. **Model Rule 1.7(a)(2)**; **Chapter 22.A at 626**. That significant risk of **material** limitation prohibits the individual lawyer with the personal **interest** or connection from being involved in the engagement. But that personal prohibition will *not* be **imputed** to other lawyers in the **practice organization** so long as, on the facts of the situation, those **interests** or connections don't create a significant risk of **materially** limiting the services of the *other* lawyers in the **practice organization** as well. **Model Rule 1.10(a)(1)**. ◅ TAMING THE TEXT

Model Rule 1.10 Comment [3] provides an excellent example of a personal interest **conflict** that would not be imputed to other lawyers in the same **practice organization**, and an excellent example of one that would be. Please take a moment to read through **Model Rule 1.10 Comment [3]** and be sure that you can explain why each is a good example of how the Rule should be applied.

---

[41] These conclusively **imputed** personal-**interest conflicts of interest** include the restrictions on nonprohibited transactions with clients (**Model Rule 1.8(a)**; **Chapter 22.A at 617**); the restrictions on gifts and bequests from clients (**Model Rule 1.8(c)**; **Chapter 22.A at 612**); the prohibition on acquiring literary or media rights related to the engagement while the engagement is pending (**Model Rule 1.8(d)**; **Chapter 22.A at 615**); the prohibition on financial assistance to litigation clients (**Model Rule 1.8(e)**; **Chapter 22.A at 606**); the restrictions on accepting compensation for services from someone other than the client (**Model Rule 1.8(f)**; **Chapter 9.B at 273**); the restrictions on clients' prospective waivers of a lawyer's malpractice liability and on settling a malpractice claim with a **current** or **former client** who is not independently represented (**Model Rule 1.8(h)**; **Chapter 9.C at 285**); and the prohibition on acquiring a proprietary interest in the client's cause of action or the subject matter of the litigation (**Model Rule 1.8(i)**; **Chapter 22.A at 616**).

Problem 22D-2: In each situation described below, which lawyers or **practice organizations** are subject to professional discipline or **disqualification** and, as to each **consequence**, on what ground or grounds? Please explain your answers.

a. Refamiliarize yourself with the Peggy Plaintiff hypothetical (**Chapter 22.A at 604**). Suppose that, in response to Peggy's request for a loan to cover her medical and living expenses during her litigation, litigation partner Happy Trials arranges for Frank's firm (rather than any individual lawyer in the firm) to extend the loan to Peggy once Peggy agrees to hire Frank's firm. Does your analysis change if Happy persuades tax and estate planning partner Willie Willmaker, who will not be involved in Peggy's representation in any way, to extend the loan to Peggy from Willie's own personal funds? What if there's a secret understanding that the firm will repay Willie if for any reason Peggy does not repay the loan? If any of the additional facts would change your analysis, please explain how and why; and if not, why not.

b. Same as (a), except that Peggy arranges a loan for medical and living expenses from a lender other than Frank's firm or any lawyer in it. In the course of the discussions, Willie Willmaker (who is older, and who lost his wife to cancer a few years ago) becomes quite smitten with Peggy. She feels the same way, and the two of them begin an intimate relationship while Peggy's case is pending. Does your analysis change if Willie is still married and his relationship with Peggy is an extramarital affair? If so, please explain how and why; and if not, why not.

c. Take another look at **Problem 22A-6(d) at 631** (Frank's firm is planning to take on a products liability case against Garage Gear; partner Barney Blackacre has just told litigation partner Happy Trials that Garage Gear's president and majority shareholder is his lifelong best friend). **May** the firm take on the products liability case against Garage Gear? **Should** it?

d. Maya's firm represents law firm Quick & Nimble in connection with its office lease and some ongoing issues with its landlord. Maya's firm is upgrading some of the computers that it supplies to its lawyers, but the old ones are still relatively new and in good shape. One of the lawyers at Maya's firm working on Quick & Nimble's leasehold issues mentions this fact to her contact at Quick & Nimble, and Quick & Nimble expresses an interest in buying the used computers for its own office use. The sale is consummated at a fair price. Does your analysis change if the buyer of the used computers is the Quick & Nimble partner who is the contact person for the work that Maya's firm is doing, and if he plans to donate them to his children's school? What if the contact person at Quick & Nimble plans to resell them to Quick & Nimble for office use? If any of the additional facts would change your analysis, please explain how and why; and if not, why not.

ii. No Imputation to a Lawyer Who Has Left the Practice Organization That Acquired the Confidential Information That Is the Basis for the Conflict of Interest, and That Departed Lawyer Has No Actual Knowledge from Any Source of That Confidential Information

Aside from non-**imputed** personal-**interest conflicts**, the Rules have identified two other situations in which the general rule of **imputation** imposes excessively broad **disqualification** under circumstances in which the risk to client **interests** is low, and thus allows the presumption of **imputation** to be rebutted by proof that those circumstances exist. Both involve situations in which lawyers are changing jobs, and so they also bring into play the general public policy interest in employee mobility (that is, the general public policy leaving workers free to change employers whenever they wish unless there is a really good reason to limit it) on top of the concerns we've already discussed.

REASON FOR THE RULE ▶ To see why these exceptions are justified, think about what happens if we let **imputation** run amok. Imagine a situation in which lawyer Gulliver (we call him that because he travels)[42] works at Firm 1 but is thinking about moving to Firm 2. Firm 1 is a big firm, and because of the general rule of **imputation**, Gulliver is *deemed* to know *all* of the **confidential information** to which *any* lawyer at Firm 1 has ever been exposed, among all the many thousands or tens of thousands of **prospective**, **current**, and **former clients** in its history. Of course, Gulliver *actually* knows only a tiny fraction of all that **confidential information**, but that's how **imputation** works.

Now Gulliver leaves Firm 1 to seek his fortune at Firm 2. Gulliver brings with him all the **imputed confidential information** of Firm 1. And the day that he starts work at Firm 2, all of Firm 1's **confidential information** that Gulliver is deemed to know (but doesn't actually know) is **imputed** to every lawyer in Firm 2, each of whom is deemed to know all of it, too, even though none of them actually knows any of it, either.

The result of these compounding fictions is that tons of **confidential information** to which Gulliver was never exposed is magically ascribed to hundreds of lawyers at his new firm who, of course, don't know it any more than Gulliver does. Now every lawyer in Firm 2 is **disqualified** from any matter in which any **confidential information** was known to any lawyer at Firm 1 at the time that Gulliver left, which could be used against a **prospective**, **current**, or **former client** of Firm 1 that confided it to some lawyer at Firm 1 at some point in history.

This oddity is referred to as the "double **imputation**" or "Typhoid Mary" problem ("Typhoid Gulliver" in our hypothetical). The disease metaphor is a good one here because Gulliver has been "infected" with **confidential information** at his old workplace and is an asymptomatic "carrier" of the "infection" when he arrives at his new workplace. Such a rule would mean that lawyers with any prior work experience would arrive at any new employer "infected" with vast amounts of potentially **disqualifying confidential information**, even though they actually knew only the tiniest bit of it. If that were the law, Firm 2 would be a lot less likely to hire Gulliver, and so would any other firm. (Do you see why? Explain it out loud.) And then, whether Gulliver is a junior associate or a senior partner, it's become unreasonably difficult for him to

---

[42] We really will be here all term, folks. Don't forget to tip your professor, especially if it's one of us. And if you hear a rimshot in your head as you read this footnote, so much the better. All three of us like stand-up comedy, though we can offer no warranties as to the quality of our own.

continue his career with a new employer, all because of huge amounts of **confidential information** that he has no realistic possibility of ever misusing, because he never actually knew it in the first place. *See* **Model Rule 1.9 Comment [4]**. REASON FOR THE RULE

Because such a rule would make it unreasonably difficult for lawyers to change jobs while preventing no discernible client risk, no jurisdiction of which we are aware has adopted a rule of double imputation when a lawyer moves from one legal employer to another. The applicable rule in this situation is codified in **Model Rule 1.9(b):**

> A lawyer shall not knowingly represent a person in the same or a **substantially related** matter in which a firm with which the lawyer formerly was associated had previously represented a client
>
> (1) whose **interests** are **materially** adverse to that person; and
> (2) about whom the lawyer had acquired information protected by Rules 1.6 and 1.9(c)
> that is **material** to the matter; unless the former client gives **informed consent, confirmed in writing**.

TAMING THE TEXT This is another example of the kind of roundabout drafting we find in the Model Rules regarding **conflicts of interest,** and we've quoted it at length so that we can show you how it works. Start by going back to our explanation of **Model Rule 1.9(a)** (**Chapter 22.C at 679**), which states the **successive client rule** as that rule applies to individual lawyers. (Take a look at the Rule and show yourself why **Model Rule 1.9(a)** is addressed only to personal **disqualification**. Then explain it out loud.) **Model Rule 1.10(a)** tells us that, while individual lawyers such as Gulliver stay at their **practice organization,** each lawyer's **successive conflicts of interest** are **imputed** to every other lawyer in the **practice organization**. What **Model Rule 1.9(b)** does is tell us how far **imputation** goes when someone like Gulliver changes jobs.

How does it do that? Well, it states a prohibition a lot like the one in **Model Rule 1.9(a),** but the prohibition in **Model Rule 1.9(b)** has two big differences. One difference is that the prohibition is based *not* just on the previous engagements in which *Gulliver himself* was involved, but on *any* engagement "in which a firm [that is, a **practice organization**] with which [Gulliver] formerly was associated" was involved. In other words, this Rule deals with **confidential information** that was learned *by anyone at Gulliver's former* **practice organization**.

The other difference is how that information is **imputed** after Gulliver changes jobs. Although the Rule starts with all of the **confidential information** at Gulliver's former firm, the prohibition is limited to engagements in which *Gulliver himself actually knows* the relevant **disqualifying confidential information**. That limitation is stated in the prohibition against "knowingly" taking on an engagement in which "*the lawyer*" (emphasis added)—that is, Gulliver himself, not just others at Gulliver's former firm—"had acquired information protected by Rules 1.6 and 1.9(c) [that is, **confidential information**] that is **material** to the matter . . . ."

Model Rule 1.9(b)(2). *See* **Model Rule 1.9 Comment [5]**. ‹CONSEQUENCES› Although this principle is stated in a disciplinary Rule, it is also widely applied when courts are considering **disqualification**. ‹CONSEQUENCES›

This interpretation leads to the following practical paraphrase for **Model Rule 1.9(b)**: *Lawyers who change jobs bring to, and **impute** within, the lawyers' new **practice organization** only that **confidential information** of which they personally have (or had) actual knowledge.*

Some interpretive pointers:

- **Model Rule 1.9(b)** rules out "double imputation." (Do you see how and why? Pause and explain it out loud in terms of the language of the Rule.) **Confidential information** is imputed only once when a lawyer changes jobs—from whatever has ever actually been in the mobile lawyer's head to everyone in his new **practice organization**.

- We used the formulation "whatever has ever actually been in the mobile lawyer's head" deliberately. The **confidential information** that a mobile lawyer carries to his new job is any **confidential information** to which the lawyer was *ever* exposed at his former firm, in *any* context and from *any* source. So Gulliver (and his new **practice organization**) cannot argue that Gulliver may have previously known **confidential information** but that he has forgotten it. Similarly, most courts are inclined to assume that, if the lawyer was *exposed* to the information, then he knew it; thus, those courts will not be receptive to arguments that Gulliver may have been exposed to particular **confidential information** but didn't pay much attention to it. And it's important to remember that Gulliver could have been exposed to **confidential information** not only by directly working on a matter, but in the course of friendly conversation with colleagues, "off-bill" informal consultation, training or discussion within Gulliver's former **practice organization**, or Gulliver's managerial or supervisory responsibilities at his former employer. *See* **Model Rule 1.9 Comment [6]**.

- The **imputation** of the **confidential information** that a mobile lawyer actually knows within his new **practice organization** is also only rebuttably presumed. Under a different Rule (**Model Rule 1.10(a)(2)**), the presumption can be rebutted with a timely implemented and properly maintained **ethical screen**. We'll discuss how that works below in **Chapter 22.D at 721**.

- The **Model Rule 1.9(b)** exception addresses only a limited category of **successive conflicts of interest** based on information protected by the **duty of confidentiality**. It has no application to **concurrent conflicts of interest**, whose **imputation** remains conclusively presumed. ‹TAMING THE TEXT›

Problem 22D-3: Of the following lawyers, who is or is not subject to professional discipline, and which lawyers or **practice organizations** are or are not subject to **disqualification**? Please explain your answers.

a. The Intake Committee at Maya's firm allows Ron Rainmaker to go ahead with the plan that he proposes in the **Introduction to this subchapter at 701** (to sideline himself and the **confidential information** that he knows regarding Petrified so that other lawyers at his firm can represent Mojo against Petrified in commercial litigation). Does anything that we learned in this section help him or his firm? Why or why not?

b. Danielle's office hires a new prosecutor, Nestor New, who has spent the last several years working as the only associate for a prominent private criminal defense lawyer in town, Delbert Defender. One of Delbert's regular clients is Wally "the Weasel" Wyzanski, an alleged organized-crime figure. Delbert has had remarkable success keeping Wally out of prison despite Wally's several indictments. As it happens, Danielle's boss has been presenting a new case against Wally to a grand jury. The new case includes some better information about Wally's criminal enterprise than the DA's office had last time, and an indictment likely will be handed up in the next couple of weeks.

c. Maya's firm hires a lateral associate, Gulliver Gettinghere. Gulliver has spent three years in the litigation department of another large firm in town, and the litigators in Maya's office have decided that they could use some additional help. Maya's firm represents Randy's Candies in a variety of matters, one of which is an employee-raiding case that Randy's is currently litigating with its competitor, Toots' Sweets. ("Employee raiding" is a general term encompassing claims for trade-secret misappropriation and other business torts arising out of one competitor's hiring of a competing company's employees who know valuable confidential business information.) Gulliver's former firm represented Toots' Sweets in a variety of matters, including the employee-raiding case. Gulliver did not work on any of his former firm's matters for Toots' Sweets.

d. Same as (c), except that Gulliver did work on a matter for Toots' Sweets at his former firm—specifically, a commercial dispute with a supplier of flavoring agents.

e. Same as (d), except that Gulliver worked on the Toots' Sweets employee-raiding case. He will not be working on that case at Maya's firm.

f. Same as (e), except that Gulliver's involvement in the Toots' Sweets employee-raiding case was a single research memo regarding the elements of a cause of action that has since been dismissed out of the case.

g. Same as (c) (Gulliver didn't work on any matters for Toots' Sweets at his former firm), except that last spring, Gulliver attended a department lunch at which some litigators gave the department a presentation about trade secret law with examples drawn from a number of cases they had worked on, including the Toots' Sweets employee-raiding case.

iii. No Imputation When the Sole Holders of a Client's Confidential Information Leave the Practice Organization in Which They Acquired the Confidential Information and Leave No Confidential Information Behind

Because **confidential information** is generally conclusively presumed to be **imputed** within a **practice organization**, a factual showing that such **information** was not shared in a particular situation will usually not even be considered. But there are a few exceptions, one of which we just discussed.

Another such exception is the situation in which the *only* lawyer or lawyers in a **practice organization** who have ever been exposed to a particular client's **confidential information** leave the **practice organization** and leave no trace of the **confidential information** behind. That is the situation described by **Model Rule 1.10(b)**. Please pause, take a careful look at the Rule, and explain out loud why its specific language is the same as the paraphrase we gave you at the beginning of this paragraph.

REASON FOR THE RULE ▸ This exception fits the reason for the general rule of **imputation** in that, in these circumstances, the legal system and the affected client can have a high degree of confidence that the client's **confidential information** is not in a position to be misused. After all, if the **practice organization** meets its burden of proving what **Model Rule 1.10(b)** requires, then any **confidential information** that could be used against the client to which it belongs is safely out of the **practice organization's** reach. ◂ REASON FOR THE RULE

TAMING THE TEXT ▸ A few practical pointers that emerge from the Rule's language:

■ All of the lawyers who have been exposed to the client's **confidential information must** have "terminated [their] association" with the **practice organization**. If even one remains, the presumption of **imputation** has not been rebutted. It generally doesn't matter *how* the knowledgeable lawyers terminated their association—they can have retired, died, or simply switched jobs. But the Rule says that it has to be a clean break ("terminated [their] association").

■ **Model Rule 1.10(b)(2)** requires that the **practice organization must** show that there is not "any lawyer remaining in the firm [who] has information protected by Rules 1.6 and 1.9(c) that is **material** to the matter."[43] What it means for "any lawyer" remaining in the **practice organization** to "ha[ve]" **confidential information** is subject to interpretation, but most authority takes a "zero tolerance" approach: If *any* trace of the relevant **confidential information** remains at the **practice organization** in *any* form, the terms of **Model Rule 1.10(b)** are not satisfied and the general presumption of **imputation** throughout the **practice organization** remains in place, unrebutted. The traces of **confidential information** could remain within the **practice organization** because there is still one lawyer within the **organization** who was exposed to the relevant **confidential information**, whether by having been involved in the relevant matter for the **prospective** or **former client**, or by having been exposed to the **confidential information** through friendly conversation, "off-bill" informal consultation, training or discussion within the **practice organization**, or managerial or supervisory duties. The remaining traces also could exist in

---

[43] Remember that "information protected by Rules 1.6 and 1.9(c)" is how the Model Rules often refer to **confidential information**. *See* **Chapter 8.A at 211**. And "firm" is the term that the Rules use to mean any **practice organization**. **Model Rule 1.0(c); Chapter 19.A at 506**.

the form of client files or other records containing **confidential information** in the relevant matter that remain in the **practice organization's** custody. Regardless of how or why any **confidential information** may remain, the burden is on the remaining lawyers and the **practice organization** to prove affirmatively that no **confidential information** from the relevant matter is left anywhere.

■ Like the **Model Rule 1.9(b)** exception discussed in the previous section, the **Model Rule 1.10(b)** exception applies *only* to an imputed **conflict of interest** based on the **successive client rule**—that is, based on a **practice organization's** exposure to a **prospective** or **former client's confidential information**. It has no effect on any **concurrent conflict of interest**. *See* **Model Rule 1.10 Comment [5]**. ◄ TAMING THE TEXT

Problem 22D-4: Which of the following lawyers is or is not subject to professional discipline, and which lawyers or **practice organizations** are or are not subject to **disqualification**? Please explain your answers.

a. The Intake Committee at Maya's firm allows Ron Rainmaker to go ahead with the plan that he proposes in the **Introduction to this subchapter at 701** (to sideline himself and the **confidential information** that he knows regarding Petrified so that other lawyers at his firm can represent Mojo against Petrified in commercial litigation). Does anything that we learned in this section help Ron or his firm? Why or why not?

b. Maya's firm represents Scooter's Computers, which owns a regional chain of retail computer stores (and an online retail site). The partner at Maya's firm who has the principal relationship with Scooter's is Gulliver Going. Gulliver announces that he's leaving Maya's firm for a competing law firm. Everyone in Gulliver's practice group who has ever worked on any matter for Scooter's ends up following Gulliver from Maya's firm to Gulliver's new firm. When Gulliver and his group left the firm, one of the things on which Gulliver was working for Scooter's was its acquisition of Chip's Chips, a local computer, accessories, parts, and service retailer with several stores and a website. A couple of weeks after the departures, Chip Chaplin (the principal of Chip's Chips) contacts one of Maya's supervising partners, Celia Deal. Chip has decided to switch lawyers and would like Celia to take over representing Chip's Chips in its acquisition by Scooter's. Celia asks Maya to help out; Maya is delighted. Is there anything else that you'd want to know to analyze this problem?

c. Same as (b), except that one lawyer who worked for Gulliver on Scooter's matters, Lefty Leftout, is not invited to join Gulliver at his new firm. Lefty was working with Gulliver on the Chip's acquisition for Scooter's when Gulliver left. Does your analysis change if Lefty hadn't done any work on the Chip's acquisition, but he had worked on other Scooter's matters? Is there anything more that you'd want to know to analyze this latter part of the problem?

d. Same as (c), except that Lefty, who had been finding that he did not care for the work or the stress at a big law firm, leaves Maya's firm for a small firm that works mostly with small businesses. Does your analysis change if, instead, Lefty unfortunately discovers that he has cancer and goes on medical leave to get treatment? What if, instead, a healthy Lefty takes a 12-month leave of absence from Maya's firm to pursue enlightenment at an ashram in India? If any of the additional facts would change your analysis, please explain how and why; and if not, why not.

e. Same as (d), except that after Gulliver departs, Scooter's writes Maya's firm and directs it to send all of Scooters's files for all of its active matters to Gulliver's new firm. Maya's firm promptly complies (*see* **Chapter 9.D at 303**). That leaves about 20 shelf-feet of hard-copy client files and several gigabytes of digital files pertaining to Scooter's matters that were completed and closed prior to Gulliver's departure. Because the Chip's acquisition is an active matter, all its files were among those transferred to Gulliver's new firm. Is there anything more you'd like to know to analyze this part of the problem? Does your analysis change if, shortly after shipping the active files off to Gulliver's new firm, Maya's firm writes Scooters's general counsel, asking her whether the firm should return or securely destroy the closed files that Maya's firm still possesses?

c. Situations in Which the Presumption of Imputation May Be Rebutted by a Timely Implemented and Properly Maintained Ethical Screen[44]

i. What Is an Ethical Screen?

An **ethical screen** or **ethical wall** (frequently shortened by dropping the "ethical" modifier) is not a literal screen or wall; it is a set of prophylactic measures designed to restrict **confidential information** to a single lawyer or small group of lawyers and staff and prevent its dissemination to others in the same **practice organization**.[45] In a very limited set of defined circumstances, the Model Rules (and related state civil law governing **disqualification**) allow **practice organizations** to **screen** personnel who have been exposed to **disqualifying confidential information** (as well as any means by which such **confidential information** may have been recorded or stored) in order to permit other personnel in the same **practice organization** to proceed with what otherwise would have been a **conflicted** engagement. In other words, a timely and proper **screen** can rebut the presumption of **imputation** in a few limited circumstances.

What features make an **ethical screen** an effective means of addressing a **confidentiality**-based **conflict of interest** in the limited circumstances in which the Rules allow it to do so? **Model Rule 1.0(k)**, which defines the term, offers only that it **must** involve "the timely imposition of procedures within a [**practice organization**]

---

[44] The **conflicts** rules regarding lawyers who are in government service are somewhat different from those in private practice. In particular, some **successive conflicts** that could be resolved only by client consent may be resolved by an **ethical screen** alone where current or former government lawyers are involved, and a few require no action at all. These rules will be discussed in **Chapter 25.D at 925**.

[45] In older authority, you may see an **ethical screen** referred to as a "Chinese wall." This was a phrase that lawyers borrowed from their investment-banking clients, who used it to describe informational barriers that were supposed to be erected between (among others) the underwriting and brokerage functions at the same financial institution. The phrase "Chinese wall" is now widely viewed as racially biased and disrespectful and should no longer be used. *See, e.g., Peat, Marwick, Mitchell & Co. v. Superior Court*, 200 Cal. App. 3d 272, 293-94 (Low, J., concurring) (Cal. Ct. App. 1988).

that are reasonably adequate under the circumstances to protect information that the isolated lawyer is obligated to protect under these Rules or other law." So we know that what is required **must** be responsive to the details of each situation ("reasonably adequate under the circumstances"; *see also* **Model Rule 1.0 Comment [9]**). That said, the Comments and some other Rules, as well as common professional practice, suggest some measures that are *never* sufficient and others that are always or usually required in order for a **screen** to be effective:

- **Formality**: It is *not* sufficient to attempt to prove simply that the **conflict**-creating **confidential information** has not been "leaked" from those who know it to others within the **practice organization**. In other words, "I haven't discussed this with anyone in my new firm, and I promise that I won't" is never enough. Formal measures within the **practice organization must** be implemented.

- **Timing**: "In order to be effective, screening measures must be implemented as soon as practical after a lawyer or law firm knows or reasonably should know that there is a need for screening." **Model Rule 1.0 Comment [10]**. If a **screen** isn't implemented in a timely manner, it simply doesn't count. Think "locking the barn after the horse has run away" here, except that you won't be allowed to try and prove that the horse is still in there—proof that a delay did not allow a "leak" to occur will typically not even be considered. In cases in which a **successive conflict of interest** will be created by a new lawyer or a new matter, caselaw typically insists that the screen be in place before or on the day that the new lawyer arrives, or before or on the day that the new engagement begins. The case reporters are littered with decisions **disqualifying practice organizations** that were not extremely prompt and proactive about putting a **screen** in place as soon as reasonably practicable after the organization **should have known** that there was a need for one.

- **Notification to and separation of personnel on opposite sides of the screen**: The **practice organization must** give formal notice to all lawyers affected by the **screen** that the **screen** is in place, and of what it forbids each of them from doing. In a typical situation, there will be lawyers (and possibly nonlawyer staff) who have been exposed to **confidential information** (and possibly physical or digital documents or files containing **confidential** information) on one side of the **screen**, and other lawyers (and nonlawyer staff, as well as files and documents) assigned to the new matter adverse to the person to whom the **duty of confidentiality** is owed (and who thus **must not** be exposed to the **screened confidential information** on the other side of the **screen**). Both groups **must** be formally notified (typically, at a minimum, by written memo) that a **screen** is in place and what their obligations are in maintaining the screen's efficacy. At a minimum, screened lawyers **must not** ever communicate with one another regarding the **screened** matters (that is, any of the matters on the opposite side of the **screen**). Personnel on one side of the **screen should** (and arguably **must**) have no management or supervisory authority over personnel on the other side. These directions are sometimes supplemented with the requirement of a written undertaking (a signed promise) on the part of each **screened** person to follow the directions. It is common for the **practice organization** that is employing the **screened** personnel to make it clear that serious employment **consequences** may result from negligent or deliberate violations of the **screen**. (In other words, to stress that anyone who violates the **screen** could suffer employment discipline up to and including termination.) *See* **Model Rule 1.0 Comment [9]**.

■ **Sequestration of physical and electronic files on opposite sides of the screen**: It is common for physical files subject to a **screen** to be labeled prominently on the outside of the file "No Access to" the persons who are **screened** from reviewing any of the file's contents. (This is an effective reminder of the **screened** persons' obligations, and a means of avoiding mistaken exposure.) In especially sensitive cases, hard-copy files containing **confidential information** may be sequestered in separate, locked file cabinets or storage rooms. Similarly, the software that the **practice organization** uses to store and manage electronic files is typically programmed to refuse to allow a **screened** person to access any electronic file or document in the matter from which that person has been **screened**. *See* **Model Rule 1.0 Comment [9]**.

■ **Internal monitoring and reminders**: Many **practice organizations** periodically remind all **screened** personnel of the existence and terms of the **screen**, usually in writing. It also is common to require **screened** personnel to report to designated management if they participate in or become aware of a "leak" of any kind, even if the leak is completely inadvertent.

■ **Notice and continuing certification of compliance to affected clients**: Some Rules allowing **screens** to rebut **imputation** require detailed written notice to all affected clients, as well as periodic certifications of compliance with the **screen** to those clients by the **practice organization** (or prompt reporting of any noncompliance; that is, prompt notification to the affected client if the **screen** is breached or if **confidential information** leaks in any way, for any reason), in order for the **screen** to be effective. The notice must include the details of the **screening** measures used, so that the affected client can judge the **screen's** adequacy, and if necessary challenge its sufficiency in court. *See* **Model Rule 1.10(a)(2); Chapter 22.D at 722**). Even in situations in which a governing Rule does not include a notice requirement, courts entertaining **disqualification** motions generally expect it, and most **practice organizations** provide it.

■ **No sharing of profits from the screened matter with the screened lawyer**: Some Rules also require the **screened** personnel in a for-profit **practice organization** who are exposed to **conflict**-creating **confidential information** to be prevented from sharing any of the profit earned on the **screened** engagement. *See, e.g.,* **Model Rule 1.10(a) (2); Chapter 22.D at 722**. Some **practice organizations** also do so when not so required, as a matter of good practice or as a gesture of good faith to the affected client. **Screening** of fees typically involves no direct sharing with the screened lawyer of a discrete fee earned from the **screened** matter, but allowing a **screened** lawyer to receive an ordinary salary, hourly wage, or previously agreed partnership profit-share that includes the firm's income from the **screened** matter is generally permitted. *See* **Model Rule 1.10 Comment [8]**.

Now you know what an **ethical screen** is and generally how to build one. Next, let's talk about what **screens** can and can't do for you. Before describing the situations in which a timely implemented and properly maintained **ethical screen** will rebut the presumption of **imputation** and neutralize a **conflict of interest** without any affected client's **informed consent**, we need to stress that these situations are small in number and limited in scope. Most **conflicts of interest** can't be avoided by a **screen**, no matter how carefully constructed and maintained. More specifically, **screens** have *no* effect on *any* **concurrent conflict of interest**. Those kinds of **conflicts must** be addressed in other ways. And among **successive conflicts of interest**, only four narrowly defined situations **may** be adequately addressed by a **screen** alone. We'll discuss them one by one.

ii. No Imputation When the Conflict Is Based on Confidential Information Known Only to a Nonlawyer in the Practice Organization, and the Knowledgeable Nonlawyer Is Timely and Properly Screened

Exposure to clients' **confidential information** during law practice is not limited to lawyers, of course. Administrative assistants, legal assistants, nonlawyer business managers, file clerks—lots of nonlawyer personnel are exposed to and handle **confidential information** in the course of a **practice organization's** daily operations. These skilled and valuable workers could not do their jobs otherwise. Nonlawyer staff change jobs, too, and when they do, they carry the **confidential information** to which they were exposed in their prior employment with them. **Successive conflict**-creating **confidential information** known to nonlawyer staff **must** also be addressed, though less aggressively than when that **information** was acquired by a lawyer.

Model Rule 1.10 Comment [4] informs us that **confidential information** to which nonlawyer personnel have been exposed will not be **imputed** to anyone else at the firm, so long as the relevant nonlawyer is timely and properly **screened** from any matter as to which the **confidential information** would create a **successive conflict**. The details of the **screen** required are not specified, but it **should** and arguably **must** include the features just discussed (*see* **Chapter 22.D at 716**).

iii. No Imputation When the Conflict Is Based on Confidential Information Acquired by a Lawyer in the Practice Organization Before That Person Became a Lawyer, and the Knowledgeable Lawyer Is Timely and Properly Screened

Model Rule 1.10 Comment [4] takes a similar approach when a lawyer was exposed to **confidential information** before becoming a lawyer—for example, while working as a legal assistant or law clerk, or in another line of work altogether, before or during law school. **Confidential information** to which a lawyer was exposed before becoming a lawyer is not **imputed** to others in the lawyer's **practice organization** so long as the lawyer is timely and properly **screened** from any matter as to which the **confidential information** would create a **successive conflict**. Again, the details of the **screen** are not defined, but **should** and arguably **must** include the features discussed above (*see* **Chapter 22.D at 716**).[46]

Problem 22D-5: Which of the following lawyers is or is not subject to professional discipline, and which lawyers or **practice organizations** are or are not subject to **disqualification**? What, if anything, could the lawyers or **practice organizations** do to prevent any problems? Please explain your answers.

a. The Intake Committee at Maya's firm allows Ron Rainmaker to go ahead with the plan that he proposes in the **Introduction to this subchapter at 701** (to sideline himself and the **confidential information** that he knows regarding Petrified, so that other lawyers at his firm can represent Mojo against Petrified in commercial litigation). Does anything that we learned in this section or the one before it help Ron or his firm? Why or why not?

b. Roberto Ramirez got a master's degree in petrochemical engineering about ten years ago and then went to work for Petrified Petroleum. He worked in Petrified's Quality Control Department and learned a lot about the ways in which Petrified's manufacturing processes could go wrong. Five years ago, Roberto started attending law school at night, continuing to work part-time at Petrified. He graduated about a year ago, left Petrified, passed the bar exam, and took a job with Maya's firm in the firm's patent prosecution practice.

c. Da'isha Davis was a police officer for seven years. She then took a job as an investigator for a leading criminal defense lawyer in town. The money was good, but Da'isha found herself uncomfortable working for some of the clients. Recently, Da'isha took a job as an investigator for Danielle's office. Da'isha's former boss, the criminal defense lawyer, has a number of cases pending against Danielle's office that Da'isha worked on.

d. Same as (c), except that Danielle is working on one of the cases being defended by Da'isha's former boss. Shortly after Da'isha joins the DA's office, Danielle asks Da'isha to lunch to welcome her to the office. In the course of a friendly conversation about their backgrounds, Danielle asks Da'isha what it was like to work for "the bad guys" (that is, for a criminal defense lawyer and his clients). Da'isha tells Danielle some funny stories about her work for the criminal defense lawyer, one of which, Danielle suddenly realizes, is about her dealings with some potential witnesses in the case that Danielle has against Da'isha's former boss.

---

[46] Those of you keeping score at home (including you, alert student!) will have noticed that this section and the prior section describe additional examples of a significant modification of a Rule of Professional Conduct carried out in the Comments.

iv. No Imputation When the Conflict Is Based on Actual Knowledge of Confidential Information That a Lawyer Acquired at a Former Firm, and the Knowledgeable Lawyer Is Timely and Properly Screened at Her New Firm

We know that there are a lot of rules and exceptions in this chapter, and it can be an effort to keep them all straight. Nevertheless, let us ask you to think back to **Chapter 22.D at 709**, where we discussed the exception to **imputation** that when lawyers change jobs, they bring to their new **practice organizations** only the **confidential information** to which they were actually exposed at their old jobs. Thus, the very large amounts of **confidential information** at their former **practice organizations** to which the departing lawyers were never actually exposed cannot create **conflicts of interest,** and they accordingly can have no effect on the activities of the departing lawyers or anyone else at the departing lawyers' new **practice organization**.

But what happens when lawyers in fact *were* exposed at their former **practice organization** to **confidential information** that could now be used against the person to whom the **duty of confidentiality** is owed in a new engagement at the new **practice organization**? To make this a little more concrete, let's suppose that our friend Gulliver was exposed to **confidential information** of client C1 while he was working at Firm 1. (It doesn't matter how.) Now Gulliver has moved to Firm 2, and Firm 2 wants to take on a new engagement in which Firm 2's client (or **prospective client**), C2, will be suing C1. And suppose further that the **confidential information** to which Gulliver was exposed at his old firm is relevant ("**substantially related**") to the new engagement (*C2 v. C1*) and could be used against C1 in the new engagement.

Based on these facts, we know that, because Gulliver had actual exposure to C1's **confidential information** while he was at Firm 1, that **confidential information** comes with him to Firm 2 when he changes jobs. And we also know that, for the same reason, that **confidential information** would ordinarily be **imputed** from Gulliver to every other lawyer at Firm 2. (*See* **Model Rule 1.10(a)**; **Chapter 22.D at 702**.) But there is a special exception to the conclusive presumption of **imputation** of **confidential information** specifically applicable to **confidential information** known to a specific lawyer who changes jobs. The presumption that the **confidential information** to which Gulliver was exposed is **imputed** to every lawyer in Firm 2 **may** be rebutted if Gulliver is subjected to a timely and proper **ethical screen** at his new firm. In that case, Firm 2 may proceed with its new engagement for C2 in *C2 v. C1—even if C1 does not consent.*

This exception is codified in **Model Rule 1.10(a)(2)**. Please pause and read the Rule right now; you'll see that it has a fair bit of important detail that we need to understand.

TAMING THE TEXT If you examine **Model Rule 1.10(a)(2)**, you'll see that it starts in subsection (a) by stating that the general rule of **imputation** applies "unless" either of two exceptions is established. We've already discussed the first exception, dealing with personal-**interest conflicts**, in **Chapter 22.D at 707. Model Rule 1.10(a)(2)** states the second exception, which arises when three conditions are met: (1) "the prohibition is based upon Rule 1.9(a) or (b)"—that is, the **conflict** is a **successive conflict** based on **confidential information** (look back at **Model Rule 1.9**); (2) that the **confidential information** "arises out of the [personally] **disqualified** lawyer's association with a prior firm"; and (3) "the disqualified lawyer"—that is, the individual lawyer who was exposed to the **disqualifying confidential information** at a prior job—"is timely **screened** from any participation in the [new] matter . . . ."

What's more, this is one situation in the Model Rules that allows **screening** to rebut the presumption of **imputation** in which many (though not all) details of the **screen** are expressly prescribed. Specifically, the **screen** allowed by this particular exception **must** include all of the following features:

- "[T]he disqualified lawyer"—again, the individual lawyer who was exposed to the **disqualifying confidential information** at a prior job—"is apportioned no part of the fee" from the new matter (**Model Rule 1.10(a)(2)(i)**).

- "[W]ritten notice is promptly given to any affected **former client** to enable the **former client** to ascertain compliance with the provisions of this Rule, which shall include a description of the **screening** procedures employed; a statement of the firm's and of the **screened** lawyer's compliance with these Rules; a statement that review may be available before a tribunal; and an agreement by the firm to respond promptly to any written inquiries or objections by the former client about the **screening** procedures" (**Model Rule 1.10(a)(2)(ii)**). In addition, the notice "generally **should** include a description of the **screened** lawyer's prior representation and be given as soon as practicable after the need for **screening** becomes apparent. It also should include a statement by the **screened** lawyer and the firm that the client's **material confidential information** has not been disclosed or used in violation of the Rules." **Model Rule 1.10 Comment [9]**.

- "[C]ertifications of compliance with these Rules and with the **screening** procedures are provided to the **former client** by the screened lawyer and by a partner of the firm, at reasonable intervals upon the **former client**'s written request and upon termination of the **screening** procedures" (**Model Rule 1.10(a)(2) (iii)**). When the **practice organization** implementing the **screen** cannot truthfully certify compliance, it **must** disclose any noncompliance that has occurred. *See* **Model Rule 1.10 Comment [10]**.

Notice how strikingly detailed the requirements for notification and certification of continuing compliance are in this instance. This is a great deal more detail than in the exceptions discussed in the two preceding sections, which simply refer to a disqualified person's being "**screened** from personal participation in the matter" in a Comment to the Rule. **Model Rule 1.10 Comment [4]**.

It remains unclear whether **screens** in situations other than the one described in **Model Rule 1.10(a)(2)** **must** comply with these detailed notice and continuing certification requirements (or, for that matter, the non-apportionment to the **screened** lawyer of any part of the fee from the **screened** matter). One thing that *is* clear is that the detailed requirements of **Model Rule 1.10(a)(2)(i)-(iii)** are *necessary* but not *sufficient* (that is, they're required, but they're not enough all by themselves) to comprise an effective screen even in the circumstances that the Rule describes. **Model Rule 1.10(a)(2)** does not mention, for example, formal notification and sequestration of people and materials within the **practice organization** on opposite sides of the **screen** (*see* **Chapter 22.D at 717**), but **Model Rule 1.0(k)** (defining "**screened**") still requires "timely imposition of procedures within a firm that are reasonably adequate under the circumstances to protect information that the isolated lawyer is obligated to protect," and internal notification and sequestration are widely viewed as indispensable parts of virtually any effective **screen** authorized by the Rules. *See* **Model Rule 1.0 Comment [9]**. ⟨ TAMING THE TEXT

> **Problem 22D-6:** Which of the following lawyers is or is not subject to professional discipline, and which lawyers or **practice organizations** are or are not subject to **disqualification**? Please explain your answers.
>
> a. The Intake Committee at Maya's firm allows Ron Rainmaker to go ahead with the plan that he proposes in the **Introduction to this subchapter at 701** (to sideline himself and the **confidential information** that he knows regarding Petrified so that other lawyers at his firm can represent Mojo against Petrified in commercial litigation). Does anything that we learned in this section help Ron or his firm? Why or why not?
>
> b. Same as **Problem 22D-3(b) at 713** (Danielle's office hires a new prosecutor, Nestor New, who has worked for several years as the sole associate for Delbert Defender, a local private criminal defense lawyer who regularly represents alleged organized crime kingpin Wally "the Weasel" Wyzanski; Danielle's boss is presenting new charges against Wally to a grand jury when the new prosecutor arrives; those charges are based on more information about Wally's criminal enterprise than the DA's office had the last time). After Wally is indicted, Danielle's boss assigns Nestor to help him prepare for Wally's trial. Nestor alertly points out that he previously worked on a case for Delbert Defender representing Wally the Weasel. Danielle's boss then **screens** Nestor from the Wyzanski case.
>
> c. Same as **Problem 22D-3(d) at 713** (Gulliver Gettinghere starts as a lateral litigation associate at Maya's firm, moving from another law firm at which he worked on an employee-raiding case for Toots' Sweets against Randy's Candies, which is represented in that case by Maya's firm). Before Gulliver starts at Maya's firm, the firm's general counsel sends a memo to all lawyers and staff working on the Randy's Candies employee-raiding case and to Gulliver informing them that Gulliver worked on the Randy's Candies case at his former firm, that Gulliver is **screened** from the Randy's Candies case at this firm, and that no one on either side of the **screen** must ever communicate regarding the case with someone on the

other side of the **screen** in any way. All recipients of the memo sign it at the bottom, next to a statement that they have read and understood the memo and that they promise to comply with it. Gulliver confirms that he has told no one at Maya's firm anything about the case, and the litigators and staff on the Randy's Candies case each confirm that they have learned nothing from Gulliver about it.

d. Same as (c), except that in addition to the **screening** measures described in (c), the firm's general counsel also notifies Gulliver's former law-firm employer in writing about Gulliver's employment and the measures taken to **screen** Gulliver from the Randy's Candies case, and promises to review and report on the integrity of the **screen** upon the former employer's written request but no more frequently than every six months. Does anything change if Gulliver joins the softball team fielded by Maya's office in the local lawyer league, which includes two litigation associates working on the Randy's Candies case? Why or why not? And if those facts change something, what **must** or **should** be done about it?

e. Same as (d), except that in addition to the **screening** measures described in (c) and (d), all of the files in the Randy's Candies matter at Maya's firm are labeled "NO ACCESS TO GULLIVER GETTINGHERE," and the firm's file-management software blocks Gulliver's access to any documents created or received in the Randy's Candies case.

f. Same as (e), except that now the case has been resolved on terms sufficiently favorable that they have triggered a special bonus fee agreed to as part of the engagement agreement between Randy's Candies and Maya's firm. A part of that special bonus is divided among the firm's associates in Maya's office, according to their seniority.

v. No Imputation When the Conflict Is Based on Actual Knowledge of Confidential Information That a Lawyer Acquired from a Prospective Client, and the Knowledgeable Lawyer Is Timely and Properly Screened

Model Rule 1.10(a)(2), which we just discussed, tells us when a **practice organization may** use a screen to neutralize a **successive conflict of interest** that would otherwise exist because of **confidential information** to which one of its lawyers was exposed relating to a **former client** at a former job. A comparable situation can arise if a lawyer is exposed to **confidential information** from a **prospective client**, no engagement with the **prospective client** results, and the **practice organization** now wants to take on a new engagement adverse to the **prospective client** in which the earlier-conferred **confidential information** is **material**. That's the last of the situations in which a timely and properly implemented **screen** of the personally **disqualified** lawyer (that is, the one who was exposed to the **prospective client's confidential information)** will prevent **imputation** of that **confidential information** to other lawyers in the **practice organization**, and thus prevent a broader **conflict of interest**, even without the **prospective client's** consent.

This exception is codified in **Model Rule 1.18(d)**. Let's take a look at how the exception is structured. [TAMING THE TEXT] **Model Rule 1.18(c)** states the general rule that "significantly harmful" **confidential information** received from a **prospective client** can't be used against the **prospective client** in a new engagement, even if no attorney-client relationship was ever formed with the **prospective client**—in other words, the **successive client rule** as applied to **prospective clients**. (*See* **Chapter 22.C at 681.**) **Model Rule 1.18(c)** also states the general rule that **confidential information** received from a **prospective client** by any lawyer in a **practice organization** is **imputed** to all other lawyers in the **organization**, "except as provided in paragraph (d)."

Model Rule 1.18(d) provides two exceptions: The first is if all affected clients give **informed consent, confirmed in writing**. **Model Rule 1.18(d)(1)**. We'll talk about that avenue for addressing **conflicts of interest** in **Chapter 22.E at 738**. The other exception is if the lawyer who received the **confidential information** from the **prospective client** is **screened** from the new matter adverse to the **prospective client**, but only if three important conditions are met:

- "[T]he **disqualified** lawyer"—that is, the individual lawyer who was exposed to the **disqualifying confidential information** from the **prospective client**—"is apportioned no part of the fee" from the new matter adverse to the **prospective client** (**Model Rule 1.18(d)(2)(i)**). We've seen this condition before. **Model Rule 1.18 Comment [7]** confirms that it should be treated the same way as the similar condition under **Model Rule 1.10(a)(2)**.

- "[W]ritten notice is promptly given to the **prospective client**" (**Model Rule 1.18(d)(2)(ii)**). This notice requirement does not contain the details about what the notice **must** contain, or an explicit requirement of continuing certification of compliance, that are part of **Model Rule 1.10(a)(2)**. **Model Rule 1.18 Comment [8]** clarifies that the notice to the **prospective client must** include "a general description of the subject matter about which the lawyer was consulted, and of the screening procedures employed," and that it should be given as promptly as reasonably practicable. But it is unclear whether the implication is that the additional elements listed in **Model Rule 1.10(a)(2)** are also required despite their omission here, or are not required, in order for the **screen** to be effective in this situation. Prudence suggests including them.

- "[T]he lawyer who received the information took reasonable measures to avoid exposure to more **disqualifying** information than was reasonably necessary to determine whether to represent the **prospective client**" (**Model Rule 1.18(d)(2)**). This is a major difference from other situations in which **screening may** be used to address a **conflict of interest**. The **screen may** be used in lieu of the **prospective client's** consent only if the lawyer being consulted in contemplation of possible representation limited the **confidential information** conveyed only to the minimum "reasonably necessary to determine whether to represent the **prospective client**." That minimum would virtually always include the names of all interested parties involved in and a general description of the **prospective** matter, so that the **practice organization** could check to see if it had any **conflicts**

of interest. *See* **Chapter 22.F at 753**. It would usually include information that the lawyer needed to know to determine if she had the time, expertise, and interest to take on the engagement, and whether the client was willing and able to pay the lawyer's fees. *See* **Model Rule 1.18 Comments [3]-[4]**. Anything beyond that minimum would need to be justified as "reasonably necessary to determine whether to represent the **prospective client**" under the circumstances. The effect of this requirement is clear from its context: If the lawyer has elicited more than the minimum **confidential information** reasonably necessary from the **prospective client**, **screening** that lawyer will not prevent **imputation** of the **confidential information**, and the **successive conflict of interest** that it creates, to every other lawyer in the **practice organization**. ◁ TAMING THE TEXT

▶ REASON FOR THE RULE ▷ Why, you may be wondering, is there a condition that **confidential information** received from a **prospective client** be minimized in order for a **screen** to be effective, when other situations in which a **screen** is authorized don't require it? The explanation starts from the perspective that a **screen** by itself, unilaterally implemented by the **conflicted practice organization** (that is, without the affected client's consent), is a solution to **successive conflicts** in only a few limited situations (and is *never* a solution to **concurrent conflicts** by itself). Usually, the client's **informed consent, confirmed in writing**, is required to overcome a **conflict of interest**. In order to protect **prospective clients**, we require lawyers to limit their exposure to a **prospective client's confidential information** until both the **prospective client** and the lawyer are sure that they want to form an attorney-client relationship. Once that happens, the lawyer and the client are free to (and **should**) exchange all the **confidential information** that might be helpful to the engagement. But until it does, we limit what a lawyer may gather so that any **screen** that may eventually be authorized involves as little **confidential information**, and thus as little risk to the **prospective client** in the event of a "leak," as reasonably possible. *See* **Model Rule 1.18 Comments [3]-[4]**. ◁ REASON FOR THE RULE

▶ TIPS & TACTICS ▷ We wouldn't be surprised if, by this point, you were a little frustrated with the proliferating details of these different rules and exceptions. Just in considering how to rebut the presumption of **imputation** of **confidential information** within a **practice organization**, we've seen three scenarios in which the presumption of **imputation** can be rebutted by situational facts, and four situations in which the presumption of imputation can be rebutted by a timely and proper **screen**. And out of those four situations, the Model Rules describe the details of the **screen** required in three different ways. (Quick—can you name them? Go back and find them. *Hint: See* **Chapter 22.D at 719**; **Chapter 22.D at 722**; **Chapter 22.D at 725**.) "Why me?" you may be wondering.

If it's any comfort, it's not about you. **Conflicts of interest** is an area of the law governing lawyers that has developed piecemeal; the disciplinary rules and **disqualification** doctrines have evolved unevenly, the caselaw is convoluted and inconsistent, and the pieces don't always fit together snugly. But the stakes in compliance are quite high; very embarrassing and expensive things happen to lawyers who don't recognize or respond to **conflicts of interest** properly.

The good news about **conflicts of interest** is that, if you and your **practice organization** do your jobs with reasonable care, you can see them coming. We'll talk about how to do that in **Chapter 22.F at 753**. Once you see a **conflict** coming, you can figure out whether you have to stay out in order to avoid **consequences**, or whether the **conflict** can be addressed, and if so, how. And when in doubt about the applicable standard for compliance (which happens with some frequency in this area of the law), *choose the most restrictive standard* and comply with that. For example, if you can address a particular **conflict** with a **screen** but the standards for an effective **screen** are not completely clear, implement a **screen** that encompasses every element that *might* be required. This tactic will make your **screen** much more likely to survive a challenge, and just as important, it may discourage any challenge in the first place, because there will be no serious argument that anything is missing. TIPS & TACTICS

vi. CONSEQUENCES What Happens If You Rebut the Presumption of Imputation by Adopting a Screen as Permitted by Rule, But Then the Screen Is Violated?

Suppose you find yourself in one of the situations in which a timely and proper **ethical screen** will rebut the presumption of **imputation**, and you and your **practice organization** put the **screen** together in the right way at the right time. Then, weeks, or months, or maybe even years later (if the **screen** is still needed for that long), something goes wrong: Somebody mislabels a file, or blurts out a **confidence** from the **screened** engagement without thinking, or fails to confirm compliance promptly upon request, or (much worse) succumbs to temptation and deliberately provides **screened confidences** to colleagues? What happens now?

Strikingly (and perhaps as a reflection of how seriously the practicing bar takes **screening** measures when they're imposed), the answer is unclear. Authority is sparse to nonexistent. Since most if not all **screens** include some kind of notice to the client protected by the **screen**, breaches can often be brought to a supervising court's (and the licensing bar's) attention. The party that the **screen** protected would likely argue that the Rules say that an unconsented **conflict of interest** exists in the absence of a proper and timely screen, so if the screen fails, the **conflict** exists and **must** be remedied with the tools the law provides—professional discipline and **disqualification**. It might turn out that way.

That said, we could imagine that a court confronted with a broken screen might take a more equitably measured view, and adopt remedies both tailored and proportional to the breach. A technical but harmless breach (say, failure to circulate required periodic reminders to comply, or an inadvertent failure to program the **screening** firm's document-management software to exclude **screened** personnel, coupled with proof that no such personnel actually accessed a **screened** document or file), might be met with requirements for more active monitoring or more frequent reporting, but nothing as disruptively explosive as **disqualification**. By contrast, a deliberate violation, even if relatively harmless, might provoke a strong remedial reaction. And any "leak" of **material confidential information** would likely be met with strong protective and compensatory measures, whether or not inadvertent. Similarly, a disciplinary authority that decided to prosecute such a violation would have discretion to impose a level of discipline proportional to the intent and practical consequences of the violation.

But the truth is, there is very little authority, so it's hard to say. Our best advice: Don't be the person on whose back new law in this area is built. ⟨CONSEQUENCES⟩

Problem 22D-7: Which of the following lawyers is or is not subject to professional discipline, and which lawyers or **practice organizations** are or are not subject to **disqualification**? Please explain your answers.

a. The Intake Committee at Maya's firm allows Ron Rainmaker to go ahead with the plan that he proposes in the **Introduction to this subchapter at 701** (to sideline himself and the **confidential information** that he knows regarding Petrified, so that other lawyers at his firm can represent Mojo against Petrified in commercial litigation), provided that Ron takes steps to **screen** himself from Mojo's representation by the firm against Petrified. What measures **must** or **should** that **screen** include (and which are **musts** and which are **shoulds**)?

b. Same as (a), but now assume that the firm implements a timely and proper **screen** between Ron and the litigators who seek to represent Mojo against Petrified. Will that **screen** adequately address Ron's **conflict of interest**? Why or why not?

c. Gigantothon Corporation is an industry leader in squibbles (that's an imaginary product like a widget). In fact, the company has been so successful that it controls 72 percent of the squibbles market. Gigantothon's next-most-successful competitor sues Gigantothon for monopolization of the squibbles market in violation of Section 2 of the Sherman Antitrust Act. This will be a large, protracted, and very expensive (from the lawyers' side, that means very profitable) lawsuit to defend. Gigantothon wants to pick the defense counsel best suited for this big and important job and decides to hold what has colloquially been known as a "beauty contest" or "bake-off" (these are now generally viewed as gender-biased terms and disfavored, but you will still hear them occasionally from older lawyers). Gigantothon invites six law firms with experienced antitrust lawyers to participate in a competition. Each firm gets an identical set of materials, about three binders' worth, accompanied by a detailed memo describing anticipated claims and defenses and a range of concerns regarding anticipated business, discovery, public relations, and other issues. All the materials are prominently labeled "CONFIDENTIAL AND PRIVILEGED." Each invited firm is asked to propose a specific litigation team for the case, and three members of each team will meet with a committee that includes Gigantothon's general counsel, CEO, and a member of its board of directors for two hours, during which they will have the opportunity to introduce the members of their team and discuss their anticipated approach to defending the case. Maya's firm is invited.

Although the competition law team from Maya's firm makes a strong showing, Gigantothon ultimately selects another firm to defend it in the antitrust case. Two months later, one of Gigantothon's competitors in the squibbles market other than the plaintiff in the pending case approaches Maya's firm to represent that competitor in a similar monopolization case against Gigantothon. **May** Maya's firm take on the engagement? What **must** or **should** the firm do to take on the engagement properly, if that's possible? Please be detailed and explain your answer.

Big-Picture Takeaways from Chapter 22.D

1. The general rule, which is codified in **Model Rule 1.10(a)** and incorporated in the civil **disqualification** law of every jurisdiction, is that, if *any* lawyer in a **practice organization** has a **conflict of interest** (or a relationship or knowledge that could create one), then *every* lawyer in the same **practice organization** (and the **practice organization** itself) is deemed to have the same **conflict of interest** (or relationship or knowledge). *See* **Chapter 22.D at 702**. In most situations, the **imputation** of **conflicts of interest** within a **practice organization** is not only presumed, it is presumed *conclusively*. *See* **Chapter 22.D at 704**.

2. There are several situations in which the presumption that **conflicts of interest** are **imputed** throughout the **conflicted** lawyer's **practice organization** is *rebuttable*—that is, other lawyers in the **practice organization**, and the **practice organization** itself, may show facts that will cut off **imputation** from the **conflicted** lawyer to others within the **practice organization**, allowing other lawyers in the **practice organization** to proceed with an engagement that would otherwise be prohibited, even without the consent of any affected client. These exceptions are codified in portions of **Model Rule 1.9**, **Model Rule 1.10**, and **Model Rule 1.18**, and they block the imposition of professional discipline that would otherwise be based on an **imputed conflict of interest**. Most jurisdictions have also adopted the same exceptions on the same terms as a defense to **disqualification**. *See* **Chapter 22.D at 705**.

3. The Rules of Professional Conduct have identified seven specific situations in which the conclusive presumption of **imputation** is relaxed. In these situations, the presumption of **imputation** remains, but it is rebuttable, and the party seeking to rebut it bears the burden of proving facts defining a situation identified in the Rules in which we can feel reasonably sure that the affected clients' legitimate **interests** remain protected. In situations in which one lawyer's **conflict of interest** is *not* **imputed**, any other lawyer in the same **practice organization** **may** go ahead with the **conflicted**

engagement, as long as the personally **disqualified** lawyer is not involved. No client consent of any kind is required. *See* **Chapter 22.D at 705**.

4. The exceptions, generally speaking, break down into two groups: Those in which the presumption of **imputation may** be rebutted by specific situational facts, and those in which the presumption of **imputation may** be rebutted by proof of a timely implemented and properly maintained **ethical screen**. *See* **Chapter 22.D at 705**.

5. The situations in which the presumption of **imputation may** be rebutted by specific situational facts include the following:

   a. **Model Rule 1.10(a)(1)** provides that there is no **imputation** when "the **conflict** is based on a personal **interest** of the **disqualified** lawyer and does not present a significant risk of **materially** limiting the representation of the client by the remaining lawyers in the firm." This exception is a lot narrower than it sounds, because most of the "personal-**interest**" **conflicts** are already *conclusively* presumed to be **imputed** within the **practice organization** under **Model Rule 1.8(k)** and related civil law. The ones that are not conclusively presumed to be **imputed** are the restrictions on sex with a client (**Model Rule 1.8(j)**; *see* **Chapter 5.C at 108**), and the personal-**interest conflict** created when an individual lawyer's personal **interests** or connections create a "significant risk of **materially** limiting" a client's representation (**Model Rule 1.7(a)(2)**; *see* **Chapter 22.A at 626**). *See* **Chapter 22.D at 707**.

   b. **Model Rule 1.9(b)** provides that lawyers who change jobs bring to, and **impute within**, a new **practice organization** employer only that **confidential information** of which they personally have (or had) actual knowledge. The **Model Rule 1.9(b)** exception addresses only a limited category of **successive conflicts of interest** based on information protected by the **duty of confidentiality**. It has no application to **concurrent conflicts of interest**. *See* **Chapter 22.D at 709**.

   c. **Model Rule 1.10(b)** describes an exception to **imputation** when the *only* lawyer or lawyers in a **practice organization** who have ever been exposed to a particular client's or **prospective client's confidential information** leave the **practice organization** and leave no trace of the **confidential information** behind. All of the lawyers who have been exposed to the client's **confidential information must** have "terminated [their] association" with the **practice organization**. If even one remains, the presumption of **imputation** has not been rebutted. And if *any* trace of the relevant **confidential information** remains at the **practice organization** in *any* form (including paper or digital files), the terms of **Model Rule 1.10(b)** are not satisfied and the general presumption of **imputation** throughout the **practice**

organization remains in place, unrebutted. The **Model Rule 1.10(b)** exception applies *only* to an **imputed conflict of interest** based on the **successive client rule**—that is, based on a **practice organization's** exposure to a **prospective** or **former client's confidential information**. It has no effect on any **concurrent conflict of interest.** *See* **Chapter 22.D at 713.**

6. An **ethical screen** or **ethical wall** is a set of prophylactic measures designed to restrict **confidential information** to a single lawyer or small group of lawyers and staff and prevent its dissemination to others in the same **practice organization.** In a very limited set of defined circumstances, the Model Rules (and related state civil law governing **disqualification**) allow **practice organizations** to **screen** personnel who have been exposed to **disqualifying confidential information** (as well as any means by which such **confidential information** may have been recorded or stored) in order to permit other personnel in the same **practice organization** to proceed with what otherwise would have been a **conflicted** engagement. Most **conflicts of interest** cannot be avoided by a **screen**, no matter how carefully constructed and maintained—and **screens** have *no* effect on *any* **concurrent conflict of interest. Model Rule 1.0(k),** which defines a "**screen**," offers only that the **screen must** involve "the timely imposition of procedures within a [**practice organization**] that are reasonably adequate under the circumstances to protect information that the isolated lawyer is obligated to protect under these Rules or other law." Specific Rules require specific measures in the circumstances that they address. Common practice has given us a list of widely used **screening** measures, and there are a number of features that are widely viewed as essential to any effective **screen**, in addition to any particular measures specified by an applicable Rule. *See* **Chapter 22.D at 716.**

    Among **successive conflicts of interest**, only four narrowly defined situations **may** be adequately addressed by a **screen** alone:

    a. **Model Rule 1.10 Comment [4]** informs us that **confidential information** to which nonlawyer personnel have been exposed will not be **imputed** to anyone else at the **practice organization**, so long as the relevant nonlawyer is timely and properly **screened** from any matter as to which the **confidential information** would create a **successive conflict.** *See* **Chapter 22.D at 719.**

    b. **Model Rule 1.10 Comment [4]** takes a similar approach when a lawyer was exposed to **confidential information** before becoming a lawyer; for example, while working as a legal assistant or law clerk, or in another line of work altogether, before or during law school. *See* **Chapter 22.D at 719.**

    c. **Model Rule 1.10(a)(2)** provides that the **confidential information** to which a lawyer who changes jobs was actually exposed will not be **imputed** to every lawyer in the mobile lawyer's new firm if the mobile lawyer is subjected to a timely and proper **ethical screen**. *See* **Chapter 22.D at 721**.

d. **Model Rule 1.18(d)** provides that there is no **imputation** when the **conflict** is based on actual knowledge of **confidential information** that a lawyer acquired from a **prospective client**, provided that the "lawyer who received the information took reasonable measures to avoid exposure to more **disqualifying** information than was reasonably necessary to determine whether to represent the **prospective client**," and the knowledgeable lawyer is timely and properly **screened**. *See* **Chapter 22.D at 724**.

Multiple-Choice Review Questions for Chapter 22.D

1. Abigail, Victor, Chrissy, and Keisha all work for a large law firm. Abigail works in the Keystone office. Victor, Chrissy, and Keisha work in the firm's office in the neighboring State of Garden. Keisha represents BirdCo. in a trademark dispute against BirdWorld. Although Keisha is counsel of record on the case, Chrissy assists with research for the case.

   Under the general rule in **Model Rule 1.10(a)**, who is conflicted from representing BirdWorld in a matter related to the trademark dispute?
   a. Keisha.
   b. Keisha and Chrissy.
   c. Keisha, Chrissy, and Victor.
   d. Keisha, Chrissy, Victor, and Abigail.

2. A church asks a law firm to defend it against claimed health code violations in the church's soup kitchen. When the firm discusses handling the case, one of the firm's partners, Amir, objects. Amir explains that the church refuses to engage in same-sex marriage ceremonies. Amir refuses to handle a case for an organization that he believes discriminates on the basis of sexual orientation. Another partner, Leona, offers to handle the case so that Amir need not handle it.

   Can Leona handle the case, or is she **conflicted** due to Amir's beliefs?
   a. Yes. Amir's **conflict** is not **imputed** to Leona.
   b. Yes. Amir's **conflict** is irrelevant because the legal issues in the case involve health code violations and not the church's stand on same-sex marriage.
   c. No. Amir's **conflict** would be **imputed** to Leona.
   d. No. If something happens to Leona, Amir may be forced to assume responsibility for the case, and this would cause a **conflict** between the church's objectives in the litigation and Amir's personal beliefs.

3. Lulu worked at Small Law LLC. The firm had been handling a breach of contract case on behalf of Bullseye Corp. Bullseye is being sued by one of

its suppliers, Boxes Etc. Another Small Law attorney, Conan, had a **conflict of interest** caused by his knowledge of **confidential information** from Boxes. Conan was instructed not to work on the case. Unfortunately, the lawyer handling the matter for Bullseye, Beatrice, consulted with Conan about litigation strategy on the case. Opposing counsel discovered this fact and successfully moved to **disqualify** Small Law from representing Bullseye. Bullseye then retained counsel from Big Law LLC, another law firm in the city.

Lulu was not involved in the Bullseye case and learned nothing **confidential** about Bullseye.

Lulu left Small Law and went to work for Big Law. If Big Law fails to **screen** Lulu, is Big Law subject to being **disqualified** from representing Bullseye?

    a. Yes, because Lulu's **disqualifying** exposure to **confidential information** is **imputable** to all the other lawyers at Big Law unless she is **screened**.

    b. Yes, unless Boxes gives **informed consent, confirmed in writing**.

    c. No, as long as Lulu does not receive any fees flowing from the representation of Bullseye.

    d. No, because Lulu did not have **confidential information** about Bullseye.

4.   What does **Model Rule 1.0(k)** require of an **ethical screen**?

    a. It must be reasonably adequate under the circumstances to protect the information that the **screened** lawyer is obligated to protect.

    b. It must successfully protect the information that the **screened** lawyer is obligated to protect.

    c. It must remove any appearance of impropriety.

    d. It must be managed by a non-lawyer employee of the firm.

5.   An **ethical screen** is ineffective for what type of **conflict of interest**?

    a. A **successive conflict of interest**.

    b. A **concurrent conflict of interest**.

    c. An **imputed conflict of interest**.

    d. A potential **conflict of interest**.

E. Addressing Conflicts of Interest Through Abstention or Client Consent

Ron Rainmaker looks up as Maya walks in. "Ah, there you are!" he says. "I'd like you to take a look at something I've drafted." "Okay," says Maya, pleased that she's earned this show of trust. "What's the background?"

"I haven't given up on this Mojo-Petrified thing," Ron starts. Maya smiles, thinking that Ron's perseverance probably has a lot to do with his success. "I think the Intake Committee is probably sick of me," Ron continues, "but I don't care. This one is just too good to pass up. You know I've tried every which way to get the firm *some* piece of the upcoming *Petrified v. Mojo* prizefight. The Intake Committee has been stuck on the **conflicts of interest** that the firm seems to have. I haven't been able to persuade the Committee that there's any way around or through the **conflicts**, though I got close when I volunteered to **screen** myself if we represented Mojo." Maya nods, encouraging him to continue. "I was about to give up," Ron goes on, "and then I thought, wait, why have my plans all been so confrontational? Someone can almost always consent to a **conflict of interest**."

Maya jumps in: "But I thought that the Committee told you that we wouldn't even *ask* Mojo to consent, because we want to preserve Mojo's goodwill. You're not going to go behind the Committee's back, are you?" "No," Ron replies. "I admit that I was tempted, but that would just cost me a ton of grief with my partners. We *do* have ground rules around here." Maya is relieved. "Then what?" she asks. "Well," Ron says, "the Committee says that I can't ask Mojo for consent. But they didn't say that I couldn't ask Petrified. So I drafted a waiver to send over to the general counsel who called me the other day. That's what I want you to take a look at. If Petrified waives, then we can go ahead and represent Mojo." "But I've never seen a **conflicts** waiver before," Maya says, tentatively. "That's okay," says Ron. "I just want your first impression. Put yourself behind the Petrified GC's desk, and imagine how he might react to this." Ron hands Maya a piece of paper:

Dear Roscoe:

It was great to catch up with you the other day. The fly-fishing in Montana sounded amazing—take me along next time! And again, congratulations on your daughter's upcoming wedding!

I also really enjoyed talking with you about Petrified's possible dispute with Mojo Manufacturing. I looked into it, and unfortunately it turns out that Mojo is a long-standing client of our firm.

I would have liked to see us start working together on this more than you can imagine, and I'm still hopeful that we'll find something else to work on together soon. I was hoping that you'd let me come by sometime and talk to your securities group about the new amendments to the SEC regs—no charge, of course. In the meantime, I'm sure that you'll find aggressive lawyers up to the task of pursuing Petrified's claims.

I also should let you know that Mojo has approached us and asked us to represent it in the dispute with Petrified that seems to be coming. Mojo being a longtime client of our firm, the litigators would really like to do that. As you know, Petrified never hired us, so we have no concurrent conflict of interest. Naturally, I would have nothing to do with the litigators' work for Mojo, so there's no concern there.

I know that you're planning to be away this week and next for your daughter's wedding, and your life is really full right now. To make this easy for you, if I don't hear from you by next Wednesday, I'll assume that you have no concerns with the situation. I look forward to catching up with you again when you return.

Keep the faith!

Best,

Ron

What should Maya say about Ron's draft **conflicts** waiver? If you were Petrified Petroleum's general counsel, what would you say?

* * *

We've covered an awful lot of information regarding **conflicts of interest** in the last few subchapters. In gratitude for your patience, and to give you a chance to catch your breath, here's a quick recap of what you already know:

- There are three kinds of **conflicts of interest** (we know, we've said this before, but stick with us through the recap; it couldn't hurt):
  - **Conflicts of interest** between your own personal **interests** and the **interests** of a client. *See* **Chapter 22.A at 603**.
  - **Conflicts of interest** based on *whom* you know and have ongoing relationships with, and the temptation to favor one client over another. These **conflicts** are grounded in the **duty of loyalty** and are addressed by the **concurrent client rule**. *See* **Chapter 22.B at 645**.
  - **Conflicts of interest** based on *what* you know in **confidence**, and the possible temptation to share that **confidential information** with (or use that **information** on behalf of) another client, to the original client's disadvantage. These **conflicts** are grounded in the **duty of confidentiality** and are governed by the **successive client rule**. *See* **Chapter 22.C at 678**.
- Generally speaking, **conflicts of interest** are presumed to be **imputed** within a **practice organization**, but there are several narrow exceptions.
  - The general rule of **imputation** provides that, if one lawyer in a **practice organization** has a **conflict of interest** (or a relationship or knowledge that could create one), then every lawyer in the **practice organization**, and the **organization** itself, will be deemed to have the same **conflict of interest** (or relationship, or knowledge). **Imputation** is usually presumed *conclusively*. See **Chapter 22.D at 704**.
  - However, there are seven specific situations defined by the Model Rules of Professional Conduct, and incorporated into most jurisdictions' civil law of **disqualification**, in which the presumption of **imputation may** be rebutted by showing particular facts that meet the requirements of the exception. If the presumption of **imputation** is rebutted, then the **conflict of interest** is confined to those lawyers within the **practice organization** who are personally **disqualified** (that is, who are personally involved in whatever created the **conflict of interest**). In that case, other lawyers within the **practice organization** who are not personally **disqualified** may proceed with the **conflicted** engagement without any affected client's consent. All

the exceptions address circumstances in which the **conflict of interest** is based on exposure to **confidential information**; none of them is effective in addressing a **concurrent conflict of interest**. *See* **Chapter 22.D at 705**.

■   CONSEQUENCES With only a few exceptions, all of these principles are applied in the same way to professional discipline and to efforts to **disqualify** a **conflicted** lawyer or **practice organization** from an engagement. CONSEQUENCES

A **conflict of interest** ordinarily triggers serious **consequences**. It's a basis for professional discipline. It's grounds for a court to enter an order of **disqualification**, excluding the **conflicted** lawyers (and their **practice organization**) from the **conflicted** engagement, whether or not the **conflict** has caused any actual harm. If the **conflict** is sufficiently serious, the **conflicted** lawyers and **practice organization** may forfeit their fees (including fees already paid if they were incurred while the **conflict of interest** existed). And if the **conflict** results in actual monetary harm to any affected client, then that client may recover compensatory damages. Informally, **conflicts** often do long-term damage to client relations and lawyers' professional reputations. Nasty stuff.

All of this can be prevented if a **conflict of interest** is recognized in advance and is either avoided or properly addressed. You can *avoid* (or at least avoid continuing) the **conflict** by abstaining or withdrawing—that is, by staying out or getting out of the **conflicted** engagement. You can *address* the **conflict** in one of two ways. One way is if you can determine that you are facing a situation in which your **practice organization** is allowed to rebut the presumption of **imputation** and can staff the matter with lawyers who are not personally **disqualified**. *See* **Chapter 22.D at 705**. The other way to address a **conflict of interest** is to obtain all affected clients' **informed consent** in the form and substance required by the Rules (and any parallel state law governing **disqualification**). If you have proper client consent, then you and your **practice organization** may proceed with what otherwise would have been a **conflicted** engagement, without **consequences**, according to whatever terms you and the affected clients have agreed.

With that in mind, first we'll talk briefly about abstention and withdrawal. Then we'll discuss when client consent is an effective means of addressing a **conflict of interest**—in other words, which **conflicts** are **consentable**. Finally, we'll discuss what formal and substantive characteristics a client's consent to a **consentable conflict of interest must** or **should** have.

1. Abstaining or Withdrawing from a Conflicted Engagement

One solution to a **conflict of interest** is to *avoid* the **conflict of interest** by abstaining or withdrawing. Let's be clear about the difference between abstaining and withdrawing, and when each is available.

Abstention is the simplest solution. It can be summarized in two words—*stay out*. If you or your **practice organization** is considering a new engagement, and you discover that it would create a **conflict of interest** if you took it on, you can (and, indeed, **must**) simply decline to do so. **Conflicts of interest** don't trigger **consequences** until and unless a lawyer has taken on the **conflicted** engagement.

REAL WORLD Abstention is effective, but it's not very rewarding. It requires you to turn down an engagement that you wanted to undertake (or at least had been considering seriously enough to see if it created **conflicts of interest**). That means giving up the revenue or other things you care about (supporting the client's cause, public attention from a high-profile engagement, etc.) that spurred your interest in the engagement in the first place. From where you sit right now, that sacrifice may seem somewhat abstract and not all that difficult to accept. But a few years from now, when you may have a family, a mortgage, or other pressing obligations or ambitions, it may very well feel like you were robbed of your birthright. After all, it's not *your* fault that some **conflict of interest** has gotten in the way; all *you* (or your firm) ever did was to properly represent some other client who asked you to do so. And that kind of thinking can bend your perspective in the moment and pressure you to disregard serious risks of serious **consequences**, or to develop excessively "creative" arguments that there is no problem or that there is an easy solution that somehow costlessly gives you everything you want.

This phenomenon is often referred to as "motivated reasoning." Like the other cognitive biases we discussed in **Chapter 4 at 70**, it's an extremely common cognitive bias to whose tempting distortions you need to remain alert. Beware. REAL WORLD

Abstention is available only if you plan it in advance. Simply put, you can't *stay out* unless you *never got in.* That's why all responsible lawyers and **practice organizations** do **conflicts** checks *before* accepting any new engagement (*see* **Chapter 22.F at 753**). If you check for **conflicts of interest** carefully and thoroughly before accepting any new engagement, you'll know when a new engagement creates or may create a **conflict of interest**, and you can respond proactively.

But what if you make a mistake (it happens) and find yourself actually representing a client in a **conflicted** engagement? Then you have to address the **conflict** as promptly as possible. One possible way to address the **conflict** (which is much better if you do it *before* taking on the **conflicted** engagement but **may** be used to address an actually subsisting **conflict** as well) is to obtain every affected client's (or other affected person's) **informed consent, confirmed in writing**. We'll discuss that solution in the next section. Because it requires each affected person's voluntary and **informed consent**, and clients (and others) **may** withhold such consent for any reason or no reason, consent simply may not be possible.

What then? Well, if you've already *gotten into* a **conflicted** engagement from which you should have abstained, then you have to *get out.* In other words, you **must** withdraw.[47] The alert student (good to see you again!) is asking from *which*

---

[47] Why? As we discussed in **Chapter 22.B at 647, Model Rule 1.16(a)(1)** (*see* **Chapter 9.D at 295**), says that you **must not** "represent a client or, where representation has commenced, shall withdraw from the representation of a client if . . . the

engagement you must withdraw, given that many **conflicts** involve more than one actual or prospective engagement. In the case of a **successive conflict**, the affected person is the **former** or **prospective client** who provided you (or someone else in your **practice organization**) with **confidential information** at some point in the past—that is, someone you don't currently represent. In that case, you **must** withdraw from the engagement that created the **successive conflict**—namely, the new engagement adverse to the **former** or **prospective client** in which you are in a position to use the **former** or **prospective client's confidential information** against it.

In the case of a **concurrent conflict** that you have failed to avoid, you find yourself representing two **current clients** whose **interests conflict** (whether in related or unrelated matters, and it doesn't matter which). If you withdraw from one **current client** to avoid the **conflict** while continuing with the other, then you have violated the **hot-potato rule** (*see* **Chapter 22.B at 650**), and you will still be subject to **disqualification** in the engagement that you didn't terminate. As a result, once you have actually stepped into a **concurrent conflict**, you typically **must** withdraw from *both* engagements creating the **conflict**, unless you have **informed consent, confirmed in writing**, from *both* (or if more than two, then from *all*) affected clients as to which engagement(s) you may continue. You will also need the permission of any involved tribunal to withdraw, of course (*see* **Chapter 9.D at 288**), but in these circumstances that permission is usually available.

2. Addressing a Conflict of Interest Through All Affected Clients' Informed Consent

Instead of avoiding a **conflict** by abstaining or withdrawing, and instead of addressing the **conflict** by determining that there is an available exception to the general rule of **imputation** that allows you to rebut the presumption of imputation and proceed, you also **may** address a **conflict of interest** by obtaining all affected clients' **informed consent** in the form and substance required by the Rules (and any parallel state law governing **disqualification**).

[Taming the Text] Where do we find that in the Rules? **Model Rule 1.7(a)**, which codifies the **concurrent client rule**, forbids **concurrent conflicts** "except as provided in paragraph (b)." **Model Rule 1.7(b)** provides that "[n]otwithstanding the existence of a **concurrent conflict of interest** under paragraph (a), a lawyer **may** represent a client" if the **conflict** is **consentable** and "each affected client gives **informed consent, confirmed in writing**." Similarly, **Model Rules 1.9(a) and (b)** and **Model Rule 1.18(c)** codify the **successive client rule**, which forbids a lawyer from representing a client in a new matter against a **prospective** or **former client** whose **confidential information** could be

---

representation will result in violation of the rules of professional conduct or other law . . . ." In this case, the taking on or continuation of a **conflict of interest** is a "violation of the rules of professional conduct." This is a *mandatory* withdrawal rule, so if you failed to abstain, you **must** withdraw (subject to the approval of any involved tribunal which, under these circumstances, will likely be given). And if you don't, then a court will almost certainly **disqualify** you upon an aggrieved party's motion, and additional unpleasant **consequences** will likely follow (*see* **Chapter 22.B at 663**; **Chapter 22.C at 690**).

used against that **prospective** or **former client** in the new matter, unless the affected clients give **informed consent, confirmed in writing**. And **Model Rule 1.10(c)** provides that any **conflict of interest imputed** under that Rule "**may** be waived by the affected client under the conditions stated in Rule 1.7." From these Rules, we can also see that "consent" and "waiver" are interchangeable terms for the same thing in this context—namely, a fully informed and voluntary agreement on the client's part, documented with the proper formalities, to allow a **conflicted** engagement to proceed. ◁ Taming the Text

Will a proper consent *always* solve a **conflicts** problem? Not always, but usually: "Ordinarily, clients may consent to representation notwithstanding a **conflict.**" **Model Rule 1.7 Comment [14]**. But there are limited circumstances in which no consent, however voluntary or fully informed, will serve to waive a **conflict of interest** and allow the **conflicted** engagement to proceed without **consequences**. We'll talk about those circumstances next.

3. When Is a Conflict of Interest Consentable?

The limits of client consent are set out in **Model Rule 1.7(b)** and **Model Rule 1.8**. The Rules enumerate four different kinds of **nonconsentable conflicts**:

One is when "the representation is . . . prohibited by law" (**Model Rule 1.7(b) (2)**). That's unusual, but not unheard of. **Model Rule 1.7 Comment [16]** provides a few examples. Take a look at them right now.

A second category of **conflicts of interest** that can't be addressed by waiver is all of the personal-**interest conflicts** addressed in **Model Rule 1.8**. We know that they're **nonconsentable** because—unlike all the **consentable conflicts**—their prohibition or restriction does not include the phrase "unless all affected clients give **informed consent, confirmed in writing**"—the language that the Model Rules use when client consent is allowed. Most of the examples in this category were addressed in **Chapter 22.A at 603**. They include the restrictions on nonprohibited transactions with clients (**Model Rule 1.8(a)**; **Chapter 22.A at 617**); the restrictions on gifts and bequests from clients (**Model Rule 1.8(c)**; **Chapter 22.A at 612**); the prohibition on acquiring literary or media rights related to the engagement while the engagement is still pending (**Model Rule 1.8(d)**; **Chapter 22.A at 615**); the prohibition on financial assistance to litigation clients (**Model Rule 1.8(e)**; **Chapter 22.A at 606**); the restrictions on accepting compensation for services from someone other than the client (**Model Rule 1.8(f)**; **Chapter 9.B at 273**); the restrictions on clients' prospective waivers of a lawyer's malpractice liability and on settling a malpractice claim with a **current** or **former client** who is not independently represented (**Model Rule 1.8(h)**; **Chapter 9.C at 285**); and the prohibition on acquiring a proprietary interest in the client's cause of action or the subject matter of the litigation (**Model Rule 1.8(i)**; **Chapter 22.A at 616**). All of these personal-**interest conflicts** are conclusively deemed **imputed** to the personally **disqualified** lawyer's **practice organization**, and all the lawyers in it. **Model Rule 1.8(k)**.

The third category of **nonconsentable conflict** arises if "the representation . . . involve[s] the assertion of a claim by one client against another client represented by the lawyer in the same . . . proceeding before a tribunal" (**Model Rule 1.7(b) (3)**). This prohibition is narrow, but not surprising: No amount of disclosure or consent would justify the parties' agreement to have the same lawyer represent the plaintiff *and* the defendant in the same case, which is basically the prohibited situation that the Rule describes. No lawyer could be expected to represent opposite sides at the same time responsibly, and no client should be allowed to put herself in such a bind.

Last, the fourth category of **nonconsentable conflict** is a little more general and a little more loosely described: "[T]he lawyer [does not] reasonably believe[] that the lawyer will be able to provide competent and diligent representation to each affected client" (**Model Rule 1.7(b)(1)**). TAMING THE TEXT Notice that the wording of this prohibition has both a subjective and an objective element: In order for the **conflict** to be **consentable**, the lawyer must "*reasonably believe*" that she can handle the **conflict** effectively (emphasis added). In other words, the lawyer **must** subjectively "believe" that she can "provide competent and diligent representation to each affected client," *and* that subjective belief **must** be objectively "reasonabl[e]." The touchstone in evaluating **consentability** on this ground is "whether the **interests** of the clients will be adequately protected if the clients are permitted to give their **informed consent** to representation burdened by a **conflict of interest**." **Model Rule 1.7 Comment [15]**. Put slightly differently, if no reasonable client would agree to the terms of the waiver, then it's **nonconsentable**. Like the extreme case of one lawyer representing both the plaintiff and the defendant in the same lawsuit, there are some **conflicts** that are so pervasive, disabling, or unavoidable that it would be unreasonable for a reasonable client to allow the **conflict** to occur, and any consent that the lawyer may have obtained in those circumstances must be presumed to be the result of either the lawyer's undue influence or the client's failure to appreciate the implications of the consent. Such circumstances are not common, but they do occur.[48] TAMING THE TEXT

> Problem 22E-1: Which of the following are or are not **consentable**, and why or why not?
>
> a. The situation described in **Problem 22B-2(a) at 665** (Maya's firm proposes to represent Scooter's Computers and two of its managers jointly in securities fraud litigation).

---

[48] One of the peculiar artifacts of the way that the Model Rules on **conflicts of interest** are drafted is that, by their terms, **consentability** is only a question as to **concurrent conflicts** (which are governed by **Model Rule 1.7(b)**) and **imputed conflicts** (which are generally governed by **Model Rule 1.10**, but **Model Rule 1.10(c)** says that any **imputed conflict** "**may** be waived by the affected client under the conditions stated in Rule 1.7"). **Successive conflicts**, governed by **Model Rule 1.9** and **Model Rule 1.18**, are all subject to waiver if done with full disclosure and voluntary consent ("the **former client** gives **informed consent, confirmed in writing**"). It's difficult to explain this division other than as a drafting glitch, though an argument can be made that, if a client is really told about and understands all of the costs and dangers of putting at risk almost any **confidential information** to an adversary, that consent is probably voluntary and rational enough that the legal system should not step in and prevent it.

b. Maya's firm represents Scooter's Computers in the securities fraud litigation described in (a). Ron Rainmaker is asked to represent Jiffy Janitorial, a regional janitorial company, in negotiating a contract with Scooter's for Jiffy to service all of Scooter's retail locations in Jiffy's service area.

c. The situation described in **Problem 22B-2(c) at 666** (Frank's firm agrees to advise three machinists who want to pool their skills and equipment to form a single business organization).

d. The family law partner in Frank's firm, Sally Splitsville, is asked to represent a divorcing husband and wife in their efforts to develop a consensual, out-of-court agreement on the details of their marital dissolution.

e. Danielle's office is prosecuting an organized-crime case. Indicted in the case, and set to be tried together, are Mr. Bigfish and Mr. Littlefish. Bigfish is a *capo*, a high-level leader in the organized crime "family," and Littlefish is a low-level, on-the-street operator. Danielle's office intends to prove that Bigfish directed and oversaw various acts of extortion and violence that Littlefish carried out. Delbert Defender, a local criminal defense lawyer who turns up regularly in organized-crime cases, has appeared in the case on behalf of both defendants.

f. Think back to the *Wanda Worker v. BCraftyCo* sexual harassment case in Chapter 11 (*see* **Problem 11B-2(a) at 347**). Wanda alleges that her supervisor, BCrafty store manager Gary Grabby, said and did inappropriate things to her, and it appears that Wanda may not have been alone in this regard. BCrafty has retained counsel to defend it in the likely future lawsuit. BCrafty's counsel now proposes also to represent Gary Grabby personally in the matter.

g. The situation described in **Problem 22C-3(e) at 691** (after ten years as in-house general counsel for ice-cream maker Frannie's Frozen Frolics, Rocky Rhoades is practicing on his own, and has been asked to represent Mary's Dairies in negotiating a long-term supply contract with Frannie's).

4. What's Required to Make Client Consent to a Conflict of Interest Effective?

Now let's assume that you've identified a **conflict of interest**, concluded that it is **consentable**, discussed it with the affected clients, and received indications from them that they are prepared to consent to the **conflict** and allow you (or your **practice organization**) to go ahead despite the **conflict**. (And because you're doing everything right, you haven't taken on the **conflicted** engagement yet, and won't do so until you have the proper consents in the proper form.) It's time to prepare a **conflicts** waiver. So what does one look like, and how is it done?

As we'll see in the sections that follow, there are some essential substantive requirements, and some equally essential formal requirements, for the waiver to be effective. Before we catalogue each, though, we need to stress two introductory points:

First, although some of the features we'll lay out for you are the better or best practices in which you **should** engage, most are mandatory, and thus **must** be met in order for the waiver to be effective. If *any* of the required substantive or procedural elements is omitted or insufficient, the consent is void (or voidable), the waiver doesn't count, and you have fallen into an unconsented **conflict of interest**, with all of the nasty **consequences** that follow. So it really matters that you get it right.

And *second*, the terms of a **conflicts** waiver are (within the limits the law sets) broadly negotiable. The affected client or clients **may** simply consent unconditionally, and often they will. But within the bounds of what is legally permitted, the lawyer and the client can agree to a wide range of different terms, if they choose to do so. For example, in a case in which a small number of lawyers in a **practice organization** have been exposed to **material confidential information**, the **practice organization** can agree with the client owed the **duty of confidentiality** that the knowledgeable lawyers will be **screened**, and they can agree on the details of the **screening** measures in ways that provide greater or less protection than the Rules themselves might dictate, even though any **screen** by itself (that is, without the affected clients' consent) would not have been sufficient to address the **conflict**. Similarly, in a case in which there is a **concurrent conflict**, the affected clients and the **practice organization** might agree that no single lawyer within the practice organization will work on both **conflicting** matters, a measure that, though not contemplated by any Rule, might give the client greater comfort that the client's own team of lawyers will not be distracted by **conflicting** loyalties. So long as the terms of the agreement are not against public policy, the range of possible arrangements is broad, giving parties inclined to work things out opportunities to address the situation's practical needs.

One corollary of the principle that a **conflicts** waiver **may** contain terms additional to the client's consent if the parties so agree is that (in addition to the usual imperative of clear drafting) it is important to have an understanding of what happens if a party violates the deal. For example, suppose that a **former client's** consent to a **successive conflict** includes a commitment from the **practice organization** to **screen** the knowledgeable lawyers. What happens if one of the **screened** lawyers inadvertently violates the **screen**, and the **confidential information** that the **screen** was designed to protect is "leaked" to lawyers who could use it against the consenting **former client**?

The short answer is that a **conflicts** consent with additional terms or conditions is a contract, and it will be interpreted and enforced as the law of contracts dictates. But that makes it imperative that the consent document be clear about the **consequences** of a breach—for example, does any breach, or do some particular breaches, automatically terminate or revoke the client's consent, leaving the **conflict** suddenly unconsented, and the lawyers thus subject to all available **consequences**? Or is some lesser remedy sufficient? Because the lawyer usually does the drafting in these circumstances (and for that reason the document likely will be construed against you), the completeness and clarity of any agreement is going to be up to you.

a. Substantive Requirements for an Effective Conflicts Waiver: Informed Consent, Including Full Disclosure and Explanation of All Information Necessary to Make an Informed Decision, Such as the Risks of Consent and the Client's Right to Withhold Consent

First, let's talk about what *substance* has to be in a **conflicts** waiver for the waiver to be effective. What's required is summed up in the term used in all the relevant Rules of Professional Conduct: **informed consent**. Remember, that's a defined term in the Rules, so let's review the definition and then see how it applies in this particular context. **Model Rule 1.0(e)** defines **informed consent** as "agreement by a person to a proposed course of conduct after the lawyer has communicated adequate information and explanation about the material risks of and reasonably available alternatives to the proposed course of conduct." **Model Rule 1.0 Comment [6]** elaborates: "Ordinarily, this will require communication that includes a disclosure of the facts and circumstances giving rise to the situation, any explanation reasonably necessary to inform the client or other person of the **material** advantages and disadvantages of the proposed course of conduct and a discussion of the client's or other person's options and alternatives." And, obviously, what you disclose has to be not only complete, but accurate. One **material** misrepresentation puts the validity of the entire consent at risk (and may also violate **Model Rule 4.1** and **Model Rule 8.4(c)** *and* constitute civil fraud or negligent misrepresentation).

Tips & Tactics You're not obligated to explain anything that the person from whom you're seeking consent already knows or understands, but you assume the risk that that person will end up inadequately informed (or later claim that he or she was), resulting in the consent's being invalid. **Model Rule 1.0 Comment [6]**. As a practical matter, then, the more you disclose and explain, the better protected the validity of the waiver, and the safer you and your **practice organization** will be. So the better practice is to err on the side of disclosing and explaining everything that you can imagine a reasonable client (or this particular client) might rationally consider.

Real World Lawyers nevertheless sometimes find themselves feeling reticent in these circumstances, fearing that the more that they disclose and explain, the more reasons they are supplying the client to withhold a consent that the lawyer wants and needs. Remember the **don't-wanna test**: The more that you're inclined not to disclose something because you fear it could change the client's mind, the clearer it probably is that you **must** disclose it in order for the disclosure to be complete and for the client's **consent** to be fully **informed**. **Real World**

Drafting complete and effective **conflicts** waivers is an art; the result is rarely beautiful, but it nevertheless requires real skill and attention. Bearing in mind that "[t]he communication necessary . . . will vary according to . . . the circumstances giving rise to the need to obtain **informed consent**" (**Model Rule 1.0 Comment [6]**), and that the consent that you obtain is only as good as the disclosure and explanation supporting it, an enforceable waiver **should** and arguably **must** include:

- "[T]he facts and circumstances giving rise to the situation" (**Model Rule 1.0 Comment [6]**): It's generally not enough to say simply that a **conflict of interest** has arisen (or would arise if the **practice organization** accepted a new proposed engagement); you **should** and arguably **must** explain the facts giving rise to the **conflict**, and what the **conflict** is—that is, what **interests** are in **conflict**. (This requirement is yet another reason to begin your own analysis of any potentially **conflicted** situation by asking yourself, "What's the **conflict**?")

- "[T]he material risks of . . . the proposed course of conduct" (**Model Rule 1.0(e)**): The law governing lawyers requires us to address **conflicts of interest** because they put clients' **interests** at risk. The nature and details of the risk posed by the specific **conflict** to which you seek consent **must** be disclosed. Many lawyers find themselves tempted to minimize possible risks and disadvantages—to say that there isn't really a **conflict of interest**, or that it presents no real risk, which (they then argue) is why consent can easily be granted. This is usually bad practice, and it threatens the validity of any consent that you're given.

- "[T]he . . . reasonably available alternatives to the proposed course of conduct" (**Model Rule 1.0(e)**): One alternative always available to the client is to withhold consent, which the client **may** do for any reason or no reason. Accordingly, clients **should** and arguably **must** be told that they have that right (and thus are under no obligation to grant the consent). If there are other reasonable alternatives to unconditional consent and those alternatives are not disclosed, you risk the validity of your waiver.

- "In some circumstances it may be appropriate for a lawyer to advise a client or other person to seek the advice of other counsel" regarding whether to consent (**Model Rule 1.0 Comment [6]**): If the **conflict** presents significant and unavoidable risks, it may be appropriate, or even necessary, to urge the client to seek the advice of independent counsel. In our view, a well-drafted waiver **should** almost always remind the persons from whom consent is sought that they have the right to seek any independent legal or other advice they wish and **may** take all the time they need to do so. Urging the client to actually take advantage of those rights is often wise. TIPS & TACTICS

The alert student, keeping all of us honest, points out that a proper waiver requires a lawyer to disclose quite a lot of information regarding the proposed **conflicted** engagement to which she is seeking the other client to consent. What if some of the information that **must** be disclosed is **confidential information**? After all, *anything* that the lawyer has learned from the **prospective client** in **confidence** is **confidential information**—even the simple fact that the **prospective client** has approached the lawyer and contemplated being represented in the proposed engagement. (Do you see why? Explain it out loud. *See* **Chapter 8.A at 211** if you're not sure.) Superbly acute observation, alert student, and three cheers for your making the connection between these two pieces of the course!

The short answer is that the lawyer's need for disclosure and **informed consent** in order to get an effective waiver to a **conflict of interest** is simply *not* an exception to a lawyer's **duty of confidentiality**. Of course, the client's *permission* to disclose *is* an exception to the **duty of confidentiality** (*see* **Model Rule 1.6(a)**; **Chapter 8.B at 238**), so the client who is owed the **duty of confidentiality may** always give the lawyer permission to disclose the **confidential information** necessary to obtain a properly **informed consent** to the **conflict** from the other client. But if the client "refuses to consent to the disclosure necessary to permit the other client to make an informed decision, the lawyer cannot properly ask the latter [that is, the client who needs to give **informed consent** in order for the new engagement to go forward] to consent" to the new engagement. **Model Rule 1.7 Comment [19]**. Why? Because then the lawyer is **duty**-bound *not* to provide the information necessary in order for the **consent** to be properly **informed**. And consent that is not **informed consent** is never sufficient to waive a **conflict of interest**.

i. Informed Consent Issues That Are Common in Joint Representations

Joint representations (which, we stress, are quite common for good reason and, properly documented and conducted, provide clients very significant cost savings and tactical advantages in many circumstances) often create other issues that **must** be reflected in the disclosures and **informed consent** that they virtually always require. (If you don't recall why pretty much every joint representation presents a **concurrent conflict of interest** that **must** be disclosed to and waived by each of the joint clients, *see* **Chapter 22.B at 656**.)

(A) Disclosing the Absence of Attorney-Client Privilege or Confidentiality Among the Joint Clients

One complication inherent in all joint representations arises out of the fact that, in the law of evidence and the law governing lawyers, jointly represented clients generally have no **attorney-client privilege** vis-à-vis one another and, in most jurisdictions, no right of **confidentiality** vis-à-vis one another either. Information remains **privileged** and **confidential** as to any third party outside the joint client group, but not among those within it. Thus, any information that joint counsel learns from any source in connection with the engagement, including from any joint client, **must not** be withheld from any other joint client.

Put slightly differently, joint clients have no secrets from one another, at least if they tell those secrets to their lawyer. This is a potentially significant departure from the common understanding that lawyers **must** keep their clients' secrets, and for that reason, this particular risk **must** be disclosed and explained to each of the joint clients as part of the **informed consent** that **must** be obtained from each joint client at the beginning of a joint representation. *See* **Model Rule 1.7 Comments [18], [30], [31]**.

(B) Anticipating and Disclosing the Complications That May Arise If the Joint Clients' Interests Diverge Later in the Engagement

Another issue that joint representations present is the need to anticipate, disclose, and explain the complications that may arise if the joint clients' **interests** diverge later in the engagement. Think back to the issues presented in **Problem 22B-2(a) at 665**: Maya's firm is going to represent a company (Scooter's Computers) and two of its senior managers (the Chief Financial Officer and the Regional Sales Manager) in defending claims of securities fraud that have been asserted against all three. Right now, at the beginning of the litigation, all of the **prospective clients' interests** seem fully aligned: Everyone on the defense side agrees that no one did anything wrong, and that the shared goal of all three **prospective clients** is to defeat liability and minimize damages. No **conflict** here (for now).

But what if that were not true—if, say, the company and the CFO thought that the Sales Manager had been falsifying sales records and concealing the truth from them? In that case, Maya's firm could not represent all three **prospective clients** jointly. Why? Easy: The firm would have two clients (the company and the CFO) accusing the third client (the Sales Manager) of serious wrongdoing, which the Sales Manager would deny; in representing all three clients jointly, the same lawyers would have to both blame and defend one of the joint clients (the Sales Manager). That's obviously unworkable, and this **conflict** is so serious and irremediable that the joint representation is **nonconsentable** (*see* **Model Rule 1.7(b)**; **Chapter 22.E at 740**)).

At the beginning of a typical joint representation, however, this divergence of **interests** among the proposed joint clients hasn't occurred (or hasn't yet become apparent), and maybe it never will. Right now everyone agrees about what happened and how the defense should be conducted, though that could conceivably change as the engagement proceeds and unexpected facts start to emerge. As we discussed in **Chapter 22.B at 657**, the reasonable possibility of future actual, **direct conflicts** among the joint clients that don't exist now creates a situation in which there is a "significant risk" of "**materially** limiting" the joint representation—specifically, the risk that the joint clients' **interests** later diverge so that a single **practice organization** can't effectively represent the clients jointly anymore. That potential future **conflict** among the joint clients requires disclosure and consent right now, at the outset, before any current, **direct conflict** has emerged, so that each client can decide whether to proceed with the joint representation *now*, given the risk that it might fall apart *later* and create difficulties and disruptions at that time.

Now assume that the potential future **conflict** just discussed is fully disclosed and explained, and the clients give **informed consent** (with all the proper formalities) at the beginning of the joint representation. What happens if that actual, **direct conflict** does emerge among the joint clients later? The only thing to which the joint clients consented at the beginning was that some **conflict of interest** among the joint clients *might* develop later and that, despite that risk, each client was willing to go ahead with the joint representation *for the time being*. If the potential future **conflict** becomes actual and *direct*, the situation has changed in some very important ways: Now there are new, **direct conflicts of interests** among the joint clients that **must** be addressed. Sometimes, the **conflicts** among the joint clients are manageable and can be addressed by everyone's joint consent to the changed circumstances, in which case the joint representation can continue as before with appropriate supplemental disclosures and **informed consents**. More often, however, the **conflict** among the joint clients is serious enough that the joint representation can't continue with all the joint clients (it's **nonconsentable**, or someone won't consent).

If the circumstances make joint counsel's continuing to represent all the joint clients unworkable, what happens then? Can't joint counsel simply withdraw from representing one or more of the joint clients and continue with the others? Absolutely not, or at least not without every joint client's **informed consent**. Why? Well, think about how the principles that you already know apply to this situation. You now have two or more joint clients with a **concurrent conflict of interest**. If you unilaterally drop one of those clients in order to neutralize the **conflict**, you've violated the **hot-potato rule**, and you remain subject to **disqualification** by the dropped client (*see* **Chapter 22.B at 650**). Independently and just as important, when you represented the joint client that you no longer wish to represent, you acquired **confidential information** about that client. If you drop and take any actions adverse to that client (which is inevitable, because you've reached the point at which that client's **interests** overtly and **directly conflict** with the other clients' **interests**), you are in a position to use that **confidential information** against the dropped client, and that's a classic **successive conflict of interest** that requires the dropped client's **informed consent, confirmed in writing** (*see* **Chapter 22.C at 682**). *See* **Model Rule 1.7(b); Model Rule 1.7 Comment [33]; Model Rule 1.9(a)**.

Can the situation be resolved while leaving joint counsel representing *someone*? Yes, but only with the **informed consent** of *all* of the joint clients, voluntarily given at a time when their **interests** are at war with one another. And, as you've probably already guessed, there's no guarantee that's going to happen. The joint client who's getting tossed out of the lifeboat may not feel particularly inclined to do his former counsel and former co-clients any favors and voluntarily consent to being left at sea while the others sail on as before. One or more, and possibly all, of the joint clients will have to obtain new counsel and incur the costs and possible delays of getting that counsel "up to speed." *See* **Model Rule 1.7 Comments [4], [29]**.

For these reasons, when you're disclosing and explaining the risks and potential adverse consequences of a joint representation at the beginning, you must disclose and explain not only the possibility that the joint clients' **interests** may diverge later in the engagement, but *what will happen to everyone if they do*—that if an actual, **direct conflict** among the joint clients emerges, joint counsel will have to withdraw from representing everyone in the matter unless everyone voluntarily agrees which of the joint clients that counsel may represent going forward.

ii. The Problem of the Advance Waiver

One particularly challenging **conflicts** waiver to draft effectively is the so-called "advance waiver"—that is, a consent to a **conflict of interest** that does not yet exist but that could arise in the future. The basic problem with advance waivers is that, because the **conflicts** that the client is being asked to waive haven't materialized yet, it's difficult to provide the full disclosures and explanations necessary to support **informed consent**. For example, it's difficult to describe "the facts and circumstances giving rise to" the **conflict** (**Model Rule 1.0 Comment [6]**) when you don't know what they are yet. Advance waivers of possible future **conflicts** may be useful in many different situations, but there are two common ones that we can use as examples.

(A) Example: An Advance Waiver Providing How Later-Arising Conflicts Within a Joint Representation Will Be Resolved If and When They Arise

Probably the most common situation in which an advance waiver is sought is in connection with a joint representation. As just discussed, if actual **direct conflicts of interest** materialize among joint clients as an engagement proceeds, joint counsel will have to withdraw from representing *all* the joint clients unless they can reach an agreement, at a time when their **interests** are in frank and **direct conflict**, on who stays in the jointly represented group and who gets left behind.

Can this blowout be avoided? Possibly: The consent to which the joint clients agree at the outset could *also* try to address this later-materializing problem at the beginning of the joint representation. How? Well, in addition to the disclosures and consents necessary to go ahead with the joint representation right now given the possibility of **direct conflicts of interest** among the joint clients materializing later, the initial consent could also try to anticipate and obtain the joint clients' **informed consent** as to what will happen if any future **conflict** arises—in other words, add an advance waiver.

It's not uncommon when company counsel represents company **constituents** jointly with the company in litigation (as in our Scooter's Computers securities-fraud case, **Problem 22B-2(a) at 665**) for the joint clients all to agree that, if any of the jointly represented **constituents'** interests diverge from those of the other joint clients, each **constituent** agrees, in advance, that joint counsel may withdraw from representing one or more of the joint clients while continuing with the others. Other joint representation arrangements may suggest other pre-agreed resolutions to future **conflicts**. But remember that this advance waiver requires **informed consent** by all joint clients, and it will take a lot of disclosures and explanations to be effective. Each of the consenting **constituents** needs to understand in detail the implications of possibly being dropped from the joint client group in the middle of the case (or deal). These will include (among others) the need to find new counsel, possibly under time pressure and on different economic terms, and the fact that the dropped joint client's former counsel may then take actions **directly adverse** to the dropped client's interests, possibly even including asserting claims against the dropped client in litigation, informed by **confidential information** that the dropped client imparted to that counsel while that counsel was representing him.

REAL WORLD You may be wondering why any joint client would rationally agree to such frightening terms in advance. It's a good and very important question; after all, the **consent** is only enforceable if it's voluntary and fully **informed**. The practical reason is that, usually, the joint clients really do think they're all going to stick together (and in reality, they often do). Perhaps even more important, in the common situation (like the Scooter's example) in which the company is defending itself and the accused constituents with one set of lawyers, the company is paying the bills and providing the individuals with representation free of charge. Given the cost of independent counsel, that concession is extremely valuable and important to many organizational **constituents** on the receiving end of a summons and complaint. REAL WORLD

(B) Example: The Advance "Blanket" Waiver

Another recurring instance of advance waivers sometimes sought by large law firms is referred to as a "blanket" waiver. Because of the sheer number of clients that they represent across many lawyers and offices, large law firms with national or international presence regularly find themselves asked to undertake new matters against existing clients in matters unrelated to the substance of the existing client's engagement. This is, of course, a classic **concurrent conflict**. (Do you see why? Check **Model Rule 1.7(a)(1)** and **Chapter 22.B at 646** if you're not sure.) In an effort to be available to as many clients as they reasonably can, some of these firms routinely ask new clients to consent, in advance, to the firm's representing other clients against the new client in the future so long as the new matter is not **substantially related** to the firm's representation of the new client (and thus puts no **confidential information** at risk).

Notice what this request involves: Often at the time of the request, the new client has not yet been represented by the large firm. There would not currently be any **conflicts of interest** created if the large firm took on the new client as a client.

The situation that the advance waiver contemplates is one in which, at some as-yet unidentified time in the future, the large firm will take on an engagement for some as-yet unidentified client in suing or negotiating against the new client in some as-yet unidentified matter limited only by the fact that the future matter against the new client will not involve the new client's **confidential information**.[49] The future adverse matter could be modest, but it could just as easily be huge and existentially threatening. And if and when that happens at some future point, the large firm will not need to ask the new client to consent at that time, because the client has *already* consented, in advance, to the **conflicted** engagement. In fact, the "blanket" waiver may include a waiver of the new client's right even to be *informed* of the new engagement against it.

REAL WORLD   You may again be wondering why a client would voluntarily agree to such terms. Again, there are practical reasons. The new client remains free to withhold the requested consent, but the law firm remains equally free to decline to represent the new client unless the new client consents. The dynamics are entirely, and perhaps brutally, pragmatic: If the new client's engagement is big and lucrative enough, the large firm may be willing to proceed without the blanket waiver and risk being **conflicted** out of some future engagements. If the large firm has some special skill or expertise that the client particularly wants or needs, the blanket waiver may be the price that the client has to pay to get access to it.   REAL WORLD

(C) Obtaining Enforceable Informed Consent to an Advance Waiver

How do you make advance waivers enforceable? The Model Rules and consistent state **disqualification** law generally allow advance waivers, but with particular attention to the adequacy of the **informed consent**; that is, to the adequacy of the disclosures and explanations that ground and define the advance waiver. **Model Rule 1.7 Comment [22]** provides some guidelines for when client consent to an advance waiver will be sufficiently **informed** to be enforceable:

> The effectiveness of [advance] waivers is generally determined by the extent to which the client reasonably understands the **material** risks that the waiver entails. The more comprehensive the explanation of the types of future representations that might arise and the actual and reasonably foreseeable adverse consequences of those representations, the greater the likelihood that the client will have the requisite understanding. Thus, if the client agrees to consent to a particular type of **conflict** with which the client

---

[49] To be clear, it is theoretically possible that the large firm could try to ask the new client to consent, in advance, to *any* future adverse engagement, even one in which the lawyers were in a position to use the client's **confidential information** against it. As a practical matter, large firms rarely (if ever) request a consent so sweeping, both because well-advised clients would refuse to agree to it and because its enforceability would be doubtful, given the firm's inability to give the new client some sense of what **confidential information** would be at risk in that future engagement, resulting in what most courts would consider inadequate supporting disclosure, leading to a lack of adequately **informed consent**.

is already familiar, then the consent ordinarily will be effective with regard to that type of **conflict**. If the consent is general and open-ended, then the consent ordinarily will be ineffective, because it is not reasonably likely that the client will have understood the **material** risks involved. On the other hand, if the client is an experienced user of the legal services involved and is reasonably informed regarding the risk that a **conflict** may arise, such consent is more likely to be effective, particularly if, e.g., the client is independently represented by other counsel in giving consent and the consent is limited to future **conflicts** unrelated to the subject of the representation. In any case, advance consent cannot be effective if the circumstances that materialize in the future are such as would make the **conflict nonconsentable** under [**Model Rule 1.7(b)**].

TIPS & TACTICS We quoted this Comment at length because it provides important guidance on advance waivers. Please pause and read it again carefully. As a practical matter, what the Comment suggests is that the more that a later-materializing **conflict** looks like something that you warned about in your advance waiver or that you can persuasively argue that this particular client's sophistication would have led the client to anticipate, the more likely it is that a court considering **disqualification** will find that the advance waiver supplies **informed consent** to the currently emerging **conflict**. Ironically, one thing that this general principle suggests is that the more general and sweeping the terms of your advance waiver, the *less* likely it is to withstand scrutiny when consent actually matters later, because sweeping generalities often don't give clients a clear enough idea of what they may be letting themselves in for.

The general lesson? Although you usually want to include some generalities in your descriptions of possible future **conflicts** to try and capture the less expected ones, you **should** think long and hard about the kinds of **interest**-divergences or other **conflicts** that you consider most plausibly might materialize and the risks and downsides that they present. Describe those risks and downsides in real detail, in particular the kinds of potential future conduct adverse to the client's **interests** that you are asking her to consent to in advance. When that adversity could involve the assertion of claims or defenses, or other **directly adverse** action against the client in litigation (such as cross-examination, propounding discovery, or making arguments adverse to the consenting client's **interests**), many courts will not enforce a waiver that does not directly warn of this possibility. Remember, the waiver is only as good as your disclosure. **TIPS & TACTICS**

b. Formal Requirements for an Effective Conflicts Waiver: The Disclosure and Consent Must Be Confirmed in Writing and Should Be Made in a Writing Signed by the Client

Now that we have a general understanding of the substance of the disclosures and consents necessary to address a **conflict of interest**, let's discuss the formalities. All of the Rules of Professional Conduct discussing waiver as a means of addressing a **conflict of interest** describe that waiver as **informed consent, confirmed in writing**. See **Model Rule 1.7(b)**; **Model Rule 1.9(a), (b)**; **Model Rule 1.10(c)**; **Model Rule 1.18(c), (d)(1)**. State law governing **disqualification** generally takes the same approach as that state's Rules.

The "**informed consent**" part tells you what the client has to know and understand before consenting, which was addressed in the preceding sections. But the Rules require formalities as well: Most states require the **informed consent** to be **confirmed in writing**. Your House; Your Rules A few states require **conflicts** waivers to be in **a writing signed by the client** which, as discussed below, is the better practice in any event. Your House; Your Rules The formalities are tremendously important, because the general rule is that if you didn't get the waiver in the proper form and manner, it doesn't count.

Confirmed in writing is a term defined in **Model Rule 1.0(b)** and "denotes **informed consent** that is given in writing by the person [consenting] or a writing that a lawyer promptly transmits to the person [consenting] confirming an oral informed consent." Two things are reasonably clear from the definitions of **informed consent** and **confirmed in writing**: One is that, although a client's consent may be inferred from conduct, "[o]btaining informed consent will usually require an affirmative response by the client or other person. In general, a lawyer may not assume consent from a client's or other person's silence." **Model Rule 1.0 Comment [7]**. The other is, for the client's consent to be "**informed**" and thus effective, the consent must be given "*after* the lawyer has communicated adequate information and explanation about the **material** risks of and reasonably available alternatives to the proposed course of conduct." **Model Rule 1.0(e)**. Consent given before disclosure and explanation is no consent at all.

Much less clear from the Rule's definitions or any Comment informing them is any clarification about whether the only thing that has to be **confirmed in writing** (or for that matter **in a writing signed by the client**) is the client's *consent* ("I agree to allow counsel to go forward notwithstanding the **conflict of interest**"), or whether the writing also must include the disclosures and explanations that make the client's consent **informed**. The practical significance of the difference is great. Though you **must** supply the disclosures and explanations to the client under either interpretation, under one interpretation you may do so only orally, and then **confirm** the client's **informed consent in writing** by confirming in writing only the client's consent by sending an email afterwards, saying (for example), "This will confirm that this afternoon, in our meeting, I explained to you in detail a **conflict of interest** that has arisen in your engagement, and after that explanation, you consented to go forward with our continuing to represent you, despite the **conflict of interest**. Thank you for your confidence in us." Under the other interpretation, all of the necessary disclosures and explanations discussed above, as well as the consent, must be in the writing too, or it's as if the disclosures and explanations never occurred.

TIPS & TACTICS Regardless of what the law may be in this regard (authority is sparse), the much better (and widely followed) practice is to put everything in a writing and to obtain the client's signature on that writing after answering all of her questions—and giving her the time to seek any other, independent advice that she may wish. The reason is that many **conflicts** waivers require detailed and extended disclosure and explanation in order to be enforceable. It's too easy for clients to fail to appreciate the significance of some part of the explanation (or later disclaim that they did), putting your waiver—and the viability of your continued engagements—at risk. You've heard it before: When in doubt, speak out; then **inquire; explain; confirm** (*see* **Chapter 6.A at 139**). It couldn't be better advised here. TIPS & TACTICS

> **Problem 22E-2:** Take a careful look at the **conflicts** waiver that Ron Rainmaker proposes to send to the general counsel of Petrified Petroleum in the **Introduction to this subchapter at 733**.
>
> a. What defects, if any, do you see in the *formalities* (that is, in the process by and the form in which the consent will be obtained) that Ron proposes in order to obtain Petrified's consent to the **conflict of interest**? How (if at all) would you advise him to adjust his course of action to address any possible *formal* infirmities?
>
> b. What defects, if any, do you see in the *substance* of the disclosures that Ron makes in his proposed email to support the consent that he seeks? How (if at all) would you advise him to change his email to address any possible substantive infirmities?

> **Problem 22E-3:** Go back and re-examine each of the situations described in **Problem 22E-1 at 740**. For each of those situations in which you conclude that the **conflict of interest** described is **consentable**, describe in bullet-point fashion each of the facts and risks that you conclude that you **must** or **should** disclose to the affected client or clients in order to obtain a properly **informed consent**.

> **Problem 22E-4:** For each of the situations described in **Problem 22E-1 at 740** that involves a joint representation, explain why you would or would not include, in addition to the waiver necessary to proceed at the outset of the engagement, given the possible future **conflicts of interest** among two or more of the joint clients, an advance waiver addressing what will happen if any actual **conflict of interest** later materializes. Describe the future solution to which you would want the advance waiver to provide consent and why you consider it the better or best solution. What additional disclosures or explanations would your proposed solution in each case make necessary or advisable?

F. TIPS & TACTICS How to See Conflicts of Interest Coming

After all that discussion on **conflicts of interest**, several things should be clear:

■ Any **practice organization**, from a one-lawyer solo practice to a megafirm to an in-house law department to a government agency, can and will have **conflicts of interest**.

■ Failure to avoid or properly address a **conflict of interest** will have serious and costly **consequences**.

■ Legally and practically effective management of **conflicts** requires timely action—before (or at the latest, promptly after) the **conflict's** development. By the time someone outside your **practice organization** brings a **conflict of interest** up with you, it's often too late to avoid some real ugliness.

So keeping your eyes open and being able to see these kinds of issues coming is the best—and usually the only—way to stay out of ethical and legal harm's way.

The Rules of Professional Conduct and state **disqualification** law both impose a duty on lawyers to anticipate **conflicts of interest** and to manage them proactively. "Resolution of a **conflict of interest** problem . . . requires the lawyer to: 1) clearly identify the client or clients; 2) determine whether a **conflict of interest** exists; 3) decide whether the representation may be undertaken despite the existence of a **conflict**, i.e., whether the conflict is **consentable**; and 4) if so, consult with the clients affected . . . and obtain their **informed consent, confirmed in writing**." **Model Rule 1.7 Comment [2]**. **Model Rule 1.7 Comment [3]** further cautions:

> To determine whether a **conflict of interest** exists, a lawyer **should** adopt reasonable procedures, appropriate for the size and type of firm and practice, to determine in both litigation and non-litigation matters the persons and issues involved. . . . Ignorance caused by a failure to institute such procedures will not excuse a lawyer's violation of this Rule.

Similarly, **Model Rule 5.1 Comment [2]** makes clear that the "internal policies and procedures" that lawyers with managerial duties in a **practice organization** are obligated to establish and maintain (*see* **Chapter 19.C at 514**) "include those designed to detect and resolve **conflicts of interest** . . . ."

REAL WORLD Almost all law graduates' first practice jobs will be with an existing **practice organization**. Your employer will almost certainly have policies and procedures in place for things like recognizing and responding to **conflicts of interest**, calendaring deadlines, preserving and organizing client information, and so on. You should make a point of understanding right away how those policies and procedures work and of using them to the extent that your responsibilities call for it. If you discover that your **practice organization** doesn't have basic office systems for **conflicts** checking, calendaring, and the like, you should very seriously consider not going to work there. The managers of such an **organization** are already in violation of their **duty to manage** under **Model Rule 5.1**. If they are disregarding as basic a duty as **conflicts** checking or calendaring, they are probably compromising other important duties as well. They will likely prove to be ineffective practice models and supervisors, and the **organization** itself is a professional responsibility disaster waiting to happen. Don't get entangled. While no job or workplace is perfect, some jobs really are worse than no job. REAL WORLD

But let's assume that you've landed in a reasonably well-organized and well-regulated **practice organization**. How do its "procedures . . . designed to detect and resolve **conflicts of interest**" typically work? Well, they all start with some way of keeping track of every person or organization to whom any person in the **practice organization** owes duties. In the digital age, virtually every practice organization uses computer software of some kind for this purpose. There are numerous commercial software products specifically designed to help **practice organizations** keep track of and use **conflicts** information. There's no literal requirement that you use any of them; they're just a lot faster, easier, and more reliable, and whatever you do instead needs to be comparably good. But one way or another, a **practice organization must** have systematic procedures to detect and respond to **conflicts of interest**. No matter how small or simple you may believe your practice to be, trying to keep it all in your head and searching your memory, if and when you remember to do so, is most definitely *not* what the Rules have in mind.

What goes into your **conflicts** database? Every **practice organization** varies the information it keeps in its **conflicts** database to some degree to reflect the nature of its practice. **Practice organizations** that regularly represent other lawyers or **practice organizations** as clients, for example, tend to keep track of the identity of all the lawyers involved in their engagements as counsel, because they might find themselves having to take action **directly adverse** to opposing counsel, who might be a client. *See* **Chapter 22.A at 626; Problems 22B-1(h)-(i) at 654.**

Nevertheless, there is a range of information that virtually all responsible **practice organizations** keep track of. In broad outline, it includes information from every contact between your **practice organization** and the outside world that results in anyone within your **organization** owing anyone else a professional duty. For any potential new matter, that includes the names of any people or organizations whose interests could be **materially** affected by the potential new engagement, along with a description of their relation to the matter and to your **organization**—for example, a client, an adverse party, or a **materially** interested party who may not be one of your clients or directly adverse to them. The same information **must** be recorded any time that your **practice organization** has contact with a **prospective client**, because the involved lawyers and the **organization** owe such **prospective clients duties of confidentiality** "[e]ven when no client-lawyer relationship ensues." **Model Rule 1.18(b); Chapter 8.A at 207.** And this information must be added not only from potential new matters, but from other sources of professional or fiduciary duties—for example, if a lawyer in your **organization** sits on the board of directors of a nonprofit (or for-profit) organization, or acts as a trustee, executor, or other fiduciary. *See* **Model Rule 1.7 Comment [9].**

The database must also include a brief description of the substance of the matter or potential matter and the individual lawyers involved. Why? Because when you're determining whether your **duties of confidentiality** to a **former client** or **prospective client** create a **successive conflict of interest**, you have to determine whether you have **material**

confidential information from your prior contact—that is, **substantially related confidential information** that can be used against the **former** or **prospective client** in the new engagement. And that requires you to know the subject matter of the prior engagement or earlier proposed engagement so that you can determine what's **substantially related** to it. *See* **Chapter 22.C at 684**. You also may need to get more information to make your determination, so knowing which individual lawyers in your **practice organization** know about the contact is essential, especially in an **organization** of any size.

You also have to keep your **conflicts** database updated. New parties enter cases and deals all the time; third-party discovery in litigation is often **directly adverse** to the third party. In short, the **conflicts** profile of any matter continues to evolve until it's completely over. And your **conflicts** database is only as protective and useful as it is complete and up-to-date.

All that said, despite every reasonable effort, no **practice organization's conflicts** database is ever absolutely complete. Why? Because the kinds of personal **interests** that can create "significant risk" of "material limitation" **conflicts** include such connections as close personal relationships and family relations (*see* **Model Rule 1.7(a)(2)**; **Chapter 22.A at 626**), which hardly any real-world **conflicts** databases track. The good news is that these kinds of personal-**interest conflicts** are (as the name suggests) *personal* to the lawyer involved, and that lawyer is usually in a good position to recognize the issue (hey—opposing counsel is my spouse!) and alert the **practice organization** so that it can be dealt with.

Now that you know that every responsible **practice organization** has a **conflicts** database of some kind, let's discuss how it's used. Every time that someone in the **practice organization** interacts with a **prospective client**, or a new party enters a case or deal, you do a **conflicts** check—you query your database and see if any of the people and organizations **materially** interested in your matter match the names of any people or organizations with which your **practice organization** has dealt before. If there are any matches (often referred to as "hits"), you must determine whether your **practice organization's** prior dealings with the person or organization identified in the database hit create a **conflict of interest**.

Often, they don't: For example, your **conflicts** check may show that a party to whom your client is adverse in your proposed new matter has been adverse to the same or some different client of your **practice organization** before. That's not a **conflict of interest**—the Rules generally allow you to act adversely to the same party as many times as your clients wish, simultaneously or serially. (Do you see why?) Of course, the fact that you know that your **practice organization** has been adverse to this party before allows you to consult the involved lawyers and the file from the older matter, and see if your **practice organization** learned anything last time that would be useful this time (and that you can use without disadvantaging your **former client** in the earlier matter, *see* **Chapter 8.A at 217**). So **conflicts** checking is not only good (and necessary) legal ethics; it's good lawyering.

Sometimes, your **conflicts** check uncovers something that might be a **conflict of interest**. The database hit may require more investigation on your part to determine whether **substantially related confidential information** of a **former** or **prospective client** is at risk, or whether someone your potential client is adverse to is still a **current client**. If you determine that a **conflict** is presented, you must decide how to address it: Abstain from (stay out of) the new engagement? Implement an **ethical screen,** if the Rules allow one, to address the **conflict**? Seek the affected clients' **informed consent**, and confirm it **in writings signed by the clients** (the better practice)? There are often many potential paths, and deciding which ones to pursue and how to pursue them can be complex judgments.

Finally, *when* **must** you do all this? When possible (and it is almost always possible, the only exception being a new engagement so drastically urgent there is literally no time to do a **conflicts** check), *before* accepting any new engagement. The timing is critical. If you do your **conflicts** checking and assessment *before* agreeing to represent a new client (or an existing client in a new matter), you will always have the option of abstaining from the new engagement and avoiding any **conflict** that it might have created. Because the existence of an attorney-client relationship depends on the client's reasonable and actual understanding, it's up to you to make it clear to the **prospective client** that you are *not* taking on the proposed engagement until you have checked for **conflicts** (and also fully and accurately documented the terms of the new engagement **in a writing signed by the client**).

> REAL WORLD Your pleasure at the compliment of being offered new work and your normal entrepreneurial drive may prompt you to convey that you've accepted an engagement well before you should. Be aware of this temptation and avoid it. If the **prospective client** reasonably believes that you're his lawyer, then you are. *See* **Chapter 9.A at 261**. If you then discover that the new engagement creates a **conflict of interest**, your options for addressing it are much more constrained than they would have been if you had known before accepting the engagement. *See* **Chapter 22.E at 736**. You may need to try and withdraw from the new engagement immediately after accepting it. You also may be forced to withdraw from another ongoing engagement that, you should have known, created the **conflict**. That will not endear you to the other client, and if it imposes monetary costs on that client, you may be liable for them. (Do you see why? Explain it out loud.)

Any client experienced with lawyers will understand the necessity of a **conflicts** check before starting work, and any client unfamiliar enough with lawyers not to be aware of the need should understand your explanation. A **prospective client** who cannot wait for a **conflicts** check and an engagement letter and is not in the midst of an obvious, hair-on-fire emergency is showing you a "red flag" warning of future similarly unreasonable demands and cautioning you to stay away. In every respect, forewarned is forearmed. REAL WORLD TIPS & TACTICS

Big-Picture Takeaways from Chapter 22.E.-F

1. You can *avoid* a **conflict** of interest by abstaining from (staying out of) the **conflicted** engagement: No **conflict**; no **consequences**. *See* **Chapter 22.E at 736**.

2. You can abstain from a **conflicted** engagement only if you never took it on. Once the **prospective client** reasonably believes you are his lawyer, you are. If the new engagement is **conflicted**, you then **must** withdraw. Unlike the result if you had properly abstained from the **conflicted** new engagement, you likely will be forced to withdraw from *all* engagements creating the **conflict of interest**, unless all affected clients provide **informed consent, confirmed in writing**, as to which engagements will continue and on what terms. *See* **Chapter 22.E at 737**.

3. You can *address* a **conflict** in one of two ways: (a) by determining that the situation is one in which your **practice organization** can rebut the presumption of **imputation** and staff the matter with lawyers who are not personally **disqualified**, or (b) if the **conflict** is **consentable**, by obtaining all affected clients' **informed consent** in the form and substance required by the Rules (and any parallel state law governing **disqualification**). If you have proper client consent, then you and your **practice organization may** proceed with what otherwise would have been a **conflicted** engagement, without **consequences**, according to whatever terms you and the affected clients have agreed. *See* **Chapter 22.E at 738**.

4. Although most **conflicts of interest may** be addressed by client consent, some cannot be. The limits of client consent are set out in **Model Rule 1.7(b) and Model Rule 1.8**. The Rules enumerate four different kinds of **nonconsentable conflicts**:
   a. When "the representation is . . . prohibited by law" (**Model Rule 1.7(b)(2)**).
   b. When the **conflict** is one of the personal-**interest conflicts** addressed in **Model Rule 1.8**.
   c. When the "the representation . . . involve[s] the assertion of a claim by one client against another client represented by the lawyer in the same . . . proceeding before a tribunal" (**Model Rule 1.7(b)(3)**).
   d. When "the lawyer [does not] reasonably believe[] that the lawyer will be able to provide competent and diligent representation to each affected client" (**Model Rule 1.7(b)(1)**). The lawyer **must** subjectively believe that the lawyer can handle the **conflict** appropriately, and that belief **must** be objectively reasonable. If no reasonable client would consent, then any belief is objectively unreasonable, and the **conflict** is **nonconsentable**.
   See **Chapter 22.E at 739**.

5. In order for a waiver to be effective, all affected clients must give not just consent, but **informed consent**. In this context, an enforceable waiver **should** and arguably **must** include detailed disclosure of all of the following:
   a. "[T]he facts and circumstances giving rise to the situation" (**Model Rule 1.0 Comment [6]**).

    b. "[T]he material risks of . . . the proposed course of conduct" (**Model Rule 1.0(e)**).

    c. "[T]he . . . reasonably available alternatives to the proposed course of conduct (**Model Rule 1.0(e)**), including (among others) the client's right to refuse consent.

    d. "In some circumstances it may be appropriate for a lawyer to advise a client or other person to seek the advice of other counsel" (**Model Rule 1.0 Comment [6]**).

  See **Chapter 22.E at 743**.

6. Joint representations create other issues that **must** be reflected in the disclosures and **informed consent** that they virtually always require. One of the issues that joint representations present arises out of the fact that, in the law of evidence and the law governing lawyers, jointly represented clients have no **attorney-client privilege** vis-à-vis one another and, in most jurisdictions, no right of **confidentiality** vis-à-vis one another either. *See* **Chapter 22.E at 745**. An additional issue that must be addressed in joint representations is the need to anticipate the complications that may arise if the joint clients' **interests** diverge later in the engagement. *See* **Chapter 22.E at 746**.

7. **Model Rule 1.7 Comment [22]** provides some guidelines for when an advance waiver will be enforceable: "The effectiveness of [advance] waivers is generally determined by the extent to which the client reasonably understands the **material** risks that the waiver entails." This will typically require a description of the nature of the **conflict** that materializes later for the advance waiver to be sufficient to address that **conflict**. *See* **Chapter 22.E at 750**.

8. Most states require the **informed consent** to a **conflict of interest** to be **confirmed in writing**. A few states require **conflicts** waivers to be **in a writing signed by the client**, which is the better practice, and should be followed whenever possible. Although a client's consent may be inferred from conduct, "[o]btaining informed consent will usually require an affirmative response by the client or other person. In general, a lawyer may not assume consent from a client's or other person's silence." **Model Rule 1.0 Comment [7]**. In addition, for the client's consent to be "**informed**" and thus effective, the consent must be given "*after* the lawyer has communicated adequate information and explanation about the **material** risks of and reasonably available alternatives to the proposed course of conduct." **Model Rule 1.0(e)** (emphasis added). Consent given before disclosure and explanation is no consent at all. *See* **Chapter 22.E at 751**.

9. **Practice organizations must** maintain policies, procedures, and systems for recognizing and responding to **conflicts of interest**. Those procedures

typically require the **practice organization** to assess the possibility that a new engagement may create **conflicts of interest** *before* the **organization** agrees to take on the new engagement. **Conflicts**-checking systems typically keep track of every interaction between the **practice organization** and the outside world that may have created professional duties the **practice organization** or any of its lawyers owes to anyone. Any potential new engagement and the persons or organizations involved **must** be checked against this **conflicts** database to see if any of the duties the **practice organization** already owes may **conflict** with the duties that would be created by taking on the new engagement. *See* **Chapter 22.F at 753**.

Multiple-Choice Review Questions for Chapter 22.E-.F

1. Maru and Neo have been charged as co-defendants in a robbery case filed in the United States District Court for the District of Raptor. According to the indictment filed by the Assistant United States Attorney, Maru and Neo together conspired to rob a federally chartered bank. According to the prosecution, Maru planned the heist and drove the getaway vehicle, but Neo was the one who went into the bank and demanded money from the bank teller. The two were arrested a few blocks away from the bank and a single gun was found in the car.

   Maru and Neo meet with a lawyer, Oscar. For several decades, Oscar had been an Assistant United States Attorney before he became a solo practitioner defending criminal cases.

   Maru and Neo express their interest in having Oscar represent them both, to save on defense costs. Oscar later meets with Maru and Neo separately.

   During their meeting, Maru tells Oscar that he knew nothing about the robbery. "It was all Neo," Maru says "He told me he was running in to cash a check. I had no idea about the robbery until afterwards. The gun was his."

   Oscar then meets with Neo. Neo explains, "The whole plan was Maru's. I didn't want to rob the bank but he threatened to kill me if I didn't. He had a gun so I did what he said."

   May Oscar represent both Maru and Neo?
   a. Yes, so long as the prosecution consents.
   b. Yes, because both Maru and Neo have a mutual **interest** in arguing that the prosecution failed to meet its burden of proof.
   c. No, because Maru's and Neo's **interests** will **conflict** due to the discrepancies between their versions of the facts.
   d. No, because Oscar has a **conflict of interest** due to his former employment.

2. Peyton is driving her car on the highway when she is suddenly rear-ended by a car driven by Ron. At the time of the accident, Peyton's husband Quade is in the passenger seat. Both Peyton and Quade are injured, and their car is totaled. Peyton's injuries are more severe than Quade's are. Quade suffered only minor whiplash, but Peyton suffered a concussion and dislocated her shoulder.

   A few weeks after the accident, Peyton and Quade go to see Shiva, a lawyer. They ask Shiva whether she would be willing to represent them both in litigation against Ron. Shiva interviews them both, and they tell similar versions of the story; however, Peyton does not remember braking before the collision, and Quade recalls that she hit the brakes a few seconds before the impact.

   May Shiva represent Peyton and Quade?
   a. Yes, because their **interests** are generally aligned. Shiva **must** explain the implications of joint representation and get **informed consent, confirmed in writing** from both Peyton and Quade.
   b. Yes, because they will both be plaintiffs in the litigation and therefore will have perfectly aligned interests. Shiva is only prohibited from representing Ron, who will be the defendant and whose interests will be adverse.
   c. No, because their **interests** are generally adverse. Quade's version of events suggests that Peyton may be partially at fault for the accident.
   d. No, because although they will both be plaintiffs, they are not similarly situated. Peyton will be entitled to a larger share of damages because her injuries are more extensive.

3. Cleo is currently representing the restaurant Tequilaville in an intellectual property dispute with a rival restaurant, Tacotown. Tequilaville claims that Tacotown copied Tequilaville's decor for its restaurants and that, as a result, there is a likelihood of consumer confusion. Cleo files a trade dress complaint on behalf of Tequilaville in the Commonwealth of Keystone. She argues that its red, yellow, and orange décor is distinctive and unique to Tequilaville.

   Unbeknown to Cleo, Tacotown owns one restaurant in the neighboring State of Raptor, but its restaurant in Raptor is called Burritoborough.

   The general manager of Burritoborough asks Cleo to represent Burritoborough in filing for protection of its trade dress for Burritoborough. She agrees. She files an application to register Burritoborough's trade dress with the United States Patent and Trademark Office. In the application, she argues that its red, yellow, and orange décor is distinctive and unique to Burritoborough.

Cleo realizes that Burritoborough and Tacotown are owned by the same company only after she files the application. What should Cleo do?

  a. Decline to represent Burritoborough in any future cases but finish the work related to the pending application before the USPTO.

  b. Withdraw from representing Burritoborough before the USPTO and withdraw from representing Tequilaville in the district-court litigation.

  c. Withdraw from representing Tequilaville and instead represent Tacotown in the Keystone litigation.

  d. Nothing; there is no actual or potential **conflict of interest** here.

4. Same as Question 3, except that Burritoborough and Tacotown are owned by companies that are completely unrelated to each other or to Tequilaville, and Burritoborough has just approached Cleo and asked her to assist it in filing the application to register its trade dress. What should Cleo do?

  a. Accept the Burritoborough engagement. Because Burritoborough and Tacotown are owned by companies that are unrelated to each other, Cleo would have no **concurrent conflict of interest** in representing Tequilaville in the trademark suit against Tacotown and representing Burritoborough in its registration application.

  b. Accept the Burritoborough engagement if Tequilaville and Burritoborough each give **informed consent, confirmed in writing**.

  c. Decline the Burritoborough engagement unless Tacotown gives **informed consent, confirmed in writing**.

  d. Decline the Burritoborough engagement. Tequilaville and Burritoborough have a **nonconsentable concurrent conflict of interest**.

5. Under **Model Rule 1.7**, can a client waive a **concurrent conflict of interest** when there is **direct adversity** between two **current clients**?

  a. Yes, if one of the two **directly adverse** clients gives **informed consent, confirmed in writing**.

  b. Yes, if both of the **directly adverse** clients give **informed consent, confirmed in writing**.

  c. No, even if both clients give **informed consent, confirmed in writing**.

  d. No, even if the lawyer gives **informed consent, confirmed in writing**.

6. Amity and Buzz are a married couple who meet with lawyer Chuck and ask him to draft their wills. Chuck agrees to do so, and the couple leaves. A few days later, before Chuck has finished the work, he receives a phone call from Buzz. Buzz explains that he, Buzz, has been having an affair, that Amity knows nothing about it, and that he has a child with his paramour about whom Amity also does not know. Buzz asks Chuck to keep their conversation a secret from Amity.

Chuck realizes that this information is critical and that there now may be **conflicts of interest** between Amity and Buzz that Chuck did not previously anticipate. Among other things, if Buzz dies before Amity, Buzz's illegitimate child may challenge aspects of Buzz's will, or Buzz's illegitimate child may inherit parts of the marital estate that Amity would not have agreed to had she known the child existed when the wills were drafted. The child may also seek support while Buzz is alive, thereby depleting some of the marital assets.

Would it be proper for Chuck to nonetheless draft the wills for Amity and Buzz, as he initially agreed to do?

    a. Yes. This is not a litigation matter, so Amity and Buzz will never be adverse.

    b. Yes, if both Amity and Buzz provide **informed consent, confirmed in writing** after being informed of the **conflicts of interest** that can arise in dual representation.

    c. No, because Buzz is dishonest, and any will that Chuck drafts will be against Amity's interests. Chuck cannot take action in favor of one client to the detriment of another. The **conflict of interest** between the spouses is **nonconsentable**.

    d. Maybe, but doing so would require Chuck to get **informed consent, confirmed in writing,** from both spouses. That **informed consent** would require Chuck to disclose to Amity the existence of Buzz's illegitimate child and its implications for their joint estate plan before she consented.

7. Lawyer Perry is a solo practitioner in the Commonwealth of Keystone. He represents Queenie, a plaintiff in a civil rights case who claims that an unidentified Federal Bureau of Investigation agent used excessive force during an arrest, dislocating Queenie's arm. As is allowed for this type of case, the named defendant is referred to in Queenie's complaint as "John Doe," because neither Perry nor Queenie knows the identity of the agent.

In discovery during Queenie's case, Perry learns that the agent is Roy. Perry is currently representing Roy in a wrongful termination case in which Roy claims that the FBI improperly fired him. As part of this litigation, Perry has learned significant information about Roy's discipline record at the FBI, including the fact that Roy had been accused of excessive force twice before the incident involving Queenie occurred. Perry has been representing Roy for two years. He only began representing Queenie six months ago.

What **must** Perry do?

    a. Withdraw from representing Queenie, because her representation was more recent.

    b. Withdraw from representing Roy, because he is less likely to prevail in his case.

    c. Withdraw from representing both Queenie and Roy as soon as possible.

    d. Continue to represent Queenie and Roy, but refrain from using any information from one case in the other.

8. Morris is a general contractor who does commercial projects all over the city of Grittydelphia. He usually retains lawyer Lori, who practices at a large local law firm, to handle any construction disputes in which Morris becomes involved. Lori is currently litigating a dispute on behalf of Morris relating to his work on an elementary school. Another partner at Lori's firm, Nicole, has been asked to represent Orin, who is negotiating to purchase a used crane from Morris. Morris has hired counsel from a different firm to handle the sale of the crane. Can Nicole represent Orin in the purchase of the crane?

    a. Yes, because the purchase of the crane and elementary school construction case are unrelated.

    b. Yes, because Lori is handling the construction dispute and Nicole will handle the purchase of the crane.

    c. No, because this would create a **direct conflict of interest** that cannot be waived.

    d. No, unless both Morris and Nicole give **informed consent, confirmed in writing**.

9. Jenny is a patent attorney at a large law firm. She has several clients with existing patents on medical devices, including Nuts'n'Bolts, Inc., a manufacturer of bone screws. Last year, she helped Nuts'n'Bolts patent its best-selling titanium bone screw. She is currently assisting Nuts'n'Bolts in securing a patent for an unrelated device.

    Jenny is approached by a potential new client, Screwy Co. Screwy is developing a bone screw and is nearing the time when it would be ready to patent it. Screwy asks Jenny if she would be willing to research all other bone screws and assist Screwy in drafting a patent that will avoid infringing on the existing patents, including the one held by Nuts'n'Bolts.

    Jenny sees a potential **conflict**. Which of the following may she safely do without revealing **confidential information**?

    a. Inform Screwy that she represents Nuts'n'Bolts. Disclose to Screwy **confidential information** that she learned while representing Nuts'n'Bolts to discourage Screwy from infringing on Nuts'n'Bolts's patent.

    b. Inform Nuts'n'Bolts that she will be representing Screwy. Provide sufficient time for Nuts'n'Bolts to secure other counsel before beginning the work for Screwy.

    c. Inform Screwy that she represents Nuts'n'Bolts. Seek Screwy's permission to disclose information to Nuts'n'Bolts so that she can seek **informed consent** from Nuts'n'Bolts.

    d. Inform Nuts'n'Bolts that she may seek to represent Screwy. Disclose information to Nuts'n'Bolts about Screwy's patent so that Nuts'n'Bolts can give **informed consent**.

10. Naima represents two co-defendants in a medical malpractice case, Dr. Kirk and Dr. Peters. Prior to beginning the engagement, both clients were duly informed of possible future **conflicts** and gave **informed consent** to the joint representation, **confirmed in writing**, after consulting with independent counsel.

    Things were going well until Dr. Kirk's deposition. During the deposition, Dr. Kirk unexpectedly blamed Dr. Peters for the alleged malpractice. What **must** or **may** Naima do now?

    a. Naima **may** continue representing Dr. Kirk or Dr. Peters, but not both.

    b. Nama **may** continue representing Dr. Kirk or Dr. Peters if the client getting continuing representation from Naima provides **informed consent, confirmed in writing**.

    c. Naima **may** continue to represent both doctors if each provides **informed consent, confirmed in writing**.

    d. Naima **must** withdraw from representing both doctors unless each client gives **informed consent, confirmed in writing**, to Naima's continuing to represent one client and not the other.

11. Same facts as Question 10, but after the deposition Dr. Peters, furious at being stabbed in the back by Dr. Kirk, "revoked" his consent to the joint representation and demanded that Naima withdraw from representing Dr. Kirk and continue representing Dr. Peters alone. What **must** or **may** Naima do in response? (*Hint: See* **Model Rule 1.7 Comment [21]**.)

    a. If Dr. Peters does not want Naima to represent him, he **may** discharge her.

    b. Naima **may** withdraw from representing Dr. Kirk (and continue representing Dr. Peters) unless there would be a **material** detriment to Dr. Kirk if Naima withdrew.

    c. Naima **must** withdraw from representing Dr. Kirk (and continue representing Dr. Peters) unless there would be a **material** detriment to Dr. Kirk if Naima withdrew.

    d. Naima **must not** withdraw from representing Dr. Kirk (and continue representing Dr. Peters) unless Dr. Kirk gives **informed consent, confirmed in writing**.

12. Sania generally represents general contractors in construction disputes. As a result, to reduce **conflicts**, she generally declines to represent property owners in disputes with contractors. By doing so, she has developed a book of business that includes Ernie Bock LLC, the largest general contractor in the area.

    One day, she is approached by general counsel for the City of Grittydelphia. The city is seeking to terminate a contractor working on one of its public works projects. The city asks Sania to handle the matter.

    Although Bock has no involvement in this particular project, Sania is concerned that taking the matter may create **conflicts** in the future.

    Do the Rules prohibit Sania from asking the City to preemptively waive a future **conflict** in the event that Sania represents a contractor against the City in a future, different, and unrelated dispute?

    a. Yes. A client cannot give **informed consent** to a **conflict** that does not yet exist.

    b. Maybe. It depends whether the City is aware of any projects in progress where it will likely be adverse to Bock.

    c. Maybe. It depends whether Sania is aware of any projects in progress where the city has retained Bock as a contractor.

    d. No. A client may waive a future conflict, but the effectiveness of the waiver depends on the extent to which the lawyer's disclosures and explanations allow the client to understand the **material** risks and alternatives.

13. Remi is approached by a new client, Helen. Remi realizes almost immediately that if she agrees to represent Helen, it will create a **conflict of interest** with existing client Leopold.

    Remi has known Leopold for many years and feels confident that he will agree to waive the **conflict**. So Remi tells Helen, "I will represent you."

    A few days later, Remi calls Leopold and asks for his consent. Surprisingly, Leopold refuses. It turns out that he knows Helen from their book club and he can't stand her. "Under no circumstances can you represent her," he insists.

    Remi calls Helen back and says "I misspoke earlier, and I can't handle your case after all. Sorry for wasting your time."

    Has Remi resolved any **conflicts of interest**?

    a. Yes. A **conflict** only existed while Remi represented both Leopold and Helen. Now that she has terminated Helen, the **conflict** no longer exists.

    b. Yes. A **conflict** only exists where it causes harm to a client. Remi withdrew after only a few days, so there was no prejudice to Helen.

    c. No. A **conflict** was created once Helen reasonably believed that Remi was her lawyer. Remi has not resolved the **conflict** by saying she can't help Helen.

    d. No. A **conflict** was created once Leopold refused to consent. Remi must now withdraw from representing Leopold so that she can represent Helen.

14. Lawyer Donald represents Ann-Marie, who is suing Yousef, a car dealer, in a breach of contract case after Yousef sold Ann-Marie a used car that Ann-Marie alleges had its odometer "rolled back" so that it reflected much lower mileage than the car actually had. In the applicable jurisdiction, it is against the law for a government lawyer to represent nongovernmental clients. Which of the following **conflicts of interest** are ones to which Ann-Marie **may** consent?

    a. Donald representing Yousef in the breach of contract case.

    b. Donald continuing to litigate the breach of contract case after he leaves his firm and becomes a state prosecutor.

    c. Donald representing Yousef in a dispute with the Department of Motor Vehicles over Yousef's alleged sales of used cars with rolled-back odometers.

    d. Donald representing Yousef in a real estate dispute with Yousef's neighbor Amira.

15. For a waiver to be effective, what should it include?

    a. The facts and circumstances giving rise to the situation.

    b. The **material** risks of the proposed course of action.

    c. Both a and b.

    d. Neither a nor b.

16. Most states require **informed consent** to a **conflict of interest** to be:

    a. **Confirmed in writing**.

    b. **In a writing signed by the client**.

    c. Notarized.

    d. Filed with the court.

23

Representing Organizations and Their Constituents

MAYA FINDS RON Rainmaker frowning, deep in thought. "Not Petrified and Mojo again?" she asks. "Nah," Ron replies, grinning ruefully. "I'm over that. Can't win 'em all." "Then what's up now?" Maya wants to know.

"Ted Tech," says Ron. "One of my first clients. He's been with me for years. I love the guy. He's what you call a serial entrepreneur—he's had a string of bright ideas and founded a string of companies to develop them, each one of which has been successful enough that he's been able to sell the company to a big player in its industry and make a substantial return. Ted's hired me to represent every one of those winners. It's been a great run. He already has way more money than he needs, but he loves the game, so he keeps playing."

"I don't hear a problem," Maya observes. "Patience, young padawan, patience," jokes Ron. "A while back, during one of those nice long vacations that he likes to take between ventures, Ted came up with another idea. He figured that it would require some serious research and development, but that if it worked, it would have potential applications in a very broad range of industries and products. Might turn out to be his biggest thing ever. So Ted came back to me, like he always does, to form this new company and get it up and running.

"We've been representing the company for the last year and half. Ted's the CEO—the 'E' stands for both 'Executive' and 'Engineering,' which is how he usually does it. The last six months, though, Ted has been calling to talk about friction among the members of his team. At first, it was the usual stuff—little spats about turf and budgeting and design choices. But now the personalities have gotten out of hand, and it's brought product development to a standstill. Ted's tried every which way to manage this, and he's gotten nowhere. He's disgusted."

"Why doesn't he just fire the troublemakers?" Maya asks. "He *is* the chief of pretty much everything, isn't he?" "Not that easy," Ron replies. "Ted used venture capital—outside investors—to fund this company. The money people are on his board of directors, and two of the problem children are people they brought in. He's tried, but the board members won't intervene; they're siding with the people they brought in. The whole thing is in gridlock."

"So what's Ted going to do?" Maya asks. "Well, that's what we've been discussing lately," says Ron. "Ted still really likes the basic idea he started with and thinks he could do a lot with it in a less toxic environment. He's been asking me questions about who has what kinds of rights in which technology, what kinds of things he could take with him to start something new, whether the people he calls the 'not-crazies' can join him. We're working up a plan."

"Where does that leave the existing company?" Maya inquires. "Paralyzed, I guess; possibly dead," Ron shrugs. "Look, Ted's my guy. I'll help him figure this out, and we'll see where it goes."

Where *is* this going? Has Ron thought through the situation fully, or could something go wrong?

A. Knowing Who (or What) Your Client Is

We don't always represent individual human beings. Sometimes, we represent organizations—corporations, partnerships, limited liability companies, unincorporated associations—the whole bestiary of creatures whose existence, powers, characteristics, and governance are defined by state law. At this point in your legal education, you may or may not have taken a Business Organizations or similarly named course. If you have, then some of this chapter will be old hat, but you'll still learn some essential things about how we lawyers approach representing an organizational client—things that may surprise you. If you haven't had a detailed introduction to the law of business organizations yet, that's okay—we'll tell you what you need to know about organizations and their **constituents** to apply the law governing lawyers to engagements in which your client (or your adversary in litigation or negotiation) is not a human being.[1]

The single most important principle that we want you to take away from this chapter is that you always need to know, and keep in mind, exactly who (or what) your client is (or who or what your clients are). That probably sounds ridiculously obvious, and yet lawyers—good, thoughtful, well-intentioned lawyers just like you—regularly lose track of it. How could that happen? It's easier than you think.

The reason that this confusion happens has to do with the fundamental nature of organizations. A business (or other) organization is an abstract legal object defined by state (or occasionally federal) law. Yet most organizations can do most of the things that people can—they can sue and be sued in their own names, make

---

[1] If you were thinking of skipping your law school's Business Organizations course because you figured that it was about big business issues that don't interest you, fuhgeddaboudit. In every conceivable legal career, lawyers regularly deal with business organizations. Lawyers represent clients who form and operate organizations, make deals with them, work for them, sue them, etc.—all legal careers need a basic working knowledge of the common organizational forms and their characteristics.

and enforce contracts, own property, employ people, commit torts, you name it. In fact, most state and federal law that refers to a "person" intends "person" to include organizations. And yet, unlike physical human beings, organizations have no minds, bodies, or mouths of their own and thus, in the most basic sense, can't decide, act, or speak for themselves. They can't do any of these things except through the decisions, acts, or words of living, breathing human beings. Indeed, one of the fundamental purposes of the laws defining and regulating the various different kinds of organizations (as well as some freestanding areas of the law such as agency, *see* **Chapter 6 at 131**) is to define *which* of the human beings who are associated with the organization have the power to do *which* kinds of things on the organization's behalf (and under what circumstances).

Most commonly, organizations act through their agents, just as clients frequently act through their agent-lawyers. Those agents can be officers, directors, employees, lawyers, independent contractors, and even owners or part-owners of the organization. Their authority to act may come from the organic law defining and governing the organization, the law of agency, the law of contracts, or some other law. The Rules of Professional Conduct and the law governing lawyers generally refer to those individuals who are associated with an organization and who may have the power to act or speak on its behalf in some regard as the organization's "**constituents**."

REAL WORLD The critical point here, and the one that lawyers sometimes lose track of, is that an organization is a thing distinct from its **constituents**. Again, this seems obvious, so why do sensible people get confused about it? When we represent organizations, we are hired on behalf of the organization by, and take instructions and give advice to the organization through, its **constituents**. We often develop personal relationships with the **constituents** with whom we regularly interact—relationships that cultivate feelings of connection and loyalty. And when we think of "the client," we think of these individuals, who become for us, in a very real sense, the avatars of the abstract and impersonal organization we actually represent. So if the **interests** of our human *client contact* start to diverge from the **interests** of our organizational *client*, we can quite naturally find ourselves tempted to overlook the distinctions between the organization and its **constituents**, and feel inclined to counsel or assist the **constituent** client contact in ways that may not be in the organizational client's best **interests**. REAL WORLD

This confusion is so common, and so easy to fall into, that there is a Rule of Professional Conduct specifically directed to avoiding it: "A lawyer employed or retained by an organization represents the organization acting through its duly authorized **constituents**."[2] **Model Rule 1.13(a)**. In fact, the whole of **Model Rule 1.13** is

---

[2] TAMING THE TEXT "[E]mployed or retained" is a careful word choice designed to remind us that these principles apply equally to, and are at least as easy to confuse for, an in-house lawyer "employed" by an organization that he or she represents as they are to (or for) an outside lawyer "retained" by an organization. TAMING THE TEXT

devoted to the confusions and challenges that can arise when your client is an organization, and we're going to walk through it, piece by piece, in the course of this chapter.

When we lawyers represent an organization, as we frequently do, our duties are owed exclusively to the organizational client. Our **duties of loyalty** are owed to the organizational client, not to any of its **constituents**. Our **duties of confidentiality** are similarly owed to the organizational client. That principle means that communications with **constituents** acting on behalf of the organization are **confidential** and **attorney-client privileged,** but that the **privilege** and the control of the client's **confidential information** are held by the organizational client, *not* by the human **constituent** who engaged in the communication or furnished the **confidential information**. By the same token, we have *no* authority to disclose an organizational client's **confidential information** to any organizational **constituent** (or anyone else) except to the extent that the disclosure is authorized (expressly or by implication, *see* **Chapter 8.B at 238**) by the organization itself (that is, by a **constituent** who has the organizational power to authorize the disclosure). *See* **Model Rule 1.13 Comments [1]-[2]**.

How do we know which organizational **constituents** have the power to direct us on behalf of the organizational client in some particular respect (for example, to hire us, to tell us to file an a lawsuit, to take a position in litigation or negotiation, to agree to something on the organization's behalf, or to waive an organizational **privilege**)? The answer lies *not* in the law governing lawyers, but in the law governing the organization and its operations. All that the law governing lawyers tells us to do is to consult *other* law to determine which **constituents** have the power to decide and speak for the organization, and to follow those **constituents'** instructions on the organization's behalf, within the limits of the law.

The potential confusion for an organization's lawyer between the organization's **interests** and those of its **constituents** comes up in many different contexts, some so common that sections of **Model Rule 1.13** address them directly. As we walk through the Rule, we'll see that these situations call on your hard-won knowledge about a range of other ethical issues, including **conflicts of interest**, the lawyer's fiduciary duties, the law of agency, the rules governing interactions with unrepresented persons, the **duty of confidentiality** and its exceptions, and the rules governing formation of and withdrawal from the attorney-client relationship. Get ready to put the pieces together.

1. Can You Represent an Organization and One or More of Its Constituents at the Same Time?

So far, we know that lawyers **may** and often do represent organizations, and that when they do, their duties are owed to the client organization itself, and not to any of its **constituents**, even though it will always be the **constituents** who speak and act for the client organization. By the same reasoning, lawyers **may** represent a particular organizational **constituent** for some particular purpose, in which case their duties are owed exclusively to the **constituent**, and not to the organization.

But can we do both at once—that is, can we represent both an organization and one or more of its **constituents** at the same time? Sure. It happens all the time—but it **must** be done under the right circumstances and in the right way. Prepare to see some payoff for all the sweat and tears that you lavished on **conflicts of interest** in **Chapter 22 at 599** as we examine **Model Rule 1.13(g)**:

> A lawyer representing an organization **may** also represent any of its directors, officers, employees, members, shareholders or other **constituents**, subject to the provisions of Rule 1.7. If the organization's consent to the dual representation is required by Rule 1.7, the consent shall be given by an appropriate official of the organization other than the individual who is to be represented, or by the shareholders.

TAMING THE TEXT What the first sentence of the Rule tells us is that we **may** represent an organization and one or more of its **constituents** at the same time, so long as we properly recognize and address any **conflicts of interest** that may be created. The language does that by granting the permission ("**may** also represent . . .") "*subject to the provisions of Rule 1.7*" (emphasis added). Quick—what's in **Model Rule 1.7**? As we discussed in **Chapter 22.B at 646**, **Model Rule 1.7(a)** defines when we have a **concurrent conflict of interest**—a **conflict** that arises between two clients whom we represent **concurrently**—that is, at the same time. TAMING THE TEXT

Whether the **concurrent** representation creates any **conflicts of interest** that must be recognized and addressed depends on the circumstances, of course. Could a lawyer simultaneously represent an organization and one of its **constituents** without creating a **conflict of interest**? Of course: Imagine that the real estate partner in Frank's firm, Barney Blackacre, is representing a real estate development company in connection with a land-use project, and the CEO of the development company needs to redo her estate plan. Barney sends her to his estate-planning partner, Willie Willmaker. There is no **conflict** between these two engagements (do you see why?); each partner **may** go ahead without any additional steps.

But representing an organization and one of its **constituents** can create **conflicts**, too. **Model Rule 1.7(a)(1)** says that we have a **concurrent conflict** when we represent two clients at the same time whose **interests** are "directly adverse" to one another, with "directly" generally understood to mean "nose-to-nose" adversity in the same matter. *See* **Chapter 22.B at 651**. Could that happen if you simultaneously represented an organization and one of its **constituents**? Sure: Imagine that Barney Blackacre is representing that same real estate development company in the same land-use project, and an employee of the development company comes to Barney's litigation partner, Happy Trials, seeking representation in claims that she's been sexually harassed at work. Does it matter that the two engagements have no substantive connection with each other? No—**concurrent conflicts** don't have to be related to each other to be actionable **conflicts**. The problem is that the employee wants Happy to represent her in suing a **current client** of his firm (the development company). *See* **Chapter 22.B at 651**. Does it matter that two different partners of the firm are on either side of the **conflict**? Nope—the rule of **imputation** says that, if one lawyer in a **practice organization** has a **conflict** (or a piece of one), then every lawyer in the **practice organization** does, too. **Model Rule 1.10(a)**; **Chapter 22.D at 702**. The situation squarely presents a **concurrent conflict of interest**, and Frank's firm must either abstain from the new proposed engagement for the harassed employee or get the **informed consent, confirmed in writing**, of both affected clients. If the development company refuses to waive the **conflict**, as it has every right to do (and under these circumstances probably will as a practical matter), then Frank's firm cannot take on the new engagement.

Similarly, you'll recall that **Model Rule 1.7(a)(2)** says that you have a different kind of **concurrent conflict** if your representation of, or your personal connections with, someone else creates a "significant risk" of "**materially** limiting" your representation of an existing client. *See* **Chapter 22.A at 626** (personal connections); **Chapter 22.B at 654** (attorney-client relationship). And remember that there are two kinds of "significant risk" **concurrent conflicts**—ones in which the **conflict** is indirect (not "nose-to-nose") but still currently strong enough to create that "significant risk" right now, and ones in which there is no **conflict** at all right now, but it's reasonably possible that one could develop down the road. *See* **Chapter 22.B at 655**.

Could that happen if you simultaneously represented an organization and one or more of its **constituents**? Absolutely: Imagine that Ron Rainmaker represents a minority shareholder in a closely held business, FunCo, advising the shareholder about her rights and duties as a minority shareholder. FunCo itself approaches Ron's partner, Celia Deal, seeking her assistance in raising money for the company by selling a block of newly issued shares to a new investor. The sale of shares may (or may not) be good for the company; that's for the company to decide. But if the company goes ahead, it will be bad for Ron's client, because it will "dilute" her minority position—that is, she'll own a smaller percentage of the company's outstanding shares when the deal is over, giving her less power to elect directors and influence the company's affairs. Is this "**direct**" **adversity**? No. The company is taking steps that happen to be bad for this minority shareholder, but they're not negotiating or litigating with each other **directly** (nose-to-nose) right now. Is there a significant risk of **materially** limiting the representation of the company? Sure: The company's and the minority shareholder's **interests** are in real and substantial **conflict** over this financing possibility—Ron's duties to his client make it quite likely that his client will need him to start a negotiation of some kind with Celia to see if he can get FunCo to accommodate his client's **interests**. It's a classic example of a current **indirect conflict**. Maya's firm will have to figure out what to do about it. *See* **Chapter 22.B at 655**.

Can you create possible future **conflicts** when you represent an organization and one or more of its **constituents**? Again, absolutely: Remember, virtually *any* joint representation (that is, a simultaneous representation in the same engagement of more than one client pursuing common **interests**) will create possible future **conflicts**. *See* **Chapter 22.B at 657**. Take, for example, **Problem 22.B-2(a)**, in which Maya's firm will be defending Scooter's Computers and two of its managers in securities fraud litigation. At the beginning of the engagement, everyone on the defense side agrees that none of the defendants did anything wrong, and all the joint clients want to be defended on similar grounds. Maybe things will stay that way. But down the road, it's possible that the joint clients may start disagreeing about whether some of them are more blameworthy than others, or about what may have happened. The possible future **conflict** will then have become **direct** and actual. If the original engagement agreement didn't contain an enforceable advance waiver that anticipated this situation, Maya's firm will need to figure out with the joint clients what happens next. *See* **Chapter 22.B at 657**; **Chapter 22.E at 746**.

To complete the picture, it's also possible that a completed engagement representing an organization or one or more of its **constituents** could create a **successive conflict** with a new engagement that begins after the representation of the organization is over. See if you can find one in the problems below.

Summing up, we now know that one or more of the different kinds of **conflicts of interest** may arise when you represent an organization and one or more of its **constituents**. Now let's suppose that we've identified such a **conflict**. What now? Well, we know that in deciding how to address a **conflict of interest**, one choice that is always available is to abstain—that is, to stay out of the **conflicted** engagement. *See* **Chapter 22.E at 736**. And if you're already in the **conflicted** engagement and can't resolve it any other way, you can limit (and maybe even altogether avoid) the **consequences** by getting out—that is, by withdrawing as promptly as possible. *See* **Chapter 22.E at 737**.

Other options? Sure: If it's one of the few **successive conflicts** that can be addressed fully by rebutting the presumption of **imputation**, either through situational facts or with an **ethical screen**, you can avail yourself of those options. *See* **Chapter 22.C at 716**. Or you can determine whether the **conflict** is **consentable** (**Model Rule 1.7(b)**; **Chapter 22.E at 739**), and, if it is, then see if you can obtain each affected client's **informed consent, confirmed in writing** (or better yet, **in a writing signed by the client**) (*see* **Chapter 22.E at 741**).

The alert student has noticed that we haven't yet talked about the second sentence of **Model Rule 1.13(g)** and is wondering how it fits in. (The three of us are doing the wave for you, alert student!) REASON FOR THE RULE▸ That second sentence of the Rule focuses on another situation in which the rights of organizations and the powers and duties of their **constituents** can get confused—when **concurrent** representation of an organization and a **constituent** would create a **conflict of interest**, and a waiver on behalf of both is needed to proceed. What if the **constituent who is to be jointly represented** would ordinarily have the organizational authority to give the necessary consent on the organization's behalf? The temptation is to have the **constituent** consent for himself and then, separately, consent on behalf of the organization. It's quick and easy, right?

Quick and easy, but probably not effective. The reason that we need consent in the first place is because there is a **conflict** between the **interests** of the organization and those of the **constituent**. If the **constituent** consents to one **practice organization's concurrent** representation of both, then no one has provided any independent judgment as to whether the organization's **interests** are going to be adequately protected while it and the **constituent** are represented by the same counsel. The **constituent** can't be depended on to provide independent judgment on behalf of the organization—his **interests** and the organization's **conflict**. The shared counsel has a **conflict**, too, which is why the waiver is necessary in the first place. So when client consent is required to waive a **conflict** involving the organization and a **constituent, Model Rule 1.13(g)** requires that "the consent shall be given by an appropriate official of the organization *other than the individual who is to be represented*, or by the shareholders" (emphasis added). This requirement ensures that the organization's consent is independent, voluntary, and informed.

Reason for the Rule

How do we determine the identity of that "appropriate official of the organization other than the individual who is to be represented" who will provide the necessary independent consent on the organization's behalf? In just the same way that we determine any issue of organizational authority pertaining to a question of legal ethics: According to the law and internal policies governing the organization itself, which will generally tell us who can be endowed with the necessary organizational authority, and what steps (if any) are required to accomplish it. The law governing lawyers does not address the question other than to instruct us to look to the law governing the organization.

In novel or complex situations, determining which **constituents may** or **should** consent on the organization's behalf can take careful analysis and formal organizational action (for a corporation, that could include a board of directors meeting and a board resolution or, sometimes, a formal shareholder vote). If that seems inconvenient, that's because it sometimes is. **Conflicts of interest** are serious business: They are, by definition, situations in which a client's valuable and important rights are at risk. For the client to be allowed to proceed with **conflicted** counsel, we want to be sure that an independent decisionmaker with only the organizational client's **interests** at heart assesses whether the requested consent will leave the organization's **interests** adequately protected. That's what **Model Rule 1.13(g)** does here.

Problem 23A-1: Which of the following situations create **conflicts of interest** that require recognition and a response? In each case, explain why or why not, and for those that present a **conflict**, describe what steps the **conflicted** lawyers and **practice organizations must** or **should** take to respond to the **conflict**. If there is more than one alternative for addressing a **conflict**, describe all the alternatives, identify the best one available, and explain why you believe it's the best:

a. Same as the first part of **Problem 22B-1(f)** (Frank's firm represents Diaper Dan, LLC in general business-law advice, and also represents the company's general manager, Dan DeLivers, in connection with Dan's estate plan and ongoing tax consultations).

b. The hypothetical in the **Introduction to this chapter at 769.**

c. Same as the rest of **Problem 22B-1(f)** (Baby World acquires Diaper Dan, LLC, and instructs Frank's firm to assist Diaper Dan, LLC in firing Dan DeLivers from his position as the company's general manager).

d. Same as **Problem 22B-2(a)** (Maya's firm will be defending Scooter's Computers and two of its managers in securities fraud litigation). We gave you some help in the preceding section regarding what kind of **conflict** this might be. What **must** or **should** Maya's firm do about it?

e. Let's elaborate on the FunCo hypothetical, **Chapter 23.A at 774** above. FunCo is going to raise some capital by selling a block of newly issued shares to a new investor. FunCo consults Celia Deal in Maya's firm to assist in that transaction. Pricing of those new shares is a complex and difficult task. It depends on (among other things) whether the buyer will end up with a majority interest, as well as the company's market share, and its business performance and prospects. Celia hires a valuation expert to assist the company in determining a proper price (a common practice in engagements of this kind). Ron's client (the minority shareholder) gives up on FunCo and sells her shares to the new buyer. The buyer now has a majority ownership interest in FunCo. The new majority owner hires new management and decides that the company will use a law firm other than Maya's. A group of FunCo minority shareholders other than Ron's client believes that the new majority shareholder is engaging in "freezeout" tactics designed to devalue the minority's stake in the company and lessen their influence on company business. This group approaches a business litigator in Maya's firm to bring a lawsuit against the majority shareholder for breach of the majority shareholder's fiduciary duties to the minority shareholders—a duty that is recognized in the relevant state.

2. A Common Problem in Choosing and Identifying Your Client(s): Organizational Formation

Take another look at the hypothetical in the **chapter Introduction at 769.** Now let's walk ourselves back in time to the day when Ted Tech and the two people with whom Ted has decided he's going to start his next venture sit down with Ron Rainmaker in a conference room at Maya's firm. The future looks bright, and everybody's friendly.

But who in that conference room is Ron's client? The answer is that Ron's client *could* be any one or any combination of the people in the room, and even one that's not really there. Consider:

■   Ted Tech is (as Ron put it to Maya) "[Ron's] guy," having retained Ron in connection with several prior ventures. Ron and Ted may both believe that Ron represents Ted.

■   The other two founders have been invited to "the lawyer's office" to form the company. To the extent that they are thinking about it at all, they probably think that Ron represents everybody in the room, or that, whoever else Ron may represent, he's "looking out for" the individual who may be thinking about Ron's role.

■   In addition, lawyers have invented a concept that comes up in organization formation, which many jurisdictions have incorporated into their law: The "entity-in-formation." Bear in mind that at this point the founders have not even picked an organizational form, let alone formed an organization. You might think that the organization's literal nonexistence would preclude it from being considered a lawyer's client. But many states indulge the fiction that, in a context like the one described here (several individuals meeting with a lawyer in contemplation of forming an organization), the lawyer may represent the as-yet-nonexistent organization—the "entity-in-formation"— often to the exclusion of some or all of the individual founders.[3]

At such an early point in this venture, does it really matter whom the lawyer represents? You bet it does. Think about this question in terms of what you already know about lawyers' fiduciary duties (**Chapter 5.D at 112**), the formation of the attorney-client relationship (**Chapter 9.A at 257**), and **conflicts of interest** (**Chapter 22 at 599**), and you can start to see why it matters, and how much.

Let's think it through: The three founders are meeting to structure and form their business organization. That means that they're going to decide who is contributing what to the organization, and how much ownership and management authority each of them gets. There's only one ownership pie and one control pie to cut up; if one person gets more ownership or control, someone else gets less. So the founders are effectively negotiating with one another over this division of a finite amount of management and control, whether they are thinking about it that way or not. What each founder wants or thinks he or she deserves is almost certain to differ from the others' views and even if it doesn't, the founders' respective **interests** are in immediate and **direct conflict**.

What's more, each of the founders may have unique personal needs or preferences based on their individual tax or financial positions or governance style. The

---

[3]   YOUR HOUSE; YOUR RULES ▶ The notion of representing an entity-in-formation is not universally accepted, so before you consider doing it, make sure that it's allowed in your licensing jurisdiction. ◀ YOUR HOUSE; YOUR RULES

choice of organizational form and the division of ownership and control could have significant effects, good or bad, affecting any of those preferences or needs.

So what happens depending on the identity of Ron's client or clients?

- If Ron Rainmaker represents only one founder (likely Ted, as a practical matter, but it doesn't matter which one), Ron's role is relatively straightforward. Given his **duty of loyalty** to his single client, he **must** advocate for the best deal for that client, and that client only. In order to get a deal done (which is a goal that his client wishes to pursue), he will probably have to advocate various kinds of compromises, but he will always be pushing for the best deal he can get for his client (Ted). The other founders will have to fend for themselves, with or without counsel of their own. And one thing the other founders can't expect Ron to do is to advocate for their personal preferences or needs, or even to know what they are. After the organization that will conduct the venture is formed, Ron will continue to represent the single client he represented during formation unless some other arrangement is made. If Ron is asked to represent the newly formed organization as well, it will call **Model Rule 1.13(g)** into play, as Ron will be representing the organization *and* one of its **constituents** at the same time. He will need to assess (and continually reassess) possible **conflicts** that may exist or arise between his **concurrently** represented clients. Ron might avoid this issue by terminating his representation of the founder (Ted) once the company is formed, but he and the founder may not wish to do so.

- If Ron represents more than one founder jointly, he can advocate for the jointly represented clients' shared interests against any founder he doesn't represent (if there are any; Ron might well represent all three founders jointly). As for his joint clients, there are **direct concurrent conflicts** among their interests: The more ownership or control that one jointly represented founder gets, the less another gets. As among his jointly represented founder-clients, then, Ron will have to adopt the role of "scrivener," advising the joint clients evenhandedly about possible solutions and their effects without advocating for any particular client's benefit over any other's, allowing the clients to work out any differences in their positions, and documenting the outcome. *See* **Chapter 22.B at 659**. And before he can do that, of course, he will need to obtain the **informed consent, confirmed in writing,** of each of his joint clients to the waiver of the **conflicts of interest** among them and the limited nature of the scrivener's role that those **conflicts** will require. *See* **Chapter 22.E at 743**. The same approach is dictated if one of Ron's joint clients includes the entity-in-formation, which (if you think about it) doesn't have any particular preference among the founders' positions on division of ownership or control. (If we think of the discussions among the founders as dividing up the pie of ownership and the pie of control, then the entity-in-formation *is* the pie.) Again, if Ron is asked to represent the newly formed organization, there will be **Model Rule 1.13(g)** issues, and Ron will need to assess (and continually reassess) possible **conflicts** that may exist or arise between the **concurrently** represented clients that now include the organization itself as well as several of its **constituent** founders.

- If Ron represents *only* the entity-in-formation, and not any of the founders, it (rather oddly) puts Ron in a position similar to the one he occupies if he represents all three of the founders. Why? Because as just noted, the entity-in-formation has no identifiable preference of its own among the founders' positions. If we indulge the legal fiction of considering the entity-in-formation to be anything at all, the only interest it might hold that we can even theorize is that it "wants" the founders to reach agreement so that the organization can be formed and come into being. In those circumstances, Ron should not be advocating for or negotiating on behalf of any founder in preference to any other, and again his role effectively amounts to that of a scrivener. In this case, once the organization is formed, Ron represents the organization *only*, not any of its **constituents** (do you see why?). Because Ron has only had one client throughout, he can represent the organization in taking actions adverse to one or more of the founders (or other **constituents**), though the founders who find themselves the object of these adverse actions may resent it.

Whichever client or clients Ron comes to represent (and remember, any of the arrangements discussed above are permissible with the proper preparation and conduct), two needs are paramount: *First*, Ron needs to know who is, and who is not, his client. Otherwise, he won't know for whom, if anyone, he is supposed to advocate, and he could disserve the **interests** of someone whom he is supposed to serve, either during the formation negotiations or later.

And *second*, *everyone else* needs to know who is, and who is not, Ron's client, and the implications of those client identities. From the preceding discussion, you can see why: Each person in that conference room has a sensible reason, based on the surrounding circumstances, to believe that Ron is looking out for (that is, representing) him or her. And if *that's* true, then Ron is considered to represent all of them, even if he doesn't mean to, unless he makes it clear to each of them (preferably in writing, so that the notice will be clear and durable) that he doesn't. *See* **Chapter 9.A at 261**. If Ron fails affirmatively to disclaim representation of any of these folks, he runs serious risks of later being accused of having violated his professional obligations by not protecting their **interests** in the formation negotiations or in later operations and by failing to have made proper disclosures and obtained proper consents to the **conflicts of interest** that the inferred joint representation created. He could easily be sued if anything in the venture goes badly, and he risks professional discipline as well.

What's more, any nonclients in the room who don't have lawyers of their own have rights under **Model Rule 4.3** (*see* **Chapter 12 at 374**): Ron **must not** "state or imply that [he] is disinterested"; **must** make reasonable efforts to ensure that the unrepresented persons don't misunderstand his role; and **must not** give any unrepresented persons legal advice other than to seek counsel of their own. Failure to comply could not only subject Ron to professional discipline, it could make the terms of the organization's formation subject to challenge in litigation.

> Problem 23A-2: Assume the three prospective founders of Ted Tech's next venture are meeting with Ron Rainmaker in a conference room in Ron's offices. In each of the following circumstances, what steps **must** or **should** Ron Rainmaker and his firm take in order to comply with the Rules of Professional Conduct and minimize civil liability risks, and why?
>
> a. Ron represents Ted Tech only. Does your analysis change if Ted has insisted that Ron act as his lawyer alone, but instructs Ron not to tell the other two founders that this is the case? If so, how and why; and if not, why not? Do the additional instructions require some additional response from Ron?
> b. Ron represents all three founders jointly.
> c. Ron represents the entity-in-formation only (which is recognized as proper in the relevant state).

> Problem 23A-3: Now assume that the founders in **Problem 23A-2** have formed a business organization, and work on the venture is underway. Six months later, Ted contacts Ron with a problem: He is having "engineering differences" with one of the other founders, who will not focus on developing the technology that Ted has in mind. Ted tells Ron that Ted wants the dissenting founder "out."
>
> a. In each of the client-choice scenarios presented in **Problem 23A-2(a)**, **(b)**, and **(c)**, what **must** or **should** Ron do, and why? If there is additional information you would want in any of the three scenarios, what is it, and why?
> b. Does your analysis change in any of these scenarios if Ted's concern is that one of the other founders contracted COVID-19, became seriously ill, and although she has now been discharged from the hospital after an extended stay, it is unclear when, if ever, she'll be able to resume her work for the company? If so, how and why; and if not, why not?

3. How We Must Interact with Organizational Constituents Whom We *Don't* Represent: The "Corporate *Miranda*" or "*Upjohn* Warning"

Now we know what we need to worry about if we're thinking about representing an organization and one or more of its **constituents**. More often, though, we represent the organization alone, but we still interact with various of its **constituents**. Some of those **constituents** may be our client contacts—**constituents** who speak and act for the organization in requesting our services and implementing our advice. Others may be sources of information that we need in order to do our work. Yet others may be potential organizational adversaries, for example, employees whom the organization wants to discipline or terminate, or potential participants in misconduct that the organization wants to uncover and stop. As **Model Rule 1.13(a)** reminds us, none of these **constituents** is our client, and most of the time, these **constituents** don't have lawyers of their own, either.[4]

a. What Triggers the Requirement for an *Upjohn* Warning?

So what **must** we do when we're interacting with non-client **constituents** of a client organization? It turns out there's a Rule about that. (Coincidence? We think not.) **Model Rule 1.13(f)**, which we're quoting here because it's quite important and comes up frequently, explains:

> In dealing with an organization's directors, officers, employees, members, shareholders or other **constituents**, a lawyer shall explain the identity of the client when the lawyer knows or reasonably should know that the organization's interests are adverse to those of the **constituents** with whom the lawyer is dealing.

TAMING THE TEXT This Rule is relatively easy to follow, but let's walk through it. It says that whenever you're dealing with **constituents** of a client organization (providing a handy list of examples of commonly encountered **constituents**—"directors, officers," etc.), you have to "explain" something to the **constituent**. What do you have to explain? "[T]he identity of the client." When do you have to explain it? "[W]hen"—and that means *whenever*—"the lawyer knows or reasonably should know that the organization's **interests** are adverse to those of the **constituents** with whom the lawyer is dealing." So any time that you ought to know that the individual **constituent** with whom you're interacting has **interests** that are adverse to those of your client organization, you **must** take affirmative steps to make sure that the non-client **constituent** understands that you represent the organization and are *not* his or her lawyer. And the Rule is mandatory ("shall"). TAMING THE TEXT

With a gleam of recognition in their eyes, the alert students are sensing that this reminds them of something. Hooray for all of you! But what? If you guessed **Model Rule 4.3**, feel free to light a figurative cigar. What's the connection? Well, as we discussed in **Chapter 12 at 374** (and briefly mentioned in the preceding section), **Model Rule 4.3** is about what you **must** and **must not** do when you're interacting with people who are not represented by their own lawyers (or by you). You must not "state or imply that [you're] disinterested," because you're not—you're there representing a client, and your job is to pursue your client's **interests** with undivided **loyalty**. When you "know or reasonably should know that the unrepresented person misunderstands [your] role in the matter," you **must** "make reasonable efforts to

---

[4] Individual **constituents** are, of course, free to have their own lawyers, and sometimes they do. The most common situations in which they do are when they are actively in conflict with their organizational employer—for example, if they are likely to be disciplined or fired or if they believe that they have been subjected to harassment or discrimination in the workplace. When individual **constituents** are represented with respect to some issue that they have with the organization, as company counsel you **must** comply with **Model Rule 4.2** (the **no-contact rule**) in your dealings with them. *See* **Chapter 11 at 339**.

correct the misunderstanding." And if you know or reasonably should know that the unrepresented person's **interests** "are or have a reasonable possibility of being in conflict with the interests of [your] client," you **must not** give the unrepresented person any "legal advice . . . , other than the advice to secure counsel."

Do all of **Model Rule 4.3**'s commandments apply when you're representing an organization and dealing with one of the client organization's unrepresented **constituents**? Of course they do: **Model Rule 4.3** applies *any* time that you're representing a client and dealing with an unrepresented person. The alert students who saw the connection between this Rule and **Model Rule 1.13(f)** are now puzzled—if we already have a Rule that tells us how to interact with unrepresented persons, why do we need another one? (We view puzzlement as a state of grace, by the way: Puzzlement leads to questions, and whether or not those questions lead directly to answers, they usually lead to enlightenment. In our experience, the very best lawyers are all constantly curious. So any time that you're confused and know it, consider yourself on the path to enlightenment.)

REASON FOR THE RULE Bearing in mind the principle that we try to construe a single integrated statute or set of rules to avoid redundancy,[5] let's see whether there are any differences between **Model Rule 4.3**'s generally applicable directions for dealing with unrepresented persons and **Model Rule 1.13(f)**'s directions specific to the situation of dealing with an unrepresented organizational **constituent** when acting as the lawyer for the organization. Pause and look at the two Rules. Do you see any differences?

We're sure that you do. The generally applicable Rule (**Model Rule 4.3**) says that, if you know or should know that an unrepresented person is confused about your role, you **must** clarify it. In contrast, the organization-specific Rule (**Model Rule 1.13(f)**) says that, once you see (or should see) any **conflict** between your client's **interests** and the unrepresented **constituent**'s, you **must** clarify your role immediately ("shall explain the identity of the client") *whether or not you have any reason to believe that the unrepresented **constituent** might be confused about it.*

Why would the Rules require this more sensitive trigger for the obligation to clarify your role in this specific context? Well, experience has shown that the organizational context is a fertile breeding ground for uncertainty about company counsel's role. Company counsel wander freely within the company (often, though not always, as welcome guests). **Constituents** are encouraged to cooperate with "our lawyers." Many company **constituents** have no reason to possess any legal sophistication about who company counsel is and to whom that counsel's **loyalty** is exclusively owed. So the Rule that specifically applies to this situation requires company counsel to get out in front of any uncertainty (whether or not they have any reason to believe there actually is any confusion) in any situation

---

[5] *See, e.g., Tex. Dep't of Hous. & Cmty. Affairs v. Inclusive Cmtys. Project, Inc.*, 576 U.S. 519, 538 (2015); *Commander Oil Corp. v. Barlo Equip. Corp.*, 215 F.3d 321, 329 (2d Cir. 2000).

in which the unrepresented **constituent's interests** might be at risk. Thus, if you see (or should see) **conflicts** between the **interests** of the organization client and the unrepresented **constituent**, you still have to follow **Model Rule 4.3**'s direction to refrain from giving any legal advice other than to seek independent counsel. But under those circumstances, you also have to speak up about who you are and whom you do and do not represent immediately, without waiting for any sign of confusion. ⟨ REASON FOR THE RULE

Two interchangeable nicknames refer to the admonition contemplated by **Model Rule 4.3** and **Model Rule 1.13(f)**: One nickname is the "**corporate *Miranda* warning**," drawn from the landmark Supreme Court decision in *Miranda v. Arizona*,[6] which (as anyone who has ever watched a TV cop show knows) requires law enforcement officers to remind suspects who are under arrest of their constitutional rights. *Miranda* shares with the organization-counsel situation that we're discussing here the reality that "anything you [the unrepresented **constituent**] say can and will be used against you [by the organization that the lawyer represents]." The other nickname is the ***Upjohn* warning**, again drawn from a landmark Supreme Court decision, *Upjohn Co. v. United States*.[7] *Upjohn*, you may recall (*see* **Chapter 11.B at 348**), revised and clarified the scope of an organization's **attorney-client privilege**. *Upjohn* redefined the circumstances under which particular organizational **constituents** could have communications with organization counsel protected by the organization's **attorney-client privilege**, broadening it to any circumstance in which any **constituent**, whether or not one with formal management titles or responsibilities, needs to communicate with company counsel to seek or use legal advice for the company's benefit. The warning is named for the *Upjohn* decision because it is often delivered in response to a **constituent**'s request to speak with organization counsel in **confidence**—a circumstance that we'll discuss in a moment.

As just discussed, the warning is required any time that the organization's counsel is interacting with an unrepresented **constituent** whose **interests** are adverse to the organization's. But often, company counsel may simply be seeking needed information from an employee or responding to a **constituent's** request for services or advice relating to ordinary company business. So when would a **constituent's** interest diverge from the company's? There are three general situations in which this divergence most commonly tends to happen, which we provide here to give you a sense of what to be alert for when you're company counsel and you're dealing with a **constituent** for any reason:

■ The **constituent** may be contemplating, or actually engaging in, conduct that is directly inimical to the company's interests for personal benefit; for example, embezzlement or the theft of company funds or property;

---

[6] 384 U.S. 436 (1966).
[7] 449 U.S. 383 (1981).

- The **constituent** may be contemplating, or actually engaging in, conduct *on behalf of the company* that would cause, or is causing, the company to violate the law, such as the manufacture or distribution of dangerous products, environmental damage, regulatory noncompliance, fraud on trading partners or the public, antitrust violations, or the like; or
- The **constituent** may be experiencing personal difficulties, such as depression, addiction, or other mental or physical illness, that interfere with the ability to do his or her job. (Quick—why would this tend to create **conflicts** between the organization's **interests** and the **constituent's**? Briefly describe the **conflicting interests** that might arise.)

In all these circumstances, the **constituent's** own actual or perceived personal **interest** is not consistent with the organization's. And your job as company counsel is to protect the **interests** of the company. Make no mistake: It can be heartbreakingly difficult to have to step back and warn **constituent** client contacts with whom you've dealt regularly on a friendly basis for a considerable period, and perhaps have even socialized with outside of work, that despite all that you may have shared personally, you can't advise or otherwise help that person right now (and, in fact, may have to report the person's conduct to company management). But anything else is a violation of your obligations to your organization client and will subject you to serious **consequences**.

b. What Information Must an *Upjohn* Warning Contain?

So what does an ***Upjohn* warning** look like in these circumstances? Well, it has to be tailored to the circumstances, giving enough context to make your role and **loyalties** clear and addressing any possible practical misunderstanding that may be lurking. It always includes, in one form or another, the information that you represent the company and that you don't represent the **constituent**. Beyond that, the warning needs to address any implications of your role suggested by the circumstances. For example:

- If the **constituent** seems concerned about **confidentiality**, she must be warned that you can't keep anything the **constituent** tells you secret from the company (do you see why?), and that although your communications may be (depending on the circumstances) within the *company's* **attorney-client privilege**, the company may choose to waive that privilege at any time and disclose the **constituent's** communications to you to anyone it chooses (again, do you see why?). *See* **Model Rule 1.13 Comments [2], [10]**.
- If the **constituent** may be requesting advice for personal benefit that may be in **conflict** with the **interests** of the company, you must provide the standard **Model Rule 4.3** response that you can't advise the **constituent** about that, and that all you *can* advise is for the **constituent** to get her own lawyer for that advice.

■ And remember, if the **constituent** starts volunteering information that the company seems likely to hold against the **constituent**, then if you haven't warned the **constituent** already, you must pause the conversation and make sure that the **constituent** understands your role and **loyalties**.

See **Model Rule 1.13 Comments [10]-[11]**.

c. At What Point in Organization Counsel's Interaction with an Unrepresented Constituent Must an *Upjohn* Warning Be Given?

When **must** or **should** you give an *Upjohn* warning? If the conversation is one in which you *expect* the **constituent** may be contemplating or engaging in conduct contrary to the organization's **interests**, you **must** administer it at the beginning of the conversation. Why? Because **Model Rule 1.13(f)** says you **must** clarify your role whenever you know or reasonably should know that the organization's **interests** are in **conflict** with the **constituent's**. If you're talking to this **constituent** because you are concerned that the **constituent** is contemplating or engaging in misconduct (for example, when your engagement involves investigating possible wrongdoing within or by the company), then you already reasonably should know that the **constituent's interests conflict** with your client's.

Sometimes, however, you can be surprised by something the **constituent** unexpectedly raises during what you anticipated would be an ordinary exchange. The moment that happens, you must pause and clarify your role. Bear in mind that this may result in your not getting all the information regarding the situation that your client organization would like to know. You still have to stop and warn the **constituent**. Why? Because your **duty of loyalty** to your client never requires you to violate the law. And here the Rules of Professional Conduct and parallel civil law both require you to administer the *Upjohn* warning.

d. In What Form Must or Should an *Upjohn* Warning Be Given?

What about the *form* of the *Upjohn* warning? Neither **Model Rule 4.3** nor **Model Rule 1.13(f)** states any formal requirement (nor does any parallel civil duty), so the **warning may** be administered orally. TIPS & TACTICS But in any situation in which you go into an interaction anticipating **conflicting interests** between the organization and the **constituent** (for example, an investigation on the company's behalf into potential wrongdoing), administering the **warning** in writing, and giving the **constituent** time to review it and ask questions before you begin, is the best course to avoid any future claim by the **constituent** that she was not apprised of her rights. TIPS & TACTICS

e. CONSEQUENCES What Consequences Can Result from the Failure to Give a Timely or Complete *Upjohn* Warning?

As in the more general situation of dealing with any unrepresented person, the **consequences** of failing to administer a timely and effective *Upjohn* warning can be numerous and serious. Because **Model Rule 1.13(f)** and **Model Rule 4.3** are disciplinary rules, their violation can result in professional discipline.

But the improper acquisition of information that proper conduct would have prevented can and often does have civil **consequences** as well. If you have accepted **confidences** from the **constituent** under circumstances in which the **constituent** reasonably believed that you would keep them **confidential**, then you may have assumed a **duty of confidentiality** to the **constituent** (*see* **Chapter 9.B at 268**). That duty is in **conflict** with your **duties of loyalty** and **candor** to your organization client, which require you to tell the organization what you implicitly promised the **constituent** that you would keep secret. You have a **conflict of interest**. Unless you can obtain the **constituent's informed consent, confirmed in writing**, to disclose the **confidences** to the organization (which is unlikely, because the **constituent** has told you things that will get the **constituent** in trouble if disclosed), you **must** withdraw from representing the organization, or the **constituent** may be able to **disqualify** you (and, if you are an in-house lawyer, the whole in-house law department by **imputation**).

If you disclose the **constituent's confidences** to your client (the organization), you have violated the **duty of confidentiality** that you assumed to the **constituent**. Not only may the **constituent** be able to **disqualify** you, she may sue you for any monetary damages that your disclosure has proximately caused. And if there is litigation between the **constituent** and the organization, the organization may be precluded from using as evidence anything whose disclosure by the **constituent** was improperly induced.

To the extent that the **constituent** has made decisions or taken action in reliance on advice you should not have given (remember, no legal advice to the **constituent** is allowed, except the advice to get her own lawyer), those decisions may be undone if, as a practical matter, they can be; and if they can't be undone, then the **constituent** may be able to recover any damages caused by the irreversible decision. *See* **Chapter 12.B at 385**. As you can see, *Upjohn* **warnings** are serious business. ⟨CONSEQUENCES⟩

Problem 23A-4: Maya's friend, Leo Litigator, is on a team of litigators at Maya's firm defending Dorkotron Industries, a consumer electronics manufacturer, from civil claims of conspiring with other manufacturers to fix prices for inkjet printheads, a key part of a whole class of computer printers, in violation of Section 1 of the Sherman Antitrust Act and related state law. Dorkotron denies any price-fixing conspiracy and argues that the reason that printhead prices are so uniform is that they have become a standardized commodity in the industry. Leo is assigned the task of gathering information by reviewing company emails and then speaking to the employees involved in the communications of interest.

In each of the following situations, please explain (1) *when* (if at all) the lawyer representing the organization **must** or **should** deliver an *Upjohn* **warning**; (ii) what *information* the *Upjohn* **warning must** or **should** contain and in what *form*; and (iii) what **consequences** could ensue if the lawyer fails to do what you conclude he or she **must** or **should** do in (i) and (ii), and who will be affected by those consequences. In each case, please explain your analysis.

a. Leo interviews the assistant director of Dorkotron's information technology department in order to learn how the company's email system works and what communications are saved in some form.

b. Leo interviews the administrative assistant for Dorkotron's vice president for marketing, who is involved in the company's product-pricing decisions, in order to determine what kind of devices the VP uses to communicate with others for work purposes, and what kinds of electronic and hard-copy files she maintains.

c. Same as (b), but during the interview, the administrative assistant mentions to Leo that he was diagnosed with early-onset Alzheimer's Disease last year and that his memory about a number of topics relevant to the case has gotten a bit hazy.

d. Same as (b), but during the interview, the administrative assistant informs Leo that the VP has a company-issued smartphone that she uses for work. When Leo asks the administrative assistant whether he has seen the VP use any other phones, the admin gets uncomfortable. "Don't tell my boss I told you, okay?" he says. Leo persists gently to find out what's on the administrative assistant's mind, and he learns that the administrative assistant has seen the VP texting on a different phone that she apparently keeps in a locked drawer in her desk.

e. In gathering documents from the company email server, Leo discovers among the VP for marketing's deleted emails (which many employees do not realize are retained in recoverable form for a period of time) an email to the VP's counterpart at a competitor. "Loving our profits on printheads," the marketing VP's email says. "What about you?" The reply from the competitor's VP says "Wrong email account. Delete this." Leo will include this email among numerous emails about which he needs to ask the VP when he interviews her. Leo sends the VP an invitation to set up the first session of their interview, which will require multiple sessions to complete.

Problem 23A-5: Take another look at **Problem 12A-5** (Maya advises an investment advisory company; one of its employees with whom Maya regularly communicates calls Maya to inform her that he is expecting to be laid off and asks for her advice on how to negotiate his severance). Please explain (i) *when* the lawyer representing the organization **must** or **should** deliver an *Upjohn* **warning**; (ii) what *information* the *Upjohn* **warning must** or **should** contain, and in what *form*; and (iii) what **consequences** could ensue if the lawyer fails to do what you conclude he **must** or **should** do in (i) and (ii), and to whom. In each case, please explain your analysis.

Problem 23A-6: Review the hypothetical in the **Introduction to this chapter at 769**. Please explain (i) *when* the lawyer representing the organization **must** or **should** deliver an *Upjohn* **warning**; (ii) what *information* the *Upjohn* **warning must** or **should** contain, and in what *form*; and (iii) what **consequences** could ensue if the lawyer fails to do what you conclude he **must** or **should** do in (i) and (ii), and to whom. In each case, please explain your analysis.

4. Acting as Organization Counsel When Constituents Are in Conflict

Usually, business and other organizations function according to the allocation of management and control authority among **constituents** under governing law. Most of the time, there's little controversy about which **constituents** have the authority to make particular decisions or direct particular actions on behalf of the organization. Occasional, focused disagreements about who has the authority to do something specific are typically resolved within the existing and recognized organizational structure. In other words, even though most organizations are populated and animated by many distinct **constituents**, usually they work together more or less smoothly according to ground rules provided by the law and the internal agreements (bylaws, operating agreements, shareholder agreements, etc.) that govern the organization.

Every now and then, however, organizations descend into civil war. Different factions of **constituents** develop fundamental differences about what the organization should be doing or who should be in charge, and each faction claims the authority to have the organization follow its instructions.

These are excruciatingly difficult times to be counsel to the organization: Different warring factions are all insisting, often at the top of their lungs, that they, and they alone, have the power to tell the organization what it **must** be doing. They show no interest in resolving their differences with their rivals. And you, as the organization's lawyer, are stuck in the middle. Your job is to follow your client's instructions (within the limits of the law) and to assist your client in achieving its objectives, but different factions—each often having a colorable claim to being right—are insisting that they have the power to instruct you, often in starkly different terms, about what those objectives are and what you **must** do to help achieve them.

REAL WORLD When things within an organization devolve to this state, your (and your **practice organization's**) safest and most effective course of action may well be simply to withdraw—and if you represent the organization in more than one matter, to withdraw either from all of them or from any of them in which your instructions going forward are disputed among the warring factions. (For example, you could be defending a specific lawsuit against the company that all the disputing **constituents** agree needs to be defended on terms on which they don't disagree. In that case, though, you would need to be clear that you are withdrawing from any other matters in which you are receiving conflicting instructions and limiting your engagement to the matters that are not internally disputed.)

In situations like these, each faction generally has independent counsel of its own, and the factions and their lawyers usually end up fighting out their differences in a court or some other tribunal. Under these circumstances, it's often difficult for company counsel to provide useful advice or service to the company as a whole.

Faced with conflicting instructions, your job is to determine who, under the law governing the organization, has the power to tell you and the organization what to do. **Model Rule 1.13(a)** *see* **Chapter 23.A at 772**. The faction that you conclude (after careful research and analysis, and in perfectly good faith) lacks authority will typically claim that you're wrong, will disregard or undermine your decision and actions, and quite possibly will sue you for malpractice or breach of fiduciary duty as well. Even if you're right, your vindication may not come until after a lengthy and bruising stretch of litigation. ⟨Real World⟩

> Problem 23A-7: Assume that you find yourself in a situation like the one described in the immediately preceding four paragraphs. On what basis or bases **must** or **may** you withdraw (please consider all colorable options), and what practical steps would you need to take to accomplish the withdrawal? Please explain your answer.

⟨Tips & Tactics⟩ What if, despite our advice, you decide to remain in the middle as organization counsel during an organizational civil war? What **must** or **should** you do?

- The first thing you have to do is determine whether you have a **disqualifying conflict of interest**. If you represent the organization, and the organization alone, then receiving differing instructions from competing factions of **constituents** does *not* create a **conflict of interest**. Why? You have only one client—the organization. The competing factions are making it difficult to determine how to serve that one client, but that's not a **conflict of interest** (though it is a risky and complicated professional predicament, which is why we just advised you to consider withdrawing). If, however, you also happen to represent any of the warring **constituents**—whether in connection with their **interests** in the organization or in something unrelated—then you *do* have a **conflict of interest** that you **must** avoid or address. (Do you see why? Explain it out loud. *Hint*: See **Chapter 23.A at 773**.) And you also have a **conflict of interest** if you have personal connections with a warring **constituent** that are close enough that they create a significant risk of materially limiting what you can or want to do as organization counsel. (Again, do you see why? Cite and apply the relevant Model Rule. *Hint*: See **Chapter 22.A at 626**.)

- If the competing factions seeking your advice have arguable claims to be informed of the organization's **confidential information** (which, if they have colorable claims to be directing you and the company, they likely do), then be sure to be transparent with both (or all) sides. Don't give anyone the opportunity to claim that you were acting improperly by "secretly conspiring" with one faction (the disappointed faction's likely accusation). Tell both sides that you intend to share all communications that you have with either side regarding the issues in dispute—as well as your responses—with both sides. Then do so. As you can imagine, this process can get messy and contentious.

One faction may claim the right to communicate with you in **confidence** from the other faction. *See* **Model Rule 1.13 Comment [2]**. You'll need to evaluate that claim and respond to it accordingly.

- Be sure that you limit your participation to issues that are appropriate for the organization's lawyer, rather than the organization's business advisor, or the lawyer for one faction or the other. Your job is hard enough without complicating it further.

- Keep evaluating whether it makes any sense for you to remain in the middle of the situation or whether the organization would be no worse off if you withdraw. TIPS & TACTICS

Problem 23A-8: Go back and review the hypothetical in the **chapter Introduction at 769** one more time. Assume that Ted Tech has not yet given up on the venture and has started to make the plans that Ron describes at the end of the hypothetical. The chair of the company's board of directors (it is a corporation) calls a special meeting of the board to address the differences among the managers that Ted has described to Ron. The board chair asks Ron to attend the meeting as the corporation's lawyer. Analyze the concerns that Ron must consider and address as he prepares to respond to this request and attend the meeting. Describe the specific concrete steps that Ron **must** or **should** take. For each step, explain whether it is a **must** or a **should**, and explain why.

B. Reporting Trouble "Up" or "Out"

In our job as counsel to an organization, we sometimes discover trouble within the organization. Sometimes we're specifically asked to investigate and determine whether one or more employees or other **constituents** is engaging in misconduct. Other times, we just stumble across trouble within the organization in the course of our ordinary responsibilities.

Quite frequently, the trouble that we discover within an organization can be (and is) addressed straightforwardly within the company's existing management and governance structure. For example, if management has directed you, as company counsel, to investigate potential wrongdoing within the company, then management usually really wants to find out if anything is going wrong, and to fix it. Similarly, questions from organizational **constituents** about contemplated or ongoing courses of action are often motivated by a desire to ensure that they and the organization are properly operating within the constraints of the law (or putting it slightly less charitably, what they can get away with without getting in trouble). And if you discover that your regular client contacts are engaging in practices that violate the law or company policies, part of your job is to let them know about the problem and help them correct it. Usually, they'll want to do so; in most well-run organizations, most **constituents** understand that unlawful or inhumane conduct is not a pathway to success and will make good use of your advice on how to do things right.

Every now and then, though, the organization's systems don't work. For example, personal crises may drive otherwise honest **constituents** into unlawful conduct from which they cannot see any practical escape. Or a **constituent** may have discovered ways to game the organization's rules so as to look successful while cheating, and refuses to accept your advice to stop (or, worse, promises to follow your advice and then doesn't). Or abusive behavior, lawlessness, or corruption may have become an established practice in some portion of the company, and your concerns about correcting course are met with bemused deflection or outright hostility. These are not very common situations, but they do occasionally come up in organizations large and small. What **must** or **should** you do if you find yourself in such circumstances?

1. "Reporting Up"

As so often happens, there's a Rule for that, too—one that defines the duty of the lawyer for an organization to bring trouble to the attention of higher management within the organization—a practice often referred to (though not in the Rule itself) as "**reporting up**." Take a look at **Model Rule 1.13(b)**. It's another somewhat long and circuitous Rule, so please read it slowly and carefully, and then we'll make sense of it together.

TAMING THE TEXT Let's start by focusing on the first lengthy sentence of the Rule. It takes the form of an "If . . . then" proposition (take another look and confirm that for yourself). What's more, the "if" part has several pieces:

If

(1) a lawyer for an organization knows

(2) that an officer, employee or other person associated with the organization is

- engaged in action, or
- intends to act, or
- refuses to act

(3) in a matter related to the representation

(4) and that is

- a violation of a legal obligation to the organization, or
- a violation of law that reasonably might be imputed to the organization,

(5) and that is likely to result in substantial injury to the organization,

then

the lawyer shall proceed as is reasonably necessary in the best **interest** of the organization.

Let's break down the "if" part of the Rule's first sentence. It defines the situation that triggers a requirement for action on the organization lawyer's part, and it has five pieces, all of which must be satisfied for action to be required. The lawyer for the organization has to (1) "know" (that is, have actual knowledge of) something. What does the organization's lawyer need to know? That an organization's **constituent** ("an officer, employee or other person associated with the organization") is (2) doing or not doing something (or planning to); *and* that something has to be (3) "in a matter related to the representation" (so not something that isn't related to the lawyer's services for the organization). What's more, that something has to be (4) *either* a wrong to the organization itself (such as stealing from it), *or* a wrong that would be considered to have been committed on behalf of the organization (such as a tort that "reasonably might be imputed to the organization" under any principle of vicarious liability, such as general rules of agency or *respondeat superior*). And finally, that something has to be (5) sufficiently serious that it's "likely to result in substantial injury to the organization," such as significant monetary loss or legal liability, or serious reputational harm.

Now, if all five elements are satisfied, what does the organization lawyer have to do? To "proceed as is reasonably necessary in the best **interest** of the organization." "Duh," we hope you're thinking—of course, as a fiduciary, the lawyer *always* **must** proceed "as is reasonably necessary in the best **interests** of the [client]." What's the point here?

The point comes in the second sentence of **Model Rule 1.13(b)**, which tells you what the organization's lawyer presumptively has to do under these circumstances in order to proceed in the client's best **interests**. Read that second sentence again. What does it tell us that the organization lawyer presumptively **must** do? "[T]he lawyer shall refer the matter to higher authority in the organization." The "shall" means that it's a **must** rule and, read as a whole, the Rule says that, if an organization's lawyer knows that a **constituent** is doing (or is planning to do) something that could cause "substantial injury to the organization," either by committing a wrong against the organization or by causing the organization to commit a wrong against someone else, the organization's lawyer **must** take it up with the **constituent's** boss within the organization ("higher management"). This response is often referred to colloquially as "bucking the issue up the ladder" or, more simply, "**reporting up**."

Must the organization's lawyer *always* **report up** in the circumstances defined by the first sentence of the Rule? Ordinarily, yes, "[u]nless the lawyer reasonably believes that it is not necessary in the best interest of the organization to do so." When might that happen? **Model Rule 1.13 Comment [4]** suggests that, "[i]n some circumstances . . . it may be appropriate for the lawyer to ask the **constituent** to reconsider the matter; for example, if the circumstances involve a constituent's innocent misunderstanding of law and subsequent acceptance of the lawyer's advice, the lawyer may reasonably conclude that the best interest of the organization does not require that the matter be referred to higher authority."

And what happens if the lawyer doesn't see a satisfactory resolution of the issue after **reporting** it **up**? The second sentence of **Model Rule 1.13(b)** goes on to say that the lawyer **must** *continue* **reporting up** to the next higher level of management within the organization, level by level, "including, if warranted by the circumstances[,] to the highest authority that can act on behalf of the organization as determined by applicable law." The "applicable law" here is the law governing the organization, and the "highest authority" in the organization under governing law will depend on the type of organization and the state's law governing it. In corporations, for example, the highest management authority under state corporate law is typically the corporation's board of directors. In a limited liability company, it might be the managing member. You'll learn these details in the Business Organizations course that we keep urging you to take, but what **Model Rule 1.13(b)** requires is that you determine the pathway to top management and pursue a qualifying issue along that path until you either see the issue satisfactorily addressed or reach the highest management in the organization.

Model Rule 1.13(e) articulates another feature of the duty to **report up** that comes up only occasionally. Every now and then you discover trouble that would require **reporting up** (or allow **reporting out**, which is discussed in the following section), but discover it under circumstances that cause you to withdraw from the engagement (either because you **must** withdraw under **Model Rule 1.16(a)**, or because you **may** withdraw under **Model Rule 1.16(b)** and you decide that you **should**). Or your discovery of trouble and your obligation to **report** it **up** (or your power to **report** it **out**) may cause a **constituent** involved in the misconduct who has the organizational authority to do so to discharge you as the organization's counsel—it's a predictable, if rather crude, reaction to getting caught. You might think that, once you are no longer counsel to the organization, your duties to **report up** end, too; that's likely what any **constituent** who fired you was thinking (though that person will probably dress the discharge up in some other excuse). But in either of these circumstances, **Model Rule 1.13(e)** creates a duty that survives your discharge to "proceed as [you] reasonably believe[] necessary to assure that the organization's highest authority is informed of [your] discharge or withdrawal." In other words, whatever other steps your withdrawal or discharge might require or allow under these circumstances (*see* **Chapter 9.D at 298** on the "noisy withdrawal"), you **must** alert the highest management authority in the organization that you quit or got fired because you learned of unlawful conduct that **must** be **reported up** or that **may** be **reported out**.

REASON FOR THE RULE Why do we have a Rule requiring lawyers representing an organization to **report up**? After all, **reporting up** is awkward; it's difficult; it puts us in a position where we sometimes have to "rat out" to their bosses those organizational **constituents** who send us work or have become our friends (and yes, you really **must** do that when such a situation arises, or suffer the **consequences**).

Well, remember that, although we interact with and sometimes become personally attached to an organization's **constituents**, our client is the organization itself, and it is to the organization that we owe our **duties of loyalty**, **candor**, and **care**. But organizations are frequently made up of many **constituents**, often so many that managers can't know everything that their subordinate **constituents** are doing. If we become aware that a **constituent** is violating legal obligations to the organization or causing the organization to violate legal obligations to others such that the organization stands to suffer "substantial harm," our job is to protect our client, the organization. And that means bringing the fact or risk of the harm to the attention of other **constituents** who, under the law governing the organization, are in a position to limit or avert that harm. Thus, our **duties of loyalty**, **candor**, and **care** to the organization require us to **report up** and to keep **reporting up** until the problem is addressed or there is nowhere higher up to **report**, so that the organization has every reasonable opportunity to protect itself from the wrongful actions of some of its **constituents**. ⟩REASON FOR THE RULE⟨

⟩REAL WORLD⟨ **Model Rules 1.13(b) and (e)** state affirmative duties—**musts**. But even when the circumstances don't present all the multiple requirements that have to be met to trigger these duties, you may still be looking at a situation that poses real risks to the well-being of your organization client. In that regard, it's worth keeping in mind that, though you sometimes **must report up**, you virtually always **may** do so, and not infrequently, you **should**. The **consequences** of doing so will likely be informal: Some **constituents** may consider your efforts to take problem conduct (even when it's not serious enough to invoke an enforceable legal duty to **report up**) up the ladder to be wise and courageous service to your organization client. Other **constituents** up the ladder may dislike it because your reporting the issue will force on them a problem that they might have preferred to continue ignoring. Still others—mostly those whose wrongful conduct has been dragged out into the light—will resent it bitterly. Whether and how to traverse this political minefield when you are not required to do so is a challenge that doesn't lend itself to easy generalizations. We suggest that you seek advice from someone whose judgment you respect, taking care to consult under the shield of the **attorney-client privilege** while formulating your strategy (*see* **Chapter 8.B at 244**). ⟩REAL WORLD⟨

⟩CONSEQUENCES⟨ **Model Rules 1.13(b) and (e)** are Rules of Professional Conduct, and their violation is a basis for professional discipline. ⟩RULE ROLES⟨ In addition, however, these Rules are widely understood to inform the civil standards for professional conduct in the particular contexts they address. As a result, a failure to **report up** when required that causes the organization harm is also generally actionable by the organization client as legal malpractice (a breach of the **duty of loyalty**, **candor**, or **care** causing damages) or a breach of fiduciary duty. ⟩RULE ROLES⟨ Given that the duty to **report up** arises only when a **constituent**'s violations of the law are "likely to result in substantial injury to the organization," the harm, and thus the damages, when a lawyer fails to **report up** as required can be quite substantial as well. Consequences

> Problem 23B-1: What **must** or **should** the lawyer for the organization do in each of the situations described below? Please identify which steps are **musts** and which are **shoulds** and explain why each step is required or recommended.
>
> a. Maya and a partner in her firm, Celia Deal, are helping their client contact prepare for an important contract negotiation in which the client contact will be the client company's lead negotiator. The businessperson on the other side of the deal is Fortis Ferrara. Ferrara is so famous in the industry for being unreliable and dishonest that he's widely referred to as "Forked-Tongue" Ferrara. Ferrara has suggested that "just the two businesspeople" initially meet privately "to hash out the principal terms of the deal before we turn the lawyers loose." Celia explains emphatically to the client contact that the path behind Ferrara is littered with broken promises and strategically "differing recollections" of important issues, so that a private meeting with him to "hash out the principal terms of the deal" is an absolutely terrible idea that not only will make the negotiation much longer, more complicated, and more expensive than it otherwise would be, but may jeopardize the odds of successfully reaching any agreement at all. The client contact, who is rather full of himself, assures Celia, "Don't you worry, I can handle myself," and accepts Ferrara's proposal. (*Hint: See* **Model Rule 1.13 Comments [3]-[4]**.)
>
> b. Frank is working on a commercial dispute between two businesses. He goes to the client's premises to prepare a key witness—the salesperson who made the disputed deal for the client company—for her deposition. On their way to a conference room, the salesperson stops into the supply room and loads several boxes of pens, two reams of printer paper, a dozen lined pads, a stapler and staples, two boxes of envelopes, and multiple sizes and colors of Post-It notes into a box. When Frank looks at the box quizzically, the salesperson remarks offhandedly, "Oh, it's nothing; just some stuff I need for the side business I run out of my home selling essential oils."
>
> c. Same as (b), but during Frank's conversation with the salesperson, someone stops into the room, and says to the salesperson, "United Way?" The salesperson pulls her wallet out of her handbag and gives the person what looks like about a dozen $20 bills. "I didn't know the United Way collected donations in April," Frank observes. "It doesn't," says the salesperson. "At least not *that* United Way. The sales manager here says we have to give him a part of our commissions. He calls it 'the United Way,' because he says it makes us 'united—my way.'" "What do you mean you 'have to'?" Frank asks, trying to conceal his surprise. "Well, I gotta do it if I want to keep my job," replies the salesperson.
>
> d. Same as (b), but now Frank and the witness are working their way through some documents, which include the salesperson's travel records related to the disputed transaction. Frank has noticed some odd details in the witness's expense-reimbursement forms and asks about them. "Y'know," says the witness, "sales is a really hard job, and I'm on the road 200 days a year. Do you have any idea what that does to your family life? So I make

sure the company pays me for that heartache by adjusting the numbers on my credit card receipts so I get reimbursed for everything these trips are really costing me. At least that extra nine grand will make for a super merry Christmas this year. I'm thinking that we'll go on a family ski trip."

Frank explains, as gently as he can, that the law views practices like those the witness has just described as embezzlement—that is, theft from the company. The salesperson seems genuinely concerned. "Wow, I never thought about it that way," she says. "Tell you what: I'll only submit half my actual travel expenses for reimbursement, starting now, until I make up the expense 'write-ups' I already took. Then I'll be all square with the company."

e. Maya's firm represents a large real estate brokerage with multiple offices all over the state. The realty company's management has heard rumors about inappropriate work-place conduct in one of its offices and asks an employment lawyer in Maya's firm to look into it. The employment lawyer interviews some of the agents in the office in question, and several of the women (privately after gentle prompting) express discomfort with the behavior of one of the male agents. He makes off-color jokes, regularly comments on the women agents' physical attributes, has repeatedly asked two of them out (they have declined), and has insisted on kissing both of those agents on the mouth to "celebrate" closings. The employment lawyer brings these issues to the office manager to inquire if he knows and what he's tried to do about it. The office manager says that he understands that the realtor in question is "a bit of a pig," but protests that he's "my most productive agent. He's responsible for half this office's profits all by himself. I can't mess with that."

f. Maya's firm represents Infinity Investing, Inc., an investment advisory firm. Various advisor-employees of Infinity call Maya and a couple of other associates in her depart-ment for advice about complying with securities and investment advisory regulation. Maya communicates regularly with Artie Advisor in this regard. Artie wants to recom-mend a particular annuity (a kind of investment) to one of his investors, but he's not sure that it meets the requirements of the account. "Any reason why you want this particular annuity?" Maya asks. "Yeah," Artie replies, cheerfully. "They promised an all-expense-paid trip to Jamaica to anyone who sells eight of these to customers, and I'd really like to go." Maya explains patiently that Infinity's internal rules and investment advisory law would consider that an improper inducement (effectively, a kickback), so Artie needs to find another annuity for these customers. "Okay, got it, thanks!" says Artie. "Good thing I haven't placed any of these yet." Then he hangs up.

Maya hasn't heard from Artie for months when, during coffee with one of her colleagues, he mentions Artie Advisor. Apparently, Artie has called him several times in the last few months for regulatory advice. "Has he mentioned any annuities?" Maya asks. "Not that I recall," says her colleague.

Does your analysis change if, in Maya's original conversation with Artie about the annuity, Artie disagrees with Maya's advice and says, "That's not what the lawyers at Obsequious & Pushover say about this. Know what? Forget we had this conversation. I'm consulting them from now on." If so, how does your analysis change and why; and if not, why not?

2. "Reporting Out"

If you find yourself in a position in which you **must report up**, usually you will find management up the ladder willing to take your concerns seriously and to do what's necessary to protect the organization. But what if you can't? Again, there's a Rule for that. Take a look at **Model Rule 1.13(c)**. Spoiler alert: This Rule gives you the option, in limited and rather extreme circumstances, to disclose the organization's **confidential information** *outside the organization* despite your **duty of confidentiality** in order to prevent serious harm to the organization. This option is often referred to (though, again, not in the Rule itself) as "**reporting out**."

TAMING THE TEXT ▶ Like the Rule on **reporting up**, the Rule on **reporting out** is stated as an "If . . . then" proposition. The "if" again has several parts. *If* (1) you've **reported up** all the way to the highest management authority in the organization as required by **Model Rule 1.13(b)**; and (2) "the highest authority that can act on behalf of the organization" won't address (insists on continuing or fails to stop "in a timely and appropriate manner") conduct "that is clearly a violation of the law"; and (3) you reasonably believe[] that the violation is reasonably certain to result in substantial injury to the organization," *then* you "**may** reveal information relating to the representation [that is, the organization's **confidential information**] whether or not Rule 1.6 permits such disclosure, but only if and to the extent [you] reasonably believe[] necessary to prevent substantial injury to the organization."

Another mouthful. So let's chew on it a little: You've got to start with a situation that required **reporting up** under **Model Rule 1.13(b)**. *And* you have to have **reported up**, all the way to "the highest authority that can act on behalf of the organization." *And* the highest authority has to have failed or refused to address the problem you've brought to its attention, *and* that problem has to "clearly [be] a violation of the law"—a standard that suggests that the problem that you're raising is one where there is no reasonable basis for doubt that the conduct in question is unlawful. "It is not necessary that the lawyer's services be used in furtherance of the violation [as would be the case for the **confidentiality exceptions** stated in **Model Rule 1.6(b)(2) and (3)**; *see* **Chapter 8.B at 242**], but it is required that the matter be related to the lawyer's representation of the organization." **Model Rule 1.13 Comment [7]**.

That covers the first part of the Rule—**Model Rule 1.13(c)(1)**. But we're still not done with the "if"—the Rule goes on to require that you also "reasonably believe[] that the violation is reasonably certain to result in substantial injury to the organization." Thus you must *subjectively* "believe[]" that the problem that you're raising "is reasonably certain to result in substantial injury to the organization" (not just any injury, but "substantial" injury); and that the "substantial injury" is not just possible, but "reasonably certain." *And* that belief has to be *objectively* "reasonable." **Model Rule 1.13(c)(2)**.

In addition to satisfying all the elements of the "if," there are also exceptions to the power to **report out: Model Rule 1.13(c)** begins by saying "[e]xcept as provided in paragraph (d)." **Model Rule 1.13(d)** states two exceptions to the power to **report out**: When the organization has hired you specifically "[1] to investigate an alleged violation of law, or [2] to defend the organization or an officer, employee or other **constituent** associated with the organization against a claim arising out of an alleged violation of law." REASON FOR THE RULE ▶ Why these circumstances? Well, in those situations, it is expected that you may discover unlawful conduct as part of the engagement for which you were hired—the organization has hired you to address a problem that it already knows or suspects to exist. If you find a problem, then you still have obligations to **report *up*** under **Model Rule 1.13(b)**, in order to make sure that the organization has every opportunity to use the fruits of your labor to address the problems that you were hired to find. But you're not permitted to report these problems *out* of the organization. Why? "This is necessary in order to enable organizational clients to enjoy the full benefits of legal counsel in conducting an investigation or defending against a claim." In other words, in the specific situation in which organization management has hired you to look for unlawful conduct, we don't want the threat of later **reporting out** to compromise the candor that you will need to have from your client and its **constituents** in order to accomplish your job, and in order for the client to get the full benefit of your informed advice. ◀ REASON FOR THE RULE

Okay, what about the "then"? Here's how it works: If, and only if, *all* those things in the "if" portion of **Model Rule 1.13(c)** are true, and no **Model Rule 1.13(d)** exception applies, then you **may** report out. That's a long, hard climb with many steep steps before you reach the authority to **report out**, right? What's the big deal? REASON FOR THE RULE ▶ The big deal is that **reporting out** is an exception to the **duty of confidentiality** ("**may** reveal information relating to the representation [that is, **confidential information**] whether or not Rule 1.6 permits such disclosure"). **Confidentiality** is widely viewed as one of your gravest and most serious duties as a lawyer. As we discussed in **Chapter 8.B at 235**, there aren't very many exceptions to the **duty of confidentiality**, and the ones that do exist tend to arise in serious circumstances, where the policy interest counterbalancing the interest in preserving the client's **confidences** is quite weighty. That's true here: You've pointed out unlawful conduct within a client organization to the highest management available—unlawful conduct with potentially devastating **consequences** ("substantial injury") for the organization. Those devastating **consequences** could well hurt not only the organization itself but many people who depend on the organization in all kinds of ways, such as those who depend on the safety of its products, those who depend on the organization for their employment, or those who have invested their savings in the organization. In the face of all that, the response of the organization's highest management was, in effect, "So what?" ◀ REASON FOR THE RULE

Even then, the power to **report out** is narrow and limited. To start with, it is entirely within your discretion ("**may** reveal information relating to the representation") whether to report out at all. And if you do decide to **report out**, the Rule expressly limits the disclosures that you **may** make "to the extent [you] reasonably believe[] necessary to prevent substantial injury to the organization." **Model Rule 1.13(c)(2)**. This formulation (which, the alert student has already pointed out, parallels the general limitations on the exceptions to the **duty of confidentiality** stated in the introductory language of **Model Rule 1.6(b)**—take a look back at that Rule and confirm that for yourself) means that, if you decide to report out, then you must disclose *as little* **confidential information** to *as few people* as you reasonably believe will suffice to address the problem that the organization has refused to address itself. Over-**reporting out** will destroy the **confidentiality** exception, and leave you open to discipline and civil liability for violating your **duty of confidentiality**. TAMING THE TEXT

REAL WORLD If you've gotten to the point where **reporting out** is even arguably an option, you **should** seriously consider withdrawing, whether you decide to **report out** or not. Why? Because if you've reached the point where you can consider **reporting out**, then you're representing an organization in which "clearly unlawful" conduct is happening or about to happen—clearly unlawful conduct that is causing or likely will cause "substantial injury to the organization," and quite possibly to its **constituents** or to third parties as well. What's more, you've not only brought this impending disaster to management's attention, you've forced it to the attention of the highest management in the organization. And no one is willing to do anything about it. Under these circumstances, you need to ask yourself whether there is anything that you can realistically do to help this organization, and (a little closer to home), whether the organization, some of its **constituents**, or affected third parties might try to hold you responsible for what the organization was allowing or doing when it all falls apart, unless you step aside and do whatever the law allows to distance yourself from the coming implosion (again, *see* **Chapter 9.D at 298** on "noisy withdrawal"). REAL WORLD

CONSEQUENCES The duty to **report** *up* is a duty—a **must**. Failure to do so when required is a Rules violation and breach of the civil standard of conduct. **Reporting** *out* is different. Even when its predicates are met, **reporting out** is a discretionary option—a **may**. As discussed above, what **reporting out** really amounts to is another discretionary exception to the **duty of confidentiality** supplementing **Model Rule 1.6(b)**—something that allows you to do the right thing when you want to because you consider it the right thing to do, or may need to as a matter of self-protection (for example, as part of a noisy withdrawal), provided that all the requirements are met. Because you never *have to* **report out**, you can't be professionally disciplined or civilly liable for *failing* to do so, even when you could have (and perhaps from a moral standpoint, **should** have). But keep in mind that when you do have the power under the Rules and governing law to **report out**, you are likely in a complicated and difficult situation in which some kind of extraordinary action on your part may be the morally right thing to do, or even required.[8] Consequences

> Problem 23B-2: What **must** or **should** the lawyer for the organization do in each of the situations described below? Please identify which steps are **musts** and which are **shoulds** and explain why each step is required or recommended.
>
> a. Frank's firm represents Clancy's Clamshack, a local informal seafood restaurant. Clancy's is a closely held corporation, and Clancy Clammer is the sole shareholder, officer, and director. Clancy's walk-in freezer breaks during a summer weekend. Times are hard, and Clancy can't afford to pay the technician overtime, so he waits until Monday morning to call for repairs. Clancy then calls Frank to ask what state and local health and safety regulations say he should do with the frozen seafood that he kept in the broken freezer over the weekend. Frank looks it up and confirms what he feared: "You've got to throw it away," he tells Clancy. "But I kept the door closed, and it stayed pretty cold in there all weekend," Clancy protests. Frank explains, "I'm sorry, Clancy; the rules don't have an exception. You might make people really sick." Clancy pushes back: "I can't afford to throw away 1,200 pounds of frozen seafood. Don't worry, I'll check it by smell before I serve it." "Still against the law," says Frank, sadly, "and it's dangerous. I really hate to bring you bad news, but there it is." "Okay, I'll do what I have to," says Clancy, and rings off.
>
> b. Maya's firm has a food and drug practice as well as a white-collar criminal defense practice. The firm is currently representing Fanny Pharma, a large pharmaceutical company. The company has been indicted for marketing fraud. According to the indictment, the company marketed one of its drugs for a non-FDA-approved use, which is a federal crime. (This is called "off-label marketing.") The vice president for marketing, who reports to the CEO and the board of directors, recently confided to a member of the defense team that he is aware of emails in which top management (including the CEO and two other executives who are on the company's board of directors) encouraged the sales team to market off-label, but that he can no longer find those emails on the company email server.

---

[8] We would be remiss if this chapter did not at least mention the Sarbanes-Oxley Act of 2002, Pub. L. 107–204, 116 Stat. 745, enacted July 30, 2002, not entirely affectionately known as "SOX." SOX is a federal law designed to encourage disclosure and eradication of fraud and fiduciary abuse within publicly traded companies. The statute creates specific obligations for lawyers "appearing and practicing" before the Securities and Exchange Commission, which generally amounts to any lawyer representing a company that is publicly traded or otherwise regulated by the SEC, whether in-house or as outside counsel. Simplifying a bit, such lawyers **must report up** within the organization any **material** violation of securities law, breach of fiduciary duty, or similar violation by the company or any of its agents to the company's chief legal officer or chief executive officer. And if that officer does not appropriately address the issue, then counsel **must report up** further to an independent committee of the company's board of directors or to the board itself. The SEC has promulgated regulations allowing (but not requiring) counsel to **report out** to the SEC itself any such violations that the company has not adequately addressed internally. *See SEC Adopts Attorney Conduct Rule Under Sarbanes-Oxley Act*, https://www.sec.gov/news/press/2003-13.htm (Jan. 23, 2003). The statute and the implementing regulations contain elaborate antifraud and internal reporting and governance requirements that are beyond the scope of this book, but bear in mind that this additional layer of regulation is imposed on both companies regulated by the SEC *and* their lawyers, both in-house and outside.

The company's defense to the off-label marketing charges at this point is that the off-label marketing was done ad hoc by a few rogue sales personnel trying to drum up business, rather than as something that the company was encouraging. The emails that the VP has described would be badly inconsistent with that defense and could also subject the managers who wrote the emails to personal criminal charges. The partner in charge of the defense engagement has raised the fact to the CEO and to the board of directors that the emails by top management might exist and might have been deleted from the company server (which would itself be a crime). So far, no one has directed the partner to do anything about it.

c. The white-collar defense group in Maya's firm is contacted by a longtime firm client, a closely held company that sells gravel, concrete, and other paving materials. The main owner of the company believes that the company's comptroller has been embezzling. The owner asks Maya's firm to oversee an audit of the company's records. The firm hires outside forensic accountants, conducts the audit, and discovers that the owner's suspicions are unfortunately correct. The company collected $500,000 from employee payroll for employment taxes but rather than remit these funds to the IRS as the law requires, the comptroller transferred these funds to an offshore account in his own name. It is unclear how much of the money will ever be recovered.

The owner fires the comptroller. Despite the firm's urging, the company refuses to report the theft to the authorities because, as a result of the comptroller's theft, the company still owes $500,000 in employment taxes to the government, and the company does not have nearly that much extra cash on hand. The company owner is not persuaded by the fact that the company could be subject to additional penalties and fines if it does not come clean. He would rather roll the dice and hope that the IRS does not discover the unpaid taxes.

Big-Picture Takeaways from Chapter 23

1. When we lawyers represent an organization, as we frequently do, our duties are owed exclusively to the organizational client, not to any of its **constituents.** *See* **Model Rule 1.13(a); Chapter 23.A at 770**.

2. When we represent an organization, our **duties of confidentiality** are owed to our organizational client. That fact means that communications with **constituents** acting on behalf of the organization can be **confidential** and **attorney-client privileged**, but that the **privilege** and the control of the client's **confidential information** is held by the organizational client, not the human **constituent** who engaged in the communication or furnished the **confidential information**. By the same token, we have *no* authority to disclose an organizational client's **confidential information** to any organizational **constituent** (or anyone else) except to the extent that the disclosure is authorized (expressly or by implication, *see* **Chapter 8.B at 238**) by the organization

itself (that is, by a **constituent** who has the organizational power to authorize the disclosure). *See* **Model Rule 1.13 Comment [2]; Chapter 23.A at 772**.

3. **Model Rule 1.13(g)** tells us that we **may** represent an organization and one or more of its **constituents** at the same time, so long as we properly recognize and address any **conflicts of interest** that may be created.

    a. Representation of an organization and one or more of its **constituents**, whether **concurrently** or **successively**, may create no **conflict of interest**, but it also may create any of the different kinds of **conflicts of interest** about which we learned in **Chapter 22 at 597**. *See* **Chapter 23.A at 773**.

    b. When client consent is required to waive a **conflict** involving the organization and a **constituent**, **Model Rule 1.13(g)** requires that "the consent shall be given by an appropriate official of the organization *other than the individual who is to be represented*, or by the shareholders" (emphasis added). This requirement ensures that the organization's consent is independent, voluntary, and informed. *See* **Chapter 23.A at 775**.

4. You **must** always be clear, both in your own understanding and with respect to the people involved in or on the periphery of an engagement, who your clients are, and who they are not. That can be especially challenging and subject to misunderstanding in the context of organizational formation. *See* **Chapter 23.A at 777**.

5. What **must** we do when we're interacting with nonclient **constituents** of a client organization?

    a. Because you're interacting with someone who is not represented, you must comply with **Model Rule 4.3**. *See* **Chapter 12 (at 373)**. **Model Rule 4.3** provides that, when dealing with an unrepresented person,

    i.   You **must not** "state or imply that [you're] disinterested";

    ii. When you "know or reasonably should know that the unrepresented person misunderstands [your] role in the matter," you **must** "make reasonable efforts to correct the misunderstanding"; and

    iii. If you know or reasonably should know that the unrepresented person's interests "are or have a reasonable possibility of being in conflict with the interests of [your] client," you **must not** give the unrepresented person any "legal advice . . . , other than the advice to secure counsel."

    See **Chapter 23.A at 782**.

    b. In addition, **Model Rule 1.13(f)** says that whenever you're dealing with nonclient **constituents** of a client organization, you **must** explain to the **constituent** who your client is whenever you "know[] or reasonably should know that the organization's **interests** are adverse to those of the **constituents** with whom [you're] dealing." So any time that you ought to know that the individual **constituent** with whom you're interacting has **interests** that are adverse to those of your client organization, you **must** take affirmative steps to make sure that the nonclient **constituent** understands that you represent the organization and are *not* his or her lawyer, as well as the implications of that fact under the circumstances. This makes your obligation to speak up and clarify your role apply, even if there is no indication that the nonclient **constituent** is confused, if the **constituent's** interests are adverse to the client organization's. *See* **Chapter 23.A at 783**.

c. There are three general kinds of situations in which a **constituent's** interest might diverge from the company's interest:

  i. The **constituent** may be contemplating, or actually engaging in, conduct that is directly inimical to the company's interests for personal benefit, such as embezzlement or the theft of company funds or property;

  ii. The **constituent** may be contemplating, or actually engaging in, conduct *on behalf of the company* that would cause, or is causing, the company to violate the law, such as the manufacture or distribution of dangerous products, environmental damage, regulatory noncompliance, fraud on trading partners or the public, antitrust violations, or the like; or

  iii. The **constituent** may be experiencing personal difficulties, such as depression, addiction, or other mental or physical illness, that interfere with the ability to do his or her job.

See **Chapter 23.A at 784**.

d. In any circumstances in which you are dealing with a nonclient **constituent** whose interests are adverse to the client organization's, you **must** provide what is often referred to as a **corporate *Miranda* warning** or an ***Upjohn* warning**. *See* **Chapter 23.A at 782**.

  i. The ***Upjohn* warning must** be tailored to the circumstances, giving enough context to make your role and **loyalties** clear and addressing any possible practical misunderstanding that may be lurking. It always includes, in one form or another, the information that you represent the company and that you don't represent the **constituent**. Beyond that, the warning needs to address the implications of your role that are suggested by the circumstances. *See* **Chapter 23.A at 785**.

  ii. If the conversation is one in which you expect the **constituent** may be contemplating or engaging in conduct contrary to the organization's **interests**, you **must** administer it at the beginning of the conversation because **Model Rule 1.13(f)** says you **must** clarify your role whenever you know or reasonably should know that the organization's **interests** are in **conflict** with the **constituent**'s. If you're talking to this **constituent** because you are concerned that the **constituent** is contemplating or engaging in **misconduct**, then you already reasonably should know that **constituent**'s **interests conflict** with your client's. Sometimes, however, you can be surprised by something the **constituent** unexpectedly raises during what you anticipated would be an ordinary exchange. The moment that happens, you must pause and clarify your role. *See* **Chapter 23.A at 786**.

 iii. Neither **Model Rule 4.3** nor **Model Rule 1.13(f)** states any formal requirement (nor does any parallel civil duty), so the **warning** may be administered orally. But in any situation in which you go into an interaction anticipating **conflicting interests** between the organization and the **constituent** (for example, an investigation on the company's behalf into potential wrongdoing), administering the **warning** in writing, and giving the **constituent** time to review it and ask questions before you begin, is the best course to avoid any future claim by the **constituent** that she was not apprised of her rights. *See* **Chapter 23.A at 786**.

e. The **consequences** of failing to administer a timely and effective *Upjohn* **warning** can be numerous and serious. Because **Model Rule 1.13(f)** and **Model Rule 4.3** are disciplinary rules, their violation can result in professional discipline. But the improper acquisition of information that proper conduct would have prevented can and often does have civil **consequences** as well. If you have accepted **confidences** from the **constituent** under circumstances in which the **constituent** reasonably believes that you will keep the communication **confidential**, then you may have assumed a **duty of confidentiality** to the **constituent**. That duty is in **conflict** with your **duties of loyalty** and **candor** to your organization client, which require you to tell the organization what you implicitly promised the **constituent** you would keep secret. You have a **conflict of interest**. Unless you can obtain the **informed consent, confirmed in writing**, of the **constituent** to disclose the **confidences** to the organization (which is unlikely, because the **constituent** has told you things that will get the **constituent** in trouble if disclosed), you **must** withdraw from representing the organization, or the **constituent** may be able to **disqualify** you (and your **practice organization**, which could include the organization's entire in-house law department if you are an in-house lawyer). If you disclose the **constituent's confidences** to your client (the organization), you have violated the **duty of confidentiality** that you assumed to the **constituent**. Not only may the **constituent** be able to **disqualify** you (and your **practice organization**), she may sue you for any monetary damages that your disclosure has proximately caused. And if there is litigation between the **constituent** and the organization, the organization may be precluded from using as evidence anything whose disclosure by the **constituent** was improperly induced. To the extent that the **constituent** has made decisions or taken action in reliance on advice that you should not have given (remember, no legal advice to the **constituent** is allowed, except the advice to get her own lawyer), those decisions may be undone if, as a practical matter, they can be, and if they can't be undone, then the **constituent** may be able to recover any damages caused by the irreversible decision. *See* **Chapter 23.A at 786**.

6.　What do you do if you find yourself, as company counsel, stuck in the middle during an organizational civil war? The first thing you **must** do is to determine whether you have a **disqualifying conflict of interest**. If you represent the organization, and the organization alone, then receiving differing instructions from competing factions of **constituents** does *not* create a **conflict of interest**, because you have only one client—the organization. If, however, you also happen to represent any of the warring **constituents**—whether in connection with their **interests** in the organization or in something unrelated—then you *do* have a **conflict of interest** that you **must** avoid or address. And you also have a **conflict of interest** if you have personal connections with a warring **constituent** that are close enough that they create a significant risk of materially limiting what you can or are willing to do as organization counsel. If the competing factions seeking your advice have arguable claims to be informed of the organization's **confidential information** (which, if they have colorable claims to be directing you and the company, they likely do), then be sure to be transparent with both (or all) sides. Be sure that you limit your participation to issues that are appropriate for the organization's lawyer, rather than the organization's business advisor or the lawyer to one faction or the other. Keep evaluating whether it makes any sense for you to remain in the middle of the situation, or whether the organization would be no worse off if you withdrew. *See* **Chapter 23.A at 789**.

7.　**Reporting up:**

　　a. **Model Rule 1.13(b)** says that, if an organization's lawyer knows that a **constituent** is doing (or is planning to do) something that could cause "substantial injury to the organization," either by committing a wrong against the organization or by causing the organization to commit a wrong against someone else, the organization's lawyer **must** take it up with the **constituent**'s boss within the organization ("higher management"), and **must** *continue* **reporting up** to the next higher level of management within the organization, level by level, "including, if warranted by the circumstances[,] to the highest authority that can act on behalf of the organization as determined by applicable law." *See* **Chapter 23.B at 792**.

b. In addition to triggering professional discipline for a failure to **report up** when required, such behavior—if the failure to report causes the organization harm—is also generally actionable by the organization client as legal malpractice (a breach of the **duty of loyalty**, **candor**, or **care** causing damages) or as a breach of fiduciary duty. Given that the duty to **report up** arises only when a **constituent**'s violations of the law are "likely to result in substantial injury to the organization," the harm, and thus the damages, when a lawyer fails to **report up** as required can be quite substantial as well. *See* **Chapter 23.B at 795**.

8. **Reporting out:**

a. **Model Rule 1.13(c)** also provides that, if (1) you've reported up all the way to the highest management authority in the organization as required by **Model Rule 1.13(b)**; and (2) "the highest authority that can act on behalf of the organization" won't address (insists on continuing or fails to stop "in a timely and appropriate manner") conduct "that is clearly a violation of the law"; and (3) you "reasonably believe[] that the violation is reasonably certain to result in substantial injury to the organization," then you "**may** reveal information relating to the representation [that is, the organization's **confidential information**] whether or not Rule 1.6 permits such disclosure, but only if and to the extent [you] reasonably believe[] necessary to prevent substantial injury to the organization." *See* **Chapter 23.B at 798**.

b. **Model Rule 1.13(d)** states two exceptions to the power to **report out:** When the organization has hired you specifically "[1] to investigate an alleged violation of law, or [2] to defend the organization or an officer, employee or other **constituent** associated with the organization against a claim arising out of an alleged violation of law." *See* **Chapter 23.B at 799**.

c. If, and only if, *all* those things in the "if" portion of **Model Rule 1.13(c)** are true, and no **Model Rule 1.13(d)** exception applies, then you **may** report out. If you decide to report out, then you must disclose *as little* **confidential information** to *as few people* as you reasonably believe will suffice to address the problem that the organization has refused to address itself. Overreporting will destroy the **confidentiality** exception and leave you open to discipline and civil liability for breach of your **duty of confidentiality**. *See* **Chapter 23.B at 800**.

Multiple-Choice Review Questions for Chapter 23

1. Under **Model Rule 1.13(a)**, a lawyer representing a corporation generally owes duties to which of the following:
   a. The corporation itself as an entity.
   b. The board of directors of the corporation.
   c. The shareholders of the corporation.
   d. All of the above.

2. James is a solo practitioner who primarily handles employment discrimination cases. He receives a call from Kim, one of the directors of BigCorp. Kim says that she is calling to retain counsel for the corporation. She asks James if he will conduct an internal investigation. The board is concerned that the corporation's CEO, Lonnie, discriminated against an employee, Meredith, based on her gender. As Kim explains, if the allegations are true, the corporation could be sued.

   If James agrees to handle the investigation, who will be his client?
   a. Kim.
   b. BigCorp.
   c. BigCorp.'s board of directors.
   d. Meredith.

3. Lawyer Nico represents the Commonwealth of Keystone Department of Transportation. Does he represent an organizational client as defined by **Model Rule 1.13**?
   a. Yes. The term "organization" is defined broadly to include governmental organizations.
   b. Maybe. It depends whether his duties are defined by statute and regulation.
   c. Maybe. It depends on the structure of the department.
   d. No. The term "organization" refers to only entities with a corporate form of organization.

4. BigBox Corp. hires lawyer Oakley to investigate whether its employees have been stealing inventory. BigBox suspects, but is not sure, that the theft is occurring during the night shift.

   Oakley meets with BigBox employees to interview them, in an effort to determine if there has been theft.

   Which statement is true about these meetings?

a. The interviews are **confidential** and are therefore protected by Rule 1.6. Oakley **may** disclose to the employees that BigBox suspects that the theft has occurred on the night shift.

b. The interviews are **confidential** and therefore protected by Rule 1.6. Oakley **must not** disclose to the employees that BigBox suspects that the theft has occurred on the night shift unless he receives BigBox's permission for the disclosure.

c. The interviews are not **confidential** and therefore are not subject to the protections of Rule 1.6. Oakley **may** disclose to the employees that BigBox suspects that the theft has occurred on the night shift.

d. The interviews are not **confidential** and therefore are not subject to the protections of Rule 1.6. Oakley **must not** disclose to the employees that BigBox suspects that the theft has occurred on the night shift unless he receives BigBox's permission for the disclosure.

5. Lawyer Patricia represents a large chain of clothing stores. The VP of marketing reveals to her that the company intends to embark on a new marketing campaign. The VP shows her some mock-up print advertisements that Patricia believes are borderline racist. When Patricia points this out to the VP, the VP explains that this is intentional—the company wants to be viewed as "edgy" and hopes that the ads will go viral.

Patricia thinks the plan will backfire, will drive away customers, and could seriously damage the company's bottom line.

What obligations does Patricia have under **Model Rule 1.13**?

a. She **must** ask the VP to reconsider the marketing strategy.

b. She **must** share her concerns with a higher authority within the company.

c. She **may** raise her concerns with the VP or with a higher authority within the company.

d. She **must not** question this decision even though she believes that it poses a financial risk to the company.

6. In determining whether to refer a matter to a higher authority in an organization when the lawyer for that organization discovers a **constituent**'s wrongdoing, the lawyer **must** consider:

a. The seriousness of the violation.

b. The motivation of the **constituent**.

c. The organization's policies and procedures.

d. All of the above.

7. A lawyer **may** represent an organization client named as a defendant in litigation and which other party to that same litigation?

    a. The plaintiff.

    b. A **constituent** named as a defendant whose interests are adverse to the organization's.

    c. A **constituent** named as a defendant whose interests are not adverse to the organization's.

    d. No other person.

8. Pedro has been retained by Bullnose Corp. to defend it in a breach of contract case. The company's CEO, Amy, is being deposed about statements she made to the other party reflecting her interpretation of the contract. Whom does Pedro represent at this deposition?

    a. Amy.

    b. Bullnose.

    c. Bullnose and Amy.

    d. Neither Bullnose nor Amy.

9. DM Paper Company is a small, privately-owned office supply company located in Scranton, Pennsylvania. Its lawyer for over a decade has been Michael.

    Last year, Michael assisted DM in acquiring a $1.5 million business loan. The loan was for a three-year period, at the end of which the loan was to be fully repaid to the lender. Michael negotiated the terms of the loan and drafted the loan agreement between DM and the lender. Prior to the closing, Michael drafted an opinion for the lender stating that DM's finances were in good order. Before rendering this opinion, Michael reviewed DM's financial statements, which Michael did not prepare. These were prepared by Dwight, CEO of DM. The financial statements showed that the company was in sound financial condition.

    The lender cited Michael's opinion as a basis for extending the loan. The lender was not provided with the financial statements. The statements were neither audited nor publicly filed.

    Unknown to Michael, Dwight had falsified DM's financial statements. Michael only learned this fact four months after the loan had closed. In actuality, DM was doing poorly, and the company was hemorrhaging money. Dwight promised to stop falsifying the statements going forward, but he refused to notify the lender. He pointed out that no one had seen those statements but Michael. He forbade Michael from telling the lender anything about the company's finances or the financial statements. He further forbade Michael from withdrawing his opinion. Dwight pointed out that the loan was not due for nearly three more years. He reasoned that there was plenty of time to turn the company's finances around and repay the lender.

What **must** Michael do?

a. Michael **must** call the lender and disclose the fraud. He **must** also send copies of the fraudulent financial statements.

b. Michael **must** withdraw from representing DM in any and all matters. He **must** also notify the court.

c. Michael **must** inform a member of the board of directors who was uninvolved with the fraud. He **must** also attempt to protect DM's interests.

d. Michael **must** notify the U.S. Securities and Exchange Commission. He **must** also offer to testify regarding the fraud.

24

Ethics in Advocacy

DANIELLE IS TRYING a "snatch-and-grab" robbery that occurred in a rough part of town. It's only her second solo trial, and she's both nervous and excited. The defendant appears to be responsible for a rash of violent personal robberies, and the DA's office wants him incarcerated. The crime victim and principal witness for the prosecution is Wendy Witness. Wendy is not an ideal witness—she has a history of drug use, and a criminal record that includes a recent guilty plea for breaking and entering a car to steal its contents. The DA's office has bargained down the sentence on the car break-in to probation in expectation of Wendy's truthful cooperation in the robbery case and has postponed sentencing until after her testimony.

Danielle has decided to "pull the teeth" on Wendy's history by eliciting the bad facts on direct examination, rather than waiting for the defense to do something dramatic on cross. Accordingly, after getting some basic background on the record, Danielle asks, "What experience, if any, have you had with illegal drugs, Ms. Witness?" "I used to be addicted to oxy and heroin," Wendy answers, "but a couple of years ago I got into rehab, and I've been clean ever since." Danielle knows from the police arrest report that, when Wendy was arrested for the car break-in a few months ago, she had fresh needle marks on her arms.

Flustered, Danielle continues her examination: "Can you tell us about the last time you had an encounter with the police?" "Yeah," answers Wendy. "A few months ago, my welfare check ran out, and I was hungry. I've been trying to get a job for months. So I broke into a car to get something to sell for food. I got caught." "What arrangement, if any, did you make with the DA's office regarding sentencing in that case?" Danielle asks. "I don't know if I have an arrangement," Wendy answers. "I pleaded guilty."

What, if anything, **must** or **should** Danielle do now?

* * *

We resolve legal disputes in the United States through an adversary system. The structure of that system assumes that the best way to get to the proper application of the law to the truth in matters consequential enough to find themselves in our judicial system is for advocates to make the best case that they can on each side and then let a neutral judge or jury figure out who gets what.

No justice system populated by human beings will ever be anywhere close to perfect, but our adversary system has many good qualities and is, in all events, the system that we have and that you must learn to use. Lawyers who advocate within the system are expected to make the best case that they can, within the limits of the law, on their clients' behalf. Thus, calling someone's advocacy "aggressive" is often a compliment. "Aggressive" doesn't mean nasty or mean-spirited; but it does mean pushing whatever law and facts you have as far as the law will allow you to take them. Those of us who work within the advocacy system find endless reasons to complain that our adversaries have pushed things too far; part of being an advocate is policing your adversaries' aggressions to within proper limits.

All that being said, there are some hard limits on advocacy tactics, and transgression of those limits is a very serious matter. Consistent with the nature of our adversary system, these limits generally proscribe obvious misconduct, leaving ample room for honest advocates to do their best. Some of those limits are found within existing criminal or civil law (for example perjury; obstruction of justice; malicious prosecution; civil sanctions for advocacy or discovery misconduct under, *e.g.*, **Fed. R. Civ. P. 11**, **Fed. R. Civ. P. 26**, or **Fed. R. Civ. P. 37**), but several important ones are found in the Rules of Professional Conduct. Those limits are the subject of this chapter.

A. Working in an Adversary System as an "Officer of the Court"

The **Preamble to the Model Rules** is a general statement of principles and aspirations, filled with **shoulds**, that is meant to provide context and background for the Rules themselves. The **Preamble (¶ [1])** begins by describing three distinct roles lawyers fill:

> A lawyer, as a member of the legal profession, is a representative of clients, an officer of the legal system and a public citizen having special responsibility for the quality of justice.

We've spent most of this book exploring your obligations as a "representative of clients." Your role as a "public citizen having special responsibility for the quality of justice" is quite important too, but the Rules themselves have little to say about this "public citizen" role, and the Preamble's attention to it is limited to the exhortation to "seek improvement of the law, access to the legal system, the administration of justice and the quality of service rendered by the legal profession." **Preamble ¶6**. Nevertheless, many lawyers bring to bear the skills they have honed while representing clients on seeking to improve our laws and our legal system, for example through *pro bono* work (in which the Rules themselves urge us to engage, *see* **Model Rule 6.1**), by supporting worthy causes, and by serving as judges, legislators, or other public officials or employees. We hope that you will, too.

But what about your role as an "officer of the legal system" or, as it is often phrased, an "officer of the court"? Strikingly, neither the Preamble nor any of the Rules explains what this role entails. Like the important but cloudy notion of "professionalism," there is no clear definition, even though the phrase is frequently invoked. We would say (and, in fairness, many thoughtful views on this subject differ from ours) that, without attempting a definition, being "an officer of the court" at minimum brings three important ideas into play—ideas that inform this course.

First, the role and its description hint that lawyers' behavior in advocacy may be subject to some additional degree of scrutiny beyond that accorded other lawyer conduct. Business lawyers and others who never set foot in court have demanding conventions of behavior too, of course, and they should. And some people disagree that litigation-related conduct is or should be examined more closely than other types of lawyer conduct and disagree as well about the rationale for focusing on ethics in advocacy. Perhaps it's because litigation is a public process presided over by a public officer. Perhaps it's because litigation conduct is generally recorded and preserved "on the record," so there's a lasting, even historical, feature to the process. Perhaps it's because litigation is one of the main arenas in which the processes and forces of the law impinge on unwilling citizens—as you know, at least one party has been dragged into court involuntarily, and both parties have to live with the result, whether they like it or not. Perhaps this involuntary aspect of litigation inspires stricter scrutiny. But for better or worse, as you've seen by now, we have a lot of rules about lawyers' dispute-oriented behavior.

Second, in its actual use, the phrase "officer of the court" implies some ill-defined expectation of behavior beyond the minimum demands of the professional disciplinary rules or the rules of court procedure. You will likely soon observe that the phrase "officer of the court" is most commonly used in conjunction with the assertion that the person being reminded of this status hasn't lived up to it (as in, "How could you do that? You're an officer of the court!"). Often, the phrase is used when the expectation that has been disappointed is one that lacks formal **consequences**, suggesting some "higher standard" of conduct that judges may expect of advocates, or that advocates may expect of each other, though that higher standard may not be formally enforceable.[1]

The *third* idea that the notion of being an "officer of the court" brings into focus is the one to which we're going to devote most of this chapter. That idea

---

[1] There are, however, disciplinary opinions suggesting that these duties are more than precatory. For example:

All lawyers, by virtue of their licenses, enjoy the status of officers of the court. That status brings with it the responsibility to refrain from conduct unbecoming such officers, to uphold the rule of law, and to enhance public confidence in that rule and the legal system set up to safeguard it. . . . [**Model Rule 8.4(d)**] can be violated by conduct unbecoming an officer of the court, even if a legal proceeding has ended and even if the lawyer stops somewhere short of spreading outright lies.

is that, in and around formal dispute resolution processes, the advocate's **duty of loyalty** to his or her client is constrained by other enforceable duties—duties with **consequences**—that are sometimes viewed as ones that lawyers owe directly to the court or to the legal system itself. Some of those duties are enforced by the professional disciplinary system; some are enforced by the court; and some also carry with them civil remedies to third parties who have been injured by the breach of duty. But the ethical duties in advocacy that we'll discuss in the sections that follow are ones focused on promoting a fair, rational, and at least somewhat efficient process of resolving disputes. And that makes thinking of them as duties to the court or to the legal system a helpful frame of reference.[2]

Let's get to work.

B. Gathering and Handling Evidence

Many of the Rules of Professional Conduct concerning gathering and handling evidence are straightforward and predictable—the kinds of things that you would have guessed were in there even before you opened the rulebook. But the details are important and sometimes surprising. Let's walk through those Rules to get the lay of the land.

1. Investigation Must Be Conducted Lawfully

Model Rule 4.4(a) provides, in part, that "[i]n representing a client, a lawyer shall not . . . use methods of obtaining evidence that violate the legal rights of [a third] person."[3] The Rule provides professional discipline for violation of others' legal rights in this context, but those rights may be defined by the Rules of Professional Conduct or some other local, state, or federal law. The principle probably strikes you as self-evident, but sometimes the heat of battle and the fog of war will cause lawyers to forget that investigation of a civil, criminal, or administrative case, no matter how momentous, confers no license to violate the law.

So allow us to belabor the obvious for a moment, and point out that nothing in the legal system allows you "investigate" by means of (for example) burglary,

---

In re Pyle, 283 Kan. 807, 830-31 (2007) (emphasis in original). **Model Rule 8.4(d)** says that it is professional misconduct subject to discipline to engage in "conduct prejudicial to the administration of justice." It is difficult to say how far this principle goes as an enforceable norm of professional conduct; disciplinary authorities tend to resort to it as a catchall when a lawyer has denigrated or interfered with a tribunal's orderly processes in a way that strikes the authority as disrespectful, disruptive, or dishonest. This notion's coexistence with the First Amendment is not always comfortable. *See* **Chapter 14.C at 420**.

[2] Some ethical rules seek to advance these goals for the dispute-resolution process generally. For example, **Model Rule 3.2** requires lawyers to "make reasonable efforts to expedite litigation consistent with the interests of the client." And as discussed in the preceding footnote, **Model Rule 8.4(d)** generally defines as professional misconduct "conduct that is prejudicial to the administration of justice." Other general rules governing lawyer conduct are applied in disciplinary cases to behavior that also violates one or more of the specific limits on advocacy we'll be discussing in the chapter, for example **Model Rule 8.4(c)'s** prohibition on conduct involving "dishonesty, fraud, deceit or misrepresentation" (*see* **Chapter 3.A at 43**; **Chapter 10.A at 324 & n.2**) or **Model Rule 4.1's** prohibitions on misrepresentation (*see generally* **Chapter 10 at 321**).

[3] The remainder of **Model Rule 4.4(a)** forbids lawyers from using "means that have no substantial purpose other than to embarrass, delay, or burden a third person. . . ." We talked about this portion of the Rule in detail in **Chapter 14.A at 415**, and about the related civil **consequences** it can evoke in **Chapter 14.B at 420**.

theft, wiretapping, computer hacking, or bribery, all of which are not only bases for professional discipline, but are also punishable as felonies. Similarly, "investigations" that comprise an invasion of privacy, intrusion into seclusion, or unauthorized access to or disclosure of confidential medical, legal, financial, or other records are actionable torts as well as bases for discipline under **Model Rule 4.4(a)**. Nor can you make factual misrepresentations in order to induce a witness to divulge information or share documents (or for any other purpose). *See* **Model Rule 4.1; Chapter 10 at 321.**[4]

In addition, although jurisdictions vary, many consider it improper to induce third parties to violate their **confidentiality** obligations, for example by eliciting from them **attorney-client privileged** information, trade secrets, or otherwise privileged, private, or **confidential** information or documents. Besides violating **Model Rule 4.4(a)**, such tactics are sometimes viewed as tortious and may result in civil **consequences**, including **disqualification**, evidentiary sanctions, and monetary sanctions or damages. This concern sometimes arises in the context of a lawyer's interactions with a represented or deemed-represented person protected by the **no-contact rule** of **Model Rule 4.2** (*see* **Chapter 11.G at 365**), or with an unrepresented person protected by **Model Rule 4.3** or **Model Rule 1.13(f)** (*see* **Chapter 12.B at 385; Chapter 23.A at 786**), in a manner contrary to those Rules, which is itself a "method[] of obtaining evidence that violate[s] the legal rights" of the witness or the person or organization to whom the witness owes **duties of confidentiality**.

Finally, don't forget how these principles apply in a **practice organization**. The **no-puppetry rule** (**Model Rule 8.4(a)**) makes clear that you can't get someone else to do something for you that you can't do yourself. And **Model Rule 5.1(b)** and **Model Rule 5.3(b)** require you to ensure that any attorney under your supervision doesn't violate the Rules or other governing law, and that any nonattorney under your supervision does nothing that you yourself wouldn't be allowed to do. *See* **Chapter 19.C at 515.**

> **Problem 24B-1:** In which of the following situations could the lawyer be subject to **consequences**, and what **consequences** could those be? Please explain your answers.
>
> a. Danielle has recently handed up an indictment against a defendant accused of sexually abusing child.
>   i. The police detective assigned to the case is anxious to search the defendant's home, believing that there will be child pornography on the defendant's computer. He

---

[4] Law enforcement officers have more latitude to be untruthful with crime suspects than you do in investigating your own matters. *See, e.g., Frazier v. Cupp*, 394 U.S. 731 (1969). But don't assume that just because local, state, and federal law enforcement officers (such as police officers and FBI agents) have some latitude to be untruthful with crime suspects, *prosecutors* and other government *lawyers* have that latitude. Most jurisdictions hold that government lawyers (including prosecutors) are held to the same ethical standards regarding truthfulness as any other lawyer, including the constraints discussed in this chapter. *See* **Chapter 25.D at 941**. The **consequences** for violation of these principles (beyond professional discipline for violation of an ethical rule), and the permitted interactions between prosecutors and law enforcement officers regarding officers' untruthfulness with suspects is better reserved for your Criminal Procedure course.

suggests entering the home immediately and secretly, without a warrant, while the defendant is at work, before the defendant has a chance to delete any files. Danielle says, "Go for it."

ii.   To avoid any concerns about entering the defendant's home, the detective suggests hacking into the defendant's computer remotely. Danielle says to go ahead.

iii. Now suppose that Danielle gets a warrant permitting a search of the defendant's home. The warrant does not authorize a forensic search of the defendant's computer. The defendant's computer is seized, and Danielle directs a forensic search of its memory. Now assume that Danielle does not authorize the forensic search? What **must** or **may** she do instead?

iv.   Same as (a)(iii), but assume that an absolute spousal privilege is applicable in Danielle's state, and that it protects all communications made during a marriage. Danielle directs the detective to interview the defendant's spouse. Does it matter whether the spouse consents to the interview?

v.   Same as (a)(iv), but now assume that the defendant has been arrested and is in custody. He is permitted to meet with his defense counsel in a room in the prison. Danielle arranges to have that room bugged so she can record any conversations.

vi.   Same as (a)(v), but add that prisoners are told that all their phone calls are monitored. Defendant calls his attorney, and Danielle listens to the jail's recording of the call. What if the defendant called a nonlawyer friend? What if the defendant called his wife?

vii. Same as (a)(vi), but assume also that there is no evidence to implicate the defendant's spouse in any criminal activity. Danielle threatens to have the defendant's spouse arrested if the defendant does not accept a plea bargain.

viii. Same as (a)(vii), but now assume that the defendant works for a well-known social media company. Danielle offers the defendant a lesser plea if he agrees to disclose confidential business information that he learned during the course of his employment, information that Danielle thinks might be helpful in building a racketeering case against the defendant's employer (specifically, a case that alleges that the company was knowingly involved in the distribution of child pornography). Does it matter if the defendant, as a condition of his employment, signed a nondisclosure agreement (an "NDA," which is a contract) regarding confidential company information that forbids him from disclosing the information that Danielle seeks? What if the information is protected by federal and state trade-secret law?

b. Frank is representing an employee who claims that she tripped on a crack in the sidewalk and fell outside the local grocery store that employs her. Frank has filed a complaint on the employee's behalf, and the grocery store, through its counsel, has filed an answer.

i.   Frank asks the store's general manager for permission to visit the store and take some photos. Does it matter whether Frank explains that the purpose of those photos would be to further the plaintiff's case against the grocery store? What if Frank goes to the grocery store to pick up some milk and bread, and while he's there, he pays extra attention as he enters the store: He jots down some notes about the general condition of the sidewalk and snaps a quick picture with his phone. In the checkout line, he exchanges pleasantries with the cashier. Does it matter whether Frank actually needs milk or bread? What if Frank has a firm paralegal do these tasks instead of doing them himself?

ii. Frank learns in discovery that a general contracting company may be jointly and severably liable for the condition of the area in which his client tripped and fell. He calls up the company and asks to speak to the contractor's manager. Without identifying himself or explaining that there is ongoing litigation, Frank questions the manager about the company's process for repairing sidewalks.

iii. The manager in (b)(ii) asks, "Is it possible that we might get sued?" Frank says, "No, the statute of limitations has run." Frank knows that a claim against the general contracting company would still be timely.

iv. Frank amends the complaint to add claims against the general contracting company. He serves a copy on the company. The manager to whom Frank previously spoke in (b)(ii) and (iii) calls Frank and asks for an explanation. Frank explains at length his theory of liability and advises the manager that it would be in the company's best interest to pay some money to settle the case.

v. The general contracting company hires its own counsel, files a motion to dismiss, and is dismissed from the case. Frank continues to litigate against the grocery store. One Saturday, Frank is golfing, and he sees the manager of the grocery store. The manager pulls Frank aside and says, "I hear that you're handling that trip-and-fall case; can we maybe work something out without having to get all the other lawyers involved?" Frank sits down with him to discuss it.

c. Same trip-and-fall case as in (b). Frank is deposing the grocery store's chief of maintenance, who is responsible for maintaining the area outside the store.

i. Opposing counsel has been defending the deponent as a client. (Can opposing counsel do this? Why or why not? *Hint: See* **Chapter 23.A at 772.**) During a break in the deposition, opposing counsel goes to the restroom. Frank engages in small talk with the deponent. What if Frank asks him substantive questions relating to the litigation?

ii. Early in the deposition, Frank asks the witness, "What have you done to prepare for your deposition?"

iii. Instead of the question in (c)(ii), Frank asks, "Did you speak with your lawyer in preparing for your deposition?" Opposing counsel says, "Objection; privilege. You may answer that question 'yes' or 'no.'"

iv. Same as (c)(iii), except that, before opposing counsel can state any objection, the witness blurts out, "Yeah, I told him how upset I was that the store manager wouldn't listen to me about fixing that crack."

v. Same as (c)(iii), except that now the witness answers, "Yes." Frank asks, "Please describe that conversation with your lawyer."

d. **Mess in the Press:** In the 1990s and early 2000s, a number of high-powered Los Angeles-area lawyers with celebrity clients retained private investigator Anthony Pellicano.

Mr. Pellicano was well known in legal circles for his ability to turn up powerful evidence against adversaries. The FBI ultimately charged that Pellicano had conducted illegal wiretaps and made unauthorized use of law enforcement records as a means of gathering information for the lawyers who retained him. Pellicano (along with one of the lawyers for whom he had worked, who was the managing partner of a prominent Los Angeles entertainment law firm) was convicted of wiretapping and related crimes. Pellicano was sentenced to 15 years and served about 10; the lawyer was sentenced to three years. Several other Los Angeles power lawyers were investigated for their work with Mr. Pellicano, but ultimately none of them was prosecuted. Those lawyers professed to have no knowledge of any illegal activities that Mr. Pellicano might have undertaken on their and their clients' behalf.[5] How does that contention fit into those lawyers' exposure to **consequences**, which **consequences**, and how?

e. Frank's firm is representing one of two partners against the other in a bitter small-business breakup. The business employs about 20 people, but it has only one longtime employee other than the two partners, and the client believes that this employee is a witness to a lot of disputed facts. His name is Mortimer Middle. Mort has personal relationships with both partners, and he has been very reluctant to take sides in the dispute. Nevertheless, the firm's client has persuaded him to sit down with Happy Trials and Frank. During the interview, Mort is not forthcoming, claiming bad memory regarding or noninvolvement in numerous important events. Frustrated, Happy exclaims, "Mort, I just don't understand why you're protecting [the partner on the other side]. *He* claims you've been skimming from the till for years." Mort, visibly upset, finally opens up about some of the disputed issues, and what's more, his views tend to favor Frank and Happy's client. Happy is in fact unaware of any claim by the partner on the other side of the dispute that Mort has been taking money from the business without authority. Does your analysis change if Happy's client has shared with Happy a well-grounded suspicion that Mort has been skimming? If so, how and why; and if not, why not?

f. Frank's firm represents Olegbu Olekumwa, a naturalized American citizen who emigrated from Nigeria as a young adult, in claims that he was discriminated against at work (passed over for promotion and later let go) on account of his race and national origin. The case is pending, and the employer (Consolidated Lint) has retained counsel. Olegbu tells Frank that the Director of Human Resources for the division of Consolidated for which Olegbu worked, Hannah Human, has recently left the company. Frank arranges to meet with her. Hannah was not happy at Consolidated, and is willing to share her frustrations with what she describes as "really backwards attitudes" in her division of the company. Frank asks Hannah what she means. She describes a meeting that she had during the time at issue in Olegbu's case with the division chief and "the lawyer" about hiring and promotion. "What lawyer?" Franks asks. "The company lawyer assigned to deal with employment issues in

---

[5] *See* Brooks Barnes, *Pellicano and a Lawyer Convicted in Wiretapping,* https://www.nytimes.com/2008/08/30/business/30pellicano.html (Aug. 29, 2008); David M. Halbfinger & Allison Hope Weiner, *Celebrity Lawyer in Talks About Wiretapping Evidence,* https://www.nytimes.com/2006/02/25/movies/MoviesFeatures/celebrity-lawyer-in-talks-about-wiretapping-evidence.html (Feb. 25, 2006).

our division," Hannah answers. "So what happened at that meeting?" Frank asks. Hannah goes on to describe the division manager's generalizations about racial minorities and immigrants being "bad workers" and his discussion with Hannah and the lawyer about the extent to which he could "keep them down" in lower level positions.

2. Discovery Conduct and Misconduct

This is not a procedure or litigation skills course, so we'll keep our discussion of discovery issues brief. In addition to the various civil remedies for discovery misconduct described in **Chapter 3.C at 53** (**Fed. R. Civ. P. 26(g)**, **Fed. R. Civ. P. 37**, courts' "inherent authority" to govern the proceedings before them, **28 U.S.C. § 1927**, and possible tort claims for abuse of process, among others, all of which may impose **consequences** directly on lawyers), discovery misconduct by a lawyer is also a disciplinary violation.[6] **Model Rule 3.4(d)** provides that "[a] lawyer shall not . . . in pretrial procedure, make a frivolous discovery request or fail to make reasonably diligent effort to comply with a legally proper discovery request by an opposing party." Relatedly, **Model Rule 3.4(c)** provides that a lawyer **must not** "knowingly disobey an obligation under the rules of a tribunal except for an open refusal based on an assertion that no valid obligation exists." This Rule obviously covers discovery obligations, which are typically imposed by a tribunal's procedural rules. The existence of these Rules is a frank statement that discovery misconduct is not only an interference with court processes that is remediable by the court itself, but an act calling into question the perpetrating lawyer's fitness to practice law.

3. Retaining and Handling Evidence

a. Refraining from Unlawfully Obstructing Access to, Hiding, Altering, or Destroying Evidence

Model Rule 3.4(f) forbids you from "request[ing]" someone other than a client (or a relative, employee, or other agent of a client whose **interests** you reasonably believe will not be adversely affected by doing so) "to refrain from voluntarily giving relevant information to another party." The Rule is designed to facilitate informal investigation, and applying it can depend on making some subtle distinctions surrounding what might amount to a "request to refrain from voluntarily providing relevant information." We discussed this prohibition back in **Chapter 12.A at 384**, and recommend that you go back and review the discussion and associated problems, as this is an issue that comes up in litigation with some frequency.

---

[6] In extreme cases, discovery misconduct, such as knowingly misrepresenting the completeness of a party's discovery responses or falsifying responsive documents, can be prosecuted criminally as obstruction of justice, a false-statement crime, or criminal contempt for violation of a court's discovery order. Think it never happens? Think again: Hannah Elliott, *Artist Shepard Fairey Pleads Guilty in Criminal Case, Faces Prison Time*, https://www.forbes.com/sites/hannahelliott/2012/03/07/artist-shepard-fairey-pleads-guilty-in-criminal-case-could-face-prison-time/?sh=a7446b82fdfe (March 7, 2012). *See also* **Chapter 4.A at 73, 81** for the story of a respected big-firm lawyer who went to prison for misrepresentations in discovery.

More generally, and unsurprisingly, **Model Rule 3.4(a)** provides that you **must not** "unlawfully obstruct another party's access to evidence or unlawfully alter, destroy or conceal a document or other material having potential evidentiary value," or "counsel or assist another person to do any such act." Such conduct is often criminal or tortious and subject to court sanctions, as well as comprising a disciplinary violation.

TAMING THE TEXT But look at **Model Rule 3.4(a)**'s prohibition carefully, because its limitations are as important as its reach. It says you **must not** "*unlawfully* obstruct . . . access to evidence" or "*unlawfully* alter, destroy or conceal a document or other material having potential evidentiary value" (emphasis added). Lawyers frequently *lawfully* refuse to disclose the existence of or refuse to provide documents or information, or counsel or assist others to do so, for example, when properly objecting to a discovery request, instructing a client not to answer a question calling for privileged information during a deposition, or advising clients to exercise their right to refuse to speak with law enforcement. The Rule requires you to refrain from doing so only when such conduct is "unlawful[]." The source of the legal prohibition making the activity "unlawful" can come from any applicable legal obligation, including other Rules of Professional Conduct, court procedural or discovery rules, or civil or criminal prohibitions on obstruction of justice or spoliation (a topic discussed below), but the lawyer's conduct interfering with access to the document or information must be independently illegal to violate the Rule.

Note also that the second part of the Rule says that you **must not** "unlawfully alter, destroy or conceal a document or other material having *potential evidentiary value*" (emphasis added). That word "potential" is important and significantly broadens the Rule: The concealed, altered, or destroyed "document or other material" does *not* have to be "evidence" in the sense of something that would be admissible in evidence if offered in some pending proceeding, nor does it even have to be subject to a pending discovery request, subpoena, or search warrant to fall within the Rule. In fact, there does not need to be a pending proceeding of any kind in which the material *could* be evidence for it to have "potential evidentiary value" within the meaning of **Model Rule 3.4(a)**, nor does the material in question need to be admissible under the rules of evidence in any proceeding that might eventually be brought. All that is needed is that the material be something that *could* be *relevant to* or *useful in* some *reasonably foreseeable* proceeding, and that some existing legal norm in the relevant jurisdiction forbids concealing, altering, or destroying it. **TAMING THE TEXT**

b. Counsel's Role in Avoiding Spoliation

Most jurisdictions have laws forbidding "spoliation"—a term commonly used to describe unlawful destruction or alteration of material that could have evidentiary or investigative value in some pending or reasonably foreseeable future proceeding. The proliferation of electronically stored information ("ESI") has intensified the focus on spoliation. ESI is often widely distributed within an organization, is under multiple **constituents'** control, and is often subject to automatic computerized protocols for deletion after periods of time, pursuant to what are ironically called "document retention policies." In response, law has been developing at a rapid pace over the last 20 years regarding what kinds of documents and information **must** be preserved, starting when, who is responsible for doing so, and what the **consequences** for failure may be.[7] Because this is a book about professional ethics, we don't intend to delve too deeply into these obligations here, but we strongly recommend that you invest time and effort in a skills course covering ESI and related discovery practice if you have any intention of litigating document-intensive cases.

CONSEQUENCES The **consequences** to the client when information preservation or production obligations are not met can be extremely serious. Failure to produce documents or information responsive to proper requests or disclosure obligations can result in monetary sanctions, and upon failure to comply with an order compelling the discovery can lead to evidentiary or even terminating sanctions. *See* **Fed. R. Civ. P. 37(a)-(d)**. As for preservation issues, even without any bad faith or intent to deprive an adversary of documents or information, courts are generally authorized to impose remedial measures for the prejudicial destruction of material that should have been preserved, for example by failing to halt automatic deletion measures present in many document-management systems after documents in that system become relevant to pending or reasonably foreseeable disputes. Those remedial measures may include adverse jury instructions or evidentiary sanctions to level the playing field. And with a finding of the destroying party's intent to deprive the other party of the information, the court **may** instruct the factfinder to presume that the lost information was unfavorable to the destroying party or even enter terminating sanctions against the destroying party. *See* **Fed. R. Civ. P. 37(e)**.

In addition, many courts and court systems have imposed independent personal obligations and **consequences** on *lawyers* and their **practice organizations** with respect to their *clients'* compliance with preservation and discovery obligations. Courts often find the authority to impose those obligations and **consequences**

---

[7] *Zubulake v. UBS Warburg LLC*, 229 F.R.D. 422 (S.D.N.Y. 2004), and a series of related decisions in the same case, have proved extremely influential in setting standards for the preservation of ESI during and in anticipation of litigation, and for the terms of discovery and cost-sharing for retrieving and producing ESI, in the federal court system as well as in many state systems. The Federal Rules of Civil Procedure have been amended in multiple respects regarding these issues. *See, e.g.,* **Fed. R. Civ. P. 26(f)(3)(C)** (requiring the parties to confer early in the case and inform the court of their views regarding, among other things, "any issues about disclosure, discovery, or preservation of electronically stored information, including the form or forms in which it should be produced"); **Fed. R. Civ. P. 16(b)(3)(B)(iii)** (authorizing the court to enter early case-management orders regarding the "disclosure, discovery, or preservation of electronically stored information"); **Fed. R. Civ. P. 37(e)** (providing **consequences** for failure to preserve ESI when required).

directly on counsel in such sources as **Fed. R. Civ. P. 26(g)** and **Fed. R. Civ. P. 37(a)**, which allow the court to impose discovery sanctions on the party found to be in the wrong, on its lawyer, or on both. Sometimes sanctions are imposed on counsel on the basis of a court's conclusion that counsel advised or directed the discovery or preservation misconduct, but sometimes courts seem to impose an independent duty on counsel to take reasonable care to ensure, or perhaps even guarantee, that their clients are complying. CONSEQUENCES

This means that you **should**, and arguably **must**, become actively involved in your clients' efforts to preserve information and documents that **must** be preserved, and to produce in discovery documents and information that **must** be located and produced, immediately upon your retention. Otherwise, you may be held personally responsible for sanctions for your clients' errors or omissions in preserving, locating, and producing documents and information.[8]

That involvement includes learning the legal requirements in your jurisdiction for when documents and information **must** be preserved from deletion or destruction. But it also includes affirmatively working with your client to ensure that the client and (if the client is an organization) all of its involved **constituents** know about and comply with document and information preservation requirements relative to pending and impending proceedings. This outreach usually requires the circulation of written notification to anyone who could have relevant material of something often called a "document preservation memo" or a "litigation hold notice" directing the non-destruction of anything that might be relevant to the pending or possible future dispute. Direct involvement in your clients' preservation and production efforts also requires you (and this is where litigation counsel often fall short) to become sufficiently familiar with your clients' information technology systems and architecture so that you can work with them to suspend the ongoing automatic deletion of potentially relevant electronic records, or routine destruction of other records, that is often a part of organization's document retention policies.[9] Similarly, when a disclosure obligation presents itself (by rule such as **Fed. R. Civ. P. 26(a)(1)** or by discovery request or subpoena), you must work with clients to ensure that they understand the extent of their obligations to look for responsive material and help them determine the form in which it

---

[8] Notice how these duties are structured: While they could be viewed as responsibilities to the opposing party to safeguard your client's compliance with its discovery obligations, they can also be seen as duties owed directly to the court. *See* **Chapter 24.A at 814**. In addition, if your client gets in trouble for failing to preserve or produce documents or information, your client may independently blame you for violating your **duty of care** to the client by failing to inform the client about its preservation or discovery observations and may seek to have you bear any loss or damage the client suffered as a result. (Do you see why this is a viable claim?)

[9] This is a substantial topic, but for a quick introduction *see, e.g., Data Preservation and Legal Hold: A Guide to Litigation Holds*, https://www.logikcull.com/guide/legal-holds-data-preservation (last visited Dec. 7, 2020); Stefanie F. Stacy, *Litigation Holds: Ten Tips in Ten Minutes*, https://www.ned.uscourts.gov/internetDocs/cle/2010-07/LitigationHoldTopTen.pdf (last visited Dec. 7, 2020).

will be produced. In an organization of any size, these efforts can be both logistically and technologically complex and may require expertise from within the client or from outside professionals.

Problem 24B-2: Frank's firm represents Clancy's Clamshack, an informal seafood restaurant. As to each event identified below, is that event sufficient to trigger the client's obligations to preserve potentially relevant documents and information? Why or why not? As to each event, what steps **must** or **should** Frank and his firm take, and why?

a. A customer posts a highly critical one-star review of Clancy's on Yelp, which includes the assertion that the customer got food poisoning from eating there.

b. Clancy's gets an angry email from a customer in which the customer claims to have gotten food poisoning from eating there and says, "You guys really need to clean up your act."

c. Clancy is informed that the local public health department has received a complaint from a customer that the customer got food poisoning from eating there.

d. Clancy's receives a demand letter from a lawyer who says that she represents the customer, seeking monetary damages for negligence for the food poisoning the customer claims to have gotten from eating at Clancy's. No complaint has been filed.

e. Change the facts so that each of the events in (a) through (d) involves a customer who claims to have gotten food poisoning at Clancy's during the week following the events described in **Problem 23B-2(a) at 801** (Clancy has informed Frank that his restaurant's freezer broke down over the weekend and that he couldn't afford to get it fixed until Monday; Frank informs Clancy that Clancy must discard the food that was in the freezer; Clancy protests that he can't afford to do that and is equivocal about whether he will). Does that change your answer as to any of the events? If so, how and why; and if not, why not?

Problem 24B-3: Frank is handling a trip-and-fall case on behalf of a client who claims that she tripped over a mat inside the post office because it was worn and wrinkled. The client goes to see Frank's firm within a week of falling. Frank immediately sends a letter to the United States Postal Service ("USPS") identifying the accident's time and place and notifying the agency to initiate a litigation hold. Three months later, Frank presents an administrative claim to the agency as required under the Federal Tort Claims Act. After the claim is denied, Frank files suit in federal district court.

a. As part of his discovery requests, Frank asks to inspect the mat on which his client tripped. The USPS replies that the mat was destroyed shortly before he filed the complaint. Can Frank argue that this conduct constitutes spoliation? Why or why not?

b. Assume that the USPS asserts, truthfully, that its ordinary practice is to throw out floor mats after they've been used for two months, and that it followed that practice with respect to the mat at issue. How does this affect the plaintiff's claim that the discarding of the mat is spoliation, and why?

c. As part of his discovery requests, Frank sends a document request calling for all images of the mat at issue. USPS's counsel tells the postmaster at the station in question to print out any emails and attachments sent from that station during the week the plaintiff fell. Is this sufficient to meet the lawyer's obligation?

d. USPS personnel responding to Frank's discovery requests find a thumb drive in a drawer. They're not sure what's on it, so they throw it away. Is this consistent with USPS's obligations? What about USPS's counsel's obligations? Why or why not? If not, what should each have done additionally or instead, and why?

e. USPS's counsel sends an email to the postmaster at the station where Frank's client tripped and fell, telling the post office to retain any documents related to the accident. USPS's counsel never discusses the letter with the postmaster in the station. The postmaster doesn't interpret the term "document" to apply to videotapes, so the postmaster records over the only copy of the post office's surveillance video of the fall. Is this consistent with USPS's obligations? What about USPS's counsel's obligations? Why or why not? If not, what should each have done additionally or instead, and why?

Problem 24B-4: Frank is representing the plaintiff in a slip-and-fall case. The plaintiff claims that he slipped on a spilled liquid in the grocery store, fell backwards, and injured his lower back so seriously that he has been unable to work and barely able to walk since the accident.

Before filing the complaint, Frank visits the plaintiff's Facebook page. The plaintiff doesn't limit access to his page (that is, anyone with a Facebook account can access everything that the plaintiff has posted on his page). To Frank's horror, among the plaintiff's photos is a picture of the plaintiff playing Twister with a child. (Just in case you don't know, Twister is a game in which the players are required to put their hands and feet on various points on a large mat until contortion and hilarity ensue. Its manufacturer markets it as "the game that ties you up in knots.") Unless those photos were taken before the accident, the plaintiff's position in the pictures and his position in the lawsuit seem impossible to reconcile.

Frank calls the plaintiff and asks for an explanation. The plaintiff volunteers that his wife took a couple of pictures on her phone of him playing Twister with his son, and they were so sweet that he posted them on Facebook. When Frank asks when the photos were taken, the plaintiff pauses, and then says, "I, um, don't remember." Another pause. "Any suggestions?" he asks.

a. **Must** or **may** Frank advise the plaintiff to delete the Twister photos from his Facebook page? Why or why not?

b. **Must** or **may** Frank advise the plaintiff to adjust the privacy settings on his Facebook page to the highest levels, so that only the people the plaintiff has "friended" can see his photos? Why or why not?

c. Instead of immediately offering any advice in response to the plaintiff's inquiry, Frank says that he'll need to think about it. The next day, the plaintiff calls back and announces, "No worries." "What do you mean?" Frank asks. "No pictures," the plaintiff replies. "I'm not sure I understand," says Frank. "Well," the plaintiff explains, "those pictures were so . . . I dunno, I just . . . well, they're not there anymore." How **must**, **may**, and **should** Frank respond to this news?

c. Counsel's Obligations as a Custodian of Material with Potential Evidentiary Value

Although usually we find ourselves advising our clients about the documents and information in *their* possession, custody, or control, or in the possession, custody, or control of third parties, sometimes we find *ourselves* holding material with potential evidentiary value in our clients' matters. Discerning our obligations in these circumstances can be challenging. The Model Rules furnish a general rule for these situations, and a specific rule applicable in limited circumstances.

The general rule is the one we've already discussed: **Model Rule 3.4(a)** which, as we'll remind you (because that's the way we roll), provides that you **must not** "unlawfully obstruct another party's access to evidence or unlawfully alter, destroy or conceal a document or other material having potential evidentiary value," or "counsel or assist another person to do any such act." The Rule still sounds painfully obvious until you start imagining how to comply with it in a situation in which the client or a third party entrusts you, or asks your advice about what to do, with evidence that is harmful to your client's **interests**. Take another look at **Model Rule 3.4(a)** and then try to apply it to the following two problems.

> **Problem 24B-5:** The family law partner in Frank's firm, Sally Splitsville, is shepherding Bettina Blowout through an exceptionally bitter divorce. One evening, Sally is at home with her family when the doorbell rings. It's Bettina, looking disheveled and frantic. Sally (wondering how Bettina got her home address) leads Bettina into Sally's study. "I think I just shot my husband," Bettina says, breathlessly, once they're alone. "I don't know what to do." "My God, is he all right?" Sally asks. "I don't know. I don't know. I can't think," Bettina replies. Bettina reaches into her handbag and pulls out a .22-caliber pistol. She puts it on Sally's desk and says, "Here. Hold this for me, okay?" Then she runs out of Sally's study and out the front door. Sally can't catch up before Bettina speeds away.
>
> This situation raises many ethical and strategic challenges that you may wish to discuss in class or with your classmates, but for now, please focus on these specific questions:
>
> a. **Must** or **may** Sally dispose of the pistol? Why or why not? If not, where **must** or **should** she put it, and why? Would your answers change if Bettina had instead said, "Get rid of this for me, okay?" If so, how and why; and if not, why not?
>
> b. Assume Sally decides to hold onto the pistol for the time being. How (if at all) **must, may,** or **should** Sally handle the gun, and why? **May** or **must** Sally wipe the pistol off or clean it? Why or why not?
>
> c. The police stop by Sally's house later that night. They ask about whether Sally has seen Bettina that evening, and if so, what Bettina was doing. What **must, may,** and **should** Sally say to the police? **Must** or **may** Sally give the police the pistol that Bettina left, and why or why not?

d. Assume that Bettina doesn't run out the door after putting down the pistol and asking Sally to hold it for her. What **must**, **may**, and **should** Sally say to Bettina and do in response to Bettina's request to hold the pistol for her, and why?

e. Same as (d), except Bettina puts the gun down on the desk and instead says, "What should I do with this?" What **must**, **may**, and **should** Sally say and do in response, and why?

Problem 24B-6: Happy Trials does some criminal defense work. He is representing Rodney Kolodny, who has been accused of assault and robbery, specifically with having knocked out Vince Victim and then having taken his wallet. Vince has a concussion and can't remember who hit him. Rodney tells Happy that he didn't do it, but he knows who did: His friend Sneaky Sullivan stopped by Rodney's apartment the day of the robbery and told Rodney that he'd ripped off some guy he'd run into on the street. He gave Rodney a wallet he said that he'd taken from the victim, and told him, "I took what I want. Take whatever you want from that." Rodney looked through the wallet, but found nothing of value. Leaving several of Vince's business cards in the wallet, Rodney had dropped it into the dumpster outside his apartment building.

a. Happy goes to Rodney's building and, in the dumpster in back of the building, he sees a wallet. What **must**, **may**, and **should** Happy do now?

b. Same as (a), but now Happy takes the wallet out of the dumpster, has an investigator dust it for fingerprints, and finds there are no prints left on the wallet good enough to identify them. What **must**, **may**, and **should** Happy do now?

d. Counsel's Obligations Upon Receipt of Material That Appears to Have Been Inadvertently Disclosed

We also promised you a special Rule that applies to a limited situation, and we would never let you down. The limited situation in question is when you receive material that appears not to have been deliberately disclosed. The question in that situation is what your obligations and options are; the answers may surprise you. This topic is controversial and its treatment has evolved over time; buckle up and ride with us while we sort it out.

We start with **Model Rule 4.4(b)**, which addresses the situation explicitly:

A lawyer who receives a document or electronically stored information relating to the representation of the lawyer's client and knows or reasonably should know that the document or electronically stored information was inadvertently sent shall promptly notify the sender.

TAMING THE TEXT What do we see here? The facts invoking the Rule are clearly stated—the Rule applies if all of the following are true:

- You "receive" a document or ESI—note that the Rule does *not* specify the source, so it doesn't necessarily have to come from opposing counsel or the opposing party (though it often does). It could land on your desk from anywhere. **Model Rule 4.4 Comment [2]** helpfully elaborates that ESI includes any form of electronically stored information, "including embedded data (commonly referred to as 'metadata'), that is subject to being read or put into readable form," so long as it was inadvertently included.[10]

- The document or ESI "relat[es] to the representation of [your] client." If you somehow receive inadvertently disclosed material that does not relate to a pending engagement, **Model Rule 4.4(b)** doesn't apply (though you may have other obligations regarding the material).

- You "know[] or reasonably should know that the document or [ESI] was inadvertently sent." And what does "inadvertently sent" mean? "A document or electronically stored information is inadvertently sent when it is accidentally transmitted, such as when an email or letter is misaddressed or a document or electronically stored information is accidentally included with information that was intentionally transmitted." **Model Rule 4.4 Comment [2]**. The Rule thus covers only "inadvertently" (that is, accidentally) sent material; legally protected material sent to you on purpose but in violation of someone else's rights is *not* covered by the Rule, though other law likely governs what you **must** or **may** do with it. *See* **Model Rule 4.4 Comment [2]**. You make the inference of inadvertence based on the contents of the document and the surrounding circumstances. Often, an inference of inadvertence can be based simply on the fact that the material that you've received appears to be **attorney work product, attorney-client privileged,** or **confidential**, but nothing in the Rule says that "inadvertently sent" is limited to inadvertently disclosed *attorney work product, attorney-client privileged*, or *confidential* material; *any* material that you reasonably should know was not intended by its sender for you falls within the Rule. *See, e.g.*, ABA Formal Ethics Op. No. 11-460 (2011).

If all these predicates are satisfied, then what do you have to do? First, let's notice what **Model Rule 4.4(b)** does *not* require: It does *not* require you to delete,

---

[10] Metadata, commonly defined as "data about data," is information that reveals the history, tracking, or management of an electronic document. Metadata can tell you when a document was created, who accessed the document, and when and sometimes how that document has been edited. Most metadata is invisible when a document is printed or converted to an image file, but unless it is "scrubbed" from an electronic file, it usually remains accessible. Metadata can be quite valuable to an adversary. Suppose that an attorney and client are using "track changes" to comment on a draft contract, or perhaps that attorneys within the **practice organization** representing one side are exchanging comments on the draft. The metadata might reveal the client's position or the lawyers' **attorney work product**. If opposing counsel had access to those comments, it would provide significant negotiating advantages by revealing privileged communications or by revealing evidence in a later dispute about the interpretation of the contract.

TIPS & TACTICS The moral of the story: Make sure that you understand what kinds of metadata are ordinarily incorporated into the electronic documents that you create or edit with the word processing and document management software your **practice organization** uses and how to remove the metadata from the document. When you send any electronic document outside your **practice organization**, remove metadata unless there is a good reason not to do so. The best way to avoid a fight over inadvertently disclosed **confidential** or privileged materials is not to disclose it in the first place. TIPS & TACTICS

destroy, or return the document. It does *not* require you to refrain from examining the entire document. It does *not* prohibit you from using the document's contents for any purpose that you or your client might find productive, for example to examine or impeach a witness in deposition or at trial, to guide new discovery, or to introduce as evidence for any permissible purpose. But—and this "but" is important—**Model Rule 4.4(b)** is a dead-minimum response to the receipt of material that apparently was sent inadvertently. Other law that may apply (which we'll discuss in a minute) may require a good deal more, so don't stop with **Model Rule 4.4(b)**.

But what *does* **Model Rule 4.4(b)** require? Simple: You **must** "promptly notify the sender." TAMING THE TEXT

What happens after that is not simple at all. The purpose of the notification requirement is "to permit [the sender] to take protective measures." **Model Rule 4.4 Comment [2]**. If there are colorable arguments that the material was sent inadvertently and remains protectable by the **attorney work product doctrine**, the **attorney-client privilege**, or other **confidentiality** regimes, then you can expect the sender to seek protective measures, sometimes referred to as efforts to "claw back" the information. This process typically begins with a demand to the receiving lawyer to segregate the document or ESI and its contents by deleting or returning the material or, at the very least, to hold it out of anyone's view; and to refrain from reviewing or using the document for any purpose pending the court's determination of the parties' rights and duties. The demand is often accompanied or followed by a motion for a protective order under, for example, **Fed. R. Civ. P. 26(c)** or similar provisions in state law. Depending on the importance of the material, the sender may seek emergency interim relief (that is, a temporary restraining order or equivalent), keeping the material out of reach and out of use until the merits can be heard.

Again depending on the potential value of the material to the recipient and the ruling anticipated from a court, the recipient's response may be anything from voluntarily returning and agreeing not to use the material to refusing any cooperation and arguing that the material is not protected, or that the sender's disclosure or other circumstances have waived any protection that otherwise might apply. The dynamics here are unpredictable and fact-specific, but when the parties believe that significant information is at stake, the fight can be elaborate and complex.

And don't forget that other applicable law may also be in play. If the disclosure was made in a proceeding governed by the Federal Rules of Civil Procedure (or comparable state procedural rules), **Fed. R. Civ. P. 26(b)(5)(B)** imposes additional obligations. Take a moment to read that Rule now.

TAMING THE TEXT Notice how different this provision is from **Model Rule 4.4(b)**:

■ Although **Model Rule 4.4(b)** applies to *any* material inadvertently disclosed in any context, **Fed. R. Civ. P. 26(b)(5)(B)** applies *only* if

- the disclosure occurs in a proceeding governed by the Federal Rules (or comparable state law incorporating the same or a similar Rule);
- *and* if the disputed material has been "produced in discovery" and not sent or received on any other basis, for example, if counsel inadvertently copied to opposing counsel an email that she sent to her client;
- *and* if the holder of the privilege claims that the disclosed material is protected by a privilege or the **work product doctrine** ("protection as trial-preparation material").

- Inadvertent production of nonprivileged material, or of privileged material outside the discovery process, does not fall within the literal terms of the Federal Rule.
- Once the recipient is notified that the holder of the privilege claims the privilege, **Fed. R. Civ. P. 26(b)(5)(B)** requires the recipient to "promptly return, sequester, or destroy the specified information and any copies it has"; to "not use or disclose the information until the claim is resolved"; and to "take reasonable steps to retrieve the information if the [recipient] disclosed it before being notified."
  - Notice that, under the Federal Rule, the recipient of the apparently inadvertently produced privileged materials has *no* obligation to notify the disclosing party of the receipt; instead, the receiving party **must** handle the materials in the manner dictated by the Rule only after the receiving party is notified by the holder of a privilege that the holder claims the privilege and demands that the recipient treat the materials accordingly. But because **Model Rule 4.4(b)** requires the receiving party to notify the disclosing party regardless of the source of the apparently inadvertently disclosed materials, the receiving party will be obligated to notify the disclosing party even when **Fed. R. Civ. P. 26(b)(5)(B)** also applies.
  - **Model Rule 4.4(b)**, in contrast, requires the recipient to "promptly notify the sender." But that's *all* it requires. It's silent on what should happen after the sender is notified. **Model Rule 4.4 Comment [2]** emphasizes this silence by pointing out that "[w]hether the lawyer is required to take additional steps, such as returning the document or electronically stored information, is a matter of law beyond the scope of these Rules, as is the question of whether the privileged status of a document or electronically stored information has been waived. Similarly, this Rule does not address the legal duties of a lawyer who receives a document or electronically stored information that the lawyer knows or reasonably should know may have been inappropriately obtained by the sending person."
- **Fed. R. Civ. P. 26(b)(5)(B)** also authorizes (but does not require) the recipient to "promptly present the information to the court under seal for a determination of the claim [of privilege]. This permission is not intended to supplant the

privilege-holder's right to seek a protective order or similar relief itself. The Federal Rule's authorization of the recipient to seek court guidance while keeping the information under seal is helpful to both sides, as otherwise the Federal Rules would not be entirely clear on how the recipient could seek such guidance, and keeping confidential documents under seal without an express authorization like the one in the Rule is not always easy.

- **Fed. R. Civ. P. 26(b)(5)(B)** also requires that "[t]he producing party **must** preserve the information until the claim is resolved," another subject on which **Model Rule 4.4(b)** is silent. TAMING THE TEXT

YOUR HOUSE; YOUR RULES Besides the additional obligations that federal or state procedural rules may impose, please bear in mind that there is significant variation among jurisdictions on what's required when a lawyer is faced with inadvertently disclosed information. In the 1990s, before the ABA added **Model Rule 4.4(b)** to the Model Rules, two ABA Formal Ethics Opinions expressed the view that a lawyer receiving inadvertently disclosed materials should review them only to the extent necessary to determine what to do with them, and then should return or segregate them without using them until a court had provided "definitive" guidance.[11]

The ABA Ethics opinions proved highly controversial, and in 2002, the ABA adopted the much less demanding provisions of **Model Rule 4.4(b).** Several jurisdictions, including lawyer-heavy California and Washington, D.C., have retained in their version of Rule 4.4 the approach dictated in the 1990s Formal Ethics Opinions, stringently limiting review and use of inadvertently disclosed material until the parties receive court guidance. Some jurisdictions, including New York, have left to the state's courts the determination of what happens after the sender is notified. Yet others, including Florida, have decided to adhere to **Model Rule 4.4(b)**, while still others, including Illinois, are even more lenient, requiring notification only if the receiving lawyer actually knows that the material was inadvertently sent. Wherever your practice ends up, be sure you know what your jurisdiction does and does not require, because the **consequences** of violation in more stringent jurisdictions can be quite serious. YOUR HOUSE; YOUR RULES

---

[11] The two opinions took somewhat different approaches. ABA Formal Ethics Op. No. 92-368 (1992) stated that any material that was transmitted inadvertently sent should not be reviewed at all, and that the receiving lawyer should abide by the sender's directions regarding destruction or return. The opinion's peculiar vagueness (how can you know if the material might have been sent inadvertently if you don't look at it?) provoked sufficient resistance that, two years later, ABA Formal Ethics Op. No. 94-382 (1994) relaxed the earlier opinion's prescriptions. The 1994 opinion advised that a lawyer receiving material that was apparently inadvertently sent could review it to the limited extent necessary to determine what it was and what to do with it, and was not required to follow the sender's instructions regarding the document, but instead could retain the material without using it until a court had provided "definitive" guidance. The ABA withdrew the 1992 opinion in 2005 (ABA Formal Ethics Op. No. 05-437 (2005)), and the 1994 opinion in 2006 (ABA Formal Ethics Op. No. 06-440 (2006)). Both opinions refer to the 2002 revision of the Rule as the reason for withdrawing the earlier opinions.

CONSEQUENCES Violation of your jurisdiction's version of **Model Rule 4.4(b)** is a basis for professional discipline. There are often civil **consequences** as well. Some jurisdictions that have adopted the more stringent version of the Rule also enforce it by **disqualifying** counsel who have obtained **confidential** or **privileged** information in violation of the restrictions on review and use. Evidentiary sanctions also may be available. In addition, as noted above, when disagreements break out over whether the receiving party **may** review or use the materials, they are often litigated in the context of motions for protective orders. The Federal Rules and corresponding procedural rules of many states provide that the losing party in such disputes **must** pay the prevailing party's attorneys' fees and costs in the dispute, which can be substantial. *See, e.g.,* **Fed. R. Civ. P. 26(c)(3)**; **Fed. R. Civ. P. 37(a)(5)**. The practical upshot is that both the party that discovers that it has mistakenly disclosed something that it wishes it hadn't and the party that receives it should think carefully about the value and uses of the materials and the **consequences** of overreaching in advocating what happens next—before launching into what can prove to be a lengthy and expensive distraction. CONSEQUENCES

> **Problem 24B-7:** In each of the situations below, what **must**, **may**, and **should** the lawyer receiving the materials described do, and why?
>
> a. Frank receives a large production of ESI in a pending case. Among the documents produced is a scanned .pdf with handwriting on it. Frank can't tell whose handwriting it is, but from the context, it's possible that the handwriting is actually opposing counsel's notes. Would your analysis change if the notes included information strongly indicating that they were written by opposing counsel? If so, how and why; and if not, why not?
>
> b. Same as (a), but now Frank finds a memorandum that was not within the scope of his discovery requests, but that is helpful to his case. The memo was written by a businessperson within the opposing party (which is an organization), and there is no indication that the memorandum is subject to any legitimate claim of privilege.
>
> c. Frank is negotiating a commercial lease for a retail store. He receives a document via email from opposing counsel. Only after Frank reads most of the document does he realize that it is a status update concerning the open issues in the negotiation—an update that the opposing lawyer meant to send only to her client.
>
> d. Same as (c), but now Frank has notified opposing counsel. What, if anything, **must** or **should** opposing counsel communicate to her client?
>
> e. Same as (d), but in response to Frank's notification to opposing counsel regarding the email, opposing counsel demands that Frank and his firm **disqualify** themselves and that their client obtain new counsel.
>
> f. Frank is tasked with reviewing several thousand emails for privilege before producing them in discovery. He asks the client for a list of all in-house attorneys involved in the project. The client mistakenly omits the name of one in-house lawyer, so Frank does not mark any communications to or from this lawyer as privileged. Frank produces all of these communications.

Big-Picture Takeaways from Chapter 24.A-.B

1. Being "an officer of the court" at minimum brings three important ideas into play: (1) The role and its description hint that lawyers' behavior in advocacy may be subject to some additional degree of scrutiny beyond that accorded other lawyer conduct; (2) In its actual use, the phrase "officer of the court" implies some ill-defined expectation of behavior beyond the minimum demands of the professional disciplinary rules or the rules of court procedure; and (3) In and around formal dispute resolution processes, the advocate's **duty of loyalty** to his or her client is constrained by other enforceable duties—duties with **consequences**—that can be seen as being owed to the court or to the legal system itself. *See* **Chapter 24.A at 814.**

2. Investigation **must** be conducted lawfully. **Model Rule 4.4(a)** provides, in part, that "[i]n representing a client, a lawyer shall not . . . use methods of obtaining evidence that violate the legal rights of [a third] person." *See* **Chapter 24.B at 816.**

3. In addition to the various civil remedies for discovery misconduct described in **Chapter 3.C at 53**, discovery misconduct by a lawyer is also a disciplinary violation. **Model Rule 3.4(d)** provides that "[a] lawyer shall not . . . in pretrial procedure, make a frivolous discovery request or fail to make reasonably diligent effort to comply with a legally proper discovery request by an opposing party." **Model Rule 3.4(c)** provides that a lawyer **must not** "knowingly disobey an obligation under the rules of a tribunal except for an open refusal based on an assertion that no valid obligation exists." *See* **Chapter 24.B at 821.**

4. **Model Rule 3.4(f)** forbids you from "request[ing]" someone other than a client (or a relative, employee, or other agent of a client whose **interests** you reasonably believe will not be adversely affected by doing so) "to refrain from voluntarily giving relevant information to another party." *See* **Chapter 12.A at 384. Model Rule 3.4(a)** provides that you **must not** "unlawfully obstruct another party's access to evidence or unlawfully alter, destroy or conceal a document or other material having potential evidentiary value," or "counsel or assist another person to do any such act." Such conduct is often criminal or tortious and subject to court sanctions, as well as comprising a disciplinary violation. But focus on the modifiers in that subsection: "*unlawfully* obstruct . . . access to evidence" or "*unlawfully* alter, destroy or conceal a document or other material having potential evidentiary value" (emphases added). Lawyers frequently *lawfully* refuse to disclose the existence of or refuse to provide documents or information, or counsel or assist others to do so, for example, when properly objecting to a discovery request,

instructing a client not to answer a question calling for privileged information during a deposition, or advising clients to exercise their right to refuse to speak with law enforcement. The Rule requires you to refrain from doing so only when such conduct is "unlawful[]." *See* **Chapter 24.B at 821.**

5. The second part of **Model Rule 3.4(a)** says that you **must not** "unlawfully alter, destroy or conceal a document or other material having *potential evidentiary value*" (emphasis added). The modifier "potential" is important: The concealed, altered, or destroyed "document or other material" does *not* have to be "evidence" in the sense of something that would be admissible in evidence if offered in some pending proceeding, nor does it even have to be subject to a pending discovery request, subpoena, or search warrant to fall within the Rule. It just has to be *relevant to* or *potentially useful in* a *pending or reasonably foreseeable* proceeding. *See* **Chapter 24.B at 822.**

6. Most jurisdictions have laws forbidding "spoliation"—a term commonly used to describe unlawful destruction or alteration of material that could have evidentiary or investigative value in some pending or reasonably foreseeable future proceeding. The proliferation of electronically stored information ("ESI") has intensified the focus on spoliation. *See* **Chapter 24.B at 822.**

7. The **consequences** to the client when information preservation or production obligations are not met can be extremely serious. Failure to produce documents or information responsive to proper requests or disclosure obligations can result in monetary sanctions and, upon failure to comply with an order that compels the discovery, in evidentiary or even terminating sanctions. As for preservation issues, even without any bad faith or intent to deprive an adversary of documents or information, courts are generally authorized to impose remedial measures for the prejudicial destruction of material that should have been preserved, for example when a party fails to halt automatic deletion measures. *See* **Chapter 24.B at 823.**

8. Many courts and court systems have imposed independent personal obligations, and **consequences**, on *lawyers* and their **practice organizations** with respect to their *clients'* compliance with preservation and discovery obligations. You **should**, and arguably **must**, immediately upon your retention, become actively involved in your clients' efforts to preserve information and documents that **must** be preserved and to produce in discovery documents and information that **must** be located and produced. Otherwise, you may be held personally responsible for your clients' errors or omissions in preserving, locating, and producing documents and information. This outreach to the client to ensure compliance usually requires the circulation of written notification to anyone who could have relevant material of something often called a "document preservation memo" or

a "litigation hold notice" directing the non-destruction of anything that might be relevant to the pending or future dispute. *See* **Chapter 24.B at 823**.

9. Take special care when a client (or anyone else) gives you potential evidence to hold. Remember, **Model Rule 3.4(a)** provides that you **must not** "unlawfully obstruct another party's access to evidence or unlawfully alter, destroy or conceal a document or other material having potential evidentiary value," or "counsel or assist another person to do any such act." *See* **Chapter 24.B at 827**.

10. **Model Rule 4.4(b)** requires a lawyer who receives material not intended for her eyes and that "relat[es] to the representation of [the lawyer's] client"—something that the lawyer should have reasonably known wasn't intentionally sent to her—to notify that material's sender of the unintended receipt. If the disclosure was made in a proceeding governed by the Federal Rules of Civil Procedure (or comparable state procedural rules), **Fed. R. Civ. P. 26(b)(5)(B)** imposes additional obligations. *See* **Chapter 24.B at 828**.

    a. The ABA's own views on the obligations of a lawyer who receives what apparently may be inadvertently disclosed information or documents have evolved significantly over the years. There is also significant inter-state variation in the form of **Model Rule 4.4(b)** adopted by different states and in the extent of the obligations and **consequences** for their violation that the Rule and associated civil law can impose. *See* **Chapter 24.B at 832**.

    b. Violation of your jurisdiction's version of **Model Rule 4.4(b)** is a basis for professional discipline. There are often civil **consequences** as well, including consequences arising under **Fed. R. Civ. P. 26(b)(5)(B)**. Some jurisdictions that have adopted the more stringent version of the Rule also enforce it by **disqualifying** counsel who have wrongfully obtained **confidential** or **privileged** information in violation of the restrictions on review and use. Evidentiary sanctions also may be available. *See* **Chapter 24.B at 833**.

11. To avoid your own disclosure of such information, make sure that you understand what kinds of metadata are ordinarily incorporated into the electronic documents you create or edit with the word processing and document management software that your **practice organization** uses and how to remove it from the document. When you send any electronic document outside your **practice organization**, remove metadata unless there is a good reason not to do so. *See* **Chapter 24.B at 829 n.10**.

Multiple-Choice Review Questions for Chapter 24.A-.B

1. Which of the following is a true statement about a lawyer's **duty of loyalty** to the client?
    a. The **duty of loyalty** preempts all others.
    b. The **duty of loyalty** may be constrained by duties owed to the court.

    c. The **duty of loyalty** may be constrained by duties that the lawyer owes to his or her firm.

    d. The **duty of loyalty** does not exist.

2. Lawyer James is defense counsel in a personal injury lawsuit filed against his client. He believes that the plaintiff is lying about her injuries. The plaintiff claims that she is unable to walk and, as a result, that she is entirely housebound.

    If James hires a nonlawyer private investigator, Kayne, to sit on the street outside the plaintiff's house and surreptitiously video-record her when she goes out in public in order to prove that the plaintiff is not injured, would James be violating **Model Rule 4.4(a)**?

    a. Yes. This type of surveillance involves an element of dishonesty and, therefore, it is inconsistent with the proper conduct of an officer of the court. James cannot ask Kayne to record the plaintiff.

    b. Maybe. It depends on whether James intends to use the video to impeach the witness or as substantive evidence. If he intends to use it as substantive evidence, he should gather the evidence through a discovery request rather than through surveillance.

    c. Probably not. Unless this jurisdiction forbids this type of surveillance with the equipment that Kayne is using in the place in which Kayne is using it, James **may** bolster his client's case by gathering evidence this way.

    d. No. Kayne is not a lawyer. Nonlawyers are not subject to the professional conduct rules that apply to lawyers. A lawyer like James is not responsible for the conduct of a nonlawyer like Kayne.

3. Lennie is a prosecutor. He is interviewing Meg. The government believes that Meg and Nasir robbed a bank. They intend to charge both Meg and Nasir. Lennie hopes to "flip" Meg so that she'll testify against Nasir. He offers to drop the charges against Meg if she cooperates. When she balks, he tells Meg, "We have you dead to rights—there was a surveillance video that shows you in the bank. You're going to prison if you don't cooperate."

    Lennie's statement is not entirely true. Although there is a video of the robbery, it is at an awkward angle. As a result, it is impossible to tell if Meg is the woman shown on the video. Has Lennie violated his professional obligations?

    a. Yes. This statement is a factual misrepresentation, and it is therefore prohibited.

    b. Yes. He **must not** communicate with a potential defendant. This creates a **conflict of interest**.

    c. No. His statement is misleading but not false. This sort of puffery is permitted under the Rules of Professional Conduct.

    d. No. He is allowing Meg to decide whether to cooperate or not. He is entitled to offer her leniency in exchange for her testimony.

4. Laszlo Cravensworth is litigating a complex civil financial fraud case. His opposing counsel is Colin Robinson. The two have agreed to a discovery plan that includes the production of large volumes of electronically stored information in native format (meaning whatever original format the document had in the ordinary course of business). Due to the sheer volume of documents, an associate at his firm, Nadja, has been assisting in the review of the electronic documents produced to Laszlo's firm.

    Nadja opens a Word document and, on a whim, she turns "track changes" on. This adjustment reveals some edits and comments made by Colin. Upon further inspection, many of the comments reflect **attorney-client privileged** communications.

    Assuming **Model Rule 4.4** applies, and there is no other applicable law in this jurisdiction, what **must** Nadja do to comply with her obligations?
    a. Withdraw from handling the case because she cannot "unsee" the **attorney-client privileged** information. The firm must then **screen** Nadja from Laszlo. If it does not, both are **disqualified** from handling the case.
    b. Stop reviewing the tracked changes but otherwise do nothing more. Colin negotiated and agreed to produce the documents in native format and he had the responsibility to remove any metadata before turning the documents over to Laszlo and his team. Nadja cannot use the metadata in litigation but she has no obligation to notify Colin.
    c. Promptly notify Colin that he has inadvertently disclosed **attorney-client privileged** information. Under the circumstances, Nadja reasonably should know that the production of tracked changes was unintentional.
    d. Continue to review the documents, including the metadata, and use that information to the benefit of her client. By producing the metadata, Colin waived any **attorney-client privilege** and therefore Nadja can have no obligation to do anything to notify Colin about the disclosure.

5. District Attorney Fred is prosecuting a case that arose after two parents, Michaela and Jerry, allowed their minor daughter, Ali, to throw a party where alcohol was served to minors. Ali passed out and was photographed topless during the party.

    Fred feels that Michaela and Jerry are not taking the charges seriously. He threatens to send the topless photos of Ali to the parents of other under-aged minors who attended the party.

    Does this threat violate **Model Rule 4.4(a)?**

a. Yes. The threat served no substantial purpose other than to embarrass Ali, Michaela, and Jerry.

b. Maybe. It depends whether the other parents requested to see the photos. If they did, they were entitled to see them.

c. Maybe. It depends whether Ali suffered pecuniary harm by the disclosure of the photographs.

d. No. The threat was conditional. Michaela and Jerry could prevent disclosure by cooperating with Fred.

6. Joey represents Popsi Co. in a trademark dispute filed against it by rival company Koch Inc. Counsel for Koch serves a discovery request seeking, among other things, the secret formula for Popsi's best-selling soda. Joey objects on the basis that the formula is a protected trade secret.

   Counsel for Koch files a motion to compel. Joey opposes the motion, arguing again that his client is not obligated to disclose the information because it is protected.

   The judge grants the motion and orders Joey to turn over the formula. Available appellate remedies are refused, but Joey advises Popsi that it **may** continue to refuse to produce the formula because it is a trade secret. Popsi takes Joey's advice, and Joey informs the court and opposing counsel of Popsi's intentions. Has Joey violated his professional obligations?

   a. Yes. He advised a client to violate the law.

   b. Yes. He violated his discovery obligations.

   c. No. He has openly asserted that there is no legal obligation to disclose the formula.

   d. No. The court only has the power to sanction litigants, not lawyers.

7. Allie represents Better Cakes, a bakery. Better recently received tainted flour from its supplier, Queen Mary Flour. The snafu cost Better a major account, and Allie reached out to Queen Mary to see if an informal resolution could be reached before commencing litigation. Queen Mary's owner, Cynthia, responded by directing Allie to lawyer Bao, who represents Queen Mary.

   Allie and Bao knew each other even before the litigation, and the two have a collegial relationship. They serve on the same committee of their local bar association and often work together to plan CLEs and other events.

   One day, Allie opens her inbox and discovers an email from Bao. The email has no subject line, so Allie assumes it is about committee events. Allie opens the email and her eyes scan the first line. It says, "Dear Cynthia, I have discovered several incriminating emails that I fear will cause you to lose if Better sues you . . ."

What **must** Allie do to fulfil her obligation under **Model Rule 4.4(b)**?
a. Notify Cynthia that her lawyer, Bao, was careless.
b. Notify Better Cakes that, based upon the email, it has a strong case and it should file suit.
c. Notify Bao that she sent an email to Allie instead of Cynthia.
d. Notify no one.

8. Lawyer Allison receives a call from one of her longtime clients, Ben. Ben asks if he can come in to see Allison. She agrees. Ben arrives ten minutes later. He looks distraught. Before she can say anything, Ben takes a bloody knife out of his backpack and hands it to her. "I did . . . something . . . ," he stammers.

   Allison tells him to stop talking. "Give that to me," she says. "You're in no state to discuss anything right now. Go home. We'll talk tomorrow."

   After Ben leaves, Allison drives to the next town and throws the knife away in a dumpster that she finds in an alley. Has Allison violated her professional obligations?
   a. Yes, by throwing away the knife.
   b. Yes, by failing to ask Ben what happened and by failing to call the police.
   c. No, because the knife has not actually been destroyed.
   d. No, because she does not know with certainty that Ben committed a crime.

9. A lawyer representing a party in a civil case pending in federal district court receives in her in-box an email that appears to be **attorney-client privileged** and to have been sent to the lawyer in error. The court has adopted the Model Rules of Professional Conduct to define lawyers' professional conduct obligations in matters before the court. The lawyer may have obligations under which of the following?
   a. The Model Rules of Professional Conduct.
   b. The Federal Rules of Civil Procedure.
   c. Both a and b.
   d. Neither a nor b.

10. A lawyer representing a party in a civil case pending in federal district court receives as part of a document production an email that appears to be **attorney-client privileged** and to have been produced in error. The court has adopted the Model Rules of Professional Conduct to define lawyers' professional conduct obligations in matters before the court. The lawyer may have obligations under which of the following?

a. The Model Rules of Professional Conduct.

b. The Federal Rules of Civil Procedure.

c. Both a and b.

d. Neither a nor b.

C. Limits on Advocacy

In the **chapter Introduction at 813**, we pointed out that there are some hard limits on advocacy tactics. You'll find many of them unsurprising. But the application of a few of the most obvious ones in the circumstances in which they most commonly arise will prove surprisingly difficult. We'll work our way through all of these with you now.

1. Preserving the Impartiality and Decorum of the Tribunal

Model Rule 3.5 focuses on the lawyer's duty to preserve the impartiality and the decorum of tribunals. It contains requirements that are also found in the civil and criminal law. For example, **Model Rules 3.5(a) and (b)** prohibit "seek[ing] to influence a judge, juror, prospective juror or other official by means prohibited by law" or "communicat[ing] ex parte with such a person during the proceeding unless authorized to do so by law or court order."[12] We hope that no one is surprised to find that bribing a judge or tampering with a juror (or any of the lesser offenses that the Rule also describes) is considered unethical. The Rule makes such misconduct a basis for professional discipline, which is likely to be the least of your concerns if you're caught engaging in these kinds of tactics. **Model Rule 3.5(c)** also recapitulates as a basis for professional discipline juror protections already established in other law, prohibiting lawyers from contacting jurors after the jury is discharged (which is generally allowed) if the communication is "(1) prohibited by law or court order; (2) the juror has made known to the lawyer a desire not to communicate; or (3) the communication involves misrepresentation, coercion, duress or harassment." Again, no surprises.

Model Rule 3.5(d) provides that a lawyer **must not** "engage in conduct intended to disrupt a tribunal." TAMING THE TEXT ▸ "Tribunal" includes a court or any other

---

[12] "*Ex parte*" is one of those phrases that lawyers use in different contexts to mean different things. The most common and important use (and the one intended in **Model Rule 3.5(b)**, discussed in the text, and **Model Rule 3.3(d)**, which we'll discuss in **Chapter 24.C at 882**) is to describe a hearing, motion, or communication with a tribunal or factfinder undertaken without opposing counsel (or, if the opposing party is unrepresented, the opposing party himself or herself) involved. Though generally forbidden, *ex parte* communications and proceedings are allowed under limited and defined circumstances. A few examples: Many courts allow counsel to communicate *ex parte* with court staff regarding purely procedural matters (such as scheduling), though you should find out what is considered acceptable in the courts in which you practice. An application for a search warrant is a classic *ex parte* proceeding. And **Fed. R. Civ. P. 65(b)(1)** allows a court to issue a limited-duration temporary restraining order on an *ex parte* basis (that is, without notice of the application to the party to be restrained) if "specific facts in an affidavit or a verified complaint clearly show that immediate and irreparable injury, loss, or damage will result to the movant before the adverse party can be heard in opposition." (Can you think of an example that would qualify?)

adjudicative body (*see* **Model Rule 1.0(m)**). The Rule has generally been interpreted to apply to *any* official proceeding of the tribunal, even if the adjudicating officer is not present, such as at depositions. **Model Rule 3.5 Comment [5]**. It prohibits "conduct *intended* to disrupt a tribunal" (emphasis added), which suggests that the intent that motivates counsel's conduct matters. But because we generally infer intent from words and behavior, behavior that is actually disruptive is likely to be interpreted as having been intended to disrupt. But by focusing on behavior *intended* to disrupt, the Rule also makes clear that *attempts* to disrupt that fail are still disciplinary violations. Taming the Text

Similarly, **Model Rule 8.2(a)** provides that a lawyer **must not** "make a statement that the lawyer knows to be false or with reckless disregard as to its truth or falsity concerning the qualifications or integrity of a judge, adjudicatory officer or public legal officer, or of a candidate for election or appointment to judicial or legal office." The speaker's required knowledge of the statement's falsity or reckless disregard for its truth or falsity is a standard borrowed from United States Supreme Court authority determining such statements to be beyond First Amendment protections (mostly in defamation cases).[13] However, at least one Circuit Court of Appeal and several states have rejected this formulation as unsuited for lawyer discipline; they have adopted instead an objective standard based on whether the lawyer's statement was factually false and the lawyer lacked any "reasonable basis" for the judicial criticism, including "whether the attorney pursued readily available avenues of investigation" before speaking.[14] Unlike some other Rules (such as **Model Rule 3.5(d)**, discussed above, or **Model Rule 3.6**, discussed below), **Model Rule 8.2(a)**'s reach is not limited by the context or the breadth of dissemination of the lawyer's statement.

Consequences **Model Rule 3.5(d)** and **Model Rule 8.2(a)** are, of course, disciplinary rules. Disruptive or disrespectful conduct in or near open court is also punishable by the judge as a "summary" or "direct" contempt (*see* **Fed. R. Crim. P. 42(b)**; the terms are interchangeable), and most tribunals have similar rules giving the presiding

---

[13] *E.g., New York Times Co. v. Sullivan*, 376 U.S. 254 (1964). As you may have learned in a Torts, Media Law, or First Amendment course, "knowledge or reckless disregard of falsity" has come to be referred to as the "actual malice," "constitutional malice," or "*New York Times*" standard. A nuanced and sophisticated jurisprudence has developed regarding its application, again largely in defamation cases. Given the choice of wording identical to the *New York Times* standard in **Model Rule 8.2(a)**, it seems likely that the drafters of the Model Rules, and those state authorities adopting the Model Rules, intended to import that jurisprudence along with the standard. Among other features of this jurisprudence, disparaging statements reasonably understood as general expressions of disapproval rather than specific assertions of fact, and colorful language not reasonably understood to be taken literally, are examples of statements that the Supreme Court has held to be constitutionally protected, and thus presumably outside the scope of **Model Rule 8.2(a)** as well. On the other hand, general statements that would reasonably be understood in context to imply specific facts known to the speaker to be false (or whose falsity the speaker has recklessly disregarded) are not constitutionally protected. *See, e.g.,* Restatement (Second) of Torts § 566 (1977). Such statements presumably would be within the scope of the Rule as well.

[14] *See, e.g., Standing Committee v. Yagman*, 55 F.3d 1430, 1437 & nn.12-13 (9th Cir. 1995), and cases cited therein. This alternative standard also imports a great deal of *New York Times* jurisprudence about how to determine whether a statement is factually false or whether it should be interpreted to imply factually false assertions. *Id.* at 1436-42.

officer some power to police lawyer conduct in the presence of the officer during the proceedings. The First Amendment limits on this prohibition are not entirely clear, but it seems well accepted that your freedom of expression as a lawyer appearing in court or other official proceedings is more constrained than it is outside such official proceedings. *See* **Model Rule 3.5 Comment [4]** ("Refraining from abusive or obstreperous conduct is a corollary of the advocate's right to speak on behalf of litigants"). And as just discussed, the scope of **Model Rule 8.2(a)**, though not limited to statements made during official proceedings, is meant to be limited to statements that the First Amendment does not protect. CONSEQUENCES

TIPS & TACTICS In another one of those infuriating asymmetries, you are expected to remain controlled and respectful even if a witness, opposing counsel, or the judge is behaving wrongfully or even abusively. As **Model Rule 3.5 Comment [4]** counsels, "[a] lawyer may stand firm against abuse by a judge but should avoid reciprocation; the judge's default is no justification for similar dereliction by an advocate. An advocate can present the cause, protect the record for subsequent review and preserve professional integrity by patient firmness no less effectively than by belligerence or theatrics." TIPS & TACTICS

Problem 24C-1: Which of the lawyers in the following situations could be subject to **consequences**, and what might those **consequences** be? Please explain your answers.

a. Happy and Frank are litigating a slip-and-fall claim. The defendant moves to dismiss the complaint for failure to state a claim. Frank calls up the judge's clerk, who was a couple of years behind him in law school, for an informal discussion of the caselaw cited in the motion.

b. Happy regularly golfs at a country club frequented by the judge who is assigned to the slip-and-fall case. In the locker room, the judge runs into Happy and says, "I see that I got a new one with your name on it. What's it about?" Happy informally describes his client's claims.

c. Opposing counsel in the slip-and-fall case is "Swifty" Smith. Swifty sends a letter to the judge regarding a discovery issue in the case—a letter of the kind that in this jurisdiction is sometimes used to raise a discovery issue with the court. The letter reflects on its face a "cc" indicating that Swifty simultaneously sent it to Happy and Frank. Does your analysis change if Swifty instructs his legal assistant to "forget" to send the "cc" to opposing counsel? What if, instead, Swifty tells the legal assistant to wait a week before sending the copy to opposing counsel? If any of these facts change your analysis, how and why; and if not, why not?

d. Now the slip-and-fall case is being tried to a jury. Frank is in the restroom during a break in trial. He sees a juror enter the next stall. The juror asks, "Can you pass me some toilet paper?" Can Frank respond? How?

e. Frank sees a juror in the hall during a recess. The juror says "Hi," and smiles. Frank says "Hi," and smiles back. Does your answer change if Frank says, "Hi, how are things going?" and waits for a response? If so, why and how; and if not, why not?

f. Counsel and many of the jurors eat lunch at the deli across the street from the courthouse. Swifty Smith anonymously picks up the bill for the jurors. Does your analysis change if Swifty brandishes his credit card and his intentions more publicly? If so, how and why; and if not, why not?

g. During lunch at the deli one day during trial (with jurors and counsel each eating at their own separate tables), Swifty carries on a conversation with his paralegal, at a volume level that can be heard across the room, about a story he read in the local newspaper. The story explained that lawsuits alleging injuries on business premises are proliferating, and are driving many small businesses bankrupt.

h. During the trial, Swifty repeatedly objects during Happy's direct examination of an important witness. Frank thinks that all of Happy's questions are clearly proper, and the judge is overruling all of Swifty's objections. Does your analysis change if the judge cautions Swifty to stop interfering with the witness's examination, and Swifty persists in objecting to nearly every question? What if Swifty's objections are mostly well taken, and the judge is pretty clearly wrong in overruling them? If any of these facts change your analysis, why and how; and if not, why not?

i. Same as the first part of (h) (Swifty interposes multiple meritless objections during Happy's direct), but after Swifty's objections are repeatedly overruled, he turns to his paralegal at counsel table and says, in a stage whisper, "What. An. Idiot." Does your analysis change according to whether Swifty also gestures in the direction of Happy? The judge? What if, as in the second part of (h), Swifty's objections are mostly well taken, and the judge is pretty clearly wrong in overruling them? If any of these facts change your analysis, why and how; and if not, why not?

j. One juror seems very skeptical of the defendant's case during trial. Swifty suggests to his client that they get his cousin Joey, a real "tough guy," to come sit in during the next few days of trial. Swifty thinks that a little sustained eye contact from Joey might make the juror think twice about making a "hasty decision."

k. The cross-examination of Swifty's client representative is not going well for the defense. Happy begins coughing loudly, spreads his arms wide while theatrically gasping for breath, and knocks the water pitcher off counsel table onto the floor. The judge calls a recess.

l. Happy sends a $100 bottle of champagne to the judge while the trial is ongoing. Would your analysis change if it happened to be the judge's birthday? What if Happy and the judge had been friends ever since they attended law school together, and they regularly exchanged birthday gifts? Would it change your analysis if Happy had sent the judge a less expensive gift? As to each of these, if so, why and how; and if not, why not?[15]

m. The trial ends in a plaintiff's verdict. Swifty is hoping that he can find some evidence of juror misconduct that might allow a retrial. Swifty sends his "tough-guy" cousin, Joey

---

[15] See *Attorney Kevin Gleason Suspended for 60 Days*, https://www.bizjournals.com/southflorida/news/2011/09/20/attorney-gleason-suspended-for-60-days.html#:~:text=Last%20spring%2C%20Gleason%20filed%20a,to%20%E2%80%9Cresolve%20our%20differences.%E2%80%9D (Sept. 20, 2011). Don't be misled by the headline: What did attorney Gleason do to earn a suspension?

(*see* (j)), to visit several of the jurors and see if he can get any of them to agree that any juror acted improperly during trial or deliberations and to sign a statement to that effect.

n. The trial is over. Swifty is presenting at a CLE convened by the local trial lawyers' organization and is asked about his experience with the judge who presided over his recent slip-and-fall trial. Which of Swifty's statements could be problematic, and why?

   i.   Swifty says, "I disagree with the judge's approach to evidentiary issues."
   ii.   Swifty says, "His evidentiary rulings were frequently wrong."
   iii. Swifty says, "An ignorant, ill-tempered buffoon. A midget among giants. They have an express window just for his cases at the Court of Appeals."[16]
   iv.   Swifty says, "He repeatedly ruled against me because he's in the pocket of the plaintiff's bar. Totally corrupt."
   v.   Swifty says, "A martinet. The courthouse Nazi."
   vi.   In (i) through (v), would your analysis differ if Swifty made the statement in question not at a CLE but in open court? If so, why and how; and if not, why not?

o. Danielle is trying an assault case. While sitting at counsel table and during his examinations, defense counsel visibly arranges his hand into a gesture associated with certain white-supremacist organizations.

p. The Executive Deputy DA (that is, the number two administrator in Danielle's office) is giving a brown-bag lunch talk on trial tactics. "I get a Redweld® (that is, a file folder) and label it 'Incriminating Evidence' in big letters with a black marker," says the Exec. "Then at trial I leave it on counsel table, where the jury can see. If things seem like they're going badly for me, I make some noise rifling through the Redweld®." Danielle tries this tactic.

q. The Executive Deputy DA also suggests that Danielle wear short skirts and low-cut tops when she is trying jury cases that have mostly male jurors. Danielle tries it. Suppose, instead, that Danielle does not wish to try that sartorial approach. How should she respond to the suggestion? Does your answer depend on the gender of the Executive Deputy DA? Why or why not?

2. Limits on Asserting or Contesting Claims, Defenses, or Legal or Factual Issues

Please pause and read **Model Rule 3.1.**

TAMING THE TEXT There are several limits on advocacy in here, all of which hopefully struck you as straightforward. What kinds of advocacy activities are covered? Pretty much all of them: "[B]ring[ing] or defend[ing] a proceeding" or "assert[ing] or controvert[ing] an issue therein." What's the limit? There must be "a basis in law and fact for doing so that is not frivolous, which includes a good faith argument for an extension, modification or reversal of existing law." The minimum standard is very low—"not frivolous." REASON FOR THE RULE That's a deliberate effort to

---

[16] *See Yagman, supra* note 14, 55 F.3d at 1440-41; *State Bar v. Semaan,* 508 S.W.2d 429, 431-32 (Tex. Civ. App. 1974).

leave room to "account [for] the law's ambiguities and potential for change," as well as for legitimate creative advocacy. **Model Rule 3.1 Comment [1]**. REASON FOR THE RULE

But when is the assertion of a claim or defense, or the steps taken to assert or controvert an issue, "frivolous"? Frivolousness tends to be one of those things that people feel they know when they see it.[17] Advocates tend to see it a lot more frequently than the judges before whom they appear, which in turn tends to irritate the judges, so we'd advise you to refrain from accusations of frivolousness unless you're sure that your adversary's advocacy would outrage the calmest and most unflappable observer. Nevertheless, **Model Rule 3.1 Comment [2]** tries to help:

> The filing of an action or defense or similar action taken for a client is not frivolous merely because the facts have not first been fully substantiated or because the lawyer expects to develop vital evidence only by discovery. What is required of lawyers, however, is that they inform themselves about the facts of their clients' cases and the applicable law and determine that they can make good faith arguments in support of their clients' positions. Such action is not frivolous even though the lawyer believes that the client's position ultimately will not prevail. The action is frivolous, however, if the lawyer is unable either to make a good faith argument on the merits of the action taken or to support the action taken by a good faith argument for an extension, modification or reversal of existing law.

The alert students who noticed this standard's similarity to the minimum standards for advocacy stated in **Fed. R. Civ. P. 11(b)**, which is grounded in the same reasons, are hereby accorded a round of applause. The Comment's explanation suggests that, while you're always free to make "a good faith argument for an extension, modification or reversal of existing law" (and many great moments in American legal history are the result of dedicated lawyers' having done exactly that), you should be clear with the court that that's what you're doing when you do it. Otherwise, you'll appear to be arguing that the law currently is something other than what you know that it actually is, which is, well, frivolous.

Model Rule 3.1 also makes room for broader advocacy in criminal proceedings as allowed by the Constitution, recognizing the right of a criminal defendant or other "respondent in a proceeding that could result in incarceration" to "defend the proceeding as to require that every element of the case be established." REASON FOR THE RULE Why is criminal defense called out specially for broader latitude? Well, remember that the Bill of Rights gives every criminal defendant the right simply to put the government to its proof, offering no defense at all and arguing that the prosecution has not met its burden, even if the prosecution's case is objectively and obviously overwhelming. This portion of the Rule simply acknowledges what the Constitution always allows. That doesn't mean that the

---

[17] *Cf. Jacobellis v. Ohio*, 378 U.S. 184, 197 (1964) (Stewart, J. concurring).

defense can ignore governing law or procedural rules or make up facts that lack a good faith basis, but it does give criminal defense counsel more latitude than prosecutors and the advocates in civil disputes. ◄ Reason for the Rule ◄ Taming the Text

Consequences ▶ **Model Rule 3.1** is a Rule of Professional Conduct, and thus is a basis for professional discipline. Civil **consequences**, such as court-imposed sanctions, are governed by **Fed. R. Civ. P. 11** and related law, which (as discussed above and in **Chapter 3.C at 53**) operate on similar standards, but in a different forum and context. Consequences

> Problem 24C-2: Frank represents a homeowner who is dissatisfied because the walls of his house leak. Frank retains a structural engineer to evaluate the construction. Assuming that the following happens, what **must** or **should** Frank do? Please explain your answers.
>
> a. The structural engineer's evaluation reveals that there is no flaw in the design of the walls or in the actual vapor barrier that was installed during construction. To the contrary, the engineer's opinion is that the leaking is caused by faulty installation of the vapor barrier. Frank's research reveals that the contractor who installed the vapor barrier is insolvent and has filed for bankruptcy protection. Happy Trials suggests that Frank file an action against the architect who designed the home and the manufacturer of the vapor barrier hoping that these "deep pockets" will settle the case early on before they conduct a similar evaluation or discover Frank's.
>
> b. Assume instead that the engineer's evaluation is inconclusive. Based on the evaluation alone, it's impossible to say whether it was the design, the vapor barrier itself, or the installation of that barrier that caused the leaking. Happy suggests suing the architect and manufacturer.
>
> c. Frank has sued the architect and the manufacturer of the vapor barrier. Initial evaluations were inconclusive as to the cause of the leak. Six months into discovery, the cause remains unclear. Although the evidence does indicate that there were some errors made by the architect, it is still inconclusive as to whether those errors alone caused the leaking. Happy urges Frank to continue litigating.
>
> d. Frank has sued the architect and the manufacturer of the vapor barrier. Although the engineer's initial evaluation was inconclusive, six months into discovery, Frank discovers evidence from a third party strongly indicating that the vapor barrier itself was not the cause of the leaking. Frank discusses this development with the homeowner-client, who suggests quickly settling with the manufacturer for a nominal amount before disclosing the evidence. Happy agrees. What if, instead, Frank discloses the evidence and continues to litigate against the manufacturer? If you don't think that either approach is the best course of action, what would you recommend that Frank do instead?
>
> e. Frank has sued the architect and the manufacturer. Discovery is inconclusive as to the cause of the leak. Frank settles with the architect. The homeowner uses the money to repair the walls. In the process of undertaking the repair, the homeowner discovers irrefutable evidence that proves that the contractor, not the architect, was at fault for the leaks. What obligation, if any, does Frank have now?

Problem 24C-3: Danielle's law school classmate, Irene, calls to ask for some "off the record" advice. (Is Irene seeking this advice in the way that's best for her and her client? Explain why or why not. *Hint: See* **Chapter 8.B at 243.**) Irene litigates civil rights cases. She recently filed a complaint under **42 U.S.C. § 1983** on behalf of a former government employee who was fired for political statements that the employee had made on her personal social media accounts. (Irene practices in another state, so Danielle has no **conflict of interest** in offering her some informal advice on this matter. Do you see why? Explain it out loud. *Hint: See* **Chapter 22.B at 655.**) The complaint that Irene filed contained one claim for violation of the former employee's First Amendment right to free expression. The First Amendment rights of government employees are complicated, and this is a case of first impression in Irene's circuit.

The government agency responded to Irene's complaint by filing a motion to dismiss on the basis of qualified immunity. Irene did some research and discovered that the controlling Supreme Court case on the issue is *Pearson v. Callahan*, 555 U.S. 223 (2009). Like most cases addressing qualified immunity, *Pearson* involved Fourth Amendment claims asserted against law enforcement. According to the test announced in *Pearson*, qualified immunity for a government actor is unavailable only when the constitutional right at issue is "clearly established." The Supreme Court has never decided precisely what it means for a right to be "clearly established," and the circuit courts are split on the definition. Irene has called Danielle for some feedback on arguments that she might make in her brief opposing the government's motion to dismiss. Should Danielle advise against any of these arguments? Why or why not? Please explain your answers.

a. Irene is thinking about arguing that *Pearson* was not a First Amendment case, and the standard for qualified immunity is different in First Amendment cases. She is also thinking about arguing that qualified immunity should be limited to cases involving alleged violation of constitutional rights by law enforcement. **May** Irene make these arguments, either separately or in combination? **Should** she?

b. Assume that the term "clearly established" has been defined in Irene's circuit to mean that a right is only "clearly established" when it has previously been recognized by a court within that circuit. **May** Irene argue that her client's First Amendment right is "clearly established"? **Should** she?

c. Same as (b) (the term "clearly established" has been defined in Irene's circuit to mean that a right is only "clearly established" when it has previously been recognized by a court within that circuit). **May** Irene argue that the court in her case should depart from this narrow view and join the circuits that find that a right may be "clearly established" without prior in-circuit precedent so long as the government actor is on notice that his or her conduct is unconstitutional? **Should** she? (*Hint:* Identify how this argument is different from the argument that Irene is considering in (b), and explain why that difference does or does not change your analysis.)

d. **May** Irene argue that the entire doctrine of qualified immunity should be abolished? **Should** she?

Problem 24C-4: Danielle is prosecuting a robbery case against Donnie Defendant. Which of defense counsel's arguments might result in defense counsel being subject to **consequences**, and what might those **consequences** be? Please explain your answers.

a. During trial, Danielle called the bank teller, Telly, to testify. Telly identified Donnie as the robber. During trial, no evidence was offered to suggest that Telly had any prior history of dishonesty. In closing argument, defense counsel stated, "Ladies and gentlemen of the jury, you cannot believe Telly. He has admitted to cheating on his taxes and lying to get a job. He's clearly lying to you today as well."

b. During trial, Danielle also called Donnie's co-conspirator, Coco. Coco is cooperating with the prosecution. During cross-examination, Coco admitted that she had previously been convicted for perjury. In closing, defense counsel argued that that Coco was a "liar" and that her testimony should not be believed.

c. During the defense case, Donnie himself testified. Donnie's version of events was quite different from Coco's. In closing, defense counsel argued that the jury should believe Donnie.

d. In Danielle's jurisdiction, one of the elements of robbery involves the use of "violence, intimidation, or threat." There was no evidence introduced during trial to suggest that the robber had a weapon or made any threats. In closing, defense counsel argued that the prosecution had not established its case.

Problem 24C-5: In the trial in **Problem 24C-4**, Donnie was found guilty. Defense counsel filed a motion for a new trial. The motion centered on exactly when Coco's prior conviction for perjury had been disclosed. Danielle had waited to disclose the conviction until a few weeks before trial. This timing comported with the prevailing law in her circuit as well as with her discovery obligations under the applicable rules of procedure in her state. Both the law and the rules simply required that impeachment evidence of this type be disclosed "before trial." Danielle had possession of the conviction months prior and could have disclosed it earlier. Which of defense counsel's arguments might result in defense counsel's being subject to **consequences**, and what might those **consequences** be? Please explain your answers.

a. In his motion for a new trial, defense counsel argues that Danielle violated the disclosure rules and prevailing law in the circuit.

b. Instead of the argument in (a), defense counsel argues that, even if Danielle's conduct met the state disclosure rules and the law in the circuit, that prevailing law was inconsistent with the Constitution and the Bill of Rights and should be overturned, and that his client was entitled to a new trial in the interest of fairness. How is this argument different from the argument in (a)? Does it matter that the argument is being posed to a trial court and that only a higher appellate court can overturn existing caselaw? Why might we want to allow such an argument before a trial court, even if that court cannot itself overturn existing law?

3. Limits on Miscitation of Legal Authority

Lawyers constantly accuse one another of misciting legal authority or of failing to cite authority that matters. The Rules provide limits for misuse of legal authority, though they are demanding to prove. **Model Rule 3.3(a)(1)** provides that you **must not** "knowingly . . . make a false statement of . . . law to a tribunal." Discipline under this Rule is limited to those situations in which you *actually know* that you are misciting the law, not when you are merely careless or sloppy, even inexcusably so. That doesn't mean you should feel free to be careless or sloppy in legal argument, of course; you still have **duties of competence** and **care** to consider (*see* **Model Rule 1.1**; **Chapter 7.A at 172**; **Chapter 7.B at 180**), as well as your credibility before the court.

Model Rule 3.3(a)(1) is about *affirmative misrepresentations* of the law. There is also a Rule about *omissions*: **Model Rule 3.3(a)(2)** provides that you **must not** "knowingly . . . fail to disclose to the tribunal legal authority in the controlling jurisdiction known to the lawyer to be directly adverse to the position of the client and not disclosed by opposing counsel."

TAMING THE TEXT Read that language carefully; it is closely circumscribed. Discipline under this Rule is available only if you

- "fail to disclose . . . legal authority"; that is, leave it out altogether (as opposed to, say, citing it but distinguishing it on grounds that are objectively untenable, though this approach runs afoul of other Rules that we've already discussed);
- *and* that authority was "not disclosed by opposing counsel," either;
- *and* that authority comes from the "controlling jurisdiction";
- *and* you "know[]" that it is "directly adverse to the position of the client";
- *and* you "knowingly . . . fail to disclose" it, meaning that you actually knew about it and decided not to disclose it, rather than just having missed finding it (even if you reasonably should have found it). TAMING THE TEXT

Like any other standard involving actual knowledge, the knowledge that these Rules require for discipline can be inferred from the circumstances (*see* **Model Rule 1.0(f)**). But actual knowledge is required.

REAL WORLD The fact that you will be professionally disciplined only if you deliberately misstate the law or knowingly fail to cite directly adverse controlling authority is, as a practical matter, almost beside the point. When you're arguing the law, it is for the purpose of persuading someone, usually a judge, to rule in your favor. That means that you need the judge to agree with you; and to agree with you, the judge generally needs to trust and accept your analysis. If you fail to address adverse authority providing strong analogical or persuasive arguments, or you fail to distinguish or discredit persuasive authority that runs contrary to your client's position, most judges will conclude that you are either sloppy or dishonest and, in either case, that you're not trustworthy, and therefore not persuasive. You may win this time anyway—any fool can win the easy ones, even on lousy or incomplete papers or argument. But you will have lost the judge's trust. The next time that you appear in that courtroom (or in that courthouse, as most judges talk freely with one another about the lawyers who appear before them), you'll start at the bottom of a steep slope in the judge's mind labeled (figuratively) "What's wrong *this* time?" And in future appearances in which your credibility or the court's discretion makes a difference, you'll be much more likely to lose. As we've said before, your reputation is your stock in trade. The way to keep its value high is by being thorough and reliable in your advocacy. In short, disingenuous, misleading, or haphazardly researched legal argument creates its own **consequences.** REAL WORLD

Problem 24C-6: Frank wins a slip-and-fall case litigated in the State of Garden on behalf of a client who fell and was injured after he tripped over a doormat. The property owner appeals.

On appeal, opposing counsel argues that the jury was given an improper instruction on whether a property owner is liable if a tripping hazard is "open and obvious." The jury was instructed that no such defense is recognized in the State of Garden.

Frank is preparing his answering brief on appeal. How **must** Frank deal with each of the authorities described below in the context described? In situations in which Frank has a choice, what **should** Frank do? Please explain your reasoning.

a. A decision involving a trip-and-fall over a doormat, decided by the Supreme Court of Garden. In the case, the court affirmed that the "open and obvious" defense is recognized in Garden. Opposing counsel did not cite this case.

b. Same as (a), but Frank's argument on appeal is that opposing counsel failed to properly preserve (and therefore waived) his objection to the trial court's jury instruction regarding the absence of an "open and obvious" defense.

c. A case involving a trip-and-fall over a doormat, decided by the Supreme Court of Garden. In the case, the court affirmed that the "open and obvious" defense is recognized in Garden. Opposing counsel cited this case in passing, with no explanation, in a footnote.

d. A case involving a trip-and-fall over a doormat, decided by a Garden trial court. In the case, the court discussed in dicta the "open and obvious" doctrine before dismissing the case on the grounds that it was filed outside the statute of limitations. Opposing counsel did not cite this case.

e. A case involving a slip-and-fall on ice, decided by a Garden trial court, where the court granted summary judgment for the property owner because the ice was open and obvious. Opposing counsel did not cite this case.

f. A case involving a trip-and-fall over a doormat, decided by a federal court in Keystone. In the case, applying Garden law, the court confirmed that the "open and obvious" defense is recognized in Garden. Opposing counsel did not cite this case.

g. A law journal article citing years of cases in support of the application of the "open and obvious" defense in Garden.

Problem 24C-7: Next week, Frank and his firm's litigation partner, "Happy" Trials, are trying a case involving a covenant not to compete between their client, a travel agency, and one of its former executives who left to start a rival company. The noncompete agreement prohibited the executive from competing in the travel agency business in the same state within one year of leaving the agency. The travel agency requires that all its employees sign the same noncompete agreement.

The final pretrial memorandum (which included proposed conclusions of law citing all key legal authority) was submitted to the court on Thursday and a bench trial is scheduled to start on Monday. In this jurisdiction (like many), the state supreme court issues decisions that are considered binding precedent, the intermediate appellate court may designate its decisions as available for future citation as authority or not, and trial-level decisions and verdicts are nonprecedential.

When he was first assigned to the case, Frank subscribed to a legal news feed sent daily to his email inbox that sends alerts about new decisions and cases. The news update that he opens on the Friday before trial includes the authority described below, issued after the pretrial memorandum was submitted. What, if anything, **must** Frank disclose to the court? In situations in which Frank has a choice, what **should** he disclose and how? Please explain your reasoning.

a. A decision by the state supreme court in the state where Frank's case is being tried in which the supreme court held enforceable all noncompete agreements in the travel industry.

b. A state statute in the state where Frank's case is being tried invalidating all noncompete agreements longer in duration than two years.

c. A decision by the state supreme court in the state where Frank's case is being tried in which the supreme court invalidated all noncompete agreements longer in duration than two years.

d. A decision by the state supreme court in the state where Frank's case is being tried in which the supreme court invalidated all noncompete agreements longer in duration than six months.

e. A decision by the state supreme court where Frank's case is being tried in which the supreme court criticized a statewide noncompete in dicta but dismissed the case as untimely filed.

f. A decision by the intermediate appellate court in the state where Frank's case is being tried in which the appellate court invalidated all noncompete agreements longer in duration than six months. The case is marked as "not for citation."

g. A decision by a state supreme court in a different state from the one where Frank's case is being tried invalidating the exact same noncompete agreement in litigation between the travel agency and different employee.

h. A decision by a trial court in the state where Frank's case is being tried in which that trial court held unenforceable a statewide noncompete agreement on the basis that such an agreement could have no larger than a 50-mile radius.

i. A decision following a bench trial in the same court in which Frank's case is being tried in which the judge found in favor of a former employee who had signed a year-long, statewide noncompete agreement.

j. A law-journal article criticizing noncompete agreements as against public policy.

Problem 24C-8: Would your analysis of any of the parts of **Problem 24C-7 at 851** change if counsel for the defendant former executive identified the authority to the court before Frank had a chance to decide what to do? If so, how and why; and if not, why not?

Problem 24C-9: What **consequences** might Frank and Happy face if they fail to disclose any of the authority outlined in **Problem 24C-7 at 851** that they were required to disclose?

Problem 24C-10: Assume that Frank and Happy determine that some of the authority that they've found in the parts of **Problem 24C-7 at 851 must** be disclosed to the court. Also assume that the authority has not been disclosed by counsel for the defendant former executive.

a. **May** Frank and Happy wait until trial begins to see whether opposing counsel discloses the adverse authority, and then disclose the authority before the trial starts only if opposing counsel fails to do so? **Should** they?

b. **May** Frank and Happy disclose the adverse authority by discussing it for the first time in closing argument? **Should** they?

c. **May** Frank and Happy wait until trial is concluded, and then submit an updated set of conclusions of law, disclosing any adverse authority? **Should** they?

Problem 24C-11: Same facts as **Problem 24C-7 at 851**, but Frank never checked his email between the time that he submitted the pretrial memorandum and the time that trial began. Would Frank have violated his ethical obligations based on the fact that he had received (but not read) an email disclosing adverse authority?

Problem 24C-12: Same facts as **Problem 24C-7 at 851**, but now Frank has a friend clerking for the state supreme court in the state where the case is being tried, and the friend alerts him to a case that has been decided squarely against the position Frank and Happy are asserting in their case but that has not yet been publicly released. According to Frank's friend, no one outside the supreme court and its staff knows about the decision. What, if anything, **must** or **should** Frank and Happy do, and when? Does it change your analysis if the decision will be published next week, while the trial is pending? How about if Frank's friend tells him that one dissenting justice is still preparing her dissent, and she is a notoriously slow writer, so the decision likely will not be published until after Frank's trial ends? If so, how and why; and if not, why not?

4. Publicity Before and During Trial

Although litigation is, by constitutional mandate, a public process, most cases elicit little interest among the public at large. When the occasional celebrated crime, fraud, or other litigated dispute generates wide public interest, however, the media pays close attention to the proceedings and to the people involved in them, including the advocates. Press coverage, in turn, creates the opportunity for advocates to influence potential decision makers in the case, such as potential or presiding judges, or the jury pool in the area in which the case will be tried (or sitting jurors), by amplifying ideas that an advocate may wish to cultivate.[18]

There is a delicate balance that must be struck between preserving a litigant's First Amendment rights to speak freely regarding a pending dispute and safeguarding the integrity of the jury process. This balance is struck in the application of bodies of law governing judicial management of venue, jury selection, and jury processes, as well as **Model Rule 3.6**. It is not always easy to find the balance point in specific cases, but the Rule provides some useful guidance should you find yourself involved in the rare case that draws the public spotlight.[19]

Other law or a specific court order may limit public statements of any kind (or of specific kinds) in appropriate circumstances, for example in cases involving juveniles or the disabled. *See* **Model Rule 3.6 Comment [2]**. But **Model Rule 3.6** addresses pretrial publicity in all cases not subject to these special strictures.

TAMING THE TEXT Take a look at **Model Rule 3.6(a), (b), and (d)**, and then let's break them down:

- **Model Rule 3.6(a)** says that the Rule applies to "[a] lawyer who is participating or has participated in the investigation or litigation of a matter. . . ." What does it mean to "participate"? It's enough to be involved in the same **practice organization** or otherwise associated with a lawyer who is actively involved. We know that because **Model Rule 3.6(d)** clarifies that any lawyer "associated in a firm [which is the Model Rules' term for any **practice organization**] or government agency" with a lawyer actively involved in the investigation or litigation is covered by the Rule.

- A lawyer covered by the rule **must not** ("shall not") "make an extrajudicial statement that the lawyer knows or reasonably should know will be disseminated by means of public communication . . ." that has additional characteristics discussed next. "Extrajudicial" means outside the courtroom or other site of official proceedings; thus, anything that you say in court (or other official proceedings) is not governed by **Model Rule 3.6**, though it is subject to the other constraints applicable to statements made in court. And what's "public communication"? It includes any communication to the general public, most commonly by the media, but also including social media.

- Statements that will be publicly disseminated are still okay, *unless* they "will have a substantial likelihood of **materially** prejudicing an adjudicative proceeding in the matter." Not just some possibility, but a "substantial likelihood." And not just any effect on the "adjudicative proceeding," but

---

[18] Beware: Dealing with the media is an art that requires skill and mindfulness. Public attention can turn otherwise practiced advocates not accustomed to it into burbling idiots. *See, e.g.,* **Problem 8.A-6 at 212**; *see also* pretty much every legal novel ever written.

[19] *See generally Gentile v. State Bar of Nev.,* 501 US 1030 (1991); **Model Rule 3.6 Comment [1]**. Model Rule 3.6 is informed by the decision and underlying analysis in *Gentile,* specifically but not uniquely *Gentile's* standard for proscribable pretrial publicity—communications with a "substantial likelihood of **materially** prejudicing an adjudicative proceeding."

"**material[ ]** prejudic[e]." To be sure, "substantial likelihood" and "**material[ ]** prejudic[e]" are fuzzy terms, but they are meant to convey that the public statement must be more than speculatively likely to have a real and significant effect. How could the public statement affect the "adjudicative proceeding"? By far the most common concern is prejudicing potential jurors, but a veiled (or not-so-veiled) threat directed to, say, a judge that had a substantial likelihood of significantly influencing him or her would also violate the Rule (and, depending on its content, could independently violate criminal laws against threatening judicial officers, as well as **Model Rule 8.4(d)** ("conduct prejudicial to the administration of justice")). Because of the constitutional protections at stake, the Rule is most concerned about potential jurors in a criminal case, and is somewhat less concerned about potential jurors in a civil case. It is least concerned in those situations in which no jury is involved, because judges and arbitrators are generally seen as more difficult to influence. *See* **Model Rule 3.6 Comment [6].**

- To clarify the application of the fuzzy "substantial likelihood" of "**material[ ]** prejudic[e]" standards, **Model Rule 3.6(b)** provides a nonexclusive "safe harbor" list of things that you **may** always communicate to the public without violating the Rule. **Model Rule 3.6 Comment [4].** There are six kinds of statements acceptable in civil or criminal cases, and four more that are deemed acceptable only in criminal cases. Please pause and review those ten categories of statements, which are self-explanatory, so that we don't have to write them out for you here. (Yes, you really do need to know them, because they cover the range of topics that you **may** talk about in this situation, and because the MPRE often tests on the details of this Rule.)

- **Model Rule 3.6 Comment [5]** also provides a list of "subjects that are more likely than not to have a **material** prejudicial effect on a proceeding." Unlike the topics enumerated in **Model Rule 3.6(b)** (the safe harbor), **Model Rule 3.6 Comment [5]** does not go so far as to say that the topics that it lists will *always* be considered *improper* subjects of pretrial publicity, but it indicates that chances are good that these six categories of statements will be found to be unduly prejudicial in many cases. The prudent practice, then, is to avoid them. Again, they are largely self-explanatory, but please take a few moments to review them, because you need to know what they are.

Finally, **Model Rule 3.6(c)** allows "a statement that a reasonable lawyer would believe is required to protect a client from the substantial undue prejudicial effect of recent publicity not initiated by the lawyer or the lawyer's client"; that is, a right to speak out to the extent necessary to *correct* prejudice with which an adversary may have infected the public in violation of the Rule. Such statements can only go so far as is reasonably necessary to "mitigate" the harm; overcorrecting will destroy the Rule's permission and leave you in violation. Care and thought (and a conscious effort to cool down angry reactions) should always be devoted to whether or how to respond to an adversary's improper publicity.

Problem 24C-13: Which of the lawyers in the following situations could be subject to **consequences**, and what might those **consequences** be? Please explain your answers.

a. Danielle's office is about to unseal an indictment against a well-respected local college football coach, accusing the coach of child exploitation involving local high school students who want to play for the coach. The DA himself, who enjoys the limelight and has higher political ambitions, is personally involved in the case. The DA leaks to the media that the indictment is going to be unsealed and notifies them of the time and date of the coach's expected arrest.

b. The DA expects that, once the coach learns of the charges, he will quickly hire a team of experienced lawyers and public relations specialists. Can the DA preempt any statement that the defendant's defense team might make by holding his own press conference to describe the evidence that was submitted to the grand jury (which is not yet public)?

c. After the coach is arraigned, the DA holds a press conference on the courthouse steps and discusses the contents of the now-unsealed indictment.

d. Defense counsel purchases social media advertisements targeted at possible jurors, hoping to remind them of how successful the football team has been under the coach's tenure. Would it change your analysis if the coach's PR firm purchased the targeted advertisements? If so, how and why; and if not, why not?

e. A well-known local criminal defense lawyer not personally involved in the case gives a radio interview in which she discusses the indictment. What if she gives her view of the likelihood that the prosecution will prevail in the case (she thinks the defense is strong)? How about her personal opinion as to the coach's guilt or innocence?

f. Same as (e), but now the DA has an experienced criminal defense lawyer in town—one who owes him a favor—call into the radio show to provide a more pro-prosecution view.

g. The DA sends a letter to the editor of the local newspaper stating his opinion that the coach will be convicted.

h. After the pretrial conference, the DA holds a press conference on the courthouse steps in which he describes the expected testimony from victims at trial, most of whom are high school football players under the age of 18. He is careful not to identify any witness by name.

i. The DA suggests to a local blogger who is posting about the scandal that there were multiple victims over a period of years, but he has charged the coach only with assaulting a single minor on a single occasion. Does it change your analysis if the investigation is ongoing? If so, how and why; and if not, why not?

j. The DA tells the media that the coach has refused to submit to a polygraph test. Does it change your analysis if the coach did indeed refuse? If so, how and why; and if not, why not?

k. Defense counsel releases a statement that the coach denies all charges and that his accuser is a scorned ex-spouse seeking revenge. In response, the DA releases a statement truthfully asserting that the case against the coach was initiated not by the coach's former spouse, but by an alleged victim.

l. The case goes to trial, and the coach is convicted and sentenced. Afterward, his defense firm describes its work on the case on the firm's website. Does it matter whether the coach could still appeal? If so, how and why; and if not, why not?

5. Lawyer as Witness

Generally speaking, you cannot be a witness and an advocate in the same trial. **Model Rule 3.7** states the prohibition as forbidding a lawyer to be an advocate "at a trial in which the lawyer is *likely* to be a *necessary* witness" (emphases added). **TAMING THE TEXT** The emphasized words make it possible to determine the issue before the trial begins, so that the trial is not disrupted by the issue midstream, and to avoid an adversary's opportunistic efforts to **disqualify** opposing trial counsel simply by putting trial counsel on the adversary's witness list when trial counsel's testimony likely won't really be necessary (or even likely). (Do you see why these additions were necessary?) **TAMING THE TEXT**

CONSEQUENCES Although **Model Rule 3.7** is a disciplinary rule, it (or the version of the Rule adopted in a particular jurisdiction) is widely viewed also to state the standard for **disqualifying** a lawyer-witness when the terms of the Rule are met. **CONSEQUENCES**

REASON FOR THE RULE As **Model Rule 3.7 Comment [2]** explains, "A witness is required to testify on the basis of personal knowledge, while an advocate is expected to explain and comment on evidence given by others. It may not be clear whether a statement by an advocate-witness should be taken as proof or as an analysis of the proof." The possibilities for confusion of this kind animate the Rule. **REASON FOR THE RULE**

There are three exceptions to this Rule, and one very important limitation. The exceptions are:

1. If the advocate's testimony relates only to an "uncontested issue" (**Model Rule 3.7(a)(1)**);
2. If the advocate's testimony relates to "the nature and value of legal services rendered in the case" (**Model Rule 3.7(a)(2)**); for example, if the advocate's client is claiming statutory or contractual attorneys' fees, or claiming attorneys' fees as damages; and
3. If "disqualification of the lawyer would work substantial hardship on the client" (**Model Rule 3.7(a)(3)**); for example, if the need for the advocate's testimony arises shortly before or during trial and there is no reasonably available substitute. This exception requires "balancing . . . between the interests of the client and those of the tribunal and the opposing party." **Model Rule 3.7 Comment [4]**. The tribunal's interest is in preventing the "trier of fact [from being] confused or misled by a lawyer serving as both advocate and witness"; the opposing party's interest is in preventing "the combination of roles [from prejudicing] that party's rights in the litigation." **Model Rule 3.7 Comment [2]**.

Thus, although the Rule by its terms applies to any trial in any kind of tribunal, the concerns of the tribunal and the opposing party will be strongest when the factfinder is a jury, which is less familiar with the distinctions between the roles of witness and advocate, and when the advocate's testimony is anticipated to be more central to the merits and more contested, making it easier for the factfinder to confuse the two roles. *See* **Model Rule 3.7 Comment [4]**.

The limitation on the Rule is that generally it is not **imputed** within a **practice organization**. Thus, if one lawyer in a **practice organization** is likely to be a necessary witness on a contested issue other than the nature and value of the **practice organization's** services in the case, another lawyer from the same **practice organization** can still be trial counsel, unless the role of either lawyer creates a **conflict of interest**. **Model Rule 3.7(b)**.

The **conflict of interest** precluding this solution could be any of the kinds described in **Chapter 22 at 599**. To give just one example, the lawyer-witness might be expected to testify inconsistently with her client, which would create a **concurrent conflict** between the lawyer-witness's personal duty to testify truthfully and her **duty of loyalty** to her client. That **concurrent conflict** might not be resolved by having another lawyer in the same **practice organization** conduct the witness-lawyer's examination. *See* **Chapter 22.A at 626**. **Conflicts of interest** that arise in this context may be addressed whenever, and by whatever means, they would be in any other context, such as the client's **informed consent, confirmed in writing** (or, preferably, **in a writing signed by the client**) when the relevant **conflict** is **consentable**.

Problem 24C-14: Which of the lawyers in the following situations could be subject to **consequences**, and what might those **consequences** be? Please explain your answers.

a. Frank's friend, Emma, is taking her neighbor to court after a branch from the neighbor's tree damaged Emma's fence. Emma is proceeding *pro se*. Frank had seen the tree at a barbeque a few days before the fence was damaged. At that time, Frank noticed that the tree needed pruning. Frank agrees to testify about the location and condition of the tree.

b. Emma is discharged by her employer. She believes that she was fired because of her gender, and she asks Frank to bring an employment discrimination case on her behalf. During the trial, Emma's employer claims that Emma was fired because she stole from petty cash. Frank calls several character witnesses on Emma's behalf to testify that she is always honest. When Emma requests it, Frank agrees that he will also testify as to her character.

c. The employment discrimination statute under which Emma brought her suit in (b) allows the court to award the prevailing party reasonable attorneys' fees. After Emma prevails in her employment discrimination case, a hearing is held to determine how much in attorneys' fees Emma should be awarded. Frank testifies about the number of hours that he spent litigating the case, what he did, and his hourly rate.

Problem 24C-15: Frank is walking to the county law library and witnesses a Toyota driven by Sam Speedy run a red light and collide with a Honda driven by Uma Unlucky. No one else is present; Frank is the only nonparty eyewitness. Neither car sustains major damage. Frank remains at the scene and gives a statement to the police. He tells the police, "The Toyota caused the collision. The light was red when the Toyota came to the intersection. He did not stop. He went through the intersection and hit the Honda." Under each of the following circumstances, might Frank be subject to **consequences**, and what might those **consequences** be? Please explain your answers.

a. Frank represents neither Sam nor Uma but testifies as an eyewitness when Uma sues Sam.

b. Frank represents Uma when she sues Sam. The parties agree not to call Frank but instead to offer the police report, which includes Frank's statement.

c. Happy Trials (and Frank's firm) represent Uma when she sues Sam. The police report cannot be found. Frank is listed as a potential witness for Uma in her pretrial disclosures.

d. Frank represents Uma when she sues Sam. The police report cannot be found. Frank is listed as a potential witness for Uma in her pretrial disclosures.

e. Frank represents Uma when she sues Sam. Frank is listed as a potential adverse witness by Sam in Sam's pretrial disclosures.

f. Frank represents Sam when he is sued by Uma. Frank is listed as a potential eyewitness for Sam in his pretrial disclosures.

g. Frank represents Sam when he is sued by Uma. He offers to be deposed by Uma's counsel, and he agrees that, rather than testify live at trial, portions of his deposition transcript may be read to the jury.

h. Uma sues Sam and is awarded $50,000. Sam then sues Stop-n-Go Co., the manufacturer of the stoplight at the intersection at which the collision occurred, claiming that the stoplight malfunctioned and caused the accident. Frank represents Stop-n-Go. Neither party lists Frank as a potential witness. Sam has short-term memory loss as a result of the accident. He does not dispute the date of the accident but cannot recall when it was. Frank agrees to testify as to the date of the accident.

i. Uma sues Sam and is awarded $50,000. Sam then sues Stop-n-Go Co., the manufacturer of the stoplight at the intersection where the collision occurred. Sam claims that the accident was caused by a defective light that shifted quickly back and forth between red and green. Sam claims that Stop-n-Go is liable for contribution and indemnity and should pay Sam $50,000. Frank represents Stop-n-Go. Neither party lists Frank as a potential witness. At trial, a dispute arises about whether the light was flickering at the time of the accident. Frank testifies that it was not flickering but rather that it was red.

j. Dr. Pain treated Uma after the accident. Uma sues Dr. Pain alleging medical malpractice. Frank agrees to represent Dr. Pain in the medical malpractice case.

k. After Dr. Pain settles the malpractice case, he refuses to pay Frank's and his firm's attorneys' fees. Frank's firm, represented by Frank, sues Dr. Pain for breach of contract. At trial, Frank testifies that Dr. Pain owes him $10,000 in attorneys' fees.

l. Eight years after Sam and Uma's accident, Frank represents Barbara Backseat in a worker's compensation case. Midway through trial, during cross-examination, counsel for the employer asks Barbara about the car accident between Uma and Sam. For the first time, Frank realizes that Barbara was a passenger in Uma's car. She was a teenager at the time of the accident and now looks considerably different. A key disputed issue in Barbara's case becomes the nature of the collision between Uma and Sam. Counsel for the employer claims that both cars were totaled and that Barbara's injuries are preexisting. Uma and Sam have since died of natural causes, and the police report is missing. Barbara asks Frank to testify that neither car was badly damaged after the collision. Frank cannot find another lawyer willing to represent Barbara in the middle of her case. He testifies that neither car was badly damaged.

6. Limits on Witness Examination and Argument

Take a look at **Model Rule 3.4(e)**. It forbids a lawyer from doing several things "in trial":

1. To "allude to any matter that the lawyer does not reasonably believe is relevant or that will not be supported by admissible evidence";
2. To "assert personal knowledge of facts in issue except when testifying as a witness"; or
3. To "state a personal opinion as to the justness of a cause, the credibility of a witness, the culpability of a civil litigant or the guilt or innocence of an accused."

These prohibitions are straightforward and involve long-standing principles of trial practice. These principles, like those animating the "lawyer as witness" rule (**Model Rule 3.7**), are focused on preventing the factfinder from confusing evidence and argument. Though these Rules are well understood, lawyers occasionally lose track of (or try to evade) them in the heat of battle. More explaining isn't really necessary, so let's nail down your understanding of this Rule with some problems.

Problem 24C-16: Danielle is litigating an armed robbery case. Her key witness, Eliana Eyewitness, walked by the bank as it was being robbed. She will testify that she saw the defendant fleeing from the bank with a duffel bag and a handgun. At trial, Eliana plans to identify Donnie Defendant as the robber. Which of the lawyers in the following situations could be subject to **consequences**, and what might those **consequences** be? Please explain your answers.

a. In her opening statement, defense counsel tells the jury, "You will learn that the prosecution's key witness, Eliana, has three prior convictions for perjury." In actuality, Eliana has an entirely clean criminal record.

b. In her opening statement, defense counsel tells the jury, "You will learn that the prosecution's key witness, Eliana, has a prior conviction for retail theft (that is, shoplifting)." Although this is true, the judge already excluded all evidence of this conviction in a pretrial motion *in limine*.

c. In her opening statement, defense counsel tells the jury, "You will learn that the prosecution's key witness, Eliana, has a prior conviction for retail theft." This is true. In this jurisdiction, the admission of convictions over ten years old is within the discretion of the trial court. Neither party has moved for a pretrial ruling on the admissibility of the conviction, and the conviction is 11 years old.

d. Same facts as (c), but the judge presiding over the trial has excluded similar evidence in the last five cases in which the judge presided.

e. In her opening statement, defense counsel tells the jury, "You will have reason to doubt the testimony of the prosecution's key witness, Eliana." Although Eliana's story is generally consistent with the prosecution's case, there are some minor inconsistencies between Eliana's testimony and the testimony of defense witnesses, who will claim the robber had a blue backpack rather than a black duffel bag.

f. In her opening statement, defense counsel tells the jury, "You will have reason to doubt the testimony of the prosecution's key witness, Eliana." Eliana admitted to the police that, at the time that she had witnessed the robbery, it was dark outside, she was not wearing her glasses, and the robber ran away from her so she couldn't see his or her face.

g. In her opening statement, defense counsel tells the jury, "You will learn that the prosecution's key witness, Eliana Eyewitness, couldn't carry a tune in a bucket." It is true that Eliana is a terrible singer.

h. In her opening statement, defense counsel tells the jury, "Donnie will take the stand himself and proclaim his innocence." Defense counsel has no intention of calling Donnie to testify.

i. In her opening statement, defense counsel tells the jury, "Donnie is an upstanding member of the community who has been wrongfully accused. He and I attend the same church, and he has never missed a Sunday." Donnie does in fact regularly attend the same church his lawyer does.

j. In her opening statement, defense counsel tells the jury, "Donnie is an upstanding member of the community who has been wrongfully accused. You will hear from his church pastor, who will tell you that Donnie has never missed a Sunday." Donnie's pastor is listed as a potential defense witness.

k. Danielle calls Eliana as the first prosecution witness. During Eliana's testimony, defense counsel objects and says, "Objection; this testimony is a lie. I should know, because I was at the scene of the robbery, and I saw the whole thing myself."

l. As Eliana testifies, defense counsel shakes her head angrily and mouths the word "liar" repeatedly.

m. During the trial, defense counsel offers a photograph as an exhibit. It shows Donnie at a baseball game, allegedly at the same time as the robbery. Danielle objects to its admission on the basis that the time of the photo cannot be proven. The judge sustains the objection. Defense counsel pretends to have a "technical issue" and projects the photograph for the jury to see anyway. Defense counsel then fumbles with the computer while mumbling, "Oh, no! I've shown the photo of Donnie at the baseball game at the same time as the robbery." After the jurors have had a good look, she switches off the screen and apologizes for her clumsiness.

n. Defense counsel calls Donnie's pastor to testify as a character witness for Donnie. She asks the pastor how long he has known Donnie. The pastor replies, "Ten years." She asks the pastor, "What do you think of his moral character?" The pastor replies, "He is as honest as the day is long." Defense counsel says, "And I've known you my whole life, Pastor Pat, so I know that you're a man whose word can be trusted."

o. In her closing argument, defense counsel tells the jury, "The judge has ruled to exclude certain evidence in this case. I've seen it and, if you knew what I know, you'd know why Donnie is innocent." The judge has, in fact, excluded evidence offered by the defense, and some of that evidence would be exculpatory if credited.

p. In her closing argument, defense counsel says, "I wouldn't have accepted this case if I thought that Donnie was guilty. You are looking at an innocent man."

q. In her closing argument, defense counsel says, "How would you feel if you were sitting where Donnie is sitting now—an innocent person accused of a crime you didn't commit?"

7. The Duty of Candor to the Tribunal and the Duty to Correct

A few things are probably obvious to you already: You can't lie to a tribunal. You can't encourage or assist others to do so, either. And you can't present false evidence. CONSEQUENCES Not only are these violations of the Rules of Professional Conduct stating grounds for professional discipline, but when done knowingly and with respect to **material** information, they are false-statement crimes in every U.S. jurisdiction, bearing names like perjury, suborning perjury, and obstruction of justice. These tactics are also subject to court sanctions under multiple rules and statutes. CONSEQUENCES

Easy-peasy, right? Well, in the obvious cases, sure. But what if you're *uncertain* about the truthfulness of evidence or testimony that you could present, or that your client wants you to present, or on the basis of which you might make representations to the court yourself? Then things get a little complicated. Don't worry; we remain your faithful guides. Let's walk through the details together.

a. You Must Not Make Misrepresentations to a Tribunal Yourself

Let's start with some easy stuff: You **must not** "knowingly . . . make a false statement of fact . . . to a tribunal." **Model Rule 3.3(a)(1)**. This is Rule directed specifically to what *you* say, as an advocate, when you address the tribunal, whether orally or in writing.

REAL WORLD You can see by its terms that the Rule limits discipline to a knowing misrepresentation. As in the case of incorrect or misleading legal argument, however, the requirement that the misrepresentation be "knowing[]" is a limit only on *formal* **consequences**. Providing the tribunal with reasons to trust and believe you every single time that you speak is the best investment that you can make in your future as an advocate. Aside from lying outright, shading or shortchanging the truth with clever word games will cost you your credibility with the court—and for a long time. Hell hath no fury like a judge who believes that he or she has been "played." And simple carelessness regarding the accuracy of facts underlying the representations that you make to the court will often put you in a similarly disfavored spot. (REAL WORLD)

Problem 24C-17: Frank is appearing at a pretrial conference in a breach of contract case. His client, defendant Widgeteria Corporation, allegedly entered into a contract to supply widgets to the plaintiff, FidgetDigit, Inc. The contract was allegedly entered into on behalf of Widgeteria by its former CEO, Diana Deceased, but was discovered only after Diana's death. Now, Widgeteria is being sued for failing to supply the widgets called for under the contract. Opposing counsel, Joe Joseph, is appearing for plaintiff FidgetDigit. Which of the lawyers in the following situations could be subject to **consequences**, and what might those **consequences** be? Please explain your answers.

a. When asked by the judge at the pretrial conference, "Who signed the contract on behalf of Widgeteria?" Frank says, "Diana." Indeed, based on Frank's review of the file, the signature on the contract was Diana's. Unbeknownst to Frank and his client, the signature was a forgery.

b. When asked by the judge, "Have you compared the signature on the contract to other exemplars of Diana's signature?" Frank's face turns red—he hadn't thought to do that. He replies, "Yes, and they look similar."

c. When asked by the judge, "Have you compared the signature on the contract to other exemplars of Diana's signature?" Frank's face turns red—he hadn't thought to do that. He says, "No, that hadn't occurred to me."

d. Joe believes that the signature is a forgery. He has other exemplars of Diana's signature, and they look dissimilar. He says nothing when the judge asks Frank whether he has compared Diana's signature to any exemplars. The judge doesn't ask Joe any questions about the signature, and Joe does not volunteer any information about the topic.

e. Joe believes that the signature is a forgery. He has other exemplars of Diana's signature, and they look dissimilar. The judge asks Joe, "Do you agree that Diana signed the contract on behalf of Widgeteria?" He replies, "It has her name on it, doesn't it?"

f. Same facts as (e), except that Joe replies, in answer to the judge's question, "I'm not the trier of fact, Your Honor—you are."

g. Same facts as (e), except that Joe replies, in answer to the judge's question, "My client does not contest the authenticity of Ms. Deceased's signature."

h. Same facts as (e), except that Joe simply replies "Yes" to the judge's question.

i. Same facts as (e), except that Joe replies, in answer to the judge's question, "We have some exemplars of Ms. Deceased's signature, and would admit that they do not match exactly."

j. Joe's own client had previously admitted to Joe that an employee of FidgetDigit is the one who signed for Diana on the contract. The judge asks him, "Do you agree that Diana signed the contract?" Joe says, "It sure looks like it to me."

k. Same facts as (j), except that Joe replies, in answer to the judge's question, "Yes, Diana signed the contract."

l. Same facts as (j), except that Joe replies, in answer to the judge's question, "It's disputable. There is evidence to suggest that the signature is Ms. Deceased's, but there is also evidence to suggest that it isn't." There are a few emails from Diana in which she referred to the contract. Those emails imply that Diana was at least aware that someone else signed her name and that she may have authorized or ratified that signature on her and Widgeteria's behalf. Indeed, the position of Joe's client is that Diana authorized Joe's client to sign on Diana's and the company's behalf.

Problem 24C-18: Assuming the same general situation as in **Problem 24C-17 at 863**, would it make any difference to your analysis if the representations were made in a written brief, as opposed to being made during oral argument? If so, how and why; and if not, why not?

b. You Must Not Present False Evidence, or Encourage or Assist Others to Do So

Your **duty of candor to the tribunal** is not limited to what you say yourself. As an advocate, you are responsible for presenting or attacking evidence in all forms. The Rules of Professional Conduct and related criminal and civil law impose duties on you to safeguard the integrity of the truth-finding process.

i. Encouragement of Untruthfulness

Model Rule 3.4(b) provides that you **must not** "counsel or assist a witness to testify falsely. . . ." The prohibition applies at all stages of the proceeding, including not only testimony in court but also in a deposition or a sworn affidavit or declaration.

In contrast, nothing in the Rules of Professional Conduct or other law prohibits you from *properly preparing* a witness to testify. The *Restatement* provides numerous examples of proper witness-preparation techniques:

■ Discussing the role of the witness and effective courtroom demeanor;
■ Discussing the witness's recollection and probable testimony;
■ Discussing the applicability of the law to the events in issue;
■ Reviewing the factual context into which the witness's observations or opinions will fit;
■ Reviewing documents or other physical evidence that may be introduced;
■ Discussing probable lines of hostile cross-examination that the witness should be prepared to meet;
■ Inviting the witness to provide truthful testimony favorable to the lawyer's client;
■ Revealing to the witness other testimony or evidence that will be presented and asking the witness to reconsider the witness's recollection or recounting of events in that light;

- Rehearsing testimony; and
- Suggesting choices of words that might be used to make the witness's meaning clear and consistent with the truth.[20]

What you can't do, of course, is (in the words of the Rule) to counsel or assist a witness to testify falsely.

TIPS & TACTICS You **may** prepare any witness who will let you, whether or not that witness is your client. One important difference between client and non-client witnesses is that your communications with non-client witnesses are not protected by the **attorney-client privilege**. As a result, opposing counsel may be able to ask a non-client witness in an examination during trial or a deposition, or in an informal interview of her own, what the two of you discussed.[21] That risk cautions you to phrase what you say with extra care, and to actively manage the conditions under which you talk with a non-client witness who may be hostile, unreliable, or dishonest. Many experienced advocates begin a conversation with any non-client potential witness with explicit and emphatic admonitions that the most important thing the witness can do is to tell the truth, both in the immediate conversation and in his or her eventual testimony. (This approach can lead to a delightful exchange on cross-examination: "Did you speak with my opposing counsel?" "Yes." "What did the two of you discuss?" "She said to tell the truth.") TIPS & TACTICS

> **Problem 24C-19:** Frank is preparing his client, Patricia Plaintiff, for her deposition. Patricia claims that she slipped and fell on ice while walking through the parking lot at her local post office around 9 a.m. on a Tuesday, a condition that she contends the U.S. Postal Service negligently failed to correct. Might any of the following conduct expose Frank to **consequences**, and what might those **consequences** be? Please explain your answers.
>
> a. Frank asks Patricia if she's ever been deposed before. She says that she hasn't been. Frank explains the basic "rules of the road" and tells her who will be present in the room, where they will sit, and what they will be doing. Among other things, he explains the concept of **attorney-client privilege** and tells her that she should not answer questions about what she and Frank discussed during her witness prep.

---

[20] RESTATEMENT (THIRD) OF THE LAW GOVERNING LAWYERS § 116, Comment b (2001). The rule is quite different in England, which has imposed extremely stringent limits on witness preparation. *See* Brad Rudin & Betsy Hutchings, *England & U.S.: Contrasts in Witness Preparation Rules,* http://www.newyorklegalethics.com/england-u-s-contrasts-in-witness-preparation-rules/ (2006). Witness preparation, like the interviewing to which it is closely related, is a subtle art demanding a high level of skill, and if you anticipate devoting any portion of your career to litigation, you should pursue a skills course in law school that will address it.

[21] Some of what you say or do (for example, the identity of the documents or other tangible evidence that you might have chosen to show a non-client) may be protectable as "trial preparation materials" or "mental impressions, conclusions, opinions, or legal theories of a party's attorney or other representative concerning the litigation" under the **work product doctrine**, *see, e.g.,* **Fed. R. Civ. P. 26(b)(3)**. (Do you see why? This is an important protection when it is available, so make sure that you understand its scope and limits.) Courts' treatment of this protection in this context is inconsistent and, in prudence, you should anticipate that anything that you've said or shown to a non-client witness may be elicited by an adversary in deposition or trial testimony—or outside of court.

b. Patricia tends to look down and mumble when she talks. Frank encourages her to make eye contact with her questioner and to speak up. "It's important that the court reporter be able to hear you," he says. "And we want to make a good impression on defense counsel and show them what a strong trial witness you'll be."

c. Frank explains the basics of premises liability to Patricia. He tells her that a business invitee (for example, someone who was actually going to the post office) may be entitled to greater legal protection than would a licensee who was cutting through the parking lot as a shortcut on the way to somewhere else.

d. Same facts as (c), except that then Frank asks her, "Does that help you remember what you were doing in the parking lot that morning?"

e. Frank rehearses some questions with Patricia. He gives her feedback on her answers, pointing out places where she was unclear about the chronology of events. They practice again, and Frank praises her when she tells a more cohesive version of the morning's events leading up to the fall.

f. Frank has already deposed Scott Snowblower, who was responsible for snow removal in the parking lot on the day of Patricia's fall. Frank explains to Patricia that Scott testified that he had plowed and salted the parking lot around 8 a.m. that morning.

g. Frank shows Patricia a photo of the parking lot taken by a postal service employee after Patricia reported the fall.

h. Frank asks Patricia, "Do you remember what time you fell?" She says, "Not exactly." Frank shows Patricia the accident report drafted by the USPS immediately after the fall. The report notes the time of the fall to be "9:10 a.m." Patricia says, "That seems right; I think that it was not long after 9 a.m."

i. Same facts as (h), but instead of showing Patricia the report, Frank tells her, "The postal service's accident report said that you fell around 9 a.m."

j. Assume the same facts as (h), but when Frank shows Patricia the report, Patricia says, "I think this report is wrong, because I think that I fell closer to noon." Frank knows that Patricia fell much earlier in the day; in fact, at noon, she was already in the emergency room, as reflected by her medical records. What **must**, **may**, and **should** Frank do?

k. Frank tells Patricia, "Defense counsel is going to ask you whether you had taken any medication that could have impaired your balance on the morning of the fall." Patricia says, "I had taken a Xanax, but that's all." Frank asks, "Did it make you unsteady on your feet?" Patricia says, "No."

l. Same as the first part of (k), except that Patricia interjects, "Do illegal drugs count?" Frank says, "Yes, why do you ask?" Patricia says, "I was high on cocaine at the time of the fall." Frank tells her, "Don't admit that unless defense counsel asks you directly."

m. Same facts as in (l), but instead Frank tells Patricia, "You mustn't admit that you did any illegal drugs. If you're asked about it, say that you didn't."

n. Frank asks, "What did the asphalt look like when you started walking across it?" Patricia says, "I could see that it was covered with ice." Frank says, "We'll lose the case if you say that. I need you to say, 'I didn't see any ice before I fell.'" Frank practices this question with

Patricia by asking her the question and repeating his version of the answer until she has memorized his answer verbatim.

o. Frank asks Patricia, "What parts of your body hurt after the fall?" She says, "Just my neck." Patricia had an MRI taken in the emergency room after the accident. It showed a slipped disc in her neck and another in her lower back. Frank asks, "Are you sure that you didn't also hurt your back?" Patricia says, "I don't remember." Frank says, "Okay, if that's the truth, then tell defense counsel that you don't remember."

p. Same facts as (o), but instead Frank tells Patricia, "The MRI says that you also hurt your back." Patricia says, "Okay, but I don't remember hurting my back." Frank says, "Well, say that you did anyway, because the MRI shows that you did, and you don't remember otherwise." Patricia agrees.

q. Same facts as (o), but instead, in response to Frank's statement about Patricia's MRI, Patricia says, "That slipped disc is from a car accident that I had two months before the slip-and-fall. I'm sure that my back felt fine after the fall." Frank says, "It will really help your case if you say that you hurt your back in the fall." Patricia agrees.

r. Frank asks, "What shoes were you wearing at the time of the fall?" Patricia points to the boots that she's wearing in the prep session. They're thick-soled winter snow boots. Frank says, "That's really helpful. Wear those to the deposition and make sure to mention, in response to some question, that those sturdy snow boots are what you were wearing at the time of the fall."

s. Same facts as in (r), except that Patricia points to her four-inch stiletto heels and tells Frank that those are the shoes that she was wearing at the time of the fall. Frank says, "Tell defense counsel that you were wearing snow boots, not high heels." Patricia says, "No, I'm not going to lie." Frank responds, "Fine." He ends the prep session.

ii. Inducements to Testify

Model Rule 3.4(b) also provides that you **must not** "offer an inducement to a witness that is prohibited by law." This Rule is not limited to "inducements" to testify falsely, though all such inducements would of course be "prohibited by law." The Rule prohibits *any* "inducement to a witness that is prohibited by law."

So what's prohibited? The law treats fact witnesses and expert witnesses differently. *Fact witnesses* (that is, witnesses testifying about facts from firsthand knowledge, other than treating healthcare professionals, who are considered expert witnesses for many evidentiary purposes) **must not** be paid to testify.

While a fact witness may not be paid to testify, however, lawyers (on behalf of their clients) generally may pay a fact witness's expenses reasonably and actually incurred in testifying or preparing to testify, such as travel, lodging, and meals.

State and federal law generally require the subpoenaing party to provide a subpoenaed witness mileage and a flat fee for the time a witness spends testifying, but these amounts are typically quite modest and usually much less than the actual cost to the witness.

A recurring question is just how far the permission to reimburse a fact witness's "expenses" goes. One common problem is the fact witness who is willing to cooperate (or subject to subpoena) but will have to miss work or otherwise lose income in order to testify or prepare to do so. An ABA Formal Ethics Opinion concludes that, under **Model Rule 3.4(b)**, counsel **may** compensate a fact witness for (1) time lost from other work while attending a deposition or trial to testify; (2) time lost preparing to testify; or (3) time lost "reviewing and researching records that are germane to his or her testimony." The compensation must be reasonable (that is, comparable to what the witness would have earned if she had not been testifying or preparing to testify, or otherwise reflective of the reasonable value of the witness's time); there must be a clear understanding that the compensation is not for the fact or substance of the witness's testimony or otherwise conditioned on the substance of the testimony in any way; and the payment must be permitted under the law of the governing jurisdiction. ABA Formal Ethics Op. No. 96-402 (1996). YOUR HOUSE; YOUR RULES Some states prohibit or disfavor compensating witnesses for lost income, either generally or under defined circumstances. So be sure that you're actually allowed to reimburse the specific expenses about which a fact witness is concerned before you make any promises: **Model Rule 3.4(b)** is violated once you "offer" prohibited witness compensation, whether or not the compensation is eventually agreed to or paid. YOUR HOUSE; YOUR RULES

In contrast, *expert witnesses* **may** be paid to testify or prepare to testify (and their expenses may be reimbursed as well). Most if not all jurisdictions forbid an expert to be paid a *contingent* fee (that is, one conditioned in fact or amount on the outcome of the case, a restriction that also applies to fact witnesses), but hourly and flat fees for expert preparation and testimony are both permissible and common. **Model Rule 3.4 Comment [3]**.

REASON FOR THE RULE Why do we draw these lines? **Model Rule 3.4(b)** and related criminal and civil sanctions strike a balance between (on the one hand) not deterring testimony that is valuable or even necessary to determine the truth in litigated disputes by imposing costs on third-party witnesses, and (on the other) preventing parties from offering witnesses incentives to shade (or even falsify) their testimony. In close cases, the balance may be hard to justify. But overall, the system strives for an equilibrium between the competing values. REASON FOR THE RULE

TIPS & TACTICS Bear in mind that the permissible compensation or reimbursement that parties or counsel provide to witnesses is typically discoverable and usable for impeachment as to both fact and expert witnesses. (Quick—what's the basis for the impeachment? Say it out loud.) These discovery and evidentiary mechanisms help advocates police any effort by their adversaries to defeat the spirit while adhering to the letter of the law.

Experts are expected to be paid (they are providing a professional service that the rules of evidence recognize as helpful to the trier of fact), and most are accustomed to disarming impeachment on that ground. Fact witnesses may need to be prepared for questions of this kind. And if a fact witness from modest circumstances is given permissible but extravagant food and lodging, opposing counsel may not find it difficult to play the circumstances as an effort to influence the witness's testimony. Some lawyers find it helpful to prepare a written agreement with the witness regarding compensation for experts or lost time and expense reimbursement for fact witnesses, reciting the basis for the compensation or reimbursement and explaining why it's reasonable, and reiterating the lawyer's and her client's desire, and the witness's obligation, that the witness testify truthfully and accurately. And if you can't justify your financial arrangement with a witness on these terms, then you're probably violating the law anyway. **TIPS & TACTICS**

CONSEQUENCES The consequences for improper witness compensation are serious. **Model Rule 3.4(b)** is a basis for professional discipline; but remember that the Rule is violated only when the "inducement" offered the witness is "prohibited by law." Thus, when **Model Rule 3.4(b)** has been violated, some other law has been violated as well. The **consequences** of violating that other law can include criminal sanctions under the federal anti-gratuity statute (**18 U.S.C. § 201**) or similar state law. Procedural and evidentiary rules typically authorize the exclusion of the testimony of a witness who received improper inducements, as well as awards of attorney's fees and costs to the opposing party who successfully raised the issue; a mistrial may be declared if the improperly induced testimony has already been given and is sufficiently prejudicial. **CONSEQUENCES**

If these **consequences** seem harsh, then we haven't adequately put this offense in perspective. Improper witness inducements are seen, with considerable justification, as a species of bribe to influence the content of testimony. That's a direct assault on the integrity of our truth-finding system, and it is generally treated with the utmost gravity. Don't try this at home.

Problem 24C-20: Frank is preparing for trial in the slip-and-fall case at the post office described in **Problem 24C-19 at 865**. Might any of the following conduct expose Frank to **consequences**, and what might those **consequences** be? Please explain your answers.

a. Another postal customer, Alexa, was also in the parking lot at the time of the fall. Frank would like Alexa to testify as a corroborating eyewitness. She is reluctant to testify because she lives an hour from the courthouse. Frank offers to reimburse her for mileage and parking if she will drive in to testify.

b. Alexa continues to balk at testifying. Frank offers to put her up at a five-star hotel and take her out for an expensive sushi dinner on the night before she testifies.

c. Alexa is still uninterested in testifying. Although Alexa is an unemployed socialite, Frank offers to pay her $500 per hour for the entire time that she spends travelling to and from trial and while testifying.

d. Alexa still refuses to testify. Frank offers to buy her a designer coat. She finally agrees.

e. Frank tells Alexa that she will have to return the coat if she says anything that hurts Patricia's case.

f. Alexa says that she'll make sure that Patricia wins the case, and she's willing to put her money where her mouth is. Instead of the coat, she agrees to testify in return for an amount to reimburse her expenses from testifying—an amount equal to 5 percent of anything that Patricia recovers. Frank agrees.

g. Alexa says that, for an additional $1,000, she'll even lie on the witness stand and say that the parking lot was covered in snow, when in actuality the parking lot had been recently plowed. Frank agrees.

h. Frank has also retained a medical expert to opine on the seriousness of Patricia's injuries. The expert, a board-certified orthopedist, generally earns $650 per hour when he treats patients. Frank agrees to pay the expert $650 per hour for the time that the expert spends reviewing medical records, drafting an expert report, and testifying in deposition and at trial. Does your analysis change if the doctor charges $500 per hour when he treats patients? What if he charges $500 per hour when he treats patients, but $650 per hour for consulting and expert work? If any of those additional facts would change your analysis, why and how; and if not, why not?

i. Same as (h), except the doctor is a full-time consultant and expert witness and does not treat patients. He generally charges $650 per hour for his time doing consulting and expert work. Does your analysis change if he generally charges $500 per hour for his time doing consulting and expert work? If so, why and how; and if not, why not?

j. Same as (h), but the expert offers to do all the necessary work (reviewing records; drafting an expert report; testifying in deposition and at trial) for a fee equal to 5 percent of anything that Patricia recovers.

Problem 24.C-21: If you were defense counsel in the case described in **Problem 24C-20 at 869** and you learned that Frank has made any of these arrangements, how might you use this information in deposition or at trial?

iii. How Different Levels of Knowledge of Falsity Affect Your Obligations in Different Kinds of Cases

In addition to prohibiting you from offering unlawful inducements to witnesses and from encouraging or assisting a witness to testify falsely, **Model Rule 3.4(d)** provides that you **must not** "falsify evidence." Again, there should be no surprise that engaging in forgery or tampering with documents or tangible evidence is unethical. **Model Rule 3.3(a)(3)** extends this obligation in a predictable direction by providing that you **must not** "offer evidence that [you] know[] to be false." Notice the difference between the two Rules: **Model Rule 3.4(b)** says you **must not** tamper with or create inauthentic ("falsify") evidence; **Model Rule 3.3(a)(1)** says that you **must not** "offer" evidence that you know to be false, whether you falsified it yourself or not.

TAMING THE TEXT What kind of "evidence" is **Model Rule 3.3(a)(3)** talking about? The "evidence" referred to here is *any* kind of evidence, from testimony to documents to physical evidence. What does the Rule mean by "offer[ing]" evidence? It means any of the ways in which counsel tenders evidence to the tribunal for use in adjudicating a dispute—by examining a witness, offering an exhibit into evidence, or preparing an affidavit or declaration, with or without attached exhibits, on which it invites the tribunal to rely. And what does it mean for the evidence to be "false"? The answer is a common-sense one: The term comprises any kind of falsity that frustrates the truth-finding process, such as factually false statements (whether in or out of court) or lack of authenticity (that the proffered evidence is something other than what it purports to be). Consistent with this definition, you **may** introduce false evidence for the purpose of *proving* its falsity, for example, by introducing an email written by the opposing party that has **material** falsehoods in it if you do so in order to prove that the opposing party lied, or introducing a forged or altered document if you do so in order to prove that it was forged or altered. *See* **Model Rule 3.3 Comment [5]**. TAMING THE TEXT

Now let's focus in on the prohibition against offering false evidence. We already know from the first sentence of **Model Rule 3.3(a)(3)** that you **must not** offer evidence that you "*know[]* to be false" (emphasis added). But what if you don't actually *know* that the evidence is false? Sometimes you do know (for example, a witness you intend to call just comes out and tells you that she's going to lie on the stand). More often, however, you have an incomplete picture, but you may be concerned, or suspect, or rationally believe, without actually *knowing*, that the evidence is false. What do you do?

As it turns out, what you **must** or **may** do depends on the kind of case and the kind of evidence. The key lies in the last sentence of **Model Rule 3.3(a)(1)**, which we haven't yet discussed. That sentence says that "[a] lawyer **may** refuse to offer evidence, other than the testimony of a defendant in a criminal matter, that the lawyer reasonably believes is false."

TAMING THE TEXT This is an exceptionally important sentence, with several different pieces. Let's take it apart: This part of the Rule focuses on the situation in which you "*reasonably believe[]*," but don't *actually know*, that evidence that you might like to present (or that your client is asking you to present) is false. You now know from long experience as alert students that "reasonably believe[]" has both a subjective and an objective element, both of which must be met: Having thought about it, you *subjectively* "believe[]" that the evidence in question is false. And you have *reasons* that you believe the evidence is false that are *objectively* "reasonabl[e]." TAMING THE TEXT

The distinction between *reasonably believing* proposed evidence to be false and *knowing* that it is may seem slender and elusive. But if you think about it, our legal system makes fine distinctions under uncertainty, based on a person's state of mind, all the time. For example, you're quite familiar with the often-close distinctions between a party's actually knowing something, not knowing something that the party recklessly disregarded, not knowing something that the party reasonably should have known, and not knowing something that even a reasonable person would not have known—distinctions that make enormous differences in tort and criminal law regarding both liability and blameworthiness (affecting **consequences**). Similarly here, "although a lawyer should resolve doubts about the veracity of testimony or other evidence in favor of the client, the lawyer cannot ignore an obvious falsehood." **Model Rule 3.3 Comment [8]**.

So what **must** or **may** you do with evidence that you "reasonably believe[]" is false? Generally, you have a choice: You **may** refuse to offer that evidence, even if your client insists. (This is, of course, consistent with the general rule that what evidence to offer or not offer is usually a "means" decision that the lawyer **may** make even if the client disagrees. *See* **Chapter 6.C at 157**.) But the Rule also says that you **may** offer the evidence despite your reasonable belief that it's false, so long as you don't *know* that it is. If you *know* that the evidence is false, however, then the first part of **Model Rule 3.3(a)(3)** tells you that you **must** refuse to offer it. This set of rules applies to everything except one special category of evidence, which we'll discuss next.

iv. The Problem of the Untruthful Criminal Defendant

One category of evidence is treated differently from all the others: The testimony of a criminal defendant. Let's start with the proposed testimony of a criminal defendant that you *reasonably believe*, but do not *know*, to be false. **Model Rule 3.3(a)(3)** says that you **may** refuse to offer evidence that you reasonably believe to be false *"other than the testimony of a defendant in a criminal matter"* (emphasis added). In other words, if you reasonably believe, but do not know, that what your criminal defendant client intends to say on the stand is false, you **must** let him testify anyway. This Rule is generally consistent with the criminal defendant's Fifth Amendment rights regarding whether or not to testify in his own defense, and the understanding that the decision about whether to testify is a decision on which criminal defendant clients always get to have the final say. *See* **Model Rule 1.2(a)**; **Model Rule 3.3 Comment [9]**; **Chapter 6.C at 151**.

In all situations in which you and your client disagree about whether the defendant's testimony **should** be offered, your **duty of candor** to your client requires you to consult with the client regarding the decision, and to advise your client about the potential risks of presenting the testimony that you doubt is true—for example, whether the doubtful testimony is inconsistent with other evidence; how likely it is to be disbelieved; how likely that disbelief is to make the factfinder doubt other evidence on which the defendant relies; and so on—and to advise and try to persuade the client to change his mind if you believe that the client's intended choice is a bad one. But if, after all that, the defendant insists on presenting the doubtful testimony anyway, it's his call. *See* **Model Rule 1.4; Chapter 6.C at 154.**

That may be uncomfortable, but it's something that criminal defense lawyers live with all the time. But what if your criminal defendant client insists on giving testimony that you *actually know* is false? Although the situation does not arise frequently, it does arise, and it presents one of the most difficult and contested issues in legal ethics. The question hooks you squarely on the horns of a dilemma: For very good reasons going to the fundamental integrity of the truth-finding process, **Model Rule 3.3(a)(3)** and other law unequivocally says that you **must not** offer evidence that you "know" to be false, with no exceptions. Similarly, **Model Rule 1.2(d)** and other law forbids you from counseling or assisting a client to break the law (such as the laws against lying under oath), again for very good reasons, and again without exception. But the Fifth Amendment has been interpreted to give a criminal defendant the right to testify (or not) in his own defense, a bedrock principle in our criminal justice system. What do you do?

To illustrate how difficult the situation is to resolve, consider a few possibilities:

- You could try to remonstrate with the client and persuade him not to lie on the stand. This is not only a good idea, it is required by your **duty of candor** to the client. *See* **Model Rule 3.3 Comment [6]; Model Rule 1.4; Chapter 5.D at 117.** But it doesn't always work. Even when there are very good reasons why testifying falsely is a bad idea (such as that it's highly likely to make things worse for the defendant by opening him to harmful cross-examination and impeachment or sufficiently apparent that the jury will disbelieve everything he says), some criminal defendants find themselves in the dock because sound judgment is not their greatest strength. They have the right to decide whether to testify in their own defense, whether they exercise that right wisely or foolishly.
- You could refuse to put the defendant-client on the stand. But then you're violating **Model Rule 1.2(a)**, which says that the client has the final decision on whether or not he testifies in his criminal case. And the court will be appropriately concerned about whether the defendant's Fifth Amendment rights to make that choice are being observed.
- At the other extreme, you could "go full Fifth Amendment," so to speak, and present the false testimony on direct examination with your complete support, preparing the testimony with the witness and presenting it on direct examination just as you would testimony you believed to be true. No jurisdiction has endorsed this approach. The reasoning behind this rejection amounts to the proposition that, although the defendant may have a constitutional right to testify, and he may have a constitutional right to **effective assistance of counsel,** neither separately nor both together creates a right to have a lawyer help the defendant commit what the lawyer knows is perjury more effectively than the defendant could do on his own.

- You could seek to withdraw. After all, you're faced with the reality that you would knowingly be presenting false testimony, which would violate multiple Rules of Professional Conduct and other law. *See* **Model Rules 1.16(a)(1)**; **Model Rule 1.16(b)(2), (4), (7)**; **Chapter 9.D at 295**). Withdrawal would ordinarily be permissible and even mandatory under these circumstances. But look at the quandary that withdrawal would create for the system here: Defendant tells his counsel that he's going to lie on the stand; counsel seeks to withdraw; the court grants permission (because counsel has offered proper grounds, after all). New lawyer appears for defendant; defendant tells his new counsel that he's going to lie on the stand; new lawyer seeks to withdraw; the court grants permission. Rinse and repeat. Because of the prospect of this infinite loop preventing anyone from ever completing the defendant's trial, courts almost never grant leave to withdraw under these circumstances (not to mention that this issue typically arises immediately before or during trial, so excusing defense counsel at this point also disrupts the court's calendar and might require a mistrial).

- You could decide to tell the court about the problem and have it decide what you should do. But to start with, in many jurisdictions, you would violate your **duty of confidentiality** to carry out this plan. (Think about it: None of the Model Rules exceptions fit. *See* **Chapter 8.B at 235**.) And, to do so, you would have to incriminate your client (by exposing his plans to commit perjury; and in explaining why it's perjury, you might have to disclose **confidential** facts that are prejudicial to your client's case—or flat-out incriminating). What's more, all that this approach does is take the dilemma off your back and lay it on the court's. And the court has no better options here than you do.

- The court could hold a hearing outside the presence of the jury about whether the defendant's intended testimony is false, but the constitutionality of that approach is very doubtful (and, to our knowledge, no jurisdiction does it). The whole point of the jury trial that the Bill of Rights guarantees to criminal defendants is that a jury of the defendant's peers decides whether the prosecution has proven its case beyond a reasonable doubt, including determining which witnesses are credible and which are not. Allowing the court to decide that the defendant must be forbidden from testifying in his own defense because the judge does not believe him cuts the heart (or at least some vital organs) out of that arrangement.

YOUR HOUSE; YOUR RULES As befits an unavoidable collision between two fundamental principles, there is no single established set of directions out of this trap. Different jurisdictions take different approaches to the problem, and you must thoroughly understand your jurisdiction's method should you choose to do any criminal defense work. **YOUR HOUSE; YOUR RULES**

So what to do? The Comments to the Model Rules point out and struggle with the issue, not quite endorsing any resolution. *See* **Model Rule 3.3 Comments [6]-[9]**.

Probably the single most common resolution of this dilemma in the United States is sometimes referred to as the "narrative direct," an approach that the Model Rules recognize as one that "some jurisdictions" take (without directly endorsing it). *See* **Model Rule 3.3 Comment [7]**. In this approach, instead of the question-and-answer form that a direct examination typically takes, defense counsel invites the defendant to present a narrative, at least as to the portion of the testimony that counsel knows to be false. This invitation commonly takes the form of "Mr. Defendant would like to address the jury now," or "Mr. Defendant, what would you like to say about that?" or "Did you have something to add, Mr. Defendant?" Some jurisdictions allow counsel to make the invitation more like an open-ended question on direct examination, such as "Please tell us what happened."

Although this is hardly an ideal solution, it is at least a solution of sorts. The defendant gets to present his testimony in his own defense, as is his right. The jury gets to decide whether to believe or disbelieve it. At least technically, defense counsel does not "offer" the defendant's perjured testimony in violation of the ethical rules and other law by eliciting the testimony with standard questioning; she simply stands back and lets the defendant offer it himself (and yes, we agree that this is an awfully thin distinction, and quite possibly an illusory one). The approach is hardly ideal: The minute that defense counsel invites a narrative, the judge knows exactly what's going on. The jurors may not understand what's happening, but they almost certainly notice that, suddenly, this direct examination is different from every other one that they've seen in the trial, likely raising questions for at least some of them about why.

In short, even the best solutions we can devise to the problem of the untruthful criminal defendant leave a great deal to be desired. Put a bit differently, it would seem that the best way to address this dilemma is to avoid it altogether. But how?

REAL WORLD The alert student, who has been following this discussion avidly, hasn't forgotten that we said that the situation is relatively uncommon and wants to know why. The reason why is that it's at least somewhat unusual for defense counsel to *know* that their clients want to testify falsely. And the reason that defense counsel rarely *know* that the defendant's intended testimony is false is that, fully educated about the requirements of the Rules forbidding counsel from offering evidence that they *know* is false, counsel carefully endeavor *not to know* the truth about some of the most important facts in many criminal cases while continuing to honor their **duties of loyalty** and zealous advocacy.

What do we mean by that, and how does it work? Take an example: If defense counsel knows that the defendant committed the crime (because the defendant has admitted it to his lawyer in **confidence**), the lawyer is now limited in the defense that she can offer. Under **Model Rule 3.3(a)(3)**, counsel can no longer put the defendant on the stand and, in an ordinary direct examination, allow the defendant to deny he did it. If counsel *suspects* or *believes* the defendant may be guilty, but doesn't *actually know* it, she can (in fact, **must**) allow the defendant to deny the crime under oath (assuming that the defendant wishes to testify, which, after consultation with counsel, he may sensibly wish to do if he's presentable and there aren't too many bullets that he'd have to take on cross-examination).

Thus, most experienced criminal defense lawyers will tell you that they make a point of *not* knowing whether their clients committed the crime in any case where factual innocence is a possible defense. They don't ask, and they caution the client not to tell them. So how do these criminal defense counsel assemble a defense? They investigate aggressively, making every effort to find all the evidence and every witness that is relevant. Any theory of the case has to square with the available evidence, because the prosecution will probably have that evidence, too. Defense counsel will speak carefully with the defendant, often explaining the law governing the crimes with which the defendant is charged and the facts that defense counsel knows can be proved, and then explaining what defenses that law and those facts allow, asking the defendant if any of those defenses are ones that the defendant thinks can be supported (or if any of the elements of the crime can't be proved or can be disproved). The defendant may offer possible theories in response ("I wasn't there; I was watching a *Law and Order* marathon with my mom at her house"). Counsel (often assisted by investigative staff) then check to see if these theories prove out ("Sorry, the *Law and Order* marathon ended the day before the crime"). Gradually, an attack on the prosecution's case or an affirmative defense emerges that is consistent with the available evidence. REAL WORLD

> Problem 24C-22: Marge Murderous is on trial for aggravated assault. The prosecution claims that she intentionally ran over her neighbor, Keith Knightly, with a riding lawnmower after several months of feuding. Might any of the following conduct expose her attorney, Dana Dilemma, to **consequences**, and what might those **consequences** be? Please explain your answers.
>
> a. Marge and Dana discuss the possibility that Marge would testify at trial. Dana explains the benefits and risks of this approach. She suggests that Marge not testify. At first, Marge disagrees, but she eventually decides that Dana is right—testifying is too risky. Marge does not testify.
>
> b. Marge and Dana discuss the possibility that Marge would testify at trial. Dana explains the benefits and risks of this approach. She suggests that Marge not testify. Marge insists on testifying. Dana and Marge rehearse the direct examination. Marge says, "I couldn't have hit Keith with a lawnmower; I don't even own one." Dana shows her Marge's own Facebook page, on which Marge has posted photos of herself riding a lawnmower. "Those photos are old," says Marge. "I sold that lawnmower before they claim that I used it on Keith." Dana doesn't think that Marge is being honest. Some of the photos were uploaded after the alleged assault, though they could have been taken earlier. Marge takes the stand and testifies that, at the time of the assault, she no longer owned a riding lawnmower.

c. Same facts as (b), except that during witness preparation, Marge tells Dana, when Dana presses Marge on her assertion that Marge doesn't own a lawnmower, "Well, I do own a lawnmower, but I also have a bill of sale from a traveling flea market that says I sold that lawnmower before I ran over Keith." Does this change your analysis from (b)? If so, how and why; and if not, why not?

d. Same facts as (c), but add that Marge also admits to Dana that she did run over Keith and also makes it clear that she intends to take the stand and deny it. Dana tries to persuade Marge to change her mind and exercise her Fifth Amendment right not to testify, but Marge insists on testifying. Dana refuses to allow Marge to testify.

e. Same facts as (d), except that after Marge tells Dana that she is going to lie, Dana resigns herself to the reality that Marge will lie. Dana asks Marge on direct examination, "What happened to your lawnmower?" Marge says, "I sold it." "When?" asks Dana. "Two weeks before Keith got hurt," Marge answers. Dana has Marge authenticate the bill of sale from the flea market as the document that she received confirming her sale of the mower at the earlier date, and offers the bill of sale into evidence. In closing argument, Dana argues vehemently that Keith is lying because Marge sold the lawnmower before the alleged assault.

f. Same facts as (d), except that after Marge tells Dana that she is going to lie, Dana urges Marge not to lie. Marge promises to tell the truth but insists that she testify. When Marge is on the witnesses stand, without any prompting from Dana, Marge blurts out, "I sold the lawnmower before the alleged assault." Dana asks the court for a recess, which is granted. She pulls Marge into the hallway and tells her, "After the break, I'm going to ask you whether you sold the lawnmower, and you need to tell the truth." After the break, Dana just does that, and Marge testifies, "I'm sorry that I misspoke earlier; I didn't sell my lawnmower. I sold my snowblower."

g. Same facts as (d), except that, after Marge tells Dana that she is going to lie, Dana asks the court for permission to withdraw from the case. As trial is not scheduled for several more weeks, the court grants Dana's request.

h. Same facts as (d), except that, after Marge tells Dana that she is going to lie, Dana asks the court for permission to withdraw from the case. The court denies Dana's request. Dana simply no-shows for the trial.

i. Same facts as (d) up to the point when Marge tells Dana that she is going to lie and insists on testifying. Dana's jurisdiction allows an attorney to offer a "narrative" direct examination under these circumstances. Dana calls Marge to testify and spends an hour asking Marge detailed questions on direct. During that questioning, Marge lies. Dana does not reference the lie during her closing argument.

j. Same as (i), except that Dana asks one single question on direct examination: "Please tell the jury what you'd like to say." She allows Marge to testify and then says, "Nothing further." Does your analysis change if, in closing argument, Dana urges the jury to believe Marge's testimony? If so, how and why; and if not, why not?

k. Marge asks Dana to meet with a potential defense witness, Evan Eyewitness. Marge tells Dana that Evan will testify that Marge appeared to lose control over the lawnmower and only hit Keith by accident. Dana meets with Evan. She asks Evan to tell her what he saw. Evan says, "Marge told me to say that she lost control of the lawnmower." "*Did* Marge lose control of the lawnmower?" Dana asks. "Um, I don't think so," Evan says, uneasily. "I saw Marge head right for Keith, and right before she hit him, she yelled, 'That'll teach you to keep your dogs out of my rose bed!'" Dana says, "Okay, so what do you plan to say if we call you to testify?" Evan says, "I'm scared of Marge. I'll say what she wants." Dana calls Evan to testify to protect Marge's Fifth Amendment right not to testify. He says Marge appeared to lose control of the lawnmower.

Problem 24C-23: Would your response to any of the parts of **Problem 24C-22 at 876** change if, instead of a criminal case, Dana was defending Marge in a civil assault and battery case initiated against her by Keith?

c. The Duty to Correct

After all that, one uncrossable line is still clear: We **must not** knowingly make misrepresentations to the tribunal (**Model Rule 3.3(a)(1)**) or offer evidence that we know is false (**Model Rule 3.3(a)(3)**). But what happens if we make a representation or offer evidence to the court *not* knowing that it's false at the time, but later discover that it is (or make a misrepresentation or offer false evidence in the heat of the moment, but understand the wrong that we've committed when the air cools)? The answer is clear: We have a **duty** to the tribunal **to correct** or otherwise remedy the falsehood. The **duty to correct** is stated in several Rules of Professional Conduct:

- **Model Rule 3.3(a)(1)** says that a lawyer **must not** "fail to correct a false statement of **material** fact or law previously made to the tribunal by the lawyer."
- **Model Rule 3.3(a)(3)** says that "[i]f a lawyer, the lawyer's client, or a witness called by the lawyer, has offered **material** evidence and the lawyer comes to know of its falsity, the lawyer shall take reasonable remedial measures, including, if necessary, disclosure to the tribunal."
- **Model Rule 3.3(b)** says that "[a] lawyer who represents a client in an adjudicative proceeding and who knows that a person [*any* person] intends to engage, is engaging or has engaged in criminal or fraudulent conduct related to the proceeding shall take reasonable remedial measures, including, if necessary, disclosure to the tribunal."

When does the **duty to correct** arise? The Rules tell us that the duty arises when you "come[] to know" the falsity of the representation or evidence. **Model Rule 3.3(b)** elaborates on that a bit by pointing out that, if you know that anyone "intends to engage" or "is engaging" in "criminal or fraudulent conduct related to the proceeding," you **must** "take reasonable remedial measures." When **must** you take "reasonable remedial measures" to address misrepresentation, crime, or fraud related to the proceeding? Reasonably promptly—a somewhat flexible practical standard focused on fixing the problem while the fix still matters. If you discover that someone intends to defraud the court, that may require taking "reasonable remedial measures" prophylactically, which may or may not include disclosure to the tribunal, depending on the circumstances.

And what are the "reasonable remedial measures" that the Rules require? The phrase is deliberately broadly worded to make clear that you **must** do whatever is reasonably necessary within your power to right the wrong. When you personally have made a **material** misrepresentation of fact or law to the tribunal, whether or not you knew it was false at the time (**Model Rule 3.3(a)(1)**), you **must** "correct" it. That virtually always involves telling the tribunal what was wrong and what the truth is, typically in some kind of pleading (that is, in a writing filed with the tribunal). And if you're communicating with the tribunal, you almost certainly have to copy any other counsel or unrepresented parties (*see* **Model Rule 3.5(b)** (no unpermitted *ex parte* contacts with a tribunal)) **Fed. R. Civ. P. 5(a)**.

If the wrong involves offering false evidence, "reasonable remedial action" may require a series of steps. The first step in addressing false evidence is to try to persuade the person who supplied the evidence (for example, the witness who you know has testified falsely, or the person who you know has forged or altered a document) to correct it, with your assistance, if that assistance is permissible (which it usually is). One strong incentive that you can offer to the person who supplied the false evidence is that you **must** report the falsity if she doesn't report it herself. *See* **Model Rule 3.3 Comment [11]**. If the person who supplied the evidence is your client and refuses to correct the falsity herself (with your assistance), you **may** and sometimes **must** withdraw.[22] If you find yourself obligated to take action adverse to your client to which your client refuses to consent, you have a **conflict of interest** (*see* **Model Rule 1.7(a)(2); Chapter 22.A at 626**). (Do you see why? What's the **conflict**?) Even without a **conflict of interest** (and almost certainly with one), the attorney-client relationship may have deteriorated over the issue so irretrievably that you **should** withdraw. And if your client has refused to correct the falsity herself, even if the falsity was originally an honest mistake, that refusal shows the client to be untrustworthy, and one from whom you **should** seriously consider distancing yourself, even if you don't literally have to. *See* **Model Rule 3.3 Comment [10], [15]**.

In addition, **Model Rule 3.3(c)** not only makes clear that your **duty to correct** is mandatory (a **must**), it also provides an exception to the **duty of confidentiality** ("even if compliance requires disclosure of information otherwise protected by

---

[22] The fact that a **duty to correct** has arisen doesn't *necessarily* mean that you **must** or **should** withdraw. For example, your client may have made a merely careless, or a completely honest, error (or had a lapse in judgment resulting in dishonesty) that the client is willing to correct herself, with your assistance. Circumstances such as these may pose no threat to the attorney-client relationship, create no ground for mandatory withdrawal under **Model Rule 1.16(a)**, and don't suggest any need for you to avail yourself of any ground for permissive withdrawal. *See* **Model Rule 3.3 Comment [15]**.

Rule 1.6"). In other words, if the "reasonable remedial measures" required by your having offered false evidence require you to disclose your client's **confidential information** in order to remedy the wrong, you **must** do so. Compliance with the **duty to correct** thus is one of the rare instances of a *mandatory* exception to your **duty of confidentiality**; in some states, it is the only exception that is not discretionary.

As with any exception to the **duty of confidentiality**, you **must** disclose only the *minimum* amount of information to the *minimum* number of people or institutions reasonably necessary to correct or prevent the wrong (specifically, the falsehood and its effects). If you overdisclose, you exceed the scope of **Model Rule 3.3(c)**'s mandate, and violate your **duty of confidentiality**; **consequences** will likely follow. These opposing Rules create a very uncomfortable tightrope for you to walk: **Model Rule 3.3(c)** says you **must** disclose enough **confidential information** to enough people as is reasonably necessary to correct the wrong; **Model Rule 1.6(a)**, **Model Rule 1.8(b)**, **Model Rule 1.9(c)**, and related civil standards continue to protect any **confidential information** not reasonably necessary to correct the wrong, requiring that you **must not** disclose anything beyond what is reasonably necessary. This bind can sometimes lead to uncomfortably close calls.

TIPS & TACTICS Telling the court that you made what turned out to be a false representation or offered what turned out to be false evidence may sound like a terrible idea. The alternative, however, is unquestionably worse. However disturbed the court may be about discovering that it has been misled, it will be much more disturbed by any delay in correcting the matter, and it will likely presume the worst (that is, that you made the misrepresentation or presented the falsified evidence knowingly and then concealed it by your silence) if you don't correct the problem until after somebody else calls you on it (that is, after you and your client get caught). Thus, anything more than minimal delay is likely to compound any **consequences** that may follow. So be sure that you know what happened and why (don't get it wrong *twice*!), but act fast. TIPS & TACTICS

Finally, how long does the **duty to correct** last? **Model Rule 3.3(c)** makes clear that it lasts only until "the conclusion of the proceeding" in which the misrepresentation was made or the false evidence was offered. **Model Rule 3.3 Comment [12]** clarifies that the "conclusion" of the proceeding does not occur until all appeals have been exhausted. CONSEQUENCES The fact that the **duty to correct** imposed by the Rules of Professional Conduct has lapsed does not mean that all other potential **consequences** are also time-barred. Criminal sanctions for perjury or obstruction of justice have their own statutes of limitation, for example. Similarly, relief from the judgment in a civil proceeding on the basis of a fraud on the court is governed by the time limits stated in **Fed. R. Civ. P. 60(b)** or comparable state law. CONSEQUENCES

And now, because you're special to us, we've prepared a graphic for you summarizing the **duty of candor to the tribunal** and the **duty to correct:**

The Duty of Candor to the Tribunal and the Duty to Correct

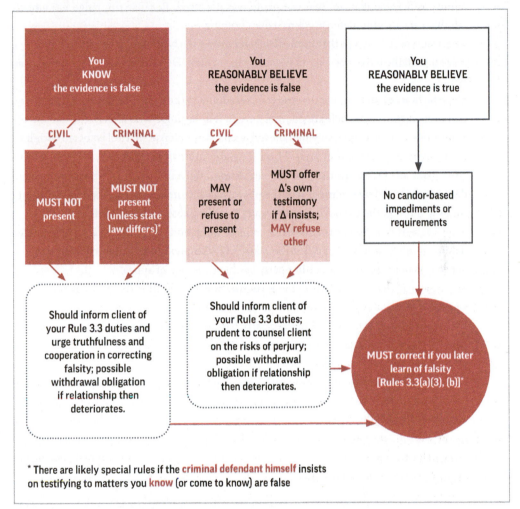

* There are likely special rules if the criminal defendant himself insists on testifying to matters you know (or come to know) are false

Problem 24C-24: Frank is trying a slip-and-fall case in which he represents Patricia Plaintiff. Assuming that the following conduct occurs, which of the lawyers in the following situations could be subject to **consequences**, and what might those **consequences** be? Please explain your answers.

a. Defense counsel offers into evidence a black-and-white photograph of the sidewalk where Patricia's fall occurred. Unbeknownst to defense counsel, his client had digitally altered the photo to remove any sign of the crack that caused the fall. Frank also fails to notice the alteration. The exhibit is admitted into evidence.

b. Same facts as (a), except that Frank thinks that something looks off about the photo, but he's not sure why.

c. Same facts as (a), except that Frank knows that the photo has been altered.

d. Same facts as (a), except that, at the next break after the exhibit is offered, the defendant admits to defense counsel that the photo was doctored. Because the judge has already admitted the exhibit, defense counsel does nothing.

e. Same facts as (d), except that immediately following the break, defense counsel asks for a sidebar with the judge and asks to withdraw the exhibit. Defense counsel does not explain why.

f. Same facts as (e), except that defense counsel admits to the judge at sidebar that the photo had been altered. Does defense counsel have to tell the judge who altered the document?

g. Same facts as (e), except that when the judge asks why defense counsel wants to withdraw the exhibit, defense counsel says, "I have a clearer, full-color copy."

h. Same facts as (a), except that, on the next break after the exhibit is offered, the defendant admits to defense counsel that the photo was doctored. Defense counsel waits until midway through the trial to notify the court that the photo was doctored.

i. Same facts as (h), except that defense counsel waits until after the jury has rendered a defense verdict and then notifies the court that the photo was doctored. The time for appeal has not expired, but neither party has filed a notice of appeal.

j. Same facts as (h), except that defense counsel waits until after the jury has rendered a verdict for the plaintiff and then notifies the court that the photo was doctored. The time for appeal has not expired, but neither party has filed a notice of appeal.

k. Same facts as (h), except that defense counsel learns that the photo was doctored only after all appeals have been exhausted.

l. A major defense theory in the case is that the crack was sufficiently obvious that Patricia had a duty to avoid it. The defense argues that, because Patricia failed to so do, she is contributorily negligent. Frank calls Patricia to testify. When he asks her what she saw before the fall, she says "Nothing." At her deposition, Patricia testified that she saw the crack before she fell. Frank is sure that Patricia is either lying now or was lying during her deposition. Frank does nothing.

Problem 24C-25: What remedial measures (if any) **must**, **may**, and **should** Frank have taken in **Problem 24C-24(l)**?

Problem 24C-26: Take another look at the **Introduction to this chapter at 813**. What remedial measures (if any) **must**, **may**, or **should** Danielle take? Start with the one that you think she **should** take first, and then go on to any additional measures, in order, that you think she should take if the previous one does not adequately remedy the problem.

d. The Special Rule of Extra Candor in *Ex Parte* Proceedings

"Ordinarily, an advocate has the limited responsibility of presenting one side of the matters that a tribunal should consider in reaching a decision; the conflicting position is expected to be presented by the opposing party." **Model Rule 3.3 Comment [14]**. There is, however, an important exception to this limited responsibility, and it arises in *ex parte* proceedings. *Ex parte* proceedings, as you'll recall (*see* **Chapter 24.B at 841 n.12**) are those conducted without the participation of an opposing party or its counsel.

In *ex parte* proceedings, you **must** "inform the tribunal of all **material** facts known to [you] that will enable the tribunal to make an informed decision, whether or not the facts are adverse." **Model Rule 3.3(d)**. This Rule applies not only in those *ex parte* proceedings that are authorized to proceed without notice to or participation of the opposing party, but in any situation in which opposing counsel is, for good reasons or bad, simply absent.[23]

Simple enough in theory, but make sure that, as you approach an *ex parte* hearing or other proceeding, you've thought through what **material** facts you know that the court might need in order to make an informed decision and how you intend to disclose them. Otherwise, you might leave something out—something that, later, your opponent can be counted on to characterize as a deliberate effort to mislead the court. Similarly, if you discover that your opposing counsel has unexpectedly failed to appear at a previously noticed hearing, think carefully about what you say about counsel's absence and the remedies you seek as a result, lest the court think later that the matter was not presented fully and fairly at the time.

CONSEQUENCES Even if your omission is only a thoughtless mistake, it's a mistake that the Rules prohibit—you have a duty of disclosure to the court, and thus the omission of known **material** facts is a basis for professional discipline. It also will inflict a serious blow to your credibility with that tribunal to leave the omission uncorrected. And if full disclosure of the facts that you knew would have resulted in a different result in the *ex parte* hearing or proceeding, in addition to undoing the original result, the court may impose sanctions or (in the case of an *ex parte* temporary restraining order) damages for a wrongful injunction, if the enjoined party can prove them. CONSEQUENCES

Big-Picture Takeaways from Chapter 24.C

1. **Preserving the impartiality and decorum of the tribunal:**
    a. **Model Rule 3.5** focuses on the lawyer's duty to preserve the impartiality and the decorum of the tribunal. It contains requirements that are also found in the civil and criminal law: Prohibitions against seeking to influence judges, juries, or other officials or trying to communicate *ex parte* with them when such communication is prohibited.

---

[23] Authority on this point is sparse, but *see Malmin v. Oths*, 126 Idaho 1024, 895 P.2d 1217 (1995) (private reprimand imposed for violation of **Model Rule 3.3(d)** when opposing counsel was notified of a hearing but failed to appear, and the disciplined lawyer sought remedies by default without informing the court of a possible misunderstanding regarding whether the matter was already settled).

It includes limited prohibitions regarding contacting jurors after a trial is over, and it has a broad-brush prohibition against all conduct intended to disrupt a tribunal (whether or not the official presiding over the tribunal is present). Tempting though it might be, you're not allowed to sass back to a judge who is being abusive. *See* **Chapter 24.C at 841**.

b. **Model Rule 8.2(a)** provides that a lawyer **must not** "make a statement that the lawyer knows to be false or with reckless disregard as to its truth or falsity concerning the qualifications or integrity of a judge, adjudicatory officer or public legal officer, or of a candidate for election or appointment to judicial or legal office." *See* **Chapter 24.C at 842**.

2. **Limits on asserting or contesting claims, defenses, or legal or factual issues: Model Rule 3.1** limits a lawyer's assertion or contest of claims, defenses, or legal or factual issues: There must be "a basis in law and fact for doing so that is not frivolous, which [**may**] include[] a good faith argument for an extension, modification or reversal of existing law." Although you're always free to make "a good faith argument for an extension, modification or reversal of existing law," you should be clear with the court that that's what you're doing when you do it. **Model Rule 3.1** also makes room for broader advocacy in criminal proceedings as required by the Constitution, allowing a criminal defendant or other "respondent in a proceeding that could result in incarceration" to "defend the proceeding as to require that every element of the case be established," even if the prosecution's case is objectively overwhelming. *See* **Chapter 24.C at 845**.

3. **Misrepresenting or misciting the law: Model Rule 3.3(a)(1)** provides that you **must not** "knowingly . . . make a false statement of . . . law to a tribunal." Discipline under this Rule is limited to those situations in which you *actually know* that you are misciting the law, not when you are merely careless or sloppy. **Model Rule 3.3(a)(2)** provides that you **must not** "knowingly . . . fail to disclose to the tribunal legal authority in the controlling jurisdiction known to the lawyer to be directly adverse to the position of the client and not disclosed by opposing counsel." These disciplinary prohibitions are very narrow, but incomplete or misleading legal argument is not only usually ineffective, it is likely to diminish your credibility with the court long after one badly framed argument is over. *See* **Chapter 24.C at 850**.

4. **Publicity before or during trial: Model Rule 3.6(a)** applies to all lawyers who are "participating or ha[ve] participated in the investigation or litigation of a matter . . ." and includes any lawyer in the same **practice organization** as a lawyer who is actively participating (or has actively participated) in the investigation or litigation. A lawyer covered by the Rule **must not** "make an

extrajudicial statement that the lawyer knows or reasonably should know will be disseminated by means of public communication . . ." if those statements "will have a substantial likelihood of **materially** prejudicing an adjudicative proceeding in the matter." **Model Rule 3.6(b)** provides a nonexclusive "safe harbor" list of things that you always **may** communicate to the public without violating the Rule. **Model Rule 3.6 Comment [5]** provides a list of "subjects that are more likely than not to have a **material** prejudicial effect on a proceeding" and are at least presumptively forbidden. **Model Rule 3.6(c)** allows "a statement that a reasonable lawyer would believe is required to protect a client from the substantial undue prejudicial effect of recent publicity not initiated by the lawyer or the lawyer's client." But be careful: Such statements can only go so far as is reasonably necessary to "mitigate" the harm; overcorrecting will destroy the Rule's permission and leave you in violation. *See* **Chapter 24.C at 853**.

5. **Lawyer as witness: Model Rule 3.7** forbids a lawyer to be an advocate "at a trial in which the lawyer is *likely* to be a *necessary* witness" (emphasis added). There are three exceptions to this Rule, and a very important limitation. The exceptions are: (1) if the advocate's testimony relates only to an "uncontested issue" (**Model Rule 3.7(a)(1)**); (2) if the advocate's testimony relates to "the nature and value of legal services rendered in the case" (**Model Rule 3.7(a)(2)**); and (3) if "disqualification of the lawyer would work substantial hardship on the client" (**Model Rule 3.7(a)(3)**). The limitation on the Rule is that its prohibition on a lawyer's acting as a trial witness is generally not **imputed** within a **practice organization**, so one lawyer in a **practice organization may** usually testify if another lawyer in the same **practice organization** serves as trial counsel. *See* **Chapter 24.C at 857**.

6. **Limits on witness examination and argument: Model Rule 3.4(e)** forbids a lawyer from doing several things "in trial": (1) to "allude to any matter that the lawyer does not reasonably believe is relevant or that will not be supported by admissible evidence"; (2) to "assert personal knowledge of facts in issue except when testifying as a witness"; or (3) to "state a personal opinion as to the justness of a cause, the credibility of a witness, the culpability of a civil litigant or the guilt or innocence of an accused." *See* **Chapter 24.C at 860**.

7. **Prohibitions on misrepresentations to the tribunal and false evidence:**
   a. Per **Model Rule 3.3(a)(1)**, you can't lie to a tribunal. You can't encourage or assist others to do so, either. And you can't present false evidence. Not only are these violations of the Rules of Professional Conduct stating grounds for professional discipline, but when done knowingly, they are false-statement crimes in every U.S. jurisdiction, bearing names like perjury, suborning perjury, and obstruction of

justice, and are also subject to court sanctions under multiple rules and statutes. *See* **Chapter 24.C at 862**.

b. **Model Rule 3.4(b)** provides that you **must not** "counsel or assist a witness to testify falsely. . . ." But nothing in the Rules of Professional Conduct or other law prohibits you from *properly preparing* a witness to testify. And you **may** prepare any witness who will let you, whether or not the witness is your client. One important difference between client and non-client witnesses is that your communications with non-client witnesses are not protected by the **attorney-client privilege**. *See* **Chapter 24.C at 864**.

c. **Model Rule 3.4(b)** also provides that you **must not** "offer an inducement to a witness that is prohibited by law." This Rule is not limited to "inducements" to testify falsely, though all such inducements would of course be "prohibited by law." The Rule prohibits *any* "inducement to a witness that is prohibited by law." *See* **Chapter 24.C at 867**.

i. *Fact witnesses* (that is, witnesses testifying about facts from first-hand knowledge, other than treating healthcare professionals, who are considered expert witnesses for many evidentiary purposes) **must not** be paid to testify. But a lawyer **may** pay a fact witness's expenses incurred in testifying or preparing to testify, such as travel, lodging, and meals. An ABA Formal Ethics Opinion concludes that, under **Model Rule 3.4(b)**, counsel **may** compensate a fact witness for (1) time lost from other work while attending a deposition or trial to testify; (2) time lost preparing to testify; or (3) time lost "reviewing and researching records that are germane to his or her testimony." The compensation must be reasonable (that is, comparable to what the witness would have earned if she had not been testifying or preparing to testify, or otherwise reflective of the reasonable value of the witness's time); there must be a clear understanding that the compensation is not for the fact or substance of the witness's testimony, or is otherwise conditioned in any way; and the payment must be permitted under the law of the governing jurisdiction. *See* **Chapter 24.C at 867**.

ii. *Expert witnesses* **may** be paid to testify or prepare to testify (and their expenses may be reimbursed as well). Most if not all jurisdictions forbid an expert to be paid a contingent fee (that is, one conditioned in fact or amount on the outcome of the case, a restriction that also applies to fact witnesses). *See* **Chapter 24.C at 868**.

iii. **Model Rule 3.4(b)** is a basis for professional discipline, but remember that the Rule is violated only when the "inducement" offered the witness is "prohibited by law." Thus, when **Model**

Rule 3.4(b) has been violated, some other law has been violated as well. The **consequences** of violating that other law can include criminal sanctions under the federal anti-gratuity statute (**18 U.S.C. § 201**) or similar state law. Procedural and evidentiary rules typically authorize the exclusion of the testimony of a witness who received improper inducements, as well as awards of attorney's fees and costs to the opposing party who successfully raised the issue; a mistrial may be declared if the improperly induced testimony has already been given and is sufficiently prejudicial. *See* **Chapter 24.C at 869**.

d. In addition to prohibiting you from offering unlawful inducements to witnesses and from encouraging or assisting a witness to testify falsely, **Model Rule 3.4(d)** provides that you **must not** "falsify evidence." **Model Rule 3.3(a)(3)** extends this obligation in a predictable direction by providing that you **must not** "offer evidence that [you] know[] to be false." Notice the difference between the two Rules: **Model Rule 3.4(b)** says you **must not** tamper with or create inauthentic ("falsify") evidence; **Model Rule 3.3(a)(1)** says that you **must not** "offer" evidence that you know to be false, whether you falsified it yourself or not. You **may**, however, introduce false evidence for the purpose of *proving* its falsity, for example, introducing an email written by the opposing party that has **material** falsehoods in it in order to prove that the opposing party lied, or introducing a forged or altered document in order to prove that it was forged or altered. *See* **Model Rule 3.3 Comment [5]**. *See* **Chapter 24.C at 870**.

e. What happens when you may be concerned, or suspect, or rationally believe without *actually knowing*, that the evidence is false? What you **must** or **may** do depends on the kind of case and the kind of evidence. The key lies in the last sentence of **Model Rule 3.3(a)(1)**: "[a] lawyer **may** refuse to offer evidence, other than the testimony of a defendant in a criminal matter, that the lawyer reasonably believes is false." *See* **Chapter 24.C at 871**.

   i. Generally, you have a choice: You **may** refuse to offer evidence that you reasonably believe is false, even if your client insists (except for the testimony of a criminal defendant). But the Rule also says that you **may** offer such evidence despite your reasonable belief that it's false, so long as you don't *know* that it is. If you *know* the evidence is false, however, then the first part of **Model Rule 3.3(a)(3)** tells you that you **must** refuse to offer it. *See* **Chapter 24.C at 871**.

   ii. One category of evidence is treated differently from all the others: The testimony of a criminal defendant. **Model Rule 3.3(a)(3)** says you **may** refuse to offer evidence you reasonably believe to be false *"other than the testimony of a defendant in a criminal matter"* (emphasis added). In other words, if you *reasonably believe*, but do not *actually know*, that what your criminal defendant client intends to say on the stand is false, you **must** let him testify anyway. *See* **Chapter 24.C at 872**.

iii. In all situations in which you and your client disagree about whether the defendant's testimony **should** be offered, your **duty of candor** to your client requires you to consult with the client regarding the decision and to advise your client about the potential risks of presenting the testimony that you doubt is true—whether it is inconsistent with other evidence; how likely it is to be disbelieved; how likely that disbelief is to make the factfinder doubt other evidence on which the defendant relies; etc.—and to advise and try to persuade the client to change his mind. But if, after all that, the defendant insists on presenting the doubtful testimony, it's his call. *See* **Chapter 24.C at 872**.

iv. What if your criminal defendant client insists on giving testimony that you *actually know* is false? Although the situation does not arise frequently, it does arise, and it presents one of the most difficult and contested issues in legal ethics. **Model Rule 3.3(a)(3)** and other law unequivocally says that you **must not** offer evidence that you "know" to be false, with no exceptions. Similarly, **Model Rule 1.2(d)** and other law forbids you from counseling or assisting a client to break the law (such as the laws against lying under oath), again without exception. But the Fifth Amendment has been interpreted to give a criminal defendant the right to testify (or not) in his own defense, a bedrock principle in our criminal justice system. There is no single established set of directions out of this trap. Different jurisdictions take different approaches to the problem, and you must thoroughly understand your jurisdiction's method should you choose to do any criminal defense work. Although none of the potential solutions to this problem is very effective, probably the single most common resolution of this dilemma in the United States is sometimes referred to as the "narrative direct," an approach that the Model Rules recognize as one "some jurisdictions" take without explicitly endorsing it. *See* **Chapter 24.C at 873**.

f. What happens if we make a representation or offer evidence to the court not knowing that it's false at the time, but later discover that it is?

i.   **Model Rule 3.3(a)(1)** says that a lawyer **must not** "fail to correct a false statement of **material** fact or law previously made to the tribunal by the lawyer." **Model Rule 3.3(a)(3)** says that "[i]f a lawyer, the lawyer's client, or a witness called by the lawyer, has offered **material** evidence and the lawyer comes to know of its falsity, the lawyer shall take reasonable remedial measures, including, if necessary, disclosure to the tribunal." **Model Rule 3.3(b)** says that "[a] lawyer who represents a client in an adjudicative proceeding and who knows that a person [*any* person] intends to engage, is engaging or has engaged in criminal or fraudulent conduct related to the proceeding shall take reasonable remedial measures, including, if necessary, disclosure to the tribunal." *See* **Chapter 24.C at 878**.

ii.   "Reasonable remedial measures" means that you must do whatever is reasonably necessary within your power to right the wrong (the wrong being the falsehood and its effects on the proceeding). *See* **Chapter 24.C at 879**.

(A) When you personally have made a **material** misrepresentation of fact or law to the tribunal, whether or not you knew it was false at the time (**Model Rule 3.3(a)(1)**), you **must "correct"** it. That virtually always involves telling the tribunal what was wrong and what the truth is, typically in some kind of pleading (that is, in a writing filed with the tribunal). And if you're communicating with the tribunal, you almost certainly have to copy (serve) opposing counsel (*see* **Model Rule 3.5(b); Fed. R. Civ. P. 5(a)**). *See* **Chapter 24.C at 879**.

(B) If the wrong involves offering false evidence, "reasonable remedial action" may require a series of steps. The first step in addressing false evidence is to try to persuade the person who supplied the evidence (for example, the witness you know to have testified falsely, or the person you know to have forged or altered a document) to correct it, with your assistance, if assistance is permissible (which it usually is). One strong incentive that you can offer to the person who supplied the false evidence is that you **must** report the falsity if she doesn't report it herself. If the person who supplied the evidence is your client and refuses to correct the falsity herself (with your assistance), you **may** and sometimes **must** withdraw. *See* **Chapter 24.C at 879**.

(C) **Model Rule 3.3(c)** makes clear, not only is your **duty to correct** mandatory (a **must**), it provides an exception to the **duty of confidentiality** ("even if compliance requires disclosure of information otherwise protected by Rule 1.6"). You **must** disclose, but you **must** disclose only the minimum necessary to **correct** the wrong. *See* **Chapter 24.C at 879**.

(D) **Model Rule 3.3(c)** makes clear that the **duty to correct** lasts only until "the conclusion of the proceeding" in which the misrepresentation was made or the false evidence was offered. **Model Rule 3.3 Comment [12]** clarifies that the "conclusion" of the proceeding does not occur until all appeals have been exhausted. *See* **Chapter 24.C at 880**.

(E) The fact that the **duty to correct** imposed by the Rules of Professional Conduct has lapsed does not mean that all other potential **consequences** are also time-barred. Criminal sanctions for perjury or obstruction of justice have their own statutes of limitation, for example. Similarly, relief from the judgment in a civil proceeding is governed by the time limits stated in **Fed. R. Civ. P. 60(b)** or comparable state law. *See* **Chapter 24.C at 880**.

g. In *ex parte* proceedings, **Model Rule 3.3(d)** requires that you **must** "inform the tribunal of all **material** facts known to [you] that will enable the tribunal to make an informed decision, whether or not the facts are adverse." *See* **Chapter 24.C at 882**.

Multiple-Choice Review Questions for Chapter 24.C

1. The CEO of a company being sued for discrimination is being deposed. Felix is defending the deposition. Despite Felix's attempts to prepare the CEO, the CEO is performing miserably. When opposing counsel asks, "Why did you fire my client?" The CEO says, "Because she was Hispanic."

   Felix asks to take a break. During the break, Felix follows the court reporter into the bathroom. Felix offers the court reporter $1,000 to change the answer in the transcript so it appears the CEO said, "Because of her attendance." The court reporter refuses.

   Has Felix violated his professional obligations under **Model Rule 3.5(a)**?
   a. Yes, because he failed to **correct** his client's misstatement on the record.
   b. Yes, because he attempted to bribe a court official.
   c. No, because a court reporter is neither a judge nor juror.
   d. No, because a deposition is not an official proceeding.

2. Attorney Acrimony would like to threaten to break the windows in Witless Witness's car unless Witness agrees to lie under oath in a way that will help Acrimony's client, Culpable Client, in a breach of contract case. What ethical rule prevents Acrimony from making this threat?
   a. **Model Rule 1.2(a)**.
   b. **Model Rule 1.14(a)**.

c. **Model Rule 3.4(b).**
d. **Model Rule 3.5(a).**

3. Tristan is a young lawyer who recently successfully litigated his first jury trial—a slip-and-fall case. After the verdict is read, the judge asks the jurors whether they consent to speak with counsel. All of the jurors agree except for Juror Number 4, who states that she is unwilling to speak with counsel.

    The judge excuses Juror Number 4 and the remaining jurors stay in the courtroom. Although Tristan would like to speak with them, his client is thrilled at the win and insists they celebrate with a round of drinks at a local bar. To appease the client, who is plainly impatient, Tristan tells the judge that he has no questions. Opposing counsel asks only one question. The judge then thanks and excuses the jury.

    A month later, Tristan walks into a coffee shop and sees Juror Number 4 sitting by herself. He asks if he can join her, and she says yes. Tristan strikes up a conversation with the juror. Although she does not immediately recognize him, once he starts describing the trial, her facial expression reflects recognition. Tristan asks her nothing substantive about the trial. He simply asks for feedback on his performance as an advocate. She frowns and says, "I've got to get going." Then she leaves.

    Has Tristan violated **Model Rule 3.5(c)**?

    a. Yes. This juror clearly communicated that she did not wish to speak with counsel, and therefore Tristan was prohibited from speaking with her about the trial.
    b. Yes. Discussions with jurors must occur in the courtroom. Any discussion outside of that context is *ex parte* and prohibited.
    c. No. Tristan asked her only about his performance. Only substantive discussions about trial evidence are addressed by the rule.
    d. No. All communication with former jurors is permitted once a trial has concluded. Tristan bumped into the juror by accident and did not intentionally contact her.

4. Rishi is defending a deposition. The deposition is held in opposing counsel's office. Present at the deposition are Rishi, the witness, opposing counsel, and a court reporter. Rishi knows that opposing counsel is inexperienced and a little nervous, so she objects to every question that counsel makes on the basis of hearsay, even when she has no valid basis to do so. She also instructs her witness not to answer on the basis of her hearsay objections, despite the fact that the applicable rules of civil procedure prohibit an instruction not to answer on this basis.

    Rishi's tactics are effective. Opposing counsel concludes the deposition after an hour, having gleaned no information from the witness.

Has Rishi violated her professional obligations?

a. Yes, because Rishi lacked a valid basis for her objections, and her conduct was disruptive.

b. Maybe. The standard is objective. Whether Rishi acted inappropriately depends on whether a reasonable attorney would have known to instruct the witness to answer regardless of the objections.

c. Maybe. It depends whether opposing counsel was able to get the same information through other means of discovery that he would have elicited through the witness.

d. No. This conduct occurred outside a formal tribunal, and no judge was present.

5. Amir handles asylum cases. He appears in court in front of an immigration judge who has a reputation for being openly hostile to asylum seekers and their counsel. At one point during a hearing, the judge curses at Amir. The judge is wholly professional toward counsel for the Department of Homeland Security. At the conclusion of the hearing, the judge reluctantly grants Amir's client asylum, but not before making several additional disparaging remarks about Amir.

What should Amir do?

a. Chastise the judge, stating that she is unprofessional and demanding that his cases be reassigned.

b. Finish the hearing and thereafter report the judge to an appropriate authority.

c. Accuse DHS counsel of benefiting from favorable treatment and move to disqualify DHS counsel in the future.

d. Appeal the judge's decision and ask in the appeal that she be removed from the bench.

6. Kalina is a lawyer who handles employment discrimination cases. She meets with a **prospective client**, Linus, who asks if she will handle his case. Linus claims that he has been fired because of his religion. At the time he was fired, Linus was classified as an unpaid intern, but he was given a stipend for living expenses.

Kalina does some research and learns that district courts in her circuit have held that an intern like Linus is not covered by Title VII because unpaid workers are not considered "employees" under the statute. Courts in other circuits, including circuit courts, have held otherwise. The Supreme Court has never addressed the issue. District court decisions and cases from outside the circuit are persuasive but not binding authority in Kalina's court.

Kalina files a Title VII claim against the employer. The employer moves to dismiss for failure to state a claim. What **must** Kalina so in her opposition to the motion?

a. State clearly that she is seeking a modification of existing law so as not to run afoul of **Model Rule 3.1**.

b. Cite the adverse district court cases from within her circuit if opposing counsel does not disclose them so as not to run afoul of **Model Rule 3.3**.

c. Both a and b.

d. Neither a nor b.

7. Mitch is a fourth-year associate at a boutique firm. He is preparing an appellate brief in a major, "bet the company" case. The brief is due at midnight. Mitch is still working on the brief long after the firm's partners have gone home.

At 11:30 p.m., Mitch discovers an extremely helpful, unpublished case on Westlaw. He checks the court rules, which prohibit citation to unpublished cases. It is too late to call the clerk's office, which closed hours earlier. He does not want to wake up any of the partners at home, either.

Mitch cites the case in his brief, making it clear in the brief that the opinion was unpublished. He files the brief at 11:59 p.m., just before the filing deadline.

Has Mitch violated any Model Rule of Professional Conduct?

a. Yes. He violated **Model Rule 3.4(c)**. He knowingly disobeyed a court rule without a valid reason for doing so.

b. Yes. He violated **Model Rule 1.3**. He waited until the last minute to finish the brief, and therefore did not leave time to contact the clerk's office for clarification.

c. No. He did not violate **Model Rule 3.3(a)**. He made a point of identifying the case as unpublished, and he did not make any effort to hide this fact from the court.

d. No. He did not violate **Model Rule 3.1**. Although unpublished, the case gave him a basis in law for the argument in his brief. He was permitted to argue for an extension of the law and ask the court to adopt the holding of the unpublished case.

8. In what type of proceeding **must** a lawyer inform the tribunal of all **material** facts known to the lawyer that will enable the tribunal to make an informed decision, whether or not the facts are adverse?

a. *Ex parte*.

b. *In limine*.

c. Criminal.

d. Immigration.

9. Candice is writing a brief. She finds a case that is 100 percent factually similar to hers, in which the court found exactly opposite of how

Candice hopes that her judge will rule. What **must** Candice do under **Model Rule 3.3**?

   a. Disclose the case.
   b. Disclose the case if it is in the controlling jurisdiction.
   c. Distinguish the case.
   d. Distinguish the case as being outside the controlling jurisdiction.

10. On which basis is an attorney always allowed to defend his or her client?
   a. In a civil case, the plaintiff may argue that it is entitled to judgment in its favor because the law is unconstitutional.
   b. In a civil case, the defendant may argue that it is entitled to judgment in its favor because the law is unfair.
   c. In a criminal case, the prosecution may argue that the defense failed to meet its burden of proof to demonstrate the defendant's innocence.
   d. In a criminal case, the defense may argue that the prosecution failed to meet its burden of proof to demonstrate every element of the charge.

11. Anwar is cross-examining a witness. He asks, "Isn't it true that, 11 years ago, you were convicted of possession with intent to distribute marijuana?" Before the witness can answer, opposing counsel objects on the basis that the question calls for inadmissible character evidence. The judge sustains the objection. No other evidence is admitted about the witness's prior history with dealing drugs.

   Can Anwar argue in closing that the witness lacks credibility because he is a drug dealer?
   a. Yes, as long as Anwar has a certified copy of the conviction.
   b. Yes, if the judge's ruling was in error and Anwar is confident he will prevail on appeal.
   c. No, because the evidence was excluded, and therefore Anwar cannot reference it in his closing.
   d. No, because dealing drugs is not a crime of dishonesty, so even if the witness was convicted, it does not demonstrate he lacks credibility.

12. Annie, a hotshot young prosecutor, is cross-examining Todd, who is accused of murder. Annie is aware that Todd is a well-respected father who is happily married and who has a spotless criminal record. While looking at the jury, she says, "Aren't you a wife-beating, pill-popping alcoholic?" Several jurors gasp in dismay. Before Todd can answer and before defense counsel can object, she says, "Withdrawn." The judge calls a recess and admonishes Annie in chambers. After the recess, the judge instructs the jurors to disregard the question entirely. Todd is ultimately acquitted.

Could Annie's conduct subject her to referral to a disciplinary authority?

a. Yes, because she committed malpractice resulting in Todd's acquittal.

b. Yes, because the question lacked a good-faith basis.

c. No, there are no limitations on cross-examination, and Todd is free to deny the allegation.

d. No, because the judge's limiting instruction cured any prejudice.

13. Brenda is a solo practitioner who handles criminal defense. She hopes to attract more white-collar crime clients. As part of her marketing strategy, she sits in on trials and blogs about them on her firm website. The trials are open to the public.

Is Brenda limited by **Model Rule 3.6(a)** when she posts her blog entries?

a. Yes, because the Rule applies to all lawyers.

b. Yes, because the Rule applies to all advertising regardless of form.

c. No, because the trials are open to the public.

d. No, because she is not actively involved in the trials.

14. Raymond is prosecuting a high-profile murder case. The evidence against the defendant is overwhelming and includes the defendant's confession, which is read to the jury during the trial. The courtroom is packed with reporters. During his closing argument, Raymond says, "The defendant is a cold-blooded killer and deserves the death penalty." After making the statement, Raymond sees several reporters furiously scribbling in their notepads. This quote appears in several news articles the following day. The jury deliberates several days more and then convicts Raymond of first-degree murder.

Has Raymond violated **Model Rule 3.6**?

a. Yes, because the statement was **materially** prejudicial, and the case was ongoing at the time the statement was made.

b. Yes, because the statement was an improper *ex parte* communication with jurors.

c. No, because although the statement was publicly disseminated, it was an argument made during the proceeding itself.

d. No, because there is no evidence that the statement led to the conviction in light of the other evidence indicative of guilt.

15. Jodi is litigating a patent dispute between two pharmaceutical companies. On her way out of the courtroom one day near the end of the bench trial, a reporter stops Jodi and asks, "Do you think you'll be done calling witnesses tomorrow?" Jodi says, "I think so. Likely the closing arguments

will be tomorrow afternoon." The reporter quotes Jodi in an article reporting on the trial but does not use Jodi's name. The article is posted online behind a paywall at a publication with limited readership.

Why is Jodi's statement likely to be deemed permissible under **Model Rule 3.6**?

    a. Because the statement is not **materially** prejudicial.

    b. Because few people are likely to read the article under the circumstances.

    c. Because the comment contains no threat or veiled threat.

    d. Because the quotation is not attributed in the article.

16. Which of the following types of statements is not covered by a "safe harbor" set forth in **Model Rule 3.6(b)**?

    a. The fact that an investigation is ongoing.

    b. The claims set forth in a publicly filed complaint.

    c. The fact that a motion to compel was granted.

    d. The lawyer's opinion as to guilt or innocence of a defendant.

17. Katie is prosecuting a criminal tax-fraud case. Following the arraignment, a reporter stops her on the steps of the courthouse and asks what information Katie can share for a newspaper article.

Which of the following true facts may Katie not disclose to the reporter?

    a. The fact that the defendant was arrested a week earlier at his home in the Hamptons.

    b. The fact that the IRS and FBI jointly investigated the case.

    c. The fact that several other defendants have been indicted under seal by a grand jury, including the defendant's spouse.

    d. That the defendant works as a certified public accountant.

18. Jessie is a prosecutor handling a DUI case brought against the mayor of the city in which the case is being tried. A jury has been selected and opening statements are scheduled for the next day.

Back in her office, Jessie receives a call from a reporter working on an article about the case. The reporter asks, "Does the state have strong evidence that the mayor was under the influence when he was pulled over?" Jessie says, "He wouldn't submit to a blood alcohol test. You tell me what that means." The subsequent article notes that the mayor refused to take a blood alcohol test. The article concludes that this behavior shows that the mayor was likely drunk.

Did Jessie violate **Model Rule 3.6**?

    a. Yes. She was prohibited from making any public statement about the trial until the verdict was reached.

    b. Maybe. She disclosed the mayor's refusal to submit to a blood alcohol test, and this was likely **materially** prejudicial information.

    c. Maybe. It depends whether the failure to submit to blood alcohol testing would have eventually been admitted at trial. If it would have been, there was no prejudice and therefore no violation of the rule.

    d. No. She did not affirmatively state her belief in the mayor's guilt; the reporter independently reached that conclusion.

19. Pursuant to **Model Rule 3.7**, when may a lawyer be a witness and an advocate in the same trial?

    a. When the client consents.

    b. When the lawyer is testifying about an uncontested issue.

    c. When the lawyer's testimony is admissible.

    d. When the lawyer is called as an adverse witness.

20. Javier is trial counsel in a wrongful termination case in which he represents a lawyer, Bruce, who claims that he was fired for blowing the whistle on his employer's fraud. Six months before trial, Javier realizes that he needs an expert witness to value the damages in the case by testifying about what a salaried lawyer like Bruce would typically earn in a year. To reduce fees, Javier offers to testify.

    Does the exception in **Model Rule 3.7(a)(2)** apply?

    a. Yes. Javier is testifying as an expert and therefore is not testifying from personal knowledge.

    b. Maybe. It depends whether the case is a jury trial or not.

    c. Maybe. It depends whether finding a different expert would work a substantial hardship to Bruce.

    d. No. Javier is not testifying about the value of his own fees in litigating Bruce's case.

21. Glinda is prosecuting an assault case arising from a vicious attack in a dark alleyway. There are no eyewitnesses. The victim suffered a concussion as a result of his injuries. His in-court eyewitness identification will be a key piece of evidence at trial. Which of the following tactics is something that defense counsel **must not** do to question the identification without disrupting the tribunal?

    a. Call the defendant to testify that he was not the assailant.

    b. Call an alibi witness to prove that the defendant was elsewhere at the time of the assault.

    c. Cross-examine the victim and argue in closing that his identification is flawed due to the darkness of the alley and the victim's brain injury.

    d. Hire an actor to sit at defense counsel table and ask the victim to identify his assailant, hoping that the witness identifies the actor in error.

22. Shirley owns a bakery and is sued by a customer, Britta, who claims that she got food poisoning from one of Shirley's pies. Shirley hires Dean to represent her. In answering interrogatories, Dean writes that Shirley never left her pies out of the refrigerator. Dean knows that this statement is untrue, because Shirley has admitted to Dean that she accidently left the pie out on the counter overnight before Britta bought it. Dean asks Shirley to review the interrogatory answers and verify them. As a nonlawyer, it all seems like legal mumbo-jumbo to Shirley. She signs the verification, and Dean serves the answers.

    Has Dean violated his obligations under **Model Rule 3.3(a)**?

    a. Yes. He served a paper in a proceeding that he knew contained a false statement of fact.

    b. Yes. He encouraged Shirley to make a false statement. Had she drafted the answer, Dean could have filed it without violating his own obligations. He is only responsible here because the misrepresentation originated with him.

    c. No. Shirley is the one who verified the interrogatory answers, not Dean.

    d. No. An interrogatory answer is not a statement to the court; it is a response to the other party's discovery request.

23. Michael represented a homeowner, Ellen, when she sued a landscaper. Ellen subsequently refused to pay Michael's legal fees. Michael initiated a case against Ellen for breach of contract. At the bench trial, Michael testifies that Ellen agreed to pay him $300 per hour and that he spent 45 hours working on her case. In support of this testimony, he offers three exhibits: his retainer agreement with Ellen; his final bill to her for $13,500; and a summary showing the tasks that he had performed as part of the representation. Michael also calls his paralegal, Andra. She explains in further detail some of the tasks that were performed.

    Has Michael violated his obligations under **Model Rule 3.7**?

    a. Yes. The exhibits alone were sufficient, so there was no need for Michael to testify.

    b. Maybe. Michael is violating the rule unless it would be an undue hardship for Michael not to be trial counsel.

    c. No. The rule only applies to testimony before a jury.

    d. No. The rule allows a lawyer to testify from personal knowledge in a case where the lawyer is a witness, when the lawyer is testifying about his fees.

24. Tasha is litigating an employment discrimination case. A witness, Jared, is on the stand. Tasha has a written statement from Bessie, Jared's former

accountant, in which Bessie states that she had uncovered evidence that Jared had cheated on his taxes for years. Bessie is not a trial witness, and the statement itself is inadmissible hearsay. For this reason, Tasha does not offer the statement itself into evidence. At the end of cross-examination, Tasha asks Jared, "You cheated on your taxes, didn't you?" He says, "No." She concludes her cross-examination, frustrated that Jared did not admit to the tax fraud.

In her closing, Tasha argues to the jury, "You can't believe a word that Jared says because he's a liar. He lied right in front of you. He told you that he never cheated on his taxes but his former accountant, Bessie, says otherwise. She says that Jared had cheated on his taxes for years!"

Has Tasha violated her obligations under **Model Rule 3.4(e)**?

   a. Yes. Her cross-examination was permissible, but she should not have referred to Bessie's statement in the closing argument because the statement was not admitted at trial.

   b. Yes. In her closing argument, Tasha was improperly vouching for Bessie's testimony by suggesting Bessie was more believable than Jared.

   c. No. Evidence need not be admissible for that evidence to be used to impeach. Here, Bessie's statement was simply used for impeachment purposes, not as substantive evidence.

   d. No. She was entitled to question Jared about his prior bad act, but she was not permitted to introduce extrinsic evidence to contradict his answer.

25. Janice is a criminal defense attorney. She handles high-profile white-collar crime cases. Dr. Teeth, a world-renowned dentist, is accused of health-care fraud. The government alleges that Dr. Teeth had accepted bribes from Zoot Inc. in exchange for recommending Zoot's prescription tooth-whitening device to patients. The case is being tried before a jury, and the trial is nearly over.

During her direct examination of Dr. Teeth, while standing in the well of the court, Janice asks Dr. Teeth to describe at length his many academic and professional accomplishments. The prosecutor, Floyd, objects on the basis that this line of questioning involves improper bolstering of the witness. The judge overrules the objection.

Janice then asks Dr. Teeth whether he's the kind of person who would risk his entire career for a few measly dollars. Again, Floyd objects and again, the judge overrules the objection. Dr. Teeth emphatically denies the allegations against him. In response to the question, Janice remarks, "Thank you for your honest testimony." She then concludes her questioning.

Has Janice violated her obligations under **Model Rule 3.4(e)**?

a. Yes. She stated a personal opinion as to Dr. Teeth's credibility when she characterized his testimony as "honest."

b. Yes. She bolstered his testimony by asking him to detail irrelevant academic and professional accomplishments so that the jury would be inclined to believe Dr. Teeth's testimony.

c. No. The judge overruled both of Floyd's objections, which is itself evidence that Janice acted ethically.

d. No. Janice was not sworn and under oath nor was she sitting on the witness stand. The rule only applies to formal testimony, and nothing Janice said constituted formal testimony.

26. Renaldo is a first-year lawyer drafting an opening brief in a federal appeal. In his research, he discovers a case, *United States v. Smith*, that is adverse and controlling. He cannot think of a way to distinguish the case, so he buries it in a long string cite with no parenthetical. The string cite addresses a wholly different aspect of the case than the part of *Smith* that is adverse to his argument.

When Renaldo is finished with his draft, he submits it to the partner for review. The partner copyedits the brief but does not check any of the citations. In an effort to reduce the overall length of the brief, the partner eliminates most string cites. In doing so, all references to the *Smith* case are removed.

After he had completed the editing, the partner hands the brief back to Renaldo and asks Renaldo to review and file the brief. Renaldo reviews it and notices that the *Smith* case is no longer cited. Figuring that the partner knows best, Renaldo files the brief, using his electronic case filing account.

Has Renaldo violated his obligations under **Model Rule 3.3**?

a. Yes. Renaldo failed to flag the *Smith* case as adverse and controlling and therefore misrepresented the importance of this case to the partner.

b. Yes. Renaldo knowingly filed a brief that omitted controlling adverse authority that Renaldo had a duty to disclose.

c. No. Renaldo was supervised by a partner, and it was the partner, not Renaldo, who ultimately decided to eliminate all citation to *Smith*.

d. No. Renaldo had no obligation to disclose the case because he could rely on the court discovering the case independently.

27. Yasmin is preparing her client, Trinh, for a deposition. Trinh has sued Cecily, claiming that Cecily ran a red light and caused an auto collision

that injured Trinh. During the preparation, Yasmin asks Trinh, "What color was the light when you arrived at the intersection?" Trinh says, "It's been so long, I honestly can't remember."

Yasmin shows Trinh the police report that was taken at the scene of the accident. The police officer interviewed both Trinh and Cecily at the scene. In the report, the police officer wrote, "Trinh claims that the light was green when she reached the intersection." Yasmin asks Trinh, "Now do you remember what color the light was?" Trinh says, "Yes, the light was green."

At her deposition, Trinh is asked what color the light was at the time she reached the intersection. Without hesitation, she answers "green."

Did Yasmin's preparation of Trinh violate **Model Rule 3.4(b)**?

a. Yes. The truth was that Trinh did not remember the color of the light. Yasmin coerced her into falsely testifying that the light was green.

b. Yes. The report was not authored by Trinh; it was authored by the police officer. It therefore was inappropriate for Yasmin to refresh Trinh's recollection with the report.

c. No. Neither a deposition nor the preparation for one constitutes a "proceeding" as defined by the Rule. The Rule does not apply.

d. No. The testimony was not false. Although Trinh initially forgot the color of the light, her recollection was refreshed, and she testified consistently with that recollection at the deposition.

28. Wai is defending Daisy in a civil assault case arising out of a bar fight. Daisy insists on taking the stand in her own defense. Wai counsels Daisy, "You told me that you hit the plaintiff over the head with a beer bottle. If you take the stand and admit that at trial, you will likely be found liable. I advise you not to testify because, if you're asked, you'll have to admit that you were the one who hit the plaintiff." Daisy refuses to follow Wai's advice and insists on testifying.

Did Wai violate **Model Rule 3.4(b)** when he counseled Daisy?

a. Yes, because he encouraged Daisy to lie by telling her that she would lose the case if she told the truth.

b. Yes, because he allowed Daisy to testify, knowing that she would be tempted to lie.

c. No, because he did not encourage Daisy to lie; in fact, he discouraged her from testifying entirely.

d. No, because a defendant may always testify in her own defense.

29. Dolores slipped and injured her back while walking down the dairy aisle of the grocery store. Another customer, Wyatt, saw the entire thing. Dolores's counsel would like Wyatt to testify at trial, but Wyatt is a busy

architect who lives 50 miles away. He typically charges his clients $250 per hour when he works on construction projects.

Which of the following may counsel offer to pay Wyatt if he agrees to testify?

    a. The cost of a train ticket and a room at a hotel so he can arrive the day before trial and stay overnight.

    b. Five percent of whatever amount Dolores recovers at trial.

    c. Both a and b.

    d. Neither a nor b.

30. Stevie, the owner of the Rosebud Motel, is sued by her former handyman, Roland. Roland claims that he was owed a $40,000 severance that Stevie never paid. Stevie claims that she never signed a severance agreement and that the signature on the purported agreement is forged. She has filed a counterclaim for fraud. She asks her attorney, Johnny, to offer the agreement into evidence at trial as evidence that Roland is engaging in fraud.

    Can Johnny offer the exhibit without violating **Model Rule 3.3(a)**?

    a. Yes, because the exhibit is being offered for the effect on the listener, so it is not being used for its truth.

    b. Yes, because he is offering it as evidence for the purpose of proving its falsity.

    c. No, because offering the exhibit would be placing false evidence before the trier of fact.

    d. No, because he is offering it to prove the truth of the matter asserted within—namely, whether the $40,000 severance is owed.

31. Which of the following types of evidence is governed by **Model Rule 3.3(a)(3)**?

    a. Testimony.

    b. Documents.

    c. Physical evidence.

    d. All of the above.

32. Jean-Ralphio is plaintiff's counsel in a slip-and-fall case. The plaintiff, Mona Lisa, is on the stand. He hands her a photograph and asks, "Do you know what this is?" She says, "Yes." He asks, "What is it?" She says, "It's a photograph of the stairwell where I fell." He asks, "Does this fairly and accurately depict the stairwell at the time that you fell?" She says, "Yes, this looks like the photo that I took with my cell phone right after the accident."

Although Mona Lisa doesn't realize it, Jean-Ralphio has had the photo edited with Photoshop to make the stairs appear steeper in the photo than they actually are in real life.

Would this be considered false evidence, as defined by **Model Rule 3.3(a)(3)**, if Jean-Ralphio offered it into evidence at trial?

a. Yes, because the evidence is inauthentic.

b. Yes, because the evidence is not being offered through a witness with personal knowledge.

c. No, because the evidence has been authenticated.

d. No, because the evidence does show the stairwell where the accident occurred.

33. Marley is defending Cleo in a criminal assault case arising out of a bar fight. Cleo insists on taking the stand in her own defense. Marley counsels Cleo, "You told me that you hit the victim over the head with a beer bottle. If you take the stand and admit that at trial, you will likely be found guilty. I advise you not to testify because, if you're asked, you'll have to admit that you hit the victim." Marley was not at the scene of the fight and does not know exactly what happened, but all the evidence suggests that Cleo did hit the victim. Despite Marley's advice, Cleo says that she still wants to testify.

Does **Model Rule 3.3** give Marley grounds to oppose Cleo's request?

a. Yes, if Marley thinks that Cleo will lie, he can refuse to call her to testify.

b. Yes, if Marley has a reasonable suspicion that Cleo is guilty, he may refuse to call her to testify.

c. No; Cleo has the right to testify in her own defense, and Marley can't prevent her from doing so simply because he believes that she may lie.

d. No; Marley **must** call Cleo to testify. He simply can't ask her a question that will affirmatively elicit a lie, and he must object if the prosecution asks such a question.

34. Barry is on trial, accused of murdering his girlfriend, Sally. Barry badly wants to testify in his own defense because he claims to be innocent of the murder. His counsel, Fuches, asks Barry what he was doing at the time of the murder. Barry reluctantly admits that he was committing a contract killing (of someone other than Sally) at that time. Fuches tells Barry that he will incriminate himself further if he admits that his alibi to Sally's murder was that he was busy committing a different murder. Barry thinks for a minute and then says, "I'll lie. I'll say I was at my acting class at the time of the murder." Fuches is also in Barry's acting class, and he knows that Barry was not in class on the night of the murder.

Which of the following actions in response would violate Fuches's ethical obligations?

a. Fuches points out to Barry that the prosecution will call other students from the acting class who will testify that Barry missed class on the night of the murder, in an effort to convince Barry not to lie.

b. Fuches discourages Barry from testifying at all by reminding him how effectively the prosecution's star witness, Detective Moss, was impeached.

c. Fuches tells Barry point-blank that the jury will disbelieve Barry's testimony because the jury has already learned that acting class was on Monday nights and the murder happened on a Saturday.

d. Fuches refuses to allow Barry to testify entirely on the theory that, if Barry does testify, he will commit perjury.

35. What is the difference between a narrative direct examination and a more traditional direct examination, and why might a lawyer use a narrative direct examination?

a. During a narrative direct examination, the lawyer controls the manner in which testimony occurs, asking specific questions to elicit the facts. This type of direct examination is used when the lawyer knows that a defendant in a civil case is lying.

b. During a narrative direct examination, the lawyer does not control the manner in which testimony occurs. The lawyer asks a broad, open-ended question and simply allows the defendant to speak. This type of direct examination is used when the lawyer knows that a defendant in a civil case is lying.

c. During a narrative direct examination, the lawyer controls the manner in which testimony occurs, asking specific questions to elicit the facts. This type of direct examination is used when the lawyer knows that a defendant in a criminal case is lying.

d. During a narrative direct examination, the lawyer does not control the manner in which testimony occurs. The lawyer asks a broad, open-ended question and simply allows the defendant to speak. This type of direct examination is used when the lawyer knows that a defendant in a criminal case is lying.

36. Pursuant to the language of **Model Rule 3.3(a)(3)**, when **must** a lawyer take remedial measures to **correct** a falsehood?

a. When the lawyer offered any evidence that the lawyer comes to know is false.

b. When the lawyer offered impeachment evidence that the lawyer comes to know is false.

c. When the lawyer offered **material** evidence that the lawyer comes to know is false.

    d. When the lawyer offered inadmissible evidence that the lawyer comes to know is false.

37. Janet represents Maggie, a former employee, who claims that she was fired by her former employer because of her race. Janet calls Maggie's former supervisor, Lynn, as an adverse witness. In response to Janet's questioning, Lynn makes a statement of **material** fact that Janet knows to be false.

    Does Janet have a duty to take remedial measures?

    a. Yes, because although Lynn is an adverse witness, Janet called Lynn to testify, and therefore Janet is responsible for having offered **material** false evidence.

    b. Yes, because lying under oath can constitute perjury, and all lawyers representing parties in a trial have a duty to remedy such conduct.

    c. Both a and b.

    d. Neither a nor b.

38. What is the typical first step that a lawyer must take to remedy false testimony when a witness called by that lawyer lies under oath during trial?

    a. Urge the witness to correct his or her false testimony.

    b. Disclose **confidential information** to the court.

    c. Move that the testimony by stricken.

    d. Withdraw.

39. Victor is an assistant United States attorney. He handles *qui tam* complaints, which are cases about defrauding the government that are initially filed under seal. The defendant in these types of cases does not know about the case until the seal is lifted.

    After six months of investigation, Victor feels that he needs additional time before the seal is lifted. He files a motion asking that the case remain sealed.

    The judge presiding over the case calls Victor into chambers to discuss the seal extension. No one else is present in chambers aside from Victor and the judge. (The defendant doesn't know the case exists, which is why he or his lawyer isn't present at the conference.)

    The judge asks whether Victor has found any evidence showing that the defendant committed fraud, as alleged in the complaint. Victor had found some evidence of fraud that is good for his case. Victor has also found some evidence that suggests the defendant may not have committed fraud and might simply have made an innocent error. That evidence is bad for Victor's case.

    What must Victor disclose to the judge?

    a. Only the evidence of fraud, because that's what the judge specifically requested.

b. Both the good and bad evidence, so the judge can make a fully educated decision about whether to extend the seal.
c. Only the evidence that is good for the government, because Victor represents the government and must advocate zealously in the government's interest.
d. He need not disclose any information to the judge.

40. Alphonso represents Gonzo in a breach of contract case. Gonzo is suing Doris, who is represented by Norris. Norris moves to dismiss the complaint for failure to state a claim on Doris's behalf. Alphonso calls Norris to discuss the case, and they agree that Alphonso will have 30 days to amend Gonzo's complaint. Alphonso accordingly does not oppose the motion to dismiss. Norris forgets to take his motion off calendar, and he happens to be in court when the motion is called for hearing. The judge asks Norris, "Am I correct in understanding that your motion to dismiss is not opposed?" Norris answers, "Yes, Your Honor." The judge dismisses Gonzo's case with prejudice.

Has anyone violated the Rules of Professional Conduct?
a. Yes. Alphonso, for not opposing the motion to dismiss.
b. Yes. Alphonso, for failing to inform his client that he intended to amend the complaint.
c. Yes. Norris, for failing to take his motion off calendar.
d. Yes. Norris, for failing to volunteer to the judge that the motion had been resolved by agreement between counsel.

25

The Government Lawyer

DANIELLE HAS BEEN PREPARING for a sexual assault trial for weeks. After the office let her "cut her teeth" on some smaller misdemeanor cases, they've finally assigned her a felony. It's a big opportunity, and Danielle understandably feels tremendous pressure to do everything right, and to win the case for the victim, her office, and the people of her state.

The case should be a slam dunk. DNA evidence links the defendant to the crime. Danielle has an analysis from the forensics lab proving that DNA left on the victim by the perpetrator is the defendant's. Danielle has prepared diligently, trying to anticipate anything and everything that could come up at trial. She has met multiple times with the lead detective and the victim, her two main witnesses. They are both prepared and ready to testify. Danielle has organized and re-organized her exhibits. She's practiced her opening until she can recite it by heart. Over the past few weeks, her colleagues and her Supervising Deputy DA have stopped by to offer moral support and encouragement. The Medium County District Attorney even popped his head into her office last week to say "good luck." Trial starts tomorrow. Danielle is ready.

Although jury selection doesn't start until 9:30 a.m., Danielle can't sleep, and gets to the office at 7:30. Awash with nervous energy and feeling too jittery to review her notes one more time, she decides to do something mindless. She starts sorting through the stack of mail that piled up while she was preparing for the trial. It's mostly junk mail—copies of legal newsletters and non-time-sensitive intra-office communications—but then she sees an envelope that makes her heart skip a beat. It's a letter addressed to her from the forensics lab that did the DNA analysis in the trial she's starting today.

Danielle's hands shake as she opens the envelope. Inside is a one-page statement of clarification. According to the statement, the forensic lab's initial analysis was in error—the DNA evidence found on the victim was *not* the defendant's as the lab had originally reported. Danielle's pulse starts racing. If she discloses the letter to the court and defense counsel, she will certainly lose the case. But if she puts the letter back in the pile and tries the case anyway—who will ever be the wiser?

* * *

This chapter is about the role and special duties of the government lawyer. Are government lawyers' professional responsibilities really different from those in private or public interest practice? Well, yes and no. Government lawyers face many of the same professional challenges that lawyers face in private practice or in the nonprofit sector. In most respects, those challenges are governed by the same Rules of Professional Conduct, and are subject to the same analysis, regardless of whether your employer or your client is a government agency. Sometimes, however, representing the government comes with factual or legal complications common in governmental matters (but not elsewhere) that affect how a professional conduct problem must be analyzed. And in a few instances, the ethical rules and professional expectations to which government lawyers are subject are substantively different from those that apply to other lawyers.

This chapter will highlight some of those complications and differences. It's not meant to be an exhaustive analysis of how each and every Model Rule applies to those representing government. Nor is it meant to address every state and federal law that applies to government practice. Rather, we'll focus in on one Model Rule that applies exclusively to the conduct of criminal prosecutors (**Model Rule 3.8**, in **Chapter 25.D at 940**), one that imposes some special **conflict of interest** rules on government lawyers that are different from those applicable to everybody else (**Model Rule 1.11**, in **Chapter 25.D at 927**), and several others that create additional wrinkles unique to government practice because of the kinds of matters that government lawyers often handle (in **Chapter 25.C at 911**). We'll start with a quick overview of government lawyering and the source of the ethical rules that regulate it.

Let's get to it.

A. What Do Government Lawyers Do?

What do government lawyers do? Anything and everything! Part of what makes government practice so appealing is the sheer variety of the work. In some capacity, lawyers are involved in every aspect of federal, state, and local government. They work in and for every arm and agency of government and often also represent governmental officers and employees. They handle cases and deals running the gamut of substantive areas of the law. If the government does something, you can bet that there's a government lawyer in the mix somewhere.

Many lawyers who represent governmental agencies or actors are employed by the government itself, from the state prosecutors who are employed by their state and work in local district attorneys' offices to the thousands of lawyers in the

United States Department of Justice, which provides representation to virtually every branch and agency of the federal government and their associated officers and employees. Many state and federal agencies also have their own in-house lawyers specializing in issues specific to the agency and its business. Lawyers in private practice are also occasionally retained to represent a governmental agency or actor, sometimes when a matter demands special skills or talents, and sometimes when the government authority involved is so small (such as a small town) that its needs don't support having a full-time lawyer on staff.

Some lawyers, such as prosecutors, handle exclusively criminal cases. Others have a civil docket. Yet others handle both types of disputes. Some government lawyers focus on a narrow area of the law, such as the inside counsel at specialized state or federal administrative agencies who advise the agency on its functions and defend or enforce its rules and regulations. Other government lawyers have broader areas of expertise. For example, assistant United States attorneys working for the Department of Justice who are assigned to the civil division of their office may defend the United States and federal agencies and their employees in tort, employment discrimination, or immigration cases, or represent the United States as a claimant in tax or contract cases. The same is true of municipal counsel, who may either handle a broad variety of cases or who may be assigned to subject-specific units, depending on the city or county's size and needs. Yet other government lawyers have entirely transactional practices, such as the military judge advocates general who draft estate-planning documents for service members (while other JAGs prosecute or defend criminal or civil claims on behalf of the military and its personnel). Like their civil counterparts, prosecutors and public defenders may specialize in particular areas of the criminal law, or they may be generalists.

There is as much variety in government practice as there is variety in law practice as a whole. You need not even practice law to work for the government with a law degree: Lawyers are regularly hired to serve in advisory and public policy roles in government, too. And although no one is required to have a law degree to be elected to public office, many elected officials do, and they make good use of it in drafting, revising, and debating the wisdom of legislation and other official acts. This book would never end if we tried to describe everything government lawyers do (but don't worry—we'll stop here).

B. What Ethical Rules Apply to Government Lawyers?

Generally speaking, government lawyers are subject to the same ethical rules as all other lawyers. (We'll cover the main exceptions to that general principle in the rest of this chapter.) Lawyers representing state and local government agencies and actors tend to be licensed and practice in a single state, whose Rules of Professional Conduct and related law governing lawyers regulate their work. Like nongovernmental lawyers, state and local government lawyers are not authorized to practice in any state in which they are not licensed unless that other state allows them to do so (for example, by admission in a single case *pro hac vice, see* **Chapter 3.A at 42 n.20**).

For federal government lawyers, the answer is a bit more complicated. The federal government requires its lawyers to be licensed to practice in at least one American state or the District of Columbia. But by federal statute, any federal government lawyer may appear in any state or federal court anywhere in the nation, regardless of where that lawyer is licensed.[1] Although federal government lawyers are authorized to practice anywhere, however, they also **must** comply with the professional conduct rules of the jurisdiction or court in which they are appearing.[2] If a federal government lawyer is practicing in a matter for which there is no tribunal or other authority imposing rules governing lawyers, then the lawyer generally **must** follow the rules of his or her licensing jurisdiction.[3] This multiplication of regulatory authority can occasionally create issues when there is a difference between the ethics rules of the jurisdiction in which the federal government lawyer is practicing and the ethics rules of the jurisdiction in which that lawyer is licensed. This problem is not unique to government lawyers, however; nongovernmental lawyers can also encounter similar problems when they are licensed or otherwise authorized to practice law in more than one jurisdiction. *See* **Model Rule 8.5**.

> **Problem 25B-1:** Attorney Julia is licensed to practice in the State of California. California offers licensing reciprocity with no other states.
>
> a. Julia applies for and is hired as an assistant United States attorney in the District of New Jersey. Assuming that her license is in good standing in California, does she need to be admitted to practice, either *pro hac vice* or by passing the New Jersey bar exam, to litigate on behalf of the United States in New Jersey federal courts? How about New Jersey state courts? Why or why not?
>
> b. Same as (a): Assume that Julia accepts the job as an AUSA in New Jersey, and that there are differences between the California and New Jersey rules of professional conduct. What jurisdiction's rules of professional conduct **must** Julia follow when she appears on behalf of the United States in federal courts located in New Jersey? How about the state courts in New Jersey? Please explain your answers.
>
> c. Now assume Julia instead accepts a job as a New Jersey state prosecutor. What, if anything, does she need to do to appear in the federal courts located in New Jersey? How about New Jersey's state courts? Why?

---

[1] **28 U.S.C. § 517** (1966).
[2] **28 U.S.C. § 530B** (known as the "McDade Amendment"); **28 C.F.R. § 77.3**.
[3] **28 C.F.R. § 77.4(c)**.

Beyond the baseline requirements just described, there are a number of special rules and standards applicable to government lawyers that are supplemental to or different from those applicable to nongovernmental ones. We'll get to those later in the chapter (*see* **Chapter 25.D at 925**). First, though, let's talk about a few situations that government lawyers confront with some regularity—situations that complicate the application of professional conduct rules that govern all lawyers, and with which you're already familiar.

C. Situations Common to Government Practice That Complicate the Application of Generally Applicable Professional Conduct Rules

1. Identifying Your Client

Much of the time, it's relatively straightforward to determine whether you have a client, and who (or what) that client is. During this course, we've identified a number of situations in which the answers to those questions can be harder to figure out, or can be mistaken because a lawyer isn't adequately focused on that issue. *See, e.g.,* **Chapter 9.A at 259** (knowing when you've formed an attorney-client relationship); **Chapter 9.B at 267** (assuming duties to non-clients); **Chapter 23.A at 770** (representing organizations and/or their **constituents**). These same issues also arise in government practice, but in a somewhat different form because of the different nature and structure of some governmental clients and engagements.

Often, it's clear who your government client is—a specific state or political subdivision of a state (a county; a city) or a federal or state administrative agency, for example. But in some contexts, a government lawyer may broadly represent an interest or function of government, or may nominally represent the apex appointee (that is, the top dog) at a particular agency when the lawyer is in practical substance representing the **interests** of that agency as a whole, or of particular agency employees. Conversely, a government lawyer may personally represent a government employee, but is doing so with the purpose of protecting the **interests** of the individual's government employer as well as those of the individual. For these reasons, the *Restatement (Third) of the Law Governing Lawyers* rather unhelpfully announces in Section 97, comment (c) that there is no "universal definition of the client of a government lawyer."

To take a common example, who are Danielle's clients? No clients walk into her office and ask her to represent them, as often happens in private practice. No court assigns her to represent a particular party in a particular case, as happens with public defenders. Prosecutors work directly and extensively with crime victims and law enforcement officers every day. When Danielle directs a police officer to seek witnesses or evidence, or prepares that officer or a crime victim to testify at trial, is she acting as their lawyer?

What's more, Danielle is a deputy district attorney in the office of the District Attorney for Medium County in the State of Confusion. Depending on prevailing law and practice in her state and in her office, the pleadings that she files and the appearances that she states in court may describe her as representing the State of Confusion, Medium County, or the People of the State or of the County. Her ultimate boss could plausibly be identified as the Governor of the State of Confusion (who is the chief executive officer of the state), the Attorney General of the State of Confusion (who is the chief law enforcement officer of the state), or the Medium County District Attorney. So who is her client? To whom or what does she owe her **duties of loyalty**, **confidentiality**, **care**, and **candor**? And who has the final word as to what her client's goals and objectives are—for example, what should Danielle do if she gets conflicting instructions from two or more of those officials?

This is an area in which you may find the Model Rules somewhat frustrating to apply because there are few Rules specific to government work. In most areas of the Model Rules, the nomenclature and concepts discussed are those most common in private practice. Nevertheless, most of the time the questions you need to ask and analyze are the same questions you would ask and analyze for a private-sector lawyer. In the private sector, these questions are sometimes difficult to analyze or need special attention and active management in order to avoid confusion, but we still know what the questions are and how to analyze them as clearly as the law may allow. The same is true in government work.

a. Witnesses, Helpers, and Victims (Oh My!)

Let's talk about a few commonly recurring examples in government practice. For example, does Danielle represent the police officers and crime victims with whom she regularly works? We already know the way to go about answering this question: Generally, people who actually and reasonably believe that they are your clients are your clients. *See* **Chapter 9.A at 259.**

How does that work here? Well, prosecutors and law enforcement work together all the time. (Remember that introductory spiel before every episode of *Law and Order* about the "two separate but equally important groups"?) Police officers and other law enforcement officials understand that prosecutors don't act as their lawyers and that their communications are not **attorney-client privileged**. They act accordingly. (There is an easy analogy here to the nonattorney investigators employed full-time by some private law firms, or the private investigators retained for particular engagements by lawyers in private practice. These personnel effectively act as agents on behalf of the lawyers employing or retaining them; properly conducted, the communications between lawyers and their investigators thus may be protected by the **attorney work product doctrine,** but not by the **attorney-client privilege.** *See* **Chapter 8.A at 226** to remind yourself of some of the differences.) Experienced private-sector investigators understand the contours of this arrangement, and in all events, the lawyers retaining the investigator must supervise the investigator and ensure that the investigator complies not only with all applicable law, but also with the lawyer's own ethical obligations. (*See* **Model Rule 5.3**; **Chapter 19.C at 515**.)

Crime victims and other witnesses are often less legally knowledgeable and sophisticated, and prosecutors generally approach them differently: When interviewing victims or witnesses or preparing them to testify, prosecutors will generally make it clear that they are not the witness's lawyer and that their communications are neither **confidential** nor **attorney-client privileged**. As we've previously discussed, making clear the lack of any attorney-client relationship between the prosecutor and the victim or other witness makes it unreasonable for the witness to believe there is one, and thus prevents an attorney-client relationship from forming contrary to the prosecutor's intentions. *See* **Chapter 9.A at 261**. And as we've also discussed, the absence of an attorney-client relationship between the prosecutor and these witnesses often influences the scope and substance of the prosecutor's witness preparation. *See* **Chapter 24.C at 865**.

b. The Identity of a Government Client, and of the Government Official Ultimately Empowered to Direct and Speak for the Client

Now we know who Danielle's clients are *not*. But who *is* her client? And who has the authority to speak for that client?

Again, we already know how to go about answering this question, though it may not always be easy. We start with **Model Rule 1.13(a)**: "A lawyer employed or retained by an organization represents the organization acting through its duly authorized **constituents**." The Model Rules don't define "organization," but **Model Rule 1.13 Comment [9]** makes clear that "[t]he duty defined in this Rule applies to governmental organizations." In other words, for purposes of the Model Rules, a governmental entity is just as much an "organization" as is a private business organization. The same Comment goes on to make the important observation that "[d]efining precisely the identity of the [governmental] client and prescribing the resulting obligations of [government] lawyers may be more difficult in the government context and is a matter beyond the scope of these Rules." *See also* **Model Rules Scope ¶ [18]**.

As we discussed in **Chapter 23.A at 770**, the definition of an organizational client is supplied by the state or federal law that creates and structures the organization; similarly, the individual **constituents** of any organization with the authority to speak for the organization and instruct its counsel are identified by that same law (and not the Model Rules or any other rules governing professional conduct). The same is true of governmental agencies and functions: Federal or state constitutions, statutes, and administrative regulations define various governmental branches, organizations, and functions, and the elected or appointed officials who are empowered to speak for them or cause them to do things. Just as in a private business organization, such as a corporation or a partnership, determining exactly what individual or group of **constituents** in a government organization has the authority to make certain decisions is often easy, but may in some limited circumstances be difficult to determine. *Cf.* **Chapter 23.A at 772.** Nevertheless, the *source* of the answer is reasonably well identified even if the answer it yields in a particular situation may be difficult to discern: The state or federal law defining and regulating the government entities or functions at issue.

REAL WORLD How does that work in real life? Well, think about Danielle. Who is her client? For most purposes, whatever her office's pleadings and form of court appearance typically say is going to be a sufficient answer (for the basic practical reason that no one disagrees, and everyone understands what governmental function she is carrying out). For similar reasons, it's usually easy for her to know what her client wants. She confers with her supervisor, who was duly appointed as her supervisor by the DA or the state Attorney General, and who advises and where needed directs her on significant decisions in her practice.

Who's got the ultimate authority to tell Danielle what to do (that is, to speak for her client)? Fortunately, that question hardly ever comes up. Most of the time, her supervisor knows what needs to be done, and he confers with his boss, the DA, when difficult questions or policy issues arise. But what if there's a controversy? Say Danielle lives in a liberal city in a conservative state, in which the state legislature has adopted harsh criminal sanctions on possessing small amounts of marijuana for personal use. The local DA understands that this law is very unpopular among those who elected him, and instructs his line prosecutors not to prosecute small-quantity possession cases. The Attorney General, elected statewide, disagrees, and tells the DA and his staff to charge and prosecute such cases as the law allows. Danielle just got handed a file in which a gram of marijuana turned up in a driver's pocket during a routine traffic stop. Who must Danielle listen to in deciding how to charge the case? If the DA and the AG insist on a formal tug-of-war about it, the question will be answered through a process of political infighting and, if necessary, by a state court's decision on what state law says about that—in the same way that if there's a control dispute among **constituents** of a business organization, a court may be called upon to resolve the warring parties' disagreements over who gets to call the shots. *See* **Chapter 23.A at 789.** But if you think about it, this kind of conflict among government authorities is quite unusual, so most of the time, responsible prosecutors like Danielle don't have to worry about it. REAL WORLD

Government and private practice are also treated the same under the Model Rules with respect to each individual government lawyer's nondelegable personal obligation to adhere to all applicable ethical rules and other governing law in doing their jobs. Just as in private practice—many would say especially in government practice—government lawyers can almost never excuse unethical or illegal conduct by claiming that they were acting as their client or supervisor instructed. *See* **Model Rule 5.2**; **Chapter 19.B at 507.**

c. The Identity of Your Client When You're Defending Government Actors

Among their responsibilities, many government lawyers often find themselves defending claims against government. These claims are of countless different kinds, but especially common are claims against government for torts (*e.g.*, the plaintiff alleges that she was negligently run over by a mail truck), employment discrimination (*e.g.*, the plaintiff alleges that she was discriminated against in government employment because of her race or gender), and civil rights violations (*e.g.*, the plaintiff alleges that she was subjected to excessive force by a police officer). Different kinds of claims become the liability of the government itself under different circumstances (government entities are often liable for the torts of government employees where the government has waived sovereign immunity, for example, but government entities do not have *respondeat superior* liability for civil rights violations under **42 U.S.C. § 1983**). But like nongovernmental organizations, governmental organizations are legal abstractions that commit torts or violate employment or other civil rights only through the acts of their human agents.

In these defensive cases, identifying the government lawyer's client may be especially challenging. Procedural and substantive rules designating necessary, proper, or improper parties in certain claims against government can make it difficult to discern the persons or organizations to whom the government lawyer owes the fiduciary duties due a client. For example, under certain anti-discrimination statutes (including Title VII, an important federal anti-employment-discrimination law), a plaintiff alleging discrimination cannot state a claim directly against a government agency, or even against the government employee who may have acted in a discriminatory fashion. Instead, by statute, such a claim is properly stated only against the head of the agency acting in his or her official capacity, though any damages assessed are the responsibility of the agency. The Advisory Committee Notes to the 1961 Amendment to **Fed. R. Civ. P. 25(d) (1)** (which addresses the automatic party substitution of successor government officers in cases of this kind after the incumbent officer leaves office for any reason) describe such actions as "in form against a named officer, but intrinsically against the government or the office or the incumbent thereof whoever he may be from time to time during the action." In other words, the procedurally proper named defendant in such a case is a government employee—the agency head. But the true client is the agency itself, acting through the agency head—whether or not the agency head had anything to do with the alleged discrimination, and even though the agency head will face no personal liability at all if the plaintiff prevails.[4]

A government official is not always sued in a representative capacity, however. There are times when government lawyers represent individual government employees personally. Generally, government lawyers represent individual government employees personally only to the extent that such a representation advances the interests of the government more broadly.[5] For example, suppose that a plaintiff in Medium County, where Danielle lives and works, claims that he was subjected to excessive force during an arrest by two Medium County sheriff's deputies in violation of his constitutional rights and **42 U.S.C. § 1983**, as well as state tort law. He claims that his injuries were the result of the County's policy or practice of violent policing in low-income neighborhoods in the County, articulated by an outspokenly "law and order" County Sheriff.

Such a lawsuit might very well name the County and the deputies employed by the County who delivered the beating. Can County counsel represent both the County and the individual deputies named in the case? Well, remember **Model Rule 1.13(g)**: A lawyer representing an organization (including a government organization) **may** also represent one or more of its **constituents** at the same time, provided that proper attention is given to disclosure to, and properly **informed consent** to any **conflicts of interest** by, all affected clients. *See* **Chapter 23.A at 772**.

In this particular case, the individual sheriff's deputies are not being sued as representatives of the sheriff's department or the County. Their personal interests are at stake, as they are alleged to have personally committed torts and civil rights violations. As a result, the accused employees are no longer involved merely as **constituents** of the County—County counsel directly represents them as clients, alongside the County, in their individual and personal capacities. *See, e.g.*, ABA Informal Ethics Op. No. 1413 (1978) ("a Government lawyer assigned

---

[4] Similarly, for complex jurisdictional reasons rooted in (among other things) the Eleventh Amendment, claims for injunctive relief against state or local government to stop violations of the federal Constitution must be stated against a governmental officer rather than the government itself. (And to make it even weirder, in these specific circumstances, the officer must be named in his or her individual rather than official capacity.) The lawsuit is nevertheless understood to be directed against unconstitutional state action, and the injunctive relief, if justified and granted, is nevertheless binding on the state or local government the officer serves. *Ex parte Young*, 209 U.S. 123 (1908). (We know, we know; just go with it for now. These rules reflect a difficult and complicated body of law that you will learn about if you take a Federal Courts course.) You don't have to understand all the details for our purposes here. The point for now is that, sometimes, for a number of different reasons and under a number of different legal doctrines, the legally proper defendant in a case seeking relief from the government is an individual, even though the thrust and gist of the case is "really" to get relief from the government organization that the individual serves.

[5] For this reason, personal representation of government employees by government counsel is subject to conditions and limitations not ordinarily encountered in private practice. For example, generally the personal representation of individual government employees is limited to defense—a government lawyer will not undertake any affirmative litigation on an individual employee's personal behalf. The distinction exists for the simple reason that such affirmative individual claims would hardly ever advance the interests of the government itself, and therefore **must** be pursued (if at all) by the government official with her own nongovernment counsel.

to represent a litigant . . . has an attorney-client relationship with the litigant, and . . . the lawyer's status as a Government employee does not exempt him or her from professional obligations, including those to preserve a client's **confidences** and secrets, that are imposed upon other lawyers").

Why do we care who the government lawyer's clients are when a government official or employee is sued? The difference is enormous, and has profound effects on several practical features of the lawyer's engagement. If the named defendant is the agency head in her official capacity as representative of the agency, then the government lawyer's **duties of loyalty, confidentiality, care**, and **candor** are owed *not* to the agency head *personally*, but to the *entire agency* as an *organization* (because the "true" client in this engagement is "really" the agency, with the agency head serving a purely procedural representative role dictated by statute). Because the entire agency as an organization is the true client in the engagement, the **attorney-client privilege** at stake is held by the agency, and not by the individual official: The lawyer thus may have **attorney-client privileged** communications not only with the agency head, but also with any agency managers authorized to seek or receive legal advice on the agency's behalf as described in the *Upjohn* case and its many progeny. *See* **Chapter 23.A at 784**. If the named-defendant agency head personally were the sole client, those communications with other agency **constituents** generally would not be **attorney-client privileged**, and thus often would be subject to discovery.

In our alleged police brutality case, on the other hand, the lawyer represents not only the County, but also the accused sheriff's deputies in their personal capacities. In this case, the lawyer owes not only the County but also those individual defendants all the fiduciary duties that a lawyer owes any client, and can communicate with the deputies on an **attorney-client privileged** basis.

Government lawyers handling these types of personal representation cases must always be sensitive to the distinction between the interests of the government and those of any individual government employee involved. As discussed above (*see* **Chapter 25.C at 911**), individual employees must never be left in any reasonable doubt as to whether government counsel represents them personally. And as we'll address in the next section of this chapter, when government counsel does represent an individual employee, there is a possibility that the individual's **interests** may **conflict** with the **interests** of the government organization in ways that **must** be recognized and addressed.

Even when the only client in a personal-capacity suit is an accused employee, that does not end the analysis. Government lawyers must always remember that representation of the individual employee is authorized only for the purpose of serving the **interests** of the government as a whole. For this reason, the government organization is also always a client whose **interests** must be considered, *even in suits involving only individual government-employee defendants*.

Problem 25C-1: Who is the government lawyer's client in each situation below? Be sure to explain your answer in each case.

a. An assistant United States attorney prosecuting a criminal embezzlement case styled *United States v. Smith*. According to the indictment, over the course of three years, Mr. Smith stole $1 million from his former employer, private-sector retailer Snacks Sixth Avenue.

b. A state public defender appointed to represent Fineas Flinders in the case of *State of Confusion v. Flinders*. According to the information, Mr. Flinders committed arson to defraud an insurance company, Liberty Betchuwill, which insured the building that Mr. Flinders allegedly torched.

c. A deputy district attorney litigating a civil health-care fraud case styled *State of Confusion v. Jones*. According to the complaint, Dr. Jones submitted false claims to the state's Medicaid program for medical equipment that he never supplied to his patients, defrauding the state's health-care system out of over $500,000.

d. An assistant city attorney defending a civil employment discrimination case styled *Rodriguez v. Carson*. In her complaint, Plaintiff Rona Rodriguez, an employee at the state's department of energy, sued the head of her department, Carlton Carson, in his official capacity, claiming that she was passed over for promotion on account of her religion in violation of Title VII.

e. An assistant United States attorney litigating a prisoner civil rights claim asserted against a prison warden under *Bivens v. Six Unknown Named Agents*, 403 U.S. 388 (1971). *Bivens* is a U.S. Supreme Court decision authorizing claims for damages against federal officials personally for violating an individual's rights under the federal Constitution. According to the complaint, the warden is liable in his personal capacity to pay damages to the plaintiff prisoner for failing to timely decide the prisoner's grievance.

f. A State Department of Social Services attorney drafting agency guidelines for the vaccination of the state's senior citizens during a pandemic.

g. Abbie is a prosecutor for the Commonwealth of Pennsylvania. She handles assault and battery cases involving victims who live within Pennsylvania. Does your analysis change if Abbie prosecutes a case involving an assault of a resident and domiciliary of New Jersey that took place in a Pennsylvania bar? If so, how and why; and if not, why not?

h. Bart is a public defender for the State of Connecticut. He is appointed to represent a defendant charged with a felony in Connecticut state court.

i. Chelsea is agency counsel for the Texas Department of Energy. She drafts regulations for the agency as well as "white papers" setting forth the agency's position on various regulatory and policy issues. These white papers are relied upon by many in the oil and gas industry seeking to do business in the state.

j. Dionne is an assistant solicitor for the United States Department of Labor. She litigates on behalf of the agency to collect wages that are due workers under the Fair Labor Standards Act (which sets the federal minimum wage and related wage and hour requirements). When the wages are collected, they are remitted to the workers.

k. Elouise is senior litigation counsel for the United States Equal Employment Opportunity Commission. In Title VII of the Civil Rights Act of 1964, Congress gave the EEOC authority to commence or intervene in litigation against private-sector employers to enforce employment discrimination laws for the benefit of individuals, groups, or classes of employees whose rights to discrimination-free workplaces and employment have been violated. Elouise handles these "enforcement actions," some (but not all) of which were initially filed by private plaintiffs before the EEOC joined each case as an intervenor.

l. Farrah is an assistant United States attorney litigating a civil slip-and-fall tort case styled *Patel v. United States*. According to the complaint, Ms. Patel tripped over a crooked mat in the lobby of a post office, causing her to fall and break an arm. The case is filed under the Federal Tort Claims Act, which waives sovereign immunity for tort claims against the United States of America but not against federal agencies or employees.

m. Gary is an assistant United States attorney in the Civil Division of the Los Angeles office of the U.S. Attorney's Office for the Central District of California. He defends federal government agencies in employment discrimination cases filed in the general geographic area where he works. By statute, these cases must be filed naming only the head of the agency employer acting in his or her official capacity.

n. Harriet is an assistant United States attorney in the Civil Division of the Philadelphia office of the U.S. Attorney's Office for the Eastern District of Pennsylvania. She handles *qui tam* whistleblower cases. By statute, these cases may be filed by private citizens on behalf of the United States, alleging that a person or organization has defrauded the United States. Harriet's cases primarily involve health-care fraud and interpretation of United States Department of Health and Human Services rules and regulations. If a private citizen is successful, this citizen, called a "relator," may share in a portion of any judgment or settlement, with the remainder going to the federal government.

o. Ingrid is counsel for the governor of New Jersey. She works directly with and was appointed by the governor. She is paid by the state of New Jersey, and her Form W-2 each year lists her employer as the State of New Jersey. Ingrid advises the governor on legal matters pertinent to the governor's official actions to ensure that his actions comply with the law.

Problem 25C-2: Anna works in the city attorney's office for Big City. She is defending the Big City School District from a retaliation suit brought by the parents of a student who claim that the student was given a low grade by his history teacher after he criticized the teacher's use of a racial slur in class. The complaint names both the teacher and the school district as defendants. The teacher stands by his use of the term, arguing that he used it in a contextualized manner for educational purposes. The school district urges an early settlement of the case, worried about the bad press. The teacher refuses to back down and insists on having his "day in court" to explain his side of the story. Whose direction **must** or **should** Anna follow?

Problem 25C-3: A **Mystery from History** (which is just a "Mess in the Press" that happened a long time ago): The "Saturday Night Massacre." In 1972, Washington, D.C., police arrested several men burglarizing and planting listening devices in the headquarters of the Democratic National Committee headquarters in the Watergate Office Building. The burglars were linked to President Richard Nixon's re-election campaign, and a Special Prosecutor—former Solicitor General and Harvard law professor Archibald Cox—was appointed to investigate. When congressional hearings on the Watergate break-in disclosed that President Nixon routinely taped conversations with his aides in the Oval Office, Mr. Cox subpoenaed recordings of the President's conversations relevant to his investigation. President Nixon, knowing that those recorded conversations would, if produced, prove his personal involvement in the cover-up of his campaign's involvement in the burglary—conduct that comprised multiple felonies on the President's part, and about which he had brazenly lied—instructed his Attorney General, Elliott Richardson, to fire the special prosecutor on a Saturday in October 1973. That evening, Mr. Richardson resigned rather than comply. The same evening, President Nixon then instructed Mr. Richardson's chief deputy, William Ruckelshaus, to fire Cox. Mr. Ruckelshaus also resigned rather than comply. President Nixon then ordered the Solicitor General, Robert Bork, to fire Cox, which Mr. Bork did as directed. The two top Justice Department officials' resignations and Special Prosecutor Cox's firing became famous as the "Saturday Night Massacre."

Whether the President had the raw governmental power to require the Attorney General (or his successor, after Mr. Richardson had resigned) to fire Special Prosecutor Cox was (and remains today) an arguable question of constitutional law, focusing on the President's powers as the head of the executive branch of the federal government. Perhaps you discussed this issue in your Constitutional Law class. For now, however, let's assume for purposes of argument that the question was arguable, that there was a serious legal basis to conclude that President Nixon had that power (irrespective of the wisdom of exercising it), and that Solicitor General Bork was acting within the law when he followed the President's instruction. The Model Rules did not exist at the time of these events, but the relevant rules of lawyer ethics then prevailing were the same as the Model Rules. Explain the conduct of Attorney General Richardson, Deputy Attorney General Ruckelshaus, and Solicitor General Bork on that Saturday night in terms of their duties as lawyers under the principles articulated today in the Model Rules. Did each act consistently with his ethical duties? Why or why not?

Problem 25C-4: Another **Mystery from History:** Take a look back at **Chapter 3's Multiple-Choice Question No. 7 at 62** (which is based on a real case, *see* **Chapter 3 at 62 n.38**). In the question, Deputy DA Anna has been instructed to investigate the propriety of Ivan's prior criminal conviction in light of newly discovered evidence. She concludes that the evidence shows that Ivan's conviction was clearly wrongful, but she is instructed by her supervisors to oppose Ivan's motion to vacate the conviction. What **must** or **should** Anna do in this situation? Specify whether any course of action that you identify is a **must** or a **should**, and of course explain your answer. In the question (and in the actual case on which it is based), Anna goes through the motions (so to speak) of opposing Ivan's lawyers, but quietly supplies them with evidence and arguments sufficient for them to present a winning position. Was the approach that Anna chose required or permissible? If so, specify which steps and why; and if not, why not?

2. Recognizing and Responding to Conflicts of Interest

Having trudged through **Chapter 22 at 599** in all its excruciatingly glorious detail, you no doubt remember that **conflicts of interest** result when a lawyer acquires or experiences **conflicting** duties to (or other **conflicting interests** regarding) two or more persons or organizations, usually clients (or experiences **conflicts** between the lawyer's own **interests** and the **interests** of or duties that the lawyer owes to someone else, often a client). For the reasons discussed in the preceding section, it can be difficult for government lawyers to discern the identity of the government organizations or **constituents** whose **interests** they **should** or **must** protect or disregard. As a result, it can be difficult for government lawyers to determine the existence or basis of **conflicts of interest**. As with other ethical questions that can arise in government practice, the rules regarding **conflicts of interest** are—with some important exceptions described in a later section of this chapter (*see* **Chapter 25.D at 927**)—generally the same for government lawyers as they are for everyone else, but those rules can sometimes be harder to apply in certain situations uniquely common in government practice.

a. Avoiding Direct Adversity to a Current Government Client

Under the **concurrent client rule**, you'll recall, a lawyer **must not** act adversely to a **current client** without all affected clients' **informed consent, confirmed in writing** (*see* **Model Rule 1.7(a)(1); Chapter 22.B at 646**). Many government lawyers serve more than one government agency or **interest** in their work—for example, a state Attorney General's office represents many different facets of state government, just as the U.S. Department of Justice represents many different federal government offices, officials, and agencies. And sometimes government entities sue or negotiate with one another. As just discussed, in government practice, it's not always easy to identify precisely which government agency or **interest** a government lawyer represents in a particular engagement. To make things more complicated still, among the many **interests**, agencies, and subdivisions in (for example) state government, it is often difficult to determine whether one of those divisions is the "same" organization as another for the purpose of deciding whether one government lawyer or government law office has a **conflict of interest** in suing one arm of state government while defending another one in some unrelated matter. In other words, there may be questions about whether the lawyer may be acting adversely to a **current client** in suing or negotiating with a government agency or actor that the same lawyer represents in something else. (And remember that **concurrent conflicts** don't have to have anything to do with one another substantively to be **disqualifying**, *see* **Chapter 22.B at 648**.)

Sometimes, substantive law provides answers about which agencies of federal, state, or local government are sufficiently distinct from one another to be considered different "clients" and thus don't offend **conflict of interest** rules when the same government lawyer represents one while acting against the other. Sometimes government officials come to some understanding about which government lawyers are going to work on either side of an intra-governmental dispute or negotiation; written **informed consents** resolve any lingering concern. In the absence of an express agreement, the identity of the government client may be inferred from the reasonable understandings and expectations of the lawyer and responsible government officials, taking into account such realistic considerations as how the government client presented to the lawyer is legally defined and funded, whether it has independent legal authority with respect to the matter for which the lawyer has been retained, and the extent to which the matter involved in the proposed representation has broader implications for the government. Uncertainty in identifying the government client **should** be resolved in favor of disclosure to all affected persons or organizations, with detailed written disclosures and consents all around.

> Problem 25C-5: The real estate partner in Frank's firm, Barney Blackacre, is asked by the Town of Turnkey, a small town located outside of the city in which the firm is located, to make demand and, if necessary, file suit against a neighboring town, the Village of Vanguard, to make Vanguard stop assessing and collecting property taxes on property that Turnkey claims is located in Turnkey rather than in Vanguard. Barney and the firm have no relationship with the Village of Vanguard, but both Turnkey and Vanguard are political subdivisions of the state in which they are located. Identify any possible **conflicts of interest**, and describe what (if anything) **must** or **should** be done about them. Be sure to explain your reasoning. Does your analysis change if Barney is also currently advising the Department of Real Estate of the state in which both cities are located regarding potential changes to state laws governing residential real estate closings? If so, how and why; and if not, why not?

b. Avoiding a Significant Risk of a Material Limitation on the Representation of a Government Client

Even if two engagements involving government entities are not **directly adverse** because the two government entities involved are not considered the same client for **conflict of interest** purposes, government lawyers also **must not** create **concurrent conflict** based on a "significant risk" that the representation of one or more **current clients** will be "**materially** limited" by the lawyer's responsibilities to others (*see* **Model Rule 1.7(a)(2); Chapter 22.B at 654**).

Whether or not the lawyer's representation of a government client in one matter may be "**materially** limited" by responsibilities to other government clients (or vice versa) depends on the extent to which either client could be affected by the process or the outcome of the other's matter, and on whether the lawyer's diligence or judgment on behalf of one client could be compromised by her relationship or identification with the other. This in turn may depend upon the issues at stake in a matter, the particular role the lawyer is playing in the matter and the intensity and duration of her relationship with the lawyers she is opposing.

Conflicts issues of this kind become even more difficult when the government attorney represents an individual government employee sued in her individual capacity. When a government employee is sued in her individual capacity, she is a personal target of the lawsuit. The plaintiff is seeking to recover money damages from the employee personally as opposed to (or in addition to) any separate claim against the employing agency.[6] As discussed above, when a government lawyer represents a government employee in her individual capacity, the employee is no longer merely a **constituent** of the government organization; she is the government lawyer's client, and is owed all of the duties that a lawyer owes any client. But at the same time, because a government lawyer may represent a government employee only for the purpose of protecting the **interests** of the government, the government lawyer has obligations to the employing agency, even in situations in which the agency is not itself a party to the litigation. *See* **Chapter 25.C at 915**. The potential divergence of **interests** between the government employee and her employer can cause problems similar to those that can plague the private-practice lawyer who represents both an organization and one or more of its **constituents**. *See* **Chapter 23.A at 772**.

Like any responsible private-sector lawyer embarking on a joint representation of a business organization and one or more of its **constituents** (*see* **Chapter 22.B at 656**; **Chapter 23.A at 772**), a government lawyer evaluating representation of an individual government employee must explore potential future conflicts at the very outset of the relationship. During this process, the government lawyer and the government employee must both have a clear understanding of whether preliminary discussions are **attorney-client privileged** and who controls the **attorney-client privilege**—the agency or the employee. Before the employee-client divulges any information, he or she must know whether the government lawyer can share that information with the employing agency (which the lawyer almost always expects to do). If information will be shared with the agency, the government lawyer must consider whether it is even possible to have a "full and frank" conversation with the employee client sufficient to provide a reliable basis for a **conflicts** determination.

A different potential problem arises when there are legal or factual arguments that might be justified by the record in the case that could advance the employee's case but that could harm the agency. Conversely, and of even greater concern, the lawyer must consider the possibility that the employee will be discovered to have engaged in conduct that will have to be reported to the employing agency. Having gathered the facts available at the outset (and remembering that the record

---

[6] In most such situations, it is part of the government employee's employment arrangement that the government will indemnify (pay any damages assessed against) the individual employee for any personal liability that the employee incurs for most kinds of wrongs committed in the course and scope of her employment. But the legal and practical structure of the lawsuit is a claim against the employee personally.

develops as a dispute proceeds), the government lawyer must decide whether it's possible to represent the employee-client, or whether **conflicts** between their **interests** in the conduct and outcome of the matter are too likely to allow prudent representation of the individual employee.

For example, when an agency and an employee **constituent** are both defendants, the availability of different defenses for governmental entities may render a **conflict of interest** between the two defendants inevitable. Even when the agency is not a named defendant, the government lawyer must consider potential **conflicts** between represented employees and the **interests** of the agency that are implicitly presented in the case. For example, the lawyer may be barred from raising arguments in defense of an employee that the agency disavows. (*See* Problem 25C-6 below.) This may **materially** limit the lawyer to the degree that representing the employee is no longer possible.

Notwithstanding best efforts at the outset of a representation, a government lawyer must be prepared to deal with **conflicts** that arise in the midst of an engagement. If that occurs, the lawyer must consider whether the **conflict** requires limiting or terminating representation of the individual employee. Disclosures and **informed consents** properly formulated at the outset and involving all potentially **interested** persons and organizations can simplify this issue considerably when it arises. *See* **Chapter 22.E at 745**; **Chapter 23.A at 772**. But predicting them at the outset and recognizing them when they materialize require subtle judgment and constant vigilance.

> **Problem 25C-6:** Late one night, New Garden State police officers force their way into Danica Disoriented's house to execute a search warrant. Awakened from a sound sleep, Danica stumbles toward the front door demanding to know what the heck is going on. One of the officers immediately tackles and handcuffs Danica, dislocating her shoulder in the process. It all turns out to be a case of mistaken identity: The police were at the wrong address. Danica files a civil lawsuit under **42 U.S.C. § 1983**, claiming the police officer who tackled her, Jim Plumb, used excessive force. She also claims that the New Garden State Police Department is liable for failing to promulgate internal policies and train officers regarding the proper use of force. Section 1983 provides that an individual like Danica may sue state government employees and others for violating her civil rights while acting "under color of state law." In her complaint, Danica seeks damages from both Officer Plumb (for his use of force) and from the state police department (for its policies and practices regarding use of force). Officer Plumb and the Department are represented by the same government attorney—a lawyer in the New Garden State Attorney General's office. Discovery reveals that the Department in fact had a sound policy prohibiting excessive force, that it regularly trained its officers in the use of force, and that Officer Plumb had twice before been disciplined for violating the policy. What possible **conflicts of interest** may arise for the government lawyer this case? What **must** or **should** she do to address them, and when?

D. Special Rules of Professional Conduct Uniquely Applicable to Government Lawyers

The previous section was about features of government practice that make generally applicable ethics rules difficult to apply in contexts that government lawyers regularly confront. This section focuses on special Rules of Professional Conduct and other law that, by their terms, apply uniquely to lawyers in (or formerly in) government service instead of the ordinary Rules applicable to all other lawyers.

1. Special Obligations for Government Lawyers Found Outside the Rules of Professional Conduct

As just discussed, government lawyers of course **must** follow all applicable Rules of Professional Conduct just as private-sector lawyers **must**. But in a special sense recognized in general terms by judges and other public officials, government service is unique. Everything that government lawyers do reflects on the government as a whole. Government lawyers are often in the public eye because they are public servants, whether they are elected or appointed.

For this reason, the leaders of government **practice organizations** as well as courts and other tribunals often articulate a "higher standard" of conduct that they expect from government lawyers: "A government lawyer 'is the representative not of an ordinary party to a controversy,' the Supreme Court said long ago in a statement that has been chiseled on the walls of the Justice Department, 'but of a sovereignty whose obligation . . . is not that it shall win a case, but that justice shall be done.'"[7] Although all lawyers are "officers of the court" (*see* **Chapter 24.A at 814**), you will see judges and **practice organization** leaders rely on this status more often in reference to government practitioners than in reference to other lawyers.

In addition to generally heightened scrutiny and expectations, there are a variety of specific laws (enforceable with various different **consequences** depending on the law) applicable to government lawyers that do not apply to lawyers in the private sector. These include a broad array of specialized **conflict of interest** rules, "ethics in government" laws, codes of conduct, and other personnel regulations focused on the hiring agency's areas of authority, as well as constraints generally applicable to all, or large subgroups of, government employees including lawyers. To give just one example, the Hatch Act (5 U.S.C. §§ 7321-7326), a federal law passed in 1939, limits certain political activities of many government officials and employees, including government lawyers. The Hatch Act is aimed at protecting

---

[7] *Berger v. United States*, 295 U.S. 78, 88 (1935); *see also Freeport-McMoRan Oil & Gas Co. v. FERC*, 962 F.2d 45 (D.C. Cir. 1992); *Reid v. INS*, 949 F.2d 287, 288 (9th Cir. 1991).

the nonpartisan nature of government programs as well as shielding government employees from coercion. It applies to employees of the executive branch of the federal government as well as to state and local government employees who participate in federally funded programs. The Act generally prohibits such employees from engaging in political activity while on duty, in a government room or building, while wearing an official uniform, or while using a government vehicle. Under the Hatch Act, "political activity" is defined as any activity directed toward the success or failure of a political party, candidate for partisan political office, or partisan political group. Violations of the Hatch Act can carry serious **consequences**, and may result in disciplinary action or removal from government employment.

There are also innumerable local, state, and federal laws and regulations restricting government employees' ability to seek or accept gifts—often including shared meals and similar hospitality common in the private sector—from persons or organizations having business with the agency that they serve. These laws apply generally to classes of government employees, but those classes often include government-employed lawyers. The details vary, but you will need to be familiar with every aspect of the ones that apply to you should you elect to enter government service.

Finally, depending on the jurisdiction and practice, government lawyers may have ethical or practice obligations in addition to those in the Rules of Professional Conduct. These obligations may arise from state or federal law or from government office policies and procedures. To give just one example that we'll discuss later in this chapter (*see* **Chapter 25.D at 945**), **Model Rule 3.8(d)** requires that a prosecutor disclose to the defense evidence or information known to the prosecutor that "tends to negate the guilt of the accused or mitigates the offense." This requirement includes admissible evidence that the accused could use at trial to demonstrate that the prosecution has failed to meet its burden to prove all elements of the charged crime beyond a reasonable doubt. But it does not include mere impeachment evidence—evidence that does not directly address guilt, but rather can be used to question the credibility of a prosecution witness—unless that impeachment evidence is so devastating that it creates the reasonable probability that its disclosure would change the result in the entire case.[8]

Yet the Justice Manual, a guidebook that contains the major United States Department of Justice policies and procedures pertaining to the investigation, litigation, and prosecution of violations of federal law, requires that assistant

---

[8] As you may have learned (or will learn) in your Criminal Procedure class, *Brady v. Maryland*, 373 U.S. 83, 87 (1963) and *Giglio v. United States*, 405 U.S. 150, 154 (1972) hold that **material** exculpatory evidence **must** be disclosed by the prosecution to the defense prior to trial as a matter of due process. The Supreme Court has not required as broad a disclosure of impeachment evidence. *See United States v. Ruiz*, 536 U.S. 622, 629 (2002) (no due process violation when impeachment evidence was withheld by the prosecution prior to a plea bargain); *Strickler v. Greene*, 527 U.S. 263 (1999) (limiting constitutionally mandated disclosure of impeachment material).

United States attorneys take a "broad view of **materiality** and err on the side of disclosing exculpatory *and impeaching* evidence," including information "beyond that which is '**material**' to guilt . . . ." Justice Manual § 9-5.001(B)-(C) (emphasis added). In this and many other respects, the Justice Manual requires more of federal government attorneys than the minimum that substantive law or the Rules of Professional Conduct require.

Many government **practice organizations** at all levels of government have adopted specialized guidelines similar to (if less elaborate than) the Justice Manual. The **consequences** for violation of these rules vary, but at the least would include employment **consequences** up to and including termination in appropriate cases.

2. Special Rules of Professional Conduct Governing Conflicts of Interest for Lawyers Moving from Government Work into Private Practice or Vice Versa (Sometimes Referred to as "Revolving Door" Rules)

As you'll remember from **Chapter 22.D at 701**, in private practice, there is a general rule of **imputation** for **conflicts of interest** providing that any client relationship of one member of a **practice organization** is presumed to apply to all other members of the same **practice organization**, and that **confidential information** known to one member of a **practice organization** is presumed to be known by every other member of the **practice organization**. *See* **Chapter 22.D at 702**. Often, that presumption is *conclusive*—for **conflicts** purposes, we presume that each lawyer in a **practice organization** has all of the client relationships of every other lawyer in the **practice organization**, even when those lawyers may be separated by thousands of miles (and many practice specialties) and may never have met each other's clients. Similarly, we presume **imputation** of **confidential information** within a **practice organization** without any proof that it's been disseminated, and often we won't even *consider* evidence to the contrary (no matter how persuasive). *See* **Chapter 22.D at 704**. In a few limited situations, however, we consider the presumption of **imputation** rebuttable, and we offer a lawyer or **practice organization** the opportunity to show specific facts that, in those limited circumstances, will rebut the presumption of **imputation**. When the presumption is properly rebutted, the individual lawyer with the **conflict** remains **disqualified**, but other lawyers in the **conflicted** lawyer's **practice organization** are not. *See* **Chapter 22.D at 705**. A number of those situations involve a lawyer who has changed (or is in the process of changing) jobs, and most of them involve **successive conflicts** based on **confidential information**. *See* **Chapter 22.D at 707**.

But *those* rules apply to *private-sector* **conflicts**. For current and former *government* lawyers, the **conflicts** rules are in some important respects very different. In some situations, the special **conflicts** rules applicable to current and former government lawyers are more restrictive; in others, they are less so. Most important, in determining whether a government lawyer has a **conflict of interest** that **must** be addressed, the **imputation** of **conflicts** within a current or former government lawyer's **practice organization** is substantially reduced. *See* **Model Rule 1.11 Comment [2]** ("**[Model] Rule 1.10** [which states the general rule of **imputation** and most of its exceptions] is not applicable to the **conflicts of interest** addressed by this Rule"). This creates tremendous practical differences in the way that many **conflicts of interest** are addressed when a current or former government lawyer is involved.

The relevant Rule of Professional Conduct for current and former government lawyers' **conflicts of interest** is **Model Rule 1.11**.[9] Pause and take a look. Bear in mind that it is rather long and is written in the same almost-impenetrable style of the other **conflicts** Rules that we've studied, so for now, just get a big-picture sense of the Rule's general terms and overall layout. One thing that you should notice is that this Rule applies to **conflicts of interest** that may be created by current or former service to the government not only as a practicing lawyer, but also as any other kind of "public officer or employee," so it applies to things that you did (or are doing) while you held (or hold) a law license, even if you were (or are) not necessarily acting as a lawyer. We'll get into the details below.

a. Concurrent Conflicts for Government Lawyers

For an individual lawyer in government service, **concurrent conflicts** are treated the same as they are for private-sector lawyers—you can't act adversely to a **current client**, whether that client is a private-sector client (which some lawyers who don't represent government full-time may have in addition to their government clients) or is another government agency. *See* **Model Rule 1.11(d)(1)** (a lawyer "currently serving as a public officer or employee . . . is subject to Rule[] 1.7 . . . ," which codifies the **concurrent client rule**); **Model Rule 1.11 Comments [1], [5]**; *see also* **Model Rule 1.7; Chapter 22.B at 646**.

But there is a big difference in the **imputation** of **concurrent conflicts** for government lawyers: **Concurrent conflicts** are *not* **imputed** to other members of the **conflicted** lawyer's **practice organization** as they are in the private-sector under **Model Rule 1.10(a)**. **Model Rule 1.11 Comment [2]**. What this means, as a practical matter, is that an individual government lawyer **must not** participate in an engagement adverse to a **current client** of that lawyer's, *but other lawyers in the conflicted government lawyer's practice organization may*. This Rule would allow one lawyer in (for example) a state Attorney General's office to defend a state

---

[9] There is some question about whether **Model Rule 1.11** applies only to lawyers who are or have been government officers or employees, or whether it also supplies the **conflicts** rules for private-sector lawyers who have one or more government agencies among their "book" of clients. An ABA opinion from the 1990s suggests that "a viable argument can be made" that, as to **successive conflicts of interest, Model Rule 1.11** applies only to current or former government employees or officers, while **Model Rule 1.9** addresses private-sector lawyers who have (or had) a government client or two. ABA Formal Ethics Op. No. 97-409 (1997) at 5 n.4 (construing an earlier version of **Model Rule 1.11** that is similar in the respects relevant here).

agency against claims by a private citizen, but would allow a different lawyer in the same government **practice organization** to sue that same state agency on behalf of another state agency in an unrelated matter, without any client's **informed consent**. That would obviously be impermissible in a private-sector law firm unless both clients gave **informed consent, confirmed in writing**. *See* **Chapter 22.B at 646; Chapter 22.D at 702**.

> **Problem 25D-1:** What effect, if any, would any of the following situations have on the government lawyer described and on his or her **practice organization**? Please be specific about what the lawyer and the **practice organization must, must not, may**, and **should** do, and why.

a. Pat Peterson works for the city attorney's office in Big City. Samantha is the Superintendent of the Big City School District, and Pat's office is currently defending Samantha in a civil suit alleging that Samantha failed timely to report a suspicion of child abuse by a teacher employed by the School District. Pat has no substantial or personal involvement in that case, and in fact handles only condemnation cases (in which the city government takes private land for public use, and must compensate the owner of the land).

   Samantha lives next door to Pat's sister, Pamela. Pamela is at her wit's end with Samantha. Samantha owns three large, menacing dogs that regularly terrorize the neighborhood. Then one of Samantha's dogs slips out of the house and attacks Pamela's cat. Pamela rushes the cat to the vet and spends several thousand dollars saving the cat's life. Pamela asks Pat to file suit against Samantha in civil court, seeking damages for the veterinary costs. Assuming that there are no limits generally on this type of outside employment (that is, lawyers in this city attorney's office are, by office policy, free to accept engagements from nongovernmental clients who are members of their family if they have the time and if the new nongovernmental client does not create any **disqualifying conflict of interest**), is Pat **conflicted** out of representing Pamela in this case?

b. Same as (a), except that Pat is defending Samantha in the "failure to report" case described above. Assuming again that there are no limits generally on this type of outside employment, is Pat **conflicted** out of representing Pamela in these circumstances? If there is a problem with Pat representing her sister in this situation, is there anything that Pat can do to resolve the problem? Please explain your answer.

c. Akio Advocate works for the County Counsel's office. He has handled a number of cases defending claims against the County Sheriff's Department and individual sheriff's deputies alleging excessive force, and is currently defending a case of this kind in which two individual deputies are the only named defendants. Now a whistleblower has come forward and alleged a bribery scheme in which individual officers have been accepting money to refrain from arresting and charging criminal activity. The whistleblower alleges that the officers share the "take" with the Sheriff. County Counsel (the person who heads the office) would like to investigate these charges, and would like Akio to participate in the investigation.

b. Successive Conflicts for Government Lawyers

Successive conflicts are also treated differently for current and former government lawyers than they are in private practice. The response required by a possible **successive conflict of interest** involving a current or former government lawyer depends on whether the **conflict** arises because something in that lawyer's former government service may be connected with something in the lawyer's current private practice—or, conversely, because something in the lawyer's former employment may **conflict** with something in that lawyer's current government service. We'll discuss each in turn.

i. Successive Conflicts of Interest Arising as a Result of a Move from Government Service into Private Practice

The first group of **successive conflicts** arise because of **confidential information** the potentially **conflicted** lawyer acquired in prior government service that may create a **conflict** with a new matter under consideration at the now-ex-government lawyer's private law firm. The possible **conflict must** be addressed differently based on the former government lawyer's level of involvement in and knowledge about the prior government matter while she was in government service. There are four such levels of knowledge or participation, each of which requires a different response.

(A) The Former Government Lawyer "Participated Personally and Substantially" in the Prior Government "Matter"

The most intensive level of prior involvement is met when a former government lawyer "participated personally and substantially" in a prior government "matter" currently at issue. TAMING THE TEXT What does it mean to have "participated personally and substantially" in a "matter"? The two quoted terms must each be examined separately.

Neither the Rule nor the Comments elaborate on what it means to "participate[] personally and substantially," so we should use those words in their ordinary sense. The phrase tells us that the lawyer has to have "participated" in the matter, and the participation has to have been "personal." That implies that acquiring **confidential information** by means other than personal participation—for example, by means of informal hallway conversation or hearing a presentation for informational or training purposes—would not suffice. (Notice how different this is from the usual rule, when *any* means of having obtained **confidential information** is sufficient to be **disqualifying**. *See* **Chapter 22.D at 712**.) The phrase also tells us that this personal participation has to be "substantial." That is not the most precise word, but it does connote something more significant in depth and involvement than, say, a passing consultation or a manager's general awareness of a matter within her purview.

Also critical to this highest level of involvement is that *what* the lawyer "participated [in] personally and substantially" must satisfy **Model Rule 1.11's** special definition of a "matter." To emphasize, even if a government lawyer "participated personally and substantially" in some kind of engagement, it does not qualify for this highest level of involvement, and the response that this highest level requires, unless *what* the former government lawyer participated in meets the special definition of a "matter." For purposes of this Rule alone, "matter" has a different and narrower meaning than it does in other parts of the Rules. That meaning is set out in **Model Rule 1.11(e)**—principally, "any judicial or other proceeding, application, request for a ruling or other determination, contract, claim, controversy, investigation, charge, accusation, arrest or other particular matter involving a specific party or parties . . . ."

In other words, in private practice, we think of a "matter" as a synonym for "engagement"—any definable set of services that a client can hire a lawyer to perform—but "matters" in government service are defined more narrowly, at least for purposes of determining the proper response to a possible **conflict of interest**. For **conflicts** purposes, a "matter" is narrowly defined to include only "a discrete and isolatable transaction or set of transactions between identifiable parties."[10] This would typically *exclude*, for example, policy formulation or agency rulemaking, tasks in which government lawyers are frequently involved, but that are not generally undertaken against specific persons or organizations, and instead apply to everyone within the scope of the policy or rule.[11] Individual government agencies are always free to tighten these requirements for the lawyers who serve them, of course, so **Model Rule 1.11(e)(2)** makes clear that a government agency client may promulgate **"conflict of interest** rules" binding on the government lawyers representing that agency that sweep more broadly than the specific *inter partes* matters called out in **Model Rule 1.11(e)(1)**. *See* **Model Rule 1.11 Comment [1]**. Taming the Text

If the former government lawyer "participated personally and substantially" in a "matter" during prior government service that is the same as the "matter" in connection with which the lawyer is being asked to "represent" a private client, the lawyer **must** keep all **confidential information** learned in the prior government matter secret ("is subject to **[Model] Rule 1.9(c)**"—the Rule that says you **must not** disclose or use a **former client's confidential information** except as otherwise allowed; take a quick look and remind yourself of its wording), and **must not** be personally involved in the new matter in private practice, "unless the appropriate government agency gives its **informed consent, confirmed in writing. . . .**" **Model Rule 1.11(a)**. This portion of the Rule amounts to a prohibition on switching to the private party's side in a pending government matter after working directly on the matter

---

[10] ABA Formal Ethics Op. No. 97-409 (1997) at 6 n.5 (quoting ABA Model Code of Professional Responsibility DR 9-101(B)).

[11] *Id.*

for the government, but it is broader in the sense that the private party's **interests** need not be in **conflict** with the government's **interests** for the prohibition to apply. In addition, some authorities construe what the former government lawyer is barred from doing—"represent[ing] a client"—broadly to include any professional or consulting service to the private client whether or not the lawyer contends she is acting as a lawyer.

As just noted, in a significant change from the treatment of ordinary **successive conflicts**, the new "matter" creating the **conflict** need not be adverse to the **interests** of the **former** government **client**. (Compare **Model Rule 1.9(a)**, which defines a disqualifying **conflict** with the **interests** of a private-sector **former client** as forbidden only if the new matter is, among other things, "**materially** adverse" to the **interests** of the **former client**.) This broader prohibition is "to prevent a lawyer from exploiting [prior] public office for the advantage of another client." **Model Rule 1.11 Comment [3]**. (Do you see how this feature of the Rule serves that goal? Explain it out loud. *Hint:* Imagine a situation in which a former government lawyer "participated personally and substantially" in a "matter" and now proposes to get involved in the same or a **substantially related** "matter" at her new private firm in a way that is not adverse to the lawyer's former government employer. How could this arrangement give someone an unfair advantage?)

Although the former government lawyer who "participated personally and substantially" in the prior government "matter" is *personally* **disqualified** from working on the new matter at her new private firm, the lawyer's private **practice organization** and its other lawyers may take on the new connected matter if "(1) the disqualified [former government] lawyer is timely **screened** from any participation in the matter and is apportioned no part of the fee therefrom; and (2) written notice is promptly given to the appropriate government agency to enable it to ascertain compliance with the provisions of this rule." **Model Rule 1.11(b)**.

The steps that comprise a proper **ethical screen** are discussed in **Chapter 22.D at 716**. TIPS & TACTICS It's not clear how many of the common features of an **ethical screen** beyond those specifically called out in **Model Rule 1.11(b)** (namely, no apportionment of fees from the **screened** matter to the **screened** lawyer and notice to the former government client; *see* **Chapter 22.D at 718**) are required to avoid either discipline or the various civil **consequences** available for inadequately addressed **conflicts of interest. Model Rule 1.11 Comment [6]** refers to the definition of "**screen**" in **Model Rule 1.0(k)**, which dictates **screening** requirements no more specifically than "the isolation of a lawyer from any participation in a matter through the timely imposition of procedures within a [**practice organization**] that are reasonably adequate under the circumstances to protect information that the isolated lawyer is obligated to protect under these Rules or other law." Given the drastic **consequences** of an improperly addressed **conflict of interest** (*see* **Chapter 22 at 603** to remind yourself how big a world of hurt that can be), erring on the side of including as many commonly used **screening** features as reasonably practicable is the prudent course. *See* **Chapter 22.D at 716**. Tips & Tactics

(B) The Former Government Lawyer Did Not "Participate[] Personally and Substantially" in a Connected "Matter," but Obtained "Confidential Government Information" During Former Government Service That May Be Used by the Private Client Against a Third Party

The next-less-intensive level of involvement in a government "matter" is that a former government lawyer did not "participate[] personally and substantially" in a prior "matter" while in government service, but did obtain "confidential government information." What's more, that "confidential government information" has to be usable by a private client against a third party (other than the lawyer's former government employer). **Model Rule 1.11(c)**. Let's break that down.

Taming the Text "Confidential *government* information" is not the same as the **confidential information** generally protected by the **duty of confidentiality** and **Model Rule 1.6**, **Model Rule 1.9**, and **Model Rule 1.18**. It is a much narrower category of knowledge gained in government service that includes *only* "information that has been obtained under governmental authority and which, at the time this Rule is applied, the government is prohibited by law from disclosing to the public or has a legal privilege not to disclose and which is not otherwise available to the public." In other words, although **confidential information** includes anything you've learned in the course of representing the client from any source unless it's "generally known" (*see* **Chapter 8.A at 214**), "confidential government information" really has to be a legally protected government secret. An example of "confidential government information" would be the fact that an individual had secretly been under government investigation in a matter that never (or had not yet) eventuated in charges, or was currently subject to an as-yet unsealed indictment.

In addition, that "confidential government information" triggers this level of involvement only if it could be used to the disadvantage of a third party (not the former government client, and not the new private client) whose **interests** are adverse to those of the new private client. Taming the Text

If the former government lawyer did not "participate[] personally and substantially" in a relevant "matter" during prior government service, but did acquire "confidential government information" pertinent to a new matter that can be used "to the **material** disadvantage" of the new private **client's** adversary, then the former government lawyer is again personally **disqualified** from involvement in the matter, but once again other lawyers in her private **practice organization may** take on the new matter "if the **disqualified** lawyer is timely **screened** from any participation in the matter and is apportioned no part of the fee therefrom." **Model Rule 1.11(c)**. Tips & Tactics As with the screen required by substantial personal participation, it's not clear how many of the common features of an **ethical screen** beyond those specifically called out in this portion of the Rule are required to avoid **consequences**. **Model Rule 1.11(c)** mentions only that no part of the fees from the **screened** matter may be apportioned to the **screened** lawyer. Notice is not mentioned, which doesn't necessary mean that it is not required, despite the textual difference from **Model Rule 1.11(b)(2)**. *See* **Chapter 22.D at 718**. Again, prudence dictates adopting as many **screening** measures as reasonably feasible. TIPS & TACTICS

(C) The Former Government Lawyer Did Not "Participate[] Personally and Substantially" in a Prior "Matter," But Does Have Personal Knowledge of Some Confidential Information About It That Is Not "Confidential Government Information"

The next-less-intensive involvement level after that is that the government lawyer did not "participate[] personally and substantially" in a prior "matter," or did participate in any way up to and including "personally and substantially" in something that did not amount to a "matter" (for example, agency rulemaking), but does have personal knowledge of some **confidential information** that is not "confidential government information." In this case, in a significant deviation from the regular **conflicts** rules, not only does the former government lawyer not need to be **screened** from the new law firm's engagement (though some private **practice organizations** may **screen** the former government lawyer anyway as a matter of prudence), but neither the former government lawyer nor any other lawyer in her private **practice organization** is **disqualified**. *See* **Model Rule 1.11 Comment [4]** ("a former government lawyer is **disqualified** only from particular matters in which the lawyer participated personally and substantially").

Notice how different this approach is from the regular **conflicts** rules, which would at a minimum require a timely and effective **screen** of the individual lawyer with **confidential information** from former employment. *Cf.* **Model Rule 1.10(a)(2)**; **Chapter 22.D at 721**. The former government lawyer must of course still adhere to all her **confidentiality** obligations under **Model Rule 1.9(c)**. Thus the former government lawyer is forbidden from using any **confidential information** that she may have acquired in her former government service to the former government client's disadvantage, or from disclosing the **confidential information** to anyone. If the former government lawyer can't be personally involved without disclosing or using the **confidential information** in the new private matter, then she **must** refrain from personal involvement. *See* ABA Formal Ethics Op. No 97-409 (1997) at 12-15.

(D) The Former Government Lawyer Had No Involvement in or Knowledge About the Relevant Former Government Matter

The least intensive level of involvement is (unsurprisingly) no involvement at all: The government lawyer neither participated in nor personally knows any

confidential information about the prior matter. This one is easy: If the former government lawyer has no relevant **confidential information** or "confidential government information" from the prior government matter, no **conflict of interest** is presented, and no response is required. This result is the same as the one under the regular **conflicts** rules.

> Problem 25D-2: What effect, if any, would each lawyer's former government service have on his or her current private firm's involvement in each matter described? Please be specific about what the lawyer and the firm **must, must not, may,** and **should** do, and why.
>
> a. When Molly Municipal worked in the City Attorney's office, she oversaw a major revision of the city's building code, which the City Council eventually adopted. Recently, Molly moved to a local law firm's real estate and land use department. One of the firm's clients is a local developer that has been constructing a substantial new hotel and conference center in town. Now the facility is nearly complete, but the city's Bureau of Building Inspection has significant concerns about the structural integrity of the building and its compliance with the revised building code. The Bureau has refused to issue the Certificate of Occupancy necessary to open and operate the facility that the property owner has spent years and millions of dollars developing. The client would like the firm to seek to persuade the city that the facility is in compliance with the building code, and if that fails then to initiate litigation requiring the city to issue the Certificate of Occupancy. The client would like Molly to take the lead on the engagement. Would your analysis change if the client merely wanted Molly to consult with the firm's lawyers who have already been working on the project? If so, how and why; and if not, why not?
>
> b. Same as (a), except that, in addition to overseeing the revision of the city's building code, while she was in the City Attorney's office Molly handled a few pieces of litigation on behalf of the city enforcing various aspects of the new code.
>
> c. Same as (b), except that, in addition, while Molly was in the City Attorney's office, she consulted with inspectors at the city's Bureau of Building Inspection regarding the application of the new building code to the developer's hotel and conference center.
>
> d. Demitri's sons were expelled from public school. Demitri hired two attorneys, Mary and Susan, to sue the school district and force it to reinstate the children. Both lawyers had previously been staff attorneys for the school district. Before switching to private practice, Mary had spent over a decade as a supervisor reviewing the work of line staff attorneys representing the school district in expulsion hearings and related litigation. Some of those expulsions had been made on grounds very much like the ones that the school district had applied to Demitri's sons. She was also involved in policy matters, helping to develop internal rules and guidelines to streamline and implement the expulsion procedure. Before switching to private practice, Susan had reported to Mary. Susan had not represented the school district in any expulsion hearings or litigation. Rather, she defended the district in employment-related claims brought against the district by

teachers and staff. Susan had been a staff attorney for only a few years before leaving government work. Are Susan and Mary **conflicted** out of representing Demitri? Why and how might the analysis differ for each lawyer?[12]

ii. Successive Conflicts of Interest Arising as a Result of a Move from Private Practice into Government Service (or from One Government Job to a Different Government Job)

Model Rule 1.11(d) addresses **conflicts of interest** for current government lawyers differently from those of former government lawyers, and also differently (in some respects, at least) from private-sector **conflicts**.[13]

As a starting point, **Model Rule 1.11(d)(1)** states plainly that current government lawyers are "subject to Rule[] . . . 1.9."[14] You are already an authority on **conflicts** under **Model Rule 1.9**, having absorbed the details of **Chapter 22.C at 678**. In honor of your perseverance into the penultimate chapter of this book (for which you have earned our great respect), here's a quick recap of the highlights:

- You have a continuing **duty of confidentiality** after an engagement ends not to use or disclose a **former client's confidential information** unless the **former client** authorizes it, the **confidential information** becomes "generally known," or there is another available exception to the **duty of confidentiality**. **Model Rule 1.9(c)**; **Chapter 8.A at 224**.

- Under the **successive client rule**, when a lawyer has a **duty of confidentiality** to anyone (whether a **prospective client**, **current client**, **former client**, or someone else), the lawyer **must not** take on or continue an engagement in which the lawyer might reasonably be able to use any **confidential information** protected by that **duty of confidentiality** against the person to whom the lawyer owes that **duty of confidentiality**. **Model Rule 1.9(a)**; **Chapter 22.C at 679**.

- That prohibition extends not only to **confidential information** that you've learned in your own client engagements, but to any **confidential information** to which you were actually exposed in previous employment in matters in which you did not personally participate. **Model Rule 1.9(b)**; **Chapter 22.D at 709**.

All of these Rules are fully applicable to a lawyer currently serving in government, just as they are to all lawyers in private practice.

---

[12] *See Dugar v. Bd. of Educ.*, Dist. 299, NO. 92 C 1621, 1992 U.S. Dist. LEXIS 8650 (N.D. Ill. June 17, 1992).

[13] The alert student, looking puzzled, is wondering whether, when a lawyer leaves one government job for a job with a different government agency, her **conflicts** in the new government job are governed by **Model Rule 1.11(a)**, which refers to "a lawyer who has formerly served as a public officer or employee," or **Model Rule 1.11(d)**, which refers to "a lawyer currently serving as a public officer or employee." Because the lawyer was formerly at one government job and now is at another, both descriptions apply. (Do you see why?) **Model Rule 1.11 Comment [5]** says that this situation is governed by **Model Rule 1.11(d)**. The answer that the Comment provides is clear, even though the Rule itself is anything but.

[14] **Model Rule 1.11(d)(1)** also says that current government lawyers are "subject to Rule[] 1.7." In other words, current government lawyers are personally subject to the **concurrent client rule**. But you knew that already. *See* **Chapter 25.D at 928**.

In addition, a current government lawyer **must not** "participate in a matter in which the lawyer participated personally and substantially while in private practice or nongovernmental employment, unless the appropriate government agency gives its **informed consent, confirmed in writing**." **Model Rule 1.11(d)(2)(i).** TAMING THE TEXT Let's break that down: After having left private practice or other nongovernmental employment for government service, you **must not** be involved ("participate") in any "matter" (in that special sense applicable to government lawyers described above, *see* **Chapter 25.D at 931**) in your government job in which you previously "participated personally and substantially" (another phrase discussed above, *see* **Chapter 25.D at 930**) in your nongovernmental job.

The alert student, eyes aglow, is wondering what this provision adds to the prohibition already stated in **Model Rule 1.9(a)** and **Model Rule 1.11(d)(1)** just discussed. (The alert student remembers that we usually assume that a rule or statute is not intended to be redundant and, having studied **Model Rule 1.9(a)** and **Model Rule 1.11(d)(2)(i)**, has noticed that **Model Rule 1.11(d)(2)(i)** seems to prohibit the same things that **Model Rule 1.9(a)** already forbids. Now that the alert student has pointed it out, can you see the overlap?) Outstanding question! If you look at **Model Rule 1.9(a)** closely, however, you will see that the **successive client rule** that it articulates prohibits a lawyer from using a former client's **confidential information** only *against* the **interests** of that **former client** ("in the same or a **substantially related** matter in which [a new client's] interests are *materially* adverse to the interests of the **former client**" (emphasis added)). **Model Rule 1.11(d)(2)(i)** takes that concept a step further and adds that, as to any "matter" in which you "participated personally and substantially" in nongovernmental employment, you can't participate in that "matter" while in government service *under any circumstances*, even if you believe that you will be acting for the government in a manner that will *advance* your **former client's interests**. TAMING THE TEXT REASON FOR THE RULE The reason that **Model Rule 1.11(d)(2)(i)** forbids the government lawyer's participation in the same matter even when it is not adverse to the government lawyer's **former client** is to mitigate "the risk . . . that power or discretion vested in [the government lawyer's] agency might be used for the special benefit of the [government lawyer's **former] client**"—that is, to guard against abuse of (or the temptation to abuse) government power *in favor of* as well as *against* the government lawyer's **former client**. **Model Rule 1.11 Comment [4]**; *see also* **Model Rule 1.11 Comment [3]**. REASON FOR THE RULE

Although **Model Rule 1.11(d)** broadens the scope of the "matters" in which the government lawyer is personally **disqualified**, it also significantly narrows the effects of that personal disqualification. Unlike private-sector **conflicts**, there is no **imputation** of the government lawyer's **conflict** to other members of the government **practice organization**, and there is no requirement that the personally **disqualified** government lawyer be **screened** to rebut the presumption, either. **Model Rule 1.11 Comment [2]** confirms that **screening** a government lawyer personally **disqualified** under **Model Rule 1.11(d)(2)** is not required, but suggests that **screening** would be "prudent."

> **Problem 25D-3:** What effect, if any, would each lawyer's former employment have on his own or his government employer's involvement in each matter described? Please be specific about what the lawyer and the firm **must**, **must not**, **may**, and **should** do, and why.
>
> a. A commercial developer applied to the municipal zoning board for a construction permit. Another developer, Skyline, objected. Lawyer Michael, an attorney in private practice, represented Skyline at the zoning board hearings. Ultimately, the permit was issued over Skyline's objections. Skyline appealed. While the appeal was pending, Michael was hired by the City Attorney's office. He withdrew from representing Skyline in the appeal. Can he now represent the city in Skyline's appeal? Why or why not? Now suppose that Michael (having moved to the City Attorney's office) has **recused** himself from any involvement in the appeal on behalf of either Skyline or the city. Could Michael still supervise the government attorney directly handling Skyline's appeal on behalf of the city?
>
> b. Same as (a), except that, under the city's ordinances, Michael's signature is necessary for any settlement with Skyline to be valid and enforceable against the city. Assuming that Michael had no **material** involvement in any litigation or settlement negotiations after joining the City Attorney's office, could he sign off on a settlement resolving the appeal? Why or why not?[15]
>
> c. Same as (a), except that Skyline's engagement was handled by another lawyer at Michael's firm, and Michael never had any personal involvement in representing Skyline while he was in private practice. **May** Michael represent the City in Skyline's appeal? Why or why not?

c. Conflicts Created as Government Lawyers Leave Government Service

Although many lawyers devote whole careers to government service, many more cycle into and out of government practice at different points in their careers, some more than once. That's one reason why these special **conflict of interest** rules for current and former government lawyers exist, and why they're sometimes referred to as "revolving door" rules.

One of the "revolving door" rules is focused specifically on the personal **interests** that may complicate a government lawyer's practice when she is *preparing* to leave government service. Many lawyers take the specialized knowledge of particular areas of government practice they have acquired during their years of government service, and offer it to private law firms for the benefit of their clients, or directly to private clients. There is, of course, nothing intrinsically wrong with this kind of employment change, so long as no **confidential information** or "confidential government information" is compromised after the switch; that's the reason for the Rules we just discussed.

---

[15] *See Kane Props., LLC v. City of Hoboken*, 214 N.J. 199, 68 A.3d 1274 (2013).

But because a government lawyer is likely to address the same subjects and government agencies in private practice that she did in government service, a particular kind of personal-**interest conflict** may develop as a government lawyer prepares to move to the private-sector. Specifically, the government lawyer may be inclined to work for the people and organizations that do business with the government agency she currently serves, or the private law firms that represent them, because they are most likely to be interested in the expertise that the lawyer has acquired in government service. This situation can create the temptation to curry favor with a possible future employer or client with a matter pending before the lawyer's government client in order to pave the way for the lawyer's switch to private practice.

To address this concern, **Model Rule 1.11(d)(2)(ii)** forbids any lawyer currently in government service from "negotiat[ing] for private employment with any person who is involved as a party or as lawyer for a party in a matter in which the lawyer is participating personally and substantially . . . ." The alert student (we knew you were still there!) correctly points out that this is just a specific instance of **Model Rule 1.7(a)(2)** — a **conflict of interest** that arises when a lawyer's personal **interest** creates a "significant risk" of "**materially** limit[ing]" a client's (here, the current government client's) representation. As the alert student still recalls from **Chapter 22.A at 629** and **Problem 22A-6(i) at 632**, the same concerns are addressed by the general terms of **Model Rule 1.7(a)(2)** when a lawyer in private practice may be negotiating to move from one law firm to another, or to an in-house law department, that is currently an adversary in a pending matter. This is an example of a specific Rule drafted to supplement a more general one and address a commonly recurring problem with special focus. (Do you see why?)

Model Rule 1.11(d)(2)(ii) also contains a special exception for law clerks serving judges or other adjudicators. Because many law-clerk positions are designed to be temporary one- or two-year positions that benefit both the judge and the law clerk, and because most law clerks work under very close supervision (the judge is, after all, the decider, and most take that role quite seriously), law clerks may negotiate for private employment while in government employment under the much more modest restrictions of **Model Rule 1.12(b)**. That Rule allows law clerks to "negotiate for employment with a party or lawyer involved in a matter in which the clerk is participating personally and substantially, but only after the lawyer has notified the judge or other adjudicative officer." REAL WORLD Many courts and individual judges have their own special restrictions regarding their law clerks' private employment negotiations that are more strict than **Model Rule 1.12(b)**, so if you have the good fortune to work as a judicial law clerk (a position that many lawyers will tell you is the best job you'll ever have, much as we hate to think of you peaking so early), check what your court and your judge want you to do before sending out any resumés.[16] REAL WORLD

> **Problem 25D-4:** Take another look at **Problem 22A-6(a) at 631 & n.24.** Read the short news stories linked in the footnote. Explain what the government lawyer described in the problem and the news stories actually did, and what Model Rule(s), if any, his conduct violated. Identify any **consequences** that the lawyer risked or suffered, and explain on what basis they were (or were not) imposed. Then describe what (if anything) the lawyer **must** or **should** have done differently, and why.

> **Problem 25D-5:** A classmate of Danielle's, Claretta Clerk, is finishing a two-year clerkship with federal district judge Grumpador B. Cranky. She's interested in applying for a position at two or three firms in the area that regularly appear in the local federal district court, and that often have one or more matters pending before Judge Cranky. Claretta has not yet taken the bar exam, and she reasons that because she is not yet a licensed lawyer, she is not subject to the Rules of Professional Conduct. As a result, she does not inform Judge Cranky about the employment applications that she's sending to the firms that interest her, and does not discover that the judge has a policy (one not uncommon among sitting judges) of not allowing law clerks to work on matters involving **practice organizations** or parties to which the clerk has applied for (or accepted an offer of) employment. What **consequences** (if any) might Claretta be subject to? What (if anything) **must** or **should** she have done differently, and why?

3. Rules of Professional Conduct Delineating the Special Role and Duties of Prosecutors

Generally, prosecutors are subject to the same rules and other law as all other lawyers. They must concern themselves with **competence**, **diligence**, **confidentiality**, **conflicts of interest**, and all the other topics you've covered in this course. But in addition, prosecutors are the only category of government attorneys subject to their own special Rule of Professional Conduct: **Model Rule 3.8** creates a number of ethical obligations for prosecutors that are different from or additional to those applicable to all other lawyers.

Why are prosecutors treated differently? The stakes are high in criminal cases, both for the defendants and for the legitimacy of the system as a whole, so integrity is essential to the administration of criminal justice. The government's power to take away an individual's property, liberty, and even life must

---

[16] In the federal judiciary, the Code of Conduct for Judicial Employees ("CCJE") takes a similar approach: Before seeking post-clerkship employment, "the law clerk or staff attorney should first consult with the appointing authority and observe any restrictions imposed by the appointing authority. If any law firm, lawyer, or entity with whom a law clerk or staff attorney has been employed or is seeking or has obtained future employment appears in any matter pending before the appointing authority, the law clerk or staff attorney should promptly bring this fact to the attention of the appointing authority." **CCJE § 320 Canon 4 § C.4.**

be exercised with great care. And unlike defense lawyers, whose professional responsibility is focused on their clients alone, prosecutors represent the interests of the public. ("Danielle Dutton for the People, Your Honor.")

Ordinarily, our adversary system asks nothing more of counsel than zealous advocacy within the limits of the law, and it depends on the process to sort truth and justice out of the fray. Prosecutors, however, don't have this luxury. They must do the "right thing," even when it may hurt their case. Prosecutors must of course pursue the guilty with every bit as much zeal as any other advocate, but also must always be mindful of the need to temper their zeal with justice when circumstances require. Sometimes the just outcome is dropped charges, an acquittal, or a confession of error on appeal, and a prosecutor must never prioritize professional ambitions (or the procedural equivalent of bloodlust) above securing justice.

References to the American prosecutor as a minister of justice date back at least to the nineteenth century and continue today.[17] Canon 5 of the 1908 American Bar Association Canons of Professional Ethics (*see* **Chapter 3.A at 30**) stated that "[t]he primary duty of a lawyer engaged in public prosecution is not to convict, but to see that justice is done." ABA Model Code of Professional Responsibility EC 7-13 (*see* **Chapter 3.A at 31**) also emphasized this difference between prosecutors and other lawyers. And the principle remains alive and well today: The **ABA Criminal Justice Standards for the Prosecution Function** ("Crim. Just. Stds."), a set of guidelines widely relied on for ethical direction and affirmatively adopted into some states' laws, reiterates in **Crim. Just. Std. 3-1.2(b)** that "[t]he primary duty of the prosecutor is to seek justice within the bounds of the law, not merely to convict." *See also* **Model Rule 3.8 Comment [1]**.

A prosecutor's special ethical obligations pervade every stage of a criminal case. **Model Rule 3.8's** eight subsections each identify a juncture in the criminal process when a prosecutor may have to make decisions favoring justice over simply winning. Many of these principles may seem self-evident in the abstract, but they present challenges when they must be applied to incomplete and uncertain facts, as they often must be.

a. Charging Only Those Defendants and Crimes for Which the Prosecutor Has a Proper Legal and Factual Basis

Model Rule 3.8(a) requires a prosecutor to "refrain from prosecuting a charge that the prosecutor knows is not supported by probable cause." This requirement seems obvious—what blow could be more foul than charging someone with a crime when it's clear that the evidence necessary to prove it is insufficient? But

---

[17] *See, e.g., Hurd v. People*, 25 Mich. 405, 416 (1872) ("The prosecuting officer represents the public interest, which can never be promoted by the conviction of the innocent. His object like that of the court, should be simply justice; and he has no right to sacrifice this to any pride of professional success").

how does a prosecutor "know" what evidence is (or eventually might be) available to support charging a case? And how does a prosecutor know that the evidence is sufficient?

There are no bright-line rules that expressly tell prosecutors when they should charge defendants and when they should not; no bright-line rules are possible. Nor are charging decisions generally subject to judicial review (other than in extreme cases). For these reasons, prosecutorial discretion must be exercised even more carefully when it comes to charging decisions than in other more regulated areas of criminal practice. Because one of the most significant responsibilities of a prosecutor is the exercise of discretion in deciding which crimes to charge (or whether to charge at all), prosecutorial discretion in charging decisions is the subject of the first subsection of **Model Rule 3.8**.

Remember, **Model Rule 3.8(a)** says a prosecutor **must** "refrain from prosecuting a charge that the prosecutor knows is not supported by probable cause." So what is "probable cause?" This is a matter of substantive law more properly the subject of your Criminal Procedure course, but let's address it briefly. Probable cause is a legal standard that requires prosecutors to reasonably believe, on a rational and factual basis, that a crime was committed, and that the accused committed it, before bringing charges. But even with this limitation, prosecutors have considerable power to choose which, and how many, crimes to charge.

The **ABA Criminal Justice Standards for the Prosecution Function** has an entire section devoted to investigation and charging decisions (Part IV) that identifies factors that a prosecutor **should** consider before charging or continuing the prosecution of a crime. **Crim. Just. Std. 3-4.4(a)** includes (among numerous others):

- the prosecutor's reasonable doubt that the accused is guilty (taking into account whether admissible evidence will be sufficient to support conviction beyond a reasonable doubt, *see* **Crim. Just. Std. 3-4.3(a)**);
- the extent of the harm caused by the offense;
- whether the authorized or likely punishment (or other collateral effects) is disproportionate to the harm caused by the offense;
- any improper motives of victims or complaining witnesses;
- whether the accused is cooperating with law enforcement towards the apprehension of others;
- the possible influence of any cultural, ethnic, socioeconomic, or other improper biases; and
- whether another jurisdiction will prosecute the offense (some crimes can be prosecuted in either the federal or state systems, or both).

The same standard (**Crim. Just. Std. 3-4.4(b)**) emphasizes that prosecutors making charging decisions **should not** consider:

- partisan or other improper political or personal considerations;
- prejudice based upon race, sex, religion, national origin, disability, age, sexual orientation, gender identity, or socioeconomic status (*see* **Crim. Just. Std. 3-1.6(a)**); or
- personal animus.

Charging decisions are highly factual and situationally dependent, and they are not always easy. But the decision not to charge or indict can be the right choice when the merits are in doubt, and even in some situations in which there may be probable cause to believe that the potential defendant committed a crime. Where resources are scant, it may not be possible to litigate all meritorious cases. Some issues may be better left for the interested parties to sort out in the civil justice system. Nor are all cases meritorious, and it is incumbent upon the prosecutor to ensure that nonmeritorious cases are stopped in their tracks. On the other hand, prosecutors should not be afraid to indict, and to charge fully, in cases that merit it and where resources support it. The decision is a balancing act, sometimes on a high-wire.

Problem 25D-6: Danielle's colleague in the DA's Office, Marnie, has been waiting for weeks for a forensic analysis to be returned so that she can file a criminal information (that is, a criminal complaint that is sometimes used to initiate a prosecution) against a particular defendant charging him with robbery. There are no eyewitnesses, and the video surveillance footage is inconclusive. The robbery is similar to several others to which the defendant pled guilty in the past, and the police recovered a partial fingerprint from the scene that is being compared to known exemplars from the defendant. Filing the criminal information is the last thing that Marnie needs to do before she can leave on vacation. She is fairly confident that the fingerprint will be a match for the defendant's print, but until the analysis is back, she won't know for sure. Can she file the complaint now and agree to drop the charges after her vacation if the print is not a match?

Problem 25D-7: Danielle's office keeps statistics on each deputy district attorney, ranking them in various categories, including the number and type of cases charged. Danielle's supervisor hands her a file and asks her to draft an information. Danielle reviews the file. The evidence currently available supports, at best, one charge of "snatch and grab" robbery against the defendant. But the police note that the well-supported charge bears some similarities to four other recent robberies, with which the police recommend also charging the defendant. Danielle knows it will improve her "stats" (and improve the police's "clearance" record, which they would appreciate) if she charges all five robberies, even though the evidence tying the defendant to the other four robberies is, at least at this point in the investigation, tenuous. **Must** Danielle charge all five robberies as the police recommend, reasoning that evidence could be found later to support the charges (notwithstanding that the evidence is currently absent or weak)? **May** she? **Should** she?

b. Assuring That the Defendant Has a Fair Opportunity to Exercise Pretrial Constitutional and Other Procedural Rights

The next three subsections of **Model Rule 3.8** address times during the litigation of a criminal case when a prosecutor might benefit unfairly from having disproportionately greater knowledge and power than the accused. We'll address each in turn.

i. Right to Counsel

Model Rule 3.8(b) provides that a prosecutor **must** "make reasonable efforts to assure that the accused has been advised of the right to, and the procedure for obtaining, counsel and has been given reasonable opportunity to obtain counsel." This requirement is an essential part of the prosecutor's role in ensuring the integrity of the judicial process. The *Miranda* admonition upon arrest that the accused has a right to a lawyer, and that if he cannot afford one, then one will be appointed for him by the court, is just the beginning of ensuring the accused's right to counsel. You may be asking why it's the ethical responsibility of the accused's opposing counsel to ensure that the accused is aware of and able to exercise his right to a lawyer. After all, lawyers other than prosecutors have a duty not to give legal advice, other than the advice to seek counsel, to an unrepresented person, and **may** refrain from giving any advice at all (*see* **Model Rule 4.3**; **Chapter 12.A at 379**). But the prosecutor is a minister of justice and a guardian of the integrity of the criminal process. As such, the prosecutor's responsibility is not to give the defendant advice, but rather to ensure that it is available. Generally, the court explains to the accused how to apply for court-appointed counsel, but the prosecutor can't sit idly by if the court doesn't do so. In this regard, the prosecutor is a safety net, ensuring that justice is done by the other participants in the process.

ii. "Important Pretrial Rights"

Model Rule 3.8(c) prohibits a prosecutor from "seek[ing] to obtain from an unrepresented accused a waiver of important pretrial rights, such as the right to a preliminary hearing."[18] An accused, whether represented or not, will have many important decisions to make throughout a criminal case. These include whether to waive constitutional and other procedural rights and whether to plead guilty

---

[18] For those who have not yet studied pretrial criminal procedure, a preliminary hearing is a procedural right furnished to a criminal defendant in the federal system under **Fed. R. Crim. P. 5.1**, and in virtually all state systems by rule or statute, to a hearing in which the prosecution **must** present evidence (in many jurisdictions under modified or relaxed rules of evidence) sufficient to persuade a judge that there is probable cause to believe that a crime was committed and that the defendant committed it. The defendant has a right to counsel at such a hearing, and that counsel is entitled to cross-examine witnesses and may (but is not required to) introduce evidence on the defendant's behalf. The defendant has a right to such a hearing in many circumstances, but may waive that right, and often does so. **Model Rule 3.8(c)** is intended to help ensure that any such waiver is appropriately knowing and voluntary.

(which involves waiver of numerous constitutional and other rights, such as the right to indictment, to a preliminary hearing, to a jury trial, and sometimes to appeal).

When a criminal defendant is represented, his lawyer can explain all the rights available to the accused and the pros and cons of waiving them in exchange for something offered by the government, such as a guilty plea to a lesser charge in return for truthful cooperation with the prosecution regarding other parties. But a prosecutor **must not** pressure, advise, or induce the acceptance of a plea or the waiver of the right to counsel (or any other substantial right) after an unrepresented accused has been informed of the right to counsel and is deciding whether to invoke (or has initiated the process to invoke) that right. Even asking an unrepresented accused if she wishes to waive the right to counsel or accept a plea is improper if it is clear from the circumstances that the accused does not understand the consequences. Independent legal advice may be necessary to clarify any such misunderstanding and, consistent with **Model Rules 3.8(b) and (c)**, and as required by **Model Rule 4.3** (*see* **Chapter 12.A at 379**), a prosecutor is precluded from offering legal advice other than the advice to seek counsel.

In fact, because guilty pleas are such an overwhelmingly prevalent means of resolving charges in the criminal justice system, the Supreme Court has included them among the "critical phases" of the criminal process during which the accused has a constitutional right to **effective assistance of counsel** (*see* **Chapter 7.C at 184**),[19] and the ABA has promulgated special prosecutorial standards for plea bargaining. **Crim. Just. Stds. 3-5.6 to 8.** Although waiving constitutional or other rights, including the right to trial, may ultimately be in the accused's best interest, **Model Rule 3.8(c)** ensures that these decisions are made only after the accused has been properly informed of and has considered the consequences of waiving his rights by either his counsel or the court.

iii. Right to Timely Disclosure of Exculpatory and Mitigating Evidence

Model Rule 3.8(d) ensures a level playing field by requiring the "timely disclosure to the defense of all evidence or information known to the prosecutor that tends to negate the guilt of the accused or mitigates the offense, and, in connection with sentencing, disclose to the defense and to the tribunal all unprivileged mitigating information known to the prosecutor," unless the tribunal orders otherwise. TAMING THE TEXT "Timely" means early enough in the proceedings so that the accused can make effective use of the information.

How exculpatory or mitigating must evidence in the prosecutor's possession be before it must be disclosed? This is not always an easy call, and the constitutional and ethical standards are different. Under the Due Process Clauses of the Fifth and

---

[19] *Missouri v. Frye*, 566 U.S. 134 (2012); *Lafler v. Cooper*, 566 U.S. 156 (2012).

Fourteenth Amendments, the evidence must be "**material**," which the United States Supreme Court has defined in this context as presenting a "reasonable probability" that its disclosure would have changed the result of the proceeding.[20]

However, **Model Rule 3.8(d)** "is more demanding than the constitutional case law, in that it requires the disclosure of evidence or information favorable to the defense without regard to the anticipated effect of the evidence or information on a trial's outcome. The rule thereby requires prosecutors to steer clear of the constitutional line, erring on the side of caution." ABA Formal Ethics Op. No. 09-454 (2009). The Rule thus seeks to avoid the kind of "what if" speculation required by the constitutional standard that exculpatory or mitigating evidence **must** be disclosed only if it presents a reasonable probability of changing the result in the case, and it reduces the inquiry to the simpler question of whether the evidence "tends to" weigh to *any* degree against guilt, or mitigate the offense or punishment (that is, to make the alleged crime less serious or blameworthy) in any way.

As discussed above, the standard for required disclosure of impeachment material under the Constitution and the Rule is more demanding than it is for exculpatory or mitigating material: The Constitution requires "**materiality**"—that is, impeachment so devastating that it creates a reasonable probability of a different result in the case; and **Model Rule 3.8(d)** by its terms applies only to material that "tends to negate the guilt of the accused or mitigate the offense," and thus impeachment material is not subject to mandatory disclosure unless it meets the constitutional standard. ⟨ TAMING THE TEXT ⟩

In addition, the Rule acknowledges, and at least arguably encourages, an opportunity for prosecutors to obtain the court's guidance or protection of vulnerable third parties. **Model Rule 3.8(d)** says that exculpatory and mitigating material **must** be disclosed to the defense "except when the prosecutor is relieved of this responsibility by a protective order of the tribunal." Such guidance may be sought, under seal or *in camera* as appropriate, in close cases or "if disclosure of information to the defense could result in substantial harm to an individual or to the public interest." **Model Rule 3.8 Comment [3]**. Even if an appellate court later finds that the trial court's protective order was in error and the protected material had to be disclosed, the prosecutor would have satisfied her ethical obligations by asking for and receiving the trial court's permission not to disclose.

> **Problem 25D-8:** Danielle appears for a preliminary hearing in an assault case. The defendant is not represented by counsel. The case is assigned to a relatively new judge, who forgets to notify the defendant of his right to counsel. After the preliminary hearing, the defendant approaches Danielle asking whether she might entertain a plea agreement. What should Danielle do?

---

[20] *United States v. Bagley*, 473 U.S. 667, 682 (1985); *Giglio v. United States*, 405 U.S. 150, 154 (1972); *Brady v. Maryland*, 373 U.S. 83, 87 (1963).

Problem 25D-9: Danielle's colleague in the DA's Office, Marnie, is prosecuting a retail theft charge against a defendant who stole clothing from a store at the mall. The defendant has three prior retail theft convictions, and Marnie prosecuted one of them. The defendant has refused to accept representation from the public defender and has not retained his own counsel. Marnie walks by the defendant sitting on a bench outside the courtroom. He is waiting outside for his preliminary hearing. "Are we really going to do this?" Marnie says to him. "It's a waste of time. You were caught red-handed, and you know that the evidence is overwhelming. Making me call the security guard to testify at this hearing isn't going to change anything." Is there anything that Marnie should have done differently? If so, what and why; and if not, why not?

Problem 25D-10: Return to the situation that Danielle was facing in the **Introduction to this chapter (at 907)**. What **must** or **should** she do? Please identify whether each step that you recommend is a **must** or a **should**, and why, including the Rules or other authority on which you base your answer.

Problem 25D-11: Danielle is helping her supervisor investigate a burglary case against Donnie Defendant. She hears rumors from witnesses that a third party, Stuart, has confessed to the burglary and is bragging that Donnie is going to take the fall for it. Danielle sends a police officer to look into it. The officer returns and tells Marnie that, although Stuart (unsurprisingly) did not personally confess to the police officer, there is hearsay evidence that Stuart has in fact said the things reported. However, the police office also says that Stuart made the reported statements in circumstances that leave the officer in real doubt that what Stuart said is true. Do Danielle and her supervisor have to disclose Stuart's purported confession to defense counsel?

Problem 25D-12: Danielle and her supervisor just indicted several individuals on charges relating to their operation of a gambling and prostitution ring. One member of the operation has agreed to cooperate with the government in exchange for immunity. Danielle and her boss are delighted and immediately prepare a plea agreement. The plea agreement contains a waiver of issues by the defendant relating to **ineffective assistance of counsel** and prosecutorial misconduct. They plan to call the cooperating witness to testify at trial. This witness will be vital to proving the case.

While preparing for trial, Danielle and her supervisor learn that the cooperating witness had been having an affair with an undercover police officer during the investigation of the case. They also learn that the officer was addicted to and regularly using cocaine during the investigation. The officer has since ended the relationship with the cooperating witness on cordial terms, has sought medical treatment, and is no longer using drugs.

a. What obligations do Danielle and her supervisor have with respect to disclosure of this information, and based on what legal authority?

b. Danielle's supervisor informs her that it is his considered decision that the information about the undercover officer and the cooperating witness need not be disclosed to the defense. What, if anything, **must**, **may**, and **should** Danielle do in response?

c. If the cooperating witness's affair with the undercover police officer is disclosed or otherwise discovered by the defense, the cooperating witness will certainly be asked about it on cross-examination. What **must** Danielle and her boss do if the cooperating witness lies while testifying about the affair?

c. Limiting Intrusion into Others' Attorney-Client Relationships

Compelling the defendant's (or someone else's, such as a witness's) lawyer to testify or produce documents before a grand jury or at trial can be tempting for a lot of the wrong reasons. It is disruptive to the attorney-client relationship, undermines the client's confidence in his lawyer, requires the lawyer to make complex judgments on the scope and effect of the **attorney-client privilege** and the **work product doctrine** on the fly and, in the grand jury context, without having counsel of her own present (counsel for witnesses generally not being allowed into the grand jury room), and may force the lawyer to invoke privileges before a grand or petit jury, encouraging adverse inferences despite proper instructions to the contrary. **Model Rule 3.8(e)** limits the opportunities for abuse in the criminal context by forbidding prosecutors from subpoenaing lawyers "in a grand jury or other criminal proceeding to present evidence about a past or present client" unless three conditions are met that together make it clear that the lawyer's testimony must be admissible, essential to the merits, and the only available source of the evidence sought:

- "the information sought is not protected from disclosure by any applicable privilege" (**Model Rule 3.8(e)(1)**);
- "the evidence sought is essential to the successful completion of an ongoing investigation or prosecution" (**Model Rule 3.8(e)(2)**); and
- "there is no other feasible alternative to obtain the information" (**Model Rule 3.8(e)(3)**).

CONSEQUENCES All three of these conditions can be raised as grounds for quashing, limiting, or delaying the subpoena as well as professional discipline.

Many jurisdictions have similar statutory or judge-made rules in civil cases as limits on discovery or testimony from lawyers, but in criminal practice, it is also a matter of prosecutorial ethics enforceable by professional discipline. CONSEQUENCES

Problem 25D-13: Danielle is working with her supervisor on a murder case. The defendant, Myrna Murderous, is accused of having stabbed her soon-to-be-ex-husband with a kitchen knife and left him to bleed out in the kitchen. Myrna told the police that she was asleep upstairs the whole time, but witnesses have identified a car of the same make and model as Myrna's driving erratically and parking outside her divorce lawyer's house that evening. The divorce lawyer has refused to answer any questions from the police about the night of the murder. Danielle would like to subpoena the lawyer to testify before the grand jury convened regarding the murder of Myrna's husband. **May** she do so? Is there anything that Danielle **must** or **should** do in connection with such a subpoena?

d. Trial Publicity

You will recall from **Chapter 24.C at 853** that **Model Rule 3.6** limits pretrial and trial publicity to protect the jury pool, within the limits of the First Amendment, from induced bias. Prosecutors have even more stringent duties regarding publicity than other advocates do. **Model Rule 3.8(f)** supplements prosecutors' duties under **Model Rule 3.6** and provides that prosecutors **must** "refrain from making extrajudicial comments that have a substantial likelihood of heightening public condemnation of the accused." These limits are designed not only to preserve the integrity of the criminal jury process and ensure that the defendant enjoys the benefit of the presumption of innocence, but also to prevent prosecutors from inflaming public sentiment against a defendant, even after conviction, that could result in extrajudicial retribution against the defendant or those close to him. The Rule includes an exception for "statements that are necessary to inform the public of the nature and extent of the prosecutor's action and that serve a legitimate law enforcement purpose."

TAMING THE TEXT The standard for neither the prohibition nor its exception neatly dovetails with **Model Rule 3.6(a)'s** existing prohibition of communications likely to be disseminated by the media that have a "substantial likelihood of **materially** prejudicing an adjudicative proceeding in the matter." Certainly nothing in **Model Rule 3.8(f)** suggests that prosecutors have *more* latitude for public comment about pending matters than other lawyers do; to the contrary, the message of the Rule is for prosecutors to be *more circumspect* in their communications out of respect for the rights and safety of the accused, both before and after conviction.

In addition, prosecutors must include among their managerial and supervisory responsibilities the "exercise [of] reasonable care to prevent investigators, law enforcement personnel, employees or other persons assisting or associated with the prosecutor in a criminal case from making an extrajudicial statement that the prosecutor would be prohibited from making under **[Model] Rule 3.6** or this Rule." This is just a specific application of the **duties to manage** and **supervise** nonlawyers codified in **Model Rule 5.3** (*see* **Chapter 19.C at 516**) to emphasize the responsibility of prosecutors to train and direct the nonlawyer personnel working under their management or supervision, such as those listed in **Model Rule 3.8(f)**, not to engage in any inappropriately prejudicial publicity that would be forbidden to the prosecutor herself. *See* **Model Rule 3.8 Comment [6]**.

> **Problem 25D-14:** Danielle's colleague Sarah has litigated a gruesome, high-profile murder case to final judgment. The defendant was convicted of torturing and murdering several children. Sarah secured the conviction and prevailed on all the subsequent appeals. Over drinks to celebrate the U.S. Supreme Court's denial of *certiorari*, which finally and completely ends the case, Sarah tells Danielle that she is giving an exclusive "tell all" interview to a local television station. "I'm going to lay out everything," she tells Danielle. "All the gory details, including the really awful stuff that the court excluded as more prejudicial than probative. The way he stalked his victims, the way they suffered—he's a monster. I still have nightmares about what he did."
>
> Would this interview violate **Model Rule 3.6**? Would it violate **Model Rule 3.8(f)**? Why might the analysis be different under each Rule? Please explain your answers.

e. Remedying Unjust Convictions

Model Rules 3.8(g) and (h) address a prosecutor's obligations upon discovering evidence tending to show that a defendant may have been wrongfully convicted. The nature and extent of those obligations depends on the strength of the evidence, and whether the conviction was obtained in the jurisdiction in which the prosecutor practices. Take a moment to read those two Rules now.

TAMING THE TEXT When a prosecutor knows of "clear and convincing evidence" (a heightened standard conventionally viewed as greater than a preponderance but less than beyond a reasonable doubt) that a defendant did not commit a crime of which he was convicted, *and* that conviction was obtained in the jurisdiction in which the prosecutor practices, the prosecutor **must** ("shall") "seek to remedy the conviction." **Model Rule 3.8(h)**. The Rule refers only to "a prosecutor"; thus there is no requirement that the prosecutor with the relevant knowledge have had anything to do with the original conviction. Nor does the Rule specify what the prosecutor **must** do to "remedy the conviction" under these circumstances. "Necessary steps may include disclosure of the evidence to the defendant, requesting that the court appoint counsel for an unrepresented indigent defendant and, where appropriate, notifying the court that the prosecutor has knowledge that the defendant did not commit the offense of which the defendant was convicted." **Model Rule 3.8 Comment [8]**.

What if the evidence the prosecutor knows is less than "clear and convincing," or the defendant was convicted in a jurisdiction other than the one in which the prosecutor practices? Then **Model Rule 3.8(g)** comes into play. A prosecutor has obligations under **Model Rule 3.8(g)** if she "knows of new, credible and **material** evidence creating a reasonable likelihood that a convicted defendant did not commit an offense of which the defendant was convicted." Let's start by breaking that down:

- Like **Model Rule 3.8(h)**, this Rule also refers in general terms to "a prosecutor." Again, that literally means *any* prosecutor. And because the Rule goes on to describe what the prosecutor **must** do if the potentially wrongful conviction occurred in a jurisdiction other than the one in which the prosecutor practices, it literally means *any* prosecutor *anywhere* who is governed by this Rule and comes to know the information that the Rule describes. In other words, there is no requirement for the prosecutor to have had any connection with the original conviction for the Rule to obligate her to act. The prosecutor doesn't even have to be in the same state.

- The evidence (or at least the prosecutor's knowledge of it) has to be "new." A prosecutor could discover another prosecutor's failure to disclose exculpatory evidence, and the evidence and its nondisclosure would be "new" to the discovering prosecutor. What about the prosecutor who already knew about the undisclosed exculpatory evidence? It would not be "new" to the prosecutor who failed to disclose it, and would not be covered by **Model Rule 3.8(g)**. But the prosecutor is still subject to **Model Rule 3.8(d)**, which would continue to require the disclosure as long as the defendant could make use of it, which the defendant presumably could by way of postconviction remedy.

- The evidence has to be "credible." "Credible" just means believable, in the sense that a reasonable factfinder could have believed it had it been presented at trial.

- The evidence has to be "**material**." As explained in the Rule's next phrase, "**material**" is given a sense here similar to the meaning of the same word under *Brady* and its progeny, namely that it "creat[es] a reasonable likelihood that a convicted defendant did not commit an offense of which the defendant was convicted." (**Model Rule 3.8(g)**; *cf.* **Chapter 25.D at 946**).

- Because the evidence **must** tend to show "that a convicted defendant did not commit an offense of which the defendant was convicted," it must be relevant to guilt or innocence. Evidence pertinent to impeachment or mitigation are not included (except in the extreme case of impeachment so devastating that it "create[s] a reasonable likelihood the defendant did not commit an offense of which the defendant was convicted"). Those materials are still covered by **Model Rule 3.8(d)**, however. *See* **Chapter 25.D at 945**.

Okay, now a prosecutor knows "new, credible, and **material** evidence creating a "reasonable likelihood that a convicted defendant did not commit an offense of which the defendant was convicted." What does the prosecutor have to do?

- First of all, the prosecutor **must** "promptly disclose that evidence to an appropriate court or authority." That disclosure could be to the court in which the conviction occurred or, under appropriate circumstances, could be to the prosecutorial authorities who obtained the original conviction, whether that is the prosecutor's office in another office in the state or in another jurisdiction, or an appropriate lawyer in the prosecutor's own office.

See **Model Rule 3.8 Comment [7]**. The prosecutors notified would now themselves be obligated to take further action under the same Rule.

■ In addition, if the conviction was in the prosecutor's own jurisdiction, then the prosecutor **must**

  ■ "promptly disclose that evidence to the defendant unless a court authorizes delay" (**Model Rule 3.8(g)(2)(i)**); and

  ■ "undertake further investigation, or make reasonable efforts to cause an investigation, to determine whether the defendant was convicted of an offense that the defendant did not commit" (**Model Rule 3.8(g)(2)(ii)**).

Because the new evidence may be no more than credible (as opposed to clear and convincing), and may create nothing more than a reasonable probability that the original conviction was wrongful, the prosecutors in charge of the office may reasonably conclude that the new evidence does not justify vacatur of the original conviction. Because the defendant has been informed, the defendant may challenge that conclusion by putting the new evidence before the relevant court.

In sum, **Model Rule 3.8(g)** simply requires the prosecutor to make the evidence known to those who ought to know it, and lets normal processes take the matter from there. Only if the new evidence is clear and convincing and the conviction is in the prosecutor's own jurisdiction is the knowledgeable prosecutor herself obligated by **Model Rule 3.8(h)** to seek to remedy the wrongful conviction. And "[a] prosecutor's independent judgment, made in good faith, that the new evidence is not of such nature as to trigger the obligations of sections (g) and (h), though subsequently determined to have been erroneous, does not constitute a violation of this Rule." **Model Rule 3.8 Comment [9]**. Taming the Text

Compare these obligations to those of a non-prosecutor in similar circumstances. Non-prosecutors who discover new evidence calling into question a result in their client's favor **must** do something about it under only limited circumstances. (We are *not* discussing the situation in which a lawyer discovers new evidence that could change a *bad* result for her client. That situation would create all kinds of natural incentives for the wronged party and her counsel to exploit available remedies. Here, we are talking about the situation in which a non-prosecutor discovers that a *good* result for her client may not have been properly supportable.) As you'll remember from **Chapter 24.C at 878**, under **Model Rule 3.3(a)**, you have a **duty to correct** any representation that you made to the court, or any evidence you offered, that you know or later discover was false. And under **Model Rule 3.3(b)** if you know that "a person"—any person—"intends to engage, is engaging or has engaged in criminal or fraudulent conduct related to the proceeding," you **must** "take reasonable remedial measures, including, if necessary, disclosure to the tribunal."

That sounds very broad and far-reaching, but:

- You (the lawyer) must *actually know* of the falsity of your representation to the tribunal or of the evidence you sponsored (**Model Rule 3.3(a)**); or must *actually know* "that a person intends to engage, is engaging or has engaged in criminal or fraudulent conduct related to the proceeding" (**Model Rule 3.3(b)**). In contrast, **Model Rule 3.8(g)** requires action when a prosecutor has "new, credible and **material** evidence creating a reasonable likelihood that a convicted defendant did not commit an offense of which the defendant was convicted." That is a much less demanding standard.

- And your **duties of candor to the tribunal** and **to correct** under these circumstances last only until final judgment in the case (**Model Rule 3.3(c)**). A prosecutor's duties under **Model Rules 3.8(g) and (h)** apply *after* final judgment, and continue to exist at least as long as there is an available post-conviction remedy. In most jurisdictions and most cases of potential actual factual innocence, that's at least until the wrongfully convicted defendant dies.

In sum, non-prosecutors' duties to address a wrongful result in their clients' favor are much more limited in both scope and time, and require a significantly higher degree of knowledge, than the duty of a public prosecutor who discovers a potentially wrongful conviction (even one she did not obtain herself). These differences are another illustration of how the prosecutor's obligations to protect the integrity of the criminal justice process exceed those of the other participants in the adversary process.

> **Problem 25D-15:** What steps, if any, **must** or **should** the lawyer in each situation described below take with respect to the case described, and why? Be sure to explain your answers, and tie them to specific authority that informs what the lawyer **must** or **should** do.
>
> a. A **Mystery from History:** After a high school student and standout athlete, Brian, was accused of rape by a classmate, Wanetta, he pled guilty and was sentenced to five years in prison. Although he had pled guilty, Brian maintained his innocence, insisting he had taken the plea only to avoid risking the much longer sentence the prosecutor had threatened to seek. The only evidence against Brian was Wanetta's testimony. Post-conviction, the prosecutor who handled the case learns that Wanetta has recanted her statement. Other evidence also suggests that Wanetta has been lying. The more he learns, the more the prosecutor doubts the conviction was just.[21]
>
> b. Danielle has been assigned half a dozen files for cases that were prosecuted by one of her colleagues, Marty, before he left to take a job at a nearby private law firm. Most of

---

[21] This is a simplified version of the story of Brian Banks from the early 2000s. Mr. Banks was eventually exonerated with the help of the California Innocence Project and students from California Western School of Law. The story was eventually the basis for a feature film. *See* https://californiainnocenceproject.org/read-their-stories/brian-banks/.

the cases are "inactive," meaning that trial is complete and the office is just waiting for the appeal period to expire before closing the files. Danielle is going through the files, ensuring the pleadings are up to date before they are sent offsite for storage.

As she is flipping through the files from the conviction of Elias Olubenga, a name catches her eye—Amos DeBruno. Amos is a defendant in one of Danielle's other cases. Intrigued, she reads more closely. Apparently Elias was accused of downloading child pornography. The police seized Elias's laptop computer and found child pornography on it. Elias claimed it was his roommate, Amos, who actually downloaded the files, a defense the jury presumably rejected in convicting him.

In the case Danielle is handling, Amos has admitted to downloading child pornography. What's more, he has admitted that he had sometimes used his roommate's computer to avoid detection. Putting two and two together, Danielle realizes that Elias's defense may have been true—and she now has a confession from Amos that makes her doubt that Elias indeed knowingly possessed child pornography. On the other hand, Danielle is not fully convinced Elias was totally innocent. Forensic evidence shows that the pornography was downloaded to a folder that also contained documents that Elias himself accessed. So it's possible that Elias was actually the one who downloaded the images, or even if he didn't, that he knew they were on his computer and kept them. Looking at the evidence in the case file, Danielle is simply not sure. But she is troubled nonetheless that evidence in her case may be exculpatory to Elias.

c. One of the other cases Danielle inherited from Marty (*see* (b)) is a very old case that has been up and down between the appellate courts and the trial court for over a decade. In the case, the defendant, Sam Donald, was accused of rape. The evidence in the case was relatively thin—he had no alibi, and the victim identified him in a lineup. Although a rape kit was performed on the victim, the hospital misplaced the kit, so it was never processed. For years Sam has been arguing that it is a case of mistaken identity and that he was not the rapist. At the time charges were filed, Sam voluntary provided his DNA for comparison.

Recently the news has been covering the fact that hundreds of old rape test kits were found, unprocessed, by an area hospital. Some are still viable and have been run. The rape kit in Sam's case was collected during the time period of the recently discovered kits, so on a whim Danielle calls the hospital lab. It turns out that the victim's kit was recently found and tested. The DNA in the kit was not a match for Sam, and the evidence fully exonerates him. Does your analysis change in any way if Sam's case was charged and tried in the county just on the other side of the state line from the county in which Danielle lives and works, and Danielle ran across the previously misplaced rape kit while investigating a different case of her own? If so, how and why; and if not, why not?

d. There is one public defender Danielle dreads dealing with. He always seems to be underwater on his caseload and Danielle worries that his clients are not getting well defended, or sometimes even **effective assistance of counsel**, as a result. In a case she has against this defender, Danielle discovers evidence that a jailhouse informant has confessed to the crime for which Danielle has indicted the defendant. She timely turns this evidence over to defense counsel. Danielle figures it will be up to the jury at trial whether to believe that the jailhouse informant actually committed the crime. It's possible, but there is other evidence that points to the defendant. What's more, the informant has not always been truthful in his dealings with the criminal justice system, and here coupled his "confession" with a request for specific changes in the conditions of his confinement. The case is not a slam dunk for either side, but Danielle feels comfortable that her office has a case that is more than strong enough to take to a jury.

Danielle is quite surprised at trial when defense counsel never introduces the informant's confession. She suspects it is because he is overwhelmed and somehow overlooked the **materiality** of this purported confession. The jury convicts.

The case continues to nag at Danielle. She decides to go to the jail to speak with the informant herself. When she does, she is shocked at the nature and detail of his confession. He describes aspects of the crime that were never public knowledge. She is now convinced that he, not the defendant, is the perpetrator. She asks the informant whether defense counsel ever interviewed him, and he replies that defense counsel never spoke to him.

e. Frank's firm recently tried a personal injury case to a jury verdict in favor of its client, Wackadoo Coffee. Wackadoo operates a coffee shop next door to the town library. Polly Pedestrian, the plaintiff in the case, alleged that she slipped and fell on ice on the sidewalk near the library. Sally sued both Wackadoo and the town because there was uncertainty about whether the ice was in front of the coffee shop or the library. (The town has an ordinance requiring business owners to clear ice and other hazards on the sidewalks in front of their businesses.)

Throughout the litigation, the township argued that the accident happened next door, on Wackadoo's property. Wackadoo argued that the fall happened on the library's part of the sidewalk. In discovery, it was revealed that the town had liability insurance with significantly higher claims limits than Wackadoo's, which as a small business could afford insurance with only modest limits. There was no outside video surveillance camera at the library or at Wackadoo, and no Wackadoo or library employee saw the fall. The entirety of the evidence that the fall happened on township property was Sally's own testimony, and Sally testified she fell in front of the library. Specifically, Sally testified that there was water dripping from the library roof that puddled and froze into a sheet of ice, on which she slipped and fell. The library introduced evidence that the building next door often had water dripping off its roof and the library did not, but the jury was convinced that the fall happened on township property. Sally was seriously injured in her fall, and the jury awarded her nearly half a million dollars, much more than Wackadoo's insurance would have covered.

The township's appeal is pending. Out of the blue, Frank receives a call from the owner of another adjacent property, who is concerned that the town's paying Sally's big judgment is going to raise her local taxes. It turns out that there was video footage of the slip-and-fall after all. Frank goes to review it. It shows clearly that the accident happened on Wackadoo's portion of the sidewalk, and not in front of the library. Sally was either mistaken or lied during her testimony, which was elicited entirely by Sally's counsel.

Big-Picture Takeaways from Chapter 25

1. Generally speaking, and with a few exceptions, government lawyers are subject to the same ethical rules as all other lawyers. However, government lawyers have a range of obligations outside the Rules of Professional Conduct that apply to them because they are government employees. In addition, there are a few situations that come up often in government practice (but much less frequently in private practice) that can make generally applicable ethical rules difficult to apply. And there are two Rules of Professional Conduct that apply to current or former government lawyers that do not apply to other lawyers—**Model Rule 1.11**, regarding **conflicts of interest** for current or former government lawyers, and **Model Rule 3.8**, regarding the special duties of criminal prosecutors. *See* **Chapter 25 at 908.**

2. Like nongovernmental lawyers, state and local government lawyers are not authorized to practice in any state in which they are not licensed unless that other state allows them to do so. The federal government requires its lawyers to be licensed to practice in at least one American state or in the District of Columbia. But by federal statute, any federal government lawyer may appear in any state or federal court anywhere in the nation, regardless of where that lawyer is licensed. Although federal government lawyers are authorized to practice anywhere, they also **must** comply with the professional conduct rules of the jurisdiction or court in which they are appearing. If a federal government lawyer is practicing in a matter for which there is no tribunal or other authority imposing rules governing lawyers, then the lawyer generally **must** follow the rules of his or her licensing jurisdiction. *See* **Chapter 25.B at 909.**

3. Often, it's clear who your government client is—a specific state or political subdivision of a state (a county; a city) or a federal or state administrative agency, for example. But in some contexts, a government lawyer may broadly represent an interest or function of government, or may nominally represent the apex appointee (that is, the top dog) at a particular agency when the lawyer is "really" representing the **interests** of that agency as a whole, or may represent a particular agency employee. Conversely, a government lawyer may personally represent a government employee, but is doing so with the purpose of protecting the **interests** of

the individual's government employer as well as those of the individual. *See* **Chapter 25.C at 911**.

4. The definition of an organizational client is supplied by the state or federal law that creates and structures the organization; similarly, the individual **constituents** of any organization with the authority to speak for the organization and instruct its counsel are identified by that same law. The same is true of governmental agencies and functions: Federal or state constitutions, statutes, and administrative regulations define various governmental branches, organizations, and functions, and the elected or appointed officials who are empowered to cause them to do things, or speak on their behalf. So when you need to know how a government agency decides something, or who calls the shots on a particular matter, you consult that law. The Rules of Professional Conduct won't tell you the answer. *See* **Chapter 25.C at 911**.

5. Among their responsibilities, many government lawyers often find themselves defending claims against government. Like nongovernmental organizations, governmental organizations are legal abstractions that commit torts or violate employment or other civil rights only through the acts of their human agents. In these defensive cases, identifying the government lawyer's client may be especially challenging. Government lawyers must always remember that representation of an individual employee is authorized only for the purpose of serving the **interests** of the government agency as a whole. For this reason, the government organization is also always a client whose **interests** must be considered, *even in suits involving only individual government-employee defendants*. *See* **Chapter 25.C at 915**.

6. As just discussed, it can be difficult for government lawyers to discern the identity of the government organizations or **constituents** whose **interests** they **should** or **must** protect or disregard. As a result, it can be difficult for government lawyers to determine the existence or basis of **conflicts of interest**. Sometimes, substantive law provides answers about which agencies of federal, state, or local government are sufficiently distinct from one another to be considered different "clients" and thus don't offend **conflict of interest** rules when the same government law office represents one against the other. Sometimes government officials come to some understanding about which government lawyers are going to work on either side of an intra-governmental dispute or negotiation; written **informed consents** resolve any lingering concern. In the absence of an express agreement, the identity of the government client may be inferred from the reasonable understandings and expectations of the lawyer and responsible government officials, taking into account such realistic

considerations as how the government client presented to the lawyer is legally defined and funded, whether it has independent legal authority with respect to the matter for which the lawyer has been retained, and the extent to which the matter involved in the proposed representation has broader implications for the government. Uncertainty in identifying a government client **should** be resolved in favor of disclosure to all affected persons or organizations, with detailed written disclosures and consents all around. Even if two engagements involving government entities are not **directly adverse** because the two government entities involved are not considered the same client for **conflict of interest** purposes, government lawyers also **must not** create **concurrent conflict** based on a "significant risk" that the representation of one or more **current clients** will be "**materially** limited" by the lawyer's responsibilities to others. *See* **Chapter 25.C at 921**.

7.   When a government lawyer represents a government employee in her *individual* capacity, the employee is no longer a mere **constituent** of the government organization; she is the government lawyer's client, owed all of the duties that a lawyer owes any client. But at the same time, because a government lawyer may represent a government employee only for the purpose of protecting the **interests** of the government, the government lawyer has obligations to the employing agency, even in situations in which the agency is not itself a party to the litigation. The potential divergence of **interests** between the government employee and her employer can cause problems similar to those that can plague the private-practice lawyer who represents both an organization and one or more of its **constituents**. Notwithstanding best efforts at the outset of a representation, a government lawyer must be prepared to deal with **conflicts** that arise in the midst of an engagement. If that occurs, the lawyer must consider whether the **conflict** requires limiting or terminating representation of the individual employee. Disclosures and **informed consents** properly formulated at the outset and involving all potentially **interested** persons and organizations can simplify handling this issue considerably. *See* **Chapter 25.C at 923**.

8.   The leaders of government **practice organizations** as well as courts and other tribunals often articulate a "higher standard" of conduct that they expect from government lawyers. There are a variety of specific laws (enforceable with various different **consequences** depending on the law) applicable to government lawyers that do not apply to lawyers in the private-sector. These include a broad array of **conflict of interest** rules, "ethics in government" laws, codes of conduct, and other personnel regulations specialized to the hiring agency's areas of authority, as well as constraints generally

applicable to all, or subgroups of, government employees including lawyers. As an example, there are also innumerable local, state, and federal laws and regulations restricting government employees' ability to seek or accept gifts—often including shared meals and similar hospitality common in the private-sector—from persons or organizations having business with the agency that they serve. *See* **Chapter 25.D at 925**.

9. In determining whether a current or former government lawyer has a **conflict of interest** that **must** be addressed, the **imputation** of **conflicts** within the government lawyer's **practice organization** is substantially reduced. The relevant Rule of Professional Conduct for current and former government lawyers' **conflicts of interest** is **Model Rule 1.11**. This Rule applies to **conflicts of interest** that may be created by current or former service to the government not only as a practicing lawyer, but also as any other kind of "public officer or employee," so it applies to things that you did (or are doing) while you held (or hold) a law license, even if you were (or are) not necessarily acting as a lawyer. *See* **Chapter 25.D at 927**.

10. There is a big difference in the **imputation** of **concurrent conflicts** for government lawyers: **Concurrent conflicts** are *not* **imputed** to other members of the **conflicted** lawyer's **practice organization** as they are in the private-sector under **Model Rule 1.10(a)**. What this means, as a practical matter, is that an individual government lawyer **must not** participate in an engagement adverse to a **current client** of that lawyer's, *but other lawyers in the **conflicted** government lawyer's **practice organization** may*. *See* **Chapter 25.D at 928**.

11. When **successive conflicts** crop up because of a lawyer's prior government service, there are four levels of potential knowledge or participation that the now-ex-government lawyer may have had in a specific piece of government work. The level of knowledge or participation determines the necessary and proper response to a possible **conflict of interest** that the former government work may create for the former government lawyer's new firm. *See* **Chapter 25.D at 930**.

    a. The most intensive level of prior involvement is met when a former government lawyer "participated personally and substantially" in the prior government "matter" currently at issue. For purposes of this Rule alone, "matter" has a different and narrower meaning than it does in other parts of the Rules. That meaning is set out in **Model Rule 1.11(e)**—principally, "any judicial or other proceeding, application, request for a ruling or other determination, contract, claim, controversy, investigation, charge, accusation, arrest or other *particular matter involving a specific party or parties . . .*" (emphasis added). If the former government lawyer "participated personally and substantially" in a "matter" during prior government service that is the same as the "matter" in connection with which the lawyer is being asked to "represent" a private client, the lawyer **must** keep all **confidential information** learned in the prior government matter secret and **must not** be involved in the new matter in private practice, "unless the appropriate government agency gives its **informed consent, confirmed in writing**. . . ." This portion of the Rule amounts to a prohibition on switching to the private party's side in a pending government matter after working directly on the matter for the government, but is broader in the sense that the private party's **interests** need not be in **conflict** with the government's **interests** for the prohibition to apply. Although the former government lawyer who "participated personally and substantially" in the prior government "matter" is *personally* **disqualified** from working on the new matter at her new private firm, the lawyer's private **practice organization** and its other lawyers may take on the new connected matter if "(1) the disqualified [former government] lawyer is timely **screened** from any participation in the matter and is apportioned no part of the fee therefrom; and (2) written notice is promptly given to the appropriate government agency to enable it to ascertain compliance with the provisions of this rule." Additional measures are probably necessary to make the **screen** effective. **Model Rule 1.11(b)**. *See* **Chapter 25.D at 930**.

b. The next-less-intensive level of involvement in a government "matter" is that the government lawyer did not "participate[] personally and substantially" in a prior "matter" for the government, but did obtain "confidential government information" about a third party. What's more, that "confidential government information" has to be about someone other than the former government employer or the new private client, and it has to be usable against the third party. "Confidential *government* information" is not the same as **confidential information** protected by the **duty of confidentiality** and **Model Rule 1.6**, **Model Rule 1.9**, and **Model Rule 1.18**. It is a much narrower category of knowledge, defined in **Model Rule 1.11(c)** as "information that has been obtained under governmental authority and which, at the time this Rule is applied, the government is prohibited by law from disclosing to the public or has a legal privilege not to disclose and which is not otherwise available to the public." An example of "confidential government information" would be the fact that an individual had secretly been under government investigation in a matter that never (or had not yet) eventuated in charges, or was currently subject to an as-yet unsealed indictment. In addition, that "confidential government information" triggers this level of involvement only if it is about a third party (not the former government client and not the new private client) whose **interests** are adverse to those of the new private client and to the **material** disadvantage of whom that information could be used. If the former government lawyer did not "participate[] personally and substantially" in a relevant "matter" during prior government service, but did acquire "confidential government information" pertinent to a new matter that can be used "to the **material** disadvantage" of the **prospective** new **client's** adversary, the former government lawyer is again personally **disqualified** from involvement in the matter, but once again her private **practice organization** and other lawyers in it **may** take on the new matter "if the disqualified lawyer is timely **screened** from any participation in the matter and is apportioned no part of the fee therefrom." Again, additional measures are probably necessary to make the **screen** effective. *See* **Chapter 25.D at 933**.

c. The next-less-intensive involvement level after that is that the government lawyer did not "participate[] personally and substantially" in a prior "matter," or did participate in any way up to and including "personally and substantially" in something that did not amount to a "matter" (for example, agency rulemaking), but does have personal knowledge of some **confidential information** that is not "confidential government information." In this case, in a significant deviation from the regular **conflicts** rules, not only does the former government lawyer not need to be **screened** from the new law firm's engagement (though some private **practice organizations** may **screen** the former government lawyer anyway as a matter of prudence), but neither the former government lawyer nor any other lawyer in her private **practice organization** is **disqualified**. The former government lawyer is forbidden from using any **confidential information** that she may have acquired in her former government service to the former government client's disadvantage or from disclosing the **confidential information** to anyone. If the former government lawyer can't be personally involved without disclosing or using the **confidential information** in the new private matter, then she **must** refrain from personal involvement. *See* **Chapter 25.D at 934**.

d. The least intensive level of involvement is (unsurprisingly) no involvement at all: The government lawyer neither participated in nor personally knows any **confidential information** about the prior matter. This one is easy: If the former government lawyer has no relevant **confidential information** or "confidential government information," from the prior government matter no **conflict of interest** is presented, and no response is required. This result is the same as the one under the regular **conflicts** rules. *See* **Chapter 25.D at 934**.

12. **Model Rule 1.11(d)** addresses **successive conflicts of interest** for current government lawyers differently from those of former government lawyers, and also differently (in some respects, at least) from private-sector **conflicts**. A current government lawyer **must not** "participate in a matter in which the lawyer participated personally and substantially while in private practice or nongovernmental employment, unless the appropriate government agency gives its **informed consent, confirmed in writing**." After having left private practice or other nongovernmental employment for government service, you **must not** be involved ("participate") in any "matter" in your government job in which you "participated personally and substantially" previously in your nongovernmental job. The **successive client rule** of **Rule 1.9(a)** prohibits a lawyer from using a former client's **confidential information** only *against* the **interests** of that **former client** ("in the same or a **substantially related** matter in which [a new client's] interests are *materially* adverse to the interests of the **former client**" (emphasis added)). **Model Rule 1.11(d) (2)(i)** takes that concept a step further and adds that, as to any "matter" in which you "participated personally and substantially" in nongovernmental employment, you can't participate in that "matter" while in government service *under any circumstances*, even if you believe that you will be acting for the government in a manner that will *advance* your **former client's interests**. The reason that **Model Rule 1.11(d)(2)(i)** forbids the government lawyer's participation in the same matter even when it is not adverse to the government lawyer's **former client** is to mitigate "the risk . . . that power or discretion vested in [the government lawyer's] agency might be used for the special benefit of the [government lawyer's **former**] **client**"—that is, to guard against abuse of (or the temptation to abuse) government power *in favor of* as well as *against* the government lawyer's **former client**. *See* **Chapter 25.D at 936**.

13. Although many lawyers devote whole careers to government service, many more cycle into and out of government practice at different points in their careers, some more than once. That's one reason why special **conflict of interest** rules for current and former government lawyers exist, and why they're sometimes referred to as "revolving door" rules. **Model Rule 1.11(d)(2)(ii)** forbids any lawyer currently in government service from "negotiat[ing] for private employment with any person who is involved as a party or as lawyer for a party in a matter in which the lawyer is participating personally and substantially . . . ." **Model Rule 1.11(d)(2)(ii)** also contains a special exception for law clerks serving judges or other adjudicators. Law clerks may negotiate for private employment while in government employment under the much more modest restrictions of **Model Rule 1.12(b)**. That Rule allows a law clerk to negotiate for or accept

employment outside the judiciary with a party or **practice organization** in a matter in which the law clerk is involved, but requires the clerk to tell her judicial boss before doing so. *See* **Chapter 25.D at 938**.

14. Prosecutors are the only category of government attorneys subject to their own Rule of Professional Conduct: **Model Rule 3.8**. Each of the eight subsections in **Model Rule 3.8** identifies a juncture in the criminal process when a prosecutor may have to make decisions favoring justice over merely winning. *See* **Chapter 25.D at 940**.

   a. **Model Rule 3.8(a)** requires a prosecutor to "refrain from prosecuting a charge that the prosecutor knows is not supported by probable cause." *See* **Chapter 25.D at 941**.

   b. **Model Rule 3.8(b)** provides that a prosecutor **must** "make reasonable efforts to assure that the accused has been advised of the right to, and the procedure for obtaining, counsel and has been given reasonable opportunity to obtain counsel." *See* **Chapter 25.D at 944**.

   c. **Model Rule 3.8(c)** prohibits a prosecutor from "seek[ing] to obtain from an unrepresented accused a waiver of important pretrial rights, such as the right to a preliminary hearing." *See* **Chapter 25.D at 944**.

   d. **Model Rule 3.8(d)** ensures a level playing field by requiring the "timely disclosure to the defense of all evidence or information known to the prosecutor that tends to negate the guilt of the accused or mitigates the offense, and, in connection with sentencing, disclose to the defense and to the tribunal all unprivileged mitigating information known to the prosecutor," unless the tribunal orders otherwise. This Rule requires broader disclosure than the constitutional doctrines on which it is based. *See* **Chapter 25.D at 945**.

   e. **Model Rule 3.8(e)** forbids prosecutors from subpoenaing lawyers "in a grand jury or other criminal proceeding to present evidence about a past or present client" unless three conditions are met that *together* make it clear that the lawyer's proposed testimony must be (1) admissible and not privileged, (2) essential to the merits, and (3) the only available source of the evidence sought. *See* **Chapter 25.D at 948**.

   f. In terms of trial publicity, **Model Rule 3.8(f)** supplements prosecutors' duties under **Model Rule 3.6** and provides that prosecutors **must** "refrain from making extrajudicial comments that have a substantial likelihood of heightening public condemnation of the accused." *See* **Chapter 25.D at 949**.

   g. **Model Rules 3.8(g) and (h)** address a prosecutor's obligations upon discovering evidence tending to show that a defendant may have been wrongfully convicted. The nature and extent of those obligations depends on the strength of the evidence, and whether the conviction was obtained in the jurisdiction in which the prosecutor practices.

    i.   When a prosecutor knows of "clear and convincing evidence" that a defendant did not commit a crime of which he was convicted, *and* that conviction was obtained in the jurisdiction in which the prosecutor practices, **Model Rule 3.8(h)** provides that the prosecutor **must** "seek to remedy the conviction." *See* **Chapter 25.D at 950**.

    ii. If the evidence the prosecutor knows is less than "clear and convincing," or the defendant was convicted in a jurisdiction other than the one in which the prosecutor practices, then **Model Rule 3.8(g)** comes into play. A prosecutor has obligations under **Model Rule 3.8(g)** if she "knows of new, credible and **material** evidence creating a reasonable likelihood that a convicted defendant did not commit an offense of which the defendant was convicted." The prosecutor **must** "promptly disclose that evidence to an appropriate court or authority." In addition, if the conviction was in the prosecutor's own jurisdiction, then the prosecutor **must** "promptly disclose that evidence to the defendant unless a court authorizes delay" (**Model Rule 3.8(g)(2)(i)**); and "undertake further investigation, or make reasonable efforts to cause an investigation, to determine whether the defendant was convicted of an offense that the defendant did not commit" (**Model Rule 3.8(g)(2)(ii)**). *See* **Chapter 25.D at 950**.

Multiple-Choice Review Questions for Chapter 25

1. One day, after the conclusion of trial, Patty Prosecutor is invited out to lunch by opposing defense counsel Derrick. He offers to take her to a fancy steakhouse. Derrick tells Patty that lunch is "his treat" in appreciation for the hard work that she does on behalf of the public. Patty reviews the applicable rules of professional conduct and sees none that would prohibit allowing Derrick to pay for the lunch. Can Patty accept the offer and allow him to pay?

    a. Yes. So long as this is not prohibited by the applicable rules of professional conduct, Patty can accept the offer.

    b. Yes. Lawyers always have the right to associate with anyone they choose, thanks to the First Amendment.

    c. Maybe. In addition to the professional ethics rules, government lawyers are subject to other ethical obligations. Patty must ensure that there are no other rules that would prohibit her from accepting Derrick's offer.

    d. No. Accepting the offer would create a direct **conflict of interest** because Patty represents the government and Derrick represents the defendant.

2. George is an Assistant District Attorney in the State of Garden. He is assigned cases by his boss, District Attorney Rogers. George has indicted Defendant Joe for shoplifting from a store owned by Vanessa Victim. His principal witness is Officer Stanley, who investigated the case. Who is George's client? (Choose any or all that apply.)

    a. The State of Garden.

    b. District Attorney Rogers.

    c. Vanessa Victim.

    d. Officer Stanley.

3. Solicitor Sam is assigned to defend an employment discrimination case filed against Secretary Alina, the head of the state Environmental Protection Agency, who has been sued in her individual capacity by Percy Plaintiff. Percy Plaintiff had applied for a position with the agency and was not selected. Who is Sam's client?

    a. Percy.

    b. Alina.

    c. The agency.

    d. Alina and the agency.

4. For a decade, Josh served as senior litigation counsel for the Department of Justice. His job was to review the briefs filed by line-level assistant United States attorneys. Josh's name was in the signature block for each brief, even if he only copyedited or just read the work product. Now Josh has taken a job with a private law firm doing white-collar criminal defense. Which cases involving federal criminal charges against a client of Josh's new private-law-firm employer is Josh now personally **conflicted** out of? (Choose any and all that apply.)

    a. Cases in which Josh's new law firm's client is **directly adverse** to the federal government.

    b. Cases in which Josh participated personally and substantially while he was employed by the Department of Justice.

    c. Cases about which Josh learned "confidential government information" while he was employed by the Department of Justice.

    d. Cases about which Josh learned **confidential information** other than "confidential government information" while he was employed by the Department of Justice.

5. Same facts as question 4. In which cases involving federal criminal charges against a client of Josh's new private-law-firm employer may other lawyers in Josh's new law firm handle the matter only if Josh is **screened** from the matter? (Choose any and all that apply.)
    a. Cases in which Josh's new law firm's client is **directly adverse** to the federal government.
    b. Cases in which Josh participated personally and substantially while he was employed by the Department of Justice.
    c. Cases about which Josh learned "confidential government information" while he was employed by the Department of Justice.
    d. Cases about which Josh learned **confidential information** other than "confidential government information" while he was employed by the Department of Justice.

6. You are a prosecutor representing the State during a defendant's arraignment. The judge indicates that she is ready to move to the next case after advising the defendant of the charges against her and asking the defendant to enter a plea. The judge has not advised the defendant of her right to counsel and her right to have the court appoint an attorney if she cannot afford one. What should you, as the prosecutor, do?
    a. Move on to the next case. Make a mental note that the judge is pro-prosecution.
    b. Move on to the next case but visit the defendant later and advise the defendant of her right to counsel.
    c. Gently remind the judge that the defendant was not advised of her right to counsel and that her financial status should be assessed to determine whether the court should appoint counsel.
    d. Withdraw from the case as prosecutor and switch sides to represent the defendant.

7. Rachel accepts a job as a federal prosecutor in the Eastern District of Keystone. She will appear exclusively in federal court on behalf of the United States of America. Rachel is licensed in the neighboring state of Garden, which does not offer reciprocity with Keystone. May Rachel appear in Keystone federal court?
    a. Yes, provided she is admitted *pro hac vice* in each case on motion by a licensed Keystone attorney.
    b. Yes, because she is a federal government lawyer and need not be licensed in Keystone to appear in courts located there.
    c. No, unless she takes and passes the Keystone bar exam and is admitted to practice in the state.
    d. No, because Garden offers no reciprocity with Keystone and she therefore cannot waive into the Keystone bar.

8. Micah is a prosecutor in the State of Peach. He handles assault and domestic violence cases. These cases are investigated by the Peach State Police. One case involves Valerie Victim, who was beaten by her spouse, Cameron. Who is Micah's client when he prosecutes Cameron? (Choose any and all that apply.)

   a. The people of the State of Peach.
   b. Valerie.
   c. The Peach State Police.
   d. Cameron.

9. Gertrude is a private attorney in the State of Peach. After Cameron pleads guilty to spousal battery (*see* question 8), Valerie asks Gertrude to file a civil tort case against Cameron for battery. Who is Gertrude's client? (Choose any and all that apply.)

   a. The people of the State of Peach.
   b. Valerie.
   c. The Peach State Police.
   d. Cameron.

10. When a government employee is sued in his or her official capacity as head of a government agency, who is the real client in the case?

    a. The government employee.
    b. Every employee of the agency in his or her individual capacity.
    c. The government agency, which acts through its **constituents**, including the head of the agency.
    d. None of the above.

11. Katayun was a former prosecutor for the state district attorney's office. She left government service to join the white-collar defense group of a law firm in town. Her new firm has asked her to serve on the defense team for a defendant being prosecuted by her former office. Absent consent from the district attorney's office, is Katayun personally **conflicted** out of defending this firm client?

    a. Yes, if she participated personally and substantially in the prosecution before leaving the district attorney's office to join the firm.
    b. Yes, regardless of whether she learned anything about the representation or was personally involved because she would be "switching sides."
    c. No, so long as there has been a year-long "cooling-off period" between when she left the district attorney's office and joined the firm.
    d. No, because one reason the firm may have hired her is for her expertise in understanding how the district attorney's office prosecutes cases.

12. Adina worked as a solicitor for the United States Department of Labor where she prosecuted wage and hour cases. Before she left, she was handling a case brought against a manufacturing company that failed to properly pay its workers overtime at one of its factories. In the midst of the case, Adina received an offer to join a boutique law firm in its toxic tort group. Looking to switch gears, Adina accepted the offer. Although the firm currently represents the manufacturing company in the wage and hour case, it assured Adina that she would not be assigned to work on this case. Is this sufficient for compliance with **Model Rule 1.11**?

    a. Yes, so long as Adina does not work on the case the firm has complied.
    b. Yes, because the rule applies only when a lawyer leaves private practice and joins the government, not vice versa.
    c. No, because Adina must also be **screened** from the wage and hour case, with notice given to the Department of Labor.
    d. No, because all attorneys at the firm are tainted by Adina joining the firm and must withdraw from representing the manufacturing plant.

13. After graduation, Praveen joined the U.S. Attorney's Office as a one-year civil division honors program fellow. In this capacity, he worked on healthcare fraud investigations. His team used nonpublic Medicare data to identify physicians whose billing practices were atypical of doctors with similar medical practices, and then subpoenaed those physicians to determine if there was fraud in government billing. Where there was, the government filed a complaint against the physician seeking to recover treble damages under the False Claims Act. Praveen was responsible for reviewing the data and making recommendations for subpoenas. He recommended that a dozen physicians be sent subpoenas, but his supervisor disagreed with the recommendation as to Dr. Hildenbrant. After Praveen's fellowship ended, he joined a firm. That firm was suing Dr. Hildenbrant on behalf of one of his patients alleging medical malpractice. Praveen was assigned to litigate the case along with one of the firm's partners. Praveen shared the information he learned from his fellowship with the partner and the partner used the information to impeach Dr. Hildenbrant during his deposition. Did Praveen violate any Rules of Professional Conduct?

    a. Yes, because when he moved to the law firm, he violated the **concurrent client rule**.
    b. Yes, because he used "confidential government information" to Dr. Hildenbrant's **material** disadvantage.
    c. No, because the government failed to bring a case against Dr. Hildenbrant when Praveen was a fellow.

d. No, because during his fellowship Praveen was adverse to Dr. Hildenbrant and he was similarly adverse to Dr. Hildenbrant in his new firm's medical malpractice case.

14. Abdullah is an assistant district attorney in the state of Michigan. He is prosecuting a robbery case against Norman. Norman claims he was out of town on a road trip when the robbery occurred. Abdullah has requested information from the Michigan Department of Transportation regarding Norman's use of state toll roads on his claimed road trip to refute Norman's alibi. The department reports that it has no information that Norman used those toll roads that day. Abdullah tries the case and secures a conviction. The following day, he receives a frantic call from the Department of Transportation. It actually had records and did not initially find them due to a computer glitch. The records show that Norman's car was scanned through a toll booth several counties away at the time of the robbery. The evidence is not clear and convincing, to be sure, but it does seem to be **material** and credible. At least in Abdullah's mind, it creates a reasonable likelihood that Norman was telling the truth and did not commit the robbery. What should Abdullah do?
    a. Disclose the evidence to the court.
    b. Disclose the evidence to Norman and undertake additional investigation into whether the conviction was proper.
    c. Nothing because the trial is over.
    d. Nothing because someone else could have been driving the car.

15. What kind of evidence that a defendant was wrongfully convicted requires a prosecutor to seek to remedy the conviction in his or her own jurisdiction?
    a. Evidence showing the defendant's innocence beyond a reasonable doubt.
    b. Clear and convincing evidence that the defendant was wrongly convicted.
    c. Evidence making it more likely than not the defendant was wrongly convicted.
    d. Evidence creating a reasonable doubt of the defendant's guilt.

UNIT VI

Judicial Ethics

YOU MAY BE WONDERING why there's a unit on *judicial* ethics in this book. It's a fair question—after all, though we hope and expect that some of you will become judges, that happy day won't come right away. Nevertheless, long before you ever don the robe, and even if you never do, there are a number of concerns relating to judicial ethics that are more immediately important to you. There are four basic reasons that you need to attend to this subject.

First, judicial ethics is tested on the Multistate Professional Responsibility Examination. On average, between one and four questions on each administration of the MPRE (out of 60) include issues arising under the ABA Model Code of Judicial Conduct. And in almost every state, you have to pass the MPRE to obtain a license to practice. The MPRE tests on the ABA Model Code of Judicial Conduct ("MCJC"), which is the basis for most states' rules governing the conduct of state-court judges and similar judicial officers. Principally for this reason, although we will occasionally compare the rules governing federal judges and their employees to the MCJC, the next chapter will focus predominantly on the ABA Model Code.

Second, judges' ethics will likely influence your life as a practicing lawyer: You will have specific ethical duties that govern your interactions with judicial officers and their staff—duties that come into effect the day that you get your bar card. Violation of those duties is a disciplinary offense that can affect your ability to practice law, and of course may result in other serious formal and informal **consequences**. We'll point out as we go issues where the rules of judicial ethics have corresponding obligations in the rules of lawyer ethics.

Third, if any portion of your personal or practice life involves interaction with adjudicators or those who work for them, whether socially or professionally, you'll need to understand the basic restrictions on their conduct so that you don't inadvertently put them in the awkward position of wondering if you're pressuring them to do something improper, or of having to rebuff your innocent (but impermissible) courtesies because accepting them might violate the rules of judicial ethics.

And *fourth*, regardless of where your career may eventually lead, a number of you are going to begin your lawyer life working for the state or federal judiciary as a law clerk or staff attorney. Others of you will serve as judicial interns or externs during law school. In those capacities, your job includes helping the court or judge you serve do everything properly. What's more, many courts and judicial systems have codes of conduct specifically applicable to the people who aren't addressed as "Your Honor" but who work with or for the people who are. The federal judicial system, for example, has a **Code of Conduct for Judicial Employees** ("CCJE") that governs a wide range of court employees, including staff attorneys, law clerks, externs, and interns. **CCJE § 310.10(a)**. Violation of those codes may result in **consequences** in your employment or internship, and also may affect your ability to be admitted to practice law or to keep your license.

Like many of the ethical rules we've explored up to this point, some of these principles are going to be the obvious sorts of things that you would have come up with yourself if someone had locked you in an empty room and told you to make up some rules for judges. Others, either in their substance or in their application, may be subtle or counterintuitive. Either way, we've got some ground to cover before you've finished this book, so let's get to it.

26

Judicial Ethics

DANIELLE HAS APPEARED numerous times before Judge Grumpador B. Cranky. In every case, she has found him to be cordial and predictable. He has a decent reputation among members of the bar, and Danielle's office prides itself on its professional relationship with Judge Cranky and the other judges who preside over the office's cases.

Danielle currently has a retail theft (shoplifting) case assigned to Judge Cranky. She has a pending motion in limine in that case that addresses an unsettled question of state evidence law over a key piece of evidence. The motion is fully briefed and needs to be decided, though no trial date is set; it has been pending for a few weeks and Judge Cranky has denied Danielle's request for oral argument. With this background, Danielle is surprised to receive a phone call, out of the blue, from Judge Cranky's chambers. She answers it, expecting it to be the judge's law clerk, and is surprised to hear the judge himself.

"How are you doing?" the judge asks. "I'm fine," stammers Danielle. "I hope I didn't overlook a deadline, your honor."

"No, no," the judge assures her, "nothing like that. I'm calling to ask a favor."

"A favor from me?" Danielle asks, incredulous, but pleased to be asked and eager to help.

"Yes," the judge explains. "You see, my son is currently a first-year law student. He's got his heart set on becoming a prosecutor like you, and he'd like to do a summer internship with your office."

"That's great," Danielle replies. "We have a formal summer program here. If you send me his resume, I can forward it to the summer program committee."

"I was hoping for something more," Judge Cranky responds, cheerfully. "Maybe a personal letter of recommendation from you?"

Danielle ponders this request. "I've never met him, your honor. What would I even say?"

"I'll have someone at my staff ghostwrite it for you. All you'll have to do is sign your name. And in exchange, I'll grant your motion as a token of my appreciation," says the judge.

Danielle pauses. "Can I think about this?" she asks.

"Well, if you really need to," replies the judge, sounding a little peeved. "But don't think too long. I'm going to decide your motion this week."

Danielle hangs up the phone with the sinking feeling that something is wrong with this situation. If she agrees to submit the letter, she'll be recommending someone she doesn't know. What that really amounts to, she begins to realize, is that she'll be lying to her own office by vouching for a stranger. What's worse, she'll have traded a favorable decision in one of her cases for submitting that letter. But what if she says no? Her stomach starts to churn. If she says no, she'll have lost all the goodwill built up with a judge before whom she has a case right now, and is likely to have others in the future—and who seems likely to deny her pending motion in limine in retaliation for her refusal to play along. Danielle's trepidation begins to turn to frustration—why would a judge put her in a spot like this in the first place? Yet here she is. What should she do?

A. Regulation of Judicial Conduct

Our friends at the American Bar Association have developed and periodically updated a **Model Code of Judicial Conduct** ("MCJC"), intended to have a role analogous to the one that the Model Rules have for lawyers and state lawyer-disciplinary authorities. Like the Model Rules, the MCJC has no legal force of its own, and is enforceable only when adopted by a particular jurisdiction as its governing law.

Also like the Model Rules in their domain, the MCJC has been quite influential. In one form or another, it has been adopted as the principal set of rules governing judicial conduct in at least 37 states. At least another nine have adopted their own Codes of Judicial Conduct that are substantively similar to the MCJC. Our focus in this chapter will be the MCJC, both because of its similarity to the actual law of most jurisdictions in most respects, and because it is the body of law on judicial conduct tested on the MPRE.

The governmental authority adopting a state's code of judicial conduct is usually the state's highest court which, under separation-of-powers principles in the state's Constitution similar to those found in the federal Constitution, claims authority to govern the conduct of the officers who exercise the state's judicial power. But legislatures in many jurisdictions are also involved in formulating and adopting related rules, such as those governing procedures and standards for judicial **recusal**.

Almost every state has a judicial disciplinary commission that administers and enforces the state's code of judicial conduct. The judicial disciplinary process is typically initiated by some sort of complaint, which can come from anyone—another judge; a litigant; a member of the public. **CONSEQUENCES** After investigation and adversary factfinding, the commission is typically empowered to impose **consequences** on offending judges ranging from private or public censure to financial penalties to suspension or removal from office. CONSEQUENCES

Federal judges are governed by a different set of ethical rules—the **Code of Conduct for United States Judges** ("CCUSJ"), which has been adopted and occasionally revised by the United States Judicial Conference, a policymaking agency of the federal judiciary. The federal Code of Conduct, which bears many substantive similarities to the MCJC, governs all judicial officers appointed under Article III of the Constitution, as well as many judicial officers appointed under Article I, such as magistrate judges, bankruptcy judges, and Court of Federal Claims judges.[1] But there's one important exception: The Code of Conduct for United States Judges does *not* govern the justices of the United States Supreme Court. Supreme Court justices have chosen not to adopt any ethics rules for themselves, and instead to allow individual justices to make their own personal ethical decisions case by case.[2]

CONSEQUENCES Enforcement of the code of conduct for federal judges is complicated by the fact that Article III judges (federal district court judges, circuit court of appeal judges, and justices of the United States Supreme Court) may not be removed from office except by impeachment or voluntary resignation, nor may they have their compensation reduced during their term of service.[3] These constitutional restrictions deprive Congress and the federal judiciary of the power to impose the most significant **consequences** on Article III judges that are common in state systems of judicial discipline (namely, financial penalties and suspension or removal). In 1980, Congress enacted the Judicial Conduct and Disability Act,[4] setting up a judicial disciplinary system that has a broader range of available **consequences** for Article I judges. The disciplinary authority that the statute

---

[1] The ABA has also promulgated a separate Model Code of Judicial Conduct for Federal Administrative Law Judges, and the individual administrative agencies within which such judges serve often have their own rules governing their adjudicators as well.

[2] This policy has not been without controversy. One prominent example was Justice Antonin Scalia's denial of a motion to **recuse** himself from a case before the Supreme Court involving official actions of then-sitting Vice President Dick Cheney, whom Justice Scalia had persuaded a third-party host to include in a duck-hunting outing in the winter before the adjudication of the case, and to which the Vice President supplied Justice Scalia and two members of his family transportation in a government-owned jet. *Cheney v. United States District Court*, 541 U.S. 913 (2004). For a criticism of Justice Scalia's decision, *see* Lawrence J. Fox, *I Did Not Sleep With That Vice-President*, 15 THE PROFESSIONAL LAWYER 1 (2004). (The title of Mr. Fox's article is drawn from Justice Scalia's assertion in his decision not to **recuse** himself that he might have decided differently if he had shared sleeping quarters with the Vice-President in the hunting camp's bunkhouse, as well as an arch reference to President Clinton's misleading denial of sexual activity with White House intern Monica Lewinsky a few years before, the latter being one in a series of ethical mishaps that led to only the second Senate impeachment trial of a president in American history.) *See also* Steven Lubet, *Why Won't John Roberts Accept an Ethics Code for Supreme Court Justices?* https://slate.com/news-and-politics/2019/01/supreme-court-ethics-code-judges-john-roberts.html (Jan. 16, 2019). Ironically, Supreme Court *staff* are subject to all kinds of ethics rules even as the justices have left themselves to the mores of their individual consciences, guided to the extent they wish to be by their perceptions of the Court's traditions. For example, Supreme Court law clerks may not appear before the Court for two years after their service. U.S. Sup. Ct. R. 7 (2003). Yes, we're aware of *all* the ironies here, and we bet you are, too.

[3] *See* **U.S. Const. Art. III § 1**.

[4] **28 U.S.C. § 351**.

creates may privately or publicly censure or reprimand, and may certify disability or recommend retirement or impeachment for, Article III judges.

Outside of judicial discipline, judges are subject to criminal **consequences** under the same standards and procedures as anyone else. Judges are, however, absolutely immune from civil **consequences** for their official actions, even for ones undertaken in excess of their authority and even for malicious actions, unless taken "in clear absence of all jurisdiction."[5] ⟨Consequences⟩

> **Problem 26A-1:** Judge Grumpador B. Cranky, a judge of the court of general jurisdiction in the State of Confusion, engages in the following conduct. What **consequences** could he face, and why?
>
> a. Judge Cranky misapplies a state statute at issue in a case before him, resulting in an incorrect disposition of the case.
>
> b. Judge Cranky, sitting in the juvenile court, adjudicates numerous accused juvenile offenders "delinquent," and sentences them to lengthy stays in a particular residential facility run by a private operator. The private operator is secretly paying Judge Cranky $5,000 per child sent to the facility.[6]
>
> c. Judge Cranky takes offense at a lawyer's repeated evidentiary objections during trial. Despite the fact that the objections are meritorious, Judge Cranky holds the lawyer in summary contempt and has his bailiff imprison him in the County Jail for the remainder of the day.
>
> d. Judge Cranky accidentally hits a pedestrian with his car. The pedestrian was crossing in a crosswalk with the light at the time.
>
> e. Same as (d) except that, at the time of the accident, Judge Cranky was conducting a virtual hearing on his cell phone.

B. The ABA Model Code of Judicial Conduct

Now we turn our attention to the ABA Model Code of Judicial Conduct. The discussion that follows is not intended to be comprehensive. Instead, we'll try to focus on the most basic and commonly arising judicial obligations.

The MCJC's structure is not unlike that of the Model Rules or the Model Code of Professional Responsibility that preceded the Model Rules (*see* **Chapter 3.A at 31**). After a Preamble, a Scope discussion, some defined Terminology, and a short section on Application of the MCJC, the substantive rules of judicial conduct

---

[5] *Stump v. Sparkman*, 435 U.S. 349 (1978). The principles in *Stump* apply to both to federal judges and to state judges sued for violating federal law, including claims that the judge deprived a plaintiff of civil rights under color of state law pursuant to **42 U.S.C. § 1983**. State judges' immunity from claims arising under state law is a question of state law, but the states generally grant judges immunity in breadth comparable to federal law.

[6] *See* Eyder Peralta, *Pa. Judge Sentenced to 28 Years In Massive Juvenile Justice Bribery Scandal*, https://www.npr.org/sections/thetwo-way/2011/08/11/139536686/pa-judge-sentenced-to-28-years-in-massive-juvenile-justice-bribery-scandal (Aug. 11, 2011).

are divided under four "Canons." The Canons each articulate a general principle, which is elaborated in Rules under the Canon, and explanatory Comments designed to assist in understanding each Rule. "[A] judge may be disciplined only for violating a Rule" in the MCJC, other than a Rule designated as discretionary by use of the terms "may" or "should." **MCJC Scope ¶ [2]**. The Rules are not intended to ground any **consequence** other than judicial discipline. **MCJC Scope ¶ [7]**.

1. Canon 1: Independence, Integrity, and Impartiality

MCJC Canon 1 provides: "A judge shall uphold and promote the independence, integrity, and impartiality of the judiciary, and shall avoid impropriety and the appearance of impropriety." The Rules under Canon 1 begin with the unobjectionable principles that a judge **must** "comply with the law, including the Code of Judicial Conduct" (**MCJC Rule 1.1**). Does this mean that a judge is subject to discipline if she commits reversible error? Of course not. Appellate courts exist because judging is hard, and even the best judges don't always get the law right. Implicit in **MCJC Rule 1.1** is a requirement that the violation of the law while acting as a judge be knowing, or at least reckless, before judicial discipline will be imposed. This Rule also requires judges' compliance with governing law in their private lives, on pain of discipline that could be as serious as removal from office in the case of a sufficiently blameworthy violation.[7] (Note the similarity to **Model Rule 8.4(b)**, which authorizes professional discipline for any lawyer who "commit[s] a criminal act that reflects adversely on the lawyer's honesty, trustworthiness or fitness as a lawyer in other respects.")

MCJC Rule 1.3 focuses on abuse of office for personal advantage. That Rule provides that judges **must not** "abuse the prestige of judicial office to advance the personal or economic interests of the judge or others, or allow others to do so." This means not using the judge's office or powers outside the courtroom improperly to influence anyone else's personal, business, or official conduct, whether by implicit (or explicit) threat or by encouraging (or demanding) treatment of the judge or her friends or family that is unequal to others similarly situated simply because the judge holds judicial office.

An important indication of the special status of the judicial role in our society is reflected in **MCJC Rule 1.2**, which says that a judge **must** "act at all times in a manner that promotes public confidence in the independence, integrity, and impartiality of the judiciary, and shall avoid impropriety and the appearance of impropriety." Note how different this Rule is from the other two under this Canon. **MCJC Rule 1.1** focuses on judges' performance of their official duties in applying the law, and in their private lives in following it, and **MCJC Rule 1.3**

---

[7] Remember that we are talking mostly about state-court judges, and federal judges who have been appointed under authority deriving from Article I of the Constitution. Article III federal judges may be removed only by impeachment. *See* **Chapter 26.A at 975**.

forbids judges from exploiting their public office for private advantage. **MCJC Rule 1.2**, by contrast, focuses predominantly on *public perception* of the judge's conduct, including all extrajudicial conduct, and requires the judge to avoid not only any kind of "impropriety," but "the *appearance* of impropriety" (emphasis added), for the explicit purpose of "promot[ing] public confidence in . . . the judiciary."

This prohibition is especially striking because the law governing lawyers has evolved over the last 50 years *away* from a view that "the appearance of impropriety" is a proper basis for invoking **consequences** such as discipline and **disqualification**, and toward the view that formal **consequences** may be grounded only in actual impropriety defined by a legal or ethical rule. Though the Model Code of Professional Responsibility (first promulgated in 1969) continued the 1908 Canons of Professional Ethics' long-standing reliance on the appearance of impropriety (*see* Model Code Canon 9), the Model Rules (first promulgated in 1983) make no reference to it. You will still see occasional references in more recent lawyer ethics decisions to the appearance of impropriety as a basis for discipline or civil **consequences**, but they represent a minority view and are often reversed.[8] The principle remains very much alive in government ethics, however—which is part of the point of the current discussion.

REASON FOR THE RULE The message here—and it is an important one for all of us, not just our judges—is that a judge is a judge 24/7, and serves in her public role not just by doing her job right, but by both appearing and being a trustworthy person in every other aspect of her life: "act[ing] *at all times* in a manner that *promotes public confidence* in the independence, integrity, and impartiality of the judiciary" (emphases added). Why? Because the public's perception of those endowed with the powers of government affects the perceived legitimacy and integrity of the government itself. And that is especially so with the judiciary, where nonpartisanship, fairness, and impartiality are the branch's defining characteristics. *See* **MCJC Rule 1.2 Comments [1]-[3]**.[9] REASON FOR THE RULE TAMING THE TEXT "This principle applies to both the professional and personal conduct of a judge." **MCJC Rule 1.2 Comment [1]**. "The test for appearance of impropriety is whether the conduct would create

---

[8] *See, e.g., Worley v. Moore*, 370 N.C. 358, 807 S.E.2d 133 (N.C. 2017); *Marcum v. Scorsone*, 457 S.W.3d 710 (Ky. 2015); Bruce A. Green, *Conflicts of Interest in Legal Representation: Should the Appearance of Impropriety Rule Be Eliminated in New Jersey—Or Revived Everywhere Else*, 28 SETON HALL L. REV. 315 (1997).

[9] *See* Fox, **Chapter 26.A at 975 n.2**, 15 THE PROFESSIONAL LAWYER at 6:

> Imagine you are a lawyer. You are handling a major case for a distraught client. The case will be tried next month to a judge. Your client, on your advice, takes a weekend of rest and relaxation at the Homestead. The client enters the elegant dining room with his wife and, as they are escorted to their table, they notice the judge, the adversary and the adversary's wife hoisting martini glasses filled with a silver liquid, laughing boisterously. As your client passes their fraternizing way, there is an embarrassed silence followed by the judge's halting comment, "Great to see you, Mr. Jones. Just down here for some trout fishing. Of course, we haven't discussed that little matter."
>
> How does that client feel? How do you feel? What has this done to the system of justice? Can the client ever be convinced that the judge will still be impartial? Should there be a need to convince the client of that fact? Even if you know the judge will be impartial, the appearance of bias is both profound and destructive.

in reasonable minds a perception that the judge violated this Code or engaged in other conduct that reflects adversely on the judge's honesty, impartiality, temperament, or fitness to serve as a judge." **MCJC Rule 1.2 Comment [5]**.[10] TAMING THE TEXT

What creates an appearance of bias requiring corrective action is to some degree situation- and community-dependent, however. As we'll discuss in more detail below, judges are allowed to have friends and a social life, and because judges were once lawyers, many have lawyers as acquaintances and friends. When one of your authors was practicing in California, it was quite common in many of California's rural counties (and for those unfamiliar with the state, large parts of California are rural areas devoted principally to farming, ranching, and forestry) for local judges and local lawyers, both few in number, to socialize in the judges' chambers before or after an appearance. It thus was not uncommon for counsel to walk out of the judge's chambers into the courtroom just ahead of the judge as court was called, something that simply never happened in larger cities where prevailing practice differed. In the outlying rural counties, however, it was widely accepted judicial behavior. As many rural judges were as scrupulously fair as urban judges were, although many urban lawyers learned that only after having picked their jaws up off counsel table and stammered their way through their first appearance while recovering from the sight of their local opposing counsel accompanying the judge out of his or her chambers into the courtroom.

> **Problem 26B-1:** Judge Cranky engages in the following conduct. What **consequences** could he face?
>
> a. Judge Cranky routinely dismisses employment discrimination cases on motion under his state's equivalent of **Fed. R. Civ. P. 12(b)(6)** on the ground that the claims are stated under "dumb laws."
>
> b. Judge Cranky has a couple too many at a retirement party for a fellow judge and is driving erratically on his way home. A local police officer pulls him over and asks if he has been drinking. Judge Cranky says, "Do you know who I am?" (*Hint: See* **MCJC Rule 1.3 Comment [1]**.)
>
> c. Judge Cranky has had a very good law clerk this year. When it comes time for the clerk to seek a job near the end of her clerkship, the judge writes a letter of recommendation to her prospective employers on court letterhead, speaking highly of her abilities, reliability, and trustworthiness. (*Hint: See* **MCJC Rule 1.3 Comment [2]**.)

---

[10] The code of conduct for federal judges speaks in the same terms. *See* **CCUSJ Canon 2 §§ (A)-(B), Comment on Canon 2(A)** ("A judge must expect to be the subject of constant public scrutiny and accept freely and willingly restrictions that might be viewed as burdensome by the ordinary citizen"). The code governing federal judicial employees similarly requires them not to "engage in any activities that would put into question the propriety of the judicial employee's conduct in carrying out the duties of the office." **CCJE § 320 Canon 2**.

   d. Judge Cranky has a niece who has just graduated from a local law school. The judge writes her a recommendation for employment in the local district attorney's office. The letter, which is addressed personally to the District Attorney, closes, "I would look quite favorably on her receiving your special consideration." Does your analysis change depending on the strength of the niece's law school record? If so, how and why; and if not, why not?

   e. The police conduct a raid on a local strip club based on tips that some of the club's employees and some of its customers are violating various state and local laws. Judge Cranky is one of the customers rounded up in the raid. He is not charged with any crime, but the local newspaper publishes a photo of him among the customers being led out of the establishment by police, identifying him by name in the caption.

2. Canon 2: Competence, Diligence, and Impartiality (Again)

MCJC Canon 2 provides that "[a] judge shall perform the duties of judicial office impartially, competently, and diligently." These general principles probably fall in your "duh" department, but as we'll see shortly, applying them in some real-world situations isn't always easy.

a. Competence and Diligence

The judicial duties of competence and diligence should remind you of your own ethical duties bearing the same names (*see* **Chapter 7.A at 172**), and in fact the duties of lawyers and of judges have a great deal in common in these respects, taking into account the differing nature of the jobs.

MCJC Rule 2.5(A) describes judges' duties of competence and diligence generally, using only those two words. The Comments and some other Rules elaborate on these two concepts. In terms strikingly similar to those defining the lawyer's **duty of competence** in **Model Rule 1.1**, **MCJC Rule 2.5 Comment [1]** describes the judge's duty of competence as requiring "the legal knowledge, skill, thoroughness, and preparation reasonably necessary to perform a judge's responsibilities of judicial office." Similarly, judges' duties of diligence include:

- ensuring "[p]rompt disposition of the court's business" by "devot[ing] adequate time to judicial duties, [being] punctual in attending court and expeditious in determining matters under submission, and tak[ing] reasonable measures to ensure that court officials, litigants, and their lawyers cooperate with the judge to that end" (**MCJC Rule 2.5 Comment [3]**);

- "demonstrat[ing] due regard for the rights of parties to be heard and to have issues resolved without unnecessary cost or delay" (**MCJC Rule 2.5 Comment [4]**; *see also* **MCJC Rule 2.6(A)**.);

- ensuring that the duties of judicial office always take precedence over personal and extrajudicial activities (**MCJC Rule 2.1**); and

- hearing and deciding the matters assigned to them (unless they **must recuse** themselves, a topic we'll discuss below) (**MCJC Rule 2.7**).

Problem 26B-2: Judge Cranky engages in the following conduct. What **consequences** could he face, and why?

a. Judge Cranky plays video games on his phone during bench trials. Unsure what to do, some counsel simply wait in silence for him to look up before introducing key evidence, while others continue their presentations assuming that Judge Cranky will review the transcript later.

b. Judge Cranky likes to sleep in. He arrives at chambers most mornings around 11 a.m. He also likes to golf, so on some days he leaves chambers around 2 p.m. to take advantage of the remaining daylight. Because he spends so little time on the bench, his calendar is unusually congested, and he often has to continue hearings and trials. Substantive motions take weeks or months longer than other judges to decide when assigned to his docket.

c. Judge Cranky takes a *lassez-faire* (hands-off) approach to scheduling his cases. He never imposes discovery deadlines and allows the parties extensions whenever one is requested. Certain lawyers have begun to exploit this system by intentionally dragging cases out in hopes that the opposing party will settle out of frustration. When the judge's law clerk gently asks why the judge maintains this approach, Judge Cranky replies that the parties are best able to determine the timing in their own cases.

d. Anytime Judge Cranky is assigned a complex, multiparty case, he pressures counsel to agree to have the case referred to a magistrate for disposition rather than have the case handled by Judge Cranky himself.

b. Decorum

MCJC Rule 2.8 requires that judges **must**:

- "require order and decorum in proceedings before the court" (**MCJC Rule 2.8(A)**);
- "be patient, dignified, and courteous to litigants, jurors, witnesses, lawyers, court staff, court officials, and others with whom the judge deals in an official capacity" (**MCJC Rule 2.8(B)**);[11]
- "require similar conduct of lawyers, court staff, court officials, and others subject to the judge's direction and control" (*id.*); and
- neither "commend [n]or criticize jurors for their verdict other than in a court order or opinion in a proceeding" (**MCJC Rule 2.8(C)**).[12]

---

[11] Complementing judges' managerial and supervisory responsibilities to require court staff to live up to the standards of courtesy and decorum required of judges, the federal **Code of Conduct for Judicial Employees** applies similar standards directly to court staff. *See, e.g.,* **CCJE § 320 Canon 3 § C.**

[12] The Code of Conduct for United States Judges unsurprisingly imposes similar duties of competence, diligence, and decorum on federal judges. **CCUSJ Canon 3 §§ (A)(1)-(3), (5), (B).**

The judicial duties to require decorous conduct by counsel correspond neatly to those of lawyers not to "engage in conduct intended to disrupt a tribunal," *see* **Model Rule 3.5(b); Chapter 24.C at 841**. But unlike lawyers, who are free within the rules of the jurisdiction and the willingness of individual jurors to meet with jurors after the case to discuss the merits (*see* **Model Rule 3.5(c); Chapter 24.C at 841**), judges may meet with jurors after discharging them, but may not discuss the merits of the case they just heard. **MCJC Rule 2.8 Comment [3]**.

> Problem 26B-3: Judge Cranky engages in the following conduct. What **consequences** could he face, and why? In each instance, what (if anything) **must** or **should** the judge have done differently?
>
> a. During oral argument, Judge Cranky allows lawyers to talk over each other. When things get particularly raucous and the court reporter indicates that she can't record all the crosstalk, Judge Cranky yells at everyone to "simmer down" and storms off the bench.
>
> b. Plaintiff's counsel arrive early before a hearing. Judge Cranky walks into the courtroom to hear the two lawyers making derogatory comments about the physical appearance of opposing counsel, who has not yet arrived. Judge Cranky joins in, figuring there's no real harm since the conversation isn't on the record and opposing counsel isn't there. Does your analysis change if Judge Cranky instead says nothing? If so, how and why; and if not, why not?
>
> c. Judge Cranky is presiding over a personal injury trial. During deliberations, the jury submits a question about one of the exhibits admitted into evidence during trial. Judge Cranky calls the jury back into the courtroom and tells them, "This is a stupid question. Either you paid attention during trial or you didn't." He then sends them back to deliberate without answering the question.

c. Management and Supervision of Court Staff, and Oversight of Other Judges and Counsel

Judges have duties of management and supervision in their domain similar to lawyers in theirs. Just as lawyers must take reasonable steps to ensure that other lawyers under their management or supervision comply with those lawyers' professional responsibilities (*see* **Model Rule 5.1; Chapter 19.C at 514**), similarly judges with administrative authority over other judges **must** "take reasonable measures to ensure that those judges properly discharge their judicial responsibilities, including the prompt disposition of matters before them." **MCJC Rule 2.12(B)**. Just as lawyers **must** take reasonable steps to ensure that nonlawyers under their management or supervision comply with the lawyer's own professional responsibilities (*see* **Model Rule 5.3; Chapter 19.C at 515**), judges **must** also "require court staff, court officials, and others subject to the judge's direction and control to act in a manner consistent with the judge's obligations under this Code." **MCJC Rule 2.12(A)**.

And just as lawyers may not have a nonlawyer do something for them that they **must not** do themselves (*see* **Model Rule 8.4(a)** (the **no-puppetry rule**)), judges **must not** have nonjudicial personnel do anything forbidden for the judge. **MCJC Rule 2.12 Comment [1]**.

Judges also have "rat on" or "tattletale" rules that are similar to **Model Rule 8.3**. In the roughly 35 states that have adopted **Model Rule 8.3**, lawyers **must**, unless prevented by the lawyer's **duty of confidentiality**, promptly report to "the appropriate authority" another lawyer's "violation of the Rules of Professional Conduct that raises a substantial question as to that lawyer's honesty, trustworthiness or fitness as a lawyer in other respects" (*see* **Model Rules 8.3(a), (c); Chapter 16.D at 446**). Lawyers **must** also promptly report to "the appropriate authority" (the state's judicial disciplinary authority or, for a federal judge, the clerk of the court for the federal judicial circuit within which the judge sits, *see* **28 U.S.C. § 351(a)**) a violation of applicable rules of judicial conduct that raises a substantial question as to the judge's fitness for office" (again, unless the information is **confidential**, *see* **Model Rules 8.3(b), (c)**). And, of course, lawyers **must not** "knowingly assist a judge or judicial officer in conduct that is a violation of applicable rules of judicial conduct or other law." **Model Rule 8.4(f)**.

Judges have similar "tattletale" obligations of their own: If a judge actually knows of violations by another judge of the Code of Judicial Conduct or by a lawyer of the Rules of Professional Conduct that raise "a substantial question" about the fitness of either to serve, the judge **must** report the violation to the appropriate authority. **MCJC Rule 2.15(A), (B)**; *see also* **MCJC Terminology, "Appropriate authority."** And if a judge does not *actually know* of a violation of the relevant set of Rules but "receives information indicating a substantial likelihood" of a violation, then the judge **must** "take appropriate action." "Appropriate action may include, but is not limited to, communicating directly" with the judge or lawyer, "communicating with a supervising judge" when a judge is involved, or reporting the suspected violation to the appropriate authority or other agency or body," the latter presumably so that the appropriate authority may investigate further and decide whether action is needed. **MCJC Rule 2.15 Comment [2]**. In addition, because substance abuse and mood disorders are so prevalent among lawyers and judges (*see* **Chapter 4.C at 91**), "[a] judge having a reasonable belief that the performance of a lawyer or another judge is impaired by drugs or alcohol, or by a mental, emotional, or physical condition, shall take appropriate action, which may include a confidential referral to a lawyer or judicial assistance program." **MCJC Rule 2.14**. As with lawyers, the failure of a judge to report or take appropriate action as required is itself a ground for judicial discipline of the nonreporting judge. And, of course, judges **must** cooperate with any inquiry of a judicial or lawyer disciplinary authority (including one regarding themselves), and **must** never "retaliate, directly or indirectly, against a person known or suspected to have assisted or cooperated with an investigation of a judge or a lawyer." **MCJC Rule 2.16**.[13]

> **Problem 26B-4:** Judge Cranky engages in the following conduct. What **consequences** could he face, and why? In each instance, what (if anything) **must** or **should** the judge have done differently?
>
> a. Judge Cranky assigns his law clerk, who recently graduated from law school, to draft all of his opinions. Judge Cranky proofreads the drafts, but never checks them for substance. Judge Cranky issues the opinions as written, sometimes with legal errors.
>
> b. Judge Cranky has a staff attorney who has been working in his chambers for over a decade. He tasks this staff attorney with presiding over case management conferences and deciding substantive legal issues during these conferences. When the staff attorney is unsure how to rule, she checks with Judge Cranky, and he advises her. Otherwise, he allows her to run the conferences independently.
>
> c. Judge Genial learns that Judge Cranky has a three-day jury trial calendared. Judge Genial has a new law clerk who asks to sit in. Judge Genial checks with Judge Cranky who voices no opposition. At the end of the first day, Judge Genial's clerk reports back to Judge Genial about what he saw during trial. According to the clerk, Judge Cranky was extremely bombastic, refused to decide several oral motions posed by counsel, and commented in front of the jury that the defendant was a "jerk." Does it change your analysis if Judge Genial sits in on the next day of trial herself, and observes behavior from Judge Cranky similar to what her clerk reported the day before? If so, how and why; and if not, why not? Be sure to tie your answers to specific language in the Model Code of Judicial Conduct.

d. Impartiality

Impartiality—the commitment to administering justice evenhandedly, without fear or favor, according to the rule of law—is the essence of the judicial role. **MCJC Rule 2.2** states that duty plainly: Judges **must** "uphold and apply the law, and shall perform all duties of judicial office fairly and impartially." *See also* **MCJC Terminology, "Impartial."**

---

[13] The Code of Conduct for United States Judges imposes similar obligations. **CCUSJ Canon 3 §§ (B)(2), (5), (6), Comment on Canon 3B(6)**. The Code of Conduct governing federal judicial employees, such as law clerks, dictates that a judicial employee "should report to the appropriate supervising authority any attempt to induce the judicial employee to violate these canons" and "take appropriate action upon receipt of reliable information indicating a likelihood of conduct contravening this Code." **CCJE § 320 Canon 3 §§ (A), (C)(1)**. The references to "these canons" and "this Code" are to the CCJE, suggesting that judicial employees have no *duty* to report the misconduct of judges, or of lawyers except to the extent that a lawyer's misconduct seeks to involve the judicial employee. Judicial employees of course remain free to report misconduct by lawyers or judges, and we would say that they **should** do so for reasons that we hope are apparent. We do, however, understand the power asymmetry that might prompt a reluctance to do so.

i. Circumstances Creating Risks of the Actuality or Appearance of Judicial Bias

Given its centrality both to the judicial function and to the preservation of the perceived legitimacy of our court system (*see* **Chapter 26.B at 978**), it's not surprising that the Model Code of Judicial Conduct identifies multiple different circumstances that can reflect, or create the possibility or appearance of, bias in favor of or against particular litigants or classes of litigants.

(A) Avoiding the Effect or the Appearance of Outside Influences

"An independent judiciary requires that judges decide cases according to the law and facts, without regard to whether particular laws or litigants are popular or unpopular with the public, the media, government officials, or the judge's friends or family." **MCJC Rule 2.4 Comment [1]**. Accordingly, **MCJC Rule 2.4** makes clear that a judge **must not**

- "be swayed by public clamor or fear of criticism" (**MCJC Rule 2.4(A)**);
- "permit family, social, political, financial, or other **interests** or relationships to influence the judge's judicial conduct or judgment" (**MCJC Rule 2.4(B)**); or
- convey or permit others to convey the impression that any person or organization is in a position to influence the judge" (**MCJC Rule 2.4(C)**). In this regard, lawyers are similarly forbidden from "stat[ing] or imply[ing] an ability to influence improperly a government agency or official or to achieve results by means that violate the Rules of Professional Conduct or other law" (**Model Rule 8.4(e)**).[14]

(B) Avoiding Any Manifestation or Appearance of Bias

The fact and appearance of fairness and impartiality are central to the judicial function, so it should come as no surprise that **MCJC Rule 2.3(A)** confirms that judges **must** "perform the duties of judicial office, including administrative duties, without bias or prejudice." But avoiding the manifestation, suggestion, or appearance of bias is also basic to the integrity and the legitimacy of the justice system as a whole. In recognition of continuing issues in need of attention, **MCJC Rule 2.3(B)** provides that judges **must not** "by words or conduct manifest bias or prejudice, or engage in harassment, including but not limited to bias, prejudice, or harassment based upon race, sex, gender, religion, national origin, ethnicity, disability, age, sexual orientation, marital status, socioeconomic status, or political affiliation, and shall not permit court staff, court officials, or others subject to the judge's direction and control to do so." Judges also **must** prevent the lawyers appearing

---

[14] The federal judiciary's code of conduct is again similar. **CCUSJ Canon 2(B), Canon 3(A)(1)**.

before them from engaging in such conduct "against parties, witnesses, lawyers, or others" in the proceedings before them. **MCJC Rule 2.3(C)**.

The forbidden conduct is defined very broadly, and it includes anything that "could reasonably be perceived as prejudiced or biased." "Examples of manifestations of bias or prejudice include but are not limited to epithets; slurs; demeaning nicknames; negative stereotyping; attempted humor based upon stereotypes; threatening, intimidating, or hostile acts; suggestions of connections between race, ethnicity, or nationality and crime; and irrelevant references to personal characteristics. Even facial expressions and body language can convey to parties and lawyers in the proceeding, jurors, the media, and others an appearance of bias or prejudice." **MCJC Rule 2.4 Comment [2]**; *see also* **MCJC Rule 3.1 Comment [3]**. "Harassment . . . is verbal or physical conduct that denigrates or shows hostility or aversion toward a person on bases such as race, sex, gender, religion, national origin, ethnicity, disability, age, sexual orientation, marital status, socioeconomic status, or political affiliation." **MCJC Rule 2.4 Comment [3]**.[15] And "[s]exual harassment includes but is not limited to sexual advances, requests for sexual favors, and other verbal or physical conduct of a sexual nature that is unwelcome." **MCJC Rule 2.4 Comment [4]**.[16]

The prohibition on manifesting or appearing to manifest bias also limits what judges may publicly (and in many situations privately) discuss. This aspect of the ban highlights an important tension in the judicial role: The First Amendment broadly (though not absolutely) guarantees public access to the courts and court records.[17] The judiciary does its job in the public eye regarding matters that are by definition in controversy and sometimes widely and publicly controversial. And a

---

[15] Although a great many state and federal judges are scrupulously careful to avoid any conduct of this kind, compliance is by no means universal; hence the need for the Rule. Regrettably, examples crop up regularly. *See, e.g.*, Gabrielle Banks & Lise Olsen, *Houston Federal Judge Bars Female Prosecutor from Trial, Sparking Standoff with U.S. Attorney's Office*, https://www.houstonchronicle.com/news/houston-texas/houston/article/Houston-federal-judge-bars-female-prosecutor-from-13610959.php (Feb. 12, 2019). Similarly, the Chief Judge in the District of Montana retired after having been found to have sent hundreds of racist emails to friends and colleagues. John Adams, *Former Judge Violated Ethics Rules, Panel Rules*, https://www.usatoday.com/story/news/nation/2014/01/17/judge-montana-cebull-racist-obama/4592315/ (Jan. 17, 2014).

[16] Again, as surprising as it may seem, the judiciary is no more immune to this species of abuse than other legal workplaces. One of your authors was subjected to unwelcome sexual advances by a federal appellate judge during her clerkship for a different judge (the judge for whom she clerked was not the one who made the advances), and her relatively recent recounting of the episode made national news. At the time of those events, it was difficult if not impossible to report or seek recourse for such misconduct, and less may have changed since then than most would have wished. *See* Dahlia Lithwick, *What Has the Judiciary Learned Since Kozinski?* https://slate.com/news-and-politics/2018/01/after-kozinski-court-employees-cant-get-clarity-on-how-to-report-judicial-abuse.html (Jan. 29, 2018). Congress held hearings in 2020 regarding the need to strengthen the oversight of the federal judiciary in this regard. *See, e.g.*, Dylan Hedtler-Gaudette & Sarah Turberville, *Sexual Harassment by Judges Operating with Impunity Shows Courts Need Their Own #MeToo*, https://www.nbcnews.com/think/opinion/olivia-warren-s-testimony-sexual-harassment-judges-shows-courts-need-ncna1137321 (Feb. 15, 2020). The federal judicial employees' code of conduct now provides that its strict and "general restriction on use or disclosure of confidential information does not prevent, nor should it discourage, an employee or former employee from reporting or disclosing misconduct, including sexual or other forms of harassment, by a judge, supervisor, or other person." **CCJE § 320 Canon 3 § D(3)**.

[17] *See Press-Enterprise Co. v. Superior Court*, 478 U.S. 1 (1986).

significant part of a court's work is done in public and on the public record, and involves speaking or writing about pending matters in the course of considering or deciding them. Judges also are encouraged to, and often do, speak publicly about the law and the legal system for purposes of civic education, including regarding law reform. *See* **MCJC Rule 3.1 Comment [1]**. Yet comments about issues that are or are reasonably likely to come before the court **must** avoid either the fact or the appearance of prejudgment, before all the proof and arguments from all interested parties are heard and considered. Thus, **MCJC Rule 2.10(A)** provides that judges **must not** "make any public statement that might reasonably be expected to affect the outcome or impair the fairness of a matter pending or impending in any court, or make any nonpublic statement that might substantially interfere with a fair trial or hearing." (Most judicial disciplinary authorities to have considered the question consider social media public expression.) Similarly, judges **must not**, "in connection with cases, controversies, or issues that are likely to come before the court, make pledges, promises, or commitments that are inconsistent with the impartial performance of the adjudicative duties of judicial office." **MCJC Rule 2.10(B)**.

This does not mean that judges are gagged at all times or for all purposes. These prohibitions obviously don't affect a judge's power to "affect the outcome . . . of a matter" by speaking or writing words that go to consideration or decision of an issue in the proper procedural course. More broadly, the First Amendment gives judges a significant measure of freedom to express their views about legal issues, particularly in the context of standing for election in those states that elect their judges.[18] That's why the constraints on judicial speech regarding legal issues limit only statements "that might reasonably be expected to affect the outcome or impair the fairness of a [specific] matter pending or impending in any court," and, more generally, "pledges, promises, or commitments that are inconsistent with the impartial performance of . . . adjudicative duties . . . ." Judges also "**may** make public statements in the course of official duties, may explain court procedures, and may comment on any proceeding in which the judge is a litigant in a personal capacity" (**MCJC Rule 2.10(D)**), and defensively "**may** respond directly or through a third party to allegations in the media or elsewhere concerning the judge's conduct in a matter" (**MCJC Rule 2.10(D)**, though most judges will tell you that this is usually a bad idea, even when it is allowed).[19] And judges **must not** ever disclose or use nonpublic information acquired in a judicial capacity for any purpose other than their official duties. **MCJC Rule 3.5**.[20]

---

[18] *Republican Party of Minnesota v. White*, 536 U.S. 765 (2002).

[19] "In cases in which the judge is a litigant in an official capacity, such as a writ of mandamus, the judge must not comment publicly." **MCJC Rule 2.10 Comment [2]**. (Do you see the difference? Think of an example of the situation described in the text and the one described in this footnote.)

[20] As you would expect, federal judges are subject to similar constraints. *See* **CCUSJ Canon 2(C), Canon 3(A)(6), (B)(4), Comment on Canon 3B(4), Canon 4(D)(5)**. Indeed, the restraints on the extrajudicial expression of federal judges are broader than those articulated in the ABA Model Code: Federal judges are discouraged from "making public comment on the merits

(C) *Ex Parte* Contacts

In an adversary process, contacts with the decision maker by parties or lawyers on one side without the other side present or at least given an opportunity to be, or in the case of a writing to the court contemporaneously provided a copy of the written communication, create the opportunity for mischief, and the appearance of favoritism or secret influence. Such *ex parte* contacts thus are barred in the absence of a very good legal or procedural reason allowing them. We've already seen that lawyers are barred from *ex parte* contacts with judicial officers regarding a client matter "unless authorized to do so by law or court order." **Model Rule 3.5(b)**; **Chapter 24.C at 841 & n.12**. Judicial conduct rules also stringently restrict *ex parte* contacts.

MCJC Rule 2.9(A) states the general rule—that judges **must not** "initiate, permit, or consider ex parte communications, or consider other communications made to the judge outside the presence of the parties or their lawyers, concerning a pending or impending matter . . . ." The rule against *ex parte* contacts also forbids judges from independently investigating the facts of a pending or impending matter. **MCJC Rule 2.9(C)**. Judges are limited to the facts they are permitted to review by the rules of evidence (including judicial notice), and they may not seek out the facts from any other source, including the Internet. **MCJC Rule 2.9 Comment [6]**. The Rule enumerates five exceptions to the general prohibition on *ex parte* contacts:

- "[E]x parte communication with the court for scheduling, administrative, or emergency purposes, which does not address substantive matters," when circumstances require, but only if "(a) the judge reasonably believes that no party will gain a procedural, substantive, or tactical advantage as a result of the ex parte communication; and (b) the judge makes provision promptly to notify all other parties of the substance of the ex parte communication, and gives the parties an opportunity to respond" (**MCJC Rule 2.9(A)(1)**).
- Receipt by the judge of "the written advice of a disinterested expert" on the applicable law, but only "if the judge gives advance notice to the parties of the person to be consulted and the subject matter of the advice to be solicited, and affords the parties a reasonable opportunity to object and respond to the notice and to the advice received" (**MCJC Rule 2.9(A)(2)**). **MCJC Rule 2.9 Comment [3]** emphasizes that the general bar on *ex parte* contacts forbids "communications [about a pending or impending proceeding] with lawyers, law teachers, and other persons who are not participants in the proceeding, except to the limited extent permitted" by **MCJC Rule 2.9**. However, a judge may properly

---

of a matter pending or impending in any court," and should make reasonable efforts to impose similar restraints on their staff. **CCUSJ Canon 3(A)(6)**. Federal judicial employees are similarly constrained, both during and after their employment. *See* **CCJE § 320 Canon 3 §§ C-D**.

seek advice *ex parte* from "ethics advisory committees, outside counsel, or legal experts concerning the judge's compliance" with the Code of Judicial Conduct. **MCJC Rule 2.9 Comment [7]**.

- Conferring with court staff and other judges, so long as "the judge makes reasonable efforts to avoid receiving factual information that is not part of the record," and retains the power and responsibility to decide the matter (**MCJC Rule 2.9(A)(3)**). This authorization to confer with other judges does *not* include judges who have been disqualified from hearing the matter, or who have appellate jurisdiction over it. **MCJC Rule 2.9 Comment [5]**.

- With the consent of the parties, meeting with parties and their counsel separately in an effort to settle a matter pending before the judge (**MCJC Rule 2.9(A)(4)**).

- "[W]hen expressly authorized by law" (**MCJC Rule 2.9(A)(5)**; *see* **Chapter 24.C at 841 n.12** for a few examples of legally authorized *ex parte* proceedings).

What if, despite the judge's reasonable efforts to avoid it (or if, in a moment of weakness or lapsed judgment, the judge allows it), she receives an unpermitted *ex parte* contact or a fact outside the court record? In either case, the judge must promptly "notify the parties of the substance of the communication [or factual information] and provide the parties with an opportunity to respond." **MCJC Rule 2.9(B)**. In other words, if something sneaks into the adversary process without being to subjected to the usual limits and contextualization that the adversary process provides, the judge **must** give the party who was deprived of the protections of the adversary system the opportunity to bring them into play.[21]

> **Problem 26B-5:** Assume the judges below engage in the following conduct. What **consequences** could each judge face, and why? What, if anything, **must** or **should** each judge have done differently?
>
> a. Before ascending to the bench, Judge Cranky worked for Big, Bigger & Biggest, a law firm. Although he has not been with the firm for many years, he still attends firm networking events and goes to lunch with the firm's hiring partner. Most of Judge Cranky's term law clerks go to work for the firm after they finish their clerkships. Among the legal community there's a general sense that you'll do better in a case pending before Judge Cranky if you retain counsel from Big, Bigger & Biggest.
>
> b. Same as (a), except that an empirical analysis of Judge Cranky's decisions reveals that Judge Cranky has been more likely to grant a motion filed by counsel from Big, Bigger, and Biggest than an identical motion filed by any other lawyer or law firm.
>
> c. Judge Cranky is more than a little old-fashioned. He refuses to allow female lawyers to wear pants in his courtroom. He has no attire rules for male lawyers.

---

[21] Again, the code of conduct governing federal judges is similar. *See* **CCUSJ Canon 3(A)(4)**.

d. Judge Cranky also believes that women should not be primary breadwinners for their families. When presiding over bench trials where women plaintiffs seek damages for lost income due to injuries, he always reduces the amount on the theory that women's labor isn't worth that much. On loss of consortium claims filed by women, however, he always increases the amount he awarded on the theory that losing a male breadwinner is a serious imposition on a family.

e. Judge Juvenile is a family court judge. After many years on the bench, she became cynical about many of the parents who appeared before her. She saw case after case involving children who suffered abuse at the hands of their parents—yet the law required family reunification whenever possible. If she deems a child's parents unfit to care for a child, Judge Juvenile is required to place a child with a fit and willing relative in "kinship care." Under the law in Judge Juvenile's jurisdiction, foster care is a last resort only if kinship care is impossible.

Judge Juvenile presided over a case involving a child who suffered broken ribs. Child protective services had removed the child from her parents' custody after a physician reported a suspicion that the child was being abused. In hearing after hearing, Judge Juvenile asked the parents for an explanation. Neither could explain the child's injuries. Judge Juvenile refused to return the child to her parents, pressuring the parents to "confess" about the injuries. Although the child's grandmother has volunteered to take the child, Judge Juvenile refuses to order kinship care, reasoning that foster-care placement provides an incentive to make the parents "fess up."

f. Consider Danielle's predicament in the **chapter Introduction at 973**. Identify any defects in Judge Cranky's conduct and the bases for your conclusions. Up to the point at which the hypothetical ends, has Danielle done anything improper? If so, what and why; and if not, why not?

g. Judge Cranky has pending before him a complex business dispute that will take over a month to try. After a routine status and scheduling conference in the case, he calls counsel into chambers.

   i. He eyes the lawyers severely, and asks, "Okay, counsel, what's it gonna take to settle this case?" (*Hint: See* **MCJC Rule 2.6(B); MCJC Rule 2.6 Comments [2]-[3]**).

   ii. The plaintiff's lawyer proposes a settlement amount. Judge Cranky responds, "That's way too high. You've got to do better."

   iii. The defendants' lawyer proposes a very low settlement amount, arguing that the strength of a pending motion for summary judgment makes any recovery unrealistic. "I'm going to deny that motion," the judge replies.

h. Judge Cranky has a newly filed case before him based on a recently enacted statute regarding data privacy. The defendant has filed a motion to dismiss for failure to state a claim, raising several issues regarding the interpretation of the statute. Judge Cranky is unfamiliar with this subject matter, and having looked at the statute at issue, finds it extremely hard to understand. He calls the dean of a local law school, who is an old friend, and asks for an introduction to a member of the faculty who is an expert in cyberlaw and data privacy. He meets with that faculty member, Prof. Clever, and asks her for "a download" on the new data privacy statute. Does your analysis change if, in the course of their discussion, the judge raises with Prof. Clever the statutory construction questions addressed in the pending motion to dismiss? If so, how and why; and if not, why not?

ii. Judicial Recusal (Also Referred to as Disqualification)

(A) What Recusal Is

"**Recusal**" is a term commonly used for the process or result of removing a judicial or other adjudicative officer from presiding over a particular pending matter. ("**Disqualification**" is also used to denote this process or result, and in fact is the term principally used in the Model Code of Judicial Conduct and the federal judicial recusal statute. Similarly, **recusal** is sometimes used for the process or result of **disqualifying** a lawyer from acting as counsel. Overall, the terms may be used interchangeably in both contexts. *See* **MCJC Rule 2.11 Comment [1]**.)

Recusal is *not* always required any time that a judge violates the Code of Judicial Conduct. Instead, it is a **consequence** called for in the limited circumstances in which a judge's impartiality may reasonably be called into question in a particular pending matter. **MCJC Rule 2.11** defines the circumstances in which judges **must recuse** themselves, and we'll discuss those circumstances below. If judges fail to **recuse** themselves when they are required by Rule to do so, a party may raise the issue by motion, and it will be adjudicated under procedures typically set by procedural rule or statute. Generally, unless the grounds for the motion are facially insufficient, the motion to recuse **must** be heard by a judge other than the one whose impartiality is challenged, a simple application of the timeless principle that no one may be a judge in her own case (*nemo iudex in causa sua* for the Latin mavens). *See, e.g.,* **28 U.S.C § 144.**

Before we get into the details of the proper grounds for **recusal**, let's pause and appreciate what a tightrope-walk **recusal** issues present for the affected judge and court. On the one hand, the parties and the judiciary as an institution have strong and legitimate interests in seeing each controversy adjudicated by an officer whose impartiality is not reasonably subject to question. But on the other, "[t]he dignity of the court, the judge's respect for fulfillment of judicial duties, and a proper concern for the burdens that may be imposed upon the judge's colleagues require that a judge not use **disqualification** to avoid cases that present difficult, controversial, or unpopular issues." **MCJC Rule 2.7 Comment [1]**. And litigants must not be allowed to judge-shop. This tension amounts to the principle that judges generally **should not recuse** themselves unless they **must** do so. But as we'll see, although some grounds for **recusal** are bright-line rules that are easy to apply, others are fuzzy standards that leave plenty of room for judgment—and argument.

(B) The Basic Standard for Recusal: When the Judge's "Impartiality Might Reasonably Be Questioned"

The basic standard for **recusal** is stated in **MCJC Rule 2.11(A)**, which provides that a judge **must** "disqualify himself or herself in any proceeding in which the judge's impartiality might reasonably be questioned . . . ." Obviously this is a fuzzy standard, and there is a fair amount of room for reasonable people to disagree about when a judge's impartiality "might reasonably be questioned."[22]

(C) Examples in the Recusal Rule of Specific Situations in Which a Judge's Impartiality Might Reasonably Be Questioned, Requiring Recusal

The MCJC's **recusal** Rule puts a little meat on these rather bare bones by providing a short list of specific circumstances intended as a nonexclusive set of examples of situations in which a judge's impartiality might reasonably be questioned, and in which **recusal** is therefore required. TAMING THE TEXT How do we know the list is nonexclusive? Because **MCJC Rule 2.11(A)** introduces the list with the phrase "including but not limited to the following circumstances." If there were any remaining doubt, **MCJC Rule 2.11 Comment [1]** explains that "[u]nder this Rule, a judge is **disqualified** whenever the judge's impartiality might reasonably be questioned, regardless of whether any of the specific provisions of paragraphs (A) (1) through (6) apply." TAMING THE TEXT The nonexclusive list of examples includes:

- "The judge has a personal bias or prejudice concerning a party or a party's lawyer, or personal knowledge of facts that are in dispute in the proceeding" (**MCJC Rule 2.11(A)(1)**). This, too, is a fuzzy standard, or at least the first half is. What kind of "bias or prejudice," how strong it is, and what evidence is competent to prove it are all subject to argument. Nevertheless, we still have the basic **recusal** standard to guide us—the Rule requires bias or prejudice of a kind and intensity, and substantiated by such evidence, that the judge's impartiality might reasonably be questioned. That, too, is more than a little vague. Sorry, but the only advice that we can give you here is to look for cases in your jurisdiction that are analogous to the one that is worrying you, so that you can find facts in those cases that either do or don't lend credence to an argument that the judge has that kind or degree of personal bias or prejudice.
- "The judge knows that the judge, the judge's spouse or domestic partner, or a person within the third degree of relationship to either of them, or the spouse or domestic partner of such a person is . . . (a) a party to the proceeding, or an officer, director, general partner, managing member, or trustee of a party; (b) acting as a lawyer in the proceeding; (c) a person who has more than a de minimis

---

[22] The basic standard for recusal of federal judges is the same. *See* **28 U.S.C. § 455**; **CCUSJ Canon 3(C)**.

interest that could be substantially affected by the proceeding; or (d) likely to be a **material** witness in the proceeding" (**MCJC Rule 2.11(A)(2)**). TAMING THE TEXT There's a lot going on here. Let's look at a few of the important terms:

- "Domestic partner" means "a person with whom another person maintains a household and an intimate relationship, other than a person to whom he or she is legally married." Thus a "domestic partner" includes, but does not have to be, someone with whom the person in question has a formal and legally recognized domestic partnership as authorized under the laws of some states. The definition simply requires that the judge and the domestic partner be "intimate," and "maintain[] a household" together, regardless of any legal recognition of their relationship. **MCJC Terminology, "Domestic partner."**

- "'De minimis,' in the context of interests pertaining to disqualification of a judge, means an insignificant interest that could not raise a reasonable question regarding the judge's impartiality." **MCJC Terminology, "De minimis."**

- The "third degree of relationship" (also referred to as the third degree of consanguinity) is a term borrowed from the civil law of Europe, and "includes the following persons: great-grandparent, grandparent, parent, uncle, aunt, brother, sister, child, grandchild, great-grandchild, nephew, and niece." **MCJC Terminology, "Third degree of relationship."** To help visualize those within the third degree of relationship, here's a handy chart:

Your great-grandparents

Your grandparents

Your parents — Your parents' siblings

YOU — Your siblings — Their kids

Your kids — Your siblings' kids

Their kids (your grandchildren)

Their kids (your great-grandchildren)

- Please remember that the **recusal** Rule includes not only those within the third degree of relationship to the *judge*, but any spouse or domestic partner of any of those persons within the third degree of relationship, as well as anyone within the third degree of relationship to the judge's spouse or domestic partner (including the spouse's or domestic partner's parents, grandparents, siblings, etc.). That list can get pretty long when the judge has a big family.

■ **MCJC Rule 2.11(A)(1)(b)** says that judges **must recuse** themselves if they have a **disqualifying** relationship with a lawyer in the proceeding. But what if a lawyer in the proceeding does not herself have such a relationship with the judge, but is part of the same **practice organization** as someone who has a **disqualifying** relationship with the judge? **MCJC 2.11 Comment [4]** reasons that this situation is not **disqualifying** *unless* there is something in particular about the judge's relationship in the specific circumstances presented for which the judge's impartiality might reasonably be questioned, or if "the relative [whose colleague is counsel in the proceeding] is known by the judge to have an interest in the law firm that could be substantially affected by the proceeding under paragraph (A)(2)(c)." An example of the latter might arise if the lawyer's firm stands to earn a large contingent fee (that is, a fee whose size depends on the outcome) in the matter at issue, of which the judge's relation would stand to receive a substantial portion. (Do you see why this could matter?) ⊲ Taming the Text

■ "The judge knows that he or she, individually or as a fiduciary, or the judge's spouse, domestic partner, parent, or child, or any other member of the judge's family residing in the judge's household, has an economic interest in the subject matter in controversy or in a party to the proceeding" (**MCJC Rule 2.11(A)(3)**). Taming the Text ⊳ This is the portion of the rule that defines economic interests of the judge or his or her family that require **recusal**. There are some defined terms:

■ The judge's own economic interests can be **disqualifying** if the interest is held for the judge's own account, or on behalf of others if the judge is serving as a fiduciary. "Fiduciary" for these purposes "includes relationships such as executor, administrator, trustee, or guardian." **MCJC Terminology, "Fiduciary."** Because that definition begins with the word "includes," we can infer that it means any position of trust in which the judge is managing things of value for someone else that might be characterized under state law as a "fiduciary" or "confidential" relationship with the beneficiary (*see* **Chapter 5.B at 106**).

■ "Member of a judge's family residing in the judge's household" means "any relative of a judge by blood or marriage, or a person treated by a judge as a member of the judge's family, who resides in the judge's household." **MCJC Terminology, "Member of a judge's family residing in the judge's household."** This term defines a much smaller group than those within the third degree of relationship. To qualify, a person must be *both* related to the judge by blood or marriage (or treated by the judge as if she were) *and* reside in the judge's household.

▪ The definition of "economic interest" is obviously the fulcrum of this ground for **recusal**. The baseline definition is "ownership of more than a de minimis legal or equitable interest." **MCJC Terminology, "Economic interest."** So, generally, ownership of anything involved in the proceeding of more than negligible value can be **disqualifying**. (Do you see why this makes sense? Go ahead and explain it out loud in terms of the general **recusal** standard of something that might create reasonable questions about the judge's impartiality.) The definition then carefully sorts out the kinds of ordinary economic relationships that generally *don't* raise questions about impartiality, adding the caution that, in unusual situations, the stakes could be high enough in one of those relationships to raise concerns: "Except for situations in which the judge participates in the management of such a legal or equitable interest, or the interest could be substantially affected by the outcome of a proceeding before a judge, it does not include: (1) an interest in the individual holdings within a mutual or common investment fund; (2) an interest in securities held by an educational, religious, charitable, fraternal, or civic organization in which the judge or the judge's spouse, domestic partner, parent, or child serves as a director, an officer, an advisor, or other participant; (3) a deposit in a financial institution or deposits or proprietary interests the judge may maintain as a member of a mutual savings association or credit union, or similar proprietary interests; or (4) an interest in the issuer of government securities held by the judge." TAMING THE TEXT

▪ In order to ensure that relevant economic information is reflected in the judge's **recusal** decisions, judges have a duty to remain informed about their own "fiduciary and economic interests," and to make "a reasonable effort to keep informed about the personal economic interests of the judge's spouse or domestic partner and minor children residing in the judge's household." **MCJC Rule 2.11(B)**.

■ "The judge knows or learns by means of a timely motion that a party, a party's lawyer, or the law firm of a party's lawyer has within the previous [insert number] year[s] made aggregate contributions to the judge's campaign in an amount that [is greater than $[insert amount] for an individual or $[insert amount] for an entity] [is reasonable and appropriate for an individual or an entity]" (**MCJC Rule 2.11(A)(4)**). TAMING THE TEXT This is the Rule that addresses the concern that contributions to a judge's election or re-election campaign by a party, a lawyer, or a law firm involved in a pending matter could reasonably call the judge's impartiality into question.[23] You will notice that the model form

---

[23] For an example so extreme that the United States Supreme Court found that it amounted to a due process violation for a judge *not* to have been recused, *see Caperton v. A. T. Massey Coal Co.*, 556 U.S. 868 (2009).

of the Rule leaves it to individual states to identify what amount of campaign contributions over what period of time is definitively or presumptively **disqualifying**, or whether the state instead adopts the fuzzier standard of an amount that is more than "reasonable and appropriate." The Rule refers to "aggregate contributions." "Contribution" means any kind of contribution, financial or in-kind, and can include goods, professional or volunteer services, or anything else that the judge-candidate would otherwise have to pay for. **MCJC Terminology, "Contributions."** "Aggregate" means adding up all the different kinds of contributions a person or organization makes, "whether the contributions are made directly to the judge's campaign committee" or "indirectly with the understanding that they will be used to support the election of a candidate or to oppose the election of the candidate's opponent." **MCJC Terminology, "Aggregate."** TAMING THE TEXT

■   "The judge, while a judge or a judicial candidate, has made a public statement, other than in a court proceeding, judicial decision, or opinion, that commits or appears to commit the judge to reach a particular result or rule in a particular way in the proceeding or controversy." **MCJC Rule 2.11(A)(5)).** TAMING THE TEXT A "judicial candidate" is anyone "who is seeking selection for or retention in judicial office by election or appointment." **MCJC Terminology, "Judicial candidate."** This ground for **recusal** is expressly limited to extrajudicial statements. (Do you see which language in the Rule states this limitation and why it's necessary?) TAMING THE TEXT

■   The judge has or had a personal connection to or role in the pending matter, specifically:

■   The judge "served as a lawyer in the matter in controversy, or was associated with a lawyer who participated substantially as a lawyer in the matter during such association" (**MCJC 2.11(A)(6)(a)**).

■   The judge "served in governmental employment, and in such capacity participated personally and substantially as a lawyer or public official concerning the proceeding, or has publicly expressed in such capacity an opinion concerning the merits of the particular matter in controversy" (**MCJC Rule 2.11(A)(6)(b)**). TAMING THE TEXT Notice the difference between the standards for a judge's prior government service and prior service in private practice. In private practice, the judge merely had to be "associated with"—that is, part of the same **practice organization** as—a lawyer who participated substantially as counsel in the matter for the matter to be **disqualifying**. In contrast, prior government service is **disqualifying** only if the judge *herself* "participated personally and substantially as a lawyer or public official concerning the proceeding," or *personally* made a public statement about the merits as part of that government service. TAMING THE TEXT

- The judge "was a **material** witness concerning the matter" (**MCJC Rule 2.11(A)(6)(c)**).
- The judge "previously presided as a judge over the matter in another court" (**MCJC Rule 2.11(A)(6)(d)**).[24]

(D) When the Parties May Waive a Judge's Recusal

Must a judge *always* be **recused** when circumstances meet any of the standards of **MCJC Rule 2.11**? In a word, no. In many situations, if all the parties and counsel to the proceeding freely and voluntarily give their **informed consent** to having the **recusable** judge continue to preside, the judge **may** continue.

But are the parties *always* free to consent? Again, no. If a judge is subject to **recusal** for bias or prejudice under **MCJC Rule 2.11(A)(1)**, no amount of consent, no matter how voluntary or informed, will be sufficient to keep the judge properly involved in that particular case. **MCJC Rule 2.11(C).** ┤REASON FOR THE RULE├ The situation is comparable to a **nonconsentable conflict of interest**: There are some situations in which the risk to the parties and to the integrity of the proceeding is so great that we simply don't give the parties the choice. *See* **Chapter 22.E at 739.** ┤REASON FOR THE RULE├

Other than this single category of analogies to **nonconsentable conflicts**, however, a judge's **recusal may** be voluntarily waived if all the parties and lawyers agree. **MCJC Rule 2.11(C)** specifies a series of procedural requirements that **must** be met for the waiver to be effective, all designed to support the purpose that the waiver be fully voluntary and informed:

- The judge must believe, reasonably and in good faith, that she can adjudicate the matter fairly and impartially. ┤TAMING THE TEXT├ This requirement is not literally stated in the Rule. So how do we know that it's there? Because **MCJC Rule 2.11(C)** says that the process of party consent begins when the judge "disclose[s] on the record the basis of the judge's disqualification and . . . ask[s]the parties and their lawyers to consider . . . whether to waive disqualification." And the Rule says the judge "**may**" do those things, which means the judge doesn't have to. What would induce a judge *not* to offer the parties the option of waiving her **disqualification**? Concern about her own ability to judge fairly and impartially, most likely. So the first step as a practical matter is the judge's own determination that, despite circumstances that could cause her impartiality

---

[24] The standards governing **recusal** of federal judges are similar to those in the Model Code. *See* **28 U.S.C. § 455; CCUSJ Canon 3(C)**. Federal judicial employees (such as law clerks) are not subject to **recusal**, but they are cautioned broadly against **conflicts of interest** in working on matters defined in general terms that would require their **recusal** if they were federal judges. *See* **CCJE § 320 Canon 3 § F**. Members of a judge's "personal staff" are subject to more exacting **conflict-of-interest** standards than general court employees. **CCJE § 320 Canon 3 § F(2), (4)**. When a judicial employee encounters such a **conflict of interest,** "the judicial employee should promptly inform his or her appointing authority. The appointing authority, after determining that an actual **conflict** or the appearance of a **conflict of interest** exists, should take appropriate steps to restrict the judicial employee's performance of official duties in such matter so as to avoid a **conflict** or the appearance of a **conflict of interest**." **CCJE § 320 Canon 3 § F(3).** *See also* **Chapter 25.D at 938.**

reasonably to be questioned, she is nevertheless willing and able to act fairly and impartially in the cause.

■ If the judge is willing and believes she is able to continue, the judge must then "disclose on the record the basis of the judge's **disqualification**" and "ask the parties and their lawyers to consider, outside the presence of the judge and court personnel, whether to waive **disqualification**." "On the record" means in a writing served on the parties and saved in the court's public file, or stated orally in open court and recorded or transcribed. REASON FOR THE RULE The record requirement preserves a basis for review of any waiver the parties give to ensure that it was properly given. And the disclosure requirement (analogous to the disclosure requirement for **informed consent** to a lawyer's **conflict of interest**, *see* **Chapter 22.E at 743**) ensures that the parties are fully informed about what factual grounds for judicial **disqualification** they are agreeing to waive. In fact, **MCJC Rule 2.11 Comment [5]** advises that "[a] judge **should** disclose on the record information that the judge believes the parties or their lawyers might reasonably consider relevant to a possible motion for **disqualification**, even if the judge believes there is no basis for **disqualification**." REASON FOR THE RULE

■ Then the parties have to consider the waiver without any express or implicit influence from the judge. "If, following the disclosure, the parties and lawyers agree, without participation by the judge or court personnel, that the judge should not be **disqualified**, the judge may participate in the proceeding." REASON FOR THE RULE Notice the Rule's repeated insistence on the right of the parties and their counsel to consider the waiver outside the presence of the judge and court staff. The judge and her staff are a powerful presence in a courtroom, even if they don't say anything, and the Rule thus insists on giving the parties and their counsel the opportunity to consider the proffered waiver privately.[25] REASON FOR THE RULE

■ Finally, "[t]he agreement **must** be incorporated into the record of the proceeding."[26] TAMING THE TEXT

(E) The "Rule of Necessity"

To close out our consideration of **recusal**, we need to discuss a rarely invoked doctrine by which an otherwise mandatory judicial **disqualification** may be overridden. It's called the "rule of necessity," and it comes into play either when *every* judge who would otherwise be available to hear and decide a matter is subject to **recusal** for the same reason, or when *only one* judge who would otherwise be

---

[25] Ask yourself, though, how "willing" that waiver might be: "Do any of you think that I might be biased in this matter?" "Of *course* not, Your Honor." A close analogy (with much lower stakes) might be the willingness of those in the courtroom to laugh at a judge's jokes, whether they're funny or not.

[26] The code governing federal judges is once again similar, though significantly fewer facts justifying **recusal** are waivable by the lawyers and parties. *See* **CCUSJ Canon 3(D)**.

recused is available under the urgent circumstances presented. **MCJC Rule 2.11 Comment [3]**.

An example of the former kind of problem (every judge is **disqualified**) would be if there were litigation filed regarding, say, the compensation of every judge in the jurisdiction. Every available judge would have a personal economic interest in the outcome of the matter, and thus be subject to **recusal**. That would mean that no judge could hear the case. The effect of the rule of necessity in those circumstances is that if *every* judge is **disqualified** from hearing the matter then, perversely, *any* judge so **disqualified** can hear it anyway. *Id.* The oddly paradoxical nature of this solution can't be denied, but it's hard to think of a better one.

An example of the other kind of problem (there is only one judge available in the time or other circumstances required) might arise if the single judge assigned to night duty is presented with an urgent request for a warrant or temporary restraining order under circumstances that create a real likelihood of a harmful outcome if the matter has to wait until another judge can be found, but the judge on the spot is subject to **recusal** under the Rule (say, the restraining order is sought by or against a company in which the judge owns some stock). In such cases, the judge **may** decide the urgent issue, but "**must** disclose on the record the basis for possible **disqualification** and make reasonable efforts to transfer the matter to another judge as soon as practicable." *Id.*

> **Problem 26B-6:** Think of an example of each of the four categories of situations enumerated in **MCJC Rule 2.11(A)(3)** (*see* **Chapter 26.B at 994**) that would *not* be **disqualifying**, and then imagine some circumstances in which each one of those categories could rise to the level of a **disqualifying** interest.

> **Problem 26B-7:** In each of the following circumstances, is the judge subject to **recusal**? If so, under what provision(s) of the Model Code of Judicial Conduct, and why; and if not, why not?
>
> a. When Judge Cranky was in private practice, he made a disciplinary referral concerning another practitioner, Lonnie Lazy. Lonnie found out, and there has been acrimony between the two ever since. In a case recently assigned to Judge Cranky, Lonnie represents one of the litigants.
>
> b. Judge Cranky's family owns and operates a real estate company, which owns many rental units. Judge Cranky recently helped the company draft a complaint against Handy Dandy, a local contractor, alleging negligent repair work on one of the family company's buildings. Handy Dandy is a litigant in one of the cases on Judge Cranky's docket (but not the one in which he helped draft the complaint, and not one involving his family company).
>
> c. Before being elected to the bench, Judge Cranky represented a bank. As a result of this representation, he learned that the bank was extremely sloppy about recording its mortgages and remitting to the taxing authority property tax payments it collected from

borrowers as part of their loan arrangements. Several times during his legal work for the bank, Judge Cranky had to appear at a tax-lien sale to bid on a property on the bank's behalf because of the bank's sloppiness. Judge Cranky has recently been assigned a case involving claims by a plaintiff who took out a home loan from the same bank, and now alleges that the plaintiff's home was sold at a tax-lien sale because the bank failed to remit property taxes it collected from the plaintiff-borrower.

d. When Judge Cranky was in law school, he competed in moot court. His partner was Lisette Lawyer. The two have not kept in touch since graduation, which was several decades ago. Lisette now has a case pending before Judge Cranky in which she represents one of the parties. Would your analysis change if Lisette personally were one of the parties? If so, how and why; and if not, why not?

e. Judge Cranky was an eyewitness to a car accident. A dispute between two insurance companies relating to the accident is now pending before him. The companies dispute who caused the accident. Judge Cranky saw the entire thing and believes it was the driver of the Toyota who ran a red light and caused the accident, and that the other driver was not at fault. Would your analysis change if, instead, the companies do not dispute who caused the accident, but rather are litigating over the interpretation of an indemnity agreement between them that would determine each company's share of the liability?

f. A small retail boutique has been sued in an employment discrimination case that is pending before Judge Cranky. The boutique is owned and operated by a limited liability company. Judge Cranky's spouse is one of several members of the company. (A member of an LLC is analogous to a shareholder in a corporation; the member holds an ownership interest in the LLC.) Would your analysis change if the member were Judge Cranky's ex-spouse? The ex-spouse's second husband? An adult child of the ex-spouse and the second husband? If so, how and why; and if not, why not?

g. Judge Cranky is presiding over a slip-and-fall case brought by a customer who fell in a supermarket. Unbeknownst to Judge Cranky, the supermarket is owned by his distant cousin, whom Judge Cranky met once years ago at a family reunion.

h. Judge Cranky's daughter is a lawyer who works for the American Civil Liberties Union ("ACLU," a nonprofit that represents people and pursues causes claiming violations of civil rights or civil liberties). Judge Cranky is presiding over a civil rights case that will make law in the jurisdiction. Neither the ACLU nor Judge Cranky's daughter is involved in the case. If the judge rules in favor of the plaintiff, it will set a precedent helpful to the ACLU in future cases.

i. Judge Cranky is handling a contract dispute between two large companies. On the eve of trial, he learns that one company made a significant contribution to his re-election campaign.

j. In Judge Cranky's state, several different trial courts have split on the question of whether a consumer has standing to bring a claim for damages under a recently enacted consumer-protection statute when the consumer received a single, unsolicited, commercial text message in violation of the statute, but the consumer alleges no harm beyond the receipt of the text message. Last year, Judge Cranky co-authored a law journal article on the topic with one of his law clerks, endorsing the view that receipt of the text message alone is sufficient to confer standing on a plaintiff. A case is now pending before the judge in which he must decide this issue.

k. Before leaving private practice for the bench, Judge Genial handled a class action lawsuit, representing one of the defendants. Judge Genial handled only some discovery in the case, and he left to join the judiciary before the case was tried. Judge Genial was recently elevated to the state's intermediate appellate court. Pending in that court is the appeal of the trial verdict in the class action. Judge Genial is assigned to the panel designated to hear that appeal.

Problem 26B-8: Mess in the Press: Go back and take another look at the circumstances surrounding the Sierra Club's request to United States Supreme Court Justice Antonin Scalia that he recuse himself in a matter to which the Sierra Club was a party then pending before the Supreme Court. **Chapter 26.A at 975 n.2**. Briefly, Justice Scalia had persuaded a third-party host to include then-sitting Vice President Dick Cheney in a duck-hunting outing during the winter before the adjudication of the case, which concerned the Vice President's actions in convening a task force concerning energy policy, the members of which he refused to identify publicly. The Vice President accepted the invitation (which the host had encouraged Justice Scalia to convey) and supplied Justice Scalia and two members of his family transportation in a government-owned jet. Justice Scalia declined to recuse himself on grounds explained in *Cheney v. United States District Court*, 541 U.S. 913 (2004).

Although there is no rule or statute regarding **recusal** of individual justices of the Supreme Court, and such questions are left to each justice's individual discretion, the standard that Justice Scalia apparently applied to the motion was drawn from the **recusal** statute applicable to all other Article III judges, **28 U.S.C. § 455(a)**, which like **MCJC Rule 2.11(A)** requires a judge to disqualify himself "in any proceeding in which the judge's impartiality might reasonably be questioned." Consider the facts listed below. Is any of them sufficient, individually or in combination with any or all of the others, to require or excuse **recusal**? If so, why; and if not, why not? (Each of these facts is discussed in Justice Scalia's opinion. You're invited to read that opinion, but not required to do so unless your professor says that you are. You are also invited to read the article by Lawrence Fox critical of Justice Scalia's opinion cited in **Chapter 26.A at 975 n.2**, but again you are not required to do so unless your professor says so. Needless to say, Justice Scalia's and Mr. Fox's opinions, which are both extremely well written and argued, are two differing points of view on a challenging subject on which there is room for argument.)

a. That Justice Scalia was an Associate Justice of the United States Supreme Court which, unlike the lower federal courts, does not have numerous other judges available to take his place if he recuses himself.

b. That the case concerned the Vice President's actions in his official capacity, not his actions as a private individual, and its outcome would govern his official conduct, but would not affect his individual liberty, property, or family.

c. That the duck-hunting excursion was arranged before *certiorari* was sought in the case.

d. That Justice Scalia knew Vice President Cheney from the time that they had both served in President Gerald Ford's administration, some 30 years before the events at issue.

e. That the host of the outing sold equipment and services to oil rigs, but did not produce oil or energy.

f. That the government spent nothing additional transporting Justice Scalia and two members of his family in the Vice President's government jet one-way to the outing (for the economists among us, the marginal cost of transporting the additional passengers was zero), nor did Justice Scalia or his family members save any money on airfare, as for various reasons they had purchased round-trip airline tickets to the outing.

g. That during the two days the Vice President attended, he and Justice Scalia spent no time together in the same duck-blind (a small, enclosed space that accommodates only two or three people).

h. That Justice Scalia and the Vice President took their meals together, but others were present as well.

i. That Justice Scalia and the Vice President did not share sleeping quarters in the bunkhouse at the hunting retreat.

Problem 26B-9: **Another Mess in the Press:** In 2008, before the United States Supreme Court settled the constitutional right to same-sex marriage in *Obergefell v. Hodges*, 576 U.S. 644 (2015), California voters passed an initiative measure (Proposition 8) amending the California Constitution to forbid same-sex marriage in that state. Opponents of the ban filed a constitutional challenge to Proposition 8 in the federal district court for the Northern District of California. That case was randomly assigned to U.S. District Judge Vaughn R. Walker. Judge Walker allowed extensive discovery and then conducted a thorough bench trial, after which he issued a lengthy opinion finding that Proposition 8 violated both the Due Process and Equal Protection Clauses of the Fourteenth Amendment. *Perry v. Schwarzenegger*, 704 F. Supp. 2d 921 (N.D. Cal. 2010).

After retiring from the bench the year after deciding *Perry*, Judge Walker publicly discussed the fact that he was a gay man in a long-term relationship with another man. At that point, the defenders of Proposition 8 moved to vacate Judge Walker's decision in *Perry* on the ground that his sexual orientation and relationship status (and his alleged failure to disclose them during the litigation, though there was dispute about how widely known these facts were at the time of the litigation) had **disqualified** him from hearing the case. A different district judge heard that motion and denied it on the ground that Judge Walker had had no obligation to disclose or **recuse**. *Perry v. Schwarzenegger*, 790 F. Supp. 2d 1119 (N.D. Cal. 2011). The U.S. Supreme Court affirmed Judge Walker's decision on the ground that the parties that had appealed the decision to the Ninth Circuit and then sought *certiorari* in the Supreme Court (which did not include the State of California itself or any of its official representatives) lacked standing to appeal. *Hollingsworth v. Perry*, 570 U.S. 693 (2013).

The public policy, standing, and constitutional issues raised in this important case are genuinely fascinating (and remain controversial), but they are not our focus in this problem. Our focus here is **recusal**. Make the best arguments on both sides as to why Judge Walker was or was not required to publicly disclose his sexual orientation and relationship status and/or to **recuse** himself. Do you think the district court was correct in denying the later motion to vacate? Why or why not?

3. Canon 3: Personal and Extrajudicial Activities

Canon 2 and its subsidiary Rules focused on how judges **must** conduct their official activities—competently, diligently, and impartially. Canon 3 focuses on how judges' *extrajudicial* activities can interfere with the proper execution of their official duties, and when and how they **must** avoid such interference. Canon 3 provides: "A judge shall conduct the judge's personal and extrajudicial activities to minimize the risk of conflict with the obligations of judicial office."

MCJC Rule 3.1 provides some guidelines, affirming that judges are generally free (and, in fact, encouraged, *see* **MCJC Rule 3.1 Comments [1]-[2]**) to engage in extrajudicial activities except as prohibited by law and the Code of Judicial Conduct. This encouragement is constrained by a number of limiting principles. Generally, a judge **must not**:

- "participate in activities that will interfere with the proper performance of the judge's judicial duties" (**MCJC Rule 3.1(A)**);
- "participate in activities that will lead to frequent **disqualification** of the judge (**MCJC Rule 3.1(B)**);
- "participate in activities that would appear to a reasonable person to undermine the judge's independence, integrity, or impartiality" (**MCJC Rule 3.1(C)**);
- "engage in conduct that would appear to a reasonable person to be coercive" (**MCJC Rule 3.1(D)**); or
- "make use of court premises, staff, stationery, equipment, or other resources, except for incidental use for activities that concern the law, the legal system, or the administration of justice, or unless such additional use is permitted by law" (**MCJC Rule 3.1(E)**).

The remaining Rules under Canon 3 address the limits on different personal and extrajudicial activities to which judicial officers are subject. Let's take a look.

a. Extrajudicial Interactions with Government

In their own dealings with the government, the principle of the rule of law (that everyone is equal before the law) requires that judges address government in their own affairs on a footing equal to that of any other citizen. Thus, judges must be careful not to leverage their office for their own or someone else's advantage, or appear to do so. To avoid this appearance, judges are generally forbidden from appearing voluntarily at public hearings or otherwise consulting with an executive or legislative official, except in matters concerning the law or the legal system, or when acting in their own personal **interest** or as a fiduciary for someone else (in which cases they must not refer to or otherwise leverage the prestige of their office). **MCJC Rule 3.2; MCJC Rule 3.2 Comment [3]**. Similarly, judges are forbidden from serving as character witnesses or otherwise vouching for another's character "except when duly summoned" (**MCJC Rule 3.3**), and they should "discourage" others from subpoenaing them for this purpose (*see* **MCJC Rule 3.3 Comment [1]**). And they are likewise forbidden from accepting appointment to "any governmental position" except one concerning the law or the legal system. **MCJC Rule 3.4**.[27]

> **Problem 26B-10:** In each of the following circumstances, is the judge subject to **consequences**? What **consequences** and why (or why not)?
>
> a. Each summer, Judge Genial accepts a handful of law students to serve as summer externs in his chambers. One student, Albert, confides to the judge that he had a substance abuse problem prior to law school. Albert attended a treatment program and is now clean. He performs well over the summer. At the conclusion of the summer, Albert explains to Judge Genial that he anticipates he will have a character and fitness hearing before being admitted to the bar. Judge Genial tells Albert that he will testify in Albert's favor at the hearing. Does your analysis change if the judge tells Albert that he will testify in Albert's favor at the character and fitness hearing if he is subpoenaed? If so, how and why; and if not, why not?
>
> b. The governor appoints Judge Genial to the board of regents for the state's university, reasoning that having a judge on the board will improve the outlook for graduates of the affiliated law school. The board is responsible for passing bylaws, rules, and regulations necessary for the day-to-day operations of the university.

b. Financial, Business, or Remunerative Activities

Given the many opportunities for the appearance of impropriety or the inadvertent or deliberate receipt of unfair benefits of office, the commercial activities permitted to judges are sharply restricted. Judges **may** hold and manage their own investments and those of their families (defined for this purpose as "a spouse, domestic partner, child, grandchild, parent, grandparent, or other relative or person with whom the judge maintains a close familial relationship"; *see* **MCJC Terminology, "Member of the judge's family"**). **MCJC Rule 3.11(A)**. They may similarly manage or participate in a closely held business or investment concern owned by the judge and members of the judge's family, except to the extent that such

---

[27] The federal judicial conduct rules are similar. *See* **CCUSJ Comment on Canon 2B, Canons 4, 4(A)(2), (F), (G)**.

activities will interfere with the judge's duties, such as by requiring "frequent **disqualification**" or requiring frequent interactions with persons likely to come before the judge in his or her official capacity. **MCJC Rule 3.11(B)-(C)**. Except for these limited permissions, judges **must not** "serve as an officer, director, manager, general partner, advisor, or employee of any business entity" (**MCJC Rule 3.11(B)**).

Similarly, judges **must not** serve in a fiduciary capacity, except for a member of the judge's family (or a family member's estate or trust), and then "only if such service will not interfere with the proper performance of judicial duties." **MCJC Rule 3.8(A)**. More specifically, otherwise permissible fiduciary service is prohibited if, in the course of that service, the judge "will likely be engaged in proceedings that would ordinarily come before the judge, or if the estate, trust, or ward becomes involved in adversary proceedings in the court on which the judge serves, or one under its appellate jurisdiction." **MCJC Rule 3.8(B)**. When judges are acting as fiduciaries, the same limits on compensation, expense reimbursement, and financial or commercial activities apply to them as to judges' extrajudicial activities on their own behalf. And if a person who is already acting as a fiduciary becomes a judge, he or she must terminate any fiduciary service inconsistent with the Rule "as soon as reasonably practicable, but in no event later than [one year] after becoming a judge," with the bracketed term leaving adopting states leeway to choose their deadline. **MCJC Rule 3.8(D)**.

In addition, judges **must not** practice law except to act *pro se* or to give legal advice to, or draft or review documents for (but not appear as a lawyer in litigation on behalf of), family members without compensation (**MCJC Rule 3.10**). Nor may judges act as arbitrators or mediators other than as part of their official judicial duties (**MCJC Rule 3.9**).

Judges may accept "reasonable compensation" for any permitted extrajudicial activity (including speaking and writing) "unless such acceptance would appear to a reasonable person to undermine the judge's independence, integrity, or impartiality." **MCJC Rule 3.12; MCJC Rule 3.12 Comment [1]**. Similarly, judges **may** accept reimbursement for their own and, where appropriate, the judge's spouse, domestic partner, or guest's actual, reasonable, and necessary travel, lodging, and meal expenses associated with permitted extrajudicial activity, unless that reimbursement amounts to a forbidden gift under **MCJC Rule 3.13** (which we'll discuss in a moment, *see* **Chapter 26.B at 1010**) or transgresses the general limiting principles of **MCJC Rule 3.1** (*see* **Chapter 26.B at 1003**). **MCJC Rule 3.14**. Similarly, judges **may** accept waivers of fees or tuition for conferences or educational events under similar restrictions. *Id.* Before accepting any such benefits, judges **must** carefully assess all the facts and circumstances to determine whether accepting "would appear to a reasonable person to undermine the judge's independence, integrity, or impartiality." **MCJC Rule 3.14 Comment [3]** provides a long and nonexclusive list of potentially relevant circumstances, including:

- "whether the sponsor is an accredited educational institution or bar association rather than a trade association or a for-profit entity";
- "whether the funding comes largely from numerous contributors rather than from a single entity and is earmarked for programs with specific content";
- "whether the content is related or unrelated to the subject matter of litigation pending or impending before the judge, or to matters that are likely to come before the judge";
- "whether the activity is primarily educational rather than recreational, and whether the costs of the event are reasonable and comparable to those associated with similar events sponsored by the judiciary, bar associations, or similar groups";
- "whether information concerning the activity and its funding sources is available upon inquiry";
- "whether the sponsor or source of funding is generally associated with particular parties or interests currently appearing or likely to appear in the judge's court, thus possibly requiring **disqualification** of the judge under **[MCJC] Rule 2.11**";
- "whether differing viewpoints are presented"; and
- "whether a broad range of judicial and nonjudicial participants are invited, whether a large number of participants are invited, and whether the program is designed specifically for judges."[28]

> Problem 26B-11: Take another look at each of the factors that a judge **should** consider before accepting expense reimbursements or fee or tuition waivers in connection with extrajudicial activities (listed just above this problem and in **MCJC Rule 3.14 Comment [3]**). For each factor:

---

[28] Again, the limits on federal judges are generally similar. *See* **CCUSJ Canon 4(A)(4)-(5), (D)(1)-(3), (E), (H)**. Federal judicial employees likewise "**should** refrain from outside financial and business dealings that tend to detract from the dignity of the court, interfere with the proper performance of official duties, exploit the position, or associate the judicial employee in a substantial financial manner with lawyers or other persons likely to come before the judicial employee or the court or office the judicial employee serves." **CCJE § 320 Canon 4 § C(1)**. Any outside activities by a member of a judge's "personal staff" (such as a law clerk or extern) about which questions might be raised **should** be reviewed with the employee's supervising judge, and the judge's recommendations **should** be followed. *Id.* The practice of law by federal judicial employees is restricted similarly to that of judges, with some minor exceptions. **CCJE § 320 Canon 4 § D**. Likewise with compensation or expense reimbursement for outside activities. **CCJE § 320 Canon 4 § E**.

One issue that comes up for judicial employees such as law clerks and externs is how to address the impression of influence that may be created by seeking or accepting post-clerkship employment with a **practice organization** that appears before the judge for whom you're working. We addressed this in **Chapter 25.D at 939** in the context of **Model Rules 1.11(d) and 1.12(b)**, which allow law clerks to seek or accept employment during government service but require them to inform the judge for whom they work. The judge **may** then adopt prophylactic measures, such as preventing a clerk from working on matters involving a prospective employer. *See* **CCJE § 320 Canon 4 § C(4)**. This can get even more complicated if a future employer offers to advance moving or bar-study expenses to a law clerk before or during a clerkship, something that could be viewed as a gift or loan from a party or counsel before or likely to come before the court, and in some courts could be forbidden. If you have or wish to seek a law job before or during a clerkship or judicial externship, or if an employer offers benefits of any kind before or during your work for the judiciary, you must research the rules in your jurisdiction and disclose the matter promptly and fully to your judicial employer.

a. Formulate a likely reason as to why the drafters included that factor in the Comment by identifying a policy value that the factor promotes, and then explaining how the factor supports that policy; and

b. Come up with an example of a situation in which the factor weighs against a judge's accepting the proffered benefit and a situation in which the factor weighs in favor of accepting the benefit. Be factually specific.

Problem 26B-12: Assume the judges below engage in the following conduct. What **consequences** could each judge face, and why (or why not)?

a. Judge Bias presides in landlord-tenant court. Her family's company owns a large housing development in town, and she serves as the executive vice president of the family company. She faithfully **recuses** herself from any cases involving the company or its properties. On average, she **recuses** herself from approximately a quarter of the cases assigned to her docket.

b. As a municipal-level judge, Judge Bias's official salary is modest. She supplements her income by ghostwriting pleadings and briefs for other lawyers. She ghostwrites only in criminal cases, and as a landlord-tenant judge, she handles only civil cases. She charges lawyers an hourly rate for her work that is reasonable in her community.

c. Judge Bias's sister Mary lives in a different state from the one in which Judge Bias lives and works. Mary is sued in a slip-and-fall case. Judge Bias reviews the complaint, drafts an answer, and directs her sister to file the answer *pro se*.

d. Judge Bias has been asked to speak by her law school's alumni association at their yearly banquet. The alumni association pays the cost for Judge Bias to fly to the banquet and stay in a hotel.

e. Judge Bias receives an offer to speak at a continuing education program hosted by a pro-landlord lobbying group that will be held out-of-state at a luxury hotel and casino in Las Vegas, Nevada.

c. Educational, Religious, Charitable, Fraternal, or Civic Organizations and Activities

Judges often involve themselves in educational, religious, charitable, fraternal, or civic organizations or activities (by which we and the Model Code of Judicial Conduct mean a broad range of more or less organized group activities outside judging that are not conducted for profit, *see* **MCJC Rule 3.1 Comment [1]**). Many judges are members of such organizations or participate in their activities, from religious services to charitable fundraising and giving to participating in community benefit projects. But because the fact and appearance of impartiality are so central to the judicial role, and because of the risk in some activities of actual or apparent coercion, undue influence, or abuse of the prestige of the office, Rules under Canon 3 carefully regulate the kinds of organizations and activities in this sphere in which judges are permitted to participate.

Although affiliation with most organizations is within a judge's reasonable discretion, judges **must not** hold membership in any organization "that practices invidious discrimination on the basis of race, sex, gender, religion, national origin, ethnicity, or sexual orientation." **MCJC Rule 3.6(A)**. "A judge's membership in an organization that practices invidious discrimination creates the perception that the judge's impartiality is impaired." **MCJC Rule 3.6 Comment [1]**. (Membership in a religious organization "as a lawful exercise of the freedom of religion" is allowed, as is service in or to the military. **MCJC Rule 3.6 Comments [4]-[5]**.)

In addition, judges' participation in extrajudicial activities associated with educational, religious, and other nonprofit organizations is limited as follows:

- Judges **may** participate in *planning* related to fundraising for nonprofit organizations, and **may** participate in the management and investment of a nonprofit organization's funds (**MCJC 3.7(A)(1)**), but **must not** *solicit contributions* to the organization from anyone other than members of their own family, or other judges over whom they have no supervisory or appellate authority (**MCJC 3.7(A)(2)**). The contributions whose solicitation is restricted include money, property in kind, volunteer services, or anything else for which the organization would otherwise have to pay (*see* **MCJC Terminology, "Contributions"**).

- Judges **may** solicit others to *join* an organization (even if there are membership dues or the like that the organization would devote to its purposes), but only if the organization "is concerned with the law, the legal system, or the administration of justice." **MCJC Rule 3.7(A)(3)**.

- Judges **may** make recommendations to public or private fund-granting organizations in connection with their programs or activities (for example, advising a charitable trust or other charitable organization how or where to grant its funds), but again only if the organization is concerned with the law, the legal system, or the administration of justice. **MCJC Rule 3.7(A)(5)**.

- The nature and degree of publicity attending a judge's involvement in an organization or one of its events must be carefully measured as to the nature of the affiliation publicized, how it is publicized, the degree of the judge's publicized involvement, and the kind of organization or event at issue. Judges **may** "appear[] or speak[] at, receiv[e] an award or other recognition at, be[] featured on the program of, [or] permit[] [their] title[s] to be used in connection with an [organization's] event . . . , but if the event serves a fund-raising purpose, the judge may participate only if the event concerns the law, the legal system, or the administration of justice." **MCJC Rule 3.7(A)(4)**. "Mere attendance at an event, whether or not the event serves a fund-raising purpose, does not constitute a violation . . . . It is also generally permissible for a judge to serve as an usher or a food server or preparer, or to perform similar functions, at fund-raising events sponsored by educational, religious, charitable, fraternal, or civic organizations. Such activities are not solicitation and do not present an element of coercion or abuse the prestige of judicial office." **MCJC Rule 3.7 Comment [3]**. Similarly, "[i]dentification of a judge's position in educational, religious, charitable, fraternal, or civic organizations on letterhead used for fund-raising or membership solicitation does not violate this Rule. The letterhead may list the judge's title or judicial office if comparable designations are used for other persons." **MCJC Rule 3.7 Comment [4]**.

■ And judges generally **may** serve as an officer, director, trustee, or nonlegal advisor of a nonprofit organization, unless it is likely that the organization or entity "will be engaged in proceedings that would ordinarily come before the judge"; or "will frequently be engaged in adversary proceedings in the court of which the judge is a member, or in any court subject to the appellate jurisdiction of the court of which the judge is a member." **MCJC Rule 3.7(A)(6)**.[29]

Problem 26B-13: In each of the following circumstances, is Judge Cranky subject to **consequences**? What **consequences** and why (or why not)? What, if anything, **must** or **should** the judge have done differently?

a. Judge Cranky (who sometimes jokingly describes himself as a "radical moderate") has been a member of the Federalist Society and the American Constitution Society since his early years of practice. The Federalist Society cultivates and supports what is conventionally viewed as "conservative" or "right of center" thought and policy. The American Constitution Society describes itself as "the leading progressive legal organization." Judge Cranky has retained both memberships since being elevated to the bench and attends events sponsored by both societies. Does your analysis change if the Judge dropped his membership in one of the two societies upon being elevated to the bench, but kept the other, and attended events sponsored only by the society in which he was a member? What if he had always been a member of only one of the two? If so, how and why; and if not, why not?

b. Judge Cranky is a member of a local elite country club. The judge is an avid golfer, and the club has the most interesting and well-tended golf course in the state. He has no involvement in the club other than being a member, playing golf there, and occasionally eating at the club's restaurant. The club refuses membership to Jews and women. Many

---

[29] Again, the restrictions on federal judges are similar overall, with some scattered differences in the details (for example, the MCJC allows a judge to give a nonprofit investment advice, while the CCUSJ provides that a federal judge **should not** do so). *See* **CCUSJ Canon 2(C) & Comment on Canon 2C, Canons 4(A)(1), (3), (B), (C)**. Federal judicial employees generally "may engage in such activities as civic, charitable, religious, professional, educational, cultural, avocational, social, fraternal, and recreational activities, and may speak, write, lecture, and teach," except for such activities that "detract from the dignity of the court, interfere with the performance of official duties, or adversely reflect on the operation and dignity of the court or office the judicial employee serves." However, "if such outside activities concern the law, the legal system, or the administration of justice, the judicial employee should first consult with the appointing authority to determine whether the proposed activities are consistent with the foregoing standards and the other provisions of this code." **CCJE § 320 Canon 4 § A**. Unlike judges, federal judicial employees may participate in fundraising activities for charitable and civic nonprofit organizations, except that they should not "use or permit the use of the prestige of the office in the solicitation of funds," should not solicit subordinates or, if a member of a judge's personal staff, solicit any court personnel, and "should not solicit or accept funds from lawyers or other persons likely to come before the judicial employee or the court or office the judicial employee serves, except as an incident to a general fund-raising activity." **CCJE § 320 Canon 4 § B**.

local "movers and shakers" belong to the club. Conversations in the clubhouse frequently concern business and professional matters, and membership in the club offers significant business and professional advantages.

c. Judge Cranky is of Polish ethnicity. He is a member of the Polish Heritage Foundation, a nonprofit organization that serves as a resource for Poles and Polish Americans to educate the community about, and promote the traditions, history, and culture of, Poland and Polish-Americans. The Foundation funds its activities through fundraising and membership dues. Although the nonprofit has no rule against exclusion of members on the basis of ethnicity, all its members are Polish or Polish American.

d. Same as (c), except that now the foundation is conducting a membership drive in the county's substantial Polish-American community. Judge Cranky serves on the Foundation's Membership Committee, and he holds an event at his home to which numerous potential new members are invited. The invitations refer to the judge as "Hon. Grumpador B. Cranky, Judge of the Superior Court." Judge Cranky gives a short speech at the event, extolling the value of embracing one's ethnic heritage and urging those in attendance to join the foundation.

e. Judge Cranky attended an all-boys preparatory high school. He serves as a member of the board of directors of the school's alumni association. Only graduates of the school may serve on the board, so the board is exclusively male. The object of the organization is to raise money for the school. Judge Cranky and the other members of the board plan the alumni association's annual fundraising drive. As part of that drive, Judge Cranky sends out a letter to all living alumni of the school, encouraging their generosity. His signature line on the letter reads, "Hon. Grumpador B. Cranky, Judge of the Superior Court." Does your analysis change if the letter is signed by another board member, but the alumni association's stationery lists the members of the board in a column at the top right of the page, and includes Judge Cranky's name and title? If so, how and why; and if not, why not?

f. Judge Cranky belongs to a neighborhood prayer circle, which limits its membership to 12 persons who are members of a local church. Judge Cranky attends the church. The object of the club is to meet every Sunday morning after services for prayer and study of religious writings. Does your analysis change if the church is a Catholic church, whose official teachings assert that abortion is a mortal sin, and Judge Cranky has before him a case challenging the constitutionality of the state legislature's recent imposition of an unconditional ban on abortion? If so, how and why; and if not, why not?

d. Receipt of Gifts, Bequests, Loans, Benefits, and Other Things of Value

Whenever a judge is treated differently from similarly situated people with respect to receiving things of value, we need to worry about whether his or her integrity has been, or appears to have been, compromised. Accordingly, the general rule is that judges **must not** "accept any gifts, loans, bequests, benefits, or other things of value, if acceptance is prohibited by law or would appear to a reasonable person to undermine the judge's independence, integrity, or impartiality."

MCJC Rule 3.13(A). (As you've undoubtedly noticed, that standard is the same as the general standard for **recusal** in **MCJC Rule 2.11(A)**, the general standard for when a judge may accept compensation for extrajudicial activities in **MCJC Rule 3.12**, and other Rules as well. Pop quiz: Why does this pattern exist? What recurring policy interest does it serve?)

The remainder of the Rule on this subject lists an array of different kinds of transfers to judges that are generally permitted unless they are specifically barred by law or (because of their size or significance) rise to the general level of concern that they would "appear to a reasonable person to undermine the judge's independence, integrity, or impartiality." The Rule divides these generally permissible categories of transfers into two categories: Those that **must** be publicly disclosed, and those that need not be.

The transfers that need not be publicly disclosed comprise what might at first seem to be a contradictory combination: Some are so innocuous and commonplace that no one could reasonably worry about their effect on a judge's impartiality; others are so obviously prejudicial that they will require **recusal** (and the lack of a disclosure requirement will allow the judge properly to step aside without having to disclose her personal affairs unnecessarily). *See* **Rule 3.13 Comments [1]-[2]**. These transfers that need not be disclosed include:

- "[I]tems with little intrinsic value, such as plaques, certificates, trophies, and greeting cards" (**MCJC Rule 3.13(B)(1)**).
- Items that are modest and commonplace, or equally available to everyone on the same terms (*see* **MCJC Rule 3.13 Comment [3]**), such as "ordinary social hospitality" (**MCJC Rule 3.13(B)(3)**); "commercial or financial opportunities and benefits" that are made available on the same terms to "similarly situated persons who are not judges" (**MCJC Rule 3.13(B)(4)**); "rewards and prizes" awarded in random drawings or contests that are open to nonjudges (**MCJC Rule 3.13(B)(5)**); "scholarships, fellowships, and similar benefits or awards" that are available to similarly situated persons who are not judges on the same terms and criteria (**MCJC Rule 3.13(B)(6)**); and books, magazines, and similar resource materials "supplied by publishers on a complimentary basis for official use" (**MCJC Rule 3.13(B)(7)**).
- "[G]ifts, awards, or benefits associated with the business, profession, or other separate activity of a spouse, a domestic partner, or other family member of a judge residing in the judge's household, but that incidentally benefit the judge" (**MCJC Rule 3.13(B)(8)**). That the benefit to the judge in these circumstances is merely "incidental[]" is important; a gift or benefit given to a member of the judge's family in an effort to influence the judge would appear to a reasonable person to undermine the judge's independence, integrity, or impartiality, and accordingly would be forbidden. *See* **MCJC Rule 3.13 Comment [4]**.
- Included in the transfers that need not be disclosed are those so plainly prejudicial that they will require **recusal**: "[G]ifts, loans, bequests, benefits,

or other things of value from friends, relatives, or other persons, including lawyers, whose appearance or interest in a proceeding pending or impending before the judge would in any event require **disqualification** of the judge under **[MCJC] Rule 2.11**" (**MCJC Rule 3.13(B)(2)**).

The other category of extrajudicial transfers must be publicly disclosed consistent with the regulating jurisdiction's rules regarding disclosure (which we'll discuss in the next section). They generally include transfers that litigants in specific cases, and the public in general, reasonably ought to know about in order to determine whether they justify a request for **recusal** or related relief. These transfers include:

- "[G]ifts incident to a public testimonial" (**MCJC Rule 3.13(C)(1)**).
- Invitations for the judge (and the judge's spouse, domestic partner, or guest) to attend without charge an event associated with a "bar-related function or other activity relating to the law, the legal system, or the administration of justice," or with "any of the judge's [permissible] educational, religious, charitable, fraternal or civic activities, if the same invitation is offered to nonjudges who are engaged in similar ways in the activity as is the judge" (**MCJC Rule 3.13(C)(2)**).
- "[G]ifts, loans, bequests, benefits, or other things of value, if the source is a party or other person, including a lawyer, who has come or is likely to come before the judge, or whose **interests** have come or are likely to come before the judge" **MCJC Rule 3.13(C)(3)**). TAMING THE TEXT Note the difference between this reportable category and the nonreportable category described in **MCJC Rule 3.13(B)(2)**. The nonreportable category involves gifts that are necessarily going to result in **recusal** because they involve a gift or other benefit from a lawyer or party in a case "pending or impending" before the judge. The reportable category involves lawyers or parties who "ha[ve] come before or [are] likely to come before the judge"—that is, lawyers or parties who have been before the judge in the past or are likely to do so in the future, but are not involved in any proceeding pending (or impending) before the judge right now. The focus on lawyers or parties who "ha[ve] come before . . . the judge" reflects a concern that a gift to a judge after a matter is over may be (or reasonably be viewed as) an improper reward after the fact for the result. The focus on lawyers or parties who are "likely to come before the judge" reflects a concern that the lawyer or party is trying improperly to curry favor with an adjudicator they expect to see in the future. In either case, the disclosure is needed to assess whether and when a request for **recusal** or related relief might be necessary. *See* **MCJC Rule 3.13 Comment [2]**.[30] TAMING THE TEXT

---

[30] Federal judges are cautioned to comply with the **Judicial Conference Regulations on Gifts** ("JCRG"), and to endeavor to prevent any member of the judge's family living in the judge's household from soliciting or accepting a gift that the judge would be prohibited from accepting herself. **CCUSJ Canon 4(D)(4)**. The Regulations on Gifts take a general approach similar

Problem 26B-14: In each of the following circumstances, is Judge Cranky subject to **consequences**? What **consequences** and why (or why not)? What, if anything, **must** or **should** the judge have done differently?

a. Judge Cranky attended an all-boys preparatory high school. He serves as a member of the board of directors of the school's alumni association. The board wishes to present him with a plaque in recognition of his service to the alumni association and of his public accomplishments.

b. Same as (a), except that, in addition to the plaque, the board wishes to award Judge Cranky a $1,000 check as a token of the alumni association's gratitude.

c. Same as (b), except that, if the alumni association can't award Judge Cranky the check, then the board wishes to invite him to give a two-minute speech at the award ceremony for which the alumni association will pay him a $1,000 "honorarium." Would your analysis change if (b) had never happened, and the board's plan from inception had been a speech and an honorarium? If so, how and why; and if not, why not?

d. The state bar association invites Judge Cranky to speak at its annual meeting in the state capital. The bar reimburses his travel expenses. Does your analysis change if Judge Cranky brings his spouse to the state bar meeting, and the state bar reimburses her travel expenses as well? If so, how and why; and if not, why not?

e. Judge Cranky is serving by assignment as a settlement judge in a case pending before another judge on his court, as the judge presiding over the case and the parties have requested. The settlement conference is expected to last all day, and the law firm representing one of the parties has offered to host the conference. At lunch, the firm provides sandwiches and sodas for everyone involved. Judge Cranky also eats a sandwich and drinks a soda. He does not reimburse the law firm.

f. Same as (e), except that instead of sandwiches and soda, the law firm has agreed to provide a $200 Kobe steak for Judge Cranky's lunch to accommodate his "special dietary needs." Judge Cranky does not reimburse the firm for the meal.

g. Judge Cranky's spouse volunteers for a local nonprofit. They send her a $200 bottle of wine as a thank-you for her work. She shares the wine with Judge Cranky over dinner.

h. Judge Cranky is presiding over a construction dispute between a supplier, Bolts-R-Us, and a general contractor, Build Inc. Counsel for Build sends Judge Cranky a holiday card.

i. Same as (h), except that, at the holidays, counsel for Build sends Judge Cranky a fruit basket valued at around $40.

j. Same as (h), except that counsel for Build sends Judge Cranky a $500 bottle of wine.

k. Same as (h), except that counsel for Build arranges for Build to repaint Judge Cranky's house at no cost to the judge.

---

to the MCJC in determining which gifts a judge may accept, with some differences in the details. *See* **JCRG §§ 620.25-.45**. Disclosure of benefits for federal judges and judicial employees is the subject of separate law, including the Ethics in Government Act (5a U.S.C. § 101 *et seq.*) and other Judicial Conference Regulations. *See* **JCRG § 620.50**. Federal judicial employees are restricted from seeking or accepting gifts on terms similar to those governing the judges whom they serve. *See* **CCJE § 320 Canon 4 § B(2).**

l.　Same as (h), except that counsel for Build sends Judge Cranky a $150-off coupon for services from Build. That coupon is also available to the general public at any local building supply store.

m.　Judge Cranky's best friend Igor buys him a $100 cashmere scarf for the holidays. Igor is not a litigant or counsel in any case pending before the judge.

n.　Judge Cranky plays bingo (which is legal in his state) every Sunday night at his church. He wins $200.

o.　The publisher of *International Geographic* magazine sends Judge Cranky a complimentary subscription for him to leave in the waiting area of his chambers.

p.　Judge Cranky's spouse is sent a deli platter by a vendor to her business. Judge Cranky eats some of the cold cuts.

e. Reporting (Public Disclosure) of the Fruits of Extrajudicial Activities

Most states and the federal judiciary have a system for public disclosure of the extrajudicial benefits that judges receive. Many jurisdictions also have broader schemes requiring disclosure of judges' personal and family assets. These mechanisms exist to allow individual litigants to assess the possibility of **recusable** bias or the appearance of bias, and correspondingly to increase public confidence in the independence, integrity, and impartiality of the judiciary.

MCJC Rule 3.15, which varies a fair bit among the jurisdictions according to their respective reporting schemes, requires judges to report extrajudicial compensation allowed by **MCJC Rule 3.12** (*see* **Chapter 26.B at 1005**), disclosable gifts and other transfers of value permitted under **MCJC Rule 3.13** (*see* **Chapter 26.B at 1012**), and expense reimbursements and fee waivers permitted under **MCJC Rule 3.14** (*see* **Chapter 26.B at 1005**).[31] The model form of the Rule leaves room for individual states to provide for a minimum amount in each category per reporting period that, if not exceeded, excuses reporting of that category for that period (*see* **MCJC Rule 3.15(A)**), and suggests the details to be disclosed and reporting periods (*see* **MCJC Rule 3.15 (B)-(C)**).

Problem 26B-15: Assume that in Judge Cranky's jurisdiction, the dollar amounts in **MCJC Rule 3.15(A)** are each $4,500. **Must** the judge report each of the following, and why or why not?

a.　The $3,000 payment Judge Cranky receives for serving as an adjunct faculty member at a local law school. Does your analysis change if the judge teaches at two different law schools and is paid $3,000 by each school? If so, how and why; and if not, why not?

---

[31] TAMING THE TEXT The alert student has observed that the Rule's specific wording creates the somewhat odd situation that a judge need not disclose receipt of prohibited or illegal payments. (Do you see why? Identify the specific words in the subsections of **MCJC Rule 3.15(A)** that lead to this result.) Of course, the judge is still subject to judicial discipline (and possibly much worse) for receiving the forbidden payments if they are discovered. TAMING THE TEXT As mentioned in **Chapter 26.B at 1012 n.30**, disclosure of gifts and similar benefits by federal judges and their employees is governed by law outside their codes of conduct.

b. The payment Judge Cranky earns as a part-time golf coach for a few of his neighbors' children which, over the course of a year, totals $5,000.

c. The $5,000 reimbursement Judge Cranky received to pay his expenses for traveling to a state bar association conference at which he was requested to speak.

d. A used car worth $5,000 given to Judge Cranky by a close friend who has no involvement in any cases pending before Judge Cranky. Does your analysis change if the friend gave the judge the car for the use of his daughter? If so, how and why; and if not, why not?

4. Canon 4: Limits on the Conduct of Candidates for Judicial Office

Judges enter office by either election or appointment. A majority of states elect at least some of their judges, and a number of states that appoint judges require them to face the electorate in occasional nonpartisan votes on whether they should be retained in office.[32] (As you probably know, the federal system appoints all of its judicial officers. Article III judges are appointed by the President and confirmed by the Senate; Article I judges are appointed by various authorities designated by federal statute.) In the Model Code of Judicial Conduct, a "candidate" for judicial office is "any person, including a sitting judge, who is seeking selection for or retention in judicial office by election or appointment." **MCJC Terminology, "Judicial candidate."**

Candidates for judicial office walk a tightrope. Like other candidates for government positions, judicial candidates will naturally wish to speak to the electorate or the appointing authority in terms that those deciding whom to choose can feel reflect their political values and preferences. But unlike most other candidates for government positions, the essence of judging (at least as conventionally conceived) is to set aside political values and preferences, to follow the law and, in the memorable analogy used by Chief Justice John Roberts in his own confirmation hearings, to "call balls and strikes, and not to pitch or bat."[33]

---

[32] Despite the ubiquity of judicial elections for state judgeships, the wisdom of the practice has been debated for a long time. The debate has become even more pointed as judicial elections have become more like political elections in their tone, partisanship, and funding. *See, e.g.,* David E. Pozen, *The Irony of Judicial Elections*, 108 COLUM. L. REV. 265 (2008). After retiring from the Supreme Court, Justice Sandra Day O'Connor became outspoken about what she considered the corrosive force of judicial fundraising and election, and advocated abolition of the practice. Bill Mears, *Former Justice O'Connor Leads Push to End Judicial Elections*, https://www.cnn.com/2009/CRIME/12/15/judicial.elections/index.html (Dec. 15, 2009). As we will see, a great many of the rules restricting judicial candidates' speech and conduct are grounded in the temptations created by judicial elections.

[33] https://abcnews.go.com/Archives/video/sept-12-2005-john-roberts-baseball-analogy-10628259 (Sept. 12, 2005). In the same statement, the future Chief Justice pointed out, quite rightly, that "[j]udges are not politicians, who can promise to do certain things in exchange for votes." *Id.* The completeness of the Chief Justice's public conceptualization of the judicial role (which was not original to him) has been widely and productively debated for a long time—it likely understates the inevitability of the intrusion of cognitive and implicit biases into judicial decision-making, and what can or should be done about that. But at the very least, Chief Justice Roberts states an essential *subjective* premise of judging (that is, he describes what most thoughtful people want judges honestly to *think* that they're doing). What's more, this premise is predominant in many aspects of the Model Code of Judicial Conduct ("independence, integrity, and impartiality," remember?).

Canon 4 and its Rules address this tension directly. The Canon provides: "A judge or candidate for judicial office shall not engage in political or campaign activity that is inconsistent with the independence, integrity, or impartiality of the judiciary." The Rules under Canon 4 set various limits on the speech and conduct of judges and judicial candidates to achieve this end. *See* **MCJC Rule 4.1 Comments [1], [3]**. REASON FOR THE RULE ▶ If Canon 4 is about judicial candidates, why do most of its Rules apply to sitting judges as well? Well, if you think about it, many sitting judges will be candidates for re-election, retention, or re-appointment at some point. The Rules thus simply anticipate the temptation to engage in political or campaign-oriented behavior that would be unacceptable for a judicial candidate before a sitting judge's formal "candidacy" might begin.[34] ◀ REASON FOR THE RULE

The overall structure of the Rules under Canon 4 is that **MCJC Rule 4.1** contains a catalogue of conduct in which judges and judicial candidates generally **must not** engage, with the later Rules mostly providing limited modifications or exceptions to the prohibitions in **MCJC Rule 4.1**. Because a great many states elect some or all of their judges, and every state has its own complex laws governing election campaigns and campaign finance (and in some states, specific aspects of judicial elections or appointments), all of the Canon 4 Rules are subject to local election and other regulation. Unless otherwise provided by other law or other judicial conduct rules, however, **MCJC Rule 4.1** provides the following restrictions (with some exceptions noted as relevant), and requires the judge or candidate to make reasonable efforts to have others refrain from undertaking the restricted activities on the judge or candidate's behalf (**MCJC Rule 4.1(B)**):

■ **No or limited public partisanship.** Judges and judicial candidates generally **must not** engage in public partisanship. Accordingly, they generally **must not** "publicly identify [themselves] as . . . candidate[s] of a political organization" (**MCJC Rule 4.1(A)(6)**); **must not** "seek, accept, or use endorsements from a political organization" (**MCJC Rule 4.1(A)(7)**); and **must not** "act as a leader in, or hold an office in, a political organization" (**MCJC Rule 4.1(A)(1)**). "'Political organization' means a political party or other group sponsored by or affiliated with a political party or candidate, the principal purpose of which is to further the election or appointment of candidates for political office." **MCJC Terminology, "Political organization."** Similarly, judges and judicial candidates **must not** "make speeches on behalf of a political organization" (**MCJC Rule 4.1(A)(2)**); **must not** "publicly endorse or oppose a candidate for any public office" (**MCJC Rule 4.1(A)(3)**, including even a family member running for a different public office, *see* **MCJC Rule 4.1 Comment [5]**); **must not** "solicit funds for, pay an assessment to, or make

---

[34] The Model Code informs us that "[a] person becomes a candidate for judicial office as soon as he or she makes a public announcement of candidacy, declares or files as a candidate with the election or appointment authority, authorizes or, where permitted, engages in solicitation or acceptance of contributions or support, or is nominated for election or appointment to office." **MCJC Terminology, "Judicial candidate."**

a contribution to a political organization or a candidate for public office" (**MCJC Rule 4.1(A)(4)**); and **must not** "attend or purchase tickets for dinners or other events sponsored by a political organization or a candidate for public office" (**MCJC Rule 4.1(A)(5)**). These general bans have a number of exceptions:

■ Legally and logically, the general prohibition on supporting or opposing a candidate for public office does not apply to the judge's own campaign. *See* **MCJC Rule 4.1 Comment [4]**. Thus judges are generally free to speak in support of their own candidacy, and against the candidacy of any of their opponents, within the other limits imposed by the Rules, such as truthfulness (*see* **MCJC Rule 4.1(A)(11)**) or, except when permitted in a partisan judicial election, to identify themselves with a political party or another candidate for a different office (*see* **MCJC Rule 4.1(A)(3), (6)**). **MCJC Rule 4.2(B)(2)-(3)**.

■ Similarly, judges and judicial candidates **must not** assume any leadership position in a political organization or campaign except their own campaign committee. *See* **MCJC Terminology, "Political organization."** Candidates **may** form campaign committees to "manage and conduct" their campaigns for judicial office (**MCJC Rule 4.4(A); MCJC Rule 4.2(B)(1)**). Judicial candidates are responsible for making reasonable efforts to ensure their campaign committees' compliance with applicable law (**MCJC Rule 4.2(A)(4); MCJC Rule 4.4(A)**), and they **must** personally "review and approve the content of all campaign statements and materials produced by the candidate or his or her campaign committee . . . before their dissemination" (**MCJC Rule 4.2(A)(3)**).

■ Some states allow partisan judicial elections; some states do not. In states that allow partisan judicial elections, judges and candidates **may** publicly identify themselves as members of a political party and seek, accept, and use endorsements from partisan political organizations. **MCJC Rule 4.2(C); MCJC Rule 4.2 Comment [3]**.

■ Even in jurisdictions in which partisan judicial candidacy is prohibited, a judge or judicial candidate **may** register to vote as a member of a political party, and **may** vote in any election in which he or she is qualified to vote. **MCJC Rule 4.1 Comments [3], [6]**. Many states that prohibit partisan judicial elections also allow candidates for nonpartisan judicial election to accept endorsements from anyone "other than a partisan political organization" (**MCJC Rule 4.2(B)(5)**); to "attend or purchase tickets for dinners or other events sponsored by a political organization or a candidate for public office" once the election season is underway (**MCJC Rule 4.2(B)(4)**; notice how much of **MCJC Rule 4.1(A)(5)** this undoes); and to make contributions to a political party or a campaign other than the judge's own, sometimes subject to limits on timing or amount (**MCJC Rule 4.2(B)(6)**). As an overarching principle, however, judicial candidates running for election, whether the election is "partisan, nonpartisan, or retention," **must** "act at all times in a manner consistent with the independence, integrity, and impartiality of the judiciary" (**MCJC Rule 4.2(A)(1)**). TAMING THE TEXT The permissions stated in **MCJC Rule 4.2(B) and (C)** are limited specifically to candidates seeking judicial office by *election*, and would not generally apply to candidates for judicial *appointment*. Candidates for judicial appointment are also generally free to seek and use endorsements from anyone other than a partisan political organization. **MCJC Rule 4.3(B).** TAMING THE TEXT

- **Limits on fundraising.** Judges and judicial candidates **must not** "personally solicit or accept campaign contributions other than through a campaign committee authorized by **[MCJC] Rule 4.4**" (**MCJC Rule 4.1(A)(8)**).
- **Prohibition on use of campaign funds for private benefit.** Judges and judicial candidates **must not** "use or permit the use of campaign contributions for the private benefit of the judge, the candidate, or others" (**MCJC Rule 4.1(A)(9)**).
- **Prohibition on use of public or government resources for campaign purposes.** Judges and judicial candidates **must not** "use court staff, facilities, or other court resources in a campaign for judicial office" (**MCJC Rule 4.1(A)(10)**).
- **Limits on statements during candidacy.**

    - Judges and judicial candidates **must not** "knowingly, or with reckless disregard for the truth, make any false or misleading statement" (**MCJC Rule 4.1(A)(11)**).

    - Judges and judicial candidates **must not** "make any statement that would reasonably be expected to affect the outcome or impair the fairness of a matter pending or impending in any court" (**MCJC Rule 4.1(A)(12)**); and **must not,** "in connection with cases, controversies, or issues that are likely to come before the court, make pledges, promises, or commitments that are inconsistent with the impartial performance of the adjudicative duties of judicial office" (**MCJC Rule 4.1(A)(13)**). REASON FOR THE RULE These limits are the same as those applicable to sitting judges, and they protect both the fact and the appearance of open-mindedness and impartiality, while limiting the restrictions on speech to those allowed by the First Amendment (*see* **MCJC Rule 2.10(B)**; **Chapter 26.B at 986**). REASON FOR THE RULE

    - TAMING THE TEXT How do we know when a candidate's statement crosses this line? "The making of a [prohibited] pledge, promise, or commitment is not dependent upon, or limited to, the use of any specific words or phrases; instead, *the totality of the statement must be examined to determine if a reasonable person would believe that the candidate for judicial office has specifically undertaken to reach a particular result.* Pledges, promises, or commitments must be contrasted with statements or announcements of personal views on legal, political, or other issues, which are not prohibited. The difference between the two is not always easy to discern. When making such statements, a judge **should** acknowledge the overarching judicial obligation to apply and uphold the law, without regard to his or her personal views." **MCJC Rule 4.1 Comment [13]** (emphasis added). On the other hand, campaign promises "related to judicial organization, administration, and court management" don't fall in the zone in which impartiality and its appearance are paramount, such as promises to "dispose of a backlog of cases, start court sessions on time, or avoid favoritism in appointments and hiring. A candidate may also pledge to take action outside the courtroom, such as working toward an improved jury selection system, or advocating for more funds to improve the physical plant and amenities of the courthouse." **MCJC Rule 4.1 Comment [14]**. ◄ TAMING THE TEXT

- **Avoiding incompatible candidacies**. Judges who become candidates for *non*judicial elective office must resign their judicial offices (unless otherwise permitted by law). **MCJC Rule 4.5(A)**. Judges who become candidates for nonjudicial *appointive* office are generally not required to resign so long as they continue to comply with the rules of judicial ethics. **MCJC Rule 4.5(B)**.

CONSEQUENCES ► A number of these restrictions (though not all) are also punishable under (among other laws) fair political practice laws by civil fines and in some cases even criminal fines and imprisonment. Why also make them violations of the rules of judicial ethics, and extend the reach of those rules to nonjudge candidates for judicial office? Well, first remember that the **consequences** of a violation of the rules of judicial ethics is judicial discipline, which, depending on the jurisdiction and the office, can include public censure as well as suspension or removal from office. *See* **Chapter 26.A at 974**. Remember also that these Rules apply mostly during the rather brief period when a judge is up for election or appointment. Misconduct may not be definitively condemned, or in the case of financial misconduct even discovered, until after the election is over or the appointment has been made. The **consequence** of suspension or removal allows the correction of a selection process that was unlawfully manipulated; the **consequence** of censure allows not only for the education and correction of a judge inclined to learn, but also informs the public and the politically accountable appointing authorities so that they know about the issue in assessing future choices. The result is, ideally, a better informed and more publicly accountable process for allocation of the awesome powers of the judiciary to the all-too-human vessels who wield it.[35]
◄ CONSEQUENCES

---

[35] Federal judges are broadly discouraged from engaging in "any . . . political activity," including the sorts of political activities barred under the ABA Model Code. Because no federal judge stands for election, the scope of political activity allowed them is nearly nonexistent. *See* **CCUSJ Canon 5**. Federal judicial employees are generally forbidden from participating in "partisan political activity," such as "act[ing] as a leader or hold[ing] any office in a partisan political organization"; "mak[ing] speeches for or publicly endors[ing] or oppos[ing] a partisan political organization or candidate"; "solicit[ing] funds for or contribut[ing] to a partisan political organization, candidate, or event"; or "becom[ing] a candidate for partisan political office." **CCJE § 320 Canon 5 § A.** Law clerks and staff attorneys, among others, may not participate in *non*partisan

Problem 26B-16: In each of the following circumstances, is Judge Cranky subject to **consequences**? What **consequences** and why (or why not)? What, if anything, **must** or **should** the judge have done differently?

a. Judge Cranky is running for re-election. He calls all of the partners in his former law firm and asks them to contribute personally to his campaign. Would your analysis change if the judge had his law clerk make the phone calls rather than making the calls personally? If so, how and why; and if not, why not?

b. Judge Cranky lends himself $500 from his re-election campaign funds to pay a personal bill that is overdue, and then pays the campaign back a few days later when he receives his state paycheck. Does your analysis change if Judge Cranky accidentally picked up the campaign committee checkbook and used it to pay the personal bill by mistake, and then reimbursed the campaign committee promptly upon discovering his error? If so, how and why; and if not, why not?

c. Judge Cranky uses a portion of his re-election campaign funds for a facelift on the theory that he will be a better candidate if he looks younger.

d. Judge Cranky asks his law clerk to photocopy campaign fliers for the judge's re-election on the court's copy machine. Does it matter whether the clerk is on or off the clock when doing the copying?

e. On the campaign trail and in his campaign advertising, Judge Cranky pledges to be "tough on crime" if re-elected. Does your analysis change if Judge Cranky handles only civil cases? If so, how and why; and if not, why not?

f. In a speech at an event to support his re-election campaign, Judge Cranky says that voters can count on him to be "pro-business" in cases like *Sparkley v. Consolidated Machine Tools*, a closely followed products liability case currently pending before him.

g. In the same speech as in (f), Judge Cranky expresses the view that "astronomical punitive damage awards are just a waste and a windfall." Does your analysis change if the judge adds that he considers punitive damage awards of more than 100 percent of the actual damages awarded in any case "excessive"? If so, how and why; and if not, why not?

h. During Judge Cranky's re-election campaign, he gives a press interview in which he disparages his opponent based on gossip that he read in an anonymous post on an Internet message board, and about which he has no other information. Does your analysis change if the judge repeats a disparaging rumor then extant about his opponent that the judge knows is untrue, prefacing it with "people are saying that . . ."? If so, how and why? If not, why not?

---

political activity either. **CCJE § 320 Canon 5 § B.** For those of you who may clerk or extern for a federal judge, it's important to understand how broad this prohibition is: No signs on your lawn or in your window; no signing petitions; no being listed as a donor; no introducing candidates at public events; and nothing that might be construed as public support for or opposition against any political candidate or ballot measure on social media. No kidding. If you work for a state judge or state court during law school or after graduating, make sure you understand the rules for court staff in your jurisdiction regarding this kind of activity. During your stint in public service, your life is not entirely your own.

i. Judge Cranky's opponent in the approaching judicial election is an experienced public defender in the county. In a press interview regarding the election, the judge remarks, "My opponent represents criminals and tries to help them escape responsibility for their crimes. Is that who you want as a judge?"

Big-Picture Takeaways from Chapter 26

1. The ABA Model Code of Judicial Conduct ("MCJC") is intended to have a role for judges analogous to the one that the Model Rules has for lawyers. Like the Model Rules, the MCJC has no legal force of its own, and is enforceable only when adopted by a particular jurisdiction as its governing law. The substantive rules of judicial conduct are divided under four "Canons." The Canons each articulate a general principle, which is elaborated in Rules under the Canon and explanatory Comments designed to assist in understanding each Rule. Judicial discipline may be imposed only for violation of a mandatory Rule. The Rules are not intended to form a basis for any **consequence** other than judicial discipline. Federal judges are governed by a separate set of ethical rules, the Code of Conduct for United States Judges, which has been adopted and occasionally revised by the United States Judicial Conference. *See* **Chapter 26.A at 974**.

2. Outside of judicial discipline, judges are subject to criminal **consequences** under the same standards and procedures as anyone else. Judges are, however, absolutely immune from civil **consequences** for their official actions, even for ones undertaken in excess of their authority and even for malicious actions, unless taken "in clear absence of all jurisdiction." *See* **Chapter 26.A at 976**.

3. **MCJC Canon 1** provides: "A judge shall uphold and promote the independence, integrity, and impartiality of the judiciary, and shall avoid impropriety and the appearance of impropriety." *See* **Chapter 26.B at 977**.

4. **MCJC Canon 2** requires that "[a] judge shall perform the duties of judicial office impartially, competently, and diligently." **MCJC Rule 2.5 Comment [1]** describes the judge's duty of competence as requiring "the legal knowledge, skill, thoroughness, and preparation reasonably necessary to perform a judge's responsibilities of judicial office." *See* **Chapter 26.B at 980**.

   a. Unlike lawyers, who are free within the rules of the jurisdiction and the willingness of individual jurors to meet with jurors after the case to discuss the merits, judges may meet with jurors after discharging them, but may not discuss the merits of the case they just heard. *See* **Chapter 26.B at 982**.

b. Judges have duties of management and supervision over the subordinates in their domain similar to lawyers in theirs. *See* **Chapter 26.B at 982**.

c. Judges also have "rat on" or "tattletale" rules that are similar to lawyers' obligations under **Model Rule 8.3**. *See* **Chapter 26.B at 983**.

d. Impartiality—the commitment to administering justice evenhandedly, without fear or favor, according to the rule of law—is the essence of the judicial role. **MCJC Rule 2.2** expresses that duty plainly, stating that judges **must** "uphold and apply the law, and shall perform all duties of judicial office fairly and impartially." *See* **Chapter 26.B at 984**.

   i. **MCJC Rule 2.3(B)** provides that judges **must not** "by words or conduct manifest bias or prejudice, or engage in harassment, including but not limited to bias, prejudice, or harassment based upon race, sex, gender, religion, national origin, ethnicity, disability, age, sexual orientation, marital status, socioeconomic status, or political affiliation, and shall not permit court staff, court officials, or others subject to the judge's direction and control to do so." Judges also **must** prevent the lawyers appearing before them from engaging in such conduct "against parties, witnesses, lawyers, or others" in the proceedings before them. **MCJC Rule 2.3(C)**. *See* **Chapter 26.B at 985**.

   ii. Judges are encouraged to, and often do, speak publicly about the law and the legal system for purposes of civic education, including regarding law reform. But **MCJC Rule 2.10(A)** provides that judges **must not** "make any public statement that might reasonably be expected to affect the outcome or impair the fairness of a matter pending or impending in any court, or make any nonpublic statement that might substantially interfere with a fair trial or hearing." Similarly, judges **must not**, "in connection with cases, controversies, or issues that are likely to come before the court, make pledges, promises, or commitments that are inconsistent with the impartial performance of the adjudicative duties of judicial office." **MCJC Rule 2.10(B)**. *See* **Chapter 26.B at 986**.

e. **MCJC Rule 2.9(A)** states the general rule that judges **must not** "initiate, permit, or consider ex parte communications, or consider other communications made to the judge outside the presence of the parties or their lawyers, concerning a pending or impending matter. . . ." *See* **Chapter 26.B at 988**.

   i. The rule against *ex parte* contacts also forbids judges from independently investigating the facts of a pending or impending matter. **MCJC Rule 2.9(C)**. *See* **Chapter 26.B at 988**.

    ii. If, despite the judge's reasonable efforts to avoid it (or if, in a moment of weakness or lapsed judgment, the judge allows it), she receives an unpermitted *ex parte* contact or a fact outside the court record, then the judge must promptly "notify the parties of the substance of the communication [or factual information] and provide the parties with an opportunity to respond." **MCJC Rule 2.9(B)**. *See* **Chapter 26.B at 989**.

f. "**Recusal**" is a term commonly used for the process or result of removing a judicial or other adjudicative officer from presiding over a particular pending matter. ("**Disqualification**" is also used for this process or result, and in fact is the term principally used in the Model Code of Judicial Conduct and the federal judicial **recusal** statute. Similarly, **recusal** is sometimes used for the process or result of **disqualifying** a lawyer from acting as counsel.) **Recusal** is *not* always required any time that a judge violates the Code of Judicial Conduct. Instead, it is a **consequence** called for in the limited circumstances in which a judge's impartiality may reasonably be called into question in a particular pending matter. *See* **Chapter 26.B at 991**.

    i. The basic standard for **recusal** is stated in **MCJC Rule 2.11(A)**, which provides that a judge **must** "disqualify himself or herself in any proceeding in which the judge's impartiality might reasonably be questioned . . . ." The Rules also provide numerous examples of common situations that usually do or do not meet the standard for **recusal**. *See* **Chapter 26.B at 992**.

    ii. In many situations, if all the parties and counsel to the proceeding freely and voluntarily give their **informed consent** to having a **recusable** judge continue to preside, the judge **may** continue. But if a judge is subject to **recusal** for bias or prejudice under **MCJC Rule 2.11(A)(1)**, no amount of consent, no matter how voluntary or informed, will be sufficient to keep the judge properly involved in that particular case. **MCJC Rule 2.11(C)**. Other than this single exception, however, a judge's **recusal may** be voluntarily waived if all the parties and lawyers agree. **MCJC Rule 2.11(C)** specifies a series of procedural requirements that **must** be met for the waiver to be effective. *See* **Chapter 26.B at 997**.

    iii. A rarely invoked doctrine by which an otherwise mandatory judicial **disqualification** may be overridden is the "rule of necessity." It comes into play either when *every* judge who would otherwise be available to hear and decide a matter is subject to **recusal** for the same reason, or when *only one* judge who would otherwise be **recused** is available under the urgent circumstances presented. **MCJC Rule 2.11 Comment [3]**. *See* **Chapter 26.B at 998**.

5. Canon 3 provides: "A judge shall conduct the judge's personal and extra-judicial activities to minimize the risk of conflict with the obligations of judicial office." *See* **Chapter 26.B at 1003**.

   a. Judges are generally forbidden from appearing voluntarily at public governmental hearings or otherwise consulting with an executive or legislative official, except in matters concerning the law or the legal system, or when acting in their own personal **interest** or as a fiduciary for someone else (in which case they **must not** refer to or otherwise leverage the prestige of their office). **MCJC Rule 3.2; MCJC Rule 3.2 Comment [3]**. Similarly, judges are forbidden from serving as character witnesses or otherwise vouching for another's character "except when duly summoned" (**MCJC Rule 3.3**), and they should "discourage" others from subpoenaing them for this purpose (*see* **MCJC Rule 3.3 Comment [1]**). And they are likewise forbidden from accepting appointment to "any governmental position" except one concerning the law or the legal system. **MCJC Rule 3.4**. *See* **Chapter 26.B at 1003**.

   b. The commercial activities permitted to judges are sharply restricted. *See* **Chapter 26.B at 1004**.

   c. Judges may accept "reasonable compensation" for any permitted extrajudicial activity (including speaking and writing) "unless such acceptance would appear to a reasonable person to undermine the judge's independence, integrity, or impartiality." Before accepting any such benefits, judges **must** carefully assess all the facts and circumstances to determine whether accepting "would appear to a reasonable person to undermine the judge's independence, integrity, or impartiality." *See* **Chapter 26.B at 1005**.

   d. Although affiliation with most nonprofit organizations is within a judge's reasonable discretion, judges **must not** hold membership in any organization "that practices invidious discrimination on the basis of race, sex, gender, religion, national origin, ethnicity, or sexual orientation." Membership in a religious organization "as a lawful exercise of the freedom of religion" is allowed, as is service in or to the military. Judges **may** participate in *planning* related to fundraising for nonprofit organizations, and they **may** participate in the management and investment of a nonprofit organization's funds, but they **must not** *solicit contributions* to the organization from anyone other than members of their own family or other judges over whom they have no supervisory or appellate authority. Judges **may** solicit others to *join* the organization (even if there are membership dues or the like that the organization would devote to its purposes), but only if the organization "is concerned with the law, the legal system, or the administration of justice." Judges **may** make recommendations to public or private fund-granting organizations in connection with their programs or activities (for example, advising a charitable trust or other charitable organization how or where to grant its funds), but again only if the organization is concerned with the law, the legal system, or the administration of justice. *See* **Chapter 26.B at 1007**.

e. Judges **must not** "accept any gifts, loans, bequests, benefits, or other things of value, if acceptance is prohibited by law or would appear to a reasonable person to undermine the judge's independence, integrity, or impartiality." The Rule divides generally permissible kinds of transfers into two categories: Those that **must** be publicly disclosed, and those that need not be. The transfers that need not be publicly disclosed comprise what might at first seem to be a contradictory combination: Some are so innocuous and commonplace that no one could reasonably worry about them; others are so obviously prejudicial that they will require **recusal** (and the lack of a disclosure requirement will allow the judge properly to step aside without having to disclose her personal affairs unnecessarily). The other category of extrajudicial transfers **must** be publicly disclosed consistent with the regulating jurisdiction's rules regarding disclosure. They generally include transfers that litigants in specific cases, and the public in general, reasonably ought to know about in order to determine whether they justify a request for **recusal** or related relief. *See* **Chapter 26.B at 1010**.

6. Canon 4 provides: "A judge or candidate for judicial office shall not engage in political or campaign activity that is inconsistent with the independence, integrity, or impartiality of the judiciary." The Rules under Canon 4 set various limits on the conduct of judges and judicial candidates to achieve this end. **MCJC Rule 4.1** contains a catalogue of conduct in which judges and judicial candidates generally **must not** engage, with the later Rules mostly providing limited modifications or exceptions. *See* **Chapter 26.B at 1015**.

Multiple-Choice Review Questions for Chapter 26

1. What are the likely **consequences** if a judge violates the ABA Model Code of Judicial Conduct?
   a. The judge may be subject to judicial discipline.
   b. The judge may be **disqualified**.
   c. The judge may incur civil liability.
   d. No **consequences**.

2. Judge Jones is handling a case filed by a *pro se* prisoner. According to the prisoner's complaint, the FBI has implanted a chip in his brain

that the government is using to read his mind. Judge Jones dismisses the action *sua sponte* (that is, on his own motion) because he believes that the claims are not plausible and therefore that the complaint does not meet the applicable pleading standard. The prisoner then files a civil action against Judge Jones, claiming damages for the judge's violation of the prisoner's constitutional rights in dismissing his first case. Which of the following is a correct argument that Judge Jones could make to avoid liability?

   a. He is immune from all **consequences** because he is a judge.

   b. He is immune from criminal **consequences** because he acted without malice.

   c. He is immune from civil **consequences** because of judicial immunity.

   d. He is immune from all **consequences** because a *pro se* litigant may not sue a judge.

3. Judge Perez recently presided over an employment discrimination trial. At the conclusion of the trial, she permitted counsel to remain in the courtroom and discuss the substance of the trial with any jurors willing to remain. Two jurors elected to remain. Counsel for the plaintiff employee and the defendant employer also remain to ask the jurors questions about the claims and defenses raised during trial. May Judge Perez join in the discussion?

   a. Yes, because she presided over the case and is already familiar with the claims and defenses.

   b. Yes, because the jurors were willing to discuss the case and volunteered to remain for the discussion.

   c. No, because she may not discuss the merits of a case with the jurors even after the case has been decided.

   d. No, because this would be an improper *ex parte* contact.

4. Judge Cohen presides in landlord-tenant court. Before taking the bench, she had been a lawyer who exclusively represented tenants. As a result of this work, she has formed the opinion that landlords often exploit tenants and that the judicial system is stacked in favor of landlords. She decides that she will "level the playing field" by finding in favor of tenants even when the law suggests that the landlord should prevail. What Rule in the Model Code of Judicial Conduct does this violate?

   a. **MCJC Rule 1.3**.

   b. **MCJC Rule 2.2**.

   c. **MCJC Rule 3.1**.

   d. **MCJC Rule 4.2**.

5. Judge Sullivan is presiding over a high-profile criminal case. The defendant is accused of shooting and killing a police officer while committing

a robbery. The trial was accompanied by large public protests, decrying the "lawless crime wave" sweeping the city. The day of sentencing is no different—hundreds of protestors line the courthouse steps. At sentencing, Judge Sullivan sentences the defendant well in excess of the statutory minimum, explaining, "If I give you a lenient sentence, I'm worried that the protests will turn violent." Is this rationale acceptable under the Model Code of Judicial Conduct?

    a. Yes, because Judge Sullivan is accepting the pragmatic reality that a lenient sentence could cause greater harm.

    b. Yes, because Judge Sullivan is permitted to consider public opinion of the defendant in fashioning a sentence.

    c. No, because Judge Sullivan is admitting to exercising discretion.

    d. No, because Judge Sullivan is admitting to being swayed by public clamor.

6. Judge Beckman walks into the courtroom to discover defense counsel making a sexist joke about the female plaintiff's appearance. Although Judge Beckman is a woman, she is not personally offended. What should Judge Beckman do?

    a. Nothing. If she intervenes, she risks showing bias against defense counsel.

    b. Admonish the lawyers and ensure that they do not continue their discussion along those lines.

    c. Join in the joking so long as the plaintiff herself is not present to hear it.

    d. **Recuse** herself from the case because she is a woman.

7. Judge Farley is currently presiding over a high-profile class action brought by investors who claim that they were defrauded as part of a Ponzi scheme. A jury trial is scheduled to commence in a few weeks. Judge Farley is speaking at a continuing education program open only to members of the bar, and an audience member asks her about the case. Judge Farley says, "Off the record, I think that the defendants are guilty as sin, but we'll see what the jury decides at the conclusion of trial." Is this statement permissible?

    a. Yes, so long as it is truthful.

    b. Yes, because it was off the record and at a members-only event.

    c. No, because it may affect the outcome of the case.

    d. No, because she does not yet know what evidence will be offered at trial.

8. Judge Chen is newly appointed to the bench. When she was in private practice, she never handled a case under her state's open-records law (analogous to the federal Freedom of Information Act). Such a case is

assigned to her. In the case, the plaintiff newspaper, represented by private counsel, seeks to compel the production of documents from the State Bureau of Investigation. A deputy Attorney General enters an appearance as counsel for the defendant agency. Judge Chen invites the deputy AG to chambers for a private, untranscribed meeting so that the deputy AG can explain the basics of the open records law and the SBI's specific objection to the newspaper's records request. Judge Chen reasons that this tutorial will allow her to appear prepared the first time that she holds a hearing in open court with all counsel. Why is this meeting improper?

   a. It demonstrates bias, because Judge Chen elected to meet with the government lawyer rather than the private practice lawyer. Had she chosen to meet with only plaintiff's counsel, the meeting would have been permissible.

   b. This is an *ex parte* meeting about a pending matter.

   c. This meeting is off the record, in chambers, and a judge may never meet with counsel except in open court.

   d. It demonstrates a lack of competence, because Judge Chen could herself contact the SBI to determine the grounds for its objection.

9. When **must** a judge **recuse** herself?

   a. In any case in which the judge has been accused of partiality.

   b. In any case in which the judge's impartiality might reasonably be questioned.

   c. In any case in which the judge has violated the Code of Judicial Conduct.

   d. Only in cases in which a lawyer or party requests **disqualification**.

10. Which of the following is *not* a ground for **recusal** that the parties and counsel may waive?

   a. Bias or prejudice.

   b. Economic interest.

   c. The judge previously served as a lawyer in the matter.

   d. The judge is a **material** witness in the matter.

11. In Judge Ruby's jurisdiction, judicial salaries are set by statute. A group of concerned citizens has challenged the legislature's recent revision of the pay scale, arguing that it violates the state Constitution. Can Judge Ruby handle this case?

   a. Yes, because this is a constitutional challenge, not a question of statutory interpretation.

   b. Yes, because this is a situation invoking the rule of necessity.

   c. No, because he has a personal stake in the outcome of the litigation.

    d. No, **because** it will create the appearance of bias if he rules the statute to be constitutional.

12. Judge Davis, **who** is appointed to the bench in Pennsylvania, receives a subpoena compelling his testimony as a character witness for one of his former employees who is on trial for embezzlement in federal court in New Jersey, a short distance from his home in Pennsylvania. **May** Judge Davis testify?

    a. Yes, but only because the trial is in a different state.

    b. Yes, but only because he has been compelled to testify.

    c. No, because judges may not appear at public hearings.

    d. No, because a judge can never serve as a character witness.

13. Can a judge be paid for public speaking?

    a. Yes, but only so long as the payment is reasonable and accepting the speaking engagement would not appear to a reasonable person to undermine the judge's independence, integrity, or impartiality.

    b. Yes, but only if the judge donates any payment to charity.

    c. No, because a judge can never engage in outside activities.

    d. No, because accepting any speaking engagement would demonstrate bias.

14. Which organization **must** a judge **not** join?

    a. A religious organization that is open to all faiths but whose members all happen to be practitioners of that organization's religion.

    b. An alumni association for the judge's single-sex school that is composed only of members who are that gender.

    c. A social organization that excludes people from membership on the basis of race.

    d. A legal organization that charges membership dues.

15. Judge Green is handling a slip-and-fall case filed against ShopRight grocery store. He himself buys groceries at ShopRight. One day while shopping there, he notices a buy-one, get-one-free sale on canned peaches, which happen to be his favorite treat. Can he take advantage of the sale?

    a. Yes, so long as he has his spouse or another household member buy the peaches for him.

    b. Yes, because the sale price is offered to the entire public and would not reasonably appear to undermine the judge's impartiality.

    c. No, because this would constitute a bribe that would disqualify the judge from handling the slip-and-fall case.

    d. No, because this would be an improper gift from a litigant appearing before Judge Green.

Glossary of Recurring Defined Terms

Account, duty to: The lawyer's **duty to account** has three principal components. One is the duty to "promptly deliver to the client or third person any funds or other property that the client or third person is entitled to receive . . ." except as otherwise provided by the Rules, other law, or by agreement with the client or third person. *See* **Model Rule 1.15(d)**; **Chapter 21.D at 586**. The second is to "promptly notify" anyone who has an interest in money or property "[u]pon receiving" that money or property. **Model Rule 1.15(d)**; **Chapter 21.D at 586**. And the third is to maintain detailed records regarding the money or property of others (or subject to dispute) that the lawyer is holding, and disclose those records to those legitimately **interested** upon request. **Model Rule 1.15(d)**; **Chapter 21.D at 587**. *See also* **safeguard, duty to**; **segregate, duty to**.

Attorney-client privilege: An evidentiary privilege (that is, an immunity from compelled disclosure) that protects **confidential** communications between attorney and client (or **prospective client**) or anyone acting on behalf of either for the purpose of seeking, receiving, or transmitting legal advice. *See* **Chapter 8.A at 226**. *Cf.* **confidentiality, duty of**; **attorney work product doctrine**.

Attorney work product doctrine (also referred to as the **work product doctrine**): A conditional immunity from compelled disclosure for **confidential** information created or compiled by or on behalf of a party in anticipation of litigation or in preparation for trial and currently codified in **Fed. R. Civ. P. 26(b)(3)** and comparable state rules. *See* **Chapter 8.A at 226**. *Cf.* **confidentiality, duty of**; **attorney-client privilege**.

Be supervised, duty to: There is no **duty to be supervised** literally stated in the Rules of Professional Conduct or in tort law. But it is an important implication of the **duties of competence, diligence**, and **care**. No matter how junior or inexperienced, lawyers have a personal, nondelegable duty owed directly to their clients to ensure that they get whatever supervision, backstopping, and support they may need to develop or obtain "the legal knowledge, skill, thoroughness and preparation reasonably necessary for the representation" (**Model Rule 1.1**), and that a reasonable lawyer would bring to the task. *See* **Chapter 19.D at 520**.

Candor, duty of: The basic fiduciary duty of a lawyer to fully, honestly, and promptly provide the client with all the information concerning the engagement that the client reasonably requests or reasonably needs to make informed decisions about the engagement. *See* **Model Rule 1.4**; **Chapter 5.D at 117**. Lawyers have a separate and different **duty of candor to tribunals** before which they appear that in general terms forbids them from making factual or legal misrepresentations to the court or offering false evidence. *See* **candor to the tribunal, duty of; Model Rule 3.3**; **Chapter 24.C at 862**.

Candor to the tribunal, duty of: The duty lawyers owe to the tribunals before which they appear not to make knowing misrepresentations of fact or law, not to falsify evidence or encourage or assist others to do so, not to offer evidence that they know is false, and not to fail to disclose facts known to the lawyer that the tribunal needs to make an informed decision in *ex parte* matters. *See* **Model Rule 3.3**; **Chapter 24.C at 862**. *See also* **correct, duty to.**

Care, duty of: The general duty every lawyer owes to clients and to those non-clients to whom the lawyer undertakes such a duty to exercise a level of skill, diligence, and care—and possess (or acquire) a level of knowledge—that a reasonably careful and prudent lawyer would exercise or possess under the same or similar circumstances. This duty, when breached, is enforced principally by civil liability sounding in professional negligence for damages payable to the person to whom the duty is owed. *See* **Chapter 7.B at 180**. *Cf.* the **duties of competence** and **diligence**, codified in **Model Rule 1.1** and **Model Rule 1.3**, respectively, which are enforced by professional discipline. *See* **Chapter 7.A at 172**.

Chinese wall: An anachronistic term for an **ethical screen** whose use is currently strongly discouraged. *See* **ethical screen.**

Competence, duty of: The general duty that every lawyer owes to have or develop "the legal knowledge, skill, thoroughness and preparation reasonably necessary for the representation." This duty is enforced principally by professional discipline. *See* **Model Rule 1.1**; **Chapter 7.A at 172**. *Cf.* the **duty of care**, which is enforced by civil liability sounding in professional negligence for damages payable to the person to whom the duty is owed.

Concurrent client rule; concurrent clients: The **concurrent client rule**, codified in **Model Rule 1.7(a)**, and adopted in similar terms as a basis for various civil remedies including **disqualification**, provides that a lawyer **must not** represent two clients at the same time (**concurrent clients**) whose **interests conflict** in one or both of the matters in which the lawyer represents the clients, even if those matters are unrelated to one another. *See* **Model Rule 1.7(a)(1)**; **Chapter 22.B at 646**. The **concurrent client rule** also provides that a lawyer **must not** represent **concurrent clients** when there is a "significant risk" that their **interests** are in or could come into **conflict** in a way that could "**materially limit**" the lawyer's representation of either client. *See* **Model Rule 1.7(a)(2)**; **Chapter 22.B at 654**. **Concurrent conflicts may** often be waived (or as the Model Rules put it, consented to), by the affected clients. Which **conflicts of interest** are **consentable** and how that consent must be obtained and documented is provided for in **Model Rule 1.7(b)**. *See* **Chapter 22.E at 738**.

Confidential information (sometimes referred to as **client confidences** or just **confidences**): Information protected by the **duty of confidentiality**, which generally includes any information that the lawyer learns from any source in connection with representing a client, or learns from a **prospective client** when consulting with that **prospective client** in contemplation of possible representation. **Confidential information** is referred to in the Model Rules as "information relating to the representation of a client," "information protected by Rule 1.6" (as to **current clients**), "information protected by Rule 1.9" (as to **former clients**), or "information protected by Rule 1.18" (as to **prospective clients**). *See* **Chapter 8.A at 210**.

Confidentiality, duty of: One of the most basic and pervasive of the lawyer's fiduciary duties, it generally forbids a lawyer from voluntarily disclosing or using **confidential information**. *See* **Chapter 8.A at 217**.

Confirmed in writing: One of the levels of formality that the Model Rules require of some disclosures, consents, or agreements. **Model Rule 1.0(n)** defines "writing" as "a tangible or electronic record of a communication or representation, including handwriting, typewriting, printing, photostating, photography, audio or video-recording, and electronic communications"; and a "signed" writing as a writing including "an electronic sound, symbol or process attached to or logically associated with a writing and executed or adopted by a person with the intent to sign the writing." **Model Rule 1.0(a)** defines **confirmed in writing** as "consent that is given in writing . . . or a writing that a lawyer promptly transmits . . . confirming an oral . . . consent" transmitted at or within a reasonable time after the consent is given. An agreement or consent that is **confirmed in writing may** be, but is not required to be, signed by the person agreeing or consenting; it **may** simply confirm the terms agreed or consented to orally in a writing transmitted after the fact. *See* **Chapter 20.B at 537 n.2; Chapter 22.E at 752**. *See also* **in a writing signed by the client; informed consent.**

Conflict of interest (sometimes shortened to "**conflict**"; to identify a **conflict of interest**, we often identify the **interests** in **conflict**, and when we determine that a lawyer is subject to a **conflict of interest**, we say that he or she is "**conflicted**"): A person's "**interests**" amount to what that person wants or needs, or may reasonably be assumed to want or need, in the situation presented. One person's **interests conflict** with another's when the two people want or need, or may reasonably be presumed to want or need, any **materially** inconsistent things. A lawyer is said to have a **conflict of interest** when the lawyer is subject to two or more **conflicting interests** or duties and it will be difficult or impossible to satisfy both or all of them. The **conflict** can be between the personal **interests** of the lawyer and the **interests** of a client, or it can be between duties to two or more clients in which the lawyer has become entangled. *See* **Chapter 22 at 600**. *See also* **concurrent client rule**; **successive client rule**.

Consent: *See* **informed consent**.

Consentable: A term used in the Model Rules to describe those **conflicts of interest** that **may** be addressed by all affected clients' **informed consent, confirmed in writing.** Most **conflicts of interest** are **consentable**; some are not. *See* **Model Rule 1.7(b) & Comment [14]**; **Chapter 22.E at 739**.

Consequences: A term embracing all the different unwelcome things that can happen to you if you act contrary to legal, customary, or personal norms. Formal **consequences** are remedies imposed by authorities with the legal power to do so, such as professional discipline or civil liability. Informal **consequences** involve unofficial responses to conduct that others find objectionable, such as damage to reputation, loss of or termination by clients, or the dispute of fees. *See* **Chapter 1 at 11**. Common **consequences** are catalogued in **Chapter 3.F at 56**.

Constituent: An individual who is employed by, has an ownership or management interest in, or is otherwise associated with a business or other organization and who may have the power to speak or act on the organization's behalf in some regard. **Constituents**, and their **interests**, are distinct from their organization and the organization's **interests**. *See* **Model Rule 1.13(a); Chapter 23.A at 770**.

Corporate *Miranda* warning: *See* ***Upjohn* warning**.

Correct, duty to: The duty that all lawyers owe the tribunals before which they appear to correct any misrepresentation that they have made to the tribunal or any false evidence that they have offered to the tribunal, even if the falsity of the representation or of the evidence is not discovered until after the representation was made or the evidence was offered. The **duty to correct** creates a mandatory exception to the **duty of confidentiality** and lasts until the conclusion of the proceedings. *See* **Model Rule 3.3; Chapter 24.C at 878**.

Current client: A client that a lawyer or **practice organization** currently represents in an ongoing engagement. **Current clients** are generally owed the full panoply of duties arising out of the attorney-client relationship. *See* **Chapter 8.A at 206; Chapter 9.A at 257**.

Diligence, duty of: The general duty that every lawyer owes to clients to exercise "reasonable diligence and promptness" in providing legal services. This duty is enforced principally by professional discipline. *See* **Model Rule 1.3; Chapter 7.A at 178**. *Cf.* the **duty of care**, *supra*, which is enforced by civil liability sounding in professional negligence for damages payable to the person to whom the duty is owed for harm caused by a breach.

Direct adversity: A term used in analyzing **concurrent conflicts of interest**. One way that a **concurrent conflict** can be created is by "**direct adversity**" between two **current clients** of the same lawyer or **practice organization**. The term is generally under-stood to mean head-on, "nose-to-nose" adversity, for example by suing a **current client**, or negotiating against a **current client**. *See* **Model Rule 1.7(a)(1)**; **Chapter 22.B at 651**. Adversity that does not qualify as **direct adversity** is sometimes referred to as **indirect adversity**. Whether **indirect adversity** creates a **concurrent conflict of interest** is judged by a different standard, namely whether there is a "significant risk" that the adversity will "**materially** limit" the lawyer's representation of the client. *See* **Model Rule 1.7(a)(2)**; **Chapter 22.B at 654**.

Disqualification: An injunctive court order directing a lawyer or **practice organization** to get out or stay out of a particular engagement, or the process seeking such an order. **Disqualification** is most commonly ordered to address an unwaived or unwaiv-able **conflict of interest** from which a lawyer fails or refuses to withdraw (*see* **Chapter 22.B at 664**; **Chapter 22.C at 690**) but is occasionally ordered in other situations in which a lawyer or **practice organization** needs to be removed from an engagement to mitigate an undue risk of future harm (*see* **Chapter 11.G at 363**; **Chapter 12.B at 385**). A lawyer who is subject to **disqualification** is sometimes described as being **disqualified** even before the remedy is applied. The process or result of removing a lawyer from serving as counsel in a particular matter is also sometimes referred to **recusal**. Simi-larly, **disqualification** is also used to describe the process or result for removing a judicial or other adjudicative officer from presiding in a pending matter. *See* **recusal**.

Don't-wanna test: A practical thought experiment to help determine whether infor-mation is **material** and thus **must** be disclosed pursuant to some applicable duty: The more you *don't wanna* disclose something, the more likely it is as a practical matter to be something **material** that you **must** disclose. The **don't-wanna test** is a good way to alert yourself to the need to examine carefully the reasons why you feel disinclined to bring something up. The test is not established legal doctrine; it is a practical way of helping you assess your obligations when a duty to disclose may be in play. *See* **Chapter 5.D at 119**; **Chapter 22.B at 630**; **Chapter 22.E at 743**.

Effective assistance of counsel: A special set of competency, diligence, and care obliga-tions imposed on criminal defense counsel by the Sixth Amendment (and similar provisions in many state constitutions). **Effective assistance of counsel** is governed by two alternative tests. The *Strickland* "deficiency and prejudice" test requires crim-inal defense clients who are claiming **ineffective assistance of counsel** to prove (1) that their counsel did (or failed to do) something in defending the accused that no reasonable defense lawyer would have done (or failed to do); *and* (2) that there was a reasonable probability that the case would have come out differently had counsel done what any reasonable defense lawyer would have done. *See* **Chapter 7.C at 185**. The *Cronic* test looks at whether the defendant was in (or defense counsel created) a situation in which *no* competent lawyer could have provided constitutionally **effective assistance**—but such cases are rare. *See* **Chapter 7.C at 191**.

Ethical screen: An **ethical screen** or **ethical wall** (frequently shortened by dropping the "ethical" modifier) is a set of prophylactic measures designed to contain **confidential information** to a single lawyer or small group of lawyers and nonlawyer staff within a **practice organization** and to prevent its dissemination to others in the same **practice organization**. In a few narrowly defined circumstances, an **ethical screen** may allow a **practice organization** to proceed with an engagement that otherwise would be subject to a **disqualifying successive conflict of interest** without any affected client's **informed consent**. *See* **Chapter 22.D at 716**.

Ethical wall: *See* **ethical screen**.

Former client: A client that a lawyer or **practice organization** represented previously, but for whom that engagement has ended. **Former clients** continue to be owed certain duties, most notably the **duty of confidentiality**. *See* **Chapter 8.A at 206**.

Former client rule: *See* **successive client rule**.

Front-page test: A thought experiment to help you discern when your thinking may be distorted by cognitive dissonance or another cognitive bias. To conduct the test, imagine the conduct you're assessing described in a simple, factual manner on the front page (or the digital home page) of the most widely read newspaper in your community. How would you feel if you saw it there? How would your nonlawyer friends and relatives react? If the conduct looks bad from that perspective, then it probably *is* bad. If you start thinking about whether the newspaper would ever find out, you've got something to hide. And if you start trying to edit the imaginary coverage rather than living with the plainly stated facts, then you know something's probably not right. *See* **Chapter 4.A at 83**.

Hot-potato rule: A corollary of the **concurrent client rule**, which provides that a lawyer **must not** terminate an ongoing engagement with a **current client** for the purpose of changing that **current client** into a **former client** to whom the lawyer owes no **duty of loyalty** for the purpose of avoiding what would otherwise be a **concurrent conflict of interest**. The nickname for the rule comes from the observation that the lawyer **must not** "drop a client like a hot potato" to avoid a **concurrent conflict**. The rule is used to impose **disqualification** on a lawyer who has violated the rule in an attempt to avoid what would otherwise have been a **disqualifying concurrent conflict of interest**; violation of the **hot-potato rule** is generally not a basis for professional discipline. *See* **Chapter 22.B at 650**.

Imputation: The attribution of one lawyer's **conflict of interest** to other lawyers in the same **practice organization** and to the **practice organization** itself. Generally, the relationships and **confidential information** of each lawyer in a **practice organization**, and the

conflicts of interest they may create, are **imputed** to all the others (and to the **practice organization**), but there are exceptions for some **conflicts** based on the personal **interest** of one lawyer, and for situations in which **Model Rule 1.9** and **Model Rule 1.10** allow **screening** to cut off **imputation** without client consent. *See* **Chapter 22.A at 628; Chapter 22.D at 702**. **Imputation** is significantly reduced in determining and responding to the **conflicts of interest** of current or former government lawyers. *See* **Chapter 25.D at 927**.

In a writing signed by the client: The most demanding level of formality that the Model Rules require of some disclosures, consents, or agreements. **Model Rule 1.0(n)** defines "writing" as "a tangible or electronic record of a communication or representation, including handwriting, typewriting, printing, photostating, photography, audio or videorecording, and electronic communications"; and a "signed" writing as a writing including "an electronic sound, symbol or process attached to or logically associated with a writing and executed or adopted by a person with the intent to sign the writing." *See* **Chapter 20.B at 537 n.2**. *See also* **confirmed in writing**; **informed consent**.

Indirect adversity: *See* **direct adversity**.

Ineffective assistance of counsel: *See* **effective assistance of counsel**.

Informed consent: A recurring term in the Model Rules, defined in **Model Rule 1.0(e)**. **Informed consent** must be based on (in the words of the Rule) "adequate information and explanation about the material risks of and reasonably available alternatives to the proposed course of conduct." For a description of the formalities that may be required in some circumstances to make **informed consent** effective, *see* **confirmed in writing**; **in a writing signed by the client**. *See* **Chapter 22.E at 743**.

Interest: A person's **interests** are anything that person wants or needs, or may reasonably be assumed to want or need, in the situation presented. *See* **Chapter 22 at 600**. *See* **conflict of interest**.

Loyalty, duty of: The most basic and overarching of all the duties imposed on fiduciaries. Fiduciaries (including lawyers) **must** treat their beneficiaries (in the case of lawyers, their clients) at least as well as they would treat themselves (or perhaps more accurately, at least as well as reasonable people would treat themselves). Thus, lawyers **must not** act in a manner adverse to the **interests** of their clients, and they **must not** act for their own benefit in relation to the engagement, except to receive reasonable compensation for their services, if that is the parties' understanding. *See* **Chapter 5.D at 113; Chapter 22.B at 648**.

Manage, duty to: The duty, codified in **Model Rule 5.1(a)** and **Model Rule 5.3(a)**, for lawyers with managerial authority within a **practice organization** to adopt and train lawyers and nonlawyer staff to follow "measures [that is, "internal policies and procedures"] giving reasonable assurance" that lawyers within the **practice**

organization will comply with the Rules of Professional Conduct, and that nonlawyers will comply with the lawyers' duties. *See* **Chapter 19.C at 514**. *See also* **supervise, duty to**; **be supervised, duty to**.

Material: A modifier that comes up in a number of different contexts and whose meaning varies by context. Generally, it refers to something that matters for a particular purpose in a particular context. *See* **Chapter 10.B at 325**; *see also* **Chapter 5.D at 118**; **Chapter 6.C at 158**.

May: Refers to things that, under governing law, you have personal discretion to do or not to do, as you choose. Things that you **may** do may lead to informal **consequences** but will not lead to formal ones. *See* **Chapter 1.E at 13**; *see also* **must** (or **must not**); **should** (or **should not**).

Must (or **must not**): Refers to things that you have an *enforceable legal obligation* to do (or not to do)—that is, an obligation whose violation can result in a formal **consequence** imposed by an authority legally empowered to do so—whether that obligation arises out of criminal law or procedure; civil statute, rule, or common law; or an obligation stated in the applicable Rules of Professional Conduct. *See* **Chapter 1.E at 13**; *see also* **may**; **should** (or **should not**).

No-contact rule: A common nickname for the rule, codified in **Model Rule 4.2**, that provides that a lawyer **must not** communicate directly with a non-client the lawyer knows to be represented by his or her own lawyer, if that lawyer is representing the non-client on the subject of the intended communication, unless that other lawyer gives permission. The **no-contact rule** also protects certain employees and managers of an organization that is represented regarding the subject of the intended communication; which organizational employees and managers are so protected varies from state to state. *See* **Chapter 11 at 341**; *see generally* **Chapter 11 (at 339)**.

Nonconsentable: *See* **consentable**.

No-puppetry rule: This principle is codified in **Model Rule 8.4(a)**; it provides that if you as a lawyer **must not** do something, you also **must not** get someone else to do it for you. A similar idea is expressed in civil and criminal doctrines of secondary and vicarious liability, such as the principal's liability for the agent's actions in the course and scope of the agency (including *respondeat superior*), conspiracy, and aiding and abetting, so you already know something about this topic. **Model Rule 8.4(a)** tells you that this same principle applies to professional conduct and discipline, too. *See* **Chapter 1.E at 13**.

Playbook information: Playbook information creates an issue that can arise in applying the **substantial relationship test** to determine whether a lawyer has a **successive conflict of interest** grounded in the **duty of confidentiality** (**Model Rule 1.9(a)**; **Model Rule 1.18(b)**). **Playbook information** refers to general information about the original client or about a *type* of dispute or deal, rather than information *specific* to a *particular* dispute or deal. The general rule regarding **playbook information** is that it is *not* sufficient to create a **substantial relationship** between the old engagements in which the **playbook information** was acquired and the new one that might create a **conflict of interest** unless the **playbook information** is so voluminous, detailed, or specifically applicable in the new engagement that it creates a substantial unfair advantage. *See* **Model Rule 1.9 Comments [2-3]; Chapter 22.C at 688.** *See also* **conflict of interest; successive client rule; substantial relationship.**

Positional conflicts: Potential **conflicts of interest** that may arise when a single lawyer or **practice organization** takes inconsistent positions on a specific issue of law or fact in two different proceedings on behalf of two different clients. The general rule is that a **positional conflict** does not create a **concurrent conflict of interest** unless "there is a significant risk that a lawyer's action on behalf of one client will **materially** limit the lawyer's effectiveness in representing another client in a different case." **Model Rule 1.7 Comment [24].** *See* **Chapter 22.B at 655.** *See also* **concurrent client rule; conflict of interest.**

Practice organization: The term referring to anything defined as a "firm" or "law firm" in **Model Rule 1.0(c).** It includes any form of private law firm (including a solo practitioner) as well as any group or organization that provides legal services, such as district attorneys' offices, public defenders' offices, city or county attorneys' offices, and the legal departments of for-profit and nonprofit companies, as well as the legal departments of government agencies. *See* **Chapter 19.A at 506.**

Prospective client: A person or organization "who consults with a lawyer about the possibility of forming a client-lawyer relationship with respect to a matter . . ." but who is not yet the lawyer's client, and may never become one. **Model Rule 1.18(a).** Even if no client-lawyer relationship ensues, the lawyer and all lawyers within the consulting lawyer's **practice organization**, as well as the **practice organization** itself, owe the **prospective client** a **duty of confidentiality**. *See* **Chapter 8.A at 207; Chapter 22.C at 681.**

Recusal: The removal of a judge or other adjudicative officer from presiding over a particular pending matter, or the process of seeking such removal. Judges **may** (and under circumstances defined in the Model Code of Judicial Conduct, **must**) **recuse** themselves, or **may** be **recused** by another judge or the court that they serve, under procedures typically defined by statute. *See* **Chapter 26.B at 976.** This process or result of removing a judge from presiding over a pending case is also referred to as **disqualification**. Similarly, **recusal** is also used to describe the process or result by which a lawyer is **disqualified** from serving as counsel in a particular matter. *See* **disqualification.**

Reporting out: The discretionary option that a lawyer representing an organization has to report outside the organization, notwithstanding any constraints that the

duty of confidentiality might impose, clearly unlawful conduct the lawyer knows that **constituents** are committing against the organization or on its behalf to the limited extent necessary to address that unlawful conduct and its likely harm to the organization. **Reporting out** is an option only after the lawyer representing the organization has **reported up** the unlawful conduct all the way to the highest authority in the organization, and the highest authority has failed or refused to address it. *See* **Model Rule 1.13(c), (d)**; **Chapter 23.B at 798**.

Reporting up: The duty of a lawyer representing an organization to report unlawful conduct that the lawyer knows that the organization's **constituents** are committing against the organization or on its behalf "up the ladder" to higher management. *See* **Model Rules 1.13(b), (e)**; **Chapter 23.B at 792**.

Safeguard, duty to: The basic duty imposed on all lawyers to keep safe and secure any money or property that is in their care but belongs to others (or whose owner-ship is disputed). **Model Rule 1.15 Comment [1]** explains that "[a] lawyer should hold property of others with the care required of a professional fiduciary." *See* **Chapter 21.B at 577**; *see also* **account, duty to**; **segregate, duty to**.

Screen: *See* **ethical screen**.

Segregate, duty to: The **duty to segregate** requires lawyers to keep clients' and third parties' money and property separate from the lawyer's own money and property. Many jurisdictions have detailed rules about precisely how a lawyer **must** segre-gate others' money or property, and what kinds of records a lawyer **must** create and maintain regarding others' money and property in the lawyer's custody. A breach of the **duty to segregate** is often referred to as "commingling." *See* **Model Rule 1.15(a)**; **Chapter 21.C at 578**; *see also* **account, duty to**; **safeguard, duty to**.

Should (or **should not**): Refers to things that you **may** do (or not do), and that in the exercise of prudence and good judgment you deem it the better or best practice to do (or not do). A **should** judgment may be based on any or all of the available competing reasons to do or not do something, including (among many others) your personal moral or ethical values about what is or is not the right thing to do, or simple self-interest (such as making a profit, avoiding potential disputes or liability, or enhancing your own reputation). *See* **Chapter 1.E at 13**; *see also* **must** (or **must not**); **may**.

Substantial relationship: An issue that arises in determining whether a **successive conflict of interest** based on the **duty of confidentiality** has arisen (**Model Rule 1.9(a)**; **Model Rule 1.18(b)**). The Model Rules and the civil law governing **disqualification** have developed a **substantial relationship test** for determining whether there is suffi-cient risk of a lawyer's misuse of **confidential information** to create a **conflict of interest** that must be addressed: That test asks whether the engagement in which the lawyer obtained the **confidential information** is "the same [as] or . . . substantially similar [to]" a new engagement in which the lawyer is to represent a client whose interests in that engagement are "**materially** adverse" to the client in the original engagement. The **substantial relationship test** provides the ground rules for determining when the old engagement and the new, adverse one are **substantially related** and therefore require the lawyer's abstention from, or the affected client's waiver of, the **conflict of interest.** *See* **Chapter 22.C at 684.**

Successive client rule: A rule, also known as the **former client rule**, defining a category of **conflicts of interest** based on the **duty of confidentiality.** The rule is codified in **Model Rules 1.9(a)-(b)** and **Model Rule 1.18(b)** for professional discipline purposes, and also defines in similar terms those civil duties that may be enforced by **disqualification** or claims for damages or restitution. The rule generally provides that, when a lawyer or **practice organization** has a **duty of confidentiality** to anyone (whether a **prospective client, current client,** or **former client**), the lawyer or **practice organization must not** take on or continue an engagement in which the lawyer or **practice organization** might reasonably be able to use the **confidential information** protected by that **duty of confidentiality** against the person to whom the **duty of confidentiality** is owed. *See* **Chapter 22.C at 679.**

Supervise, duty to: The duty, codified in **Model Rule 5.1(b)** and **Model Rule 5.3(b)**, for lawyers with "direct supervisory authority" over another lawyer or over nonlawyer staff to "make reasonable efforts to ensure" that a supervised lawyer's conduct "conforms to the Rules of Professional Conduct," and that a supervised nonlawyer's conduct "is compatible with the professional obligations of the lawyer." *See* **Chapter 19.C at 515.**

***Upjohn* warning:** Also referred to as a **corporate *Miranda* warning**, it is the admonition required by **Model Rule 1.13(f)** and **Model Rule 4.3** that a lawyer representing an organization **must** give to any unrepresented organizational **constituent** with whom the organization's lawyer is interacting in any circumstances in which the lawyer knows or reasonably should know that the **constituent's interests** are adverse to the organization client's **interests.** The admonition must be tailored to the circumstances, but it generally requires that the organization counsel clarify to the **constituent** the counsel's role as a lawyer for the organization and not as a lawyer for the **constituent,** along with the implications of that difference for the **constituent,** most particularly that the lawyer will be required to disclose anything learned from the **constituent** to the organization. *See* **Chapter 23.A at 781.**

Wall: *See* **ethical screen.**

Weasel-words: Words that we may use to try to mask (from ourselves or others) the real practical import of our conduct—for example, euphemisms; technical jargon; funny nicknames. *See* **Chapter 4.A at 86.**

Work product doctrine: *See* **attorney work product doctrine.**

Table of Cases

Index